S0-AEM-917

CLASS,

STATUS,

and POWER

Social Stratification in Comparative Perspective

SECOND EDITION

Edited by

Reinhard Bendix *and* Seymour Martin Lipset

THE FREE PRESS, NEW YORK

Collier-Macmillan Limited, London

Copyright © 1966 by The Free Press

A DIVISION OF THE MACMILLAN COMPANY

Printed in the United States of America

Earlier Edition Copyright © 1953 by The Free Press

All rights reserved. No part of this book may be reproduced or utilized in any form or by any means, electronic or mechanical, including photocopying, recording, or by any information storage and retrieval system, without permission in writing from the Publisher.

Collier-Macmillan Canada, Ltd., Toronto, Ontario

Library of Congress Catalog Card Number: 65-23025

First Printing

To the Memory of Stanislaw Ossowski

A TRUE SCHOLAR AND TEACHER

CONTENTS

Introduction   xiii

I   Theories of Class Structure

A Classical View   1
        ARISTOTLE

Factions in American Society   2
        THE FEDERALIST

A Note on Classes   5
        KARL MARX

Karl Marx's Theory of Social Classes   6
        REINHARD BENDIX and SEYMOUR MARTIN LIPSET

Estates and Classes   12
        FERDINAND TOENNIES

Class, Status and Party   21
        MAX WEBER

The Development of Caste   28
        MAX WEBER

The Theory of the Leisure Class   36
        THORSTEIN VEBLEN

The Problem of Classes   42
        JOSEPH SCHUMPETER

The Continuing Debate on Equality

Some Principles of Stratification (1945)   47
        KINGSLEY DAVIS and WILBERT E. MOORE

Some Principles of Stratification: A Critical Analysis (1953)   53
        MELVIN M. TUMIN

Reply to Tumin (1953)   59
        KINGSLEY DAVIS

Comment (1953)   62
        WILBERT E. MOORE

Reply to Kingsley Davis (1953)   62
        MELVIN M. TUMIN

Some Notes on the Functional Theory of Stratification (1962)   64
WŁODZIMIERZ WESOŁOWSKI

Some Empirical Consequences of the Davis-Moore Theory of Stratification (1963)   69
ARTHUR L. STINCHCOMBE

Social Stratification and the Political Community   73
REINHARD BENDIX

Different Conceptions of Social Class   86
STANISLAW OSSOWSKI

II   Historical and Comparative Studies

Stages in the Social History of Capitalism   97
HENRI PIRENNE

How Democracy Affects the Relations of Masters and Servants   107
ALEXIS DE TOCQUEVILLE

The Class Structure of Revolutionary America   111
JACKSON T. MAIN

The Historical Peculiarities of the Social and Economic Development of Russia   121
BORIS BRUTZKUS

Japan's Aristocratic Revolution   135
THOMAS C. SMITH

Social Stratification and Economic Processes in Africa   141
LLOYD A. FALLERS

Social Stratification in Two Equalitarian Societies: Australia and the United States   149
KURT B. MAYER

Value Patterns, Class, and the Democratic Polity: The United States and Great Britain   161
SEYMOUR MARTIN LIPSET

Social Mobility and Stratification in China   171
WOLFRAM EBERHARD

Agricultural Enterprise and Rural Class Relations   182
ARTHUR L. STINCHCOMBE

Economic Development and Class Structure   190
GLAUCIO A. D. SOARES

III   Power and Status Relations

Patterns of Power

Social Class, Political Class, Ruling Class   201
RAYMOND ARON

"Power Elite" or "Veto Groups"?   210
WILLIAM KORNHAUSER

Power in Local Communities   218
WILLIAM SPINRAD

The Corporation: How Much Power? What Scope?   231
CARL KAYSEN

Contents

On the Concept of Political Power   240
TALCOTT PARSONS

Patterns of Status

"Who's Who in America" and "The Social Register": Elite and Upper Class Indexes in Metropolitan America   266
E. DIGBY BALTZELL

The Middle Classes in Middle-Sized Cities   275
C. WRIGHT MILLS

Local Industrial Structures, Economic Power, and Community Welfare   282
IRVING FOWLER

The Disreputable Poor   289
DAVID MATZA

The Degree of Status Incongruence and Its Effects   303
ANDRZEJ MALEWSKI

Occupational Prestige

A Comparative Study of Occupational Prestige   309
ROBERT W. HODGE, DONALD J. TREIMAN, and PETER H. ROSSI

Occupational Prestige in the United States: 1925–1963   322
ROBERT W. HODGE, PAUL M. SIEGEL, and PETER H. ROSSI

Race and Class

Residential Segregation of Social Classes and Aspirations of High School Boys   335
ALAN B. WILSON

The Position of the Jews in English Society   342
HOWARD BROTZ

IV Differential Class Behavior

Population

Trends in Class Fertility in Western Nations   353
DENNIS H. WRONG

Family

Socialization and Social Class through Time and Space   362
URIE BRONFENBRENNER

Marital Satisfaction and Instability: A Cross-Cultural Class Analysis of Divorce Rates   377
WILLIAM J. GOODE

Religion

Social Class, Religious Affiliation, and Styles of Religious Involvement   388
N. J. DEMERATH III

Roman Catholic Sainthood and Social Status   394
KATHERINE and CHARLES H. GEORGE

Fashion

A Note on the "Trickle Effect"   402
    LLOYD A. FALLERS

Physical and Mental Illness

Social Class and the Experience of Ill Health   406
    CHARLES KADUSHIN

Political Attitudes and Behavior

Elections: The Expression of the Democratic Class Struggle   413
    SEYMOUR MARTIN LIPSET

The Appeal of Communism to the Peoples of Underdeveloped Areas   428
    MORRIS WATNICK

Education

The Second Transformation of American Secondary Education   437
    MARTIN TROW

Modes of Social Ascent through Education   449
    RALPH H. TURNER

The Growth of the Professions and the Class System   459
    JOSEPH BEN-DAVID

The Social Psychology of Job and Class

Work Satisfaction and Industrial Trends in Modern Society   473
    ROBERT BLAUNER

The Value Systems of Different Classes   488
    HERBERT H. HYMAN

V   Social Mobility

Structural Trends and Value Premises in the United States

The "Rags to Riches Story": An Episode of Secular Idealism   501
    R. RICHARD WOHL

Where Do You Fit in the Income Picture?   506
    HERMAN P. MILLER

Reference Group Theory and Social Mobility   510
    ROBERT K. MERTON and ALICE KITT ROSSI

Structural Trends and Value Premises in Communist Countries

Social Stratification and Mobility in the Soviet Union   516
    ALEX INKELES

Toward the Classless Society?   527
    ROBERT A. FELDMESSER

Economic Growth, Social Structure, Élite Formation: The Case of Poland 534
    ZYGMUNT BAUMAN

Contents

Structural Trends and Value Premises in Asian Countries

The Middle Classes in Japan   541
KUNIO ODAKA

A Note on Sanskritization and Westernization   552
M. N. SRINIVAS

Vertical Mobility

A Theory of Social Mobility   561
SEYMOUR MARTIN LIPSET and HANS L. ZETTERBERG

Intra-Country Variations: Occupational Stratification and Mobility   574
THOMAS FOX and S. M. MILLER

Family and Mobility   582
WILLIAM J. GOODE

Class and Mobility in a Nineteenth-Century City: A Study of Unskilled Laborers   602
STEPHAN THARNSTROM

VI Pending Issues

The Other America: Definitions   617
MICHAEL HARRINGTON

What's Happening to Our Social Revolution?   623
HERMAN P. MILLER

The Problem of Group Membership: Some Reflections on the Judicial View of Indian Society   628
MARC GALANTER

Social Selection in the Welfare State   640
T. H. MARSHALL

Social Stratification in Industrial Society   648
J. H. GOLDTHORPE

List of Some Contributors as of 1965–66   661
Name Index   663
Subject Index   671

INTRODUCTION

THE FIRST EDITION of this *Reader* was published in 1953. At that time no comprehensive treatment of social stratification was available, though there was considerable writing and research on the subject. Our sampling of that literature has been well received: the *Reader* has been reprinted nine times. During the last twelve years the study of stratification has burgeoned, and several textbooks on social stratification have appeared which attempt to treat the subject more or less systematically, as we had not. The decision to bring out a second edition would be justified only if substantial grounds exist for a major shift of emphasis in this field of study. We believe such grounds exist in the growth of comparative studies, which constitutes a major reorientation in American sociology. Whatever its accomplishments or deficiencies, before World War II American sociology had a parochial orientation. Its mainstay was the empirical study of American society. At the beginning of the 1950's, when the earlier edition was prepared, one could find large numbers of studies dealing with almost every aspect of behavior in the United States. No other society had ever been subjected to such detailed examination. To be sure, there had been interesting beginnings of empirical research in Germany, Italy, Poland, and Japan, but totalitarian regimes prevented further developments in this direction. In Great Britain sociology still appeared suspect, politically or culturally, and had no academic base outside the Fabian premises of the London School of Economics and a few "red brick" universities. In the Commonwealth, universities in Australia and New Zealand followed the lead of Oxford and Cambridge by resisting the blandishments of sociology. Even Canada, though linked in many ways with American university life, had only a limited development of sociological studies at Toronto, McGill and Laval. In France, the homeland of Emile Durkheim and his school, sociology was almost as little favored as in Britain. There were few chairs in the field and empirical studies were rare. South of the Rio Grande, there have been many sociologists teaching in the universities in the grand style of nineteenth-century social philosophy, but few empirically oriented sociologists in the American manner. And outside the world of Western civilization the study of society was typically the province of the anthropologist, whose field studies in depth concerned a tribe or village rather than problems of the "national" social structure.

Much has changed since this broad characterization applied more than a decade ago. In the United States World War II brought about a major shift of emphasis. In the course of the war and its aftermath millions of Americans went abroad, apparently acquiring an awareness of American involvements overseas which differs markedly from the effects of military service on the Continent in World War I. During the war language schools of the armed services provided linguistic training for a whole generation of American scholars, who used that training subsequently in their academic careers. Government agencies and private foundations recognized a national interest in the study of foreign cultures in view of America's new international obligations. Philanthropic and intellectual interests in non-Western cultures developed apace. As a result, there are today few major American academic institutions which fail to cultivate these new endeavors. While the majority of North American sociologists certainly continue their preoccupation with the study of American society, they now have an increasing number of colleagues who spend considerable time abroad and specialize in foreign-area studies of some kind.

The shift of emphasis in American sociology has been accompanied in the 1950's and 1960's by a sudden burgeoning of the discipline in other countries. In Britain, several appointments in sociology have been made at Oxford and Cambridge, as well as at most other universities. And as new universities are planned, programs in sociology have become a regular part of these plans. In France, the national government undertook the support of sociological research institutes on the same basis as research institutes in the natural sciences. The Centre d'Étude Sociologique in Paris employs over 70 full-time senior scholars on government salary. Other institutes concentrate on industrial sociology, rural sociology and the sociology of education. In Germany, several universities offer separate degree programs in sociology, and the number of research institutes in sociology is increasing. All the Scandinavian universities sponsor programs in sociology, and some of them also have special research institutes. Also, in the countries of the Commonwealth, earlier restrictions have been abandoned. Most Canadian universities now have sociology departments, Australia is moving in the same direction, as are newer members of the Commonwealth. Japanese sociologists are now second only to their American colleagues in number, and many are engaged in empirical studies of Japanese society, applying concepts and theories which are also used by sociologists in other countries. Even in Latin America, where the interest in social philosophy continues to be strong, there is nevertheless an increasing number of empirically oriented scholars, who study their own society and extend the range of comparative research by their use of theories or hypotheses also employed by their colleagues abroad.

If these developments indicate a growing interest, where little interest existed before, the most marked departure from previous practice has certainly occurred in the Communist countries, where until recently sociology was denounced as a "bourgeois science" furthering imperialism. The most significant change has occurred in Poland, which had had a rich sociological tradition. Since the end of the Stalinist period in 1956, sociology has developed rapidly. At the University of Warsaw five chairs have been established in this field, and many young scholars are attached to each of them; within the Academy of Science, considerable sociological work is under way. A number of sociological research units have also been established in various government ministries. A national opinion survey organization, attached to the State Radio, is available to scholars for their own work. Sociology has expanded rapidly in Yugoslavia as well, both within the universities and in institutes supported by the government. In Poland and in Yugoslavia many empirical studies of stratification have been published, dealing, among other things, with mobility, occupational status, and the relations between status-position and patterns of behavior or attitudes. In other Communist countries sociological investigations are less developed, although some beginning has been made in most — except for China and its satellites. In the Soviet Union research units have been established to deal with industrial sociology, education, and criminology, and in some Russian universities there are courses in which the writings of Western sociologists are discussed.

This record of expansion has brought with it a curious reversal, although its extent should not be exaggerated. Outside the United States, the empirical study of society is a relatively novel undertaking — despite some earlier developments in this direction as in England, Japan, Poland, Germany, France and elsewhere. Accordingly, the recent burgeoning of interest in such studies gives the impression that for a time scholars in these countries are catching up with their American colleagues — especially with regard to techniques of research. At the same time American sociologists are becoming preoccupied — for some of the reasons cited earlier — with the generalizability of findings based on studies of American society. For example, linkages between class position and religious practice vary with the character of religion in different societies, and cannot be understood as invariant relationships on the basis of the American experience. Again, some relations between class position and attitudes found in American society with its relatively flexible pattern of status-distinctions are reversed in some parts of Europe with their more rigidly defined status differences. Then again American sociologists are developing a greater historical and comparative awareness which their foreign colleagues have previously found wanting in studies devoted to the here and now. Correlations between class position and birthrate or illness, which existed at earlier periods of American history, no longer hold true in a period of affluence, but do apply now in poorer and less economically developed countries. The comparative perspective has also challenged previously held assumptions concerning differences between societies. Studies in over a dozen countries have shown that the prestige of occupations tends to be ranked in a similar order — irrespective of different levels of economic development. Related studies have shown also that the idea of the United States as a uniquely "open" society in terms of its opportunities for upward social mobility is false. If mobility is assessed in terms of comparing the occupational status of parents and children, then every society studied so far appears to have significant minorities of offspring whose status is higher or lower than that of their parents. As a result of such findings, as well as the changed climate of opinion mentioned before, American sociology has shed its earlier, parochial orientation. This second edition of the *Reader* is meant to reflect and encourage the shift of emphasis.

But as an increasing number of American scholars devote themselves to comparative research with an historical dimension, they also face unaccustomed methodological problems. In what sense are phenomena in different societies comparable? Can concepts of social stratification be "exported" across national or linguistic or cultural lines? Even abstract, analytic categories remain culture-bound and time-bound to an extent. For example, the proper translation of the German word *Stand* is estate, and the original meaning of the term was that status-differences between persons were legally defined, so that changes in status required legal sanction. Accordingly, where differences in social rank no longer have such a legal basis, the term "status" seems more appropriate, but it is so general as to be applicable to "estate-societies" as well. Similarly, the concept of "class" may not be generally applicable, even aside from its intrinsic ambiguities. Some Africans, for example, insist that many African languages do not possess concepts of stratification such as those familiar to us. This may be related to the fact that in many societies bonds of kinship, religion, language, race, locality and tradition are major sources of personal and social identity which overshadow in importance differences in wealth or occupation. In the past such bonds have played a major role in European societies as well, they are frequently relevant today, but there is a sense in which their appeal has become attenuated so that ties based on economic interest, prestige and civic loyalty have become relatively more important. Thus, while social differentiation occurs in all societies, its incidence varies with time and place in terms of the bonds which provide the most significant bases for group-action.

The difficulties of conceptualization just referred to are compounded by the fact that social scientists cannot easily avoid concepts current in general discourses. Terms like state, nation, class, status and others must be defined abstractly, in order to become generally applicable. Yet social scientists must also take account of the ways in which these concepts are understood in everyday life, since such understandings are themselves determinants of behavior of men in society. The two imperatives are perhaps not fully reconcilable. To operationalize concepts for purposes of comparative study calls for highly abstract formulations; in sociology neologisms are created so frequently because they provide universally applicable definitions. But such definitions are pointless unless they are useful analytically and this utility is impaired, if in the process of defining terms we ignore their meaning in everyday life and the variations of these meanings in different social contexts. Social scientists thus tread an uneasy path between the construction of generally applicable concepts and the use of everyday terms in scientific discourse, frequently turning from one level to the other in order to minimize the twin dilemmas of excessive abstraction or empiricism.[1]

As long as American sociology worked primarily at an empirical level within a single culture, it could operate with common-sense concepts and hence at low levels of abstraction. But in comparative studies this is more difficult to do and less satisfactory. At a minimum, cross-national research requires concepts which can subsume descriptive materials and common-sense ideas in two or more societies. For example, status-discrepancy or incongruity is a useful concept, because it is a very general, if not universal experience that men in society are ranked in terms of prestige, economic achievements or possessions, political office, educational attainments and many others, but that any one individual (or groups of individuals) may rank high on one dimension and relatively low on another. The concept thus provides a perspective applicable to many societies, but to be useful it must be combined with a study of the particulars. While status-discrepancies have been found to provide important clues for the understanding of collective behavior, societies vary both in the rank-orders and the status-discrepancies that characterize them. In the United States variations between educational and occupational attainments are a major source of status-discrepancy, while in Germany, for example, this is much less the case, since most of those whose occupational attainments are high also rank high educationally. Thus, any hypothesis which would predict consequences from the observation of status-discrepancies, must first specify the context or structure to which it will be applied.

Comparative studies in sociology have received their greatest impetus perhaps from the change of the world-political scene since World War II. This second edition of the *Reader* reflects the change by its emphasis on comparative and historical materials along with the retention of studies of stratification in American society. We recognize, of course, that many readers of the book will be concerned primarily with understanding their own society. We believe, however, that a comparative approach will contribute to their liberal education as well as enhance that understanding. Social processes and institutions in one country should be compared and contrasted with similar processes and institutions in other countries. By common consent Alexis de Tocqueville's *Democracy in America* is one of the greatest works written on

[1] Titles of books are not the place to resolve difficulties of conceptualization and we have decided to retain our original title in this second edition. But we are uncomfortably aware that in choosing it originally we were swayed by its euphonious appeal and failed to pay attention to the fact that classes and status-groups are themselves bases of aggregations of power.

the United States, yet in a letter to a friend Tocqueville says that he had not written a page without thinking about France. Similarly, if one wishes to understand the American stress on equalitarianism and opportunity, one can achieve more insight and perspective, if one also knows something of the way in which other cultures treat such orientation. It has been pointed out, for example, that American culture strongly emphasizes equalitarian standards and individual achievement, but that nevertheless preferential treatment and family influence play an important role in politics, industry and education. One may compare this setting with Japan, where all personal relations tend to involve socially prescribed and well-defined obligations, while admission to the universities and entrance upon a business or government career is fiercely competitive and largely based on individual merit. Japan as well as the United States has achieved a high degree of industrialization which is greatly facilitated by a stress on individual achievement. Comparison gives us a better insight into both societies. In American society the great general stress on achievement is not jeopardized by preferential treatment in particular situations, while in Japanese society the general stress on personal and familial obligations is so great that the most rigidly objective methods of selection are employed at certain points, in order to achieve a high level of performance. In this way, a comparative frame of reference sensitizes us to the balancing of conflicting imperatives, which is an important attribute of the social structure, at the same time that it facilitates our assessment of differential national patterns of behavior. And accordingly we believe that this edition, though containing less material on American society than the previous one, provides a better introduction to the study of American stratification.

Since this new edition reflects the impact of historical change upon the intellectual perspectives of American sociology, it may not be amiss to comment briefly on the record of past and the possibility of further reorientations — with special reference to the study of social stratification. During much of the nineteenth century that study was part and parcel of the struggle for human rights and economic well-being which accompanied the growth of industrial societies in Europe. One major objective of that struggle was the extension of the franchise, and the early achievement of a universal franchise in the United States may have been one reason why the concern with social stratification was less intense in America than in Europe. The burgeoning of interest in sociological studies of stratification up to the 1940's still reflects the earlier concerns and especially the influence of Marxist theory, but its dominant emphasis seems to be a preoccupation with inequality in a modern welfare-state. Proximate as this thematic characterization must remain here, it is noteworthy that the new emphasis on comparative studies during the past decade reflects international happenings in addition to national concerns. It is quite possible that events abroad will prompt still further reorientations in the years to come. We noted earlier that in the so-called developing nations of the world groups based on lineage, religion, language, race, locality and tradition are more significant than social classes. And we would add here that in the great ideological conflict between Soviet Russia and China, the Russians are still adhering to the old vocabulary of the class-struggle between capitalists and the proletariat, while the Chinese are speaking of the unity between all classes of the population in their common struggle against Western imperialism. In recent years studies have been published dealing with "international stratification" between rich and poor countries, rather than the stratification with societies. Perhaps, ten years hence, a third edition may become appropriate, in which the study of stratification will be reoriented further to take account of the increasing degree to which the social differentiation of societies has become an object of political manipulations, both within social structures and in international relations. Scholars can seek to understand and even anticipate such changes, but the record to date does not encourage the view that they can keep pace with the rapid transformations of modern society.

In the Introduction to the earlier edition we pointed out that a book such as this must omit more material than it can include. The rapid rate of publication during the past fifteen years has made the task of selection even more difficult. The desire to obtain a certain coverage of various sub-fields has necessitated the omission of many excellent studies for reasons of space. But a *Reader* is an introduction, not an Encyclopedia. If our readers are led to look for further materials into the many journals and books now published in sociology, we will feel that we have done our job, even if the judgment should be in a number of instances that other writings would have been as worthy or more worthy of inclusion. One purpose has been to provide a representative sampling of the best literature in this field.

While this volume was in preparation, both editors pursued comparative studies of their own, adding their bit to the new mobility of the academic profession but detracting somewhat from the attention needed for stylistic details. Small inconsistencies in the footnotes, some over-sights concerning publications which have appeared since the original appearance of the material reprinted here, and some lapses in cross-referencing the articles of this volume have been the result. We are indebted to the editorial work of Mrs. Barbara Busch of The Free Press for keeping these blemishes to a minimum, and those that remain are outweighed by the fact that in this second edition the footnotes appear on each page rather than at the end of the volume.

We want to express our sincere appreciation to Richard Roman, Charles Leinenweber, and Eliezer Rosenstein for helping us with the many intellectual and editorial tasks involved in preparing this second edition. We are also grateful to the Institute of International Studies of the University of California, Berkeley, for valuable assistance.

Reinhard Bendix
Seymour Martin Lipset

Berkeley, California

CLASS, STATUS, *and* POWER

Second Edition

One

Theories of Class Structure

A Classical View

Aristotle

NOW IN ALL STATES there are three elements: one class is very rich, another very poor, and a third is a mean. It is admitted that moderation and the mean are best, and therefore it will clearly be best to possess the gifts of fortune in moderation; for in that condition of life men are most ready to follow rational principle. But he who greatly excels in beauty, strength, birth, or wealth, or on the other hand who is very poor, or very weak, or very much disgraced, finds it difficult to follow rational principle. Of these two the one sort grow into violent and great criminals, the others into rogues and petty rascals. And two sorts of offences correspond to them, the one committed from violence, the other from roguery. Again, the middle class is least likely to shrink from rule, or to be over-ambitious for it; both of which are injuries to the state. Again, those who have too much of the goods of fortune, strength, wealth, friends, and the like, are neither willing nor able to submit to authority. The evil begins at home; for when they are boys, by reason of the luxury in which they are brought up, they never learn, even at school, the habit of obedience. On the other hand, the very poor, who are in the opposite extreme, are too degraded. So that the one class cannot obey, and can only rule despotically; the other knows not how to command and must be ruled like slaves. Thus arises a city, not of freemen, but of masters and slaves, the one despising, the other envying; and nothing can be more fatal to friendship and good fellowship in states than this: for good fellowship springs from friendship; when men are at enmity with one another, they would rather not even share the same path. But a city ought to be composed, as far as possible, of equals and similars; and these are generally the middle classes. Wherefore the city which is composed of middle-class citizens is necessarily best constituted in respect of the elements of which we say the fabric of the state naturally consists. And this is the class of citizens which is most secure in a state, for they do not, like the poor, covet their neighbours' goods; nor do others covet theirs, as the poor covet the goods of the rich; and as they neither plot against others, nor are themselves plotted against, they pass through life safely. Wisely then did Phocylides pray — "Many things are best in the mean; I desire to be of a middle condition in my city."

Thus it is manifest that the best political community is formed by citizens of the middle class, and that those states are likely to be well-administered, in which the middle class is large, and stronger if possible than both the other classes, or at any rate than either singly; for the addition of the middle class turns the scale, and prevents either of the extremes from being dominant. Great then is the good fortune of a state in which the citizens have a moderate and sufficient property; for where some possess much, and the others nothing, there may arise an extreme — either out of the most rampant democracy, or out of an oligarchy; but it is not so likely to arise out of the middle constitutions and those akin to them. I will explain the reason of this hereafter, when I speak of the revolutions of states. The mean condition of states is clearly best, for no other is free from faction; and where the middle class is large, there are least likely to be factions and dissensions. For a similar reason large states are less liable to faction than small ones, because in them the middle class is large; whereas in small states it is easy to divide all the citizens into two classes who are either rich or poor, and to leave nothing in the middle. And democracies are safer and more permanent than oligarchies, because they have a middle class which is more numerous and has a greater share in the government; for when there is no middle

Reprinted from Aristotle, *Politics*, tr. by Benjamin Jowett (New York: Modern Library, 1943), pp. 190–193.

class, and the poor greatly exceed in number, troubles arise, and the state soon comes to an end. A proof of the superiority of the middle class is that the best legislators have been of a middle condition; for an example, Solon, as his own verses testify; and Lycurgus, for he was not a king; and Charondas, and almost all legislators.

These considerations will help us to understand why most governments are either democratical or oligarchical. The reason is that the middle class is seldom numerous in them, and whichever party, whether the rich or the common people, transgresses the mean and predominates, draws the constitution its own way, and thus arises either oligarchy or democracy. There is another reason — the poor and the rich quarrel with one another, and whichever side gets the better, instead of establishing a just or popular government, regards political supremacy as the prize of victory, and the one party sets up a democracy and the other an oligarchy. Further, both the parties which had the supremacy in Hellas looked only to the interest of their own form of government, and established in states, the one, democracies, and the other, oligarchies; they thought of their own advantage, of the public not at all. For these reasons the middle form of government has rarely, if ever, existed, and among a very few only. One man alone of all who ever ruled in Hellas was induced to give this middle constitution to states. But it has now become a habit among the citizens of states, not ever to care about equality; all men are seeking for dominion, or if conquered, are willing to submit.

Factions in American Society

The Federalist

To the People of the State of New York:
Among the numerous advantages promised by a well-constructed Union, none deserves to be more accurately developed than its tendency to break and control the violence of faction. The friend of popular governments never finds himself so much alarmed for their character and fate, as when he contemplates their propensity to this dangerous vice. He will not fail, therefore, to set a due value on any plan which, without violating the principles to which he is attached, provides a proper cure for it. The instability, injustice, and confusion introduced into the public councils, have, in truth, been the mortal diseases under which popular governments have everywhere perished; as they continue to be the favorite and fruitful topics from which the adversaries to liberty derive their most specious declamations. The valuable improvements made by the American constitutions on the popular models, both ancient and modern, cannot certainly be too much admired; but it would be an unwarrantable partiality, to contend that they have as effectually obviated the danger on this side, as was wished and expected. Complaints are everywhere heard from our most considerate and virtuous citizens, equally the friends of public and private faith, and of public and personal liberty, that our governments are too unstable, that the public good is disregarded in the conflicts of rival parties, and that measures are too often decided, not according to the rules of justice and the rights of the minor party, but by the superior force of an interested and overbearing majority. However anxiously we may wish that these complaints had no foundation, the evidence of known facts will not permit us to deny that they are in some degree true. It will be found, indeed, on a candid review of our situation, that some of the distresses under which we labor have been erroneously charged on the operation of our governments; but it will be found, at the same time, that other causes will not alone account for many of our heaviest misfortunes; and, particularly, for that prevailing and increasing distrust of public engagements, and alarm for private rights, which are echoed from one end of the continent to the other. These must be chiefly, if not wholly, effects of the unsteadiness and injustice with which a factious spirit has tainted our public administrations.

By a faction, I understand a number of citizens, whether amounting to a majority or minority of the whole, who are united and actuated by some common impulse of passion, or of interest, adverse to the rights of other citizens, or to the permanent and aggregate interests of the community.

There are two methods of curing the mischiefs of faction: the one, by removing its causes; the other, by controlling its effects.

There are again two methods of removing the causes of faction: the one, by destroying the liberty which is essential to its existence; the other, by giving to every citizen the same opinions, the same passions, and the same interests.

Reprinted from *The Federalist* (New York: Modern Library, n.d.), pp. 53–62.

It could never be more truly said than of the first remedy, that it was worse than the disease. Liberty is to faction what air is to fire, an ailment without which it instantly expires. But it could not be less folly to abolish liberty, which is essential to political life, because it nourishes faction, than it would be to wish the annihilation of air, which is essential to animal life, because it imparts to fire its destructive agency.

The second expedient is as impracticable as the first would be unwise. As long as the reason of man continues fallible, and he is at liberty to exercise it, different opinions will be formed. As long as the connection subsists between his reason and his self-love, his opinions and his passions will have a reciprocal influence on each other; and the former will be objects to which the latter will attach themselves. The diversity in the faculties of men, from which the rights of property originate, is not less an insuperable obstacle to a uniformity of interests. The protection of these faculties is the first object of government. From the protection of different and unequal faculties of acquiring property, the possession of different degrees and kinds of property immediately results; and from the influence of these on the sentiments and views of the respective proprietors, ensues a division of the society into different interests and parties.

The latent causes of faction are thus sown in the nature of man; and we see them everywhere brought into different degrees of activity, according to the different circumstances of civil society. A zeal for different opinions concerning religion, concerning government, and many other points, as well of speculation as of practice; an attachment to different leaders ambitiously contending for pre-eminence and power; or to persons of other descriptions whose fortunes have been interesting to the human passions, have, in turn, divided mankind into parties, inflamed them with mutual animosity, and rendered them much more disposed to vex and oppress each other than to co-operate for their common good. So strong is this propensity of mankind to fall into mutual animosities, that where no substantial occasion presents itself, the most frivolous and fanciful distinctions have been sufficient to kindle their unfriendly passions and excite their most violent conflicts. But the most common and durable source of factions has been the various and unequal distribution of property. Those who hold and those who are without property have ever formed distinct interests in society. Those who are creditors, and those who are debtors, fall under a like discrimination. A landed interest, a manufacturing interest, a mercantile interest, a moneyed interest, with many lesser interests, grow up of necessity in civilized nations, and divide them into different classes, actuated by different sentiments and views. The regulation of these various and interfering interests forms the principal task of modern legislation, and involves the spirit of party and faction in the necessary and ordinary operations of the government.

No man is allowed to be a judge in his own cause, because his interest would certainly bias his judgment, and, not improbably, corrupt his integrity. With equal, nay with greater reason, a body of men are unfit to be both judges and parties at the same time; yet what are many of the most important acts of legislation, but so many judicial determinations, not indeed concerning the rights of single persons, but concerning the rights of large bodies of citizens? And what are the different classes of legislators but advocates and parties to the causes which they determine? Is a law proposed concerning private debts? It is a question to which the creditors are parties on one side and the debtors on the other. Justice ought to hold the balance between them. Yet the parties are, and must be, themselves the judges; and the most numerous party, or, in other words, the most powerful faction must be expected to prevail. Shall domestic manufactures be encouraged, and in what degree, by restrictions on foreign manufacturers? are questions which would be differently decided by the landed and the manufacturing classes, and probably by neither with a sole regard to justice and the public good. The appointment of taxes on the various descriptions of property is an act which seems to require the most exact impartiality; yet there is, perhaps, no legislative act in which greater opportunity and temptation are given to a predominant party to trample on the rules of justice. Every shilling with which they overburden the inferior number, is a shilling saved to their own pockets.

It is in vain to say that enlightened statesmen will be able to adjust these clashing interests, and render them all subservient to the public good. Enlightened statesmen will not always be at the helm. Nor, in many cases, can such an adjustment be made at all without taking into view indirect and remote considerations, which will rarely prevail over the immediate interest which one party may find in disregarding the rights of another or the good of the whole.

The inference to which we are brought is, that the *causes* of faction cannot be removed, and that relief is only to be sought in the means of controlling its *effects*.

If a faction consists of less than a majority, relief is supplied by the republican principle, which enables the majority to defeat its sinister views by regular vote. It may clog the administration, it may convulse the society; but it will be unable to execute and mask its violence under the forms of the Constitution. When a majority is included in a faction, the form of popular government, on the other hand, enables it to sacrifice to its ruling passion or interest both the public good and the rights of other citizens. To secure the public good and private rights against the danger of such a faction, and at the same time to preserve the spirit and the form of popular government, is then the great object to which our inquiries are directed. Let me add that it is the great desideratum by which this form of government can be rescued from the opprobrium under which it has so long labored, and be recommended to the esteem and adoption of mankind.

By what means is this object attainable? Evidently by one of two only. Either the existence of the same passion or interest in a majority at the same time must be prevented, or the majority, having such coexistent passion or interest, must be rendered, by their number and local situation, unable to concert and carry into effect schemes of oppression. If the impulse and the opportunity be suffered to coincide, we well know that neither moral nor religious motives can be relied on as an adequate control. They are not found to be such on the injustice and violence of individuals, and lose their efficacy in proportion to the number combined together, that is, in proportion as their efficacy becomes needful.

From this view of the subject it may be concluded that a pure democracy, by which I mean a society consisting of a small number of citizens, who assemble and administer the government in person, can admit of no cure for the mischiefs of faction. A common passion or interest will, in almost every case, be felt by a majority of the whole; a communication and concert result from the form of government itself; and there is nothing to check the inducements to sacrifice the weaker party or an obnoxious individual. Hence it is that such democracies have ever been spectacles of turbulence and contention; have ever been found incompatible with personal security or the rights of property; and have in general been as short in their lives as they have been violent in their deaths. Theoretic politicians, who have patronized this species of government, have erroneously supposed that by reducing mankind to a perfect equality in their political rights, they would, at the same time, be perfectly equalized and assimilated in their possessions, their opinions, and their passions.

A republic, by which I mean a government in which the scheme of representation takes place, opens a different prospect, and promises the cure for which we are seeking. Let us examine the points in which it varies from pure democracy, and we shall comprehend both the nature of the cure and the efficacy which it must derive from the Union.

The two great points of difference between a democracy and a republic are: first, the delegation of the government, in the latter, to a small number of citizens elected by the rest; secondly, the greater number of citizens, and greater sphere of country, over which the latter may be extended.

The effect of the first difference is, on the one hand, to refine and enlarge the public views, by passing them through the medium of a chosen body of citizens, whose wisdom may best discern the true interest of their country, and whose patriotism and love of justice will be least likely to sacrifice it to temporary or partial considerations. Under such a regulation, it may well happen that the public voice, pronounced by the representatives of the people, will be more consonant to the public good than if pronounced by the people themselves, convened for the purpose. On the other hand, the effect may be inverted. Men of factious tempers, of local prejudices, or of sinister designs, may, by intrigue, by corruption, or by other means, first obtain the suffrages, and then betray the interests, of the people. The question resulting is, whether small or extensive republics are more favorable to the election of proper guardians of the public weal; and it is clearly decided in favor of the latter by two obvious considerations.

In the first place, it is to be remarked that, however small the republic may be, the representatives must be raised to a certain number, in order to guard against the cabals of a few; and that, however large it may be, they must be limited to a certain number, in order to guard against the confusion of a multitude. Hence, the number of representatives in the two cases not being in proportion to that of the two constituents, and being proportionally greater in the small republic, it follows that, if the proportion of fit characters be not less in the large than in the small republic, the former will present a greater option, and consequently a greater probability of a fit choice.

In the next place, as each representative will be chosen by a greater number of citizens in the large than in the small republic, it will be more difficult for unworthy candidates to practice with success the vicious arts by which elections are too often carried; and the suffrages of the people being more free, will be more likely to centre in men who possess the most attractive merit and the most diffusive and established characters.

It must be confessed that in this, as in most other cases, there is a mean, on both sides of which inconveniences will be found to lie. By enlarging too much the number of electors, you render the representative too little acquainted with all their local circumstances and lesser interests; as by reducing it too much, you render him unduly attached to these, and too little fit to comprehend and pursue great and national objects. The federal Constitution forms a happy combination in this respect; the great and aggregate interests being referred to the national, the local and particular to the State legislatures.

The other point of difference is, the greater number of citizens and extent of territory which may be brought within the compass of republican than of democratic government; and it is this circumstance principally which renders factious combinations less to be dreaded in the former than in the latter. The smaller the society, the fewer probably will be the distinct parties and interests composing it; the fewer the distinct parties and interests, the more frequently will a majority be found of the same party; and the smaller the number of individuals composing a majority, and the smaller the compass within which they are placed, the more easily will they concert and execute their plans of oppression. Extend the sphere, and you take in a greater variety of parties and interests; you make it less probable that a majority of the whole will have a common motive to invade the rights of other citizens; or if such a common motive exists, it will be more difficult for all who feel it to discover their own strength, and to act in unison with each other. Besides other impediments, it may be remarked that, where there is a consciousness of unjust or dishonorable purposes, communication is always checked by distrust in proportion to the number whose concurrence is necessary.

Hence, it clearly appears, that the same advantage which a republic has over a democracy, in controlling the effects of faction, is enjoyed by a large over a small republic — is enjoyed by the Union over the States composing it. Does the advantage consist in the substitution of representatives whose enlightened views and virtuous sentiments render them superior to local prejudices and to schemes of injustice? It will not be denied that the representation of the Union will be most likely to possess these requisite endowments. Does it consist in the greater security afforded by a greater variety of parties, against the event of any one party being able to outnumber and oppress the rest? In an equal degree does the increased variety of parties comprised within the Union, increase this security. Does it, in fine, consist in the greater obstacles opposed to the concert and accomplishment of the secret wishes of an unjust and interested majority? Here, again, the extent of the Union gives it the most palpable advantage.

The influence of factious leaders may kindle a flame within their particular States, but will be unable to spread a general conflagration through the other States. A religious sect may degenerate into a political faction in a part of the Confederacy; but the variety of sects dispersed over the entire face of it must secure the national councils against any danger from that source. A rage for paper money, for an abolition of debts, for an equal division of property, or for any other improper or wicked project, will be less apt to pervade the whole body of the Union than a particular member of it; in the same proportion as such a malady is more likely to taint a particular country or district, than an entire State.

In the extent and proper structure of the Union, therefore, we hold a republican remedy for the diseases most incident to republican government. And according to the degree of pleasure and pride we feel in being republicans, ought to be our zeal in cherishing the spirit and supporting the character of Federalists.

A Note on Classes

Karl Marx

THE OWNERS merely of labour-power, owners of capital, and landowners, whose respective sources of income are wages, profit, and ground-rent, in other words, wage-labourers, capitalists, and land-owners, constitute the three big classes of modern society based upon the capitalist mode of production.

In England, modern society is indisputably most highly and classically developed in economic structure. Nevertheless, even here the stratification of classes does not appear in its pure form. Middle and intermediate strata even here obliterate lines of demarcation everywhere (although incomparably less in rural districts than in the cities). However, this is immaterial for our analysis. We have seen that the continual tendency and law of development of the capitalist mode of production is more and more to divorce the means of production from labour, and more and more to concentrate the scattered means of production into large groups, thereby transforming labour into wage-labour and the means of production into capital. And to this tendency, on the other hand, corresponds the independent separation of landed property from capital and labour,[1] or the transformation of all landed property into the form of landed property corresponding to the capitalist mode of production.

The first question to be answered is this: What constitutes a class?—and the reply to this follows naturally from the reply to another question, namely: What makes wage-labourers, capitalists, and landlords constitute the three great social classes?

At first glance—the identity of revenues and sources of revenue. There are three great social groups whose members, the individuals forming them, live on wages, profit, and ground-rent respectively, on the realization

[1] F. List remarks correctly: "The prevalence of a self-sufficient economy on large estates demonstrates solely the lack of civilization, means of communication, domestic trades and wealthy cities. It is to be encountered, therefore, throughout Russia, Poland, Hungary and Mecklenburg. Formerly, it was also prevalent in England; with the advance of trades and commerce, however, this was replaced by the breaking up into middle estates and the leasing of land." (*Die Ackerverfassung, die Zwergwirtschaft und die Auswanderung*, 1842, p. 10.)

Unfinished chapter from *Capital: A Critique of Political Economy*, Vol. III (Moscow: Foreign Languages Publishing House, 1962), pp. 862–863.

of their labour-power, their capital, and their landed property.

However, from this standpoint, physicians and officials, e.g., would also constitute two classes, for they belong to two distinct social groups, the members of each of these groups receiving their revenue from one and the same source. The same would also be true of the infinite fragmentation of interest and rank into which the division of social labour splits labourers as well as capitalists and landlords—the latter, e.g., into owners of vineyards, farm owners, owners of forests, mine owners, and owners of fisheries.

(HERE THE MANUSCRIPT BREAKS OFF.)

Karl Marx's Theory of Social Classes
Reinhard Bendix and Seymour Martin Lipset

KARL MARX'S THEORY of social classes was of great importance in his work and it has had a profound influence on modern social thought. Yet the writings of Marx, voluminous as they are, do not contain a coherent exposition of that theory. They contain, instead, many scattered fragments on this topic. We have tried to assemble some of these fragments; and by writing a commentary on this series of quotations we attempt to give a view of the theory as a whole. We should add that such a procedure neglects Marx's own intellectual development, for it treats as part of one theory ideas which he expressed at various times in his career. However, in the case of Marx's theory of social classes this difficulty is not a serious one in our judgment.

According to Marx history may be divided roughly into several periods, for example, ancient civilization, feudalism, and capitalism. Each of these periods is characterized by a predominant mode of production and, based upon it, a class structure consisting of a ruling and an oppressed class. The struggle between these classes determines the social relations between men. In particular, the ruling class, which owes its position to the ownership and control of the means of production, controls also, though often in subtle ways, the whole moral and intellectual life of the people. According to Marx, law and government, art and literature, science and philosophy: all serve more or less directly the interests of the ruling class.

In the period of its revolutionary ascendance each class is "progressive" in two senses of that word. Its economic interests are identical with technical progress and hence with increased human welfare. And its efforts to pursue these interests align this class on the side of liberating ideas and institutions and against all who retard technical progress and human welfare. But in time an ascending class may become a ruling class, such as the feudal lords or the capitalists, and then it comes to play a different role. Its economic interests, which originally favored technical progress, call for opposition to it when further change would endanger the economic dominance which it has won. Upon its emergence as a ruling class, it turns from a champion of progress into a champion of reaction. It resists increasingly the attempts to change the social and economic organization of society, which would allow a full measure of the progress that has become technically possible. Such changes would endanger the entrenched position of the ruling class. Hence, tensions and conflicts are engendered that eventually lead to a revolutionary reorganization of society.

. . . the means of production and of exchange, which served as the foundation for the growth of the bourgeoisie, were generated in feudal society. At a certain stage in the development of these means of production and of exchange, the conditions under which feudal society produced and exchanged, the feudal organization of agriculture and manufacturing industry, in a word, the feudal relations of property became no longer compatible with the already developed productive forces; they became so many fetters. They had to be burst asunder; they were burst asunder.

Into their place stepped free competition, accompanied by a social and political constitution adapted to it, and by the economic and political sway of the bourgeois class.

A similar movement is going on before our own eyes. Modern bourgeois society with its relations of production, of exchange, and of property, a society that has conjured up such gigantic means of production and of exchange, is like the sorcerer who is no longer able to control the powers of the nether world whom he has called up by his spells. For many a

---

This is an original article prepared for the first edition of *Class, Status and Power.*

decade past the history of industry and commerce is but the history of the revolt of modern productive forces against modern conditions of production, against the property relations that are the conditions for the existence of the bourgeoisie and its rule. It is enough to mention the commercial crises that by their periodical return put the existence of the entire bourgeois society on trial, each time more threateningly. In these crises a great part not only of the existing products, but also of the previously created productive forces, are periodically destroyed. In these crises there breaks out an epidemic that, in all earlier epochs, would have seemed an absurdity — the epidemic of overproduction. Society suddenly finds itself put back into a state of momentary barbarism; it appears as if a famine, a universal war of devastation had cut off the supply of every means of subsistence; industry and commerce seem to be destroyed. And why? Because there is too much civilization, too much means of subsistence, too much industry, too much commerce. The productive forces at the disposal of society no longer tend to further the development of the conditions of bourgeois property; on the contrary they have become too powerful for these conditions, by which they are fettered, and no sooner do they overcome these fetters than they bring disorder into the whole of bourgeois society, endanger the existence of bourgeois property. The conditions of bourgeois society are too narrow to comprise the wealth created by them. And how does the bourgeoisie get over these crises? On the one hand by enforced destruction of a mass of productive forces; on the other, by the conquest of new markets, and by the more thorough exploitation of the old one. That is to say, by paving the way for more extensive and more destructive crises, and diminishing the means whereby crises are prevented.

The weapons with which the bourgeoisie felled feudalism to the ground are now turned against the bourgeoisie itelf.

But not only has the bourgeoisie forged the weapons that bring death to itself; it has also called into existence the men who are to wield those weapons — the modern working class — the proletarians.[1]

This conception of class conflict and historical change lent itself to a dogmatic interpretation. In particular, the materialist conception of history was often used in a manner which implied that only technical and economic factors were *really* important and that the whole social, political and intellectual realm (what Marx called the "superstructure") was of secondary significance. In two letters, written in 1890, Friedrich Engels, the lifelong collaborator of Marx, opposed this "vulgar" interpretation:

Marx and I are ourselves partly to blame for the fact that the younger writers sometimes lay more stress on the economic side than is due it. We had to emphasize this main principle in opposition to our

adversaries, who denied it, and we had not always the time, the place or the opportunity to allow the other elements involved in the interaction to come into their own rights. . . .

. . . the materialist conception of history also has a lot of friends nowadays, to whom it serves as an excuse for *not* studying history. . . .

In general the word *materialistic* serves many of the younger writers in Germany as a mere phrase with which anything and everything is labelled without further study; they stick on this label and they think the question disposed of. But our conception of history is above all a guide to study, not a lever for construction after the manner of the Hegelians. All history must be studied afresh, the conditions of existence of the different formations of society must be individually examined before the attempt is made to deduce from them the political, civil-legal, aesthetic, philosophic, religious, etc., notions corresponding to them. . . .[2]

It is well to keep these reservations in mind. They suggest that Marx and Engels often felt compelled by the exigencies of the social and political struggle, to cast their ideas in extremely pointed formulations. Had they been scholars of the traditional type, they might have avoided at least some of the dogmatic interpretations of their work, though they would have had far less success in spreading their ideas and getting them accepted. Much of the difficulty in obtaining a concise view of Marxian theory stems from the fact that it was meant to be a tool for political action. In reviewing briefly Marx's theory of history and his theory of social class, we shall at first disregard this political implication. We shall consider this implication more directly in the concluding paragraphs of this essay.

A social class in Marx's terms is any aggregate of persons who perform the same function in the organization of production. "Freeman and slave, patrician and plebeian, lord and serf, guild-master and journeyman, in a word, oppressor and oppressed" (Communist Manifesto) are the names of social classes in different historical periods. These classes are distinguished from each other by the difference of their respective positions in the economy. Since a social class is constituted by the function, which its members perform in the process of production, the question arises why the organization of production is the basic determinant of social class. Marx's answer is contained in his early writings on philosophy, especially in his theory of the division of labor.

Fundamental to this theory is Marx's belief that work is man's basic form of self-realization. Man cannot live without work; hence the way in which man works in society is a clue to human nature. Man provides for his subsistence by the use of tools; these facilitate his labor

[1] Karl Marx and Friedrich Engels, *Manifesto of the Communist Party* (New York: International Publishers, 1932), 14-15.
[2] Karl Marx and Friedrich Engels, *Selected Correspondence, 1846-1894* (New York: International Publishers, 1942), 477, 472-473.

and make it more productive. He has, therefore, an interest in, and he has also a capacity for, elaborating and refining these tools, and in so doing he expresses himself, controls nature and makes history. *If human labor makes history*, then an understanding of the conditions of production is essential for an understanding of history. There are four aspects of production, according to Marx, which explain why man's efforts to provide for his subsistence underlie all change in history.

a) "... life involves before everything else eating, and drinking, a habitation, clothing and many other things. The first historical act is thus the production of the means to satisfy these needs, the production of material life itself."[1]

b) "The second fundamental point is that as soon as a need is satisfied (which implies the action of satisfying, and the acquisition of an instrument), new needs are made."[2]

c) "The third circumstance which, from the very first, enters into historical development, is that men, who daily remake their own life, begin to make other men, to propagate their kind: the relation between man and wife, parents and children, the FAMILY. The family which to begin with is the only social relationship, becomes later, when increased needs create new social relations and the increased population (creates) new needs, a subordinate one...."[3]

d) "The production of life, both of one's own in labor and of fresh life in procreation, now appears as a double relationship: on the one hand as a natural, on the other as a social relationship. By social we understand the cooperation of several individuals, no matter under what conditions, in what manner and to what end. It follows from this that a certain mode of production, or industrial stage, is always combined with a certain mode of cooperation, or social stage, and this mode of cooperation is itself a 'productive force.' Further, that the multitude of productive forces accessible to men determines the nature of society, hence that the 'history of humanity' must always be studied and treated in relation to the history of industry and exchange."[4]

There is a logical connection between these four aspects. The satisfaction of man's basic needs makes work a fundamental fact of human life, but it also creates new needs. The more needs are created the more important is it that the "instruments" of production be improved. The more needs are created and the more the technique of production is improved, the more important is it that men cooperate, first within the family, then also outside it. Cooperation implies the division of labor and the organization of production (or in Marx's phrase "the mode of cooperation" as a "productive force") over and above the techniques of production

which are employed. It is, therefore, the position which the individual occupies in the social organization of production, that indicates to which social class he belongs. The fundamental determinant of class is the way in which the individual cooperates with others in the satisfaction of his basic needs of food, clothing, and shelter. Other indexes such as income, consumption patterns, educational attainment, or occupation are so many clues to the distribution of material goods and of prestige-symbols. This distribution is a more or less revealing consequence of the organization of production; it is not identical with it. Hence, the income or occupation of an individual is *not*, according to Marx, an indication of his class-position, i.e., of his position in the production process. For example, if two men are carpenters, they belong to the same occupation, but one may run a small shop of his own, while another works in a plant manufacturing pre-fabricated housing; the two men belong to the same occupation, but to different social classes.

Marx believed that a man's position in the production process provided the crucial life experience, which would determine, either now or eventually, the beliefs and the actions of that individual. The experience gained in the effort of making a living, but especially the experience of economic conflict, would prompt the members of a social class to develop common beliefs and common actions. In analyzing the emergence of these beliefs and actions Marx specified a number of variables which would facilitate this process:

1) Conflicts over the distribution of economic rewards between the classes;

2) Easy communication between the individuals in the same class-position so that ideas and action-programs are readily disseminated;

3) Growth of class-consciousness in the sense that the members of the class have a feeling of solidarity and understanding of their historic role;

4) Profound dissatisfaction of the lower class over its inability to control the economic structure of which it feels itself to be the exploited victim;

5) Establishment of a political organization resulting from the economic structure, the historical situation and maturation of class-consciousness.

Thus, the organization of production provides the necessary but not a sufficient basis for the existence of social classes. Repeated conflicts over economic rewards, ready communication of ideas between members of a class, the growth of class-consciousness, and the growing dissatisfaction with exploitation which causes suffering in psychological as much as in material terms: these are the conditions which will help to overcome the differences and conflicts between individuals and groups within the class and which will encourage the formation of a class-conscious political organization.

Marx's discussions of the development of the bourgeoisie and of the proletariat give good illustrations of the manner in which he envisages the emergence of a social class.

---

[1] Karl Marx and Friedrich Engels, *The German Ideology* (New York: International Publishers, 1939), 16.

[2] *Ibid.*, 16–17.

[3] Marx and Engels, *loc. cit.*

[4] *Ibid.*, 18.

In the Middle Ages the citizens in each town were compelled to unite against the landed nobility to save their skins. The extension of trade, the establishment of communications, led the separate towns to get to know other towns, which had asserted the same interests in the struggle with the same antagonist. Out of the many local corporations of burghers there arose only gradually the burgher *class*. The conditions of life of the individual burghers became, on account of their antagonism to the existing relationships and of the mode of labour determined by these conditions which were common to them all and independent of each individual. The burghers had created the conditions in so far as they had torn themselves free from feudal ties, and were created by them in so far as they were determined by their antagonism to the feudal system which they found in existence. When the individual towns began to enter into associations, these common conditions developed into class conditions. The same conditions, the same antagonism, the same interests necessarily called forth on the whole similar customs everywhere. The bourgeoisie itself, with its conditions, develops only gradually, splits according to the division of labour into various fractions and finally absorbs all earlier possessing classes (while it develops the majority of the earlier non-possessing, and a part of the earlier possessing, class into a new class, the proletariat) in the measure to which all earlier property is transformed into industrial or commercial capital.

The separate individuals form a class only in so far as they have to carry on a common battle against another class; otherwise they are on hostile terms with each other as competitors. On the other hand, the class in its turn achieves an independent existence over against the individuals, so that the latter find their conditions of existence predestined, and hence have their position in life and their personal development assigned to them by their class, become subsumed under it. This is the same phenomenon as the subjection of the separate individuals to the division of labour and can only be removed by the abolition of private property and of labour itself. . . . [1]

This passage makes it apparent that Marx thought of social class as a condition of group-life which was constantly generated (rather than simply given) by the organization of production. Essential to this formation of a class was the existence of a common "class enemy," because without it competition between individuals would prevail. Also, this is a gradual process, which depends for its success upon the development of "common conditions" and upon the subsequent realization of common interests. But the existence of common conditions and the realization of common interests are in turn only the necessary, not the sufficient bases for the development of a social class. Only when the members of a "potential" class enter into an association for the

organized pursuit of their common aims, does a class in Marx's sense exist.

In discussing the development of the proletariat under capitalism Marx described a process which was essentially similar to that which he had described for the development of the modern bourgeoise.

The first attempts of the workers to *associate* among themselves always take place in the form of combinations (unions).

Large-scale industry concentrates in one place a crowd of people unknown to one another. Competition divides their interests. But the maintenance of wages, this common interest which they have against their boss, unites them in a common thought of resistance — combination. Thus combination always has a double aim, that of stopping the competition among themselves, in order to bring about a general competition with the capitalist. If the first aim of the general resistance was merely the maintenance of wages, combinations, at first isolated, constitute themselves into groups as the capitalists in their turn unite in the idea of repression, and in the face of always united capital, the maintenance of the association becomes more necessary to them than that of wages. This is so true that the English economists are amazed to see the workers sacrifice a good part of their wages in favor of associations, which in the eyes of the economists are established solely in favor of wages. In this struggle — a veritable civil war — are united and developed all the elements necessary for the coming battle. Once it has reached this point association takes on a political character.

Economic conditions had first transformed the mass of the people of the country into workers. The domination of capital has created for this mass a common situation, common interests. This mass is thus already a class as against capital, *but not yet for itself*. In this struggle, of which we have noted only a few phases, this mass becomes united, and constitutes itself as a class for itself. The interests it defends become class interests. But the struggle of class against class is a political struggle.[2]

Thus in the case of the proletariat, as in the case of the bourgeoisie, Marx cited several conditions which were essential for the development of a social class: conflict over economic rewards, physical concentration of masses of people and easy communication among them, the development of solidarity and political organization (in place of competition between individuals and organization for purely economic ends). The antagonism of the workers to the capitalist class and to the prevailing economic system was to Marx not simply a consequence of the struggle for economic advantage. In addition to the conditions mentioned he laid great stress on the human conse-

[1] *German Ideology*, 48–49.
[2] Karl Marx, *The Poverty of Philosophy* (New York: International Publishers, n.d.), 145–146.

quences of machine production under capitalism. The social relations which capitalist industry imposed deprived the workers of all opportunities to obtain psychological satisfaction from their work. This complete want of satisfaction Marx called the alienation of human labor. He attributed it to the division of labor in modern industry, which turned human beings into the appendages of the machine.

The knowledge, the judgment and the will, which though in ever so small a degree, are practiced by the independent peasant or handicraftsman, in the same way as the savage makes the whole art of war consist in the exercise of his personal cunning — these faculties (?) are now required only for the workshop as a whole. Intelligence in production expands in one direction, because it vanishes in many others. What is lost by the detail laborer, is concentrated in the capital that employs them. It is a result of the division of labor in manufactures, that the laborer is brought face to face with the intellectual potencies of the material process of production, as the property of another, and as a ruling power. This separation begins in simple cooperation, where the capitalist represents to the single workman, the oneness and the will of the associated labor. It is developed in manufacture which cuts down the laborer into a detail laborer. It is completed in modern industry, which makes science a productive force distinct from labor and presses it into the service of capital.

In manufacture, in order to make the collective laborer, and through him capital, rich in social productive power, each laborer must be made poor in individual productive powers. 'Ignorance is the mother of industry as well as of superstition. Reflection and fancy are subject to err; but a habit of moving the hand or the foot is independent of either. Manufactures, accordingly, prosper most where the mind is least consulted, and where the workshop may ... be considered as an engine, the parts of which are men.' (A. L. Ferguson, p. 280.)[1]

... within the capitalist system all methods for raising the social productiveness of labor are brought about at the cost of the individual laborer; all means for the development of production transform themselves into means of domination over, and exploitation of the producers; they mutilate the laborer into a fragment of a man, degrade him to the level of an appendage of a machine, destroy every remnant of charm in his work and turn it into a hated toil; they estrange from him the intellectual potentialities of the labor-process in the same proportion as science is incorporated in it as an independent power; they distort the conditions

[1] Karl Marx, *Capital* (New York: Modern Library, 1936), 396–397.
[2] Marx, *op. cit.*, 708–709. (Our emphasis.)
[3] *Ibid.*, 709.
[4] Karl Marx, "Wage, Labor and Capital," in *Selected Works* (Moscow: Cooperative Publishing Society of Foreign Workers in the U.S.S.R., 1936), I, 273.

under which he works, subject him during the labor-process to a despotism the more hateful for its meanness; they transform his life time into working-time and drag his wife and child under the wheels of the Juggernaut of capital. But all methods for the accumulation of surplus value are at the same time methods of accumulation; *and every extension of accumulation becomes again a means for the development of those methods. It follows therefore that in proportion as capital accumulates, the lot of the laborer, be his payments high or low, must grow worse.*[2]

Marx believed that the alienation of labor was inherent in capitalism and that it was a major psychological deprivation, which would lead eventually to the proletarian revolution. This theory of why men under capitalism would revolt, was based on an assumption of what prompts men to be satisfied or dissatisfied with their work. Marx contrasted the modern industrial worker with the medieval craftsman, and — along with many other writers of the period — observed that under modern conditions of production the worker had lost all opportunity to exercise his "knowledge, judgment and will" in the manufacture of his product. To Marx this psychological deprivation seemed more significant even than the economic pauperism to which capitalism subjected the masses of workers. At any rate, two somewhat conflicting statements can be found in his work. In one he declared that the physical misery of the working classes would increase with the development of capitalism.

Accumulation of wealth at one pole is, therefore, at the same time accumulation of misery, agony of toil, slavery, ignorance, brutality, mental degradation, at the opposite pole....[3]

But in the other he maintained that capitalism could result in an absolute increase of the standard of living for the workers, but that it would result nevertheless in the experience of mounting personal deprivation.

When capital is increasing fast, wages may rise, but the profit of capital will rise much faster. The material position of the laborer has improved, but it is at the expense of his social position. The social gulf which separates him from the capitalist has widened.[4]

And, as we have seen, Marx summarized his analysis of the oppressive effects of capitalism with a long list of striking phrases, only to conclude this eloquent recital with the sentence: "It follows therefore that in proportion as capital accumulates, the lot of the labourer, *be his payment high or low*, must grow worse."

It will be apparent from the preceding discussion that Marx did not simply identify a social class with the fact that a large group of people occupied the same objective position in the economic structure of a society. Instead, he laid great stress on the importance of subjective awareness as a precondition of organizing the class successfully for the economic and the political struggle. Marx felt certain that the pressures engendered by capitalism would determine its development in the future. And he believed it to be inevitable that the masses of industrial workers would come to a conscious realization of their class interests. Subjective awareness of class interests was in his view an indispensable element in the development of a social class, but he believed that his awareness would inevitably arise along with the growing contradictions inherent in capitalism. In the preceding discussion we have cited two of the conditions which made Marx feel sure of this prediction: the concentration of workers in towns and the resulting ease of communication between them, and the psychological suffering engendered by the alienation of labor. By way of summarizing Marx's theory of class we cite his views on the French peasants who occupy a similar position in the economic structure but do not thereby provide the basis for the formation of a social class.

> The small peasants form a vast mass, the members of which live in similar conditions, but without entering into manifold relations with one another. Their mode of production isolates them from one another, instead of bringing them into mutual intercourse. . . . In so far as millions of families live under economic conditions of existence that divide their mode of life, their interests and their culture from those of other classes, and put them into hostile contrast to the latter, they form a class. In so far as there is merely a local interconnection among these small peasants, and the identity of their interests begets no unity, no national union, and no political organization, they do not form a class.[1]

That is to say, the peasants occupy the same position in the economic structure of their society. But in their case this fact itself will *not* create similar attitudes and common actions. The peasants do not form a social class in Marx's sense, because they make their living on individual farms in isolation from one another. There is no objective basis for ready communication between them.

In the case of the industrial workers, however, such an objective basis for ready communication existed. They were concentrated in the large industrial towns, and the conditions of factory production brought them into close physical contact with one another. Yet, even then Marx did not believe that the political organization of the working class and the development of class-consciousness in thought and action would be the automatic result of these objective conditions. In this view these objective conditions provided a favorable setting for the development of political agitation. And this agitation was in good part the function of men, who were not themselves workers, but who had acquired a correct understanding of historical change, and who were willing to identify themselves with the movement of those who were destined to bring it about.

> . . . in times when the class struggle nears the decisive hour, the process of dissolution going on within the ruling class, in fact within the whole range of old society, assumes such a violent, glaring character, that a small section of the ruling class cuts itself adrift and joins the revolutionary class, the class that holds the future in its hands. Just as, therefore, at an earlier period, a section of the nobility went over to the bourgeoisie, so now a portion of the bourgeoisie goes over to the proletariat, and in particular, a portion of the bourgeois ideologists, who have raised themselves to the level of comprehending theoretically the historical movement as a whole.[2]

There is little question that Marx conceived of his own work as an example of this process. The scientific analysis of the capitalist economy, as he conceived of it, was itself an important instrument by means of which the class consciousness and the political organization of the workers could be furthered. And because Marx conceived of his own work in these terms, he declared that the detachment of other scholars was spurious, was merely a screen thrown up to disguise the class-interests which their work served. Hence he denied the possibility of a social science in the modern sense of that word. The "proof" of his theory was contained in the actions of the proletariat.

It is apparent that Marx's theory of social classes, along with other parts of his doctrine, involved a basic ambiguity which has bedevilled his interpreters ever since. For, on the one hand, he felt quite certain that the contradictions engendered by capitalism would inevitably lead to a class conscious proletariat and hence to a proletarian revolution. But on the other hand, he assigned to class-consciousness, to political action, and to his scientific theory of history a major role in bringing about this result. In his own eyes this difficulty was resolved because such subjective elements as class-consciousness or a scientific theory were themselves a by-product of the contradictions inherent in capitalism. The preceding discussion has sought to elucidate the meaning of this assertion by specifying the general philosophical assumptions and the specific environmental and psychological conditions on the basis of which Marx felt able to predict the *inevitable* development of class-consciousness.[3] To the critics this claim to predict an inevitable future on the basis of assumptions and conditions, which may or may not be valid, has always seemed the major flaw in Marxian theory.

[1] Karl Marx, *The Eighteenth Brumaire of Louis Bonaparte* (New York: International Publishers, n.d.), 109.

[2] Karl Marx and Friedrich Engels, *Manifesto of the Communist Party* (New York: International Publishers, 1932), 19.

[3] On a few occasions Marx allowed for the possibility that the development from capitalism to socialism might occur without a proletarian revolution, especially in England, Holland, and the United States. Properly understood the statement to this effect did not mean that this development was a mere possibility, but that it might take several forms, depending upon the historical situation of each country. By his analysis of the capitalist economy Marx sought to predict major changes, not specific occurrences; but while he allowed for the latter he did not expect them to alter the central tendency of the former.

Estates and Classes

Ferdinand Toennies

Social collectives

I INTERPRET THE TERM *social collectives* to mean groups of individuals or families, who are tied to one another by virtue of shared traditions or because of their common interests and their common perspective. They are aware of a certain ideological unity, though this would not result by itself in a collective will, because they are not (as individuals or families) capable to decide and act by means of established organizations. These social collectives are capable merely of a tacit consensus, which may manifest itself, though it need not, in a variety of ways, given certain conditions or occasions. This consensus remains a latent one, as long as there are no stimuli which would force it into consciousness. I regard the political party as the ideal type of a *societal* collective. In taking sides for or against a given issue many people are brought together by a party to which they are consciously committed. This is to be regarded as a typical example of the societal collective which originates from, and depends upon, the free decision of its members. The societal collective is also the rational collective, and it is most easily understood for this reason. The party is, as it were, the criterion by which the other collectives should be judged, which are not societal in the sense of a political party and which are therefore *communal* collectives.[1] The party is serviceable in this respect because the decision which formed it, or which holds it together, is given a rational articulation (party programs and organization) that clarifies the decision in turn.

All collectives must have a rational component, an articulated purpose which gives meaning to them, whatever may be the reasons for their origin. This meaning or purpose is always and inevitably an awareness, and an affirmation, of solidarity, regardless of whether this is felt more or less unconsciously, or whether it is expressly regarded as good and useful. And this purpose is most conscious, when the collective is regarded as a useful tool for the achievement of the common or joint goals of its members. The *political* party is the prototype of a socetial collective because the will of the individuals is directly related to the will of the party. The will of both aims at certain purposes and weighs and chooses the means for their attainment. Through its political struggle the party seeks to enhance and exercise its power, just as the state pursues these same goals on behalf of its more comprehensive purposes.

Collectives may be subdivided like all other social groupings into: (*a*) economic, (*b*) political, (*c*) intellectual-moral. More *communal* or more *societal* collectives occur side by side in each of these categories. We should add, however, that a description of a collective as societal does *not* mean that such a collective has been chosen as average or typical. It means rather that its chance to be so selected is relatively great in the sense that it contains significant societal tendencies.

Estates and classes distinguished

Estates and *classes* are based essentially on the facts of economic life. But their significance reaches over into political affairs and into the intellectual and moral sphere. Estates are related to one another like the organs or limbs of a body; classes are engaged in a contractual relationship. Classes look upon, and deal with, one another basically as opponents, who depend on one another nevertheless as a result of their mutual interests. The relation between classes turns immediately into enmity, when one class is dissatisfied with the actions of the other, when one accuses the other that the contract is inadequate or that its conditions have not been observed. Hence, estates change over into classes, when they engage in hostile actions or engage one another in war. These struggles are class-struggles, even if they are called struggles between estates.

The terms "estate" and "class" are synonyms which are often used interchangeably. But scientifically we want to distinguish these terms in the sense that estates are conceived as *communal* and classes as *societal* collectives. Another distinction between them consists in the

---

[1] According to Toennies, the concepts of societal and of communal collective are subsidiary to the more general concept of social collective.

Reprinted from "Stände und Klassen" in Alfred Vierkandt, ed., *Handwörterbuch der Soziologie* (1931), pp. 617–628 by permission of Mrs. Franziska Toennies Heberle and the Ferdinand Enke Verlag. (Copyright, 1931, by Ferdinand Enke Verlag.) Translation by Reinhard Bendix. All footnotes have been added by the translator. Some of the factual information which Toennies uses, has special reference to Germany in the 1920's, but the range of problems which he considers, is of general interest. The original article included a discussion of certain political problems and a survey of the relevant literature, which have been omitted from this translation. Some of the sub-titles have also been added for the sake of clarity.

greater rigidity of estates as against the often extreme fluidity of classes. Classes are more frequently determined by environmental conditions, which as a rule remain the same for generations, but which become more changeable in the course of social development and which cause individuals and families to rise or fall to a higher or lower class. It follows, on the other hand, that an estate becomes more identical with a class, the more it disintegrates, i.e. the more the mobility of its members increases. But such a development, like all social developments is conditioned also by changes in political and in the moral and intellectual life, although these in turn are significantly influenced by economic changes.

Ruling estates

Ruling estates are the prototype of an estate with regard to their economic, political, intellectual as well as moral characteristics. We refer in the first place to those *ruling estates* (Herrenstände), whose activities are generally of a war-like or priestly character, and who lead and command as a result of these two functions. Estates are divided into a secular and a clerical nobility, although the term "nobility" is reserved for the former. The great mass of the "third" or peasant estate is distinguished from the ruling estates according to its principal occupation. The peasant-estate is distinguished in turn from the estate of craftsmen and of merchants, which together form the bourgeoisie (Bürgerstand) of the towns.

Consciousness of status[1] is a characteristic feature of the ruling estates which is manifest in many different social forms. Pride is an especially noteworthy aspect of this consciousness, i.e. a heightened awareness of prominence, of adornment and beauty, which are based on one's estate, though in a petty way such pride may appear as vanity. Aristocratic pride is especially significant when it turns into an arrogance of status that has an effect on the lower strata of the governed.

The pride of the clerical estate is of a different kind, though it becomes more akin to aristocratic pride as its position and influence approximate or even surpass the great of this world and to the extent that the members of the two estates are in close personal contact. Clerical pride is derived from the presumption of, or the claim to, divine favor and grace. The priest feels that he is the representative, the delegate, and the confidant of supernatural powers and that he is sanctified by them. Therefore he wants to see his whole estate recognized as holy, even though his pride may be disguised by a denial of pride. By this humility the priest subordinates himself to those powers whose essence and will he alone can know and interpret, and if not completely then at any rate much better than laymen could. As a rule, this ability of the priest is readily trusted. In some relatively rare cases the priestly estate is not hereditary, but depends on election and appointment. In such cases its consciousness of status may be intensified, because members of the estate are not recruited through procreation

and inheritance. Hence the replacement of the members seems to be based on supernatural sanction, in so far as it is attributed to the will of the Gods, or of one God.

Ever since the beginning of culture, this holiness of men has been the most favorable legitimation of authority, based on the reverence and humility of the people. And something of this holiness remains as an attribute of the secular ruling estates and their consummation, the princely estates and kingship. Closely related as it is to the original dignity of age, this element of holiness lends dignity to these estates. Moreover, the separation of the two ruling estates has always developed out of a common origin, from which they derived a natural affinity and a common magnificence, though this did not preclude the most bitter hatred and the most acute enmity between them. The self-assurance which goes with a consciousness of status has also moral effects, especially when it coincides with distinctive gifts. It can facilitate and encourage the development of these gifts, because it arouses and strengthens self-confidence and a sense of responsibility. This is true of all "higher" social strata as well as of estates in the narrow sense; it is true, for example, of the remnants of the aristocracy, and of the higher clergy, in so far as they claim their high position or prove their worth through education and achievements. Analogous statements are true of any ruling class, in which the characteristics of the ruling estates are preserved.

Status honor

Estates in the sense discussed above have acquired a connotation of dignity as a result of the preeminent position of the ruling estates, both secular and clerical. And this connotation has been transferred easily to other preeminent strata or to their select circles, especially when these held privileged rank or possessed political power under the constitutional provisions of an estate-society. Ruling estates claim a special honor, they want to be honored by others. (A clerical estate wants to be honored especially by all those whom it represents and who worship its Gods.) But they also want to have and enjoy this honor as an inalienable possession that is highly prized, a *character indelebilis*. Consequently, ruling estates demand of their members that they should live in accordance with a code of honor which they must not violate, if they want to be members in good standing. A ruling estate, to a greater extent than other collectives, must insist on a certain level of performance and on a certain measure of dignified restraint. Such an estate must control or eliminate impropriety and lack of dignity, although it is not

[1] The term "Standesbewusstein" may be translated literally as *consciousness of estate*. Unfortunately, this term is meaningless to the American reader. I, therefore, rely on the context of this discussion of estates, to have the term consciousness of status understood to mean "consciousness of status by a member of an estate."

organized so as to decide and formally act upon the exclusion of people who belong to it. The public opinion of an estate has other means of ostracism; these are the more effective the more that opinion is unified.

But the conduct which is "proper" to the estate (Standesgemäss) is not the only mark of honor. Another such mark is the way of life which is "proper" in this sense and which finds special expression in the life of the family, especially as regards marriage. The nobility is *endogamous*. In the strict sense of the word, only the "high" nobility is endogamous, and among its families hereditary succession depends upon equality of birth. But even the lower ranks of the nobility show the same tendency, although it is not really regarded as lacking in chivalrous conduct, if the family tree is "enriched" by a bourgeois, or even by a Jewish marriage.

Estates of birth and of occupation

The two ruling estates have played a leading role throughout many centuries of European history. It is evident that we must distinguish between estates of birth and occupational estates, although estates of birth are often similar to occupational estates. Estates of birth depend on the assumption that the qualities which really or presumably entitled a man and a woman to a position of authority, are perpetuated through the generations. This is often the case with regard to physical traits and those physical and moral qualities which are affected by them. It is much less true of qualities of the mind and their intellectual and moral correlates; indeed these are often associated with a slender body-build and an effeminate character of thought and imagination, even if it is found in men. Hence, in a certain sense the clerical estate has always been a representative of the female sex. Within the confines of its thought-ways and its way of life, this estate has devoted itself for a long time to art and science, in addition to the espousal of the faith and to the performance of its priestly functions. Its reputation with, and its influence on, the female sex has always been strongest, in contrast to the specifically male character of the medieval knight and of the secular aristocracy.

The clerical estate is thought to depend on election, though this election takes the form of divine grace and as such often depends on vows which would dedicate even a child to the dignity of this calling. During the Middle Ages the calling or vocation of a person was based on an election, though as a rule this election took place *within* an occupational estate. Even so, an election was often made impossible for extraneous reasons. *Pride* of status prevailed in offices or guilds to such an extent that the estate would exclude from membership children born out of wedlock as well as whole trades (masters and sons) such as the linen-weavers. Today, it has become indispensable that the individual choose a trade and apprentice in it, so that only the vocation of the rulers depends upon birth where the monarchy has

been maintained, i.e., it devolves upon the first-born. To be sure, even today Great Britain has the *Peers* as an hereditary estate of the realm, which is entitled to participate in legislation and adjudication. The same was true until recently with reference to legislation in Prussia and in some other German states. Until the last few decades it was also rare for women to choose a career; their natural vocation was thought to be that of wife and mother, especially in the upper social strata. Their task was to keep house, to rear and educate children, but also to care for the sick, the aged, to act as a Good Samaritan or as a teaching sister (Lehrschwester) in a nunnery.

When the choice of occupation is free, it manifests a social regularity, in that it is determined in large measure by social origin and depends for the most part on the economic situation from which a young person originates. But occupational choice is also affected by social conditions, relatives, family-tradition and other factors which have a moral significance. Thus, the occupations depending on higher education stand in contrast to those that do not require it. The people with a higher education, who comprise a great portion of the upper stratum, also originate from it with few exceptions. And among the people in occupations which do not require a higher education, the choice of occupation depends in the first instance on the possession or non-possession of wealth. Among the masses of people without wealth, this choice depends again on the availability of means which will enable the boy or girl to learn a trade. This need not mean that apprenticeship fees must be paid, which is becoming rarer nowadays, but it does mean that the family is satisfied with the meager earnings of an apprentice. The various crafts are still recruited on the basis of this ability of families to make do, although they have been transformed in large measure into industrial labor of the factory-type. The inheritance of estate can be clearly recognized even within the working class in the sense that as a rule the sons of semi-skilled and of skilled workers become semi-skilled and skilled workers in turn. In this respect the retail trades are similar to manual labor because of their stable location, mainly in small cities which also include villages and market places.

However, the retail trades also extend into the large cities, and they are economically healthier than the handicrafts. A large portion of the latter turns into a retail trade with manufactured goods with which the craftsman is acquainted and on which he makes minor repairs. The estate of craftsmen must be regarded as a survival of an occupational grouping. This estate is accustomed to think of itself with great pride of status as the so-called *middle estate* (Mittelstand). As such the estate claims to be the core of the *bourgeois estate* (Bürgerstand). The retail tradesman also regards himself as part of this latter estate. Recently in Germany a so-called new middle estate has appeared, which is said to have developed especially from the ranks of salaried employees of large industrial and commercial enterprises.

This "estate" is to be regarded in a different light, however. The craftsman or merchant has a sense of pride on account of his independence. He thinks of himself and his fellows as entrepreneurs, even if his independence is often spurious. On the other hand, salaried employees know that they are completely dependent upon capital and its representatives. A small minority of these employees feel that they belong to the status-position of the capitalist and that they are destined to become capitalists, even if at first only as commercial or technical managers in the higher positions of an enterprise. On the other hand, he may feel akin to the proletariat and be in close contact with its higher strata.

What is the proletariat? What are the capitalists, the entrepreneurs, the merchant princes, the bank directors, etc.? The proletariat has often been considered the "fourth estate," as if the three estates: the military, the academic, and the agrarian, were still in existence in the sense in which they may be thought of historically. The term "fourth estate," however, has no historical or sociological basis, though it conveys more meaning than a further term, the "fifth" estate. This latter group is more appropriately called the "Lumpenproletariat": it consists of the "scum of the earth" which is drawn from all strata of society, somewhat like the *outcasts* of India, who are made up from all the declassed elements in the society. Capitalists, like the proletariat, can hardly be regarded as an estate. Both may be considered more appropriately as classes.

Castes in India

Today, a society of an estate-like character survives in a noteworthy form in India, a land of ancient culture which is much admired. The society is composed of "castes" whose nature is often misunderstood. A caste combines the characteristic elements of both, estates of birth and of occupation. Moreover, the caste often coincides with the "clan," a still older type of collective which assumes the functions of an association. The traditional doctrine, still scarcely challenged a century ago, holds that there are four strata, which nowadays are called castes in the classic sense. These four castes consist of three which rule and the fourth which serves. They are: the Brahmans or priests, the Kshatryjas or warriors, the Vaishyjas or merchants and peasants, and the Sudras, also known as the Parias. The Sudras are, however, only one of the many lower castes which the higher castes consider to be unclean. Today the four castes, as they are described in the Veda, are regarded as mythical and as having been introduced by the Brahmans. The Brahmans represent themselves as the highest stratum, while the remaining people take up positions more or less close to them. The lowest stratum is regarded as unclean, the Brahmans reject all association or intermarriage with it; they do not wish even to accept water from its members, and indeed reject any physical contact whatsoever with them. Still, the correspondence between this caste-system and the division

into three estates in Europe is so striking that one may easily suspect the existence of something primitively Aryan behind it all. Today the castes of India number in the thousands if one includes the sub-castes. In the central provinces which have about sixteen million inhabitants, the census of 1901 identified nearly nine hundred caste names, which were subsumed, however, by classification under two hundred "real" castes. "The correct view of India is that as a whole it is divided into an infinite number of independent, organized groups which act autonomously. These organized groups are those of the peasant, craftsman and merchant" (Sir H. S. Maine). Maine did not think it appropriate to mention the lowest of all the strata: the castes which are described as consisting of thieves or robbers, religious mendicants, vagabonds and gypsies, beggars and itinerant musicians, vagrants, criminals, and prostitutes. Yet, all of these castes belong to the whole picture together with the lower strata of the people from which they come. A similar stratum has existed in Europe from early times. Its members, degenerate and destitute, could not, or did not wish to, fit into the pattern of social life. Such people must not be thought of as constituting an estate, if we establish status-consciousness as a basic characteristic.

It is apparent that, apart from the groups whose activities lie outside the accepted forms of social life, the castes as well as the occupational estate of Europe were originally based on the division of labor. In Europe, however, the resulting associations never took on as rigid a form as they did in India, where they have defied the centuries. For in principle each caste is endogamous and perpetuates itself as such. Also, the castes are scattered locally throughout the entire area, and as a rule they constitute communities at the same time. In India a truly urban civilization has hardly existed until the most recent phase of development under English influence. This represents the great difference between the Indian and European cultures. It follows from this that in ancient India one scarcely finds the beginnings of a "state." Nor can one detect the beginnings of a capitalistic society, which is both a condition and consequence of the state.

Estates and cities in ancient civilization

In ancient civilization the early and significant development of the urban community hindered and limited the development of the estates in Greece and Rome. In the Homeric reports we still find mention of the elements of knighthood, whose leaders, called "shepherds of the people," gathered something of a court about them in their castle strongholds. We also find mention of an estate of priests and prophets, figures like Kalchas and Teiresias who were shrouded in something of a sacred halo. But in historical times a society stratified by estates occurred only in the Doric cities. Apparently Rome was also organized aristocratically since primitive times, though apparently without any influence having come from the Doric cities. Struggles for rank and political feuds between the patrician and plebeian groups fill the history of centuries of this community which rose to world domination. In the later period of the Roman Empire a transformation took place through an aristocracy of office; up to the most recent times the aristocracy of all Latin countries has received its name from this Roman nobility. A knightly estate arose at first on the basis of a law of Gajus Gracchus. This estate consisted for the most part of tax-farmers, an estate of the wealthy which maintained its position in the Roman Principate and even gained new significance, though it was wholly dependent upon the emperor as the commander-in-chief. The clerical estate acquired no importance in the ancient religions or lost early what importance it had had. In Rome only the individual *Collegia* of priests had a stable rank-order. Including the Collegia of women, Rome had no less than twenty-three such Collegia and each had a certain influence on social and political life. But the Collegia as a group did not have any influence. It is significant to note that the Pontifex Maximus and the eight higher Pontifices occupy positions of the highest rank. The enactments of the Imperium and the Christian church which was created in accordance with them became the determinants of all Europe for about twelve centuries. And these are the antecedents of the estates which have given form and substance to our entire cultural life up to the most recent times.

For this reason our culture is quite different from that of ancient India. Sir H. S. Maine writes: "The real India has a caste of priests which is in a certain, though very limited, sense the highest caste of all." Through most of its history, Europe has had secular and clerical ruling estates, which have been the most powerful factors in political life, and which have exerted thereby a powerful influence on economic affairs and on the moral and intellectual development. In these respects the two estates stand next to the monarchy, which was always both supported and restricted by the estates. The history of the past four centuries is the story of the gradual but increasingly rapid collapse of this aristocratic grandeur. The strongholds of the knights are destroyed. But before and during World War I the regiments of the Guards, particularly those of the Cavalry Guards, still recruited their officers almost exclusively from the nobility. The privileged claim of the nobility to high administrative offices could not be maintained anywhere. Nevertheless, congeries of cliques, drawn to be sure from a young "plutocratic" stratum rather than from the old nobility, still preserved for the nobility as a whole a preferred position in diplomacy and higher administration. This position is maintained in various ways in day-to-day politics. The traditional cultivation of personal qualities which are significant for diplomatic and administrative posts favors the privileged position of the nobility in these respects as much as they do in the army.

Occupational estates

Estates still exist to the degree that their members think of them as such and want them to exist. Objective analysis can correct this subjective view only inasmuch as the conscious image of the estate contains elements which have no adequate empirical basis but rest solely upon self-esteem, personal claims, and imaginary constructs. When we trace back the image of the estates to the realm of social fact, we must consider the occupations first of all. The question arises what present-day occupational estates have in common with the old ruling estates which were characteristic of an earlier time. Obviously, the word "vocation" or "calling" suggests the answer. The estates of earlier times believed themselves to be answering the call of their God. Today, the groups who hold fast to this belief consist at most of a considerable portion of the clergy and of several backwoods-monarchs. In general people feel and think of themselves as having a vocation for a given activity after the manner of the craftsman. One has learned his trade and can hope to become a master of his craft if he has not become one already. There is an old saying of the masons that only those who already show their "capability" shall be apprenticed. In this sense each occupation can establish something in the nature of an estate. However, it is more probable that kindred occupational groups join together and develop an awareness of their collective skills, desires, and aspirations. Today innumerable *Congresses* are evidence of this fact. They discuss and deliberate their common affairs, purposes and concerns, their aspirations and interests. Often, associations are organized as a result of these conferences. They have a permanent board of directors, set up their own newspapers and sometimes seek to attain political influence.

Class and class-consciousness

The estates have been superseded more and more by the awareness of belonging to a "class." A class is intent upon developing effective power through the strength of the mass, i.e., through the large number of those who belong to this collective; it depends to a lesser extent on the skills of the individuals. This is true of collectives of every sort. But the farmers, the craftsmen, the civil servants, and the academicians still feel themselves to be occupational estates even today. The first two groups claim to be of the middle class; but the status-consciousness of the latter two groups is usually weak or not entirely genuine because it is not uniform throughout the group. There are certain sub-groups which are exceptions, such as the elementary school teachers in the public schools. Moreover, soldiers constitute an estate which stands in notable contrast to the "civilians." This is a product of the standing army, and as such a product of the modern state. The self-esteem of soldiers as a group is often greatly favored and promoted by the state through its laws and institutions. In this sense, soldiers approximate a new, secular ruling-estate, at least insofar as the higher ranks and officers are concerned. This officer-corps actually tends to be hereditary, although this is always compatible with freedom of occupational choice. Finally, there is an estate of civil servants; and although an army officer is nothing but a public official himself, the term estate (Beamtenstand) is used only with reference to civil servants.[1] But civil servants do not constitute an estate in the sense we have described above, for there is hardly a shared consciousness of status among higher government administrators, let alone among the middle and lower ranks.

But it is the development of capitalism which is the moving force, that is the influence of commerce and trade, the formation of large and increasingly larger cities, the individualization of all rights, and the principles of freedom and equality in their effects on legislation. If we consider the factor which promotes the cohesion of social classes most strongly, namely the distribution of wealth and income, we find that there is a simple division into two groups. On the one hand there are individuals and families, who are wealthy and earn a high income, though they may have high income without considerable wealth. On the other hand there are those without wealth and with little income. This is the traditional division of rich and poor. Of course, there are today countless individuals and families who cannot be regarded as either rich or poor in the strict sense of the word. Nevertheless, further observation makes it apparent that these people lean more or less to one or the other of the two main groups. This comes about partly through their emotions or ideas, but even more because of the circumstances and conditions of their lives. Some persons are in constant danger of sinking to the level of the poor; others at least hope and continually strive to rise to the level of the rich. And many others, despite their complete impoverishment, still retain and cultivate the comforting thought of belonging to "Society," or of belonging to the better class of people, which amounts to the same thing in this connection. These people think more in terms of education and concepts of honor than in terms of wealth, though as a rule wealth provides a foundation for education and honor.

Individualism

The development cannot be understood without recourse to the concept of "individualism." As a rule, this concept is interpreted as an opinion or as a doctrine, which people like to refute as erroneous. They also like to contrast "individualism" with the correct opinion or doctrine of "universalism." And then it is declared that social life would be rid of all its evils and shortcomings, if only this correct doctrine were taught and believed by all. In this view, the manifest evils and shortcomings have certainly arisen from the error of individualism.

But individualism is first of all a fact of social life

itself. That is, "there is no individualism in history or culture except as it emerges from the community and remains conditioned by it, or except as individualism produces and supports a society." To put it differently: every human being, male or female, adult or child, is by nature an individual. If one regards the individual in a special sociological sense, then this can only mean that men act as individuals and prove themselves as such to a greater or lesser extent; they are aware of and they express their individualism more or less strongly. It is true that in this sense the adult is more of an individual than the child, the man more than the woman, and the mature man more than the youth or the old man. But more important than these distinctions are the differences of social activity, social position and status which are already apparent in an essentially communal phase of the development of culture. Here, the master is more of an individual than the servant, the commander more so than the common soldier, the master craftsman more so than the journeyman. *Individualism grows along with power and with wealth.* But it also grows together with the *responsibility* which the single individual has towards himself and towards others, especially towards those individuals and groups which *make* him responsible. Therefore, there arise a great many kinds of individualism. But certain kinds of individualism stand out particularly when we regard the over-all trends of social development. These are exemplified by persons who are capable of handling their resources with a special degree of freedom. To attain their goals, these persons must dispose over their resources in such a way that they achieve their purposes to the fullest extent possible.

Occupation and business

We must consider first of all the merchant. His business is a matter of simple calculation. He risks his resources in the form of a sum of money. His intention and his more or less well-founded expectation is to get back the initial outlay and an additional increment after a certain length of time. In order to make sure of his success as much as possible, he needs a certain knowledge of men, their inclinations, capabilities, and weaknesses. He also needs a knowledge of living conditions and of social institutions, a knowledge of the market, of customs, of laws, and of the courts. He further needs a certain boldness in order to risk a business venture. Above all he needs circumspection, cleverness, and cunning, and not infrequently ruthlessness against prevailing opinions and inhibitions. In this respect also he must take certain risks and as a rule he will do so more readily, the greater the probability of success and the higher the prize of victory. It has long been customary, therefore, to compare the work and activity of businessmen with a race. Indeed human life itself has often been represented as a struggle much like a race between competitors. Thus, in recent times it is often thought that

[1] There is no American equivalent for this usage.

everyone is like a business man chasing after profits. This is like saying that everyone is bent on the acquisition of riches like the merchant, only with less success because he is weaker in the qualities which distinguish the merchant. Or the success is attributed to luck, to an advantageous chance, which lifts some individuals above mediocrity, others less or not at all.

Thus, each person who has wealth may be regarded as more or less similar to a merchant, especially if this wealth is invested in a business enterprise (i.e., as shares). It is of no relevance in this respect if such a person has a negative attitude toward this enterprise or towards business in general. In fact, it has long been recognized that if such an outsider is knowledgeable, he enjoys a special advantage in this race, which has also been called the struggle for existence. This is seen particularly in the aptitude of the stranger to become a great capitalist entrepreneur, and the entrepreneur is but the consummation of the merchant. Werner Sombart has described the share which the "stranger" has had in the development of the capitalist economy, especially with regard to the migration of individuals and of emigrants generally. In his work, *Der Bourgeois*,[1] he devotes a special section to the Jews. Their role as strangers is one of the five conditions to which Sombart attributes the adaptability of Jews to capitalism. As a supplement to this deduction we should point out that there is a mixture of many national elements in every important commercial city. The larger the city becomes, the more general becomes the alienation of the inhabitants from one another. The individuals, who come into contact through business transactions like creditor and debtor, landlord and tenant, entrepreneur and worker, have little in common by virtue of the diminished importance of occupational groupings for each of them.

The worker is characterized mainly by the fact that he has little money, hence no capital. But frequently he has this much in common with the merchant and entrepreneur that he is a stranger. As such he is not bound as a rule to his employer, either by any bond of kinship, of home, of occupation, or yet by any bond of religion which in any case diminishes in importance under these conditions. But all these people are dependent on one another; the retail merchant upon the customer, the customer upon the retailer who acts frequently also as a creditor, above all the entrepreneur upon the worker, and the worker upon the entrepreneur as the customer and consumer of his labor-power. Thus social relationships are established, by far the most important one being that of the work contract. But no estate or class arises out of such relationships, though temporarily a nominal membership in an occupation does result.

Individuals get together much more readily, how-

ever, on the basis of a similarity of their living conditions: they have in common economic, political, and intellectual interests. This leads to the establishment of a great variety of associations. There are many individuals, on the other hand, who are prompted to join together because of their awareness of belonging to a collective. This collective has its own particular characteristics as a "class," and as such it is distinct from associations. The simplest division is that between propertied and property-less classes, although many individuals and families fall between these two groups. By and large the countries of present-day Europe have developed in this direction.

The persistence of medieval ways of life in England is a remarkable exception in this respect. Both ruling estates are still vigorously alive and they are still strongly represented politically. The middle class is made up of capitalists and of the entire stratum which is known as the bourgeoisie in France and Germany. But in Great Britain a middle stratum between the bourgeoisie and the working class is hardly worth mentioning. This is explained simply by the diminished significance for centuries past of the artisan and even more of the peasantry. English language and literature does not recognize the organization of the people in "estates," whether these are ruling estates or a bourgeois estate, estates of birth or of occupation. Only three classes are recognized: upper, middle, and lower. The differentiation of estates is neither established linguistically nor theoretically, even though the social position or rank, to which someone belongs, is often discussed. Such discussion points at least to the existence of estates, partly of birth and partly of occupation.

Present-day occupational estates

Let us now consider the existence of occupational estates in modern society. If we turn to Germany or to some other state, we find that occupational estates persist, although they are not hereditary, and although freedom of occupational choice prevails. Occupations in their manifold manifestations have the character of collectives. There are organizations of occupations and estates, as for instance those of lawyers and doctors. Such organizations presuppose the existence of occupations, which are clearly defined. There are agencies representing occupational interests such as chambers of commerce, trade associations, and craft-unions. There are also occupational associations under public law which insure the workers belonging to them against the accidents to which they are exposed in the course of their work.

Furthermore, there are "occupational statistics": those of the German statistical office distinguish carefully between divisions, groups and types of occupations. Only the last category comprises the traditional occupations which are freely chosen. These occupations include especially the farmers, gardeners, foresters, fishermen, numerous craftsmen such as the shoemakers,

---

[1] *Der Bourgeois* (1913) translated as *The Quintessence of Capitalism*. Toennies also refers to an earlier work by Sombart, *The Jews and Modern Capitalism*, which has been republished by the Free Press, New York.

tailors, carpenters, weavers, plumbers, and printers. The newer, semi-professional occupations such as druggists and photographers may also be included. Next come the occupations in commerce and the service trades, such as transportation, hotels, and restaurants. Finally there are the free professions, persons employed by state and church, who are concerned with teaching, adult education, public health services, and the arts.

Occupational estates do not figure in occupational statistics. But the following distinctions do: *1)* division into gainfully employed, domestic servants, (non-working) family-members; *2)* among the gainfully employed (which category is alone relevant for the study of occupations) it is important to distinguish between *a)* the self-employed, *b)* salaried employees, and *c)* wage-earners. The official commentary indicates that the self-employed *a)* include also the higher civil servants and business executives. Within this group of the self-employed the following distinctions are made parenthetically: property owners, proprietors, owners, joint proprietors or owners, tenants, hereditary tenants, master craftsmen, entrepreneurs, directors, and administrators. The apparent implication of this classification is that these higher positions within the several occupations represent the consummation of an occupational career. And the independence of these positions is regarded as characteristic of an "occupational estate." Some of these occupations of the "self-employed" are obviously the result of choice, such as those of agriculture and handicrafts. No one, however, chooses the occupation of owner, proprietor, entrepreneur, director, and administrator. And yet such positions are seen as consummating an occupational career. The explanation of this is easy. The occupational activity itself plays a subordinate role: *the occupation has been submerged by business.*

By its nature business is a commercial undertaking; already Adam Smith said that in this sense the commercial society makes "everyone" into a merchant. Consequently, the occupational division which comprises commerce and transportation as well as the hotel and restaurant-industries, is the division that includes the more significant of the occupations which remain. For neither agriculture nor the handicrafts any longer determine the character of occupations. Instead, the commercial element has become the decisive factor in the management of both large-scale agriculture and large-scale industry. Capital, complemented and represented by credit, exercises the function of the occupation. And even for the operation of the capital market, the decisive factor is no longer to learn "the enterprise," to acquire knowledge of commercial transactions, but to have the ability and the outlook appropriate for the most advantageous investment of capital, i.e., the pursuit of gain. This is seen in the generalized meaning of the term "enterprise," especially with regard to the individual who has wealth and who has invested it. He belongs to the class of self-employed to the extent that he has invested in profitable enter-

prises. Otherwise, this division of the self-employed class consists only of "those living from their own wealth, from rents or pensions." This division includes the small number of leisured millionaires or at any rate of well-to-do persons, especially of women who are dependent upon income from their properties and wealth together with pensioned civil servants, etc. and the large number of former workers who receive a small substitute for wages from the proceeds of insurance.

It is easily seen from this discussion that in present-day society occupational estates have a questionable existence. They survive for the most part in those who are dependent upon capital rather than upon other estates and individuals. Of these persons a portion carry on an occupational activity which has been learned, but they can do so only as employees, that is, to the extent that they are given work. Ostensibly, they are given work so as to cooperate in some work project; but in reality they help in the utilization of capital, i.e., in order to realize a gain of sufficient magnitude. Occupations and occupational estates become less significant in the very large number of relations where this [substitution of commercial for occupational considerations] has become decisive. Instead, there exist now within that grouping which is still called "occupation" a characteristic division between active and inactive persons, between employed and unemployed, between persons who belong to the capitalist and those who belong to the working class. Those large numbers of persons who find it necessary to make a living by utilizing their labor-power or their skills prefer to consider themselves part of a class rather than of an occupational estate. Class exerts its influence more through the strength of the masses and less through the abilities of individuals. Its influence depends on the great number of persons belonging to a collective. The object of this influence is of an economic, political, and intellectual-moral nature.

The facts just presented may also be interpreted in the sense that the division of labor in society is reflected in occupations which are either hereditary or freely chosen. Yet, the occupational hierarchy has been disrupted both at the bottom and at the top. Each individual can become a capitalist, a property owner, or a gentleman farmer, without having chosen or learned any occupation whatsoever. Even a newly-born child as well as a senile old woman can become a capitalist. What is more, the common unskilled worker is differentiated from the capitalist only through the happenstance that he does not possess means of subsistence which are secure under the law but can acquire these means only by selling his labor-power.

Parties

The decisive characteristic of class is class-consciousness, just as that of the estate is status-consciousness among members of an estate. Class and estate have thus a characteristic in common with the party which has been posited as the rational proto-type of societal reality.

Party-consciousness is an integral element of the "party." However, class-consciousness, even though it comes close to the act of choosing a party, still is not a matter of choice. To join a party happens regularly because of conviction — or so it seems. The opinion, which I acknowledge to be my own, appears to me as the "correct" one. It may be regarded as the only correct opinion, such as the views regarding the existence and being of God, which are "foreordained" for the orthodox Christian, Jew, or Moslem, who consider it their duty to declare allegiance to their party. Or it may be regarded as the correct opinion in terms of some purpose, based on utilitarian considerations. Then its content is determined by the end, which the individual has in view in joining a party: such as affairs of state, of the church, of the community, of an association. In such cases it always appears, and this impression may be strengthened, as if the individual has in mind the welfare of the state, the church, etc., and as if he is considering or has considered this high and necessary goal. Thus, by joining a certain party he devotes himself to this cause, this institution, to the best of his knowledge and in keeping with his conscience. However, there are good reasons to doubt that this is really true. The fact that such doubt arises follows readily from the strife and struggle among the parties. The following reproaches are made by all factions: *1*) the other party only pursues its own advantage or the advantage of its leaders or of a greater portion of its followers; *2*) one's own party is only the representative of "class-interests," i.e., of material interests, or it always has in mind the interests of an institution, such as the state, which is indispensable for the people and for mankind. In short, "we" are noble and think accordingly, while the opponent is "common," even villainous. The observer will conclude that in all probability each faction reproaches the other for what is human and natural. It is a consequence of the urge for self-preservation, and of the idea that association with one's equals, that is an alliance with them, is the appropriate means for maintaining and advancing one's self in the struggle for existence. However, it must be admitted that man strives to give a noble garb to his patently egoistic striving, and that he may do so in good faith and in order to relieve his conscience. He does so, not often perhaps in order to deceive the public as to his real intentions, but rather in order to counter the reproaches which seem justified even to the individual himself, and which he himself makes whenever he can expect advantages from so doing.

Class struggle

It is undeniable that party-affiliation in political matters is conditioned as a rule by the economic position of individuals and by their status or class consciousness. It has long been recognized as an elementary, even trivial truism that the poor think differently (*if* they think) from the rich with regard to legislation when they know and understand that such legislation is significant for their well-being and daily existence. This truth is confirmed by experience although appearances and interests often obscure it. But several preconditions must be fulfilled in order that this truth is given a genuine expression in legal terms, as for example in political elections. Do the poor have a voice? As is well known, the franchise for the poor is an innovation of the 19th and in part of the 20th century, and it has not yet been introduced in all states. But once this extension of suffrage has occurred, do the poor then know what they are doing when they cast their ballots? To be poor means to be dependent, very often to be dependent upon the grace and good-will of the rich. Therefore it is dangerous, perhaps even ruinous, to vote in a way which does not please the rich or which appears to them as something detestable. In the case of a public ballot this danger is clear and imminent, but it is also present in the case of a secret ballot. That which is not seen and heard may still be surmised — and reasons for surmise are readily available. Countless voters, especially in rural and small-town areas, consider it absolutely right or necessary to make use of their franchise in a way which pleases, or at least does not displease too much, the masters (Herren), whether these are landowners, home-owners, higher civil servants, or just gentlemen, regular customers, or employers. This they do even if such masters have not made their wishes known directly, although this occurs naturally in the election-campaign.

But the contrast between rich and poor is not the only thing which is conditioned by the economic position of one's fellows. There are other contrasts such as those between creditor and debtor, between people in urban and in rural areas, between advocates of tariff protection and those who champion free trade, between producers and consumers, between monopolists and those engaged in free competition. In general there are contrasts between those who have been blessed with good fortune and those who have been less favored in this respect, between businessmen who advance and those who stand still or who are on the downgrade. Thus there are many economic contrasts and struggles which are more or less sharply reflected in political life. But these contrasts and struggles are obscured by the *class struggle*, if this has found room to develop, as has been the case increasingly during the last one hundred years. The class struggle itself must be recognized as developing and subject to continuous change. If the class struggle is ever culminated, it will be because all persons are ranged on one side who have been engaged in gainful work or have been so engaged as long as they were able. These persons may acquire a common conviction that they desire a social organization of property other than that represented by the actual owners of land and capital who control the means of production and of trade. A unified social structure represented by the state would have to take the place of these owners, if a large majority of those pursuing gainful employment possessed political power. Even in the present stage of its development this majority aspires to the exercise of power, and in several of the important states has already acquired a part of that power. The completion of this movement in highly developed capitalistic states is only conceivable in a process which would last more than a century.

Class, Status and Party

Max Weber

Economically determined power and the social order

LAW EXISTS when there is a probability that an order will be upheld by a specific staff of men who will use physical or psychical compulsion with the intention of obtaining conformity with the order, or of inflicting sanctions for infringement of it.[1] The structure of every legal order directly influences the distribution of power, economic or otherwise, within its respective community. This is true of all legal orders and not only that of the state. In general, we understand by "power" the chance of a man or of a number of men to realize their own will in a communal action even against the resistance of others who are participating in the action.

"Economically conditioned" power is not, of course, identical with "power" as such. On the contrary, the emergence of economic power may be the consequence of power existing on other grounds. Man does not strive for power only in order to enrich himself economically. Power, including economic power, may be valued "for its own sake." Very frequently the striving for power is also conditioned by the social "honor" it entails. Not all power, however, entails social honor: The typical American Boss, as well as the typical big speculator, deliberately relinquishes social honor. Quite generally, "mere economic" power, and especially "naked" money power, is by no means a recognized basis of social honor. Nor is power the only basis of social honor. Indeed, social honor, or prestige, may even be the basis of political or economic power, and very frequently has been. Power, as well as honor, may be guaranteed by the legal order, but, at least normally, it is not their primary source. The legal order is rather an additional factor that enhances the chance to hold power or honor; but it cannot always secure them.

The way in which social honor is distributed in a community between typical groups participating in this distribution we may call the "social order." The social order and the economic order are, of course, similarly related to the "legal order." However, the social and the economic order are not identical. The economic order is for us merely the way in which economic goods and services are distributed and used. The social order is of course conditioned by the economic order to a high degree, and in its turn reacts upon it.

Now: "classes," "status groups," and "parties" are phenomena of the distribution of power within a community.

Determination of class-situation by market-situation

In our terminology, "classes" are not communities; they merely represent possible, and frequent, bases for communal action. We may speak of a "class" when 1) a number of people have in common a specific causal component of their life chances, in so far as 2) this component is represented exclusively by economic interests in the possession of goods and opportunities for income, and 3) is represented under the conditions of the commodity or labor markets. [These points refer to "class situation," which we may express more briefly as the typical chance for a supply of goods, external living conditions, and personal life experiences, in so far as this chance is determined by the amount and kind of power, or lack of such, to dispose of goods or skills for the sake of income in a given economic order. The term "class" refers to any group of people that is found in the same class situation.]

It is the most elemental economic fact that the way in which the disposition over material property is distributed among a plurality of people, meeting com-

[1] *Wirtschaft und Gesellschaft*, part III, chap. 4, pp. 631–640. The first sentence in paragraph one and the several definitions in this chapter which are in brackets do not appear in the original text. They have been taken from other contexts of *Wirtschaft und Gesellschaft*.

Reprinted from *Max Weber: Essays in Sociology* (1946), translated by H. H. Gerth and C. Wright Mills, pp. 180–195 by permission of the translators and publishers. (Copyright, 1946, by Oxford University Press, Inc.)

petitively in the market for the purpose of exchange, in itself creates specific life chances. According to the law of marginal utility this mode of distribution excludes the non-owners from competing for highly valued goods; it favors the owners and, in fact, gives to them a monopoly to acquire such goods. Other things being equal, this mode of distribution monopolizes the opportunities for profitable deals for all those who, provided with goods, do not necessarily have to exchange them. It increases, at least generally, their power in price wars with those who, being propertyless, have nothing to offer but their services in native form or goods in a form constituted through their own labor, and who above all are compelled to get rid of these products in order barely to subsist. This mode of distribution gives to the propertied a monopoly on the possibility of transferring property from the sphere of use as a "fortune," to the sphere of "capital goods"; that is, it gives them the entrepreneurial function and all chances to share directly or indirectly in returns on capital. All this holds true within the area in which pure market conditions prevail. "Property" and "lack of property" are, therefore, the basic categories of all class situations. It does not matter whether these two categories become effective in price wars or in competitive struggles.

Within these categories, however, class situations are further differentiated: on the one hand, according to the kind of property that is usable for returns; and, on the other hand, according to the kind of services that can be offered in the market. Ownership of domestic buildings; productive establishments; warehouses; stores; agriculturally usable land, large and small holdings — quantitative differences with possibly qualitative consequences —; ownership of mines; cattle; men (slaves); disposition over mobile instruments of production, or capital goods of all sorts, especially money or objects that can be exchanged for money easily and at any time; disposition over products of one's own labor or of others' labor differing according to their various distances from consumability; disposition over transferable monopolies of any kind — all these distinctions differentiate the class situations of the propertied just as does the "meaning" which they can and do give to the utilization of property, especially to property which has money equivalence. Accordingly, the propertied, for instance, may belong to the class of rentiers or to the class of entrepreneurs.

Those who have no property but who offer services are differentiated just as much according to their kinds of services as according to the way in which they make use of these services, in a continuous or discontinuous relation to a recipient. But always this is the generic connotation of the concept of class: that the kind of chance in the *market* is the decisive moment which presents a common condition for the individual's fate. "Class situation" is, in this sense, ultimately "market situation." The effect of naked possession *per se*, which among cattle breeders gives the non-owning slave or serf into the power of the cattle owner, is only a fore-runner of real "class" formation. However, in the cattle loan and in the naked severity of the law of debts in such communities, for the first time mere "possession" as such emerges as decisive for the fate of the individual. This is very much in contrast to the agricultural communities based on labor. The creditor-debtor relation becomes the basis of "class situations" only in those cities where a "credit market," however primitive, with rates of interest increasing according to the extent of dearth and a factual monopolization of credits, is developed by a plutocracy. Therewith "class struggles" begin.

Those men whose fate is not determined by the chance of using goods or services for themselves on the market, e.g. slaves, are not, however, a "class" in the technical sense of the term. They are, rather, a "status group."

Communal action flowing from class interest

According to our terminology, the factor that creates "class" is unambiguously economic interest, and indeed, only those interests involved in the existence of the "market." Nevertheless, the concept of "class-interest" is an ambiguous one: even as an empirical concept it is ambiguous as soon as one understands by it something other than the factual direction of interests following with a certain probability from the class situation for a certain "average" of those people subjected to the class situation. The class situation and other circumstances remaining the same, the direction in which the individual worker, for instance, is likely to pursue his interests may vary widely, according to whether he is constitutionally qualified for the task at hand to a high, to an average, or to a low degree. In the same way, the direction of interests may vary according to whether or not a *communal* action of a larger or smaller portion of those commonly affected by the "class situation," or even an association among them, e.g. a "trade union," has grown out of the class situation from which the individual may or may not expect promising results. [Communal action refers to that action which is oriented to the feeling of the actors that they belong together. Societal action, on the other hand, is oriented to a rationally motivated adjustment of interests.] The rise of societal or even of communal action from a common class situation is by no means a universal phenomenon.

The class situation may be restricted in its effects to the generation of essentially *similar* reactions, that is to say, within our terminology, of "mass actions." However, it may not have even this result. Furthermore, often merely an amorphous communal action emerges. For example, the "murmuring" of the workers known in ancient oriental ethics: the moral disapproval of the work-masters' conduct, which in its practical significance was probably equivalent to an increasingly typical phenomenon of precisely the latest industrial development, namely, the "slow down" (the deliberate limiting of work effort) of laborers by virtue of tacit agreement. The degree in which "communal action," and possibly "societal action," emerges from the "mass actions" of the members of a class is linked to general cultural conditions, especially to those of an intellectual sort. It is also linked to the extent of the contrasts that have already evolved, and is especially linked to the *transparency* of the connections between the causes and the consequences of the "class situation." For however different life chances may be, this fact in itself, according to all experience, by no means gives birth to "class action" (communal action by the members of a class). The fact of being conditioned and the results of the class situation must be distinctly recognizable. For only then the contrast of life chances can be felt not as an absolutely given fact to be accepted, but as a resultant from either 1) the given distribution of property, or 2) the structure of the concrete economic order. It is only then that people may react against the class structure not only through acts of an intermittent and irrational protest, but in the form of rational association. There have been "class situations" of the first category (1), of a specifically naked and transparent sort, in the urban centers of Antiquity and during the Middle Ages; especially then, when great fortunes were accumulated by factually monopolized trading in industrial products of these localities or in foodstuffs. Furthermore, under certain circumstances, in the rural economy of the most diverse periods, when agriculture was increasingly exploited in a profit-making manner. The most important historical example of the second category (2) is the class situation of the modern "proletariat."

Types of "class struggle"

Thus every class may be the carrier of any one of the possibly innumerable forms of "class action," but this is not necessarily so. In any case, a class does not in itself constitute a community. To treat "class" conceptually as having the same value as "community" leads to distortion. That men in the same class situation regularly react in mass actions to such tangible situations as economic ones in the direction of those interests that are most adequate to their average number is an important and after all simple fact for the understanding of historical events. Above all, this fact must not lead to that kind of pseudo-scientific operation with the concepts of "class" and "class interests" so frequently found these days, and which has found its most classic expression in the statement of a talented author, that the individual may be in error concerning his interests but that the "class" is "infallible" about its interests. Yet, if classes as such are not communities, nevertheless class situations emerge only on the basis of communalization. The communal action that brings forth class situations, however, is not basically action between members of the identical class; it is an action between members of different classes. Communal actions that

directly determine the class situation of the worker and the entrepreneur are: the labor market, the commodities market, and the capitalistic enterprise. But, in its turn, the existence of a capitalistic enterprise presupposes that a very specific communal action exists and that it is specifically structured to protect the possession of goods *per se*, and especially the power of individuals to dispose, in principle freely, over the means of production. The existence of a capitalistic enterprise is preconditioned by a specific kind of "legal order." Each kind of class situation, and above all when it rests upon the power of property *per se*, will become most clearly efficacious when all other determinants of reciprocal relations are, as far as possible, eliminated in their significance. It is in this way that the utilization of the power of property in the market obtains its most sovereign importance.

Now "status groups" hinder the strict carrying through of the sheer market principle. In the present context they are of interest to us only from this one point of view. Before we briefly consider them, note that not much of a general nature can be said about the more specific kinds of antagonism between "classes" (in our meaning of the term). The great shift, which has been going on continuously in the past, and up to our times, may be summarized, although at the cost of some precision: the struggle in which class situations are effective has progressively shifted from consumption credit toward, first, competitive struggles in the commodity market and, then, toward price wars on the labor market. The "class struggles" of antiquity — to the extent that they were genuine class struggles and not struggles between status groups — were initially carried on by indebted peasants, and perhaps also by artisans threatened by debt bondage and struggling against urban creditors. For debt bondage is the normal result of the differentiation of wealth in commercial cities, especially in seaport cities. A similar situation has existed among cattle breeders. Debt relationships as such produced class action up to the time of Cataline. Along with this, and with an increase in provision of grain for the city by transporting it from the outside, the struggle over the means of sustenance emerged. It centered in the first place around the provision of bread and the determination of the price of bread. It lasted throughout antiquity and the entire Middle Ages. The propertyless as such flocked together against those who actually and supposedly were interested in the dearth of bread. This fight spread until it involved all those commodities essential to the way of life and to handicraft production. There were only incipient discussions of wage disputes in antiquity and in the Middle Ages. But they have been slowly increasing up into modern times. In the earlier periods they were completely secondary to slave rebellions as well as to fights in the commodity market.

The propertyless of antiquity and of the Middle Ages protested against monopolies, pre-emption, forestalling, and the withholding of goods from the market in order to raise prices. Today the central issue is the determination of the price of labor.

This transition is represented by the fight for access to the market and for the determination of the price of products. Such fights went on between merchants and workers in the putting-out system of domestic handicraft during the transition to modern times. Since it is quite a general phenomenon we must mention here that the class antagonisms that are conditioned through the market situation are usually most bitter between those who actually and directly participate as opponents in price wars. It is not the rentier, the share-holder, and the banker who suffer the ill will of the worker, but almost exclusively the manufacturer and the business executives who are the direct opponents of workers in price wars. This is so in spite of the fact that it is precisely the cash boxes of the rentier, the share-holder, and the banker into which the more or less "unearned" gains flow, rather than into the pockets of the manufacturers or of the business executives. This simple state of affairs has very frequently been decisive for the role the class situation has played in the formation of political parties. For example, it has made possible the varieties of patriarchal socialism and the frequent attempts — formerly, at least — of threatened status groups to form alliances with the proletariat against the "bourgeoisie."

Status honor

In contrast to classes, *status groups* are normally communities. They are, however, often of an amorphous kind. In contrast to the purely economically determined "class situation" we wish to designate as "status situation" every typical component of the life fate of men that is determined by a specific, positive or negative, social estimation of *honor*. This honor may be connected with any quality shared by a plurality, and, of course, it can be knit to a class situation: class distinctions are linked in the most varied ways with status distinctions. Property as such is not always recognized as a status qualification, but in the long run it is, and with extraordinary regularity. In the subsistence economy of the organized neighborhood, very often the richest man is simply the chieftain. However, this often means only an honorific preference. For example, in the so-called pure modern "democracy," that is, one devoid of any expressly ordered status privileges for individuals, it may be that only the families coming under approximately the same tax class dance with one another. This example is reported of certain smaller Swiss cities. But status honor need not necessarily be linked with a "class situation." On the contrary, it normally stands in sharp opposition to the pretensions of sheer property.

Both propertied and propertyless people can belong to the same status group, and frequently they do with very tangible consequences. This "equality" of social esteem may, however, in the long run become quite precarious. The "equality" of status among the American "gentlemen," for instance, is expressed by the fact that outside the subordination determined by the different functions of "business," it would be considered strictly repugnant — wherever the old tradition still prevails — if even the richest "chief," while playing billiards or cards in his club in the evening, would not treat his "clerk" as in every sense fully his equal in birthright. It would be repugnant if the American "chief" would bestow upon his "clerk" the condescending "benevolence" marking a distinction of "position," which the German chief can never dissever from his attitude. This is one of the most important reasons why in America the German "clubbyness" has never been able to attain the attraction that the American clubs have.

Guarantees of status stratification

In content, status honor is normally expressed by the fact that above all else a specific *style of life* can be expected from all those who wish to belong to the circle. Linked with this expectation are restrictions on "social" intercourse (that is, intercourse which is not subservient to economic or any other of business's "functional" purposes). These restrictions may confine normal marriages to within the status circle and may lead to complete endogamous closure. As soon as there is not a mere individual and socially irrelevant imitation of another style of life, but an agreed-upon communal action of this closing character, the "status" development is under way.

In its characteristic form, stratification by "status groups" on the basis of conventional styles of life evolves at the present time in the United States out of the traditional democracy. For example, only the resident of a certain street ("the street") is considered as belonging to "society," is qualified for social intercourse, and is visited and invited. Above all, this differentiation evolves in such a way as to make for strict submission to the fashion that is dominant at a given time in society. This submission to fashion also exists among men in America to a degree unknown in Germany. Such submission is considered to be an indication of the fact that a given man *pretends* to qualify as a gentleman. This submission decides, at least *prima facie*, that he will be treated as such. And this recognition becomes just as important for his employment chances in "swank" establishments, and above all, for social intercourse and marriage with "esteemed" families, as the qualification for dueling among Germans in the Kaiser's day. As for the rest: certain families resident for a long time, and, of course, correspondingly wealthy, e.g. "F. F. V., i.e. First Families of Virginia," or the actual or alleged descendants of the "Indian Princess" Pocahontas, of the Pilgrim fathers, or of the Knickerbockers, the members of almost inaccessible sects and all sorts of circles setting themselves apart by means of any other characteristics and badges . . . all these elements usurp "status" honor. The development of status is essentially a question of stratification resting upon usurpation. Such usurpation is the normal origin of almost all status honor. But the road from this purely conventional situation to legal privilege, positive or negative, is easily traveled as soon as a certain stratification of the social order has in fact been "lived in" and has achieved stability by virtue of a stable distribution of economic power.

"Ethnic" segregation and "caste"

Where the consequences have been realized to their full extent, the status group evolves into a closed "caste." Status distinctions are then guaranteed not merely by conventions and laws, but also by *rituals*. This occurs in such a way that every physical contact with a member of any caste that is considered to be "lower" by the members of a "higher" caste is considered as making for a ritualistic impurity and to be a stigma which must be expiated by a religious act. Individual castes develop quite distinct cults and gods.

In general, however, the status structure reaches such extreme consequences only where there are underlying differences which are held to be "ethnic." The "caste" is, indeed, the normal form in which ethnic communities usually live side by side in a "societalized" manner. These ethnic communities believe in blood relationship and exclude exogamous marriage and social intercourse. Such a caste situation is part of the phenomenon of "pariah" peoples and is found all over the world. These people form communities, acquire specific occupational traditions of handicrafts or of other arts, and cultivate a belief in their ethnic community. They live in a "diaspora" strictly segregated from all personal intercourse, except that of an unavoidable sort, and their situation is legally precarious. Yet, by virtue of their economic indispensability, they are tolerated, indeed, frequently privileged, and they live in interspersed political communities. The Jews are the most impressive historical example.

A "status" segregation grown into a "caste" differs in its structure from a mere "ethnic" segregation: the caste structure transforms the horizontal and unconnected coexistences of ethnically segregated groups into a vertical social system of super- and subordination. Correctly formulated: a comprehensive societalization integrates the ethnically divided communities into specific political and communal action. In their consequences they differ precisely in this way: ethnic coexistences condition a mutual repulsion and disdain but allow each ethnic community to consider its own honor as the highest one; the caste structure brings about a social subordination and an acknowledgment of "more honor" in favor of the privileged caste and status groups. This is due to the fact that in the caste structure ethnic distinctions as such have become "functional" distinctions within the political societalization (warriors, priests, artisans that are politically important for war and for building, and so on). But even pariah people who are most despised are usually apt to continue cultivating in some manner that which is equally peculiar to ethnic and to status communities: the belief in their own specific "honor." This is the case with the Jews.

Only with the negatively privileged status groups does the "sense of dignity" take a specific deviation. A sense of dignity is the precipitation in individuals of social honor and of conventional demands which a positively privileged status group raises for the deportment of its members. The sense of dignity that characterizes positively privileged status groups is naturally related to their "being" which does not transcend itself, that is, it is to their "beauty and excellence." Their kingdom is "of this world." They live for the present and by exploiting their great past. The sense of dignity of the negatively privileged strata naturally refers to a future lying beyond the present, whether it is of this life or of another. In other words, it must be nurtured by the belief in a providential "mission" and by a belief in a specific honor before God. The "chosen people's" dignity is nurtured by a belief either that in the beyond "the last will be the first," or that in this life a Messiah will appear to bring forth into the light of the world which has cast them out the hidden honor of the pariah people. This simple state of affairs, and not the "resentment" which is so strongly emphasized in Nietzsche's much admired construction in the *Genealogy of Morals*, is the source of the religiosity cultivated by pariah status groups. In passing, we may note that resentment may be accurately applied only to a limited extent; for one of Nietzsche's main examples, Buddhism, it is not at all applicable.

Incidentally, the development of status groups from ethnic segregations is by no means the normal phenomenon. On the contrary, since objective "racial differences" are by no means basic to every subjective sentiment of an ethnic community, the ultimately racial foundation of status structure is rightly and absolutely a question of the concrete individual case. Very frequently a status group is instrumental in the production of a thoroughbred anthropological type. Certainly a status group is to a high degree effective in producing extreme types, for they select personally qualified individuals (e.g. the Knighthood selects those who are fit for warfare, physically and psychically). But selection is far from being the only, or the predominant, way in which status groups are formed: Political membership or class situation has at all times been at least as frequently decisive. And today the class situation is by far the predominant factor, for of course the possibility of a style of life expected for members of a status group is usually conditioned economically.

Status privileges

For all practical purposes, stratification by status goes hand in hand with a monopolization of ideal and material goods or opportunities, in a manner we have come to know as typical. Besides the specific status honor, which always rests upon distance and exclusiveness, we find all sorts of material monopolies. Such honorific preferences may consist of the privilege of wearing special costumes, of eating special dishes taboo to others, of carrying arms — which is most obvious in its consequences — the right to pursue certain non-professional dilettante artistic practices, e.g. to play certain musical instruments. Of course, material monopolies provide the most effective motives for the exclusiveness of a status group; although, in themselves, they are rarely sufficient, almost always they come into play to some extent. Within a status circle there is the question of intermarriage: the interest of the families in the monopolization of potential bridegrooms is at least of equal importance and is parallel to the interest in the monopolization of daughters. The daughters of the circle must be provided for. With an increased inclosure of the status group, the conventional preferential opportunities for special employment grow into a legal monopoly of special offices for the members. Certain goods become objects for monopolization by status groups. In the typical fashion these include "entailed estates" and frequently also the possessions of serfs or bondsmen and, finally, special trades. This monopolization occurs positively when the status group is exclusively entitled to own and to manage them; and negatively when, in order to maintain its specific way of life, the status group must *not* own and manage them.

The decisive role of a "style of life" in status "honor" means that status groups are the specific bearers of all "conventions." In whatever way it may be manifest, all "stylization" of life either originates in status groups or is at least conserved by them. Even if the principles of status conventions differ greatly, they reveal certain typical traits, especially among those strata which are most privileged. Quite generally, among privileged status groups there is a status disqualification that operates against the performance of common physical labor. This disqualification is now "setting in" in America against the old tradition of esteem for labor. Very frequently every rational economic pursuit, and especially "entrepreneurial activity," is looked upon as a disqualification of status. Artistic and literary activity is also considered as degrading work as soon as it is exploited for income, or at least when it is connected with hard physical exertion. An example is the sculptor working like a mason in his dusty smock as over against the painter in his salon-like "studio" and those forms of musical practice that are acceptable to the status group.

Economic conditions and effects of status stratification

The frequent disqualification of the gainfully employed as such is a direct result of the principle of status stratification peculiar to the social order, and of course, of this principle's opposition to a distribution of power which is regulated exclusively through the market. These two factors operate along with various individual ones, which will be touched upon below.

We have seen above that the market and its processes "knows no personal distinctions": "functional" interests dominate it. It knows nothing of "honor." The status order means precisely the reverse, viz.: stratification in terms of "honor" and of styles of life peculiar to status groups as such. If mere economic acquisition and naked economic power still bearing the stigma of its extra-status origin could bestow upon anyone who has won it the same honor as those who are interested in status by virtue of style of life claim for themselves, the status order would be threatened at its very root. This is the more so as, given equality of status honor, property *per se* represents an addition even if it is not overtly acknowledged to be such. Yet if such economic acquisition and power gave the agent any honor at all, his wealth would result in his attaining more honor than those who successfully claim honor by virtue of style of life. Therefore all groups having interests in the status order react with special sharpness precisely against the pretensions of purely economic acquisition. In most cases they react the more vigorously the more they feel themselves threatened. Calderon's respectful treatment of the peasant, for instance, as opposed to Shakespeare's simultaneous and ostensible disdain of the *canaille* illustrates the different way in which a firmly structured status order reacts as compared with a status order that has become economically precarious. This is an example of a state of affairs that recurs everywhere. Precisely because of the rigorous reactions against the claims of property *per se*, the "parvenu" is never accepted, personally and without reservation, by the privileged status groups, no matter how completely his style of life has been adjusted to theirs. They will only accept his descendants who have been educated in the conventions of their status group and who have never besmirched its honor by their own economic labor.

As to the general *effect* of the status order, only one consequence can be stated, but it is a very important one: the hindrance of the free development of the market occurs first for those goods which status groups directly withheld from free exchange by monopolization. This monopolization may be effected either legally or conventionally. For example, in many Hellenic cities during the epoch of status groups, and also originally in Rome, the inherited estate (as is shown by the old formula for indiction against spendthrifts) was monopolized just as were the estates of knights, peasants, priests, and especially the clientele of the craft and merchant guilds. The market is restricted, and the power of naked property *per se*, which gives its stamp to "class formation," is pushed into the background. The results of this process can be most varied. Of course, they do not necessarily weaken the contrasts in the economic situation. Frequently they strengthen these contrasts, and in any case, where stratification by status permeates a community as strongly as was the case in all political communities of antiquity and of the Middle Ages, one can never speak of a genuinely free market competition as we understand it today. There are wider effects than this direct exclusion of special goods from the market. From the contrariety between the status order and the purely economic order mentioned above, it follows that in most instances the notion of honor peculiar to status absolutely abhors that which is essential to the market: higgling. Honor abhors higgling among peers and occasionally it taboos higgling for the members of a status group in general. Therefore, everywhere some status groups, and usually the most influential, consider almost any kind of overt participation in economic acquisition as absolutely stigmatizing.

With some over-simplification, one might thus say that "classes" are stratified according to their relations to the production and acquisition of goods; whereas "status groups" are stratified according to the principles of their *consumption* of goods as represented by special "styles of life."

An "occupational group" is also a status group. For normally, it successfully claims social honor only by virtue of the special style of life which may be determined by it. The differences between classes and status groups frequently overlap. It is precisely those status communities most strictly segregated in terms of honor (viz. the Indian castes) who today show, although within very rigid limits, a relatively high degree of indifference to pecuniary income. However, the Brahmins seek such income in many different ways.

As to the general economic conditions making for the predominance of stratification by "status," only very little can be said. When the bases of the acquisition and distribution of goods are relatively stable, stratification by status is favored. Every technological repercussion and economic transformation threatens stratification by status and pushes the class situation into the foreground. Epochs and countries in which the naked class situation is of predominant significance are regularly the periods of technical and economic transformations. And every slowing down of the shifting of economic stratifications leads, in due course, to the growth of status structures and makes for a resuscitation of the important role of social honor.

Parties

Whereas the genuine place of "classes" is within the economic order, the place of "status groups" is within the social order, that is, within the sphere of the distribution of "honor." From within these spheres, classes and status groups influence one another and they influence the legal order and are in turn influenced by it. But "parties" live in a house of "power."

Their action is oriented toward the acquisition of social "power," that is to say, toward influencing a communal action no matter what its content may be. In principle, parties may exist in a social "club" as well as in a "state." As over against the actions of classes and status groups, for which this is not necessarily the case, the communal actions of "parties" always mean a societalization. For party actions are always directed toward a goal which is striven for in planned manner. This goal may be a "cause" (the party may aim at realizing a program for ideal or material purposes), or the goal may be "personal" (sinecures, power, and from these, honor for the leader and the followers of the party). Usually the party action aims at all these simultaneously. Parties are, therefore, only possible within communities that are societalized, that is, which have some rational order and a staff of persons available who are ready to enforce it. For parties aim precisely at influencing this staff, and if possible, to recruit it from party followers.

In any individual case, parties may represent interests determined through "class situation" or "status situation," and they may recruit their following respectively from one or the other. But they need be neither purely "class" nor purely "status" parties. In most cases they are partly class parties and partly status parties, but sometimes they are neither. They may represent ephemeral or enduring structures. Their means of attaining power may be quite varied, ranging from naked violence of any sort to convassing for votes with coarse or subtle means: money, social influence, the force of speech, suggestion, clumsy hoax, and so on to the rougher or more artful tactics of obstruction in parliamentary bodies.

The sociological structure of parties differs in a basic way according to the kind of communal action which they struggle to influence. Parties also differ according to whether or not the community is stratified by status or by classes. Above all else, they vary according to the structure of domination within the community. For their leaders normally deal with the conquest of a community. They are, in the general concept which is maintained here, not only products of specially modern forms of domination. We shall also designate as parties the ancient and medieval "parties," despite the fact that their structure differs basically from the structure of modern parties. By virtue of these structural differences of domination it is impossible to say anything about the structure of parties without discussing the structural forms of social domination *per se*. Parties, which are always structures struggling for domination, are very frequently organized in a very strict "authoritarian" fashion....

Concerning "classes," "status groups," and "parties," it must be said in general that they necessarily presuppose a comprehensive societalization, and especially a political framework of communal action, within which they operate. This does not mean that parties would be confined by the frontiers of any individual political community. On the contrary, at all times it has been the order of the day that the societalization (even when it aims at the use of military force in common) reaches beyond the frontiers of politics. This has been the case in the solidarity of interests among the Oligarchs and among the democrats in Hellas, among the Guelfs and among Ghibellines in the Middle Ages, and within the Calvinist party during the period of religious struggles. It has been the case up to the solidarity of the landlords (international congress of agrarian landlords), and

<hr>

[1] The posthumously published text breaks off here. We omit an incomplete sketch of types of "warrior estates."

has continued among princes (holy alliance, Karlsbad decrees), socialist workers, conservatives (the longing of Prussian conservatives for Russian intervention in 1850). But their aim is not necessarily the establishment of new international political, i.e. *territorial*, dominion. In the main they aim to influence the existing dominion.[1]

<hr>

The Development of Caste

Max Weber

Caste and tribe

As long as a tribe has not become wholly a guest or a pariah people, it usually has a fixed tribal territory. A genuine caste never has a fixed territory. To a very considerable extent, the caste members live in the country, segregated in villages. Usually in each village there is, or was, only one caste with full title to the soil. But dependent village artisans and laborers also live with this caste. In any case, the caste does not form a local, territorial, corporate body, for this would contradict its nature. A tribe is, or at least originally was, bound together by obligatory blood revenge, mediated directly or indirectly through the sib. A caste never has anything to do with such blood revenge.

Originally, a tribe normally comprised many, often almost all, of the possible pursuits necessary for the gaining of subsistence. A caste may comprise people who follow very different pursuits; at least this is the case today, and for certain upper castes this has been the case since very early times. Yet so long as the caste has not lost its character, the kinds of pursuits admissible without loss of caste are always, in some way, quite strictly limited. Even today "caste" and "way of earning a living" are so firmly linked that often a change of occupation is correlated with a division of caste. This is not the case for a "tribe."

Normally a tribe comprises people of every social rank. A caste may well be divided into subcastes with extraordinarily different social ranks. Today this is usually the case; one caste frequently contains several hundred subcastes. In such cases, these subcastes may be related to one another exactly, or almost exactly, as are different castes. If this is the case, the subcastes, in reality, are castes; the caste name common to all of them has merely historical significance, or almost so, and serves to support the social pretensions of degraded

subcastes towards third castes. Hence, by its very nature, caste is inseparably bound up with social ranks within a larger community.

It is decisive for a tribe that it is originally and normally a political association. The tribe is either an independent association, as is always originally the case, or the association is part of a tribal league; or, it may constitute a *phyle*, that is, part of a political association commissioned with certain political tasks and having certain rights: franchise, holding quotas of the political offices, and the right of assuming its share or turn of political, fiscal, and liturgical obligations. A caste is never a political association, even if political associations in individual cases have burdened castes with liturgies, as may have happened repeatedly during the Indian Middle Ages (Bengal). In this case, castes are in the same position as merchant and craft guilds, sibs, and all sorts of associations. By its very nature the caste is always a purely social and possibly occupational association, which forms part of and stands within a social community. But the caste is not necessarily, and by no means regularly, an association forming part of only one political association; rather it may reach beyond, or it may fall short of, the boundaries of any one political association. There are castes diffused over all of India. Of the present Hindu castes (the chief ones), one may say that twenty-five are diffused throughout most of the regions of India. These castes comprise about 88 million Hindus out of the total of 217 million. Among them we find the ancient priest, warrior, and merchant castes: the Brahmans (14.60 million); Rajputs (9.43 million); Baniya (3.00 or only 1.12 million—according to whether or not one includes the split subcastes); Cayasts (ancient caste of official scribes 2.17 million); as well as ancient tribal castes like the Ahirs (9.50 million); Jats (6.98 million); or the great, unclean,

<hr>

Reprinted from Max Weber, *The Religion of India* (The Free Press of Glencoe, 1958), translated and edited by Hans H. Gerth and Don Martindale.

occupational castes like the Chamar, the leather workers (11.50 million); the Shudra caste of the Teli, the oil pressers (4.27 million); the genteel trade caste of the goldsmiths, the Sonar (1.26 million); the ancient castes of village artisans, the Kumhar (potters) (3.42 million) and Lohar (blacksmiths) (2.07 million); the lower peasant caste of the Koli (cooli, derived from *kul*, clan, meaning something like "kin" — *Gevatter*) (3.17 million); and other individual castes of varying origin. The great differences in caste names as well as several distinctions of social rank which, in the individual provinces, derive from castes obviously equal in descent, make direct comparisons extremely difficult. Yet today, each of the subcastes and also most of the small castes exist only in their respective small districts. Political division has often strongly influenced the caste order of individual areas, but precisely the most important castes have remained interstate in scope.

With regard to the substance of its social norms, a tribe usually differs from a caste in that the exogamy of the totem or of the villages co-exist with the exogamy of the sibs. Endogamy has existed only under certain conditions, but by no means always, for the tribe as a whole. Rules of endogamy, however, always form the essential basis of a caste. Dietary rules and rules of commensality are always characteristic of the caste but are by no means characteristic of the tribe.

We have already observed that when a tribe loses its foothold in its territory it becomes a guest or a pariah people. It may then approximate caste to the point of being actually indistinguishable from it. The Banjaras, for instance, are partly organized as castes in the Central Provinces. In Mysore, however, they are organized as an (Animist) tribe. In both cases they make their living in the same way. Similar instances frequently occur. The differences that remain will be discussed when we determine the positive characteristics of caste. In contrast to the tribe, a caste is usually related intimately to special ways of earning a living, on the one hand, and, on the other, to social rank. Now the question arises, how is caste related to the occupational associations (merchant and craft guilds) and how is it related to status groups? Let us begin with the former.

Caste and guild

Guilds of merchants, and of traders who figured as merchants by selling their own produce, as well as craft guilds, existed in India during the period of the development of cities and especially during the period in which the great salvation religions originated. As we shall see, the salvation religions and the guilds were related. The guilds usually emerged within the cities, but occasionally they emerged outside; survivals of these are still in existence. During the period of the flowering of the cities, the position of the guilds was quite comparable to that occupied by guilds in the cities of the medieval Occident.

The guild association (the *mahajan*, literally, the same as *popolo grasso*) faced the prince on one hand and, on the other, the economically dependent artisans. These relations were about the same as those of the great guilds of literati and of merchants with the lower craft-guilds (*popolo minuto*) of the Occident. In the same way, associations of lower craft guilds existed in India (the *panch*). Moreover, the liturgical guild of Egyptian and late Roman character was perhaps not entirely lacking in the emerging patrimonial states of India. The uniqueness of the development of India lay in the fact that these beginnings of guild organization in the cities led neither to the city autonomy of the Occidental type nor, after the development of the great patrimonial states, to a social and economic organization of the territories corresponding to the "territorial economy"[1] of the Occident. Rather, the Hindu caste system, whose beginnings certainly preceded these organizations, became paramount. In part, this caste system entirely displaced the other organizations; in part, it crippled them; it prevented them from attaining any considerable importance. The "spirit" of this caste system, however, was totally different from that of the merchant and craft guilds.

The merchant and craft guilds of the Occident cultivated religious interests as did the castes. In connection with these interests, questions of social rank also played a considerable role among guilds. Which rank order the guilds should follow, during processions, for instance, was a question occasionally fought over more stubbornly than questions of economic interest. Furthermore, in a "closed" guild, that is, one with a numerically fixed quota of income opportunities, the position of the master was hereditary. There were also quasi-guild associations and associations derived from guilds in which the right to membership was acquired in hereditary succession. In late Antiquity, membership in the liturgical guilds was even a compulsory and hereditary obligation in the way of a *glebae adscriptio*, which bound the peasant to the soil. Finally, in the medieval Occident there were "opprobrious" trades, which were religiously déclassé; these correspond to the "unclean" castes of India. The fundamental difference, however, between occupational associations and caste is not affected by these circumstances.

First, that which is partly an exception and partly an occasional consequence for the occupational association is truly fundamental for the caste; the magical distance between castes in their mutual relationships.

In 1901 in the "United Provinces" roughly ten million people (out of a total of about forty million) belonged to castes with which physical contact is ritually polluting. In the Madras Presidency, roughly thirteen million people (out of about fifty-two million) could infect others even without direct contact if they ap-

---

[1] "Territorial economy" designates a stage in economic development. The term was coined by Gustav Schmoller, who distinguished between "village economy" — "city economy" — "territorial economy" — "national economy." (Gerth and Martindale, eds.)

proached within a certain, though varying, distance. The merchant and craft guilds of the Middle Ages acknowledged no ritual barriers whatsoever between the individual guilds and artisans, apart from the aforementioned small stratum of people engaged in opprobrious trades. Pariah peoples and pariah workers (for example, the knacker and hangman), by virtue of their special positions, come close sociologically to the unclean castes of India. And there were factual barriers restricting the connubium between differently esteemed occupations, but there were no ritual barriers, such as are absolutely essential for caste. Within the circle of the "honorable" people, ritual barriers to commensalism were completely absent; but such barriers belong to the basis of caste differences.

Furthermore, caste is essentially hereditary. This hereditary character was not, and is not, merely the result of monopolizing and restricting the earning opportunities to a definite maximum quota, as was the case among the absolutely closed guilds of the Occident, which at no time were numerically predominant. Such quota restriction existed, and still exists in part, among the occupational castes of India; but restriction is strongest not in the cities but in the villages, where a quota restriction of opportunities, insofar as it has existed, has had no connection with a guild organization and no need for it. As we shall see, the typical Indian village artisans have been the hereditary "tied cottagers" of the village.

The most important castes, although not all castes, have guaranteed the individual member a certain subsistence, as was the case among our master craftsmen. But not all castes have monopolized a whole trade as the guild at least strove to do. The guild of the Occident, at least during the Middle Ages, was regularly based upon the apprentice's free choice of a master and thus it made possible the transition of the children to occupations other than those of their parents, a circumstance which never occurs in the caste system. This difference is fundamental. Whereas the closure of the guild toward the outside became stricter with diminishing income opportunities, among the castes the reverse was often observed, namely, they maintained their ritually required way of life, and hence their inherited trade, most easily when income opportunities were plentiful.

Another difference between guild and caste is of even greater importance. The occupational associations of the medieval Occident were often engaged in violent struggles among themselves, but at the same time they evidenced a tendency towards fraternization. The *mercanzia* and the *popolo* in Italy, and the "citizenry" in the north, were regularly, organizations of occupational associations. The *capitano del popolo* in the south and, frequently, though not always, the Bürgermeister in the north were heads of oath-bound organizations of the occupational associations, at least according to their original and specific meaning. Such organizations seized political power, either legally or illegally. Irrespective of their legal forms, the late medieval city

in fact rested upon the fraternization of its productive citizenry. This was at least the case where the political form of the medieval city contained its most important sociological characteristics.

As a rule the fraternization of the citizenry was carried through by the fraternization of the guilds, just as the ancient *polis* in its innermost being rested upon the fraternization of military associations and sibs. Note that the base was "fraternization." It was not of secondary importance that every foundation of the occidental city, in antiquity and the Middle Ages, went hand in hand with the establishment of a cultic community of the citizens. Furthermore, it is of significance that the common meal of the *prytanes*, the drinking rooms of the merchant and craft guilds, and their common processions to the church played such a great role in the official documents of the occidental cities, and that the medieval citizens had, at least in the Lord's Supper, commensalism with one another in the most festive form. Fraternization at all times presupposes commensalism; it does not have to be actually practiced in everyday life, but it must be ritually possible. The caste order precluded this.

Complete fraternization of castes has been and is impossible because it is one of the constitutive principles of the castes that there should be at least ritually inviolable barriers against complete commensalism among different castes. As with all sociological phenomena, the contrast here is not an absolute one, nor are transitions lacking, yet it is a contrast which is essential features has been historically decisive.

The commensalism existing between castes really only confirms the rule. For instance, there is commensalism between certain Rajput and Brahman subcastes which rests upon the fact that the latter have of yore been the family priests of the former. If the member of a low caste merely looks at the meal of a Brahman, it ritually defiles the Brahman. When the last great famine caused the British administration to open public soup kitchens accessible to everyone, the tally of patrons showed that impoverished people of all castes had in their need visited the kitchens, although it was of course strictly and ritually taboo to eat in this manner in the sight of people not belonging to one's caste. A separate lower caste (the Kallars) has arisen in Bengal among people who had infracted the ritual and dietary laws during the famine of 1866, and in consequence been excommunicated. Within this caste, in turn, the minority separate themselves as a subcaste from the majority. The former maintaining a price ratio of six seers for the rupee, separated themselves from those maintaining a price ratio of ten seers for the rupee.

At the time of the famine the strict castes were not satisfied with the possibility of cleansing magical defilement by ritual penance. Yet under threat of excommunicating the participants, they did succeed in securing employment only of high-caste cooks; the hands of these cooks were considered ritually clean by all the castes concerned. Furthermore, they made certain that often a sort of symbolic *chambre séparée* was created for each caste by means of chalk lines drawn around the tables and similar devices. Apart from the fact that in the face of starvation even strong magical powers fail to carry weight, every strictly ritualist religion, such as the Indian, Hebrew, and Roman, is able to open ritualistic back doors for extreme situations.

Yet, it is a long way from this situation to a possible commensalism and fraternization as they are known in the Occident. To be sure, during the rise of the kingdoms, we find that the king invited the various castes, the Shudra included, to his table. They were seated, however, at least according to the classic conception, in separate rooms; and the fact that a caste that claimed to belong to the Vaishya was seated among the Sudra in the Vellala Charita occasioned a famous (semi-legendary) conflict, which we shall have to discuss later.

Let us now consider the Occident. In his letter to the Galatians (11:12, 13ff.) Paul reproaches Peter for having eaten in Antioch with the gentiles and for having withdrawn and separated himself afterwards, under the influence of the Jerusalemites. "And the other Jews dissembled likewise with him." That the reproach of dissimulation made to this very Apostle has not been effaced shows perhaps just as clearly as does the occurrence itself the tremendous importance this event had for the early Christians. Indeed, this shattering of the ritual barriers against commensalism meant a destruction of the voluntary ghetto, which in its effects is far more incisive than any compulsory ghetto. It meant to destroy the situation of Jewry as a pariah people, a situation that was ritually imposed upon this people.

For the Christians it meant the origin of Christian "freedom," which Paul celebrated triumphantly again and again; for this freedom meant the universalism of Paul's mission, which cut across nations and status groups. The elimination of all ritual barriers of birth for the community of the eucharists, as realized in Antioch, was, in connection with the religious pre-conditions, the hour of conception for the occidental "citizenry." This is the case even though its birth occurred more than a thousand years later in the revolutionary *conjurationes* of the medieval cities. For without commensalism — in Christian terms, without the Lord's Supper — no oathbound fraternity and no medieval urban citizenry would have been possible.

India's caste order formed an obstacle to this, which was unsurmountable, at least by its own forces. For the castes are not governed only by this eternal ritual division. A nabob of Bankura, upon the request of a Chandala, wished to compel the Karnakar (metal workers) caste to eat with the Chandala. According to the legend of the origin of the Mahmudpurias, this request caused part of this caste to flee to Mahmudpura and to constitute itself as a separate subcaste with higher social claims. Even if there are no antagonisms of economic interests, a profound estrangement usually exists between the castes, and often deadly jealousy and hostility as well, precisely because the castes are completely oriented towards social rank. This orientation stands in contrast to the occupational associations of the Occident. Whatever part questions of etiquette and rank have played among these associations, and often it has been quite considerable, such questions could never have gained the religiously anchored significance which they have had for the Hindu.

The consequences of this difference have been of considerable political importance. By its solidarity, the association of Indian guilds, the *mahajan*, was a force which the princes had to take very much into account. It was said: "The prince must recognize what the guilds do to the people, whether it is merciful or cruel." The guilds acquired privileges from the princes for loans of money, which is reminiscent of our medieval conditions. The *shreshti* (elders) of the guilds belonged to the mightiest notables and ranked equally with the warrior and the priest nobility of their time. In the areas and at the time that these conditions prevailed, the power of the castes was undeveloped and partly hindered and shaken by the religions of salvation, which were hostile to the Brahmans. The later turn in favor of the the monopoly rule of the caste system not only increased the power of the Brahmans but also that of the princes, and it broke the power of the guilds. For the castes excluded every solidarity and every politically powerful fraternization of the citizenry and of the trades. If the prince observed the ritual traditions and the social pretensions based upon them, which existed among those castes most important for him, he could not only play off the castes against one another — which he did — but he had nothing whatever to fear from them, especially if the Brahmans stood by his side. Accordingly, it is not difficult even at this point to guess the political interests which had a hand in the game during the transformation to monopoly rule of the caste system. This shift steered India's social structure — which for a time apparently stood close to the threshold of European urban development — into a course that led far away from any possibility of such development. In these world-historical differences the fundamentally important contrast between "caste" and "guild," or any other "occupational association," is strikingly revealed.

If the caste differs fundamentally from the guild and from any other kind of merely occupational association, and if the core of the caste system is connected with social rank, how then is the caste related to the status group, which finds its genuine expression in social rank?

Caste and status group

What is a "status group?" "Classes" are groups of people who, from the standpoint of specific interests, have the same economic position. Ownership or nonownership of material goods, or possession of definite skills constitutes a class situation. "Status," however, is a quality of social honor or a lack of it, and is in the main conditioned as well as expressed through a specific style of life. Social honor can adhere directly to a class situation, and it is also, indeed most of the time, determined by the average class situation of the status-group members. This, however, is not necessarily the case. Status membership, in turn, influences class situation in that the style of life required by status groups makes them prefer special kinds of property or gainful pursuits and reject others. A status group can be closed (status by descent) or it can be open.[1]

A caste is doubtless a closed status group. All the obligations and barriers that membership in a status group entails also exist in a caste, in which they are intensified to the utmost degree. The Occident has known legally closed "estates," in the sense that intermarriage with nonmembers of the group was lacking. But, as a rule, this bar against connubium held only to the extent that marriages contracted in spite of the rule constituted *mésalliances*, with the consequence that children of the "left-handed" marriage would follow the status of the lower partner.

Europe still acknowledges such status barriers for the high nobility. America acknowledges them between whites and Negroes (including all mixed bloods) in the southern states of the union. But in America these barriers imply that marriage is absolutely and legally inadmissible, quite apart from the fact that such intermarriage would result in social boycott.

Among the Hindu castes at the present time, not only intermarriage between castes but even intermarriage between subcastes is usually absolutely shunned. Already in the books of law mixed bloods from different castes belong to a lower caste than either of the parents, and in no case do they belong to the three higher ("twice-born") castes. A different state of affairs, however, prevailed in earlier days and still exists today for the most important castes. Today one occasionally encounters full connubium among subcastes of the same caste, as well as among castes of equal social standing. According to Gait's general report for 1911,[2] this was the case for the equally genteel castes of the Baidya and Kayastha in Bengal, the Kanet and the Khas in the Punjab, and, sporadically, among the Brahmans and Rajputs, and the Sonars, Nais, and the Kanets (women). Enriched Maratha peasants may avail themselves of Moratha women for a sufficient dowry.

In earlier times this was undoubtedly more often the case. Above all, originally connubium was obviously not absolutely excluded, but rather hypergamy was the rule. Among the Rajputs in Punjab, hypergamy often still exists to such an extent that even Chamar girls are purchased. Intermarriage between a girl of higher caste

and a lower-caste man was considered an offense against the status honor of the girl's family. However, to own a wife of lower caste was not considered an offense, and her children were not considered degraded, or at least only partially so. According to the law of inheritance, which is certainly the product of a later period, the children had to take second place in inheritance (just as in Israel the sentence that the "children of the servant" — and of the foreign woman — "should not inherit in Israel" has been the law of a later period, as is the case everywhere else).

The interest of upper-class men in the legality of polygamy, which they could afford economically, continued to exist, even when the acute shortage of women among the invading warriors had ended. Such shortages have everywhere compelled conquerors to marry girls of subject populations. The result in India was, however, that the lower-caste girls had a large marriage market, and the lower the caste stood the larger was their marriage market; whereas the marriage market for girls of the highest castes was restricted to their own caste. Moreover, by virtue of the competition of the lower-caste girls, this restricted marriage market was by no means monopolistically guaranteed to upper-caste girls. And this caused the women in the lower castes, by virtue of the general demand for women, to bring high prices as brides. It was in part as a consequence of this dearth of women, that polyandry originated. The formation of marriage cartels among villages or among special associations, Golis, as frequently found, for instance, among the Vania (merchant) castes in Gujarat and also among peasant castes, is a countermeasure against the hypergamy of the wealthy and the city people, which raised the price of brides for the middle classes and for the rural population. If in India[3] the whole village — the unclean castes included — consider themselves to be interrelated, that is, if the new marriage partner is addressed by all as "son-in-law" and the older generation is addressed by all as "uncle," it is evident that this has nothing whatsoever to do with derivation from a "primitive group marriage"; this is indeed as little true in India as elsewhere.

Among the upper castes, however, the sale of girls to a bridegroom of rank was difficult and the more difficult it became, the more was failure to marry considered a disgrace for both the girl and her parents. The bridegroom had to be bought by the parents with incredibly high dowries, and his enlistment (through professional matchmakers) became the parents' most important worry. Even during the infancy of the girl it was a sorrow for the parents. Finally, it was considered an outright "sin" for a girl to reach puberty without being married. This has led to grotesque results: for example, the marriage practice of the Kulin Brahmans, which enjoys a certain fame. The Kulin Brahmans are much in demand as bridegrooms; they have made a business of marrying *in absentia*, upon request and for money, girls who thus escape the ignominy of maidenhood. The girls, however, remain with their families

---

[1] It is incorrect to think of the "occupational status group" as an alternative. The "style of life," not the "occupation," is always decisive. This style may require a certain profession (for instance, military service), but the nature of the occupational service resulting from the claims of a style of life always remain decisive (for instance, military service as a knight rather than as a mercenary). (Gerth and Martindale, eds.)

[2] *Census of India*, 1911. Report, I, 378.

[3] *Census Report*, 1901, XIII, 1, 193.

and see the bridegroom only if business or other reasons accidentally bring him to a place where he has one (or several) such "wives" in residence. Then he shows his marriage contract to the father-in-law and uses the father's house as a "cheap hotel." In addition, without any costs, he has the enjoyment of the girl, for she is considered his "legitimate" wife.

Elsewhere infanticide is usually a result of restricted opportunities for subsistence among poor populations. But in India female infanticide was instituted precisely by the upper castes. This occurred especially among the Rajputs. Despite the severe English laws of 1829, as late as 1869, in twenty-two villages of Rajputana there were twenty-three girls and 284 boys. In an 1836 count, in some Rajput areas, not one single live girl of over one year of age was found in a population of 10,000 souls! Infanticide existed alongside child marriage. Child marriage has determined, first, the fact that in India some girls five to ten years old are already widowed and that they remain widowed for life. This is connected with widow celibacy, an institution which, in India as elsewhere, was added to widow suicide. Widow suicide was derived from the custom of chivalry: the burial of his personal belongings, especially his women, with the dead lord. Secondly, marriages of immature girls has brought about a high mortality rate in childbed.

All of this makes it clear that in the field of connubium, caste intensifies "status" principles in an extreme manner. Today hypergamy exists as a general caste rule only within the same caste, and even there it is a specialty of the Rajput caste and of some others that stand close to the Rajput socially, or to their ancient tribal territory. This is the case, for instance, with such castes as the Bhat, Khatri, Karwar, Gujar, and Jat. However, the rule is strict endogamy of the caste and of the subcaste; in the case of the latter, this rule is, in the main, broken only by marriage cartels.

The norms of commensalism are similar to those of connubium: a status group has no social intercourse with social inferiors. In the southern states of America, social intercourse between a white and a Negro would result in the boycott of the former. As a status group, caste enhances and transposes this social closure into the sphere of religion, or rather of magic. The ancient concepts of taboo and their social applications were indeed widely diffused in India's geographical environs and may well have contributed materials to this process. To these taboos were added borrowed totemic ritualism and, finally, notions of the magical impurity of certain activities, such as have existed everywhere with widely varying content and intensity.

The Hindu dietary rules are not simple in nature and by no means do they concern merely the questions *1)* what may be eaten, and *2)* who may eat together at the same table. These two points are covered by strict rules, which are chiefly restricted to members of the same caste. The dietary rules concern, above all, the further questions: *3)* Out of whose hand may one take food of a certain kind? For genteel houses this means above all: Whom may one use for a cook? And a further question is: *4)* Whose mere glance upon the food is to be excluded? With *3)* there is a difference to be noted between food and drink, according to whether water, and food cooked in water (*kachcha*) is concerned, or food cooked in melted butter (*pakka*). *Kachcha* is far more exclusive. The question with whom one may smoke is closely connected with norms of commensality in the narrower sense. Originally, one smoked out of the same pipe, which was passed around; therefore, smoking together was dependent upon the degree of ritual purity of the partner. All these rules, however, belong in one and the same category of a far broader set of norms, all of which are status characteristics of ritual caste rank.

The social rank positions of all castes depend upon the question of from whom the highest castes accept *kachcha* and *pakka* and with whom they dine and smoke. Among the Hindu castes the Brahmans are always at the top in such connections. But the following questions are equal in importance to these, and closely connected with them: Does a Brahman undertake the religious services of the members of a caste? And possibly: to which of the very differently evaluated subcastes does the Brahman belong? Just as the Brahman is the last, though not the only authority in determining, by his behavior in questions of commensalism, the rank of a caste, so likewise does he determine questions of services. The barber of a ritually clean caste unconditionally serves only certain castes. He may shave and care for the "manicure" of others, but not for their "pedicure." And he does not serve some castes at all. Other wageworkers, especially laundrymen, behave in a similar manner. Usually, although with some exceptions, commensalism is attached to the caste; connubium is almost always attached to the subcaste; whereas usually, although with exceptions, the services by priests and wageworkers are attached to commensality.

The discussion above may suffice to demonstrate the extraordinary complexity of the rank relations of the caste system. It may also show the factors by which the caste differs from an ordinary status order. The caste order is oriented religiously and ritually to a degree not even partially attained elsewhere. If the expression "church" was not inapplicable to Hinduism, one could perhaps speak of a rank order of church estates.

Caste and sib

There remains to be examined still another important peculiarity of Indian society which is intimately interrelated with the caste system. Not only the formation of castes but the heightened significance of the sib belongs to the fundamental traits of Indian society. The Hindu social order, to a larger extent than anywhere else in the world, is organized in terms of the principle of *clan charisma*. "Charisma" means that an extraordinary, at least not generally available, quality adheres to a person. Originally charisma was thought of as a magical quality. "Clan charisma" means that this extraordinary quality adheres to sib members per se and not, as originally, to a single person.

We are familiar with residues of this sociologically important phenomenon of clan charisma particularly in the hereditary "divine right of kings" of our dynasties. To a lesser degree the legend of the "blue blood" of a nobility, whatever its specific origin, belongs to the same sociological type. Clan charisma is one of the ways personal charisma may be "routinized," (i.e., made a part of everyday social experience).

In contrast to the hereditary chieftain in times of peace who, among some tribes, could also be a woman, the warrior king and his men were heroes whose successes had proven their purely personal and magical qualities. The authority of the war leader, like that of the sorcerer, rested upon strictly personal charisma. The successor also originally claimed his rank by virtue of personal charisma. (The problem, of course, is that more than one "successor" may raise such claims.) The unavoidable demand for law and order in the question of successorship forces the followers to consider different possibilities: either the designation of the qualified successor by the leader; or the selection of a new leader by his disciples, followers, or officials. The progressive regulation of these originally spontaneous and nonprocedural questions may lead to the development of elective bodies of officials in the manner of "princes," "electors," and "cardinals."

In India a suggestive belief won out: that charisma is a quality attached to the sib per se, that the qualified successor or successors should be sought within the sib. This led to the *inheritance* of charisma, which originally had nothing to do with heredity. The wider the spheres to which magical belief applied, the more consistently developed such beliefs became, the wider, in turn, the possible field of application of clan charisma. Not only heroic and magico-cultic abilities, but any form of authority, came to be viewed as determined and bound by clan charisma. Special talents, not only artistic but craft talent as well, fell within the sphere of clan charisma.

In India the development of the principle of clan charisma far surpassed what is usual elsewhere in the world. This did not occur all at once; clan charisma was in conflict with ancient genuine charismatism which continued to uphold only the personal endowment of the single individual, as well as with the pedagogy of status cultivation.

Even in the Indian Middle Ages, many formalities in the apprenticeship to and practice of handicraft show strong traces of the principle of personal charisma. These are evident in the magical elements of the novitiate and the assumption by the apprentice of journeyman status. However, since, originally, occupational differentiation was largely interethnic and the practitioners of many trades were members of pariah tribes, there were strong

[1] Cf. Max Weber, *The Religion of China*, Trans. by H. H. Gerth (Glencoe: The Free Press, 1951), Chapter VII and VIII.

forces for the development of charismatic clan magic.

The strongest expression of clan charisma was in the sphere of authority. In India the hereditary transmission of authority, i.e., on the basis of family ties, was normal. The further back one traces the more universal the institution of the hereditary village-headship is found to be. Merchant and craft guilds and castes had hereditary elders; anything else was normally out of the question. So self-evident was priestly, royal, and knightly office charisma that free appointment of successors to office by patrimonial rulers, like the free choice of urban occupations, occurred only during upheavals of the tradition or at the frontiers of social organization before the social order was stabilized.

The exceptional quality of the sib was (note!) realized "in principle." Not only could knightly or priestly sibs prove to be barren of magical qualities and thus lose them as an individual does, but a *homo novus* could prove his possession of charisma and thereby legitimatize his sib as charismatic. Thus, charismatic clan authority could be quite unstable in the single case.

In the study of W. Hopkins of present-day Ahmadbad, the Nayar Sheth — the counterpart of the medieval Lord Mayor of the Occident — was the elder of the richest Jain family of the city. He and the Vishnuite Sheth of the clother's guild, who was also hereditary, jointly determined public opinion on all social, i.e., ritualistic and proprietary questions of the city. The other hereditary Sheths were less influential beyond their guilds and castes. However, at the time Hopkins made his study a rich manufacturer outside all guilds had successfully entered the competition.

If a son was notoriously unfit his influence waned — be it the son of a craft, guild or caste elder or the son of a priest mystagogue or artist. His prestige was channelized either to a more adequate member of the particular sib or to a member (usually the elder) of the next richest sib. Not new wealth alone, but great wealth combined with personal charisma legitimatized its possessor and his sib in social situations where status conditions were still or once again fluid. Although in single cases charismatic clan authority was quite unstable, everyday life always forced compliance with sib authority once it was established. The sib always reaped the benefits of individually established charisma.

The economic effects of sib integration through magical and animistic beliefs in China was described in a previous work.[1] In China the charismatic glorification of the sib, countered by the examination system of patrimonial dominion, had economic consequences similar to those in India. In India, the caste organization and extensive caste autonomy and the autonomy of the guild, which was still greater because it was ritually unfettered, placed the development of commercial law almost completely in the hands of the respective interest groups. The unusual importance of trade in India would lead one to believe that a rational law of trade, trading companies, and enterprise might well have developed.

However, if one looks at the legal literature of the Indian Middle Ages one is astonished by its poverty. While partially formalistic, Indian justice and the law of evidence were basically irrational and magical. Much of it was formless in principle, because of hierocratic influence. Ritually relevant questions could only be decided by ordeals. In other questions the general moral code, unique elements of the particular case, tradition (particularly), and a few supplementary royal edicts were employed as legal sources.

Yet, in contrast to China, a formal trial procedure developed with regulated summons (*in jus vocatio*, under the Mahratts summons were served by clerks of the court). The debt-liability of heirs existed but was limited after generations. However, the collection of debts, although debt bondage was known, remained somewhat in the magical stage or in that of a modified billet system. At least as a norm, joint liability of partners was lacking. In general, the right of association appeared only late in Indian development and then only in connection with the right of religious fraternities. The law of corporations remained inconsequential. All sorts of corporations and joint property relationships received mixed treatment. There was a ruling on profit sharing which, incidentally, extended also to artisans coöperating under a foreman, hence in an *ergasterion*.[1] Above all, however, the principle, recognized also in China, that one should grant unconditional credit and pawn objects only among personally close members of the phratry, among relatives and friends, held also in India. Debts under other circumstances were recognized only under provision of guarantors or witnessed promissory notes.[2]

The details of later legal practice, to be sure, were adequate to implement trading needs but they hardly promoted trade on its own. The quite considerable capitalistic development which occurred in the face of such legal conditions can be explained only in terms of the power of guilds. They knew how to pursue their interests by use of boycott, force, and expert arbitration. However, in general, under conditions such as those described, the sib fetters of credit relationships had to remain the normal state of affairs.

The principle of clan charisma also had far-reaching consequences outside the field of commercial law. Because we are prone to think of occidental feudalism, primarily as a system of socio-economic ties, we are apt to overlook its peculiar origins and their significance.

Under the compelling military needs of the time of its origin, the feudal relationship made a free contract among sib strangers basic for the faith-bound relation between the lord and his vassals. Increasingly feudal lords developed the in-group feeling of a unitary status group. They developed eventually into the closed hereditary estate of chivalrous knights. We must not forget that this grew on the basis of sib estrangement among men who viewed themselves not as sib, clan, phratry, or tribe members but merely as status peers.

Indian development took quite a different turn. It is true that individual enfeoffment of retainers and officials with land or political rights occurred. Historically, this is clearly discernible. But it did not give the ruling stratum its stamp, and feudal status formation did not rest on land grants. Rather, as Baden-Powell[3] has correctly emphasized, the character of Indian developments was derived from the sib, clan, phratry, and tribe.

Before continuing we shall have to clarify our terminology. The Irish term "clan" is ambiguous. In our terminology the typical organization of warrior communities consists of: *1*) the tribe or a collectivity of "phratries" — in our terminology, primarily always associations of (originally, magically) trained warriors; *2*) the sib, i.e., charismatically outstanding agnatic descendants of charismatic chieftains. The plain warrior did not necessarily have a "sib" but belonged to a "family" or a totemic (or quasi-totemic) association besides his phratry and possibly unitary age group.

A gens of overlords, however, had no totem; it had emancipated itself from it. The more the ruling tribes of India developed into a ruling class the more survivals of the totem (*devaks*) vanished and "sibs" emerged (or better, continued to exist). A blurring of charismatic clan differences occurred when the phratry began to develop "we-feeling" on the ground of common descent, rather than of joint defense, and hence became a quasi-sib.

In India the charismatic head of the phratry distributed conquered land; manorial prerogatives among fellow-sib members; open fields among the ordinary men of the phratry. The conquering classes must be conceived of as a circle of phratries and sibs of lords dispersing over the conquered territory under the rule of the tribe.

Prerogatives were enfeoffed by the head of the phratry (*raja*) or where one existed by the tribal king (*maharaja*) only, as a rule, to his agnates. It was not a freely contracted trusteeship. Fellow-sib members claimed this grant as a birthright. Each conquest produced, in the first place, new office fiefs for the sib of the king and its subsibs. Conquest was, therefore, the *dharma* of the king.

However different some details of the Indian from its occidental counterpart, the ascendency of the secular overlords and their estates had similar basis. No matter how often individual charismatic upstarts and their freely recruited followings shattered the firm structure of the sibs, the social process always resumed its firm course of charismatic clan organization of tribes, phratries, and sibs. Among the Aryans the ancient sacrificial priests, even at the time of the early Vedas, had become a distinguished priestly nobility. The various sibs of the priestly nobility divided according to hereditary function and appropriate clan charisma

[1] Brihaspati, Tr. by Jolly, *Sacred Books of the East* 33, XIV, 28, 29.

[2] *Ibid.*, XIV, 17

[3] In his *Indian Village Community* (1896). In details many of the conclusions of Baden-Powell are perhaps questionable.

into hereditary "schools." Given the primacy of magical charisma claimed by the clans, they and their heirs — the Brahmans — became the primary propagators of this principle through Hindu society.

It is clear that the magical charisma of the clans contributed greatly to the establishment of the firm structure of caste estrangement, actually containing it in *nuce*. On the other hand, the caste order served greatly to stabilize the sib. All strata which raised claims to distinction were forced to become stratified on the pattern of the ruling castes. The exogamous kinship order was based on the sib. Social situation, ritual duty, way of life and occupational position in the end were determined by the charismatic clan principle which extended to all positions of authority. As clan charisma supported the caste so the caste, in turn, supported the charisma of the sib.

The Theory of the Leisure Class

Thorstein Veblen

Pecuniary emulation

IN THE SEQUENCE of cultural evolution the emergence of a leisure class coincides with the beginning of ownership. This is necessarily the case, for these two institutions result from the same set of economic forces. In the inchoate phase of their development they are but different aspects of the same general facts of social structure.

It is as elements of social structure — conventional facts — that leisure and ownership are matters of interest for the purpose in hand. An habitual neglect of work does not constitute a leisure class; neither does the mechanical fact of use and consumption constitute ownership. The present inquiry, therefore, is not concerned with the beginning of the appropriation of useful articles to individual consumption. The point in question is the origin and nature of a conventional leisure class on the one hand and the beginnings of individual ownership as a conventional right or equitable claim on the other hand.

The early differentiation out of which the distinction between a leisure and a working class arises is a division maintained between men's and women's work in the lower stages of barbarism. Likewise the earliest form of ownership is an ownership of the women by the able bodied men of the community. The facts may be expressed in more general terms, and truer to the import of the barbarian theory of life, by saying that it is an ownership of the woman by the man. . . .

Wherever the institution of private property is found, even in a slightly developed form, the economic process bears the character of a struggle between men for the possession of goods. It has been customary in economic theory, and especially among those economists who adhere with least faltering to the body of modernized classical doctrines, to construe this struggle for wealth as being substantially a struggle for subsistence. Such is, no doubt, its character in large part during the earlier and less efficient phases of industry. Such also is its character in all cases where the "niggardliness of nature" is so strict as to afford but a scanty livelihood to the community in return for strenuous and unremitting application to the business of getting the means of subsistence. But in all progressing communities an advance is presently made beyond this early stage of technological development. Industrial efficiency is presently carried to such a pitch as to afford something appreciably more than a bare livelihood to those engaged in the industrial process. It has not been unusual for economic theory to speak of the further struggle for wealth on this new industrial basis as a competition for an increase of the comforts of life, — primarily for an increase of the physical comforts which the consumption of goods affords.

The end of acquisition and accumulation is conventionally held to be the consumption of the goods accumulated — whether it is consumption directly by the owner of the goods or by the household attached to him and for this purpose identified with him in theory. This is at least felt to be the economically legitimate end of acquisition, which alone it is incumbent on the theory to take account of. Such consumption may of course be conceived to serve the consumer's physical wants — his physical comfort — or his so-called higher wants — spiritual, aesthetic, intellectual, or what not; the latter class of wants being served indirectly by an expenditure of goods, after the fashion familiar to all economic readers.

But it is only when taken in a sense far removed from

Reprinted from *The Theory of the Leisure Class* (1931) by permission of The Viking Press. (Copyright, 1931, by The Viking Press.)

its naïve meaning that consumption of goods can be said to afford the incentive from which accumulation invariably proceeds. The motive that lies at the root of ownership is emulation; and the same motive of emulation continues active in the further development of the institution to which it has given rise and in the development of all those features of the social structure which this institution of ownership touches. The possession of wealth confers honor; it is an invidious distinction. Nothing equally cogent can be said for the consumption of goods, nor for any other conceivable incentive to acquisition, and especially not for any incentive to the accumulation of wealth.

It is of course not to be overlooked that in a community where nearly all goods are private property the necessity of earning a livelihood is a powerful and ever-present incentive for the poorer members of the community. The need of subsistence and of an increase of physical comfort may for a time be the dominant motive of acquisition for those classes who are habitually employed at manual labour, whose subsistence is on a precarious footing, who possess little and ordinarily accumulate little; but it will appear in the course of the discussion that even in the case of these impecunious classes the predominance of the motive of physical want is not so decided as has sometimes been assumed. On the other hand, so far as regards those members and classes of the community who are chiefly concerned in the accumulation of wealth, the incentive of subsistence or of physical comfort never plays a considerable part. Ownership began and grew into a human institution on grounds unrelated to the subsistence minimum. The dominant incentive was from the outset the invidious distinction attaching to wealth, and, save temporarily and by exception, no other motive has usurped the primacy at any later stage of the development. . . .

Gradually, as industrial activity further displaces predatory activity in the community's everyday life and in men's habits of thought, accumulated property more and more replaces trophies of predatory exploit as the conventional exponent of prepotence and success. With the growth of settled industry, therefore, the possession of wealth gains in relative importance and effectiveness as a customary basis of repute and esteem. Not that esteem ceases to be awarded on the basis of other, more direct evidence of prowess; not that successful predatory aggression or warlike exploit ceases to call out the approval and admiration of the crowd, or to stir the envy of the less successful competitors; but the opportunities for gaining distinction by means of this direct manifestation of superior force grow less available both in scope and frequency. At the same time opportunities for industrial aggression, and for the accumulation of property by the quasi-peaceable methods of nomadic industry, increase in scope and availability. And it is even more to the point that property now becomes the most easily recognized evidence of a reputable degree of success as distinguished from heroic or signal achievement. It therefore becomes the conventional

basis of esteem. Its possession in some amount becomes necessary in order to acquire any reputable standing in the community. It becomes indispensable to accumulate, to acquire property, in order to retain one's good name. When accumulated goods have in this way once become the accepted badge of efficiency, the possession of wealth presently assumes the character of an independent and definitive basis of esteem. The possession of goods, whether acquired aggressively by one's own exertion or passively by transmission through inheritance from others, becomes a conventional basis of reputability. The possession of wealth, which was at the outset valued simply as an evidence of efficiency, becomes, in popular apprehension, itself a meritorious act. Wealth is now itself intrinsically honourable and confers honour on its possessor. By a further refinement, wealth acquired passively by transmission from ancestors or other antecedents presently becomes even more honorific than wealth acquired by the possessor's own efforts; but this distinction belongs at a later stage in the evolution of the pecuniary culture and will be spoken of in its place. . . .

So soon as the possession of property becomes the basis of popular esteem, therefore, it becomes also a requisite to that complacency which we call self-respect. In any community where goods are held in severalty it is necessary, in order to his own peace of mind, that an individual should possess as large a portion of goods as others with whom he is accustomed to class himself; and it is extremely gratifying to possess something more than others. But as fast as a person makes new acquisitions, and becomes accustomed to the resulting new standard of wealth, the new standard forthwith ceases to afford appreciably greater satisfaction than the earlier standard did. The tendency in any case is constantly to make the present pecuniary standard the point of departure for a fresh increase of wealth; and this in turn gives rise to a new standard of sufficiency and a new pecuniary classification of one's self as compared with one's neighbours. So far as concerns the present question, the end sought by accumulation is to rank high in comparison with the rest of the community in point of pecuniary strength. So long as the comparison is distinctly unfavourable to himself, the normal, average individual will live in chronic dissatisfaction with his present lot; and when he has reached what may be called the normal pecuniary standard of the community, or of his class in the community, this chronic dissatisfaction will give place to a restless straining to place a wider and ever-widening pecuniary interval between himself and this average standard. The invidious comparison can never become so favourable to the individual making it that he would not gladly rate himself still higher relatively to his competitors in the struggle for pecuniary reputability

In the nature of the case, the desire for wealth can scarcely be satiated in any individual instance, and evidently a satiation of the average or general desire for wealth is out of the question. However widely, or equally, or "fairly," it may be distributed, no general increase of the community's wealth can make any approach to satiating this need, the ground of which is the desire of every one to excel every one else in the accumulation of goods. If, as is sometimes assumed, the incentive to accumulation were the want of subsistence or of physical comfort, then the aggregate economic wants of a community might conceivably be satisfied at some point in the advance of industrial efficiency; but since the struggle is substantially a race for reputability on the basis of an invidious comparison, no approach to a definitive attainment is possible.

What has just been said must not be taken to mean that there are no other incentives to acquisition and accumulation than this desire to excel in pecuniary standing and so gain the esteem and envy of one's fellowmen. The desire for added comfort and security from want is present as a motive at every stage of the process of accumulation in a modern industrial community; although the standard of sufficiency in these respects is in turn greatly affected by the habit of pecuniary emulation. To a great extent this emulation shapes the methods and selects the objects of expenditure for personal comfort and decent livelihood.

Besides this, the power conferred by wealth also affords a motive to accumulation. That propensity for purposeful activity and that repugnance to all futility of effort which belong to man by virtue of his character as an agent do not desert him when he emerges from the naïve communal culture where the dominant note of life is the unanalysed and undifferentiated solidarity of the individual with the group with which his life is bound up. When he enters upon the predatory stage, where self-seeking in the narrower sense becomes the dominant note, this propensity goes with him still, as the pervasive trait that shapes his scheme of life. The propensity for achievement and the repugnance to futility remain the underlying economic motive. The propensity exchanges only in the form of its expression and in the proximate objects to which it directs the man's activity. Under the régime of individual ownership the most available means of visibly achieving a purpose is that afforded by the acquisition and accumulation of goods; and as the self-regarding antithesis between man and man reaches fuller consciousness, the propensity for achievement — the instinct of workmanship — tends more and more to shape itself into a straining to excel others in pecuniary achievement. Relative success, tested by an invidious pecuniary comparison with other men, becomes the conventional end of action. The currently accepted legitimate end of effort becomes the achievement of a favourable comparison with other men; and therefore the repugnance to futility to a good extent coalesces with the incentive of emulation. It acts to accentuate the struggle for pecuniary reputability by visiting with a sharper disapproval all shortcoming and all evidence of shortcoming in point of pecuniary success. Purposeful effort comes to mean, primarily, effort directed to or resulting

in a more creditable showing of accumulated wealth. Among the motives which lead men to accumulate wealth, the primacy, both in scope and intensity, therefore, continues to belong to this motive of pecuniary emulation.

In making use of the term "invidious," it may perhaps be unnecessary to remark, there is no intention to extol or depreciate, or to commend or deplore any of the phenomena which the word is used to characterize. The term is used in a technical sense as describing a comparison of persons with a view to rating and grading them in respect of relative worth or value — in an æsthetic or moral sense — and so awarding and defining the relative degrees of complacency with which they may legitimately be contemplated by themselves and by others. An invidious comparison is a process of valuation of persons in respect of worth.

Conspicuous leisure

If its working were not disturbed by other economic forces or other features of the emulative process, the immediate effect of such a pecuniary struggle as has just been described in outline would be to make men industrious and frugal. This result actually follows, in some measure, so far as regards the lower classes, whose ordinary means of acquiring goods is productive labour. This is more especially true of the labouring classes in a sedentary community which is at an agricultural stage of industry, in which there is a considerable subdivision of property, and whose laws and customs secure to these classes a more or less definite share of the product of their industry. These lower classes can in any case not avoid labour, and the imputation of labour is therefore not greatly derogatory to them, at least not within their class. Rather, since labour is their recognized and accepted mode of life, they take some emulative pride in a reputation for efficiency in their work, this being often the only line of emulation that is open to them. For those for whom acquisition and emulation is possible only within the field of productive efficiency and thrift, the struggle for pecuniary reputability will in some measure work out in an increase of diligence and parsimony. But certain secondary features of the emulative process, yet to be spoken of, come in to very materially circumscribe and modify emulation in these directions among the pecuniarily inferior classes as well as among the superior class.

But it is otherwise with the superior pecuniary class, with which we are here immediately concerned. For this class also the incentive to diligence and thrift is not absent; but its action is so greatly qualified by the secondary demands of pecuniary emulation, that any inclination in this direction is practically overborne and any incentive to diligence tends to be of no effect. The most imperative of these secondary demands of emulation, as well as the one of widest scope, is the requirement of abstention from productive work. This is true in an especial degree for the barbarian stage of culture.

During the predatory culture labour comes to be associated in men's habits of thought with weakness and subjection to a master. It is therefore a mark of inferiority, and therefore comes to be accounted unworthy of man in his best estate. By virtue of this tradition labour is felt to be debasing, and this tradition has never died out. On the contrary, with the advance of social differentiation it has acquired the axiomatic force due to ancient and unquestioned prescription.

In order to gain and to hold the esteem of men it is not sufficient merely to possess wealth or power. The wealth or power must be put in evidence, for esteem is awarded only on evidence. And not only does the evidence of wealth serve to impress one's importance on others and to keep their sense of his importance alive and alert, but it is of scarcely less use in building up and preserving one's self-complacency. In all but the lowest stages of culture the normally constituted man is comforted and upheld in his self-respect by "decent surroundings" and by exemption from "menial offices." Enforced departure from his habitual standard of decency, either in the paraphernalia of life or in the kind and amount of his everyday activity, is felt to be a slight upon his human dignity, even apart from all conscious consideration of the approval or disapproval of his fellows.

The archaic theoretical distinction between the base and the honourable in the manner of a man's life retains very much of its ancient force even to-day. So much so that there are few of the better class who are not possessed of an instinctive repugnance for the vulgar forms of labour. We have a realizing sense of ceremonial uncleanness attaching in an especial degree to the occupations which are associated in our habits of thought with menial service. It is felt by all persons of refined taste that a spiritual contamination is inseparable from certain offices that are conventionally required of servants. Vulgar surroundings, mean (that is to say, inexpensive) habitations, and vulgarly productive occupations are unhesitatingly condemned and avoided. They are incompatible with life on a satisfactory spiritual plane — with "high thinking." From the days of the Greek philosophers to the present, a degree of leisure and of exemption from contact with such industrial processes as serve the immediate everyday purposes of human life has ever been recognized by thoughtful men as a prerequisite to a worthy or beautiful, or even a blameless, human life. In itself and in its consequences the life of leisure is beautiful and ennobling in all civilized men's eyes.

This direct, subjective value of leisure and of other evidences of wealth is no doubt in great part secondary and derivative. It is in part a reflex of the utility of leisure as a means of gaining the respect of others, and in part it is the result of a mental substitution. The performance of labour has been accepted as a conventional evidence of inferior force; therefore it comes itself, by a mental short-cut, to be regarded as intrinsically base.

During the predatory stage proper, and especially during the earlier stages of the quasi-peaceable development of industry that follows the predatory stage, a life of leisure is the readiest and most conclusive evidence of pecuniary strength, and therefore of superior force; provided always that the gentleman of leisure can live in manifest ease and comfort. At this stage wealth consists chiefly of slaves, and the benefits accruing from the possession of riches and power take the form chiefly of personal service and the immediate products of personal service. Conspicuous abstention from labour therefore becomes the conventional mark of superior pecuniary achievement and the conventional index of reputability; and conversely, since application to productive labour is a mark of poverty and subjection, it becomes inconsistent with a reputable standing in the community. Habits of industry and thrift, therefore, are not uniformly furthered by a prevailing pecuniary emulation. On the contrary, this kind of emulation indirectly discountenances participation in productive labour. Labour would unavoidably become dishonourable, as being an evidence of poverty, even if it were not already accounted indecorous under the ancient tradition handed down from an earlier cultural stage. The ancient tradition of the predatory culture is that productive effort is to be shunned as being unworthy of able-bodied men, and this tradition is reinforced rather than set aside in the passage from the predatory to the quasi-peaceable manner of life.

Even if the institution of a leisure class had not come in with the first emergence of individual ownership, by force of the dishonour attaching to productive employment, it would in any case have come in as one of the early consequences of ownership. And it is to be remarked that while the leisure class existed in theory from the beginning of predatory culture, the institution takes on a new and fuller meaning with the transition from the predatory to the next succeeding pecuniary stage of culture. It is from this time forth a "leisure class" in fact as well as in theory. From this point dates the institution of the leisure class in its consummate form....

Abstention from labour is not only an honorific or meritorious act, but it presently comes to be a requisite of decency. The insistence on property as the basis of reputability is very naïve and very imperious during the early stages of the accumulation of wealth. Abstention from labour is the conventional evidence of wealth and is therefore the conventional mark of social standing; and this insistence on the meritoriousness of wealth leads to a more strenuous insistence on leisure. *Nota notae est nota rei ipsius.* According to well-established laws of human nature, prescription presently seizes upon this conventional evidence of wealth and fixes it in men's habits of thought as something that is in itself substantially meritorious and ennobling; while productive labour at the same time and by a like process becomes in a double sense intrinsically unworthy. Prescription ends by making labour not only disreputable in the eyes of the community, but morally impossible to the noble, freeborn man, and incompatible with a worthy life.

This tabu on labour has a further consequence in the industrial differentiation of classes. As the population increases in density and the predatory group grows into a settled industrial community, the constituted authorities and the customs governing ownership gain in scope and consistency. It then presently becomes impracticable to accumulate wealth by simple seizure, and, in logical consistency, acquisition by industry is equally impossible for high-minded and impecunious men. The alternative open to them is beggary or privation. Wherever the canon of conspicuous leisure has a chance undisturbed to work out its tendency, there will therefore emerge a secondary, and in a sense spurious, leisure class — abjectly poor and living a precarious life of want and discomfort, but morally unable to stoop to gainful pursuits. The decayed gentleman and the lady who has seen better days are by no means unfamiliar phenomena even now. This pervading sense of the indignity of the slightest manual labour is familiar to all civilised peoples, as well as to peoples of a less advanced pecuniary culture. In persons of delicate sensibility, who have long been habituated to gentle manners, the sense of the shamefulness of manual labour may become so strong that, at a critical juncture, it will even set aside the instinct of self-preservation. . . .

It has already been remarked that the term "leisure," as here used, does not connote indolence or quiescence. What it connotes is non-productive consumption of time. Time is consumed non-productively *1*) from a sense of the unworthiness of productive work, and *2*) as an evidence of pecuniary ability to afford a life of idleness. But the whole of the life of the gentleman of leisure is not spent before the eyes of the spectators who are to be impressed with that spectacle of honorific leisure which in the ideal scheme makes up his life. For some part of the time his life is perforce withdrawn from the public eye, and of this portion which is spent in private the gentleman of leisure should, for the sake of his good name, be able to give a convincing account. He should find some means of putting in evidence the leisure that is not spent in the sight of the spectators. This can be done only indirectly, through the exhibition of some tangible, lasting results of the leisure so spent — in a manner analogous to the familiar exhibition of tangible, lasting products of the labour performed for the gentleman of leisure by handicraftsmen and servants in his employ.

The lasting evidence of productive labour is its material product — commonly some article of consumption. In the case of exploit it is similarly possible and usual to procure some tangible result that may serve for exhibition in the way of trophy or booty. At a later phase of the development it is customary to assume some badge or insignia of honour that will serve as a conventionally accepted mark of exploit, and which at the same time indicates the quantity or degree of exploit of which it is the symbol. As the population increases in density, and as human relations grow more complex and numerous, all the details of life undergo a process of elaboration and selection; and in this process of elaboration the use of trophies develops into a system of rank, titles, degrees and insignia, typical examples of which are heraldic devices, medals, and honorary decorations.

As seen from the economic point of view, leisure, considered as an employment, is closely allied in kind with the life of exploit; and the achievements which characterize a life of leisure, and which remain as its decorous criteria, have much in common with the trophies of exploit. But leisure in the narrower sense, as distinct from exploit and from any ostensibly productive employment of effort on objects which are of no intrinsic use, does not commonly leave a material product. The criteria of a past performance of leisure therefore commonly take the form of "immaterial" goods. Such immaterial evidences of past leisure are quasi-scholarly or quasi-artistic accomplishments and a knowledge of processes and incidents which do not conduce directly to the furtherance of human life. So, for instance, in our time there is the knowledge of the dead languages and the occult sciences; of correct spelling; of syntax and prosody; of the various forms of domestic music and other household art; of the latest proprieties of dress, furniture, and equipage; of games, sports, and fancy-bred animals, such as dogs and race-horses. In all these branches of knowledge the initial motive from which their acquisition proceeded at the outset, and through which they first came into vogue, may have been something quite different from the wish to show that one's time had not been spent in industrial employment; but unless these accomplishments had approved themselves as serviceable evidence of an unproductive expenditure of time, they would not have survived and held their place as conventional accomplishments of the leisure class.

These accomplishments may, in some sense, be classed as branches of learning. Beside and beyond these there is a further range of social facts which shade off from the region of learning into that of physical habit and dexterity. Such are what is known as manners and breeding, polite usage, decorum, and formal and ceremonial observances generally. This class of facts are even more immediately and obtrusively presented to the observation, and they are therefore more widely and more imperatively insisted on as required evidences of a reputable degree of leisure. It is worth while to remark that all that class of ceremonial observances which are classed under the general head of manners hold a more important place in the esteem of men during the stage of culture at which conspicuous leisure has the greatest vogue as a mark of reputability, than at later stages of the cultural development. The barbarian of the quasi-peaceable stage of industry is notoriously a more high-bred gentleman, in all that concerns decorum, than any but the very exquisite among the men of a later age. Indeed, it is well known, or at least it is currently believed, that manners have progressively deteriorated as society has receded from the patriarchal stage. Many a gentleman of the old school has been provoked to remark regretfully upon the under-bred manners and bearing of even the better classes in the modern industrial communities; and the decay of the ceremonial code — or as it is otherwise called, the vulgarization of life — among the industrial classes proper has become one of the chief enormities of latter-day civilization in the eyes of all persons of delicate sensibilities. The decay which the code has suffered at the hands of a busy people testifies — all deprecation apart — to the fact that decorum is a product and an exponent of leisure-class life and thrives in full measure only under a regime of status.

The origin, or better the derivation, of manners is, no doubt, to be sought elsewhere than in a conscious effort on the part of the well-mannered to show that much time has been spent in acquiring them. The proximate end of innovation and elaboration has been the higher effectiveness of the new departure in point of beauty or of expressiveness. In great part the ceremonial code of decorous usages owes its beginning and its growth to the desire to conciliate or to show good-will, as anthropologists and sociologists are in the habit of assuming, and this initial motive is rarely if ever absent from the conduct of well-mannered persons at any stage of the later development. Manners, we are told, are in part an elaboration of gesture, and in part they are symbolical and conventionalized survivals representing former acts of dominance or of personal service or of personal contact. In large part they are an expression of the relation of status, — a symbolic pantomime of mastery on the one hand and of subservience on the other. Wherever at the present time the predatory habit of mind, and the consequent attitude of mastery and of subservience, gives its character to the accredited scheme of life, there the importance of all punctilios of conduct is extreme, and the assiduity with which the ceremonial observance of rank and titles is attended to approaches closely to the ideal set by the barbarian of the quasi-peaceable nomadic culture. Some of the Continental countries afford good illustrations of this spiritual survival. In these communities the archaic ideal is similarly approached as regards the esteem accorded to manners as a fact of intrinsic worth.

Decorum set out with being symbol and pantomime and with having utility only as an exponent of the facts and qualities symbolized; but it presently suffered the transmutation which commonly passes over symbolical facts in human intercourse. Manners presently came, in popular apprehension, to be possessed of a substantial utility in themselves; they acquired a sacramental character, in great measure independent of the facts which they originally prefigured. Deviations from the code of decorum have become intrinsically odious to all men, and good breeding is, in everyday apprehension, not simply an adventitious mark of human excellence, but an integral feature of the worthy human soul. There are few things that so touch us with instinctive revulsion as a breach of decorum; and so far have we pro-

gressed in the direction of imputing intrinsic utility to the ceremonial observances of etiquette that few of us, if any, can dissociate an offence against etiquette from a sense of the substantial unworthiness of the offender. A breach of faith may be condoned, but a breach of decorum can not. "Manners maketh man."

None the less, while manners have this intrinsic utility, in the apprehension of the performer and the beholder alike, this sense of the intrinsic rightness of decorum is only the proximate ground of the vogue of manners and breeding. Their ulterior, economic ground is to be sought in the honorific character of that leisure or non-productive employment of time and effort without which good manners are not acquired. The knowledge and habit of good form come only by long-continued use. Refined tastes, manners, and habits of life are a useful evidence of gentility, because good breeding requires time, application, and expense, and can therefore not be compassed by those whose time and energy are taken up with work. A knowledge of good form is *prima facie* evidence that that portion of the well-bred person's life which is not spent under the observation of the spectator has been worthily spent in acquiring accomplishments that are of no lucrative effect. In the last analysis the value of manners lies in the fact that they are the voucher of a life of leisure. Therefore, conversely, since leisure is the conventional means of pecuniary repute, the acquisition of some proficiency in decorum is incumbent on all who aspire to a modicum of pecuniary decency.

So much of the honourable life of leisure as is not spent in the sight of spectators can serve the purposes of reputability only in so far as it leaves a tangible, visible result that can be put in evidence and can be measured and compared with products of the same class exhibited by competing aspirants for repute. Some such effect, in the way of leisurely manners and carriage, etc., follows from simple persistent abstention from work, even where the subject does not take thought of the matter and studiously acquire an air of leisurely opulence and mastery. Especially does it seem to be true that a life of leisure in this way persisted in through several generations will leave a persistent, ascertainable effect in the conformation of the person, and still more in his habitual bearing and demeanour. But all the suggestions of a cumulative life of leisure, and all the proficiency in decorum that comes by the way of passive habituation, may be further improved upon by taking thought and assiduously acquiring the marks of honourable leisure, and then carrying the exhibition of these adventitious marks of exemption from employment out in a strenuous and systematic discipline. Plainly, this is a point at which a diligent application of effort and expenditure may materially further the attainment of a decent proficiency in the leisure-class proprieties. Conversely, the greater the degree of proficiency and the more patent the evidence of a high degree of habituation to observances which serve no lucrative or other directly useful purpose, the greater the consumption of time and substance impliedly involved in their acquisition, and the greater the resultant good repute. Hence, under the competitive struggle for proficiency in good manners, it comes about that much pains is taken with the cultivation of habits of decorum; and hence the details of decorum develop into a comprehensive discipline, conformity to which is required of all who would be held blameless in point of repute. And hence, on the other hand, this conspicuous leisure of which decorum is a ramification grows gradually into a laborious drill in deportment and an education in taste and discrimination as to what articles of consumption are decorous and what are the decorous methods of consuming them.

In this connection it is worthy of notice that the possibility of producing pathological and other idiosyncrasies of person and manner by shrewd mimicry and a systematic drill have been turned to account in the deliberate production of a cultured class — only with a very happy effect. In this way, by the process vulgarly known as snobbery, a syncopated evolution of gentle birth and breeding is achieved in the case of a goodly number of families and lines of descent. This syncopated gentle birth gives results which, in point of seviceability as a leisure-class factor in the population, are in no wise substantially inferior to others who may have had a longer but less arduous training in the pecuniary properties. . . .

The Problem of Classes

Joseph Schumpeter

WE HERE MEAN by classes those social phenomena with which we are all familiar — social entities which we observe but which are not of our making. In this sense every social class is a special social organism, living, acting, and suffering as such and in need of being understood as such.[1] Yet the concept of class occurs in the social sciences in still another meaning — a meaning shared with many other sciences. In this sense it still corresponds to a set of facts, but not to any specific phenomenon of reality. Here it becomes a matter of classifying different things according to certain chosen characteristics. Viewed in this sense, class is a creation of the researcher, owes its existence to his organizing touch. These two meanings are often annoyingly mixed up in our social-science thinking, and we therefore emphasize what should be self-evident, namely, that there is not the slightest connection between them as a matter of necessity. Whenever there is any actual coincidence of their contents, this is either a matter of chance, or — if it is really more than that — must be demonstrated, generally or specifically, by means of pertinent rules of evidence. It can never be assumed as a matter of course. This word of caution applies especially to the field in which theoretical economics operates. In theoretical economics, a landlord — the very term implies the confusion we oppose — is anyone who is in possession of the services of land. But not only do such people not form a social class. They are divided by one of the most conspicuous class cleavages of all. And the working class, in the sense of economic theory, includes the prosperous lawyer as well as the ditch digger. These classes are classes only in the sense that they result from the scholar's classification of economic subjects. Yet they are often thought and spoken of as though they *were* classes in the sense of the social phenomenon we here seek to investigate. The two reasons that explain this situation actually make it more troublesome than it would otherwise be. There is, first, the fact that the characteristic by which the economist classifies does have some connection with the real phenomenon. Then there is the fact that the economic theorist finds it exceedingly difficult to confine himself strictly to his problems, to resist the temptation to enliven his presentation with something that fascinates most of his readers — in other words, to stoke his sputtering engine with the potent fuel of the class struggle. Hence the amusing circumstance that some people view any distinction between economic theory and the facts of social class as evidence of the most abysmal failure to grasp the point at issue; while others see any fusion of the two as the most abysmal analytical blundering. Hence, too, the fact that the very term class struggle, let alone the idea behind it, has fallen into discredit among the best minds in science

[1] We also mean to imply that a class is no mere "resultant phenomenon," [*Resultaterscheinung*] such as a market, for example (for the same viewpoint, from another theoretical orientation, see Spann, *loc. cit.*). We are not concerned with this here, however. What does matter is the distinction between the real social phenomenon and the scientific construct.

Reprinted from *Imperialism and Social Classes* (1951), pp. 137–147, 209–211, by permission of Mrs. Elizabeth B. Schumpeter, and the publisher, Augustus M. Kelley, Inc. (Copyright, 1951, by Mrs. Schumpeter.)

and politics alike — in much the same way that the overpowering impression of the Palazzo Strozzi loses so much by its inescapable juxtaposition with the frightful pseudo-architecture of modern apartment houses.

Of the many sociological problems which beset the field of class theory — the scientific rather than the philosophical theory, the sociological rather than the immediately economic — four emerge distinctly. First, there is the problem of the *nature* of class (which is perhaps, and even probably, different for each individual scientific discipline, and for each purpose pursued within such a discipline) — and, as part of this problem, the function of class in the vital processes of the social whole. Fundamentally different, at least theoretically, is the problem of class *cohesion* — the factors that make of every social class, as we put it, a special living social organism, that prevent the group from scattering like a heap of billiard balls. Again fundamentally distinct is the problem of class *formation* — the question of why the social whole, as far as our eye can reach, has never been homogeneous, always revealing this particular, obviously organic stratification. Finally, we must realize — and we shall presently revert to this point — that this problem is again wholly different from the series of problems that are concerned with the *concrete causes and conditions* of an individual determined, historically given class structure — a distinction that is analogous to that between the problem of the theory of prices in general and problems such as the explanation of the level of milk prices in the year 1919.

We are not, at this point, seeking a definition that would anticipate the solution of our problem. What we need, rather, is a characteristic that will enable us, in each case, to recognize a social class and to distinguish it from other social classes — a characteristic that will show on the surface and, if possible, on the surface alone; that will be as clear or as fuzzy as the situation itself is at first glance. Class is something more than an aggregation of class members. It is something else, and this something cannot be recognized in the behavior of the individual class member. A class is aware of its identity as a whole, sublimates itself as such, has its own peculiar life and characteristic "spirit." Yet one essential peculiarity — possibly a consequence, possibly an intermediate cause — of the class phenomenon lies in the fact that class members behave toward one another in a fashion characteristically different from their conduct toward members of other classes. They are in closer association with one another; they understand one another better; they work more readily in concert; they close ranks and erect barriers against the outside; they look out into the same segment of the world, with the same eyes, from the same viewpoint, in the same direction. These are familiar observations, and among explanations which are traditionally adduced are the similarity of the class situation and the basic class type.

To this extent the behavior of people toward one another is a very dependable and useful *symptom* of the presence or absence of class cohesion among them — although it does not, of course, go very deeply, let alone constitute a cause. Even more on the surface — a symptom of a symptom, so to speak, though it hints at a far-reaching basic orientation — is the specific way in which people engage in social intercourse. These ways are decisively influenced by the degree of "shared social *a priori*," as we might say with Simmel. Social intercourse within class barriers is promoted by the similarity of manners and habits of life, of things that are evaluated in a positive or negative sense, that arouse interest. In intercourse across class borders, differences on all these points repel and inhibit sympathy. There are always a number of delicate matters that must be avoided, things that seem strange and even absurd to the other classes. The participants in social intercourse between different classes are always on their best behavior, so to speak, making their conduct forced and unnatural. The difference between intercourse within the class and outside the class is the same as the difference between swimming with and against the tide. The most important symptom of this situation is the ease or difficulty with which members of different classes contract legally and socially recognized marriages. Hence we find a suitable definition of the class — one that makes it outwardly recognizable and involves no class theory — in the fact that intermarriage prevails among its members, socially rather than legally.[1] This criterion is especially useful for our purposes, because we limit our study to the class phenomenon in a racially homogeneous environment, thus eliminating the most important additional impediment to intermarriage.[2]

Our study applies to the third of the four questions we have distinguished — to the others only to the extent that it is unavoidable. Let us begin by briefly discussing three difficulties in our way — a consideration of each of them already constituting an objective step toward our goal.

Firstly: We seek to interpret the class phenomenon in the same sense in which we understand social phenomena generally, that is, as *adaptations* to existing needs, grasped by the observer — ourselves — as such. We shall pass over the logical difficulties inherent in even this simple statement, such as whether it is admissible to apply our own conceptual modes to cultures remote from us. There is also the question of the extent to which the condition of culturally primitive peoples in our own time may be taken as a clue to the past state of modern civilized peoples, and the even more important question of the extent to which historical data are

[1] In support of this criterion we may now also invoke the authority of Max Weber, who mentions it in his sociology, though only in passing.

[2] We do not use the term "estate" since we have no need of it. Technically it has fixed meaning only in the sense of status and in connection with the constitution of the feudal state. For the rest, it is equated, sometimes with "profession," and sometimes with "class." Caste is merely a special elaboration of the class phenomenon, its peculiarity of no essential importance to us.

at all valid for theoretical purposes. One difficulty, however, we must face. Unless specifically proven, it is an erroneous assumption that social phenomena to which the same name has been applied over thousands of years are always the same things, merely in different form. This is best seen in the history of social institutions. Anyone will realize that common ownership of land in the ancient Germanic village community — supposing, for the moment, that its existence had been proven — is something altogether different from common land ownership in present-day Germany. Yet the term ownership is used as though it always implied the same basic concept. Obviously this can be true only in a very special sense, to be carefully delimited in each case. When taken for granted, it becomes a source of one-sided and invalid constructions. The fact that there may occur in the language of law and life of a given period expressions that we regard as equivalent to our chosen concept, proves nothing, even when those expressions were actually used in an equivalent sense. Similarly, the actuality of the institution we call marriage has changed so greatly in the course of time that it is quite inadmissible to regard that institution always as the same phenomenon, from a general sociological viewpoint and without reference to a specific research purpose. This does not mean that we renounce the habit, indispensable in analysis, of seeking, wherever possible, the same essential character in the most diverse forms. But the existence of that character must be a fact, its establishment the result of study, not a mere postulate. This applies to our problem as well. When we speak of "the" class phenomenon and take it to mean that group differences in social values, found everywhere, though under varying conditions, are everywhere explained by the same theory, that is not even a working hypothesis, but merely a method of presentation in which the result is anticipated — a result that has meaning only from the viewpoint of the particular theory in question. "Master classes," for example, do not exist everywhere — if, indeed, the concept of "master" has a precise content at all.

Secondly: The class membership of an individual is a primary fact, originally quite independent of his will. But he does not always confirm that allegiance by his conduct. As is well known, it is common for non-members of a class to work with and on behalf of that class, especially in a political sense, while members of a class may actually work against it. Such cases are familiar from everyday life — they are called fellow travelers, renegades, and the like. This phenomenon must be distinguished, on the one hand, from a situation in which an entire class, or at least its leadership, behaves differently from what might be expected from it class orientation; and, on the other hand, from a situation in which the individual, by virtue of his own functional position, comes into conflict with his class. There is room for differences of opinion on these points. For example, one may see in them aberrations from the normal pattern that hold no particular interest, that

have no special significance to an understanding of society, that are often exceptions to the rule more apparent than real. Those who view the class struggle as the core of all historical explanation will generally incline to such opinions and seek to explain away conflicting evidence. From another viewpoint, however, these phenomena become the key to an understanding of political history — one without which its actual course and in particular its class evolution become altogether incomprehensible. To whatever class theory one may adhere, there is always the necessity of choosing between these viewpoints. The phenomena alluded to, of course, complicate not only the realities of social life but also its intellectual perception. We think that our line of reasoning will fully answer this question, and we shall not revert to it.

Thirdly: Every social situation is the heritage of preceding situations and takes over from them not only their cultures, their dispositions, and their "spirit," but also elements of their social structure and concentrations of power. This fact is of itself interesting. The social pyramid is never made of a single substance, is never seamless. There is no single *Zeitgeist*, except in the sense of a construct. This means that in explaining any historical course or situation, account must be taken of the fact that much in it can be explained only by the survival of elements that are actually alien to its own trends. This is, of course, self-evident, but it does become a source of practical difficulties and diagnostic problems. Another implication is that the coexistence of essentially different mentalities and objective sets of facts must form part of any general theory. Thus the economic interpretation of history, for example, would at once become untenable and unrealistic — indeed, some easily demolished objections to it are explained from this fact — if its formulation failed to consider that the manner in which production methods shape social life is essentially influenced by the fact that the human protagonists have always been shaped by past situations. When applied to our problem, this means, first, that any theory of class structure, in dealing with a given historical period, must include prior class structures among its data; and then, that any general theory of classes and class formation must explain that fact that classes coexisting at any given time bear the marks of different centuries on their brow, so to speak — that they stem from varying conditions. This is in the essential nature of the matter, an aspect of the nature of the class phenomenon. Classes, once they have come into being, harden in their mold and perpetuate themselves, even when the social conditions that created them have disappeared.

In this connection it becomes apparent that in the field of our own problem this difficulty bears an aspect lacking in many other problems. When one seeks to render modern banking comprehensible, for example, one can trace its historical origins, since doubtless there were economic situations in which there was no banking, and others in which the beginnings of banking can be observed. But this is impossible in the case of class, for there are no amorphous societies in this sense — societies, that is, in which the absence of our phenomenon can be demonstrated beyond doubt. Its presence may be more or less strongly marked, a distinction of great importance for our solution of the class problem. But neither historically nor ethnologically has its utter absence been demonstrated in even a single case, although there has been no dearth either of attempts in that direction (in eighteenth-century theories of culture) or of an inclination to assume the existence of classless situations.[1] We must therefore forego any aid from this side, whatever it may be worth,[2] though the ethnological material nevertheless retains fundamental significance for us. If we wanted to start from a classless society, the only cases we could draw upon would be those in which societies are formed accidentally, in which whatever class orientations the participants may have either count for nothing or lack the time to assert themselves — cases, in other words, like that of a ship in danger, a burning theater, and so on. We do not completely discount the value of such cases, but quite apparently we cannot do very much with them. Any study of classes and class situations therefore leads, in unending regression, to other classes and class situations, just as any explanation of the circular flow of the economic process always leads back, without any logical stopping point, to the preceding circular flow that furnishes the data for the one to follow. Similarly — though less closely so — analysis of the economic value of goods always leads back from a use value to a cost value and back again to a use value, so that it seems to turn in a circle. Yet this very analogy points to the logical way out. The general and mutual interdependence of values and prices in an economic situation does not prevent us from finding an all-encompassing explanatory principle: and the fact of regression in our own case does not mean the non-existence of a principle that will explain the formation, nature, and basic laws of classes — though this fact naturally does not necessarily furnish us with such a principle. If we cannot derive the sought-for principle from the genesis of classes in a classless state, it may yet emerge from a study of how classes function and what happens to them, especially from actual observation of the changes in the relationship of existing classes to one another and of individuals within the class structure — *provided* it can be shown that the elements explaining such changes also include the reason why classes exist at all. . . .

The facts and considerations that have been presented or outlined may be summarized as follows:

Shifts of family position within a class are seen to take place everywhere, without exception. They cannot be explained by the operation of chance, nor by automatic mechanisms relating to outward position, but only as the consequences of the different degree to which families are qualified to solve the problems with which their social environment confronts them.

Class barriers are always, without exception, surmountable and are, in fact, surmounted, by virtue of the same qualifications and modes of behavior that bring about shifts of family position within the class.

The process by which the individual family crosses class barriers is the same process by which the family content of classes is formed in the first instance, and this family content is determined in no other way.

Classes themselves rise and fall according to the nature and success with which they — meaning here, their members — fulfill their characteristic function, and according to the rise and fall in the social significance of this function, or of those functions which the class members are willing and able to accept instead — the relative social significance of a function always being determined by the degree of social leadership which its fulfillment implies or creates.

These circumstances explain the evolution of individual families and the evolution of classes as such. They also explain why social classes exist at all.

We draw the following conclusions from these statements:

The ultimate function on which the class phenomenon rests consists of individual differences in aptitude. What is meant is not differences in an absolute sense, but differences in aptitude with respect to those functions which the environment makes "socially necessary" — in our sense — at any given time; and with respect to leadership, along lines that are in keeping with those functions. The differences, moreover, do not relate to the physical individual, but to the clan or family.

Class structure is the ranking of such individual families by their social value in accordance, ultimately, with their differing aptitudes. Actually this is more a matter of social value, once achieved, becoming firmly established. This process of entrenchment and its perpetuation constitutes a special problem that must be specifically explained — at bottom this is the immediate and specific "class problem." Yet even this entrenched position, which endures in group terms, offering the picture of a class made secure above and beyond the individual, ultimately rests on individual differences in aptitude. Entrenched positions, which constitute the class stratification of society, are attained or created by

[1] The theory of the "original" classless society is probably headed for a fate similar to that which has already overtaken the theory of primitive communism and primitive promiscuity. It will prove to be purely speculative, along the line of "natural law." Yet all such conceptions do receive apparent confirmation in the conditions of the "primitive horde." Where a group is very small and its existence precarious, the situation necessarily has the aspects of classlessness, communism, and promiscuity. But this no more constitutes an organizational principle than the fact that an otherwise carnivorous species will become vegetarian when no meat is available constitutes a vegetarian principle.

[2] The explanatory value of historically observable genesis must not be overrated. It does not always lead to an explanation and never offers an explanation *ipso facto*, not even when a phenomenon appears immediately in its "pure" form, which is neither inevitable nor even frequent.

behavior which in turn is conditioned by differential aptitudes.[1]

[1] It is only this process of entrenchment that creates a special cultural background, a greater or lesser degree of promptness in concerted action, one aspect of which is expressed in the concept of the class struggle. We refrain here from passing any judgment on the actual significance of this factor.

From other points of view — some of them still in the field of sociology, others beyond it and even beyond the field of science altogether — the essence of social classes may appear in a different light. They may seem organs of society, legal or cultural entities, conspiracies against the rest of the nation. From the explanatory viewpoint they are merely what we have described them to be.

THE CONTINUING DEBATE ON EQUALITY

Some Principles of Stratification

Kingsley Davis and Wilbert E. Moore

IN A PREVIOUS PAPER some concepts for handling the phenomena of social inequality were presented.[1] In the present paper a further step in stratification theory is undertaken — an attempt to show the relationship between stratification and the rest of the social order.[2] Starting from the proposition that no society is "classless," or unstratified, an effort is made to explain, in functional terms, the universal necessity which calls forth stratification in any social system. Next, an attempt is made to explain the roughly uniform distribution of prestige as between the major types of positions in every society. Since, however, there occur between one society and another great differences in the degree and kind of stratification, some attention is also given to the varieties of social inequality and the variable factors that give rise to them.

Clearly, the present task requires two different lines of analysis — one to understand the universal, the other to understand the variable features of stratification. Naturally each line of inquiry aids the other and is indispensable, and in the treatment that follows the two will be interwoven, although, because of space limitations, the emphasis will be on the universals. .

Throughout, it will be necessary to keep in mind one thing — namely, that the discussion relates to the system of positions, not to the individuals occupying those positions. It is one thing to ask why different positions carry different degrees of prestige, and quite another to ask how certain individuals get into those positions. Although, as the argument will try to show, both questions are related, it is essential to keep them separate in our thinking. Most of the literature on stratification has tried to answer the second question (particularly with regard to the ease or difficulty of mobility between strata) without tackling the first. The first question, however, is logically prior and, in the case of any particular individual or group, factually prior.

The functional necessity of stratification

Curiously, however, the main functional necessity explaining the universal presence of stratification is precisely the requirement faced by any society of placing and motivating individuals in the social structure. As a functioning mechanism a society must somehow distribute its members in social positions and induce them to perform the duties of these positions. It must thus concern itself with motivation at two different levels: to instill in the proper individuals the desire to fill certain positions, and, once in these positions, the desire to

[1] Kingsley Davis, "A Conceptual Analysis of Stratification," *American Sociological Review*, 7: 309–321, June, 1942.

[2] The writers regret (and beg indulgence) that the present essay, a condensation of a longer study, covers so much in such short space that adequate evidence and qualification cannot be given and that as a result what is actually very tentative is presented in an unfortunately dogmatic manner.

Reprinted from *The American Sociological Review*, V. 10, No. 2 (1945), pp. 242–249, by permission of the authors and the publisher.

perform the duties attached to them. Even though the social order may be relatively static in form, there is a continuous process of metabolism as new individuals are born into it, shift with age, and die off. Their absorption into the positional system must somehow be arranged and motivated. This is true whether the system is competitive or non-competitive. A competitive system gives greater importance to the motivation to achieve positions, whereas a non-competitive system gives perhaps greater importance to the motivation to perform the duties of the positions; but in any system both types of motivation are required.

If the duties associated with the various positions were all equally pleasant to the human organism, all equally important to societal survival, and all equally in need of the same ability or talent, it would make no difference who got into which positions, and the problem of social placement would be greatly reduced. But actually it does make a great deal of difference who gets into which positions, not only because some positions are inherently more agreeable than others, but also because some require special talents or training and some are functionally more important than others. Also, it is essential that the duties of the positions be performed with the diligence that their importance requires. Inevitably, then, a society must have, first, some kind of rewards that it can use as inducements, and, second, some way of distributing these rewards differentially according to positions. The rewards and their distribution become a part of the social order, and thus give rise to stratification.

One may ask what kind of rewards a society has at its disposal in distributing its personnel and securing essential services. It has, first of all, the things that contribute to sustenance and comfort. It has, second, the things that contribute to humor and diversion. And it has, finally, the things that contribute to self respect and ego expansion. The last, because of the peculiarly social character of the self, is largely a function of the opinion of others, but it nonetheless ranks in importance with the first two. In any social system all three kinds of

[1] Unfortunately, functional importance is difficult to establish. To use the position's prestige to establish it, as is often unconsciously done, constitutes circular reasoning from our point of view. There are, however, two independent clues: *a*) the degree to which a position is functionally unique, there being no other positions that can perform the same function satisfactorily; *b*) the degree to which other positions are dependent on the one in question. Both clues are best exemplified in organized systems of positions built around one major function. Thus, in most complex societies the religious, political, economic, and educational functions are handled by distinct structures not easily interchangeable, In addition, each structure possesses many different positions, some clearly dependent on, if not subordinate to, others. In sum, when an institutional nucleus becomes differentiated around one main function, and at the same time organizes a large portion of the population into its relationships, the *key* positions in it are of the highest functional importance. The absence of such specialization does not prove functional unimportance, for the whole society may be relatively unspecialized; but it is safe to assume that the more important functions receive the first and clearest structural differentiation.

rewards must be dispensed differentially according to positions.

In a sense the rewards are "built into" the position. They consist in the "rights" associated with the position, plus what may be called its accompaniments or perquisites. Often the rights, and sometimes the accompaniments, are functionally related to the duties of the position. (Rights as viewed by the incumbent are usually duties as viewed by other members of the community.) However, there may be a host of subsidiary rights and perquisites that are not essential to the function of the position and have only an indirect and symbolic connection with its duties, but which still may be of considerable importance in inducing people to seek the positions and fulfil the essential duties.

If the rights and perquisites of different positions in a society must be unequal, then the society must be stratified, because that is precisely what stratification means. Social inequality is thus an unconsciously evolved device by which societies insure that the most important positions are conscientiously filled by the most qualified persons. Hence every society, no matter how simple or complex, must differentiate persons in terms of both prestige and esteem, and must therefore possess a certain amount of institutionalized inequality.

It does not follow that the amount or type of inequality need be the same in all societies. This is largely a function of factors that will be discussed presently.

The two determinants of positional rank

Granting the general function that inequality subserves, one can specify the two factors that determine the relative rank of different positions. In general those positions convey the best reward, and hence have the highest rank, which *a*) have the greatest importance for the society and *b*) require the greatest training or talent. The first factor concerns function and is a matter of relative significance; the second concerns means and is a matter of scarcity.

DIFFERENTIAL FUNCTIONAL IMPORTANCE

Actually a society does not need to reward positions in proportion to their functional importance. It merely needs to give sufficient reward to them to insure that they will be filled competently. In other words, it must see that less essential positions do not compete successfully with more essential ones. If a position is easily filled, it need not be heavily rewarded, even though important. On the other hand, if it is important but hard to fill, the reward must be high enough to get it filled anyway. Functional importance is therefore a necessary but not a sufficient cause of high rank being assigned to a position.[1]

DIFFERENTIAL SCARCITY OF PERSONNEL

Practically all positions, no matter how acquired, require some form of skill or capacity for performance. This is implicit in the very notion of position, which implies that the incumbent must, by virtue of this incumbency, accomplish certain things.

There are, ultimately, only two ways in which a person's qualifications come about: through inherent capacity or through training. Obviously, in concrete activities both are always necessary, but from a practical standpoint the scarcity may lie primarily in one or the other, as well as in both. Some positions require innate talents of such high degree that the persons who fill them are bound to be rare. In many cases, however, talent is fairly abundant in the population but the training process is so long, costly, and elaborate that relatively few can qualify. Modern medicine, for example, is within the mental capacity of most individuals, but a medical education is so burdensome and expensive that virtually none would undertake it if the position of the M.D. did not carry a reward commensurate with the sacrifice.

If the talents required for a position are abundant and the training easy, the method of acquiring the position may have little to do with its duties. There may be, in fact, a virtually accidental relationship. But if the skills required are scarce by reason of the rarity of talent or the costliness of training, the position, if functionally important, must have an attractive power that will draw the necessary skills in competition with other positions. This means, in effect, that the position must be high in the social scale — must command great prestige, high salary, ample leisure, and the like.

HOW VARIATIONS ARE TO BE UNDERSTOOD

In so far as there is a difference between one system of stratification and another, it is attributable to whatever factors affect the two determinants of differential reward — namely, functional importance and scarcity of personnel. Positions important in one society may not be important in another, because the conditions faced by the societies, or their degree of internal development, may be different. The same conditions, in turn, may affect the question of scarcity; for in some societies the stage of development, or the external situation, may wholly obviate the necessity of certain kinds of skill or talent. Any particular system of stratification, then, can be understood as a product of the special conditions affecting the two aforementioned grounds of differential reward.

Major societal functions and stratification

RELIGION

The reason why religion is necessary is apparently to be found in the fact that human society achieves its unity primarily through the possession by its members of certain ultimate values and ends in common. Although these values and ends are subjective, they influence behavior, and their integration enables the society to operate as a system. Derived neither from inherited nor from external nature, they have evolved as a part of culture by communication and moral

pressure. They must, however, appear to the members of the society to have some reality, and it is the role of religious belief and ritual to supply and reinforce this appearance of reality. Through belief and ritual the common ends and values are connected with an imaginary world symbolized by concrete sacred objects, which world in turn is related in a meaningful way to the facts and trials of the individual's life. Through the worship of the sacred objects and the beings they symbolize, and the acceptance of supernatural prescriptions that are at the same time codes of behavior, a powerful control over human conduct is exercised, guiding it along lines sustaining the institutional structure and conforming to the ultimate ends and values.

If this conception of the role of religion is true, one can understand why in every known society the religious activities tend to be under the charge of particular persons, who tend thereby to enjoy greater rewards than the ordinary societal member. Certain of the rewards and special privileges may attach to only the highest religious functionaries, but others usually apply, if such exists, to the entire sacerdotal class.

Moreover, there is a peculiar relation between the duties of the religious official and the special privileges he enjoys. If the supernatural world governs the destinies of men more ultimately than does the real world, its earthly representative, the person through whom one may communicate with the supernatural, must be a powerful individual. He is a keeper of sacred tradition, a skilled performer of the ritual, and an interpreter of lore and myth. He is in such close contact with the gods that he is viewed as possessing some of their characteristics. He is, in short, a bit sacred, and hence free from some of the more vulgar necessities and controls.

It is no accident, therefore, that religious functionaries have been associated with the very highest positions of power, as in theocratic regimes. Indeed, looking at it from this point of view, one may wonder why it is that they do not get *entire* control over their societies. The factors that prevent this are worthy of note.

In the first place, the amount of technical competence necessary for the performance of religious duties is small. Scientific or artistic capacity is not required. Anyone can set himself up as enjoying an intimate relation with deities, and nobody can successfully dispute him. Therefore, the factor of scarcity of personnel does not operate in the technical sense.

One may assert, on the other hand, that religious ritual is often elaborate and religious lore abstruse, and that priestly ministrations require tact, if not intelligence. This is true, but the technical requirements of the profession are for the most part adventitious, not related to the end in the same way that science is related to air travel. The priest can never be free from competition, since the criteria of whether or not one has genuine contact with the supernatural are never strictly clear. It is this competition that debases the priestly position below what might be expected at first glance. That is why priestly prestige is highest in those societies where membership in the profession is rigidly controlled by the priestly guild itself. That is why, in part at least, elaborate devices are utilized to stress the identification of the person with his office — spectacular costume, abnormal conduct, special diet, segregated residence, celibacy, conspicuous leisure, and the like. In fact, the priest is always in danger of becoming somewhat discredited — as happens in a secularized society — because in a world of stubborn fact, ritual and sacred knowledge alone will not grow crops or build houses. Furthermore, unless he is protected by a professional guild, the priest's identification with the supernatural tends to preclude his acquisition of abundant wordly goods.

As between one society and another it seems that the highest general position awarded the priest occurs in the medieval type of social order. Here there is enough economic production to afford a surplus, which can be used to support a numerous and highly organized priesthood; and yet the populace is unlettered and therefore credulous to a high degree. Perhaps the most extreme example is to be found in the Buddhism of Tibet, but others are encountered in the Catholicism of feudal Europe, the Inca regime of Peru, the Brahminism of India, and the Mayan priesthood of Yucatan. On the other hand, if the society is so crude as to have no surplus and little differentiation, so that every priest must be also a cultivator or hunter, the separation of the priestly status from the others has hardly gone far enough for priestly prestige to mean much. When the priest actually has high prestige under these circumstances, it is because he also performs other important functions (usually political and medical).

In an extremely advanced society built on scientific technology, the priesthood tends to lose status, because sacred tradition and supernaturalism drop into the background. The ultimate values and common ends of the society tend to be expressed in less anthropomorphic ways, by officials who occupy fundamentally political, economic, or educational rather than religious positions. Nevertheless, it is easily possible for intellectuals to exaggerate the degree to which the priesthood in a presumably secular milieu has lost prestige. When the matter is closely examined the urban proletariat, as well as the rural citizenry, proves to be surprisingly god-fearing and priest-ridden. No society has become so completely secularized as to liquidate entirely the belief in transcendental ends and supernatural entities. Even in a secularized society some system must exist for the integration of ultimate values, for their ritualistic expression, and for the emotional adjustments required by disappointment, death, and disaster.

GOVERNMENT

Like religion, government plays a unique and indis-

pensable part in society. But in contrast to religion, which provides integration in terms of sentiments, beliefs, and rituals, it organizes the society in terms of law and authority. Furthermore, it orients the society to the actual rather than the unseen world.

The main functions of government are, internally, the ultimate enforcement of norms, the final arbitration of conflicting interests, and the overall planning and direction of society; and externally, the handling of war and diplomacy. To carry out these functions it acts as the agent of the entire people, enjoys a monopoly of force, and controls all individuals within its territory.

Political action, by definition, implies authority. An official can command because he has authority, and the citizen must obey because he is subject to that authority. For this reason stratification is inherent in the nature of political relationships.

So clear is the power embodied in political position that political inequality is sometimes thought to comprise all inequality. But it can be shown that there are other bases of stratification, that the following controls operate in practice to keep political power from becoming complete: *a)* The fact that the actual holders of political office, and especially those determining top policy must necessarily be few in number compared to the total population. *b)* The fact that the rulers represent the interest of the group rather than of themselves, and are therefore restricted in their behavior by rules and mores designed to enforce this limitation of interest. *c)* The fact that the holder of political office has his authority by virtue of his office and nothing else, and therefore any special knowledge, talent, or capacity he may claim is purely incidental, so that he often has to depend upon others for technical assistance.

In view of these limiting factors, it is not strange that the rulers often have less power and prestige than a literal enumeration of their formal rights would lead one to expect.

WEALTH, PROPERTY, AND LABOR

Every position that secures for its incumbent a livelihood is, by definition, economically rewarded. For this reason there is an economic aspect to those positions (e.g. political and religious) the main function of which is not economic. It therefore becomes convenient for the society to use unequal economic returns as a principal means of controlling the entrance of persons into positions and stimulating the performance of their duties. The amount of the economic return therefore becomes one of the main indices of social status.

It should be stressed, however, that a position does not bring power and prestige *because* it draws a high income. Rather, it draws a high income because it is functionally important and the available personnel is for one reason or another scarce. It is therefore superficial and erroneous to regard high income as the cause of a man's power and prestige, just as it is erroneous to think that a man's fever is the cause of his disease.[1]

The economic source of power and prestige is not

---

[1] The symbolic rather than intrinsic role of income in social stratification has been succinctly summarized by Talcott Parsons, "An Analytical Approach to the Theory of Social Stratification." *American Journal of Sociology*, 45: 841–862, May, 1940.

income primarily, but the ownership of capital goods (including patents, good will, and professional reputation). Such ownership should be distinguished from the possession of consumers' goods, which is an index rather than a cause of social standing. In other words, the ownership of producers' goods is properly speaking, a source of income like other positions, the income itself remaining an index. Even in situations where social values are widely commercialized and earnings are the readiest method of judging social position, income does not confer prestige on a position so much as it induces people to compete for the position. It is true that a man who has a high income as a result of one position may find this money helpful in climbing into another position as well, but this again reflects the effect of his initial, economically advantageous status, which exercises its influence through the medium of money.

In a system of private property in productive enterprise, an income above what an individual spends can give rise to possession of capital wealth. Presumably such possession is a reward for the proper management of one's finances originally and of the productive enterprise later. But as social differentiation becomes highly advanced and yet the institution of inheritance persists, the phenomenon of pure ownership, and reward for pure ownership, emerges. In such a case it is difficult to prove that the position is functionally important or that the scarcity involved is anything other than extrinsic and accidental. It is for this reason, doubtless, that the institution of private property in productive goods becomes more subject to criticism as social development proceeds toward industrialization. It is only this pure, that is, strictly legal and functionless ownership, however, that is open to attack; for some form of active ownership, whether private or public, is indispensable.

One kind of ownership of production goods consists in rights over the labor of others. The most extremely concentrated and exclusive of such rights are found in slavery, but the essential principle remains in serfdom, peonage, encomienda, and indenture. Naturally this kind of ownership has the greatest significance for stratification, because it necessarily entails an unequal relationship.

But property in capital goods inevitably introduces a compulsive element even into the nominally free contractual relationship. Indeed, in some respects the authority of the contractual employer is greater than that of the feudal landlord, inasmuch as the latter is more limited by traditional reciprocities. Even the classical economics recognized that competitors would fare unequally, but it did not pursue this fact to its necessary conclusion that, however it might be acquired, unequal control of goods and services must give unequal advantage to the parties to a contract.

TECHNICAL KNOWLEDGE

The function of finding means to single goals, without any concern with the choice between goals, is the exclusively technical sphere. The explanation of why positions requiring great technical skill receive fairly high rewards is easy to see, for it is the simplest case of the rewards being so distributed as to draw talent and motivate training. Why they seldom if ever receive the highest rewards is also clear: the importance of technical knowledge from a societal point of view is never so great as the integration of goals, which takes place on the religious, political, and economic levels. Since the technological level is concerned solely with means, a purely technical position must ultimately be subordinate to other positions that are religious, political, or economic in character.

Nevertheless, the distinction between expert and layman in any social order is fundamental, and cannot be entirely reduced to other terms. Methods of recruitment, as well as of reward, sometimes lead to the erroneous interpretation that technical positions are economically determined. Actually, however, the acquisition of knowledge and skill cannot be accomplished by purchase, although the opportunity to learn may be. The control of the avenues of training may inhere as a sort of property right in certain families or classes, giving them power and prestige in consequence. Such a situation adds an artificial scarcity to the natural scarcity of skills and talents. On the other hand, it is possible for an opposite situation to arise. The rewards of technical position may be so great that a condition of excess supply is created, leading to at least temporary devaluation of the rewards. Thus "unemployment in the learned professions" may result in a debasement of the prestige of those positions. Such adjustments and readjustments are constantly occurring in changing societies; and it is always well to bear in mind that the efficiency of a stratified structure may be affected by the modes of recruitment for positions. The social order itself, however, sets limits to the inflation or deflation of the prestige of experts: an over-supply tends to debase the rewards and discourage recruitment or produce revolution, whereas an under-supply tends to increase the rewards or weaken the society in competition with other societies.

Particular systems of stratification show a wide range with respect to the exact position of technically competent persons. This range is pershaps most evident in the degree of specialization. Extreme division of labor tends to create many specialists without high prestige since the training is short and the required native capacity relatively small. On the other hand it also tends to accentuate the high position of the true experts — scientists, engineers, and administrators — by increasing their authority relative to other functionally important positions. But the idea of a technocratic social order or a government or priesthood of engineers or social scientists neglects the limitations of knowledge and skills as a basic for performing social functions. To the extent that the social structure is truly specialized the prestige of the technical person must also be circumscribed.

Variation in stratified systems

The generalized principles of stratification here suggested form a necessary preliminary to a consideration of types of stratified systems, because it is in terms of these principles that the types must be described. This can be seen by trying to delineate types according to certain modes of variation. For instance, some of the most important modes (together with the polar types in terms of them) seem to be as follows:

A) THE DEGREE OF SPECIALIZATION

The degree of specialization affects the fineness and multiplicity of the gradations in power and prestige. It also influences the extent to which particular functions may be emphasized in the invidious system, since a given function cannot receive much emphasis in the hierarchy until it has achieved structural separation from the other functions. Finally, the amount of specialization influences, the bases of selection. Polar types: *Specialized, Unspecialized.*

B) THE NATURE OF THE FUNCTIONAL EMPHASIS

In general when emphasis is put on sacred matters, a rigidity is introduced that tends to limit specialization and hence the development of technology. In addition, a brake is placed on social mobility, and on the development of bureaucracy. When the preoccupation with the sacred is withdrawn, leaving greater scope for purely secular preoccupations, a great development, and rise in status, of economic and technological positions seemingly takes place. Curiously, a concomitant rise in political position is not likely, because it has usually been allied with the religious and stands to gain little by the decline of the latter. It is also possible for a society to emphasize family functions — as in relatively undifferentiated societies where high mortality requires high fertility and kinship forms the main basis of social organization. Main types: *Familistic, Authoritarian* (*Theocratic* or sacred, and *Totalitarian* or secular), *Capitalistic.*

C) THE MAGNITUDE OF INVIDIOUS DIFFERENCES

What may be called the amount of social distance between positions, taking into account the entire scale, is something that should lend itself to quantitative measurement. Considerable differences apparently exist between different societies in this regard, and also between parts of the same society. Polar types: *Equalitarian, Inequalitarian.*

D) THE DEGREE OF OPPORTUNITY

The familiar question of the amount of mobility is different from the question of the comparative equality or inequality of rewards posed above, because the two criteria may vary independently up to a point. For instance, the tremendous divergences in monetary income in the United States are far greater than those found in primitive societies, yet the equality of opportunity to move from one rung to the other in the social scale may also be greater in the United States than in a hereditary tribal kingdom. Polar types: *Mobile* (open), *Immobile* (closed).

E) THE DEGREE OF STRATUM SOLIDARITY

Again, the degree of "class solidarity" (or the presence of specific organizations to promote class interests) may vary to some extent independently of the other criteria, and hence is an important principle in classifying systems of stratification. Polar types: *Class organized, Class unorganized.*

External conditions

What state any particular system of stratification is in with reference to each of these modes of variation depends on two things: *1*) its state with reference to the other ranges of variation, and *2*) the conditions outside the system of stratification which nevertheless influence that system. Among the latter are the following:

A) THE STAGE OF CULTURAL DEVELOPMENT

As the cultural heritage grows, increased specialization becomes necessary, which in turn contributes to the enhancement of mobility, a decline of stratum solidarity, and a change of functional emphasis.

B) SITUATION WITH RESPECT TO OTHER SOCIETIES

The presence or absence of open conflict with other societies, of free trade relations or cultural diffusion, all influence the class structure to some extent. A chronic state of warfare tends to place emphasis upon the military functions, especially when the opponents are more or less equal. Free trade, on the other hand, strengthens the hand of the trader at the expense of the warrior and priest. Free movement of ideas generally has an equalitarian effect. Migration and conquest create special circumstances.

C) SIZE OF THE SOCIETY

A small society limits the degree to which functional specialization can go, the degree of segregation of different strata, and the magnitude of inequality.

Composite types

Much of the literature on stratification has attempted to classify concrete systems into a certain number of types. This task is deceptively simply, however, and should come at the end of an analysis of elements and principles, rather than at the beginning. If the preceding discussion has any validity, it indicates that there are a number of modes of variation between different systems, and that any one system is a composite of the society's status with reference to all these modes of variation. The danger of trying to classify whole societies under such rubrics as *caste, feudal,* or *open class* is that one or two criteria are selected and others ignored, the result being an unsatisfactory solution to the problem posed. The present discussion has been offered as a possible approach to the more systematic classification of composite types.

Some Principles of Stratification
A CRITICAL ANALYSIS[1]   *Melvin M. Tumin*

THE FACT of social inequality in human society is marked by its ubiquity and its antiquity. Every known society, past and present, distributes its scarce and demanded goods and services unequally. And there are attached to the positions which command unequal amounts of such goods and services certain highly morally-toned evaluations of their importance for the society.

The ubiquity and the antiquity of such inequality has given rise to the assumption that there must be something both inevitable and positively functional about such social arrangements.

Clearly, the truth or falsity of such an assumption is a strategic question for any general theory of social organization. It is therefore most curious that the basic premises and implications of the assumption have only been most casually explored by American sociologists.

The most systematic treatment is to be found in the well-known article by Kingsley Davis and Wilbert Moore, entitled "Some Principles of Stratification."[2] More than twelve years have passed since its publication, and though it is one of the very few treatments of stratification on a high level of generalization, it is difficult to locate a single systematic analysis of its reasoning. It will be the principal concern of this paper to present the beginnings of such an analysis.

The central argument advanced by Davis and Moore can be stated in a number of sequential propositions, as follows:

1) Certain positions in any society are functionally more important than others, and require special skills for their performance.

2) Only a limited number of individuals in any society have the talents which can be trained into the skills appropriate to these positions.

3) The conversion of talents into skills involves a training period during which sacrifices of one kind or another are made by those undergoing the training.

4) In order to induce the talented persons to undergo these sacrifices and acquire the training, their future positions must carry an inducement value in the form of differential, i.e., privileged and disproportionate access to the scarce and desired reward which the society has to offer.[3]

5) These scarce and desired goods consist of the rights and perquisites attached to, or built into, the positions, and can be classified into those things which contribute to *a)* sustenance and comfort, *b)* humor and diversion, *c)* self-respect and ego expansion.

[1] The writer has had the benefit of a most helpful criticism of the main portions of this paper by Professor W. J. Goode of Columbia University. In addition, he has had the opportunity to expose this paper to criticism by the Staff Seminar of the Sociology Section at Princeton. In deference to a possible rejoinder by Professors Moore and Davis, the writer has not revised the paper to meet the criticisms which Moore has already offered personally.

[2] *American Sociological Review,* X (April, 1945), pp. 242–249. An earlier article by Kingsley Davis, entitled, "A Conceptual Analysis of Stratification," *American Sociological Review,* VII (June, 1942), pp. 309–321, is devoted primarily to setting forth a vocabulary for stratification analysis. A still earlier article by Talcott Parsons, "An Analytical Approach to the Theory of Social Stratification," *American Journal of Sociology,* XLV November, 1940), pp. 849–862, approaches the problem in terms of why "differential ranking is considered a really fundamental phenomenon of social systems and what are the respects in which such ranking is important." The principal line of integration asserted by Parsons is with the fact of the normative orientation of any society. Certain crucial lines of connection are left unexplained, however, in this article, and in the Davis and Moore article of 1945 only some of these lines are made explicit.

[3] The "scarcity and demand" qualities of goods and services are never explicitly mentioned by Davis and Moore. But it seems to the writer that the argument makes no sense unless the goods and services are so characterized. For if rewards are to function as differential inducements they must not only be differentially distributed but they must be both scarce and demanded as well. Neither the scarcity of an item by itself nor the fact of its being in demand is sufficient to allow it to function as a differential inducement in a system of unequal rewards. Leprosy is scarce and oxygen is highly demanded.

Reprinted from *The American Sociological Review,* V. 18 (August, 1953), pp. 387–393, by permission of the author and the publisher.

6) This differential access to the basic rewards of the society has as a consequence the differentiation of the prestige and esteem which various strata acquire. This may be said, along with the rights and perquisites, to constitute institutionalized social inequality, i.e. stratification.

7) Therefore, social inequality among different strata in the amounts of scarce and desired goods, and the amounts of prestige and esteem which they receive, is both positively functional and inevitable in any society.

Let us take these propositions and examine them *seriatim.*[1]

1) CERTAIN POSITIONS IN ANY SOCIETY ARE MORE FUNCTIONALLY IMPORTANT THAN OTHERS AND REQUIRE SPECIAL SKILLS FOR THEIR PERFORMANCE

The key term here is "functionally important." The functionalist theory of social organization is by no means clear and explicit about this term. The minimum common referent is to something known as the "survival value" of a social structure.[2] This concept immediately involves a number of perplexing questions. Among these are: *a*) the issue of minimum vs. maximum survival, and the possible empirical referents which can be given to those terms; *b*) whether such a proposition is a useless tautology since any *status quo* at any given moment is nothing more and nothing less than everything present in the *status quo.* In these terms, all acts and structures must be judged positively functional in that they constitute essential portions of the *status quo; c*) what kind of calculus of functionality exists which will enable us, at this point in our development, to add and subtract long and short range consequences, with their mixed qualities, and arrive at some summative judgment regarding the rating an act or structure should receive on a scale of greater or lesser functionality? At best, we tend to make primarily intuitive judgments. Often enough, these judgments involve the use of value-laden criteria, or, at least, criteria which are chosen in preference to others not for any sociologically systematic reasons but by reason of certain implicit value preferences.

Thus, to judge that the engineers in a factory are functionally more important to the factory than the unskilled workmen involves a notion regarding the dispensability of the unskilled workmen, or their replaceability, relative to that of the engineers. But this is not a process of choice with infinite time dimensions. For at some point along the line one must face the prob-

lem of adequate motivation for *all* workers at all levels of skill in the factory. In the long run, *some* labor force of unskilled workmen is as important and as indispensable to the factory as *some* labor force of engineers. Often enough, the labor force situation is such that this fact is brought home sharply to the entrepreneur in the short run rather than in the long run.

Moreover, the judgment as to the relative indispensability and replaceability of a particular segment of skills in the population involves a prior judgment about the bargaining-power of that segment. But this power is itself a culturally shaped *consequence* of the existing system of rating, rather than something inevitable in the nature of social organization. At least the contrary of this has never been demonstrated, but only assumed.

A generalized theory of social stratification must recognize that the prevailing system of inducements and rewards is only one of many variants in the whole range of possible systems of motivation which, at least theoretically, are capable of working in human society. It is quite conceivable, of course, that a system of norms could be institutionalized in which the idea of threatening withdrawal of services, except under the most extreme circumstances, would be considered as absolute moral anathema. In such a case, the whole notion of relative functionality, as advanced by Davis and Moore, would have to be radically revised.

2) ONLY A LIMITED NUMBER OF INDIVIDUALS IN ANY SOCIETY HAVE THE TALENTS WHICH CAN BE TRAINED INTO THE SKILLS APPROPRIATE TO THESE POSITIONS (I.E., THE MORE FUNCTIONALLY IMPORTANT POSITIONS)

The truth of this proposition depends at least in part on the truth of proposition *1* above. It is, therefore, subject to all the limitations indicated above. But for the moment, let us assume the validity of the first proposition and concentrate on the question of the rarity of appropriate talent.

If all that is meant is that in every society there is a *range* of talent, and that some members of any society are by nature more talented than others, no sensible contradiction can be offered, but a question must be raised here regarding the amount of sound knowledge present in any society concerning the presence of talent in the population.

For, in every society there is some demonstrable ignorance regarding the amount of talent present in the population. *And the more rigidly stratified a society is, the less chance does that society have of discovering any new facts about the talents of its members.* Smoothly working and stable systems of stratification, wherever found, tend to build-in obstacles to the further exploration of the range of available talent. This is especially true in those societies where the opportunity to discover talent in any one generation varies with the differential resources

---

[1] The arguments to be advanced here are condensed versions of a much longer analysis entitled, *An Essay on Social Stratification.* Perforce, all the reasoning necessary to support some of the contentions cannot be offered within the space limits of this article.

[2] Davis and Moore are explicitly aware of the difficulties involved here and suggest two "independent clues" other than survival value. See footnote 1 on p. 48 of their article.

of the parent generation. Where, for instance, access to education depends upon the wealth of one's parents, and where wealth is differentially distributed, large segments of the population are likely to be deprived of the chance even to *discover* what are their talents.

Whether or not differential rewards and opportunities are functional in any one generation, it is clear that if those differentials are allowed to be socially inherited by the next generation, then, the stratification system is specifically dysfunctional for the discovery of talents in the next generation. In this fashion, systems of social stratification tend to limit the chances available to maximize the efficiency of discovery, recruitment and training of "functionally important talent."[1]

Additionally, the unequal distribution of rewards in one generation tends to result in the unequal distribution of motivation in the succeeding generation. Since motivation to succeed is clearly an important element in the entire process of education, the unequal distribution of motivation tends to set limits on the possible extensions of the educational system, and hence, upon the efficient recruitment and training of the widest body of skills available in the population.[2]

Lastly, in this context, it may be asserted that there is some noticeable tendency for elites to restrict further access to their privileged positions, once they have sufficient power to enforce such restrictions. This is especially true in a culture where it is possible for an elite to contrive a high demand and a proportionately higher reward for its work by restricting the numbers of the elite available to do the work. The recruitment and training of doctors in modern United States is at least partly a case in point.

Here, then, are three ways, among others which could be cited, in which stratification systems, once operative, tend to reduce the survival value of a society by limiting the search, recruitment and training of functionally important personnel far more sharply than the facts of available talent would appear to justify. It is only when there is genuinely equal access to recruitment and training for all potentially talented persons that differential rewards can conceivably be justified as functional. And stratification systems are apparently *inherently antagonistic* to the development of such full equality of opportunity.

3) THE CONVERSION OF TALENTS INTO SKILLS INVOLVES A TRAINING PERIOD DURING WHICH SACRIFICES OF ONE KIND OR ANOTHER ARE MADE BY THOSE UNDERGOING THE TRAINING

Davis and Moore introduce here a concept, "sacrifice", which comes closer than any of the rest of their vocabulary of analysis to being a direct reflection of the rationalizations, offered by the more fortunate members of a society, of the rightness of their occupancy of privileged positions. It is the least critically thought-out concept in

the repertoire, and can also be shown to be least supported by the actual facts.

In our present society, for example, what are the sacrifices which talented persons undergo in the training period? The possibly serious losses involve the surrender of earning power and the cost of the training. The latter is generally borne by the parents of the talented youth undergoing training, and not by the trainees themselves. But this cost tends to be paid out of income which the parents were able to earn generally by virtue of *their* privileged positions in the hierarchy of stratification. That is to say, the parents' ability to pay for the training of their children is part of the differential *reward* they, the parents, received for their privileged positions in the society. And to charge this sum up against sacrifices made by the youth is falsely to perpetrate a bill or a debt already paid by the society to the parents.

So far as the sacrifice of earning power by the trainees themselves is concerned, the loss may be measured relative to what they might have earned had they gone into the labor market instead of into advanced training for the "important" skills. There are several ways to judge this. One way is to take all the average earnings of age peers who did go into the labor market for a period equal to the average length of the training period. The total income, so calculated, roughly equals an amount which the elite can, on the average, earn back in the first decade of professional work, over and above the earnings of his age peers who are not trained. Ten years is probably the maximum amount needed to equalize the differential.[3] There remains, on the average, twenty years of work during each of which the skilled person then goes on to earn far more than his unskilled age peers. And, what is often forgotten, there is then still another ten or fifteen year period during which the skilled person continues to work and earn when his unskilled age peer is either totally or partially out of the labor market by virtue of the attrition of his strength and capabilities.

One might say that the first ten years of differential pay is perhaps justified, in order to regain for the trained person what he lost during his training period. But it is difficult to imagine what would justify continuing such differential rewards beyond that period.

Another and probably sounder way to measure how

---

[1] Davis and Moore state this point briefly on p. 51 but do not elaborate it.

[2] In the United States, for instance, we are only now becoming aware of the amount of productivity we, as a society, lose by allocating inferior opportunities and rewards, and hence, inferior motivation, to our Negro population. The actual amount of loss is difficult to specify precisely. Some rough estimate can be made, however, on the assumption that there is present in the Negro population about the same range of talent that is found in the White population.

[3] These are only very rough estimates, of course, and it is certain that there is considerable income variation within the so-called elite group, so that the proposition holds only relatively more or less.

much is lost during the training period is to compare the per capita income available to the trainee with the per capita income of the age peer on the untrained labor market during the so-called sacrificial period.) If one takes into account the earlier marriage of untrained persons, and the earlier acquisition of family dependents, it is highly dubious that the per capita income of the wage worker is significantly larger than that of the trainee. Even assuming, for the moment, that there is a difference, the amount is by no means sufficient to justify a lifetime of continuing differentials.

What tends to be completely overlooked, in addition, are the psychic and spiritual rewards which are available to the elite trainees by comparison with their age peers in the labor force. There is, first, the much higher prestige enjoyed by the college student and the professional-school student as compared with persons in shops and offices. There is, second, the extremely highly valued privilege of having greater opportunity for self-development. There is, third, all the psychic gain involved in being allowed to delay the assumption of adult responsibilities such as earning a living and supporting a family. There is, fourth, the access to leisure and freedom of a kind not likely to be experienced by the persons already at work.

If these are never taken into account as rewards of the training period it is not because they are not concretely present, but because the emphasis in American concepts of reward is almost exclusively placed on the material returns of positions. The emphases on enjoyment, entertainment, ego enhancement, prestige and esteem are introduced only when the differentials in those which accrue to the skilled positions need to be justified. If these other rewards were taken into account, it would be much more difficult to demonstrate that the training period, as presently operative, is really sacrificial. Indeed, it might turn out to be the case that even at this point in their careers, the elite trainees were being differentially rewarded relative to their age peers in the labor force.

All of the foregoing concerns the quality of the training period under our present system of motivation and rewards. Whatever may turn out to be the factual case about the present system — and the factual case is moot — the more important theoretical question concerns the assumption that the training period under *any* system must be sacrificial.

There seem to be no good theoretical grounds for insisting on this assumption. For, while under any system certain costs will be involved in training persons for skilled positions, these costs could easily be assumed by the society-at-large. Under these circumstances, there would be no need to compensate anyone in terms of differential rewards once the skilled positions were staffed. In short, there would be no need or justification for stratifying social positions on *these* grounds.

4) IN ORDER TO INDUCE THE TALENTED PERSONS TO UNDERGO THESE SACRIFICES AND ACQUIRE THE TRAINING, THEIR FUTURE POSITIONS MUST CARRY AN INDUCEMENT VALUE IN THE FORM OF DIFFERENTIAL, I.E., PRIVILEGED AND DISPROPORTIONATE ACCESS TO THE SCARCE AND DESIRED REWARDS WHICH THE SOCIETY HAS TO OFFER

Let us assume, for the purposes of the discussion, that the training period is sacrificial and the talent is rare in every conceivable human society. There is still the basic problem as to whether the allocation of differential rewards in scarce and desired goods and services is the only or the most efficient way of recruiting the appropriate talent to these positions.

For there are a number of alternative motivational schemes whose efficiency and adequacy ought at least to be considered in this context. What can be said, for instance, on behalf of the motivation which De Man called "joy in work," Veblen termed "instinct for workmanship" and which we latterly have come to identify as "intrinsic work satisfaction?" Or, to what extent could the motivation of "social duty" be institutionalized in such a fashion that self interest and social interest come closely to coincide? Or, how much prospective confidence can be placed in the possibilities of institutionalizing "social service" as a widespread motivation for seeking one's appropriate position and fulfilling it conscientiously?

Are not these types of motivations, we may ask, likely to prove most appropriate for precisely the "most functionally important positions?" Especially in a mass industrial society, where the vast majority of positions become standardized and routinized, it is the skilled jobs which are likely to retain most of the quality of "intrinsic job satisfaction" and be most readily identifiable as socially serviceable. Is it indeed impossible then to build these motivations into the socialization pattern to which we expose our talented youth?

To deny that such motivations could be institutionalized would be to overclaim our present knowledge. In part, also, such a claim would seem to derive from an assumption that what has not been institutionalized yet in human affairs is incapable of institutionalization. Admittedly, historical experience affords us evidence we cannot afford to ignore. But such evidence cannot legitimately be used to deny absolutely the possibility of heretofore untried alternatives. Social innovation is as important a feature of human societies as social stability.

On the basis of these observations, it seems that Davis and Moore have stated the case much too strongly when they insist that a "functionally important position" which requires skills that are scarce, "must command great prestige, high salary, ample leisure, and the like," if the appropriate talents are to be attracted to the position. Here, clearly, the authors are postulating the unavoidability of very specific types of rewards and, by implication, denying the possibility of others.

5) THESE SCARCE AND DESIRED GOODS CONSIST OF RIGHTS AND PERQUISITES ATTACHED TO, OR BUILT INTO, THE POSITIONS AND CAN BE CLASSIFIED INTO THOSE THINGS WHICH CONTRIBUTE TO A) SUSTENANCE AND COMFORT; B) HUMOR AND DIVERSION; C) SELF RESPECT AND EGO EXPANSION

6) THIS DIFFERENTIAL ACCESS TO THE BASIC REWARDS OF THE SOCIETY HAS AS A CONSEQUENCE THE DIFFERENTIATION OF THE PRESTIGE AND ESTEEM WHICH VARIOUS STRATA ACQUIRE. THIS MAY BE SAID, ALONG WITH THE RIGHTS AND PERQUISITES, TO CONSTITUTE INSTITUTIONALIZED SOCIAL INEQUALITY, I.E., STRATIFICATION

With the classification of the rewards offered by Davis and Moore there need be little argument. Some question must be raised, however, as to whether any reward system, built into a general stratification system, must allocate equal amounts of all three types of reward in order to function effectively, or whether one type of reward may be emphasized to the virtual neglect of others. This raises the further question regarding which type of emphasis is likely to prove most effective as a differential inducer. Nothing in the known facts about human motivation impels us to favor one type of reward over the other, or to insist that all three types of reward must be built into the positions in comparable amounts if the position is to have an inducement value.

It is well known, of course, that societies differ considerably in the kinds of rewards they emphasize in their efforts to maintain a reasonable balance between responsibility and reward. There are, for instance, numerous societies in which the conspicuous display of differential economic advantage is considered extremely bad taste. In short, our present knowledge commends to us the possibility of considerable plasticity in the way in which different types of rewards can be structured into a functioning society. This is to say, it cannot yet be demonstrated that it is *unavoidable* that differential prestige and esteem shall accrue to positions which command differential rewards in power and property.

What does seem to be unavoidable is that differential prestige shall be given to those in any society who conform to the normative order as against those who deviate from that order in a way judged immoral and detrimental. On the assumption that the continuity of a society depends on the continuity and stability of its normative order, some such distinction between conformists and deviants seems inescapable.

It also seems to be unavoidable that in any society, no matter how literate its tradition, the older, wiser

and more experienced individuals who are charged with the enculturation and socialization of the young must have more power than the young, on the assumption that the task of effective socialization demands such differential power.

But this differentiation in prestige between the conformist and the deviant is by no means the same distinction as that between strata of individuals each of which operates *within* the normative order, and is composed of adults. The *latter* distinction, in the form of differentiated rewards and prestige between social strata is what Davis and Moore, and most sociologists, consider the structure of a stratification system. The *former* distinctions have nothing necessarily to do with the workings of such a system nor with the efficiency of motivation and recruitment of functionally important personnel.

Nor does the differentiation of power between young and old necessarily create differentially valued strata. For no society rates its young as less morally worthy than its older persons, no matter how much differential power the older ones may temporarily enjoy.

7) THEREFORE, SOCIAL INEQUALITY AMONG DIFFERENT STRATA IN THE AMOUNTS OF SCARCE AND DESIRED GOODS, AND THE AMOUNTS OF PRESTIGE AND ESTEEM WHICH THEY RECEIVE, IS BOTH POSITIVELY FUNCTIONAL AND INEVITABLE IN ANY SOCIETY

If the objections which have heretofore been raised are taken as reasonable, then it may be stated that the only items which any society *must* distribute unequally are the power and property necessary for the performance of different tasks. If such differential power and property are viewed by all as commensurate with the differential responsibilities, and if they are culturally defined as *resources* and not as rewards, then, no differentials in prestige and esteem need follow.

Historically, the evidence seems to be that every time power and property are distributed unequally, no matter what the cultural definition, prestige and esteem differentiations have tended to result as well. Historically, however, no systematic effort has ever been made, under propitious circumstances, to develop the tradition that each man is as socially worthy as all other men so long as he performs his appropriate tasks conscientiously. While such a tradition seems utterly utopian, no known facts in psychological or social science have yet demonstrated its impossibility or its dysfunctionality for the continuity of a society. The achievement of a full institutionalization of such a tradition seems far too remote to contemplate. Some successive approximations at such a tradition, however, are not out of the range of prospective social innovation.

What, then, of the "positive functionality" of social stratification? Are there other, negative, functions of institutionalized social inequality which can be identified, if only tentatively? Some such dysfunctions of stratification have already been suggested in the body of this paper. Along with others they may now be stated, in the form of provisional assertions, as follows:

1) Social stratification systems function to limit the possibility of discovery of the full range of talent available in a society. This results from the fact of unequal access to appropriate motivation, channels of recruitment and centers of training.

2) In foreshortening the range of available talent, social stratification systems function to set limits upon the possibility of expanding the productive resources of the society, at least relative to what might be the case under conditions of greater equality of opportunity.

3) Social stratification systems function to provide the elite with the political power necessary to procure acceptance and dominance of an ideology which rationalizes the *status quo*, whatever it may be, as "logical," "natural" and "morally right." In this manner, social stratification systems function as essentially conservative influences in the societies in which they are found.

4) Social stratification systems function to distribute favorable self-images unequally throughout a population. To the extent that such favorable self-images are requisite to the development of the creative potential inherent in men, to that extent stratification systems function to limit the development of this creative potential.

5) To the extent that inequalities in social rewards cannot be made fully acceptable to the less privileged in a society, social stratification systems function to encourage hostility, suspicion and distrust among the various segments of a society and thus to limit the possibilities of extensive social integration.

6) To the extent that the sense of significant membership in a society depends on one's place on the prestige ladder of the society, social stratification systems function to distribute unequally the sense of significant membership in the population.

7) To the extent that loyalty to a society depends on a sense of significant membership in the society, social stratification systems function to distribute loyalty unequally in the population.

8) To the extent that participation and apathy depend upon the sense of significant membership in the society, social stratification systems function to distribute the motivation to participate unequally in a population.

Each of the eight foregoing propositions contains implicit hypotheses regarding the consequences of

[1] Davis and Moore, *op. cit.*, p. 243.

unequal distribution of rewards in a society in accordance with some notion of the functional importance of various positions. These are empirical hypotheses, subject to test. They are offered here only as exemplary of the kinds of consequences of social stratification which are not often taken into account in dealing with the problem. They should also serve to reinforce the doubt that social inequality is a device which is uniformly functional for the role of guaranteeing that the most important tasks in a society will be performed conscientiously by the most competent persons.

The obviously mixed character of the functions of social inequality should come as no surprise to anyone. If sociology is sophisticated in any sense, it is certainly with regard to its awareness of the mixed nature of any social arrangement, when the observer takes into account long as well as short range consequences and latent as well as manifest dimensions.

Summary

In this paper, an effort has been made to raise questions regarding the inevitability and positive functionality of stratification, or institutionalized social inequality in rewards, allocated in accordance with some notion of the greater and lesser functional importance of various positions. The possible alternative meanings of the concept "functional importance" has been shown to be one difficulty. The question of the scarcity or abundance of available talent has been indicated as a principal source of possible variation. The extent to which the period of training for skilled positions may reasonably be viewed as sacrificial has been called into question. The possibility has been suggested that very different types of motivational schemes might conceivably be made to function. The separability of differentials in power and property considered as resources appropriate to a task from such differentials considered as rewards for the performance of a task has also been suggested. It has also been maintained that differentials in prestige and esteem do not necessarily follow upon differentials in power and property when the latter are considered as appropriate resources rather than rewards. Finally, some negative functions, or dysfunctions, of institutionalized social inequality have been tentatively identified, revealing the mixed character of the outcome of social stratification, and casting doubt on the contention that

Social inequality is thus an unconsciously evolved device by which societies insure that the most important positions are conscientiously filled by the most qualified persons.[1]

Reply to Tumin

Kingsley Davis

TUMIN'S CRITIQUE, almost as long as the article it criticizes, is unfortunately intended not to supplement or amend the Davis-Moore theory but to prove it wrong. The critique also sets a bad example from the standpoint of methodology. Nevertheless, it does afford us a meager opportunity to clarify and extend the original discussion. The latter, limited to eight pages, was so brief a treatment of so big a subject that it had to ignore certain relevant topics and telescope others. In the process of answering Tumin, a partial emendation can now be made.

General considerations

Our critic seems to labor under four major difficulties, two of a methodological and two of a substantive character. First, he appears not so much interested in understanding institutionalized inequality as in getting rid of it. By insinuating that we are "justifying" such inequality, he falls into the usual error of regarding a causal explanation of something as a justification of it: He himself offers no explanation for the universality of stratified inequality. He argues throughout his critique that stratification does not have to be, instead of trying to understand why it is. Our interest, however, was only in the latter question. If Tumin had chosen to state our propositions in our own words rather than his, he could not have pictured us as concerned with the question of whether stratification is "avoidable."

Second, Tumin confuses abstract, or theoretical, reasoning on the one hand with raw empirical generalizations on the other. Much of his critique accordingly rests on the fallacy of misplaced concreteness. Our article dealt with stratified inequality as a general property of social systems. It represented a high degree of abstraction, because there are obviously other aspects of society which in actuality affect the operation of the prestige element. It is therefore impossible to move directly from the kind of propositions we were making to descriptive propositions about, say, American society.

Third, in concentrating on only one journal article, Tumin has ignored other theoretical contributions by the authors on stratification and on other relevant aspects of society. He has thus both misrepresented the theory and raised questions that were answered elsewhere.

Fourth, by ignoring additions to the theory in other places, Tumin has failed to achieve consistency in his use of the concept "stratification." The first requirement, in this connection, is to distinguish between stratified and non-stratified statuses. One of the authors under attack has shown the difference to hinge on the family. "Those positions that may be combined in the same legitimate family — viz., positions based on sex, age, and kinship — do not form part of the system of stratification. On the other hand those positions that are socially prohibited from being combined in the same legal family — viz., different caste or class positions — constitute what we call stratification."[1] This distinction is basic, but in addition it is necessary to realize that two different questions can be asked about stratified positions: *a*) Why are different evaluations and rewards given to the different *positions*? *b*) How do *individuals* come to be distributed in these positions? Our theory was designed to answer the first question by means of the second. But much confusion results, as illustrated by Tumin's ambiguities, if the term "stratification" is used in such a way as to overlook the distinction between the two.

The specific criticisms

It will be seen that these four difficulties plague Tumin throughout his remarks and lead to much obfuscation. In answering his criticisms, we shall follow his sequence in terms of the propositions attributed to us.

1) DIFFERENTIAL FUNCTIONAL IMPORTANCE OF POSITIONS

Tumin criticizes the idea of unequal functional importance on the grounds that the concept is unclear, unmeasurable, and evaluative, and that other systems of motivation are conceivable. The latter point is irrelevant, since the proposition in question says nothing whatever about motivation. So is the remark about "value-laden criteria," since no such criteria are advanced by us. As for the difficulty of measuring functional importance, we stated this before Tumin did, but he does not elect to discuss the two criteria suggested in our article. The difficulty of exact empirical measure-

[1] Kingsley Davis, *Human Society*, New York: Macmillan, 1949, p. 364.

Reprinted from *The American Sociological Review*, V. 18 (August, 1953), pp. 394–397, by permission of the authors and the publisher.

ment does not itself make a concept worthless; if so we should have to throw away virtually all theoretical concepts. Rough measures of functional importance are in fact applied in practice. In wartime, for example, decisions are made as to which industries and occupations will have priority in capital equipment, labor recruitment, raw materials, etc. In totalitarian countries the same is done in peacetime, as also in underdeveloped areas attempting to maximize their social and economic modernization. Individual firms must constantly decide which positions are essential and which not. There is nothing mystical about functional importance.

Tumin points out that the unskilled workmen in a factory are as important as the engineers. This is of course true, but we have maintained that the rating of positions is not a result of functional importance alone but also of the scarcity of qualified personnel. Any concrete situation is a product of both. It requires more capital to train an engineer than to train an unskilled worker, and so engineers would not be trained at all unless their work were considered important.

Actually Tumin does not deny the differential functional importance of positions. He disguises his agreement with the proposition by tendentious argumentation.

2) THE STRANGULATION OF TALENT BY "STRATIFICATION"

Tumin's objection to the idea of a scarcity of trained and talented personnel rests on the argument *a)* that societies do not have a "sound knowledge" of talents in their populations and *b)* that stratification interferes with, rather than facilitates, the selection of talented people. The first point is inconsequential, because a selective system—e.g., organized baseball—does not require a pre-existing knowledge of talent to be effective. The second point is crucial, but Tumin strangely fails to refer to a later treatment of this very problem by Davis.[1] In introducing the problem, Davis says: "One may object to the foregoing explanation of stratification [as contained in the Davis-Moore article] on the ground that it fits a competitive order but does not fit a non-competitive one. For instance, in a caste system it seems that people do not get their positions because of talent or training but rather because of birth. This criticism raises a crucial problem and forces an addition to the theory." The addition takes the following form: The theory in question is a theory explaining the differential prestige of *positions* rather than individuals. Even though a high-caste person occupies his rank because of his parents, this fact does not explain the high evaluation of the caste's *position* in the community. The low estate of sweeper as compared with priestly castes cannot be explained by saying that the sons of sweepers become sweepers and the sons of Brahmins become Brahmins. The explanation of the differential evaluation of strata

[1] *Human Society*, pp. 369–370.
[2] K. Davis, "A Conceptual Analysis of Stratification," *American Sociological Review*, 7 (June, 1942), pp. 309–321.

must be sought elsewhere, in the survival value of drawing qualified people into the functionally most important positions. But since this is not the only functional necessity characterizing social systems, it is in actuality limited by certain other structures and requirements. Among the latter is the family, which limits vertical mobility by the mechanism of inheritance and succession. The family's limiting role, however, is never complete, for there is some vertical mobility in any society. Thus the selective effect of the prestige system exists in its pure form only abstractly, not concretely; and the same is true of the inheritance of status. Consequently, to say that in a given society there is partial inheritance of high positions is not to deny that at the same time the prestige system is operating to draw capable people into these positions.

One source of confusion in this argument is the ambiguity, mentioned above, of the term "stratification." On the one hand it is used by us to designate the institutionalized inequality of rewards as between broad strata.[2] On the other hand, it is used (as Tumin does implicitly) to mean the inheritance of class status. With the latter definition, of course, the idea that stratification contributes to upward mobility is incongruous. One cannot expect a theory designed to account for the universal existence of institutionalized inequality as between positions to be, at the same time, an explanation of the inheritance of class status. However, it is possible to extend the theory by combining with it a general analysis of the family's articulation with the differential reward system in society. This has been done by Davis, and the result is that one can understand the combined existence in the same society of *a)* a differential ranking of stratified positions, *b)* a certain amount of verticle mobility, and *c)* a certain amount of inheritance of status. It is this extension of the theory that Tumin ignores.

3) THE "NO SACRIFICE" CRITICISM

Tumin contends, in effect, that no differential rewards are necessary to induce individuals to qualify for functionally important positions, because they make no "sacrifices." In support of his view he says *a)* that the family often makes the sacrifice for the offspring, *b)* that the loss of earning power during the training period is negligible, and *c)* that the prestige during the training period is high.

But point *a* confirms rather than denies the theory. It makes no essential difference that the family assumes some of the burden of training; the fact is that there is a burden. The differential ability of families to make such sacrifices of course comes back to the role of the family in limiting competition for status, which has already been discussed. The claim under point *b* that the loss of earning power during training is more than made up in the years following again confirms the theory, for we have said there is a differential reward for those attaining functionally important positions. As for point *c*, the fact that the trainee may enjoy a standard of living higher than that of his already working age peers comes back to the family's status, already discussed. Nor does the claim that the psychic rewards are high during training offer any objection to the theory, because these psychic rewards are mainly a reflection of the anticipated rewards of an ultimately high status to be attained through training. It is amusing that throughout his discussion of "sacrifice" Tumin, though thinking in terms of professional training, never once mentions the onerous necessity of studying. It is unfortunately true that most individuals regard hard study as burdensome, and it is something that the family cannot do for them. Many youths are unwilling to make this sacrifice and also many are incapable of doing it well enough to succeed. There are, however, many other kinds of hurdles to high position that would discourage an individual if it were not for the rewards offered. So difficult is it to get enough qualified personnel in good positions that the modern state undertakes to bear some of the costs, but it cannot bear them all.

4) ALTERNATIVE MOTIVATIONAL SCHEMES

Our critic contends that there are "a number of alternative motivational schemes" as efficient as differential rewards in motivating people to strive for important positions. Actually he mentions three: joy in work, sense of social service, and self interest. The third is obviously a ringer. Concerning it he asks, "To what extent could the motivation of 'social duty' be institutionalized in such a fashion that self interest and social interest come closely to coincide?" The answer is that such coinciding is not only possible but is actually accomplished — and our theory of social inequality explains how. This leaves, then, only two alternatives that offer any possible criticism of our views. In the eight-page article under attack, it was mentioned that one consideration is the unequal pleasantness of activities required by different positions, but space did not allow us to follow out the implications of this fact. The truth is that if everybody elected to do just what he wanted to do, the whole population would wind up in only a few types of position. A society could not operate on this basis, because it requires performance of a wide range of tasks. Surviving societies therefore evolve some system of inducements over and above the joy of work which motivates people to do what they would otherwise not do. Finally, as for the sense of social service, any sociologist should know the inadequacy of unrewarded altruism as a means of eliciting socially adequate behavior. It must be remembered that the differential rewards characterizing the status scale are not all material; they also lie in the good opinion and expectations of others and in the feeling of self-satisfaction at having stood well in others' eyes. No one will deny that joy of work and a sense of social service are actual motives, any more than one will deny the reality of the desire for esteem (in contrast to prestige) but in any society they are supplementary rather than alternative to the positional reward mechanism.

5–6) TYPES OF REWARDS

The Davis-Moore article mentioned a rough tripartite classification of types of rewards occurring in stratified positions. Tumin says these may be unequally employed, that one society may emphasize one type more than another. This is true; we said nothing to the contrary. Tumin goes on to say that societies give approval to behavior that conforms with norms. This we certainly never disputed; indeed, in connection with positions, Davis has given a name to it — *esteem*, the kind of approval that comes with the faithful fulfillment of the duties of a position.[1] The approval that comes with *having* a position, i.e., approval attached to the position and not to the degree of faithfulness in performing its duties, is called *prestige*. Whatever the words used, the distinction is important, but Tumin has confused the two. A social system, though it certainly utilizes esteem, is not entirely built on it, because there must be motivation not only to conform to the requirements of positions held but also to strive to get into positions. Esteem alone tends to produce a static society, prestige a mobile one. Tumin's statement that the position of the parent vis-a-vis the child is not part of the stratified system is true, but it agrees perfectly with Davis's distinction between stratified and non-stratified status, already mentioned as an essential part of the theory overlooked by Tumin.

7) INEVITABILITY AND DISFUNCTIONALITY

As the grand climax of his restatement of our views, Tumin has us concluding that social inequality is *inevitable* in society. Let it be repeated, we were not concerned with the indefinite or utopian future but with societies as we find them. No proof or disproof of a proposition about inevitability is possible. As "evidence" of his view of inevitability, Tumin *hopes* to see a society based on "the tradition that each man is as socially worthy as all other men so long as he performs his appropriate tasks conscientiously." But this is, once again, the idea of a society based exclusively on esteem. The question would still remain, how do people in the first place get distributed in their different positions with their "appropriate tasks?" One can hardly criticize a theory by ignoring the problem with which it deals.

Tumin goes on to point out ways in which stratification is disfunctional. In most of what he says, however, "stratification" is being used in the sense of inheritance of status. In so far as his assertion of disfunctionality is true, then, the culprit is the family, not the differential positional rewards. He also mentions unfavorable self-images, but the disfunctionality of these is not clear, because an unfavorable self-image may be a powerful stimulus to competitive and creative

[1] "Conceptual Analysis of Stratification," *loc. cit.*, pp. 312–313; *Human Society*, pp. 93–94.

activity. The same comment can be made about the alleged disfunctionality of class conflict. Incidentally, in this part of his critique Tumin makes pronouncements of functionality with firm confidence, although in the early part he doubted the functionality could be determined.

The truth is that any aspect of society is functional in some ways and disfunctional in others. Our theory was designed to suggest some of the ways in which institutionalized positional inequality contributes to societies as going concerns. Otherwise it seems difficult if not impossible to explain the universal appearance of such inequality. Excrescencies and distortions certainly appear, but they do not completely negate the principle. Tumin's analysis of the disfunctions is unsophisticated because of his confusion as to what it is that *has* the disfunctions, because of his uncritical concept of function, and because of his lack of any clear notion of a social system as an equilibrium of forces of which the stratified positional scale is only one.

Comment
Wilbert E. Moore

I GENERALLY CONCUR with Professor Davis's reply, which is somewhat more comprehensive than the comments I had prepared independently. However, I should like to emphasize that there is no reason to deny to Professor Tumin the right and even the propriety of a theoretical approach to an equalitarian system, as long as relevant principles of social structure are somehow taken into account. I do not believe Professor Tumin has met the latter qualification. With regard to the relevance of his criticism of our paper, I suggest that Professor Tumin made the major mistake of not explicitly defining social stratification, which in turn led him to assume that differential rewards and inequality of opportunity are the same thing. Neither theory nor evidence will support this equation, and making it true by implicit definition can only stand in the way of theoretically significant research.

Reply to Kingsley Davis
Melvin M. Tumin

WE ADVANCE OUR SCIENCE by developing and expanding the existing theoretical statements formulated by our fellow scientists. It was with this aim in mind that I took the article by Davis and Moore as the best statement of a given theoretical position. I, therefore, regret that Mr. Davis has viewed my efforts in a somewhat different light. That I chose the Davis-Moore article should be ample evidence of my respect for it.

In view of Davis' objections to my suggested revisions, it now becomes possible to point up the central issues which ought to be joined.

1) Does the fact that a given institutional pattern is universal necessarily imply that it is positively functional? Are there not numerous universals which represent structurally built-in limits on human efficiency? It is important that this alternative characterization of universal patterns be offered, since Mr. Davis insists that only those patterns survive which prove to be "best for society." Clearly, he cannot use this argument in

Reprinted from *The American Sociological Review*, V. 18 (December, 1953), pp. 672–673, by permission of the author and the publisher.

accounting for existing stratification systems without applying it equally to such other matters as institutionalized human ignorance, war, poverty and magical treatment of disease.

2) Does the universality of an institutional pattern necessarily testify to its indispensability? In the case of stratification, does Mr. Davis really mean to imply that the functions of locating and allocating talent cannot be performed by any other social arrangement? Since a theoretical mode *can* be devised in which all other clearly indispensable major social functions are performed, but in which inequality as motive and reward is absent, how then account for stratification in terms of structural and functional necessities and inevitabilities?

3) An essential characteristic of all known kinship systems is that they function as transmitters of inequalities from generation to generation. Similarly, an essential characteristic of all known stratification systems is that they employ the kinship system as their agent of transmission of inequalities. In effect, of course, this is saying the same thing in two apparently different ways. The fact is that kinship and stratification overlap in all known societies. One cannot fully describe any given kinship system without implicitly including the transmission of inequalities if one assigns the function of "status-placement" to kinship. Similarly, one cannot describe any stratification system in operation without implying the generational transmission of inequalities, if one includes the dynamics of inequality.

To the extent that this is true, then it is true by definition that the elimination from kinship systems of their function as transmitters of inequalities (and hence the alteration of the definition of kinship systems) would eliminate those inequalities which were generation-linked.

What puzzles me, therefore, is how one can assign the "villainy" of the act of transmission of inequalities to the kinship system and insist, in turn, that the stratification system is pristine in this regard.

4) Obviously, the denial to parents of their ability and right to transmit both advantages and disadvantages to their offspring would require a fundamental alteration in all existing concepts of kinship structure. At the least, there would have to be a vigilant separation maintained between the unit which reproduces and the unit which socializes, maintains and places. In theory, this separation is eminently possible. In practice, it would be revolutionary.

One of its likely consequences would be a thoroughgoing alteration in the motives which impel men to high effort. It was precisely to this point of alternative possible motives that I addressed much of my original argument. Dr. Davis argues against the motive of "esteem" as being inadequate on the grounds that esteem alone tends to produce a static society. This may be true by definition. Aside from that possible source of verity, there is no empirical evidence which will support Dr. Davis' contention.

Further regarding alternative motivations, Davis argues that *a)* if everybody elected to do just what he wanted to do, the whole population would wind up in only a few types of position; and *b)* any sociologist should know the inadequacy of unrewarded altruism as a means of eliciting socially adequate behavior. These statements are not true even by definition; and certainly we have no sound empirical studies which will support them as Davis puts them.

It does not seem to be the best thing for a growing science to shut the door on inquiry into alternative possible social arrangements.

5) Finally, my central argument was to the effect that there are strategic functions of stratification systems which were overlooked in the Davis-Moore article. I tried to identify a number of the operations of stratification which seemed clearly to render inefficient the process of location and allocation of talent. Davis chooses in his rejoinder either to ignore these disfunctions or to attribute them to kinship rather than to stratification. But they are there clearly to be seen. Added in with the positive functions which have been identified, we get a *mixed* net result of inequality in operation.

Of course, all institutional arrangements of any complexity are bound to be mixed in their instrumentality. It is the recognition of this mixture, and the emphasized sensitivity to the undesired aspects, which impels men to engage in purposeful social reform. In turn, social scientists have been traditionally concerned with the range of possible social arrangements and their consequences for human society. One is impelled to explore that range after probing deeply into whether a given arrangement is unavoidable and discovering that it is not. One is even more impelled to such exploration when it is discovered that the *avoidable* arrangement is probably less efficient than other possible means to the stated end. It was toward such further probing that I directed my original remarks. Joining the issues here here raised will, perhaps, help probe more deeply.

Some Notes on the Functional Theory of Stratification

Włodzimierz Wesołowski

ONE MIGHT BE TEMPTED to find many reasons for the length and pertinacity of discussion aroused by the articles of K. Davis and W. Moore. No doubt one reason would be the abbreviated and abstract form in which the theory is presented, making it subject to various interpretations, as well as the "ideological overtone" attached to it. In my view, however, the most important reason for the length of discussion is the importance of the problem itself.

In the form in which it was presented in *The American Sociological Review*,[1] the theory would seem to contain three main assertions:

1) Social stratification (uneven distribution of material rewards and of prestige) is functionally necessary and is therefore a universal and permanent feature of society;

2) Stratification is functionally necessary because every society needs a mechanism inducing people to occupy positions which are socially important and require training; material rewards and prestige act as stimuli towards the occupation of such positions;

3) The existence of the above mechanism ensures that "the most important positions are conscientiously filled by the most qualified persons" ("the most qualified" here means: the ablest and best trained).

During the discussion following the articles,[2] and even earlier, (in K. Davis' book, *Human Society*) the third assertion, suggesting the "perfection" of this social mechanism of selection, was withdrawn by the authors owing to its blatant inconsistency with many sociological facts. Attention was drawn to the fact that the occurrence of cases where *1)* status is ascribed, *2)* status is "prepared" by the position and efforts of the parents, and *3)* the status and career of the individual are influenced by various group and clique determinants, means that *a)* not all those who have equal ability have equal opportunity to acquire training, *b)* not all those who are equal in training have equal opportunity to occupy positions bringing high prestige and income. For these reasons I shall not deal with the third assertion.[3] I should like, however, to make some comment on the first two assertions, which seem to me the core of the theory.

These assertions are concerned not so much with the system of selection, as with the system of motivation. When the third assertion is rejected, the theory asserts only that if positions which are important and require training are to be filled, then they must provide greater prestige and higher income; otherwise no-one would bother to train himself to fill them. Nevertheless, the theory does not say that everyone occupies a position suitable to his talents and his training. There are some people who, although capable, had no chance to acquire a training. There are others, who, although trained, had no opportunity to gain high positions. But the very fact that there is differentiation of prestige and differentiation of income nevertheless acts as a stimulus encouraging people to make the effort to win a higher position.

The central point of the theory, then, is the hypothesis concerning motivation. According to this hypothesis, the striving for high income and high prestige is an indispensable and principal motive which drives people to make the effort to occupy positions which are important and require training. It is this assertion which will be the subject of our comment. Before we come to this, however, a certain concept which is used in the theory calls for explanation. This is the concept of "importance" of position.

---

[1] K. Davis, "A Conceptual Analysis of Stratification," *The American Sociological Review*, Vol. 7, 1942, No. 3; K. Davis and W. Moore, "Some Principles of Stratification," *The American Sociological Review*, Vol. 10, 1945, No. 2.

[2] M. M. Tumin, "Some Principles of Stratification: A Critical Analysis," *The American Sociological Review*, Vol. 18, 1953, No. 4; K. Davis and W. Moore, "Reply and Comment," *The American Sociological Review*, Vol. 18, 1953, No. 4; M. M. Tumin, "Reply to K. Davis," *The American Sociological Review*, Vol. 18, 1953, No. 6. Among the large number of contributions to the discussion, the following should be especially noted: W. Buckley, "Social Stratification and the Functional Theory of Social Differentiation," *The American Sociological Review*, Vol. 23, 1958, No. 3; D. H. Wrong, "The Functional Theory of Stratification: Some Neglected Considerations," *The American Sociological Review*, Vol. 24, 1959, No. 6. The theory is also discussed in the following books: J. F. Cuber and W. F. Kenkel, *Social Stratification in the United States*, New York 1954; J. A. Kahl, *The American Class Structure*, New York, 1957; M. M. Gordon, *Social Class in American Society*, North Carolina 1958; L. Reissman, *Class in American Society*, Glencoe 1959.

[3] The present author discusses this at greater length in an article: "Davis' and Moore's Functional Theory of Stratification," *Studia Socjologiczne*, 1962, No. 4.

Reprinted from *The Polish Sociological Bulletin*, No. 3–4 (5–6), (1962), pp. 28–38, by permission of the author and the publisher.

"Importance" of position

According to this theory, greater prestige and greater material rewards give positions which have greater importance for society and require greater training or talent. It is more or less clear what the authors mean by "training or talent". In this article I will take training into account and by it I will mean education (general and specific) which in modern industrial society is the chief means of attaining basic knowledge and skill required for most highly valued jobs (e.g. doctor, lawyer, engineer).[1] It is less clear, however, what should be regarded as making importance of position. Here we are left to our own suppositions and interpretation.

The authors write: "Unfortunately, functional importance is difficult to establish. To use the position's prestige to establish it, as is often unconsciously done, constitutes circular reasoning from our point of view. There are, however, two independent clues: a) the degree to which a position is functionally unique, there being no other positions that can perform the same function satisfactorily; b) the degree to which other positions are dependent on the one in question. Both clues are best exemplified in organized systems of positions built round one major function. Thus, in most complex societies the religious, political, economic, and educational functions are handled by distinct structures not easily interchangeable. In addition, each structure possesses many different positions, some clearly dependent on, if not subordinate to, others. In sum, when an institutional nucleus becomes differentiated around one main function, and at the same time organizes a large portion of the population into its relationships, the key positions in it are of the highest functional importance."[2]

Let us examine these assertions.

As "functionally unique" (see point a above) one can regard those positions that call for specific training. The "specific" character of this training and talent may consist in its "quality" or "quantity." The training of a doctor and of an engineer are qualitatively different and yet quantitatively similar (high educational level). Likewise, the training of a fitter in a factory and that of a nurse are qualitatively different, yet quantitatively similar.

The engineer cannot be replaced in his duties by the doctor; neither can the fitter be replaced by the nurse. Owing to their different "qualitative" training, both the doctor and engineer are equally "irreplaceable." Likewise with the fitter and the nurse. On the "horizontal" plane, therefore, it would be difficult to find differences in extent of "irreplaceability" between the various occupations. Such differences can only be found in the "vertical" plane. The doctor is more irreplaceable than the nurse because he can carry out the nurse's duties (although less efficiently), but the nurse cannot carry out the doctor's duties. Similarly, it would be easier for the engineer to carry out the duties of the fitter, than for the fitter to carry out the duties of the engineer; and easier for the manager to carry out the clerk's duties than the clerk to carry out the duties of the manager. Thus those occupational positions which call for higher specialized training (in industrial societies it means chiefly higher education) are more "irreplaceable." Thus the first clue indicating the "functional importance" of a position does not seem to contribute any new element to the theory, since the role of training is mentioned as the first determinant of the height of position (besides "functional importance" as the second determinant).

But the second clue indicating "functional importance" (mentioned in point b) does seem to introduce a new element. Explanations given by Davis and Moore suggest that the second factor determining the functional importance of position is authority. For — according to them — those positions are important, which other positions are subordinate to, or which they depend on; formulated differently, they are "key positions." Examples given by the authors point out to the highest positions in hierarchic structures of social institutions.[3]

The above analysis leads us to the conclusion that, according to this theory, unequal distribution of material advantages and prestige is needed to make people train for positions requiring higher occupational skills and, perhaps, positions of high occupational skill and of authority. A good example of the first position is the position of a medical doctor; examples of the second would be the position of a business executive or of a general.

The mechanism of motivation

The authors regard their theory as being universally applicable to all known societies throughout history. But this is a view which is easy to disprove. It is very doubtful, for example, if ever differences of prestige

---

[1] Attention given here to the training and not to the talent seems to me in accordance with the main features of the theory under discussion since it is dealing with the mechanism of motivation to attain the positions that require training. This attention is also justified by the author's assertions that: a) gaining the doctor's training is in capacity of anyone with average talent (the same is probably true about lawyer, engineer and many other occupations); b) in cases of many occupations talents are fairly abundant in the population, but only training is long and costly. One can add also that even the artistic occupations in which inborn talents play a greater role, demand today not only talents but training.

[2] K. Davis and W. Moore, "Some Principles of Stratification," *The American Sociological Review*, Vol. 10, 1945, No. 2, p. 243, footnote 3.

[3] Authority is a kind of power — "institutionalized" power. Authority belongs to a person who as a result of his position in some institutional structure has the right to issue orders to other people who also occupy a position in that structure. These orders are carried out because of the customs or laws concerning the functioning of the structure as a whole. In any modern organization (industrial or political), the hierarchy of positions is the simplest example of the hierarchical system of positions in which authority, as here understood, is to be found. See R. Bierstedt, "An Analysis of Social Power," *The American Sociological Review*, Vol. 15, 1950, No. 6.

and differences of income were "functionally necessary" for the filling of positions in stabilized societies where statuses were ascribed. And it should be remembered that societies of this type have been predominant throughout by far the greater part of history.

But the theory does seem to grasp the essential connections which occur in societies where statuses are achieved. This would appear to be the reason for the great liveliness of discussion on the articles by Davis and Moore. For modern industrial societies — both capitalist and socialist — are societies with achieved statuses. And in these societies are to be found may facts confirming the existence of the motivational mechanism described by the authors of this theory. The question arises, therefore, whether the theory holds good for all industrial societies where there is far-reaching division of labour and where statuses are attainable.

In Davis' and Moore's theory, it is this problem which is of the greatest interest. It seems possible, however, that a number of weighty theoretical arguments, as well as certain factual data, can be brought up against the theory.

SOME GENERAL ARGUMENTS

The main theoretical argument against Davis' and Moore's conception is that their theory contains three erroneous assumptions. These are concerned with *a*) the human nature, *b*) the pattern of society, *c*) the structure of values.

It has already been pointed out that in many respects Davis' and Moore's theory recalls the classical theory of political economy, for example its implicitly assumed conception of unchanging "human nature." According to Davis and Moore, human nature is characterized, on the one hand by a drive towards personal advantages, and on the other by laziness. In a society where human nature is such, then stratification (the unequal distribution of material rewards and prestige) is an unavoidable necessity if important positions requiring training are to be filled properly. It must be said, however, that whereas such a concept of human nature has not yet completely disappeared from the economic text-books, it does not occur at all in modern text-books of sociology, psychology, or cultural anthropology. In fact it may be said that the psychological content of Davis' and Moore's theory is inconsistent with modern theory of social psychology.

Here is what T. Newcomb says on this very subject: "Many motives which we, as members of our own society, think of as being part of human nature, are by no means dependable the world over. Motives of wanting prestige, wanting to be free from the dominance of authority of others, jealousy in love relationships as well as motives of acquiring property, seem utterly

natural to us. They are, in fact, fairly dependable in large sections of American society. Their dependability rests, however, upon the dependability of the cultural conditions under which they are acquired. They may, perhaps, be said to represent "contemporary middle-class American nature," but they do not correspond to anything dependable in human nature" (dependable = universal).[1]

The statement that the motives of people's behaviour depend on the type of culture in which they were brought up and in which they live is today universally accepted by sociologists, social anthropologists, and social psychologists. The same is true of the thesis that motives of behaviour are affected by two essential elements in any culture — the system of values and the objective living conditions.[2]

It can be said that each culture has its own specific values. But it is possible to hold less extreme view, that certain cultures have similar, or even identical, set of accepted values, but that these cultures differ from each other in the importance they attach to the various values. In other words, they differ as to the position of the various values in the structure of values as a whole. Both in the first and in the second case it is at least theoretically possible to have a culture in which the motive of personal material advantage and prestige is not one of the fundamental motives of human behaviour, nor one of the fundamental motives underlying choice of occupation and job training (or, as a result, choice of social position.)

I should like to put forward the hypothesis that in industrial societies which differ in their social organization (e.g. capitalist societies and socialist societies), it is possible that at least the inner structure of their system of values differs. The difference in this structure may consist not only of the different "weight" given to the diverse values in their whole system, but perhaps in the different "character" of the separate values.

Some values may be recognized as desirable because they themselves represent something desired; others may be recognized because they are a good means of attaining some other values. According to Davis and Moore, in the motivation of individuals education (knowledge, skill) and authority occur as values which are means of attaining the other values, material reward and prestige. In my opinion, the relationship between the values education and authority, and material reward and prestige, may be different. I also think that the striving for education or the striving for authority may be the chief motives of human behaviour. Generally speaking, there is not any fixed constelation of values in their division between values-means and values-ends: there is not any universally pursued end-value either.

In Davis' and Moore's theory not only it is assumed that the motivation of the human individual is unchanging. It also assumes a certain unchanging "pattern" of society, or at least it assumes that some of the characteristics of that society are universal and permanent (this

---

[1] T. M. Newcomb, *Social Psychology*, New York 1950, p. 137.
[2] Cf. J. W. Atkinson (Ed.), *Motives in Fantasy, Action and Society. A Method of Assessment and Study*. Part V. "Motivation and Society."

pattern again reminds us of classical political economy). If the authors assert that unequal distribution of material goods and of prestige must exist because otherwise people would not take the trouble to prepare for positions requiring training, then they assume that the acquisition of training is a matter of individual choice and effort, and that the acquisition of training also demands a certain amount of sacrifice. They also assume an insufficiency of products, the unequal distribution of these products according to position, and an insufficiency of trained personnel.

But other patterns of industrial societies are also possible. This may be illustrated by certain trends in the socialist countries or the *kibbutz* in Israel, although certain tendencies towards change can also be observed in contemporary capitalist societies. Trends towards the planned training and employment of qualified cadres, or towards the award of scholarships which relieve parents of the cost of educating their children, are becoming more and more marked in the modern world, especially in the socialist countries, but in the capitalist countries as well.

MATERIAL ADVANTAGES

The values which drive people to acquire a training are material advantage and prestige. Both occur together in Davis' and Moore's theory. But they are separate values. They should therefore be examined separately. Let us first deal with material advantages.

Let us assume the existence of a society with the following attributes: *a)* income differences are small, and the basic needs of most families are met; *b)* education is assured without any sacrifice either on the part of the parent or of the child; the level of education of the community as a whole is relatively high; *c)* the dominant ideas in the system of values are equality, social service, education and full development of personality.

In such a society, even where certain differences of income exist according to qualifications, it is possible that material advantages are not the main stimulus to education and training. Although the differences in material advantages exist, they may not result in significant differences in the standard of living. The system of values may not attach much importance to these differences, whereas the desire for full development of personality, and awakened interest in learning may make the desire to acquire education suiting the person's talents the principal motive for acquiring training. Education (knowledge, skill) which in Davis' and Moore's theory are values that are a means to an end, may in themselves become ends.

Certain elements in the situation described above are to be found in some contemporary societies. For example, in Poland (and similarly in Norway) there has been a distinct curtailment of the range of income. In Poland free education is open to all. At the same time, in propaganda more and more emphasis is being placed on education. Education, as some researches show, is very high on the scale of values accepted by the people for our country. Egalitarianism also has wide support — both in the sphere of postulates and in everyday behaviour.[1]

Like education, "authority" may appear as a value in itself and not as a means to an end. We assumed, that in Davis' and Moore's theory, material advantage and prestige are regarded as rewards for those who occupy positions of authority. But authority itself may be such a reward. Max Weber and Harold Lasswell wrote of this convincingly. In this connection it is worth noting that in industrial societies planning, and the general organizing of society, is becoming more common. In such a situation positions of authority provide an immense opportunity for the individual to express his own personality, his talents and ideas, quite apart from the opportunity such an individual has of satisfying his thirst for power, his desire to direct others.

Examples may be given illustrating the high value placed on authority by many people, even if it is not accompanied by material advantage or prestige. In present day conditions in Poland the factory foreman would seem to provide a good example. Neither in earnings nor in prestige is he superior to those under his authority. But the very fact that a foreman does have people under him is one of the assets of such a position, even although in other respects it does not stand very high.

Thus it seems quite possible to have an industrial society in which the differentiation of material advantages is not a "functional necessity." Positions calling for education and training, as well as positions of authority, may be filled not because they offer material advantages, but because their principal attributes — skill, knowledge and power — prove to be sufficiently attractive. Those values, which in Davis' and Moore's theory are treated as intermediate values, may appear as end-values.

PRESTIGE

As in the case when we analysed income differentiation, likewise in the case of prestige differentiation must we distinguish between: *a)* the very existence of such differentiation, and *b)* the role it fulfils as a stimulus for the occupation of "important positions requiring training." From the empirical point of view, such a differentiation may turn out to be extremely difficult; from the point of view of analysis, however, it is extremely important.

[1] Cf. W. Wesołowski and A. Sarapata, "Hierarchia zawodów i stanowisk" ["Hierarchy of Jobs and Occupations"], *Studia Socjologiczne* 1961, No. 2. In recent research carried out in Łódź by Dr. A. Sarapata, 50% of the respondents replied "No" when asked if some occupations were more important than others — which should be regarded as a sign of an egalitarian attitude. In a new survey carried out by the present author on a sample of the rural population throughout Poland, the respondents were asked what should be the difference between incomes. About 65% declared that differences of income should be small. When asked who should earn more than the others, the majority of the respondents said "people whose work is the hardest."

If differences of prestige were to be eliminated entirely, then we would have to have such a system of values in which "equality" would be a value completely outweighing all the other values (probably this would also necessitate the complete disappearance of differences in income, education, power and other social attributes). Even if we take it that egalitarian values are growing in favour and that more practical steps are being taken towards ensuring objective equality between people, one can hardly imagine that a world without differences of prestige is imminent.

Yet the very fact that differences of prestige exist does not mean that Davis and Moore are right. For their theory states that prestige must occur as one of the main motives leading people to prepare for and fill social positions. Thus their theory would not hold true where education and authority were end-values, sufficiently strong to induce people to occupy certain positions in society. Differences in prestige connected with these positions would then cease to be "functionally necessary."

It is true that then there would be certain difficulties of interpretation.

If we accept the view that a desire for education (knowledge, skill) and a desire for authority act as motives for the occupation of important positions requiring training, then we must accept that education and authority are important values. And it would be difficult to imagine differences of education and differences of authority disappearing completely. In this situation, on the basis of differences of education and authority, there may arise different estimates as to the prestige of positions which have varying elements of skill and power.

The question therefore arises: should prestige differentiation then be treated as an epiphenomenon incapable of acting as principal stimulus, or should it be treated as an important stimulus giving rise to the desire to occupy positions which despite everything have greater prestige?

It is impossible at present to give an answer to this question. The whole situation is hypothetical. If ever such a situation were to exist, this question could be settled by means of research on the strength of various motives on the choice of social positions.[1]

The functional aspect of power and stratification

Material advantage and prestige are the two ele-

ments of stratification on which Davis and Moore concentrate their attention. They are inclined to relegate authority to the background. But from the functional point of view authority may be regarded as an important stratificatory element — perhaps even more fundamental than material advantage or prestige.

The "functionalism" of Davis' and Moore's theory consists mainly in the fact that it places stratification in the group of phenomena which in "functional analysis" are called "functional requirements," or "functional prerequisites" of every society.

There is no divergence of views that biological reproduction, the production of consumer goods, the socialization of the younger generation (together with indoctrination in some system of values), and social organization are functional prerequisites. The functionalists, however, tend to add the number of these prerequisites. Because of the tendency to expand the "functional requirements" of any social system, and in this way to attribute universality and permanence to the various elements of social life, the idea of these "functional requirements" has been fairly severely criticized. There has been a suggestion that "functional alternatives" should be sought and studied, that is, phenomena which may occur as the equivalents of other phenomena.[2] Davis and Moore may be criticized because they declare stratification is universal by including it among the "functional prerequisites" of social life, and do not take into account the possibility that other phenomena may occur in its place, in the form of functional alternatives (e.g. such a system of values as would cause people to train and to fill positions of skill or authority without reckoning on future material advantages or prestige).

It is worth noting, however, that among the functional prerequisites of social life it would be difficult not to take social organization into account. Social life is group life. And group life involves the inner structuralization of the group. This structuralization consists among others in the emergence of positions of command and subordination (as well as of "intermediate" positions at further stages of development.) In such a structure, authority is unevenly distributed. For as soon as the positions of authority are filled, those who occupy the positions have the right (and duty) to give orders, while the others have the duty to obey them.

The inevitable occurrence of power relations of this kind in every complex social structure was long ago pointed out by social thinkers of very divergent theoretical orientations (quite independently of how they differed as to how positions of authority are, or should be, filled, or in whose interest authority is wielded, or what connection exists between the distribution of authority and the distribution of other values which occur as factors stratifying society, etc.). Engels, for example, who said that in a communist system the State as a weapon of class domination would wither away nevertheless declared that it would be impossible to think of any great modern industrial enterprise or of

[1] In our discussion we have avoided the question of divergence of motives of human behaviour, since this is a separate and extensive subject. It may only be mentioned that the values accepted in present-day societies are very varied and rather "autonomous" and in consequence there is a great variety of motive in choice of education and career. When a sufficiently high standard of living would be assured, this variety might be much more marked.

[2] Cf. R. K. Merton, "A Paradigm for Functional Analysis in Sociology," in *Social Theory and Social Structure*, Glencoe 1949.

the organization of the future communist society without authority — or superiority-subordination relationships.[1] G. Mosca wrote, "There can be no human organization without rankings and subordination. Any sort of hierarchy necessarily requires that some should command and others obey."[2] M. Weber gave a number of reasons for the necessity of a functional division of authority in large administrative and political structures.[3] W. L. Warner is a contemporary author who explains in the brief form but explicitly the functional inevitability of stratification, pointing out that positions of authority are bound to occur.[4]

Davis and Moore seem to perceive the functional inevitability and stratifying role of authority relationships. Remarks on that are to be found in their considerations on "major societal functions" and the institutions fulfilling these functions. For example when they discuss "government" they say that "stratification is inherent in the nature of political relationships."[5] Yet they make no use of such a kind of observations in the construction of their theory. Neither do they explain how such statements are to be connected with the main propositions of their theory. Meanwhile it seems that these observations may lead us to quite a different explanation of the "functional inevitability" of stratification.

This explanation may be as follows: The existence of great social structures creates social hierarchies built on authority. Thus if we are to take stratification to mean the occurrence of social positions among which there is an unequal distribution of some value, then it can be said that in the given structures there are positions among which the value which we call authority is unevenly distributed; in such cases, then, there is stratification along the dimension of authority.

In consequence it may be said that if there is any functional necessity for stratification, it is the necessity of stratification according to the criterium of authority and not according to the criterium of material advantage or prestige. Nor does the necessity of stratification derive from the need to induce people for the acquirement of qualifications, but from the very fact that humans live collectively.

[1] F. Engels, "O zasadzie autorytetu" ["On the Principle of Authority"] in: K. Marx and F. Engels, *Dziela Wybrane* [*Selected Works*], vol. I, Warszawa 1949.

[2] G. Mosca, *The Ruling Class*, New York 1939, p. 397.

[3] Cf. H. H. Gerth and C. W. Mills, *From Max Weber: Essays in Sociology*, New York 1958.

[4] W. L. Warner, M. Meeker and K. Eels, *Social Classes in America*, Chicago 1949, p. 8.

[5] Davis and Moore, op. cit., p. 245.

Some Empirical Consequences of the Davis-Moore Theory of Stratification[1]

Arthur L. Stinchcombe

DAVIS AND MOORE's theory of stratification,[1] though frequently discussed, has stimulated remarkably few studies. Perhaps this is due to the lack of derivations of empirical propositions in the original article. I would like in this note to outline some empirical implications of the theory.

Davis and Moore's basic argument is that unequal rewards tend to accrue to positions of great importance to society, provided that the talents needed for such positions are scarce. "Society" (i.e. people strongly identified with the collective fate) insures that these functions are properly performed by rewarding the talented people for undertaking these tasks. This implies that the greater the importance of positions, the less likely they are to be filled by ascriptive recruitment.[2]

It is quite difficult to rank tasks or roles according to

their relative importance. But certain tasks are unquestionably more important at one time than at another, or more important in one group than another.

[1] Kingsley Davis and Wilbert E. Moore, "Some Principles of Stratification," *American Sociological Review*, 10 (April, 1945), pp. 242–249.

[2] The theory holds that the most important positions, if they require unusual talents, will recruit people who otherwise would not take them, by offering high rewards to talent. This result would take place if one assumed a perfectly achievement-based stratification system. Some have asserted that Davis and Moore's argument "assumes" such a perfectly open system, and hence is obviously inadequate to the facts. Since the relevant results will be obtained if a system recruits more talented people to its "important" positions but ascribes all others, and since this postulate is not obviously false as is the free market assumption, we will assume the weaker postulate here. It seems unlikely that Davis and Moore ever assumed the stronger, obviously false, postulate.

Reprinted from *The American Sociological Review*, V. 28 (October, 1963), pp. 805–808, by permission of the author and the publisher.

This note was stimulated by a seminar presentation by Renate Mayntz, who focused attention on the problem of empirical investigation of functional theories.

For instance, generals are more important in wartime than in peacetime. Changes in importance, or different importance in different groups, have clear consequences according to the theory. If the importance of a role increases, its rewards should become relatively greater and recruitment should be more open.

The following empirical consequences of the theory are "derivations" in a restricted sense. We identify supposed changes in the importance of roles, or identify groups in which certain roles are more important. Then we propose measures of the degree of inequality of reward and openness of recruitment which are consequences of such changes. If changes in importance are correctly identified, and if the measures of inequality of reward are accurate, then the consequences are logical derivations from the theory. If it turns out that generals are not more recruited according to talent in wartime, then it may be because the theory is untrue. But it may also be that generals are not in fact more important in wartime, or that our measures of recruitment do not work.

Consequence 1

In time of war the abilities of generals become more important than in time of peace. According to the theory, this should result in the following types of re-structing of the stratification system during wartime (and the reverse with the onset of peace):

a) The rewards of the military, especially of the elite whose talents are scarce, should rise relative to the rewards of other elites, especially those which have nothing to do with victory (e.g., the medical and social service elite charged with care of incurables, the aged, etc.).[1]

b) Within the military, the degree of inequality of rewards should become greater, favoring generals, for their talents are particularly scarce.

c) Even standardizing for the increase in sheer numbers of high military officials (which of itself implies that more formerly obscure men will rise rapidly) there should be pressure to open the military elite to talent, and consequently, there should be a higher proportion of Ulysses S. Grant type careers and fewer time-servers.

d) Medals, a reward based on performances rather than on the authority hierarchy, should behave the same way. They should be more unequally distributed in wartime within any given rank; new medals, particularly of very high honor, should be created in wartime rather than peacetime, etc.

Consequence 2

The kingship in West European democratic monarchies has consistently declined in political importance

[1] This very interesting case is treated in Willard Waller, "War and Social Institutions," 478–532, esp. 509–511, in W. Waller (ed.), *War in the Twentieth Century*, New York, Dryden, 1940.

as the powers of parliament have increased (this does not apply, for instance, to Japan, where apparently the Emperorship was largely a ritual office even in medieval times). Modern kings in rich countries now perhaps have other functions than political leadership. Certainly the role requirements have changed — for instance, a modern king's sex life is much more restricted than formerly. Their rewards have also changed, emphasizing more ceremonial deference and expressions of sentiment, less wealth and power. It is not clear whether the ceremonial element has actually increased, or whether the rewards of wealth and power have declined. Investitures in the Presidency in the United States and Mexico seem to have nearly as much pomp as, and more substance than, coronations in Scandinavia and the Low Countries. Changes in the nature of the role-requirements and of the rewards indicate a shift of functions. At the least these changes indicate that some ceremonial functions of the kingship have declined much less in importance than the political functions. But to have a non-political function in a political structure is probably to be less important in the eyes of the people. Consequently, historical studies of the kingship in England, Scandinavia, and the Low Countries should show:

a) The decline of the rewards of kingship relative to other elites.

b) Progressively more ascriptive recruitment to the kingship. This would be indicated by *I*) fewer debates over succession rules, less changing of these rules in order to justify getting appropriate kings, and fewer successions contested by pretenders; *II*) fewer "palace revolutions" or other devices for deposing incompetent or otherwise inappropriate kings; and *III*) less mythology about good and bad kings, concerning performance of the role, and more bland human interest mythology focused on what it is like to occupy an ascribed position.

Consequence 3

In some industries individual talent is clearly a *complementary* factor of production, in the sense that it makes other factors much more productive; in others, it is more nearly *additive*. To take an extreme case of complementarity, when Alec Guiness is "mixed" with a stupid plot, routine supporting actors, ordinary production costs, plus perhaps a thousand dollars for extra makeup, the result is a commercially very successful movie; perhaps Guiness increases the value of the movie to twice as much by being three times as good as the alternative actor. But if an equally talented housepainter (three times as good as the alternative) is "mixed" with a crew of 100 average men, the value of the total production goes to approximately 103 per cent. Relatively speaking, then, individual role performance is much more "important" in the first kind of enterprise. Let us list a few types of enterprises in which talent is a complementary rather than additive factor, as compared with others which are more nearly additive, and make the appropriate predictions for the whole group of comparisons:

1. Talent Complementary Factor

Research
   Universities
Entertainment
Management
Teams in athletics and other "winner-take-all" structures
Violin concertos

2. Talent Nearly Additive

Teaching
   Undergraduate colleges
   High schools
Manufacturing
Manual work
Groups involved in ordinary competition in which the
   rewards are divided among the meritorious
Symphonies

For each of these comparisons we may derive the following predictions:

a) The distribution of rewards (e.g., income distributions) should be more skewed for organizations and industries in 1, whereas the top salaries or honors should be nearer the mean in 2. In organizations with ranks, there should be either more ranks or greater inequality of rewards within ranks in 1.

b) Since the main alternative to pure achievement stratification in modern society is not ascription by social origin, but rather ascription by age and time-in-grade, seniority should determine rewards less in the systems on the left than on the right. There are of course many ways to measure it. For instance, men at the top of the income distribution in groups in 1 should have reached the top at an earlier age than those in 2. There should also be a higher proportion of people whose relative income has declined as time passes in the talent-complementary industries and groups.

Other easily accessible empirical consequences of the theory are suggested by the increased importance of the goal of industrialization in many countries since World War II, the rise in the importance of international officials during this century, and the increased importance of treatment goals in mental hospitals. Since these consequences are easy to derive, we may omit their explication here.

Another set of derivations can be made if we add a postulate that a bad fit between functional requirements and the stratification system makes people within the group (and particularly those strongly identified with the group) perceive the system as unfair. For example, this postulate together with the others would imply that where talent is a complementary factor, those organizations with seniority stratification systems should create more sense of injustice than those in which the young shoot to the top. In addition, the alienation should be greatest among those *more* committed to group goals in seniority dominated talent-complementary groups, whereas it should be greatest among those *less* committed to the group where there is an achievement system. All these consequences ought to be reversed, or at least greatly weakened, for groups where talent is an additive factor.

It may be useful to present briefly a research design which would test this consequence of the theory. Suppose we draw a sample of colleges and universities, and classify (or rank) them on the importance of research within them. Perhaps a good index of this would be the number of classroom contact hours divided by the number of people of faculty rank on the payroll, which would be lower, the greater the importance of research relative to teaching.

Within each of the institutions we compute a correlation coefficient between age and income of faculty members. (Since the relation between age and income strikes me in this case as being curvilinear, some transformation of the variables will be appropriate.) The

TABLE 1. *Hypothetical Proportion Thinking "Most Faculty Promotions Go to the People Who Deserve Them Most"*

	INSTITUTIONS WITH			
	SUBSTANTIAL RESEARCH FUNCTIONS AND		MOSTLY TEACHING FUNCTIONS AND	
	Achievement systems	*Seniority systems*	*Achievement systems*	*Seniority systems*
	Proportion thinking the system is fair			
Faculty with				
Strong commitments	High	Low	Low	High
Weak commitments	Low	High	High	Low

higher the correlation coefficient, the more seniority-dominated the stratification system of the institution.[1] The first hypothesis that we can immediately test is that this correlation coefficient should be generally smaller in research-dominated institutions. This is a direct consequence of the functional theory as originally stated.

Then we could divide institutions into four groups, according to whether they are research or teaching institutions and whether they are seniority-dominated or not. We could ask the faculty within a sample of

[1] An elimination system, in which young people are either fired or given raises, depending on their performance, will also produce a high correlation between age and income within an institution, and yet may produce (if the institutions with such elimination systems have markedly higher salary scales), in the higher educational system as a whole, a lower correlation. I doubt if the appropriate adjustments for this would substantially affect the analysis except for a very few institutions, but this is, of course, an empirical question. The adjustments could be made, theoretically, by including the people who have been fired, with their current incomes, in the institutions which fired them.

such institutions a series of questions which would sort out those highly devoted to their work and to staying in the system, and those not highly devoted. At the same time we could ask them to agree or disagree with some such statement as "Most faculty promotions in this school go to the people who deserve them most." According to the functional theory with the added postulate on the sense of justice, we could predict results approximately according to the pattern in Table 1.

But adding postulates goes beyond the original theory into the mechanisms by which the functional requirements get met, which is an undeveloped aspect of functional theory generally.

I do not intend to investigate the truth of any of these empirical consequences of the theory here. The only purpose of this note is to point out that functional theories are like other scientific theories: they have empirical consequences which are either true or false. Deciding whether they are true or false is not a theoretical or ideological matter, but an empirical one.

Social Stratification and the Political Community

Reinhard Bendix

IN THE DEVELOPING AREAS of the world new class-relations emerge, as one after another country adopts democratic institutions and initiates industrial growth. In the "developing areas" of Europe a comparable process took place since the French Revolution and during much of the nineteenth century. This essay seeks to enhance our understanding of the modern problem by a re-examination of the European experience with special reference to the relation of social stratification and the political community in the nation-state.[1]

This re-examination has a theoretical purpose. The social and political changes of European societies provided the context in which the concepts of modern sociology were formulated. As we turn today to the developing areas of the non-Western world, we employ concepts that have a Western derivation. In so doing one can proceed in one of two ways: by formulating a new set of categories applying to all societies or by rethinking the categories familiar to us in view of the transformation and diversity of the Western experience itself. This study adopts the second alternative in the belief that the insights gained in the past should not be discarded lightly and that a reassessment of the Western experience may aid our understanding of the developing areas of the non-Western world.

The problem before us is the transformation of Western Europe from the estate-societies of the Middle Ages to the absolutist regimes of the eighteenth century and thence to the class-societies of plebiscitary democracy in the nation-states of the twentieth century. In the course of this transformation new class-relations emerged, the functions and powers of centralized national governments increased and all adult citizens acquired formal legal and (at a later time) political equality. Attempts to understand this transformation gave rise to social theories that were necessarily a part of the society they sought to comprehend. Though their scientific value is independent of this fact, our understanding is aided when we learn how men come to think as they do about the society in which they live. Such self-scrutiny can protect us against the unwitting adoption

[1] The two terms used in the title of this paper were chosen in preference to the more conventional terms "society" and "state", although the latter are used in the text as well. My reason is that "social stratification" emphasizes (as "society" does not) the division of individuals into social ranks which provide the basis of group-formation that is of interest here. The term is used in this very general sense with the understanding that individuals who differ from one another are united into groups by a force that overrides the differences existing between them, as T. H. Marshall put it in his definition of "class". "Political community" in turn emphasizes the consensus between governors and governed within the framework of a polity while the term "state" puts the emphasis upon the administrative aspect of government, at any rate in English usage. Both aspects must be considered together, but I did not wish to emphasize the latter in the title.

Reprinted from the *European Journal of Sociology*, V. 1, No. 2, 1960, by permission of the publisher.

of changing intellectual fashions; it can alert us to the limitations inherent in any theoretical framework. Since the present essay deals with social stratification in relation to the political community, a critical assessment of some of the assumptions implicit in studies of this relationship constitutes a part of our inquiry.

A glance at the history of social thought since the Renaissance suggests that this relation has been viewed in terms of three perspectives: that society is an object of government, that politics and government are a product of society, and thirdly that society and government are partly interdependent and partly autonomous spheres of social life.[1]

Inevitably, this division of social theories since the Renaissance is arbitrary. Each of the three orientations can be traced back much farther; and there are many linkages among these orientations which blur the distinctions between them. But it is also true that these perspectives have recurred in the history of social theory and that they provide us with useful benchmarks for the reconsideration of "society and the state" which is the particular purpose of this essay.

1. Theoretical perspectives

The idea that society is an object of state-craft goes back in the Western tradition to the medieval tracts containing "advice to princes". From an education of

[1] For easy identification it would be desirable to label these three approaches, but it is awkward to do so since every label has misleading connotations. "Society as an object of state-craft" may be considered a Machiavellian approach, but this perspective is also characteristic of the social-welfare state which is not "Machiavellian" in the conventional meaning of that term. Government considered as a "product of society" might be called the sociological perspective, but this is also characteristic of Marxism which should not be identified with sociology, and then there are sociologists like Max Weber and Robert MacIver who do not adhere to this view. The theory of a partial dualism between society and government is a characteristic feature of European liberalism, but to call it the "liberal orientation" carries overtones of a specific political theory which need not be associated with this approach. In view of such difficulties I have decided to avoid convenient labels and repeat the three phrases mentioned in the text.

[2] The development suggested here is traced in Friedrich Meinecke, *Die Entstehung des Historismus* (München, R. Oldenbourg, 1946) ch. III. The partly scientific orientation of Machiavelli and Montesquieu is discussed in Leonard Olschki, *Machiavelli the Scientist* (Berkeley, The Gillick Press, 1945) and Emile Durkheim, *Montesquieu and Rousseau* (Ann Arbor, University of Michigan Press, 1960).

[3] See Friedrich Meinecke, *Die Idee der Staatsräson* (München, R. Oldenbourg, 1925), *passim*. The work is available in English translation under the title *Machiavellism*. The relation between this concern with "reasons of state" and the development of factual knowledge about society is discussed in Eli Heckscher, *Mercantilism* (New York, Macmillan Co., 1955), II, pp. 13–30, 269 ff. and Albion Small, *Origins of Sociology* (Chicago, University of Chicago Press, 1925). See also C. J. Friedrich, *Constitutional Reasons of State* (Providence, Brown University Press, 1957).

[4] Quoted in Frank E. Manuel, *The New World of Henri de Saint-Simon* (Cambridge, Harvard University Press, 1956), p. 135. Professor Manuel shows how this theme recurs in ever new formulations throughout Saint-Simon's writings.

character designed for the sons of rulers this idea was developed into an instrument of state council by Machiavelli. In the eighteenth century Montesquieu drew upon this tradition in his theory of law in which he combined the old precepts of state-craft by a personal ruler with an analysis of the social and physical conditions which would facilitate or hinder the exercise of authority under different systems of rule.[2] A view of society as an object of state-craft was closely related to the rise of absolutism in Europe, as Friedrich Meinecke has shown in his study of ideas concerning "reasons of state" and the rights and duties of rulers.[3] In this intellectual perspective a high degree of passivity on the part of society had been presupposed. The masses of the people were excluded from all political participation and became an object of governmental attention primarily as a source of tax revenue and military recruitment. Accordingly, this intellectual perspective lost its appeal wherever absolutism declined and political participation on the part of the people at large increased, although in inchoate form it has come back into fashion through the growth of the welfare-state.

As attention came to be focused on the conditions facilitating or hindering the ruler's purpose, "Machiavellism" gradually blended with the second perspective, the idea that politics and government are products of society. In post-Renaissance Europe this idea came to the fore in the attacks of the Enlightenment philosophers on the established privileges of the church and the aristocracy. These privileges were seen as unjust usurpations arising from the vested interests of established institutions, while politics appeared as a by-product of established prerogatives. If this orientation tended to sociologize politics, its application to the past politicized history. With unabashed forthrightness writers like Voltaire surveyed and judged past events in terms of the eighteenth century concept of a universal human nature and its inherent morality. By distributing praise or blame among contestants of the past they made history appear as a story of ever-changing conflicts among vested interests, suggesting that all governments are mere by-products of contemporary partisanship.

During the eighteenth century such judgments were made in the belief that "man" was endowed by God with certain universal moral attributes. During the nineteenth century this belief and the theory of natural law were replaced increasingly by attempts to develop a scientific study of human nature and the political community. A key figure in this transition was Henri de Saint-Simon who proposed to make morals and politics into a "positive science" by basing both on the study of physiology which concerned the truly universal properties of man. In this way speculation would be replaced by precise knowledge with the result that political problems would be solved as simply as questions of hygiene.[4] The outstanding feature of this approach was the tendency to reduce the manifest diversity of social and political life to some underlying, basic element, that presumably could be understood with scientific precision. During the nineteenth century ever new elaborations of this reductionist approach were advanced, from proposals of a "sociology" based upon biological facts through various explanations in terms of climate, race and the struggle for survival to Marx's theory of history as ultimately determined by the imperative that men "must be able to live, if they are to 'make history'." Many of these theories of society accepted the scientific optimism of the nineteenth century and assumed that a knowledge of the "underlying" forces of society or nature provided the clue to human power and that in one way or another such knowledge could be translated into action.

The third intellectual perspective, that society and government are partly interdependent and partly autonomous spheres of social life, deserves more extended consideration, since it reflects (and provides insight into) the structural transformation of Western societies which is the focus of this essay. Here again we may begin with the Enlightenment, especially with those philosophers who emphasized the cleavage between bourgeois *society* and the *state*. That cleavage existed as long as each man's private concerns were at variance with his duties as a citizen. It was towards a solution of this problem that Rousseau made his many attempts to reconcile man in the "state of nature" whose virtues and sentiments were as yet unspoiled by civilization, and man as a citizen who must subordinate himself to the community but without doing violence to his dignity as a man.[1] This speculative contrast between man's potential morality and his actual conduct, and this effort to base the political community on the first rather than the second, were replaced in the nineteenth century by explanations which accounted for man's ethical capacities *and* his actual behavior in terms of human nature in society.

An outstanding example of such an explanation is found in the work of Emile Durkheim, which illuminates both the theoretical perspective of liberalism and the transformation of Western society which is examined below. As a sociologist Durkheim wished to study morality empirically, as a phenomenon arising "naturally" from the group-affiliations of the individual. But as a political liberal Durkheim also knew that such group-affiliation would obliterate the personality of the individual, unless the state intervened to guarantee his freedom. It will be seen that in this way Durkheim altered and continued the tradition of the Enlightenment; for him society itself was the "state of nature" for each individual, but as such it was also differentiated from the legal order and representative government of the "civil state".

From the beginning of his work Durkheim was concerned with a scientific analysis of the moral problems raised by the Enlightenment. He praised Rousseau for developing a construct of the *civil state* or society that was superimposed on the "state of nature" *without doing violence to the latter*. But he also criticized Rousseau's conception of the individual person as isolated,

which made it difficult to see how any society was possible.[2] Durkheim applied a similar criticism to the utilitarian doctrine, which indeed he regarded as inferior to the Enlightenment tradition in that it made the social nexus entirely dependent upon the exchange relationship on the market while abandoning the earlier concern with the moral pre-conditions of the civil state.[3] The supposition underlying these approaches, that a basic conflict existed between "man in nature" and "man in society," appeared to Durkheim to be factually incorrect. By a study of the exterior social constraints which compel individuals to act alike regardless of personal motivation he proceeded to demonstrate that society was possible because man was naturally social. In a series of studies of suicide, the family, crime, religion, and the division of labor he showed that the moral norms governing individual behavior originated in each person's group-affiliation and hence that Rousseau had been wrong in postulating a conflict between man in a "state of nature" and man in society. In other words, Durkheim "solved" Rousseau's problem by making the individual completely subordinate to society.

> Every society is despotic, at least if nothing from without supervenes to restrain its despotism. Still, I would not say that there is anything artificial in this despotism: it is natural because it is necessary, and also because, in certain conditions, societies cannot endure without it. Nor do I mean that there is anything intolerable about it: on the contrary, the individual does not feel it any more than we feel the atmosphere that weighs on our shoulders. From the moment the individual has been raised on this way by the collectivity, he will naturally desire what it desires and accept without difficulty the state of subject to which he finds himself reduced.[4]

Thus, if society is jeopardized, this is due not to a hypo-

---

[1] Karl Löwith has shown that this contrast goes back to ancient Greek and Christian ideas and he has traced the development of this theme during the nineteenth century. See his book *Von Hegel zu Nietzsche* (Zürich, Europa Verlag, 1941), pp. 255–265 and ff. See also the judicious restatement of Rousseau's position in R. R. Palmer, *The Age of the Democratic Revolution* (Princeton, Princeton University Press, 1959), pp. 119–127.

[2] Emile Durkheim, *Montesquieu and Rousseau*, pp. 65, 137, and *passim*.

[3] See Emile Durkheim, *The Division of Labor in Society* (Glencoe, The Free Press, 1947), pp. 200–206 and *passim*.

[4] Emile Durkheim, *Professional Ethics and Civic Morals* (Glencoe, The Free Press, 1958), p. 61. Published for the first time in 1950 in a Turkish edition of the French manuscript, these lectures were delivered by Durkheim in 1898, 1899 and 1900 at Bordeaux and in 1904 and 1912 at the Sorbonne. As will be shown below, these lectures contain Durkheim's political theory and their repeated delivery together with the well-known preface to the second edition of *The Division of Labor* (published in 1902) indicate that for Durkheim this aspect of his work was of great importance. It is a symptom of the "sociologizing" tendency of our own time that this political aspect has been neglected or ignored by most scholars who have been influenced by Durkheim's sociological theories.

thetical conflict between society and the individual, but to a state of *anomie* in which his group-affiliations no longer provide the individual with norms regulating his conduct in a stable fashion. Where such group-norms are weakening as in modern society, the social order can be rebuilt only on the basis of strengthened group-norms. Accordingly, Durkheim concluded his studies with the proposal of a new corporatism, based on modern occupational groups, so that "the individual is not to be alone in the face of the State and live in a kind of alternation between anarchy and servitude."[1]

As these studies progressed Durkheim continued to espouse the "moral existence of the individual". As a life-long liberal he was not willing to postpone this humanistic component to the indefinite future, as Marx had done. And as a sociologist he had demonstrated both man's fundamentally social nature and the seemingly inevitable tendency of increasing "individual variations" as the division of labor increased and the "common conscience" of the group became more general and permissive.[2] But if individualism is inevitable sociologically, why be concerned with safeguarding it politically? This combination of a sociological determinism with political liberalism arose, because like Tocqueville, Durkheim became concerned with the *secular transformation of group-constraint.* The associational ties of the province, the parish and the municipality one after another lost their significance for the individual. "In the structure of European societies", he observed, a "great gap" had been created between the state and the individual.[3] Durkheim's proposal to bridge this "gap" by a new corporatism did not provide a political solution to the problem, as he himself recognized. The

individual would be saved in this way from anomie and loneliness vis-à-vis the state, but he would also be oppressed by the secondary group to which he belonged.

Durkheim's answer to this question deserves extensive quotation, since it is not generally familiar.

> In order to prevent this happening, and to provide a certain range for individual development, it is not enough for a society to be on a big scale; the individual must be able to move with some degree of freedom over a wide field of action. He must not be curbed and monopolized by the secondary groups, and these groups must not be able to get a mastery over their members and mould them at will. There must therefore exist above these local, domestic — in a word, secondary — authorities, some overall authority which makes the law for them all: it must remind each of them that it is but a part and not the whole and that it should not keep for itself what rightly belongs to the whole. The only means of averting this collective particularism and all it involves for the individual, is to have a special agency with the duty of representing the overall collectivity, its rights and its interests, vis-à-vis these individual collectivities [. . .]
>
> Let us see why and how the main function of the State is to liberate the individual personalities. It is solely because, in holding its constituent societies in check, it prevents them from exerting the repressive influences over the individual that they would otherwise exert. So there is nothing inherently tyrannical about State intervention in the different fields of collective life; on the contrary, it has the object and the effect of alleviating tyrannies that do exist. It will be argued, might not the State in turn become despotic? Undoubtedly, provided there were nothing to counter that trend [. . .] The inference to be drawn from this comment, however, is simply that if that collective force, the State, is to be the liberator of the individual, it has itself need of some counter-balance; it must be restrained by other collective forces, that is, by those secondary groups [. . .] *And it is out of this conflict of social forces that individual liberties are born.*[4]

For these reasons Durkheim defined the political society as "one formed by the coming together of a rather large number of secondary social groups, subject to the same one authority which is not itself subject to any other superior authority duly constituted."[5]

Durkheim's sociological theories do not prepare us for this political solution of his problem.[6] The emancipation of the individual from the "despotism of the group" appears in the bulk of his work as a result of the increasing division of labor and the related attenuation of custom and law. Though as a political liberal Durkheim valued this "range of individual development," as a social philosopher he feared its consequences for

---

[1] I take this telling phrase from Marcel Mauss's introduction to Emile Durkheim, *Socialism and Saint-Simon* (Yellow Springs, The Antioch Press, 1958), p. 2. Durkheim's elaboration of his views on the corporate society may be found in the second preface to his *The Division of Labor*, pp. 1–31. Cf. especially the following summary statement of his position: "A society composed of an infinite number of unorganized individuals, that a hypertrophied state is forced to oppress and contain, constitutes a veritable sociological monstrosity [. . .]. Where the State is the only environment in which men can live communal lives, they inevitably lose contact, become detached, and thus society disintegrates. A nation can be maintained only if, between the State and the individual, there is intercalated a whole series of secondary groups near enough to the individual to attract them strongly in their sphere of action [. . .]" *ibid.*, p. 28. In the preceding account I have only restated in the briefest compass the familiar themes of Durkheim's work. The best analytical exposition of these themes is contained in Talcott Parsons, *The Structure of Social Action* (Glencoe, The Free Press, 1949), ch. VIII–XI, though this statement was written before Durkheim's unpublished lectures on the state became available.

[2] Emile Durkheim, *The Division of Labor*, pp. 283 ff.

[3] *Ibid.*, pp. 27–28, 218–219.

[4] Emile Durkheim, *Professional Ethics and Civic Morals*, pp. 61–63. My italics.

[5] *Ibid.*, p. 45. This formulation is indebted to Montesquieu and Tocqueville.

[6] Cf. the reference to this paradox in E. Benoit-Smullyan. *The Sociologism of Emile Durkheim and His School*, in H. E. Barnes, ed., *An Introduction to the History of Sociology* (Chicago, University of Chicago Press, 1948) pp. 518–520.

social morality where these consisted in the isolation of the individual and the loss of regulative norms of conduct (anomie). Accordingly he sought to safeguard the individual against the dangers of anomie by his reintegration in the "secondary groups" of society (corporations based on the occupational division of labor). Yet at the same time he called on the aid of the state to preserve individual liberties against the "despotism" with which these groups would seek to control the individual. Implicit in this approach is, therefore, a "dualism" whereby man's psychological and moral attributes are explained in terms of his membership in the society, while the society as a whole is characterized by an overall process (the increasing division of labor), which accounts among other things for man's capacity to alter these attributes through state-intervention in the interest of justice.[1]

This incongruity between Durkheim's sociological and political theories was symptomatic of the liberal tradition in the nineteenth century. Even the classic formulation of this tradition contained, as Elie Halévy has shown, two contradictory principles. Arising from the division of labor in a market-economy man's "propensity to truck, barter and exchange one thing for another" tended to reveal a "natural identity of interests" which enhanced unaided the general interest of society. Yet the quantity of subsistence is insufficient to allow all men to live in abundance and this insufficiency is aggravated by the failure of men voluntarily to limit their numerical increase. Hence it follows, by an exception to the first principle, that the State should protect the property of the rich against the poor as well as educate the latter so that they will restrain their instinct of procreation. In this way the State acts to ensure the "artificial identification of interests."[2]

Thus, the liberal tradition in its classic or its Durkheimian version is characterized by a "dualism" according to which society and government constitute two interdependent, but partially autonomous spheres of thought and action. From a theoretical standpoint this tradition is unsatisfactory because it constantly shifts from the empirical level, as in the analysis of market-behavior or the individual's group-affiliation, to the ethical and political level, as in the demand that the state should act to prevent the undesired consequences of market-behavior or group-affiliation. Still, historically, this perspective can be explained by the unquestioned fact that the societies of nineteenth and twentieth century Europe witnessed a juxtaposition between society as an aggregate of interrelated groups and the nation-state with its identifiable culture and institutional structure.

2. Structural perspectives

A) MEDIEVAL POLITICAL LIFE

In turning now from theoretical perspectives to problems of social structure it will prove useful to begin, however sketchily, with the pre-conditions of representative government in the West.[3] In the problematic relations between the "estates" and the power of royal government, say since the eleventh and twelfth centuries, we have to do with group-formations in society and the exercise of legitimate authority and hence with the relation between society and government which was discussed above in theoretical terms.[4]

Characteristic of the political communities of this early period was the fundamental assumption that the personal ruler of a territory is a leader who exercises his authority in the name of God and with the consent of the "people."[5] Because he is the consecrated ruler and represents the whole community, the "people" are obliged to obey his commands; but he in turn is also responsible to the community. This idea of a reciprocal obligation between ruler and ruled was part of an accepted tradition; it can be traced back to ancient Roman and Germanic practices, was greatly strengthened by Christian beliefs, but became formal law only very gradually.[6]

These characteristics of medieval kingship were closely related to the political conditions of royal administration. Each ruler possessed a domain of his own which he governed as the head of a very large household. On the basis of the economic resources derived from this domain, and in principle, on the basis of his consecrated claim to legitimate authority, each ruler

---

[1] See *Division of Labor*, pp. 386–388.

[2] Elie Halévy, *The Growth of Philosophical Radicalism* (London, Faber and Faber, 1928), pp. 90–91, 118–120, 489–491 and *passim*.

[3] The following statement relies on the work of Otto Hintze, Weltgeschichtliche Bedingungen der Repräsentativverfassung, *Historische Zeitschrift*, CXLIII (1930) pp. 1–47 and by the same author, Typologie der ständischen Verfassungen, *Historische Zeitschrift*, CXLI (1929), pp. 229–248. Hintze's contributions are corroborated and extended in Dietrich Gerhard's Regionalismus und Ständisches Wesen als ein Grundthema Europäischer Geschichte, *Historische Zeitschrift*, LCXXIV (1952), pp. 307–337.

[4] This characteristic feature of medieval political life will be contrasted below with the problematic relation between social stratification and the political community in modern Western societies.

[5] The quotation marks refer to the ineradicable ambiguity of this term in medieval society. The "people" were objects of government who took no part in political life. Yet kings and estates frequently couched their rivalries in terms of some reference to the "people" they claimed to represent. In fact, "consent of the people" referred to the secular and clerical notables whose voice was heard in the councils of government. See the discussion of this issue in Otto Gierke, *Political Theories of the Middle Ages* (Boston, Beacon Press, 1958), pp. 37–61. It may be added that this ambiguity is not confined to the Middle Ages, since all government is based in some degree on popular consent and since even in the most democratic form of government the "people" are excluded from political life in greater or lesser degree. These differences of degree, as well as the qualities of consent and participation are all-important, of course, even though it may be impossible to do more than formulate proximate typologies.

[6] Cf Max Weber, *Law in Economy and Society* (Cambridge, Harvard University Press, 1954), ch. v and *passim*.

then faced as his major political task the extension of his authority over a territory beyond his domain. In their efforts to solve this task secular rulers necessarily had to rely upon those elements of the population which by virtue of their possessions and local authority were in a position to aid the ruler financially and militarily, both in the extension of his territory and the exercise of his rule over its inhabitants. From a pragmatic political standpoint this was a precarious expedient, since such aid of local notables could enhance their own power as well as that of the ruler.

As a result, secular rulers typically sought to offset the drive towards local autonomy by a whole series of devices which were designed to increase the personal and material dependence of such notables on the ruler and his immediate entourage.[1] This typical antinomy of the pre-modern political community in Western Europe became manifest with every demand by secular rulers for increased revenue and military service. And to the extent that such demands were followed up by administrative measures, local notables typically responded by uniting into estates that could exact further guarantees or increases of their existing privileges by way of compensating for the greater services demanded of them.

A second characteristic of medieval political life was, therefore, that certain persons and groups were exempted from direct obedience to the commands issued by, or in the name of, the ruler. This "immunity" guaranteed that within the delimited sphere of their authority these persons and groups were entitled to exercise the legal powers of government. This institution goes back to the privileged legal position of the royal domains in Imperial Rome, a privilege which was subsequently transferred to the possessions of the church, the secular local rulers (i.e. the landed nobility under feudalism) and during the eleventh and twelfth centuries to the municipalities. This system of negative and positive privileges (which may be called "immunities" and "autonomous jurisdiction") became the legal foundation

of representative government in Western Europe, because it accorded positive, public rights to particular persons and groups within the political community. This institution of public rights on the part of certain privileged subjects is more or less unique to Western Europe. Perhaps the most important factor contributing to this development was the fundamental influence of the church, which through its consecration of the ruler and through the autonomy of its organization restrained the power of secular rulers and re-enforced the political autonomy of the secular estates.[2]

In this setting a political life in the modern sense could not exist. Rather, the political community consisted of an aggregate of more or less autonomous jurisdictions, firmly or precariously held together by a king to whom all lords and corporate bodies owed allegiance, and under whose strong or nominal rule they fought or bargained with him and with each other over the distribution of fiscal and administrative preserves. Consequently, politics at the "national" level consisted for the most part of a species of "international" negotiations among more or less autonomous jurisdictions, within the confines of a country that sometimes possessed only a precarious cultural and political unity. In such a community the coalescence of interests among individuals was not based on voluntary acts, but on rights and obligations determined by birth, such that each man was — at least in principle — bound to abide by the rules pertaining to his group lest he impair the privileges of his fellows. Classes or status-groups in the modern sense could not exist, because joint action occurred as a result of common rights and obligations imposed on each group by law, custom, or special edict. Thus, every group or social rank encompassed the rights and obligations of the individual person. Under these conditions a man could modify the personal and corporate rule to which he was subject only by an appeal to the established rights of his rank and to the benevolence of his lord, although these rights might be altered collectively in the course of conflicts and adjustments with competing jurisdictions. As Max Weber has stated,

the individual carried his *professio juris* with him wherever he went. Law was not a *lex terrae*, as the English law of the King's court became soon after the Norman Conquest, but rather the privilege of the person as a member of a particular group. Yet this principle of 'personal law' was no more consistently applied at that time than its opposite principle is today. All volitionally formed associations always strove for the application of the principle of personal law on behalf of the law created by them, but the extent to which they were successful in this respect varied greatly from case to case. At any rate, the result was the coexistence of numerous 'law communities', the autonomous jurisdictions of which overlapped, the compulsory, political association

---

[1] In his analysis of traditional domination Max Weber distinguished patrimonial from feudal administration, i.e., the effort of rulers to extend their authority and retain control by the use of "household officials" or by their "fealty-relationship" with aristocratic notables of independent means. These two devices are by no means mutually exclusive, since "household officials" were usually of noble birth and in territories of any size demanded autonomy, while "feudal" notables despite their independence frequently depended upon the ruler for services of various kinds. Contractual obligations as well as elaborate ideologies buttressed the various methods of rule under these complementary systems. For an exposition of Weber's approach cf. R. Bendix, *Max Weber, An Intellectual Portrait* (Garden City, Doubleday and Co., 1960), pp. 334–79, which is based on Weber, *Wirtschaft und Gesellschaft* (Tübingen, J. C. B. Mohr, 1925), II, pp. 679–752. These sections are not available in translation.

[2] A systematic analysis of this role of the church is contained in Max Weber, *op. cit.*, II, pp. 779–817. A brief résumé of this chapter is contained in Reinhard Bendix, *Max Weber*, pp. 320–326. For a detailed historical treatment of the consecration of secular rule cf. Ernst Kantorowicz, *The King's Two Bodies* (Princeton, Princeton University Press, 1957).

being only one such autonomous jurisdiction in so far as it existed at all [...].[1]

In Western Europe this medieval political structure of more or less loosely united congeries of jurisdictions was superseded gradually by absolutist regimes marked by a relative concentration of power in the hands of the king and his officials and by a gradual transformation of the king's relation to the privileged estates.[2] The variety and fluidity of conditions under these absolutist regimes were as great as under the feudal political structure. For example, the nation-wide powers of the king developed much earlier in England than on the Continent, partly as a legacy of the Norman conquest. However, the insular condition with its relative ease of communication together with legal tradition antedating the conquest both in Normandy and in England also made for an early and effective growth of "countervailing" powers. None of the Continental countries achieved a similar balance with the result that their absolutist political structures revealed either a greater concentration of royal power and correspondingly a greater destruction of the estates as in France or an ascendance of many principalities with some internal balance between king and estates but at the expense of overall political unity, as in Germany. Still, by the eighteenth century, most European societies were characterized by absolutist regimes in which the division of powers between the king and oligarchic estates as represented by various "constituted bodies" was at the center of the political struggle.[3]

The French Revolution with its Napoleonic aftermath destroyed this system of established privileges and initiated the mass democracies of the modern world. We can best comprehend this major transformation of the relation between society and the state if we leave the complicated transitional phenomena to one side and focus attention on the contrast between medieval political life and the modern political community which has emerged in the societies of Western civilization. To do so, it will prove useful to take the work of Tocqueville as our guide.

B) TOCQUEVILLE'S INTERPRETATION OF "THE GREAT TRANSFORMATION"

Tocqueville's analysis has power because it covered a very long time-period, because the French Revolution unquestionably marked a transition despite all equally unquestioned continuities, and because in his admittedly speculative fears about a tyranny of the future he used a "logic of possibilities" that enabled him to cope intellectually with contingencies he could not predict. By extending the scope of his analysis he made sure that he was dealing with genuine distinctions between different patterns of social relations and political institutions at the beginning and end of the time-span he chose to consider.

In his famous study of the French Revolution Tocqueville showed how the *ancien régime* had destroyed the century-old pattern of medieval political life by concentrating power in the hands of the king and his officials and by depriving the various autonomous jurisdictions of their judicial and administrative functions.[4] In pointed contrast to Burke's great polemic against the French Revolution Tocqueville demonstrated that in France the centralization of royal power and the concomitant decline of corporate jurisdictions had developed too far to make the restoration of these jurisdictions a feasible alternative. The nobility no longer enjoyed the rights it had possessed at one time, but its acquiescence in royal absolutism had been "bought" by a retention of financial privileges like tax-exemption, a fact which greatly intensified anti-aristocratic sentiment. Through the royal administrative system of the *intendants* the rights of municipal corporations and the independence of the judiciary had been curtailed in the interest of giving the government a free hand in the field of taxation with the result that the urban *bourgeoisie* was divested of local governmental responsibility and the equitable administration of justice was destroyed. Noblemen thus preserved their pride of place in the absence of commensurate responsibilities, urban merchants aped aristocratic ways while seeking preferential treatment for themselves, and both combined social arrogance with an unmitigated exploitation of the peasants. In lieu of the balancing of group-interests in the feudal assemblies of an earlier day each class was now divided from the others and within itself with the result that "nothing had been left that could obstruct

[1] Weber, *Law in Economy and Society*, p. 143. In this connection it should be remembered that the privileges or liberties of medieval society were associated with duties that would appear very onerous to a modern citizen. Also, these individual or collective "privileges" frequently resulted from compulsion rather than a spontaneous drive for freedom, as is vividly described in Albert B. White, *Self-government at the King's Command* (Minneapolis, University of Minnesota Press, 1933). The title itself illuminates the combination of royal power *and* compulsory local autonomy, which was typical of England, but not found to the same extent elsewhere in Europe. Still, the privileges of an estate also had the more ordinary meaning of rights (rather than duties), and this was true to some extent even of the lower social orders. Cf. the discussion of this problem by Herbert Grundmann, Freiheit als religiöses, politisches und persönliches Postulat im Mittelalter, *Historische Zeitschrift*, CLXXXIII (1957), pp. 23–53. A detailed case-study of medieval political life is contained in Otto Brunner, *Land und Herrschaft* (Brünn, Rudolf M. Rohrer Verlag, 1943).

[2] Cf. note 22 above for a reference to Weber's distinction between feudalism and patrimonialism as the two aspects of "traditional domination" which were present throughout the European Middle Ages. The development towards absolutist régimes is best seen, therefore, as a relative shift of emphasis in Western European institutions, which varied from country to country.

[3] For a comparative account of this political structure in eighteenth century Europe cf. Palmer, *The Age of the Democratic Revolution*, ch. III and *passim*.

[4] Alexis de Tocqueville, *The Old Regime and the Revolution* (Garden City, Doubleday and Co., 1955), pp. 22–77. For a modern appraisal of the survival of corporate and libertarian elements under the absolutist regimes of the eighteenth century cf. Kurt von Raumer, Absoluter Staat, Korporative Libertät, Persönliche Freiheit, *Historische Zeitschrift*, CLXXXIII (1957), pp. 55–96.

the central government, but, by the same token, nothing could shore it up."[1]

Tocqueville's analysis was concerned explicitly with the problem of the political community under the conditions created by the French Revolution. He maintained that in the medieval societies of Western Europe, the inequality of ranks was a universally accepted condition of social life. In that early political structure the individual enjoyed the rights and fulfilled the obligations appropriate to his rank; and although the distribution of such rights and duties was greatly affected by the use of force, it was established contractually and consecrated as such.[2] The Old Regime and the French Revolution destroyed this system by creating among all citizens a condition of abstract equality, but without providing guarantees for the preservation of freedom. Hence, Tocqueville appealed to his contemporaries that a new community, a new reciprocity of rights and obligations, must be established and that this could be done only if men would combine their love of equality and liberty with their love of order and religion. This admonition arose from his concern with the weakness and isolation of the individual in relation to government. Because he saw the trend towards equality as inevitable, Tocqueville was deeply troubled by the possibility that men who are equal would be able to agree on nothing but the demand that the central government assist each of them personally. As a consequence the government would subject ever new aspects of the society to its central regulation. I cite one version of this argument:

> As in periods of equality no man is compelled to lend his assistance to his fellow men, and none has any right to expect much support from them, everyone is at once independent and powerless. These two conditions, which must never be either separately considered or confounded together, inspire the citizen of a democratic country with very contrary propensities. His independence fills him with self-reliance and pride among his equals; his debility makes him feel from time to time the want of some outward assistance, which he cannot expect from any of them, because they are all impotent and unsympathizing. In this predicament he naturally turns his eyes to that imposing power [of the central govern-

ment] [. . .] Of that power his wants and especially his desires continually remind him, until he ultimately views it as the sole and necessary support of his own weakness.[3]

Here is Tocqueville's famous paradox of equality and freedom. Men display an extraordinary independence when they rise in opposition to aristocratic privileges. "But in proportion as equality was [. . .] established by the aid of freedom, freedom itself was thereby rendered more difficult of attainment."[4] In grappling with this problem Tocqueville used as his base-point of comparison an earlier society in which men had been compelled to lend assistance to their fellows, because law and custom fixed their common and reciprocal rights and obligations. As this society was destroyed the danger arose that individualism and central power would grow apace. To counteract this threat men must cultivate the "art of associating together" in proportion as the equality of conditions advances, lest their failure to combine for private ends encourage the government to intrude — at the separate request of each — into every phase of social life.[5]

We can learn much from these insights. Tocqueville was surely right in his view that the established system of inequality in medieval society had been characterized by an accepted reciprocity of rights and obligations, and that this system had been destroyed as the *ancien régime* had centralized the functions of government. The French Revolution and its continuing repercussions levelled old differences in social rank and the resulting equalitarianism posed critical issues for the maintenance of freedom and political stability. Again, he discerned an important mechanism of centralization when he observed that each man would make his separate request for governmental assistance. In contrast to this tendency as he observed it in France, Tocqueville commended the Americans for their pursuit of private ends by voluntary association, which would help to curtail the centralization of governmental power.

It is necessary, of course, to qualify these insights in view of Tocqueville's tendency to read into modern conditions the patterns of medieval political life. At an earlier time, when landed aristocrats protected their liberties or privileges by resisting the encroachments of royal power, the centralization of that power appeared as an unequivocal curtailment of such liberties. Today, however, that centralization is an important bulwark of all *civil* liberties, though by the same token government can infringe upon these liberties more effectively than before, as Tocqueville emphasized time and again. The collective pursuit of private ends, on the other hand, is not necessarily incompatible with an increase of central government, because today voluntary associations frequently demand more rather than less government action in contrast to the medieval estates whose effort to extend their jurisdictions was often synonymous with resistance to administrative interference from the outside. In contrast to Tocqueville, Durkheim

---

[1] Alexis de Tocqueville, *op. cit.*, p. 137.

[2] *Ibid.*, pp. 15–16.

[3] Tocqueville, *Democracy in America* (New York, Vintage Books, 1945), II, p. 311. In advancing this thesis Tocqueville referred, for example, to the innovative activities of manufacturers that were characteristic of democratic eras. Such men engaged in "novel undertakings without shackling themselves to their fellows", they opposed in principle all governmental interference with such private concerns, and yet "by an exception of that rule" each of them sought public assistance in his private endeavor when it suited his purpose. Tocqueville concluded that the power of government would of necessity grow, wherever large numbers of mutually independent men proceeded in this manner. See *ibid.*, p. 311, n. 1.

[4] *Ibid.*, p. 333.

[5] Cf. *ibid.*, pp. 114–132.

clearly perceived this positive aspect of modern government and, correspondingly, the dangers implicit in group-control over the individual.

> It is the State that has rescued the child from patriarchal domination and from family tyranny; it is the State that has freed the citizen from feudal groups and later from communal groups; it is the State that has liberated the craftsman and his master from guild tyranny [. . .]
>
> [The State] must even permeate all those secondary groups of family, trade and professional association, Church, regional areas and so on . . . which tend [. . .] to absorb the personality of their members. It must do this, in order to prevent this absorption and free these individuals, and so as to remind these partial societies that they are not alone and that there is a right that stands above their own rights.[1]

Important as these qualifications are, they should not make us overlook the reason why Tocqueville's interpretation of the "great transformation" was illuminating.[2] By contrasting an earlier condition of political life, the transformation brought about by the *ancien régime*, the new condition of equality ushered in by the French Revolution, and the possibility of a new tyranny in the future Tocqueville was concerned with "speculative truths" as he called them. This simplification of different social structures enabled him to bring out the major contrasts among them, and these are not invalidated by the short-run and more deductive analyses that went astray. As I see it, Tocqueville's work becomes intellectually most useful, if we attempt to develop within his overall framework a set of categories that may enable us to handle the problem of the modern political community, which he discerned, in closer relation to the empirical evidence as we know it today.[3]

To do so it will be useful to summarize the preceding discussion. Medieval political life consisted in struggles for power among more or less autonomous jurisdictions, whose members shared immunities and obligations based on an established social hierarchy and on a fealty relation with a secular ruler consecrated by a universal church. By the middle of the eighteenth century this pattern had been replaced by a system of oligarchic rule, in which the king exercised certain nation-wide powers through his appointed officials while other important judicial and administrative powers were pre-empted on a hereditary basis by privileged status-groups and the "constituted bodies" in which they were represented. In contrast to both patterns modern Western societies are characterized by national political communities, in which the major judicial and executive functions are centralized in the hands of a national government, while all adult citizens participate in political decision-making under conditions of formal equality in the more or less direct election of legislative (and in some cases executive) representatives. Centralization, on the one hand, and formally equal political participation, on the other, have given rise to the duality between government and society discussed above in theoretical terms.

C) THE PROBLEM OF THE MODERN POLITICAL COMMUNITY

Centralization means that such major functions as the adjudication of legal disputes, the collection of revenue, the control of currency, military recruitment, the organization of the postal system and others have been removed from the political struggle in the sense that they cannot be parcelled out among competing jurisdictions or appropriated on a hereditary basis by privileged status-groups. Under these circumstances politics are no longer a struggle over the distribution of the national sovereignty; instead they have tended to become a struggle over the distribution of the national product and hence over the policies guiding the administration of centralized governmental functions.

One unquestioned corollary of such centralization is the development of a body of officials, whose recruitment and policy execution was separated gradually from the previously existing involvement of officials with kinship loyalties, hereditary privileges and

---

[1] Emile Durkheim, *Profession Ethics and Civic Morals*, pp. 64-65.

[2] A fuller critical appraisal of Tocqueville's facts and interpretations is contained in the essay by George W. Pierson, *Tocqueville in America* (Garden City, Anchor Books, Doubleday and Co., 1959), pp. 430-477, though Pierson slights Tocqueville's theoretical contribution which is emphasized in the text.

[3] A further theoretical note is in order here. No one doubts the relevance of the distinction between a feudal order and an equalitarian social structure, which Tocqueville analyzed. In any study of social change we require some such long-run distinction so that we can know whence we came and where we may be going, though distinctions of this kind may be tools of very unequal intellectual worth. But while it is the merit of long-run distinctions that they enable us to conceptualize theoretically significant dimensions of social life (within the same civilization over time or between different civilizations), it also follows that these distinctions will become blurred the more closely we examine social change in a particular setting and in the short-run. The following discussion will suggest some concepts that are designed to "narrow the gap" between the long and the short-run and hence reduce to some extent the reliance on deductions which characterized Tocqueville's work. But I doubt that the gap can be closed entirely, because in the short-run we are bound to fall back upon Tocqueville's method of logically deduced possibilities of social change, even if we can go farther than he did in comparing actual changes with these artificial benchmarks. Two rules of thumb should be kept in mind, however. One is that this partly inductive and partly deductive study of social change in the short-run should not lose sight of the long-run distinctions, for without them we are like sailors without compass or stars. The other is that this retention of the long-run distinctions imparts a dialectical quality to the analysis of short-run changes. Since we do not know where these changes may lead in the long-run we must keep the possibility of alternative developments conceptually open and we can do this by utilizing the dichotomous concepts so characteristic of sociological theory. For suggestions along these lines cf. Reinhard Bendix and Bennett Berger, Images of Society and Problems of Concept-Formation in Sociology, *in* Llewellyn Gross, ed., *Symposium on Sociological Theory*, pp. 92-118. This perspective is greatly indebted, of course, to the work of Max Weber.

property interests.[1] A second corollary of centralization has been a high degree of consensus at the national level. In the political communities of Western nation-states no one questions seriously that functions like taxation, conscription, law enforcement, the conduct of foreign affairs, and others, belong to the central government, even though the specific implementation of such functions is in dispute.[2] The "depersonalization" of governmental administration and the national consensus on the essential functions of government have resulted in national political communities characterized by a *continuous* exercise of central authority. This continuity is not affected by the individuals filling governmental positions or the conflicts of interest among organized groups which affect the legislative process. Accordingly, a national government of the modern type represents a more or less autonomous principle of decision making and administrative implementation.[3] For Durkheim it was the state which alone could guarantee the "moral existence" of the individual, and in his judgment the state was capable of having this effect because it is "an organ distinct from the rest of society."[4] Presumably, people as members of a political community regard the overall jurisdiction of this organ as inviolate, because they believe in the achievement and orderly revision of an overall reciprocity of rights and duties, whatever the particular political vicissitudes of the moment.

[1] Max Weber's well known concept of "bureaucracy" is based on the assumption that this process of separation of modern from patrimonial administration has been completed. See his *Essays in Sociology* (tr. and ed. by H. H. Gerth and C. W. Mills; New York, Oxford University Press, 1946), ch. VIII. For an exposition of the contrast between patrimonial and bureaucratic administration see R. Bendix, *Max Weber*, pp. 419–420. An admirably clear, comparative study of administrative history, in which this process of separation is traced since the middle of the seventeenth century, is contained in Ernest Barker, *The Development of Public Services in Western Europe, 1660–1930* (New York, Oxford University Press, 1944).

[2] Admittedly, these matters are in flux and in this respect significant differences exist within Western civilization. Still, no one can be in doubt in the instances in which this fundamental assumption has come into question, as in the American Civil War or more recently in the critical conflict between the national government in France and the French settlers in Algeria. The Southern opposition to school-integration is *not* a comparable development, I believe, since even in the more extreme cases it is combined with an acceptance of national jurisdiction on which there is no sharp disagreement. But the political reintegration of the South has been and may continue to be painfully slow, because the American political structure appears to militate against the type of statesmanship that combines principled firmness with tactical flexibility.

[3] Neither medieval political life nor the absolutist regimes of the eighteenth century nor yet many of the "developing areas" of the modern world knew or know a government of this type, because adjudication and administration were and are decentralized, personal, intermittent, and subject to a fee for each governmental service.

[4] E. Durkheim, *Professional Ethics and Civic Morals*, pp. 64, 82.

[5] For a survey of this line of thought, disguised as it is in theoretical disquisitions, cf. Robert A. Nisbet, *The Quest for Community* (New York, Oxford University Press, 1953).

In the modern political community consensus (or a workable reciprocity of rights and obligations) is strongest at this national level, although as such it possesses an impersonal quality that does not satisfy the persistent craving for fraternity or fellow-feeling. But this emergence of a national consensus concerning the functions of the national government has been accompanied also by a decline of social solidarity at all other levels of group formation. Classes, status groups and formal associations arise from the coalescence of social and economic interests, other groups are formed on the basis of ethnic and religious affiliation: in some measure these collectivities are reflected in voting behavior. Yet none of them involves a consensus comparable to the acceptance by all citizens of the idea that the national government possesses sovereign authority.

This is not a new issue. From the very beginning of the modern political community, say, since the great debates of the eighteenth century, social and political theorists have complained of the loss of social solidarity, for which the vast proliferation of associations did not appear to be a proper palliative. When writers like Tocqueville and Durkheim stressed the importance of "secondary groups", they did so in the belief that such groups could counteract both the isolation of each man from his fellows *and* the centralization of government. Yet much of this analysis remained at a level where considerations of policy and an element of nostalgia merged with considerations of fact, especially in the ever-recurring, invidious contrasts between traditionalism and modernity.[5] Despite the eminent names associated with it, we should discard this legacy of obfuscation. The "great transformation" leading to the modern political community made the decline of social solidarity inevitable, because (if so complex a matter can be stated so simply) no association based on a coalescence of interests or on ethnic and religious affiliation could recapture the intense reciprocity of rights and duties that was peculiar to the "autonomous jurisdictions" of an estate society. The reason is that in these "jurisdictions", or "law communities" (*Rechtsgemeinschaften*) as Max Weber called them, each individual was involved in a "mutual aid" society, which protected his rights only if he fulfilled his duties. This great cohesion within social ranks was above all a counterpart to the very loose integration of a multiplicity of jurisdictions at the "national" political level. In this respect the absolutist regimes achieved a greater integration through centralized royal administration and the people's loyalty to the king, although the hereditary privileges appropriated by Church and aristocracy also subjected the ordinary man to the autocratic rule of his local master. Where such hereditary privileges replaced the "law communities" of an earlier day, the privileged groups achieved considerable social cohesion, but the people were deprived of what legal and customary protection they had enjoyed and hence excluded even from their former, passive participation in the reciprocity of rights and obligations.[1] Modern political communities have achieved a greater centralization of government than either the medieval or the absolutist political systems, and this achievement has been preceded, accompanied, or followed by the participation of all adult citizens in political life (on the basis of the formal equality of the franchise). The price of these achievements consists in the diminished solidarity of all "secondary groups".

This "price" is a by-product of the separation between society and government in the modern political community. Whereas solidarity had been based on the individual's participation in a "law community" or on his membership in a privileged status group possessing certain governmental prerogatives, it must arise now from the social and economic stratification of society aided by the equality of all adult citizens before the law and in the electoral process.[2] On this basis exchange relations and joint actions may develop to the exclusion of "governmental interference" or in quest of governmental assistance or with the aim to achieve representation in the decision making bodies of government.[3] Though it certainly has an impact on the national government, individual and collective action on this basis does not account for the governmental performance of administrative tasks, or, in the larger sense, the continuous functioning of the national political community.

In the societies of Western civilization we should accept, therefore, the existence of a genuine hiatus between the forces making for social solidarity independently of government and the forces accounting for the continuous exercise of central authority in the national political community.[4] This existing pattern is the result of a slow and often painful process. As the central functions of the national government became gradually accepted, organized groups within the society demanded representation in this national political community. Accordingly, "political community" refers not only to the central functions of government and the consensus sustaining them, but to the much more problematic question whether and how the groups arising within the society have achieved a national reciprocity of rights and obligations. For at the beginning of European industrialization in the nineteenth century new social groups were in the process of formation and had yet to learn (in the words of Tocqueville) what they were, what they might be or what ought to be in the emerging national community of their country.

3. Implications for a comparative study of social structures

During the eighteenth and nineteenth centuries the societies of Western civilization industrialized and became democratic. We should utilize the knowledge gained from this experience as we turn today to a study of the "developing areas" of the non-Western world. This task is difficult because our theories of the "great transformation" in the West have been inevitably a part of that transformation as well. In an effort to disentangle these theories of change from the change itself the preceding discussion has separated the theoretical reflections on this transformation from a consideration of changes in the institutional structure. While retaining the contrast between medieval and modern society it has discarded the nostalgia so often associated with that contrast. And it has utilized the distinction between society and the state in view of its analytical utility and the institutional duality which exists in this respect in the "developing areas" of yesterday and today.[5] In this concluding section I attempt to reformulate this contrast in general terms so as to facilitate a comparative study of social structures.

[1] Tocqueville tended to obscure this distinction by identifying this reciprocity in the earlier estate societies of medieval Europe with the later symbiosis of absolutist rule and aristocratic privilege, though he was quick to point out how absolutism tended to undermine the aristocratic position. On the increase of aristocratic privileges just prior to the French Revolution cf. Palmer, *op. cit.*, ch. II–IV.

[2] Max Weber has characterized the contrast as follows: "In the legal systems of the older type all law appeared as the privilege of particular individuals or objects or of particular constellations of individuals or objects. Such a point of view had, of course, to be opposed by that in which the state appears as the all embracing coercive institution [. . .] The revolutionary period of the 18th century produced a type of legislation which sought to extirpate every form of associational autonomy and legal particularism [. . .] This [. . .] was effected by two arrangements: the first is the formal, universally accessible, closely limited, and legally regulated autonomy of association which may be created by anyone wishing to do so; the other consists in the grant to everyone of the power to create law of his own by means of engaging in private legal transactions of certain kinds." Max Weber, *Law*, pp. 145–146.

[3] Demands for representation are difficult to distinguish from demands for privileged jurisdictions or outright benefits, because representation in decision-making bodies may be used to obtain these privileges or benefits. It is clear at any rate that voluntary associations are not the unequivocal counter-weight to centralized power for which Tocqueville was searching in his study of American society. Instead, voluntary associations frequently demand governmental assistance even where they reject it in principle, and in this respect they act in much the same way as individual manufacturers tended to do a century ago according to Tocqueville's observations. Voluntary associations are a protean phenomenon. They are evidence of consensus within the society, especially where they pursue private ends as an alternative to governmental assistance and regulation. But they may also be evidence of dissensus within the national political community, in so far as they enlist the national government in the service of parochial interests, and hence seek to secure from the government privileges that are denied to other groups.

[4] Incidentally this hiatus is reflected in the very widespread and sanguine juxtaposition of patriotism with the most extreme selfishness of individuals and groups.

[5] The term "state" is needed to designate the continuing political identity of the nation irrespective of the governments embodying this identity from time to time. Where monarchical institutions have survived they represent this identity separately from the ruling government. Such institutional separation is not possible under democracies. In this discussion the terms "state" and "political community" or "polity" are used interchangeably, since all three refer with different emphasis to the apparatus and the consensus sustaining the continuous political identity of the modern nation.

My thesis is that for our understanding of "society" and "the state" in the nations of Europe since the French Revolution the third perspective (mentioned before in Part I) is most useful, if it is considered as an analytical framework rather than as the political theory of liberalism. In the utilitarian contrast between the "natural identity" and the "artificial identification of interests", in Durkheim's concern with group-integration and state-interference, or, to cite an American example, in W. G. Sumner's distinction between "crescive" and "enacted" institutions we have repeated references to two types of human associations. One of these consists in affinities of interest which arise from relations of kinship, the division of labor, exchanges on the market place and the ubiquitous influence of custom. The other consists in relations of super- and sub-ordination which arise from the exercise of instituted authority and compliance with its commands.[1] The distinction refers to a universal attribute of group-life in the sense that, however interrelated, these two types of human association are not reducible to each other.[2] From an analytical viewpoint it is necessary to consider "society" and "the state" as interdependent, but autonomous, spheres of thought and action which coexist in one form or another in all complex societies, although the separation of these "spheres" is perhaps greatest in modern Western societies.[3]

The generality of this distinction suggests that it lends itself to a comparative study of types of interrelation between social structure and the political community. In medieval Europe two such types were "competing" with each other as Machiavelli pointed out:

> Kingdoms known to history have been governed in two ways: either by a prince and his servants, who, as ministers by his grace and permission, assist in governing the realm; or by a prince and by barons, who hold positions not by favour of the ruler but by antiquity of blood. Such barons have states and subjects of their own who recognize them as their lords, and are naturally attached to them. In those states which are governed by a prince and his servants, the prince possesses more authority, because there is no one in the state regarded as a superior other than himself, and if others are obeyed it is merely as ministers and officials of the prince, and no one regards them with any special affection.[4]

Government as an extension of the royal household and government based on the fealty between landed nobles and their king and leader thus represented two types of social structure as well as two types of instituted authority. Again, in the societies of Western civilization at the beginning of the present era this duality between society and the state is reflected in two far-reaching developments, which were eventually followed by a third. A market economy emerged based on contract or the ability of individuals to enter into legally binding agreements, while gradually the exercise of governmental authority was separated from kinship ties, property interests and inherited privileges. These developments occurred at a time when the determination of governmental policies and their administrative implementation were confined to a privileged few, but in the course of the nineteenth century this restriction was reduced and eventually eliminated through the extension of the franchise. If we consider these developments in retrospect we can summarize their effects on society and the state. The growth of the market economy and the adoption of universal franchise have given rise to interest groups and political parties which mobilize collectivities for economic and political action and thereby "facilitate the interchange between [. . .] the spontaneous groupings of society" and the exercise of authority.[5] On the other hand, the "depersonalization" of governmental functions has accompanied a centralization of legislative, judicial and administrative

---

[1] Like all such distinctions there is a good bit of overlap between the two types. Affinities of interest which arise from the social structure forever engender relations of super- and sub-ordination, while the exercise of instituted authority forever produces, and is affected by, affinities of interest.

[2] Hence, the ideas that society is an object of state-craft or that all governmental institutions are the product of social forces represent perspectives which are useful only as long as their partiality is recognized.

In a recent article Raymond Aron stated the case against the Comtean as well as Marxian tendency to reduce all politics and government to forces arising from the socio-economic substructure. "Contre l'un et l'autre, nous avons appris que la politique est une catégorie éternelle de l'existence humaine, un secteur permanent de toute société. Il est illégitime de se donner, par hypothèse, l'élimination de la politique en tant que telle ou de caractériser une société par sa seule infrastructure." See Raymond Aron, Les sociologues et les institutions représentatives, *Archives européennes de sociologie*, I (1960), p. 155. The present analysis is in agreement with this position and I assume that Professor Aron would agree that the sociological level of analysis likewise possesses a certain autonomy. Perhaps it is symptomatic for the modern climate of opinion in the social sciences that the most elaborate systematization of social theory to date acknowledges society, culture and personality, *but not politics*, as relatively autonomous levels of analysis. Cf. Talcott Parsons, E. A. Shils *et al.*, *Toward a General Theory of Action* (Cambridge, Harvard University Press, 1951), pp. 28–29. Cf. also the learned critique of this reductionist tendency in Sheldon S. Wolin, *Politics and Vision* (Boston, Little, Brown & Co., 1960), chs. IX–X.

[3] As I see it, this is the viewpoint from which Max Weber developed the analytical framework of his posthumously published work *Wirtschaft und Gesellschaft*. The fundamental distinction of that work is not the one between "economy" and "society", but between society and domination and hence between groups arising from the pursuit of "ideal and material interests", on the one hand, and relations of super- and sub-ordination arising from beliefs in legitimacy, administrative organization, and the threat of force. For details of this interpretation cf. my book *Max Weber*, *passim*. A lucid exposition of the fundamental assumptions of this approach is contained in Robert MacIver, *The Web of Government* (New York, Macmillan and Co., 1947), ch. XIII.

[4] Niccolò Machiavelli, *The Prince and the Discourses* (New York, The Modern Library, 1940), p. 15.

[5] See S. M. Lipset, Party Systems and the Representation of Social Groups, *Archives européenes de sociologie*, I (1960), p. 51. In this article Professor Lipset presents comparative materials on the interrelation of different representative systems with different social structures.

decision-making and implementation which now facilitates the "reverse interchange" between the state and society.[1] The efficacy of these "interchanges" will vary not only with social cleavages and party-structures as Lipset has shown, but also with the "depersonalization" of government and the propensities of rule-abiding behavior among the people at large. On the whole Western societies are characterized in these respects by a cultural tradition which ensures the containment of group-conflicts within a gradually changing constitutional framework and a high degree of probity in office and popular compliance with rules. But it is well to remember that even in the West the centralization of government and the democratization of political participation have on occasion created a hiatus that has proved more or less intractable. A striking case in point is the Italian experience with its "negative interchange" between society and the state, as exemplified by the "anti-government organization" of the Sicilian *Mafia* which among other things "protects" the society against governmental encroachments.[2] An extreme case like this serves to remind us that all Western societies have had to grapple with a duality that ranges from the juxtaposition of private concerns and public obligation in each citizen to the juxtaposition of solidary groups based on common interest and appointed officials acting in their authorized capacity.

To say that this hiatus is bridged by "interchange" from both sides only refers to the end-product of a prolonged balancing of group interests and formal institutions. In this respect the great issue of the nineteenth century had to do with the question whether and on what terms the disfranchised masses would be accorded the rights of national citizenship. The resolution of this issue could be eased *or* complicated through the continued confinement of politics to an elite of notables and through the natural as well as legal obstacles standing in the way of effective political organization. The balance between oligarchic resistance and popular political activation, the rise of central power and the later development of citizenship on the part of all adults posed the problem of how a new reciprocity of rights and obligations could be established *at the national level*. In several European countries this problem of a national political community came to the fore at a time when the "new" social classes of employers and workers began to make their bid for political participation and to cope as well with the problem of their reciprocal rights and obligations. Ideological controversy was at its height as these and other groups became capable of organized action and as long as they were denied their bid for equal participation in the political process. But as one after another social group has been admitted to such participation, they have in each case used their newly acquired power to pressure the national government into enacting and implementing a guaranteed minimum of social and cultural amenities. In this way a new reciprocity of rights and obligation among conflicting groups could be established by the "welfare state" at the national level and where this has occurred ideological controversy has declined.[3]

Clearly, this statement does not apply to the "developing areas" of the world today. Instead, we are witnessing ever new attempts to mobilize the "voiceless masses" through democratic ideas and institutions and at the same time provide these masses with the amenities of the "welfare state". This means that all the cleavages of the social structure are given political articulation simultaneously, while governments attempt to plan economic development and provide the minimum essentials of a welfare state. If it be argued that such governments possess only an uncertain authority and relatively little experience, it will be answered that they must make the attempt nevertheless because only on this basis will the mobilized masses positively identify themselves with the new nation.[4] As a consequence of these conditions, ideological controversy is waged with unparalleled intensity, while political leaders attempt to establish a functioning governmental machinery and protect it against the continuous assault of politics and corruption.

In their increasing preoccupation with the "developing areas" of Asia and Africa since World War II Western scholars have had to grapple with the applicability of concepts which had been formulated in the context of Western experience. Since a simple application of these concepts is found wanting the further we move away from that experience, it is not surprising that some scholars decide to discard them altogether in an attempt to comprise in one conceptual scheme all political phenomena, Western and non-Western. The spirit of this enterprise is best conveyed in the following quotation:

> [. . .] the search for new concepts [. . .] reflects an underlying drift towards a new and coherent way of

[1] Cf. Philip Selznick, *TVA and the Grass Roots* (Berkeley, University of California Press, 1949), which may be considered a case-study of this "reverse interchange".

[2] Cf. the analysis by E. J. Hobsbawm, *Social Bandits and Primitive Rebels* (Glencoe: The Free Press, 1959), ch. III. See also Roger Vailland's novel *The Law* which illustrates the anarchical propensities through which either formal compliance with, or the symbolic re-enactment of, the law is used to subvert all "rule-abiding behavior".

[3] There is, thus, a close relationship between this *gradual* establishment of "social rights" and the decline of ideology, although it must be kept in mind that this decline in the West may be the consequence of the Cold War and the rise of ideology in the rest of the world as much as it is the result of the welfare-state. Different aspects of this complex phenomenon are discussed in T. H. Marshall, *Citizenship and Social Class* (Cambridge, at the University Press, 1950) ch. I; Otto Brunner, Das Zeitalter der Ideologien, *Neue Wege der Sozialgeschichte* (Göttingen, Vandenhoeck and Ruprecht, 1956), ch. IX; E. A. Shils, Ideology and Civility, *Sewanee Review*, LXVI (1958), pp. 450–480; Daniel Bell, *The End of Ideology* (Glencoe: The Free Press, 1960), Part II; and S. M. Lipset, *Political Man* (New York, Doubleday and Co., 1960), pp. 403–417.

[4] For a comparative analysis of the cleavages facing the "new nations" and the related liabilities of government cf. E. A. Shils, Political Development in the New States, *Comparative Studies in Society and History*, II (1960), pp. 268–282, 379–411.

thinking about and studying politics that is implied in such slogans as the 'behavioral approach'. This urge towards a new conceptual unity is suggested when we compare the new terms with the old. Thus, instead of the concept of the 'state', limited as it is by legal and institutional meanings, we prefer 'political system'; instead of 'powers', which again is a legal concept in connotation, we are beginning to prefer 'functions'; instead of 'offices' (legal again), we prefer 'roles'; instead of 'institutions', which again directs us toward formal norms, 'structures'; instead of 'public opinion' and 'citizenship training', formal and rational in meaning, we prefer 'political culture' and 'political socialization'. We are not setting aside public law and philosophy as disciplines, but simply telling them to move over to make room for a growth in political theory that has been long overdue.[1]

In this approach politics is to be considered a universal phenomenon and as a result the distinction is discarded between societies which are "states" and those which are not, and that just at a time when leading groups in the "developing areas" are directly concerned with the organization of states and the development of governmental machinery.[2]

The preceding discussion has suggested that this is not

[1] Gabriel Almond, A Functional Approach to Comparative Politics, *in* Gabriel Almond and James S. Coleman, eds., *The Politics of the Developing Areas* (Princeton, Princeton University Press, 1950), p. 4.

[2] The concept "state" is discarded on the curious ground that it is based on a dichotomy which is incompatible with the existing continuity of the phenomena. Professor Almond suggests that with reference to the "developing areas" only the political "input" functions will be analysed because the formal governmental structure ("output" function) is usually not well developed. This decision would seem to reintroduce the distinction which was discarded. Cf. *ibid.*, pp. 12, 17.

a new problem even in the Western experience. The rise of absolutism promoted the centralization of governmental power. But no one reading the record of mercantilist regimes can avoid the conclusion that the efficacy of that central power was often as doubtful as is the efficacy of highly centralized governments in the "developing areas" of today. Again, the destruction of many intermediate centers of authority and the consequent emancipation of the individual through the institution of a national citizenship inevitably accentuated all existing cleavages within the society by mobilizing the people for the electoral struggle over the distribution of the national product. Thus, centralization of power and national citizenship gave a new meaning to the duality between society and the state, as Tocqueville observed long ago, and as we have occasion to witness in the "new nations" of the non-Western world today. It may be true, of course, that some of these "developing areas" are confronted by such an accentuation of cleavages within their social structure and such a lack of effective government, that anarchy reigns, or a political community can be established only by a "tutelary democracy" or a dictatorship as safeguards against anarchy. Meagre resources in the face of staggering tasks, the relative absence of a legal and governmental tradition, and the precipitous political mobilization of all the people greatly increase the hazards even aside from the additional aggravation of the Cold War. The efforts to cope with these difficulties certainly command our earnest attention and no one can be sure of their outcome. In view of that uncertainty we should try to preserve the insights we have gained from the Western experience into the social foundations of government *and* the political foundations of society. If a balance is achieved between these perspectives we may be able to utilize our knowledge for an understanding of contemporary social change.

Different Conceptions of Social Class
Stanislaw Ossowski

IN MY ANALYSIS of the conceptions of class structure, I use the concept of class and the corresponding concept of a class-society regardless of whether or not the term "class" appears in the texts I am examining. I could not in any case take the terminological criterion into account since I am also concerned with historical periods in which the term "social class" did not yet exist.

None the less, when we come to consider modern views on the problems of social structure it is not only the concept of class that is important but the term as well. In the course of the nineteenth and twentieth centuries the term itself has acquired a considerable emotional load and a rich field of associations. It is no longer a matter of indifference which denotata receive

Reprinted from *Class Structure in the Social Consciousness* (London: Routledge & Kegan Paul, 1963), pp. 121–144, by permission of the publisher.

their share in this emotional charge. In consequence, the meaning of the term is no mere matter of semantic conventions when one is considering disputes about the concept of class.

For the moment, however, I am concerned with the semantic aspects of this matter. The ambiguity of the term "class" makes it difficult to find one's bearings among the divergencies between the different viewpoints involved. Later, I shall consider the problem of the common conceptual content to be found in different conceptions of a class-society. But before that it is well to realize the relation of the general concept of class to the two concepts with a narrower extension which are as a rule referred to by means of the same term (that is to say, the term of "class").

Therefore, I shall first deal with the overlapping of the three denotations of the term "social class", both with regard to the origin of its threefold nature, which is connected with the social changes of recent centuries, and with regard to the actual requirements of the conceptual apparatus.

A new term and a new reality

The history of the term "social class" from the second half of the XVIII century onwards is an interesting subject for sociologists. As I have not made any systematic study of it, however, I am confining myself to observations drawn mainly from sources which were consulted for other purposes.

In the *Encyclopaedia* of Diderot and d'Alembert, I could not find the term *classe sociale*, although the word "class" in the meaning of *social class* is found as early as Spinoza. I am indebted to Professor Leszek Kolakowski for drawing my attention to Proposition XLVI in the third book of the Ethics, which is of interest in this context.[1] In their description of social structure the authors of the *Encyclopaedia* found the terms *état* and *ordre* sufficient for their purpose, *état* being used in reference only to groups with a legal existence, that is to say groups which are organized in a certain way and which have some kind of political representation.

Thus the *Encyclopaedia* could maintain that there were only two estates in Poland (the *szlachta* and the priesthood), while four were noted in Sweden (nobility, priesthood, burghers and peasants) and three in France.[2] Here the term *état* is used, as we can see, in a manner very remote from the general concept of class. Turning to Mably, I was unable to find the term *classe* in his treatise of 1758, *Des droits et des devoirs du citoyen*. He did, however, employ the term in his polemic with the physiocrats, written a dozen or more years later, in a sentence referring to the conflict of class interests. In this polemic the term *classe* has a clear economic connotation.[3]

Not many years after the publication of the *Encyclopaedia*, Adam Smith divided society into basic groups, according not to legal but to economic criteria.[4] But he again did not apply the term "class" to these groups

but the term "order". We do find the word "class", in the meaning of a social group, in Smith's works, but it is applied to a more differentiated division. The three basic orders are in their turn divided into "classes".[5]

Adam Smith's followers came to apply the term class to his basic groups, and we also find it used occasionally by Madison.[6] At the beginning of the French Revolution Sieyès saw the fundamental social conflict as a struggle between the estates, and used only the latter term in his picture of contemporary social structure and of the homogeneous society of the future.[7]

Some years later, however, Babeuf was writing only of social classes, and was presenting French society as divided by a basic class antagonism. In the new conditions, a new term was essential to underline this antagonism, which Sieyès had not discerned or at least had not mentioned. Babeuf regarded France from the viewpoint of another class than did the Abbé Sieyès. Saint-Simon, however, although in this regard he held the same position as did Sieyès and although his "industrial class" (*classe industrielle* or *classe travailleuse*) approximately coincides in extension with the third estate, nevertheless applied the term "class" in his conceptions of social structure, and used a new term, *classe paresseuse*, to attack the remnants of estate privileges that persisted after the Restoration.[8]

Thus the term "class" was used in an unspecified manner by Adam Smith, Madison and the other writers of the eighteenth century as one of the possible synonyms of "group" or "estate" available in colloquial speech.

[1] "If a man has been affected pleasurably or painfully by anyone of a class or nation different from his own, and if the pleasure of pain has been accompanied by the idea of the said stranger as cause, under the general category of the class or nation; the man will feel love or hatred not only to the individual stranger, but also the whole class or nation whereto he belongs." (*Prop.* XLVI, R. H. M. Elwes' translation).

[2] "Le tiers-état", we read in the Encyclopaedia, "ne commença à se former que sous Louis le Gros, par l'affranchissement des serfs.'

[3] "Qui ne voit pas que nos sociétés sont partagées en differentes classes d'hommes, qui, grâce aux propriétés, à leur vanité, ont toutes des interèts, je ne dis différent, mais contraires?" *Doutes proposes aux philosophes économistes*, Letter VIII. There is a mention of class interests in Letter III and in Letter VIII the author refers to the concept of *class stérile* employed by the physiocrats. In general however the term *classe* appears in this work only on a handful of occasions.

[4] *Wealth of Nations*, 1776.

[5] "Three different orders of people . . . those who live by rent . . . those who live by wages . . . those who live by profit . . . Merchants and master manufacturers are, in this order, the two classes of people who commonly employ the largest capitals." (*op. cit.*)

[6] "The Scheme of Gradation", *Class Structure in the Social Consciousness*, pp. 38–57.

[7] *Qu'est-ce que le tiers-état?*, 1789.

[8] On the other hand, both Saint-Simon and his followers used the term "class" to denote narrower groups, as for instance when they speak of "various working classes" and of "the idle classes". We find the same dual use of the term in other writers of the nineteenth century. For example, Marx and his school speak of the "working class" and "working classes", of the "middle class" and the "middle classes", of the "propertied class" and the "propertied classes", etc.

For the French post-revolutionary writers, however, the word came to be a technical term. As such, its use was to spread through modern theories of social structure, through party programmes and ideological manifestos. It was to become naturalized in almost all European languages, hardly changing its sound but only its inflexion. In my view, the fact that this term requires no translation has contributed much to its international success. Marxism and the international workers' movement have of course played a great part in this international success. But the wide use of the term "class", in the sense of "social class", in the contemporary United States and in European bourgeois milieux in the nineteenth century can undoubtedly be traced to a different and pre-Marxian origin.

In Poland, as elsewhere in the first half of the nineteenth century, the two terms "class" and "estate" were often used interchangeably. People referred to the "middle estate" or the "middle class", or spoke of seeking wives from the women who belong to their own estate or their own class. In his monumental dictionary of the Polish language (published between 1807 and 1814), Bogumil Linde defined a "class in the society" in terms of "estate" or "sphere". As examples he gave "artisan, working, industrial, clerical; upper, middle, lower, lowest; wealthy, poor". In most of these expressions nobody would at that time have objected to the substitution of the term "estate", as in "clerical estate", "artisan estate" and so on. On the other hand, it would even at that early date have been difficult in some cases to substitute the term "estate" for "class", e.g. in such expressions as "working class", or "refined class".

The writings of Joachim Lelewel[1] afford us some typical instances of the way in which "estate" and "class" were used in that period. In the same study both terms appear with frequency as synonymous to designate the most general concept of class.[2] Elsewhere "class" is opposed to "estate", the latter being interpreted in the same manner as in Diderot's *Encyclopaedia*.

Thus we find Lelewel making statements that sound quite contradictory. On some pages he speaks of the "peasant estate", while on others he writes that "the peasants did not constitute an estate, they were merely a distinct class"; they did not constitute an estate because they did not have any civic rights. Finally, Lelewel uses the term "class" in the freest possible way to denote a group which is neither opposed to nor coincides with an estate.

During the nineteenth century, "class" generally replaced the older term "estate" in expressions which did not refer to legal criteria, particularly in expressions in which the term "class" was used in its most general meaning: that is to say, when it referred to the basic groups in different societies. "Class" ousted "estate" in social theories, ideological declarations and the programmes of social movements. The only complication arose from the fact that as a consequence of socialist propaganda the word "class" and its derivative expressions gradually came to be regarded as typical of certain milieux and acquired a "class flavour". For this reason, as Tawney once wrote, the use of these words in well-bred society was regarded as almost indecent.[3]

Synonymity and diversity of meanings

The social changes which took place in the era in which the term "class" became a part of the language of the social sciences and social ideologies would seem to have exerted an interesting influence on the semantic functions of this term. I am thinking of a certain fundamental ambiguity of meanings which this term can have, an ambiguity which concerns the varying degree of generality of the term and which confuses the sense of certain general statements; the point here is the three-fold denotation of the term "class", which is rather difficult to remove in the present terminology of the social sciences.

We have already noted that after the French Revolution the term "class" ousted "estate" with reference to the general concept of basic groups in a social structure. This happened in an era when the European societies were changing their social systems and when the old criteria which determined social divisions were giving place to new ones. In consequence, each of these terms, even when used in a general sense, came to represent a different period and to be associated with a different type of social structure.

In such conditions, the term "class" acquired two meanings. In certain contexts the term was synonymous with "estate", while in others it was differentiated, as in the statement that a class-structure had succeeded the estate-structure. When Adam Smith's followers spoke of three basic "classes" where he used the term "orders", or when Guizot expressed the view that there were no "classes" left in France,[4] the term "class" replaced the "order", which was previously used in similar circum-

---

[1] A Polish historian and a friend of Mazzini, Herzen and Marx.

[2] "Why is it that the Poles, who have for sixty years fought the oppressors of their country, cannot break their bonds? It may be that the walls erected and not yet broken down between the various classes of inhabitants, will prove to be the most essential cause of this failure". (From *Trzy konstytucje polskie 1791, 1807, 1815 porównał i różnice ich rozważył Joachim Lelewel w toku 1831. The three Polish constitutions of 1791, 1807 and 1815 compared and their differences evaluated by Joachim Lelewel, 1831*, Poznan, 1861, pp. 7–8. "The non-noble estate had no significance; the (urban) estate had another law than the noble estate, but the (rural) estate was subordinated to the noble estate." (*ibid*, p. 44) " . . . But although there is only one class that has a political right . . . " (*ibid.*, p. 8). "Under Prussian and Austrian rule all the classes of the old (Polish) Republic were levelled down, all its estates, for the noble and the non-noble equally lost their rights completely, were equally deprived of political life, and became equally subjects under foreign rule and enslaved." (*ibid.*, p. 100). I am indebted to Mrs. H. W. for these quotations from Lelewel.)

[3] R. H. Tawney, *Equality*, London 1931, p. 66.

[4] Cf. N. Assorodobraj: "Elements in the Class Consciousness of the Bourgeoisie" (*Elementy świadomości klasowej mieszczaństwa*) (Łódź, *Przegląd Socjologiczny 1947*).

stances (in Polish *stan*, in French *ordre* or *état*, in German *stand*). The new term came, however, to be specially associated with the social structure of bourgeois democracy, without losing its general meaning as the name of the basic groups in all societies, and this had certain consequences in the construction of general theories of social development and social structure.

The classic period of capitalism was, as we know, the period when economic power was at its peak. It was a period in which economic dependence dominated other forms of human relations to a degree never previously encountered. Money seemed to be able to buy all kinds of real privileges; the exploitation of labour was effected almost exclusively by means of the privilege of possessing the means of production, and the state was coming to be regarded, not by Marxists alone, as an executive committee of the ruling class. The representatives of big business frequently did not trouble to conceal their belief that in 'civilized countries' persons who had large sums at their disposal could buy governments like so much merchandise.

Moreover, the people of this era expected further evolution in the same direction — particularly after the American Civil War and the ending of slavery in the United States, and before the establishment of a new customary caste-structure in the American way of life. The supposition that the next century could see the triumph of the principles on which the rule of Hitler was founded would have seemed to the people of that time incompatible with the laws of history. Their vision of the future approximated to an ideal type of society in which the power of capital would be the only form of authority and the relations of ownership the only determinant of the social-status system.

Like some of his forerunners, Marx and his followers associated the concept of class with the concept of the exploitation of other men's labour. But because in the days when capitalism flourished most abundantly the only form of mass exploitation of labour was exploitation based on the ownership of the means of production, the author of *Das Kapital* defined social classes in terms of their relation to the means of production (possession, non-possession, possession to a degree insufficient to permit the employment of hired labour). At the same time, this same term "class" was used to describe the social structure of other "formations", without troubling about the fact that "class" was burdened with a meaning linked with a narrower range of phenomena.

In the latter part of his life Marx uttered a warning against the danger of applying generalizations reached after the investigation of the development of the capitalist societies of Western Europe to other periods in the history of mankind.[1] He himself did not however feel it necessary to differentiate between the two meanings of the term "class", depending on whether he meant the classes characteristic of the structure of a capitalist society or the "social classes" of every kind whose struggles were held to constitute the history of mankind

from the disappearance of the original community of primitive society.

Because this differentiation of meaning is not made, the use of the Marxian or Leninist concept of class tends to suggest — contrary to certain assertions made by both Engels and Lenin — that all class divisions have been based simply on a difference in relations to the means of production, and that all class rule, all exploitation of other men's labour, has been achieved by a class monopoly of the ownership of the means of production.

Today it seems clear that when we study the problems of social structure as problems of systems of human inter-relationships, problems concerned with the privileges of power and wealth, problems of social inequalities and exploitation, we need a distinct general term. Such a term should cover not only social classes, in the narrower, non-institutional meaning characteristic of the structure of the bourgeois democracies, but also groups entering into the composition of systems in which the relation between possession of the means of production and control of the means of power takes a different form, as in the case of estate and caste systems. Here I have in mind a term of the kind which could also be applied in the analysis of post-capitalistic societies, where the division of the national income, the rise of privileged or underprivileged groups, and membership of these groups is to a considerable extent the result of deliberate decisions by the political authorities.

A superordinate concept and a two-fold specification

In my account of the history of the relation between the terms "class" and "estate" I referred to the two-fold denotation of the term "class". This term is sometimes used in a general meaning in expressions where the term "estate" would formerly have been used; at others it is used to characterize the social structure of modern capitalism, in contradistinction to the term "estate" or to the term "caste". This contradistinction can in its turn be interpreted in two ways. In speaking of the contradistinction of terms we sometimes have in mind their correspondence to concepts which are mutually exclusive. In other cases we speak of terminological distinctions when the respective terms refer to concepts with a different content. In the first instance the extensions of the concepts are mutually exclusive, while in the second they may overlap. In the case of the term "class" both interpretations are applicable.

In its narrower meaning, in which it is opposed to estates and castes, "class" can be defined either by the negation of the attributes characterizing a caste or an estate or by criteria altogether inapplicable to what we have in mind when we speak of "estates" or "castes". When, therefore, we have to do with the denotation of the term "class" in application to problems of social

[1] Letter to the Editor published in the Russian periodical, *Octebestvennye Zapiski* (Fatherland Notes), November, 1877.

structure, I see three possibilities, each of which has been and is made use of in sociological theories and in different accounts of the system of social relations, though not always with a distinct conceptual awareness.

1) In the general sense each group which is regarded as one of the basic components of the social structure may be called a "class" of the social structure. I shall be considering the interpretation of the expression "one of the basic components of the social structure" in the following chapter. In any case such a comprehensive concept includes both estate and caste, and also class in the second and third meanings distinguished here.

2) Of the two specifying versions of the concept of class which I should like to consider here, the first shows us a social class as a group distinguished in respect of the relations of property. We formulate this criterion in a quite general way, or rather we indicate only the kind of criterion involved, because this version, i.e. the economic version of the concept of social class, may vary in content in different definitions. This framework allows room for the definitions of both Adam Smith and Madison, for the age-old division of men into rich, poor and moderately well-to-do, for the Marxian division of classes according to their relation to the means of production, and for the economic definition of social class found in the early American sociologists (Ward, Small, Giddings and Cooley).

The economic criteria which are involved in the concept of class in all varieties of this version neither coincide with nor exclude the criteria which determine the extension of such concepts as estate or caste. Some caste or estate-systems can at the same time be economic-class systems, but such a coincidence can only be empirically established. In cases where such a coincidence does apply one can speak of the "class" aspect of caste relations or the "estate" aspect of the class-system.

In a somewhat different meaning it is also possible to speak of the "class" aspect of an estate-system or a caste-system even when the coincidence does not occur, if we assume that between an estate-system and a class-system there holds some more or less complicated causal dependence. This is precisely the Marxian assumption. The view, not formulated by the Marxists, that all the historical struggles between estates, which are not separate classes in the economic sense, were in reality disguised class struggles, would correspond to the well-known view about the true nature of the religious conflicts in history.

3) In the second version specifying the concept of class, the class-system is contrasted with group-systems in the social structure in which an individual's membership of a group is institutionally determined and in which privileges or discriminations result from an individual's ascription to a certain group. In contradistinction to such groups of a caste or estate type, a class in this version is a group of which membership is not assigned by a birth-certificate nor any official docu-

[1] Cf. p. 44, *Class Structure in the Social Consciousness.*

ment, such as a title of nobility or an act of manumission, but is the consequence of social status otherwise achieved. The privileges and discriminations, which in this case require no sanction from any source, are not the effect but the cause of the individual's placement in the capitalist or proletarian class: one is reckoned among the capitalists because one possesses capital, and one belongs to the proletariat because one possesses no other sources of income than the capacity to hire out one's labour. The ideal type of privileges and discriminations that fix an individual's social status regardless of the social categories to which this individual may belong are the economic privileges and discriminations found in a system of free competition: property, income, the way in which one works for a living.

In various social systems one can observe two or more coexisting types of the relation of class dependence (using the term class in its widest sense). The two specifying versions of the concept of class are nevertheless most closely connected with an unrestricted capitalist system. In the former version, however, a class can at the same time be a caste or an estate, whereas in the latter these concepts are mutually exclusive. In contradistinction to groups whose composition and privileges have the sanction of political or religious institutions, a social class in the latter version comes into being "spontaneously", by the force of events.

This is the usual way in which the term "class" is used by contemporary sociologists of a non-Marxist persuasion. Hence we find the terms "caste" and "class" contrasted in dictionaries of the social sciences, and hence such titles as "Caste and Class in a Southern Town".

Incidentally we should note that, as seen from the viewpoint of the third conception, social classes, in the sense of so-called "high society" and in general classes in a scheme of synthetic gradation,[1] should be regarded as a sort of synthesis of caste and class — at least in societies where some estate traditions survive.

Because of the absence of terminological distinctions, "class" has different meanings in different contexts. It means one thing when one speaks of the "overlapping of a caste and a class structure", and something else when we speak of the "history of class societies" or the "history of the class struggle". In these cases the meaning of the term is determined by its context. This may not evoke misunderstandings as to the denotation of the term, but it does imply the risk mentioned above. Moreover the burdening of the term "class" with an ambiguous content makes it more difficult to analyse the structure of modern societies with nationalized means of production.

Terminological suggestions

The adjustment of the terminology to the conceptual apparatus can be affected in two ways. If we keep the term "class" for the superordinate concept, we shall have to use specifying qualifications for "class" in its second and third meanings. Thus the "overlapping of an estate and a class structure", used with reference to Poland in the great period of the *szlachta*, or to France under the last Bourbons, would be an overlapping of two different social-class systems, like the "overlapping of a caste and a class structure" in the United States or India.

On the other hand, if, following prevailing usage in modern sociology, the term "class" is reserved for the narrower concept in its first or second version, it will be necessary to find a term for the more comprehensive concept. This is no easy task if we wish to avoid introducing semantic conventions which completely disregard the usage of colloquial speech and the terminological traditions of the social sciences.

In search of a common conceptual content

In general conceptions of social structure, especially where different forms of social order are involved, we usually have to deal with the widest concept of class, just as we do in general theories concerned with the class determination of cultural phenomena. But even when matters are not complicated by the threefold denotation of the term "social class" discussed above, this has been interpreted in various ways, not only in colloquial speech but also in scientific literature, as the divergent definitions of class bring out clearly.

We now have to consider whether the conceptions which we are comparing have any common ground, and to what extent the representatives of different viewpoints are in agreement about the basic characteristics of social structure in respect of which they speak of the "class" character of societies. To put this differently, we are faced by the question: what common conceptual content can be found in definitions which disagree with each other?

It seems to me that we can point to at least three generally accepted assumptions relating to the concept of class and the "class" society. These appear most frequently in the form of implicit assumptions discoverable in the course of discussion. The main reasons why these assumptions are usually not explicitly formulated in definitions is that they seem to be self-explanatory or that they are implied by the definition. If they seem self-explanatory, it is because they are generally accepted.

The three assumptions which appear to be common to all conceptions of a "class" society can be stated in the following manner:

1) The classes constitute a system of the most comprehensive groups in the social structure.

2) The class division concerns social statuses connected with a system of privileges and discriminations not determined by biological criteria.

3) The membership of individuals in a social class is relatively permanent.

In the first assumption two elements must be distinguished: *a*) that classes are the most comprehensive groups; *b*) that classes form a system of such groups. By the most comprehensive groups in the social structure I understand here a small number of groups — two or more — differentiated in consequence of the division of society according to criteria that are important in social life. The second element introduced by this assumption involves treating a class as a member of a certain system of relations. This means that the definition of any class must take into account the relation of this class to the other groups in this system. To explain who is a proletarian in the Marxian sense we must bring in the concept of a capitalist. When we speak of a middle class we assume the existence of a lower class and an upper class. This constitutes a fundamental distinction between a social class and occupational groups, irrespective of their size. In this respect occupational groups can be compared with ethnic or religious groups; they can be described without reference to their relation with each other. Thus at the moment when we begin to regard an occupational group for example, farmers, priests, or warriors in certain social systems, as a component of the system of basic groups in a social structure, this occupational group become a social class, without ceasing — from another viewpoint — to be an occupational group. In the same way, an ethnic or religious group can also in certain cases become a social class.

The second assumption has been formulated in so general a manner as to be applicable both to divisions made with reference to the functions of the different classes in economic life and to divisions concerned with the relative share in the national income. It has also been formulated in such a way that class divisions may include divisions corresponding to a system of non-economic privileges and discriminations (some caste-systems) or to a system of privileges and discriminations dependent in different ways on economic status but not directly fixed by it. We have encountered such divisions in, for instance, conceptions of synthetic gradation. The assumption under discussion refers equally to groups differentiated, as it were, by an absolute division of privileges and discriminations (privileged and under-privileged groups) and to groups which differ from one another *in the type* of privileges and discriminations associated with them. In this way, this assumption can be applied even when it is accepted that each class has its privileges and its duties, associated with different social functions, as some supporters of the class system have tried to show with the aid of a functional interpretation of inter-class relations. The reservation with regard to biological criteria excludes the privileges and discriminations assigned directly by sexual criteria.

In the third assumption I am thinking of the sort of situation in which a transition from one group to another is made by some individuals only, and where the rule is rather to remain within one's own group throughout one's life. Herein social classes differ from levels in an official hierarchy or from the age-groups that play so important a part in the structure of pre-capitalist societies, and particularly in the so-called "primitive" societies. The relative permanence of class membership constitutes a necessary condition of a "class" society according, it would seem, to all the conceptions which we have considered.

Various criteria and common assumptions

The three common assumptions just considered are, as I have already pointed out, usually accorded tacit acceptance. On the other hand, it is other characteristics of the social-class structure that are usually mentioned as the fundamental characteristics of a class-system. On the basis of the former implicit assumptions, we can discern in the latter characteristics different criteria of social classes. In the light of the discussion so far, it would seem that out of the whole variety of ways of conceiving the social structure, out of all the differing manners of understanding class, one can elicit three or four such characteristics. They are by no means of equal importance in the history of social thought.

1) The first of these characteristics is the vertical order of social classes: the existence of superior and inferior categories of social statuses, which are superior and inferior in respect of some system of privileges and discriminations. When one accepts such a criterion, "class structure" means as much as "class stratification".

For a broader interpretation privileges and discriminations of all kinds can be involved, provided that they are socially significant. In a narrower interpretation we are concerned only with relations of wealth and power. Materially speaking, it is not very important which of these interpretations is chosen, because socially-significant privileges are usually included in the relations of wealth and power. The emphasis laid on the privileges of wealth and power seems to me advisable because of the connexion of the concept of class with the problems from which it arose, namely, the connexion with important practical problems and with the clashes

between ideologies which make use of the term. For it is this connexion that gives the concept of class a particular importance. The Marxist theory of classes uses a still narrower criterion, taking as the basis of the vertical order the privilege of exploiting other men's labour. The classes are placed in a hierarchical order with reference to this fundamental privilege, which is conditioned by the different relations of particular classes to the means of production.

2) The second characteristic is the distinctness of permanent class interests (a "class" society being regarded as a society that is divided into large groups with distinct, important and permanent interests). In a more extreme interpretation, one would speak not of the distinctness of class interests but of their conflicts: according to the traditional Smithian view, developed and popularized by the founders of Marxism, the source of these conflicts is to be found in the different modes of sharing in the national income, which are conditioned by different relations to the means of production.[1]

3) The third characteristic is class consciousness. The content of this concept may be more or less comprehensive. It may involve not only class identification but also a consciousness of the place of one's class in the class-hierarchy, a realization of class distinctness and class interests and, possibly, of class solidarity as well. A "class" society in this sense is a society in which the majority of active members possess class consciousness, and this is reflected in their behaviour.

4) Finally, the fourth of those characteristics which can provide a basis for belief that a given society is a "class" society is social isolation. The absence of closer social contacts; social distance — this is the behavioural criterion of class divisions, which undoubtedly plays an important part in the social consciousness of different milieux, and not only in caste and estate cultures. On this criterion is based the definition of class used by some social scientists in the United States: according to this definition a social class is the largest group of people whose members have intimate social access to one another.[2] Using this sort of criterion, some observers in the last quarter of the nineteenth century divided Warsaw society into five social classes. A society is a "class" society in respect of this characteristic if there exist within it distinct barriers to social intercourse and if class boundaries can be drawn by means of an analysis of inter-personal relations.

When one speaks of the "class" character of a given society from this viewpoint, one usually finds that not only is social isolation involved but also the effects of this isolation and the effects of differences in the degree of access to the means of consumption. Here I am thinking of cultural cleavages and the feeling that people belonging to different classes are strangers to each other. The members of different classes differ in customs and modes of behaviour and speech. The latter may be differences of vocabulary and pronunciation, or differences in the actual language spoken. In Haiti, the members of the upper class speak French, while lower class people speak

---

[1] We speak of the *distinctness* of class interests when what serves or does not serve the interest of one class does not affect the interest of another class. The *conflict* of interests arises when something that serves the interest of one class is to the disadvantage of another class and *vice versa*. One can obviously speak of conflicts of class interests both from the viewpoint of the classes concerned and from the viewpoint of the theorist, who may consider that the members of this or that class are not generally aware of their "essential" class interests.

[2] A. Davis and J. Dollard, *Children of Bondage*, Washington, p. 13. See also *ibid.*, p. 259. (Both quotations are taken from Myrdal, *op. cit.*, pp. 673, 1378.) J. Schumpeter accepts as a criterion of class in racially homogeneous milieux a connexion expressed by the range of marital eligibility. "We find a suitable definition of the class — one that makes it outwardly recognisable and involves no class theory (*sic*.) — in the fact that intermarriage prevails among its members, socially rather than legally." "Imperialism and Social Theory", 1951, quoted from *Class, Status and Power*, ed. Bendix and Lipset, Free Press 1953, p. 77. (The article by Schumpeter also appears elsewhere in this edition. — ed.).

Creole.[1] The feeling of class distance with which the educated strata regarded the "mob" was brought out in an arresting manner by the Polish writer Stefan Żeromski in his *Homeless People*, written in 1898. In 1936, L. W. Doob describing the "poor whites" in the Southern States, wrote that the people of this class could be distinguished even in their appearance from other inhabitants of Southern towns as easily as a Negro could be distinguished by his pigmentation.[2] In the period preceding the changes of recent years in post-war Poland, the witty Warsaw cockneys defined the two classes in socialist countries by the terms 'proletariat' and 'chevroletariat'.[3]

Disraeli compared the two social classes in England to two nations,[4] and the same comparison may be encountered in Engels' study of the conditions of the English working class published in 1845. Contemporary Soviet writers regard a distinctive "socio-political and spiritual profile"[5] as one of the fundamental class characteristics, in a similar way as those American sociologists who regard class as a socio-psychological phenomenon.[6]

The interdependence of characteristics

The class criteria enumerated above are not independent of one another. It is hard to doubt that social stratification — a class hierarchy of privileges and discriminations — implies conflicts of class interests. Class consciousness and class isolation find their explanation in class stratification and conflict of interests. Those who take class consciousness as a criterion of the class-system, as contemporary American sociologists do, do not question the "objectivity" of the conditions from which this consciousness arises.

If the characteristics which we have specified as different versions of the criterion of a class-system are inter-dependent, then various definitions of a class society may in reality differ less between themselves than one would believe in view of the different formulations. Although one or another characteristic may be used in particular definitions of a class society, the description of that society which supplements the definitions may contain all these characteristics. At this point the differences between the different conceptions may be reduced above all to differences of opinion as to which trait of a "class society" is regarded as "primary", the most important from the viewpoint of causal dependence, or the most distinctive or the most socially-significant in some other respects. Do we follow Marx in placing the main emphasis on the system of privileges and discriminations, on exploitation and in general on asymmetrical relations of dependence? Or do we follow Madison or Max Weber (when he is speaking of class structure) in stressing the distinctness of interests? Or again, are we at one with modern American sociologists in acknowledging class consciousness as the most socially-important fact in the domain of inter-group relations, and do we, in describing a "class" society — despite the suggestive terminology — give primacy to the characteristics which Weber links with his concept of an estate, not with the concept of class?[7]

[1] The Haitian *langue créole* is a peculiar mixture of French dialect and Spanish, with a few African elements. A recent book by B. Ryan affords an eloquent example of the fourth criterion of the class character of a society in post-war Ceylon. Here the two basic urban classes are "an English-educated, shoe-and-trousers-wearing, white-collar and professional upper class, and the saronged, barefooted vernacular-speaking labor class". *Caste in Modern Ceylon*, New Brunswick, 1953; quotation from the review of this study in the *American Sociological Review*, Oct. 1954.

[2] L. W. Doob: "Poor Whites: a Frustrated Class" (published as an appendix to John Dollard's book: *Caste and Class in a Southern Town*, New York, 1949, first published 1957).

In an article already cited, M. Rosenberg writes: "An important social characteristic likely to engender awareness of class differences are styles of life visibly represented by consumption items. In large parts of Europe the rich are clearly set off from the poor by items requiring a large financial investment, such as bath tubs and inside plumbing, the possession of automobiles, the wearing of a suit for weekday use. In mediaeval Europe the classes (or estates) could be visibly differentiated by the possession of horses and armor." "Perceptual Obstacles to Class Consciousness", *Social Force*, Oct. 1953.

[3] Before 1956 there was a raising of wage-scales in various sectors in Poland, in which the benefit went for the most part to those who had previously earned most. I heard this wage-policy defended on the following economic grounds. The small stocks of consumer goods available in the country — so ran the argument — make it impossible to raise the wages of the majority of employees. On the other hand, an increase in the income of those whose earnings are several times higher than the average does not constitute a threat to the stock of consumer goods which the mass of people are interested in obtaining. This is so not only because only relatively small numbers of people are affected but above all because the budget of those who earn high wages contains different items. An increase in their incomes will not produce an increase in the consumption of bread, butter, sausage or cheap clothing, nor will it swell the crowds in cheap eating-houses; instead it will be used for luxuries which could not in any case have figured in the budget of people who earn less than the average. In this connexion it was explained that the importation or production of luxury goods is essential, either because of trade agreements, or of the need to develop production techniques, or for prestige reasons. So far as I know, these arguments had a real influence on the decisions taken by the makers of economic policy in Poland, and probably in other countries with a socialist economy as well. If the premises on which the arguments are based correspond to reality, it means that in a socialist country too we could be faced with some traits of a social structure consisting of two collectivities, each living in an entirely different manner — according to the indices of consumption, as envisaged by our fourth criterion of a class system. The terms "proletariat" and "chevroletariat" used above are a way of expressing the sociological aspect of an economic harmony of this kind.

[4] *Sybil or the Two Nations*, London, 1845.

[5] T. Gubariev: 'O priodolenii klassovykh razlichii b SSSR' (About the overcoming of class differences in the U.S.S.R.), *Bolshevik*, 1951, No. 5.

[6] Those in this country who speak of the "middle class" as our largest cohesive social group . . . refer to those millions of Americans who share, in general, common values, attitudes and aspirations. Such spokesmen reiterate a view presented "scientifically" by the Sociological Fathers. Charles H. Page, *Class and American Sociology*, New York, 1940, p. 254.

[7] "In contrast to classes, status groups (*Stände*) are normally communities. They are, however, often of a rather amorphous kind. In contrast to the purely economically determined "class situation", we wish to designate as "status situation" every typical component of the life fate of men that is determined by a specific, positive or negative, social estimation of

Differences of opinion as to the essence of the "class" nature of "class" societies are not however only a matter of emphasis. If the different criteria which are taken as the basis of various definitions of a "class" society are not independent of one another, this does not mean that one can assume that they are permanently present together. The various conceptions may differ not only in respect of the particular characteristic of the class-system which they single out as fundamental but also because some take three or four conditions into consideration, while others take only two. The common basic assumptions concerned with the concept of class sometimes make it difficult to see clearly whether, when faced by discrepant definitions, we are in fact dealing with differences of conceptual apparatus or with contradictory views regarding the scope of the phenomena which is established by these common assumptions.

"Class" character as a characteristic of social structure admitting of gradation

A society may be more or less class-divided and its "class" character may be more or less rich in content. Elsewhere[1] I have pointed out that Marx, in calling a class without class consciousness a "stratum" or a "class in itself" (*Klasse an sich*), in contrast to a "class for itself" (*Klasse für sich*), was expressing his conviction that a class fully deserves the name of "class" only if its members are conscious of class interests and feel class solidarity. Without accepting any one particular characteristic as a necessary condition of a class-system, one can nevertheless regard such a characteristic as an important factor in intensifying the "class" nature of a society.

Moreover, probably all the characteristics with which we are concerned here admit of gradation. This is true of the permanence of class membership, that is to say of the stability of class divisions. In other words, in different "class" societies there exists a differing degree of probability that an individual will remain in his class until the end of his life. An extreme example of this is caste-affiliation, which is life-long, determined before the individual's birth and passed on unconditionally to his descendants. At the other extreme would be the society that satisfies the ideals of Lincoln, who approved of all the three social statuses that correspond to Marx's

[1] See Chapter V, *Class Structure in the Social Consciousness*.
[2] "I want every man to have a chance — and I believe a black man is entitled to it — in which he can better his condition — when he may look forward and hope to be a hired laborer this year and next, work for himself afterwards, and finally to hire men to work for him. That is the true system." Speech in New Haven, 6 March 1860, quoted by Myrdal, *op. cit.*, p. 670.

honor. This honor may be connected with any quality shared by a plurality.... In content, status honor is normally expressed by the fact that above all else a specific style of life can be expected from all those who wish to belong to the circle." (From Max Weber, *Essays in Sociology*, Routledge & Kegan Paul, 1947, pp. 186–187.)

three basic classes, provided that each man should be able during his lifetime to achieve each of the three statuses, beginning as a hired labourer, later working for himself, and with the hope that in the future he himself might be able to benefit from the hired labour of others.[2]

Other characteristics admitting of gradation are those concerned with the distinctness of class boundaries, the range of social inequalities, and the cleavages or conflicts of class interests. Class consciousness is also a matter of degree, both where it concerns the prevalence of class consciousness and also its content and emotional charge. Finally, "class" societies differ in the degree of social isolation and social contacts across class boundaries. There is a wide range in this respect between the *mores* of contemporary Scandinavian countries and those found in societies with estate traditions, like Spain, Hungary, or Poland in the second half of the nineteenth century. Nor should we forget caste-societies, where group separation is supported by severe formal sanctions.

In addition, a society may be regarded as more or less class-divided both with regard to the *number* of class criteria which it displays and the *degree* to which particular class characteristics can be attributed to it. From this viewpoint we can compare different societies as historical phenomena, and also different images of the same society.

The model of a class as a basic group

Like other concepts relating to social life and culture the concept of class has been formed according to a model adopted by way of exemplification. If my earlier examination is accurate in this respect, the same model corresponds closely to different conceptions of class, even when these give discrepant definitions.

The model of a class is made up of several different characteristics admitting of gradation. Several criteria overlap in it, and the absence of one criterion may be offset by a higher degree of another characteristic, just as in the evaluation of a work of art a lower level of artistic technique may be offset, for instance, by originality of idea or power of expression. A work of art can be a work of art to a greater or lesser degree, just as a social class may be a class to a greater or lesser degree.

The point now is to determine the limit: what deviations from the model are permissible? The criteria which make up the model of a social class are not commensurable, any more than the criteria which make up the model of a work of art. There is no objective measure which would enable one to establish the degree of originality in a work of art which would make up for a certain degree of technical deficiency. Nor is there an objective measure which could establish the degree of rigidity of class boundaries which could offset, say, a lack of class consciousness. As the criteria are not commensurable, the final decision as to what is and what is not a social class must ultimately be reached by intuitive judgments made in a given milieu about the importance of various criteria (compare the conceptions of American sociologists), or by considering practical consequences and the requirements of action (compare the Marxist theory of class).

Exhaustive and non-exhaustive divisions

The extension of the concept of class becomes narrower or wider according to the degree of strictness with which one regards deviations from the model of the particular class concept used, according to the degree of tolerance employed in offsetting one criterion against another. If the concept of class is strictly applied, it may not cover all the groups that are differentiated in the social structure. In that event not every member of the society will belong to a class, just as in the Indian caste system there are people who do not belong to any caste.

The division of a society into classes may therefore be either an exhaustive or a non-exhaustive one, for, depending on the way in which class is conceived, a society may be either a system of classes, or a system of classes and groups that resemble classes to a certain degree but are not comprised in the concept of class. As I have already said, the Marxists usually call these groups "strata"; thus a society may, according to the Marxist conception, be composed not only of classes but also of "strata" which do not fall under any class. In this respect, Marx in his "18th Brumaire" took up an indecisive position in respect of the French peasantry, an important component of French society which deviated from the class model in its lack of consciousness of class interests.

According to Marx and the Marxists, the *lumpenproletariat* is not a class because it does not take part in the process of production. Nor, though for quite other reasons, is the intelligentsia a class. In this case the deviation from the model is excessive. On the other hand, Stalin and his followers considered that the deviation of the "non-antagonistic classes" in the Soviet Union from the model of class, a model which after all included class antagonism as one of its characteristics, did not prevent the working class and the *kolchoz* — peasantry — in the Soviet Union from being recognized as classes. In this Stalinist conception of society, in which there are classes without class antagonisms and without class stratification, only the intelligentsia would not fall under the concept of class and would be named a "stratum".

American and West European sociologists, for whom the term "social class" does not fulfil those social functions which it was made to perform by the Marxian school of thought, have conceived the concept of class so widely that the division into classes may be an exhaustive division, that is to say, that every individual in the society may be included in a social class. Only if they conceive social structure from a different point of view do they make use of the term "stratum". Although it differs from the division of society into classes,

the division of society into strata is also an exhaustive one.

Types of deviation from the model

The deviations from the model are not only a question of defining the concept of class with a broader or narrower scope. The various conceptions which start from the same model differ not only in the degree of permissible deviations or in the exhaustive or non-exhaustive nature of the division of society into classes but also in the type of deviation. In the different conceptions the emphasis is laid on one or another of the various characteristics contained in the model of social class; one or another characteristic is regarded as the "basic" one, and the extension of the concept of class permits one or another form of compensation, both as regards the choice of characteristics chosen for such compensation and the differing degree in which these characteristics should be present. Differences of this kind occur not only when we are dealing with different schemes of social structure but also when we are concerned with the same scheme applied to different cases. We noted this in the instance of the dichotomic scheme as interpreted by the followers of Saint-Simon and, on the other hand, by Babeuf or the authors of the *Communist Manifesto*.

The model of a proletarian and the denotation of the proletariat

Indistinct images of class structure may not only have their origin in deviations from the model of a social class; they may also stem from the models of particular classes. In the Marxist view of social classes in a capitalistic system the social class *par excellence*, the class which is nearest to the general model of a class, is the proletariat, and the Marxist model of a proletarian is that of a class-conscious factory worker. The Marxist model of the proletariat does not coincide in extension with the Marxist definition, which gives as characteristics defining the proletarian the fact of working for hire and a low share in the national income (a share that does not correspond to the "surplus value" produced by the proletarian).

The definition allows manifold deviations from the model of a proletarian, for it also covers wage-workers who are not class-conscious, those who do not work in factories and those who do not do manual work. When the boundaries of the proletariat are being drawn, the first two of these 'deviant' groups do not give rise to any doubts. Marxism recognizes both proletarians who lack class-consciousness and an agricultural or cottage-industry proletariat. On the other hand, the Marxist standpoint with regard to the third category, that of hired workers who do not work with their hands, is uncertain. The founders of Marxism and their followers often use the terms 'proletariat' and 'working class' as synonyms. If manual labour is not included is the set of criteria that define a proletarian then the proletariat is not coextensive in scope with the working class; but if manual labour is included, then white-collar workers, who have a low share in the national income, do not belong to any class.

Conceptual precision and practical requirements

In sociological studies attempts to provide a precise concept of class have been expressed in a number of definitions which suggest a new usage of the term (henceforth to be called 'projecting definitions') and in suggestions proposing certain terminological distinctions.

But the concept of class has long been an *idée force* in social movements and the term "class" has become an instrument of action. In changing circumstances an instrument is more convenient when it lends itself to many uses. For a politician or for a social leader a discussion of the extension of the concept of class is academic. In general discussions he works with models: the proletariat *par excellence* is more convenient on such occasions than the proletariat determined according to one definition or another. In the same way it is more convenient in general discussions to use the concept of class *par excellence*. When one turns to concrete problems, on the other hand, the extension of the concepts is widened according to need and greatly exceeds that of the model. At the same time a suggestion is left that the designata of both terms correspond to the models originally used.

Two

Historical and Comparative Studies

Stages in the Social History of Capitalism[1]
Henri Pirenne

IN THE PAGES that follow I wish only to develop a hypothesis. Perhaps after having read them, the reader will find the evidence insufficient. I do not hesitate to recognize that the scarcity of special studies bearing upon my subject, at least for the period since the end of the Middle Ages, is of a nature to discourage more than one cautious spirit. But, on the one hand, I am convinced that every effort at synthesis, however premature it may seem, cannot fail to react usefully on investigations, provided one offers it in all frankness for what it is. And, on the other hand, the kind reception which the ideas here presented received at the International Congress of Historical Studies held at London last April, and the desire which has been expressed to me by scholars of widely differing tendencies to see them in print, have induced me to publish them. Various objections which have been expressed to me, as well as my own subsequent reflections, have caused me to revise and complete on certain points my London address. In the essential features, however, nothing has been changed.

A word first of all to indicate clearly the point of view which characterizes the study. I shall not enter into the question of the formation of capital itself, that is, of the sum total of the goods employed by their possessor to produce more goods at a profit. It is the capitalist alone, the holder of capital, who will hold our attention. My purpose is simply to characterize, for the various epochs of economic history, the nature of this capitalist and to search for his origin. I have observed, in surveying this history from the beginning of the Middle Ages to our own times, a very interesting phenomenon to which, so it seems to me, attention has not yet been sufficiently called. I believe that, for each period into which our economic history may be divided, there is a distinct and separate class of capitalists. In other words, the group of capitalists of a given epoch does not spring from the capitalist group of the preceding epoch. At every change in economic organization we find a breach of continuity. It is as if the capitalists who have up to that time been active, recognize that they are incapable of adapting themselves to conditions which are evoked by needs hitherto unknown and which call for methods hitherto unemployed. They withdraw from the struggle and become an aristocracy, which if it again plays a part in the course of affairs, does so in a passive manner only, assuming the role of silent partners. In their place arise new men, courageous and enterprising, who boldly permit themselves to be driven by the wind actually blowing and who know how to trim their sails to take advantage of it, until the day comes when, its direction changing and disconcerting their manoeuvres, they in

[1] This article represents the substance of an address delivered at the International Congress of Historical Studies held in London, April, 1913.

Reprinted from "The Stages in the Social History of Capitalism," *American Historical Review* (1914), pp. 494–515, by permission of the editor. (Copyright, 1914, American Historical Review.)

their turn pause and are distanced by new crafts having fresh forces and new directions. In short, the permanence throughout the centuries of a capitalist class, the result of a continuous development and changing itself to suit changing circumstances, is not to be affirmed. On the contrary, there are as many classes of capitalists as there are epochs in economic history. That history does not present itself to the eye of the observer under the guise of an inclined plane; it resembles rather a staircase, every step of which rises abruptly above that which precedes it. We do not find ourselves in the presence of a gentle and regular ascent, but of a series of lifts.

In order to establish the validity of these generalizations it is of course needful to control them by the observation of facts, and the longer the period of time covered thereby the more convincing will the observations be. The economic history of antiquity is still too little known, and its relations to the ages which follow have escaped us too completely, for us to take our point of departure there; but the beginning of the Middle Ages gives us access to a body of material sufficient for our purpose.

But first of all, it is needful to meet a serious objection. If it is in fact true, as seems to be usually conceded since the appearance of Bücher's brilliant *Entstehung der Volkswirtschaft*[1] — to say nothing here of the thesis since formulated with such extreme radicalism by W. Sombart[2] — that the economic organization of the Middle Ages has no aspect to which one can rightly apply the term capitalistic, then our thesis is limited wholly to modern times and there can be no thought of introducing into the discussion the centuries preceding the Renaissance. But whatever may be the favor which it still enjoys, the theory which refuses to perceive in the medieval urban economy the least trace of capitalism has found in recent times ever increasing opposition. I will not even enumerate here the studies which seem to me to have in an incontrovertible manner established the fact that all the essential features of capitalism — individual enterprise, advances on credit, commercial profits, speculation, etc. — are to be found from the twelfth century on, in the city republics of Italy — Venice,[3] Genoa,[4] or Florence[5] I shall not ask what one can call such a navigator as Romano Mairano (1152–1201), if, in spite of the hundreds of thousands of francs he employed in business, the fifty per cent profits he realized on his operations in coasting trade, and his final failure, one persists in refusing to him the name of capitalist. I shall pass over the disproof

of the alleged ignorance of the medieval merchants. I shall say nothing of the astonishing errors committed in the calculations, so confidently offered to us as furnishing mathematical proof of the naïveté of historians who can believe the commerce of the thirteenth and fourteenth centuries to have been anything more than that of simple peddlers, a sort of artisans incapable of rising even to the idea of profit, and having no views beyond the day's livelihood.[6] Important as all this may be, the weak point in the theory which I am here opposing seems to me to lie especially in a question of method. Bücher and his partisans, in my opinion, have, without sufficient care, used for their picture of the city economy of the Middle Ages, the characteristic of the German towns and more particularly the German towns of the fourteenth and fifteenth centuries. Now the great majority of the German towns of that period were far from having attained the degree of development which had been reached by the great communes of northern Italy, of Tuscany, or of the Low Countries. Instead of presenting the classical type of urban economy, they are merely examples of it incompletely developed; they present only certain manifestations; they lack others, and particularly those which belong to the domain of capitalism. Therefore in presenting as true of all the cities of the Middle Ages a theory which rests only on the observation of certain of them, and those the least advanced, one is necessarily doing violence to reality. Bücher's description of *Stadtwirtschaft* remains a masterpiece of penetration and economic understanding. But it is too restricted. It does not take account of certain elements of the problem, because these elements were not encountered in the narrow circle which the research covered. One may be confident that if, instead of proceeding from the analysis of such towns as Frankfort, this study had considered Florence, Genoa, and Venice, or even Ghent, Bruges, Ypres, Douai, or Tournai, the picture which it furnished us would have been very different. Instead of refusing to see capitalism of any kind in the economic life of the bourgeoisie, the author would have recognized, on the contrary, unmistakable evidences of capitalism. I shall later have occasion to return to this very essential question. But it was indispensable to indicate here the position which I shall take in regard to it.

Of course I do not at all intend to reject *en bloc* the ideas generally agreed upon concerning the urban economy of the Middle Ages. On the contrary, I believe them to be entirely accurate in their essential elements, and I am persuaded that, in a very large number of cases, I will even say, if you like, in the majority of cases, they provide us with a theory which is completely satisfactory. I am very far from maintaining that capitalism exercised a preponderant influence on the character of economic organization from the twelfth to the fifteenth centuries. I believe that, though it is not right to call this organization "acapitalistic," it is on the other hand correct to consider it "anticapitalistic." But to affirm this is to affirm the existence of

---

[1] First edition in 1893.

[2] *Der Modern Capitalismus* (1902).

[3] R. Heynen, *Zur Entstehung des Capitalismus in Venedig* (1905).

[4] H. Sieveking, "Die Capitalistische Entwickelung in den Italienischen Städten des Mittelalters." *Vierteljahrschrift für Sozial- und Wirtschaftsgeschichte* (1909).

[5] Davidsohn, *Forschungen zur Geschichte von Florenz*, III 36; A. Doren, *Die Florentiner Wollentuchindustrie*, p. 481.

[6] A. Schaube, "Die Wollausfuhr Englands von 1272," *Vierteljahrschrift für Sozial- und Wirtschaftsgeschichte* (1908), pp. 39 ff. Cf. F. Keutgen, "Hansische Handelsgesellschaften," *Ibid.* (1906), pp. 288 ff.

capital. That organization recognized the existence of capital since it tried to defend itself against it, since, from the end of the thirteenth century onward, it took more and more measures to escape from its abuses. It is incontestable that, from this period on, it succeeded by legal force in diminishing the role which capitalism had played up to that time. In fact it is certain, and we shall have occasion to observe it, that the power of capital was much greater during the first part of the urban period of the Middle Ages than during the second. But even in the course of the latter period, if municipal legislation seems more or less completely to have shut it out from local markets, capital succeeded in preserving and in dominating a very considerable portion of economic activity. It is capital which rules in inter-local commerce, which determines the forms of credit, and which, fastening itself on all the industries which produce not for the city market but for exportation, hinders them from being controlled, as the others are, by the minute regulations which in innumerable ways cramp the activity of the craftsmen.[1]

Let us recognize, then, that capitalism is much older than we have ordinarily thought it. No doubt its operation in modern times has been much more engrossing than in the Middle Ages. But that is only a difference of quantity, not a difference of quality, a simple difference of intensity not a difference of nature. Therefore, we are justified in setting the question we set at the beginning. We can, without fear of pursuing a vain shadow, endeavor to discern what throughout history have been the successive stages in the social evolution of capitalism.

Of the period which preceded the formation of towns, that is, of the period preceding the middle of the eleventh century, we know too little to permit ourselves to tarry there. What may still have survived in Italy and in Gaul of the economic system of the Romans has disappeared before the beginning of the eighth century. Civilization has become strictly agricultural and the domain system has impressed its form upon it. The land, concentrated in large holdings in the hands of a powerful landed aristocracy, barely produces what is necessary for the proprietor and his *familia*. Its harvests do not form material for commerce. If during years of exceptional abundance the surplus is transported to districts where scarcity prevails, that is all. In addition certain commodities of ordinary quick consumption, and which nature has distributed unequally over the soil, such as wine or salt, sustain a sort of traffic. Finally, but more rarely, products manufactured by the rural industry of countries abounding in raw materials, such as, to cite only one, the friezes woven by the peasants of Flanders, maintain a feeble exportation. Of the condition of the *negociatores* who served as the instruments of these exchanges, we know almost nothing. Many of them were unquestionably merchants of occasion, men without a country, ready to seize on any means of existence that came their way. Pursuers of adventure were frequent among these roving creatures, half traders, half pirates, not unlike the Arab

merchants who even to our day have searched for and frequently have found fortunes amid the negro populations of Africa. At least, to read the history of that Samo who at the beginning of the eighth century, arriving at the head of a band of adventuring merchants among the Wends of the Elbe, ended by becoming their king, makes one think involuntarily of certain of those beys or sheiks encountered by voyagers to the Congo or the Katanga.[2] Clearly no one will try to find in this strong and fortunate bandit an ancestor of the capitalists of the future. Commerce, as he understood and practised it, blended with plunder, and if he loved gain it was not in the manner of a man of affairs but rather in that of a primitive conqueror with whom violence of appetite took the place of calculation. Samo was evidently an exception. But the spirit which inspired him may have inspired a goodly number of *negociatores* who launched their barks on the streams of the ninth century. In the society of this period only the possession of land or attachment to the following of a great man could give one a normal position. Men not so provided were outside the regular classification, forming a confused mass, in which were promiscuously mingled professional beggars, mercenaries in search of employment, masters of barges or drivers of wagons, peddlers, traders, all jostling in the same sort of hazardous and precarious life, and all no doubt passing easily from one employment to another. This is not to say, however, that among the *negociatores* of the Frankish epoch there were not also individuals whose situation was more stable and whose means of existence were less open to suspicion. Indeed, we know that the great proprietors, lay or ecclesiastical, employed certain of their serfs or of their *ministeriales* in a sporadic commerce of which we have already mentioned above the principal features. They commissioned them to buy at neighbouring markets the necessary commodities or to transport to places of sale the occasional surplus of their grain or their wine. Here too we discover no trace of capitalism. We merely find ourselves in the presence of hereditary servants performing a gratuitous service, entirely analogous to military service.

Nevertheless commercial intercourse produced even then, in certain places particularly favored by their geographical situation, groups of some importance. We find them along the sea-coast — Marseilles, Rouen, Quentovic — or on the banks of the rivers, especially in those places where a Roman road crosses the stream, as at Maastricht on the Meuse or at Valenciennes on the Scheldt. We are to think of these *portus* as wharves for merchandise and as winter quarters for boats and boatmen. They differ very distinctly from the towns of the following period. No walls surround them; the buildings which are springing up seem to be scarcely more than wooden sheds, and the population which is found

---

[1] *Cf.* H. Pirenne, *Les Anciennes Democraties des Pays-Bas*, pp. 11 ff.

[2] I. Goll, "Samo und die Karantinischen Slaven," *Mitteilungen des Instituts für Oesterreichische Geschichtsforschung*, vol. XI.

there is a floating population, destitute of all privileges and forming a striking contrast to the bourgeoisie of the future. No organization seems to have bound together the adventurers and the voyagers of these *portus*. Doubtless it is possible, it is even probable, that a certain number of individuals, profiting by circumstances, may have little by little devoted themselves to trade in a regular fashion and have begun by the ninth century to form the nucleus of a group of professional traders. But we have too little information to enable us to speak with any precision.

The operations of credit follow much the same course. We cannot doubt that loans had been employed in the Carolingian period, and the Church as well as the State had occupied itself in combating their abuses.[1] But it would be a manifest exaggeration to deduce from this the existence of even a rudimentary capitalistic economy. Everything indicates that the loans which we are considering here were only occasional loans, of usurious nature, to which people who had met with some catastrophe, such as war, a fire, or a poor harvest, were forced to have recourse temporarily.

Thus, the early centuries of the Middle Ages seem to have been completely ignorant of the power of capital. They abound in wealthy landed proprietors, in rich monasteries, and we come upon hundreds of sanctuaries the treasure of which, supplied by the generosity of the nobles or the offerings of the faithful, crowds the altar with ornaments of gold or of solid silver. A considerable fortune is accumulated in the Church, but it is an idle fortune. The revenues which the landowners collect from their serfs or from their tenants are directed toward no economic purpose. They are scattered in alms, in the building of monuments, in the purchase of works of art, or of precious objects which should serve to increase the splendor of religious ceremonies. Wealth, capital, if one may so term it, is fixed motionless in the hands of an aristocracy, priestly or military. This is the essential condition of the patronage that this aristocracy (*majores et divites*) exercises over the people (*pauperes*). Its action is as important from the social point of view as it is important from that of economics. No part of it is directed toward the *negociatores*, who, left to themselves, live, so to speak, on the fringe of society. And so it will continue to be, for long centuries.

Landed property, indeed, did not contribute at all to that awakening of commercial activity which, after the disasters of the Norman invasion in the North and the Saracen raids on the shores of the Mediterranean, began to manifest itself toward the end of the tenth century and the beginning of the eleventh. Its preliminary manifestations are found at the two extremities of the Continent, Italy and the Low Countries. The interior seas, between which Europe was restricted in

[1] A. Dopsch, *Die Wirtschaftsentwicklung der Karolingerzeit*, II, 274. I cannot, however, accept the thesis of Mr. Dopsch on the importance of commerce in the Carolingian period. The extremely interesting texts which he has assembled seem to me to establish the existence of a sporadic commerce only.

her advance toward the Atlantic, were its first centres of activity. Venice, then Genoa and Pisa, venture on the coasting trade along their shores, and then maintain, with their rich neighbors of Byzantium or of the Mohammedan countries, a traffic which henceforward constantly increases. Meanwhile Bruges at the head of the estuary of the Zwyn, becomes the centre of a navigation radiating toward England, the shores of North Germany, and the Scandinavian regions. Thus, economic life, as in the beginning of Hellenic times, first becomes active along the coasts. But soon it penetrates into the interior of the country. Step by step it wins its way along the rivers and the natural routes. On this side and on that, it arouses the hinterland into which the harbors cut their indentations. In this process of growth the two movements finally meet, and bring into communication the people of the North and the people of the South. By the beginning of the twelfth century it is an accomplished fact. In 1127 Lombard merchants, journeying by the long route which descends from the passes of the Alps toward Champagne and the Low Countries, reach the fairs of Flanders.

If the feeble and precarious commercial activity of the Carolingian period was sufficient to create gathering-places of merchants at the points most frequented in travel, it is not difficult to understand that the steady progress of economic activity from the end of the tenth century would result in the formation, at the strategic points of regional transit, of aggregations of like character but much more important and more stable. The surface of the land, the direction and the depth of the streams, determining the routes of commerce, also determined the location of the towns. Indeed, European cities are the daughters of commerce and of industry. Unquestionably in the countries of old civilization, in Italy or in Gaul, the Roman cities had not completely disappeared. Within the circle of their walls, which had now become too large and were filled with ruins, there gathered, around the bishop resident in each of them, a whole population of clerics and monks, and beside them a lay population employed in their service or support. In the North, one found the same spectacle at the centres of the new dioceses, at Thérouanne, at Utrecht, at Magdeburg, or at Vienna. But here was no trace, properly speaking, of municipal life. A certain number of artisans, some of them serfs, a little weekly market for the most indispensable commodities, sometimes a fair visited by the merchant-adventurers of whom we have spoken above — this is the sum total of economic life.

But the situation changes from the moment when the increasing intensity of commerce begins to furnish men with new means of existence. Immediately one discovers an uninterrupted movement of migration of peasants from the country towards the places in which the handling of merchandise, the towing of boats, the service of merchants furnish regular occupations and arouse the hope of gain.

If the old cities disadvantageously placed at one side

from the highways of travel continue in their torpor, the others see their population increase continuously. Suburbs join the old enclosure; new markets are established; new churches are built for the new comers; and soon the primitive nucleus of the town, surrounded on all sides by the houses of the immigrants, becomes merely the quarter of the priests, bound to the shadow of the cathedral and submerged on all sides by the expansion of lay life. Much that at the beginning was the essential is now nothing more than the accessory. The episcopal burg disappears amid faubourgs.[1] The city has not been formed by growing with its own forces. It has been brought into existence by the attraction which it has exerted upon its surroundings whenever it has been aided by its situation. It is the creation of those who have migrated toward it. It has been made from without and not from within. The bourgeoisie of the oldest towns of Europe is a population of the transplanted. But it is at the same time essentially a trading population, and no other proof of this need be advanced than the fact that, down to the beginning of the twelfth century, *mercator* and *burgensis* were synonymous terms.

Whence came these pioneers of commerce, these immigrants seeking means of subsistence, and what resources did they bring with them into the rising towns? Doubtless only the strength of their arms, the force of their wills, the clearness of their intelligence. Agricultural life continued to be the normal life and none of those who remained upon the soil could entertain the idea of abandoning his holding to go to the town and take his chances in a new existence. As for selling the holding to get ready money, like the men of a modern rural population, no one at that time could have imagined such a transaction. The ancestors of the bourgeoisie must then be sought, specifically, in the mass of those wandering beings who, having no land to cultivate, floated across the surface of society, living from day to day upon the alms of the monasteries, hiring themselves to the cultivators of the soil in harvest time, enlisting in the armies in time of war, and shrinking from neither pillage nor rapine if the occasion presented itself. It may without difficulty be admitted that there may have been among them some rural artisans or some professional peddlers. But it is beyond question that with few exceptions it was poor men who floated to the towns and there built up the first fortunes in movable property that the Middle Ages knew.

Fortunately we possess certain narratives which enable

us to support this thesis with concrete examples. It will suffice to cite here the most characteristic of them, the biography of St. Godric of Finchale.[2]

He was born of poor peasants in Lincolnshire, toward the end of the eleventh century, and from infancy was forced to tax his ingenuity to find the means of livelihood. Like many other unfortunates of all times, he at first walked the beaches on the outlook for wreckage cast up by the sea. Then we see him, perhaps by reason of some fortunate find, setting up as a peddler and traveling through the country with a little pack of goods (*cum mercibus minutis*). At length he gathers together a small sum, and one fine day joins a troop of town merchants whom he has met in the course of his wanderings. Thenceforward he goes with his companions from market to market, from fair to fair, from town to town. Having thus become a professional merchant, he rapidly gains a sufficient sum to enable him to associate himself with other merchants, charter a boat with them, and engage in the coasting trade along the shores of England, Scotland, Denmark, and Flanders. The company is highly successful. Its operations consist in carrying to a foreign country goods which it knows to be uncommon there, in selling them there at a high price, and acquiring in exchange various merchandise which it takes pains to dispose of in the places where the demand for them is greatest and where it can consequently make the greatest gains. At the end of some years this prudent practice of buying cheap and selling dear has made of Godric, and doubtless of his associates, a man of important wealth. Then, touched by divine grace, he suddenly renounces his fortune, gives his goods to the poor, and becomes a monk.

The story of Godric, if one omits its pious conclusion, must have been that of many others. It shows us, with perfect clearness, how a man beginning with nothing might in a relatively short time amass a considerable capital. Our adventurer must have been favored by circumstances and chance. But the secret of his success, and the contemporary biographer to whom we owe the story insists strongly upon it, is intelligence.[3] Godric in fact shows himself a calculator, I might even say a speculator. He has in a high degree the feeling, and it is much more developed among minds without culture than is usually thought, for what is practicable in commerce. He is on fire with the love of gain. One sees clearly in him that famous *spiritus capitalisticus* of which some would have us believe that it dates only from the time of the Renaissance. Here is an eleventh-century merchant, associated with companions like himself, combining his purchases, reckoning his profits, and, instead of hiding in a chest the money he has gained, using it only to support and extend his business. More than this, he does not hesitate to devote himself to operations which the Church condemns. He is not disquieted by the theory of the just price; the Decretum of Gratian disapproves in express terms of the speculations which he practises: "Qui comparat rem ut illam

---

[1] Of course all the new towns did not grow up around an episcopal residence. Many of them, especially in the North and particularly in the Low Countries, had as their primitive nucleus a fortress (Ghent, Bruges, Ypres, Lille, Douai, etc.), But my purpose here is merely to recall the broad outlines of the subject.

[2] See on this subject the interesting article by W. Vogel, "Ein Seefahrender Kaufmann um 1100," *Hansische Geschichtsblätter* (1912), pp. 239 ff.

[3] "Unde non agriculturae delegit exercitia colere, sed potius, quae sagacioris animi sunt, rudimenta studuit arripiendo exercere."

ipsam integram et immutatum dando lucretur, ille est mercator qui de templo Dei ejicitur."

After this, how can we see, in Godric and any of those who led the same sort of life, anything else but capitalists? It is impossible to maintain that these men conducted business only to supply their daily wants, impossible not to see that their purpose is the constant accumulation of goods, impossible to deny that, barbarous as we may suppose them, they none the less possessed the comprehension, or, if one prefers, had the instinct for commerce on the large scale.[1] Of the organization of this commerce the life of Godric shows us already the principal features, and the description which it gives us of them is the more deserving of confidence because it is corroborated in the most convincing fashion by many documents. It shows us, first of all, the merchant coming from the country to establish himself in the town. But the town is to him, so to speak, merely a basis of operations. He lives there but little, save in the winter. As soon as the roads are practicable and the sea open to navigation, he sets out. His commerce is essentially a wandering commerce, and at the same time a collective one, for the insecurity of the roads and the powerlessness of the solitary individual compel him to have recourse to association. Grouped in guilds, in hanses, in *caritates*, the associates take their merchandise in convoy from town to town, presenting a spectacle entirely like that which the caravans of the East still furnish in our day. They buy and sell in common, dividing the profits in the ratio of their respective investments in the expedition, and the trade they carry on in the foreign markets is wholesale trade, and can only be that, for retail trade, as the life of Godric shows us, is left to the rural peddlers. It is in gross that they export and import wine, grain, wool, or cloth. To convince ourselves of this we need only examine the regulations which have been preserved to us. The statutes of the Flemish hanse of London, for example, formally exclude retail dealers and craftsmen from the company.

Moreover, the merchant associations of the eleventh and twelfth centuries have nothing exclusively local in their character. In them we find bourgeoisie of different towns, side by side. They have rather the appearance of regional than of urban organisms. They are still far from the exclusivism and the protectionism which are to be shown with so much emphasis in the municipal life of the fourteenth century. Commercial freedom is not troubled by any restrictive regulations. Public authority assigns no limits to the activity of the merchants, does not restrict them to this or that kind of business, exercises no supervision over their operations. Provided they pay the fiscal dues (*teloneum, conductus*, etc.) levied by the territorial prince and the seigneurs having jurisdiction at the passage of the bridges, along the roads and rivers, or at the markets, they are entirely free from all legal obstacles. The only restrictions which hinder the full expansion of commerce do not come from the official authority, but result from the practices of commerce itself. To wit, the various merchant associations, guilds, hanses, etc., which encounter each other at the places of buying and selling, oppose each other in brutal competition. Each of them excludes from all participation in its affairs the members of all the others. But this is merely a state of facts, resting on no legal title. Force holds here the place of law, and whatever may be the differences of time and of environment, one cannot do otherwise than to compare the commerce of the eleventh and twelfth centuries to that bloody competition in which, in the sixteenth and seventeenth centuries, the sailors of Holland, England, France, and Spain engaged in the markets of the New World. We shall conclude then that medieval commerce, at its origin, is essentially characterized by its regional quality and by its freedom. And it is not difficult to understand that it was so, if one bears in mind two facts to which attention should be drawn.

In the first place, down to the end of the twelfth century, the number of towns properly so-called was relatively small. Only those places that were favored by a privileged geographical situation attracted the merchants in sufficient number to enable them to maintain a commercial movement of real importance. After that, the attraction which these centres of business exerted upon their environs was much greater than is ordinarily imagined. All the secondary localities were subject to their influence. The merchants dwelling in these last, too few to act by themselves, affiliated themselves to the hanse or guild of the principal town. The Flemish hanse, which we have already instanced, proves this fully, by showing us the merchants of Dixmude, Damme, Oudenbourg, Ardenbourg, etc., seeking admission into the hanse of Bruges.

In the second place, at the period we have now reached the towns devoted themselves far more to commerce than to industry. Few could be cited that appear thus early as manufacturing centres. The concentration of artisans within their walls is still incomplete. If their merchants export, along with the products of the soil, such as wine and grain, a quantity of manufactured products, such, for example, as cloth, it is more than probable that these were for the most part made in the country.

Admit these two statements, and the nature of early commerce is explained without difficulty. They account in fact both for the freedom of the merchants and for that character of wholesale exporters which they exhibit so clearly and which prevents our placing them in the category in which the theory of urban economy claims to confine them. Contrary to the general belief, it appears then that before the thirteenth century we find a period of free capitalistic expansion. No doubt the capitalism of that time is a collective capitalism: groups, not isolated individuals, are its instruments. No doubt too it contents itself with very simple operations.

---

[1] One finds already in the twelfth century lenders of money undertaking veritable financial operations. See H. Jenkinson and M. T. Stead, "William Cade: a Financier of the Twelfth Century," *English Historical Review* (1913), p. 209 ff.

The commercial expeditions upon which its activity especially centres itself demand, for their successful conduct, an endurance, a physical strength, which the more advanced stages of economic evolution will not require. But they demand nothing more. Without the ability to plan and combine they would remain sterile. And so we can see that, from the beginning, what we find at the basis of capitalism is intelligence, that same intelligence which Georg Hansen has so well shown, long ago, to be the efficient cause of the emergence of the bourgeoisie.[1]

The fortunes acquired in the wandering commerce by the parvenus of the eleventh and twelfth centuries soon transformed them into landed proprietors. They invest a good part of their gains in lands, and the land they thus acquire is naturally that of the towns in which they reside. From the beginning of the thirteenth century one sees this land held in large parcels by an aristocracy of patricians, *viri hereditarii, divites, majores,* in whom we cannot fail to recognize the descendants of the bold voyagers of the guilds and the hanses. The continuous increase of the burghal population enriches them more and more, for as new inhabitants establish themselves in the towns, and as the number of the houses increases, the rent of the ground increases in proportion. So, from the commencement of the thirteenth century, the grandsons of the primitive merchants abandon commerce and content themselves with living comfortably upon the revenue of their lands. They bid farewell to the agitations and the chances of the wandering life. They live henceforward in their stone houses, whose battlements and towers rise above the thatched roofs of the wooden houses of their tenants. They assume control of the municipal administration; they and their families monopolize the seats in the *échevinage* or the town council. Some even, by fortunate marriages, ally themselves with the lesser nobility and begin to model their manner of living upon that of the knights.

But while these first generations of capitalists are retiring from commerce and rooting themselves in the soil, important changes are going on in the economic organization. In the first place, in proportion as the wealth of the towns increases, and with it their attractive power, they take on more and more an industrial character, the rural artisans flocking into them *en masse* and deserting the country. At the same time many of them, favored by the abundance of raw material furnished by the surrounding region, begin to devote themselves to certain specialties of manufacture — cloth-making or metallurgy. Finally, around the principal aggregations many secondary localities develop, so that all Western Europe, in the course of the thirteenth century, blossoms forth in an abundance of large and small towns. Some, and much the greater number of them, content themselves perforce with local commerce. Their production is determined by the needs of their population and that of the environs which extend two or three leagues around their walls and, in exchange for the manufactured articles which the city furnishes to them, attend to the food supply of the urban inhabitants. Other towns, on the contrary, less closely set together but also more powerful, develop chiefly by means of an export industry, producing, as did the cloth industry of great Flemish or Italian cities, not for their local market,[2] but for the European market, constantly extensible. Others still, profiting by the advantages of nearness to the sea, give themselves up to navigation and to transportation, as did so many ports of Italy, of France, of England, and especially of North Germany.

Of these two types of towns, the one sufficient to themselves, the other living upon the outside world, it is unquestionably the first to which the theory of the urban economy applies. Direct trade between purchaser and consumer, strict protectionism excluding the foreigner from the local market and reserving it to the bourgeoisie alone, minute regulations confining within narrow limits the industry of the merchant and the artisan; in a world, all the traits of an organization evidently designed to preserve and safeguard the various members of the community by assigning to each his place and his role, are all found and all explained without difficulty in those towns which are confined to a clientage limited by the extent of their suburban dependencies. In these one can rightly speak of an anticapitalistic economy. In these we find neither great *entrepreneurs* nor great merchants. It is true that the necessity of stocking the town with commodities which it does not produce or cannot find in its environs — groceries, fine cloths, wines in northern countries — brings into existence a group of exporters whose condition is superior to that of their fellow citizens. But on inspection they cannot be regarded as a class of great professional merchants. If they buy at wholesale in foreign markets, it is to sell at retail to their fellow-citizens. They dispose of their goods piecemeal, and like the *Gewandschneider* of the German towns, they do not rise above the level of large shopkeepers.[3]

In the towns of the second category we find a quite different condition. Here capitalism not only exists but develops toward perfection. Instruments of credit, such as the *lettre de foire*, make their appearance; a traffic in money takes its place alongside the traffic in merchandise and, despite the prohibition of loans at interest, makes constantly more rapid progress. The *coutumes* of the fairs, especially those of the fairs of Champagne, in which the merchants of the regions most advanced in an economic sense, Italy and the Low Countries, meet each other, give rise to a veritable commercial law. The circulation of money expands and becomes

---

[1] *Die drei Bevölkerungsstufen.*

[2] The *Livre de la Vingtaine d'Arras* (ed. A. Guesnon) says, in speaking of the merchants of that town, in 1222, "Emunt non ad usum civitatis, sed ut exportent et discurrant per nondinas longinquas et per Lombardiam."

[3] G. von Below, "Grosshändler und Kleinhändler im Deutschen Mittelalter," *Jahrbücher für Nationalökonomie und Statistik* (1900).

regulated; the coinage of gold, abandoned since the Merovingian period, is resumed in the middle of the thirteenth century. The security of travellers increases on the great highways. The old Roman bridges are rebuilt and here and there canals are built and dykes constructed. Finally, in the towns, the commercial buildings of the previous period, outgrown, are replaced by structures more vast and more luxurious, of which the *halles* of Ypres, with their façade one hundred and thirty-three metres long, is doubtless the most imposing specimen.

In the presence of these facts it is impossible to deny the existence of a considerable traffic. Moreover documents abound which attest the existence in the great cities of men of affairs who hold the most extended relations with the outside world, who export and import sacks of wool, bales of cloth, tuns of wine, by the hundred, who have under their orders a whole corps of factors or "sergents" (*servientes, valet,* etc.) whose letters of credit are negotiated in the fairs of Champagne, and who make loans amounting to several thousand of livres to princes, monasteries, and cities in need of money. To cite there merely a few figures, let us recall that in 1273 the company of the Scotti of Piacenza exports wool from England to the value of 21,400 pounds sterling, or 1,600,000 francs (metallic value);[1] in 1254 certain burgesses of Arras furnish 20,000 livres to the Count of Guines, prisoner of the Count of Flanders, to enable him to pay his ransom.[2] In 1339 three merchants of Mechlin advance 54,000 florins (700,000 francs) to King Edward III.[3]

Extensive, however, as capitalistic commerce has been since the first half of the thirteenth century, it no longer enjoys the freedom of development which it had before. As we advance toward the end of the Middle Ages, indeed, we see it subjected to limitations constantly more numerous and more confining. Henceforth, in fact, it has to reckon with municipal legislation. Every town now shelters itself behind the ramparts of protectionism. If the most powerful cities can no longer exclude the stranger, upon whom they live, they impose upon him a minute regulation, the purpose of which is to defend against him the position of their own citizens. They force him to have recourse in his purchases to the mediation of his "hosts" and his "courtiers"; they forbid him to bring in manufactured articles which may compete with those which the city produces; they exploit him by levying taxes of all sorts: duties upon weighing, upon measuring, upon egress, etc.

In those cities especially in which has occurred the popular revolution transferring power from the hands of the patriciate into those of the craft-guilds, distrust of capital is carried as far as it can go without entirely destroying urban industry. The craftsmen who produce for exportation — for example, the weavers and the fullers of the towns of Flanders — try to escape from their subjection to the merchants who employ them. Not only do the municipal statutes fix wages and regulate the conditions of work, but they also limit the independence of the merchant, even in purely commercial matters. It will be sufficient to mention here, as one of their most characteristic provisions, the forbidding of the cloth merchant to be at the same time a wool merchant, a prohibition inspired by the desire to prevent operations that will unfavourably affect prices and the workman's wages.[4]

But it is not solely the municipal authority which attacks the speculations born of the capitalistic spirit. The Church steps forward, and under the name of usury forbids indiscriminately the lending of money at interest, sales on credit, monopolies, and in general all profits exceeding the *justum pretium*. No doubt these prohibitions themselves attest the existence of the abuses which they endeavor to oppose, and their frequency proves that they did not always succeed. It is none the less true that they were very burdensome and that the pursuit of business on a large scale found itself much embarrassed by them.

The increasing specialization of commerce embarrassed it much more. At the beginning the merchants had devoted themselves to the most various operations at once. Wandering from market to market, they bought and sold without feeling in need of centring their activity on this or that kind of products or commodities, but from about 1250 this is no longer the case. The progress of economic evolution has resulted in localizing certain industries and in restraining certain branches of commerce to the groups of merchants best suited to their promotion. Thus, for example, in the course of the thirteenth century the trade in fine cloth became a monopoly of the towns of Flanders, and banking a monopoly of certain merchant companies of Lombardy, Provence, or Tuscany. Thenceforward commercial life ceases to overflow at random, so to speak. It has a less arbitrary, a more deliberate, and consequently a more embarrassed quality.

These limitations resting upon commerce have resulted in turning away from it the patricians, who moreover have become, as has been said above, a class of landed proprietors. The place which they left vacant is filled by new men, among whom, as among their predecessors, intelligence is the essential instrument of fortune. The intellectual faculties which they first developed in wandering commerce are used by these later men to overcome the obstacles raised in their pathway by municipal regulations of commerce and ecclesiastical regulations in respect to money affairs.[5] Many of them find a rich source of profit by devoting themselves to brokerage. Others in the industrial cities

---

[1] A Schaube, "Die Wollausfuhr Englands vom Jahre 1273," *Vierteljahrschrift für Sozial- und Wirtschaftsgeschichte* (1908), p. 183.
[2] A. Duchesne, *Histoire des Maisons de Guines, d'Ardres et de Gand*, p. 289.
[3] Rymer, *Foedera*, vol. II, part IV, p. 49.
[4] For an example, see Espinas and Pirenne, *Recueil de Documents relatifs à l'Histoire de la Draperie Flamande*, II, 391.
[5] J. Kulischer, "Warenhändler und Geldausleiher im Mittelalter." *Zeitschrift für Volkswirtschaft*, etc., XVII (1908).

exploit shamelessly and in defiance of the statutes the artisans whom they employ. At Douai, for example, Jehan Boinebroke (1280–1310) succeeds in reducing to serfdom a number of workers (and characteristically, they are chiefly women) by advancing wool or money which they are unable to repay, and which therefore place them at his mercy.[1] The richest or the boldest profit by the constantly increasing need of money on the part of territorial princes and kings, to become their bankers. It will be remembered that it was Lombard capitalists who furnished Edward III with money to prepare his campaigns against France,[2] and quite recently, the history of Guillaume Servat of Cahors (1280–1320) has shown us a man who, setting out with nothing, like Godric in the eleventh century, accumulates in a few years a considerable fortune, supplies the King of England with a dowry for one of his daughters, lends money to the King of Norway, farms the wool duties at London, and, unscrupulous as he is shrewd, does not hesitate to engage in shady speculations upon the coinage.[3] And how many other financiers do we not know whose career is wholly similar: Thomas Fin at the court of the counts of Flanders,[4] the Berniers at that of the counts of Hainaut, the Tote Guis, the Vane Guis, at that of the kings of France, not to name the numberless Italians entrusted by the popes with the various operations of pontifical finance, those *mercatores Romanam curiam sequentes* among whom are found the ancestors of the great Medici of the fifteenth century.[5]

In the course of the fifteenth century this second class of capitalists, courtiers, merchants, and financiers, successors to the capitalists of the hanses and the guilds, is in its turn drawn along toward the downward grade. The progress of navigation, the discoveries made by the Portuguese, then by the Spaniards, the formation of great monarchical states struggling for supremacy, begin to destroy the economic situation in the midst of which that class had grown to greatness, and to which it had adapted itself. The direction of the currents of commerce is altered. In the north, the English and Dutch marine gradually take the place of the hanses. In the Mediterranean, commerce centres itself at Venice and at Genoa. On the shores of the Atlantic, Lisbon becomes the great market for spices, and Antwerp, supplanting Bruges, becomes the rendezvous of European commerce. The sixteenth century sees this movement grow more rapid. It is favored at once by moral, political, and economic causes; the intellectual progress of the Renaissance, the expansion of individualism, great wars exciting speculation, the disturbance of monetary circulation caused by the influx of precious metals from the New World. As the science of the Middle Ages disappears and the humanist takes the place of the scholastic, so a new economy rises in the place of the old urban economy. The state subjects the towns to its superior power. It restrains their political autonomy at the same time that it sets commerce and industry free from the guardianship which the towns have hitherto imposed upon them. The protectionism and the exclusiveness of the bourgeoisies are brought to an end. If the craft-guilds continue to exist, yet they no longer control the organization of labor. New industries appear which, to escape the meddling surveillance of the municipal authorities, establish themselves in the country. Side by side with the old privileged towns, which merely vegetate, younger manufacturing centres, full of strength and exuberance, arise; in England, Sheffield and Birmingham, in Flanders, Hondschoote and Armentières.[6]

The spirit which is now manifested in the world of business, is that same spirit of freedom which animates the intellectual world. In a society in process of formation, the individual, enfranchised, gives the rein to his boldness. He despises tradition, gives himself up with unrestrained delight to his virtuosity. There are to be no more limits on speculation, no more fetters on commerce, no more meddling of authority in relations between employers and employed. The most skillful wins. Competition, up to this time held in check, runs riot. In a few years enormous fortunes are built up, others are swallowed up in resounding bankruptcies. The Antwerp exchange is a pandemonium where bankers, deep-sea sailors, stock-jobbers, dealers in futures, millionaire merchants, jostle each other — and sharpers and adventurers to whom all means of money-getting, even assassination, are acceptable.

This confused recasting of the economic world transfers the rôle played by the capitalists of the late Middle Ages to a class of new men. Few are the descendants of the business men of the fourteenth century among those of the fifteenth and sixteenth. Thrown out of their course by the current of events, they have not been willing to risk fortunes already acquired. Most of them are seen turning toward administrative careers, entering the service of the state as members of the councils of justice or finance and aspiring to the *noblesse de robe*, which, with the aid of fortunate marriages, will land their sons in the circle of the true nobility. As for the new rich of the period, they almost all appear to us like parvenus. Jacques Cœur is a parvenu in France. The

[1] G. Espinas, "Jehan Boine-Broke, Bourgeois et Drapier Douaisien," *Vierteljahrschrift für Sozial- und Wirtschaftsgeschichte* (1904), pp. 34 ff.

[2] For the relations of the capitalists with the English crown see: Whitwell, "Italian Bankers and the English Crown," *Transactions of the Royal Historical Society*, XVIII (1903), and Bond: "Extract from the Liberate Rolls relative to the Loans supplied by Italian Merchants to the Kings of England," *Archaeologia*, XXVII (1840). *Cf.* Hansen, "Der Englische Staatscredit unter König Edward III und die Hansischen Kaufleute," *Hansische Geschichtsblätter* (1910).

[3] F. Arens, "Wilhelm Servat von Cahors als Kaufmann zu London," *Vierteljahrschrift für Sozial- und Wirtschaftsgeschichte* (1913), pp. 477 ff.

[4] V. Fris, "Thomas Fin, Receveur de Flander," *Bulletin de la Commission Royale d'Histoire de Belgique* (1900), pp. 8 ff.

[5] Schneider, "Die Finanziellen Beziehungen der Florentinischen Banquiers zur Kirche," *Schmollers Forschungen*, vol. XVII.

[6] Pirenne, "Une Crise Industrielle au XVI Siècle," *Bulletin de l'Academia Royale de Belgique*, classe des lettres (1905).

Fuggers and many other German financiers – the Herwarts, the Seilers, the Manlichs, the Haugs – are parvenus of whose families we know little before the fifteenth century, and so are the Fescobaldi and the Gualterotti of Florence, or that Gaspar Ducci of Pistoia who is perhaps the most representative of the fortune hunters of the period.[1] Later, when Amsterdam has inherited the commercial hegemony of Antwerp, the importance of the parvenus characterizes it not less clearly. We may merely mention here, among the first makers of its greatness, Willem Usselinx,[2] Balthazar de Moucheron, Isaac Lemaire. And if from the world of commerce we turn toward that of industry the aspect is the same. Christophe Plantin, the famous printer, is the son of a simple peasant of Touraine.

The exuberance of capitalism which reached its height in the second half of the sixteenth century was not maintained. Even as the regulative spirit characteristic of the urban economy followed upon the freedom of the twelfth century, so mercantilism imposed itself upon commerce and industry in the seventeenth and eighteenth centuries. By protective duties and bounties on exportation, by subsidies of all sorts to manufactures and national navigation, by the acquiring of transmarine colonies, by the creation of privileged commercial companies, by the inspection of manufacturing processes, by the perfecting of means of transportation and the suppression of interior custom-houses, every state strives to increase its means of production, to close its market to its competitors, and to make the balance of trade incline in its favor. Doubtless the idea that "liberty is the soul of commerce" does not wholly disappear, but the endeavor is to regulate that liberty henceforward in conformity to the interest of the public weal. It is put under the control of intendants, of consuls, of chambers of commerce. We are entering into the period of national economy.

This was destined to last, as is familiar, until the moment when, in England at the end of the eighteenth century, on the Continent in the first years of the nineteenth, the invention of machinery and the application of steam to manufacturing completely disorganized the conditions of economic activity. The phenomena of the sixteenth century are reproduced, but with tenfold intensity. Merchants accustomed to the routine of mercantilism and to state protection are pushed aside. We do not see them pushing forward into the career which opens itself before them, unless as lenders of money. In their turn, and as we have seen it at each

great crisis of economic history, they retire from business and transform themselves into an aristocracy. Of the powerful houses which are established on all hands and which give the impetus to the modern industries of metallurgy, of the spinning and weaving of wool, linen, and cotton, hardly one is connected with the establishments existing before the end of the eighteenth century. Once again, it is new men, enterprising spirits, and sturdy characters which profit by the circumstances.[3] At most, the old capitalists, transformed into landed proprietors, play still an active rôle in the exploitation of the mines, because of the necessary dependence of that industry upon the possessors of the soil, but it can be safely affirmed that those who have presided over the gigantic progress of international economy, of the exuberant activity which now affects the whole world, were, as at the time of the Renaissance, parvenus, self-made men. As at the time of the Renaissance, again, their belief is in individualism and liberalism alone. Breaking with the traditions of the old régime, they take for their motto "*laissez faire, laissez passer.*" They carry the consequences of the principle to an extreme. Unrestrained competition sets them to struggling with each other and soon arouses resistance in the form of socialism, among the proletariat that they are exploiting. And at the same time that that resistance arises to confront capital, the latter, itself suffering from the abuse of that freedom which had enabled it to rise, compels itself to discipline its affairs. Cartels, trusts, syndicates of producers, are organized, while states, perceiving that it is impossible to leave employers and employees longer to contend in anarchy, elaborate a social legislation; and international regulations, transcending the frontiers of the various countries, begin to be applied to working men.

I am aware how incomplete is this rapid sketch of the evolution of capitalism through a thousand years of history. As I said at the beginning, I present it merely as an hypothesis resting on the very imperfect knowledge which we yet possess of the different movements of economic development. Yet, in so far as it is exact, it justifies the observation I made at the beginning of this study. It shows that the growth of capitalism is not a movement proceeding along a straight line, but has been marked, rather, by a series of separate impulses not forming continuations one of another but interrupted by crises.

To this first remark may be added two others, which are in a way corollaries.

The first relates to the truly surprising regularity with which the phases of economic freedom and of economic regulation have succeeded each other. The free expansion of wandering commerce comes to its end in the urban economy, the individualistic ardor of the Renaissance leads to mercantilism, and finally, our own epoch of social legislation follows the age of liberalism.

The second remark, with which I shall close, lies in the moral and political rather than the economic field. It may be stated in this form, that every class of capi-

---

[1] R. Ehrenberg, *Das Zeitalter der Fugger*, I, 311 ff.

[2] J. F. Jameson, "Willem Usselinx," in Am. Hist. Assoc., *Papers*, II.

[3] See, in Cunningham, *The Growth of English Industry and Commerce in Modern Times*, p. 618, this citation from P. Gaskell: "Few of the men who entered the trade rich were successful. They trusted too much to others, too little to themselves." Let us recall here that the founder of the largest industrial establishments of Belgium, John Cockerill, was a simple workman. See E. Mahaim, "Les Débuts de l'Etablissement John Cockerill à Seraing." *Vierteljahrschrift für Sozial- und Wirtschaftsgeschichte* (1905), p. 627.

talists is at the beginning animated by a clearly progressive and innovating spirit but becomes conservative as its activities become regulated. To conceive one's self of this truth it is sufficient to recall that the merchants of the eleventh and twelfth centuries are the ancestors of the bourgeoisie and the creators of the first urban institutions; that the business men of the Renaissance struggled as energetically as the humanists against the social traditions of the Middle Ages; and finally, that those of the nineteenth century have been among the most ardent upholders of liberalism. This would suffice to prove to us, if we did not know it otherwise, that all these have at the beginning been nothing else than parvenus brought into action by the transformations of society, embarrassed neither by custom nor by routine, having nothing to lose and therefore the bolder in their race toward profit. But soon the primitive energy relaxes. The descendants of the new rich wish to preserve the situation which they have acquired, provided public authority will guarantee it to them, even at the price of a troublesome surveillance; they do not hesitate to place their influence at its service, and wait for the moment when, pushed aside by new men, they shall demand of the state that it recognize officially the rank to which they have raised their families, shall on their entrance into the nobility become a legal class and no longer a social group, and shall consider it beneath them to carry on that commerce which in the beginning made their fortunes.

How Democracy Affects the Relations of Masters and Servants

Alexis de Tocqueville

An AMERICAN who had traveled for a long time in Europe once said to me: "The English treat their servants with a stiffness and imperiousness of manner which surprise us; but, on the other hand, the French sometimes treat their attendants with a degree of familiarity or of politeness which we cannot understand. It looks as if they were afraid to give orders; the relative position of the superior and the inferior is poorly maintained." The remark was a just one, and I have often made it myself. I have always considered England as the country of all the world where in our time the bond of domestic service is drawn most tightly, and France as the country where it is most relaxed. Nowhere have I seen masters stand so high or so low as in these two countries. Between these two extremes the Americans are to be placed. Such is the fact as it appears upon the surface of things; to discover the causes of that fact, it is necessary to search the matter thoroughly.

No communities have ever yet existed in which social conditions have been so equal that there were neither rich nor poor, and, consequently, neither masters nor servants. Democracy does not prevent the existence of these two classes, but it changes their dispositions and modifies their mutual relations.

Among aristocratic nations servants form a distinct class, not more variously composed than that of their masters. A settled order is soon established; in the former as well as in the latter class a scale is formed, with numerous distinctions or marked gradations of rank, and generations succeed one another thus, without any change of position. These two communities are superposed one above the other, always distinct, but regulated by analogous principles. This aristocratic constitution does not exert a less powerful influence on the notions and manners of servants than on those of masters; and although the effects are different, the same cause may easily be traced.

Both classes constitute small communities in the heart of the nation, and certain permanent notions of right and wrong are ultimately established among them. The different acts of human life are viewed by one peculiar and unchanging light. In the society of servants, as in that of masters, men exercise a great influence over one another: they acknowledge settled rules, and in the absence of law they are guided by a sort of public opinion; their habits are settled, and their conduct is placed under a certain control.

These men, whose destiny it is to obey, certainly do

Reprinted from *Democracy in America*, V. II (New York: A. A. Knopf, 1945), pp. 177–185, by permission of the publisher.

not understand fame, virtue, honesty, and honor in the same manner as their masters; but they have a pride, a virtue, and an honesty pertaining to their condition; and they have a notion, if I may use the expression, of a sort of servile honor.[1] Because a class is mean, it must not be supposed that all who belong to it are mean-hearted; to think so would be a great mistake. However lowly it may be, he who is foremost there and who has no notion of quitting it occupies an aristocratic position which inspires him with lofty feelings, pride, and self-respect, that fit him for the higher virtues and for actions above the common.

Among aristocratic nations it was by no means rare to find men of noble and vigorous minds in the service of the great, who did not feel the servitude they bore and who submitted to the will of their masters without any fear of their displeasure.

But this was hardly ever the case among the inferior ranks of domestic servants. It may be imagined that he who occupies the lowest stage of the order of menials stands very low indeed. The French created a word on purpose to designate the servants of the aristocracy; they called them "lackeys." This word *lackey* served as the strongest expression, when all others were exhausted, to designate human meanness. Under the old French monarchy to denote by a single expression, a low-spirited, contemptible fellow it was usual to say that he had the *soul of a lackey;* the term was enough to convey all that was intended.

The permanent inequality of conditions not only gives servants certain peculiar virtues and vices, but places them in a peculiar relation with respect to their masters. Among aristocratic nations the poor man is familiarized from his childhood with the notion of being commanded; to whichever side he turns his eyes, the graduated structure of society and the aspect of obedience meet his view. Hence in those countries the master readily obtains prompt, complete, respectful, and easy obedience from his servants, because they revere in him not only their master, but the class of masters. He weighs down their will by the whole weight of the aristocracy. He orders their actions; to a certain extent, he even directs their thoughts. In aristocracies the master often experiences, even without being aware of it, amazing sway over the opinions, the habits, and the manners of those who obey him, and his influence extends even further than his authority.

In aristocratic communities not only are there hereditary families of servants as well as of masters, but the same families of servants adhere for several generations to the same families of masters (like two parallel lines, which neither meet nor separate); and this considerably modifies the mutual relations of these two classes of

[1] If the principal opinions by which men are guided are examined closely and in detail, the analogy appears still more striking, and one is surprised to find among them, just as much as among the haughtiest scions of a feudal race, pride of birth, respect of their ancestry and their descendants, disdain of their inferiors, a dread of contact, and a taste for etiquette, precedents, and antiquity.

persons. Thus although in aristocratic society the master and servant have no natural resemblance, although, on the contrary, they are placed at an immense distance on the scale of human beings by their fortune, education, and opinions, yet time ultimately binds them together. They are connected by a long series of common reminiscences, and however different they may be, they grow alike; while in democracies, where they are naturally almost alike, they always remain strangers to one another. Among an aristocratic people the master gets to look upon his servants as an inferior and secondary part of himself, and he often takes an interest in their lot by a last stretch of selfishness.

Servants, on their part, are not averse to regarding themselves in the same light; and they sometimes identify themselves with the person of the master, so that they become an appendage to him in their own eyes as well as in his. In aristocracies a servant fills a subordinate position which he cannot get out of; above him is another man, holding a superior rank, which he cannot lose. On one side are obscurity, poverty, obedience for life; on the other, and also for life, fame, wealth, and command. The two conditions are always distinct and always in propinquity; the tie that connects them is as lasting as they are themselves.

In this predicament the servant ultimately detaches his notion of interest from his own person; he deserts himself as it were, or rather he transports himself into the character of his master and thus assumes an imaginary personality. He complacently invests himself with the wealth of those who command him; he shares their fame, exalts himself by their rank, and feeds his mind with borrowed greatness, to which he attaches more importance than those who fully and really possess it. There is something touching and at the same time ridiculous in this strange confusion of two different states of being. These passions of masters, when they pass into the souls of menials, assume the natural dimensions of the place they occupy; they are contracted and lowered. What was pride in the former becomes puerile vanity and paltry ostentation in the latter. The servants of a great man are commonly most punctilious as to the marks of respect due to him, and they attach more importance to his slightest privileges than he does himself. In France a few of these old servants of the aristocracy are still to be met with here and there; they have survived their race, which will soon disappear with them altogether.

In the United States I never saw anyone at all like them. The Americans are not only unacquainted with the kind of man, but it is hardly possible to make them understand that such ever existed. It is scarcely less difficult for them to conceive it than for us to form a correct notion of what a slave was among the Romans or a serf in the Middle Ages. All these men were, in fact, though in different degrees, results of the same cause: they are all retiring from our sight and disappearing in the obscurity of the past, together with the social condition to which they owed their origin.

Equality of conditions turns servants and masters into new beings, and places them in new relative positions. When social conditions are nearly equal, men are constantly changing their situations in life; there is still a class of menials and a class of masters, but these classes are not always composed of the same individuals, still less of the same families; and those who command are not more secure of perpetuity than those who obey. As servants do not form a separate class, they have no habits, prejudices, or manners peculiar to themselves; they are not remarkable for any particular turn of mind or moods of feeling. They know no vices or virtues of their condition, but they partake of the education, the opinions, the feelings, the virtues; and the vices of their contemporaries; and they are honest men or scoundrels in the same way as their masters are.

The conditions of servants are not less equal than those of masters. As no marked ranks or fixed subordination are to be found among them, they will not display either the meanness or the greatness that characterize the aristocracy of menials, as well as all other aristocracies. I never saw a man in the United States who reminded me of that class of confidential servants of which we still retain a reminiscence in Europe; neither did I ever meet with such a thing as a *lackey*: all traces of the one and the other have disappeared.

In democracies servants are not only equal among themselves, but it may be said that they are, in some sort, the equals of their masters. This requires explanation in order to be rightly understood. At any moment a servant may become a master, and he aspires to rise to that condition; the servant is therefore not a different man from the master. Why, then, has the former a right to command, and what compels the latter to obey except the free and temporary consent of both their wills? Neither of them is by nature inferior to the other; they only become so for a time, by covenant. Within the terms of this covenant the one is a servant, the other a master; beyond it they are two citizens of the commonwealth, two men.

I beg the reader particularly to observe that this is not only the notion which servants themselves entertain of their own condition; domestic service is looked upon by masters in the same light, and the precise limits of authority and obedience are as clearly settled in the mind of the one as in that of the other.

When the greater part of the community have long attained a condition nearly alike and when equality is an old and acknowledged fact, the public mind, which is never affected by exceptions, assigns certain general limits to the value of man, above or below which no man can long remain placed. It is in vain that wealth and poverty, authority and obedience, accidentally interpose great distances between two men; public opinion, founded upon the usual order of things, draws them to a common level and creates a species of imaginary equality between them, in spite of the real inequality of their conditions. This all-powerful opinion penetrates at length even into the hearts of those whose

interest might arm them to resist it; it affects their judgment while it subdues their will.

In their inmost convictions the master and the servant no longer perceive any deep-seated difference between them, and they neither hope nor fear to meet with either at any time. They are therefore subject neither to disdain nor to anger, and they discern in each other neither humility nor pride. The master holds the contract of service to be the only source of his power, and the servant regards it as the only cause of his obedience. They do not quarrel about their reciprocal situations, but each knows his own and keeps it.

In the French army the common soldier is taken from nearly the same class as the officer and may hold the same commissions; out of the ranks he considers himself entirely equal to his military superiors, and in point of fact he is so; but when under arms, he does not hesitate to obey, and his obedience is not the less prompt, precise, and ready, for being voluntary and defined. This example may give a notion of what takes place between masters and servants in democratic communities.

It would be preposterous to suppose that those warm and deep-seated affections which are sometimes kindled in the domestic service of aristocracy will ever spring up between these two men, or that they will exhibit strong instances of self-sacrifice. In aristocracies masters and servants live apart, and frequently their only intercourse is through a third person; yet they commonly stand firmly by one another. In democratic countries the master and the servant are close together: they are in daily personal contact, but their minds do not intermingle; they have common occupations, hardly ever common interests.

Among such a people the servant always considers himself as a sojourner in the dwelling of his masters. He knew nothing of their forefathers; he will see nothing of their descendants; he has nothing lasting to expect from them. Why, then, should he identify his life with theirs, and whence should so strange a surrender of himself proceed? The reciprocal position of the two men is changed; their mutual relations must be so, too.

In all that precedes I wish that I could depend upon the example of the Americans as a whole; but I cannot do this without drawing careful distinctions regarding persons and places. In the South of the Union slavery exists; all that I have just said is consequently inapplicable there. In the North the majority of servants are either freedmen or the children of freedmen; these persons occupy an uncertain position in the public estimation; by the laws they are brought up to the level of their masters; by the manners of the country they are firmly kept below it. They do not themselves clearly know their proper place and are almost always either insolent or craven.

But in the Northern states, especially in New England, there are a certain number of whites who agree, for wages, to yield a temporary obedience to the will of their fellow citizens. I have heard that these servants commonly perform the duties of their situations with punctuality and intelligence and that, without thinking themselves naturally inferior to the person who orders them, they submit without reluctance to obey him. They appeared to me to carry into service some of those manly habits which independence and equality create. Having once selected a hard way of life, they do not seek to escape from it by indirect means; and they have sufficient respect for themselves not to refuse to their masters that obedience which they have freely promised. On their part, masters require nothing of their servants but the faithful and rigorous performance of the covenant: they do not ask for marks of respect, they do not claim their love or devoted attachment; it is enough that, as servants, they are exact and honest.

It would not, then, be true to assert that in democratic society the relation of servants and masters is disorganized; it is organized on another footing; the rule is different, but there is a rule.

It is not my purpose to inquire whether the new state of things that I have just described is inferior to that which preceded it or simply different. Enough for me that it is fixed and determined; for what is most important to meet with among men is not any given ordering, but order.

But what shall I say of those sad and troubled times at which equality is established in the midst of the tumult of revolution, when democracy, after having been introduced into the state of society, still struggles with difficulty against the prejudices and manners of the country? The laws, and partially public opinion, already declare that no natural or permanent inferiority exists between the servant and the master. But this new belief has not yet reached the innermost convictions of the latter, or rather his heart rejects it; in the secret persuasion of his mind the master thinks that he belongs to a peculiar and superior race; he dares not say so, but he shudders at allowing himself to be dragged to the same level. His authority over his servants becomes timid and at the same time harsh; he has already ceased to entertain for them the feelings of patronizing kindness which long uncontested power always produces, and he is surprised that, being changed himself, his servant changes also. He wants his attendants to form regular and permanent habits, in a condition of domestic service that is only temporary; he requires that they should appear contented with and proud of a servile condition, which they will one day shake off, that they should sacrifice themselves to a man who can neither protect nor ruin them, and, in short, that they should contract an indissoluble engagement to a being like

themselves and one who will last no longer than they will.

Among aristocratic nations it often happens that the condition of domestic service does not degrade the character of those who enter upon it, because they neither know nor imagine any other; and the amazing inequality that is manifest between them and their master appears to be the necessary and unavoidable consequence of some hidden law of Providence.

In democracies the condition of domestic service does not degrade the character of those who enter upon it, because it is freely chosen and adopted for a time only, because it is not stigmatized by public opinion and creates no permanent inequality between the servant and the master.

But while the transition from one social condition to another is going on, there is almost always a time when men's minds fluctuate between the aristocratic notion of subjection and the democratic notion of obedience. Obedience then loses its moral importance in the eyes of him who obeys; he no longer considers it as a species of divine obligation, and he does not yet view it under its purely human aspect; it has to him no character of sanctity or of justice, and he submits to it as to a degrading but profitable condition.

At that period a confused and imperfect phantom of equality haunts the minds of servants; they do not at once perceive whether the equality to which they are entitled is to be found within or without the pale of domestic service, and they rebel in their hearts against a subordination to which they have subjected themselves and from which they derive actual profit. They consent to serve and they blush to obey; they like the advantages of service, but not the master; or, rather, they are not sure that they ought not themselves to be masters, and they are inclined to consider him who orders them as an unjust usurper of their own rights.

Then it is that the dwelling of every citizen offers a spectacle somewhat analogous to the gloomy aspect of political society. A secret and internal warfare is going on there between powers ever rivals and suspicious of one another: the master is ill-natured and weak, the servant ill-natured and intractable; the one constantly attempts to evade by unfair restrictions his obligation to protect and to remunerate, the other his obligation to obey. The reins of domestic government dangle between them, to be snatched at by one or the other. The lines that divide authority from oppression, liberty from license, and right from might are to their eyes so jumbled together and confused that no one knows exactly what he is or what he may be or what he ought to be. Such a condition is not democracy, but revolution.

The Class Structure of Revolutionary America
Jackson T. Main

THE NATURE of the class structure in early America has been much disputed. Indeed, even the existence of classes has been denied; while at the other extreme major developments such as the revolts of Bacon and Leisler, Shaysites and Regulators, have been interpreted as arising out of economic inequalities. The resolution of these differences and indeed our understanding of the colonial and Revolutionary eras depend in part upon an accurate knowledge of colonial society. Moreover any discussion of the changes that have occurred in our social structure — the increase or decrease of mobility, the distribution of wealth, the varying size of the laboring, middle, or upper classes — must rest upon a detailed description of our society as it was in the beginning; we must have a base line for comparisons. A complete analysis must await the intensive research, the numerous monographs, which support generalizations about our present class system; but the importance of the subject justifies preliminary treatment which will reveal at least in outline the character of Revolutionary society.[1]

The conclusion that classes were absent in early America is reached by two lines of argument. First, the word *class* is so defined as to require class consciousness and the presence of clearly distinguishable divisions between classes. Such a definition probably would negate the existence of classes; but there is no reason to accept either criterion as essential. Some word is needed to describe a situation in which obvious economic inequalities exist, and in which, therefore, people — whether they recognize it or not—are economically differentiated. The dictionary definition of class as "a number or body of people with common characteristics" enables us to use the term wherever differences of income, property, or even occupation, are evident. The second line of argument accepts the existence of such differences but denies that they were great enough to warrant the use of the word *class*. This conclusion can be sustained only by a careful selection of the evidence, such as studying the small villages of rural New England while ignoring the larger towns, or by omitting slaves from the southern class structure.[2]

The approach adopted here is pragmatic. The evidence of tax lists, inventories, and other sources is examined, and if economic inequalities are found, a class system is then defined as it is revealed by the data. American society was never entirely uniform, and

long before Revolutionary times it had become complex. Not only were there obvious and familiar differences between north and south, but the distinctions between the frontier and areas long settled, between isolated uplands and rich river valleys, between country and city, were already evident. In these various regions distinct societies had appeared. We can also identify groups of men at various levels of income and wealth. Many people had almost no property: such were the slaves and servants. Others were small proerty owners: such were most farmers and artisans. Still others were well-to-do or wealthy: such were large landowners and the great merchants. These constituted the basic classes, the relative proportion of which differed widely from one area to another.[3]

Two types of society developed on the frontier: the speculative and the nonspeculative. By far the more common variety was that in which the small farmers migrated, acquiring land individually or collectively. Ordinarily no men of wealth were present, although a few of the pioneers might be well-to-do. Land was cheap and easy to obtain, so that the great majority were small farmers. However, one-fourth or one-fifth of the men were landless. These included a few slaves or indentured servants belonging to the occasional man of property, especially in the South; while others were probably hired hands who had not yet secured enough money or credit to purchase land. A few never would do so, for every frontier contained drifters who

[1] Research for this study was assisted by a Sabbatical leave from San Jose State College and a fellowship from the American Council of Learned Societies. A more detailed discussion will be published by the Princeton University Press in September, 1965.

[2] The most forceful presentation of the view that classes were absent in early America is Robert E. Brown, "Economic Democracy Before the Constitution," *American Quarterly*, VII (1955), 257–274.

[3] Basic sources for this analysis are tax lists and inventories. The principal tax lists used were: Massachusetts assessment lists for 1771, Mass. Archives (selected towns); scattered records in the Connecticut State Library; New York assessment rolls, principally for 1779, New York State Library; *Pennsylvania Archives*, third series; Delaware assessment lists for the 1780's Hall of Records, Dover, Delaware; tax records principally for the same period, Virginia State Library; North Carolina tax records on microfilm as listed in William S. Jenkins and Lillian A. Hamrick, eds., *Guide to the Microfilm Collection of Early State Records* (Washington, 1950), 73–74; scattered South Carolina tax lists for 1786–1787, South Carolina Archives.

Published here for the first time, by permission of the author.

perhaps were incapable of independence. However, probably at least three out of four of those landless workers (slaves excepted) ultimately became farmers on some frontier. In Lunenburg County, Virginia, which was being occupied during the 1760's, three-fourths of the men who owned no land in 1764 are known to have done so by 1782, either in that county or farther west; and if we knew the full history of every man the proportion would approach 80 percent.[1]

The frontier supported few men other than farmers. Most of the pioneers were poor, and obliged to be as self-sufficient as possible. One of the yeomen might also keep a little store, competing with the transient peddler; another had a mill; still another could make shoes. There might be a blacksmith, perhaps a minister, and rarely a doctor. Most of the necessary nonagricultural functions were, however, performed by the farmers themselves. Therefore the society was simple and uniform rather than complex and diverse. Both real and personal property were evenly distributed, compared with the situation elsewhere: the 10 percent of the men who had the largest estates owned between one-third and two-fifths of the wealth.

The numerous frontier villages of New England illuminate this type of social structure. The town of Kent, Connecticut, carefully studied by Charles S. Grant, was settled in 1739.[2] Lots were sold for as little as £165 "old tenor" (about £24), but no cash was required. It was therefore occupied primarily by men of the yeoman farmer class, who settled down as respectable small-property holders. Grant identified no upper class, and placed between two-thirds and three-fourths of the men in the middle class. The remainder formed a lower class of poor men. Some of these soon left for other frontiers; while of those who remained, the great majority quickly improved their economic position. Similarly the pioneers of Berkshire County, Massachusetts, were principally small farmers whose land produced scarcely £4 annually, according to the assessment list of 1771 (the true income was perhaps twice that sum).[3] Indeed in the frontier villages of Sandisfield, Tyringham, and Williamstown, only two men had real estates estimated at more than £10, whereas an eastern town of comparable size would have at least ten times as many. The society of these communities consisted of two classes: the middle, practically all of whom were farmers, and the lower class of agricultural laborers, most of whom were farmers'

sons. The wealthiest 10 percent — such as they were — had about 40 percent of the real property.

This proportion was slightly higher than that in Washington County, Virginia, which included, in 1787, the southwestern corner of the state. Virginia's frontier always attracted a few men of means, and one pioneer had twenty-three slaves. There were a few other whites who owned slaves too, but over four-fifths had none. The county contained, as did Virginia generally, a considerable number of landless men, most of them poor, some with no property. These made up 30 percent of the white population. When slaves are added, the laboring class as a whole included 36 percent of the men.

The district of South Carolina called "Ninety-six" was also a frontier region during the Revolutionary era, though by 1787, from which year a tax list survives, it was rapidly being filled with settlers. The unusual feature of its society was the virtual absence of a white lower class: only 6 percent of the men lacked land, and some of these were slaveowners. Even if adult male slaves are included in the social structure, the laboring class comprised only one-third of the population. A majority were small farmers holding one or two hundred acres. Large planters were already present: 4 percent of the men had already acquired at least a thousand acres. One of them held twenty-five slaves, but most slaveowners held only a few and more than half of the men had none. The richest 10 percent of the men had about 40 percent of the wealth.

North Carolina also had a large frontier area in the Revolutionary period. Typical were the counties of Surry in the northwest and Rutherford in the southwest. Southerners had a disorderly way of settling without a land title, and in both counties one-third of the men paid no land tax. However many of these — probably one-third — were using somebody's land, and several had considerable property (one owned five slaves, four horses, and twenty-eight cattle), so that the true class of landless poor did not come to much over 20 percent. Some of the farmers were little better off than the landless workers, but the typical westerner had a couple of hundred acres, three horses, and half a dozen cows. No one in either county had more than sixteen slaves and large landowners were rare, though a few (about 2 percent) of the men did have a thousand acres. All told, including slaves, about one-fourth of the population belonged to the class of dependent poor, and almost all of the rest were free farmers. The concentration of property was the same as that usually found on the southern frontier of this sort: the wealthiest 10 percent had less than 40 percent of the land.

Frontiers in which speculation occurred differed from the usual type in several ways. Either some men of real wealth were present, or some large estates were owned by absentee proprietors. There were more landless men, and the property, especially in land, was more concentrated in a few hands. Wolfeborough, New Hampshire, contained in 1774 fifty-three resident

---

[1] See tax lists in Landon C. Bell, *Sunlight on the Southside* (Philadelphia, 1931).

[2] *Democracy in the Connecticut Frontier Town of Kent* (New York, 1961), 19.

[3] These lists recorded the value of the real estate by estimating the average annual income of the property, which probably meant 5 percent of its assessed value. Judging from land prices given in probate records, the actual worth of the land was about twice the sum fixed by the assessor. Unimproved and evidently other types of unproductive lands were not taxed. In addition to land, the value of stock in trade and money at interest, tons of shipping, houses, shops, mills, stillhouses, warehouses and the like, and certain farm animals, are included.

taxpayers of whom five held well over half of the taxable property. At the other end of the social scale, about half of the men were landless. Many of these worked on the "Abbott-Wentworth" farm which contained nearly 3,000 acres.[1] In the "Saratoga" district of New York, north of Albany, Philip Schuyler paid a tax three times that of anyone else; the district contained more men of small property and the largest taxpayers had more of the land than was the case in most frontier districts of that state. So too Virginia's "Northern Neck" (south of the Potomac and north of the Rappahannock) was from the beginning a vast speculative enterprise. As region after region was opened up, the great planters purchased large tracts which were developed by slaves or rented to tenants. Only gradually did the tenants acquire property and become free farmers. In some counties not over 30 percent of the whites had land, and a very small number of wealthy men — many of them nonresidents — held as much as 70 percent of the real property. Slaves were concentrated in like degree. Frontiers of this nature were commercial developments from the start. They were, however, unusual. Ordinarily the frontier offered almost unlimited opportunity for the man of humble origin to acquire land and become part of the dominant middle class of small farmers, in a "democratic" society of exceptional economic equality.

When the frontier stage ended, the class structure changed. Its growth and direction depended upon the nature of the land and the accessibility of markets: if the land was good and markets close by, or if transportation to markets was cheap, commercial agriculture developed. Otherwise, the members of the community had to be largely, though of course never entirely, self-sufficient, which meant that most of them must be farmers. The availability of capital had something to do with it too, since a commercial farm required a large investment and higher operating costs, especially for labor. Even where both land and transportation were good, some time might elapse before capital could be accumulated. Meanwhile the farmer must supply most of his own needs.

The subsistence farm society was the most common type in the North, though in the South it was no longer as prevalent by Revolutionary times as in earlier years because of the rapid expansion of commercial agriculture. Typically only two classes were present, as on the frontier, because the relative lack of economic opportunities prevented the growth of an upper class. A lower class of landless workers did exist but it was small, partly because most farmers were not prosperous enough to buy slaves or servants or to hire hands, partly because land was not very valuable and so was easily acquired by the poor whites. This class therefore scarcely exceeded one-fifth of the men. Most of those who started from scratch preferred to leave for more promising areas. The overwhelming majority of the residents were small farmers. Such a society included a scattering of artisans, professionals, and men in trade;

but as on the frontier, these comprised only a minor element in the population because most of the farmers had to do their own work whenever possible. Economic equality was a universal characteristic of the subsistence farm society. The wealthiest 10 percent of the men owned roughly 35 percent of the property. Most of the men, though not rich, had enough to live on; and though economic opportunities were limited the people were comfortable, owning on the average about £100 worth of personal and over £300 worth of real property.[2]

The best example of the subsistence-farm type of social structure is found in New England, such as in Worcester County, Massachusetts. The inventories of estates recorded in probate records reveal a low proportion of men with little property.[3] Only about one in ten had less than £50, and one in five owned less than £100 (equal perhaps to $5,000 today). On the other hand, scarcely one in ten held £1,000, while the well-to-do with twice that amount comprised not over 5 percent of the men. In between was the great majority of small property owners — 70 percent of the men. As a rule, those at the bottom of the economic order had no land. Most of these were laborers, who comprised a small element in the population, certainly less than one-fifth. About one in ten men were artisans, usually those with a skill or equipment that the farmers did not possess — they were blacksmiths, shoemakers, and tanners. Another 10 percent were business and professional men. All the rest were farmers, who left property ranging in value from a few pounds to the £9,631 fortune owned by Gardner Chandler, Esquire. Chandler and a few others formed a small elite which dominated their society and owned one-fourth of the property. A similar class structure is revealed by the 1782 tax list for Simsbury, Connecticut, in the northwestern upland. No one was rich or even well-to-do; the estate with the highest assessed value was £116, owned by a man who had ninety-four improved acres

---

[1] Benjamin Franklin Parker, *History of Wolfeborough (New Hampshire)* . . . (Cambridge, 1901), 144–145 *et seq.*

[2] These figures are based upon inventories in probate records. The *New Jersey Archives* and the *New Hampshire State Papers* contain valuable series of these, but only the total value of the property is given. Therefore manuscript records must be used. The generalizations here are based upon about 4,000 cases. For Massachusetts: Suffolk County Probate Office, Boston, 1764–1771 and 1782–1787 (Vols. 63–71, 81–87), Worcester County Court House, 1763–1776 and 1783–1788 (Vols. 8–11, 18–21). For Virginia: Halifax County Will Book 0 (1753–1772) and 2 (1783–1792); Lunenburg County Will Book 2 (1762–1788), and 3 (1779–1791); Spotsylvania Will Book D (1761–1772) and E (1772–1798); Chesterfield Will Book 3 (1774–1785) and 4 (1785–1800); Essex Will Book 13 (1775–1785) and 14 (1786–1792); Richmond Will Book 6 (1753–1767); Westmoreland Records and Inventories, Vol. 5 (1767–1776), Virginia State Library. For South Carolina, inventory books X (1763–1768) and A (1783–1788), South Carolina Archives. All figures are local currency except in the case of South Carolina where sterling is used.

[3] These inventories are accurate as to the evaluations made and include all sorts of people except indentured servants and slaves.

and nineteen farm animals. Only 21 percent of the men lacked land. A "faculty" tax on non-farm property was paid by fewer than one out of ten. The town had a doctor, a minister, and a few artisans, but apparently no shopkeeper. The wealthiest 10 percent of the taxpayers owned only 20 percent of the taxable wealth, compared with 36 percent in Milford, a commercial center on the coast.

Southern society everywhere included more large landowners and more slaves than did the northern — was, that is to say, more commercial; and by the Revolutionary era the regions that were limited to subsistence farming were rapidly diminishing. Still, sharp contrasts were evident between the rich river valleys which produced a large surplus for sale, and the uplands which could not export nearly as much. The subsistence areas even in the North were never entirely self-sufficient, the term "subsistence" being indeed one of degree. If the word is thus loosely defined, the extensive North Carolina backcountry may be considered as a subsistence farm area, especially when that region is contrasted with the "plantation" areas of her sister states. Although a fourth of the men did not own land, half of these had personal property which probably raised them out of the laboring class. Some of the larger farmers employed slaves, who together with the white workers made up a lower class comprising 30 percent of the population. Land was cheap, and some men had acquired sizable estates. They formed an upper class which included between 5 and 10 percent of the men. Most of the rest were small farmers. Property was equally distributed, the upper 10 percent owning less than 40 percent of the wealth. Similar class structures existed in many other parts of the South. The presence of slaves everywhere distinguished southern society from that of the North, but in other respects the subsistence farm communities were much the same throughout the country.

Commercial farm societies also showed similar characteristics wherever they existed. The greater wealth produced by the agricultural surplus led to a higher income level which benefited especially the larger farmers. Many became truly wealthy, comprising a class virtually absent on the frontier or in subsistence regions. These men hired or bought laborers who performed most of the agricultural work. Southerners relied primarily on slaves, northerners on indentured white servants, tenants, and hired hands; but all were used to some extent everywhere. This lower class of landless and often propertyless men formed anywhere from a fourth of the population in New England to considerably over half in the South. The middle class in the South was smaller than elsewhere, and the property was less evenly distributed, the wealthiest 10 percent owning more than half of the wealth. Economic opportunities for the poor men (other than slaves) were excellent while the area was first being occupied, but diminished sharply thereafter. Land then became less easily obtained because it was expensive; and the local economic elite formed, after the first generation

or so, a very nearly closed group which held so much of the property that few new men could acquire the amount necessary for admission. In the North, the society of commercial farm areas also differed from that of other rural communities because it was much more diversified. The greater wealth, and the tendency of the farmers to devote most of their time to producing some cash crop, led them to rely upon others for much that the pioneers or self-sufficient yeomen supplied for themselves; so that artisans were much more numerous and the proportion of professionals, merchants and others following non-farm occupations was greatly increased.

Detail concerning such towns is supplied by the Massachusetts assessment lists. Milton, Waltham, and Roxbury were commercial farm centers near Boston. About one-fourth of the taxpayers were landless, a fairly high percentage for that state, and one which suggests the presence of indentured servants and perhaps of tenants. There were, at the other end of the economic scale, an equal proportion who had land valued at £12 annually, which probably meant about £500 worth. Most of these were the substantial farmers characteristic of such a community. The median income of £7 was about twice that of Worcester County towns. The wealthiest 10 percent had about 46 percent of the real estate compared with less than 40 percent in Worcester. As usual, these towns had more artisans, shopkeepers, and professional men than did the subsistence farm societies; Milton in particular had several prosperous merchants and three doctors. Laborers comprised about a third of the population. However farmers were of course the principal element.

The predominance of farmers is also shown, perhaps exaggerated, by the probate records. Among the important commercial farm centers in Suffolk County were the towns near Boston such as Braintree, Cohasset, and Hull. About 60 percent of the estates inventoried during the years 1764–1771 and 1782–1788 were those of farmers, more than half of whom had substantial property worth over £500. Lawyers, doctors, ministers, merchants and the like made up about 8 percent of the population. The rest of the men were laborers and artisans, who were much more numerous than in subsistence farm towns. Among over 300 men whose estates were inventoried, 13 left property in excess of £2,000, 66 more than £1,000, and 145 owned at least £500. The last included forty-six of the men as contrasted with about 30 percent in other Suffolk and Worcester County towns. The figure may be exaggerated, since the inventories do not reveal as many small estates as we know existed, but the error occurs in both areas, so that the comparison is just. The wealthiest 10 percent owned more than half of the property.

Virginia's tidewater counties are representative of the southern commercial farm society. They contained a high proportion of landless whites, averaging indeed more than half of the men. Many of these — perhaps

15 percent of the whites — were probably tenants, often possessing considerable property, who of course were not farm laborers. Still, whites holding no land, no slaves, and few farm animals comprised at least 30 percent of the men. One-third of these were related to landowners and could make use of the family holdings, but since they had little property themselves they must be regarded as landless workers. When slaves are added, this class of laborers becomes enormous, reaching over four-fifths of the population in a rich county such as Middlesex and about two-thirds in the tidewater generally. The number of large landowners varied greatly. In the easternmost counties, land had been divided and subdivided until estates of a thousand acres were comparatively rare, but these increased in number farther west. Perhaps ownership of slaves is a better measure of wealth. If possession of twenty denoted a man of means, then about 6 percent of the men belonged to that class, as compared with 3 percent in the semi-subsistence farm region of the Piedmont. The rich upper class had a very large share of the wealth, owning 60 percent or more of the land and over half of all property.

The probate records of tidewater counties prove the great wealth of the planter class, for 15 percent of the estates inventoried exceeded £1,000 in the value of personal property. Only about one-fifth of the men had less than £50. These proportions are inaccurate, for the tax records indicate that there were really many more poor whites, so that obviously a higher percentage of the large estates than of the small were being evaluated; but the general characteristics of the society are clear. As in the North, indentured servants must be added to the lower class. Both probate records and tax lists demonstrate that there were fewer small farmers in commercial farm areas than elsewhere in the South.

The probate records also furnish some idea of the different occupations in eastern Virginia. The principal fact which emerges is the small number of men other than farmers. About one-fifth of the men lacked land, but of these many were workers on the land — perhaps indentured servants — and the proportion engaged in non-farming occupations seems not to have exceeded one-tenth. This estimate excludes skilled slaves, who often were trained as artisans. The overwhelming majority of whites were yeomen farmers, a majority of whom were substantial landholders with property worth over £500.

The rice plantation society of coastal South Carolina illustrates an extreme form of the commercial class structure. Tax records for St. Paul's and St. James's parishes in 1786 and 1787 show that about a third of the men lacked land, but since most of these were slave-owners, only one-eighth of the whites were propertyless laborers. So great was the number of slaves, however — nearly forty for each white man — that almost nine-tenths of the adult males were laborers! Two of the whites were overseers, one is identified as a shoemaker, and there was one doctor. None of these had land. Large farmers outnumbered the small by a ratio of two to one: in fact, one-third of the taxpayers had a thousand acres and more than one-fourth had fifty slaves. The richest 10 percent had about half of the land and slaves.

This dominance of the well-to-do and wealthy in South Carolina is demonstrated by a study of the probate records. The value of this data is reduced because the poor people of the commercial farm areas are not represented in proper proportion. Still, even if the source is inaccurate, it reveals unmistakably a society of great wealth, which included relatively few poor whites. Only 3 percent of the estates were evaluated at less than £100 sterling (the true percentage according to the tax records is perhaps 12 percent). In contrast, one-fifth of the upcountry estates were worth less than that sum. Men of moderate property were also fewer in the east: one-third of the westerners and only one-sixth of the easterners died with £100 to £500 in personal property. On the other hand, five-eighths of the easterners left estates of £1,000 — and this figure includes only personal property, not land. The percentages are inexact, but the inference to be drawn from them is obvious: the commercial farm areas contained a far greater proportion of wealthy men. The concentration of property too was much higher along the coast: at least half of the wealth was owned by the richest 10 percent. The probate records also demonstrate the predominantly rural nature of the society (excluding Charleston). Only some 10 percent of the men followed a non-farm occupation, and most of these lived in a few small towns. Here was the quintessence of the southern commercial farm society: a numerous laboring class, many extremely wealthy men, more large than small farmers, a high concentration of property, and a society almost entirely rural.

The class structure of the larger towns was similar to that of the commercial farm areas. Here were the largest number of wealthy men, and many poor laborers. The middle class was smaller than that of subsistence farm or frontier societies, but the far greater wealth enabled most people to raise their standard of living. The wealthiest 10 percent held more than half of the property, yet society was so fluid that economic opportunities were excellent: between one-third and one-half of the wealthy merchants were self-made men. The townsmen followed a great variety of occupations. Here were mariners, printers, ropemakers, goldsmiths, barbers, lawyers, staymakers, brewers, carters, clerks, hair dressers, and even farmers. This diversity, together with the small amount of capital needed for most enterprises, made the city a desirable residence for the ambitious young man.

Boston's society exhibited all of these characteristics. The neighboring towns in Suffolk County (which was much more extensive then) contained many large landowners, but Bostonians owned practically all of the estates in the county which were valued in probate at £5,000 and nearly three-fourths of those worth £2,000. Most of these men were merchants, but many of them had land and several, such as Jeremiah Preble, who had £6,000 worth of land in Maine, were very large landowners. The city's property was concentrated in the hands of these rich men just as was the wealth of commercial farm areas: Boston's richest 10 percent had 57 percent of the wealth. There was plenty of room at the top, and more room at the bottom. Nearly 30 percent of the Boston estates were worth less than £50, and a somewhat larger proportion of the men formed the city's laborers, including mariners, journeymen, servants, and slaves.[1] There were few of the last in Boston, but a southern city such as Charleston had so many that the proportion of dependent poor was increased to nearly two-thirds of the population. Smaller towns ordinarily had fewer men at the top and bottom, a larger middle class, less wealth, and a lower concentration of property, yet did possess all of the attributes of urban society.

The society of the Revolutionary era was characterized by class distinctions based on the unequal distribution of property. Although there were no sharp dividing lines between the economic classes, most of the men can readily be placed in one of three general categories. There was, first, a class of dependent laborers most of whom lived in the country. These men had no land and little personal property, usually less than £50 worth. About one in five whites belonged to this class, which therefore, as proletariats go, would have been extraordinarily small had it not been for the Negro slaves. These raised the proportion to over one-third of the adult men. Second, the largest element in the population consisted of small property owners almost all of whom were economically independent. Small farmers were the most numerous among this group. Blacks aside, they comprised perhaps 40 percent of the people. One out of ten whites was an artisan, and a scattering of other men—shopkeepers, innkeepers, officials, some professional men and the like—also belonged to the middle class, which included over half of the population. These people owned property worth anywhere from £50 to £500, averaging about £300 in real and £100 in personal estate. An intermediate, or upper middle class of substantial farmers, prosperous artisans, and professional men owned £500 to £1,000. Finally, some 10 percent of the whites at the top, consisting principally of large landholders and merchants, held, as a rule, £1,000 or more in personal property and the same amount in land. These men owned nearly half of the wealth of the country, including perhaps one-seventh of the country's people.

[1] In addition to tax and probate records see the tax lists published in *The Bostonian Society Publications*, IX (1912), 15–59.
[2] Material for determining the cost of living is found in newspapers, diaries, letters, account books, probate records, and various published sources. Some interesting examples are, Suffolk County Probate Records, vol. 85, pp. 33–36. Lawrence B. Romaine, "Family expenses during the Revolution," *Hobbies*, LIV (1949), 53; E. V. Wilcox, "Living High on $67.77 a Year," New York State Historical Association, *Proceedings*, XXIV (1926), 197.

The classes of Revolutionary America were distinguishable not only by the property they held but by the kind of life they led. The cost of living depended, as it does today, upon income and desires as much as upon the actual price of necessities. Most people spent little more than the basic sum needed for food, clothing, and shelter. Some, in "middling" circumstances, required a much larger amount of money to uphold their standards, while a few lived luxuriously.

The money earned and spent by the various classes can be interpreted only when its value is understood. The English pound sterling was the basic monetary unit, but each colony and state had its own "pound" which differed from that of England. The common denominator, into which these pounds were translated, was the Spanish dollar, containing (supposedly) an ounce of silver. The dollar was worth four shillings and sixpence sterling. In New England and Virginia, the dollar was legally pegged at six shillings local money; elsewhere it was commonly 7s 6d to 8s. Hereafter figures will be given in sterling unless otherwise indicated.

The value of the pound in today's dollars depends upon the particular item considered, for inflation has proceeded unevenly. In general, prices of staple food products and of inexpensive clothing have risen least, while housing costs have increased more rapidly and many other prices more rapidly still. Roughly, the pound sterling equalled forty dollars in food and clothing, fifty dollars in shelter, and from ten to one hundred dollars in other items, the general average being about fifty. The family living at the subsistence level required probably forty or fifty times as many dollars in 1960 as the 1760 family needed in pounds; but the man of wealth needed only thirty times as much. However these comparisons are not very useful because in those days almost everyone produced his own food, much of his own clothing and household equipment, and often indeed the house itself. The average income of wage and clerical families has risen as much as one hundred times, but their cash needs have risen as rapidly, partly because they now buy nearly everything, and because at least a quarter of their earnings are spent in purchasing products unknown to their forebears.

The Revolutionary family that paid cash for everything needed nearly £50 to subsist. The minimum cost of food and clothing for the man and wife was not far from £20. Each child cost £5 or so to feed, while clothes cost £2 each. Children of this class did not go to school unless a free one was within walking distance. House rent might be £5 or £10. Doctors' bills, wood, candles, taxes, and miscellaneous essentials added another £5 or more.[2]

The family that wished to live in comfort and decency needed two or three times as much. The Society for the Propagation of the Gospel in Foreign Parts regarded £100 as a "sufficient Support," and the well-informed author of *American Husbandry* believed that a "planter's" family would spend the same amount, probably excluding food.[1] An income of £150 maintained a Boston family "in credit," enabled a Maryland "gentleman" to support his family, and sufficed for a typical Georgia "planter"; while £200 permitted both Bostonians and New Yorkers to live "in a genteel manner" and save for their old age and their children. Such a standard of living included a good house, adequate food, respectable attire, schooling for the children, and rum for the parents.[2]

The man of means spent a much larger sum to maintain himself in comfort and allow for some luxuries. £400 was the usual annual expenditure of wealthy landholders such as Charles Carroll and Landon Carter, but when most of the food had to be bought, £500 was needed.[3] Alexander Contee Hanson, a Maryland judge, itemized nearly £600 which he wrote "by no means, supposes a splendid, magnificent style of living – It affords not equipage, costly entertainments, or sumptuous fare – It provides a comfortable subsistence; but not even that, without a strict attention to expenditures.' House rent came to £75 and food for ten including five servants cost £220; while clothing for five required £120, medical bills were £15, the liquor cost £40, firewood £50, candles £8.15.0, and the five servants had been hired for £60. "There is no allowance made for casualties, or for what is called pocket money." Thus the expenses of a judge, when one added the cost of traveling, came to nearly £700. Presumably Hanson was using the Maryland currency, so that his sterling requirements were about £400.[4] Henry Knox regarded £755 as "but a slender support," while Joseph Pemberton, a Philadelphia merchant, spent £4,476 in eight years.[5]

The cost of living of a Revolutionary family varied all the way from £50 to £500. The American's economic situation and way of life therefore depended upon his income, the degree to which he could supply his needs without cash, and the manner of living to which he aspired. More than one out of four adult male Americans had almost no income or property and depended upon others for their survival. Negro slaves occasionally received tips and were sometimes allowed to raise a little food, but except in extraordinary cases they lived at the subsistence level. The master spent between £3 and £8 per slave annually, the lower figure being more general. Clothes, which were rough but adequate, came to £1 each year. The slaves ate only a little meat and lived in cheap small cabins, but as a rule the necessities were furnished them. Northern slaves, most of whom were house servants, were better treated than were those in the South.[6]

Indentured servants were in the same economic position as the slaves, temporarily. They also might have a little property and a few shillings a year, but had to rely upon their masters for almost everything. They fared a little better than the slaves did, living in separate quarters from the blacks and wearing better clothes. In the North they were often treated as members of the family. During much of the colonial period these servants were an inferior lot, but by Revolutionary times they were of much better quality, and after they had served their time they advanced economically as rapidly as did other Americans.[7]

The economic status of a free farm laborer or town worker without any special skill depended upon whether he had a family. If he did not (as was usually the case) his position was good. The average daily wage was 3s currency, or 2s sterling, which had he been steadily employed six days a week would have totaled £30, about £5 above his expenses. However this income was sporadic, not regular, for such a worker was hired only when there was some unusual demand for labor such as at harvest time. Ordinarily the worker was employed by the month or year and was "found": that is, he received board and room and a cash wage varying between £10 and £20.[8] The single man could save enough to set himself up independently in a few years. On the other hand the married man could not support his family. Fortunately there were few such persons, for the great majority quickly learned a trade or farming. The proportion of men who remained poor probably did not exceed 5 percent of the free whites. They were cared for by the "poor rate" which every town raised. Most laborers became skilled, bought

[1] Frank J. Klingberg, *An Appraisal of the Negro in Colonial South Carolina* (Washington, 1941), 79; Harry J. Carman, ed., *American Husbandry* (New York, 1939), 293.

[2] *The Massachusetts Centinel* (Boston), March 11, 1786; Donnell Owings, *His Lordship's Patronage: Offices of Profit in Colonial Maryland* (Baltimore, 1953), 2; *The Gazette of the State of Georgia* (Savannah), July 3, 1788; Sidney Kaplan, "The Reduction of Teachers' Salaries in Post-Revolutionary Boston," *New England Quarterly*, XXI (1948), 375–376; Hugh Hastings, ed., *Ecclesiastical Records. State of New York*, VI (Albany, 1905), 3855.

[3] *Maryland Historical Magazine*, XII (1917), 349; *William and Mary Quarterly*, XIII (1904–1905), 158.

[4] *The Maryland Gazette* (Annapolis), March 29, 1787.

[5] To Washington, Boston, March 24, 1785, Washington Papers, vol. 232, #7, Library of Congress; Pemberton Papers, Box 28, 1775–1776, pp. 111–114, Historical Society of Pennsylvania. See also Thomas Elfe Account Book, *South Carolina Historical Magazine*, XXXV (1934) and subsequent volumes; *American Husbandry*, 68; Walter Livingston Account Book, Robert R. Livingston papers, New York Historical Society; Thomas Lee Shippen Account Book, 1793–1797, Shippen Papers, Box 2, Library of Congress.

[6] Travel accounts contain valuable observations on slavery. See also John Spencer Bassett, *Slavery and Servitude in the Colony of North Carolina* (Baltimore, 1896); Lewis Cecil Gray, *History of Agriculture in the Southern United States to 1860* (Washington, 1932), I, 364; Klingberg, *Negro in South Carolina*; Lorenzo Johnston Greene, *The Negro in Colonial New England 1620–1776* (New York, 1942).

[7] For indentured servitude see Abbot Emerson Smith, *Colonists in Bondage* (Chapel Hill, 1947), and Warren B. Smith, *White Servitude in Colonial South Carolina* (Columbia, 1961).

[8] Information on wages is scattered. Valuable are Dr. Thomas Williams account book, New York Hist. Soc.; Benjamin Snyder account book, vol. II, *ibid.*, James Coultas' account book, 1761–1762, The Joseph Downs Manuscript Library, The Henry Francis du Pont Winterthur Museum, Winterthur, Delaware (shelf #61.64 and 61.65).

land, and advanced into the middle class of small property owners.[1]

The "artisans and mechanics" or "craftsmen" were divided into two groups: those who owned small business enterprises, such as blacksmiths, and those who worked for others, such as shipwrights. Their incomes were two or three times that of ordinary workers and most of them lived in comfort. Washington paid his joiners, masons, millers, and coopers well, offering transportation, good food, washing, and lodging; yet conditions were so favorable in Baltimore that he had trouble finding men.[2] The incomes of those who worked for wages varied from £20 to £100 or so, averaging perhaps £50. Most of them raised some of their own food and were partly self-sufficient in other ways too, so that even the more poorly paid artisans lived decently, though they suffered during hard times. Tailors, housewrights, coopers, and shoemakers earned less than the average; blacksmiths, shipwrights, weavers, and joiners had incomes near the median; while distillers, tanners, ropemakers, and goldsmiths were often men of means.[3] Most artisans owned homes worth on the average £150 in the country and £250 to £300 in the city. Ebenezer Kezar, blacksmith-farmer of Sutton, Massachusetts, is typical except that he had more real estate (£287.10) than usual. His personal property was worth £50. This included £3.9.6 in blacksmith's tools, about £5 in other implements, two cows, a calf, six sheep and a pig, one colt and a mare, and £6 or so in clothes (wife's excluded). Henry Stone, a Stoughton, Massachusetts, blacksmith, owned £80 in real estate including a small dwelling house with four acres valued at £24, an orchard with his blacksmith's shop on it, a wood lot of 150 acres (£27), and one-fourth of a sawmill (£9). His wearing apparel and books were valued at £1.14.9, four beds with their furnishings at £13.18.7. He had one horse, two cows, two swine, and personal property totalling £59.11.7. City artisans often had larger estates. The Boston tailor Ephraim Copeland was typical of many artisans of modern property. He had a house and land worth £266.13.4, a similar watch, silver buckles, a pair of gold buttons and two gold rings, six silver spoons, and furniture, including china and glass, worth over £75.[4]

Artisans who were independent businessmen might earn large incomes and become well-to-do. Certain types of enterprise required considerable capital and produced proportionate returns. A Dorchester, Massachusetts, tanner left £3,186, including £1,484 worth of real estate and notes due him of £1,238. Captain Andrew Sigourney, a Boston distiller, owned real estate valued at £1,400. His stills cost £310 and he had on hand £666.13.3 worth of molasses. The "mansion house" contained furniture appraised at £238 not counting £116 in plate. Sigourney had spent £30 for clothes and £7 for books; his three slaves were estimated at £100; and he was well supplied with £156 worth of rum and spirits. Such men could entertain as grandly as the merchants and professional men whom they doubtless emulated, but the great majority of artisans belonged to the middle class.[5]

The middle class too were mostly professional men. Teachers, however, were poorly paid especially in the subsistence farm areas where they earned hardly more than did ordinary laborers. Those who taught in a city, or in an academy which catered to wealthy sons, were more fortunate, and received the £150 to £200 that permitted a comfortable living. Nevertheless the college graduate could make more money in almost any field. Most schoolmasters therefore did not make teaching a career. Few acquired property, but spent what they earned subsisting, and those with ability soon left their jobs.[6]

---

[1] Statements concerning the ability of laborers to advance economically are based upon case studies dealing with Lunenburg, Richmond, and Lancaster Counties in Virginia, Chester County, Pennsylvania, Philadelphia, and Goshen, Connecticut. See also Grant, *Democracy in Kent*.

[2] Tench Tilghman to Washington, Baltimore, July 15, 1784, Washington papers, Vol. 230, #102, Library of Congress. See also *ibid.*, Vol. 233, #2, #4; and John C. Fitzpatrick, ed., *The Diaries of George Washington 1748–1799* (4 Vols., Boston and New York, 1925), I, 366, III, 137.

[3] Examples are, Richard Walsh, *Charleston's Sons of Liberty: A Study of the Artisans, 1763–1789* (Columbia, S.C., 1959), 143–145; U.S. Department of Labor, Bureau of Labor Statistics, *Bulletin #499, History of Wages in the United States from Colonial Times to 1928* (Washington, 1929), 53; *The Pennsylvania Journal; and Weekly Advertiser* (Philadelphia), Nov. 11, 1772; *The Pennsylvania Gazette*, April 27, 1785; *Boston Evening Post*, August 8, 1763; *The Maryland Gazette*, Dec. 13, 1787; Conn. Hist. Society, *Collections*, XX, 204; Nina Moore Tiffany and Susan I. Lesley, *Letters of James Murray Loyalist* (Boston, 1901), 81; *Diaries of Washington*, I, 178n, 282, 399; *The Columbian Herald, or the Independent Courier of South Carolina* (Charleston), Nov. 20, 23, 1786; *Penn. Journal*, Jan. 25, 1770.

[4] Kingsbury, *Sutton*, 243; Suffolk County Probate Records, Vol. 83, pp. 658–660, Vol. 65, pp. 216–217 (figures in currency) See account books of Joseph Cook, Connecticut State Library, Abiel Abbot and Benjamin Clark, Winterthur Library, and Daniel Dibble, Connecticut Historical Society.

[5] Suffolk County Probate Records, Vol. 65, pp. 190–194.

[6] Many salaries of teachers are given in Clifford K. Shipton, *Biographical Sketches of those who Attended Harvard College . . .* (Vols. IV–XII of *Sibley's Harvard Graduates*, Cambridge and Boston, 1933–1962); Walter Herbert Small, *Early New England Schools* (Boston, 1914); Kaplan, "Teachers' Salaries," *New England Quarterly*, XXI (1948), 373–379; Robert Francis Seybolt, *The Public Schoolmasters of Colonial Boston* (Cambridge, 1939), 22–25, and *The Public Schools of Colonial Boston* (Cambridge, 1935), 80–81; Robert L. McCaul, "Education in Georgia During the Period of Royal Government 1752–1776," *Georgia Historical Quarterly*, XL (1956), 103–112, 248–259; Freeman H. Hart, *The Valley of Virginia in the American Revolution 1763–1789* (Chapel Hill, 1942), 29; Willard S. Elsbree, *The American Teacher* (New York, 1939, 88–89; Douglass Adair, ed., The Autobiography of the Reverend Devereaux Jarratt, 1732–1763," *William and Mary Quarterly*, 3 series IX (1952), 363–376; *Ecclesiastical Records of New York*, VI, 4260–4261; Thomas Woody, *Early Quaker Education in Pennsylvania* (New York, 1920), 211, 243; William Webb Kemp, *The Support of Schools in Colonial New York by the Society for the Propagation of the Gospel in Foreign Parts* (New York, 1913), 56, 101–106; Edgar W. Knight, ed., *Documentary History of Education in the South before 1860* (5 vols., Chapel Hill, 1949–1955), I, 92, 95, 127, 171. Newspapers furnish many examples.

Ministers, on the other hand, usually received enough to keep them in the profession. Subsistence farm and frontier communities could not pay well, but members of the clergy were given a house, firewood, and £30 sterling; they sometimes received fees and gifts, took a few pupils, or practiced medicine. In this way they could just support a style of life that befited their superior social rank. Large towns and commercial farm communities paid from £100 exclusive of the above perquisites up to £300, salaries being highest in the South. Clergymen in these areas could live like gentlemen and a few acquired large estates. The average minister left property worth £500 or more, at least 50 percent above the general average.[1]

The income of doctors varied more than did that of ministers, but averaged about the same. A good many had no training and received what their quackery deserved. Even skilled physicians earned little in country towns, for often they were not paid at all. One of the two doctors in Ashfield, Massachusetts paid an assessment upon only a horse, owning no other farm animals, no house, and no land; the other had a house, four acres, a cow, and two pigs, paying a very low tax.[2] On the other hand the earnings of some city doctors exceeded the salaries of even the most highly-paid clergymen. One Boston physician had an annual income of £700 sterling.[3] Side by side in a Suffolk County will book are a "Physician" whose entire estate consisted of £4.2.9 in personal property, and a doctor whose books alone were worth four times as much. A South Carolina physician died worth £6,789, not including real estate, of which £5,683 was in debts; while another owned 52 slaves, a fiddle and bow, many music books, and other volumes including a set of Moliere. Ordinarily however doctors were substantial men but far from well-to-do.[4]

Lawyers, on the other hand, almost always belonged to the upper class. Their average income was probably £1,000 sterling a year if not more. Inventories indicate that they accumulated large estates, and the law was regarded as the most lucrative of all the professions.[5]

Commerce might be as profitable, but the risks were greater, and many men in trade were small enterprisers. The country shopkeepers and town retailers usually had above-average incomes, perhaps £200 — though this is a guess. Certainly they accumulated more property than their neighbors, owning twice as much personal estate as the ordinary citizen and more land than most farmers. In Groton, Connecticut, where the median assessed value for tax purposes was £33, "shopkeepers" and "traders" had £129, £122, £104, £95, £70, £59, £51, and £50. Country storekeepers in the South were sometimes poor, like the one in Jacksonburgh who owned only £29 worth of property; but they were more apt to be slaveowners and men of consequence, like Maurice Harvey of St. George's, Dorchester, with £2,905 (£415 sterling) in personal

estate alone, including five slaves, and in addition £25,178 currency in debts outstanding.[6]

Merchants who engaged in foreign commerce included poor men as well as rich, but characteristically they earned over £500 sterling and accumulated upwards of £2,000 worth of property. In all sections of the country commerce offered the best opportunity for success, and merchants stood at the very top of the economic class structure. Many spent £500 a year or more, buying imported clothes, fine foods, good wines, carriages for as much as £200, gold watches for £27 or so, costly silver, plate, and furniture. The family expenses of a Baltimore family with two children ran over £600 a year, including dancing lessons, membership in a fishing club, and losses at whist.[7]

Farmers constituted the largest occupational group in early America, including about 60 percent of the whites. Most of them had fairly small cash incomes, which varied from roughly £15 in New England, £25 in the middle states, and £40 or £50 in the South outside of North Carolina.[8] Pioneers on the frontier and the

[1] Shipton is again helpful, as is Franklin P. Dexter, ed., *Biographical Sketches of the Graduates of Yale College with Annals of the College History* (3 Vols., New York, 1885–1912). Much data on incomes is given in Hugh Egerton, ed., *The Royal Commission on the Losses and Services of American Loyalists 1783 to 1785* (Oxford, 1915). See also Charles Woodmason, *The Carolina Backcountry on the Eve of the Revolution* (ed. by Richard J. Hooker, Chapel Hill, 1953).

[2] Frederick G. Howes, *History of the Town of Ashfield* (n.p., n.d.), 95–96.

[3] Shipton, *Harvard Graduates*, IX, 429.

[4] Robert Stanton account book, 1755–1783, Connecticut Historical Society; Dr. Thomas Williams, Ledger, New York Historical Society; Samuel Holten Papers, Library of Congress; *The Boston Evening–Post*, Feb. 15, 1768.

[5] Diary of Jaspar Yeates, Historical Society of Pennsylvania; Thomas Burke to Mrs. Sydney Jones, c. 1778, Thomas Burke Papers, University of North Carolina Library; Dexter, *Yale Graduates*, III, 10; "Diary of James Allen, Esq., of Philadelphia," *Pennsylvania Magazine of History and Biography*, IX (1885), 183, 185; Duke de la Rochefoucault Liancourt, *Travels Through the United States of North America, . . .* (2 Vols., London, 1799), II, 38–39; John Caile account book, 1766–1770, Virginia Historical Society; John Mercer Account book 1736–1767, Mercer papers, *ibid.*; Massachusetts Historical Society, *Proceedings*, XLIX (1915–1916), 447; *Loyalist Claims*, 26, 40, 63, 86, 115, 119, 168, 175–177, 275, 282, 302, 311, 338.

[6] Examples of shopkeepers are Glenn Weaver, *Jonathan Trumbull* (Hartford, 1956); Charles C. Crittenden, *The Commerce of North Carolina, 1763–1789* (New Haven, 1936), 101–102; Thomas Rutherford Letter Book, Virginia Historical Society; Isaiah Tiffany Account Book 1763–1767, Connecticut Historical Society; Benjamin Snyder account book, New York Historical Society.

[7] John Davidson account books, Maryland Historical Society. Helpful are Frances Norton Mason, ed., *John Norton & Sons Merchants of London and Virginia* (Richmond, 1937) and the papers of prominent merchants such as the Caleb Davis papers, Massachusetts Historical Society, the Jeremiah Wadsworth papers, Connecticut Historical Society, and the Galloway-Marcoe-Maxie Collection, Library of Congress.

[8] Assessment lists and probate records are useful in determining the profits made by farmers. See also Douglas S. Robertson, ed., *An Englishman in America 1785 Being the Diary of Joseph Hadfield* (Toronto, 1933), 219; *The Connecticut Gazette* (New Haven), Feb. 7, 1767; *The American Mercury* (Hartford), Aug. 27, 1787; George Dangerfield, *Chancellor Robert R.*

yeomen of subsistence farm areas, who were nearly self-sufficient, probably earned less than £10 in cash; but those on commercial farms cleared several times as much. A Pennsylvanian estimated that £30 was the usual net income there.[1] Even the lowest figure, however, represents in large part clear gain, for the family spent only a few pounds for food, made almost all of its own clothing, and built its own home. The miller, the blacksmith, the shoemaker, weaver, doctor, and shopkeeper were paid in kind for a few days' labor. Only the tax collector and the creditor needed cash. Despite the low cash income of farmers, their standard of living was quite comfortable, though continuous hard work was required to maintain it.[2]

The property accumulated by the yeomen testifies to their prosperity. In Massachusetts, farmers owned nearly twice as much property as did the artisans and nearly as much as professional men, holding £100 in personal and £300 in real estate. Southerners had a higher standard of living. Samuel Carne, a typical South Carolinian, left a personal estate of £2,418 current money, or £347 sterling. He owned 2 Negro men, a wench with child, a wench with 2 children, a young wench, and a young girl, the whole amounting to £2,050. He had 24 cattle, 7 horses, and 6 hogs. His land had produced 70 bushels of rice, 150 of corn, and 12 of peas, worth about £10 sterling. William Townsend, also a representative Carolinian, had fewer slaves, but a much higher standard of living if his personal possessions are evidence. He owned, for example, an easy chair, 12 walnut chairs, 2 dining tables and a sideboard, a mahogany desk, looking glasses, napkins, 15 silver spoons, and a pair of gold sleeve buttons. The small planter Theophilus Faver of Essex County, Virginia,

who had 11 slaves and raised corn and tobacco, used pewter rather than silver, but he did own a desk, a sugar box, candlesticks and snuffers, 8 old chairs, table cloths, and a pair of sheets. His property was typical of the average farmer. He had plenty of food: 18 geese, 26 "Fat Hogs" and 19 other pigs, some honey, 3 pecks of beans, bags of fruit, onions, and 75 gallons of brandy (at 4s 6d per gallon), though his entire "waring apparrel" came to only £3.2.[3]

Large landowners made far greater profits. The great estates of such men as James DeLancey, Charles Carroll, and Robert Livingstone returned upwards of £1,000 net.[4] Southern "planters" and their northern equivalents certainly cleared well over £100 cash, not including provisions and other articles furnished by their land. Even in Massachusetts there were farmers with £5,000 worth of property, and in the South many estates were valued at more than £10,000 sterling. These men stood with the great merchants and lawyers at the apex of their society.[5]

The economic class structure of Revolutionary America was equal or unequal, democratic or undemocratic, depending upon what one means by those words and the facts one selects for emphasis. Certainly classes did exist, and economic inequalities are as obvious to us today as they were evident and alarming then. There were poor people who survived only because others provided for them, and rich people who lived in luxury, served by servants and slaves whom they exploited. In some areas considerably over half of the property was owned by a tenth of the men — men who earned fifty times as much as the common laborer and infinitely more than the slave. More than one out of five persons were held in permanent bondage; one in ten were temporarily bond servants; and at any given time another 10 percent of the whites were laborers earning little more than a subsistence wage. Furthermore, in certain parts of the country, notably the southern commercial-farm regions, these inequalities were outstanding characteristics of the society. Class antagonisms were a predictable consequence.

At the same time these class antagonisms were minimized and often entirely eliminated by opposite qualities, qualities that are especially striking when Revolutionary society is contrasted with other class structures. The proportion of servile or wage workers was small compared with that of the United States a century later, when nearly 60 percent of the people belonged to that category. In many parts of the country not over one in four or five men were laborers. Therefore a great majority belonged to the middle class of small property owners most of whom were independent enterprisers rather than dependent, salaried employees. Men of wealth, though conspicuous both for their incomes and for their style of life, yet were not to be compared with the European aristocrat or the millionaire of a later era. Moreover the proportion of property which they owned was much less than that held by the upper class of recent times, when 10 percent of the

---

[1] *Penn. Gazette*, Oct. 15, 1788.

[2] Good descriptions of the farmers are in Jedidiah Morse, *The American Geography* (2 ed., London, 1792), 313–317; *American Husbandry*, 48; Gray, *Agriculture*, I, 441–442; Schoepf, *Travels*, I, 30; *The Diary of Matthew Patten of Bedford, N.H.* (Concord, N.H., 1903); David Hickok Diary, Connecticut State Library.

[3] Inventory Book X, 356–357, 257–258, South Carolina Archives; Essex County Will Book 13, pp. 443–444, Va. State Lib.

[4] Various large incomes are, Dangerfield, *Livingston*, 29; *Loyalist Claims*, 146, 241; *Maryland Historical Magazine*, XII (1915), 27.

[5] Gray, *Agriculture*, I, 182, 218–219, 294; Schoepf, *Travels*, II, 159–160; 162; *The Journal of Nicholas Cresswell 1774–1777* (New York, 1924), 195–196; W. W. Abbot, *The Royal Governors of Georgia, 1754–1775* (Chapel Hill, 1959), 23–24; Carl Bridenbaugh, *Myths and Realities* (Baton Rouge, 1952), 67–68; *State Gazette of Georgia*, July 5, 1788; John Norton & Sons, 172.

Livingston of New York 1746–1813 (New York, 1960), 427; "Timoleon," *The Independent Gazetteer; or, the Chronicle of Freedom* (Philadelphia), Jan. 3, 1787; *An Address to the Freeholders of New Jersey* (Philadelphia, 1763), 106; Johann David Schoepf, *Travels in the Confederation* (2 Vols., Philadelphia, 1911), I, 353, *The American Museum*, II, 131–133; *North Carolina Historical Review*, II (1925), 235; *The Pennsylvania Packet*, Feb. 22, 1773; Hart, *Valley of Virginia*, 10.

people held over 60 percent of the wealth of the United States and three-fourths of that in England.[1]

Perhaps the Revolutionary American was unimpressed by this relative absence of class distinctions; but there were two circumstances that all whites regarded with satisfaction. There was a generally high level of comfort. Beggars were almost unknown; paupers were few; and the poor people were provided for. Even slaves and servants were guaranteed a minimum livelihood, while most people lived well above the subsistence level. Finally, all but the slaves could look forward to a better future. The opportunity for economic advancement was so great that probably not one out of fifteen or twenty men remained at the bottom of the economic rank order. So excellent a prospect prevented the development of a class consciousness and persuaded even the poor man that he could prosper in this land of plenty.

[1] According to a recent estimate, the wealthiest 10 percent of the people owned sixty-four percent of the wealth in 1928

and fifty-six percent in 1956. Robert J. Lampman, *The Share of Top Wealth-Holders in National Wealth* (Princeton, 1962), 215. The corresponding figure for 1776 is about forty-five percent. The following table shows the distribution of personal property (not real estate) as indicated by probate records. The sample, though it includes some 4,000 estates, is not large enough for precision, which would in any case be prevented by the different currencies used. Percentages are therefore approximate. Indentured servants and slaves are not included in probate records, so that the first column showing the general property held is accurate only for free whites. Figures are currency not sterling.

	All estates	Laborers	Teachers	Artisans	Doctors	Ministers	Traders & shopkeepers	Farmers	Merchants
£2,000+	3	0	0	0	8	7	4	4	27
£1,000–1,999	7	0	0	3	7	3	7	8	16
£500–999	10	0	0	7	15	15	13	12	13
£200–499	20	0	20	20	30	35	40	25	25
£100–199	20	2	20	20	20	15	16	20	10
£50–99	20	48	20	20	10	15	10	15	3
£1–49	20	50	40	30	10	10	10	15	6

The Historical Peculiarities of the Social and Economic Development of Russia

Boris Brutzkus

Introduction

THE POSITION OF RUSSIA in Europe appears now as it did centuries ago. Again it stands apart from the West just as it did before the reforms of Peter the Great. Indeed, it is an alien country in the occidental world, and one may well call it an enemy of that world. The real Russia lies far to the east of its old western boundaries and of its Baltic neighbors. Its capital is no longer the Europeanized Petersburg, but the ancient city of Moscow. Russia's present trade with the rest of the world, as compared with the period before World War I, has become significantly smaller, and in general its ties with the West are astonishingly weak. The work of Peter the Great, who brought the history of the old Muscovite Empire to a close by creating a new Russia and incorporating it into the European community, seems to be totally destroyed. Even his name has been taken from his magnificent capital. Another deep gulf has opened up between Russia and Europe.

The geographic environment of Russian historical development

It is immediately clear that the historic process in Russia evolved in a natural environment in many ways different from that of Europe. As the East Slavic peoples, driven by the Avars, turned toward the east in the seventh century, they had an almost unpopulated and seemingly endless expanse of plain before them.... For a long time, the Russian people had the possibility of solving their problem of a growing population through extensive expansion on the vast plain. Kljucevskij, the

Reprinted from "Die Historischen Eigentümlichkeiten der wirtschaftlichen und sozialen Entwicklung Russlands." *Jahrbücher für Kultur und Geschichte der Slaven* (1934), pp. 62–99. Translation by Reinhard Bendix. The article has been abridged somewhat, omissions from the original text have been marked by " ...." Footnotes have been added by the translator.

most observant of Russian historians, states, "The history of Russia is the history of a country that became colonized." ... The colonization of the steppes of European Russia lasted till the middle of the 19th century. Since then, great colonizing movements developed behind the Urals, in West Siberia and in Middle Asia.

The second peculiarity of Russia's geographical environment is formed by the wide zone of steppes which isolate the Russian plain along its southern boundary. The South Russian steppes are exceptionally favorable for a nomadic economy, and extend directly into the vast steppes of Middle Asia. These same steppes served as an open path for the forward progress of the nomads. The agricultural population of the Russian plain, and especially those of the wide, and extremely fertile middle zone of forests and steppes, were constantly driven out by unexpected attacks of the nomads. Only through the protection of an exceptionally strong state organization could they hold their ground. . .

And the third peculiarity of the geographical area, within which the Russian people developed, is the fact that the Russian plain lies so far distant from the centers from which all Europe's cultural development disseminated: the countries of the Mediterranean. . . .

The three most important peculiarities of Russia's geographical environment were: limitless possibilities for colonization, close proximity of the nomads, and isolation from the centers of European civilization.

However, the direct effects of these factors in the historical development of the country must have become ever less in the course of time. As the population grew rapidly and as accessible territories were fully settled, colonization decreased in significance as a means of solving the demographic problem. Since the second half of the nineteenth century, . . . intensification of agriculture and division of labor became the only answers. Danger from nomads had ceased in the eighteenth century. . . . Thirdly, transportation improved considerably when Peter the Great conquered the Baltic coast and began to build roads and canals. A permanent change in this direction took place in the 1860s and '70s when Russia was covered by a network of railroads. The country was emerging from its isolation and seemed tightly linked with the rest of Europe. It could now be truly westernized.

But the history of a people develops under peculiar, external conditions which determine its social institutions and its mental outlook. . . . In order to understand the present correctly we must turn back to the history of the old Muscovite Empire.

The rise of the Muscovite State

The Muscovite Empire freed itself from the yoke of the Tartars and it became consolidated in the second half of the fifteenth century along with the monarchies of Western Europe, England, France, and Spain. Nevertheless, the structure of the state was altogether different from that of these European countries. These Western states were formed on the basis of an already established economy, and the central power of the state strongly aided the development of the economy. On the other hand, the Muscovite state originated under conditions of complete immaturity in the economic and in the cultural sense. The old Russian forms of social and political organization, which had much in common with European feudalism, proved to be completely incapable of fighting effectively against the nomads invading from the south. . . . The formation of the Muscovite Empire was a response to the necessities which faced the people in their difficult struggle against the nomads. The Grand Dukes of Moscow, who assumed the title of Czar from the middle of the sixteenth century on, were regarded by the people as their protectors and leaders in this fight to resist the nomads. This is the historical foundation of the absolute authority granted the Czars. . . .

The formation of a great state which lacked the requisite maturity of economic development and faced such difficult military tasks, gave rise to an all-encompassing centralization of political authority and to a complete harnessing of the people's efforts. Europe had no counterpart to the absolute, iron rule which thus developed in old Russia. There were no free citizens; everyone performed arduous duties. And the position of the citizens in the society was defined by the services which they had to render their master, the Czar, whose power was unlimited.

The development of agrarian conditions in Russia

1) THE STRUCTURE OF RURAL SOCIETY IN THE MUSCOVITE STATE

Western monarchs, in their struggle against feudal lords, had but one goal: to strip them of any sovereign rights. There was no intention to nullify personal rights or to question their civil rights regarding the ownership of land. Rather, following the consolidation of the monarchies, the landed estates of the nobles were consistently extended, in keeping with the spirit of Roman Law. The Russian Bojars, who were for the most part the successors and heirs of erstwhile territorial princes, presented a far different picture. In their struggle against these nobles the rulers of Moscow had to resort to measures of much greater severity than had been the case in the West. These rulers needed immense numbers of civil and military officials. In a country which was as backward economically as Russia, the officials could not be remunerated sufficiently by money-payments; instead, they were rewarded by land-grants. An official who had not inherited any land had to be provided for by the Czar by a land-grant which was commensurate with his rank. The goal of the great confiscation of land by the Muscovite rulers in the 15th and 16th centuries was to eradicate the power of free cities and their aristocracy, and to create a pool of land with which to reward government officials. This movement reached a climax in the second half of the 16th century under Ivan the Fourth, or the Terrible, who was the first Muscovite monarch to assume the title of Czar. Ivan created a special organization, the Opricina, by means of which he sought to establish his absolute authority. The position of the Bojars was drastically weakened in politics, and a new aristocracy arose. These were the Dvorjane, or Courtiers; actually, they were officials in the Czar's government. . . .

So-called service-estates became the prevailing form of land-ownership. Yet, they were only a precarious type of landed property, because these land-grants to state officials were regulated anew from time to time in accordance with the services rendered. Inherited estates did not disappear permanently, but they declined very much in importance, and their owners were also required to perform services for the government. One loophole of this whole system was the presence of extensive and privileged landholdings by the church. However, the sixteenth century marks the beginning of ever increasing measures to halt further growth of these holdings. Free land, which was not used as grants to officials, was regarded as the property of the Czar. Peasants on this land were regarded as permanently entitled to the produce [but they did not own the land].

The concept of private ownership was severely shaken in the course of the 15th and 16th centuries. During this phase of the Muscovite state the opinion came to prevail that a civil right to property did not exist. All property belonged to the Czar. His subjects only possessed the right of usufruct, insofar as they fulfilled certain obligations to the Czar. Possession of real estate was a matter of public, not of civil law.

Serfdom also developed along different lines in Russia than in Europe. In the West all land was always supplied with workers. Dense settlement made it almost impossible for a peasant to annex free land. Russia's situation was not the same. On the vast areas of the Russian plain the peasants could be more mobile than in the West. In the second half of the 16th century, when the Russian state began to press southward, the peasants were particularly anxious to move and claim new land. The unsettled, unused and rich black earth drew the peasants irresistibly away from the forest lands in the north, which had little fertility. Officials sought to hold the peasants back through indebtedness, but this was only partially successful. Peasants often left their fields without paying their debts and without abiding by any administrative rules. The landowners always turned to the government, in order to seek out the run-aways. Due to an appalling decrease of workers competition between landholders became intense. Landlords of rank and influence pirated peasants from the landlord-officials of lesser rank. The government had to interfere ever more energetically to maintain order. Mobility was increasingly limited until, in 1647, Alexei Michailovich, second Czar of the House

of Romanov, bound all peasants permanently to the service of the aristocrat on whose land the peasant found himself at the time. . . . Serfdom originated in the main from the power of the Czar.

But the Czar did not relinquish his authority over the peasants to the land-owning aristocracy. Peasants still owed taxes to the Czar. . . . The peasants were aware that the aristocrats had received their land and the right to demand work from the peasants residing on that land as compensation for services rendered the Czar. Indeed, the peasants felt bound to the Czar only, and not to the landowners. At the end of the reign of Peter the Great, long after serfdom was well established, Pososkov, a self-taught and noteworthy social and political writer of peasant origin, expressed this basic thought very clearly. He wrote, "Land owners do not always own the peasants, and for this reason are not the most careful masters. The peasants' true ruler is the master of all the Russians, but land owners keep the peasants for a limited time only." This conviction was of exceptional importance for the further historical development. . .

2) THE DISORGANIZATION OF THE RURAL SOCIAL STRUCTURE OF THE MUSCOVITE STATE, SINCE PETER THE GREAT

The permanent serfdom of the peasants and the radical reforms of Peter the Great became firmly established through the support of the aristocracy. All other strata of the population opposed these measures, which did much, however, to strengthen the power of the aristocracy in relation to the state. Peter was successful in obtaining additional rights while freeing himself from duties, but he was soon at odds with the traditions of the old Muscovite State as well as with the convictions of the peasant population.

A change in the character of the estates of the nobles became noticeable in the second half of the seventeenth century. Development of agriculture was hindered by frequent re-divisions of already existing estates. The nobles were trying to make their lands inviolable to any power. The government took more and more cognizance of this wish, and toward the end of the seventeenth century the inheritance of landed estates was, for all practical purposes, an established fact. Peter's Decree of 1717 established fiefs as hereditary estates. . . .

Nevertheless Peter did not permit the landed aristocrats to free themselves from service. Like a true Muscovite Czar he ruthlessly punished every attempt of the nobles to evade their duties.

However, during the frequent Palace Revolutions of the eighteenth century following Peter's reign, the pressure of the aristocrats on the government became ever stronger, and they succeeded step by step in lightening their burden of governmental services. Russia's economy was by now far enough advanced so that the government could make money payments for services. Finally, in the Manifesto of 1762 by Peter the Third, the state gave up its claims to the service of the nobility. The position of the nobles was now that of a privileged estate, which possessed lands and peasants but which did not have special duties. . . .

The aristocracy used its social position to transform the rights over the peasants which the state had given them, into a proprietary right over the person of the peasant. Peasants were not bound to the soil, as was the case in most European states, but to the person of the landowner, as in Poland and in parts of Prussia. They became serfs. Landowners soon assumed the right to buy and sell peasants with or without the land. During Peter the Great's time peasant families were forcibly divided through sales of this sort. . . . Freedom for the nobility and enslavement for the peasants went hand in hand. . . .

The conceptions of the nobility and of the peasants concerning landownership were developing in opposite directions at the time when this crass difference between the freedom of the nobles and the deprivation of the peasant population was being established. For the nobles in the eighteenth century land-ownership became a matter of private property as in Roman Law. . . . During this same time the peasants developed the custom of communal land-distribution. . . .[1] In this custom the entire community rather than the individual proprietor disposes of the land. This does not mean a collective economy or communism as is often supposed. Rather, the use of this custom means that from time to time land is redistributed among families so as to utilize fully the collective effort of each family, in order to insure the greatest productivity of all the land and in order to guarantee a sufficient amount of goods for the subsistence of each family. . . .

It would be correct to say that the state and the land-owners played a significant role in firmly establishing the system of communal land-distribution. It is most important to notice here that Peter the Great, toward the end of his reign, ordered all taxes to be collected according to the actual number of males in an area. Since then "revisions" have taken place every ten to twenty years; that is to say, the number of people in the classes of each peasant community which were liable to taxation were recounted and the taxes were determined according to the results. This new head-tax strengthened considerably the position of the peasants, who were in need of land, in their fight to secure a more equal distribution of the land. It is apparent that the poor peasant could not pay as large a share of the tax load as the owners of large holdings. The latter either had to carry a tax burden which was really too heavy for any individual, or agree to land-redistribution. In so far as disputes between peasants on the public domain[2] came

before state authorities, decisions were always rendered in favor of the man needing more land and in favor of land-redistribution. Therefore, it became customary among these peasants, when no surplus of land remained, to divide land according to the number of men subject to taxation. A redistribution of the land followed each "revision" of the census.

Still another idea arose among the state-peasants, who formed a significant portion of the rural population despite the many grants of land. The government made sure that all these peasants had sufficient landholdings so that they could meet their fiscal obligations. If the peasants had too little land, the government portioned out some of its reserves, or resettled the peasants on other holdings. Also, veterans always received a portion of land upon completion of their military service. Hence, the conception arose among the peasantry on the public domain that they would always be given sufficient farmland and that they could claim a legal title to the land, in keeping with their obligations to the state.

As far as estate-owners were concerned, their peasants had no proprietary claim whatever to the land. They constantly interfered with the ownership relations of their peasants and divided land among them according to the availability of labor. In this manner communal land-distribution spread also to the peasants on the estates, although in their case this system was not developed as thoroughly as among the peasants on the public domain.

The state and the nobility prevented the development of private property among the peasants. This fact produced an unbridgeable conflict of views between aristocracy and peasantry concerning the question of landownership. The nobles regarded the ownership of land from the viewpoint of Roman Law, which was expounded systematically in the tenth volume of the Russian books of law, codified at the beginning of the nineteenth century. But the peasant had no understanding of the private ownership of land. His relation to the land was in the nature of a public right: the land must be divided among the peasants in such a way that they could feed themselves and fulfill their duties to the Czar. . . .

This opposition concealed real dangers for the smooth inner development of the Russian state. The Russian peasantry was by no means inclined to that servility, which characterized the peasants of Poland and Middle Europe. This was due in large part to the fact that in Russia the process of colonization still continued. It was always possible for the courageous peasant to escape serfdom by going to the ever-expanding frontier areas of Russia. There, the authorities needed fighting men in the struggle against the Tartars. They would enlist them as soldiers and they were reluctant to return these to the estate-owners. The most unruly portion of the population in the Muscovite state as well as in the Polish Ukraine fled from the yoke of serfdom across the border to the Steppes of the south. Here they lived in

---

[1] The author also refers to villages which adopted this system, by the term "field-communities" or "redistributive communities."

[2] The author uses the term 'Staatsbauer" or, literally, state-peasant. This refers to the peasants residing on the domain of the Czar, *i.e.*, on all land which has *not* been granted to members of the Russian aristocracy.

free communities on the basis of fishing and hunting, but in ceaseless struggle with the nomads. The Cossack areas of Southern Russia developed in this manner. The Cossacks did not shy away from raids on Russia or Poland, and under their leadership peasant mutinies could grow into real uprisings. Revolts of Ukrainian peasants under Cossack leadership played an essential part in the downfall of Poland. Such revolts occurred in Russia, too. Three of these are of particular significance. The first occurred at the time of the Great Unrest in 1607 under the leadership of a former servant, Bolotnikov, even before the definite establishment of serfdom. The second great revolt of Cossacks and peasants occurred in the Muscovite state in 1669, after the establishment of serfdom. It was led by the famous captain of brigands, Stenka Razin. That revolt, which lasted three years, was cruelly put down, but the name of Razin is glorified to the present day in Russian folk songs.

Peter the Third's Manifesto of 1762 concerning freedom from governmental service for the nobility made a strong impression on the peasantry. They were convinced the manifesto concerning the freedom of the aristocracy would soon be followed by one concerning the freedom of the peasants. When this did not take place, they grew suspicious that such a manifesto had indeed been announced but that the nobles had concealed it. The rural areas became more and more restless, until in 1773 the peasants began another tremendous revolt. The leader was Emeljan Pugachev, a Cossack, who declared himself to be Peter the Third, the legitimate Czar.

These revolts did not exercise a favorable influence on the social condition of the peasants. Rather, they deteriorated further following the suppression of the revolt under Pugachev.... These peasant revolts were repeated with each new succession to the throne, for the peasants were always awaiting for the manifesto which would give them their freedom.

3) THE EMANCIPATION OF THE PEASANTS

This unrest continued during the reign of Nikolaus the First (1825-1855). Government circles had long been convinced that a further maintenance of serfdom would endanger the state. During Nikolaus' time a number of secret commissions were developing policies for the emancipation of the peasants. But for the time being very little was done to improve their position legally. Two obstacles stood in the way of any attempts to secure freedom. First, the entire social structure of Czarist Russia was built upon serfdom. Written law applied only to a small minority of the population. The lives of the majority, i.e., the peasants, were controlled by a right founded upon custom. The abolition of serfdom would require an entire reorganization of the life of the entire population, and for a long time the government could not muster the courage needed for this task.

There was also another difficulty. It would have been possible for the government to impose a policy of emancipation upon the nobility. But the latter would not yield on one point: the land belonged to them, and peasants could never lay claim to it. Emancipation would have to come about without land. However, the government felt that on this issue the viewpoints of the two classes were in direct opposition. The peasants believed they had a right to appropriate the land, because they tilled it and because only they were bound to meet their obligations to the Czar. In this view, the nobles had forfeited their claim to the land and their right to demand services from the peasants because they had been exempted from rendering service to the Czar. Abolition of serfdom without land in the face of the existing scarcity of land, could meet with the stubborn resistance of the peasants. Hence, this project of emancipation continued to be postponed.

At the time of the unfortunate Crimean War in 1854-56 this situation came to a dangerous climax. At the moment when the armies of the enemy were standing at the border, the government was obliged to use troops against its own peasants.... The government was forced to recognize that without sweeping reforms Russia's political position could no longer be maintained. Moreover, considerations of internal security indicated that serfdom could no longer be continued. In 1857, Czar Alexander the Second declared, "It is better to abolish serfdom from above than to wait until it begins to abolish itself from below."

In 1861, serfdom was abolished at one stroke.... The conflicting interpretations of land ownership by the nobility and the peasants became immediately evident. In working out the statute of emancipation the nobles still had the idea of emancipating the peasants without land. But very soon this proved to be impractical. The nobles had to recognize that the peasants would receive the continuous use of the land which they had previously tilled, though certain limitations were imposed. Formally speaking, the peasant's land remained the property of the estate-owner, and the peasant was required to pay rent to the owner. But following the emancipation the nobles themselves were eager to sell these plots of land. Still, the peasants were by no means satisfied with the Manifesto of 1861. They believed they were entitled to all the land and that without compensation. As a result, disturbances occurred in many parts of the country when the reform was carried out. Even after the reform the peasants retained a vague hope that eventually they would receive additional land-grants....

The most important problem for the future agricultural development of Russia concerned the form which peasant land-ownership was to take. The ultimate goal of the government was to further the private ownership of land among the peasants. This goal was to be realized at some future date. In the meantime the land of the field-communities were given over to collective ownership. This all-important decision was made for two reasons. First, the payments of the peasants were to be guaranteed by the collective responsibility of all members of the community. Second, a considerable part of the former power of the estate-owners was to be vested in the peasant community, called a "Mir." This development made it especially difficult for the individual peasant to waive his claim to a part of the land and to leave the village community. And through this partial restriction of the free mobility of the peasants the nobles hoped to secure for themselves a sufficient supply of workers and tenants.

4) THE AGRARIAN CRISIS

This control of the peasants' landed property by the community was regarded as provisional in the legislative enactments of the emancipation period. Immediately after a peasant had made full payment for his piece of land he would be its free private owner. However, these regulations concerning the future disposition of the landed property of the peasants had to be abandoned in the following period. The opinion came to prevail in all parts of society that the redistributive community was a very valuable institution which should be preserved at all costs. Conservatives saw in these field communities a means of preserving the remnants of society of estates. They also felt that the field communities would prevent the rise of a landless proletariat, a social group which had proved to be revolutionary in the West. Yet the radical wing of the Russian intelligentsia, which at that time controlled public opinion, was also an ardent supporter of the redistributive community. They believed that the maintenance and development of the redistributive community was an especially advantageous way for Russia to enter directly into the stage of socialism and to escape the sufferings of capitalism. All parts of the educated public in Russia were at one in their advocacy of the so-called peasant rights as opposed to the civil code. This populist tendency so-called (Narodnichestvo), in its conservative or radical form, came to dominate public opinion completely. The Senate of the Legislature set itself the task of interpreting the law so as to work out the rights of peasants systematically. The relation of the peasants to the land was interpreted as a matter of public law. This coincided with the age-old traditions of the Russian state and of the Russian peasantry. According to these interpretations two types of communities existed in rural life: first, the individual peasant farm, and secondly, the peasant community. The farm is a cooperative; the proprietor is the representative of the farm and of the family; he is the manager of the farm-enterprise, but in no case is he the owner of the farm; this belongs to the cooperative. The peasant community is a public institution for the redistribution of land. Its activity is of a public and in no way of a private character. It supplies its members with the land they require, and the members must take responsibility in turn for the taxes which are assessed on the land.

In keeping with these views the law of 1893 put great obstacles in the way of the peasant who would waive his claim or leave the field community. The final goal of the reform of 1861, to make the peasants into free landowners, was completely dropped.

The redistributive community has proved to be a major hindrance to the progressive development of the economy. In large areas of Russia, especially in the northern regions of the "black earth" area, the peasantry suffered an economic crisis at the end of the 19th century. It was a crisis caused by over-population. The present development of agriculture did not suffice to feed the rural population. The redistributive peasant community, so highly valued by the educated classes, proved to be an institution which only corresponded to the most primitive economic conditions. It was inadequate in two ways: *1*) redistribution of land hindered the intensification of agriculture; *2*) it endangered an increase in population which could not be harmonized with the existing food supply.

In densely settled, rural areas, including the northern "black earth" regions of Russia, agrarian society must be so constituted as to promote occupational differentiation and prevent rural overpopulation. Therefore, the demographic problem must be made apparent to every peasant family. This was by no means the case in the redistributive community. A member of the redistributive community can propagate without thought for the future, because the community is obligated to provide his children with land. Since the cultivation of a large area is relatively more profitable than of a small one, even if the family is correspondingly larger, it proved to be advantageous for a member of such a community to have a large family. . . . In fact, the areas in which redistributive communities prevailed were characterized by very early marriages, very high birth and death rates, and a large natural increase of population. The whole increasing population remained in the community in the hope of receiving land from it. The individual peasant was not aware of the fact that the size of the available land stayed the same, and that with each redivision the share of each member became ever smaller. The danger of overpopulation which is obvious to the individual landowner unwittingly grows upon the peasant in the redistributive communities. The peasants also faced objective difficulties in leaving the overpopulated village because they were not permitted to sell their share of the land. As a result they could not acquire the means necessary for migration.

The redistributive community had likewise a bad effect on the economic development of the large estates. With the exception of the steppes, the lands of the plain were overpopulated; but it was nevertheless difficult for the estate-owner to obtain a steady labor supply. The son of every peasant could receive his own piece of land in the redistributive community, and he preferred to work his own farm land. The estate-owner could have more than enough tenants, therefore, but never enough steady workers. The peasants had pieces of land on which one could work but from which one could not get enough to eat. Therefore, they would try to rent some additional land from the nearby estate-owner. These owners were constantly tempted to give up running their own estates and lease the land to the peasants. They used the disparity between the supply and demand of lease-hold lands to jack up the price of rent. A majority of the owners did not engage in agriculture, but exploited the land hunger of the peasants. The impoverished peasants could only obtain annual rent contracts. On the tenant holdings the soil became exhausted. The rent of these holdings climbed rapidly while the yields diminished.

Russian agriculture was in a dead-end street. The land-shares of the peasant and their tenant holdings of the northern "black earth" area were exhausted and every drought brought a crop failure. The weakened peasant farms were in no position to cope with these failures, and the state had to intervene to prevent starvation.

5) THE AGRARIAN REVOLUTION

The agricultural economy of Russia not only brought the peasantry to a crisis situation, it also created the atmosphere for an agricultural revolution. The peasants had no understanding for private ownership of land. Everyone who worked the land with his own hands should claim as much land as he needed to live from its yield. Since the peasant communities did not have enough land, a new distribution of the land should be made. All land should be incorporated in the field-communities. These were the views of the peasants. The deeply rooted dream of the peasants concerning a general, equal distribution of the land, which must come to pass someday, took hold of the masses with renewed strength under the impact of the depression. The peasants were also animated by the idea of a self-sufficient, agricultural economy. The peasant had not created the complicated political economy; that was the work of the nobility. The poor peasant had only a few primitive needs. It was easy for him to believe that the whole division of labor within the economy was superfluous as far as he was concerned. He should be given a piece of land from which he could meet his needs *in natura*. All else was of no concern to him.

These primitive demands which emanated from the most backward of the peasants in the field-communities were accepted and elaborated by the leftist and revolutionary wing of the Populists (Narodniki). In the 20th century this wing was represented principally by the Revolutionary Socialist Party.

The Russian Populists wanted to make the Russian "Mir" the basic principle of rural society. All lands should be incorporated in the redistributive communities. But the boundaries of each field-community should lose their rigidity. A nation-wide settlement of the land question should take place. They wanted to transform all the rural areas of Russia into a single, great field-community. They wanted to create a new and subjective civil code, namely, the right to the land, the right

of every citizen to as much land as he needed in order to live from its yield. The principal task of the state should be to create the conditions under which the equal right to the land would be realized. The populists of the left hoped to eliminate all economic crises not by developing the economy, but by a permanent equalization of land-holdings. This was the idea of the socialization of the land.

Political ferment, re-enforced under the impression of the ill-fated Russo-Japanese War, also precipitated stormy agrarian movements from 1905 to 1907. Peasants burned and looted the landed estates. They were determined to "smoke out" the landowners and to incorporate their estates into the redistributive communities. However, the government managed to repress the revolts at this time. The program of the populists, which envisaged an equalizing redistribution of the land was rejected by the government, even in limited form in which the Constitutional-Democratic Party had presented this program.

Nonetheless, these significant historical problems in the realm of agrarian politics, which the aristocratic monarchy was incapable of solving peaceably, were brought significantly closer to a solution through the upheavals of the first revolution and counter-revolution.

To begin with, these agrarian revolts had liquidated and destroyed a large portion of the estates which were economically most backward. At the same time the government had decided to abandon the earlier policy of protecting the field-communities. Under the leadership of Stolypin the government now made it possible for peasants, and it encouraged them even, to sever their ties with the field-community. The economy of free exchange, which would have undermined the field-community ordinarily, was finally given free reign.

The results of the reform surpassed even the highest expectations. In the ten years before the second revolution [of 1917] over two million peasant farms withdrew from the field-community. Some did so to improve their farming methods, others to forestall a curtailment of their share of the land at the next redistribution, and still others in order to sell some or all of their land. The Russian field-community was apparently on the way out.

A rapid social differentiation set in among the peasantry. A great stream of emigrants headed for Russia's Asiatic possessions, and the government aided this migration with considerable subventions. The other peasants established new farms on land bought with the help of the Peasant Bank. Many who could not maintain themselves on their farms migrated to the cities or found employment in rural, domestic industries or on large farms. For the first time in Russia there was an extensive clearing of land and the amalgamation of many small plots. Active steps were taken to improve agricultural methods and make credit available to the peasants.

Generally speaking, the results of these reforms were very favorable. The damages to the rural economy, which had resulted from the agrarian revolts, were quickly repaired. The old routine of the peasants was broken, and the rural economy began to show real progress. A capitalistic economy developed on the large estates which remained. There was evidence of a rapid intensification of agricultural methods. The peasant began to avail himself of better means of production which were on the market, and this in turn led to the growth of Russian industry and of urban life. The position of the agricultural wage earner was markedly improved, although the agrarian reforms created a great landless proletariat. The Russian economy made such rapid progress before World War I that it was capable of absorbing the new supply of labor.

But the methods used to carry out the new reforms were too abrupt in many respects. The reforms created a sharp antagonism between different levels of the peasantry which could become dangerous under different political conditions. Nevertheless, there were no signs before World War I which presaged the collapse of the rural structure for the near future. On the contrary, the development of rural conditions seemed to indicate that the danger of a disintegration of the economy had passed. Such a danger had been inherent in the self-sufficiency of the field-community. Large masses of peasants rather than small privileged groups became involved in the transformation of agriculture on the basis of an exchange economy. Although the government was not always too careful in carrying out its new agrarian policies, and often discriminated against the peasants remaining in the field-communities, agrarian unrest had subsided by 1908, and during the years up to the second revolution the countryside was completely quiet. The peasant was otherwise preoccupied apparently, usually with taking advantage of the opportunities for economic activities within the framework of an expanding economy.

The sudden outbreak of World War I subjected the Russian state to severe tests. The state found itself unable to cope with them. Agrarian reform was far from complete. The fight between the principle of private ownership and the principle of land redistribution was still far from settled. After the overthrow of Czarist power the surviving ideas of the field-community and of a self-sufficent agriculture came to dominate the mind of the peasants, and that became a determinant of the outbreak of the Russian revolution.

The Communist Party seized power at the head of a mutinous army. It could retain this power permanently only if it could find strong support among the Russian peasantry. The Russian peasants would have been hostile to a revolutionary party, if they had had a clear conception of private property in land. This was, in fact, the case in the ceded areas of the Russian border states and in parts of the Ukraine. But the point is that the Russian peasants did not have such a conception. For 45 years after the emancipation of the peasant the Russian nobility and bureaucracy had supported the redistributive community as a conservative institution. Yet this institution

had inculcated in the peasants convictions which now proved advantageous for the unleashing of a social revolution. The peasantry used the political revolution to realize its old dream of dividing the "black earth," and this successful agrarian revolution of the peasants bound them in turn to the Communist Party, whose whole philosophy was and is entirely alien to that of the peasants. However hesitantly, the Russian peasants supported the Communist Party in the difficult fight against the counter-revolution and helped it to obtain victory. . . .

The Russian City

In the beginnings of Russian history, when Kiev was still the principal center of the Russian peoples, cities played a leading part in the economic and political life of the country. The Scandinavian sagas often referred to the Russia of the Kiev period as "Gardarijk," "the land of cities." An important trade route passed through Kievan Russia which connected Scandinavia with the Byzantine Empire. The old Russian chronicles called it the route from the Varangians to the Greeks. However, Russia was not only a country for trade in transit; she was herself active in this commerce. At that time Russia was still an unlimited, sparsely settled forest area where hunting and bee-keeping yielded produce in abundance. Such products as valuable furs, honey and wax were highly prized in the countries of the Mediterranean which had been deforested a long time ago and large quantities of them were exported from Russia. The Russian cities were situated along the rivers which constituted the only passable transportation routes through forests with thick undergrowth. The most famous cities were: Kiev on the middle Dneper River in the south and Novgorod on the Ilmen Lake at the mouth of the Volchov River in the north. There were, too, numerous other cities of significance like Rostov, Smolensk, Polock, Chernigov and others.

The cities were centers of settlement for the Normans who were gradually being assimilated by the Slavs. The Normans gathered the products of hunting and bee-keeping, which were mainly payments of tribute by subject, Slavic tribes. These products were exported to Constantinople. These Varangian rulers also carried on a large trade in Slavic slaves. Although these Russian export commodities were characteristic for a country at a low stage of economic and cultural development, this brisk trade with Byzantium was bound to produce certain positive results. From there Christianity found its way into Russia. The ruling classes of Russia came in contact with a higher culture, and their tastes lost their primitive character. Not only educated priests, but also skilled craftsmen came from the Byzantine Empire to Russia. Gradually native crafts and trades developed in Russian cities.

But this favorable economic development was interrupted by the assault of the nomads. The trade routes to the Byzantine Empire were already cut off in the twelfth century. And at the beginning of the thirteenth century the Russia of the Kiev period was permanently laid waste by the Tartars. Of the old cities, only those in North, which were in touch with the West, maintained their importance. Among them Novgorod was especially successful owing to its active trade with the German Hanseatic League. In Novgorod and in the neighboring commercial city of Pskov the bourgeoisie succeeded in occupying a governing position. Two city-republics emerged, of which Novgorod came to dominate the entire Northern part of Russia as its colony. Novgorod's trade with the Hanseatic cities remained much the same as that of the earlier Kiev-Byzantine trade, except for the slave trade which ceased. Novgorod exported products like furs, honey and wax which were exchanged principally for cloth.

The central location of the Russian peoples was shifted to the remote forest area between the Upper Volga and the Oka Rivers after the region of forests and steppes had been laid waste by the Mongols. Here, agriculture was less productive than in the Kiev area, a circumstance which was disadvantageous for the division of labor within the population. Contacts with countries of a higher culture could not be established from this isolated region. For these reasons the rapid growth of cities so characteristic of the West in the late Middle Ages did not occur in Russia during the period of the small principalities.

The autocratic Muscovite State arose in this region of economic immaturity as a necessary means of defense in the struggle of the Russian people against the nomads. The rigid military structure of the Muscovite State constituted an unbridgeable contrast to the bourgeois spirit of the city-republics in the Western areas, which had almost no contact with the Mongols. As a result, the Muscovite rulers endeavored not only to subordinate the city-republics, but also to dispossess the well-to-do bourgeoisie of these cities which was accustomed to a position of dominance. They forced the bourgeoisie to move to Moscow or to other cities, and in part they annihilated it. Two such purges took place in Novgorod, the first under Ivan III at the end of the fifteenth century, and the second one hundred years later under Ivan IV (the "Terrible"). The bourgeoisie, which had libertarian ideas, was rooted out after each of these purges. Moreover, Novgorod definitely lost its earlier importance as the main trading center of Russia, owing to the commercial decline of the German Hanseatic League in the sixteenth century.

Yet, the further expansion of the Muscovite State was not unfavorable to the development of commerce. In 1553 the English discovered the northern route to Russia by way of the White Sea and the Northern Dvina River. They received many privileges and developed an active trade in Russia. The Dutch competed successfully with the English. Products of cattle-breeding such as skins, meat, butter, tallow, etc., gained in importance in Russia's export trade in addition to the products from bee-keeping and hunting. Industrial products like weapons and cloth were imported in return. On the Caspian Sea the Muscovite State came into contact with the Transcaucasus and Persia whence it imported silk and cotton.

The significant differences between the natural and economic conditions of the areas within this vast country were favorable to the development of internal trade. The northern region of Russia is ill-suited for agriculture because of its severe climate; it is dependent on food products from the south. But the North exchanged fish, salt and furs. However, game became gradually scarce. Because of this the conquest of Siberia in the 1680s, with its trade in valuable furs, was of the greatest importance. On the other hand, the newly settled "black earth" areas produced abundant surpluses of agricultural and dairy products. Thus, a very active inter-regional trade developed within the Muscovite Empire. Moscow became a great commercial center. Cities developed on the route from the White Sea to Moscow, such as Jaroslavl, Vologda, Cholmogory, and Archangel. The same was true on the route to Siberia and on the Volga with Niznij, Novgorod, Kazan and Astrakhan.

Still, the use of money penetrated the economic life of the population of this great land only very slowly. It was only in the latter half of the seventeenth century that the state was able to obtain the greatest part of its revenue in the form of money. The large mass of the peasantry still satisfied their needs almost entirely from their own labor.

Urban development was one-sided. They were centers of trade far more than centers of production. The development of cities was insignificant where, as was the case in the "black earth" areas, there was no tie-in with international trade. In the sixteenth and seventeenth centuries the techniques of industrial production were still extraordinarily backward. The use of tools and of iron products was still very rare. The use of saws and of planes were still unknown in the sixteenth century. Even the carpentry on ships was done without the use of iron nails. Industrial products were in demand only by the state and by a very small social elite. And after the discovery of the northern route, these needs were satisfied in large measure by the English through duty-free imports. The extensive privileges of foreign merchants, especially of the English, severely hindered the native industrial development. Insofar as the country required industrial output, its production was not concentrated in the cities to the same extent as in Europe. The monasteries and the large landed estates rather avoided trading on the market; for the most part they were satisfied with the primitive products of their own craftsmen. The division between town and country was not rigid; the urban population was still partly engaged in agriculture, and there were large villages on the estates which were engaged in industrial production. And in the cities, those who were engaged in trade and industry did not only belong to the bourgeois class (posadskie); among them were also peasants, servants subject to military draft and even clergymen.

These conditions are related to the fact that the bourgeoisie of the Muscovite Empire did not succeed in creating organizations of its own in order to defend its rights, such as the craft guilds and merchant companies of the West. In the eighteenth century such organizations were created on the initiative of the government, but even then they could not assert themselves. The inner weakness of the Russian bourgeoisie was matched by its political impotence. The bourgeoisie never became strong enough to challenge the aristocracy and its ruling position in the state. As a result, the French revolution and the subsequent revolutionary movements of 1830 and 1848 had no repercussions in Russia.

Russian industry

Large-scale industry in Russia owes its origin to Peter the Great. Peter's reforms, which made deep inroads on the life of the people, resulted principally from the critical situation in foreign affairs. Russia was involved in major wars with Turkey and with Sweden. The country could not remain dependent indefinitely on imports from abroad, especially from England and Holland. In order to equip its large armies and its fleet, Russia had to learn to supply herself with weapons, munitions and metal. Also, Peter was influenced by the doctrines of mercantilism which were dominant at the time. He hoped to increase the solvency of the people and thereby the power of the State through the creation of industry on a large scale.

However, there were only very rudimentary beginnings of large-scale industry. In the seventeenth century isolated enterprises of modest size had been founded by foreigners with government support. A core of experienced workers, which usually develop out of the crafts, did not exist. But a certain amount of private capital accumulation had occurred in Muscovite Russia, although principally in trade rather than in industry. A class of entrepreneurs with considerable capital developed in the Capitol: the so-called Guests, the Guest hundred, the Cloth-hundred (*gost, gostinnaja sotnja, sukonnaja sotnja*). These entrepreneurs were wholesalers in all kinds of goods; they undertook to make large deliveries for the state, they handled the sale of liquor on a licensing basis, and they transacted the great commercial undertakings of the Czar. They also owned large salt mines. Their high profits were in no small measure the result of monopolies and privileges, and they were, therefore, disliked by the smaller merchants.

Peter the Great engaged in energetic organizing campaigns in order to create a large-scale industry. A part of the industrial enterprises which were to serve the needs of the army and navy were built, and continued to be conducted, as state enterprises. However, the entire industrial establishment could not remain exclusively a state enterprise. Thus, Peter had to enlist the rather pampered, private capital to help solve the task of industrial development. "The factories and plants which he regarded as indispensable — mines and found-ries, factories producing weapons, cloth, linen, and sail cloth — were founded by him with state capital and later turned over to private entrepreneurs. In other cases private entrepreneurs were advanced considerable sums without interest by the national treasury, and those persons who built factories on their own account were provided with tools and workers. Highly skilled craftsmen were brought from abroad. The manufacturers received important privileges. . . ." This was the origin of private industrial enterprise according to the description of Tugan-Baranovsky, the well-known Russian economist and historian of Russian industry. The state was a dependable customer for the products of these manufacturers, who were protected by high tariffs against foreign competition.

The labor management of this newly created, large-scale industry had to be organized along lines which were entirely different from those of the West. The creation of a suitable labor force for this new industry encountered great difficulties. It was impossible to find experienced and disciplined workers in Russia because of the rudimentary development of handicrafts. The sparse population of the cities could not begin to supply a sufficient number of workers for the factories. They had to be taken from the villages. But peasants on the estates were bound to the estate owner. The state-peasants usually had enough land, and they had no reason to let their farm deteriorate in order to take up the unaccustomed work in the factory. Most of the manufacturers came from the class of merchant-entrepreneurs who had no serfs of their own and were not permitted to own them, because this was a privilege of the nobility. Peter the Great found himself forced to abridge this privilege in part, despite the protests of the nobility. He ascribed villages of state-peasants to the newly-built factories, which were permitted to recruit workers forcibly from these villages. In 1721 he also permitted the manufacturers to buy serfs. But these serfs were bound to the factory, not to the manufacturer himself, in contrast to the peasant-serfs, who were bound specifically to the person of the aristocratic landowners. This was the beginning of the so-called "possessional factories."

The new possessional factories proved to be highly profitable owing to the privileges which had been granted to them. This in turn aroused the envy of the politically dominant nobility. After the death of Peter the nobles tried to curtail the privileges of the manufacturers. The nobles themselves built factories on their estates and they forced their peasant-serfs to work in these factories. The peasants, who received no wage, were ruthlessly exploited and they came to regard the building of a factory as a disaster which had befallen them. The estate-factories of the nobility generally worked up raw materials from the estate. Most of these factories produced textiles.

In the beginning the Russian factories operated at high costs, and the quality of their products left much to be desired. The lack of skilled workers and the miserable situation of the servile workers hampered their successful development. At first such an industry could not exist without high protective tariffs. Nevertheless, Russian large-scale industry made some progress in the course of the eighteenth century. Under Catherine the Second tariffs were lowered significantly; yet, the development of industry was not held back by this action.

Thus, the most valuable products of the material culture of the West were transplanted to an alien soil, thanks to the energetic initiative of a talented ruler. Measured by the standards of the West, the Russian factories were very large enterprises. There were a number of factories which employed more than 1,000 workers. Efforts were made to build the technical foundation of these factories according to the best models of the West. In her industrial development Russia occupied a major position in Europe in one fell swoop. In the eighteenth century Russian iron production, centering mainly in the Ural Mountains, was the largest in the world, and even allowed her to export iron. Russian industry was the material foundation for the military power of the Russian state which played a leading role in eighteenth century Europe.

Nevertheless, the social structure of this industry was genuinely Muscovite. It was built entirely on forced labor, which was only of minor significance in the industry of the West. And this was the underlying reason why, as Western industry changed over to machine production in the first half of the nineteenth century, Russia soon lost her industrial supremacy and economically became one of the most backward countries in Europe.

Russian industry of the eighteenth century did not yet use either motor power or machines. From a technical standpoint these enterprises were manufactures. A very singular development occurred at that time. In the West factories originated in large measure on the basis of the handicrafts and especially of the domestic industry.[1] During the second half of the eighteenth century the process which took place in Russia developed in the opposite direction, so to speak: factories proved to be most important for the dissemination of all sorts of skills in the countryside. During the reign of Catherine the Second, an important home industry developed under the direct influence of the factories, especially around Moscow. Textiles, metal and leather goods were produced cheaply and in large quantities.

It is of extraordinary significance that this domestic industry was located in the countryside and not in the cities. As a result, this development of domestic industry could not contribute to the growth of Russian cities or to the strengthening of the Russian bourgeoisie. Domestic or homeworkers were predominantly peasant-serfs. The estate owners found it advantageous to forego the compulsory services and payments in kind from those peasants who worked in the home-industry, and to substitute for these obligations a steep monetary assessment. As a result, the economic activity of their peasants could develop more freely.

Thus, the Russian factory which was based on forced labor had created a dangerous competitor for itself at the end of the 18th century. The technical advantages of the factory as compared with the home industry were not decisive. And the home-worker was far more industrious than the factory worker, for at home he worked in his own interest. In the factory the worker took no interest in the work; he was forced to work like a slave. Only the conversion of the old factories to machine technology could have helped them in their competition with the home-industry. But the use of machines is hardly compatible with the employment of forced labor. Such technical changes called for similar changes in the entire organization of production. The problem was difficult to solve in a society which was still based on serfdom. The fact that the abolition of serfdom was delayed until the 1860's proved to be unfavorable for the development of large-scale industry.

The nobility was entirely unable to reorganize its factories on the basis of machine technology and free labor. They lacked both the entrepreneurial spirit and the necessary capital. As a result, most of the factories which belonged to the nobility ceased to exist in the first half of the nineteenth century.

The owners of the possessional factories now regarded their right to use forced labor as a rather odious privilege. Their workers were bound to the factory, but the factory was in turn bound to its labor-force. The factory had to provide its labor-force with work and subsistence. Such a relationship was entirely unsuited for the progressive development of the factories. The owners of possessional factories soon decided that it would be more advantageous to get rid of this privilege. But the government hesitated until 1840 before it decided to grant the owners of possessional factories the right to set the workers free and thereby to liberate the factories from their dependence on a labor-force bound to the factory. From this date on [the 1820's and 1830's] the possessional factories gradually began to change over to the use of a free labor-force.

A new Russian factory arose in the first half of the nineteenth century which was based on machine-technology and a free labor-force. It arose out of the home-industry of the peasants and was partially independent of the old factories. Soon there developed in the villages a class of putting-out masters, with capital, who proved themselves to be far more capable than either the nobles or the possessional manufacturers. These masters brought the home-workers together in manufacture, and they began to convert the manufacture to machine-production. The workers were still peasant-serfs, but they were bound only to the estate owners to whom they had to pay certain taxes. These same workers were free wage-earners in their relation to the manufacturers. Moreover, these manufacturers themselves were still serfs at the beginning of the nineteenth century. They succeeded in obtaining their personal freedom only by overcoming many difficulties and through

[1] Also called home-industry or house-industry.

the payment of large sums of money. The families of the great industrial magnates of Moscow of the period before the First World War, such as the Morozov, Konsin, Bachrusin, and Prochorov, stemmed from these serfs who were masters in the putting-out system. This new industry was also independent of the state in a sense, because its work was done for mass-consumption rather than for the state. The great cotton-industry was a typical example of an industry which developed on the basis of free labor. This industry had become fully based on machine production long before the emancipation of the peasants. Therefore, there were two types of factories in Russia before the emancipation: one type was still based on forced labor and the other was already based on free labor. The latter type was more progressive not only socially, but also technically.

For industry emancipation of the peasants in 1861 entailed at first certain adverse repercussions. A portion of the workers felt so released from bondage or from the heavy tax-burden, that they turned their backs on the factories. It is self-evident that those factories suffered most, which had been organized on the basis of forced labor.

It took about ten years before this setback finally could be overcome. Meanwhile, certain preconditions were created for a rapid revival of industry. The emancipation of the peasants was followed by the construction of a Russian railroad network. Commerce made progress, and the market for industrial products expanded significantly. These were the economic foundations for the revival of industry in the 1870's. Now, the supply of labor no longer encountered any difficulties. In northern Russia the peasants were heavily burdened with the payments necessary to buy off their share of land and they had to seek opportunities for additional income outside of agriculture. By then large-scale industry had overcome the competition of the home industries. As a matter of fact, industrial progress led to the decline of many branches of the home-industry, especially in textiles. The peasantry became increasingly dependent on factory-work.

However, the development of industry was limited by a weak, internal market, which was caused by unfavorable agricultural conditions in central Russia. In the 1880's industry experienced a period of stagnation. In the middle 1890's the brilliant Russian minister of Finance, Sergei Julevic Witte, set himself the task of promoting the further, rapid expansion of large-scale industry. Two of his measures were of special importance. First Witte undertook new railroad-constructions on a large scale, especially the construction of the stupendous, Transsiberian railway. This project provided industry, and especially the iron-industry, with profitable orders. And it gradually incorporated in the national economy the far-flung border-areas of Russia with their inexhaustible sources of raw materials. Second, Witte proceeded to base the national economy on the gold standard, a measure of the greatest significance. In this way, the Russian economy was related more

closely to the European money-market, and as a result European capital could risk participation in the expansion of Russian industry. Russian industry, especially the iron industry, got a tremendous boost in the 1890's. Owing to the influx of foreign capital excellent coal mines, foundries and metal industries developed in southern Russia centering in the Donetz Basin and Krivoj Rog. In its economic significance this new industry became the cornerstone of the entire Russian economy far surpassing the corresponding industries in the Urals, whose organization remained backward.

The weak side of Russian industry as a whole was the excessive dependence of its heavy industry on the program of railroad construction. The large masses of peasants in their field-communities were still engaged in a subsistence economy. They did not need any improved tools yet, and the roofs of their houses were still covered with straw, not with sheet metal. The population at large, then, did not as yet constitute a market sufficiently extensive for the built-up, heavy industry. When large-scale railroad construction drew to a close at the turn of the century, the heavy industry experienced a severe trade-depression which lasted from 1900 to 1909. Light industry, and especially textile production, was less affected by the crisis, its progress continued, though at a somewhat slower pace.

But Russian agriculture had been directed into new channels, in the meantime, by the Revolution of 1905 and the reforms of Stolypin. Large numbers of single peasant farms had been rounded out and were now being developed along progressive lines. Rural cooperatives developed with great success, which encouraged the extension of modern agricultural methods even among those peasants who still remained in the field-communities. Also, those estates which remained after the upheavals of the revolution, partook of a progressive, i.e., capitalist, development. In the rural areas the division of labor developed at a rapid rate, and this led in turn to a rapid urban development. The decisive fact was that so far a hundred million Russian peasants had entered the market only to purchase necessities, and even these only in very modest quantities, while now they finally entered the market in order to purchase also means of production for their own use. They demanded hardware, sheet metal, farm machinery and tools, etc.

From 1909 to the outbreak of the First World War the entire Russian industry moved forward rapidly. There was reason to believe that this recovery had a more stable basis than that of the 1890's, because the heavy industry was no longer pushed ahead by railroad construction alone. It now produced for a large internal market. The capital market was also enriched by savings of the people to a much greater extent than in the 1890's.

The Russian working class

In spite of this great recovery on the eve of the First World War, Russian industry was still by no means capable to meet the demands of a war economy. Compared with Europe, moreover, there remained in the labor relations of Russian industry certain historic peculiarities which contained great dangers.

These peculiarities resulted from the historical fact that large-scale industry in Russia had not developed organically on the basis of handicraft-production and of small-scale industry in the cities. For this reason its labor-force was recruited principally from the villages. It was very difficult for the worker to sever his ties with the village owing to the peculiar development of agrarian conditions up to the time of Stolypin's reforms. The largest part of the labor-force belonged to the peasantry up to the end of the 19th century, and workers were actually in closest contact with the village. Each year, a worker had to obtain a new passport from his village. Either he or the members of his family had a share of land in the field-community for which a high land tax had to be paid. The community could refuse renewal of the passport, if the tax had not been paid. Most workers sent a portion of their wages to their family in the village. A worker's wife and children seldom lived together with him in the city. Usually they lived in the village where they continued farming at a primitive level in order to meet their basic needs.

This separation of families was by no means favorable for labor productivity. The worker did not feel himself to be a part of the factory, and his ties to the factory always remained tenuous. He often changed jobs. He regarded his life in the city as a passing thing. When he grew old he returned to the village. And his children grew up in a village environment which stood in no relation to the occupation of a future industrial worker.

The disruption of his family also had an adverse effect on the moral life of the worker. Drunkenness was widespread among laborers. The terrible housing shortage in the Russian cities became so bad that the worker was not even able to rent a room. Usually he rented only the corner of a room. In the industrial areas of Moscow the manufacturers usually built barracks for their workers. However inadequate, this was the only way to deal with the housing shortage. Such poor housing conditions had a depressing effect on the workers.

The productive performance of the Russian worker was very modest despite his great native talents. He was not sufficiently dependable. Large-scale industry, which had once been based exclusively on forced labor, still continued to be based on a low level of wages. This was typical of the entire industrial organization in Russia. Only highly skilled workers were well paid, often even better than abroad, because such workers continued to be rather scarce in Russia since a class of well-trained craftsmen had not existed earlier.

The general development in Russia as in the West was, nevertheless, in the direction of loosening the ties that traditionally bound the worker to the village. The majority of workers had less and less prospect of ever returning to the already overpopulated village.

Workers already had some degree of education, and their contact with urban life created new desires. However, the overpopulated countryside produced a mass-migration to the city, which destroyed every chance of higher wages for the workers. The entire organization of Russian industry would have had to undergo a basic transformation to make such higher wages possible. But the managers of industry did not yet see any pressing need to introduce such a reform.

Still, a few far-sighted manufacturers discerned the approaching danger, and others also wanted to improve the condition of their workers on humanitarian grounds. A few of these men, especially in the Moscow area, developed noteworthy provisions for their workers. They built working-class houses, schools, nurseries, and so on.

The government, too, found itself obliged to deal with the labor problem. The beginning of Russian labor legislation dates from the years 1845 and 1866. In the 80's important laws were enacted for the protection of young workers and working women. A regular inspection of factories was introduced. Finally, the law of June 2, 1897, limited the working hours of adults. It stipulated a maximum working-day of $11\frac{1}{2}$ hours, and a maximum of 10 hours before a holiday. A further law, dated June 2, 1903, made it obligatory upon the entrepreneur to indemnify the worker in case of accidents. However, the laws were enacted in the absence of an organized working class which could protect its rights. On the other hand, industrialists were organized, and they exercised a certain amount of influence on the government. Thus, the effect of this protective labor legislation was very much reduced by means of supplementary instructions.

A basic improvement in the condition of the working class could not be enacted from above. This could be achieved only through the independent activity of the workers themselves. But the demands of the workers fell on deaf ears. The Russian state continued to be strictly autocratic. The weak Russian bourgeoisie was not in a position to transform the state in the direction of liberalism. A freedom to form coalitions did not exist in this state, and any organization of workers was entirely incompatible with the whole structure of the Russian state. There was no legal way for the workers to improve their condition. The only remaining alternative for young and audacious members of the working class was to engage in revolutionary activities.

The radical Russian intelligentsia had conducted a bitter fight against autocracy for many years. In the 1870's it had already made certain isolated attempts to develop revolutionary agitation among the industrial workers. But these attempts were not yet of a systematic character. For at that time the "Populists" dominated the intelligentsia politically, and they focused their attention more on the peasantry than on the workers. In the 1890's the Marxist movement developed among members of the radical intelligentsia in a bitter ideological struggle against the populists. Various groups of the intelligentsia engaged in socialist agitation among the workers, and attempts were made to create secret organizations of workers. Finally a secret Russian Social-Democratic Party was founded in 1898, which claimed for itself the leadership of the worker-class movement. Socialistic agitation had a certain success among the workers. This created great anxiety in the autocratic government. As a result, the government decided upon the use of very dangerous means in its fight against socialism.

At the instigation of Zubatov, director of Moscow's Political Security Police, the government itself undertook to create worker-organizations, which would be led by the political police. The police was to come forth as the protector of the workers against their exploitation by the bourgeoisie. In this way the government wanted to compete with the social democrats for the favor of the workers. The hopes of the oppressed working masses were extraordinarily raised by virtue of this competing organization of the political police. Yet, the government had no positive program; its only aim was to incite the workers against the radical intelligentsia. That was playing with fire. As early as 1903 the agitation of the political police led to partly unanticipated, mass demonstrations by the workers. And on January 9, 1905, great throngs of workers in Petersburg with Gapon, a priest supported by the police, at their head, marched on the Winter Palace, carrying images of Saints, in order to ask their dear father, the Czar, for his promised help. In his deadly fear the Czar could only think of meeting these childishly naive working masses, who had been misled by his own agents, by rounds of rifle fire. Blood flowed freely in the streets of Petersburg. On that day the Czar forever lost his historically derived authority over the workers. Thus, one may say that the revolution was set ablaze by the Russian autocracy itself.

Autocracy was forced to yield on some points and after serious fighting it succeeded in subduing the first revolution.

This revolution entailed important changes in the social structure of Russia, which were bound to influence the position of the working class. Stolypin's agrarian legislation made it possible for workers to withdraw from the peasantry, to sell their share of land, and definitely to sever their ties with the village. The process of developing a real industrial work force was greatly advanced thereby. But real workers who settled with their families in the city, had to demand better wages. It was conceivable that the revolution had created certain new possibilities for the systematic improvement of the worker's position. In view of the labor movement that had developed, the government granted the workers the right to organize. But it was a vain hope to suppose that the workers, organized in trade unions, would manage to improve their economic position step by step, and to bring a corresponding influence to bear on the organization of industry. The trade union movement developed very quickly, but it also lost its mo-

mentum in a short time. Part of the fault lay with the workers, who were poorly prepared to administer their own affairs and who were moreover in a restive mood. But the government, too, was partly to blame. The autocratic tendencies within the government again increased in strength while the revolutionary momentum ebbed away. Autocracy had not been overcome definitely. Russia still merely appeared to have a constitutional regime. The bureaucracy could not reconcile itself to the existence of trade unions as a social force, and it utilized every misdemeanour of the trade unions in order to prohibit them. Hence the workers could not better their position through the trade unions. To be sure, in 1912 the government took another important step in the development of protective labor legislation: accident insurance was expanded further, and the first important measures were taken to establish health insurance. However, this could not replace the independent activities of the workers themselves, nor could it quiet them.

Moreover, the actions of the autocratic government provoked the workers time and again. In 1912 a strike broke out in the Lena gold fields, Without sufficient reason, the authorities ordered the workers fired upon, leaving five hundred dead and wounded. This provoked a storm of indignation among the workers and in the society at large. Innumerable sympathy-strikes took place accompanied by worker-demonstrations.

The mood of the working class was especially disturbed before the outbreak of the First World War. Russian industry was advancing rapidly and it was passing through a period of great prosperity. The workers wanted a share of the increased profits. Because of the weakness of the trade union organizations, the strike seemed to them the only way to realize their wishes.

A revolutionary temper was also notable among the proletariat of many other countries. The Russian proletariat differed only in terms of the characteristic intensity of this temper. This was the result of two causes, as the preceding historical survey has made evident. First, the entire Russian industry was based historically on workers who came from, and were still tied to, the village, who were unreliable and poorly paid. The process whereby industry would come to depend on a more reliable and better paid worker was still in its infancy. Secondly, the fact was that Russian absolutism could not be overcome, definitely, and as a consequence the Russian proletariat had no legal way to improve its position; the path of a revolutionary struggle remained as the only way out.

The extraordinary concentration of Russian industry facilitated the political struggle of the proletariat. This concentration was also due to the fact that Russian industry was built up from above through the initiative of the state and of large capital investments, partly from abroad, rather than on the basis of urban handicrafts and small-scale industry. The vertical concentration of different branches of production was a necessity for an industry of this kind. Compared with the size of the country, the scale of Russian industry was still moderate. But it consisted of very large, and partly of gigantic plants, in which it was relatively easy to organize the workers in political demonstrations.

Czarism fell because of its military defeat and its internal disintegration, and the Communist Party seized power with the help of mutinous troops in the rear. The party leader, Lenin, was confronted with a revolutionary proletariat which did not even need to be incited, with an impotent, politically inexperienced bourgeoisie, and with masses of peasants who had no

conception of the principle of private ownership in land. Once the peasants were promised the "black redistribution" of the land, the social revolution could be realized in the fullest extent. The Russian state, its economy and culture, which had been built up by the long and difficult historical efforts of the Russian people, lay in ruins. A victorious successor of Stenka Razin had conquered the empire of the Czars after 250 years and the red flag of world disaster, of world revolution now waves over the Kremlin of Moscow, where the Czars once ruled.

Japan's Aristocratic Revolution

Thomas C. Smith

"AN ARISTOCRACY," Alexis de Tocqueville wrote, "seldom yields [its privileges] without a protracted struggle, in the course of which implacable animosities are kindled between the different classes of society." Despite our democratic partialities, most of us would add, "And why should it?" To know the exalted pleasures of power, and the grace of refined taste with the means of satisfying it; to believe oneself superior on the only evidence that gives conviction — the behavior of others; and to enjoy all this as birthright, with no vitiating struggle, nor any doubt that one's privileges are for God, King, country and the good of one's fellow man — what happier human condition, for a few, have men devised?

Yet, not all aristocracies have behaved as one fancies they must. Japan's warrior class, a feudal aristocracy though it differed from European aristocracies in crucial respects, did not merely surrender its privileges. It abolished them. There was no democratic revolution in Japan because none was necessary: the aristocracy itself was revolutionary.

Consider the bare outlines of the case. Until 1868, Japan was ruled by a class of knights who alone had the right to hold public office and bear arms and whose cultural superiority the rest of the population acknowledged. A party within this aristocracy of the sword (and swagger) took power in 1868 and embarked on a series of extraordinary reforms. Where there had before been little more than a league of great nobles, they created an immensely powerful central government: they abolished all estate distinctions, doing away with warrior privileges and throwing office open to anyone with

the education and ability to hold it; they instituted a system of compulsory military service, although commoners had previously been forbidden on pain of death to possess arms; they established a system of universal public education; and much else. The result was a generation of sweeping and breathless change such as history had rarely seen until this century. I believe, though of course I cannot prove, that these decades brought greater changes to Japan than did the Great Revolution of 1789 to France.

Why was the Japanese aristocracy — or part of it — revolutionary? Why did it abandon the shelter of its historic privileges for the rigors of free competition, which, incidentally, many warriors did not survive? Its behavior, like that of a man who takes cold baths in the morning, requires a special explanation.

Two general lines of explanation have been offered; though no bald summary can do them justice, even on fuller account they leave much unexplained.

One might be called the prescient patriot theory. That is, the foreign crisis — to be quite specific, the unamiable Yankee, Commodore Perry, and the Americans, English, and Russians who followed him — stimulated the patriotism of the warriors and demonstrated to them the inadequacy of existing institutions, prompting them to make revolutionary innovations in the name of national salvation. This I believe is quite true in a way. But it takes for granted what most needs explaining. Communities in danger do not necessarily seek safety in innovation; commonly they reaffirm tradition and cling to it the more resolutely. Such was the first response to the challenge of the modern West in China and

Reprinted from *Yale Review*, V. 50 (1960–1961), pp. 370–383, by permission of the author and the publisher.

Korea; it also had intelligent and patriotic spokesmen in Japan.

The other explanation may be called the Western analogue theory. It emphasizes (in the century before Perry's arrival) the improvement of transport, the growth of towns, the development of trade, and the rise of a wealthy merchant class — all important developments which add much to our knowledge of pre-modern Japan. But, suggestive as they are, these developments would better explain, keeping the Western analogy in mind, an aristocracy being overthrown or reluctantly forced to share power with a rising new class, than an aristocracy conducting a social revolution.

Differences, rather than analogies, would seem more to the point. The man who takes cold baths is made of different stuff from most of us; and the Japanese warrior differed from the European aristocrat in ways that throw light on his seemingly odd class behavior. I wish to discuss three such ways that any satisfactory explanation of the aristocratic revolution, as I will call it, would have to take into account. One has to do with the relations of the warrior to the merchant class; another with social and economic distinctions within the warrior class; and the third with the relations of the warrior class to land and political power.

My earlier statement that there was no democratic revolution in Japan because the aristocracy was revolutionary has an important corollary: had there been a democratic revolution, the aristocracy would not have been revolutionary. Nothing unites an aristocracy so quickly and firmly in defense of its privileges as an attack from below, by classes in which it can perceive neither distinction nor virtue.

Unlike the Western bourgeoisie, townsmen in Japan never challenged aristocratic privileges, either in practice or theory. They were seemingly content with a secondary political role, finding apparent satisfaction in money-making, family life, and the delights of a racy and exuberant city culture. This political passivity is puzzling. It is not to be explained by numerical weakness (Tokyo was a city of a million people in the late eighteenth century, and Osaka was only slightly smaller); nor by poverty, nor illiteracy, nor political innocence. Least of all is it to be understood as reflecting an absence of resentment at the warriors' smug and strutting pretensions. There was resentment aplenty and there were many instances of private revenge; but for some reason resentment never reached the pitch of ideology, never raised petty private hurts to a great principle of struggle between right and wrong. For whatever reasons, townsmen acknowledged the political primacy of the warrior, leaving him free to experiment without fear that to change anything would endanger everything.

But, one may suppose, no ruling group ever launches on a career of radical reform merely because it is free to do so; there must be positive incentives as well. In the Japanese case these incentives were in part born of differences within the aristocracy. Such differences were not unique to Japan, of course, but they can rarely have been more pronounced anywhere.

On the one hand were a few thousand families of superior lineage and very large income, with imposing retinues and magnificent houses, who in practice, though not in law, monopolized the important offices of government; some offices in effect became hereditary. On the other hand was the bulk of the warrior class, numbering several hundred thousand families, who were cut off from high office and lived on very modest incomes; many in real poverty, pawning their armor and family heirlooms, doing industrial piecework at home to eke out small stipends, and resorting to such pitiful tricks as sewing strips of white cloth to the undersides of their collars so people might take them to be wearing proper undergarments. As warrior mothers proudly taught their children, a samurai might have an empty belly but he used a toothpick all the same.

But it was not so much the contrast between his own and the style of life of his superior that moved the ordinary warrior to fury. It was, rather, the impropriety of the merchant's wealth. Surely it was a perversion of social justice, that the warrior, who gave his life to public service, should live in want and squalor, while men who devoted themselves to money-making lived in ease and elegance, treated him with condescension and even rudeness, and in the end not infrequently found favor with the lord.

The merchant himself was not to blame since he merely followed his nature. Though he was feared and hated for that, ultimate responsibility lay with the effeminate high aristocrats who, through idleness or incompetence, failed to use their inherited power for the proper ends of government. No secret was made of the failure, either. Political writings were full of charges of the incompetence and corruption of government, of the fecklessness and indifference of princes; and the only remedy, it was said, lay in giving power to new men — men of lower rank, who were close to the people and whose characters had been formed by hardship. This was no revolutionary doctrine. It called for a change of men, not institutions; but the men it helped to power were in fact radical innovators.

This brings me to the final difference — or rather to two differences — between the Japanese warrior class and European aristocrats. Japanese warriors did not own land, and their political power was to a greater extent bureaucratic. I want to say more on these points, but first it will be helpful to see how a once feudal aristocracy had come to be without private economic or political power.

We must go back to the late sixteenth century. At that time warriors were scattered over the land in villages where they were overlords, levying taxes, administering justice, and keeping the peace. To defend their territories and lessen the hazards of life, they had long since banded together into regional military organizations consisting of a lord and his vassals. The normal state among such groups was war or preparation for war, that being the most direct means of increasing territory and territory of increasing strength and security.

Then, about the turn of the century, Tokugawa Ieyasu, a man of authentic genius, who had the remarkably good fortune of having two brilliant predecessors who had already half done what he intended, succeeded in conquering the country. Instead of destroying the feudal leagues or groups, however, he chose to use them to govern, taking care only to establish his own firm control over them. Seemingly a compromise between order and chaos, the resulting political structure, surprisingly, kept the peace for two and a half centuries.

These long years of orderly government, which favored economic growth and urban development, brought profound changes to the warrior class, altering not so much, however, the fact of warrior power (which remained uncontested) as the nature of it. I would like to mention three such changes in particular.

First was a change in the relation of warriors to the land. The lord, in order better to control his vassals and to achieve greater uniformity of administration within the territory he dominated, gradually restricted his vassals' power over their fiefs. He forbade them to administer local justice; he moved them from the land into a town which now grew up around his castle; he decreed what taxes they might collect and at what rates, then decided to collect the taxes himself and in return to pay them stipends in money or kind from his treasury.

There were local exceptions to the rule, but taking the country as a whole, fiefs in land disappeared. Land and the seignorial rights associated with it, once widely dispersed through the warrior class, were now consolidated in the hands of a few hundred noble families. The typical warrior had become a townsman living on a salary paid him by the lord, with the townsman's disdain for the country and country people. Both his juridical and social ties with the land were gone. If his fief was still an identifiable piece of land at all, it was rarely more than a unit of account, with other land, under the lord's common administration.

Second was the resulting bureaucratization of government. The lord, having taken into his hands his vassals' political and judicial functions, now governed an average population of about 100,000. To police so large a population, to collect its taxes and regulate its trade, to give it justice and maintain its roads and irrigation works, required a small army of officials and clerks. The lord, of course, used his vassals to perform these functions, to man the expanding and differentiating bureaucracy under him. The warriors who manned the bureaucracy exercised far more power over the rest of the population than warriors ever had before; but it was a new kind of power. Formerly power was personal and territorial: it pertained to a piece of land and belonged to a man as inherited right. Now it was impersonal and bureaucratic: it pertained to a specialized office to which one must be appointed and from which he might be removed.

There is unmistakable evidence of the increasingly bureaucratic nature of power in the more and more impersonal criteria for selecting officials. However writers on government might differ on other matters, by the late eighteenth century they were in astonishingly unanimous agreement that ability and specialized knowledge should take precedence over lineage and family rank in the appointment and promotion of officials. To this end they devised tests for office, job descriptions, fitness reports, official allowances, salary schedules, and pensions.

It was only in the lower ranks of officials that the ideal of impersonality came close to realization. Nevertheless, men of low rank were sometimes promoted to high office; merchants and occasionally even peasants with specialized qualifications were ennobled that they might hold office; and promotion in the bureaucracy became for warriors an important means of improving status. If the highest offices usually went to certain well-placed families, this was looked on as an abuse rather than proper recognition of rank, and an abuse that struck at the very foundations of good government. Moreover, many families of high rank were without office, and office rather than rank or wealth gave power.

Thus a group of young samurai who met on the morrow of Perry's first alarming visit to Japan, to consider what they might do for their country, were exhorted by their leader to do what they could *even though none held office.* One cried out: "But what *can* we do without office!" No one, it seems, complained of the lack of age, wealth, or high rank in the group.

The third change I would like to mention followed very largely from the second. The relationship between vassal and lord was slowly, silently, and profoundly transformed. It had been an intimate, intensely emotional relationship, based in no small part on the personal qualities of the lord, a relationship which existed between men who had fought side by side, grieved together at the loss of comrades, whose safety and families' safety depended on their keeping faith. During the centuries of peace and urban living, however, the relationship lost much of its emotional significance. It became distant and formal; it was hedged about by ceremonies and taboos; the vassal came to look on his lord less as a leader in war (for there was no war) than as an administrative head.

One sees this change in the changing concept of the ideal warrior. Once a strong, stout-hearted fellow, quick and warm in his sympathies, generous to the weak and unyielding to the strong, he becomes a man whose native intelligence has been disciplined in the classroom, who gets on harmoniously with his colleagues, who deals with matters within his jurisdiction without fear or favor. Loyalty is still the highest virtue for him; but where once it had meant willingness to follow the lord to death, now it meant giving the lord disinterested advice and conducting oneself in a way reflecting credit on his administration. Qualities of the ideal bureaucrat had come to be viewed as the very essence of the warrior.

Moreover, the power of the lord as administrative head increasingly became merely symbolic; actual power passed to lower echelons of officials. Partly this was a result of the growing complexity of government, but in greater measure it was because the lord's position was hereditary and as time passed fewer and fewer of his breed were men of force and intelligence, fit for the top job. Vassals who still looked on the lord with awe were likely to be men who regarded him from a distance; those who saw him closer, despite all outward deference, could often scarcely conceal their contempt.

Indeed some hardly tried. An anonymous author, writing about 1860, calls the lords of his day time-servers; men brought up by women deep in the interior of palaces where no sound of the outside world penetrated; surrounded from childhood by luxury and indulged in every whim, they were physically weak and innocent of both learning and practical experience. But it was not revolution that was called for, only better education for rulers, that they might choose better officials. "The secret of good government," the writer confidently declared, "lies in each official discharging his particular office properly, which in turn depends on choosing the right man for the right job."

To summarize up to this point: the two and a half centuries of peace after 1600 brought great changes to the warrior class. They brought a change in the warrior's relationship to the land, which became purely administrative; in his relationship to political power, which became bureaucratic; and in his relationship to his lord, which became distant and impersonal.

I should like now to show, as concretely as I can, the connection between these changes and some aspects of the economic and social transformation of the country after 1868 — my so-called aristocratic revolution.

Consider the creation in the years immediately after 1868 of a highly centralized government. This was a brilliant achievement which permitted the new leaders who came to power to formulate for the first time a national purpose and to call up energies that did not before exist. Political power had lain scattered in fragments over the map, each lord collecting his own taxes, maintaining his own army and navy, even following an independent foreign policy. Then, with astonishing speed, the fragments were pulled together; a central government created; the entire country subjected to a single will. Feudal lords and their miniature kingdoms were swept away and one bureaucratic empire emerged in their place.

This change was possible in part because warriors had long since been removed from the land and stripped of seignorial rights. Had these interests remained, the warrior must first have been dispossessed of them — the base of his power and source of his pride. Whoever might eventually have succeeded in this would not likely himself have been a warrior, nor have accomp-

lished the feat without a long and bitter struggle. As it was, only the great lords had to be deprived of their power, and the deed was sooner done because their powers had come to be exercised, in fact, by officials who might trade them for similar powers within a vastly larger organization.

But what of the vaunted loyalty of the samurai? One would think this must have prevented liquidation of the great territorial lords by their own vassals. The unconditional loyalty to the lord as war leader, however, had shrunk to the conditional loyalty of the administrative subordinate to his chief — a loyalty valid only so long as the chief performed his duties efficiently. That the great lords had long ceased to do this was known to all. Meanwhile a new and higher loyalty emerged, sanctioning — indeed, those who prevailed thought, demanding — the transfer of all power to a central government. This was loyalty to the Emperor, in whose name the aristocratic revolution was carried out. Nor was the emergence of this new loyalty unconnected with the decline of the older one: one suspects that men brought up in the cult of loyalty to the lord, as an absolute obligation and the noblest of human ideals, needed some escape from the disloyalty they felt in their hearts.

Second, consider how the new central government used its power to liquidate the four estates of which society was legally composed. Each estate — warrior, peasant, artisan, and merchant — was theoretically closed, and subject to detailed restrictions concerning occupation, residence, food, and dress peculiar to itself. The new government swept away such restrictions, and endowed men with extensive civic, though not political, rights. Henceforth anything that was legally permissible or obligatory for one, was permissible or obligatory for all; moreover, a system of free public schools very soon gave this new legal dispensation concrete social meaning. The warrior lost his privileges and immunities and was forced to compete in school and out with the sons of tradesmen and peasants. Even his economic privileges were done away with. Warrior stipends were commuted into national bonds redeemable in twenty years, after which time warriors, as such, had no claim on the national income.

Now, how is one to explain a ruling class thus liquidating its privileges, and not by a series of forced retreats but as a single willing stroke? Surely part of the answer lies in warrior privileges not being bound up with the ownership of land. To restrict or even abolish them, therefore, did not arouse fears for the safety of property, or stir those complicated emotions that seem to attach peculiarly to land as a symbol of family continuity and an assurance of the continuing deference of neighbors. Few ruling classes have ever been so free of economic bias against change. Warrior power was based almost exclusively on office-holding, and this monopoly was not immediately in danger because no other class had yet the experience, education, and confidence to displace warriors in administration. The striking down of barriers between estates, on the other hand, opened up to warriors occupational opportunities formerly denied them, a not insignificant gain in view of the large number of warriors who, with more than normal pride but neither property nor important office, were nearly indigent.

This brings me to a third aspect of the revolutionary transformation of Japanese society after 1868: the explosion of individual energies that followed the sudden abolition of status distinctions. Until then opportunity was very limited; men looked forward to following the occupations of their fathers, and even to living out their lives in their same villages and towns and houses. After it, everything seemed suddenly changed, and young men strove with leaping hope and fearful determination to improve their characters, to rise in the world, to become something different from their fathers.

For warriors the abolition of status restrictions meant finding new occupations and new roles in society. Few had enough property after the commutation of stipends to live without work, and not all could continue in the traditional occupations of soldier, official, policeman, and teacher. A very large number were forced either to suffer social eclipse or become merchants, industrialists, lawyers, engineers, scientists; or they saw in these occupations exciting new opportunities for wealth and fame.

In any case, there was a grand redirection of warrior talent and ambition. Despite the traditional warrior aversion to money-making and the merchant's love of it, for example, most of the first generation of modern entrepreneurs, above all the earliest and most daring, came from the warrior class. Nor is this to be explained merely by the occupational displacement of the warrior. Part of the explanation lies in the warrior's aristocratic background — his educational preferment under the old regime, his cult of action, and (at his best) his intense social idealism.

Okano Kitaro, a man born in a warrior family of low rank, who founded an important provincial bank, illustrates the point. He writes in his autobiography: "I lost my wife and third daughter in the earthquake of 1923. They were on their way to a resort hotel when the great quake struck, and their train plunged into the sea. When news of the accident reached me my courage failed, but after a while my sense of responsibility returned and I thought to myself, 'You are head of the Suruga Bank! You must discharge your duty as a banker in this time of trouble! Compared to that, your personal loss is a trifling matter!' My whole body trembled."

Other classes were scarcely less affected than warriors. Finding themselves suddenly free to become whatever wishes, effort, and ability could make them, with not even the highest positions in society closed to competition, they responded with an heroic effort at self-transcendence. Freedom of this kind must always be heady; but one wonders if it is not especially so when it comes suddenly, in societies with a strong sense of status differences, where the social rewards of success are more finely graded and seem sweeter than in societies less schooled to such distinctions.

In a charming little anecdote in his autobiography, Ito Chubei, the son of a peasant who became a leading industrialist, gives some hint of the poignancy of the hopes for success he shared with other peasant boys of his generation. Upon graduating from elementary school not long after 1868, the first boy in his village to do so, Ito called on the headmaster to take leave. He was not surprised to meet with an angry scolding, since he had been far from the model boy. After the master finished his scolding, however, he spoke glowingly of Ito's future and predicted that, despite his rebelliousness, he would be a success. "You will make your mark in the world, I know it!" he exclaimed. And at this the young boy, unable to hold back his tears, wept aloud. Years later, in recounting this incident to a reunion of his classmates, Ito was so affected that he wept again, and his gratitude to his former teacher was no less when, after the meeting, he discovered that all of his classmates had been sent off with exactly the same exhortation!

Such hopes were real because, though not everyone was equal in the competition for wealth and honor, the privileged estate under the old regime had no prohibitive or enduring advantage. In respect to income, for example, warriors were at no advantage over the rest of the population, and though they were the most literate class in society, literacy was very widespread among other classes as well, and it rapidly became more so through the new schools. But most important, perhaps, warriors could not for long claim a cultural superiority, compounded of superior education, elegance, and taste, to act as a bar to the achievement of others, or to divert others from achievement in the pursuit of aristocratic culture. Indeed, by the twentieth century, one can scarcely speak of an aristocratic culture in Japan, despite the peerage created by the government in 1885. Whether a young man came of warrior family could no longer be reliably told from his speech, manners, or social ideas; moreover, his origins were far less important to his self-esteem and the good opinion of others than whether he had a university diploma and where he was employed. I want to return to this point.

In hope of making its revolutionary behavior less puzzling than must otherwise appear, I have discussed three ways the Japanese warrior class differed from Western aristocracies — its relation to other classes, its internal divisions, and its relation to economic and political power. I should like now to suggest, very briefly, some of the ways in which Japanese society seems to be different because its modern revolution was aristocratic rather than democratic.

First, a point so obvious it need only be mentioned in passing: the aristocratic revolution, despite the civil equality and economic progress it brought, has not made for a strong democratic political tradition — but the contrary.

Second, more than any other single factor, perhaps, that revolution helps explain Japan's rapid transition from an agrarian to an industrial society. How different the story must have been had the warriors behaved as one would expect of an aristocracy, if they had used their monopoly of political and military power to defend rather than change the existing order.

Third, as there was no aristocratic defense of the old regime, there was no struggle over its survival; no class or party war in which the skirmish line was drawn between new and old, revolutionaries and conservatives. There was, of course, tension between traditional and modern, Japanese and Western, but not a radical cleavage of the two by ideology. All parties were more or less reformist, more or less traditional, and more or less modern; excepting perhaps the Communists, whose numbers were insignificant, no pre-war party thought of the past, as such, as a barrier to progress. It was a barrier in some respects, in others a positive aid. Modernization therefore appeared to most Japanese who thought about it at all, not as a process in which a life-or-death confrontation of traditional and modern took place, but as a dynamic blending of the two. I wonder if this does not account in large part for what has seemed to many people the uncommon strength of tradition in the midst of change in modern Japan.

Fourth, status-consciousness is relatively strong in Japan in part because there was no revolutionary struggle against inequality, but for that reason class-consciousness is relatively weak. These attitudes are by no means contradictory. The nervous concern of Japanese for status is quite consonant with their relatively weak feeling about classes — higher-ups to some extent being looked on as superior extensions of the self. This is an attitude familiar to us elsewhere. It is illustrated in Jane Austen by the servant who fairly bursts with pride when his master is made a baronet; and by Fielding's story of Nell Gwynn. Stepping one day from a house where she had made a short visit, the famous actress saw a great mob assembled, and her footman all bloody and dirty. The fellow, being asked by his mistress what happened, answered, "I have been fighting, madam, with an impudent rascal who called your ladyship a whore." "You blockhead," replied Mrs. Gwynn, "at this rate you must fight every day of your life; why, you fool, all the world knows it." "Do they?" the fellow said in

a muttering voice; "They shan't call me a whore's footman for all that."

Finally, and this brings me back to an earlier point about the absence of an aristocratic culture in modern Japan, since warriors were never thrown on the defensive by the hostility of other classes, they never felt the need to make a cult of their peculiar style of life, either as evidence of virtues justifying their privileges or as compensation for loss of them. One wonders if Western aristocracies did not put exceptional value on leisure, gambling, dueling, and love-making, as aspects of the aristocratic way of life, in good part because they were a dramatic repudiation of bourgeois values.

In any case the warrior did not have the means of supporting a leisurely and aesthetic style of life. The revolution found him separated from the land, living on a government salary rather than on income from property; he therefore carried no capital inheritance from his privileged past into the modern age. He had no country estates, no rich town properties, no consols to spare unbecoming compromises with the crass new world of business. On the contrary, warriors were the chief makers of this world and they scrambled for success in it to escape social and economic oblivion.

Then too, this new world was irrevocably bound up with Western culture, whence came (with whatever modifications) much of its technology and many of its conventions. Success in it had very little to do with traditional skills and tastes, and much to do with double-entry bookkeeping, commercial law, English conversation, German music, French painting, and Scotch whisky. Traditional arts were not forgotten, but they were never identified with a particular social class, least of all perhaps the upper class. It is significant, for example, that the pre-war Peer's Club in Tokyo, located within easy walking distance of the Foreign Office and the Ministry of Finance, was a great ugly stone building with marble stairways, thick carpets, mahogany bar, wallpaper, glass chandeliers, and French cuisine. In respect to such things all classes of Japanese, during the first generation or two after 1868, were born cultural equals. One could not learn of these things at home, any more than one could learn there a foreign language or the calculus. Such subjects were taught only in the schools, and the schools were open to anyone.

Social Stratification and Economic Processes in Africa

Lloyd A. Fallers

SOCIAL STRATIFICATION is a relatively complex pheno-menon. Studying it involves more than simply plotting the distribution of power and wealth in a society, and more than securing ratings by a society's members of one another's prestige. Such simplifications may for some purposes be quite appropriate, but they are unsatisfactory if we aim to reach an understanding of the various ways in which economic processes may be involved in social inequality. For this purpose, a broader conception of social stratification and its place in human societies is required.

In its essential character, social stratification is not an economic phenomenon at all. This is not to say that economic phenomena are not involved or are unimportant in stratification, but simply that the economic aspect of stratification is secondary to another, and more basic, aspect: the moral or cultural one. The heart of stratification — what makes it universal in human societies — is man's tendency to evaluate his fellows, and himself, as "better" or "worse" in terms of some cultural notion of "the good."[1] To be sure, the content of such notions varies over a wide spectrum, but the universality of moral ideas forms one of the common roots of stratification. At this most basic level, economic phenomena may be involved in varying degrees and ways; goods and services of different kinds, and goods and services as such, may be differently evaluated in different cultures.

Here we encounter the notion that "the economic" is founded upon a set of basic biological imperatives — a set of irreducible needs for food, clothing and shelter. It is true, of course, that there are some kinds of goods and services which no culture is in a position utterly to disregard, but there are relatively few areas in Africa where considerations of this sort take us very far. The admirable reports and films on the Bushmen of the Kalahari produced by the Marshalls[2] impress upon us the precariousness of life in the desert and the marvelous ingenuity of the Bushmen in solving its problems through a single-minded adjustment of all aspects of life to the food quest, but for Africa as a whole, this is an extremely unusual situation.

The vast majority of Africans have in recent centuries been reasonably prosperous agriculturalists or pastoralists, or often both, employing relatively efficient technologies. As Jones has put it: "Diets are those of poor people, but they are not necessarily poor diets. The total supply of calories appears to be adequate, and Africans rarely know hunger in the sense of persisting shortage of food energy."[3] As a matter of fact, in many areas, such as the highlands of eastern Africa, sheer subsistence requires of the ordinary man a good deal less attention than it did, let us say, of the medieval European peasant. Subsistence production can be left mainly in the hands of the female part of the labor force so that men may be largely available to work and fight for the king or chief. Consequently, "biological imperatives" do not take us very far in explaining the ways in which goods and services are evaluated in traditional Africa. Africans are relatively well off, and hence their cultures are free to give varying kinds and degrees of attention to goods and services.

On the other hand, traditional African cultures do not use the freedom which a relatively efficient technology gives them to actively *devalue* goods and services as, we are told, some traditional Asian cultures do. One must be cautious here; the stereotype of the "spiritual, non-materialistic East" can be very misleading if taken to mean a simple lack of avarice among Asian peoples. As Geertz has shown in his study of religion and economics in a Javanese town, the matter is more complex.[4] The people of Modjokuto see things — persons, modes

[1] The general approach to stratification adopted here owes a great deal to Talcott Parsons, "An Analytic Approach to the Theory of Social Stratification," in *Essays in Sociological Theory* (rev. ed.; New York: The Free Press, 1954), pp. 69–88.

[2] Lorna Marshall, "The Kin Terminology of the !Kung Bushman," *Africa*, vol. 27 (1957), pp. 1–24; "Marriage among the !Kung Bushmen," *Africa*, vol. 29 (1959), pp. 335–365; "!Kung Bushmen Bands," *Africa*, vol. 30 (1960), pp. 325–355; and E. M. Thomas, *The Harmless People* (New York: Alfred A. Knopf, 1959).

[3] W. O. Jones, "Food and Agricultural Economies of Tropical Africa," *Food Research Institute Studies*, vol. 2 (1961), p. 5.

[4] Clifford Geertz, "Religious Belief and Economic Behavior in a Central Javanese Town: Some Preliminary Considerations," *Economic Development and Cultural Change*, vol. 4 (1956), pp. 138–158.

Reprinted from Melville Jean Herskovits and Mitchell Harwitz (eds.), *Economic Transition in Africa* (Evanston: Northwestern University Press, 1964), pp. 113–130, by permission of the author, editors and publisher.

of behavior, psychic states and material objects — as ranging along a continuum of relative excellence bounded by the polar concepts *alus* and *kasar* — that is, roughly speaking, subtlety, control, inner serenity, as contrasted with crudity, awkwardness and uncontrolled animal passion. High rank, power and wealth should be held by persons who are *alus*. This does not mean that persons in Modjokuto lack the desire for goods and services, but it does mean that concern for such things receives no sanction from the cultural definitions of excellence which are associated with the élite and hence remains unregulated by them. Economic activities of a sort which involve attention to the rationalization of production and exchange tend to be devalued or ignored, even while the products themselves may be greatly desired. Such activities are the concern of the *santri*, a more fully Islamicized sub-group standing somewhat aside from the mainstream of Javanese life. No people — certainly not the people of overpopulated Java — are in a position totally to ignore the wants and needs of the biological man. But many Asian peoples do seem to have committed themselves to religious conceptions which regard the body as an unfortunate impediment to the perfection of the soul.

While recognizing that such generalizations, in the present very imperfect state of our understanding of such matters, inevitably oversimplify the cultural dynamics involved, it seems clear that this sort of cultural turning-away from things economic has not been prominent in Africa. Whatever features of traditional African life may stand in the way of more rapid economic development, an absorbing interest in achieving states of inner spiritual perfection is not among them. On the contrary, Africans seem to have, on the whole, a very utilitarian, matter-of-fact view of goods and services.

This is not to say that African cultures have made the organization of production and exchange a central concern. Except perhaps in those areas of Western Africa where trade has become a highly developed calling, this is clearly not the case. It will be argued below that, much more typically, production and exchange have been undertaken as an adjunct — a means — to the organization of power, the field in which, it appears, the African genius has really concentrated its efforts. But there is no evidence that in traditional Africa, economic concerns were rejected as spiritually unworthy. Far from viewing the biological man and his wants as base and unworthy of concern, there is a certain tendency for traditional African religions to make the health, fertility and prosperity of the living individual and the living community matters of central importance. A great deal of the ritual communication which takes place between living persons and the spirit

world has as its object the maintenance or re-establishment of individual or group well-being in a quite material, biological sense.

With all the variation that may be found in traditional African religion, this seems to be one of the more persistent themes, appearing, for example, in the intricate cosmological religion of the Dogon of the western Sudan as well as in the ancestral cults of so many Bantu peoples.[1] In the context of this sort of cultural orientation, the production and exchange of goods and services, while not the primary objects of human endeavor, are good and useful insofar as they contribute to individual and group comfort and well-being. In their recent economic contacts with the outside world Africans have on the whole responded in this essentially utilitarian way.

2

Thus far we have been discussing culture as one of the bases of social stratification. We have concluded that traditional African cultures, while not regarding economic processes as ends in themselves, have nevertheless given them definite positive value. We may now turn to the other universal root of stratificatory phenomena, the differentiation of roles in the social structure. No human community is a completely undifferentiated aggregation of like beings. The mutual expectations on the basis of which persons are enabled to interact with one another are always to some extent arranged into bundles or clusters on the basis of age, sex and kinship — and usually, of course, upon other bases as well. Again economic phenomena may be involved — perhaps they always are, since the differentiation of roles always tends to involve some differential allocation of economic tasks and thus to be, in one of its aspects, a "division of labor." In general, the more complex the technological apparatus, the more complex the division of labor may become, though the relationship is by no means a simple and direct one. The division of labor between men and women, for example, seems to be largely independent of technological complexity.

The cultural and social structural roots of stratification are not, of course, discrete "things"; instead they come together in the tendency of the differentiated roles themselves, including their economic aspects, to be culturally evaluated. Since tasks are differentially allocated, the culture evaluates persons differentially; that is to say, not just pottery-making and praying are evaluated, but also potters and priests. Obviously, varying degrees of excellence in the performance of priests' and potters' tasks are also recognized.

In traditional African societies, the complexity of the differentiation of roles varies over a wide range, but it varies within definite limits. On the one hand, some degree of economic specialization beyond that represented by the sexual division of labor is present almost everywhere. Again the Bushmen, and perhaps some Pygmy groups, provide exceptions; but these, though

---

[1] Marcel Griaule, "The Dogon of the French Sudan," in Daryll Forde, ed., *African Worlds* (London: Oxford University Press, 1954), pp. 83–110; E. Colson, "Ancestrial Spirits and Social Structure among the Plateau Tonga," *International Archives of Ethnography*, vol. 47 (1954), pp. 21–68.

they may be of great scientific interest for certain purposes, actually represent only an insignificant fragment of the population of Subsaharan Africa. In most African villages, an array of traditional crafts tends to be reflected in a corresponding array of semi-specialized craft roles: potter, smith, woodworker, musician, bark-cloth-maker or weaver, and often others as well. In recent decades the bicycle mechanic and the tailor with his treadle "Singer" have often joined the ranks of "traditional" village specialists.

On the other hand, in village Africa, as in the rest of the non-industrialized world, there is little differentiation of occupational from domestic organization. By far the greater part of the production of goods and services takes place in a domestic setting, that is, in some kind of local homestead unit. Workplace and homestead are the same and have the same inhabitants. Most homesteads in traditional Africa produce most of what they consume, and consume most of what they produce, and this probably remains true for a majority of African people today, despite the great changes of recent decades.

This relative lack of differentiation between homestead and work group has important consequences for social stratification. It means that what is stratified is not a series of autonomous occupational categories and organization, but rather a series of domestic and other kinship units whose economic functions are but one among a number of characteristics on the basis of which their relative worth, in terms of cultural values, is judged. One of the great differentiating characteristics of industrial societies, from the point of view of social stratification, is their tendency to develop such autonomous organizations in which occupational roles may be played outside the domestic context. The modern business firm and the governmental bureaucracy, in their ecological aspect, are places spatially and socially segregated from domestic and other kinship units.

It was one of Karl Marx's great contributions to social science to point out some of the consequences of this separation. The point is not, of course, that occupational and domestic roles cease in such cases to influence each other, but rather that the autonomous occupational organizations tend to become the main foci of cultural evaluation, and hence of stratification. The domestic unit of the job-holder comes to depend for its status, and even for its basic existence, upon the occupational system to which it is linked by a more or less "purely economic" tie. It is for this reason that students of stratification in industrial societies tend to focus their attention upon occupational ranking. Where occupational roles remain embedded in multifunctional domestic units, it is these latter which tend to be the units of stratification. Such units may remain economically more self-sufficient; a wider range of their characteristics and performances may remain relevant to evaluation and stratification.

Thus we have in traditional Subsaharan Africa the following range of variation: Almost anywhere there is craft specialization, but everywhere we also find that the production of goods and services is household production. Within this range, there is room for a good deal of variation in the degree to which households specialize economically. In most of Africa, craft specialization is predominantly part-time. That is to say, almost every household engages in a basic subsistence activity — usually some combination of agriculture and animal husbandry, but in some cases fishing or transhumant pastoralism — and in addition some households also engage in a part-time speciality like smithing or pottery-making.

In eastern, central and southern Africa, crafts were almost always carried out in this part-time way. Even during late colonial times, in the villages of Buganda and Busoga, for example, one would be hard put to find a really full-time specialist of any kind. Potters, smiths, bark-cloth makers and tailors, as well as modern school teachers, shop keepers and clergymen, maintained gardens, flocks and herds to supply their staple diet. Even a large part of the employed population of the modern town of Kampala found it possible to grow much of their own food.

One gains the impression that this is common throughout the continent wherever urban dwellers are not crowded into "labor lines" or housing estates whose layout makes gardening impossible. In traditional eastern, central and southern Africa really full-time craft specialists only exist at the courts of the more powerful and affluent kings, where they form part of the royal household. In Buganda, only the king's, and perhaps a few more eminent chiefs', bark-cloths, pots and music are produced by persons who work more or less full-time; those consumed by villagers are made by fellow-agriculturalists for whom the craft is a sideline.

In traditional western Africa, as Skinner points out in his discussion of the indigenous economies of this part of the continent, full-time craft specialists are more common and the crafts themselves more highly developed. The old Yoruba towns contain many — perhaps a majority — of persons who maintain farms in the surrounding countryside, but they also contain weavers, smiths, carvers and traders who are full-time professionals, dependent upon the sale of their products for basic subsistence.[1] Here, too, one finds the closest approach to the development of autonomous occupational organizations in the guilds of craftsmen and traders, which control entrance into these occupations and whose leaders represent their members' interests in the governments of the towns. It is not clear, however, how far these guilds as corporate bodies engage in production and exchange and how far they are structurally distant from the lineage organization which is prominent in Yoruba society.[2] The craft

[1] W. R. Bascom, "Urbanization as a Traditional African Pattern," *The Sociological Review*, vol. 7 (1959), pp. 29–43.
[2] Daryll Forde, "The Yoruba-Speaking Peoples of Southwestern Nigeria," *Ethnographic Survey of Africa, Western Africa, Part* 4 (London: International African Institute, 1951), pp. 10–16.

guilds of Bida, the capital of the Moslem Nupe, which tend to be hereditary and hence to be made up of a series of related kinship groups, are highly organized bodies exercising a substantial measure of control over their members.[1]

Throughout traditional Africa, however, full-time occupational specialization, in the sense of freedom from participation in subsistence production, is more commonly related to political than to economic tasks. Whereas full-time specialization in craft production or trade is relatively rare, the specialist in government is quite common. Indeed, there is in Africa a certain political efflorescence which is perhaps a corollary of the lack of the particular kind of other-worldly religious orientation found in parts of Asia. Authority is sought for and admired, both as a goal of individual ambition and as a means toward, and symbol of, group prosperity and well-being. This is reflected in the African passion for litigation, as well as in the tendency toward formalized political hierarchy. This characterization does not apply only to the great traditional kingdoms, which included much less than half the continent, and were limited to relatively restricted areas of the Guinea coast, the western Sudan, the Great Lakes area and parts of southern Africa and the Congo basin. Political specialists, such as kings and chiefs, are by definition found only in polities with a degree of political centralization, but the absorbing interest in things political of which these states are but a particularly explicit expression is common also, for example, to the decentralized, decent-organized polity of the Tiv, with its elaborate system of moots.[2] It is perhaps not going too far to assert that the *emphasis* in African systems of stratification is primarily political. The roles which are most highly regarded are usually authority roles, whether these involve the part-time political activity and adjudication of disputes which absorb the energies of the elders of a descent group, or the full-time exercise of authority engaged in by the rulers and chiefs of the great kingdoms.

One aspect of this peculiar prominence of the political in African systems of stratification, and perhaps the most important for the purposes of this discussion, is a tendency for economic structures and processes to be overshadowed by — or, perhaps better, *contained within* — political structures and processes. It would not be unreasonable to hazard the guess that in Subsaharan Africa the greater part of the exchanges of goods and services which take place outside domestic units occur as incidents to the exercise or acknowledgement of authority. Wherever there are kings or chiefs, or even petty headmen, goods and services pass upward in the form of taxes or tribute and back down again in the form of hospitality and gifts. In societies organized on the basis of descent, exchanges serve to mark the political alignment of corporate groups. Land-holding, too, is commonly, in traditional society, a political matter. "*Omwami tafuga ttaka; afuga bantu,*" runs a proverb of the Baganda: "A chief does not rule land; he rules people."

Again the matter is fundamentally the same in both centralized and decentralized societies; landholding tends to be merely the territorial aspect of political relations and groupings, not a distinct and predominantly economic relationship in itself. "Landlords" and "tenants" are exceedingly rare in traditional Africa, perhaps in part because on the whole land is not scarce. Of course we must be careful not to overstate the case. Throughout Subsaharan Africa there is also trade for its own sake, particularly, as we have noted, in western Africa. And a few peoples, perhaps most notably the Kikuyu of Kenya, seem always to have regarded land as a commodity.[3] But throughout the region, at any rate prior to the extension of the money economy in recent times, the predominant tendency has been for political structures to dominate and enclose economic ones and hence for authority to be the principle basis for stratification.

3

Thus far we have considered the two basic sources of stratificatory phenomena — the system of values and the pattern according to which roles are differentiated. There is clearly, however, much more to stratification than this. If the allocation and performance of differentially evaluated roles were a simple mechanical process, a catalog of values and roles would suffice. But societies are not machines, and the persons and groups who make up societies are not cogs and levers. Culture is not a set of engineer's drawings. Persons and groups interpret, feel and strive, and in the process they react to, manipulate and even create both the structure of social relations and the ideas which go to make up culture. All this results in certain additional complexities in stratification and in the economic processes related to it.

By differentially evaluating roles, societies secure a commitment of energy and intelligence on the part of their members to tasks embodied in the roles which are more highly regarded, but in accomplishing this they assume the burden of assuring, explaining and justifying the ways in which particular persons are selected to fill these roles. The range of possibilities here is of course very wide. Access to the more honorific roles is never entirely free and, to the degree to which it is not, culture may undertake to legitimatize inequality of access by means of an ideology of inborn differences in capacity or sanctity. Or it may attribute differential

---

[1] S. F. Nadel, *A Black Byzantium, The Kingdom of Nupe in Nigeria* (London: Oxford University Press, 1942), pp. 257–297.

[2] Paul Bohannan, *Justice and Judgement among the Tiv* (London: Oxford University Press, 1957), *passim*.

[3] Greet Sluiter, *Kikuyu Concepts of Land and Land King* (M.A. Thesis, University of Chicago, 1960), Manuscript; J. F. M. Middleton, *The Kikuyu and Kamba of Kenya* (Ethnographic Survey of Africa, East Central Africa, Part V; London: International African Institute, 1953), pp. 52–56; Jomo Kenyatta, *Facing Mount Kenya, the Tribal Life of the Kikuyu* (London: Secker and Warburg, 1938), pp. 20–40.

success to luck or the whim of the gods. Where a degree of openness is recognized, it may glorify competitive striving; and the qualities singled out for recognition may in varying degrees relate to actual superiority in the performance of the roles in question. The variations seem endless, but the problem is universal; as a result there develop what might be called "secondary cultures of stratification" — values and beliefs *about* stratification, in contrast with the basic values which give rise to stratification in the first instance.

These secondary cultures include both general public views of how stratification should or does work and also, commonly, a verdant growth of more or less "private," but typically standardized, ideas and beliefs through which persons and groups express their own aspirations, gratifications and frustrations with respect to the results. Thus in Buganda, as in contemporary United States, a public glorification of achievement is combined with an absorbing interest on the part of individuals and kinship groups in genealogy and the symbols of ascribed status, as well as in securing for their own children advantages in competition which are, from the point of view of the publicly expressed ideal, "unfair."[1]

The various elements which make up such a complex of ideas may in one sense, be "contradictory," but they relate to each other in perfectly understandable ways in the context of the problem of linking and reconciling individual and group motivation with the overall system of stratification. The example just given pertains to systems in which achievement is publicly endorsed; but systems of hereditary status also have their public and private secondary cultures of stratification which, as materials from India demonstrate, allow lower-caste persons both to "accept" the fact of low hereditary status and, at the same time, to protest and work against it.[2] One would no doubt discover similar phenomena in the few real caste societies which are found in Africa, such as those of Rwandi and Burundi.[3]

Where different groups within a society become sufficiently separate from each other, the secondary culture of stratification may develop into distinct subcultures, based upon class, of the sort which interested Robert Redfield.[4] That is to say, relatively distinct "folk" and "élite" versions of the common culture may develop, expressing the respective interests, values and beliefs of the élite and village levels of society. It has been argued elsewhere that such cultural differentiation, which is one of the marks of the true "peasant society," has not been prominent in Africa, in part because of the lack of a written religious literature of the kind which has formed the basis for élite subcultures in Europe and Asia.[5]

In this cultural sense, Africa tends to be rather strikingly egalitarian. This does not mean that Africans reject inequality of any kind; on the contrary, there is among them, as we have noted, a strong tendency toward political hierarchy. But, lacking the degree of cultural differentiation between strata which was common in medieval Europe, Africans do tend to be egalitarian about a man's class origins. The person who manages to acquire a position of authority and wealth is accepted as such; since the élite culture is not greatly differentiated from that of the villages, he can easily learn it and hence does not carry about with him linguistic and behavioral stigmata of the sort which have tended to mark the socially mobile European as a *parvenu*.

Along with this secondary culture of stratification there also develops what we may call a secondary structural aspect of stratification, an aspect commonly symbolized in the literature on the subject by the figure of a pyramid. Such figures are meant to illustrate, beyond the basic differentiation and differential evaluation of roles, the relative numbers of roles of various kinds that are actually available for allocation. The "shape" of the pyramid is clearly related in an important way to degrees of technological complexity. Thus the systems of stratification in those relatively complex, but non-industrialized, societies which are commonly called "peasant" or "feudal" tend to be broad-based, with a small political and religious élite supported by a large mass of subsistence producers.

The traditional African kingdoms may be considered "peasant societies" in this structural sense, though they lacked the cultural differentiation characteristic of their Asian, Near Eastern and European counterparts. Economic modernization of such societies tends to increase the number of "middle class" roles, and thus to "push outward" the sides of the pyramid. Insofar as this image is an accurate one, it has important implications for the working of stratification. Peasant societies may to varying degrees emphasize achievement or hereditary status in their values, but if the élite is very small and the "common man" very numerous, the opportunity for mobility will be extremely slight, no matter how much the culture may glorify it, and no matter to what degree the small élite may actually be recruited from below.

There are other secondary structural aspects of stratification which are not so easily considered in terms of the pyramid image. Perhaps among the most important are family and descent systems, which greatly influence the allocation of roles and the nature of the units which are stratified. For example, systems of corporate unilineal descent groups, though of course by no means universal in Africa, are very common there. Given the

[1] Lloyd Fallers, "Despotism, Status Culture and Social Mobility in an African Kingdom," *Comparative Studies in Society and History*, vol. 2 (1959), pp. 11–32.

[2] G. D. Berreman, "Caste in India and the United States," *American Journal of Sociology*, vol. 66 (1960), pp. 120–127; McKim Marriott, *Caste Ranking and Community Structure in Five Regions of India and Pakistan* (Deccan College Monograph Series No. 23; Poona, 1960), pp. 14 ff.

[3] Ethel Albert, "Une étude de valeurs en Urundi," *Cahiers d'Études Africaines*, vol. 2 (1960), pp. 147–160.

[4] Robert Redfield, *Peasant Society and Culture* (Chicago: University of Chicago Press, 1956).

[5] Lloyd Fallers, "Are African Cultivators to be called 'Peasants'?" *Current Anthropology*, vol. 2 (1961), pp. 108–110.

sharply "peaked" shape of traditional stratification pyramids, that is, given the tendency for the powerful and rich to be relatively few and the weak and poor to be relatively numerous, with comparatively small numbers of persons in between, then it follows that extended kinship solidarities will tend to cut across stratification hierarchies in ways which are rather startling to Europeans and Americans. Solidary extended kinship groupings will tend to contain persons of widely varying degrees of power and wealth. This is particularly so where, as is common in Africa, persons of high status have higher rates of polygny and fertility, with the result that in each generation there are many more élite children than can possibly inherit their parents' status.

In traditional European societies, although the phenomenon of the gradually declining "cadet" lines within a noble or gentry family is a familiar one, solidary kinship groups have tended to be narrower in range and more homogeneous as regards status. The kinship groups involved have been less ramified and marriage has tended to be endogamous with respect to class — or better, for the period of European history concerned, with respect to "estate." In Africa, however, solidary kinship groups tend to contain persons of widely varying power and wealth, both because they ramify widely and because marriage is seldom class-endogamous in any important sense. And this is particularly true of the kinship groups of élite persons, which status-differential polygyny and fertility tend to cause to expand more rapidly than others. Overall status distinctions, therefore, tend to be blurred and it is difficult to find clearly defined strata, even in the larger kingdoms.

African societies have worked out numerous ways of handling the apparent contradictions that result from the juxtaposition of sharp stratification of power and wealth and ramified kinship solidarity. Descent groups may be ranked, both internally and externally, by genealogical seniority, as in the southern Bantu states; or descent groups may be ranked *vis-à-vis* one another, while internal differentiation is determined by some form of election, as among the Akan peoples of the Guinea coast. Still another pattern is found in some of the interlacustrine Bantu states, where the political hierarchy, which here as elsewhere dominates stratification, is simply segregated structurally from the solidarities of descent groups. Except for the kingship, political office in these states is usually not hereditary. Chiefs are recruited by royal appointment, and thus a man's place in the state is one matter, his role in the internal domestic affairs of his lineage quite another.

Understandably, none of these ways of handling the problem entirely resolves the ultimate tension between stratification and the leveling influence of corporate

descent groups, because every person remains influenced by both. This is another reason why relatively enduring, culturally defined, "horizontal" strata of the sort familiar in traditional Europe and Asia have not been prominent in Africa. Extended kinship solidarities work against their crystallization. Of course in the uncentralized societies organized on the basis of descent, where formal stratification and differentiation of authority are in any case relatively slight, these issues tend not to arise.

In the processes by means of which persons are distributed through the system of stratification of their society, economic phenomena may be involved in various ways and at different points. We have already, in discussing the cultural and structural roots of stratification, noted how the production of goods and services may be involved at the level of the primary evaluation of differentiated roles. Roles involving production and trade may to varying degrees be differentiated out and may in varying degrees be evaluated as élite roles. In traditional Africa, as we have seen, full-time specialization in non-agricultural production or trade is relatively uncommon, though it certainly exists, and in general authority roles tend to outrank those primarily associated with economic processes.

Apart from this primary evaluation of economic processes and roles, however, goods and services are also involved in other ways in the dynamics of stratification. For stratification, and indeed any element of social structure, always tends to have an economic aspect, even though this aspect may not predominate. Interaction between persons always involves the allocation of scarce goods and services — at a minimum those of space and time, and usually other things as well. Because they are scarce, their allocation is problematical, and this limits the ways in which interaction can proceed.[1] In the case of systems of stratification, it is useful to think of such goods and services as symbols and as facilities.[2] On the one hand, all systems of stratification tend to select some scarce goods and services as symbols of status. The differential allocation of such goods and services is in itself an expression of stratification and a reward to persons thereby favored. On the other hand, there are also goods and services, possession of which is not in itself particularly honorific, whose utilization is nevertheless essential to the achievement or maintenance of high position.

It is rarely possible to classify actual goods and services as falling wholly into one or the other of these categories, for the distinction is an analytic, not a concrete descriptive one. Thus the corvée labor which so many African kings and chiefs could demand from their people was simultaneously an expression of their superiority and a means of maintaining and strengthening it through the performance of useful work. But particular goods and services may vary considerably in the degree to which they function as symbols or as facilities and it is in the purer cases that the distinction becomes most clear.

---

[1] M. J. Levy, *The Structure of Society* (Princeton: Princeton University Press, 1952), pp. 95–98, 390–467.

[2] The distinction is related to that made by Melville Herskovits, *Cultural Anthropology* (New York: Alfred A. Knopf, 1955), pp. 155–156, following DuBois, between "prestige" and "subsistence" economies, although facilities are of course not limited to subsistence goods.

Thus in eastern Africa cattle are particularly highly valued goods; indeed, they are valued to such a degree that Herskovits has given the name "East African cattle area" to the whole region.[1] But in many of these societies, cattle are very much in the nature of status symbols, while in others they are regarded as utilitarian goods. A good illustration of the contrast may be seen in the neighboring and closely related kingdoms of Rwanda and Buganda. In Rwanda, cattle are the élite symbols *par excellence*. Possession of large herds and consumption of a diet consisting as far as possible of dairy products are perhaps the most important expressions of Tutsi aristocracy.[2] Cattle are favorite subjects for poetry and exchanges of beasts validate the relationship of lord and vassal. The Baganda, also, value cattle — they are, for example, among the main objects sought in raids against neighboring peoples, just as they are in Rwanda.

But to Baganda, cattle are simply meat — the means by which king and chiefs may provide feasts for their followers. Mere possession of herds means nothing and cattle have no ritual significance in any context. Perhaps most striking of all, the tall, thin cattle people, whose Tutsi and Hima cousins in cattle kingdoms like Rwanda and Ankole form the ruling aristocracy, are in Buganda regarded simply as rustic and rather smelly herdsmen, who hire themselves out to look after the cattle of wealthy Baganda. However, the cattle of Baganda chiefs are not in any real sense more "economic" than are the more symbolic beasts of the Tutsi, though the uses to which they are put may be more mundane. Both facilities and symbols are "economic" in the sense that they are valuable and scarce and hence their allocation presents a problem in economizing for both persons and groups. The Tutsi chief in Rwanda, it is clear, allocates his cattle quite as carefully as he does his less symbolic possessions.

Here again we return to the point that in traditional Africa goods and services, both as symbols and as facilities, circulate primarily in terms of political relations, for it is the polity that dominates stratification. Persons and groups strive to control the symbols and facilities that are the expressions of authority and the means of strengthening and extending it. A good case could be made that, at least in eastern, central and southern Africa, the most important facilities are people. This does not mean that people are regarded by their rulers as mere "things", though of course various forms of slavery have sometimes been involved, but rather simply that in the production of goods and services in this part of Africa, the most problematic factor is usually human labor.

As we have seen, land is on the whole not scarce and agricultural and military technology are relatively simple. The means of production are therefore controlled by groups of village cultivators. For the chief who wishes to strengthen and extend his rule, the main problem consists in securing an adequate supply of labor. The solution of this problem lies in attracting and holding the maximum number of subjects who, as cultivators and warriors, can then produce the maximum amount of tribute and booty in craft and agricultural products. These in turn can be redistributed as largess to the maximum number of loyal supporters. The principal danger to the authority of the chief lies in the ultimate ability of his disaffected subjects simply to pick up and move away, leaving him to be "chief of the pumpkins." Thinking, as we tend to do, of land and capital goods as the problematic factors, this tribute-largess-labor-starved economy may seem a tenuous base upon which to erect a highly centralized and stratified society, but the examples of the eighteenth- and nineteenth-century kingdoms of the Zulu and Baganda show that this can be done by rulers able to manipulate shrewdly the symbols and facilities of authority.[3]

Trade has also tended to be dominated by the polity, that is, to be directed to the political ends of rulers. In eastern Africa, where trade with the coast came late, rulers strove to monopolize the trade in such new facilities as firearms, which greatly reinforced the ruler's authority if he was in fact successful in controlling it, and, through sumptuary laws, such new symbols as tailored clothing. The Reverend Batulumayo Musoke Zimbe, who as a boy served as a page at the court of King Mutesa of Buganda, describes in his memoirs how Mutesa assigned different types of clothing to various ranks.[4] Even in western Africa, where trade is more extensive, more diversified, more professionalized and of longer standing, it tends to be heavily influenced by political considerations. Rosemary Arnold's account of the domination of the port town of Whydah by the kingdom of Dahomey provides an excellent example of the tendency toward "administered trade."[5] The independent trading town of the sort described in the diary of Antera Duke of Calaba; where a kind of "lodge" or "guild" of trader-chiefs themselves ruled the town in the interest of trade, is a much rarer phenomenon in Africa.[6] Trade has most commonly been controlled in the interest of the polity.

[1] M. J. Herskovitz, "The Cattle Complex in East Africa," *American Anthropologist*, vol. 28 (1926), *passim*.

[2] J. Maquet, *The Premise of Inequality in Ruanda* (London: Oxford University Press, 1961), pp. 18–19, 129–142.

[3] Max Gluckman, in "The Rise of a Zulu Empire," *Scientific American* vol. 202 (1960), pp. 157–167, says that the crucial factor in the creation of the Zulu "empire" of Shaka was land shortage, but he does not explain how this effect was produced and one does not find his argument convincing. On the contrary, the Zulu polity, as he himself so well describes it, seems an excellent example of a state built upon military and political intelligence and charisma. Land shortage, if such existed, did not prevent the empire from disintegrating when Shaka's leadership ceased to be effective.

[4] B. M. Zimbe, *Buganda ne Kabaka* (Kampala, 1938), pp. 19–20.

[5] Rosemary Arnold, "A Port of Trade: Whydah on the Guinea Coast," in Karl Polanyi, C. M. Arensberg, and Harry Pearson, eds., *Trade and Market in the Early Empires* (New York: The Free Press, 1957), pp. 154–176.

[6] Daryll Forde, ed., *Efik Traders of Old Calabar* (London: Oxford University Press, 1956).

4

Traditional African societies, then, have characteristically exhibited patterns of role differentiation in which political specialization has been more prominent than economic. The ambitions of their members have been directed primarily toward attaining authority, and economic processes have commonly been dominated by the political needs of individuals and groups. While sharply "peaked" systems of stratification have been created in the great traditional kingdoms, even in these cases there has been relatively little cultural differentiation between élite and common folk and little concentration of the non-human means of production in élite hands. Extended kinship solidarities have worked against rigid status stratification. Keeping these indigenous patterns in mind, we may in conclusion draw attention to some of the consequences that contemporary processes of economic modernization seem to be having or, equally important in some respects, not having, for these traditional patterns.

First of all, there has been taking place all over Africa, particularly during the past half-century, an ever-increasing commercialization of land and labor. This process was often initiated in the first instance by the demand for money created by the imposition of taxation by colonial governments, but it has also, and increasingly, been stimulated by the desire for the vast array of new goods and services, both imported and locally produced, which have become available. In some areas Africans numbering in the hundreds of thousands have gone to work for wages in mines and factories and on plantations; somewhat fewer have become white-collar workers—the ubiquitous "clerks" who tend the machinery of bureaucracy in both government and business firms. Others, in still larger numbers, have become cash-crop cultivators, producing cocoa, coffee, tobacco, cotton and other crops for the export market.

Frequently cash-crop agriculture and wage work have competed for African labor, and in a great many areas vast numbers of men move back and forth between the two forms of money-making in cycles varying from daily commuting to periods of many years, combining agriculture and employment in ways that best suit their various situations and tastes.[1] Underlying all the variations in pattern, however, has been a pervasive and constantly deepening commitment to a money economy, in which both labor and land have increasingly become marketable commodities. If in very many areas traditional subsistence patterns have remained intact enough to make the money economy a rather superficial overlay, a source of "luxury" goods and services, the number for whom this is true has constantly diminished as the relationship of population to land has changed and as what were formerly merely "wants," have become "needs."

[1] Walter Elkan and Lloyd A. Fallers, "The Mobility of Labor," in Wilbert E. More and Arnold J. Feldman, eds., *Labor Commitment and Social Change in Developing Areas* (New York: Social Science Research Council, 1960), pp. 238–257.

At the same time, ever-expanding educational systems have been busily producing practitioners of the learned professions — physicians, lawyers, clergymen, engineers and teachers. Expanding literacy and the nationalist movements have encouraged the rise of politicians and publicists. Africanization of governmental and business bureaucracies has produced civil servants and junior executives. New opportunities for trade have stimulated a few real African entrepreneurs.

All this has meant a great proliferation of differentiated roles and, in particular, of occupational roles. In fact, over much of Africa, true occupational roles, in the sense of full-time roles played outside the domestic context in exchange for basic income, have essentially come into existence for the first time during this period. As a result we may confidently expect the emergence of new patterns of stratification. However, we may also expect that in these new patterns there will remain important elements of continuity with the past.

Almost without exception, direct continuity with traditional systems of stratification has been rendered nearly impossible by the lack of congruence between traditional and modern societal and cultural boundaries. Most African countries, having acquired their boundaries through the maneuvers of European diplomats, are extremely heterogeneous, and those lying south of the Moslem Sudan and Christian Ethiopia lack over-arching literate élite cultures of the sort that, for example, give some unity to the otherwise quite diverse peoples of India. Thus, traditional élites, deriving their positions from societal and cultural units that have been absorbed and superseded by the new states or proto-states, tend to have little legitimacy on a national level.

In Asia and the Near East, traditional élites can to a greater extent absorb and give birth to the new. Gandhi and Mohammed Abdu, for example, could in some measure reinterpret in modern terms traditional élite cultures that represented the common pasts of the peoples of their countries, thus contributing an essential element of continuity to the culture of new nations. In the African countries, however, there is inevitably a greater discontinuity between old and new cultures and between old and new élites. The only culture self-consciously shared by the new élites has tended to be that imported from France, Belgium or Britain — or that formed in reaction to French, Belgian or British domination. This is not to say that there are no underlying regional cultural unities in Subsaharan Africa, but these tend to be of a sort discovered by anthropological research. Not having been made explicit by being embodied in literary traditions, they are difficult for élites to utilize in the creation of new national cultures. Such concepts as "African personality" and "*négritude*" represent attempts by contemporary African leaders to solve this problem.

There are, however, other kinds of continuity between traditional and modern systems of stratification which may be even more important. Although direct cultural continuity may be difficult to achieve, some characteristic features of the traditional systems may perhaps persist and give a distinctly African character to the new independent nations. For example, in the new African nations, as in the old, political structures seem likely to continue to dominate economic ones, and political élites to retain their pre-eminence. To be sure, the place of economic processes in society has changed greatly. Whereas in traditional societies an essentially static economy was manipulated for political ends, the new independent states make rapid economic development the principal aim of public policy.

But this is precisely the point: Whereas in Europe and America economic modernization was in great measure carried out by private entrepreneurs under régimes of *laisser faire*, Africa is attempting to modernize at a speed, and under conditions, which require a more prominent role for state entrepreneurship. This means a greater prominence, both in numbers and in status, for civil servants, as compared with private business men. As a result, the élite of a country like Nigeria, recently studied by the Smythes, is perhaps as heavily political as was, say, that of the old Yoruba state of Oyo.[1] The traditional cultural emphasis upon authority coincides with, and perhaps helps to produce, modern conceptions of planning for economic development.

It may be anticipated, also, that the new African states will continue to be relatively "classless" in the same sense in which the old ones were. To be sure, occupa-

tional differentiation has greatly increased and the new educational systems hold the potentiality for creating cultural stratifications of a kind unknown in traditional societies. In the colonial period, during the early phases of educational development, many African societies seemed to be producing new solidary élites of European-educated persons, and many writers have dwelt upon the gap between such persons and the uneducated masses, often, one suspects, reading into the African situation European attitudes toward status which were not really there. We certainly should not expect egalitarianism in the sense of a lack of differentiation according to power, wealth and prestige; such differentiation was prominent in the past and is likely to remain so.

At least in the short run, however, extended kinship solidarities will tend to check the development of clearly defined strata. Welfare-state policies in education and other fields, policies which modern populist politics make almost inevitable, also will militate against the solidification of the new élites into hereditary estates or castes. Furthermore, the modernization of economies tends to increase the number of intermediate, or middle class roles, thus increasing the structural opportunities for mobility. Thus, while the new African societies may be highly stratified economically and politically, they will probably remain relatively open to talent.

[1] Hugh and Mabel Smythe, *The New Nigerian Elite* (Stanford: Stanford University Press, 1960).

Social Stratification in Two Equalitarian Societies: Australia and the United States[1]

Kurt B. Mayer

IN RECENT YEARS American sociologists have shown a growing interest in comparative analysis of the institutions of complex societies. Comparative studies were, indeed, one of the earliest preoccupations of the sociological pioneers for they recognized clearly that one can best understand a given institutional structure by comparing it with others. However, in their cross-cultural comparisons sociologists have too often been tempted to draw upon anthropological materials from non-literate societies. Comparisons of social institutions

in very different societies undoubtedly drive home the point of cultural relativity in dramatic fashion. Yet for a detailed understanding of the structural peculiarities of Western institutions, comparisons with closely related social structures would seem to be more rele-

[1] This paper was written at the Australian National University and the author is most grateful for the help and criticism offered by his colleagues W. D. Borrie, S. Encel and J. Zubrzycki who read a draft of the manuscript. They bear no responsibility, however, for errors of fact or interpretation.

Reprinted from *Social Research*, V. 31 (Winter, 1964), pp. 435–465, by permission of the author and the publisher.

vant. The study of institutional variations within a context of close cultural similarity is likely to be more fruitful than comparisons from widely differing cultures where the general divergences are so great that given variations can be explained in several different ways.[1]

For American sociologists the study of Australian society, largely neglected so far,[2] should prove particularly rewarding because there are many close similarities between the two social systems at the same time that there are also important differences which highlight the specific emphases of their institutional structures. Both countries are of very similar size and both began as British settlements in a wilderness sparsely inhabited by nomadic tribes. Both are pioneer societies, characterized by democratic political institutions, by federal forms of government and by strongly equalitarian value systems. But differences in geographic conditions and in historical and economic circumstances have resulted in noticeable variations of their social institutions. It is the purpose of this paper to trace the similarities and the contrasts of the stratification systems of Australian and American society.

I

Neither the Australian nor the American stratification systems can be understood apart from their historical contexts. From the very beginning both of these colonial societies differed sharply from the mother country in that they lacked a hereditary aristocracy and the rigidity of formal hierarchical grades. But at the same time the developing class structures on these new continents also differed from each other. From the outset American society was characterized by the predominance of a broad middle class. In the absence of feudal restrictions and privileges most of the virgin American territory was occupied by free farmers who

individually owned the land they cultivated. To be sure, American colonial society did not at any time consist of an undifferentiated mass of freeholders. There always existed definite social distinctions between small farmers and large landowners, between craftsmen, ministers and town merchants. There were also considerable numbers of propertyless men, journeymen and mechanics. In addition there were also those who not only owned no property but were themselves the property of others, the indentured servants and the Negro slaves. Yet the propertyless classes formed only a minority of the early American population and so did the upper class groups of large landowners and wealthy merchants who quickly filled the vacuum at the top of the social structure created by the absence of the nobility. Able and ambitious men of humble social origin rose to the top, amassing large acreages as planters or acquiring wealth as merchants, traders or shippers. But the number of great landowners remained small in America and was even reduced by the confiscation and breakup of large northern Loyalist estates after the American Revolution.

The relative size of the different classes varied considerably from north to south and from the eastern seaboard to the moving frontier, and changes occurred over time as well. But it is a fact of great significance that in comparison with contemporary European societies America's early society hierarchy appeared like a truncated pyramid: lacking both an hereditary aristocracy and a peasantry in the European sense, the broad middle class of independent producers was the dominant stratum socially and economically, if not politically. It has been estimated that in the first quarter of the 19th century as many as four-fifths of the free people who worked were owners of their own means of livelihood.[3] Rank and position rested upon the amount of property owned, income was derived from working with and on one's own property. Moreover, even those who worked for wages did not intend to remain wage workers all their lives. There was so much movement in and out of the small-enterpriser level that propertyless men appeared justified in believing that they, too, could acquire a competence before long. It was this middle-class society which gave birth to democratic political institutions and to a philosophy of equalitarianism which became firmly entrenched as a permanent American ideal. Even though the impact of the industrial revolution later transformed the simple society of independent small enterprisers into a nation of industrial wage earners and salaried white-collar employees, the image of America as a society where "everybody is middle class" persisted through periods when it was no longer in accordance with economic and social reality. There is considerable evidence that in recent years the discrepancy between ideology and objective reality is beginning to disappear and that the class structure of American society is once more becoming predominantly middle class. The evidence for this has been presented elsewhere;[4] for the

[1] This point has recently been made by several American sociologists. Cf Arnold M. Rose, ed. *The Institutions of Advanced Societies* (Minneapolis: University of Minnesota Press, 1958), p. vi; and Leonard Broom, "The Social Stratification of Australia: Method and First Findings," unpublished paper presented at the meetings of the American Sociological Association, New York, August 1960.

[2] Very few sociological studies of Australia have been made by Americans; Cf. Broom, *op. cit.*,; Seymour Martin Lipset, "The Value Patterns of Democracy: A Case Study in Comparative Analysis," *American Sociological Review*, 28 (August 1963), pp. 515–531; Stanley Lieberson, "The Old-New Distinction and Immigrants in Australia," *American Sociological Review*, 28 (August 1963), pp. 550–565; Robert R. Alford, *Party and Society: The Anglo-American Democracies* (Chicago: Rand-McNally, forthcoming).

[3] Cf. Lewis Corey, *The Crisis of the Middle Class* (New York: Covici-Friede, 1935), pp. 113–114; and C. Wright Mills, *White Collar* (New York: Oxford University Press, 1951), p. 7.

[4] Cf. Kurt Mayer, "Recent Changes in the Class Structure of the United States", *Transactions of the Third World Congress of Sociology* (London: International Sociological Association, 1956), Vol. III, pp. 66–80; same author, "Diminishing Class Differentials in the United States, *Kyklos*, 12 (October 1959), pp. 605–627; and "The Changing Shape of the American Class Structure", *Social Research*, Winter 1963.

present purpose it is important to keep in mind the major role which the middle class has played in American society from the beginning, because this is one of the fundamental differences between American and Australian social history.

It is well known that Australia began as a British prison colony, founded in Sydney in 1788, an inauspicious beginning very different from the landing at Plymouth, Massachusetts, more than a century and a half earlier. Yet the convict origins were perhaps less decisive in the shaping of Australia's social structure than the factors of geography, time, and technology. For the British had hoped to develop in Australia not merely a penal colony but a society of independent small farmers. Small freeholds were to be granted to ex-convicts who had served their sentences or been pardoned as well as to ex-soldiers and to free immigrants who might want to settle in the new colony. The intentions of the colonial government were frustrated, however, by the fact that farming proved very difficult in the poor soil and unfavorable environment of Australia. The farmers were continually threatened by droughts, floods, fires, insect pests and unfamiliar diseases, affecting both plants and animals. Moreover, they lacked ready markets for their products. But the land, which was inhospitable to farming with the primitive agricultural techniques prevailing at the turn of the 19th century, proved to be exceptionally well adapted for the grazing of sheep. Sheep farming was easier and more economical and therefore soon came to dominate the Australian rural scene.

It is true that this economic development originated in unique political circumstances. For the earliest years of Australian settlement were characterized by neglect from the colonial authorities in the mother country. England was preoccupied elsewhere during the Napoleonic wars. The military officers of the garrison were in control of the colony and used the opportunity to establish a complete trading monopoly. Amassing private fortunes through their monopolistic activities, the officers forced most of the newly-established small farmers into bankruptcy while they themselves obtained large land grants. Using convicts as free labor, some of them began to experiment successfully with the grazing of sheep and the exporting of wool to England. They succeeded in breeding fine Merino wool at the very time when the English textile industry had begun factory production of woolen cloth and the rapid expansion of demand permitted it to absorb all the wool Australia could produce. Thus wool became the cornerstone of Australia's economy and the basis of its social structure during the first half of the 19th century.

There is no question that the activities of the officers of the New South Wales Corps whose only desire was to get rich quickly played a very important role in Australia's early history, but the basic factors were economic: grazing proved more profitable than growing vegetables and corn. The dreams of the landhungry colonists and the intentions of the colonial power were frustrated not merely by the machinations of a handful of selfish men but by the ineluctable fact that sheep runs were more economical than small farms and that efficient growing of fine wool could in Australia not be accomplished by small freeholders. It required the holding of large pasture lands by individual owners operating with hired hands. Grazing was a big man's business, requiring considerable capital and very large holdings. The consequences were that the Australian continent was explored and occupied not by subsistence farmers but by pastoralists who drove their flocks into the unknown interior of the continent and settled down as squatters on Crown land wherever they found feed and water. Desiring systematic colonization in closely-settled communities, the government viewed these unplanned advances with distaste and tried to set boundaries that were not to be trespassed. But the pastoralists disregarded artificial boundaries and won a long struggle for cheap land and secure tenure. Between 1820 and 1850 the wave of pastoral expansion carried the squatters and their sheep to the very edges of the desert which covers the center of Australia and which has remained uninhabitable to the present day.[1]

In contrast with America, therefore, the beginnings of Australian society were not formed by a rural middle class. Instead, the Australian social structure was dominated initially by a pastoral upper class intent on emulating the English gentry and served by a class of propertyless men who furnished the labor supply. At first the rural work force consisted of convicts, later of a mixture of convicts, emancipists and free men, becoming after the end of transportation a migratory rural proletariat. However, since the labor force required by the pastoralists was relatively small, the working class increasingly drifted to the capital cities. Each of the six Australian colonies had one port city which began as an administrative center but which soon became the trading center and railway terminus for the wool industry of the entire colony. The population of Australia thus became concentrated early and to an unusually high degree in a few large cities.

In the middle of the 19th century, then, both the United States and Australia were frontier countries, but the character of the frontier differed sharply. In America it was a small man's frontier which was the mainspring of democracy and equalitarianism. In Australia, on the other hand, the origin of democracy was in the cities. The population of the seaport towns was swelled after 1831 by the arrival of free immigrants whose passage was assisted by the government by the proceeds from land sales. The townspeople became the focus of the democratic movement, demanding self-government and opposing the power of the pastoralists. The opposition of the townsmen to the grazier oligarchy received a major upthrust when the discovery of gold in 1851 suddenly brought a large wave of immi-

[1] More than two-fifths of Australia is arid. No more than one-fifth of the area has enough rainfall to permit close settlement and most of this is in the southeast.

gration into the country. Fortune-seekers and assisted immigrants flocked to the goldfields of Victoria and New South Wales from all over the world and the Australian population increased from 405,000 in 1851 to 1,145,000 in 1861. The goldfever lasted only a few years. When the surface workings were exhausted, company mines replaced the individual diggers who now had to seek other sources of employment. Once more the logical outlet seemed the land — the development of farming homesteads obtained on easy terms from the Crown. But most of the land was held on lease by the pastoralists in large blocks.

A major struggle to "unlock the land" now began. Having been granted limited self-government based on representative political institutions during the 1850's, the effective control of the Crown lands had passed into the hands of the colonial legislatures. In the early 1860's the legislatures of New South Wales and Victoria enacted laws authorizing anyone to select a block of Crown land for settlement at the price of £1 per acre. But once more the attempt to establish a middle class of propertied farmers proved largely futile. In part the failure was due to loopholes in the land selection legislation, which exempted a large part of the lands leased by the squatters and permitted them to preempt by various subterfuges the watered parts of their non-exempt holdings, thereby rendering the rest useless for would-be settlers. The squatters therefore emerged with their monopoly power not only unscathed but actually strengthened. In New South Wales 96 men managed to acquire the freehold of 8 million acres and even in Victoria, where the legislation was less defective, 100 men secured the freehold of 1½ million acres which were sold in the early sixties.[1] However, the machinations of the pastoralist were not the only cause of the failure. Most farmers were once again defeated by the exigencies of the Australian climate, the high costs of transportation and of labor, and the lack of adequate markets.

Whatever the causes of the failure of the Australian selection acts, the contrast with contemporary American legislation is most instructive. For in the United States the Homestead Act of 1862, which corresponded in purpose with the Australian legislation, was effective in providing large-scale opportunity for the establishment of family farms on productive land that was not claimed by anyone else. The Homestead Act enhanced equality of opportunity and strengthened the rural middle class in America through the late 19th century. In Australia, where legislation was unable to dislodge the big man's frontier the middle class remained weak.

The different development of the frontier and the opposite solution of the land question resulted in important divergences in both social structure and

ideology. In America the success of the small farmer tilling his own soil supported the tradition of "rugged individualism" and helped to enshrine the doctrine of laissez-faire. The tangible evidence of individual opportunity muted and largely inhibited the development of serious class antagonism. In Australia, on the other hand, the small man's struggle against conditions which favored large-scale grazing led to disappointment and frustration both of the wage earners in the towns and of the shifting landless workmen of the bush. A sense of contracting opportunity taught the Australian working man the advantages of cooperating against the economically stronger at an early date and induced them to invoke the help of the state wherever possible. The propertyless men in Australia sought salvation not in individual success-striving so much as in collective efforts and class solidarity. Most of the immigrants to Australia were of working-class origins and had tried to escape the limitations imposed upon them by the rigid British class structure. Their class solidarity gave rise to a strong trade union movement and later to a working-class political party which imparted an appearance of class divisions to Australian politics.[2] An especially militant influence was exerted by the Irish, who made up a substantial proportion of both convicts and free immigrants. Their bitterness against the English landlords put them in the vanguard of the nascent labor movement. It is interesting to note that although they are today not disproportionately represented in the working class but well spread throughout the occupational scale in both rural and urban areas, the Irish continue to dominate the leadership positions of the Australian Labour Party to the present day.

Moreover, the cohesiveness and egalitarian class solidarity had its roots not only in the working-class origins of most British immigrants but also had a native source in the life conditions of the semi-nomadic bush workers of the interior, the outback. Throughout most of the 19th century the work force of the typical grazing station consisted of an itinerant rural proletariat. Its outlook was conditioned by the brutal geographic and climatic conditions and the penetrating loneliness of the immense space which forced the bush workers to depend completely on each other for survival and companionship. This created the pattern of mateship: each man had a "mate" with whom he traveled from station to station and with whom he shared work, possessions and hardships, and for whom he expected to make any sacrifice if necessary. A sort of male marriage, the tradition of mateship was also quickly taken over by the gold diggers who likewise lacked female companionship and therefore formed teams of two or three men working and living together. From the outback and the goldfields mateship, mutual aid, and solidarity, blending with the sentiments of class consciousness of immigrants, became national traditions of the Australian working class as a whole. The ethos of mateship and of militant equalitarianism have become

[1] W. K. Hancock, *Australia* (London: Ernest Benn, 1930), p. 24.
[2] Cf. Brian Fitzpatrick, *The Australian People* (Melbourne: Melbourne University Press, 1946), pp. 54–61; and A. G. L. Shaw, "The Old Tradition," in Peter Coleman ed., *Australian Civilization* (Melbourne: F. W. Cheshire, 1962), pp. 12–25.

major ingredients of the basic value system of Australian society which have persisted well into the 20th century.[1]

The contrast between American individualism and Australian collectivism had very important consequences for the development of social and economic institutions in the two countries. The American settler needed relatively little help from the state, he wanted to be left alone in an environment of enormous natural resources which could be developed by hard-working private individuals. Local government bodies and "grass-roots democracy" seemed adequate to work out administrative problems and provide essential public services like education and police. In Australia, however, sparse settlement of wide areas made reliance on centralized governments an inevitable necessity. The Australian colonists faced greater distances and a harder environment which could not be tamed without collective action. From the beginning Australians have depended upon the government to provide most of the public services. Roads and railroads proved too costly for the scattered rural communities and unprofitable for private investors and had to be provided by the state. The state also had to take an active part in peopling the country. Since Australia's great distance from Europe put her at a disadvantage in competing for immigrants, the government had to assist migration. The outlying communities could not attract schoolteachers in competition with the capital cities, therefore the Australian states had to resort to centralized state-education systems which assign teachers to communities and also support aspirants to the profession in teachers' colleges.

The tradition of reliance on the state was eventually also extended to the field of labor relations where patterns have developed that differ sharply from those in America. The beginnings of Australian trade unionism date back to the 1820's, but the role of the unions did not become important until the 1870's and 1880's. Between 1886 and 1890 unionization was extended from the skilled crafts to the semi-skilled and unskilled workers, particularly the miners and the sheep shearers of the bush. Unionism was embraced with enthusiasm by men who believed in equality of opportunity but who saw less and less possibility of achieving economic independence. After winning a succession of victories in the boom period of the 1880's, the unions suffered shattering defeats in the early 1890's when they decisively lost a series of widespread strikes. In their distress the workers began to pay increased attention to political activities. In several colonies a labor party had already been organized in the late 1880's. The disastrous failure of the strikes now gave these parties a major impetus. The goal was to gain social reforms through legislation, which direct union activity had failed to achieve. The Labour Party quickly became the official opposition and as early as 1904, only three years after federation of the six colonies into the Commonwealth, it was able to form the national government. But in spite of this, Australian politics, like American politics,

have been characterized by the lack of sharp ideological differences such as are found in Continental Europe and at times in England.

The Australian labor movement has succeeded in strongly stamping its imprint upon the country's social institutions. The keystone is the system of industrial arbitration which operates through an elaborate mechanism of state and federal tribunals to which all industrial disputes must be submitted. The arbitration courts determine wages, salaries and conditions of work and their decisions are legally binding. The system of compulsory arbitration began in the 1890's as a method for settling wage disputes but the tribunals soon came to regulate industrial conditions generally. Arbitration emerged as the Australian device for satisfying the militant demands of the working class and through the arbitration machinery the government has intervened in the class struggle.[2] The arbitration tribunals have endeavored to guarantee the Australian worker an acceptable standard of living by developing two main concepts: the basic wage and margins. The basic wage is the minimum which must be paid for unskilled labor. The first basic wage was declared in 1907 when the Commonwealth Court of Arbitration calculated an amount of money sufficient to satisfy "the normal needs of the average employee regarded as a human being living in a civilized community." This amount, adjusted for changes in the cost of living, became an established standard from which upward variations for different degrees of skill and responsibility have been determined. These upward variations are the margins above the basic wage. These concepts are applied not only to wage earners but also to clerical, administrative and professional employees whose margins may be several times the basic wage itself.

The unions have placed great stress on margins, skill has been so broadly interpreted that only a small percentage of Australian workers are actually awarded only the basic wage. Moreover, the basic wage and the margins are merely legally prescribed minima. Actual wage rates may exceed the legal awards through the payment of bonuses or merit money. When labor is in oversupply actual wage rates and awards will coincide closely but in times of full employment earnings tend

[1] The historical origins and the development of the "Australian spirit" have been traced by Russel Ward, *The Australian Legend* (Melbourne, Oxford University Press, 1958).

[2] This is an outstanding example of the institutionalization of conflict which characterizes Australian society to an unusually high degree. Not only is industrial arbitration largely substituted for collective bargaining, but quasi-judicial boards and commissions have been established with statutory power to resolve all kinds of organizational, jurisdictional and employment issues which in other countries are fought out in open conflict by the interested parties. For example, the distribution of electoral boundaries is decided by a statutory commission, federal subsidies to competing state governments are allocated by the Commonwealth Grants Commission, likewise federal grants to the various state universities are determined by the Universities Commission. Cf. R. S. Parker, "Power in Australia," unpublished paper read at the Australian National University in Canberra, October 8, 1962.

to exceed the award rates. Despite the emphasis on margins and bonuses, the differences between rates have been kept relatively narrow, so that the differentials between wages for skilled and unskilled workers are smaller than in the United States, Canada and the United Kingdom. This reflects the nature of the Australian economy where prosperity has always depended on primary products and their export. Because manufacturing industry has not been basic until recently, incentive wages have not been of major importance. In this institutional framework the egalitarian sentiment of Australian workers who abhor inequality not only in general but also among their own ranks has been able to achieve success.

Since the formation of a union is an indispensable prerequisite to negotiations before the court, the arbitration system has encouraged the growth of unions. In Australia two-thirds of all workers belong to unions and 90 percent of all employees are covered by awards.

income [in Australia] has not increased markedly since early this century."[1] However, it is noteworthy that Australian unions have been able to place greater emphasis on shorter hours so that nearly one-third of the increase in productivity was taken in the form of shorter hours, compared to about 10 percent in the two other countries. This clearly manifests the preference of Australian workers on equality of enjoyment rather than on success-striving. Given a floor under his standard of living, the Australian worker prefers more leisure to more money.

II

Although Australia was in the vanguard of urbanization — as early as 1911, 58 percent of the population were living in urban areas — industrialization lagged behind. To be sure, the beginnings of some manufacturing industries date back to the 1860's and the 1870's but

TABLE I. *Percentage Distribution of the Australian Work Force in 1947 and 1961, and of Employed Persons in the United States in 1960*

	AUSTRALIA		UNITED STATES
	1947	1961	1960
White-collar occupations	31.4	36.0	43.2
Professional and technical	5.1	8.4	11.8
Managerial	5.4	7.0	8.8
Clerical and commercial	20.9	20.6	22.6
Manual occupations	50.4	51.6	50.4
Farm occupations	14.8	11.1	6.5
Occupation not stated	3.4	1.3	*
Total	100.0	100.0	100.0

* Workers who did not state their occupations are excluded.
Sources: *Census of the Commonwealth of Australia 1947, Statistician's Report*, p. 196. The 1961 Australian census data are preliminary and were obtained in a personal communication from the Commonwealth Bureau of Census and Statistics. The U.S. data are from the *U.S. Census of Population, 1960. General and Economic Characteristics, U.S. Summary.* Final Report PC(1)–1C, p. xxv.

Although the basic wage has established a floor below which wages are not allowed to sink, the real income of Australian workers has risen less and more slowly than in the United States. For example, real hourly wages doubled in the United States between 1914 and 1939 whereas in Australia they rose only 36 percent. In Britain the increase was about 50 percent during the same period. As Walker has pointed out, changes in real wage rates in all three countries have been tied closely to increases in productivity. "The arbitration system has not had any decisive influence on the improvement of real wages and labor's share in the national

throughout the 19th century Australia's economy depended heavily on primary production. Industrialization in the sense of the development of heavy industry and a complex and diversified type of manufacturing began about the time of the First World War.[2] But even during the interwar period Australia still continued to depend heavily on imports of manufactured products. During and after World War II, however, the process of industrialization gathered momentum very rapidly.[3] Today Australia ranks among the most highly-industrialized nations of the world with about 30 percent of its work force engaged in manufacturing activities. Yet, a large part of Australian manufacturing industry remains an offshoot of British, American and European industry. Moreover, primary industry has by no means been relegated to insignificance. Although employing only about 13 percent of the work force, primary production still contributes about one-fifth of the national income and accounts for over 90 percent of Australian exports.[4]

[1] Kenneth F. Walker, *Industrial Relations in Australia* (Cambridge: Harvard University Press, 1956), pp. 325–331. For a concise, brief account of the Australian arbitration system see also P. H. Karmel and Maureen Brunt, *The Structure of the Australian Economy* (Melbourne: F.W. Cheshire, 1962), pp. 36–42.
[2] Karmel and Brunt, *op. cit.*, pp. 88–89.
[3] Cf. Alex Hunter, ed., *The Economics of Australian Industry* (Melbourne: Melbourne University Press, 1963).
[4] Karmel and Brunt, *op. cit.*, p. 88.

Inevitably the rapid expansion of manufacturing, commerce and finance is bringing about important changes in the class structure of Australian society. Unfortunately the data are scanty and tenuous but there is definite evidence that the middle class is expanding and playing a more important role than previously. Table I shows the distribution of the Australian work force by major occupation groups for 1947 and 1961, as well as the distribution of the United States labor force in 1960. It should be pointed out that the occupational breakdowns are very rough indeed and comparisons can be made only with great caution: there are considerable differences in the occupational classifications employed by the Australian censuses of 1947 and 1961 and neither of them is fully comparable with the classifications of the United States census. Despite these important qualifications the trend is clear. The proportion of those engaged in agriculture is shrinking, the percentage of urban blue-collar workers is beginning to stabilize and the white-collar occupations are expanding rapidly. Particularly impressive is the increase in the professional and in the managerial occupations. The percentage engaged in clerical and commercial occupations is undoubtedly understated, due to changes in classification. The 1961 census included clerical and manual workers in the transportation industries in the same category, whereas in 1947 the clerical workers in the transportation industry have been grouped with all other clerical and commercial workers. If allowance is made for this, there is no doubt that the proportion of clerical and commercial workers has increased, not declined, since 1947 and that the increase in total white-collar workers has been somewhat greater than is indicated in Table I.

When the Australian data are compared with those for the United States it is evident that the shape of the occupational structure of Australia is well on the way to approaching that of the United States. At the same time certain important differentials still remain. The proportion of the farm population is still considerably larger in Australia than in the United States and the percentage in white-collar occupations, especially in the professional and technical occupations, still lags behind American developments. The expansion of the professional occupations is related to the growth of tertiary education which had been rather slow in Australia prior to World War II but which is now expanding very rapidly. In 1939 there were only 14,000 students enrolled in six universities. At present there are ten universities — and several new ones are in the process of being established — with approximately 72,000 students. Yet despite the rapid postwar increase, the proportion of Australian youngsters enrolled in secondary schools and in universities is still far below that in the United States. By 1958 approximately 20 percent of Australian youths in the age group 15–19 were attending school, as compared to 66 percent in the United States. For the age group 20–24 the corresponding proportions were 2 percent for Australia and 12 per-

cent for the United States.[1] The Australian enrollment ratios are rapidly rising every year but Australia still compares unfavorably with many other countries, especially the United States.

The lag in educational attainments reflects not only the recency of industrial development and a lower degree of economic differentiation but also the traditional spirit of Australian egalitarianism which is indifferent to all forms of special distinctions, including university degrees. Until recently a tertiary education was neither required for most managerial occupations nor for higher civil service positions. A questionnaire survey of 327 managers and directors representing 185 of Australia's leading business firms undertaken a few years ago showed that only 35 percent had tertiary education,[2] whereas 76 percent of their American counterparts had attended college and 57 percent had graduated.[3] Until recently the relatively small scale of Australia's industrial organizations did not require many university-trained professional managers. At present, however, the situation is changing; as the "managerial revolution" is extending to Australia, the demand for university graduates is growing and the corporations are actively recruiting university men in rapidly increasing numbers.

The strong emphasis on egalitarianism and the corresponding disregard for higher education clearly manifested itself in the establishment of the civil service systems of the Australian states and of the Commonwealth around the turn of the century. The Commonwealth Public Service was deliberately created as a closed bureaucracy, open on the whole only to young men who entered a civil service career at the age of sixteen. Promotion to higher positions was to be strictly from within the Service and the idea of a specially recruited corps of senior officials with advanced educational qualifications to staff the higher positions was deliberately shunned.[4] University degrees were required only for engineers, architects, lawyers and physicians. During the sixty years that have passed since the setting up of the Commonwealth Public Service, however, pressures for the appointment of university graduates to clerical and administrative positions have built up increasingly. Limited recruiting of graduates was introduced in the 1930's and considerably extended during World War II when many temporary officers had to be appointed from outside the Service. In the postwar period the legally permissible

[1] P. H. Karmel, *Some Economic Aspects of Education* (Melbourne: F. W. Cheshire, 1962), p. 13. Australia's population which was about 7 million in 1939 is now close to 11 million.

[2] S. Encel, "The Business Elite in Australia," unpublished paper.

[3] W. Lloyd Warner and James C. Abegglen, *Occupational Mobility in American Business and Industry* (Minneapolis: University of Minnesota Press, 1955).

[4] Cf. H. A. Scarrow, *The Higher Public Service of the Commonwealth of Australia* (Durham: Duke University Press, 1957); and Solomon Encel, "Recruitment of University Graduates to the Commonwealth Public Service," *Public Administration* (Summer, 1954), pp. 217–228.

quota of 10 percent for the appointment of university graduates has been filled every year. A recent study of 326 senior Commonwealth public servants showed that 56 percent had university degrees although nearly one-third of these had obtained them through part-time study after joining the public service.[1] However, the basic principle of a closed career system entered on the basis of merely an elementary or partial secondary education has never been abandoned and the various staff associations and unions have always strenuously opposed the recruitment of university graduates for higher positions as both unnecessary and evil. The Commonwealth government is currently considering reorganization proposals which might lead to increased recruitment of administrative officers from outside the Service. These proposals have drawn sharp fire from the Administrative and Clerical Officers' Association whose Canberra spokesman proclaimed: "The apparent proposals regarding a 'higher public service' might well be considered as a diabolical attempt to further fragment employee organizations within the Public Service. The efficiency of Australia's national administration depends on the preservation of the principle of democratic promotional opportunities on the basis of efficiency."[2]

The combined effects of union power, egalitarianism and until recently, a relatively undifferentiated and simple economy are clearly evident in the Australian income distribution which is much flatter than that of the United States. Great caution must be exercised in comparing the two distributions because the only available Australian data are based on income tax statistics. Income tax statistics are subject to tax evasion and tax avoidance. Moreover, the Australian data refer to individuals, the American data to "income receiving unit," i.e., families and unrelated individuals. Neither set of statistics includes capital gains and non-cash perquisites. But even keeping these important qualifications in mind, a comparison of the available data remains instructive. As Table 2 shows, 70 percent of all Australian taxpayers reported incomes between $1,000 and $3,000. Only 12 percent of the Australians had incomes above $3,000, compared to 67 percent of the Americans. Expressed in quartiles, the two middle quartiles of the Australian income distribution extend from about $1,250 to about $2,550, a range of $1,300, whereas in the United States they lie between about $2,200 and $7,200, a range of $5,000, almost four times that of Australia. The United States inter-quartile range is more than double the 25th percentile, the Australian range is about equal to its 25th percentile. Thus the span of the Australian income distribution is much narrower than the American and its peak is

much lower. The top 2 percent of Australian incomes begins at the $4,500 level, the top 2 percent in the United States at the $15,000 level.[3]

The narrow range of the Australian income distribution means that there are few paupers and few multi-millionaires. The operation of the arbitration system which controls the whole structure of wages and salaries ensures not only a subsistence level for unskilled workers but also ties to it the wages of skilled workers and the incomes of salaried employees. The relative differentials are practically frozen and changes affect all wage and salary earners in a substantially uniform manner.

The low income differentials express themselves in a pervasive homogeneity of life styles. For example, 82 percent of all Australians live in detached single-family homes and 70 percent either own their homes completely or are paying them off. Since 80 percent of Australia's population lives in urban areas and 56 percent

TABLE 2. *The Distribution of Income in Australia and in the United States*

	Australian taxpayers 1957–8	Families and unrelated individuals in the United States 1959
	Percent	
Under $1,000	17.9	12.8
$1,000–1,999	35.9	10.5
$2,000–2,999	34.5	9.2
$3,000–3,999	8.6	9.5
$4,000–4,999	1.5	10.2
$5,000–5,999	.4	10.7
$6,000–6,999	.3	8.9
$7,000–9,999	.7	16.2
$10,000 and over	.2	12.0

Sources: For Australia: *40th Report of the Commissioner of Taxation, June 1, 1961,* Table 31, p. 42. For the United States: *U.S. Census of Population, 1960,* PC(1)–1C, Table 96, p. 277.

in metropolitan areas, this means in effect that the majority of Australians are suburbanites. The metropolitan suburbs extend for many miles in every direction, consisting mainly of five-room bungalows. This does not mean, of course, that there are no visible differences between working class and middle-class suburbs but the contrasts are gradual and subdued, not stark and crass. The typical Australian working man is a homeowner, no less than the salaried employee. The main cities like Melbourne and Sydney also have their upper-class suburbs where modest bungalows give way to more stately homes and occasional mansions, but as a perceptive English journalist has pointed out, "the houses of the rich are not really very big or magnificent for the good reason that the rich can get no servants to look after them."[4] The overall impression is that of relatively small differences in the quality of housing for the great majority of the population. The ownership of automobiles and consumer goods is widespread. There is one automobile for every 3.8

[1] S. Encel, "The Bureaucratic Elite in Australia," unpublished paper.

[2] *The Canberra Times,* July 19, 1963.

[3] For these measures I am indebted to Leonard Broom, *op. cit.* I have updated the figures to the latest available data.

[4] John Douglas Pringle, *Australian Accent* (London: Chatto and Windus, 1958), p. 32.

persons in Australia, compared to 2.6 in the United States, 3.7 in Canada and 8.0 in the United Kingdom.[1]

The similarity in the material standard of living is accompanied by a similarity in tastes, dress and leisure activities. An intensive love of and preoccupation with sports and outdoor activities is shared by all strata of Australian society and is not related to social distinctions. Nor is speech a mark of class, as it is in England for instance, despite the fact that the broad Australian accent is very distinctive and reminiscent of cockney English. But the presence or absence of this accent cuts clear across the entire social hierarchy and is not a reliable indicator of social position. Differences in income and wealth divide Australians quantitatively but not qualitatively. Money does not afford a different kind of life. The rich man drives a bigger car and has a finer house than the ordinary fellow but they spend their leisure in much the same way. They go to the same films, the same beaches, they watch the same games and they drink the same beer. It is also significant that in Australia the custom of tipping with its connotation of servility has been traditionally absent. For the same reason single passengers, whether male or female, often sit beside the driver in the front of a taxi, not in the back. To sit alone in the back would imply the master-servant relationship of the rich man and his chauffeur, an impression which most Australians are anxious to avoid.

The relatively small differentials in style of life and the aggressive emphasis on social equality does not mean, of course, that status differences are altogether absent. Beneath the equalitarian surface many status distinctions do exist. A British visitor has aptly observed: "Each community, whether it is a suburb or a small town, has its recognized pecking order, in which professional people rank very high; it has its prestige symbols in the types and furnishings of the home or of the school which the children attend. It has its tendency to put people of one occupation or religion on key committees and to leave others off."[2] Indeed, the type of school attended has long been one of the most important stratification variables in Australian society. Non-government, fee-paying schools, called private schools in some states, but public schools in others (following the British custom) exist side by side with the state schools. As in the United States, the Roman Catholic church maintains an extensive system of primary and secondary schools (although no universities) whose fees are nominal. The large majority of the children not educated in the state schools attend Catholic parochial schools. But it is the non-Catholic private schools whose fees are substantial which carry social prestige. Their aim is to provide education for the social élite. These schools vary among themselves in prestige — the older-established and more expensive ones enjoy the highest status. In 1958 government schools were providing education for 76 percent of all children, Roman Catholic schools for 20 percent, and independent schools for 4 percent.[3]

The role of the independent schools has been very important. Prior to the last war the large majority of university students were alumni of these schools, and of those entering the professions three-fourths came from private schools. Encel's study of the business élite showed that 54 percent of the directors and managers included had attended independent secondary schools and that 41 percent were alumni of five of the most well known "Greater Public Schools."[4] Of the senior public servants surveyed by the same author 28 percent had attended independent schools and nearly half of these were graduates of the same five high prestige schools.[5] The postwar expansion of tertiary education has brought about a definite "democratization of higher education" so that the private schools no longer furnish the majority of university students. In 1959–60 about 28 percent of all students entering Australian universities came from independent schools.[6]

As in the United States, class distinctions are most evident in informal social association and in participation in formal organizations. The major cities have a profusion of voluntary associations and social and service clubs which form a prestige hierarchy and usually draw their membership from a rather narrow class range. In small communities which cannot support a large number of formal organizations, membership often represents a much wider cross-section of the community. Yet the highest offices of the more prestigious associations always tend to be filled by the local people of the highest class position. "There may be rivalry among the eligible candidates for these high offices, or perhaps more commonly certain offices become virtually the preserve of certain individuals; in one country town in New South Wales the matrons of the two leading families speak to each other of '*your* Red Cross' and '*my* Country Women's Association'."[7]

In rural Australia the early social distinctions between the wealthy landholders and the rest of the population have maintained themselves to a considerable extent. Many of the "old families" still retain large pastoral holdings and form a highly cohesive and self-conscious upper-class group with a distinctive style of life isolated from the rest of the community. Their children are generally sent as boarders to the high-prestige private schools and tend to marry within their own circles. Members of this group visit their friends throughout their own state and beyond and participate with them in the so-called picnic races, country shows, and weddings up and down the land. They frequently visit

[1] Karmel and Brunt, *op. cit.*, p. 9.
[2] Jean MacKenzie, *Australian Paradox* (Melbourne: W. F. Cheshire, 1961, pp. 130–131).
[3] Commonwealth Office of Education, *Statistics of Australian Education for 1958 and Earlier Years* (Sydney 1961).
[4] "The Business Elite in Australia," *op. cit.*
[5] "The Bureaucratic Elite in Australia," *op. cit.*
[6] W. C. Radford, *School Leavers in Australia* (Melbourne: Australian Council for Educational Research, 1962), p. 31.
[7] Jean I. Martin, "Marriage, the Family and Class," in A. P. Elkin, ed., *Marriage and the Family in Australia* (Sydney: Angus and Robertson, 1957), p. 34.

the metropolis or even maintain houses there for social functions and shopping. They do not form a leisure class since most of the men run their own properties but their pace as a status élite is undisputed and through their economic and social connections they exercise considerable power.[1]

In the metropolitan cities, too, there exists a recognizable social élite. The urban upper class, which was based in the 19th century on mercantile and financial wealth and which modeled itself on the English upper class, has been enlarged and partially superseded by the industrialization process which has created a new upper class of industrialists who more closely resemble the American model. Australian industry is characterized by a high degree of concentration. "A handful of firms, certainly no more than a couple of hundred, dominate the private sector of the economy."[2] and most of these firms are related to each other through interlocking directorates. Since Australian corporations are smaller than their American counterparts the separation of ownership and control has not yet proceeded as far as in the United States. It is true that an important proportion of large companies is overseas-sponsored and thus overseas-controlled — the outstanding example of this is the General Motors-Holden Company which is a wholly-owned subsidiary of General Motors and manufactures about half of Australia's automobiles. But the domestic companies are controlled by less than 200 families who form an exclusive oligarchy.[3] A high degree of concentration also prevails in banking where the three leading banks do almost two-thirds of the private banking business and in the field of mass communications which is dominated by less than half a dozen firms.

The urban upper class is small in number but wields considerable economic and political power. ". . . the success of crucial aspects of government policy may be dependent upon the co-operation of a small number of large firms; and consequently it is not uncommon on a number of issues to find Government and Business (or the relevant section of Business) bargaining on somewhat equal terms."[4] It would be wrong, however, to suppose that a handful of upper-class families forms a power élite which runs the country. For one thing, despite its rapid growth, Australian industry remains only medium-sized in comparison with other industrial countries, and the Australian economy is still largely dependent on exports of primary products and imports of many manufactured articles as well as overseas capital. Domestic Big Business therefore does not wield as much influence as it does in more highly-developed economies. Secondly, the government has traditionally played a very important role in the Australian economy. Public enterprise dominates in the field of public utilities and developmental work and is in active competition with private business in the transport and communications industries, as well as in banking and housing. Thus nearly 30 percent of all wages and salaries originate in the public sector.[5] The government bureaucracy exercises a large amount of both political and economic power and it is worth noting that both the civil servants and the politicians do not interlock very much with the business élite in terms of social background and education. They appear as three distinctive groups and not many businessmen are active in politics nor are politicians engaged in business. For these reasons the foremost student of this subject in Australia concludes that a power élite in the sense in which this term has been used in the United States, Britain or even Canada, does not exist in Australia although there are definite tendencies towards it.[6]

As in the United States, the urban upper class forms a status élite which carries on its social life in exclusive clubs and self-contained cliques. Although it can also be found in Melbourne and Adelaide, the playing of the status game is perhaps most evident in Sydney, where postwar prosperity has created groups of nouveaux riches intent on social climbing. For this purpose residence is of great importance and a recent survey has shown how the 386 suburbs of Sydney can be ranked on a status scale.[7] Under the equalitarian surface the hunt for status symbols seems to be increasing. Thus it has become fashionable to buy Australian art, active participation in philanthropic activities is rising, and the number of knighthoods conferred upon Australians has increased in recent years. By and large, however, the behavior patterns of the upper class have had little influence on the Australian style of life. The rich are less emulated than their counterparts abroad and the mass of Australians is still pretty indifferent about snobbishness and status anxieties. The perceptive appraisal made by the novelist D. H. Lawrence forty years ago still seems to apply fairly well today: "There was really no class distinction. There was a difference of money and of 'smartness.' But nobody felt *better* than anyone else, or higher; only better-off. And there is all the difference in the world between feeling better than your fellowmen, and merely feeling better-off."[8] It remains to be seen, however, whether the equalitarian tradition will be able to successfully withstand the growing pressures of an increasingly complex industrial society in future.

An important factor which is introducing additional complexity in Australian society is immigration. Prior to World War II the overwhelming majority of immigrants had always originated from the British Isles

---

[1] Cf. Martin, *op. cit.*, pp. 36 ff.; and MacKenzie, *op. cit.*, pp. 137–139.

[2] Karmel and Brunt, *op. cit.*, p. 62.

[3] Cf. E. L. Wheelwright, *Ownership and Control of Australian Companies* (Sydney: Law Book Co. of Australasia, 1957).

[4] Karmel and Brunt, *op. cit.*, p. 63.

[5] *Ibid.*, p. 104.

[6] Cf. Solomon Encel, *Is There an Australian Power Elite?* (Melbourne: Chifley Memorial Lecture, 1961, Melbourne University Australian Labour Party Club, 1961).

[7] Athol A. Congalton, *Status Ranking of Sydney Suburbs* (Sydney: University of New South Wales, 1961).

[8] D. H. Lawrence, *Kangaroo* (London: Penguin Books, 1950), p. 26.

and the Australian population had been both small and remarkably homogeneous. However, after the war Australia changed its immigration policy and accelerated the influx of immigrants from Continental European countries. Since 1945 there has been a net intake of approximately 1,400,000 migrants of whom about one-half were of non-British origins, many of them from southeastern Europe. The immigrants, particularly those from southeastern Europe, tend to enter in disproportionately large numbers into the lower levels of the Australian class structure. This tends to promote an upward movement of native Australians into higher income and occupational positions and to give the working class a distinct ethnic character. Since native Australians look down upon immigrants in general and non-British migrants in particular, this threatens

tained 49 percent manual workers. Table 3 shows class identification by occupation. Most realistic is the self-ascribed status of persons in managerial and professional occupations, very few of whom described themselves as working-class, but in all other categories the discrepancies between occupation and class identification are considerable. In particular the skilled workers appear split in their identification, not quite half of them designated themselves as working-class.

Essentially similar results were obtained in a sample survey of 265 voters of an outer suburb of Melbourne during a 1960 by-election campaign. Here no forced choice was used. An open answer to the question "If you had to say which group or section of the community you belonged to, what would you say?" resulted in 37 percent identifying themselves as working-class, 44

TABLE 3. *Class Identification by Occupation, 1961 Federal Election Gallup Poll (in percentages)*

Class	Managerial and professional	Small business	White collar	Skilled	Semi-skilled	Unskilled	Farmers	Farm Employees
Upper middle	13	5	6	2	—	4	5	4
Middle	80	45	51	38	22	17	60	20
Lower middle	5	21	15	14	10	2	17	17
Working	2	29	28	46	68	77	18	59
	100	100	100	100	100	100	100	100
Percent of total sample	11.9	5.0	24.4	22.5	16.2	6.8	9.7	3.5

Source: Australian Gallup Poll.

TABLE 4. *Class Identification by Occupation, 1960 La Trobe By-Election Survey (in percentages)*

Class	Managerial and professional	Small business	White collar	Skilled	Semi-skilled	Unskilled
Middle	84.4	51.6	52.6	28.8	31.1	11.1
Working	15.6	25.8	25.6	57.7	51.7	66.6
Other	—	22.6	21.8	13.5	17.2	22.3
	100.0	100.0	100.0	100.0	100.0	100.0
Percent of total sample	13.3	12.9	32.5	21.7	12.1	7.5

Source: A. F. Davies, "Social Class in the New Suburb", *op. cit.*, p. 16.

the working-class claims to equality. The parallel with the situation in the United States in the 1880's is quite striking.

Only a very small number of empirical studies of social stratification have been undertaken in Australia to date[1] but they include several attempts to ascertain individuals' perceptions of their position in the class structure and its relation to voting behavior. It is interesting to note that more Australians describe themselves as middle-class than as working-class. In a 1961 Federal election poll undertaken by the Australian Gallup Poll a national cross-section of prospective voters was given a forced choice of the following class categories: upper middle, middle, lower middle, and working class. Only 38.5 percent of the total identified themselves as working-class although the sample con-

percent as middle-class, 2 percent designated other class positions, and 17 percent did not identify themselves in class terms.[2] Table 4 presents the class

[1] Besides Congalton's study cited in footnote 7, on p. 158, they include the following: R. Taft, "The Social Grading of Occupations in Australia," *British Journal of Sociology* 4 (March 1953), pp. 181–188; O. A. Oeser and S. B. Hammond, eds., *Social Structure and Personality in a City* (London, Routledge and Kegan Paul, 1954), Part V; S. Encel, "The Old School Tie in Business," *Nation*, July 18, 1959, same author, "The Political Elite in Australia," *Political Studies*, 9 (February 1961), pp. 16–36; Creighton Burns, *Parties and People* (Melbourne: Melbourne University Press, 1961); A. F. Davies, "Social Class in the New Suburb," *Westerly*, 3 (1961), pp. 15–18; Athol A. Congalton, *Social Standing of Occupations in Sydney* (Sydney: University of New South Wales, 1962; and same author, *Occupational Status in Australia* (Sydney: University of New South Wales, 1963).

[2] A. F. Davies, *op. cit.*

identification of the 240 persons in the work force by occupation. None of the persons in professional or managerial occupations identified with the working class, and a majority of all categories of manual workers placed themselves in the working class. But the percentage of workers who either consider themselves middle-class or use no class designation is considerable, as is the proportion of white-collar employees and small businessmen who designate themselves as working-class or no class.

As might be expected, voting behavior was clearly related to both objective class position, as measured by occupation, and subjective class identification. Table 5 shows the voting intentions in the 1961 federal elections by occupation. A clear majority of all grades of urban manual workers intended to vote for labor parties while white-collar people and farmers favored the Liberal-Country parties.[1] The farm employees, however, appeared evenly divided. Table 6 shows the relation between party preference and class identification for both the 1961 federal election poll and the 1960 by-election survey. In both cases a clear majority of those who called themselves working-class intended to vote for the labor parties while the majority of those identifying with the middle class favored the Liberal-Country parties. However, in the Gallup Poll a majority of those who called themselves lower middle-class intended to vote for labor. A 1962 post-election survey of 150 people in three Melbourne suburbs found that two-thirds of those who called themselves working-class had actually voted for labor, while two-thirds of those identifying with the middle class had voted for the Liberal party.[2]

Although great caution is necessary in the interpretation of voting polls and the reliability of class identification obtained in such surveys is dubious, it would appear that class consciousness is neither universal nor necessarily politically compelling. Nevertheless, the majority of Australians are not only clearly aware of class divisions but act politically in accordance with both their objective occupational position and their subjective perception of the class system. As yet neither the pronounced equalitarianism, derived from firmly entrenched working-class traditions, nor the high standard of living and the relatively small differentials in life style have obliterated class awareness and class solidarity.

In summary, the Australian class structure differs from the American in several respects. Whereas in the United States the imprint of the middle class on the

stratification system has been decisive from the beginning, Australia began with a dichotomous class structure in which a pastoral upper class faced a hostile working class, and it was the working class which made the main impact on most social institutions. During the present century industrialization has brought about a rapid expansion of the Australian middle class and has also strengthened the small but influential urban upper

TABLE 5. *Voting Intentions, by Occupation, 1961 Federal Election Poll (in percentages)*

Occupation	Liberal-Country parties	Labour parties	Don't know & other
Managerial & professional	73.9	19.8	6.1
Small business	49.1	41.5	9.4
White collar	48.9	45.6	5.5
Skilled manual	32.5	59.4	8.1
Semi-skilled	23.4	70.1	6.5
Unskilled	17.1	78.5	4.4
Farmers	73.7	19.7	6.6
Farm employees	47.7	47.7	9.2

Source: Australian Gallup Poll.

class. The Australian stratification system is now becoming increasingly complex. Nevertheless the span of the contemporary Australian class structure is still much narrower than that of the United States and the style of life of the middle class differs only slightly from that of the working class. Despite the generally rising standard of living and spreading affluence, class consciousness remains more pronounced

TABLE 6. *Voting Intentions, by Class Identification, 1961 Federal Elections and 1960 LaTrobe By-Election (in percentages)*

Class	Liberal-Country parties	Labour parties	Don't know or other
	1961 Federal Election		
Upper middle	66	18.5	15.5
Middle	61	34	5
Lower middle	42	52	6
Working	25	70	5
	1960 LaTrobe By-Election		
Middle	56	31	13
Working	20	61	19

Sources: Australian Gallup Poll and Burns, *Parties and People, op. cit.*, p. 78.

in Australia than in America and this is related to the fact that the equalitarian stance of the two societies has remained different for the time being. In the United States the emphasis has always been on equality of opportunity and sharp status differences have been interpreted as individual and temporary and have therefore been tolerated with relative equanimity. In Australia the emphasis has been on equality of life style

---

[1] At the present time there are four political parties in Australia. The Australian Labor Party, based solidly on the trade unions is currently the major opposition party. In 1954 a splinter party, the Democratic Labor Party, was formed as the result of a split in the Australian Labor Party over the Communist issue. Since 1948 two Conservative parties, the Liberal Party and the Country Party have formed the federal government. The Liberal Party is the senior partner in this coalition.

[2] Unpublished paper by A. F. Davies presented at the Australian National University in Canberra, July 4, 1963.

and enjoyment, symbols of superiority are resented and the effort has been to "level up" and to "cut down the tall poppies." However, the similarities between the two social structures outweigh the differences and, as the industrialization of Australia and the expansion of her middle class proceed further, the resemblances

tend to become closer. Although it is unlikely that the differences between the two social structures will disappear altogether, similar forces are operating in both societies in the middle of the 20th century and if this process continues, it is likely that they will produce similar results.

Value Patterns, Class, and the Democratic Polity
THE UNITED STATES AND GREAT BRITAIN
Seymour Martin Lipset

To compare national value systems, we must be able to classify them and distinguish among them. Talcott Parsons has provided a useful tool for this purpose in his concept of "pattern variables." These were originally developed by Parsons as an extension of the classic distinction by Ferdinand Tönnies between "community" and "society" — between those systems which emphasized *Gemeinschaft* (primary, small, traditional, integrated) values, and those which stressed *Gesellschaft* (impersonal, secondary, large, socially differentiated) values.[1] The pattern variables to be used in the following analysis are achievement-ascription, universalism-particularism, and specificity-diffuseness. According to the achievement-ascription distinction, a society's value system may emphasize individual ability or performance or it may emphasize ascribed or inherited qualities (such as race or high birth) in judging individuals and placing them in various roles. According to the universalism-particularism distinction, it may emphasize that all people shall be treated according to the same standard (*e.g.*, equality before the law), or that individuals shall be treated differently according to their personal qualities or their particular membership in a class or group. Specificity-diffuseness refers to the difference between treating individuals in terms of the specific positions which they happen to occupy, rather than diffusely as individual members of the collectivity.[2]

The pattern variables provide us with a much more sensitive way of classifying values than the older polar concepts of sociology, such as the folk-urban, mechanical-organic, primary-secondary, or *Gemeinschaft-Gesellschaft*, etc. For instance, they make it possible for us to establish differences in value structures between two

nations that are at the same end of the *Gemeinschaft-Gesellschaft* continuum, or are at similar levels of economic development or social complexity. They are also useful for describing differences within a society. Thus the family is inherently ascriptive and particularistic while the market is universalistic and achievement oriented — the weaker the kinship ties in a given society, the greater the national emphasis on achievement is likely to be.

The manner in which any set of values is introduced will obviously affect the way the values are incorporated into a nation's institutions. In France, for instance, where the values of universalism, achievement, and specificity were introduced primarily through a political revolution, we would expect to find them most pro-

[1] Ferdinand Tönnies, *Community and Society, Gemeinschaft und Gesellschaft* (East Lansing: Michigan State University Press, 1957). A somewhat more complex specification of the component elements of these two concepts may be found in Charles P. Loomis, *Social Systems: Essays on Their Persistence and Change* (Princeton, N.J.: Van Nostrand, 1961), especially pp. 57–63. The pattern variables may also be seen as derived from Max Weber's types of social action, especially the traditional and the instrumentally rational. See Max Weber, *The Theory of Social and Economic Organization* (New York: Oxford University Press, 1947), pp. 115–118.

[2] Parsons has two other pattern variables which I ignore here, largely for reasons of parsimony: affectivity-affective neutrality, and the instrumental-consummatory distinction. For a detailed presentation of the pattern variables, see Talcott Parsons, *The Social System* (Glencoe, Ill.: The Free Press, 1951), pp. 58–67. Parsons' most recent elaboration of the relationship of pattern variable analysis to other elements in his conceptual framework is "Pattern Variables Revisited," *American Sociological Review*, 25 (1960), pp. 467–483; see also his article, "The Point of View of the Author," in Max Black, ed., *The Social Theories of Talcott Parsons* (Englewood Cliffs, N.J.: Prentice-Hall, 1961), pp. 319–320, 329–336.

Adapted from *The First New Nation*, (New York: Basic Books Inc., 1963).

minent in the political institutions; in Germany, where they have been introduced primarily through industria-

[1] Karl W. Deutsch, S. A. Burrell, R. A. Kann, M. Lee, Jr., M. Lichterman, R. E. Lindgren, F. L. Loewenheim, R. W. Van Wagenen, *Political Community and the North Atlantic Area* (Princeton, N.J.: Princeton University Press, 1957).

[2] Although all four polarity distinctions are important to the analysis of the political system, ascription-achievement and universalism-particularism seem more important than the other two. As Parsons has suggested, these are the variables which have the most reference to the total social system, rather than to subparts or to the motivation of individuals. "They are concerned . . . with the type of value-norms which enter into the structure of the social system." Combinations of these pairs are also most useful to help account for "structural differentiation and variability of social systems." See Parsons, *The Social System*, p. 106. The other two pairs, specificity-diffuseness and equalitarianism-elitism, are to a considerable degree dependent on the particular combinations of the first two.

[3] As Parsons has put it: "In a very broad way the differentiations between types of social systems do correspond to this order of cultural value pattern differentiation, but *only* in a very broad way. Actual social structures are not value-pattern types, but *resultants* of the integration of value-patterns with the other components of the system." *Ibid.*, p. 112. (Emphases in the original.) Gabriel Almond has criticized the utility of pattern-variable analysis for the study of comparative politics on the grounds that it results in exaggerations of the differences among political systems, particularly between Western and non-Western and primitive ones. He argues that "all political systems — the developed Western ones as well as the less-developed non-Western ones — are transitional systems in which cultural change is taking place." Thus they both include elements of each polarity of the pattern variables in many of their institutions. See Gabriel Almond, "Introduction: A Functional Approach to Comparative Politics," in Gabriel Almond and James S. Coleman, eds., *The Politics of Developing Areas* (Princeton, N.J.: Princeton University Press, 1960), pp. 20–25. This criticism is useful if it is considered as a warning against reifying these concepts, or tending to exaggerate the integrated character of societies, whether large or small. However, there is no reason why use of the pattern variables for analytic purposes need fall into these errors, and Parsons himself repeatedly stresses that systems and structures are never wholly one.

A detailed criticism of Parsons' analysis of politics, which, however, does not touch on the concepts dealt with here may be found in Andrew Hacker, "Sociology and Ideology," in Max Black, ed., *The Social Theories of Talcott Parsons* (Englewood Cliffs, N.J.: Prentice-Hall, 1961), pp. 289–310.

[4] It is important to note also that the pattern variables can be and have been used to distinguish among and within different orders of social systems or structures. Thus we may characterize total epochs (feudalism compared to capitalism), whole nations (the United States compared to Britain), subsystems within nations that logically may operate with different combinations of the variables (the state, or industry), subsystems within nations that logically must follow a specific set of pattern variables (the family), and subsystems within which there is conflict between different pattern variables (*e.g.*, the French business system, to be discussed later.)

[5] See S. M. Lipset, *The First New Nation* (New York: Basic Books, Inc., 1963), pp. 224–239, for a discussion of value patterns and political instability in France and Germany; there have been other efforts at using the pattern variables for political analysis. For the most part, however, they do so in the context of specifying differences between Western and agrarian societies and hence posit ideal types of integrated *Gemeinschaft* and *Gesellschaft* cultures. A paper which does attempt to use the variables to analyze contemporary differences is William Evan, "Social Structure, Trade Unionism, and Consumer Cooperation," *Industrial and Labor Relations Review*, 10 (1957), pp. 440–447.

lization, we would expect to find them most prominent in its economic institutions. The American example suggests that for democratic values to become legitimate in a post-revolutionary polity the norms of universalism, achievement, and specificity must be introduced into its economic institutions as well. This fosters rapid economic development, and encourages the underprivileged to believe that they as individuals may personally improve their status.[1]

I shall add the equalitarian-elitist distinction to the pattern variables just outlined. According to this, a society's values may stress that all persons must be given respect simply because they are human beings, or it may stress the general superiority of those who hold positions of power and privilege. In an equalitarian society, the differences between low status and high status people are not stressed in social relationships and do not convey to the high status person a general claim to social deference. In contrast, in an elitist society, those who hold high positions in any structure, whether it be in business, in intellectual activities, or in government, are thought to deserve, and are actually given, general respect and deference.[2] All ascriptively oriented societies are necessarily also elitist in this use of the term. On the other hand, achievement orientation and egalitarianism are not necessarily highly correlated, since a stress on achievement is not incompatible with giving generalized deference to all who have achieved their elite positions. To a considerable degree societies which are in the process of changing from an emphasis on ascription to one on achievement seem disposed, as we shall see later, to retain their elitist orientations and institutions when contrasted with societies in which ascriptive values have never had a preeminent role.

In actual fact, *no society is ever fully explicable by these analytic concepts, nor does the theory even contemplate the possible existence of such a society.*[3] Every society incorporates some aspect of each polarity. We may, however, differentiate among social structures by the extent to which they emphasize one or another of these polarities.[4] It should be added that classifications of the relative emphases among nations with respect to certain value polarities do not imply that such values are either prescriptive or descriptive of actual behavior. Rather, they are intended to provide base lines for comparative analysis.

I have chosen to discuss the United States and Great Britain to illustrate the relationship between values and the stability of democratic political systems.[5]

Though the United States and Great Britain are both urbanized, industrialized, and have stable, democratic political systems, they are integrated around different values and class relations. Tocqueville's *Democracy in America* and Bagehot's *The English Constitution* accurately specified these different organizing principles. According to Tocqueville, American democratic society was equalitarian and competitive (achievement oriented); according to Bagehot, Britain was deferential (elitist) and ascriptive. As both Tocqueville and Bagehot indicated, a society in which the historic ties of traditional legitimacy had been forcibly broken could sustain a stable democratic polity only if it emphasized equality and if it contained strong, independent, and competitive institutions. Conversely, if the privileged classes persisted and continued to expect ascriptive (aristocratic) and elitist rights, a society could have a stable democratic system only if the lower classes accepted the status system. A stable democracy can result from different combinations of pattern variables.

The United States, more than any other modern non-Communist industrial nation, emphasizes achievement, equalitarianism, universalism, and specificity.[1] These four tend to be mutually supportive. This does not mean that other stable combinations are not possible or that the "American" combination does not exhibit tensions. From the perspective of the polity, however, this combination of variables does encourage stable democracy. The upper classes can accept improvements in the status and power of the lower strata *without feeling morally offended*. Since all men and groups are expected to try to improve their position *vis à vis* others, success by a previously deprived group is not resented as deeply as in countries whose values stress the moral worth of ascription.[2] Similarly, the emphasis on equalitarianism, universalism, and specificity means that men can expect — and within limits do receive — fair treatment according to the merits of the case or their ability. Lower-class individuals and groups which desire to change their social position *need not be revolutionary*; consequently their political goals and methods are relatively moderate. There is little class consciousness on their part, since this consciousness is in part an adaptation to the behavior of the upper class in those societies characterized by ascription, elitism, particularism, and diffuseness. The latter values imply that men will be treated by others and will treat each other diffusely in terms of class status. American values support interaction with an individual in terms of his role as worker in one situation, as suburban dweller in another, as a member of the American Legion in a third, and so forth.

The above comments are, of course, an oversimplification. In fact, American society does display ascriptive, elitist, particularistic, and diffuse culture traits. These are not completely dysfunctional, as will be shown. They do create frictions (see the analyses of McCarthyism as a reaction to "status-panic"),[3] but in general, with the exception of race and ethnic relations, these have not affected the basic stability of the polity.

The American South, which has stressed ascriptive-elitist-particularistic-diffuse values in race relations and to some extent in its total social system, has constituted a major source of instability in the American polity. It was retained in the nation only by force, and down to the present it does not have a stable, democratic polity. To the extent that its citizens have felt the pull of the dominant value system, the South has always found it difficult to build an integrated regional social order on its own terms.[4]

Britain has come to accept the values of achievement in its economic and educational system, and to some extent in its political system, but retains a substantial degree of elitism (the assumption that those who hold high position be given generalized deference) and ascription (that those born to high place should retain it).[5] Tocqueville described the British class system as an

[1] For a discussion of the American value system, see Robin Williams, *American Society* (New York: Alfred A. Knopf, 1951), pp. 372–442; see also Talcott Parsons and Winston White, "The Link Between Character and Society," in S. M. Lipset and Leo Lowenthal, eds., *Culture and Social Character* (New York: The Free Press, 1961), pp. 98–103; on values and the political system see William Mitchell, *The American Polity* (New York: The Free Press, 1963). I deal in detail with American values and the political system in *The First New Nation*.

[2] Like all comparative generalizations, this is a relative rather than an absolute statement. It is obvious that in the United States, as in other countries, those with higher status dislike any challenge to their privileged positions, and resist and resent new claimants. The common resistance to the claims for status equality of upwardly mobile ethnic groups such as the Jews, the Irish, and the Italians illustrates this. Status resentments against rising groups have been a frequent source of social tension all through American history.

[3] Daniel Bell, ed., *The Radical Right* (Garden City, N.Y.: Doubleday, 1963).

[4] See the essays in Charles Sellers, ed., *The Southerner as American* (Chapel Hill: University of North Carolina Press, 1960), for interesting insights on the difficulties faced by Southern whites both before and after the Civil War in resolving the conflicts generated within the society and within the individuals by the sharply varying dictates of alternative value systems.

[5] The general concept of elitism explicitly affects the training given to prospective members of the British upper class. Thus a description of the English public schools (private in the American sense) reports that "learning and the getting-fit are represented as part of the 'training for leadership' which many public-schoolmasters see as their social role.... It infects the whole set-up with a certain smugness and a certain frightening *elite* concept. The word 'breeding' is often on their lips.... Many of these boys go around looking for people to lead: they actually say at the University interviews that they feel they have been trained to lead ..." John Vaizey, "The Public Schools," in Hugh Thomas, ed., *The Establishment* (New York: Clarkson Potter, 1959), pp. 28–29.

"What does the middle-class Briton mean when he says that Eton or some obscure public school in the Midlands will develop his son's character? ... I would say that he includes in character such traits as willingness to take responsibility, loyalty to the class concept of the nation's interests, readiness to lead, which implies, of course, a belief that he is fit to lead and that people are willing to be led...." Drew Middleton, *The British* (London: Pan Books, 1958), pp. 230–231.

The role of the public schools as a means of training an elitist upper class which took into itself the best of the *arrivistes* was an explicit objective of the reforms of the public school system initiated by Thomas Arnold in the 1830's. He strongly admired aristocracy, saw respect for it at the heart of England's security and freedom, and wanted to make certain that it would not be corrupted. As he saw it, public school boys were "destined to become the new masters, the epitome of all the new tendencies, annexed and made subservient to the old aristocratic order of things. 'You should feel,' he said in addressing the boys of the Sixth Form, 'like officers in the Army or Navy.' Officers! This comparison has been applied ever since to the public school men of England." G. J. Renier, *The English: Are They Human?* (New York: Roy Publishers, 1952), p. 249 and pp. 229–270; see also Asa Briggs, *Victorian People* (Chicago: University of Chicago Press, 1954), pp. 150–177; and Denis Brogan, *The English People* (New York: Alfred A. Knopf, 1943), pp. 18–56.

[1] Writing in Thomas Arnold's day in 1833, Tocqueville pointed out that what distinguished the English aristocracy "from all others is the ease with which it has opened its ranks. . . . [W]ith great riches, anybody could hope to enter into the ranks of the aristocracy. . . The reason why the French nobles were the butt of all hatreds, was not chiefly that only nobles had the right to everything, but because nobody could become a noble. . . . The English aristocracy in feelings and prejudices resembles all the aristocracies of the world, but it is not in the least founded on birth, that inaccessible thing, but on wealth that everyone can acquire, and this one difference makes it stand, while the others succumb. . . .

"[O]ne can clearly see in England where the aristocracy begins, but it is impossible to say where it ends. It could be compared to the Rhine whose source is to be found on the peak of a high mountain, but which divides into a thousand little streams and, in a manner of speaking, disappears before it reaches the sea. The difference between England and France in this manner turns on the examination of a single word in each language. 'Gentleman' and 'gentilhomme' evidently have the same derivation but 'gentleman' in England is applied to every well-educated man whatever his birth, while in France *gentilhomme* applies only to a noble by birth. . . . The grammatical observation is more illuminating than many long arguments. . . .

"[I]f you speak to a member of the middle classes, you will find he hates some aristocrats but not the aristocracy. . . .

"The whole of English society is still clearly based on an aristocratic footing, and has contracted habits that only a violent revolution or the slow and continual action of new laws can destroy. . . ." Alexis de Tocqueville, *Journeys to England and Ireland* (New Haven, Conn.: Yale University Press, 1958), pp. 59–60, 67, 70–71.

Similarly, the great French student of English history, Elie Halévy, described the English upper class as "an aristocracy in which no rank was a closed caste, an aristocracy in which the inferior regarded the superior not with envy but respect. It was not impossible to climb into a superior class and those who respected those above them were respected in turn by those below. . . ." *History of the English People in the Nineteenth Century* (London: Ernest Benn Ltd., 1961), Vol. IV, p. 345. See also Vol. I, pp. 221–222.

For a recent discussion stressing the same point, see Anthony Sampson, *Anatomy of Britain* (New York: Harper & Bros., 1962), especially pp. 3–30.

[2] For a detailed analysis of the way in which the values regulating class relations gradually changed with the rise of industry, see Reinhard Bendix, *Work and Authority in Industry* (New York: John Wiley, 1956), pp. 100–116.

[3] See C. A. R. Crosland, *The Future of Socialism* (London: Jonathan Cape, 1956), pp. 232–237; Raymond Williams, *The Long Revolution* (New York: Columbia University Press, 1961), pp. 318–321; Sampson, *Anatomy of Britain*, pp. 160–217.

[4] Writing in the early 1860's, before Bagehot laid down his thesis that the stability of the British polity rested on the strength of deferential ties, Taine predicted that these social relations would maintain the class structure even under conditions of universal suffrage: "[B]eneath the institutions and charters, the bill of rights and the official almanacs, there are the ideas, the habits and customs and character of the people and the classes; there are the respective positions of the classes, their reciprocal feelings — in short a complex of deep and branching invisible roots beneath the visible trunk and foliage. . . . We admire the stability of British government, but this stability is the final product, the fine flower at the extremity of an infinite number of living fibres firmly planted in the soil of the entire country. . . .

"For the grip of tradition, sentiment and instinct is tenacious. There is no stronger attachment than — attachment. . . . Even at the time of the rotten boroughs Parliament was representative of the people's will, as it is today although the number of people having a vote is rather small. And it will still be so in ten years' time, if the Reform Bill extends the suffrage. In my view

"open aristocracy," which can be entered by achievement but which confers on new entrants many of the diffuse perquisites of rank enjoyed by those whose membership stems from their social background.[1] Thus Britain differs from the United States in having, in terms of pattern variables, a strong emphasis on ascriptive, elitist, particularistic, and diffuse values.

In the nineteenth century the British business classes challenged the traditional pre-industrial value integration.[2] But the British upper class (in contrast to most Continental aristocracies) did not strongly resist the claims of the new business classes, and later those of the workers, to take part in politics. When pressure for political participation developed within these classes in Britain, it was members of already enfranchised classes who took the leadership in reform movements. If communication between the different strata in Britain had been blocked by jealously guarded privileges — as it had been in France — conflicts over the suffrage might have become more divisive. As Robert Michels once pointed out, the presence of upper-class leaders in a working-class party serves to reduce conservatives' hostility toward it. To the extent that the social system permits a "left" party to recruit leaders from the existing elite, it is easier for this party to become an accepted part of the polity. It is worth noting that, unlike the British Labour Party, the German socialists have recruited few, if any, leaders from the old upper classes.

Thus the *economy* and *polity* in Britain have been characterized by achievement, elitism, universalism, and diffuseness. The *social class* system, however, retains many elements of ascription, elitism, particularism, and diffuseness. The traditional upper classes and their institutions — the public schools, the ancient universities, and the titled aristocracy — remain at the summit of the social structure.[3] At the same time, achievers in job and school are not barred from securing diffuse elite status, and the lower classes feel that the political institutions operate for their benefit. Like the liberal bourgeoisie before them, the British workers have never seriously developed the objective of eliminating the old privileged classes, either socially or economically.[4] Having been allowed into the political club almost as soon as British labor developed organizations of its own, working-class leaders have supported the rules of the parliamentary game. Unlike many early continental socialist parties, they were willing, while a small minority party, to cooperate with one of the older parties. And currently they remain the only socialist party whose policies "sustain" the legitimacy of aristocracy; their leaders, like other members of the Establishment, willingly accept aristocratic titles and other honors from the Crown.[5]

The deference shown to the system by the leaders and the rank and file of the labor movement is not simply a reaction to the strength of the status system. The British upper class has long shown a high level of sophistication in handling the admission of new strata to the "club." Thus in 1923, as Labour was about to form its first government, the *Sunday Times* printed a manifesto by Richard Haldane (Viscount of Cloan) urging that the two old parties give Labour a fair chance at government.

We have to recognize that a great change is in progress. Labour has attained to commanding power and to a new status. There is no need for alarm. All may go well if as a nation we keep in mind the necessity of the satisfaction of two new demands — that for recognition of the title to equality, and for more knowledge and its systematic application to industry and to the rest of life. . . . The result of the General Election may prove a blessing to us if it has awakened us to our neglect of something momentous which has been slowly emerging for years past. . . . Three quarters of a century since, the old Whigs, wise in their limited way, refused to meet the Chartist movement merely with a blank refusal. Thereby they earned our gratitude. For while most of the nations of Europe were plunged into revolution as a result of turning deaf ears to their violent progressives, we were saved, and remained in comparative quiet. . . . We had spoken with the enemy in the gate, and he had turned out to be of the same flesh and blood as ourselves. . . . [1]

Edward Shils, in *The Torment of Secrecy*, seeks to account for the great emphasis on publicity concerning political matters in the United States, *e.g.*, congressional investigations, as contrasted with the stress on privacy and secrecy in Britain. His explanation hinges on the fact that Britain is still a deferential society as compared with the United States:

The United States has been committed to the principle of publicity since its origin. The atmosphere of distrust of aristocracy and of pretensions to aristocracy in which the American Republic spent its formative years has persisted in many forms. Repugnance for governmental secretiveness was an offspring of the distrust of aristocracy.

In the United States, the political elite could never claim the immunities and privileges of the rulers of an aristocractic society. . . .

American culture is a populistic culture. As such, it seeks publicity as a good in itself. Extremely suspicious of anything which smacks of "holding back", it appreciates publicity, not merely as a curb on the arrogance of rulers but as a condition in which the members of society are brought into a maximum of contact with each other.

. . . Great Britain is a modern, large-scale society with a politicized population, a tradition of institutionalized pluralism, a system of representative institutions and great freedom of enquiry, discussion, and reporting. . . . British political life is strikingly quiet and confined. Modern publicity is hemmed about by a generally well-respected privacy. . . .

Although democratic and pluralistic, British society is not populist. Great Britain is a hierarchical country. Even when it is distrusted, the Government, instead of being looked down upon, as it often is in the United States, is, as such, the object of deference because the Government is still diffused with the symbolism of a monarchical and aristocratic society. The British Government, of course, is no longer aristocratic . . . [But it] enjoys the deference which is aroused in the breast of Englishmen by the symbols of hierarchy which find their highest expression in the Monarchy. . . .

The acceptance of hierarchy in British society permits the Government to retain its secrets, with little challenge or resentment. . . . The deferential attitude of the working and middle classes is matched by the uncommunicativeness of the upper-middle classes and of those who govern. . . . The traditional sense of

[1] Quoted in Kingsley Martin, *The Crown and the Establishment* (London: Hutchinson, 1962), p. 88.

changes in the law relating to the suffrage do no more than perfect the system in detail, without affecting fundamentals. The important thing remains the same, public assent. And, enfranchised or not, the labourer and the 'shopkeeper' agree in wanting a man of the upper classes at the helm." On the other hand, Taine felt that "attachment" to leaders or representatives was absent in his native France; democracy could not work well there because France was characterized by "egalitarian envy," while at the same time it lacked the educated mass base which made possible "an intelligent democracy" in the United States. Hippolyte Taine, *Notes on England* (Fair Lawn, N.J.: Essential Books, 1958), pp. 162, 164–165.

[5] Clement Attlee, speaking as leader of the Labour Party in the House of Commons on July 9, 1952, opposed sweeping economies in royal expenditures on the following grounds: "It is a great mistake to make government too dull. That, I think, was the fault of the German Republic after the first World War. They were very drab and dull." Cited in Edward Shils and Michael Young, "The Meaning of the Coronation," in S. M. Lipset and Neil Smelser, eds., *Sociology: The Progress of a Decade* (Englewood Cliffs, N.J.: Prentice-Hall, 1961), p. 221.

"In 1957, three people in five throughout the country were still keeping souvenirs from the 1953 Coronation, and three in ten claimed to have a picture of a royal person in their house." Tom Harrison, *Britain Revisited* (London: Victor Gollancz, 1961), p. 232.

George Orwell suggested that elitist sentiments are strong among British workers as well. "Even in socialist literature it is common to find contemptuous references to slum-dwellers. . . . There is also, probably, more disposition to accept class distinctions as permanent, and even to accept the upper classes as natural leaders, than survives in most countries. . . . The word 'Sir' is much used in England, and the man of obviously upper-class appearance can usually get more than his fair share of deference from commissionaires, ticket-collectors, policemen, and the like. It is this aspect of English life that seems most shocking to visitors from America and the Dominions." *The English People* (London: Collins, 1947), p. 29.

The British journalist Jenny Nasmyth has pointed out that "most Labour M.P.s who can afford it, and many who cannot, send their children to the traditional [public] schools of the governing classes. They do this, perhaps, not primarily because they are snobs, but because, having themselves assumed the obligations of governing, they have an easy conscience (so easy that they seem blind to the inconsistencies between their political principles and their private lives) about partaking in the privileges of the governing classes." "Dons and Gadflies," *The Twentieth Century*, 162 (1957), p. 386.

the privacy of executive deliberations characteristic of the ruling classes of Great Britain has imposed itself on the rest of the society and has established a barrier beyond which publicity may not justifiably penetrate.[1]

The protection from populist criticism which an elitist system gives to all who possess the diffuse status of "leaders" extends not only to the political and intellectual elites but to school teachers and the school system as well. A study of the comparative position of teachers in England and America points this out well:

Conservative, Labour, and Liberal parties alike have

[1] Edward A. Shils, *The Torment of Secrecy* (Glencoe, Ill.: The Free Press, 1956), pp. 37–51. This book deserves recognition as at least a minor classic of sociological analysis of a social problem; and yet curiously is not well known. There are few other books I know of which are as illuminating concerning the interrelationships of American society and polity. The earlier article by Shils and Michael Young on the monarchy is also well worth reading in the context of problems raised in this chapter. "The Meaning of the Coronation," *op. cit.*, pp. 220–233. See also H. H. Hyman, "England and America: Climates of Tolerance and Intolerance," in Daniel Bell, ed., *The Radical Right*, pp. 227–258.

Other articles and books which present interesting case materials on significant differences between various aspects of British and American society are: Stephen Richardson, "Organizational Contrasts on British and American Ships," *Administration Science Quarterly*, 1 (1956), pp. 189–207; L. C. B. Gower and Leolin Price, "The Profession and Practice of Law in England and America," *Modern Law Review*, 20 (1957), pp. 317–346; Roy Lewis and Rosemary Stewart, *The Managers: A New Examination of the English, German, and American Executive* (New York: Mentor Books, 1961); P. S. Florence, *The Logic of British and American Industry* (Chapel Hill: The University of North Carolina Press, 1953); E. Lipson, *Reflections on Britain and the United States — Mainly Economic* (London: The Pall Mall Press, 1959), see especially Chapter 1, "The American and British Way of Life,"; C. A. R. Crosland, *The Future of Socialism*, pp. 238–257 and *passim*; and George Baron and Asher Tropp, "Teachers in England and America," in A. H. Halsey, Jean Floud, and C. A. Anderson, eds., *Education, Economy, and Society* (New York: The Free Press, 1961), pp. 545–557.

[2] Baron and Tropp, "Teachers in England and America." *op. cit.*, p. 548.

[3] Ralph Turner, "Modes of Social Ascent through Education: Sponsored and Contest Mobility," in Halsey, Floud, and Anderson, *Education, Economy, and Society*, pp. 122, 125. (Emphasis in original.) For a discussion of the elitist assumptions and consequences of the English school system by a Labour Party leader who is much impressed by the egalitarian aspects of the American educational system, see Crosland, *The Future of Socialism*, pp. 258–277 and *passim*; see also Sampson, *Anatomy of Britain*, pp. 174–194.

[4] Turner, "Modes of Social Ascent . . . ," *op. cit.*, p. 126. One of the key differences between England and the United States that has been noted as most clearly reflecting the contrast between an egalitarian society with a "common school" and an elitist society with a highly class segregated system of education is accent variations. As C. A. R. Crosland has put it: "[P]art of the reason why these differences [between classes in England] make so strong an impact is that they are associated with, and exaggerated by, the most supremely unmistakable of all symbols of social standing — differences of accent and vocabulary. In no other country is it possible in the same way to assess a person's social standing the moment he opens his mouth. . . . " *The Future of Socialism*, pp. 177–178.

consistently held to the view that the content of education and methods of instruction are not matters for popular debate and decision, but should be left in the hands of teachers themselves and of other professional educators. This being so, individuals or groups seeking to "use" the schools for their own purposes are confronted, not by the hastily constructed defenses of the teacher or of a single school or school board, as in America, but by the massive disregard of experienced politicians and administrators. This willing delegation of educational issues to educators is possible because the latter form a coherent and predictable element in the authority structure that moulds society. . . .

The relation between the school and the family also differs in the two countries. In America, for the most part, the parents hand over their child to the school system, but maintain a continuous scrutiny over progress. In England, "interference" by the parents in the school is resisted both by teachers and by educational administrators. Parents' associations and parent-teacher associations are becoming increasingly common, but they limit their activities to social functions and to meetings at which school policy is explained but not debated.[2]

Ralph Turner also shows how variations in the basic values of the two societies impinge on their educational systems. American education reflects the norms of *contest mobility*, "a system in which elite status is the prize in an open contest and is taken by the aspirants' own efforts. . . . Since the 'prize' of successful upward mobility is not in the hands of the established elite to give out, the latter are not in a position to determine who shall attain it and who shall not." Conversely, British education reflects the norms of *sponsored mobility*, in which "elite recruits are chosen by the established elite or their agents, and elite status is *given* on the basis of some criterion of supposed merit and cannot be *taken* by any amount of effort or strategy. Upward mobility is like entry into a private club, where each candidate must be 'sponsored' by one or more of the members."

The American system, with its emphasis on the common school and opportunities for further education at every level, encourages all to advance themselves through their own efforts. "Every individual is encouraged to think of himself as competing for an elite position, so that in preparation he cultivates loyalty to the system and conventional attitudes."[3] Conversely, the British system has always selected the minority who will go ahead in the educational system at a relatively early age. Those not selected, the large bulk of the population, are taught to "regard themselves as relatively incompetent to manage society. . . . The earlier that selection of the elite recruits can be made, the sooner the masses can be taught to accept their inferiority and to make 'realistic' rather than phantasy plans."[4] Those selected for the elite, on the other hand, are removed from competition and admitted to a school, either public or grammar, in which there is great emphasis on absorbing the elite's aesthetic culture, manners, and sense of paternalism toward the non-elite. Unlike the situation in America, where in the absence of a sense of a special elite culture the masses retain their right and ability to determine taste, English society operates on the assumption that only the elite may determine what is high or low quality.[1]

In his discussion of the sources of stability of English democracy, Harry Eckstein observes that authority patterns vary among the classes — authoritarian relations increase as one moves down the social ladder. Within the British elite, he suggests, social relations

> tend to be quite surprisingly democratic, or at least consultative and comradely; here . . . we might note the ubiquity of committees at every conceivable level in the higher civil service, the unusual use of staff committees in the military services, and the easy relations among officers of all ranks in military regiments, especially in elitist regiments like the Guards . . . ., while behavior among pupils [in upper-class public schools] is modeled to a remarkable extent on the political system.
>
> [Conversely, where hierarchical relations are involved, as] between members of the Administrative Class [of the Civil Service] and their underlings, officers and their men, managers and their help, relations are highly non-consultative and certainly not comradely. . . .[2]

The United States and Great Britain differ, of course, not only in these patterns, but in the extent to which the same value orientations dominate the key status, economic, and political subsystems of the society. Presumably, Eckstein would relate the stability of American populist democracy to the fact that there are egalitarian social relations within all levels. American society has more homogeneity of values than the British. On the other hand, the particular distribution of different value orientations in Britain would also seem to be congruent with the stability of an industrialized democracy, since it legitimates open participation by all groups in the economy and polity, while the diffuse elitism rewards all with a claim to high position.

Some quantitative indicators for the value differences between the United States and Great Britain particularly as it pertains to achievement, may be deduced from variations in the numbers securing higher education. Perhaps the most striking evidence of the difference between American and British values is the variation in such opportunities. In the United States, the strong and successful efforts to extend the opportunities to attend colleges and universities have, to some considerable degree, reflected both pressures by those in lower status positions to secure the means to succeed, and recognition on the part of the privileged that American values of equality and achievement require giving

the means to take part in the "race for success" to all those who are qualified.

Thus if we relate the number enrolled in institutions of higher learning to the size of the age cohort 20 to 24, we find that almost seven times as large a group was attending such schools in 1956–1957 in the United States as in England and Wales.[3] Some proof that these differences reflect variation in values, and not simply

[1] For an analysis of the way in which the variations in the status of elites, diffuse or specific, affect the position of intellectuals in England and America, see my *Political Man*, pp. 326–328. A. G. Nicholas has argued that although intellectuals do not have high status *within* the elite in England, the intellectual there receives more overt respect from the population as a whole than does his compeer in America because the former "has been in some degree sheltered by his very position in what Bagehot called a 'deferential' society. Not *very* deferential to him, perhaps; less deferential than to the landowner, the administrator, the soldier, the clergyman, or the lawyer, over all of whom the protective gabardine of the appellation 'gentleman' has fallen more inclusively, with fewer ends sticking out. Nevertheless, the [English] intellectual has shared in it too. . . ." "Intellectuals and Politics in the U.S.A.," *Occidente*, 10 (1954), p. 47; see also Gertrude Himmelfarb, "American Democracy and European Cities," *The Twentieth Century*, 151 (1952), pp. 320–327.

A clear indication of the differences in the values of those in charge of English elite education and those of comparably placed Americans may be seen in the criticism of the views of the former president of the highest status American university, Harvard, by the Master of the Manchester Grammar School: "When Professor Conant demands 'a common core of general education which will unite in one cultural pattern the future carpenter, factory workers, bishop, lawyer, doctor, salesmanager, professor and garage mechanic,' he is simply asking for the impossible. The demand for such a common culture rests either on an altogether over-optimistic belief in the educability of the majority that is certainly not justified by experience or on a willingness to surrender the highest standards of taste and judgment to the incessant demands of mediocrity." Cited from E. James, *Education for Leadership*, in Michael Young, *The Rise of the Meritocracy* (New York: Random House, 1959), p. 40.

[2] Harry Eckstein, *A Theory of Stable Democracy* (Princeton, N.J.: Monograph No. 10. Center for International Studies, Princeton University, 1961), pp. 15–16.

[3] The number attending institutions of higher learning (post-high school) has been related to the four year age category 20–24, since in most countries the bulk of such students are in this age group. The best category for such analysis would probably be 18–21, but the more or less standardized census categories are 15–19, and 20–24. Since these two groups are about the same size, using the category 20–24 probably gives as good an estimate as is needed of the national variations in the proportion of the relevant age cohort attending schools of higher education.

And in a recent report on English life, the founder of Mass Observation (an organization which has studied mass behavior through systematic observation techniques since 1937), writing about working-class life, comments that in spite of all the other major changes that have occurred since they began their observations: "No voice changes can be detected between 1937 and 1960. Radio, television and other outside impacts oriented to a more standard English appear to have had little or no effect. A tiny minority have consciously altered their voices. But elocution and speech training are still not important here. An English master at one of the big local schools . . . gave his considered opinion that if anything the standard of speaking of what he called 'King's English' had gone *down*." Harrison, *Britain Revisited*, p. 32. (Emphasis in original.)

differences in wealth or occupational structures, may be deduced from the fact that the one major former American colony, the Philippines, has a much larger proportion enrolled in colleges and universities than any country in Europe or the British Commonwealth, a phenomenon which seemingly reflects the successful effort of Americans to export their belief that "everyone" should be given a chance at college education. A comparison of the variation in enrollment in such institutions in the two major Caribbean nations long under the hegemony of Britain and the United States, Jamaica and Puerto Rico, is also instructive. Thus Jamaica, like many other former British colonies in Africa and Asia, has a higher education system which seems premised on the belief that only a tiny elite should receive such training; while the system in Puerto Rico, like the one in the Philippines, clearly reflects the continued impact of American assumptions concerning widespread educational opportunity.

The greater difference between Britain and the United States, in the extent to which populist explosions and threats to systematic due process occur, is reflected to some degree in their attitudes toward law and order. The latter is more willing to tolerate lawlessness. The reason for this may be that the absence of traditional mechanisms of social control in the United States has weakened the pressure to conform without coercion. As the Australian historian Russel Ward has well put it, the deferential "respect for the squire" which underlies the acceptance of authority and informal social controls in Britain is "based on traditional obligations which were, or had been, to some extent mutual." This was not easily transferred to new equalitarian societies which emphasized the universalistic cash nexus as a source of social relations.[1]

One indicator of the relative strength of the informal normative mechanisms of social control as compared with the restrictive emphases of legal sanctions seems to be the extent to which given nations need lawyers. Among the English-speaking democracies, the United States and Britain stand at polar extremes. As of 1955, the United States had 241,514 lawyers "of whom approximately 190,000 were engaged in private practice. This means there was one lawyer in private practice per 868 of population. . . . [T]he total English legal profession seems to number about 25,000, and those in private practice can hardly be more than 20,000 or one lawyer per 2,222 population.[2]

The emphasis on populist values derivative from equalitarianism in the United States as contrasted with the very different value emphases in Britain is reflected in the differential status and role of judge and jury in the two countries. The American system has stressed the notion of the judge as a neutral "umpire," in a

TABLE I. *Students Enrolled in Institutions of Higher Learning as Per Cent of Age Group 20-24, by Country, about 1956*

COUNTRY	
United States	27.2
Australia	12.05*
Canada	8.0
England and Wales	3.7*
Scotland	5.1*
Philippines	14.5
Jamaica	.7
Puerto Rico	11.9
Western Europe	4.5
Denmark	6.6
France	5.8
Germany (West)	4.1
U.S.S.R.	11.1

Source: The educational data for the first eight countries and the U.S.S.R. are calculated from materials in UNESCO, *Basic Facts and Figures, 1958* (Paris: 1959), and the *Demographic Yearbook 1960* (New York: Statistical Office of the United Nations, 1960). The data for the Western European countries other than Britain are taken from J. F. Dewhurst, *et al., Europe's Needs and Resources* (New York: Twentieth Century Fund, 1961), p. 315.

* The proportion of Britons and Australians attending institutions of higher education is somewhat higher than the figures given in the table proper, which include those in universities and teachers' colleges only. Both countries have a system of technical colleges, most of which are designed for vocational training in technical subjects for students who have not completed high schools. However, some of these "colleges" do give university level education in engineering and scientific subjects. No precise estimate of the size of this group has been located, but one report indicates that as of 1957, approximately 20,000 students were taking work comparable to that in universities in British technical colleges. See E. J. King, *Other Schools and Ours* (London: Methuen and Co., 1958), p. 98. If this group is added to the English total, then it would indicate about 4 per cent of the age cohort in higher education. Since there are over 200,000 students in Australian technical colleges, the "true" Australian figure may also be somewhat higher than the one presented in the table. On the other hand, it should be noted also that a higher proportion of students in English universities are foreigners (over 10 per cent) than is true in most other countries. The Russian figure is probably a low estimate since it is based on educational enrollment for 1956, but on a population cohort taken from 1959 census data.

Since definitions of higher education and methods of training for different professions vary so much from country to country, it is necessary to stress the fact that statistics such as these, though derived from official national bodies and censuses, are subject to considerable error, particularly when used comparatively.

contest which is decided by a jury drawn from the population, while the British have placed more stress on the positive role of the judge and less on the role of the jury. In a detailed study of changes in the British conception of the jury, Joseph Hamburger points out the relationship between these differences and the larger social systems:

[1] Russel Ward, *The Australian Legend* (New York: Oxford University Press, 1959), p. 27.

[2] L. C. B. Gower and Leolin Price, "The Profession and Practice of Law in England and America," *Modern Law Review*, 20 (1957), p. 317.

The main difference between England and America that led to the different status of the jury system in the estimate of public opinion arises from the differences in social and political backgrounds. America, a new country in which people had a greater freedom to form their opinions without the restraints of tradition or the influences of an established class system, allowed wider range for populistic fantasies. There were, particularly in the frontier communities, few ancient traditions or vested interests of an established society to keep people from modelling their institutions on the popular democratic beliefs that seemed to emerge almost naturally in such an atmosphere. It is not surprising, therefore, that the jury was seen, not in its English historical context, but as a microcosm of the popular will, a positive instrument of democracy. Accompanying such an image, there were hostilities to any ideas or practices that spoiled the pure, democratic character of this picture; thus, the impatience with judges who asserted more authority than an umpire needed or who insisted on the authority of a law that was not only complex but also foreign. The jury appeared to be an ideal instrument for allowing the sovereign people to form and interpret the laws that regulated their conduct.[1]

Values and the democratic process

While the stability of a democracy demands that the values of universalism and achievement be dominant in both the economic and political spheres, it does not require them to be dominant in the status hierarchies. That is, the status hierarchy may lean toward elitism, as it does in Britain, or toward equalitarianism, as in the United States, yet both of these nations are stable democracies.

However, these differences do have their effects on the ways in which the political system functions, particularly in the viability of the "rules of the game," and in such matters as the tolerance of opposition and nonconformity and in the respect shown for the due process of the law.

Although popular agreement about the importance of such rules would seem an important requisite for their effectiveness, the empirical data do not clearly sustain this expectation. The less educated and the lower strata in most countries do not accept the need for tolerance of what they consider to be "error" or "wickedness," that is, opposition to what is "clearly right." Conversely, the "rules of the game" are most respected where they are most significant, that is, among the various politically relevant and involved elites.[2] Perhaps the highest degree of tolerance for political deviance is found, therefore, in democratic systems which are most strongly characterized by the values of elitism and diffuseness. Diffuse elitism of the variety which exists in most of the democratic monarchies of

Europe tends to place a buffer between the elites and the population. The generalized deference which the latter give to the former means that even if the bulk of the electorate do not understand or support the "rules," they accept the leadership of those who do. It is deferential respect for the elite rather than tolerant popular opinion which underlies the vaunted freedom of dissent in countries like Britain and Sweden. The ability of countries to operate with an unwritten constitution which places no formal restrictions on parliamentary violations of civil liberties is in some considerable measure made possible by the emphasis on diffuseness and elitism in the system.[3] In these societies, the elites, whether those of the intellect, of business, of politics, or of mass organizations, are both protected and controlled by their membership in the "club."

The seemingly lesser respect for civil liberties and minority rights in the more equalitarian democracy such as the United States may be viewed as a consequence of a social system in which elite status is more specific, so that contending elites do not receive diffuse respect and feel less acutely the need to conform to an appropriate set of rules when in conflict with one another. They do not see themselves as part of the same club, as members of "an establishment." Hence disagreement about *the rules*, as well as over policies, are thrown to the broader public for settlement. And this entails

---

[1] See his chapter, "Trial by Jury and Liberty of the Press," in Harry Kalven, ed., *The Public Image of the Jury System* (Boston: Little, Brown, forthcoming); see also Hamburger's chapter, "Decline of the Jury Trial in England," in the same volume.

[2] See S. M. Lipset, *Political Man: The Social Bases of Politics* (Garden City, N.Y.: Doubleday, 1960), pp. 101–105, 109–114, for a summary of studies bearing on this problem. The reverse proposition will be true in countries in which democratic "rules of the game" have not been institutionalized. Where privileged classes are fighting to retain their traditional oligarchic rights and powers, they will strongly resist the claims for participation in the polity of groups based on the lower strata.

[3] In an extremely interesting paper comparing life and social organization on ships in the American and British merchant marines, Stephen Richardson indicates that variations in basic national values deeply affect authority relationships within identical economic institutions: "Comparison of British and American crews suggests that the British realize and accept the authority of competent persons and are not as fearful of the misuse of authority as Americans. This acceptance of authority is closely related to acceptance of social stratification and the symbols of these differences. Status symbols function as cues for self-regulation, in conformity with the status and role requirements of the ship. British seamen are conditioned before coming to sea to accept authority, and consequently the change in attitudes required when a man becomes a seaman is slight. . . .

"Among American crews a far greater fear and suspicion of authority appears to exist. Social stratification is not widely accepted and is often denied. Many symbols of social stratification have been removed, and, because they are suspect, the remaining symbols do little to enhance self-regulation of the man in conformity with the status and role demands of the ship's social organization." Since the norms of the social structure undermine authority on American ships, there is a necessity for a "far greater formalization of the social system than [on] the British," and American ships have many more explicit rules and regulations. Richardson, "Organizational Contrasts on British and American Ships," pp. 206–207.

appealing in some degree to a mass electorate to adjudicate on rules whose utility, in some measure, they cannot be expected to understand; appreciation of the necessity for such rules often involves a long-term socialization to the nature of the political and juridical process, secured primarily through education and/or participation. Thus, though civil liberties will be stronger in elitist democracies than in equalitarian ones, the latter may be regarded as more "democratic" in the sense that the electorate has more access to or power over the elite.

Another of Parsons' pattern variables not discussed earlier suggests specific sources of political strain in contemporary American society. His distinction between self-orientation and collectivity-orientation stresses the extent to which values emphasize that a collectivity has a claim on the individual units within it to conform to the defined interests of the larger group, as contrasted to a stress on actions predominantly reflecting the perceived needs of the units. An emphasis on particularism tends to be linked to collectivity-orientation. Moreover, the *noblesse oblige* morality inherent in aristocracy is an aspect of collectivity-orientation. Traditionally, Britain appears to have stressed collectivity obligations more than has the United States. Consequently, the rise of socialist and welfare-state concepts have placed less of a strain on British values than on American. Although modern industrial society, including the United States, appears to be moving generally toward a greater acceptance of collectivity-orientations, the American values' emphasis on self-orientation results in a stronger resistance to accepting the new community welfare concepts than occurs elsewhere. In discussing the rise of right-wing extremism in American society, Parsons has argued that they are the most self-oriented segments of the American population which currently find the greatest need for political scapegoats and which strongly resist political changes which are accepted by the upper classes in such countries as Britain and Sweden.[1] Thus, the values of elitism and ascription may protect an operating democracy from the excesses of populism and may facilitate the acceptance by the privileged strata of the welfare planning state, whereas emphases on self-orientation and anti-elitism may be conducive to right-wing populism.

Elitism in the status hierarchy has major dysfunctions

[1] See Talcott Parsons, "Social Strains in America," in Daniel Bell, ed., *The Radical Right*, pp. 183–184.

[2] For a good discussion of the dysfunctions inherent in an elitist society see C. A. R. Crosland, *The Future of Socialism*, pp. 227–237.

[3] Religious movements may also, of course, constitute a major element in secular political protest. This is the case today among American Negroes. Lower-class churches and their ministers may directly or indirectly help form class-based political movements. And, of course, sectarian groupings have often expressed the hostility of the depressed strata to the privileged order and their religion. But such forms of institutionalized protest, like radical political movements, themselves serve as means of defining lower status in forms which are palatable to those occupying lower status positions.

which should be noted here.[2] A system of differential status rankings requires that a large proportion of the population accept a negative conception of their own worth as compared with others in more privileged positions. To be socially defined as being low according to a system of values which one respects, must mean that, to some unspecified degree, such low status is experienced as "punishment" in a psychological sense. This felt sense of deprivation or punishment is often manifested in "self-hatred," a phenomenon which, when perceived as characteristic of inferior ascriptive racial or ethnic status, has often been deplored. The features of such self-hatred are: rejection of behavior patterns associated with one's own group as uncouth, negative judgments concerning the value of occupational roles characteristic of one's own group, and the desire to leave one's own group and "pass" into a dominant group. It is universally recognized that such feelings on the part of a Negro or a Jew are indicators of psychic punishment; yet the same reactions among the lower class are often not perceived in the same way.

To a considerable degree, the social mechanisms which operate to legitimate an existing distribution of status inequalities succeed in repressing such discontent, sometimes by structuring perceptions so that even low status individuals may view themselves as higher and therefore "better" than some others, or by creating bonds of vicarious identification with those in higher positions. The latter mechanism is particularly prevalent in systems which emphasize ascriptive and elitist values. However, it is doubtful that such mechanisms alone are a sufficient solution for the problem of social rejection and psychological self-punishment inherent in low status.

There are different adaptive mechanisms which have emerged to reconcile low status individuals to their position and thus contribute to the stability and legitimacy of the larger system. The three most common appear to be:

1) Religion — Belief in a religion with a transvaluational theology, one which emphasizes the possibility or even the probability that the poor on earth will enjoy higher status in heaven or in a reincarnation, operates to adjust them to their station, and motivates those in low positions to carry out their role requirements.[3]

2) Social Mobility — The belief that achievement is possible and that virtue will be rewarded by success for one's self or one's children provides stabilizing functions comparable to those suggested for religion.

3) Political Action — Participation in or support for political movements which aim to raise the position of depressed groups, and which in their ideology contain transvaluational elements — the assumption that the lower strata are morally better than the upper classes — also helps to adjust the deprived groups to their situation.

Since the three mechanisms may be regarded as functional alternatives to one another, that is, as satisfying similar needs, it may be posited that where one or more is weakly present, the other(s) will be strongly in evidence. Specifically, for example, where belief in religion or social mobility is weak, the lower strata should be especially receptive to radical transvaluational political or economic appeals.[1] Social systems undergoing major institutional changes, which weaken faith in traditional religion and which do not replace this lost faith by the value system of an open, achievement-oriented society, have experienced major extremist political movements. It has been argued by some that one of the factors sustaining the bases for Communist and anarchist movements in countries like Spain, France, and Italy has been the perpetuation in society of strong ascriptive and elitist value elements together with a "dechristianized" lower stratum.[2]

A strong societal emphasis on achievement and equalitarianism (which in part may be perceived as a secular transvaluational ideology) combined with strong religious belief, particularly among the lower strata, should maximize the legitimacy of the existing distribution of privilege, and thus minimize the conditions for extremist protest. This is, of course, the situation in the United States. The strong emphasis in American culture on the need to "get ahead," to be successful, seems to be accompanied by powerful transvaluational religions among those who have the least access to the approved means of success.

[1] The thesis that revolutionary socialism and transvaluational religion have served similar functions for oppressed groups was elaborated by Friedrich Engels, "On the Early History of Christianity," in K. Marx and F. Engels, *On Religion* (Moscow: Foreign Language Publishing House, 1957), pp. 312–320.

[2] In France, for example, ecological studies which contrast degree of religious practice with Communist strength show that the Communists are most successful in regions in which the "anti-clerical" wave had previously suppressed much of the traditional fidelity to Catholicism. See G. LeBras, "Géographie électorale et géographie religieuse," in *Etudes de sociologie électorale*, Cahiers de la fondation nationale des sciences politiques, n. 1 (Paris: Armand Colin, 1949); and François Goguel, *Géographie des élections Françaises de 1870 à 1941*, Cahiers de la fondation nationale des sciences politiques, n. 27 (Paris: Armand Colin, 1951), pp. 134–135.

Social Mobility and Stratification in China
Wolfram Eberhard

WHEN THE WESTERN WORLD began to look toward China, the term "social mobility" did not exist. Yet, it was precisely this topic which, among a few others, was of special interest to those describing the Chinese state and society. Soon it appeared that there were two opposing views.

During the 17th and 18th centuries, the absolutistic period of Europe, China was described as a country in which the wise men ruled under an enlightened emperor, in contrast to Europe which suffered under absolute kings and a rotten nobility. After the European and American revolutions of the late 18th and early 19th century, the view was different. China was now regarded as an unchanging country, ruled by a despotic emperor with the help of corrupt officials. It was believed that ability and merit did not count, only bribery and connections. With the advent of the 20th century Chinese writers began to explain China to the West. They stressed the examination system which, they stated, gave every able man the chance to move from the lowest to the highest place in society. Down to the 1930's, these two opinions continued to coexist: for some, China was an example of an unchanging society without social mobility; for others, China was an example of an open society with much social mobility stimulated and regulated by an examination system and by a bureaucracy with a merit system. However, no attempts were made to prove these beliefs by scientific methods.

2

Although Chinese thinkers of the 20th century, as a reaction against Western beliefs tried to "save" the reputation of China by asserting that China always had had more social mobility than the West, earlier Chinese thinkers were of quite different opinions.

In the 5th century B.C. ancient Chinese feudal society broke down. This society was characterized by a hereditary nobility which in itself was hierarchically structured and which was in a contractual relationship to a central king, who from the beginning had more religious, ceremonial power than real power. Below this upper class were "subjects" whose status was at first probably not much further defined and who only slowly were differentiated into farmers (who developed

This is an original article prepared for this volume.

from serfs into owners), artisans and merchants. Below this level there were slaves who were not regarded as a part of human society. Already before 500 B.C. the king and his court had lost all political power; differentiations within the nobility had broken down. Many nobles had actually become farmers, while some merchants had become wealthy. At this stage, from the 5th century B.C. on, discussions about society and the status of different groups emerged. Society was regarded as made up of four "classes": officials, farmers, artisans and merchants. This division has been retained by Chinese thinkers and as a system of classification of population down to the modern period. The early philosophers assumed that *classes* were not equal: officials, the successors of the old nobility, were the best and, therefore, had the knowledge and the right to rule. Farmers were the honest producers. Artisans produced, but mainly unessential objects, while merchants did not produce anything, but transported unnecessary luxury items from one place to another, thus corrupting the self-sufficient farmers. An individual could (depending on the philosophical system adopted) either perfect his inborn good qualities or eliminate his inborn bad qualities and move up to the stage he deserved. In this period, then, philosophers believed in social mobility and we have reasons to assume that, indeed, social mobility existed in reality. From the late 2nd century B.C. on, with the advent of a new form of society which we call "gentry society" and which was characterized by a bureaucratic system of control, philosophers proceeded to say that not all *humans* were equal. Some, whom they called "saints," were by nature superior to others, while others were by nature wicked and depraved and, therefore, at the bottom of society. These ideas were further developed in the following centuries until they found their final form in the philosophy of the Sung period during the late 12th and early 13th centuries A.D. This theory ran as follows. When the world came into existence, the chaos separated into pure and impure particles. The pure particles rose and formed the sky, while the impure particles sank down and formed the earth. Similarly, human beings contain, at the moment of their coming into existence, either more pure or more impure substance. The relative mixture determines their place in society: the individuals with the better inborn qualities are at the top of society and correctly so, while the others are below. Social classes are the "natural" result of creation and everybody should remain in the class in which he or she belongs. Social mobility is against nature. Buddhism, which came into China at approximately the beginning of our era, or perhaps even slightly earlier, did not much influence this development. Buddhism recognized social classes and explained social status as the "natural" result of actions committed in an earlier existence: a man is now a member of the upper class because of good actions done in the previous existence. He is there not because of merit in his present life; rather his mental, physical and moral structure at the moment of birth was such that he "naturally" belonged in a certain class. An apparent case of social mobility was seen to be connected with actions in a former life and not with merits in this life; merit in this life was believed to help assure social mobility only in the next rebirth. In short, Buddhistic philosophy in the form we find in China regards society as it is as just and fair and believes that adjustments occur only between different reincarnations.

The gradual hardening of the social attitudes of Chinese philosophers between 100 B.C. and A.D. 1200 was accompanied, on the part of government officials, by constant attempts to keep the citizens in their places, i.e., prevention of social mobility. One, although certainly not the only, reason that officials were against changes in social status — necessitating changes in taxation, military obligations, legal status, etc., as will be seen below — was that they were in charge of the government files. The system of bookkeeping and statistics was constantly expanded, especially in the field of population statistics, and any change of the status of a person (involving, in Chinese society, the status of his whole family) would tend to confuse the files and might open the door to all kinds of illegal practices. Over the centuries, the rights and duties of each class were defined in more and more detail. Only the officials were truly "free citizens": they had the right to send their children to special schools, to introduce them into the bureaucracy. They were subject to special laws and exempted from certain punishments, from military service, and from forced labor services. In theory farmers were not denied the right to enter the bureaucracy if they qualified, but they were subject to the common law and to harsh physical punishments; they could not change their residence without special permission; they had to do military service, corvée and pay several kinds of taxes. Artisans were not allowed to enter the bureaucracy at all, at least in some periods, for the rest they were under the same restrictions as the farmers. In addition, the sons of artisans had to remain in the same class, and all their children had to marry within that class. In theory, artisans should work only for the court and the bureaucracy, not for other classes who should produce by themselves whatever they needed. Merchants, too, could not enter the bureaucracy; they had to register whenever they had to change their residence or whenever they had to travel; in theory, they were obliged to marry within their own group and to work for the court and the bureaucracy and not for the other classes. In spite of such restrictive regulations, members of all three of these "lower" classes were still regarded as "free" or "full" citizens. Below them several categories of "unfree" or "low" people were distinguished at various times, and their status also became fixed by law. Eventually even true slaves were accepted as a part of society, at least insofar as they could be punished by the courts for crimes they had committed — although they were subject to special and much harsher laws than the other classes. Besides, until very late in history they could not bring court action against any member of the free classes.

The legal and other privileges of the different classes were accompanied by sumptuary laws, so that the status of any person was indicated by his clothing as well as by his dwelling. Certain colors, materials, and fashions were reserved to certain classes, and violations were severely punished. Changes of class status, if necessary or desired by the rulers, involved a legal act by which the old class status was officially altered in all personal files. For example, if a person wanted to enter a religious order, he had to get official permission, often accompanied by the payment of a fairly high sum of money, to have his civil social status deleted and be inscribed in the official files kept for all monks or nuns. The number of permits issued each year was restricted for long periods of Chinese history, because too high a number of nonproducing monks and nuns might, it was thought, upset the balance between producers and consumers and lead to hunger and misery.

The official attitude and government policy concerning social mobility in this period between 100 B.C. and A.D. 1200 was closely related to the attitude of philosophers, as we have seen. The 11th and 12th centuries comprise the period in which the philosophers negated the right to social mobility most strongly and in which rulers tried to make mobility well-nigh impossible. Yet in practice this was a time in which violations of these restrictions became more and more common and remained in most cases unpunished. In spite of considerable social mobility (as we shall see later) between A.D. 1000 and 1800, philosophers did not change their attitudes substantially, and most of the class legislation and the sumptuary laws were retained. There was an exception in the case of the lower classes: the status of unfree persons and slaves was raised; labor restrictions and obligations of artisans were lifted (from the 15th century on) so that they could work for anybody who ordered work, and they could pay a tax instead of working for the government.

From the 19th century on, China's contact with the material achievements of the West as well as with Western ideas became closer, consequently, both official and philosophical attitudes concerning social mobility began to change.

3

There is more or less general agreement that aside from the most recent period which is not the topic of this article, Chinese social history can be divided into three main periods: *1)* The period of antiquity which came to an end in the time between 400 and 200 B.C. If an exact date be desired, the year 256 B.C. may be mentioned, the year in which the Chou Dynasty abdicated. *2)* The period of medieval China which came to an end between A.D. 700 and 1000; as an "exact date" the year 960 might serve, the end of the period of the "Five Dynasties." *3)* The "modern" period.

There is no agreement about its duration; according to some, 1841 (The Opium War), according to others 1911 (abdication of the last dynasty), or even 1948 have been considered the time when China's recent history and with it a new period began. Marxist writers often unite our periods 2 and 3, but subdivide the first period into two or more independent periods in order to fit them into the Marx-Engels system of periodization. Chinese literary sources which could serve as a basis for a study of social mobility begin around 1450 B.C. However, for the whole first period usable data are very limited. There are no census or other population data; the only thing we know is that probably between 400 and 250 B.C., a great increase in population took place which may have brought China's population to something around 20 million people. This estimate has been calculated on the basis of increasing sizes of armies, of war casualties and of increases in the number and the sizes of cities. The main literary sources for the first period are oracles, incised in bone and tortoise shell; bronze inscriptions; philosophical texts; and two styles of historiography, one more annalistic and the other more novelistic in its style of writing. For the end of the first period, several thousand names of persons are available in these sources, but most of the persons belong to the upper class, the nobility, and their courts. Data on members of any other social class are extremely scanty.

The character of these data makes an application of statistical methods impossible. The situation changes greatly during the second, the medieval, period. For this period, we have systematic historical accounts presenting much detailed information. While for the beginning of this period we have some 500 to 1,000 names per century, we have around 3,000 per century towards the end of the period. We are more or less informed about all higher government officials over the whole period, about scholars, artists, poets, and about some lower officials. In addition, from the beginning of our era, we have census reports on the population of the country as a whole as well as of individual districts. The analysis of these reports still presents many problems, mainly because the census was not always taken in the same way; besides, errors in writing often have distorted the figures; yet, as a whole, these population data can be used. Fragments of original population registers have been found, though these fragments are not large enough to serve as an independent source for a study of population movements. We know that people in this medieval period kept genealogies, but none of them was preserved. However, historians were interested in genealogical facts, and official histories usually contain social background data on important personalities which can be used for a study of mobility. In summary, in this period, sets of data exist which are consistent and extensive as well as reliable, so that quantitative methods can be used for their interpretation. However, the data still cover mainly the leading government officials; about the lower classes, we have practically no information which can be subjected to quantitative analysis.

The third, the "modern," period is characterized by a phenomenal increase in population. While during the medieval period the population of China had reached a peak of some 50 million at the end of the 1st century B.C. and, despite considerable oscillation, remained on that level until the end of the period, the population in the modern period increased from 50 to 400 million. Information is now so massive that most scholars specialize in the study of only one or two centuries. In addition to official histories which cover the history of the whole of China, we now have innumerable local histories and personal records. We have thousands of genealogies, each one usually covering some 500 years and containing a minimum of 2,000 names. The information on government officials now includes even local officials of low rank. The census reports are now much more detailed, and — at least for the end of the "modern" period — the original census lists are preserved and can be studied. Novels, short stories, plays and other entertainment literature has become abundant and contains much information that can be used for a study of social mobility.

4

This character of the sources has determined the character of the studies of Chinese social mobility. Quantitative historical research began in the late 1930's, and Chinese scholars found that in different periods of Chinese history the several districts of China contributed to the "elite" to a markedly different extent. Up to around A.D. 800 an area covering parts of the present northern provinces of Shantung, Hopei, Konan and North Kiangsu produced the majority of Chinese leaders, while from then on most of the important persons mentioned in the texts came from the central provinces of Kiangsu (southern part), Anhui, and Chekiang.[1] The first hypothesis was that this might be connected with inherited qualities; therefore the interest soon shifted towards a study of genealogical data, and thereby to the "modern" period for which such data abound.

Systematic work on social mobility in antiquity is very recent and rare, as was to be expected. Hsü Cho-yün[2] attempted in 1962 to assess social mobility between

722 and 222 B.C. by investigating the social origins of persons mentioned in the most important historical books, mostly the *Tso-chuan*, *Kuo-yü* and *Chan-kuo-ts'e*. By dividing the period of antiquity into a number of shorter periods, he tried to show that from the beginning of his period, but increasingly so towards the end, persons of lower origin rose to high or even leading positions. His conclusions are probably correct, since upward social mobility was to be expected in this period of the breakdown of the feudal society and the birth of the centralized bureaucratic state, a period in which China consisted of a decreasing number of independent states fighting one another until only one state remained and reunited China. These, often very bloody wars, induced the rulers of the different states to look for talent in military as well as in political fields. We know of cases where rulers competed for such talented men and tried to lure them away from their native states. (The material available for Hsü's study is not uniform enough to allow true quantitative analysis. The sources for different centuries differ in their character, and different kinds of people were considered worth recording. Thus, the data are often open to doubt, especially if a person was described as of "low origin." It is difficult to find out whether such a person simply was poor but still a member of the aristocracy or whether he really came from a lower, non-noble class.) However, we should expect also a fairly strong downward social mobility because during this period many small princedoms and states were destroyed and their ruling families sank into oblivion. This tendency cannot be studied quantitatively. Only rarely do the sources indicate what happened to dispossessed noble or ruling families. An additional difficulty is that during this period the use of standardized family names became more and more general while clan units broke up; but the connections between the emerging new families among themselves and between them and the original clans are often unclear, so that it is not possible to follow the fate of a family through a longer period of time. Hsü could, therefore, mainly study the careers of individuals over their lifetime, combined with some information on their direct background. This is similar to what has been done in many Western studies of social mobility, but differs from most studies dealing with later periods of Chinese history.

It is generally agreed that during the first part of the medieval period, i.e., to about 100 B.C., social mobility was high. The founder of the famous Han Dynasty (206 B.C. to A.D. 220) was a low-ranking soldier of lower-class origin; his wife and many of his followers were similarly of lower-class, often urban, origins. No systematic analysis of all available data exists for this period, except a study dealing with the social origin of leading officials.[3] This study seems to bear out the impression of relatively high mobility. The upper class accepted numerous persons from other classes, in the beginning of the dynasty as well as during the short period between

[1] Ting Wen-chieng, "Li-shih-ti jen-wu yü ti-li-ti kuan-hsi," in *K'o-hsüeh* (Science), vol. 8, No. 1 (1923), pp. 10–24 and again in *Tung-fang tsa-chih* (The Eastern Miscellany), vol. 20, No. 5 (1923), pp. 125–134 and in *Nü-li chou-pao*, Nos. 43/44.

[2] Hsü Cho-yün, *A Study of Social Mobility in Ancient China, 722–222 B.C.* (PhD thesis, University of Chicago, 1962), published in revised form as *Ancient China in Transition, an Analysis of Social Mobility, 722–222 B.C.* (Stanford: Stanford University Press, 1965). See also his "The Transition of Ancient Chinese Society," in *Second Biennial Conference Proceedings* (Taipei, 1962), pp. 13–26.

[3] Yang Lien-sheng, "Landed Nobility of the Eastern Han Dynasty" in *Tsing-hua Journal*, vol. 11 (1936), no. 4, pp. 1007–1063 (in Chinese).

120 and 80 B.C. in which the despotic tendencies of the ruler gave special chances to persons who pleased the ruler for one reason or another. However, it seems that during this period a new privileged class began to form, the so-called gentry, which successfully prevented lower-class people from intruding into its ranks. From about the end of the 2nd century B.C. on, certain "gentry families" emerged which continued to play leading roles in Chinese politics and culture down to the end of the 9th century A.D. Each of these families had a definite family seat in a rural area where the family also had invested its wealth in the form of extensive land holdings. They were identified by their country seat (for example, "the Ch'ing-ho Ts'ui," i.e., the gentry family named Ts'ui from the district of Ch'ing-ho), a custom which has been retained until the present time. The family seat was preserved as long as this was possible and served as the ritual center of the family. During the medieval period, the family occupying the family seat was regarded as the "real" family; branches which settled in other areas were soon regarded as independent families and chose, if they had status, another new family seat whose name they attached to their family name. It seems that this system was already well established and customary in the 2nd century A.D., a period apparently of little mobility. But as yet there are no systematic statistical studies of this situation. The only comprehensive attempt to gain insight into medieval social mobility was done for the T'o-pa period (Yüan Wei period), roughly A.D. 380 to 550.[1] The official history for this period listed around 7,200 persons. They could be grouped, on the basis of information contained in the history, by families or lineages who felt that they belonged together. The text contained almost exclusively persons within the political leadership and only occasionally persons of common origin, mainly servants and some other persons attached to persons of high rank. Therefore, the analysis was an analysis of the political elite. The result of the study was that a group of about a hundred leading families, so-called "gentry families" as mentioned above, provided the personnel for the administration during this period. In most cases, the data permit us to state that these families had been in positions of political leadership already before the period under study, often since the 1st century A.D. or even B.C.; and in a number of cases, it could be shown that the families remained in such positions until the late 9th or early 10th centuries. There was practically no case in which a commoner on the basis of his merits gained a post in the administration. Within the elite, a number of shifts occurred, mainly as the result of factional fights; with the victory of one faction, the adherents of the inimical faction were often slain, and attempts were made to exterminate them. However, in all observed cases, the defeated families succeeded in saving a few members who, within some fifty years or less, reestablished the power and influence of their families and retained their membership in the political elite. In this period, no upward social mobility could

be discerned as far as entry into the elite was concerned. Apparently there was some downward mobility, but this cannot be proven. Whether there was social mobility within or between other strata of the society cannot be discussed because there are not enough data.

This period, just as other sub-periods of the medieval era, was characterized by the rule of a foreign, non-Chinese (probably Turkish-Mongolian) ethnic group over the Chinese. Social differences had existed within the conquering group before the conquest. In fact, they came equipped with a definite and well-developed aristocracy. This aristocracy remained intact during the time of their rule over China, although tensions began to develop between the aristocracy and the commoners. On the other hand, several different processes of accommodation and assimilation began to appear between the foreign aristocracy and the Chinese pre-conquest elite, the gentry. First of all, Chinese gentry families and foreign aristocrats intermarried fairly freely; secondly, gentry families here and there adopted foreign family names, and accepted certain other customs and aristocratic behavior traits. On the other hand, the foreign rulers marrying Chinese gentry women accepted Chinese names, languages, culture, customs and dress. So far as we know, no mixture of the foreign commoners with Chinese commoners occurred. By the time foreign rule ended, many formerly foreign aristocratic families had become Chinese families and continued to play leading roles in China for the next centuries. Among the aristocratic traits, introduced into China by the foreign rulers and accepted by the Chinese gentry, was the hierarchical social structure which developed in the Chinese gentry and was typical for the period between 400 and 900. Accordingly, some gentry families considered themselves of higher social rank than even the emperors of the great T'ang dynasty (618-907) and refused to give their daughters in marriage to emperors and princes. Another new trait was the compilation of lists of "good" families, listing the gentry families according to geographical districts, so that in case of meeting a person from another area or in case of an offer of marriage, the status of the other could be verified. These lists — comparable to the so-called "Gotha" handbook of European aristocracy, — mentioned explicitly that mismarriages could be avoided by their use.

The study of the gentry in the T'o-pa period was supplemented by a similar study in which another official history book, the "Annals of the Five Dynasties" was analyzed.[2] This book, which covers the period between 907 and 960, contains data on more than 3,000 persons. Again, the period is a time of conquest during which four foreign dynasties and one Chinese dynasty ruled over North China in quick succession. Here again, a number of clearly defined gentry families mono-

[1] Wolfram Eberhard, *Das Toba-Reich Nord-Chinas*, (Leiden, E. J. Brill, 1949).
[2] Wolfram Eberhard, *Conquerors and Rulers*, Second Edition, (Leiden, E. J. Brill, 1965), pp. 157-171.

polized the political leadership. Many of them had been gentry families centuries before the 10th century; in fact, many had been elite families in the T'o-pa period. But on the other hand, a fair number of new families had moved into the upper class. These were families of military leaders or successful rebels who established their position by force and victory, much to the dismay of the old elite. Although most of these newcomers from the lower classes could not retain their position for more than one or two generations, the composition of the gentry around 960, the time of the establishment of a new, long-lasting Chinese dynasty (Sung, 960–1278), was very different from that of the time around 900. Most important of all: the aristocratic tradition was broken forever. Sung rulers and Sung gentry were more "bourgeois," if this term be allowed, than any elite before.

Already at the time when China began to develop a bureaucratic system of administration, i.e., at the beginning of the medieval period, there appeared some procedures to select capable men. It is now assumed that already around 165 B.C. some form of written examination was established.[1] Chinese theory was maintained that these civil service examinations were a "democratic" institution which guaranteed upward mobility to those with the proper abilities. K. A. Wittfogel has taken the opposite position, maintaining that the examinations did not bring new blood into the upper class.[2] Already before this statement was made, Yang Lien-shang[3] had characterized the examinations of the Later Han period (25–220 A.D.) as a farce. In reality, the system of selection was that the administrator of each administrative province (*chou*) was required to recommend one man for each of several categories of posts. The recommended persons were brought to the capital and subjected to some form of examination. The recommending official was responsible for the person he sponsored: if the candidate turned out to be unworthy, the sponsor could face punishment; if the

candidate was good, the sponsor could expect some benefits. This meant, of course, that he recommended normally only members of already influential families and did not take a chance with upstarts. So it is not a surprising result that in one of the classes of candidates, for the time between 220 B.C. and A.D. 9 58 percent of the men were sons of officials, 22 percent sons of the nobility (i.e. relatives of the emperor's family), 4 percent from wealthy families, 10 percent of unknown origin (lack of information) and only 6 percent from families designated as "poor". It should be noted, however, that "poor" does not in this period necessarily mean "low-class origin," but may merely indicate that a member of a high-status family was raised in relative poverty. Among 117 persons of the same category in the time between A.D. 25 and 220, 10 percent were designated as of "poor" origin, while 77 percent were either sons of the nobility, or of officials, or of wealthy families.[4] Special studies of successful examination candidates for other parts of the medieval period do not exist; but the study of T'o-pa society implicitly proves that passing an examination was not an important factor in social mobility. In fact, the T'o-pa and their successors until the early 7th century retained the quota and recommendation system. We have, to my knowledge, no systematic study of the candidates of the T'ang period (618–906) in which the examination system was greatly improved; one gains the impression that in this period some people eventually entered the ranks of leadership by way of successful examinations, but doubtlessly, family status remained the most important factor. In the 10th century a proverbial saying stated that "for passing an examination, one need not read books,"[5] implying that if he paid bribery, everybody could pass. Wittfogel, in a study of examination candidates during the Liao period (907–1127), came to the result that examinations were not a vehicle of social mobility.[6] However, it should be kept in mind that the Liao were another dynasty of conquest, a factor which most surely worked against a fair application of the examination system. Over time, the eligibility of candidates became more and more restricted. Already before A.D. 220, foreigners were excluded from participation.[7] In A.D. 587 merchants and artisans, i.e., two of the four social classes mentioned above, were specifically excluded from participation, a practice which probably antedated that year.[8] In any case, this exclusion remained. In the early 10th century a special quota for merchants was established.[9] Eighty members of the merchant class were admitted in a total number of 25,000.[10] In the 11th century, artisans, merchants, monks and criminals as well as descendants of criminals were explicitly excluded, at the same time, descendants of the so-called dishonest classes, criminals and native tribes were admitted, with a special stipulation as to the number of generations which had to have passed since the change of the family's status.

The analysis of the state examinations has been a main tool for the study of social mobility in the third,

[1] H. G. Creel, "The Fa-chia: 'Legalists' or 'Administrators'," in *Bulletin of the Institute of History & Philology, Academia Sinica, Extra volume no. 4, Studies Presented to Tung Tso Pin on His Sixty-Fifth Birthday*, Taipei, 1961, pp. 607–636, esp. p. 633. Compare also his "The Beginnings of Bureaucracy in China" in *Journal of Asian Studies*, vol. 23, no. 2, 1964, pp. 156–184, especially p. 156, note 6.

[2] K. A. Wittfogel, *New Light on Chinese Society*, New York, Institute of Pacific Relations (1938), p. 11–12. A German version, slightly changed, is in *Zeitschrift für Sozialforschung*, vol. 7, 1938, pp. 123–132.

[3] See note 3, p. 174 (p. 1038).

[4] Data in *Bulletin of Chinese Studies*, vol. 2, 1941, p. 100 and vol. 3, 1942, p. 35 (Ch'eng-tu, 1941–1942; in Chinese).

[5] *Hou ching lu*, chapter 4, page 2a (a text of the Sung period).

[6] K. A. Wittfogel, "Public Office in the Liao Dynasty and the Chinese Examination System" in *Harvard Journal of Asiatic Studies*, vol. 10, 1947, pp. 13–40.

[7] *Hou Han shu*, chapter 67, page 7a.

[8] *Wen-hsien t'ung-k'ao*, chapter 28, page 269a.

[9] P. Buriks, *Fan Chung-yen's Versuch einer Reform des chinesischen Beamtenstaates*, Ph.D. Thesis, Universität Göttingen 1954, page 40.

[10] Chang Chung-li, *The Chinese Gentry*, Seattle 1955. p. 82–83.

the "modern," period of Chinese history. From the Sung period on (960–1278), down to the present time, we have lists of successful candidates usually together with some data on their fathers and grandfathers. It is fairly easy to find out how many successful candidates had prominent ancestors and thus to find some measure of social mobility into the leading families. E. Kracke, who was the first to use this material,[1] came to the conclusion first that during the Sung period, but even later, social mobility was fairly high; secondly, that the examination system must have functioned fairly objectively, because powerful fathers were not regularly successful in pushing their sons through the examinations and into high posts. The use of examination lists has some inherent weaknesses which make conclusions rather doubtful. During the period covered in the study just mentioned, and down to even more recent times, a high official had the right according to the Yin principle, to recommend a son or a close relative to office. This recommended person did not have to pass an examination. In the Sung period, an official could not recommend only one son, but in twenty years he could recommend twenty persons for jobs in the central administration.[2] Under the Liao dynasty (which was almost contemporaneous with the Sung dynasty, but covered North China), about 40 percent of the jobs were filled by application of this system.[3] Thus, the way through the examination was only one way to get into office, and it was not the most common way in all periods.[4] Yet, although upward mobility should be discernible in the lists of successful examination candidates, there are other methodological problems.

The lists may well mention fathers and grandfathers, but only if these had had posts of importance. Jobs at the lower end of the bureaucracy usually were not mentioned, so that the impression is created that the successful candidate came from a non-elite family. Because of the clan-cohesion and of inter-clan ties between powerful gentry families, a man who had no direct ancestors with official titles or jobs still often came from an elite family through his mother's side or through a first or second paternal uncle. Finally, similar to the situation in European noble families, a gentry family of repute not only had certain official privileges, but also enjoyed local prestige and functioned as a local elite for generations although none of its members may have aspired to a job in the bureaucracy. If a man from such a family passed the examination, one may have a spurious case of upward mobility, because no "famous" father or grandfather appeared in the list. Furthermore, the examination lists contain the names of successful candidates, but this does not mean that they were put into positions of influence. On the contrary, evidently many of them did not have any career. No analysis has been made of the men who passed the examination but had no subsequent career: did they perhaps belong to families of lower status, and was this the reason for their later failure? Finally, no analysis has been made of the men who did not pass; we know from many texts

that there was an element of chance in the examinations, but it is quite possible that there was also another element involved, for instance that persons of lower origin had a high chance of failing. While it is — with a high input of time — possible to remedy the first two weaknesses and to refine the results of studies based upon examination lists, it is probably impossible to get the necessary quantitative data for the last point. Thus, it is of limited value to study social mobility on the basis of examination lists. Only if we made the assumption (which certainly is not correct) that the distorting factors always remained the same, could we distinguish periods of higher and lower mobility by this method. On the basis of general familiarity with the period, I am of the opinion that in the case of the Sung time E. Kracke's conclusion was in general correct, i.e., that there was more social mobility in this period and later than in the periods before 960.

No attempt has been made to measure social mobility during the period of Mongol rule over China (1278–1367). During this period, the conquering Mongols and their non-Mongol allies established themselves as a new ruling class on top of Chinese society. They developed an elaborate system which was meant to prevent ethnic mixture and acculturation; it was even forbidden for Chinese to learn Mongol or any other foreign language. The Mongols had special promotion systems, including special examinations for Mongols which enabled almost any Mongol to get into the administration but made it extremely difficult for a Chinese to move up. It can be shown[5] that Chinese families who succeeded in collaborating with the conquerors at an early time retained their status or even moved up, while other families, who were opposed to the Mongol conquerors, lost their status and often also their wealth. If we consider only the Chinese the whole period, then, was one of disturbance in which individuals with initiative and without moral qualms had chances of moving upward, as is any other period of revolt, civil war or turmoil. This was especially true also for the beginning of the Ming dynasty (1368–1643) in which the new imperial house and many of its closest followers came from low-class origin and had moved up through success as bandits, rebels or popular heroes. Such a fluidity usually remained for some time after the establishment of a new order, as shown clearly by Ho Ping-ti's study.[6]

[1] E. A. Kracke, "Family Versus Merit in Chinese Civil Service Examinations Under the Empire", in *Harvard Journal of Asiatic Studies*, vol. 10, 1947, no. 2, pp. 103–123. See also his *Civil Service in Early Sung China*, Cambridge 1953.

[2] P. Buriks, l.c. page 19.

[3] K. A. Wittfogel, in H. F. MacNair, *China*, Berkeley 1946, p. 116.

[4] Chinese texts as well as theatre plays abound in often very detailed descriptions of large-scale cheating in the examinations.

[5] Wolfram Eberhard, *Social Mobility in Traditional China*, Leiden, E. J. Brill 1962, pp. 85–86.

[6] Ho Ping-ti, *The Ladder of Success in Imperial China. Aspects of Social Mobility, 1368–1911*, New York, Columbia Univ. Press 1962.

Because of the better data available for this period, Ping-ti could refine the method which had been first developed by Kracke. He could investigate whether social mobility differed regionally; the information concerning ancestors of successful candidates was much broader; the lower ranks of the bureaucracy could be included; and it was possible to establish more refined categories of classification. Although here, too, not all the weaknesses inherent in this approach could be overcome, the conclusions – which also took into consideration other non-quantitative information – can be regarded as the best estimates of social mobility available at the present time for the periods between 1368 and 1911. Ho Ping-ti agreed with Kracke that there was some mobility in the Sung period; he added the findings that mobility had a high peak at the time of the establishment of the Ming dynasty, remained fairly high during the 15th and early 16th centuries, and fell constantly from the late 16th century to the middle of the 17th century. When the new dynasty, the Ch'ing dynasty (1644–1911) created by conquering Manchu, took over, we find again a brief period of higher mobility, but very soon mobility became restricted and remained at a low level until the beginning of the 19th century, when a small increase was to be seen. The T'ai-p'ing rebellion in the middle of the 19th century again caused a brief, but considerable increase in mobility. The main weakness of the method in this study is, that the basic unit of discussion is the individual and not the family, so that a person is compared only with his father and/or grandfather, but in disregard of the situation of the family or clan to which this person belonged.

I have tried to attack the problem from this side of family continuity by a study of genealogies covering mainly the same period which was investigated by Ho Ping-ti'. Besides, these genealogies provided some insight into earlier times. As each genealogy contains several thousand names of persons and covers several centuries, and as each person has to be examined, so far it has not been possible to analyze great numbers of genealogies. Nor was and is it possible to select a "representative" or "typical" genealogy, since no one knows which factors are "typical" and which are unique in the development of Chinese families. Besides, genealogies have a tendency to veil events regarded as shameful for the family, and to overstate successes. Yet, this study of whole genealogies revealed certain long-range development tendencies of families and it seemed to indicate long-range policies on their part. Downward social mobility, mentioned already by Ho Ping-ti was clearly visible in the genealogies. An attempt to quantify the upward social mobility appearing in the genealogies[1] showed results compatible with those of Ho Ping-ti. During the 18th century, upward mobility appeared to be quite limited, but before as well as after this time it was more common. The genealogies also gave an indication of the attitude of fathers towards the training of their sons. In the Ming period fathers tried to push their first sons through the examinations, if at all possible. In the later periods, fathers tried to give an equal chance to all sons, or to have sent the most capable sons to state examinations. Furthermore, the genealogies gave insight into a special aspect of downward mobility which, however, could not be quantified. Less able sons who did not qualify for examinations, were settled on land owned by the family and became ordinary farmers. Normally, such branch families had no prominent sons for at least five generations. We can assume that, economically, these branch families were not too well-off. On the other hand, sons who were capable, but who were psychologically not fit or not willing to spend many years of study for the examinations, were often given a chance (and probably money as well) to go into business. These gentlemen-businessmen were not small shopkeepers but usually long-distance merchants, dealing in such state-controlled objects as salt, silver or silk. They set up their business in places far from the family home, but enjoyed some "protection" through the connections of their family with other influential families. The normal development for such men was either to buy land at the place of their activities and to start a new branch family of landlords, or to directly buy a title and rank for themselves or their sons. Such buying of titles or rank was a practice during most Chinese dynasties, although the scholars who got into the bureaucracy by the examination system were always against such "upstarts." In most periods, only lower ranks could be bought and a further career depended again upon the quality and the intentions of the buyer. But with a rank or title, the bearer was again in the ranks of the elite. Thus, the study of genealogies revealed that change into the class of large-scale merchants was usually not a permanent change but a change for an individual's lifetime, although it might not always have worked out this way.

The genealogies also showed that an ordinary farmer who either was not capable of passing the examination or did not have the means to acquire the necessary learning, could go into the city as a peddler and finally become a grocer. In the old time, this seemed to have been a dead-end way, because as a rule no further upward mobility from the stage of a grocer seemed possible. In recent times[2] this stage has apparently become an intermediate stage. The sons of these small businessmen tend to go into the professions or into the lower echelons of the bureaucracy. Perhaps this was so also formerly, but it cannot be proved, because we do not have any data concerning the staff and servants of lower local officials.

[1] See note 5, p. 177. The first study of social mobility in China which made use of genealogies is by P'an Kuang-tan, *Ming-Ch'ing liang-tai Chia-hsing-ti wang-tsu* (The Prominent Clans of Chia-hsing during the Ming and Ch'ing Dynasties). Shanghai, Commercial Press 1947 (in Chinese). P'an paid attention mainly to eugenic factors.
[2] W. Eberhard, "Social Mobility among Businessmen in a Taiwanese Town" in *Journal of Asian Studies*, vol. 21, no. 3 (1962), pp. 327–339.

Another study covering partly the same "modern" period, namely the Manchu period, used a different method but yielded comparable results. In his first work, R. Marsh,[1] studied "prominent men," their background and careers. He used a dictionary of prominent men compiled by a number of American and Chinese scholars[2] which, however, contains only the most important figures in politics and classical scholarship seen through the eyes of traditional Chinese scholars and persons important in connection with Chinese-Western relations. Clearly, this dictionary is in some ways biased; and clearly, the relatively small number of persons precludes statistical treatment. Marsh has tried to dig up the family background of the leaders, and in this attempt he drew his circle wider than did others. Besides, he separated the Chinese from the Manchu because the Manchu also were a privileged group. In spite of the weaknesses inherent in his data, he was able to show, for instance, that Manchu because of their privileged status had an easier and earlier start in their careers than Chinese, but that once a Chinese was in the bureaucracy, his career chances were almost equal to those of a Manchu. He came to the conclusion that for men in the bureaucracy, standards of merit were more important than social privileges.

The last study of this period is by Chang Chung-li and covers only the 19th century.[3] Chang used mainly local histories ("gazetteers") which gave data on successful candidates coming from the local area. Ho Ping-ti had shown[4] that the information in local histories was often incomplete and that the inclusion of incomplete information tended to blow up the percentage of persons from non-prominent families, and thus create a spurious impression of high mobility. Further, Chang regarded those fathers who passed a lower but not a higher examination as not belonging to the elite — whereas, as Ho and others have shown, in traditional society such fathers played a leading role, if normally only locally. As a matter of fact, Chang merely wished to know how many persons on the highest level of the Chinese bureaucracy came from high-level ancestors. When he speaks of the "gentry," he defines the gentry not as a class but as a professional group consisting of persons who had passed the higher examinations. Thus, his results could not be compared with results of studies which defined the gentry as a class and which tried to find out to which degree this class was self-reproducing. But if we evaluate Chang's work with all these points in mind, we still agree with him that there was considerable social mobility in the 19th century and even more during the T'ai-p'ing rebellion. Not only could capable military leaders make quick careers during this time, but also the harassed government tried hard to get the collaboration of able men.

Since the study of social mobility in China is a new field, it is not surprising that many potential sources of information have not yet been tapped. Finally, no attempt has been made so far to assess the size and origin of special social groups such as monks and nuns. Although they never seemed to exceed 1 or 2 percent of the total population, they constituted an avenue to limited, individual upward mobility at least from the 11th century on, when the majority of monks and nuns apparently came from the lower classes, especially farmers, while before that time, many a monk and nun seemed to be of upper-class origin. Individual mobility out of a low class was common at all times for girls of rare beauty — therefore at the same time "common" and "rare." They could become concubines of influential men and were then accepted into the upper class, though the rest of their family was never accepted officially.

In short, by far not all available material bearing on the topic of social mobility has been used, so that the results of the existing studies are preliminary, and refinements can be expected. Also, several categories of potential sources have not yet been tapped. Yet, incomplete and weak as the existing studies of social mobility in traditional China may be, they have already proved one important point: that China, just like Western traditional society, had far from a negligible amount of social mobility, perhaps not even less than America, surprising as this may sound. The conclusion is that the partly true and partly supposed absence of class barrier in an "open" society (no matter what the definition of the classes) cannot be used as an argument in the explanation of rapid social change or rapid industrialization.

Let me give only one example from my own experience. It seems conceivable to study cases of social mobility reported in short stories and, by dating the stories, to make inferences about the increase or decrease of social mobility, as reflected in the stories of various times. I have made a preliminary survey of 1,535 short stories, as shown on the following table.

TABLE I. *Social Mobility in Chinese Short Stories*

Time	Number of stories	Cases of mobility
Before 1000 A.D.	106	0
1000–1399	94	0
1400–1599	28	0
1600–1699	70	4
1700–1799	891	8
1800–1899	338	2
1900–	8	0

The results of this survey were disappointing. Not counted as social mobility were all cases in which a

[1] Robert Marsh, *Mandarin and Executive* (PhD thesis, University of Michigan, 1959). Published in revised form as *The Mandarins: Circulation of Elites in China* (Glencoe: The Free Press, 1961). See the criticism of his comparative work by E. Lahav in *American Sociological Review*, vol. 29 (1964), pp. 99–100.

[2] A. W. Hummel, *Eminent Chinese of the Ch'ing Period*, Washington, Government Printing Office, 1943, 2 volumes.

[3] Chang Chung-li, *The Chinese Gentry. Studies in their Role in 19th Century Chinese Society*. Seattle, Univ. of Washington Press 1955, and *The Income of the Chinese Gentry*, Seattle, 1962.

[4] See note 6, p. 177.

person became wealthy as a reward for a good deed in a prior incarnation, i.e., as a supernatural reward, in our terminology. Also not counted were all cases in which a man rose to prominence by studying hard and passing the examinations, because there was no clear information whether the man was simply a member of an impoverished upper-class family, in which case we cannot really speak of upward mobility, or whether he really belonged to a lower class and rose through his own efforts. Such cases, needless to say, we would have included. The cases of true social mobility which then remained were cases dealing with the acquisition of wealth. As examples, let me give some details of the eight cases reported in short stories of the 18th century.

1) A quail seller has the good luck that a prince buys one of his quails at a high price. He thus becomes wealthy.[1]

2) A man specializes in growing chrysanthemums for sale and becomes wealthy.[2]

3) A merchant finds a treasure, opens pawnshop, becomes wealthy.[3]

4) A monk engages in business and becomes very wealthy.[4]

5) A wealthy man selects a poor man with good looks as a son-in-law. This enables the young man to compete in the examinations and to become influential.[5]

6) A poor young poet through a trick makes such an impression upon a group of wealthy merchants that they give him much money. This enables him to make a successful career.[6]

7) A traveler who is stranded in a foreign country finds gold and becomes wealthy.[7]

8) A merchant who uses sharp and unscrupulous practices becomes a wealthy textile dealer.[8]

It is clear that good luck was seen as the most important way of getting wealthy, but otherwise in these stories, only those come into the elite who, coming from an upper-class background, work hard on the examinations. The collection contains a significant story in which a scholar tells a merchant in a fable that a lowly person could never hope to be socially accepted by the gentry.[9] I have not completed a similar survey of the plays, but a preliminary search in about 850 plays seems to indicate the same tendency: people remain in their class, but poor members of the gentry can move into power and wealth by the examination system. Even in folk and fairy tales, there is rarely a story of a man who became a king or a high official. Yet I think that a more intensive study of literature might yield more

insight, not, to be sure, into the size of actual mobility but into attitudes toward mobility.

5

Let us attempt to draw some conclusions from the above-mentioned studies of social mobility in traditional China. It can be stated with certainty today that the old notion of a socially immobile China versus a socially mobile West is no longer tenable. All through Chinese history there were periods of social mobility. These were first, the periods of turmoil in which new men and new groups came into power through force, and also the immediately following years in which a new group attempted to draw administrators from the circle of early collaborators or friends. Apart from such "abnormal" conditions, periods of relatively high social mobility followed periods of low mobility. In general, as far as data exist and have been analyzed, we can say that the period between 100 B.C. to around A.D. 960 was a period of relatively low mobility, a time in which a small number of families constantly supplied the state with high-level administrators and leaders. From about A.D. 1000 on, there was certainly more social mobility in general. It seemed to have been fairly high in the 11th century and again around 1400, but we must admit that the time from the middle of the 12th up toward the end of the 13th century has not yet been thoroughly studied. The 10th as well as the 14th century were both periods of turmoil and conquest, accompanied by high mobility. Mobility seemed to have remained fairly high from 1400 to 1550, but then apparently dropped except for a short interruption by conquest in the middle of the 17th century which produced higher mobility. Relatively high mobility occurred again in the early and especially in the late 19th century. This was not the result of foreign ideas or impact, but rather seemed to be the result of inner crises. Modern patterns of mobility began to appear only with the introduction of a Western educational system (before 1900), the abolition of the traditional examination system (1904) and the overthrow of the monarchy (1911).

These results are important, but in no way sufficient. Our survey has shown that many important aspects have not yet been studied. Statements about mobility refer almost exclusively to the composition of the leading class, the gentry. In the case of Chang's study[10] the gentry was defined as comprising only the top level of the bureaucracy, a few thousand persons in a nation of about 400 million, while other studies included more people, or, rather, more *families* into their definitions of the gentry. Only two studies have pointed out that there was always a considerable downward social mobility (Ho; Eberhard), since the totality of persons in the elite, or all gentry families (depending on the unit that was used) produced more children than could be absorbed by the administration of the next generation. This point may be more important than has been

---

[1] *Liao-chai chih-i*, chapter I (vol. 1, pp. 27–31).
[2] *Liao-chai chih-i*, chapter 34 (vol. 4, pp. 425–429).
[3] *Liao-chai chih-i*, vol. 8, p. 31a.
[4] *Liao-chai chih-i*, chapter 5 (vol. 5, p. 128).
[5] *Liao-chai chih-i*, chapter 8 (vol. 5, pp. 285–289).
[6] *Hsieh-to*, chapter 3, pp. 2a–4a.
[7] *Yah-t'en sui-lu*, p. 48.
[8] *Hsieh-to*, chapter 7, p. 3b.
[9] *Hsieh-to*, chapter 7, pp. 5a–5b.
[10] See footnote 3, p. 179.

recognized thus far, but in making it we have only taken account of the fact that, on the average, Chinese upper-class families seemed to produce *consistently* more children than the lower classes. But China also had a tremendous general increase of population between 1550 and 1840 from about 100 to 400 million people.[1] Yet we have the impression that the number of government officials did not increase proportionally, so that relatively speaking the gentry became smaller and smaller in every generation, thus aggravating the disadvantage of surplus sons of the elite and making the rise of new people even more difficult. This relation between the size of the population and the number of administrators has not yet been studied, so that we can speak only of impressions.

Not much else is known about social mobility in traditional China besides the few lines of study that have been pursued. We have some idea, at least for the last centuries, what possibilities a farmer's son had to change his status, but we do not have any way to calculate the size of his chance. It is probably safe to assume that it was minimal. We have some very limited insight into the situation of large-scale merchants in the last centuries, but we have only an impression about the small businessman's chances to change his status. And about the other lower classes, especially the artisans and craftsmen, there is almost no information at all. Only for the Ming period (1368–1644) do we have a few examples of individuals who came from the crafts and got a place in the bureaucracy. Most of these reports stated that those men were appointed to technical jobs connected with building and construction works.[2] We know that slaves and other social outcasts improved their status over the centuries, so that eventually they disappeared as separate classes;[3] but we do not know how such families changed their status over the generations. We know very well that China, at least since the 11th century, had fairly large-scale industries, often with several thousand workers, for example mining, porcelain and pottery, and arms factories. But we know very little about the worker's social origin. They seemed to be farmers who illegally, usually driven by hunger, left their homes individually, fled into another district in which they were not registered, and committed themselves to powerful entrepreneurs who could protect them against government officials. Other workers, especially those in state factories, apparently were indentured former criminals or relatives of criminals; their only chance to become independent again seemed to be by being forgotten and wiped off the lists, to get hold of a piece of land, and to become simple, poor farmers.[4]

Another point relevant to the problem of social mobility was geographical mobility. We know that migration and colonization played an important role in the Far East. In most periods of Chinese history, the Chinese migration was directed towards the South and gradually converted large areas inhabited by non-Chinese into solidly Chinese areas which were eventu-

ally included into the state of China. Besides, from at least the 11th century on, Chinese migrations flowed far over the borders of China into Southeast Asia — with the possible late 19th and 20th centuries also into other continents — to the effect that one day some parts of Southeast Asia may be included within the political borders of China. The study of interior migrations depends largely on the critical use of population data. Here, the work by E. Balasz,[5] H. Bielenstein,[6] and Ho Ping-ti[7] and H. van der Sprenckel constitutes the first steps. Bielenstein[8] showed that Chinese migration tended to follow trade routes, and therefore, valleys and plains; Li Chi[9] tried to trace migrations by studying the creation of new walled cities over time and area; Eberhard[10] and H. Wiens[11] studied the repression and/or assimilation of non-Chinese by Chinese settlers. We know that the Chinese settlers inside and outside of China were extremely successful economically and, therefore, that migration was one important route towards upward social mobility. However, detailed studies are still missing.[12] We know that in traditional Chinese society accumulation of wealth did not automatically mean rise of social status, as it does in recent Western society. Wealth was not regarded as permanent. There is a Chinese saying that families go through a three-generation cycle, from the industrious grand-

[1] See footnote 6, p. 177.

[2] H. Friese, "Zum Aufstieg von Handwerkern ins Beamtentum während der Ming-Zeit," *Oriens Extremus*, vol. 6 (1959), pp. 160–175.

[3] The exact time when slavery disappeared is unknown. Foreign observers often called servant-girls "slaves," because a payment was made to the parents when the girl, at the age of 4 or 6, moved to the employer. Legally, such payment was regarded as prepayment of wages. The girl had to be married off at the age of 16 to 18 and a dowry had to be given, regarded as another payment of wages. Modern laws are discussed in H. L. Haslewood, *Child Slavery in Hong Kong* (London, 1930), *passim*.

[4] Recent research seems to indicate that the entrepreneurs often were landlords rather than officials or merchants.

[5] E. Balasz, "Beiträge zur Wirtschaftsgeschichte der T'ang-Zeit", in *Mitteilungen des Seminars für Orientalische Sprachen*, Berlin, vol. 34, 1931, pp. 1–92, vol. 35, 1932, pp. 1–73, and vol. 36, 1933, pp. 1–62.

[6] H. Bielenstein, "The Census of China during the Period 2–742 A.D.", in *Bulletin of the Museum of Far Eastern Antiquities*, no. 19, Stockholm 1947, and other studies by the same author.

[7] Ho Ping-ti, *Studies on the Population of China, 1368–1953*, Cambridge, 1959, and other studies by the same author, especially his "Social Composition of Ming-Ch'ing Ruling Class", in *Second Biennial Conference Proceedings*, International Assoc. of Historians of Asia, Taipei, 1962, pp. 101–117.

[8] "The Chinese Colonization of Fukien until the End of T'ang" in *Studia Serica, Bernhard Karlgren Dedicata*, Copenhagen, 1960, pp. 98–122.

[9] Li Chi, *The Formation of the Chinese People*, Cambridge 1928.

[10] Wolfram Eberhard, *Kultur und Siedlung der Randvölker Chinas*, Leiden, 1941.

[11] Herold J. Wiens, *China's March Towards the Tropics*, Hamden, The Shoe String Press, 1954.

[12] The conditions in Taiwan are ideal for studies of this kind. Some remarks on migrations to Taiwan and settlement there were presented in a lecture by Mark Mancall on "Land Settlement and Utilization" (on Taiwan) at the 17th Annual Meeting of the Assoc. for Asian Studies, April 2, 1965.

father who rises to prominency and wealth, to the father who enjoys the wealth, to the son who dissipates it and becomes as poor as the great-grandfather had been. It has been suggested that one factor contributing to this circulation of wealth was the law of equal inheritance of all sons which supposedly made it impossible to accumulate land — the main type of investment — over generations. This is not completely correct for several reasons. First, there was always some preference for the first son. Secondly, the three-generation cycle[1] referred only to economic wealth. In traditional society, an upper-class family retained its status even if it became poor. We have many examples of this, and Chinese writers loved to describe their cultural heroes as men of good, but impoverished families. A family with status but without wealth had much better chances to move up than a wealthy family without status, as was also the case in traditional Europe. Thirdly, the saying of the three-generation cycle was just a *witty saying*, and it did not take into account what everyone surely knew, that wealth in order to be permanent, had to go together with a position in the bureaucracy or, at least, with good government connections. Yet it is desirable to study families who rose solely through acquiring wealth, but none has been undertaken until now.

All existing studies deal almost exclusively with

[1] W. Eberhard, *Social Mobility*, p. 205.

[2] Interesting and important, but non-statistical, is the book by Jacques Gernet, *Daily Life in China on the Eve of Mongol Invasion*, New York, 1962, 254 pages.

inter-generational mobility. Intra-generational changes have not yet been studied in any detail for the pre-modern period.

Another problem which has not even been mentioned yet in Chinese studies is the mobility potentially caused by the shift of whole occupational groups. We have no data to establish, for instance, whether over time there was a change in the percentage of people occupied in agriculture. We have reason to believe as indicated above that the number of persons in the top-level of the bureaucracy decreased proportionately to the population during the last centuries. On the other hand, some other shifts probably occurred too, because of the growing urbanization of China since the 11th century. For the traditional period there are still no urban studies which are based on quantitative data.[2] Probably a fairly large part of the city population was in service occupations, such as servants, helpers of government officials, hotel and shopkeepers, restaurant and theatre personnel. Others were simply coolies who worked irregularly, and finally there were artisans and craftsmen. We have no knowledge whether at different times there were more or less of these people, relative to other social classes. It seems safe to say, however, that at all times the Chinese city had more male than female citizens, because the majority of servants were male and many officials kept their wives in the rural home rather than move them from city to city during their transfers from one position to another, which usually occurred every three years.

Agricultural Enterprise and Rural Class Relations[1]

Arthur L. Stinchcombe

MARX'S FUNDAMENTAL INNOVATION in stratification theory was to base a theory of formation

[1] James S. Coleman, Jan Hajda, and Amitai Etzioni have done me the great service of being intensely unhappy with a previous version of this paper. I have not let them see this version.

[2] This formulation derives from Talcott Parsons' brief treatment in *The Structure of Social Action* (Glencoe, Ill.: Free Press, 1949), pp. 488–495.

of classes and political development on a theory of the bourgeois enterprise.[2] Even though some of his conceptualization of the enterprise is faulty, and though some of his propositions about the development of capitalist enterprise were in error, the idea was sound: One of the main determinants of class relations in different parts of the American economy is, indeed, the eco-

Reprinted from the *American Journal of Sociology*, V. 67 (1961–1962), pp. 165–176, by permission of the author and the publisher.

nomic and administrative character of the enter-prise.[1]

But Marx's primary focus was on class relations in cities. In order to extend his mode of analysis to rural settings, we need an analysis of rural enterprises. The purpose of this paper is to provide such an analysis and to suggest the typical patterns of rural class relations produced in societies where a type of rural enterprise predominates.

Property and enterprise in agriculture

Agriculture everywhere is much more organized around the institutions of property than around those of occupation. Unfortunately, our current theory and research on stratification is built to fit an urban environment, being conceptually organized around the idea of occupation. For instance, an important recent mono-graph on social mobility classifies all farmers together and regards them as an unstratified source of urban workers.[2]

The theory of property systems is very much under-developed. Property may be defined as a legally de-fensible vested right to affect decisions on the use of economically valuable goods. Different decisions (for instance, technical decisions versus decisions on dis-tributions of benefits) typically are affected by dif-ferent sets of rights held by different sets of people. These legally defensible rights are, of course, important determinants of the actual decision-making structure of any social unit which acts with respect to goods.

But a property system must be conceived as the typical interpenetration of legally vested rights to affect decisions and the factual situation which determines who actually makes what decisions on what grounds. For example, any description of the property system of modern business which ignores the fact that it is economically impossible for a single individual to gain majority stock holdings in a large enterprise, and politi-cally impossible to organize an integrated faction of dis-persed stockholders except under unusual conditions, would give a grossly distorted view. A description of a property system, then, has to take into account the internal politics of typical enterprises, the economic forces that typically shape decisions, the political situa-tion in the society at large which is taken into account in economic decisions, the reliability and cost of the judiciary, and so forth. The same property law means different things for economic life if decisions on the distribution of income from agricultural enterprise are strongly affected by urban *rentiers'* interests rather than a smallholding peasantry.

It is obviously impossible to give a complete typology of the legal, economic, and political situations which determine the decision-making structure within agri-cultural organizations for all societies and for all im-portant decisions. Instead, one must pick certain fre-quent constellations of economic, technical, legal, and labor recruitment conditions that tend to give rise to a distinct structure of decision-making within agricultural enterprises.

By an "enterprise" I mean a social unit which has and exercises the power to commit a given parcel of land to one or another productive purpose, to achieve which it decides the allocation of chattels and labor on the land.[3] The rights to affect decisions on who shall get the benefit from that production may not be, and quite often are not, confined within the enterprise, as defined here. The relation between the enterprise and power over the distribution of benefit is one of the central variables in the analysis to follow, for instance, distin-guishing tenancy systems from smallholding systems.

Besides the relation between productive decisions and decisions on benefits, some of the special economic, political, and technical characteristics which seem most important in factual decision-making structure will be mentioned, such as the value of land, whether the "owner" has police power over or kinship relations with labor, the part of production destined for market, the amount of capital required besides the land, or the degree of technical rationalization. These are, of course, some of the considerations Marx dealt with when describing the capitalist enterprise, particularly in its factory form. Plantations, manors, family-size tenancies, ranches, or family farms tend to occur only in certain cogenial economic, technical and political environ-ments and to be affected in their internal structure by those environments.

A description and analysis of empirical constellations of decision-making structures cannot, by its untheore-tical nature, claim to be complete. Moreover, I have deliberately eliminated from consideration all precom-mercial agriculture, not producing for markets, because economic forces do not operate in the same ways in precommercial societies and because describing the enterprise would involve providing a typology of extended families and peasant communities, which

---

[1] Cf. especially Robert Blauner, "Industrial Differences in Work Attitudes and Work Institutions," paper delivered at the 1960 meeting of the American Sociological Association, in which he compares class relations and the alienation of the working class in continuous-process manufacturing with that in mechanical mass-production industries.

[2] S. M. Lipset and R. Bendix, *Social Mobility in Industrial Society* (Berkeley, Calif.: University of California Press, 1959). The exceedingly high rate of property mobility which charac-terized American rural social structures when the national ideology was being formed apparently escapes their attention. Yet Lipset discusses the kind of mobility characteristic of fron-tiers and small farm systems very well in his *Agrarian Socialism* (Berkeley, Calif.: University of California Press, 1950), p. 33. In 1825 occupational mobility only concerned a small part of the population of the United States. The orientation of most nineteenth-century Americans to worldly success was that of Tennyson's "Northern Farmer, New Style": "But proputty, proputty sticks, an' proputty graws."

[3] Occasionally, the decisions to commit land to a given crop and to commit labor and chattels to cultivations are made separately, e.g., in cotton plantations in the post bellum American South. The land is committed to cotton by the land-owner, but labor and chattels are committed to cultivation by the sharecropper.

would lead us far afield. I have also not considered the "community-as-enterprise" systems of the Soviet sphere and of Israel because these are as much organizational manifestations of a social movement as they are economic institutions.[1]

Systems of commercialized manors, family-sized tenancies, family smallholdings, plantations, and ranches cover most of the property systems found in commercialized agriculture outside eastern Europe and Israel. And each of these property systems tends to give rise to a distinctive class system, differing in important respects from that which develops with any of the other systems. Presenting argument and evidence for this proposition is the central purpose of this paper.

Variations in rural class relations

Rural class structure in commercialized agriculture varies in two main ways: the criteria which differentiate the upper and lower classes and the quality and quantity of intraclass culture, political, and organizational life. In turn, the two main criteria which may differentiate classes are legal privileges and style of life. And two main qualities of class culture and organization are the degree of familiarity with technical culture of husbandry and the degree of political activation and organization. This gives four characteristics of rural class structures which vary with the structure of enterprises.

First, rural class systems vary in the extent to which classes are differentiated by legal privileges. Slaves and masters, peons and *hacendados*, serfs and lords, colonial planters and native labor, citizen farmers employing aliens as labor — all are differentiated by legal privileges. In each case the subordinate group is disenfranchised, often bound to the land or to the master, denied the right to organize, denied access to the courts on an equal basis, denied state-supported education, and so on.

Second, rural stratification systems vary in the sharpness of differentiation of style of life among the classes. Chinese gentry used to live in cities, go to school, compete for civil service posts, never work with their hands, and maintain extended families as household units. On each criterion, the peasantry differed radically. In contrast, in the northern United States, rich and poor farmers live in the country, attend public schools, consume the same general kinds of goods, work with their hands, at least during the busy seasons, and live in conjugal family units. There were two radically different ways of life in rural China; in the northern United States the main difference between rich and poor farmers is wealth.

Third, rural class systems vary in the distribution of the technical culture of husbandry. In some systems the upper classes would be completely incapable of making the decisions of the agricultural enterprise: they depend on the technical lore of the peasantry. At the other extreme, the Spanish-speaking labor force of the central valley in California would be bewildered by the marketing, horticultural, engineering, and transportation problems of a large-scale irrigated vegetable farm.

Fourth, rural classes vary in their degree of political activity and organization, in their sensitivity or apathy to political issues, in their degree of intraclass communication and organization, and in their degree of political education and competence.

Our problem, then, is to relate types of agricultural enterprises and property systems to the patterns of class relations in rural social life. We restrict our attention to enterprises producing for markets, and of these we exclude the community-as-enterprise systems of eastern Europe and Israel.

Class relations in types of agricultural enterprise

1. THE MANORIAL OR HACIENDA SYSTEM

The first type of enterprise to be considered here is actually one form of precommercial agriculture, divided into two parts: cultivation of small plots for subsistence by a peasantry, combined with cultivation by customary labor dues of domain land under the lord's supervision. It fairly often happens that the domain land comes to be used for commercial crops, while the peasant land continues to be used for subsistence agriculture. There is no rural labor market but, rather, labor dues or labor rents to the lord, based on customary law or force. There is a very poorly developed market in land; there may be, however, an active market in estates, where the estates include as part of their value the labor due to the lord. But land as such, separate from estates and from manors as going concerns, is very little an article of commerce. Estates also tend to pass as units in inheritance, by various devices of entailment, rather than being divided among heirs.[2]

The manorial system is characterized by the exclusive access of the manor lord (or *hacendado* in Latin America) to legal process in the national courts. A more or less unfree population holding small bits of land in villein or precarious tenure is bound to work on the domain land of the lord, by the conditions of tenure or by personal peonage. Unfree tenures or debts tend to be inheritable, so that in case of need the legal system of the nation will subject villeins or peons to work discipline on the manor.

---

[1] However, the origin of the *kolkhoz* or collective farm does seem to depend partly on the form of prerevolutionary agriculture. Collectivization seems to occur most rapidly when a revolutionary government deals with an agriculture which was previously organized into large-scale capitalist farms.

[2] In some cases, as in what was perhaps the world's most highly developed manorial system, in Chile, an estate often remains undivided as an enterprise but is held "together in the family as an undivided inheritance for some years, and not infrequently for a generation. This multiplies the number of actual owners [but not of haciendas], of rural properties in particular" (George M. McBride, *Chile: Land and Society* [New York: American Geographical Society, 1936], p. 139).

Some examples of this system are the hacienda system of Mexico up to at least 1920[1] some areas in the Peruvian highlands at present,[2] medieval England,[3] East Germany before the reconstruction of agriculture into large-scale plantation and ranch agriculture,[4] the Austro-Hungarian Empire, in the main, up to at least 1848,[5] and many other European and South American systems at various times.

The manorial system rests on the assumptions that neither the value of land nor the value of labor is great and that calculation of productive efficiency by the managers of agricultural enterprise is not well developed. When landowners start making cost studies of the efficiency of forced versus wage labor, as they did, for instance, in Austria-Hungary in the first part of the nineteenth century, they find that wage labor is from two to four times as efficient.[6] When landowners' traditional level of income becomes insufficient to compete for prestige with the bourgeoisie, and they set about trying to raise incomes by increasing productivity, as they did in eastern Germany, the developmental tendency is toward capitalist plantation or ranch agriculture.[7] When the waste and common become important for cattle- or sheep-raising and labor becomes relatively less important in production, enclosure movements drive precarious tenants off the land. When land becomes an article of commerce and the price and productivity of land goes up, tenancy by family farmers provides the lord with a comfortable income that can be spent in the capital city, without much worry about the management of crops. The farther the market penetrates agriculture, first creating a market for commodities, then for labor and land, the more economically unstable does the manorial economy become, and the more likely is the manor to go over to one of the other types of agricultural enterprise.

In summary, the manorial system combines in the lord and his agents authority over the enterprise and rulership or *Herrschaft* over dependent tenants. Classes are distinct in legal status. In style of life the manor lord moves on the national scene, often little concerned with detailed administration of his estate. He often keeps city residence and generally monopolizes education. Fairly often he even speaks a different language, for example, Latin among Magyar nobility, French in the Russian aristocracy, Spanish, instead of Indian dialects, in parts of Latin America.

The pattern of life of the subject population is very little dependent on market prices of goods. Consequently, they have little interest in political issues. Even less does the peasantry have the tools of political organization, such as education, experienced leadership, freedom of association, or voting power. Quite often, as, for example, in the Magyar areas of the Hapsburg monarchy or among the Indian tribes of Latin America, intraclass communication is hindered by language barriers. A politically active and competent upper class confronts a politically apathetic, backward, and disenfranchised peasantry.

2. FAMILY-SIZE TENANCY

In family-size tenancy the operative unit of agriculture is the family enterprise, but property rights in the enterprise rest with *rentier* capitalists. The return from the enterprise is divided according to some rental scheme, either in money or in kind. The rent may be fixed, with modification in years of bad harvest, or share.[8] The formal title to the land may not be held by the noncultivator — it is quite common for the "rent" on the land to be, in a legal sense, the interest on a loan secured by the land.

This type of arrangement seems to occur most frequently when the following five conditions are met: *a*) land has very high productivity and high market price; *b*) the crop is highly labor-intensive, and mechanization of agriculture is little developed; *c*) labor is cheap; *d*) there are no appreciable economies of scale in factors other than labor; and *e*) the period of production of the crop is one year or less. These conditions are perhaps most fully met with the crops of rice and cotton, especially on irrigated land; yet such a system of tenancy is quite often found where the crops are potatoes or wheat and maize, even though the conditions are not fulfilled. A historical, rather than an economic, explanation is appropriate to these cases.

The correlation of tenancy arrangements with high valuation of land is established by a number of pieces of evidence. In Japan in 1944, most paddy (rice) land was in tenancy, and most upland fields were owner-operated.[9] The same was true in Korea in 1937.[10] South China, where land values were higher and irrigated culture more practiced,[11] had considerably higher rates of tenancy than did North China.[12] In Thailand tenancy is concentrated in the commercialized farming of the river valleys in central Siam.[13] In Japan, up to World War II, except for the last period (1935–40), every time

[1] Frank Tannenbaum, *The Mexican Agrarian Revolution* (New York: Macmillan Co., 1929), pp. 91–133.

[2] Thomas R. Ford, *Man and Land in Peru* (Gainesville: University of Florida Press, 1955), pp. 93–95.

[3] Paul Vinogradoff, *The Growth of the Manor* (London: Swan Sonnenschein, 1905), pp. 212–235, 291–365.

[4] Max Weber, *Gesammelte Aufsätze zur Sozial- und Wirtschaftsgeschichte* (Tübingen: J. C. B. Mohr, 1924), pp. 471–474.

[5] Jerome Blum, *Noble Landowners and Agriculture in Austria, 1815–1848* (Baltimore: Johns Hopkins Press, 1948), pp. 23, 68–87.

[6] *Ibid.*, pp. 192–202.

[7] Weber, *op. cit.*, pp. 474–477.

[8] But share rents in commercialized agriculture are often indicators of the splitting of the enterprise, as discussed above: it most frequently reflects a situation in which land is committed to certain crops by the landlord and the landlord markets the crops, while the scheduling of work is done by the tenant and part of the risks are borne by him.

[9] Sidney Klein, *The Pattern of Land Tenure Reform in East Asia* (New York: Bookman Associates, 1958), p. 227.

[10] *Ibid.*, p. 246.

[11] See Chan Han-Seng, *Landlord and Peasant in China* (New York: International Publishers, 1936), pp. 100–103.

[12] *Ibid.*, pp. 3–4; and Klein, *op. cit.*, p. 253.

[13] Erich H. Jacoby, *Agrarian Unrest in Southeast Asia* (New York: Columbia University Press, 1949), pp. 232–235.

the price of land went up, the proportion of land held in tenancy went up.[1]

The pattern of family-size tenancy was apparently found in the potato culture of Ireland before the revolution, in the wheat culture of pre–World War I Rumania[2] and also that of Bosnia-Herzegovina (now part of Yugoslavia) at the same period.[3] The sugar-cane regions of central Luzon are also farmed in family-size tenancies, though this is so uneconomical that, without privileged access to the American market, cane culture would disappear.[4] It also characterizes the cotton culture of the highly productive Nile Valley in Egypt[5] and the cotton culture of the Peruvian coast.[6] This pattern of small peasant farms with rents to landlords was also characteristic of prerevolutionary France[7] and southwest England during the Middle Ages.[8] In lowland Burma a large share of the rice land is owned by the Indian banking house of Chettyar,[9] and much of the rest of it is in tenancy to other landlords. The landtenure system of Taiwan before the recent land reform was typical family-size tenancy.[10]

Perhaps the most remarkable aspect of this list is the degree to which this system has been ended by reform or revolution, becoming transformed, except in a few Communist states, into a system of smallholding farms. And even in Communist states the first transformation after the revolution is ordinarily to give the land to the tiller: only afterward are the peasants gathered into collective farms, generally in the face of vigorous resistance.

The system of *rentier* capitalists owing land let out in family farms (or *rentier* capitalists owning debts whose

service requires a large part of farm income) seems extremely politically unstable. The French Revolution, according to De Tocqueville, was most enthusiastically received in areas in which there were small farms paying feudal dues (commuted to rent in money or in kind).[11] The eastern European systems of Rumania and parts of Yugoslavia were swept away after World War I in land reforms. Land reforms were also carried through in northern Greece, the Baltic states, and many of the succession states of the Hapsburg monarchy (the reform was specious in Hungary). A vigorous and long-lasting civil war raged in Ireland up to the time of independence, and its social base was heavily rural. The high-tenancy areas in central Luzon were the social base of the revolutionary Hukbalahaps during and after World War II. The Communist revolution in China had its first successes in the high-tenancy areas of the south. The number of peasant riots in Japan during the interwar period was closely correlated with the proportion of land held in tenancy.[12] Peasant rebellions were concentrated in Kent and southeast England during the Middle Ages.[13] In short, such systems rarely last through a war or other major political disturbance and constantly produce political tensions.

There are several causes of the political instability of such systems. In the first place, the issue in the conflict is relatively clear: the lower the rent of the *rentier* capitalists, the higher the income of the peasantry. The division of the product at harvest time or at the time of sale is a clear measure of the relative prerogatives of the farmer and the *rentier*.

Second, there is a severe conflict over the distribution of the risks of the enterprise. Agriculture is always the kind of enterprise with which God has a lot to do. With the commercialization of agriculture, the enterprise is further subject to great fluctuation in the gross income from its produce. *Rentiers*, especially if they are capitalists investing in land rather than aristocrats receiving incomes from feudal patrimony, shift as much of the risk of failure as possible to the tenant. Whether the rent is share or cash, the variability of income of the peasantry is almost never less, and is often more, than the variability of *rentiers'* income. This makes the income of the peasantry highly variable, contributing to their political sensitization.[14]

Third, there tends to be little social contact between the *rentier* capitalists living in the cities and the rural population. The *rentiers* and the farmers develop distinct styles of life, out of touch with each other. The *rentier* is not brought into contact with the rural population by having to take care of administrative duties on the farm; nor is he drawn into local government as a leading member of the community or as a generous sharer in the charitable enterprises of the village. The urban *rentier*, with his educated and often foreign speech, his cosmopolitan interests, his arrogant rejection of rustic life is a logical target of the rural community, whose only contact with him is through sending him money or goods.

[1] Ronald P. Dore, *Land Reform in Japan* (London: Oxford University Press, 1959), p. 21.

[2] Henry L. Roberts, *Rumania: The Political Problems of an Agrarian State* (New Haven, Conn.: Yale University Press, 1951), pp. 14–17; Tables IX, X, p. 363.

[3] Jozo Tomasevich, *Peasants, Politics, and Economic Change in Yugoslavia* (Stanford, Calif.: Stanford University Press, 1955), pp. 96–101, 355.

[4] Jacoby, *op. cit.*, pp. 181–191, 203–209.

[5] Doreen Warriner, *Land Reform and Development in the Middle East* (London: Royal Institute of International Affairs, 1957), pp. 25–26.

[6] Ford, *op. cit.*, pp. 84–85.

[7] Alexis de Tocqueville, *The Old Regime and the French Revolution* ("Anchor Books" [Garden City, N.Y.: Doubleday & Co., 1955]), pp. 23–25, 30–32.

[8] George Homans, *English Villagers of the Thirteenth Century* (Cambridge, Mass.: Harvard University Press, 1941), p. 21.

[9] Jacoby, *op. cit.*, pp. 73, 78–88.

[10] Klein, *op. cit.*, pp. 52–54, 235.

[11] De Tocqueville, *op. cit.*, p. 25.

[12] Dore, *op. cit.*, p. 72 (cf. this data on tenancy disputes with the data on tenancy, p. 21).

[13] Homans, *op. cit.*, p. 119.

[14] Though they deal with smallholding systems, the connection between economic instability and political activism is argued by Lipset (*op. cit.*, pp. 26–29, 36) and by Rudolf Heberle (*Social Movements* [New York: Appleton-Century-Crofts Inc., 1951], pp. 240–248; see also Jacoby, *op. cit.*, p. 246; and Daniel Lerner, *The Passing of Traditional Society* [Glencoe, Ill.: Free Press, 1958], p. 227). Aristotle noted the same thing: "it is a bad thing that many from being rich should become poor; for men of ruined fortunes are sure to stir up revolutions" (*Politics*, 1266b).

Fourth, the leaders of the rural community, the rich peasants, are not vulnerable to expulsion by the land-owners, as they would be were the landowners also the local government. The rich peasant shares at least some of the hardships and is opposed in his class interests to many of the same people as are the tenants. In fact, in some areas where the population pressure on the land is very great, the rich peasants themselves hold additional land in tenancy, beyond their basic holdings. In this case the leadership of the local community is not only not opposed to the interests of the tenants but has largely identical interests with the poor peasants.

Finally, the landowners do not have the protection of the peasants' ignorance about the enterprise to defend their positions, as do large-scale capitalist farmers. It is perfectly clear to the tenant farmer that he could raise and sell his crops just as well with the landlord gone as with him there. There is no complicated co-operative tillage that seems beyond the view of all but the land-lord and his managers, as there may be in manorial, and generally is in large-scale capitalist, agriculture. The farmer knows as well or better than the landlord where seed and fertilizer is to be bought and where the crop can be sold. He can often see strategic investments un-known to his landlord that would alleviate his work or increase his yield.

At least in its extreme development, then, the land-owning class in systems of family-size tenancy appears as alien, superfluous, grasping, and exploitative. Their rights in agricultural enterprise appear as an unjusti-fiable burden on the rustic classes, both to the peasantry and to urban intellectuals. No marked decrease in agricultural productivity is to be expected when they are dispossessed, because they are not the class that carries the most advanced technical culture of agriculture. Quite often, upon land reform the productivity of agriculture increases.[1]

So family-size tenancy tends to yield a class system with an enfranchised, formally free lower class which has a monopoly of technical culture. The style of life of the upper class is radically different from that of the lower class. The lower class tends to develop a relatively skilled and relatively invulnerable leadership in the richer peasantry and a relatively high degree of politi-cal sensitivity in the poorer peasantry. It is of such stuff that many radical populist and nationalist movements are made.

3) FAMILY SMALLHOLDING

Family smallholding has the same sort of enterprises as does family tenancy, but rights to the returns from the enterprise are more heavily concentrated in the class of farmers. The "normal" property holding is about the size requiring the work of two adults or less. Probably the most frequent historical source of such systems is out of family-tenancy systems by way of land reform or revolution. However, they also arise through colonization of farmlands carried out under govern-ments in which large landlords do not have predomi-nant political power, for instance, in the United States and Norway. Finally, it seems that such systems tend to be produced by market forces at an advanced stage of industrialization. There is some evidence that farms either larger or smaller than those requiring about two adult laborers tend to disappear in the industrial states of western Europe.[2]

Examples of such systems having a relatively long history are the United States outside the "Black Belt" in the South, the ranch areas of the West, and the central valleys of California, Serbia after some time in the early nineteenth century,[3] France after the great revolution, most of Scandinavia,[4] much of Canada, Bulgaria since 1878,[5] and southern Greece since sometime in the nine-teenth century. Other such systems which have lasted long enough to give some idea of their long-term development are those created in eastern Europe after World War I; good studies of at least Rumania[6] and Yugoslavia[7] exist. Finally, the system of family small-holding created in Japan by the American-induced land reform of 1946 has been carefully studied.[8]

Perhaps the best way to begin analysis of this type of agricultural enterprise is to note that virtually all the costs of production are fixed. Labor in the family hold-ing is, in some sense, "free": family members have to be supported whether they work or not, so they might as well work. Likewise, the land does not cost rent, and there is no advantage to the enterprise in leaving it out of cultivation. This predominance of fixed costs means that production does not fall with a decrease in prices, as it does in most urban enterprises where labor is a variable cost.[9] Consequently, the income of smallholders varies directly with the market price of the commodities they produce and with variability in production pro-duced by natural catastrophe. Thus, the political move-ments of smallholders tend to be directed primarily at maintenance of the price of agricultural commodities rather than at unemployment compensation or other "social security" measures.

Second, the variability of return from agricultural enterprise tends to make credit expensive and, at any rate, makes debts highly burdensome in bad years. Smallholders' political movements, therefore, tend to be opposed to creditors, to identify finance capital as a class enemy: Jews, the traditional symbol of finance

---

[1] See. e.g., Dore, *op. cit.*, pp. 213–219.

[2] Folke Dovring, *Land and Labor in Europe, 1900–1950* (The Hague: Martinus Nijhoff, 1956), pp. 115–118. The median size of the farm unit, taking into consideration the type of crops grown on different sized farms, ranges from that requiring one man-year in Norway to two man-years in France, among the nations on the Continent.

[3] Tomasevich, *op. cit.*, pp. 38–47.

[4] Dovring, *op, cit.*, p. 143.

[5] Royal Institute of International Affairs, *Nationalism* (London, Oxford University Press, 1939), p. 106.

[6] Roberts, *op. cit.*

[7] Tomasevich, *op. cit.*

[8] Dore, *op. cit.*

[9] Wilfried Kahler, *Das Agrarproblem in den Industrieländern* (Göttingen: Vandenhoeck & Ruprecht, 1958), p. 17.

capital, often come in for an ideological beating. Populist movements are often directed against "the bankers." Further, since cheap money generally aids debtors, and since small farmers are generally debtors, agrarian movements tend to support various kinds of inflationary schemes. Small farmers do not want to be crucified on a cross of gold.

Third, agrarian movements, except in highly advanced societies, tend to enjoy limited intraclass communication, to be poor in politically talented leaders, relatively unable to put together a coherent, disciplined class movement controlled from below.[1] Contributions to the party treasury tend to be small and irregular, like the incomes of the small farmers. Peasant movements are, therefore, especially prone to penetration by relatively disciplined political interests, sometimes Communist and sometimes industrial capital.[2] Further, such movements tend to be especially liable to corruption,[3] since they are relatively unable to provide satisfactory careers for political leaders out of their own resources.

Moreover, at an early stage of industrial and commercial development in a country without large landowners, the only sources of large amounts of money available to politicians are a few urban industrial and commercial enterprises. Making a policy on the marketing and production of iron and steel is quite often making a policy on the marketing and production of a single firm. Naturally, it pays that firm to try to get legislation and administration tailored to its needs.

Fourth, small-farmer and peasant movements tend to be nationalistic and xenophobic. The explanation of this phenomenon is not clear.

Finally, small-farmer and peasant movements tend to be opposed to middlemen and retailers, who are likely to use their monopolistic or monopsonistic position to milk the farm population. The co-operative

movement is, of course, directed at eliminating middlemen as well as at provision of credit without usury.

Under normal conditions (that is, in the absence of totalitarian government, major racial cleavage, and major war) this complex of political forces tends to produce a rural community with a proliferation of associations and with the voting power and political interest to institute and defend certain elements of democracy, especially universal suffrage and universal education. This tends to produce a political regime loose enough to allow business and labor interest groups to form freely without allowing them to dominate the government completely. Such a system of landholding is a common precursor and support of modern liberal democratic government.

In smallholding systems, then, the upper classes of the rural community are not distinct in legal status and relatively not in style of life. Social mobility in such a system entails mainly a change in the amount of property held, or in the profitability of the farm, but not a change in legal status or a radical change in style of life.[4]

A politically enfranchised rural community is characterized by a high degree of political affect and organization, generally in opposition to urban interests rather than against rural upper classes. But, compared with the complexity of their political goals and the level of political involvement, their competence tends to be low until the "urbanization of the countryside" is virtually complete.

4) PLANTATION AGRICULTURE

Labor-intensive crops requiring several years for maturation, such as rubber, tree fruit, or coffee, tend to be grown on large-scale capitalistic farms employing either wage labor, or, occasionally, slave labor. Particularly when capital investment is also required for processing equipment to turn the crop into a form in which it can be shipped, as for example in the culture of sugar cane and, at least in earlier times, sugar beets, large-scale capitalist agriculture predominates.

The key economic factor that seems to produce large-scale capitalist culture is the requirement of long-term capital investment in the crop or in machinery, combined with relatively low cost of land. When the crop is also labor-intensive, particularly when labor is highly seasonal, a rather typical plantation system tends to emerge. In some cases it also emerges in the culture of cotton (as in the ante bellum American South and some places in Egypt), wheat (as in Hungary, eastern Germany,[5] and Poland[6]), or rice (as on the Carolina and Georgia coasts in the ante bellum American South).[7]

The enterprise typically combines a small highly skilled and privileged group which administers the capital investment, the labor force, and the marketing of the crops with a large group of unskilled, poorly paid, and legally unprivileged workers. Quite generally, the workers are ethnically distinct from the skilled core of administrators, often being imported from economically more backward areas or recruited from an

---

[1] I.e., as compared with political movements of the urban proletariat or bourgeoisie. They are more coherent and disciplined than are the lower-class movements in other agricultural systems.

[2] An excellent example of the penetration of industrial capital into a peasant party is shown by the development of the party platforms on industry in Rumania, 1921–26 (Roberts, *op. cit.*, pp. 154–156). The penetration of American populists by the "silver interests" is another example.

[3] Cf. *ibid.*, pp. 337–339; and Tomasevich, *op. cit.*, pp. 246–247. The Jacksonian era in the United States, and the persistent irregularities in political finance of agrarian leaders in the South of the United States, are further examples.

[4] The best description that I know of the meaning of "property mobility" in such a system is the novel of Knut Hamsun, *Growth of the Soil* (New York: Modern Library, 1921), set in the Norwegian frontier.

[5] Weber, *loc. cit.*

[6] Victor Lesniewski and Waclaw Ponikowski, "Polish Agriculture," in Ora S. Morgan (ed.), *Agricultural Systems of Middle Europe* (New York: Macmillan Co., 1933), pp. 260–263. Capitalist development was greatest in the western regions of Poznan and Pomerania (cf. *ibid.*, p. 264). There seem to have been many remains of a manorial system (*ibid.*, p. 277).

[7] Albert V. House, *Planter Management and Capitalism in Ante-bellum Georgia* (New York: Columbia University Press, 1954) esp. pp. 18–37.

economically backward native population in colonial and semicolonial areas. This means that ordinarily they are ineligible for the urban labor market of the nation in which they work, if it has an urban labor market.

Examples of plantation systems are most of the sugar areas in the Caribbean and on the coast of Peru,[1] the rubber culture of the former Federated Malay States in Malaya[2] and on Java[3] the fruit-growing areas of Central America, the central valleys of California, where the labor force is heavily Latin American, eastern Germany during the early part of this century, where Poles formed an increasing part of the labor force,[4] Hungary up to World War II, the pineapple-growing of the Hawaiian Islands,[5] and, of course, the ante bellum American South. The system tends to induce in the agricultural labor force a poverty of associational life, low participation in local government, lack of education for the labor force, and high vulnerability of labor-union and political leadership to oppression by landlords and landlord-dominated governments. The domination of the government by landlords tends to prevent the colonization of new land by smallholders, and even to wipe out the holdings of such small peasantry as do exist.

In short, the system tends to maintain the culture, legal and political position, and life chances of the agricultural labor force distinct both from the urban labor force and from the planter aristocracy. The bearers of the technical and commercial knowledge are not the agricultural laborers, and, consequently, redistribution of land tends to introduce inefficiency into agriculture. The plantation system, as Edgar T. Thompson has put it, is a "race-making situation"[6] which produces a highly privileged aristocracy, technically and culturally educated, and a legally, culturally, and economically underprivileged labor force. If the latter is politically mobilized, as it may be occasionally by revolutionary governments, it tends to be extremist.

5) CAPITALIST EXTENSIVE AGRICULTURE WITH WAGE LABOR: THE RANCH

An extensive culture of wool and beef, employing wage labor, grew up in the American West, Australia, England and Scotland during and after the industrial revolution, Patagonia and some other parts of South America, and northern Mexico. In these cases the relative proportion of labor in the cost of production is smaller than it is in plantation agriculture. Such a structure is also characteristic of the wheat culture in northern Syria. In no case was there pressure to recruit and keep down an oppressed labor force. In England a surplus labor force was pushed off the land. A fairly reliable economic indicator of the difference between ranch and plantation systems is that in ranch systems the least valuable land is owned by the largest enterprises. In plantation systems the most valuable land is owned by the largest enterprises, with less valuable land generally used by marginal smallholders. The explanation of this is not clear.

The characteristic social feature of these enterprises is a free-floating, mobile labor force, often with few family ties, living in barracks, and fed in some sort of "company mess hall." They tend to make up a socially undisciplined element, hard-drinking and brawling. Sometimes their alienation from society takes on the form of political radicalism, but rarely of an indigenous disciplined radical movement.

The types of agricultural enterprise outlined here are hardly exhaustive, but perhaps they include most of the agricultural systems which help determine the political dynamics of those countries which act on the world scene today. Nor does this typology pretend to outline all the important differences in the dynamics of agricultural systems. Obviously, the system of family-sized farms run by smallholders in Serbia in the 1840's is very different from the institutionally similar Danish and American systems of the 1950's.[7] And capitalistic sheep-raisers supported and made up the House of Lords in England but supported populistic currents in the United States.

However, some of the differences among systems outlined here seem to hold in widely varying historical circumstances. The production and maintenance of ethnic differences by plantations, the political fragility of family-size tenancy, the richer associational life, populist ideology, corrupt politics of smallholders, and the political apathy and technical traditionalism of the manor or the old hacienda — these seem to be fairly reliable. Characteristics of rural enterprises and the class relations they typically produce are summarized in Table 1.

This, if it is true, shows the typology to be useful. The question that remains is: Is it capable of being used? Is it possible to find indexes which will reliably differentiate a plantation from a manor or a manor from a large holding farmed by family tenancy?

The answer is that most of these systems have been accurately identified in particular cases. The most elusive is the manor or traditional hacienda; governments based on this sort of agricultural enterprise rarely take accurate censuses, partly because they rarely have

[1] Ford, *op. cit.*, pp. 57–60.

[2] Jacoby, *op. cit.*, pp. 106–108, 113.

[3] *Ibid.*, pp. 43, 45, 56–61.

[4] Weber shows that, in the eastern parts of Germany during the latter part of the nineteenth century, the proportionate decrease of the German population (being replaced by Poles) was greater in areas of large-scale cultivation (*op. cit.*, pp. 452–453).

[5] Edward Norbeck, *Pineapple Town: Hawaii* (Berkeley: University of California Press, 1959).

[6] Cf. Edgar T. Thompson, "The Plantation as a Race-making Situation," in Leonard Broom and Philip Selznick, *Sociology* (Evanston, Ill.: Row, Peterson & Co., 1958), pp. 506–507.

[7] E.g., in the average size of agricultural villages, in the proportion of the crop marketed, in the level of living, in education, in birth rate, in the size of the household unit, in the intensity of ethnic antagonism, in degree of political organization and participation, in exposure to damage by military action — these are only some of the gross differences.

TABLE I. *Characteristics of Rural Enterprises and Resulting Class Relations*

Type of enterprise	Characteristics of enterprise	Characteristics of class structure
Manorial	Division of land into domain land and labor subsistence land, with domain land devoted to production for market. Lord has police power over labor. Technically traditional; low cost of land and little market in land	Classes differ greatly in legal privileges and style of life. Technical culture borne largely by the peasantry. Low political activation and competence of peasantry; high politicalization of the upper classes
Family-size tenancy	Small parcels of highly valuable land worked by families who do not own the land, with a large share of the production for market. Highly labor- and land-intensive culture, of yearly or more frequent crops	Classes differ little in legal privileges but greatly in style of life. Technical culture generally borne by the lower classes. High political affect and political organization of the lower classes, often producing revolutionary populist movements
Family smallholding	Same as family tenancy, except benefits remain within the enterprise. Not distinctive of areas with high valuation of land; may become capital-intensive at a late stage of industrialization	Classes differ neither in legal privileges nor in style of life. Technical culture borne by both rich and poor. Generally unified and highly organized political opposition to urban interests, often corrupt and undisciplined
Plantation	Large-scale enterprises with either slavery or wage labor, producing labor-intensive crops requiring capital investment on relatively cheap land (though generally the best land within the plantation area). No or little subsistence production	Classes differ in both style of life and legal privileges. Technical culture monopolized by upper classes. Politically apathetic and incompetent lower classes, mobilized only in time of revolution by urban radicals
Ranch	Large-scale production of labor-extensive crops, on land of low value (lowest in large units within ranch areas), with wage labor partly paid in kind in company barracks and mess	Classes may not differ in legal status, as there is no need to recruit and keep down a large labor force. Style of life differentiation unknown. Technical culture generally relatively evenly distributed. Dispersed and unorganized radicalism of lower classes

an agricultural policy worthy of the name. Often even the boundaries of landholdings are not officially recorded. Further, the internal economy of the manor or hacienda provides few natural statistical indexes — there is little bookkeeping use of labor, of land, of payment in kind or in customary rights. The statistical description of manorial economies is a largely unsolved problem.

Except for this, systematic comparative studies of the structure and dynamics of land tenure systems are technically feasible. But it has been all too often the case that descriptions of agricultural systems do not permit them to be classified by the type of enterprise.[1] Perhaps calling attention to widespread typical patterns of institutionalizing agricultural production will encourage those who write monographs to provide the information necessary for comparative study.

[1] E.g., the most common measure used for comparative study is the concentration of landholdings. A highly unequal distribution of land may indicate family-tenancy, manorial, plantation, or ranch systems. Similarly, data on size of farm units confuse family smallholding with family tendency, and lumps together all three kinds of large-scale enterprise. A high ratio of landless peasantry may be involved in family-tenancy, plantation, or manorial systems. Ambiguous references to "tenancy" may mean the labor rents of a hacienda system, or the cash or share rents of family-size tenancy, or even tenancy of sons before fathers' death in smallholding systems. "Capitalistic agriculture" sometimes refers to ranches, sometimes to plantations, and sometimes to smallholdings. "Feudalism," though most often applied to manorial systems, is also used to describe family-size tenancy and plantation economies. "Absentee landlordism" describes both certain manorial and family-size-tenancy systems.

Economic Development and Class Structure
Glaucio Ary Dillon Soares

Introduction

WESTERN SOCIAL SCIENCES have paid unusual attention to the subject of social classes, and the sociological literature is crowded with articles and books on social stratification. Although social classes were conceptualized by Western social scientists as a series of superimposed strata or a series of arbitrary points on a continuum of status, rather than as discrete phenomena,

This article is based on a chapter in *Economic Development and Political Radicalism* (New York: Basic Books, forthcoming).

and although this difference in conceptualization is fairly relevant in determining what further steps should logically be taken,[1] these differences will not be treated here. It is sufficient to say that I conceive urban stratification as a discrete phenomenon, but with class lines following the manual-nonmanual dichotomy[2] rather than the ownership-nonownership of the means of production dichotomy, as in the case of orthodox Marxism. A second difference between the present conceptualization of social classes and the Marxist theory is that current thinking acknowledges the existence of strata *within* classes, rather than conceiving them as homogeneous units, and we also deny any *trend* toward intra-class homogeneity. A third difference has to do with the concept of class consciousness, which we take operationally as the sum of the individual identifications.[3] Furthermore, we consider that identification labels are often ideological by-products, without a very close connection with the economic infra-structure.[4] Thus, people may identify with many different labels, and these identifications have a varying influence upon behavior,[5] but the labels do not necessarily reflect objective status. For instance, there is a substantial proportion of manual workers identifying with the middle and upper classes and of nonmanual workers (white-collar, professionals, etc.), who identify with the working classes. Whether we call it "false" or "alienated" class consciousness or not, the fact remains that this is a persistent phenomenon which shows no tendency to disappear.

The main justification for a first dichotomic approach along the manual-nonmanual line has to do with theoretical considerations about the influence of working conditions along the office versus factory tradition and the suggestive empirical findings about behavior being stratified between classes as well as between strata within classes.[6] In this sense, it seems that there is a sharp shift in references and aspirations when one examines the strata from the top manual to the bottom nonmanual, suggesting important sociopsychological boundaries, which may, if one wishes, be dialectically interpreted as qualitative changes resulting from quantitative differences.

We feel justified, then, in giving emphasis to the manual-nonmanual boundaries and, whenever summarizing data, we will attempt to follow this dichotomy.

The analysis of the relationships between economic development and class structure will proceed on three levels: *a)* secular trends in occupational structure; *b)* differences among countries, and *c)* differences among states or provinces of a given country.

It will be argued that, contrary to the class polarization trend visualized by Marx, there is a recent visible trend toward the growth (both in absolute and relative terms) of the nonmanual occupations, which are characteristic of the middle class. Although our analytical scheme is basically dichotomous, for the sake of semantic agreement we will use the term "middle class" whenever referring to these growing occupational

strata. Conversely, we will use the term "working class" whenever referring to manual workers. It will be further argued that advanced industrial countries exhibit a larger proportion of nonmanuals in the nonagricultural labor force than the least developed nations. Finally, it will be shown that no similar trends can be observed among provinces.

Secular trends in occupational structure

One of the necessary consequences of Marx's class polarization scheme is the absorption of the middle

[1] The late Polish sociologist, Stanislaw Ossowski, has undertaken a remarkable analysis of the causes and implications of dichotomic and gradation conceptions of class structure. See his *Class Structure in the Social Consciousness* (New York: The Free Press, 1963). See also, from the same author, "La Vision Dichotomique de la Stratification Sociale," in *Cahiers Internationaux de Sociologie*, vol. XX (1956), pp. 15-29; "Old Notions and New Problems: Interpretations of Social Structure in Modern Society" in *Transactions of the Third World Congress of Sociology*, Vol. III (London: The International Sociological Association, 1956).

[2] The stream of sociological thought dealing with occupation as an indication of socioeconomic status stems from the Lynds' work in Middletown. A more recent study, by Kahl and Davis, using factor analysis, shows that occupation is at the center of the cluster of indicators of socioeconomic status. Finally, a comparative study by Inkeles and Rossi shows that there is a remarkable similarity in the prestige hierarchy of occupations in different countries, lending support and generalization to this tradition in the stratification area which is ultimately based upon occupational prestige. See Lynd, R. S. and Lynd, H. M., *Middletown* (New York: Harcourt Brace, 1929) and *Middletown in Transition* (New York: Harcourt Brace, 1937), Kahl, J., and Davis, J., "A Comparison of Indexes of Socioeconomic Status," in *American Sociological Review*, XX (June, 1955), pp. 317-325, and Inkeles, A. and Rossi, F., "National Comparisons of Occupational Prestige," in *American Journal of Sociology*, LXI (January, 1956), pp. 329-339.

[3] This, of course, follows the same line of work that Richard Centers emphasized. See his *The Psychology of Social Classes* (Princeton: Princeton University Press, 1949).

[4] See Soares, G. A. D., "Las Clases Sociales, los Estratos Sociales y las Elecciones Presidenciales de 1960 en Brasil," in *Revista Mexicana de Sociologia*, XXIV (septiembre, diciembre, 1962), pp. 895-918.

[5] I used an identification question with six categories suggested by previous qualitative interviewing in the State of Guanabara, Brazil. These classes had not only a different occupational and educational composition, but also had a different *impact* upon political behavior. See Soares, *op. cit.*

[6] There are many indications of this. Berelson *et al.* suggest that opinion leadership is class-bound: "On each side of the broad occupational dichotomy between white-collar and blue-collar workers, the upper occupational groups within each pair provided more opinion leaders than the lower. One inference is that white-collar people look more to professional and managerial people as their opinion leaders and that the semi- and unskilled workers similarly look to the skilled workers." Inkeles' data show that in the USSR, USA and West Germany, skilled workers have higher job satisfaction than the lower nonmanual strata. If one takes the manual-nonmanual dichotomy, then *within* each of these, occupational satisfaction is rectilinearly related to occupational prestige. See Berelson, B., Lazarsfeld, P. and McPhee, W., *Voting* (Chicago: The University of Chicago Press, 1956), p. 112 and Inkeles, A., "Industrial Man: the Relation of Status to Experience, Perception and Value," in *American Journal of Sociology*, LXVI (July, 1960), Table 1, p. 6.

class by the proletariat. This, of course, was the result of Marx's observation of the growing numbers of workers and of the proletarization of independent artisans, small shopkeepers, etc.

> The lower strata of the middle class — the small tradespeople, shopkeepers, and retired tradesmen generally, the handicraftsmen and peasants — all these sink gradually into the proletariat . . . thus the proletariat is recruited from all classes of the population.[1]

In Marx's days, the "new middle class" had not yet made its large-scale debut. Sections of the lower strata of the old middle class were indeed being absorbed by the proletariat. From these observations he inferred a historical tendency toward class polarization, with a small minority of capitalists on the one hand, and the proletariat on the other. In this scheme, there is no room for a middle class.

Contrary to the Marxist predictions, the middle class has not disappeared, and the upper occupational groups have not decreased in size. As early as 1899, Bernstein, using comparative occupational data in a surprisingly up-to-date way, argued that

> It is quite wrong to assume that the present development of society shows a relative or indeed absolute diminution of the number of members of the possessing classes. Their number increases both relatively and absolutely.[2]

Answering the critiques of more orthodox Marxists, who were unhappy with Bernstein's revisionist position,[3] he added the following explanation:

> . . . And if we had not before us the fact empirically proved by statistics of income and trades it could be demonstrated by purely deductive reasoning as the necessary consequence of modern economy. What characterizes the modern mode of production above all is the great increase in the productive power of labour. The result is a no less increase of production — the production of masses of commodities. Where are these riches? Or, in order to go direct to the heart of the matter: where is the surplus product that the industrial wage earners produce above their own consumptions limited by their wages? If the "capitalist magnates" had ten times as large stomachs as popular satire attributes to them, and kept ten times as many servants as they really have, their consumption would only be a feather in the scale against the mass of yearly national product . . . Where then is the quantity of commodities that the magnates and their servants do not consume? If they do not go in one way or another to the proletarians, they must be caught up by other classes. Either a relatively growing . . . number of capitalists and an increasing wealth in the proletariat, or a numerous middle class — these are the only alternatives which the continued increase of production allows.[4]

It is clear that Bernstein had already grasped the historical trends in the occupational structure and even in income distribution. For, as data consistently show, there is both a growing middle class and an increasing wealth of the proletariat.

In the 1940's the trend was already patent and studies dealing with the growing new middle class began to spring up in the United States.[5] Sibley wrote a celebrated article, where he stated that

> the transition from blue-collar to white-collar work can be taken as a rough index of upward occupational movement. . . . Considering only transfers between these two very broad categories and disregarding vertical mobility within each one, changes in the national economy between 1870 and 1930 produced a very marked upward shift of the center of occupational gravity (to coin a very dubious term). Some 9,000,000 persons who were white-collar workers in 1930 would have been engaged in manual labor if the occupational distribution of 1870 had persisted. On the average, about 150,000 workers per year ascended from blue-collar to white-collar jobs.[6]

Therefore, another important feature of modern industrial societies seems to be the relatively high percentage of nonmanual occupations in the labor force, by comparison with their preindustrial past. Furthermore, nonmanual workers tend to think of themselves as middle-class.[7]

The growth in the proportion of nonmanual occupations obeys a secular trend which can be observed in

[1] Marx, K. and Engels, F., "Manifesto of the Communist Party: in Feuer, L. (ed.), *Marx and Engels* (Garden City: Doubleday-Anchor, 1959), p. 15.

[2] Bernstein, *op. cit.*, p. 48.

[3] Especially Kautsky, who attacked Bernstein at the Stuttgart Congress of the German Social Democracy.

[4] Bernstein, *op. cit.*, pp. 50–51.

[5] See, for instance, Corey L., "The New Middle Class," in *The Antioch Review* (August, 1945), pp. 1–20.

[6] See Sibley, E., "Some Demographic Clues to Stratification," in Bendix, R. and Lipset, S. M. (eds.), *Class, Status and Power* (Glencoe: The Free Press, 1953), p. 382.

[7] There is a massive amount of research confirming the thesis that persons with nonmanual occupations tend to identify with the middle class, whereas persons with manual occupations tend to think of themselves as working class. For Brazil, see Soares, *op. cit.*, Cuadro, V, p. 905. Even when ideological connotations are removed by a simple spacial representation of social classes, those with nonmanual occupations tend more than those with manual occupations to place themselves in the upper categories. See Hutchinson, B., "Class Self-Assessment in a Rio de Janeiro Population," in *América Latina*, VI (janeiro a março de 1963), Table 4, p. 57. For identification data in the United States, cf. Berelson, *op. cit.*, pp. 56 *et passim*, which presents data from a community with weak working class consciousness, Elmira. For an interesting discussion of the role of class identification in politics, see Campbell, A., Converse, P. E., Miller, W. E., and Stokes, D. E., *The American Voter* (New York: John Wiley, 1960), Chapter 13. And, of course, the classic work dealing with class identification is that of Centers, *op. cit.*

most industrial societies, not in the United States alone.[1] One way to check this tendency has been proposed by Bendix,[2] who developed a very simple ratio of administrative employees over production workers. Administrative employees are predominantly nonmanual, enjoy a higher degree of social and occupational prestige, are thought of as middle-class, and think of themselves as such. By contrast, production workers enjoy a lower degree of occupational and social prestige, are classified as working-class, and think of themselves as such.

Taking the manufacturing industries of five industrial countries of today — USA, England, Sweden, Germany, and France — it is seen that the ratio of salaried, or administrative, employees over production workers has tended to increase from the turn of the century on. Thus, in the United States, the A/P ratio increased from 7.7% in 1899, to 12.0% in 1909, to 15.6% in 1923, to 17.9% in 1929, dropped slightly to 17.7% in 1937, reaching 21.6% in 1947; in Great Britain a similar pattern can be observed: from 8.6% in 1907, the A/P ratio increased steadily to 20.0% in 1948. Sweden is no exception either: starting in 1915, we have an A/P ratio of 6.6%, at a time when the industrial countries had already surpassed the 10% level. The immediate explanation is that Sweden was a late starter in the industrialization race; nevertheless, as Sweden "caught up" industrially, her A/P leveled with the others, reaching 21% in 1950. However, as it will be seen later on, the A/P ratio is not conceptualized in this paper as a function of industrialization and industrialization only. Other variables may intervene.

Germany also shows a steady growth from a low of 4.8% in 1895 to 7.6% in 1907, to 11.9% in 1925 and 14.0% in 1933. Finally, France started high, with 11.8% as early as 1901, followed by a small reduction to 10.4% in 1906 and then proceeding with ups and downs to 14.6% in 1936.[3]

This generally observable trend is noted in a growing number of works dealing with the subject. A recent article, by Dahrendorf, makes the point clearly:

By the end of the nineteenth century, the category of white collar employees ... amounted to roughly 5 per cent of all persons gainfully employed. There were differences between countries, of course, but by and large the similarities in both the starting point and the extraordinary rate of growth of the white-collar group since the beginning of this century are more startling than the differences. By 1910, the proportion of blackcoated employees had reached 10 per cent in the developed countries, by 1930, 15 per cent; and some of the recent figures given by the International Labour Organization are 35 per cent for Sweden (1950); 32 per cent for Austria (1951); 28 per cent for Germany (1950); 27 per cent for Belgium (1947); 25 per cent for Britain (1951). Other sources give somewhat lower figures for all these countries, but they all confirm the same trend.[4]

Thus, it is clear that industrial societies of today have shown a tendency toward growth of the intermediate occupational strata at a higher rate than the lower ones. This tendency seems to follow closely industrial maturity. Why should this be so?

It may logically be argued that advanced technology increases labor productivity. This essentially means "liberating" a growing proportion of the labor force from manual jobs. This is reflected in unemployment problems and in a tremendous pressure for increases in nonmanual jobs. In most industrialized countries, a growth in middle and higher educational facilities have provided adequate training for this growing middle class. Nevertheless, this occupational change was not solely quantitative. This growing middle class is qualitatively new; it is internally more differentiated than the old middle class because it has a different occupational composition.

However, if increasing technology and labor productivity seem to be a sufficient condition for expanding the relative size of the middle class, it does not seem to be a necessary condition. Here we deal with the possibility of "premature" bureaucratizations, which may not be based upon solid *structural* changes in the economy. Thus, a few countries which have enjoyed a favorable economic conjuncture during many years on the basis of exports (for example, Uruguay) have been able to support a relatively large middle class. The decline of this favorable conjuncture represents the beginning of serious structural problems, as these countries now have a relatively large middle class whose values and tastes for goods which are not internally produced now cannot be afforded. If, on the one hand, it is true that in countries with a large population, a relatively large middle class provides a market for certain goods, thereby stimulating their internal production, it is also true that in countries with a smaller population, the market that this middle class represents may not be sufficient to stimulate heavy investments. On the other hand, this premature market for consumption goods may divert investments from basic structural aims.[5]

[1] There are several relatively recent publications dealing with the theme of the new middle class. Among these, Mills, C. W., *White Collar* (New York: Oxford University Press, 1956), for the United States; Crozier, M., "Classes Sans Conscience," *European Journal of Sociology*, Vol. II, n. 1 (1961), pp. 18–50; Schelsky, H., "Die Bedeutung des Klassenbegriffes fur die Analyse unserer Gesellschaft" in *Jahrbuch fur Sozialwissenschaft*, XII (1963), Heft 3; Dahrendorf, R., "Recent Changes in the Class Structure of European Societies," in *Daedalus* (Winter, 1964), pp. 225–270; Lipset, S. M., "The Changing Class Structure and Contemporary European Politics," in *Daedalus* (Winter, 1964), pp. 271–303; Croner, F., *Die Angestellten in der Modernen Gesellschaft* (Frankfurt: Humboldt Verlag, 1954) and Geiger, T. *Die Soziale Schichtung des Deutschen Volkes* (Stuttgart: Ferdinand Enke, 1932).

[2] See Bendix, R., *Work and Authority in Industry* (New York: Wiley, 1956).

[3] From Bendix, *op. cit.*, Table 6, p. 214.

[4] Cf. Dahrendorf, R., "Recent Changes in the Class Structure of European Societies," in *Daedalus* (winter, 1964), p. 245.

[5] A point also made by Galenson, W., in his *Labor and Economic Development* (New York: Wiley, 1959).

Argentina is perhaps another case of premature bureaucratization and middle-class growth. Although its geographical and demographic proportions give Argentina far better industrial prospects by comparison with Uruguay, it seems that the Argentinian middle class has grown faster than the country's technological and industrial development allows. Furthermore, it has had a more impressive educational expansion than Uruguay. A recent article comparing educational mobility in Montevideo and Buenos Aires, shows that 60.2% of the Buenos Aires respondents had a higher educational status than did their parents, as opposed to 46.7% in Montevideo.[1] This growth in educational opportunities has not been followed by a corresponding growth in industrial jobs. As a consequence, in recent years, Argentina, a country traditionally favored by immigrants, has lost through emigration a substantial number of skilled workers, technicians, and professionals.[2] To what extent this accounts for Argentina's unrest is a matter of empirical research. If, on the one hand, Peronismo and leftist agitation in recent years seem to be the result of Argentina's inability to meet the heightened aspirations of urban workers, the continuous emergence of no less radical rightist movements may be the reaction of middle-class sectors to loss of status and to the country's inability to sustain the middle class's high level of consumption.

The secular trend toward bureaucratization is by no means a peculiarity of manufacturing industries alone, as previous data might have suggested. Swedish national data indicate that whereas the actual number of employers decreased from approximately 650,000 in 1940 to around 600,000 in 1950, and whereas the number of wage earners decreased from about 1,750,000 to about 1,660,000, the number of salaried employees increased from about 600,000 to about 840,000 during the same period.[3]

Data by Kahl also point to the fact that the number of nonmanuals and their relative share over the total labor force as well, tended to increase from 1870 to 1950. Thus, professionals increased from 3% to 8.5%; proprietors, managers, and officials increased slightly from 6% to 8.6%; but clerks, salespeople, and the like were the ones who showed the biggest increase: from 4% to 18.9%.

However, these figures do not tell the whole story, as the proportion of farmers and farm laborers declined substantially during this period (from 53% to 11.6%), thereby contributing to an overall increase in the nonfarm sector. Taking the nonfarm sector alone, it is seen that the manual share declined steadily from 72.3% in 1870, to 62.4% in 1910, to 56.6% in 1950. However, the proportion of unskilled workers actually *increased* from 1870 to 1910, dropping sharply from 1910 to 1950. As a percentage of the total labor force, unskilled workers increased from 9% in 1870 to 14.7% in 1910.[4] Thus, those at the bottom of the urban stratification actually increased both in absolute and in relative numbers from 1870 to 1910. Possibly the beginning of this increase antedates 1870, but the data reported by Kahl only go back to 1870. This period of relative proletarization of the labor force is also the same period that Kuznets pointed out as the one of growing inequality of income distribution.[5]

Is this curvilinear tendency found elsewhere? Early data for a Swedish firm covering the period 1845–1873 suggests that at first there may be a relative proletarization, as the A/P ratio dropped from 10% in 1845 to 3.3% in 1855, rising to 4.2% in 1865, dropping again to 3.4% in 1873.[6]

However suggestive the data bearing on the curvilinear hypothesis may be, it is insufficient to prove the point. Adequate comparable historical occupational data are indeed a scarce good. The available data suggest a continuous increase in the white-collar and other nonmanual strata in the twentieth century and, for recent decades, the data are abundant and precise enough to allow the conclusion. However, the stage in which the proportion of unskilled workers might be increasing could be tentatively placed in the second half of the nineteenth century and perhaps the first one or two decades of the twentieth century except for England, which industrialized earlier.

The industrializing countries of today may not follow the same trend. Technological diffusion is now stronger than ever. Patents of all sorts, industrial equipment, and techniques are continuously borrowed and imported from more developed countries. This means fewer jobs, especially at the unskilled level, and a wider gap between the skills of the rural migrant and the requirements of industrial occupations.

By the turn of the century, the population of the city of Sao Paulo, an extreme instance of fast urbanization, was about 240,000. Twenty years later it was 579,000. In 1940 it had more than doubled again, reaching 1,326,000. And from 1940 to 1960 it almost tripled, reaching 3,674,000. In Venezuela, the propor-

---

[1] Cf. Iutaka, S., "Mobilidade Social e Opportunidades Educacionais em Buenos Aires e Montevidéu: uma Análise Comparativa" in *América Latina*, 6 (abril de 1963), p. 22.

[2] Argentinian data show severe unemployment problems for professionals as a consequence of the country's inability to absorb the production of college and university graduates. Data for 1961 show that in 1961 there were 11,673 college graduates working in enterprises employing 100 persons or more. In 1960 alone, Argentinian universities graduated 7,350 persons. One reaction to this situation has been emigration. Thus, from 1950 to 1963, 774 physicians, 863 engineers, 191 chemists, 172 accountants, 76 lawyers, 92 architects, 77 dentists, 48 pharmacists, 756 teachers and professors, have been accepted as immigrants by the United States alone. Data from research carried out by the Centro de Investigaciones Economicas, Instituto Torcuato di Tella, from *La Prensa* of September 26, 1963, and from the U.S. Department of Justice, Immigration and Naturalization Service.

[3] Data from *Statistisk Årsbok för Sverige*, 1955 (Stockholm: Statistiska Centralbyrån, 1955), p. 29.

[4] See Kahl, J., *The American Class Structure* (New York: Rinehart, 1957).

[5] See Kuznets, S. S. "Economic Growth and Income Inequality," *American Economic Review*, 45 (March, 1955), pp. 18–19.

[6] Data reported by Bendix, *op. cit.*, p. 212.

tion of the total population living in cities and towns with over one thousand inhabitants increased from 39.4% in 1941 to 53.8% in 1950, to 67.5% in 1960. In Panama, the proportion of the total population living in cities of 10,000 or more increased 10% in one decade: from about 25% in 1950, to about 35% in 1960. Changes which required half a century in nineteenth-century Europe now are taking only one or two decades.

These high urbanization rates are not due to a higher fertility of urban dwellers. On the contrary, it has been demonstrated many times that urbanization and fertility rates are negatively correlated.[1] Although mortality rates are usually higher in rural areas, rural fertility rates are so much higher than urban ones that they compensate with advantage the mortality differentials, allowing a net population gain. Urbanization, then, is predominantly the result of rural–urban migration. Every year, hundreds of thousands move from rural and small towns to the cities. If industrialization does not keep pace with this massive increase in the urban population, the result is a high rate of urban unemployment. This seems to be a characteristic of the new industrialization.

This situation is perhaps illustrated in the following table:

TABLE I. *Economic Development and Class Structure, Panama, 1940-1960*[2] *(in percentages)*

	Urban (a)	Nonmanuals (b)	Workers (c) Excluding services	Workers (c) Including services	Un-employed
1940	25.1	11.3	23.4	34.6	1
1950	25.5	15.5	18.4	29.9	8
1960	35.3	19.3	19.4	32.4	11

(a) Urban population is defined in the Panamanian Census as the proportion living in towns and cities with 1,500 or more inhabitants, which have certain minimum urban characteristics such as electric light, paved streets, etc.

(b) Middle class, or nonmanuals, includes the following occupational groups: "profesionales, tecnicos y trabajadores afines; Gerentes, administradores y funcionarios de categoria directiva, oficinistas y trabajadores afines, vendedores y similares."

(c) Working class, or manuals, includes "trabajadores en medios de construcción de medios de transporte; artesanos, trabajadores en proceso de produción y trabajadores en ocupaciones afines; trabajadores manuales y jornaleros, no especificados en otra categoria, trabajadores en ocupaciones de mineria, de canteras y afines; trabajadores de servicios y similares." The classification leaves out "agricultores, pescadores, cazadores, madereros y trabajadores afines; otras ocupaciones y ocupaciones no identificables."

There is evidence suggesting that the growth in industrial employment has not kept pace with the speed of urbanization. Table 1 shows that between 1940 and 1950 the percentage of workers over the total economically active population actually *decreased* in Panama. This decade witnessed a rare phenomenon, which was an actual growth in the proportion of the labor force in the primary sector, and urbanization was extremely low. Nevertheless, technological unemployment rose, as the proportion of unemployed soared

from less than 1% to more than 8%. The 1950–60 decade was a period of fast social and economic change in Panama. But the proportion of the economically active population engaged in manual jobs outside of agriculture increased by a meager 1% (2.5% if service workers are included) in spite of a 10% jump in the urbanization rate. Thus, it is obvious that Panama did not provide an increase in the industrial sector which was congruent with the rate of urbanization.

Venezuela presents a similar picture. Fast urbanization was not followed by a corresponding increase in industrial jobs. The proportion of the total economically active population engaged in manual jobs outside of agriculture increased less than 4% between 1950 and 1960, from 23.7% to 27.3%. If we include service workers, actually there was a *decline* between 1950–1960.

TABLE 2. *Economic Development and Class Structure, Venezuela, 1950-1960*[3] *(in percentages)*

	Urban (a)	Nonmanuals (b)	Workers (c) Excluding services	Workers (c) Including services	Un-employed
1950	53.8	15.6	23.7	33.1	6.3
1960	67.5	21.3	27.3	32.1	13.7

(a) Urbanization is defined in the Venezuelan Census as the proportion of the population living in cities and towns with 1,000 and more inhabitants.

(b) and (c) See notes to Table 1.

Urban unemployment has been a concomitant of urbanization and industrialization in many developing countries. In Venezuela, for instance, the number of unemployed (including those looking for a first job) increased from 106,953 in 1950 to 328,675 in 1960, more than a threefold increase. As a percentage of the economically active population, this represents an increase from 6.3% to 13.7%. Panamanian data offer similar results. From a handful of 1,594 unemployed in 1940, unemployment became a major problem in ten years, for there were 21,556 unemployed reported in the

[1] See, for instance, Davis, K., *The Population of India and Pakistan* (Princeton: Princeton University Press, 1951); Taeuber, I., *The Population of Japan* (Princeton: Princeton University Press, 1958); Duncan, O. and Reiss, A., *Social Characteristics of Urban and Rural Communities* (New York: John Wiley, 1952).

[2] Data from: Republica de Panama. *Censos Nacionales de 1950. Quinto Censo de Población. Volumen III, Caracteristicas Economicas.* (Panama City, Contraloria General de la Republica: Dirección de Estadística y Censo, 1954) and from *Censos Nacionales de 1960. Vols. I, Lugares Poblados de la Republica,* and V, *Caracteristicas Economicas* (Panama City, Contraloria General de la Republica: Dirección de Estadística y Censo, January, 1962 and February, 1964.)

[3] Data from: Republica de Venezuela. *Octavo Censo General de Población. Volumen XII, Resumen General de la Republica, Parte A.* (Caracas, Ministerio de Fomento; Dirección General de Estadística y Censos Nacionales, 1957), from *Censo de Vivienda y Población of 26-2-61, Resultados Nacionales y del Area Metropolitana de Caracas* (Caracas, no date) and from *Proyección de la Población Urbana y Rural de Venezuela y de sus Ciudades más Importantes* (Caracas, 1964).

1950 census. In 1960 the corresponding figure experienced a further jump, reaching 30,432. This represents less than 1% of the economically active population in 1940, around 8% in 1950 and 11% in 1960. Brazilian data suggest the same trend, for between 1950 and 1960 industrial employment increased at a yearly rate of 3%, in spite of a 9% increase in industrial production; at the same time, the urban population experienced an approximate yearly increase of 6%.[1]

Nevertheless, middle-class occupations have not suffered a stalemate as have working-class occupations: both in absolute and relative figures, professionals, managers, salesmen, white-collar workers in general, have been growing in numbers in developing countries. In Panama, they increased from 11.3% of the total economically active population in 1940, to 15.5% in 1950, reaching 19.3% in 1960. In Venezuela the corresponding percentages for 1950 and 1960 are 15.6% and 21.3%, a 5.7% jump, which ostensibly contrasts with the manual figures (which experienced an actual decline, when service workers are included.)[2]

Thus, the new industrialization which takes place in developing countries is characterized by important changes in the class structure. A fast and continuous growth in middle-class occupations is present but the same is not true of working-class employment. This contrasts with the pattern usually seen in the European countries in the nineteenth century, for it was not until the beginning of the twentieth century that the middle class increased significantly in size.[3] This was due to the fact that urbanization was slow and the relative size of the middle class, which is predominantly urban, had its growth limited by the speed of the urbanization process.

On the other hand, unemployment is soaring in developing countries. Although there is no hard evidence that a similar phenomenon did not take place in the nineteenth century, deductively we may arrive at such a conclusion, for urbanization was slower and industrialization was labor-intensive, rather than capital-intensive.

Thus, in some developing countries, although industrial output has increased rapidly during the past decades, the number of working-class jobs has not kept pace with this growth, nor, for that matter, with

the speed of urbanization. This may help to account for the widespread urban unrest observed in these countries.

Therefore, it should not be concluded from the preceding data that industrialization has a permanent relationship to specific changes in the occupational structure. Theories which assume a linear path for industrialization may be out of place, for industrialization in the developing countries of today offers a somewhat different pattern. Contrary to conditions in the past history of today's industrial societies, the developing countries can now borrow advanced technology and thereby use a much smaller amount of semiskilled and unskilled labor. This is *not* to imply that the industrializing countries are not passing, or will not pass, through the hypothesized crucial stage when the unskilled strata grow faster than the nonmanual. On the contrary, developing countries may actually have to face a stage of unprecedented problems. The very possibility of using higher technology also means acute unemployment and underemployment problems, thus intensifying the problems that characterize this early stage.

One conclusion imposes itself: the new industrialization is fundamentally different from the old. Developing countries present themselves with a relatively developed middle class, with its taste for conspicuous consumption, and with an army of unemployed and underemployed workers. In a sense, this is a far more explosive situation than the one that was faced by the industrial societies of today during their early industrialization period.

Differences among nations

Analysis of data organized by Germani from fifteen Latin American countries reveals that three different measures of economic development are positively correlated with the relative size of the middle class. This relationship is extremely strong in the case of the total labor force, for the relative size of the middle class correlates .86 with three measures of development: urbanization, industrialization, and literacy. Thus, economic development alone explains almost three-fourths of the variance in the relative size of the middle class.

When data are broken down into primary economic sector on the one hand and secondary and tertiary sectors on the other hand, differences appear. The relative size of the middle class outside of the primary sector is much more influenced by economic development than the relative size of the middle class in the primary sector. Thus, if one equates (approximately) the secondary and the tertiary economic sectors with the "urban" category, we may conclude that the urban class structure is more dependent upon economic development than the rural class structure. Literacy alone, as expected, explains almost 70% of the variance in the proportion of the urban middle-class over the

[1] This point is discussed by Furtado, C., "Obstáculos Políticos ao Crescimento Economico do Brasil," paper presented to the Conference on Obstacles to Change in Latin America, sponsored by the Royal Institute of International Affairs, London, February, 1965.

[2] Germani, using data for Argentina, Brazil and Mexico, shows that the relative size of the middle and upper strata increased between 1870 to 1950. From this data, it is apparent that Argentina went through a fast process of middle-class growth during the last few decades of the nineteenth century. See Germani, G., "The Strategy of Fostering Social Mobility" in de Vries, E., and Medina Echavarria, J., *Social Aspects of Economic Development in Latin America*, Vol. I (UNESCO, 1963), Table I.

[3] With the exception of England, where these changes took place a little earlier. For data on the growth of middle and upper nonmanual occupations in England, see Mitchell, B. and Deane, P., *Abstract of British Historical Statistics* (New York: Cambridge University Press, 1962).

total urban class structure. This suggests that an increase in educational standards puts considerable pressure toward an increase in middle-class occupations.

On the other hand, it is seen that only 25% of the variance in the composition of the rural class structure is accounted for by economic development. The remaining 75% must be accounted for by other variables, not by economic development as measured in this paper.

Some definitional changes, as well as the inclusion of non-Latin, developed countries, do not alter the foregoing conclusions. Taking the proportion of the labor force in agricultural activities as a *negative* indicator of economic development, and a nonmanual/manual ratio (excluding agricultural activities) as an indicator of middleclassness, the results are very similar to the previous ones, as indicated in Figure 1.

It may be safely stated that the more developed nations are able to support a much larger urban middle class relative to the working class than the lesser-developed countries, for the percentage of nonmanuals over manuals correlates positively with the percentage of

nonagricultural middleclassness allows for idiosyncratic variations. Like Chile, Venezuela has a smaller than expected middle/working class ratio.

It is fairly clear, therefore, that the more developed countries have a relatively larger nonagricultural middle class, in comparison with the working class. The same results are achieved when other measures are used. When one uses income per capita, measured in U.S. dollars, similar results are obtained. Also, if one excludes the service-workers category, little change is observed.

Differences among provinces

The situation is by no means the same in intranational comparisons. In the case of Panama, for instance, there is actually a negative correlation between the relative size of the nonagricultural middle class and the proportion of the labor force outside of agriculture, the coefficient being −.54. Thus, economic development and the relative size of the middle class have a *negative* correlation in the case of Panama.

Panama City is a deviant case, however, and the

TABLE 3. *Product-Moment Correlations between Economic Development and Class Structure, Fifteen Latin American Nations, 1950*[1]

	Urbanization[1]	Industrialization[2]	Literacy[3]
Middleclassness,[4] primary sector	.50	.47	.50
Middleclassness,[3] secondary and tertiary sectors	.79	.68	.83
Middleclassness,[4] total labor force	.86	.86	.86

Note: With fifteen observations, a correlation of .50 is needed for significance at the .05 level.
[1] Proportion of the total population living in cities of 20,000 and over.
[2] Proportion of the labor force outside of the primary sector.
[3] Population ten years and older.
[4] Proportion of the labor force with high and medium occupations over corresponding total.

the labor force outside of agriculture. The United States and Canada, which stand clearly as having the proportionately smallest agricultural labor force (less than 20%), also have the highest nonmanual/manual ratio (nonmanuals being about 70% of the manuals). These nations are followed by pre-revolutionary Cuba, which stands as having a larger middle class than its degree of industrialization would suggest. This may be the consequence of either a "premature" bureaucratization or of the fact that the Cuban economy was, and still is, largely dependent on sugar-cane production, or both. Chile, on the contrary, has a smaller middle class than its degree of economic development would suggest, with some 10%–15% less than could be expected. Puerto Rico, Panama, Brazil, Venezuela, and the Dominican Republic have similar middle/working class proportions (varying from 47.1% in Venezuela, to 51.6% in Puerto Rico). Nevertheless, their degree of economic development has a wider variation, with Brazil still having 59.1% of the labor force in agricultural activities, against 35.9% in Puerto Rico, and 36.4% in Venezuela. Again, the relationship between economic development and

analysis of this deviance may help to formulate another tentative rule *vis-à-vis* the role of the national capitals in stratification and politics. Panama City, being the administrative center of the nation, concentrates a large number of federal bureaucrats, thereby increasing the nonmanual/manual proportion. Federal capitals in most Latin American countries have a politics of their own. As most of them are also the industrial center of the country, they have a large working class. They also attract a large number of rural migrants and a sizable proportion of these migrants do not readily find industrial employment. This implies the existence of large segments of the working class which are unemployed or underemployed. Public and private administration make for a sizable middle class. Thus, Latin American federal capitals play an important role in both working-class and middle-class politics. In Brazil, for instance, the city of Rio de Janeiro, which in fact still is the nation's administrative center, has given strong electoral support to the Communist and Labor parties (PCB and PTB) *and* to the very conservative

[1] Data from Germani, *op. cit.*

UDN. In some instances, such as Rio, class conflict is manifest; in other capital cities, where traditionalism still has a say, it is latent only.

In Venezuela, the situation is also far from clear-cut. Including all the provinces and the Federal District, and leaving aside the territories, an overall correlation of only −.07 is found.[1] Again, in the case of Venezuela, the Federal District stands up as a deviant case, with a very high nonmanual/manual ratio. Thus, the impression that one has from inspection of the Venezuelan

(.11) between the proportion of the labor force outside of agricultural activities and the nonmanual/manual ratio. The small size of the correlation leads in the same direction as the Venezuelan data. However, inspection of the data shows two interesting things. The former is the old pattern of the capital city, in the United States represented by the District of Columbia, which stands as having a very large middle class, reflecting the concentration of federal employees. The latter is that the southern states clearly have a *smaller* relative middle

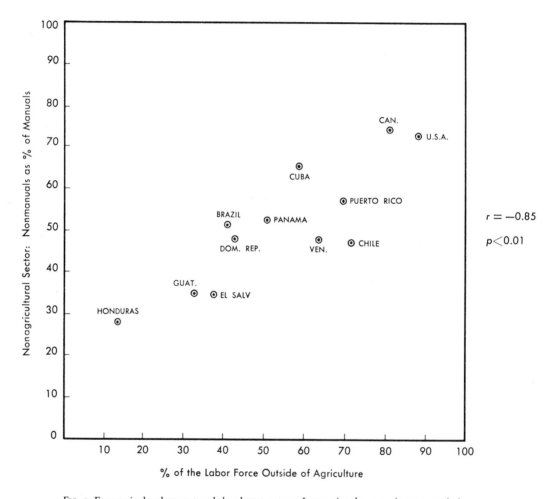

FIG. I. Economic development and the class structure. International comparisons, 1950 (32)

data is that of an actual lack of correlation between economic development and nonagricultural middleclassness.

One question that occurs immediately is: is this pattern of relationships a characteristic of underdeveloped countries, so that in the developed countries, the more developed provinces would also be the ones with a relatively larger middle class? Global data for the United States shows that there is a slight positive correlation

[1] Data from first source cited for Table 2.

class than the statistical expectation, on the basis of their level of economic development. Thus, West Virginia, Georgia, Alabama, South and North Carolina, Arkansas, Mississippi, and Tennessee stand clearly at the bottom of the middleclassness data. This leads to the idea that the South may be taken as a clearly distinct sociological setting and that this setting may influence the aforementioned relationship. Correlations were then recomputed separately for the southern states and the rest of the Union, excluding the District of

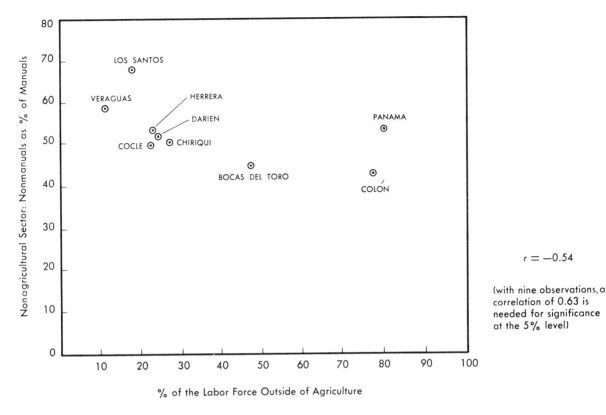

FIG. 2. Economic development and the class structure. Panamanian provinces, 1950 (33)

Columbia which is a special case. The southern states considered were Virginia, West Virginia, Florida, Louisiana, Georgia, Alabama, North Carolina, South Carolina, Kentucky, Arkansas, Mississippi, and Tennessee. The results are extremely interesting: the southern states have a small negative (−.09) correlation between the proportion of the labor force outside of agriculture and the nonmanual/manual ratio; i.e. the relationship between economic development and middleclassness is mildly *negative*. The case with the other states is even stronger: a correlation of −.65 is found, when the southern States and the District of Columbia are excluded. This correlation is significant at the .01% level. This means that, in the South as in the rest of the United States, the relationship between economic development and the relative size of the middle class is a *negative* one. The relationship for the non-southern states is fairly strong and leaves no room for arguing in favor of a random relationship.[1, 2]

One conclusion imposes itself: *the relationship between economic development and class structure varies with the level of analysis.* While data clearly point to one direction in international comparisons, in *intra*-national comparisons the data either point to the opposite direction or are very indefinite, thus suggesting that, as a first step, *separate* theories of class structure and change have to be developed for each level of analysis, in order

to account for empirical variation in the data, before we can start dreaming about a unifying theory of social classes with universal validity.

[1] Data from U.S. Bureau of the Census. *U.S. Census of the Population, 1950. Volume II, Characteristics of the Population, Part 1, United States Summary.* (Washington, D.C., U.S. Government Printing Office, 1953). Table 76, pp. 1–128.

[2] Torcuato Di Tella, in a very interesting study, shows that in Chile economic development is negatively correlated with the relative size of the urban middle class. When three geo-economic areas are considered, the same relationship is found *vis-à-vis* the relative size of the rural middle class. Brazilian data yield opposite conclusions when definitions are changed. Argentinian data are also highly inconclusive. Di Tella's conclusion that the relationship between economic development and middleclassness is a curvilinear one, which we support at the time series level when European nations and the U.S. are analyzed, does not seem to be valid at the intranational level. It seems that Di Tella places all units along a continuum of development, whereas I insist that such a procedure entails the assumption of unilinear evolution. Furthermore, our data show that when the southern states are kept separate, and the deviant case of Washington, D.C., ignored, there is a *negative* correlation between economic development and the relative size of the nonagricultural middle class. If Di Tella's hypothesis were correct, this relationship should be clearly positive. See Di Tella, T., *La Teoría del Primer Impacto del Crecimiento Económico* (Buenos Aires, mimeographed, no date). See also Soares, G. A. D., "Desenvolvimento Econômico e Radicalismo Político: Notas para uma Teoria," in *Boletim do Centro Latino-Americano de Pesquisas em Ciências Sociais,* IV (maio de 1961), pp. 117–157.

Three

Power and Status Relations

PATTERNS OF POWER

Social Class, Political Class, Ruling Class
Raymond Aron

SOCIOLOGISTS DISAGREE on the meaning of the term "class" — either they do not all use it to denote the same reality or they have different views of the reality to which it applies. At least they all admit that the concept of class is legitimate and that there are social groups which merit the name class. Even the legitimacy of concepts such as "political class" or "ruling class" or "elite" is questioned by only a fraction of sociologists. Does the ruling class exist or is it only a myth? Is the power elite created by the sullen imagination of the sociologist or does it actually dominate American society?

Most American sociologists do not like the concept of a ruling class; the very idea of a ruling class seems contradictory to the ideology of a "government of the people, by the people, for the people." Marxian sociologists are even less attracted to the concept since according to Soviet ideology, "monopolists" rule in the United States and "proletarians" rule in the Soviet Union. The existence of a ruling class is incompatible with the antithesis of the bourgeois regime (where the monopolists govern) and of the socialist regime (where the proletariat is in power): if there is a social reality which corresponds to the concept of a ruling class, it follows therefrom that it is not the monopolists in the United States nor the proletariat in the Soviet Union which exercises the higher functions of the bureaucracy and the state.

This reference to nationally accepted doctrines is not intended polemically, but only to point up an obvious fact: that any effort to discuss the problem of a ruling class is loaded with ideological implications. The objective of sociological analysis ought to be to make clear the possibilities and limits of an objective study.

The first theoreticians of sociology, at the beginning of the 19th century, Saint-Simon, Auguste Comte, Alexis de Tocqueville, and Karl Marx, stressed the contrast between the *ancien regime* and modern society, the post-Revolutionary society. Pre-Revolutionary society was composed of orders or estates. Before 1789 the French were not born free and equal; they did not all have the same rights; they were not all subject to the same obligations. Social heterogeneity was considered normal — heterogeneity not only of occupation, of income, and of living conditions but also of juridical status. Whatever social mobility there was, classes appeared hereditary; the juridical status of the noble like that of the non-noble was determined at birth. The French Revolution generated a society whose principles were fundamentally different. All the members of society became theoretically subject to the same legislation and, although limitations on the right of suffrage and the distinction between active and passive citizens were maintained in Western Europe for much of the last century, the accepted ideology recognized and

Translated from the *European Journal of Sociology*, Vol. 1 (1960), pp. 260–281, by permission of the author and the publisher.

proclaimed the universal extension of citizenship. Juridically homogeneous, composed of citizens with equal rights, modern society was nevertheless divided into groups (I purposely employ the vaguest term) which were ordered into a more or less clear hierarchy, with members of each group sharing enough traits to be discernible from members of other groups. Sociologists were in search of the right interpretation of the difference between the society of the *ancien regime* and modern society; they wanted to clarify the relationship between the estates of yesterday and the social groups of today.

One of the first interpretations could be found in the celebrated parable of Saint-Simon: suppose the elite[1] of diplomats, counselors of state, ministers, parliamentarians and generals were suddenly eliminated by a catastrophe — society would not be mortally harmed. The same quantity of riches would be produced and the living conditions of the majority would not be seriously affected. On the other hand, suppose the elite of bankers, industrialists, engineers and technicians were eliminated, then society would be paralyzed because the production of wealth would cease or be slowed down greatly. This famous text's central theme is the contrast between industrial society and politico-military society. The former is the sub-structure, the latter is nothing more than the super-structure (if we translate the Saint-Simonian distinction into Marxian terminology). The two schools — Saint-Simonian and positivist on the one hand, and Marxian on the other — give a different interpretation of the conflicts within industrial society itself. Without denying the conflicts of interests between employers and employees, Saint-Simon and Auguste Comte consider them to be secondary: the interests of the two groups are fundamentally the same but are opposed to the interests of the survivors of the theological and military age. On the other hand, according to Karl Marx, the conflict between wage-earners and capitalists, between the workers and the owners of the means of production, is decisive. They form two classes and it is their struggle that is the mainspring of historical change and, finally, of the socialist revolution.

Marxism is, so to speak, an interpretation of the society of the *ancien regime* made in the light of modern society, and of modern society made in the light of the society of the *ancien regime*. Neither juridical equality nor even political equality has substantially modified the condition of the masses. The workers are not "liberated" just because they vote once every four years. The *social groups* of modern society are not less distinct nor do they form less of a hierarchy than the pre-Revolutionary orders. And if they are comparable to these orders, in spite of juridical equality among individuals, do they not retrospectively throw light upon the true origin, that is, upon the base of the structure of

the *ancien regime*? The upper class (from now on let us employ this term in place of the term "social group") is always that which possesses the means of production — yesterday the land, today the land or the factories. The capitalists of our day are the equivalents of the feudal barons, and in their day the latter were the equivalents of the capitalists. Marx does not deny the unique character of modern society as formulated by the Saint-Simonians, but he does deny the essential solidarity of the producers as affirmed by economists, Saint-Simonians, and positivists. It is only after the socialist revolution that social classes — those of the *ancien regime* as well as those of modern society — will be eliminated and the promise offered by the prodigious development of productive capacities will be fulfilled.

This interpretation of two societies — pre-Revolutionary and post-Revolutionary — by the same scheme brings with it a parallel between the advent of the bourgeoisie and the rise of the proletariat. As the capitalist relations of production were formed in the midst of the feudal society, so socialist relations of production will form in the midst of capitalist society and the socialist revolution will give the power to the proletariat as the bourgeois revolution has given the political power to the bourgeoisie who were already holding the real social power. But this very comparison immediately illustrates the paradox, or, rather, the internal contradiction, of Marxian interpretation.

Let us consider the world of labor. Within every complex society one distinguishes among different groups according to the occupation practiced (farmers, merchants, craftsmen) and within each of these groups there is a hierarchy by property, success, luck, and income. The feudal lord and the capitalist financier or industrialist have in common the ownership of the means of production. But the function provided by the feudal lord was military; once the security of the peasants was assured, the peasants no longer needed the lord. They only needed the equivalent of a landowner in the large farm area where collective activity required managers or lawyers. In the factories or mills those who can organize or manage are obviously indispensable, although they need not be the owners. In other words, elimination of capitalists cannot mean elimination of managers; it only means the elimination of owners and the taking over of managerial functions by nonowners.

In effect, the comparison between the advent of the third and that of the fourth estate becomes especially problematic. In the eyes of Saint-Simon and Karl Marx, the bourgeoisie represented the class of workers opposed to the aristocracy of feudal origin, which was a military class. The opposition between the bourgeoisie and the proletariat, on the other hand, is situated within modern society. The aristocracy would disappear if it no longer fulfilled its military function or if this function was taken over by others. Likewise the bourgeoisie can disappear in so far as it is defined by owner-

---

[1] By "elite" I here refer to the minority which, in each of the enumerated professions, has succeeded best and occupies the highest positions.

ship of the means of production or where individual proprietors are not necessary. But the functions fulfilled by the bourgeoisie, organization and administration of collective work, must be taken up by others.

Where is the difference between the managerial group in an industrial society without private ownership of the instruments of production and the same stratum in a system in which individual ownership of the means of production exists? That is the major question which arises *à propos* of the concept of the proletariat as the dominant class.

Furthermore, in pre-Revolutionary society, the bourgeoisie constituted a privileged minority. Before the Revolution they occupied positions of command and prestige. The Revolution gave them the political power formerly exercised by the king and, in part, by the nobles. But in gaining power, the bourgeoisie remained the same. However, the proletariat must delegate power to "representatives"; the representatives cease being proletarians the day they begin directing a factory, a corporation or a ministry. The bourgeoisie in power remain the bourgeoisie. Proletarians in power are no longer proletarians.

Alexis de Tocqueville, whose thoughts were no less focussed upon the comparison between the *ancien regime* and modern society than Comte's or Marx's, also considered the social classes as the principal actors of history. In *l'Ancien Régime et la Révolution* he wrote this revealing statement: "I speak of classes, they alone should concern the historian."[1]

Neither Marx, in *The Class Wars in France* or *The 18th Brumaire of Louis Bonaparte*, nor Tocqueville systematically specified the relevant classes. The descendant of the old nobility and the prophet of socialism, both equally good observers, brought forth in the course of their accounts or analyses, the aristocracy (Marx distinguishes two factions — Legitimist-landowners and Orléanist-bankers), the high bourgeoisie of business or of law, the peasants (many landowners), the petty bourgeoisie of the cities (craftsmen or tradesmen), and the workers. Marx added the underworld or the sub-proletariat. All these groups, some survivors of the *ancien regime*, others belonging to modern society, appear in person upon the scene of history. In June 1848, it is the workers themselves who fight, alone and abandoned by their leaders. And the national guard is composed of the petty bourgeois who wish to fight for themselves and their class interests.

The existence of the State, the machinery of State — civil and military — creates difficulty for this interpretation of social and political history in terms of classes. Louis-Napoléon and his original retinue of Parisian bohemians take possession of the French State. Which class is in power? The peasant-proprietors who have voted *en masse* for the nephew of the great emperor? The high-bourgeoisie of capitalists whose interests will be safeguarded and protected by the imperial regime? Or are class relationships expressed in the imperial regime? Would similar relationships have been possible in a different type of regime; what would have been the consequences of a bourgeois republic?

Tocqueville would have been able to answer all these questions. Although he saw the classes as the principal actors of history, the State or the government is not explained entirely by classes and their struggles. Governments can be said to be representative, but neither the mode of representation nor the constitutional rules are determined strictly by the social context. Modern societies all uphold equality, but they may be liberal or despotic.

Marx observed the enormous machinery of State and the conquest of this by a clique of adventurers. He refused to derive from these facts the lesson which they contain; he refused to acknowledge the absence of a direct connection between political conflicts and social struggles. The operation of the state apparatus is never independent of the social classes but yet is not adequately explained by the power of only one class. Having dogmatically affirmed that the State is the instrument of exploitation in the service of the dominant class, Marx observed as an historian the relative autonomy of the political order. But he refused to recognize it explicitly. He sought refuge in utopia when he envisaged the proletarian revolution. The true revolution would not consist of conquering the State as is done by all revolutions which maintain a society of classes and the domination-exploitation of the masses by the bourgeoisie. The true revolution would destroy the machinery of the State.

Such a revolutionary utopia offers an easy target for the realistic theorists who think in terms of a ruling class.

The modern theoreticians of elites or oligarchies, G. Mosca, V. Pareto, R. Michels, are in part the legitimate descendants of classical political philosophy. But at the same time they are critics of parliamentarian democracy and socialist utopia. These political philosophers have never doubted the inequality of men's intellectual capacities or the inequality of citizens in wealth and power. To them, the problem was not to eliminate natural or social inequalities, but to assure the accession of the most worthy to the positions of responsibility, and, at the same time, to establish reciprocal relations — of authority and obedience, of benevolence and confidence — between the governors and the governed. Machiavelli had suggested that these relations were not always what they ought to be in the eyes of the moralists, and that the means most generally employed by rulers — force and deception — are reprehensible and necessary. But even if we put aside the pessimism of Machiavelli, the classic conception ran the risk of seeming cynical from the very moment it was used against democratic or socialist ideology. To say that all the parties, including those who claim to speak in the name of democracy and who conform to the obligations of a democratic constitution, are in fact led by a small number of men, a more or less permanent first

[1] Volume II, Chapter XII, p. 179 (edited by J. P. Mayer).

estate, is to restore the iron law of oligarchy, a law which only appears deceiving or scandalous to democrats inclined to believe that the power *of* the people is exercised *by* the people.

What is true for the party is all the more true for a regime regardless of the way the rulers are recruited. No matter how it operates — in theory or practice — government is always in the hands of a small number of men. In this respect the supposedly democratic regimes are no different from despotic or authoritarian governments. The formulas[1] may change, that is to say, the ideas or principles in whose name minorities rule, but the fact of oligarchy remains. In the first part of his life, G. Mosca indefatigably *unmasked* the liberal and bourgeois democracies by bringing to light the power of politicians, and beyond that, the intrigues and pressures of the leaders of finance and industry, all of which lay behind the letter of the law and appeals to the people. V. Pareto pursued the same enterprise in a still more polemical tone. Although he stated his agreement with Karl Marx concerning the class struggle, he predicted that the future proletarian revolution would simply be one more example of revolution made by a minority for its own gain. Marx agreed with the oligarchical interpretation of all revolutions except for the future socialist revolution. It was easy and tempting to refuse to agree that this exception was possible and to put the future revolution in the same category as the large number of its predecessors.

To designate these oligarchies, which Mosca distinguished mostly by their respective *formulas* and which Pareto characterized by their psychosocial attitudes (violence or cunning, revolutionary syndicalists or plutocrats), three terms have been used: *elite*, *political class*, and *ruling class*. It may appear that to distinguish among these three terms is not very important: after all, sociologists may legitimately use any terms which please them, provided that they define them exactly. But hesitation in choosing among the concepts reflects an ambiguity related to reality.

Pareto began by defining the elite in an objective manner, that is, by reference to facts which an outside observer is able to verify. Let us consider those — no matter what their occupation, whether they be prostitutes or scholars — all those who have succeeded and are considered by their peers and by the public as the best may be considered the elite of society. They are the *best*, not in any moral sense, but in the social, that is value neutral sense. But when Pareto spoke of the elite, he usually did not mean all those who have succeeded, but those — a small number — who exercise the political functions of administration or government, and also those who, without being officials, deputies, or ministers, influence or determine the conduct of the governing minority. Personally, I also give

these three terms, *elite*, *political class*, and *ruling class*, different meanings. For each one I specify another reality, or to put it differently, with the help of each one I pose another problem.

I use the term *elite* in the broadest sense: all those who in diverse activities are high in the hierarchy, who occupy any important privileged positions, whether in terms of wealth or of prestige. The term *political class* should be reserved for the much more narrow minority who actually exercise the political functions of government. The *ruling class* would be situated between the *elite* and the *political class:* it includes those privileged people who, without exercising actual political functions, influence those who govern and those who obey, either because of the moral authority which they hold, or because of the economic or financial power they possess.

Of these three terms, elite[2] is the one which I like least, because it has equivocal implications. Is it possible or useful to group as an entity all those who have succeeded, including the kings of the underworld? In certain occupations, such as those of craftsmen, ability is not recognized outside of a small circle, and confers neither power nor fame. To pinpoint the circle within which success insures entry to the elite is not easy nor, for that matter, is it useful. Basically this word serves no purpose other than to recall the iron law of oligarchy, and the inequality of talent and success (success is not always proportional to talent).

On the other hand, the two terms, "political class" and "ruling class" pose an important problem, that of the relations between the minority which actually exercises political power and the larger minority which exercises authority or has prestige in society at large, but is not involved in the government activities. Every regime has a political class whether its political system is democratic or Soviet. A society can not be said to have a ruling class if the heads of its industry, its trade-unions, and political parties, consider each other as enemies, when they have no feeling of solidarity.

The fact, or iron law, of oligarchy can be emphasized aggressively with respect to ideologies. Naive democrats imagine that the people govern in the West, although the electors are actually "manipulated" by the "cunning" politicians. The Communists, whether true believers or cynics, affirm that the proletariat is in power in the Soviet Union. In reality, of course, the party, the Central Committee, the Presidium, actually the secretary-general of the party, "manipulates" the masses, and in the name of the proletariat exercises a power more absolute than that of the kings or emperors of the past. This polemic and political argument is cheap. It should not interest us although it obviously carries a part of the truth. It is the problem, not the solution. It is clear that a small number governs always and everywhere; but who is this small number? What are the methods of recruitment, the organization, the formulas?

---

[1] The term *formula* comes from Mosca.

[2] On the other hand, I do not object to the use of the term "elite" used in the plural, as an equivalent of that which I call the leading categories.

How is authority exercised? What are the relations of the political class with the other groups who are privileged and have power and prestige?

These questions are all the more unavoidable as social differentiation has intensified in the course of the past century since these first sociological doctrines were proclaimed, while during the same period, claims to equality for all have become more resolute. Today, equality before the law is no longer challenged in philosophical terms, and the universal right of political participation through a general suffrage is no longer disputed. All members of society are citizens. But in a "civil society," to use Hegel's expression,[1] each citizen has an occupation. The functions of administration at the city, regional or national level, like the political functions (often elective), are exercised by men who are or become professionals. The political class is not hereditary in the East or in the West. In the East as in the West, the holders of state authority have *connections* (it remains to specify what these are) with the economically powerful and with those high in intellectual or spiritual prestige. We must analyze the various social categories which can belong to the ruling class — or again as I have explained before — the various sorts of elites, if we wish to compare societies with respect to their political class or ruling class.

Four antitheses — temporal power and spiritual power, civil power and military power, political power and administrative power, political power and economic power — illustrate the modern differentiation of the functions of control, the increase in the number of social groups actually capable of exercising the functions of control or of substantially influencing those who exercise it.

In all societies, those who establish the hierarchy of values, form the ways of thinking, and determine the content of beliefs, constitute what Auguste Comte called the spiritual power. In our day the spiritual power is shared among or disputed by three kinds of men: the priests, survivors of the spiritual power which the founder of positivism called theological; the intellectuals, writers or scholars; and the party ideologists. A look at the regimes, Soviet and Western, is sufficient to point up a fundamental difference in the structural relations of their leading groups. According to the Soviet formula, it is party ideologists who proclaim the supreme truth and teach what is sacred. Priests officially enjoy little prestige and intellectuals must subscribe to the ideological truth, more or less modified according to the time and the man.

Power in modern societies wants to be civilian in its origin and legitimacy since it bases its "title to rule," its legitimacy on popular endorsement. But it is only effective if it obtains the obedience of the commanders of the army and of the police. In fact, in our age, many regimes owe their power to the action of the army. There are many politicians who first wore the uniform and owe all or part of their moral authority and prestige to their military past.

The modern State is first of all an administrative State. Citizens, as the economic subjects, are permanently subject to the rules of officials who fix the laws of competition between individuals and determine the consequences of the laws in each circumstance. This administrative power is in a sense "de-personalized" and sometimes deprived of its political character: officials command in the capacity of officials and citizens obey the laws and the anonymous representatives of the State. But high administrators belong to the governing minority because they influence the decisions of politicians. The administrative power influences the distribution of the social product which constitutes one of the stakes in the struggle between social groups.

In the West, politicians are differentiated from administrators, although, in certain states, ministers are chosen from among the officials. They are more or less "professionals," depending upon whether or not politics is their primary career and sole source of income. They are, however, always "differentiated" in the sense that their activity, as representatives or as ministers, is inserted into a network of obligations, rights, and specific actions.

The network of these political actions is tied to other networks of social actions, more specifically to the network which can be called economic. Two categories of privileged persons, holders of two sorts of power, emerge from the economic system: *managers of collective labor*, owners of the means of production, directors, engineers, and *leaders of the masses*, heads of workers' unions, and eventually heads of political parties, anxious to organize an occupational group (the industrial workers) on the basis of a class affiliation.

These leading figures are present in any modern society, whether it is a Soviet regime or a Western regime. The relationships provided by the formula or imposed by the law or custom between the various types of privileged persons — holders of moral or legal authority, of actual economic or social power — I call the *structure of the ruling class* or of the power leaders. The Western type of regime is distinguished not only by differentiation among the heads of various power structures, but also by a free dialogue among them. The Soviet type of regime is defined by a lesser degree of differentiation and, especially, by a lesser degree of freedom of dialogue or opposition between priests and intellectuals, between intellectuals and ideologues, ideologues and heads of the party, heads of the party and government. Managers of enterprises do not constitute a category distinct from the state officials. The leaders of the masses, at the factory level, officers of local unions, are more concerned with keeping the masses in line than with expressing their grievances and are recruited because of their abilities to fulfill this function.

A regime of the Soviet type, in distinction to a regime of the Western type, tends to re-establish the confusion

[1] *Bürgerliche Gesellschaft*, ordinarily translates as "civil society."

between the concepts of society and state. Modern western systems create or accentuate the distinction by differentiating political functions from others. They tolerate legitimate conflict among professional and political organizations which are independent of each other. Furthermore, in the East, from the enterprise to the central office of the ministry, managers are State officials, whereas in the West, those responsible for the management of the economy are divided into multiple categories (owner, nonowner, manager, state official). In the East, the heads of the party are at the same time government executives, leaders of the masses, and official ideologues. In the West, the government continually has to face a more or less independent opposition, union officials, and writers, scholars, and ideologues who never cease disputing the true and the false, the sacred and the scandalous. The voices of the temporary holders of government office are not able to dominate the tumult of debate or propaganda.

These remarks do not aim at developing a theory of the ruling class in the East or West, but only at indicating the kind of problems which are posed by the study of *modern oligarchies* or, if one prefers, the study of the *oligarchical fact within modern societies*. Social differentiation has not spared the *oligarchs* but it has led to two extreme types: the regrouping of leading categories beneath the temporal and spiritual authority of the leaders of a single party, and the disintegration of the ruling class into a sort of permanent cold war (or peaceful coexistence) among the leading groups. Most Western regimes are situated between these two extremes. Great Britain seems to me to be the best example of a country whose regime is Western but which still possesses a ruling class: the higher echelons in the world of affairs, of the university, of the press, church, and of politics find themselves in the same clubs; they often have family ties, they are aware of the community they constitute, they consist in a relatively defined way of the higher interests of England. This class is open to talented persons, it absorbs individuals of lowly origin and does not reject those of high status origin who have assumed the leadership of popular movements of protest. These summits of different groups constitute a ruling class to the extent that the political class and the social elite overlap.

The empirical study of a leading stratum includes essentially four aspects: what is the social origin and manner of recruitment of the politicians (or of the high officials or of the intellectuals)? What are the qualities which seem to assure success; what are the career patterns? What is the manner of thinking and conception of existence characteristic of this category? What is the coherence and consciousness of solidarity among the members of this stratum.

When it is a question of political class, of relations between heads of industry and rulers of the State, these last questions become obviously preliminary and others will follow. The most important decisions are made by one or several men. Sometimes it is one man who must choose between peace and war. In this sense, the concentration of power is not a hypothesis but a fact. One question which should be answered is to what degree do the decisions made by the President of the United States or the members of the Cabinet directly express the interests, the will or the ideal, of a small group which has been termed "power elite" or "monopolists" or "capitalists."

First, we note that this question is more an empirical than theoretical question. The answer should result from investigation, not from theory or the analysis of concepts. The following remarks then, aim at defining the subject, not at treating it. It goes without saying that in a regime with private ownership of the means of production the measures taken by the legislators and ministers are not in fundamental opposition to the interests of the owners. Politicians are not radically hostile to the interests of those who have succeeded in the economic system. The rulers of Western democracies are not, and cannot be, at war with the economic system which the Soviets call capitalist. But this proposition is too obvious to be instructive.

It is necessary to go beyond this platitude in order to formulate the real questions. A capitalist regime, if we retain such a vague concept, may include extremely diverse patterns such as a considerable extension of collective property or public sector, of economic planning, a more or less progressive taxation system, etc. To demonstrate that western democracies are ruled by capitalists or monopolists, it would be necessary to first establish that the capitalists or monopolists have a consciousness of their own solidarity, that they have a common idea of their class and of their class interests. The available facts do not suggest that such consciousness exists or that common class interests are known and recognized by those they should unite.

Nothing would be more natural than for a director of Standard Oil or of General Motors to do his best to obtain support from the State Department against the menace of nationalization in a foreign country. But does the State Department yield to such pressures? The real problem is to determine the effect of pressure exercised by the big corporations in various fields of government, not to simply document that such pressure occurs. Do the political leaders make major decisions because they conform to the interest of large influential organizations, big corporations, monopolies, or others? This assumption has not been demonstrated and even seems implausible.

The Republican businessmen who filled the administration of Eisenhower preached and applied the doctrine of sound money and of financial rigor because it satisfied their system of values, even though, in many respects, it was less favorable for an increase in profits than the opposite set of doctrines. They were forced to reduce military expenditures in order to balance the budget. They had no common interpretation of the international situation, and they could not have said which type of diplomacy best responded to the class interest of large capitalism.

No one will dispute that the heads of the army and the rulers of industry have many close contacts today in the United States because of arms contracts, and also because of the jobs offered by industry to the generals after their retirement. But would the conduct of foreign policy actually be different if these links were less close? Do the generals recommend a program because they are thinking of possible future jobs in industry? Whatever the type regime of a given industrial society the heads of the army and industry must be intimately associated together. Is American diplomacy and the amount of armaments determined by these personal or social ties? In my opinion no one has yet documented an affirmative answer.

The relations between these leading strata and the social classes must be clarified. All the evidence indicates that these relations differ according to the type of society and the type of regime. We will only treat them here in the context of modern industrial society as it has flourished in the 20th century in the United States, in the Soviet Union, and in Western Europe.

The mass of the population is divided into occupations — agriculture, industry, and services — which economic progress has multiplied and differentiated. The income of each depends essentially upon the place occupied in the processes of production, the place being defined either by the relation to the ownership of the means of production, or by the qualifications needed for the work involved, or by these two criteria together. A Soviet type society only allows for the second criterion since it radically eliminated private ownership of the means of production. The social organization which appears basic to individuals is the system of production and exchanges, the family community is no longer a unit of production, and the religious or ideological communities, in most cases, no longer supplies the means of subsistence. "Civil society" (*die bürgerliche Gesellschaft*) in Hegel's sense, envelops the whole of society and constitutes, as it were, the substructure. Does it give rise to classes in conflict, one of which — the exploited class — has as a mission the revolutionary overthrow of the established regime? Neither in the Soviet Union, nor in the United States, is the working class revolutionary. In other words, it does not seem to think or act as if its objective or ambition were the overthrow of the economic or political regime. Neither is it in power; it has not been transformed into a "universal class" in the East or in the West. It seems revolutionary only in France and in Italy where large numbers of workers vote in favor of a regime of the Soviet type within a society of the Western type.

The industrial workers — Russian or American — are integrated into a certain administrative and technical organization. Empirical study establishes the magnitude of the differences in income within the working class. What is the differential in wages between the unskilled laborer and the skilled laborer? Do the workers as a class have the same way of living, the same convictions; do they have the consciousness of kind to constitute a social or historical unit with its own mission? In other words, when it is a question of class — and we take the example of the working class because, according to all the authors, it presents the most defined characteristics of a class — one poses two questions: To what extent does the class exist *objectively*? To what extent does it have an awareness of itself and what is the content — conservative, reformist, or revolutionary — of this awareness?

The first question may be posed both with respect to the Soviet working class and the American working class. The second question is not posed or does not allow an empirically determined answer with respect to the Soviet working class, because the authority structure forbids dealing with the question. Let us place ourselves within a modern industrial enterprise: the workers are subject to an authority which is not democratic in its origin (nomination, not election) or in its mode of exercise (commanding, not discussing). If the union members are allowed to do so, they will present with greater or lesser vehemence, economic (higher salaries, fringe benefits) or political (participation in plant decisions) demands. If the unionized workers are directed by secretaries named by or subject to the ruling Communist party, certain demands will not be made. The very existence of an interest of a specific class, possibly opposed to the interest of the directors of the enterprise, would be denied.

Let us now place ourselves on a more general level, that of industrial workers generally. The same opposition is found even more distinctly here. Class awareness, the idea of a common vocation depends more on propaganda and on organization than on the degree of objective community (to what extent are the workers the same or different from the other members of the society in general?). Workers cannot gain an awareness of themselves as a class if the economic and political regime forbids independent organizations, or to put it another way, if the structure of relations among the leading strata prevents dialogue among the intellectuals, the leaders of the masses, and the politicians.

The relations of classes are not unilaterally determined by the interactions within the leading strata. If one compares the various Western societies, it would be unreasonable to attribute the revolutionary attitude[1] of the working class, in France or in Italy, only to the action of the leaders. Do the leaders determine the attitude of the masses or are they carried along by the masses? The answer must be made according to the circumstances, and it is rarely categorical in one sense or another. We wish to show that the "class-relationships" only become clear in an industrial society on the condition that socio-economic organizations outside

[1] This formula is exaggerated simple and the revolutionary attitude has many nuances. But it is here a question of theoretical analysis or of a description.

of the machinery of the single party of the State are tolerated. What the comparison between the Soviet universe and the Western world reveals is that the structure of the ruling groups, and not class-relationships, determines the essence of the economic-political regimes.

It is true that social groups are formed differently according to whether or not private ownership of the instruments of production, of the land, or of the machines is tolerated. Distribution of wages and level and style of living of groups are influenced by the status of property, and still more by the mode of regulation (market or planning). But the major differences come from the structure of the power groups, the relations established by the regime between the society and the State. It is enough for a regime of the Soviet type to establish itself, that a Communist party, alone or with the aid of the Red Army, should take power. It is not, then, the state of the productive forces but the state of the political forces — that is the military — which is the main cause of the varying characteristics of each type of society, the cause of the rise or fall of one type of society or another.

Let us compare the results of these analyses with the sociological doctrines discussed earlier and with the interpretations — more or less justified or polemical — which each regime gives of itself and of others.

The reality of the Soviet regime does not have much in common with the myth of the "universal class" and of the "power of the proletariat." Power is exercised by the party which represents the proletariat but which is obviously no longer directed by proletarians. Certainly a Communist type revolution radically eliminates the survivors of the former privileged classes (nobles and bourgeois property-owners); the members of the power groups of the new society emerge from the popular masses and, in theory, the regime facilitates success by the best endowed, attenuating but not excluding the transmission of privileges within families through its abolition of private property and of the accumulation of familial wealth.[1]

Some merits of such a regime are, on the one hand, those which it attributes to itself, but, on the other, some are exactly opposite to those which the official ideology proclaims. The struggle of groups for the division of the national product, the clash between workers and property owners disappears as the doctrine suggests. Society ceases to be the theater of a permanent cold war. But peace is re-established, not by abolishing the occasions for, or the stakes of, the conflicts, but by preventing the organization of class armies and propaganda for class war. Saint-Simonians and Marxists both consider as basic, the cooperation of all producers — both managers and employees, since they have the same fundamental interests. But the Saint-Simonians did not believe that it was necessary

[1] The children of a member of the Politburo obviously enjoy advantages from birth.

to destroy private ownership of the instruments of production in order for all the producers to recognize their solidarity. Marxists, on the contrary, have argued that there would be a class struggle as long as there is a distinction between capitalists and proletarians. They eliminated the private ownership of the instruments of production, the capitalist class; then in accord with their doctrine, they proclaimed that there were no longer classes or that the classes were no longer antagonists. Finally, so that reality could not make a lie of their doctrine, they gave a monopoly of power to their party and its ideology. The representatives of all groups in society who must express themselves through the party, using its vocabulary, vie with each other in their affirmation of the disappearance of classes and class-struggle.

The Soviet regime is a reaction against the tendency, characteristic of the Western societies, of differentiation of functions and the dispersion of power groups. It re-establishes the unit of a ruling class, the spiritual and political unity of those in positions to lead, which in the West has been threatened by the dialogue among the politicians, intellectuals, and leaders of the masses. In this sense, it is the opposite of what it claims to be; it accentuates the oligarchical fact which it denies, it confirms the cynicism of Pareto, it represents the victory of a minority which calls upon the voice of history or the proletariat in the same way that other minorities have called upon the voice of God or of the People. The elite theory of a Pareto is better adapted to the interpretation of revolutions which claim to follow Marx than is Marxism. The revolutionary efficacy of the State has been gloriously illustrated by those who say that the State is only the instrument of the economically privileged class. It is easy for those who hold the military power to quickly assure themselves of economic authority and political power.

But the Westerner, "unmasking" the Soviet reality with the aid of the conceptions of a Pareto, would be wrong to belittle the historical accomplishments of the adverse regime. For it has actually put an end to class struggle, not, it is true, by substituting a miraculous harmony of interests in place of the contradictions of yesterday, but by first proclaiming and then refusing to doubt that such harmony exists from now on. The monopoly of a party and of an ideology, the submission by the intellectuals and the mass leaders to the orders of the leader of the party, contribute to the restoration of a ruling class. Now, the Western regimes are menaced less by the total power of monopolists than by the disintegration of the *social consensus*, by the rivalry among the major power groups.

Soviet polemicists and Western critics who believe themselves to be the heirs of Marx, "unmask" Western type democracy by exposing the sinister role of monopolists or of power elites. The existence of oligarchy once again, is not in question. But the characteristic trait of the oligarchy, within Western societies, is not the hidden power of a group of men (the heads of industry or of the army); rather it is the absence of a common will, of a common conception among the power strata who fight each other according to the rules of the game of the democratic polity. The much greater danger is that the struggle among the power groups does not necessarily give the ordinary citizen a sense of freedom. Even if the functioning of the economy and the conduct of diplomacy in the United States are not controlled, directed, or thought up by one man or by any one conscious team, the citizen does not acquire, for all that, the conviction that he is capable of influencing the course of events or the policies of industry or of the army. The mythology of hidden power elites succeeds because it expresses the impotence felt by the majority and it designates those responsible, those who "really" have power. The sense of impotence is made no less authentic by the fact that the "power elite" does not exist, or that it is everyone and no one at the same time.

The elite theorists are not wrong in "unmasking" democracy. There is no government of the people by the people. But this does not prove that the desires or the inclinations of the majority are without effect upon the conduct of the governments. The question — to what extent do those who govern manipulate the masses or are simply translating the aspirations of the masses into acts — is to a large extent a false question. In all regimes, there is a dialogue between the governed and the governing. The plurality of the parties, the regularity of elections, the freedom of debate, reinforce public opinion and reduce the margin of maneuver and manipulation by the dominant power groups. But the existence of these factors, which gives certain guarantees to the governed, does not confer the reality or the illusion of power upon them.

Even though the leading power centers treat each other as enemies and the State is not held by a resolute minority aware of a mission, the masses will not feel the exaltation of freedom; on the contrary, they will imagine a mysterious elite which in the shadows is weaving the threads of their destiny; a few must be all powerful, if so many millions of men are powerless.

The scientific and political controversy over the concepts of social class and ruling class has at its origin one specific trait of modern societies, the separation of social power and of political authority, the differentiation of functions, in particular, of political functions. The sociologists of the last century all recognized this separation of the society and the State (to employ the German antithesis *Gesellschaft und Staat*), all admitted that the development of industrial society contributed to the re-establishment of unity, the surviving parts of feudalism and of the *ancien regime* gradually disappeared and the State became the authentic expression of modern society. But none of the great sociologists on the continent had a clear idea of what the modern State would be, of what would be the true expression of modern society. Some saw it taken over by the producers, others heralded the dying out of the State after the victory of the proletariat, others questioned the respective probabilities for representative regimes or for despotism.

One of the principal causes of these uncertainties was the very ambiguity of the notion of class which was applied to privileged minorities – noble and bourgeois – and to the masses – peasants and workers. The privileged classes of the *ancien regime* were minorities who held social power (by landownership), military force (they were soldiers or army leaders), and political power (they exercised judicial and administrative functions). Before the Revolution the noble class had lost a large part of its economic power and almost all of its judicial and administrative functions. Different men exercised these functions, and these men depended more and more upon the machinery of State. But the pre-Revolutionary nobility continued to furnish the model of the "dominant class" of industrial society, a minority which is socially privileged and which actually exercises power in society and the State. This picture is inadequate for modern society which is characterized by a differentiation of functions that forbids property owners and managers of the means of production to themselves even if army officers or political executives. As this confusion between the reality of power and the way in which the summits of different structures operate, is too difficult for modern men to understand, the ideologists invented the myth of clandestine elites who have omnipotence through their ability to infiltrate the state.

Reality is at once simpler and more complex. Authority relations within modern societies are essentially multiple because the worker, the citizen, the taxpayer, the motorist are each subject to a separate set of regulations – technical, administrative, legal, political. The men who direct these organizations, who preside over these apparatuses, are inevitably different. On the basis of these facts, the diversity of power groups is the first relevant datum, the relations among these upper strata have a specific character in each regime. The Western regimes tolerate dialogue among these groups, the Soviet regimes confer a party and authority monopoly on a party and an ideology. The separation between society and State is reduced, the competition among the power groups attenuated.

All modern societies basically accept as a fundamental premise the political equality of individuals. Thus they all have as their base, democratic legitimacy. At the political summit, however, they may possess either a single party and state ideology, or multiple parties and incessant debates. Between the legitimacy base and the political summit are interposed, firstly the social groups, each defined by participation in the processes of production, a level and style of life, manner of thinking and systems of values. The relations among these groups differ according to the attitudes that the masses and the rulers adopt toward one another. The relations between union leaders and businessmen are determined in the

West by the policies of the regime (which authorizes free negotiation), by the state of mind of the masses, and by the ideological conceptions of the leaders of the masses and the managers of the economy. In the East these relations are determined more by the regime which forbids open conflict or the advocacy of opposing interests, than by the feelings of the masses although under certain limited circumstances, these may influence union leaders, and even State officials. In other words, the intermediate zone of relations among groups can only be understood by reference to given socio-economic facts and to the political regime because the government determines the structure of the leading groups and the awareness that the social groups have or do not have of themselves.

The diversity of leading strata is inseparable from the nature of modern societies, but these strata may constitute a ruling class when they are made such in a single party system or when, in a competitive party system, they preserve the sense of a common interest in the regime and in the State, when they continue to be recruited for the most part from a narrow and, as it were, an aristocratic group. The two notions of leading strata and of ruling class can and ought to be used in scientific analyses without an ideological intention. In the eyes of certain people, they pass as politically oriented, but this is

wrong. It is true that such concepts "unmask" the mythical confusion of the proletariat with the ruling class of the Soviet societies, and the hypothetical confusion of economic and political power in democratic societies. But they also unmask the *naiveté* of democratic ideology, *a la* Lincoln, "by the people and for the people." Otherwise the concepts do not settle the real problems in the East and West, of the agreement or divorce between the sentiments and interests of the large number on the one hand, and the action of the dominant minorities on the other. One may still argue that a ruling class, unified by the discipline of a party, is more efficient for the welfare of a society than is free competition among minorities.

Finally, is it the fault of sociology if one regime gives an interpretation of itself which is much farther removed from reality than the interpretation which the other regimes prefer to give of themselves? The sociologist is not making a politically determined judgement if his investigations force him to conclude that the political "myth" of one system is much more "mythical" or unrealistic than is that of the other. To have value-free scholarship does not require findings which are similar in their political consequences for every political or social system.

"Power Elite" or "Veto Groups"?

William Kornhauser

RECENTLY TWO BOOKS appeared purporting to describe the structure of power in present-day America. They reached opposite conclusions: where C. Wright Mills found a "power elite," David Riesman found "veto groups." Both books have enjoyed a wide response, which has tended to divide along ideological lines. *The Power Elite* has been most favorably received by radical intellectuals, while *The Lonely Crowd* has found its main response among liberals. Mills and Riesman have not been oblivious to their differences. Mills is quite explicit on the matter: Riesman is a "romantic pluralist" who refuses to see the forest of American power inequalities from the trees of short-run and

discrete balances of power among diverse groups.[1] Riesman has been less explicitly polemical, but he might have had Mills in mind when he spoke of those intellectuals "who feel themselves very much out of power and who are frightened of those who they think have the power," and who "prefer to be scared by the power structures they conjure up than to face the possibility that the power structure they believe exists has largely evaporated."[2]

I wish to intervene in this controversy just long enough to do two things: *1)* locate as precisely as possible the issues upon which Riesman and Mills disagree; and *2)* formulate certain underlying problems in the analysis of power which have to be considered before such specific disagreements as those between Riesman and Mills can profitably be resolved.

[1] C. Wright Mills, *The Power Elite* (New York: Oxford University Press, 1956); p. 244.

[2] David Riesman, *The Lonely Crowd* (New York: Doubleday Anchor Edition, 1953); pp. 257–258.

This is a slightly revised version of an essay that appears in S. M. Lipset and Leo Lowenthal, eds., *Culture and Social Character* (N.Y.: Free Press of Glencoe, 1961).

I

We may compare Mills and Riesman on power in America along five dimensions:

1) structure of power: how power is distributed among the major segments of present-day American society;

2) changes in the structure of power: how the distribution of power has changed in the course of American history;

3) operation of the structure of power: the means whereby power is exercised in American society;

4) bases of the structure of power: how social and psychological factors shape and sustain the existing distribution of power;

5) consequences of the structure of power: how the existing distribution of power affects American society.

1) STRUCTURE OF POWER

It is symptomatic of their underlying differences that Mills entitles his major consideration of power simply "the power elite," whereas Riesman has entitled one of his discussions "Who has the power?" Mills is quite certain about the location of power, and so indicates by the assertive form of his title. Riesman perceives a much more amorphous and indeterminate power situation, and conveys this view in the interrogative form of his title. These contrasting images of American power may be diagrammed as two different pyramids of power. Mills' pyramid of power contains three levels:

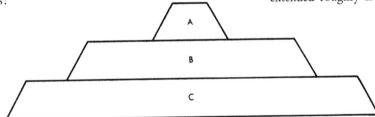

The apex of the pyramid ("A") is the "power elite": a unified power group composed of the top government executives, military officials, and corporation directors. The second level ("B") comprises the "middle levels of power": a diversified and balanced plurality of interest groups, perhaps most visibly at work in the halls of Congress. The third level ("C") is the "mass society": the powerless mass of unorganized and atomized people who are controlled from above. Riesman's pyramid of power contains only two major levels:

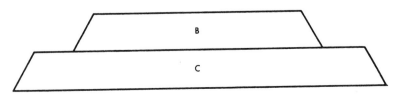

The two levels roughly correspond to Mills' second and third levels, and have been labeled accordingly. The obvious difference between the two pyramids is the presence of a peak in the one case and its absence in the other. Riesman sees no "power elite," in the sense of a single unified power group at the top of the structure, and this in the simplest terms contrasts his image of power in America with that of Mills. The upper level of Riesman's pyramid ("B") consists of "veto groups": a diversified and balanced plurality of interest groups, each of which is primarily concerned with protecting its jurisdiction by blocking actions of other groups which seem to threaten that jurisdiction. There is no decisive ruling group here, but rather an amorphous structure of power centering in the interplay among interest groups. The lower level of the pyramid ("C") comprises the more or less unorganized public, which is sought as an ally (rather than dominated) by the interest groups in their maneuvers against actual or threatened encroachments on the jurisdiction each claims for itself.

2) CHANGES IN THE STRUCTURE OF POWER

Riesman and Mills agree that the American power structure has gone through four major epochs. They disagree on the present and prospective future in the following historical terms: Mills judges the present to represent a fifth epoch, whereas Riesman judges it to be a continuation of the fourth.

The first period, according to Mills and Riesman, extended roughly from the founding of the republic to the Jacksonian era. During this period, Riesman believes America possessed a clearly demarcated ruling group, composed of a "landed-gentry and mercantilist-money leadership."[1] According to Mills, "the important fact about these early days is that social life, economic institutions, military establishment, and political order coincided, and men who were high politicians also played key roles in the economy and with their families, were among those of the reputable who made up local society."[2]

[1] *Ibid.*, p. 239.
[2] *Power Elite*, p. 270.

The second period extended roughly from the decline of Federalist leadership to the Civil War. During this period power became more widely dispersed, and it was no longer possible to identify a sharply defined ruling group. "In this society," Mills writes, "the 'elite' became a plurality of top groups, each in turn quite loosely made up."[1] Riesman notes that farmers and artisan groups became influential, and "occasionally, as with Jackson, moved into a more positive command."[2]

The third period began after the Civil War and extended through McKinley's administration in Riesman's view,[3] and until the New Deal according to Mills.[4] They agree that the era of McKinley marked the high point of the unilateral supremacy of corporate economic power. During this period, power once more became concentrated, but unlike the Federalist period and also unlike subsequent periods, the higher circles of economic institutions were dominant.

The fourth period took definite shape in the 1930's. In Riesman's view this period marked the ascendancy of the "veto groups," and rule by coalitions rather than by a unified power group. Mills judges it to have been so only in the early and middle Roosevelt administrations: "In these years, the New Deal as a system of power was essentially a balance of pressure groups and interest blocs."[5]

Up to World War II, then, Mills and Riesman view the historical development of power relations in America along strikingly similar lines. Their sharply contrasting portrayal of present-day American power relations begins with their diverging assessments of the period beginning about 1940. Mills envisions World War II and its aftermath as marking a new era in American power relations. With war as the major problem, there arises a new power group composed of corporate, governmental, and military directors.

> The formation of the power elite, as we may now know it, occurred during World War II and its aftermath. In the course of the organization of the nation for that war, and the consequent stabilization of the war-like posture, certain types of man have been selected and formed, and in the course of these institutional and psychological developments, new opportunities and intentions have arisen among them.[6]

Where Mills sees the ascendancy of a power elite, Riesman sees the opposite tendency toward the dispersal of power among a plurality of organized interests:

There has been in the last fifty years a change in the configuration of power in America, in which a single hierarchy with a ruling class at its head has been replaced by a number of "veto groups" among which power is dispersed (239). The shifting nature of the lobby provides us with an important clue as to the difference between the present American political scene and that of the age of McKinley. The ruling class of businessmen could relatively easily (though perhaps mistakenly) decide where their interests lay and what editors, lawyers, and legislators might be paid to advance them. The lobby ministered to the clear leadership, privilege, and imperative of the business ruling class. Today we have substituted for that leadership a series of groups, each of which has struggled for and finally attained a power to stop things conceivably inimical to its interests and, within far narrower limits, to start things.[7]

We may conclude that both Mills and Riesman view the current scene as constituting an important break with the past; but where one finds a hitherto unknown *concentration* of power, the other finds an emerging *indeterminacy* of power.

3) OPERATION OF THE STRUCTURE OF POWER

Mills believes the power elite sets all important public policies, especially foreign policy. Riesman, on the other hand, does not believe that the same group or coalition of groups sets all major policies, but rather that the question of who exercises power varies with the issue at stake: most groups are inoperative on most issues, and all groups are operative primarily on those issues which vitally impinge on their central interests. This is to say that there are as many power structures as there are distinct spheres of policy.[8]

As to the modes of operation, both Mills and Riesman point to increasing *manipulation* rather than command or persuasion as the favored form of power play. Mills emphasizes the secrecy behind which important policy-determination occurs. Riesman stresses not so much manipulation under the guise of secrecy as manipulation under the guise of mutual tolerance for one another's interests and beliefs. Manipulation occurs, according to Riesman, because each group is trying to hide its concern with power in order not to antagonize other groups. Power relations tend to take the form of "monopolistic competition", "rules of fairness and fellowship [rather than the impersonal forces of competition] dictate how far one can go."[9] Thus both believe the play of power takes place to a considerable extent backstage; but Mills judges this power play to be under the direction of one group, while Riesman sees it as controlled by a mood and structure of accommodation among many groups.

Mills maintains that the mass media of communication are important instruments of manipulation: the

---

[1] *Power Elite*, p. 270.   [2] *Lonely Crowd*, p. 240.
[3] *Ibid.*, p. 240.   [4] *Power Elite*, p. 271.
[5] *Ibid.*, p. 273.
[6] C. Wright Mills, "The Power Elite," in Arthur Kornhauser (ed.), *Problems of Power in American Society* (Detroit: Wayne University Press, 1958), p. 161.
[7] *Lonely Crowd*, pp. 246–247.
[8] *Ibid.*, p. 256.   [9] *Ibid.*, p. 247.

media lull people to sleep, so to speak, by suppressing political topics and by emphasizing entertainment. Riesman alleges that the mass media give more attention to politics and problems of public policy than their audiences actually want, and thereby convey the false impression that there is more interest in public affairs than really exists in America at the present time. Where Mills judges the mass media of communication to be powerful political instruments in American society,[1] Riesman argues that they have relatively less significance in this respect.[2]

4) BASES OF THE STRUCTURE OF POWER

Power tends to be patterned according to the structure of interests in a society. Power is shared among those whose interests converge, and divides along lines where interests diverge. To Mills, the power elite is a reflection and solidification of a *coincidence of interests* among the ascendant institutional orders. The power elite rests on the "many interconnections and points of coinciding interests" of the corporations, political institutions, and military services.[3] For Riesman, on the other hand, there is an amorphous power structure which reflects a *diversity of interests* among the major organized groups. The power structure of veto groups rests on the divergent interests of political parties, business groups, labor organizations, farm blocs, and a myriad of other organized groups.[4]

But power is not a simple reflex of interests alone. It also rests on the capabilities and opportunities for cooperation among those who have similar interests, and for confrontation among those with opposing interests. Mills argues in some detail that the power elite rests not merely on the coincidence of interests among major institutions but also on the "psychological similarity and social intermingling" of their higher circles.[5] By virtue of similar social origins (old family, upper-class background), religious affiliations (Episcopalian and Presbyterian), education (Ivy League college or military academy), and the like, those who head up the major institutions share codes and values as well as material interests. This makes for easy communication, especially when many of these people already know one another, or at least know many people in common. They share a common way of life, and therefore possess both the will and the opportunity to integrate their lines of action as representatives of key institutions. At times this integration involves "explicit co-ordination," as during war.[6] So much for the bases of power at the apex of the structure.

At the middle and lower levels of power, Mills emphasizes the lack of independence and concerted purpose among those who occupy similar social positions. In his book on the middle classes,[7] Mills purports to show the weakness of white-collar people that results from their lack of economic independence and political direction. The white-collar worker simply follows the more powerful group of the moment. In his book on labor leaders,[8] Mills locates the

alleged political impotence of organized labor in its dependence on government. Finally, the public is construed as composed of atomized and submissive individuals who are incapable of engaging in effective communication and political action.[9]

Riesman believes that power "is founded, in large measure, on interpersonal expectations and attitudes."[10] He asserts that in addition to the diversity of interest underlying the pattern of power in America there are widespread feelings of weakness and dependence at the top as well as at the bottom of the power structure: "if businessmen feel weak and dependent they do in actuality become weaker and more dependent, no matter what material resources may be ascribed to them."[11] In other words, the amorphousness of power in America rests in part on widespread feelings of weakness and dependence. These feelings are found among those whose position in the social structure provides resources which they could exploit, as well as among those whose position provides less access to the means of power. In fact, Riesman is concerned with showing that people at all levels of the social structure tend to feel weaker than their objective position warrants.

The theory of types of conformity that provides the foundation of so much of Riesman's writings enters into his analysis of power at this point. The "other-directed" orientation in culture and character helps to sustain the amorphousness of power.

The other-directed person in politics is the "inside-dopester," the person who possesses political competence but avoids political commitment. This is the dominant type in the veto groups, since other-direction is prevalent in the strata from which their leaders are drawn.

> Both within the [veto] groups and in the situation created by their presence, the political mood tends to become one of other-directed tolerance.[12]

However, Riesman does not make the basis of power solely psychological:

> This does not mean, however, that the veto groups are formed along the lines of character structure. As in a business corporation there is room for extreme inner-directed and other-directed types, and all mixtures between, so in a veto group there can exist complex "symbiotic" relationships among people of different political styles. . . . Despite these complications I think it fair to say that the veto groups, even when they are set up to protect a

[1] *Power Elite*, pp. 315–316. [2] *Lonely Crowd*, pp. 229–231.
[3] *Power Elite*, p. 19. [4] *Lonely Crowd*, p. 247.
[5] *Power Elite*, p. 19. [6] *Ibid.*, pp. 19–20.
[7] C. Wright Mills, *White Collar* (New York: Oxford University Press, 1951).
[8] C. Wright Mills, *The New Men of Power* (New York: Harcourt, Brace, 1948).
[9] *Power Elite*, 302 ff. [10] *Lonely Crowd*, p. 253.
[11] *Ibid.*, p. 253. [12] *Ibid.*, p. 248.

clearcut moralizing interest, are generally forced to adopt the political manners of the other-directed.[1]

Riesman and Mills agree that there is widespread apathy in American society, but they disagree on the social distribution of political apathy. Mills locates the apathetic primarily among the lower social strata, whereas Riesman finds extensive apathy among people of higher as well as lower status. Part of the difference may rest on what criteria of apathy are used. Mills conceives of apathy as the lack of political meaning in one's life, the failure to think of personal interests in political terms, so that what happens in politics does not appear to be related to personal troubles.[2] Riesman extends the notion of apathy to include the politically uninformed as well as the politically uncommitted.[3] Thus political indignation undisciplined by political understanding is not a genuine political orientation. Riesman judges political apathy to be an important *basis* for amorphous power relations. Mills, on the other hand, treats political apathy primarily as a *result* of the concentration of power.

5) CONSEQUENCES OF THE STRUCTURE OF POWER

Four parallel sets of consequences of the structure of power for American society may be inferred from the writings of Mills and Riesman. The first concerns the impact of the power structure on the interests of certain groups or classes in American society. Mills asserts that the existing power arrangements enhance the interests of the major institutions whose leaders constitute the power elite.[4] Riesman asserts the contrary: no one group or class is decisively favored over others by the cumulated decisions on public issues.[5]

The second set of consequences concerns the impact of the structure of power on the quality of politics in American society. Here Mills and Riesman are in closer agreement. Mills maintains that the concentration of power in a small circle, and the use of manipulation as the favored manner of exercising power, lead to the decline of politics as public debate. People are decreasingly capable of grasping political issues, and of relating them to personal interests.[6] Riesman also believes that politics has declined in meaning for large numbers of people. This is not due simply to the ascendancy of "veto groups," although they do foster "the tolerant mood of other-direction and hasten the retreat of the inner-directed indignants."[7] More important, the increasing complexity and remoteness of politics make political self-interest obscure and aggravate feelings of impotence even when self-interest is clear.[8]

The third set of consequences of the American power structure concerns its impact on the quality of power relations themselves. Mills contends that the concentration of power has taken place without a corresponding shift in the bases of legitimacy of power: power is still supposed to reside in the public and its elected representatives, whereas in reality it resides in the hands of those who direct the key bureaucracies. As a consequence, men of power are neither responsible nor accountable for their power.[9] Riesman also implies that there is a growing discrepancy between the facts of power and the images of power, but for a reason opposite to Mills': power is more widely dispersed than is generally believed.[10]

Finally, a fourth set of consequences concerns the impact of the power structure on democratic leadership. If power tends to be lodged in a small group which is not accountable for its power, and if politics no longer involves genuine public debate, then there will be a *severe weakening of democratic institutions*, if not of leadership (the power elite exercises leadership in one sense of the term in that it makes decisions on basic policy for the nation). Mills claims that power in America has become so concentrated that it increasingly resembles the Soviet system of power:

> Official commentators like to contrast the ascendancy in totalitarian countries of a tightly organized clique with the American system of power. Such comments, however, are easier to sustain if one compares mid-twentieth-century Russia with mid-nineteenth-century America, which is what is often done by Tocqueville, quoting Americans making the contrast. But that was an America of a century ago, and in the century that has passed, the American elite have not remained as patrioteer essayists have described them to us. The "loose cliques" now head institutions of a scale and power not then existing and, especially since World War I, the loose cliques have tightened up.[11]

If, on the other hand, power tends to be dispersed among groups which are primarily concerned to protect and defend their interests, rather than to advance general policies and their own leadership, and if at the same time politics has declined as a sphere of duty and self-interest, then there will be a *severe weakening of leadership*. Thus Riesman believes that "power in America seems to [be] situational and mercurial; it resists attempts to locate it."[12] This "indeterminacy and amorphousness" of power inhibits the development of leadership:

> Where the issue involves the country as a whole, no individual or group leadership is likely to be very effective, because the entrenched veto groups cannot be budged. . . . Veto groups exist as defense groups, not as leadership groups.[13]

---

[1] *Lonely Crowd*, p. 249.   [2] *White Collar*, p. 327.
[3] David Riesman and Nathan Glazer, "Criteria for Political Apathy," in Alvin W. Gouldner (ed.), *Studies in Leadership* (New York: Harper, 1950).
[4] *Power Elite*, 276 ff.   [5] *Lonely Crowd*, p. 257.
[6] *White Collar*, pp. 342–350.   [7] *Lonely Crowd*, p. 251.
[8] "Criteria for Political Apathy," p. 520.
[9] *Power Elite*, pp. 316–317.   [10] *Lonely Crowd*, pp. 257–258.
[11] *Power Elite*, p. 271.   [12] *Lonely Crowd*, p. 257.
[13] *Ibid.*, pp. 257, 248.

Yet Riesman does not claim that the decline of leadership directly threatens American democracy at least in the short run: the dispersion of power among a diversity of balancing "veto groups" operates to support democratic institutions even as it inhibits effective leadership. The long-run prospects of a leaderless democracy are of course not promising.

In the second part of this paper, I wish to raise certain critical questions about Riesman's and Mills' views of power. One set of questions seeks to probe more deeply the basic area of disagreement in their views. A second set of questions concerns their major areas of agreement.

than only its unequal distribution. He is especially eager to analyze common responses to power:

> If the leaders have lost the power, why have the led not gained it? What is there about the other-directed man and his life situation which prevents the transfer? In terms of situation, it seems that the pattern of monopolistic competition of the veto groups resists individual attempts at power aggrandizement. In terms of character, the other-directed man simply does not seek power; perhaps, rather, he avoids and evades it.[3]

Whereas Mills emphasizes the *differences* between

Two Portraits of the American Power Structure

Power structure	Mills	Riesman
Levels	a) unified power elite b) diversified and balanced plurality of interest groups c) mass of unorganized people who have no power over elite	a) no dominant power elite b) diversified and balanced plurality of interest groups c) mass of unorganized people who have some power over interest groups
Changes	a) increasing concentration of power	a) increasing dispersion of power
Operation	a) one group determines all major policies b) manipulation of people at the bottom by group at the top	a) who determines policy shifts with the issue b) monopolistic competition among organized groups
Bases	a) coincidence of interests among major institutions (economic, military, governmental) b) social similarities and psychological affinities among those who direct major institutions	a) diversity of interests among major organized groups b) sense of weakness and dependence among those in higher as well as lower status
Consequences	a) enhancement of interests of corporations, armed forces, and executive branch of government b) decline of politics as public debate c) decline of responsible and accountable power — loss of democracy	a) no one group or class is favored significantly over others b) decline of politics as duty and self-interest c) decline of effective leadership

Power usually is analyzed according to its distribution among the several units of a system. Most power analysts construe the structure of power as a *hierarchy* — a rank-order of units according to their amount of power. The assumption often is made that there is only one such structure, and that all units may be ranked vis-à-vis one another. Units higher in the hierarchy have power over units lower in the structure, so there is a one-way flow of power. Mills tends to adopt this approach to the structure of power.

Riesman rejects this conception of the power structure as mere hierarchy:

> The determination of who [has more power] has to be made all over again for our time: we cannot be satisfied with the answers given by Marx, Mosca, Michels, Pareto, Weber, Veblen, or Burnham.[1]

> The image of power in contemporary America presented [in the *Lonely Crowd*] departs from current discussions of power which are usually based on a search for a ruling class.[2]

Riesman is not just denying the existence of a power elite in contemporary American society; he is also affirming the need to consider other aspects of power

units according to their power, Riesman emphasizes their *similarities* in this respect. In the first view, some units are seen as dominated by other units, while in the second view, all units are seen as subject to constraints which shape and limit their use of power *in similar directions*.

The problem of power is not simply the differential capacity to make decisions, so that those who have power bind those who do not. Constraints also operate on those who are in decision-making positions, for if these are the places where acts of great consequence occur so are they the foci for social pressures. These pressures become translated into restrictions on the alternatives among which decision-makers can choose. Power may be meaningfully measured by ascertaining the range of alternatives which decision-makers can realistically consider. To identify those who make decisions is not to say how many lines of action are open to them, or how much freedom of choice they enjoy.

A major advance in the study of power is made by going beyond a formal conception of power, in which those who have the authority to make decisions are assumed to possess the effective means of power and the will to use it. Nor can it be assumed that those not in

---

[1] *Lonely Crowd*, p. 255.   [2] *Ibid.*, p. 260.   [3] *Ibid.*, p. 275.

authority lack the power to determine public policy. The identification of effective sources of power requires analysis of how *decision-makers are themselves subject to various kinds of constraint*. Major sources of constraint include *1)* opposing elites and publics, and *2)* cultural values and corresponding psychological receptivities and resistances to power. A comparison of Mills and Riesman with respect to these categories of constraint reveals the major area of disagreement between them.

Mills implies that both sources of constraint are inoperative on the highest levels of power. *1)* There is little opposition among the top power-holders. Since they are not in opposition they do not constrain one another. Instead, they are unified and mutually supportive. Furthermore, there are few publics to constrain the elite. Groups capable of effective participation in broad policy determination have been replaced by atomized masses that are powerless to affect policy since they lack the bases for association and communication. Instead, people in large numbers are manipulated through organizations and media controlled by the elite. *2)* Older values and codes no longer grip elites nor have they been replaced by new values and codes which could regulate the exercise of power. Top men of power are not constrained either by an inner moral sense or by feelings of dependence on others. The widespread permissiveness toward the use of expedient means to achieve success produces "the higher immorality," that is to say, the irresponsible exercise of power.

In sharp contrast to Mills, Riesman attaches great importance to constraints on decision-makers. *1)* There is a plethora of organized groups, "each of which has struggled for and finally attained a power to stop things conceivably inimical to its interests."[1] Furthermore, there is extensive opportunity for large numbers of people to influence elites, because the latter are constrained by their competitive relations with one another to bid for support in the electoral arena and more diffusely in the realm of public relations. *2)* The cultural emphasis on "mutual tolerance" and social conformity places a premium on "getting along" with others at the expense of taking strong stands. People are disposed to avoid long-term commitments as a result of their strong feelings of dependence on their immediate peers. "Other-directed" persons seek to maximize approval rather than power.

In general, the decisive consideration in respect to the restraint of power is the presence of multiple centers of power. Where there are many power groups, not only are they mutually constrained; they also are dependent on popular support, and therefore responsive to public demands. Now, there are many readily observable cases of regularized constraint among power groups in American society. Organized labor is one of many kinds of "countervailing power" in the market place.[2] In the political sphere, there is a strong two-party system and more or less stable factionalism within both parties, opposition among interest blocs in state and national legislatures, rivalry among executive agencies of government and the military services, and so forth.

Mills relegates these conflicting groups to the middle levels of power. Political parties and interest groups both inside and outside of government are not important units in the structure of power, according to Mills. It would seem that he takes this position primarily with an eye to the sphere of foreign policy, where only a few people finally make the big decisions. But he fails to put his argument to a decisive or meaningful test: he does not examine the pattern of decisions to show that foreign policy not only is made *by* a few people, but that it is made *for their particular interests*. Mills' major premise seems to be that all decisions are taken by and for special interests; there is no action oriented toward the general interests of the whole community. Furthermore, Mills seems to argue that because only a very few people occupy key decision-making *positions*, they are free to decide on whatever best suits their particular interests. But the degree of *autonomy* of decision-makers cannot be inferred from the *number* of decision-makers, nor from the *scope* of their decisions. It also is determined by the character of decision-making, especially *the dependence of decision-makers on certain kinds of procedure and support*.

Just as Mills is presenting a distorted image of power in America when he fails to consider the pressures on those in high positions, so Riesman presents a biased picture by not giving sufficient attention to *power differentials* among the various groups in society. When Riesman implies that if power is dispersed, then it must be relatively equal among groups and interests, with no points of concentration, he is making an unwarranted inference. The following statement conjures up an image of power in America that is as misleading on its side as anything Mills has written in defense of his idea of a power elite.

One might ask whether one would not find, over a long period of time, that decisions in America favored one group or class . . . over others. Does not wealth exert its pull in the long run? In the past this has been so; for the future I doubt it. The future seems to be in the hands of the small business and professional men who control Congress, such as realtors, lawyers, car salesmen, undertakers, and so on; of the military men who control defense and, in part, foreign policy; of the big business managers and their lawyers, finance-committee men, and other counselors who decide on plant investment and influence the rate of technological change; of the labor leaders who control worker productivity and worker votes; of the black belt whites who have the greatest stake in southern

---

[1] *Lonely Crowd*, p. 247.

[2] Riesman notes that "the concept of the veto groups is analogous to that of countervailing power developed in Galbraith's *American Capitalism*, although the latter is more sanguine is suggesting that excessive power tended to call forth its own limitation by opposing power . . ." (Riesman and Glazer, "The Lonely Crowd: A Reconsideration in 1960," in S. M. Lipset and Leo Lowenthal, editors, *Culture and Social Character*, N.Y.: The Free Press of Glencoe, 1961, p. 449).

politics; of the Poles, Italians, Jews, and Irishmen who have stakes in foreign policy, city jobs, and ethnic, religious and cultural organizations; of the editorializers and storytellers who help socialize the young, tease and train the adult, and amuse and annoy the aged; of the farmers — themselves a warring congeries of cattlemen, corn men, dairymen, cotton men, and so on — who control key departments and committees and who, as the living representatives of our inner-directed past, control many of our memories; of the Russians and, to a lesser degree, other foreign powers who control much of our agenda of attention; and so on.[1]

It appears that Riesman is asking us to believe that power differentials do not exist, but only differences in the spheres within which groups exercise control.

If Riesman greatly exaggerates the extent to which organized interests possess equal power, nevertheless he poses an important problem that Mills brushes aside. For Riesman goes beyond merely noting the existence of opposition among "veto groups" to suggest that they operate to smother one another's initiative and leadership. It is one thing for interest groups to constrain one another; it is something else again when they produce stalemate. Riesman has pointed to a critical problem for pluralist society: the danger that power may become fragmented among so many competing groups that effective general leadership cannot emerge.

On Mills' side, it is indisputable that American political institutions have undergone extensive centralization and bureaucratization. This is above all an *institutional* change wrought by the greatly expanded scale of events and decisions in the contemporary world. But centralization cannot be equated with a power elite! There can be highly centralized institutions and at the same time a fragmentation of power among a multiplicity of relatively independent public and private groups. Thus Riesman would appear to be correct that the substance of power resides in many large organizations, and that these organizations are not unified or co-ordinated in any firm fashion. If they were, surely Mills would have been able to identify the major mechanisms that could produce this result. That he has failed to do so is the most convincing evidence for their nonexistence.

To complete this analysis, we need only remind ourselves of the fundamental area of agreement between our two critics of American power relations. Both stress *the absence of effective political action* at all levels of the political order, in particular among the citizenry. For all of their differences, Mills and Riesman agree that there has been a decline in effective political participation, or at least a failure of political participation to measure up to the requirements of contemporary events and decisions. This failure has not been compensated by an increase in effective political action at the center: certainly Riesman's "veto groups" are not capable of defining and realizing the community's general aspirations; nor is Mills' "power elite" such a political agency.

Both are asserting the inadequacy of political institutions, including public opinion, party leadership, Congress, and the Presidency, even as they see the slippage of power in different directions. In consequence, neither is sanguine about the capacity of the American political system to provide responsible leadership, especially in international affairs.

If there is truth in this indictment, it also may have its source in the very images of power that pervade Mills' and Riesman's thought. They are both inclined toward a negative response to power; and neither shows a willingness to confront the idea of a political system and the ends of power in it. Riesman reflects the liberal suspicion of power, as when he writes "we have come to realize that men who compete primarily for wealth are relatively harmless as compared with men who compete primarily for power." That such assertions as this may very well be true is beside the point. For certainly negative consequences of power can subsist along with positive ones. At times Riesman seems to recognize the need for people to seek and use power if they as individuals and the society as a whole are to develop to the fullest of their capacities. But his dominant orientation towards power remains highly individualistic and negative.

Mills is more extreme than Riesman on this matter, as he never asks what the community requires in the way of resources of power and uses of power. He is instead preoccupied with the magnitude of those resources and the allegedly destructive expropriation of them by and for the higher circles of major institutions. It is a very limited notion of power that construes it only in terms of coercion and conflict among particular interests. Societies require arrangements whereby resources of power can be effectively used and supplemented for public goals. This is a requirement for government, but the use of this term should not obscure the fact that government possesses power — or lacks effectiveness. Mills does not concern himself with the *ends* of power, nor with the conditions for their attainment. He has no conception of the bases of political order, and no theory of the functions of government and politics. He suggests nothing that could prevent his "power elite" from developing into a full-blown totalitarianism. The logic of Mills' position finally reduces to a contest between anarchy and tyranny.[2]

[1] *The Lonely Crowd*, p. 257.

[2] Mills' narrow conception of power has been discussed by Talcott Parsons in his review of *The Power Elite* [Talcott Parsons, "The Distribution of Power in American Society," *World Politics*, X (October, 1957), 123–143]. Parsons notes that Mills uses a "zero-sum" notion, in that power is interpreted exclusively as a fixed quantity which is more or less unequally distributed among the various units in society. Power, however, also has a more general reference, to the political community as a whole, and to government as the agency of the total community. Viewed from this standpoint, power is a function of the integration of the community and serves general interests. Parsons argues, I think correctly, that Mills' sole concern for how power is used by some against others is associated with his tendency to exaggerate both the weight and the illegitimacy of power in the determination of social events.

The problem of power seems to bring out the clinician in each of us. We quickly fasten on the pathology of power, whether we label the symptoms as "inside-dopesterism" (Riesman) or as "the higher immorality" (Mills). As a result, we often lose sight of the ends of power in the political system under review. It is important to understand that pivotal decisions increasingly are made at the national level, and that this poses genuine difficulties for the maintenance of democratic control. It is also important to understand that a multiplicity of relatively autonomous public and private agencies increasingly pressure decision-makers, and that this poses genuine difficulties for the maintenance of effective political leadership. But the fact remains that there are many cases of increasingly centralized decision-making

and democratic control, and of multiple constraints on power *and* effective leadership. There is no simple relationship between the extent to which power is equally distributed and the efficacy of democratic order. For a modern democratic society requires strong government as well as a dispersal of power among diverse groups. Unless current tendencies are measured against both sets of needs, there will be little progress in understanding how either one is frustrated or fulfilled. Finally, in the absence of more disciplined historical and comparative research, we shall continue to lack a solid empirical basis for evaluating such widely divergent diagnoses of political malaise as those given us by Mills and Riesman.

Power in Local Communities

William Spinrad

SINCE Floyd Hunter published his study of "Regional City" about a decade ago, many social scientists have devoted their attention to the study of community power.[1] Whatever comments we will make on some of the specific material, we would initially like to welcome this trend in the allocation of the professional resources of the social science fraternity. Particularly in the area of community research, this had been a relatively neglected subject, with the conspicuous exception of the Lynds' monumental study of Middletown.[2] The detailed cataloguing of the status structure was too often the dominant, in fact sometimes the only, theme. Longing for a simple stratification model in which everyone fits, more or less, into an obviously assignable place, the students of American communities tended to avoid the more complicated task of striving to learn "who got things done," why and how. It was, therefore, especially pleasing to read that in the old New England city of New Haven very few of the "social notables," the members of status-exclusive clubs, had any crucial role

in the community decision-making process under review.[3]

The efforts at community power analysis have been many, the findings plentiful, the interpretations challenging. But, despite several suggestive attempts, thorough systematization is still wanting; the relation between the "power variable" and the entire community social structure is barely sketched. Let this preliminary appraisal not be misconstrued. The critique which follows is prefaced not only with praise for a worthwhile direction of social scientific inquiry but an appreciation of the valuable material that already exists. It is offered as a modest set of directives for future work in the area.

Several recently published volumes provide a springboard for an excursion into the field. An elaborate compendium of existing data on "public leadership" by Bell, Hill, and Wright offers little assistance to those who seek a comprehensive organization of ideas on the subject.[4] Marshalling a vast array of information, it initially classifies the methods by which leadership is located. The categories listed are: formal position, reputation, degree of social participation, opinion leadership, and role in specific decisions or events. The probability that each type will be drawn from particular demographic groups — sex, age, race, nationality, religion, social class, etc. — is assessed on the basis of reported investigations. Finally, the authors present the various findings on public attitudes towards leadership and motivations for leadership. As a catalogue of source

[1] Floyd Hunter, *Community Power Structure: A Study of Decision Makers*, Chapel Hill: The University of North Carolina Press, 1953.

[2] Robert S. Lynd and Helen M. Lynd, *Middletown in Transition*, New York: Harcourt, Brace, 1957.

[3] Robert Dahl, *Who Governs? Democracy and Power in an American City*, New Haven and London: Yale University Press, 1961, pp. 63–69.

[4] Wendell Bell, Charles J. Hill, Charles R. Wright, *Public Leadership*, San Francisco: Chandler Publishing Co., 1961.

Reprinted from *Social Problems*, V. 12 (Winter, 1965), pp. 335–356, by permission of the author and the publisher.

material, the book can serve a useful purpose. But no attempt is made to organize or interpret the information. There are thus no summary statements, no attempts to develop models, no formulated clues to assist further discussions about community power. And these are precisely what are needed.

This brief consideration of the volume includes one additional caution. In its formulations, "public leadership" becomes a gross, diffuse concept. The "opinion leader," for instance, can hardly be equated with the other categories. Directed towards locating interpersonal communication networks, one general conclusion from opinion leadership research is that many, many people influence some others on some questions.[1] Such inquiries, valuable in their own sphere, scarcely provide any insight into community "power".

A meaningful organization of the field would be a posing of the major contending analyses. This, in essence, is the function of a symposium entitled *Power and Democracy in America.*[2] Despite its rather grandiose title and the variety of subjects considered by the major contributors and the editors, the core of the book is the debate between two students of community power, Delbert Miller and Robert Dahl. Utilizing their own researches and other relevant material, the two scholars generally represent and expound the two opposite sides of the methodological and analytical conflict that has characterized recent community power discussion. Miller favors the "reputational" form of investigation and finds a pyramidal, quasi-monolithic structure dominated by a "business elite" more or less typical. He is thus quite in accord with the findings of Hunter's original study. Dahl, utilizing "event analysis," searches for evidence of specific decision makers on particular issues, and concludes that a relatively pluralistic power structure is more prevalent. Of course, the divergencies are more complex and detailed, but these are the summary statements around which the discussion evolves.

The reputational technique, which has, with many variations, become fairly widespread in use, seeks to get knowledgeable informants to select, from a list of leading figures in community organizations and institutional areas, those whom they considered most powerful in "getting things done." Those chosen were then interviewed to learn about the personal and social relations among them, and which people they would themselves solicit if they wanted something adopted or achieved. Reviewing many studies with this research emphasis, including his own "Pacific City," Miller's conclusions are, essentially, the following:[3]

1) Businessmen are overrepresented among "key influentials" and dominate community policy-making in most communities.[4]

2) Local governments are weak power centers. The elected officials are mostly small businessmen, local lawyers, and professional politicians. Policy on important questions is formulated by organized interests groups under the influence of the economic dominants. City councils merely respond to their pressures.

3) Representatives of labor, education, religious, and "cultural" groups are rarely key influentials, are underrepresented in city councils.

4) In vivid contrast, Miller reports his investigations of "English City," like "Pacific City" a seaport community of about 500,000 population. Businessmen constitute only a minority of the "key influentials." Labor is significantly represented. There is also an appreciable number from educational, religious, welfare, and "status" leaderships. Furthermore, the city council is the major arena of community decision making, the party organizations the directing groups.

Noting differences between "Regional City" and "Pacific City," Miller does not insist that the power pattern is identical in all American communities. In fact, he develops a typology of possible structures which will be later considered. But the modal type is clearly sketched, particularly in contrast with the findings of his British study.

Dahl's counter propositions are based primarily on his study of New Haven, summarized in the symposium and more fully elaborated in his book *Who Governs?*[5] The power structure of New Haven is seen as relatively pluralistic or, to use his terminology, one of "dispersed inequalities," a metamorphosis from earlier days of oligarchal dominance by "aristocratic patricians" and "entrepreneurs" successively. This is initially indicated in the change in political leadership with the rise of the "ex plebeians" from various ethnic groups, often with proletarian backgrounds. The attention is, however, more to the examination of decision-leadership in three issue areas — political nominations, public education, and urban redevelopment, which Dahl insists are both representative and salient. The method in such "event analysis" is typically one of chronological narration of who did what, when, and what effect it had, in this instance supplemented by a more precise systematic tabulation of the kinds of people who held formal positions in the organizations concerned with the above issues and of those who initiated or vetoed significant decisions.

The refutation of the business dominance thesis is quite explicit. Some two hundred "economic notables" were located. Within the issue-areas studied, a significant number occupied formal positions only in connection with urban redevelopment (about fifty), of which seven were actually considered decision leaders. None were formally involved in public education, a handful in political parties.

[1] See Elihu Katz, "The Two-Step Flow of Communication: An Up-To-Date Report of an Hypothesis," *Public Opinion Quarterly,* 21 (Spring, 1957), pp. 61–78.

[2] *Power and Democracy in America,* edited by William V. D'Antonio and Howard J. Ehrlich, Notre Dame, Indiana: University of Notre Dame Press, 1961.

[3] Actually, the major bulwarks for his thesis are his own and Hunter's research, plus a series of inquiries by Charles Loomis and his associates in Southwestern United States for which no published citations are given. The other references offered actually reveal much more complex patterns. See *Ibid.,* pp. 38–71.

[4] *Ibid.,* p. 61.   [5] Dahl, *op. cit.*

Even within the area of urban redevelopment, the decision-making role of businessmen was considered minor. Their contributions came largely through their participation in the "Citizens Action Committee," organized by the Mayor with the objective of legitimizing decisions and providing an arena in which objections to the program could be anticipated and avoided. Neither the Committee, nor individual businessmen or business groups, were responsible for many crucial decisions. Dahl believes that they could, if vigorously in opposition, have blocked proposals, but the political officials, led by the Mayor, prevented such contingencies by a "capacity for judging with considerable precision what the existing beliefs and the commitments of the men on the CAC would compel them to agree to if a proposal were presented in the proper way, time, and place."[1] In general, business groups possess many "resources," but they are also limited by many power "liabilities," so that they simply appeared as "one of the groups out of which individuals sporadically emerge to influence the policies and acts of city officials."[2] "Like other groups in the community, from the Negroes on Dixwell Avenue to teachers in the public school, sometimes the Notables have their way and sometimes they do not."[3]

In the decision areas studied, the "inequalities" are not so widely "dispersed." Only a few people make the key decisions in each issue area, but they achieve their hegemony by accepting the indirect influence of larger groups. Nominations are generally determined by a few party leaders, but with attention to the wishes of their followers within the party organizations, especially sub-leaders and representatives of ethnic groups. Most important redevelopment decisions were made by the Mayor and appropriate staff officials, with full sensitivity to the need for getting support from business and other groups. Major public education policy was directed by the Mayor and his appointees on the Board of Education; superintendents, principals, and teachers' organizations played some part, but mostly to mobilize support for public education. A few public and party officials thus constituted the directing leadership, each in his own province, with the office and personality of the dynamic Mayor, Richard Lee, supplying the unifying force. We have advisedly called the leading group a "directing" rather than a "dominating" oligarchy. It apparently got its way less from authority or influence, in the communication sense, than from the ability to please others, particularly potentially opposing groups. In fact, the political leaders favored the existence of organized groups as a means of legitimizing their decisions and mobilizing support, as well as providing an arena where various sentiments could be expressed and somewhat satisfied. The Citizens Action Committee in the urban

redevelopment field was one such example. Similarly, school principals and the Board of Education utilized PTAs "to head off or settle conflicts between parents and the school system."[4]

Dahl does not maintain that the New Haven pattern he describes is the only one possible or existent. Like Miller, he offers a model of power types which will be later discussed. But the New Haven analysis provides the basic elements around which most of the varied forms are structured.

The dispute between the two major contending approaches to American community power is thus, more or less, joined. Partly methodological, it is, at least initially, a disagreement between a business-elite dominance thesis and an acceptance of a relative pluralism. It is also a disagreement about the role of local government and political leadership. Dahl believes that mayors and their staff have increasingly become the initiators and organizers of important community decisions. Miller insists that the political leaders are uncertain about themselves and wait for the cues of others, while businessmen have a clearly defined image "and thus act with more assertion."[5]

A third recent volume further helps locate the principal disputes on the subject. Edward Banfield's *Political Influence*, utilizing event analysis, narrates, with a detailed chronology, how decisions involving six very specific community problems were arrived at or, in most cases, blocked or compromised.[6] In all cases, there was a divided opinion around significant forces and individuals. The actual list of issues should be of some interest: proposals for extending a particular hospital's facilities, reorganization of welfare administration, a state subsidy for the Chicago Transit Authority, a plan for a vast business center, the creation of a large Chicago branch of the University of Illinois, the building of an extensive Exhibition Hall. At the time of publication, only the last had been achieved. The welfare reorganization plans had produced a compromise; in all other cases, the contending elements had forced a general stalemate.

Banfield's accounts are in the nature of the best type of scholarly journalistic history. They contain extensive details, but little systematic treatment. However, his interpretations are organized around several summary ideas. Initially, he does not discount the possibility of business dominance. In essence, he believes that the resources of the leading Chicago businessmen, representing the top officials of leading national corporations and prominent regional commercial and banking institutions, offer an apparently unlimited power potential. Yet, he insists that, in his investigations, the "richest men in Chicago are conspicuous by their absence."[7] In fact, "big businessmen are criticized less for interfering in public affairs than for 'failing to assume their civic responsibilities.' "[8]

Businessmen do not dominate community decisions because of lack of unity, lack of interest, and because of the "costs" of intervening on any issue, including the

[1] Dahl, *op. cit.*, p. 137.   [2] *Ibid.*, p. 72.
[3] *Ibid.*, p. 75.   [4] *Ibid.*, p. 156.
[5] D'Antonio and Ehrlich, *op. cit.*, p. 136.
[6] Edward C. Banfield, *Political Influence*, New York: The Free Press of Glencoe, 1961.
[7] *Ibid.*, p. 288.   [8] *Ibid.*, p. 287.

encouragement of counter pressures. Their vital interests are not at stake and they are relatively satisfied with what is done. When their interests are more aroused, either because of some visible economic stake or because of personal predilections, particular business organizations may become heavily involved and be very influential. For instance, the disputed Exhibition Hall was built because it was a pet project of Colonel Robert McCormack and his successors on the Chicago *Tribune*. But, usually businessmen are only casually concerned or on all sides of most of the questions studied.

Typically, the most influential people in the community-decision making in Chicago are: "the managers of large organizations, the maintenance of which is at stake, a few 'civic leaders' whose judgment, negotiating skill, and disinterestedness are unusual and above all, the chief elected officials."[1] The organizations referred to are specified as those supported by "customers" rather than "members."[2] They may be profit-making businesses, public agencies which give free services, or public and semi-public agencies which sell services. In most cases, the involved organizations are public and the executives are civil servants, though Banfield describes them as "fighting politicians" rather than "bureaucrats."[3]

However, the most influential leaders in this megalopolis, as in the medium-sized city of New Haven, are the elected political officials, especially the Mayor. Banfield is thus on the side of Dahl against Miller. But, the leadership of Mayor Richard Daley, so frequently bracketed with Mayor Lee of New Haven as one of the "strong" mayors of our times, appears to be less forceful. Though both chief executive and official leader of the powerful Democratic machine, he is faced with many limitations on the exercise of power, even within the political realm. He needs the cooperation of other elected officials, "irregulars" within his own party, elected officials of the other party (especially the Republican Governor in the period under study). He may be, and in this study actually was, blocked by the courts. Voters may veto proposals, as on a bond referendum, and, of course, the possibility of electoral opposition in the next election must always be considered. Above all the Mayor and his associates, like anyone who seeks to wield power in specific situations, has limited resources of "working capital." These cannot be "used up" for every challenge that arises.

Like the business dominants, Banfield seems to consider the political leaders as potentially omnipotent when they go "all out" on any question. But this would require depleting their limited working capital. They have to contend with other power groups besides those mentioned – national government in some cases, businessmen, other strong community elements that may be affected or aroused. They are, therefore, in practice, slow to take up issues and seek compromises. The initiative on most questions thus comes from the maintenance and enhancement needs of the type of formal organization listed. Other organizations may

then support, oppose, or strive for modification. The following are some examples: A hospital tries to expand. Another hospital, for its own reasons, opposes. The *Tribune* wants an Exhibition Hall, the owners of another Hall oppose. The state, city, and county Welfare Departments have varying positions on reorganization plans. Attempts are made to line up different elements of the "public" on each side. The political leaders may then adjudicate or support one side or the other, but rarely with all their resources.

The varying positions of Miller, Dahl, and Banfield have been presented in some detail not so much to assess their ideas and their work at this juncture, but because their combined efforts do suggest the kinds of questions that have to be probed. These include the following:

1) Of what does community power consist and how does one locate it? This involves the general question of methodology.

2) Who attempts to wield power in which situation? Power motivation is generally ignored by Miller, is of great importance to Dahl and Banfield.

3) How are important community decisions made? Miller appears to see most community-relevant decisions as a simple reflection of the values and efforts of the business elite and its subordinates. Dahl and Banfield pay attention to the motivation, resources and tactics of specific groups and individuals.

4) What is the power position of particular groups? Emphasis has been on business and local government.

5) What is the prevailing power picture in the community? Corollary questions include the relation between power and other features of particular communities. Comparisons among communities is thus an inherent element of such analyses.

The remainder of this discussion is an attempt to elaborate and, to some extent, answer those questions, utilizing the material already reviewed as well as those of other students in the area. Our formulations are, of course, very tentative; we hope, in any case, that they can be guides for those looking for more complete answers, either in the research already undertaken or in the subsequent investigation which, we hope, is forthcoming.

Orientation and methodology: What is community power and how is it located?

What is community power? Initially, the term "community power" demands clarification. Appending the concept of "influence," which is, more or less, assumed to be synonymous, adds to the confusion. The traditional theoretical emphasis, summarized in Weber's formula – "the chance of a man or of a number of men to realize their own will in a communal action even against the resistance of others who are participating in the action" – is generally irrelevant to most discussions

[1] *Political Influence*, p. 288.   [2] *Ibid.*, p. 265.
[3] *Ibid.*, p. 266.

of American community power.[1] The orientation actually utilized is more in line with Bertrand Russell's description of power as "the production of intended effects."[2] Investigations have concentrated on the ability to and/or the practice of deciding what is to be done in, for, by the community. Power over people is thus an implicit, but rarely explicit, feature of the investigations. Furthermore, a "Machiavellian" model of power, which depicts individual power maintenance and enhancement as ends in themselves, must yield to approaches which seek to relate the exercise of power to other interests and values. Similarly, the long list of descriptions of types of power, bases of power, mechanisms of power, the distinctions among "power," "authority," "social control," et al., seem operationally outside the scope of the literature on American community power analysis.[3]

In essence, the focus is characteristically on community decisions, actual or potential, even if the methodology is "reputational." The basic question becomes who has more to say, or can have more to say, about things which are important to many people in the community. This is one of the reasons why such dissections of local power operations should be distinguished from those of the larger society, as exemplified by the nation.[4] There may be similarities between the city and the nation which can at times provide appropriate illustrations from one to develop some contentions about the other. Perhaps an ultimate comprehensive model would fit community power analysis into a more general framework of "power

in society." But, at present, it is best to stay in one's own domain. An inventory of research on communities does not furnish a ready appraisal of "Power and Democracy in America."

The extrapolation of the findings from local community studies to the national picture, as in the attempt of some of the contributors to the above-named volume, represents a casual reductionism, a view of the operations of the great society and the smaller units as, a priori, identical — a common enough fallacy in American social science. As an example, the Hunter-Miller research has frequently been interpreted as lending support to C. Wright Mills' "power elite" thesis.[5] Whatever the validity of each and their superficial similarities, the respective formulations are quite different, partially because they deal with different orders of phenomena. Mills postulates a triumvirate of national elites — business, political, and military — with co-ordinated aims and interchangeable personnel. He does not depict business "dominance" over other groups with different power motivations, but a composite grouping with similar interests. When there is conflict, the elite thesis may not hold, but he believes that the realities of American society, in toto, relegate such conflicts to "middle-range" decisions. On the local level, there is no pressing need for such coordination; all decisions there tend, in his approach, to be middle-range. In fact, those investigated in community studies appear quite minor, in terms of the future of society. If Mills' contentions were accurate, they would thus be quite compatible with any community power analysis yet offered.[6]

Methodology   The variations in the findings are often, but not always, correlated with the method of inquiry — *reputation* vs. *event* analysis. A more obvious set of criteria, *formal position*, has been attempted and rejected. One study disclosed that the economic and political "office holders" were not typically community leaders by reputation.[7] Another revealed that the formal leaders were not directly involved in decision-making.[8] Research-wise, these conclusions may be pertinent, but they are subject to further probing as analytical interpretations, as later discussed.

Both of the major approaches have obvious virtues and defects, as apparent in their application. The "reputation" material is relatively codifiable and systematic, allows for ready replication and comparison. The criticisms are also obvious and often enough noted: the arbitrary choice of informants which can initially bias the findings, the "circularity" of the interviews (influentials talking about "influentials"), the acquired information suggesting "power potential" rather than "power utilization," the vagueness of the question wording, the possibility that the informant's observations may reflect folklore rather than knowledge, the possibility that "status" is automatically identified with power.[9] The tone is frequently a kind of groping inside-dopester exposé rather than a depiction of the institutional complexities of the contemporary American community.

[1] From *Max Weber: Essays in Sociology*, translated, edited, and with an introduction by H. H. Gerth and C. Wright Mills, New York: Oxford University Press, Galaxy Book, 1958, p. 180.

[2] Bertrand Russell, *Power: A New Social Analysis*, London: Unwin Books, 1962, p. 25.

[3] Game models of decision-making, which pose analogies of combatants striving to win out over each other, are apparently as inapplicable as other orientations which emphasize "power over" rather than "power to." Dahl, for instance, has offered such a theoretical model, which he does not seem to utilize in his own community power analysis. See Robert A. Dahl, "The Concept of Power," *Behavioral Science*, 3 (July, 1957), pp. 201–215.

[4] A symposium of a few years ago on national power, which included such participants as Robert Lynd, C. Wright Mills, and Harold Lasswell, contained little overlap with most of the material on community power. See *Problems of Power in American Democracy*, edited by Arthur Kornhauser, Detroit: Wayne State University Press, 1959.

[5] C. Wright Mills, *The Power Elite*, New York: Oxford University Press, Galaxy Books, 1959, especially pp. 269–297.

[6] One scholar has postulated a particular "convergence" of such power on the local level, as later discussed. See Robert Salisbury, "Urban Politics: The New Convergence of Power," paper delivered at meetings of American Political Science Association, New York, September, 1963.

[7] Robert O. Schulze and Leonard U. Blumberg, "The Determination of Local Power Elites," *American Journal of Sociology*, 63 (November, 1957), pp. 290–296.

[8] Linton C. Freeman, Thomas J. Fararo, Warner Bloomberg Jr., and Morris H. Sunshine, "Locating Leaders in Local Communities: A Comparison of Some Alternative Approaches," *American Sociological Review*, 28 (October, 1963), pp. 791–798.

[9] For a thorough criticism see Raymond E. Wolfinger, "Reputation and Reality in the Study of Community Power," *American Sociological Review*, 25 (October, 1960), pp. 636–644.

The event analysis has more of the feel of the precise socio-political processes. It dwells on what has been done, not about what could be done, though ad hoc discussions of resources available are significantly added, in many cases, as additional variables. Some of the institutional arrangements, conflicts and coalitions, problems and issues are available to the reader. At least, up to now, the defects and dangers are also glaring. Choice of issues involves neglecting others. Are those which are chosen representative? Are they salient to the functioning of the city, to the analysis of the power structure, or even to the specific purposes of the inquiry? Are the cases generalizable to the entire city decision-making process or only to particular types of decision-making?

One study did strive for an elaborate systematization of specific decisions.[1] Examining action on almost forty issues in the city of Syracuse, the researchers, through documentation and interviews, were able to locate the crucial decision-makers in each case. The quest was for a precise statistical summation of the more relevant social characteristics of these "influentials." Through factor analysis of these characteristics, a large proportion of the decisions could be grouped, i.e., the same types of people were involved in these types of decisions. The technique warrants continued applications and the results, referred to from time to time in this paper, were suggestive. But serious deficiencies remain. All the issues seem to have been given equal weight, and the problems of generalizability, pertinence, etc. still remain.

If the reputation approach sometimes resembles a quantification of a gossip column, some event descriptions appear like detailed journalistic case histories, good and comprehensive examples of the genre, but all with inherent dangers. The New Haven and Syracuse studies do offer more precise and ordered material, but they are not constructed so as to give us a clear-cut systematic picture of power in the community. The ideas are seminal, the evidence is there, but the data are still subject to the charge of selective choice.

In summary, the reputation approach appears to be comprehensive and methodologically neat; the question to be posed is: how relevant are the answers to meaningful hypotheses about community power. Event studies present the proper queries, search in the right directions, and provide tentative answers. But the answers remain partial and, usually, insufficiently systematized. Yet the author's predilection is towards the event approach, somehow systemized. It tends to be more concrete, to be accompanied by greater attention to the socio-political life of the community, to suggest more suitable insights into such elements as motivation for power utilization and power potential and, generally, to produce more fruitful results. However, our objective is not principally to appraise methodology. The discussion which follows utilizes material however obtained, though the method of acquiring the data is, necessarily, at least an implicit feature of our evaluation.

Location of power and the social structure As a preliminary caution, it is necessary to point out that the full meaning of "power" in a community or society may not be directly available to any of the above techniques. Those who are powerful in specific crucial institutional areas of community life may neither possess the appropriate reputations nor participate in many significant community-relevant decisions. Their power comes from the functions of their institutions. The decisions they make within their apparently limited sphere may be so consequential for the rest of the community or society that they are inherently "powerful," as long as the position of their groups are maintained.

This is particularly true of "business" in a "business society." One may then speak of an ultimate "business power" on the national level, and to some extent locally, even if political leadership is not generally under their control. Dominating the economy (with appropriate veto power from other groups), they have power over the national livelihood, even if this power is less a matter of concrete decisions than of merely maintaining their institutional structures. Their power then may rest on the legitimacy of their institutions, not on how much they may control the direct decisions of government. Put another way, under the conditions of the existing economy, business must make money and businessmen must run their businesses accordingly. Secondly, no programs which involve economic activity can succeed without their participation or, at least, against their veto. Their specific roles in concrete decisions of political or other community relevance is another matter, related to specific situational factors. The varying interpretations of the power of business groups in communities are, in that sense, inadequate answers to the basic questions about the position of "business" in the social system. But this limitation may be irrelevant to the purposes of community investigations, which come back to the issue of who does or can make the important community-relevant decisions. Of course, the exercise of power within a specific institutional area, like business, may impel businessmen to strive to wield power on other community decisions.

Motivation for decision-making

In the relatively pluralistic American community, power over decisions is not an automatic reflection of a prescribed hierarchal role description. A significant variable that emerges from the literature is the motivation to intervene in a particular decision-making process. Such motivation is simply a product of the extent to which that decision is salient to the group and/or the individual.

[1] Linton C. Freeman, Warner Bloomberg Jr., Stephen S. Koff, Morris S. Sunshine, Thomas J. Fararo, "Local Community Leadership," Publications Committee of University College, Syracuse University, 15, 1960; Linton C. Freeman, Thomas J. Fararo, Warner Bloomberg Jr., Morris H. Sunshine, "Metropolitan Decision Making," Publications Committee of University College, Syracuse University, 28, 1962.

GROUP SALIENCY FACTORS

Several types of group saliency factors are listed here, not with any logical organization, which does not seem obvious at this point, but as a list of the kinds of elements observed in the literature. They include: group power maintenance or enhancement in specific areas, furtherance of economic "interests" in the traditional sense, defense and extension of values. Contrariwise, non-intervention may imply that relative power, economic interests, and values are being achieved without such decision intervention.

Group power in community   The general lines of this type of motivation are indicated in the methodological note and the review of Banfield's narratives. A community decision which may limit or enhance the relative power of groups will impel intervention by the leaders of such groups. This rather simplistic formula may be better understood by noting the converse, the non-intervention by potentially powerful groups when their power positions are not at stake. Returning again to our methodological note, this is one reason why business groups do not throw their resources into every question that arises. For instance, one of the discussants in the *Power and Democracy in America* volume, noting that businessmen collect philanthropic funds but leave the question of disbursement, the genuine decision-making aspects, to welfare professionals, remarks: "Perhaps the crucial issue is whether or not the allocation of funds is of relevance to the businessmen. If, in fact, they have no interest in, or are satisfied with, the allocation, their lack of concern may reflect not their weakness or fear of defeat but the realization that there is little power challenge involved."[1]

[1] D'Antonio and Ehrlich, *op. cit.*, p. 125.

[2] Peter H. Rossi, "The Organizational Structure of an American Community," in *Complex Organizations*, edited by Amitai Etzioni, New York: Holt, Rinehart and Winston, Inc., 1962, pp. 301–312; Ronald J. Pellegrin and Charles H. Coates, "Absentee-Owned Corporations and Community Power Structure," *American Journal of Sociology*, 61 (March, 1956) pp. 413–419; Robert O. Schulze, "The Role of Economic Dominants in Community Power Structure," *American Sociological Review*, 23 (February, 1958), pp. 3–9.

[3] Scott Greer, *Metropolitics: A Study of Political Culture*, New York: John Wiley and Sons, Inc., 1963.

[4] Peter H. Rossi, "Theory and Method in the Study of Power in the Local Community," paper presented at meetings of American Sociological Association, New York, August, 1960.

[5] Banfield, *op. cit.*, *passim*.

[6] Freeman, *et al.*, "Local Community Leadership," *op. cit.*

[7] Werner E. Mills Jr. and Harry R. Davis, *Small City Government: Seven Cases in Decision Making*, New York: Random House Studies in Political Science, 1962, pp. 31–43.

[8] Dahl, *Who Governs? op. cit.*, pp. 253–255.

[9] Peter H. Rossi and Robert A. Dentler, *The Politics of Urban Renewal: The Chicago Findings*, New York: The Free Press of Glencoe Inc., 1961; Robert C. Wood, *1400 Governments: The Political Economy of the New York Metropolitan Region*, Cambridge, Mass.: Harvard University Press, 1961, pp. 158–169; Salisbury, *op. cit.*

[10] Robert C. Wood, *Suburbia: Its People and Their Politics*, Boston: Houghton Mifflin Co., 1959, pp. 161–197, *passim*; Arthur J. Vidich and Joseph Bensman, *Small Town in Mass Society*, Princeton, New Jersey; Princeton University Press, 1958, pp. 109–136.

Similarly, the oft-noted ambivalence of officials of large absentee corporations toward participation in community activities, except when middle-management is prodded by the company for public relations reasons, is partly a reflection of the fact that their local and, of course, their national power positions, are rarely affected.[2] On the other hand, local government officials were among the few citizens actively concerned about metropolitan government reorganization plans, for the future of their "domains" might be at stake.[3]

One other power motivation may be noted, the search for power in some areas to compensate for powerlessness in other areas of the potentially powerful. The dominant role of businessmen in civic and philanthropic organizations may thus be seen as an outlet for power loss in local government.[4]

In summary, power groups will intervene in decisions when their bases of power are the issue. There seems to be little evidence of a drive towards generic power imperialism in American communities. Rather, the impulsion seems to be towards the maintenance and enhancement of the group's position in these particular "areas" of power within which it operates, which, to repeat, may involve an inherent power over many "areas."

Economic interests   The literature likewise supports the almost truistic statement that intervention in decision-making will vary with the extent to which an issue has definite economic relevance to a group. In Banfield's discussion of proposed Chicago projects, those businessmen who would clearly gain business advantages were most vigorous in pushing for them, those who might lose a competitive position thereby were actively, if sometimes surreptitiously, in opposition.[5] Absentee corporations may have little concern about local problems which have little effect on the enterprises; however, in the communities where they have large home offices they may be actively involved in redevelopment decisions. In the Syracuse study, the local "aristocratic commercial leadership" were heavily represented in "Downtown Development" decisions, the "new management" elite of industrial corporations in those of "Industrial Interest."[6] In a study of the politics of a small town, merchants who would be adversely affected by a rerouting of traffic were decisive in defeating an attempt to change a highway through town.[7] Unions may be only tangentially concerned about community problems except when the economic interests of members are directly involved.[8]

Urban renewal offers a particular area in which economic interests may be at stake. Therefore, observers, with the possible exception of Dahl, find that many business groups are, quite appropriately, conspicuously engaged in decision-making about such questions.[9] An additional type of power exercise around economic interests is the ever present striving to lower governmental expenditures and to maintain lower taxes. Much of the intervention in small town or suburban community politics is concerned with little else.[10]

Values Such "interests" may or may not be closely identified with group values, particularly those which are manifestly politically relevant, and especially when some aspect of the group's legitimacy in the social structure is at issue. Public welfare expenditures can be considered an ideological challenge to a private business approach to solving community problems. Therefore, businessmen oppose such expenditures, actively work at private philanthropic alternatives, or get into official government positions where they can combat the "welfare state" philosophy.[1] People will spend as much on private activities as it would cost in taxes if the same effort were undertaken by government agencies.[2] Businessmen will push for a tax-supported subsidy to a private bus company rather than sanction a publicly-owned bus line.[3]

Perhaps the converse again reveals the nub of the question more clearly. Intervention by potential power wielders is less likely when neither the legitimacy nor the resources of the power base is threatened. Especially is this true of businessmen. Why bother with the effort, and costs, of trying to marshal resources on every decision, even of business relevance? As long as you can run your business, let the others have their particular decision-areas. This has been part of the traditional attitude of big business towards "corrupt" municipal political machines. Such a non-intervention orientation will, of course, be even more likely when there is a general satisfaction, or at least minimal antagonism towards what others are doing, especially if it may help your "interests." Why should New Haven businessmen spend their valuable time in the details of urban renewal planning, except when prodded by the Mayor? He and his staff seem to be doing a good enough job.

Somewhat surprisingly, the literature contains few other explicit examples of intervention in decisions because of group values beyond those of business groups. There are descriptions of those who get involved in decisions because of group "tastes" (art, mental health), professional orientation (health), life style (home owners striving to maintain a neighborhood).[4] Especially surprising is the comparative absence of accounts of group "ideological" motivation, secular and religious.

Conclusion The literature emphasizes decision intervention by business groups when the issues have some direct association with maintenance or enhancement of area of power, direct economic interests, or business "values." Such an accent is, to some extent, a reflection of the nature of prevailing arguments in the field, so often focused on "business power" hypotheses. But there is enough material to suggest, and one may add plausible further speculations, that motivations for attempts to exercise power on any community-relevant decision is similar for all groups. Certainly, the activities of civil rights groups on questions salient to them implies concern about power maintenance, interests, and values. Similar analysis can be applied to religious bodies, professional organizations, etc. which are insufficiently treated in the literature, as well as specific government bodies, who receive more attention. The research and analytical directive can almost be summed up as: find out why the leaders of a particular group should care about a particular controversy, find out why it does or does not mean enough to the group to warrant marshalling resources in the light of the possible contending forces.

PERSONAL FACTORS

Role The specific individual role requirements may be as consequential as the group aspects in determining the degree of intervention in decision-making. This has been the point of the many analysts who emphasize the central power position of the Mayor, his staff, and the responsible professionals in government agencies. In the context of the problems and structure and public expectations of the contemporary American cities, to do their jobs, especially to do them well, they have to become actively involved in many important decisions, have to utilize their power resources. In former times, when their role expectations were less demanding, they could more readily avoid power utilization and decision responsibility.

Career Attempts at power utilization may not be inherent in the role, but may enhance the possibility of success in that role and resultant career opportunities. It becomes an estimate of how to "do the job well," which may mean trying to foster or alter particular decisions. This could characterize some "go-getting officials," bureaucrats, professionals, perhaps some city managers. The mayor who wants to make a "name for himself," whatever the purpose, would be such an example, as in the case of Mayor Lee of New Haven. The pressure of corporations to get middle management to participate in civic organizations has been previously described. This is apparently the principal reason why many do participate, for it can become an appropriate mechanism for a favorable judgment in the corporation hierarchy or, in some cases, the opportunity to get known and thus shift to a position outside the corporation.

Personality Because of the nature of the inquiries, there has been little explicit attention to personality factors, which are frequently central in some general models of "power striving." It is appropriate to suggest, however, that motivations for exercise of power include this variable. It may be related to career strivings, to role performance, to group power maintenance, or to some combination thereof, as, for instance, the attempted use of power by anxious individuals who feel that their individual roles and careers are threatened by an assumed threat to their group's power. How this can be meaningfully studied is not readily answerable.

Conclusion Motivation for an effort at decision-making, or power wielding, in a situation where there

[1] Pellegrin and Coates, *op. cit.;* Hunter, *op. cit.,* pp. 207–227.
[2] Vidich and Bensman, *op. cit.,* pp. 128–136.
[3] Mills and Davis, *op. cit.,* pp. 55–72.
[4] Freeman, *et al.,* "Local Community Leadership," *op. cit.,* Dahl, *op. cit.,* pp. 192–199; Banfield, *op. cit., passim.*

is controversy, or possibility of controversy, is a product of, among other things, the extent to which the issue is deemed salient to the appropriate actors. Among the elements involved, as noted in the literature, are: the possible effects on the relative power position of a group; the economic interests of a group (or individual); the relevance to legitimacy, values, and life styles; the role demands and career aspirations of individuals.

Who are the "powerful," how, and why?

As spelled out, those who have most to say about community relevant decisions are appropriately motivated to intervene in that decision. The measure of their "power," to what extent they will have their "way," requires some consideration of the following elements:

FORMAL FEATURES

Formal position The formal position of groups of individuals within the social structure involves being assigned the ultimate function of making the relevant decisions. With the popularity of "invisible government" approaches implicit in so much of the Hunter-Miller type of finding, it is important that this be initially emphasized. Even Vidich and Bensman, who frequently use the "invisible government" label in depicting the structure of a rural community, actually describe a "power elite" quartet which has important formal positions in the local government and party.[1]

The formal function of particular organizations is related to the kinds of decisions in which such organizations are involved. Thus, it should not be surprising that government officials play more of a role in decisions which have to be made by a government agency, have less to say when they are not officially assigned this responsibility. Private philanthropy projects are illustrative. Those with money collect from others with money. The money collectors, or rather the directors of money collections, are in the obvious position of deciding what is to be done with the money if they so wish. Similarly, since businessmen have to build private redevelopment and private civic projects, they will have much to say about those projects, whoever else may be involved.

If the formal position, or formal organization, require decisions on a subject, and if the issue is salient to the position or organization, the occupant is likely to be, in some manner, an important participant in the decision-making process. Thus, in the contemporary context, school superintendents are important in school decisions, expert officials in municipal departments are assigned decision responsibilities within their sphere and, above all, the "wishes" of the leaders of city governments today inherently carry great weight. In contrast, the officials of small towns and suburbs are not, by constitutional requirement or popular expectations, presumed

to have much of an independent decision role, and few issues are very salient to them.[2] Therefore, their governments tend to be "weak."

However, as already indicated, some studies reveal that the formal leaders may not be either those who have power by reputation or those directly involved in important decisions. Their roles may be limited to that of "lending prestige or legitimizing the situations provided by others."[3] Those others, labeled as the "Effectors," are generally the underlings — particularly government personnel and the employees of the large private corporations.

Such interpretations tend to confuse "formal position" with "formal organizations." Comparatively lower range personnel of organizations may be involved in the actual decision process, but it is the position in the entire social structure of their organizations which gives them the ability and the motivation to make decisions. Furthermore, this decision-making potential and impetus would not exist without and cannot, in most instances, be counter to the more formal leadership of the organization. In essence, power-wielding hardly exists outside organization role. Whether the reputation or decision approach is used, the decision-makers are thus usually found rooted in some formally organized matrix.

There remains one formally assigned decision-making entity in a democracy with open contests — the electorate. Elections for office are rarely emphasized in the literature. In most of the communities studied, the incumbents or their likely successors seem fairly secure in tenure. But there are several indications of need to make a "good showing" in elections, as a popular legitimizing of their policies, a way of enhancing careers, a method of mobilizing followers, or simply because the role of a politician requires getting more votes. The "power" of the electorate, in this widespread situation of municipal government continuity, is that of a variety of publics toward whom politicians somehow try to appeal even if any comparative lack of appeal may not mean loss of political power. Referenda present a different picture. A formal requirement for popular approval limits the decision-making capabilities of any political leader or anyone else involved in such a decision. In the extreme case of suburban school officials, the decision-making option becomes very narrow.[4] The communication "appeals" then become of vital concern, the response to those appeals a direct expression of power by the electorate or sections thereof.

As a final consideration, the background of formal decision-makers, the element so frequently emphasized in traditional "elite" analysis, is rarely emphasized in community studies. Such features are occasionally stated, more frequently implied, but are rarely explicitly considered. In essence, such an approach states that because of common interests and values, the orientation of formal decision-makers is directed towards the reference group of those of similar origin, who, there-

[1] Vidich and Bensman, *op. cit.*, especially pp. 217–221.
[2] Wood, *Suburbia, op. cit.*, pp. 153–255, *passim.*
[3] Freeman, *et al.*, "Locating Leaders," *op. cit.*, pp. 797–798.
[4] Wood, *op. cit.*, pp. 192–194.

fore, become powerful. It is not utilized because contemporary role, organization, etc. of those in formal positions seems to provide a more meaningful focus.

Access to formal decision-makers The notion of "access" to those who formally make decisions, particularly government officials, is evident in many studies of national and state politics. All discussions of "pressure groups" in local affairs dwell on, except when referenda are involved, some means of "getting to" and thus affecting those who have the official decision-making responsibility. This is the assigned task of the "effectors" in corporations.[1] But, in most reputational studies and typical accompanying business dominance emphasis, as well as in various notions of "invisible government," much more is implied. The government is assumed to be a weak power center. Businessmen, as well as other groups "behind the scenes," possess formal and informal communication channels to government officials. Since the former represents "strength," the communications will be heeded.[2] To the extent that this process does occur, it should not be interpreted as a symptom of decision by intrigue. It is merely a reflection of the existing power relationship.

Formal structure The propensity and ability to make decisions may be related to the formal *structure* of the group and the formal relations with other groups. The power of local government, for instance, may be greater if staffed by full-time rather than part-time officials, and if elections are partisan rather than "non-partisan."[3] The existence of a structure for making decisions and formal resources for implementing them may be other variables. Thus, Dahl describes how earlier attempts at urban redevelopment proved unsuccessful because there was no available political process for agreement, nor appropriate financial sources.[4] The Federal Housing Act of 1949 provided both. The "strong mayor" tendency is partly buttressed by the city charter provisions which give the chief executive authority and responsibility for so many decisions. Small towns and suburban governments frequently decide little because they are not constitutionally so assigned and would not have the formal means for executing such decisions if they were made.

Banfield describes two contrasting types of groups with varying formal decision-making potentials. "Civic organization" leaders do not have a mandate to take positions on certain controversial issues, it would be difficult to get the membership to make such decisions, and the organizations could not be readily mobilized to support them if adopted. Leaders of private corporations and the type of public bodies he describes can make such decisions and, to some degree, commit their organizations to them.[5]

The list of formal limitations to power exercise can be readily extended. Local governments have to receive state and Federal approval for many actions. As already described, electorate support is a definite limitation when referenda are required, a latent control in candidate elections. Courts may act as a check on many political

decisions. Corporation employees operating in community affairs may require corporation approval for their actions.[6] In summary, in American communities today, effective exercise of power is partially dependent on the existence of appropriate formal mechanisms and the lack of formally restricting structures.

VALUES

Legitimate position of decision-maker The legitimacy of the formal decision-maker or decision-making group in the specific area also obviously affects his likely success, i.e., his relative power. Businessmen, local government officials, school officials, professionals and experts *should*, with appropriate checks, make decisions in their respective spheres. The followers of traditional political machines grant their leaders the "right" to select nominees and officials. The decline of the machine is, among other things, a reflection of the loss of that "legitimate" function.

Extending the concept further, the "legitimate wisdom" of particular people in specific areas may influence decisions even if they are not necessarily the official decision-makers or share this function with others. This is especially evident when status is an ingredient of power, as in Hunter's "Regional City." Other examples from the literature include the University of Illinois officials in the conflict over expansion described by Banfield and the specialists in such areas as mental health and the arts in the Syracuse study.[7] A well-known individual case is that of Robert Moses in New York City and State, who has generally had so much power over many decisions because, among other reasons, officials and publics tend to accept his "record."[8]

Values of specific groups When the values of specific groups are more in accord with prevailing community values their opinions are more likely to produce the desired decisions, no matter what the formal decision mechanisms. This implies substantive value agreement, not merely acceptance of the legitimate role of particular people. Theses about business dominance are frequently accompanied by interpretations of a "broad dissemination of business values: what is good for business is good for the community."[9]

But value agreement may not be so inclusive. Differing values may prevail in different areas of disputes, and there may be value conflicts and contradictions. The business viewpoint may or may not prevail in the face of popular demands for "welfare," "justice," etc., as should be very obvious by now. These are, in effect, the values which provide a power potential for government

[1] Freeman, *et al.*, "Locating Leaders," *op. cit.*
[2] Hunter, *op. cit.*, pp. 83–113, 171–205.
[3] Rossi, "Theory and Method," *op. cit.*, pp. 26–29.
[4] Dahl, *op. cit.*, p. 116.
[5] Banfield, *op. cit.*, pp. 288–295.
[6] Pellegrin and Coates, *op. cit.*
[7] Banfield, *op. cit.*, pp. 165–166; Freeman, *et al.*, "Local Community Leadership," *op. cit.*
[8] Wood, *1400 Governments*, *op. cit.*, pp. 163–166.
[9] D'Antonio and Ehrlich, *op. cit.*, p. 126.

officials in the contemporary city, further augmented by a widespread normative consensus in favor of "community redevelopment." Educators and education officials face two conflicting popular values in achieving their aims — a strong commitment to education as a social goal and a desire for "economy."

If the sought-for decision is to be achieved by more open propagandistic appeals to many publics, either as an effort at pressure politics or to achieve a particular popular vote, "values" may be consequential in more complex fashion. It is not merely that general values are inherently associated with particular groups, but specific situational values are utilized to get support. This seems little more than a restatement of a simple dictum of communication and opinion analysis, but it implies something more: that one of the means for achieving power in a specific decision area is the ability to mobilize organized groups and unorganized publics by appeals to salient values. To use an illustration by Dahl, "right to work" referenda, even though pushed by powerful business groups, pass when farmers were sufficiently aroused and fail when labor unions were properly mobilized.[1] In this instance, "power" is closely associated with "influence" in the communication sense. The strong motivations of the would-be decision-maker are effectively transferred to a receptive audience, which, by vote or pressure on the formal decision-makers, affects what is decided. Unfortunately, systematic analysis of such processes are rare in the community literature. Description of *prior* consideration of possible value pressures in formulating policy or maneuvering to secure consensus are more evident. Certainly, any inquiry into current civil rights controversies throughout the country, almost completely absent in community studies to date, would have to accentuate communication and mobilization around values.

Concern with communication implies attention to communication channels. An assumed ingredient of a position of power is the ability to utilize such channels, whatever they may be. The local press is especially identified as an important decision-making mechanism. But, as with so many claims about opinion formation, such contentions have hardly been tested. In fact, the role of the local press has been seriously questioned.[2] Its "power" may rest more on the belief in its potential rather than any realization, as exemplified by the attention given to the opinions of the editors of the *Chicago Tribune*.[3]

OTHER FACTORS
Money and numbers as resources   The importance of money as a power variable in contemporary American

communities requires little elaboration, except for the caution that it is not all powerful, will not always be utilized except when thoroughly motivated, will not be on the same side on many questions. Even if more fully utilized it can be countered by the opposing feature of numbers, as recognized as far back as Aristotle. As important in communities as mere quantity are the mobilization around dominant values and/or interests and, sometimes, the degree of access to official decision-makers.

Sanctions   The use of "power over" to facilitate "power for," a common enough expectation, is rarely clearly indicated in the literature. Hunter does describe uses of deliberate pressures to silence or remove opposition from strategic positions.[4] Other possible examples are: removal of funds, closing down business, strikes, threats of resignation. When existent, these are typically implicit rather than stated.

Conclusion   In summary, who makes the community relevant decisions or has more say about them? First of all, those who make them are those who are supposed to make them, because of their officially assigned positions or because this is their approved legitimate bailiwick. When the decision is not directly within their formally-designed domain, the appropriate formula should be along these lines: those who are properly motivated by the saliency of an issue, capable of committing and mobilizing their groups, having access to those who have the ability and the impulsion to make the appropriate formal decisions, possessing some form of legitimacy in the decision-area, capable of and utilizing appeals to the values and interests of many publics, able further to mobilize either large numbers or those in strategic positions (using whatever resources can be called upon), and somehow having an opposition with as few as possible of these advantages, will win out, i.e., will exercise their power over a particular area around a specific decision.

Power position of business and local government

Although many groups thus can and do exercise power in American communities, the major contentions are, quite appropriately, about the two major institutional groups, business and local government. The foundations of their respective power positions are accordingly appraised in line with the previous formulations.

Business   Banfield offers this conjecture about possible behavior of leading Chicago businessmen: "In some future case — one in which their vital interests are at stake — they may issue the orders necessary to set in motion the lower echelons of the alleged influence hierarchy."[5] Whatever the results of such an effort, this would imply a crucially divisive issue in the community, a quasi "revolutionary" conflict in which some aspect of legitimacy is debated. None of this appears in the literature. Business power within its own institutional

[1] *Ibid.*, p. 106.
[2] Greer, *op. cit.*; Alvin J. Remmenga, "Has the Press Lost Its Influence in Local Affairs," in *Urban Government*, edited by Edward C. Banfield, New York: The Free Press of Glencoe, Inc., 1961, pp. 379–389.
[3] Banfield, *Political Influence, op. cit.*, pp. 212–217, 222–231.
[4] Hunter, *op. cit.*, pp. 176–179.
[5] Banfield, *Political Influence, op. cit.*, p. 288.

area is hardly an issue in contemporary American communities. Beyond this, the following emerges from the literature.

The most important resources of businessmen are obviously the possession of money — their own and of others whose money can be utilized — and status. For many who postulate business elite dominance, these are the only factors involved, for there is the casual assumption that, in American society, wealth, status, and power are automatically correlated. Additionally, there is the generally accepted legitimacy of business values and the expertise of businessmen. Material interest in the city compels concern about many decisions. There is frequently close internal communication among businessmen.

But the inherent limitations to their exercise of power are also evident, as already suggested. The legitimacy of businessmen and their values is not accepted in all areas of community life and by all people.[1] Conflict of interest and opinion among businessmen is as evident as cohesion. Communication may not be as easy as assumed, especially through their far-flung organizations.[2] The process of formal decision-making on an issue is not always readily available, and potentially divisive decisions, within business organizations or in the community, are avoided. Public relations may be more important than power wielding for its own sake. There is little desire for political activity by corporation officials unless pushed by the companies' desire for a proper public image.

Businessmen expect public officials to handle the political problems and, unless seriously dissatisfied with what is done, will rarely intervene with any vigor. When economic interests are involved, they may participate, but often as supporters and legitimizers of the outspoken proponents. Their role in political affairs may be more extensive when local government is weak or when intervention does not brook serious opposition. In essence, they would then be responding to a "power vacuum," even though it is one of long standing. Their "citizen" activity may tend to be in civic, service, and philanthropic organizations, where objectives are clear, methods "clean," and controversy minimal, and the thorny arena of political conflict avoided. The exceptions, to repeat, are situations when *direct economic interests are involved*. Small local businessmen and professional people may be more involved in political affairs, particularly in smaller communities, because of more direct material interest, status strivings, or greater value concerns about the community.

Local government The basis for the power position of local government can be sketched more briefly. Despite the growing nationalization of government and politics and the checks that automatically follow, municipal government power has grown within the following context: the necessary functions of the government in solving complex contemporary problems and the accompanying role of professionals; a popularly supported plebeian-based political organization, typically with some ties to labor organizations and ethnic groups; a formal political structure which accents the power potential of the mayor and "partisan" organizations and elections. Traditional political machines are typical, though often diminished in power and appeal, but they are rarely involved in major policy decisions. Relative lack of power of political leaders and their staff professionals is correlated with the comparative absence of the above and the power of business groups, because of specific community configurations and historical antecedents, including the dominant position of local-based business and the slowness of change.

The power structure of American communities

All that has been said tends to substantiate a pluralistic interpretation of American community power. People try to exercise power when a particular decision is salient and/or required. This obviously means that different groups in the community will be more involved in different kinds of decisions. Many groups possess appropriate resources, internal decision-making mechanisms, access to those who make the necessary formal decisions, widely accepted legitimacy and values, means for communicating to and mobilizing large publics. The investigation of power then becomes a study of discrete decision-making processes, with many sectors of the population revealing varying degrees of impact on different type decisions.[3]

But summary statements about American community power should go beyond such casual nominalism, as they must transcend facile monolithism. Some decisions are obviously more salient to the community than others. Power motivation, formal decision-making potential, resources, access, communication facilities may be widespread, but there are significant differences. To use the abused cliché, some are more equal than others. The two important dominant groups remain businessmen, of varying types, and local government officials. The pattern of American community power observed is mostly a matter of the respective positions of these two groups and their relation with the residual "all other groups."

Despite their disagreement about the prevailing power picture, Miller and Dahl offer models of possible power structure which are not too dissimilar.[4] Both allow for completely pluralistic patterns, with either particular spheres of influence for specific groups or open struggles by relatively equal groups on the same issues. To Miller,

---

[1] See Dahl in D'Antonio and Ehrlich, *op. cit.*, p. 109.

[2] Banfield, *op. cit.*, pp. 295–296.

[3] A political science text on the government of New York City thus concludes simply by listing six power groups in the city who, among others, appear to be important decision-makers in particular areas. See Wallace S. Sayre and Herbert Kaufman, *Governing New York City*, New York: Russell Sage Foundation, 1960.

[4] D'Antonio and Ehrlich, *op. cit.*, pp. 62–70; Dahl, *op. cit.*, pp. 184–189.

these are subordinate aspects in most American communities. To Dahl, they exist but are less likely possibilities than a system of comparative pluralism with *coordination by the political leadership* in different ways in different communities, a variant not specifically indicated by Miller. Finally both accept the possibility of domination by an economic elite, but Dahl generally relegates such situations to the past while Miller insists that this pattern, with all its variations, is most common in the United States today.

A more composite replica of these typologies is that of Rossi, with his simple division into "monoliths" and "polyliths."[1] The former is typically business elite dominant. In a polylith, local government is the province of the political leaders, backed by strong parties and working class associations.[2] The rest of his formulation is in accord with our previous discussion. Civic associations and community chests are in the hands of the leaders of business and staff professionals. A polylith is associated with strong political parties, based upon class political attitudes, frequently with ethnic concomitants. In response, economic leaders (and others), may advocate changes in government structure (nonpartisan elections) to thwart some of the power of political parties. Absentee corporation officials will tend to set themselves off from purely local political concerns. In monoliths, conflicts tend to take on the character of minor revolts, like the revolutionary postures of the powerless in authoritarian countries.

All this can be restated in terms of what has already been spelled out. Business elite dominance appears most characteristic of communities when the dominant businessmen are most motivated to participate in community decisions (company towns, established commercial aristocracies, etc.) and/or when there are fewer rival power centers. The polylith is characterized by both the leadership of government officials and relative pluralism. Decision-making is widespread among many groups, depending upon motivation, resources, and the other listed ingredients. Businessmen are an important part of the power picture, but only as part of the above formula. In fact, a large section avoids the arena of political decisions, except when very pressing, because of the efforts demanded and risks inherent, and concentrates on the private areas of community decision-making, such as civic associations and philanthropic activities, where there is little opposition in power or ideology. The political leaders are the necessary coordinators in such a complex pattern and their power rests on the fairly strong power position of many groups — especially political parties, trade unions, ethnic groups, staff professionals, etc. — and the importance of governmental decisions today.

To complete our review, one additional presentation

must be described. Political Scientist Robert Salisbury states that what others would consider polylithic structures are, in most cases, evidence of a "new convergence."[3] A new power triumvirate has arisen to solve the vital problems of the contemporary city. Its elements have already been sufficiently identified: the business interests directly dependent on the condition of the city, particularly the downtown area; the professionals, technicians, experts engaged in city programs; the mayor, generally secure in his tenure. What Salisbury emphasizes is that this constitutes a coordinate power group; the mayor is the most influential, but he appears to be only the first among equals.

The leadership convergence directs most mayor decisions, particularly those that involve allocation of scarce resources; some of these, like redevelopment and traffic control, can determine the future of the city. The rest of the population — other organized groups, other politicians, and unorganized publics — are part of the process in three ways: they must be "sold" on certain issues, especially if referenda are in order; their interests and needs must be somewhat satisfied and/or anticipated; some demands must be responded to, such as race relations. Salisbury, however, believes that the importance of the last process can be exaggerated. Specifically, he insists that Banfield's selection of issues tends to magnify the initiative of the groups outside the "convergence." The more vital questions should, with few exceptions such as race relations, reveal the initiating, as well as decision-making position, of the triumvirate.

Salisbury's analysis can thus supply the basis for the concluding statements of this essay. Power over community decisions remains a matter of motivation, resources, mechanisms of decision-making, mobilization of resources, etc. On many, many decisions, various groups may initiate and win out, as in Banfield's account and in some of the descriptions of Dahl and others. Current disputes about race relations offer a fitting example where this more pluralistic interpretation, including both the ideas of spheres of influence and competing pressures around a common issue, may be readily applicable. But on the most salient community issues a directing leadership can be observed. In some communities, for the reasons outlined, the decision leaders have been, and may still be, particular business interests. In most of them, a new pattern has emerged, a polylithic structure in which business groups and local government each lead in their own domains. But the urgent problems of the past World War II era in most large cities have brought some business groups into the same decision area as the local government and the ever growing crop of experts. The extent to which the businessmen are involved may vary, as in the different accounts of the role of businessmen in urban renewal in different cities.

Does the rest of the population, organized and unorganized, become merely an audience called on occasionally to affirm and applaud these "big decisions?" Salisbury may have overstated his case. Many groups

---

[1] Rossi, "Theory and Method", *op. cit.*, pp. 24–43.

[2] A good example is provided in the description of Lorain, Ohio, by James B. McKee, "Status and Power in the Industrial Community," *American Journal of Sociology*, 58 (January, 1939), pp. 364–370.

[3] Salisbury, *op. cit.*

may initiate, veto, modify, pressure in all decision areas, in accord with the ingredients frequently listed. But those who are part of the new power convergence cannot be circumvented. In some manner, they have the responsibilities and will generally have to assume a decision-making role in all major decisions.

To return to the original debate, whatever evidence is available tends to support Dahl's emphasis against Miller's. Most American communities reveal a relatively pluralistic power structure. On some community-relevant questions, power may be widely dispersed. On the most salient questions, many groups may have an effect on what is decided, but the directing leadership comes from some combination of particular business groups, local government, and, in recent developments, professionals and experts. Communities differ and communities change in the power relations among these elements. A suggestive hypothesis holds that the tendency has been towards their coordination into a uniquely composite decision-making collectivity.[1]

---

[1] One type of community does not seem to fit any model described — the ever growing residential suburb. Perhaps, the reason is that it does not constitute a genuine "community."

The Corporation: How Much Power? What Scope?

Carl Kaysen

THE PROPOSITION that a group of giant business corporations, few in number but awesome in aggregate size, embodies a significant and troublesome concentration of power is the cliché which serves this volume as a foundation stone. I propose here to analyze this proposition, both to trace out what I consider its valid content to be, and to reflect briefly on its possible implications for social action. Let me anticipate my conclusion on the first point by saying that its familiarity is no argument against its truth.

The power of any actor on the social stage I define as the scope of significant choice open to him. Accordingly, his power over others is the scope of his choices which affect them significantly. Our fundamental proposition thus asserts that a few large corporations exert significant power over others; indeed, as we shall see, over the whole of society with respect to many choices, and over large segments of it with respect to others. It is worth noting that this sense of "power" is not that in which we speak of the "power" of a waterfall or a fusion reaction, or any other transformation in a fully deterministic system; rather it is appropriate to a social system in which we see human actors, individually or in organized groups, as facing alternative courses of action, the choice among which is not fully determined without reference to the actors themselves.

We usually demonstrate the concentration of power in a small number of large corporate enterprises by showing what part of various total magnitudes for the whole economy the largest enterprises account for. The statistics are indeed impressive: I shall list a few of the more striking.[1]

---

[1] The sources for the figures quoted are listed in order below.

Total business population: 1956, 4.3 million; 1954, 4.2 million, whence my current estimate. See U.S. Department of Commerce, Bureau of the Census, *Statistical Abstract of the United States 1957* (Washington, D.C., 1957), p. 482.

Corporate share and size distribution: U.S. Department of Commerce, Office of Business Economics, *Survey of Current Business* (April 1955); figures refer to January 1, 1952, for share, and January 1, 1947, for size distribution. If anything, the figures understate the numerical preponderance of small unincorporated enterprises today.

The census figures refer to 1954. See U.S. Department of Commerce, Bureau of the Census, *Company Statistics 1954*, Bulletin CS-1 (Washington, D.C., 1958).

Asset holding of large corporations: U.S. Treasury, Internal Revenue Service, *Statistics of Income, Part 2, 1955* (Washington, D.C., 1958), Table 5, pp. 41 ff.

Research and Development Expenditures: U.S. National Science Foundation, *Science and Engineering in American Industry* Washington, D.C., 1956).

Defense Contracts: "100 Companies and Affiliates Listed According to Net Value of Military Prime Contract Awards, July 1950–June 1956." Department of Defense, Office of

---

Reprinted from Edward S. Mason, ed., *The Corporation in Modern Society* (Cambridge, Mass.: Harvard U. Press, 1960), by permission of the author, the editor, and the publisher.

1) There are currently some 4.5 million business enterprises in the United States. More than half of these are small, unincorporated firms in retail trade and service. Corporations formed only 13 per cent of the total number; 95 per cent of the unincorporated firms had fewer than twenty employees.

2) A recent census survey covered all the firms in manufacturing, mining, retail and wholesale trade, and certain service industries: in total some 2.8 million. These firms employed just under 30 million persons. The 28 giant firms with 50,000 or more employees — just 0.001 per cent of the total number — accounted for about 10 per cent of the total employment. The 438 firms with 5000 or more employees (including the 28 giants) accounted for 28 per cent of the total. In manufacturing, where large corporations are characteristically more important than in the other sectors covered, 263,000 firms reported just over 17 million employees: 23 giants with 50,000 or more employees reported 15 per cent of the total, 361 with 5000 or more, just under 40 per cent.

3) The most recent compilation of the corporation income-tax returns showed 525,000 active nonfinancial corporations reporting a total of $413 billion of assets. The 202 corporations in the largest size class — each with assets of $250 million or more — owned 40 per cent of this total.

4) The last survey of the National Science Foundation reported some 15,500 firms having research and development laboratories. The largest 7 among them employed 20 per cent of the total number of technical and scientific personnel in the whole group, and accounted for 26 per cent of the total expenditures on research and development. The largest 44, all those with 25,000 or more employees in total, accounted for 45 per cent of the total number of technicians and scientists, and more than 50 per cent of the total expenditures.

5) The one hundred companies that received the largest defense contracts over the period July 1950–June 1956 received nearly two thirds of the total value of all defense contracts during the period. The largest ten contractors accounted for just short of one third of the total value of all contracts. These were General Motors,

General Electric, American Telephone and Telegraph, and seven large aircraft manufacturers.

Large corporations are not of the same importance in all sectors of the economy.[1] In agriculture they are of no importance; in service, trade, and construction, proprietorships and partnerships and small corporations that are essentially similar in all but legal form predominate. Conversely, activity in the utility, transportation, mining, manufacturing, and financial sectors is overwhelmingly the activity of corporations, and predominantly that of corporate giants. The share of total business accounted for by corporations in these sectors ranged from 85 per cent for finance to 100 per cent of utilities; by contrast it was between 50 and 60 per cent for trade and construction, less than 30 per cent in service, and less than 10 per cent in agriculture. The five sectors in which large corporations predominate produced 51 per cent of the total national income, and 57 per cent of the privately-produced national income. Moreover, the strategic importance of these sectors as compared with trade and service — the largest part of the small-business part of the economy — is greater than their contribution to national income would indicate. The relative share of giant corporations in these sectors was larger than in the economy as a whole. The corporate income-tax returns for 1955 showed the relative importance of the largest corporations, as in the accompanying table.

The Relative Share of Giant Corporations in Various Sectors of the United States Economy

| Sector | ALL CORPORATIONS | | CORPORATIONS WITH ASSETS OF $250 MILLION OR MORE | |
	Number (thousands)	Assets (billions of dollars)	Number	Proportion of assets of all corporations (percentage)
Manufacturing	124.2	201.4	97	42
Mining*	9.7	13.3	5 (19)	17 (32)
Public utilities	4.8	62.9	56	72
Transportation	21.9	43.5	30	61
Finance	214.6	474.9	218	46

* The figures in parentheses show the number and share of corporations with assets of $100 million or more, since the number of mining corporations in the largest size class is so small.

Many more figures similar to these could be added to the list. They show clearly that a few large corporations are of overwhelmingly disproportionate importance in our economy, and especially in certain key sectors of it. Whatever aspect of their economic activity we measure — employment, investment, research and development, military supply — we see the same situation. Moreover, it is one which has been stable over a period of time. The best evidence — though far from complete — is that the degree of concentration has varied little for the three or four decades before 1947; more recent material has

[1] The figures on the relative importance of corporations come from R. A. Gordon, *Business Leadership in the Large Corporation* (Washington, D.C., 1946), p. 14, and Appendix A. These figures refer to 1939; no more recent ones are available and they almost certainly understate the relative importance of corporations. The shares of the sectors in national income are calculated from the figures for national income by industrial origin for 1956 given in *Statistical Abstract of the U.S. 1957*, p. 300. The share of large corporations in asset holdings of all corporations are from the *Statistics of Income, Part 2, 1955*, Table 5, pp. 41 ff.

Assistant Secretary of Defense (Supply and Logistics), mimeo release dated 10 April 1957.

For a fuller but slightly dated discussion, see M. A. Adelman, "The Measurement of Industrial Concentration," *The Review of Economics and Statistics*, 23: 269–296 (1951), reprinted in *Readings in Industrial Organization and Public Policy*, ed. R. B. Heflebower and G. W. Stocking (Homewood, Ill., 1958).

not yet been analyzed. Further, the group of leading firms has had a fairly stable membership, and turnover within it is, if anything, declining.[1] We are thus examining a persistent situation, rather than a rapidly changing one, and one which we can expect to continue into the future.

Disproportionate share alone, however, is not a valid basis for inferring power as I have defined it. In addition, we must consider the range of choice with respect to significant decisions open to the managers of the large corporation. The disproportionate share of the sun in the total mass of our solar system would not justify the ascription to it of "power" over the planets, since in the fully-determinate gravitational system the sun has no choice among alternative paths of motion which would change the configuration of the whole system. Though the relative weight of the sun is great, its range of choice is nil, and it is the product of the two, so to speak, which measures "power." It is to an examination of the managers' range of choice that we now turn.

Our economy is organized on a decentralized, competitive basis. Each business firm, seeking higher profit by providing more efficiently what consumers want, is faced by the competition of others, seeking the same goal through the same means. Coordination and guidance of these activities is the function of the system of markets and prices. These form the information network that tells each manager what is and what is not currently profitable, and, in turn, registers the effects of each business decision, of changes in consumers' tastes, and the availability and efficiency of productive factors. Ideally, in a system of competitive markets, the signals would indicate only one possible course for any particular manager consistent with profitability. Nor would this depend on the degree to which the manager was committed to the goal of profit-maximization; margins between costs and prices would be so narrow as to make bankruptcy the alternative to "correct" choices. In practice, of course, no real firm functions in markets operating with the sureness, swiftness, and freedom from frictions that would eliminate the discretion of management entirely and make the firm merely an instrument which registered the forces of the market. But firms operating in highly competitive markets are closely constrained by market pressures, and the range of economic decision consistent with survival and success that is open to them is narrow.

By contrast, there exist much less competitive markets in which firms are insulated from these compulsions and the range of discretionary choice in management decisions is correspondingly widened. There is a wide variety of situations which can confer such market power on firms. In practice, the most important is large size relative to the market: the situation in which a few large firms account for all or nearly all of the supply. Large size relative to the market is associated with large absolute size of firm. Other reasons, including barriers to the entry of new firms into the market provided by product differentiation and advertising, by patents, by

control over scarce raw materials, or by collusive action of existing firms, or by government limitation of competition, are also significant, but they are of less importance than the oligopolistic market structure common in those sectors of the economy that are dominated by large firms.

In manufacturing, nearly two-thirds of the identifiable markets, accounting for about 60 per cent of the value of manufacturing output, showed significant elements of oligopoly; they were especially important in the durable-goods and capital-equipment fields. In mining, the proportion of identifiable markets with oligopolistic structures was much higher, but since the largest mining industry — bituminous coal — is unconcentrated, these accounted for less than 25 per cent of total mineral output. Public utilities, transportation, and finance are all subject to more or less direct government regulation, of more or less effectiveness. But the underlying market structures in these areas are either monopolistic, as in electric and gas utilities and telephone communication, or oligopolistic, as in transportation and finance.[2] Thus, typically, the large corporation in which we are interested operates in a situation in which the constraints imposed by market forces are loose, and the scope for managerial choice is considerable. It is this scope combined with the large relative weight of the giant corporation that defines its economic power; it is substantially on its economic power that other kinds of power depend.

The powerful firm can use its power primarily to increase its profit over what it could earn in a competitive market: the traditional economic view of the drawback of market power has been the achievement of monopoly profit by the restriction of supply. But it need not do so. While the firm in the highly competitive market is constrained to seek after maximum profits, because the alternative is insufficient profit to insure survival, the firm in the less competitive market can choose whether to seek maximum profit or to be satisfied with some "acceptable" return and to seek other goals. Further, the firm in a competitive market must attend more closely to immediate problems, and leave the long future to take care of itself; while the firm with considerable market power necessarily has a longer time-horizon, and takes into account consequences of its decisions reaching further into the future. This in turn increases the range of choice open to it, for the future is uncertain, and no single "correct" reading of it is possible. Many courses of action may be consistent with reasonable expectations of the future course of events.

[1] See Adelman: "The Measurement of Industrial Concentration," S. Friedland, "Turnover and Growth of the Largest Industrial Firms, 1906–1950," *Review of Economics and Statistics* (February, 1957), and J. F. Weston, *The Role of Mergers in the Growth of Large Firms* (Los Angeles, 1953).

[2] These estimates are taken from Carl Kaysen and D. F. Turner, "Antitrust Policy, an Economic and Legal Analysis" (to be published by Harvard University Press, Cambridge, Mass,). See chap. ii and the appendices. The figures are based on data for 1954 for manufacturing, and on scattered years for other industries.

The more dominant the position of any particular firm in a single market, the further into the future will it see the consequences of its own choices as significant, and correspondingly, the wider will be its range of significant choice. The width of choice and the uncertainty of consequences combine to rob the notion of maximum profit of its simplicity; at the minimum of complexity, the firm must be viewed as seeking some combination of anticipated return and possible variation, at the same time perhaps safeguarding itself against too much variation. But even this is too simple. In the absence of the constraints of a competitive market, the firm may seek a variety of goals: "satisfactory" profits, an "adequate" rate of growth, a "safe" share of the market, "good" labor relations, "good" public relations, and so forth, and no particular combination need adequately describe the behavior of all large firms with significant market power.

The large corporations with which we are here concerned characteristically operate many plants and sell and buy in many markets. Their power in some markets can be used to reinforce their power in others; their large absolute size, and the pool of capital at their command, adds something to their power in any particular market which is not explained simply by the structure of that market. In the extreme, the operations of the firm in a particular market can be completely or almost completely insensitive to its economic fortunes in that market, and thus the range of choice of decisions with respect to it may be widened far beyond that possible to any firm confined within its boundaries. Absolute size has to a certain extent the same effect in respect to the operations of any particular short time-period: the impact of likely short-period losses or failures may bulk insufficiently large to form a significant constraint on action.

We have spoken so far of the powers of choice of the corporation and the management interchangeably. By and large, this is justified. Corporate management is typically — in the reaches of business we are examining — an autonomous center of decision, organizing the affairs of the corporation and choosing its own successors. While stockholders are significant as part of the environment in which management operates, they exercise little or no power of choice themselves. The views of stockholders, as reflected in their willingness to hold or their desire to dispose of the corporation's stock, are certainly taken into account by management, but only as one of a number of elements which condition their decisions. The ideology of corporate management which describes them as one among a number of client groups whose interests are the concern of management — labor, consumers, and the "public" forming the others — is in this particular realistic.

[1] See Otto Eckstein, "Inflation, the Wage-Price Spiral, and Economic Growth," *The Relationship of Prices to Economic Stability and Growth*, papers submitted by panelists appearing before the Joint Economic Committee, 85 Cong., 2 Sess. (Washington, D.C., March 1958).

How does the giant corporation manifest its power? Most directly, in economic terms, the noteworthy dimensions of choice open to it include prices and price-cost relations, investment, location, research and innovation, and product character and selling effort. Management choice in each of these dimensions has significance for the particular markets in which the firm operates, and with respect to some of them, may have broader significance for the economy as a whole.

Prices and price-cost relations, in turn, show at least four important aspects. First is the classic question of the general level of prices in relation to costs: are profits excessive? Second, and perhaps more important, is the effect of margins on the level of costs themselves. Where the pressure of competition does not force prices down to costs, costs themselves have a tendency to rise: internal managerial checks alone cannot overcome the tendency to be satisfied with costs when the over-all level of profit is satisfactory. Third, there is the problem of interrelations among margins on related products: does the price of a Chevrolet bear the same relation to its costs as the price of a Cadillac, or is there a tendency to earn more in the long run on resources converted into the one than into the other? This form of distortion of price-cost relations is common in the multiproduct firm, and can coexist with a modest average profit margin. Finally, there are the interrelations, both directly within a single firm and indirectly through labor and product markets, of prices and wages. Where price increases are the response to wage increases which in turn respond to price increases, the pricing policy of a firm or group of firms can be an inflationary factor of some importance. This has been the case in the steel industry in the postwar period.[1] A related problem is the behavior of prices in the face of declining demand. When a group of firms can raise prices relative to wages although unused capacity is large and increasing, they make a contribution to aggregate instability, in this case in a deflationary rather than an inflationary direction. Here again the steel industry provides a recent example.

The investment decisions of large firms are of primary importance in determining the rates of growth of particular industries, and where the role of these industries in the economy is a strategic one, their impact may be much wider. Again we may point to the steel industry. Overpessimism about expansion in the early postwar period contributed to the continuing bottleneck in steel that was apparent until the 1957 recession. In the twenties, the slowness with which aluminum capacity was expanded led to recurrent shortages in that market. The speed, or slowness, with which investment in nuclear-fueled electric power generation is now going forward, even with the aid of considerable government subsidy, is again the product of the decisions of a relatively small number of major power producers. This is not to argue that the pace chosen is the wrong one, but simply to indicate a choice of possible broad significance, lying in large part in the hands of a few corporate managements.

A particular kind of investment decision, the consequences of which may reach far into the future and beyond the specific firm or industry involved, is the decision about location. Where new plants are placed both in regional terms and in relation to existing centers of population affects the balance of regional development and the character of urban and suburban growth. Characteristically, it is the large multiplant enterprise which has the widest set of alternatives from among which to choose in making this decision; smaller firms are tied closely to their existing geographic centers.

Even more far reaching are the choices of large enterprises in respect to innovation. Decisions as to the technical areas which will be systematically explored by research and development divisions and decisions as to what scientific and technical novelties will be translated into new products and new processes and tried out for economic viability have very deep effects. Ultimately, the whole material fabric of society, the structure of occupations, the geographic distribution of economic activity and population are all profoundly affected by the pattern of technical change. Not all significant technical change springs from the activities of organized research and development departments, but they do appear to be of increasing importance. And the disproportionate share of a few large corporations in this sphere is greater than in any other. Here again, I am not arguing that the decisions now taken on these matters are necessarily inferior to those which would result from some different distribution of decision-making power, but only pointing to the locus of an important power of choice.

It is worth remarking, on a lower level of generality, that the concentration of the power of choice with respect to new products and new models of old products in a few hands has a significance which is enhanced by the large role which producers' initiative plays in determining consumers' choices in our economy. Whether the extent and character of advertising and selling in our economy is something idiosyncratically American, or simply a product of the high average level of income combined with its relatively equal distribution, it is clear that the importance of these institutions adds to the importance of the producers' power of choice in respect to product change and new products. Further, selling and advertising are likewise relatively highly concentrated, and both the pervasiveness of "sales talk" in the media of communication and the relatively large amounts of its income our rich society spends on all kinds of durable goods give decisions in the sphere of product character and selling techniques a wide impact.

The significance of the economic choices that are made by the powerful large firm can be summed up in terms of their effects on the achievement of four basic economic goals: efficiency, stability, progressiveness, and equity. Economic efficiency means producing the most of what consumers want with available supplies of resources. It involves not only the idea of technical efficiency — for example, performing any particular technical operation with the cheapest combination of inputs required for a unit of output — but the more subtle idea of not producing less of any one particular good in relation to others, and conversely, more of another, than consumers' desires indicate. In more concrete terms, whenever one particular good is priced high in relation to its costs, while another one is priced low, then too much of the second and too little of the first tends to be produced in relation to consumers' demands. When the price-cost margin on a product remains high over a period of time, this is an indication of economic inefficiency. So is continued price discrimination, in the sense in which we defined it above. In addition, of course, the lack of competitive pressure on margins may lead to inefficiency in the simpler sense as well: not producing the actual goods with the minimum amount of resources possible. The exercise of market power thus leads frequently to economic inefficiency.

Stability of output and employment at high levels, and, perhaps a little less important, of price levels, is an economic goal which is generally given great weight. The exercise of pricing discretion can contribute to destabilizing forces both in upswings and downswings of activity. As we argued before, there are examples of wage-price spirals in which a significant upward push on wage levels in general, and thus on price levels, is exercised by particular pricing decisions. The maintenance of margins in the face of declining demand is less clear and striking in its effects, but it probably makes a net contribution to further destabilization in comparison with some moderate decline. On the other hand, it is clear that stable prices and wages are far more desirable than continuous declines in both in the face of declining aggregate demand; and thus the choice typically made by the powerful firm may be less than the best but considerably better than the worst possible one.

When we come to test the economic decisions of the large firm against the standard of progressiveness, we find that we can say little that is unequivocal. That large firms spend heavily on research and development is clear. That some industries in which the application of improved techniques and growth of output of new products is spectacular are industries — such as chemicals, oil, electronics — dominated by large firms is also clear. But when we try to look deeper, obscurity replaces clarity. Is the present degree of dominance of large firms a necessary condition of the amount of progress experienced, or even a sufficient condition? Are larger firms more effective, per dollar of expenditures, in producing new ideas and new methods than smaller ones are, and over what size range is this true? Should corporations spend on research and development much more or much less than they now spend? Should the incentives of the market be allowed more or less control than they now have of the whole chain of sequential and interrelated processes from the first observation of a new natural phenomenon or the first conception of a new scientific idea to the introduction into the market of a new product or the application on the production line of a new technology? These are all questions to which well-informed and competent students do not give the same answer, if indeed they give any. However, it is enough for our present purpose to say that there are specific examples of the importance for technical progress of competition, and particularly of the kind of competition represented by new and small firms that are not heavily committed to present products and processes, in sufficient number to cast doubt on the universal correctness of the judgments of powerful dominant firms.[1] While we cannot assert that these judgments are likely to be always wrong, we also cannot say that they need no corrective. When technical change can take the spectacularly wasteful forms that it has achieved recently in the automobile industry, in which new products, introduced at considerable production and marketing expense, are not cheaper to produce, cheaper to operate, nor more durable than those they supplant, and their increase in serviceability, functional efficiency, or even aesthetic appeal is at best debatable, it is hard to deny that "progress" and "free choice in the marketplace" both become phrases of rather dubious content. All the potential gain in productive efficiency in the automobile industry over the last decade, and probably more, has gone into "more" product rather than into cost savings and price reductions. This result is the product of decisions of a small number of managements — perhaps only one — and it underlines the appropriateness of raising the question of whether there is not too much power in the hands of those responsible for the choice.

The standard of equity is at least as slippery as that of progressiveness, although for different reasons. While the importance of equity in the sense of a fair distribution of the income of society as a goal is undeniable, equity itself is not measurable by any economic standard. We have long since abandoned reliance on the notion that the reward of the marketplace is necessarily a "fair" reward, even when the market functions effectively and competitively. Indeed, some of our interferences with the functioning of markets are justified on equity grounds, reflecting our social dissatisfaction with the income distribution resulting from the unchecked operation of the market. But, although little exists in the way of comprehensive standards of equity which command wide acceptance, certain specific judgments are possible. "Excessive" property incomes are suspect: high profits based on monopoly power are widely subject to criticism. Where market power is translated into sustained high profits, the result can be described as

inequitable as well as inefficient. Further, where management decision translates a portion of the high profits into high salaries, bonuses, stock options, and generous pension plans for itself, the imputation of unfairness is strengthened. These are recorded as views that command fairly wide agreement, not as economically inevitable conclusions nor necessary moral judgments. It may be that the equally high incomes of crooners and .400 hitters are logically open to as much criticism; in fact, however, they are not so much criticized.

Any discussion of equity moves rapidly from an economic to what is essentially a political view, since equity is ultimately a value problem whose social resolution is of the essence of politics. When we make this move, a new order of equity problems connected with the power of the large firm appears. This is the problem of the relation between the large enterprise and the host of small satellite enterprises which become its dependents. These may be customers bound to it by a variety of contractual relations, such as the service stations bound to the major oil companies who are their suppliers (and frequently their landlords and bankers as well), or the automobile dealers connected with the manufacturers by franchise arrangements. Or they may be customers without explicit contractual ties, yet nonetheless dependent on the maintenance of "customary" relations with large suppliers of their essential raw material, as has been the case with small fabricators of aluminum and steel products, whose business destinies have been controlled by the informal rationing schemes of the primary producers in the frequent shortage periods of the postwar decade. Or they may be small suppliers of large firms: canners packing for the private brands of the large chain grocers, furniture or clothing manufacturers producing for the chain department stores and mail-order houses, subcontractors producing for the major military suppliers. In any case, these small firms are typically wholly dependent on their larger partners. It is worth noting that this dependence may be consistent with a fairly competitive situation in the major product market of the large purchaser, or even the over-all selling market of the large supplier, provided the particular submarket in which the transactions between large and small firm occur is segmented enough to make it costly and risky for the small firm to seek new sources or outlets.

All these relations present a double problem. First, is the treatment which the dependent firms experience "fair" in the concrete: Have there been cancellations of dealers' franchises by major automobile manufacturers for no cause, or, worse, in order to transfer them to firms in which company executives had an interest? Have aluminum companies "favored" their own fabricating operations at the expense of independent fabricators during periods of short supply?[2] Second, and more fundamental, is what might be called the procedural aspect of the problem. Whether unfair treatment by large firms of their small clients abounds, or is so rare as

---

[1] See R. Maclaurin, *Innovation and Invention in the Radio Industry* (New York, 1949); A. A. Bright, Jr., *The Electric Lamp Industry* (New York, 1949); C. Kaysen, *United States v. United Shoe Machinery Co.* (Cambridge, Mass., 1956); J. Jewkes et al., *The Sources of Invention* (London, 1958).

[2] See, on automobiles, the *Hearings on Automobile Marketing Practices* before the Interstate and Foreign Commerce Committee of the Senate, 84 Cong., 2 Sess. On aluminum, see the *Hearings* before Subcommittee No. 3 of the Select Committee on Small Business, House of Representatives, 84 Cong., 1 Sess. (1956) and the *Hearings* before the same Subcommittee, 85 Cong., 1 and 2 Sess. (1958).

to be written off as the vagary of a few executives, the question of whether it is appropriate for the large firm to possess what amount to life-and-death powers over other business remains.

And the same question arises more broadly than in respect to the patron-client relations of large firms and their dependent small suppliers and customers. All of the areas of decision in which powerful managements have wide scope for choice, with effects reaching far into the economy, that we discussed above raise the same question. Not the concrete consequences of choice measured against the economic standards of efficiency, stability, progressiveness, and equity, but the power and scope of choice itself is the problem. This view of the problem may appear somewhat abstract, and even be dismissed as a piece of academic fussiness: if the outcomes are in themselves not objectionable, why should we concern ourselves with the process of decision which led to them; and, if they are, why not address ourselves to improving them directly? But so to argue ignores the point that choice of economic goals is itself a value choice, and thus a political one; and that direct concern with the loci of power and constraints on its use may legitimately rank in importance as political goals with the attainment of desired economic values. If the regime of competition and the arguments of *laissez-faire* ever commended themselves widely, it has been primarily on political rather than economic grounds. The replacement of the all-too-visible hand of the state by the invisible hand of the marketplace, which guided each to act for the common good while pursuing his own interests and aims without an overt show of constraint, was what attracted general ideological support to the liberal cause. The elegance of the optimum allocation of resources which Walras and Pareto saw in the ideal competitive economy by contrast has remained a concept of importance only to the most academic economist. When the invisible hand of the competitive market is, in turn, displaced to a significant extent by the increasingly visible hand of powerful corporate management, the question "Quo warranto?" is bound to arise, whatever decisions are in fact made. And the fact is that the power of corporate management is, in the political sense, irresponsible power, answerable ultimately only to itself. No matter how earnestly management strives to "balance" interests in making its decisions — interests of stockholders, of employees, of customers, of the "general public," as well as the institutional interests of the enterprise — it is ultimately its own conception of these interests and their desirable relations that rules. When the exercise of choice is strongly constrained by competitive forces, and the power of decision of any particular management is narrow and proportioned to the immediate economic needs of the enterprise, the political question of the warrant of management authority and its proper scope does not arise. When, as we have argued, the scope of choice is great and the consequences reach widely into the economy and far into the future, the problem of the authority and

responsibility of the choosers is bound to become pressing.

The market power which large absolute and relative size gives to the giant corporation is the basis not only of economic power but also of considerable political and social power of a broader sort. Some of the political power of large business is of course the product of group action to defend group interests and, in this sense, presents no problems peculiar to large business, except perhaps the problem of the large availability of funds and certain nonpurchasable resources of specialized talent and prestige in support of its interest. That we pay, in the form of percentage depletion, an outrageous subsidy to the oil and gas business (which goes to many small producers as well as to the giant integrated oil firms) is a phenomenon of no different order than that we pay nearly equally outrageous ones to farmers. On the other hand, it is money rather than votes which supports the one, and votes rather than money which support the other; and the latter situation is, as the former is not, in accord with our professed political morality. More special to the position of the large firm is the power in both domestic and foreign affairs which the large oil companies have by virtue of their special positions as concessionaires — frequently on a monopoly basis in a particular country — in exploiting the oil of the Middle East and the Caribbean. Here the large firms exercise quasi-sovereign powers, have large influence on certain aspects of the foreign policy of the United States and the Atlantic Alliance, and operate in a way which is neither that of public government nor that of private business. While the oil companies are the most spectacular examples of the involvement of strong American companies with weak foreign governments in areas which are important to national policy, they are not the only ones, and other examples could be cited.

Perhaps the most pervasive influence of big business on national politics lies in the tone of the mass media. Both because of the influence of advertising — itself heavily concentrated in the largest firms, and the big-business character of many publishing and broadcasting enterprises, the political tone of the media is far from reflecting even approximately the distribution of attitudes and opinions in the society as a whole. But an influence may be pervasive without thereby being powerful, and the importance of this state of affairs is open to argument.

It is when we step down from the level of national politics to the state and local levels that the political power of the large corporation is seen in truer perspective. The large national-market firm has available to it the promise of locating in a particular area or expanding its operations there, the threat of moving or contracting its operations as potent bargaining points in its dealings with local and even state political leaders. The branch manager of the company whose plant is the largest employer in a town or the vice-president of the firm proposing to build a plant which will become the largest employer in a small state treats with local government not as a citizen but as a quasi-sovereign power. Taxes, zoning laws, roads, and the like become matters of negotiation as much as matters of legislation. Even large industrial states and metropolitan cities may face similar problems: the largest three employers in Michigan account for probably a quarter of the state's industrial employment; in Detroit the proportion is more nearly a third. At this level, the corporation's scope of choice, its financial staying power, its independence of significant local forces are all sources of strength in dealing with the characteristically weak governments at the local and often at the state levels.

The broader social power which the high executives of large corporations exercise — in part in their own positions, in part in their representative capacity as "business leaders" — is more difficult to define and certainly less definite than the kind of political power and economic power discussed above. Yet it is no less important, and to the extent that it is linked to the economic power of the large firm — a point to which I return immediately below — no less relevant to our discussion. One aspect of this broad power to which we have already referred is the position that corporate management occupies as taste setter or style leader for the society as a whole. Business influence on taste ranges from the direct effects through the design of material goods to the indirect and more subtle effects of the style of language and thought purveyed through the mass media — the school of style at which all of us are in attendance every day. Further, these same business leaders are dominant social models in our society: their achievements and their values are to a large extent the type of the excellent, especially for those strata of society from which leaders in most endeavors are drawn. This, more shortly stated, is the familiar proposition that we are a business society, and that the giant corporation is the "characteristic," if not the statistically typical, institution of our society, and, in turn, the social role of high executives is that appropriate to leading men in the leading institution.

How much is this kind of social power, as well as the political power discussed above, connected with the market power of giant firms? Is it simply a consequence of their economic power, or does it depend on deeper elements in our social structure? These are questions to which any firm answer is difficult, in part because they can be interpreted to mean many different things. To assert that any diminution in the underlying power of large firms in the markets in which they operate would lead to a corresponding decrease in their social and political power appears unwarranted; so does the assertion that universally competitive markets would end the social and political power of business. But there are important connections. Part of the power of the business leaders comes from the size of the enterprises they operate and the number of people they influence directly as employees, suppliers, customers; absolute size, in turn, is highly correlated with relative size and market power. Freedom in spending money is connected

with both absolute size, and the security of income which market power provides. The initiative in the complex processes of taste formation might shift away from smaller and more competitive businesses toward other institutions to a substantial extent; and the ability of firms to spend large resources on shaping demand would be lessened by reductions in their market power. Thus diminution of the economic power of large firms would have a more-than-trivial effect on their power in other spheres, even if we cannot state firmly the law that relates them.

The reasons for concern about the social and political power of business are also worth consideration, since they are not obviously the same as those which the concentrated economic power of large corporations raise. There are two aspects of this question which appear worth distinguishing. The first is the already-mentioned point of the irresponsibility of business power. Its exercise with respect to choices which are themselves far from the matters of meeting the material needs of society that are the primary tasks of business further emphasizes this point. The process of selection of business leaders may be adaptive with respect to their performance of the economic function of business; there is no reason to expect that it should be with respect to the exercise of power in other realms. In short, why should we entrust to the judgment of business leaders decisions of this kind, when we have neither a mechanism for ratifying or rejecting their judgments and them, nor any reason to believe them particularly suited to make these judgments? Second, we can go further than merely to raise the question of whether the training and selection of business leaders qualifies them to make the kinds of decisions and exercise the kinds of power we have discussed. In some quite important respects, it is clear that business values and business attitudes are dysfunctional in meeting our national needs. This is true both with respect to the many problems which we face in our international relations, and with respect to important domestic problems as well. If we look on our economic relations with the under-developed nations, especially those of Asia and Africa, as primarily tasks of business firms to be met through the market under the stimulus of market incentives, supported to some extent by special subsidies, it appears unlikely that we will succeed in achieving our political and security goals. If our attitudes toward other governments are heavily colored by ideological evaluations of the kind of economic organization they favor, from the standpoint of our own business ideology, our world problems will be made no easier. And in the domestic sphere, there is a range of problems from education to metropolitan organization and urban renewal which cannot be dealt with adequately if viewed in business perspectives and under business values.

We can sum up these points by saying that the position of big businesses and their leaders contributes significantly to our being a "business society." Do we want to be? Can we afford to be?

These rhetorical questions indicate clearly enough my own view on whether or not we should try to limit or control the power of large corporate enterprise. The crucial question, however, is whether such power can be limited or controlled. Broadly, there are three alternative possibilities. The first is limitation of business power through promoting more competitive markets; the second is broader control of business power by agencies external to business; the third, institutionalization within the firm of responsibility for the exercise of power. Traditionally, we have purported to place major reliance on the first of these alternatives, in the shape of antitrust policy, without in practice pushing very hard any effort to restrict market power to the maximum feasible extent. I have argued elsewhere that it is in fact possible to move much further than we have in this direction, without either significant loss in the over-all effectiveness of business performance or the erection of an elaborate apparatus of control.[1] While this, in my judgment, remains the most desirable path of policy, I do not in fact consider it the one which we will tend to follow. To embark on a determined policy of the reduction of business size and growth in order to limit market power requires a commitment of faith in the desirability of the outcome and the feasibility of the process which I think is not widespread. What I consider more likely is some mixture of the second and third types of control. Business itself has argued vehemently that a corporate revolution is now in process, which has resulted in a redirection of business goals and conscious assumption of responsibility in broad social spheres. This theme has been put forward by academic writers as well.[2] To whatever extent such a "revolution" has taken place, it does not meet the need for the institutionalization of responsibility which the continued exercise of wide power demands. It is not sufficient for the business leaders to announce that they are thinking hard and wrestling earnestly with their wide responsibilities, if, in fact, the power of unreviewed and unchecked decision remains with them, and they remain a small, self-selecting group.[3] Some of the more sophisticated accounts of the revolutionary transformation of business identify business as a "profession" in the honorific sense, and imply that professional standards can be relied on as

a sufficient social control over the exercise of business power, as society does rely on them to control the exercise of the considerable powers of doctors and lawyers. This is a ramifying problem which we cannot here explore; it is sufficient to remark that there is, at least as yet, neither visible mechanism of uniform training to inculcate, nor visible organization to maintain and enforce, such standards; and, further, that even if business decisions in the business sphere could be "professionalized" and subject to the control of a guild apparatus, it seems less easy to expect that the same would be true of the exercise of business power in the social and political spheres.

Some likely directions of development of explicit control can be seen in the kinds of actions which now provoke Congressional inquiry, and the suggestions which flow from such inquiries. Concern with the wage-price spiral has led to Congressional investigation of "administered prices" and to suggestions that proposed price and wage changes in certain industries be reviewed by a public body before becoming effective. A combination of the increase of direct regulation of some of the economic choices of powerful firms with an increase in public criticism, and perhaps even institutionalized public discussion of the choices which are not explicitly controlled, appears probable. Such a program will, in effect, do by a formal mechanism and systematically what is currently being done in a somewhat haphazard way by Congressional investigation. On the whole, it is this which has been the active front. The development of mechanisms which will change the internal organization of the corporation, and define more closely and represent more presently the interests to which corporate management should respond and the goals toward which they should strive is yet to begin, if it is to come at all.

[1] See Kaysen and Turner, "Antitrust Policy."
[2] A. A. Berle, Jr., *The Twentieth Century Capitalist Revolution* (New York, 1954); A. D. H. Kaplan, *Big Enterprise in a Competitive System* (Washington, D.C., 1954), and A. D. H. Kaplan, J. Dirlam, and R. Lanzilloti, *The Pricing Policy of Big Business* (Washington, D.C., 1958).
[3] See E. S. Mason, "The Apologetics of Managerialism," *Journal of Business, University of Chicago*, 31: 1 (1958).

On the Concept of Political Power

Talcott Parsons

POWER IS ONE of the key concepts in the great Western tradition of thought about political phenomena. It is at the same time a concept on which, in spite of its long history, there is, on analytical levels, a notable lack of agreement both about its specific definition, and about many features of the conceptual context in which it should be placed. There is, however, a core complex of its meaning, having to do with the capacity of persons or collectivities "to get things done" effectively, in particular when their goals are obstructed by some kind of human resistance or opposition. The problem of coping with resistance then leads into the question of the role of coercive measures, including the use of physical force, and the relation of coercion to the voluntary and consensual aspects of power systems.

The aim of this paper is to attempt to clarify this complex of meanings and relations by placing the concept of power in the context of a general conceptual scheme for the analysis of large-scale and complex social systems, that is of societies. In doing so I speak as a sociologist rather than as a political scientist, but as one who believes that the interconnections of the principal social disciplines, including not only these two, but especially their relations to economics as well, are so close that on matters of general theory of this sort they cannot safely be treated in isolation; their interrelations must be made explicit and systematic. As a sociologist, I thus treat a central concept of political theory by selecting among the elements which have figured prominently in political theory in terms of their fit with and significance for the general theoretical analysis of society as a whole.

There are three principal contexts in which it seems to me that the difficulties of the concept of power, as treated in the literature of the last generation, come to a head. The first of these concerns its conceptual diffuseness, the tendency, in the tradition of Hobbes, to treat power as simply the generalized capacity to attain ends

or goals in social relations, independently of the media employed or of the status of "authorization" to make decisions or impose obligations.[1]

The effect of this diffuseness, as I call it, is to treat "influence" and sometimes money, as well as coercion in various aspects, as "forms" of power, thereby making it logically impossible to treat power as a *specific* mechanism operating to bring about changes in the action of other units, individual or collective, in the processes of social interaction. The latter is the line of thought I wish to pursue.

Secondly, there is the problem of the relation between the coercive and the consensual aspects. I am not aware of any treatment in the literature which presents a satisfactory solution of this problem. A major tendency is to hold that somehow "in the last analysis" power comes down to one or the other, i.e., to "rest on" command of coercive sanctions, *or* on consensus and the will to voluntary cooperation. If going to one or the other polar solution seems to be unacceptable, a way out, taken for example by Friedrich, is to speak of each of these as different "forms" of power. I shall propose a solution which maintains that both aspects are essential, but that neither of the above two ways of relating them is satisfactory, namely subordinating either one to the other or treating them as discrete "forms."

Finally the third problem is what, since the Theory of Games, has widely come to be called the "zero-sum" problem. The dominant tendency in the literature, for example in Lasswell and C. Wright Mills, is to maintain explicitly or implicitly that power is a zero-sum phenomenon, which is to say that there is a fixed "quantity" of power in any relational system and hence any gain of power on the part of A must by definition occur by diminishing the power at the disposal of other units, B, C, D. . . . There are, of course, restricted contexts in which this condition holds, but I shall argue that it does not hold for total systems of a sufficient level of complexity.

Some general assumptions

The initial assumption is that, within the conception of society as a system, there is an essential parallelism in theoretical structure between the conceptual schemes appropriate for the analysis of the economic and the

[1] Thus E. C. Banfield, *Political Influence* (New York: The Free Press of Glencoe, 1962), p. 348, speaks of control as the ability to cause another to give or withhold action, and power as the ability to establish control over another. Similarly, Robert Dahl, "The Concept of Power," *Behavioral Scientist* 2 (July, 1957), says that "*A* has power over *B* to the extent that he can get *B* to do something that *B* would not otherwise do." C. J. Friedrich takes a similar position in his book *Man and his Government* (New York: McGraw-Hill, 1963).

Reprinted from *Proceedings of the American Philosophical Society*, Vol. 107, No. 3, June, 1963, by permission of the author and the publisher.

political aspects of societies. There are four respects in which I wish to attempt to work out and build on this parallel, showing at the same time the crucial substantive differences between the two fields.

First "political theory" as here interpreted, which is not simply to be identified with the meaning given the term by many political scientists, is thought of as an abstract analytical scheme in the same sense in which economic theory is abstract and analytical. It is not the conceptual interpretation of any concretely complete category of social phenomena, quite definitely not those of government, though government is the area in which the political element comes nearest to having clear primacy over others. Political theory thus conceived is a conceptual scheme which deals with a restricted set of primary variables and their interrelations, which are to be found operating in all concrete parts of social systems. These variables are, however, subject to parametric conditions which constitute the values of other variables operating in the larger system which constitutes the society.

Secondly, following on this, I assume that the empirical system to which political theory in this sense applies is an analytically defined, a "functional" sub-system of a society, not for example a concrete type of collectivity. The conception of the economy of a society is relatively well defined.[1] I should propose the conception of the *polity* as the parallel empirical system of direct relevance to political theory as here advanced. The polity of a given society is composed of the ways in which the relevant components of the total system are organized with reference to one of its fundamental functions, namely effective collective action in the attainment of the goals of collectivities. Goal-attainment in this sense is the establishment of a satisfactory relation between a collectivity and certain objects in its environment which include both other collectivities and categories of personalities, e.g. "citizens." A total society must in these terms be conceived, in one of its main aspects, as a collectivity, but it is also composed of an immense variety of subcollectivities, many of which are parts not only of this society but of others.[2]

A collectivity, seen in these terms, is thus clearly not a concrete "group" but the term refers to groups, i.e. systematically related pluralities of persons, seen in the perspective of their interests in and capacities for effective collective action. The political process then is the process by which the necessary organization is built up and operated, the goals of action are determined and the resources requisite to it are mobilized.

These two parallels to economic theory can be extended to still a third. The parallel to collective action in the political case is, for the economic, production. This conception in turn must be understood in relation to three main operative contexts. The first is adjustment to the conditions of "demand" which are conceived to be external to the economy itself, to be located in the "consumers" of the economic process. Secondly, resources must be mobilized, also from the environment

of the economy, the famous factors of production. Thirdly, the internal economic process is conceived as creatively combinatorial; it is, by the "combination" of factors of production in the light of the utility of outputs, a process of creating more valuable facilities to meet the needs of consuming units than would be available to them without this combinatorial process. I wish most definitely to postulate that the logic of "value added" applies to the political sphere in the present sense.[3]

In the political case, however, the value reference is not to utility in the economic sense but to effectiveness, very precisely, I think in the sense used by C. I. Barnard.[4] For the limited purposes of political analysis as such the givenness of the goal-demands of interest groups serves as the same order of factor in relation to the political system as has the corresponding givenness of consumers' wants for purposes of economic analysis — and of course the same order of qualifications on the empirical adequacy of such postulates.

Finally, fourth, political analysis as here conceived is parallel to economic in the sense that a central place in it is occupied by a generalized medium involved in the political interaction process, which is also a "measure" of the relevant values. I conceive power as such a generalized medium in a sense directly parallel in logical structure, though very different substantively, to money as the generalized medium of the economic process. It is essentially this conception of power as a generalized medium parallel to money which will, in the theoretical context sketched above, provide the thread for guiding the following analysis through the types of historic difficulty with reference to which the paper began.

The outputs of political process and the factors of effectiveness

The logic of the combinatorial process which I hold to be common to economic theory and the type of political theory advanced here, involves a paradigm of inputs and outputs and their relations. Again we will hold that the logic is strictly parallel to the economic case, i.e. that there should be a set of political categories strictly parallel to those of the factors of production

[1] *Cf.* Talcott Parsons and Neil J. Smelser, *Economy and Society* (New York: The Free Press of Glencoe, 1956), chapter I, for a discussion of this conception.

[2] E.g. the American medical profession is part of American society, but also it is part of a wider medical profession which transcends this particular society, to some extent as collectivity. Interpenetration in membership is thus a feature of the relations among collectivities.

[3] For discussions of the conception of "value-added" in spheres of application broader than the economic alone, *cf.* Neil J. Smelser, *Social Change in the Industrial Revolution* (New York: The Free Press of Glencoe, 1959), chapter II, pp. 7–20, and Neil J. Smelser, *Theory of Collective Behavior* (New York: The Free Press of Glencoe, 1963), chapter II, pp. 23–47.

[4] C. I. Barnard, *The Functions of the Executive* (Cambridge: Harvard University Press, 1938), chapter V, pp. 46–64.

(inputs) on the one hand, the shares of income (outputs) on the other.

In the economic case, with the exception of land, the remaining three factors must be regarded as inputs from the other three cognate functional subsystems of the society, labor from what we call the "pattern-maintenance" system, capital from the polity, and organization, in the sense of Alfred Marshall, from the integrative system.[1] Furthermore, it becomes clear that land is not, as a factor of production, simply the physical resource, but essentially the commitment, in value terms, of any resources to economic production in the system independent of price.

In the political case, similarly the equivalent of land is the commitment of resources to effective collective action, independent of any specifiable "pay-off" for the unit which controls them.[2] Parallel to labor is the demands or "need" for collective action as manifested in the "public" which in some sense is the constituency of the leadership of the collectivity in question — a conception which is relatively clear for the governmental or other electoral association, but needs clarification in other connections. Parallel to capital is the control of some part of the productivity of the economy for the goals of the collectivity, in a sufficiently developed economy through financial resources at the disposal of the collectivity, acquired by earnings, gift, or taxation. Finally, parallel to organization is the legitimation of the authority under which collective decisions are taken.

It is most important to note that none of these categories of input is conceived as a form of power. In so far as they involve media, it is the media rooted in contiguous functional systems, not power as that central to the polity — e.g. control of productivity may operate through money, and constituents' demands through what I call "influence." Power then is the *means* of acquiring control of the factors in effectiveness; it is not itself one of these factors, any more than in the economic case money is a factor of production; to suppose it was, was the ancient mercantilist fallacy.

Though the analytical context in which they are placed is perhaps unfamiliar in the light of traditional political analysis, I hope it is clear that the actual categories used are well established, though there remain a number of problems of exact definition. Thus control of productivity through financing of collective action is

very familiar, and the concept of "demands" in the sense of what constituents want and press for, is also very familiar.[3] The concept legitimation is used in essentially the same sense in which I think Max Weber used it in a political context.[4]

The problem of what corresponds, for the political case, to the economist's "shares of income" is not very difficult, once the essential distinction, a very old one in economic tradition, between monetary and "real" income is clearly taken into account. Our concern is with the "real" outputs of the political process — the analogue of the monetary here is output of power.

There is one, to us critically important revision of the traditional economic treatment of outputs which must be made, namely the bracketing together of "goods and services," which then would be treated as outputs to the household as, in our technical terms, a part of the "pattern-maintenance" system. The present position is that goods, i.e., more precisely property rights in the physical objects of possession, belong in this category, but that "services," the commitment of human role-performances to an "employer," or contracting agent constitute an output, not to the household, but to the polity, the type case (though not the only one) being an employing organization in which the role-incumbent commits himself to performance of an occupational role, a job,[5] as a contribution to the effective functioning of the collectivity.

There is, from this consideration, a conclusion which is somewhat surprising to economists, namely that service is, in the economic sense, the "real" counterpart of interest as monetary income from the use of funds. What we suggest is that the political control of productivity makes it possible, through combinatorial gains in the political context, to produce a surplus above the monetary funds committed, by virtue of which under specified conditions a premium can be paid at the monetary level which, though a result of the combinatorial process as a whole, is most directly related to the output of available services as an economic phenomenon, i.e. as a "fluid resource." Seen a little differently, it becomes necessary to make a clear distinction between labor as a factor of production in the economic sense and service as an output of the economic process which is utilized in a political context, that is one of organizational or collective effectiveness.

Service, however, is not a "factor" in effectiveness, in the sense in which labor is a factor of production, precisely because it is a category of power. It is the point at which the economic utility of the human factor is matched with its potential contribution to effective collective action. Since the consumer of services is in principle the employing collectivity, it is its effectiveness for collective goals, not its capacity to satisfy the "wants" of individuals, which is the vantage point from which the utility of the service is derived. The output of power which matches the input of services to the polity, I interpret to be the "opportunity for effectiveness" which employment confers on those employed or contract

---

[1] On the rationale of these attributions, see *Economy and Society, op. cit.*, chapter II.

[2] "Pay-off" may be a deciding factor in choice between particular contexts of use, but not as to whether the resources shall be devoted to collective effectiveness at all.

[3] I have in fact adopted the term "demands" from the usage of David Easton, "An Approach to the Analysis of Political Systems." *World Politics* **9** (1957): 383–400.

[4] *Cf.* Max Weber, *The Theory of Social and Economic Organization* (New York: Oxford University Press, 1947), p. 124. Translation by A. M. Henderson and Talcott Parsons; edited by Talcott Parsons.

[5] The cases of services concretely rendered to a household will be considered as a limiting case where the roles of consumer and employer have not become differentiated from each other.

offers to partners. Capital in the economic sense is one form of this opportunity for effectiveness which is derived from providing, for certain types of performances, a framework of effective organization.[1]

The second, particularly important context of "real" output of the political process is the category which, in accord with much tradition, I should like to call capacity to assume leadership responsibility. This, as a category of "real" output also is not a form of power, but this time of influence.[2] This is an output not to the economy but to what I shall call the integrative system, which in its relevance to the present context is in the first instance the sector of the "public" which can be looked on as the "constituencies" of the collective processes under consideration. It is the group structure of the society looked at in terms of their structured interests in particular modes of effective collective action by particular collectivities. It is only through effective organization that genuine responsibility can be taken, hence the implementation of such interest demands responsibility for collective effectiveness.[3] Again it should be made quite clear that leadership responsibility is not here conceived as an output of power, though many political theorists (e.g. Friedrich) treat both leadership and, more broadly influence, as "forms" of power. The power category which regulates the output of leadership influence takes this form on the one side of binding policy decisions of the collectivity, on the other of political support from the constituency, in the type case through franchise. Policy decisions we would treat as a factor in integration of the system, not as a "consumable" output of the political process.[4]

Finally, a few words need to be said about what I have called the combinatorial process itself. It is of course assumed in economic theory that the "structures" of the factors of production on the one hand, the "demand system" for real outputs on the other hand, are independent of each other. "Utility" of outputs can only be enhanced, to say nothing of maximized, by processes of transformation of the factors in the direction of providing what is wanted as distinguished from what merely is available. The decision-making aspect of this transformative process, what is to be produced, how much and how offered for consumption, is what is meant by economic production, whereas the physical processes are not economic but "technological"; they are controlled by economic considerations, but are not themselves in an analytical sense economic.

The consequence of successful adaptation of available resources to the want or demand system is an increment in the value of the resource-stock conceived in terms of utility as a type of value. But this means recombination of the components of the resource-stock in order to adapt them to the various uses in question.

The same logic applies to the combinatorial process in the political sphere. Here the resources are not land, labor, capital, and organization, but valuation of effectiveness, control of productivity, structured demands and the patterning of legitimation. The "wants" are not for

consumption in the economic sense, but for the solution of "interest" problems in the system, including both competitive problems in the allocative sense and conflict problems, as well as problems of enhancement of the total effectiveness of the system of collective organization. In this case also the "structure" of the available resources may not be assumed spontaneously to match the structure of the system of interest-demands. The increment of effectiveness in demand-satisfaction through the political process is, as in the economic case, arrived at through combinatorial decision-processes. The organizational "technology" involved is not in the analytical sense political. The demand-reference is not to discrete units of the system conceived in abstraction from the system as a whole — the "individual" consumer of the economist — but to the problem of the share of benefits and burdens to be allocated to subsystems of various orders. The "consumption" reference is to the interest-unit's place in the allocative system rather than to the independent merits of particular "needs."

The concept of power

The above may seem a highly elaborate setting in which to place the formal introduction of the main subject of the paper, namely the concept of power. Condensed and cryptic as the exposition may have been, however, understanding of its main structure is an essential basis for the special way in which it will be proposed to combine the elements which have played a crucial part in the main intellectual traditions dealing with the problems of power.

Power is here conceived as a circulating medium, analogous to money, within what is called the political system, but notably over its boundaries into all three of the other neighboring functional subsystems of a society (as I conceive them), the economic, integrative, and pattern-maintenance systems. Specification of the properties of power can best be approached through an attempt to delineate very briefly the relevant properties of money as such a medium in the economy.

Money is, as the classical economists said, both a

---

[1] In the cases treated as typical for economic analysis the collective element in capital is delegated through the *bindingness* of the contracts of loan of financial resources. To us this is a special case, employment being another, of the binding obligation assumed by an organization, whether it employs or loans, by virtue of which the recipient can be more effective than would otherwise be the case. It is not possible to go further into these complex problems here, but they will, perhaps, be somewhat illuminated by the later discussion of the place of the concept of bindingness in the theory of power.

[2] See my paper "On the Concept of Influence," *Public Opinion Quarterly* 27 (Spring, 1963), pp. 37–62.

[3] Here again Barnard's usage of the concept of responsibility seems to me the appropriate one. See Barnard, *op. cit.*

[4] In order not to complicate things too much, I shall not enter into problem of the interchange system involving legitimation here. See my paper "Authority, Legitimation, and Political Process," in *Nomos* I, reprinted as chapter V of my *Structure and Process in Modern Societies* (New York: The Free Press, 1960), chapter V, pp. 170–198.

medium of exchange and a "measure of value." It is symbolic in that, though measuring and thus "standing for" economic value or utility, it does not itself possess utility in the primary consumption sense – it has no "value in use" but only "in exchange," i.e. for possession of things having utility. The use of money is thus a mode of communication of offers, on the one hand to purchase, on the other to sell, things of utility, with and for money. It becomes an essential medium only when exchange is neither ascriptive, as exchange of gifts between assigned categories of kin, nor takes place on a basis of barter, one item of commodity or service directly for another.

In exchange for its lack of direct utility money gives the recipient four important degrees of freedom in his participation in the total exchange system. *1*) He is free to spend his money for any item or combination of items available on the market which he can afford, *2*) he is free to shop around among alternative sources of supply for desired items, *3*) he can choose his own time to purchase, and *4*) he is free to consider terms which, because of freedom of time and source he can accept or reject or attempt to influence in the particular case. By contrast, in the case of barter, the negotiator is bound to what his particular partner has or wants in relation to what he has and will part with at the particular time. The other side of the gain in degrees of freedom is of course the risk involved in the probabilities of the acceptance of money by others and of the stability of its value.

Primitive money is a medium which is still very close to a commodity, the commonest case being precious metal, and many still feel that the value of money is "really" grounded in the commodity value of the metallic base. On this base, however, there is, in developed monetary systems, erected a complex structure of credit instruments, so that only a tiny fraction of actual transactions is conducted in terms of the metal – it becomes a "reserve" available for certain contingencies, and is actually used mainly in the settlement of international balances. I shall discuss the nature of credit further in another connection later. For the moment suffice it to say that, however important in certain contingencies the availability of metallic reserves may be, no modern monetary system operates primarily with metal as the actual medium, but uses "valueless" money. Moreover, the acceptance of this "valueless" money rests on a certain institutionalized confidence in the monetary system. If the security of monetary commitments rested only on their convertibility into metal, then the overwhelming majority of them would be worthless, for the simple reason that the total quantity of metal is far too small to redeem more than a few.

One final point is that money is "good," i.e. works as a medium, only within a relatively defined network of market relationships which to be sure now has become world-wide, but the maintenance of which requires special measures to maintain mutual convertibility of national currencies. Such a system is on the one hand a range of exchange-potential within which money may be spent, but on the other hand, one within which certain conditions affecting the protection and management of the unit are maintained, both by law and by responsible agencies under the law.

The first focus of the concept of an institutionalized power system is, analogously, a relational system within which certain categories of commitments and obligations, ascriptive or voluntarily assumed – e.g. by contract – are treated as binding, i.e. under normatively defined conditions their fulfillment may be insisted upon by the appropriate role-reciprocal agencies. Furthermore, in case of actual or threatened resistance to "compliance," i.e. to fulfillment of such obligations when invoked, they will be "enforced" by the threat or actual imposition of situational negative sanctions, in the former case having the function of deterrence, in the latter of punishment. These are events in the situation of the actor of reference which intentionally alter his situation (or threaten to) to his disadvantage, whatever in specific content these alterations may be.

Power then is generalized capacity to secure the performance of binding obligations by units in a system of collective organization when the obligations are legitimized with reference to their bearing on collective goals and where in case of recalcitrance there is a presumption of enforcement by negative situational sanctions – whatever the actual agency of that enforcement.

It will be noted that I have used the conceptions of generalization and of legitimation in defining power. Securing possession of an object of utility by bartering another object for it is not a monetary transaction. Similarly, by my definition, securing compliance with a wish, whether it be defined as an obligation of the object or not, simply by threat of superior force, is not an exercise of power. I am well aware that most political theorists would draw the line differently and classify this as power (e.g. Dahl's definition), but I wish to stick to my chosen line and explore its implications. The capacity to secure compliance must, if it is to be called power in my sense, be generalized and not solely a function of one particular sanctioning act which the user is in a position to impose,[1] and the medium used must be "symbolic."

Secondly, I have spoken of power as involving legitimation. This is, in the present context, the necessary consequence of conceiving power as "symbolic," which therefore, if it is exchanged for something intrinsically valuable for collective effectiveness, namely compliance with an obligation, leaves the recipient, the performer of the obligation, with "nothing of value." This is to say, that he has "nothing" but a set of expectations, namely that in other contexts and on other occasions, he can invoke certain obligations of the part of other units. Legitimation is therefore, in power systems, the factor which is parallel to confidence in

---

[1] There is a certain element of generality in physical force as a negative sanction, which gives it a special place in power systems. This will be taken up later in the discussion.

mutual acceptability and stability of the monetary unit in monetary systems.

The two criteria are connected in that questioning the legitimacy of the possession and use of power leads to resort to progressively more "secure" means of gaining compliance. These must be progressively more effective "intrinsically," hence more tailored to the particular situations of the objects and less general. Furthermore in so far as they are intrinsically effective, legitimacy becomes a progressively less important factor of their effectiveness — at the end of this series lies resort, first to various types of coercion, eventually to the use of force as the most intrinsically effective of all means of coercion.[1]

I should like now to attempt to place both money and power in the context of a more general paradigm, which is an analytical classification of ways in which, in the processes of social interaction, the actions of one unit in a system can, intentionally, be oriented to bringing about a change in what the actions of one or more other units would otherwise have been — thus all fitting into the context of Dahl's conception of power. It is convenient to state this in terms of the convention of speaking of the acting unit of reference — individual or collective — as *ego*, and the object on which he attempts to "operate" as *alter*. We may then classify the alternatives open to ego in terms of two dichotomous variables. On the one hand ego may attempt to gain his end from alter either by using some form of control over the situation in which alter is placed, actually or contingently to change it so as to increase the probability of alter acting in the way he wishes, or, alternatively, without attempting to change alter's situation, ego may attempt to change alter's intentions, i.e. he may manipulate symbols which are meaningful to alter in such a way that he tries to make alter "see" that what ego wants is a "good thing" for him (alter) to do.

The second variable then concerns the type of sanctions ego may employ in attempting to guarantee the attainment of his end from alter. The dichotomy here is between positive and negative sanctions. Thus through the situational channel a positive sanction is a change in alter's situation presumptively considered by alter as to his advantage, which is used as a means by ego of having an effect on alter's actions. A negative sanction then is an alteration in alter's situation to the latter's disadvantage. In the case of the intentional channel, the positive sanction is the expression of symbolic "reasons" why compliance with ego's wishes is "a good thing" independently of any further action on ego's part, from alter's point of view, i.e. would be felt by him to be "personally advantageous," whereas the negative sanction is presenting reasons why noncompliance with ego's wishes should be felt by alter to be harmful to interests in which he had a significant personal investment and should therefore be avoided. I should like to call the four types of "strategy" open to ego respectively *1)* for the situational channel, positive sanction case, "inducement"; *2)* situational channel

negative sanction, "coercion"; *3)* intentional channel, positive sanction "persuasion," and *4)* intentional channel, negative sanction "activation of commitments" as shown in the following table:

Sanction type		Channel		
Positive	Intentional Persuasion	3	1	Situational Inducement
Negative	Activation of Commitments	4	2	Coercion

A further complication now needs to be introduced. We think of a sanction as an intentional act on ego's part, expected by him to change his relation to alter from what it would otherwise have been. As a means of bringing about a change in alter's action, it can operate most obviously where the actual imposition of the sanction is made contingent on a future decision by alter. Thus a process of inducement will operate in two stages, first contingent offer on ego's part that, if alter will "comply" with his wishes, ego will "reward" him by the contingently promised situational change. If then alter in fact does comply, ego will perform the sanctioning act. In the case of coercion the first stage is a contingent threat that, unless alter decides to comply, ego will impose the negative sanction. If, however, alter complies, then nothing further happens, but, if he decides on noncompliance, then ego must carry out his threat, or be in a position of "not meaning it." In the cases of the intentional channel ego's first-stage act is either to predict the occurrence, or to announce his own intention of doing something which affects alter's sentiments or interests. The element of contingency enters in in that ego "argues" to alter, that if this happens on the one hand alter should be expected to "see" that it would be a good thing for him to do what ego wants — the positive case — or that if he fails to do it it would imply an important "subjective cost" to alter. In the positive case, beyond "pointing out" if alter complies, ego is obligated to deliver the positive attitudinal sanction of approval. In the negative case, the corresponding attitudinal sanction of disapproval is implemented only for noncompliance.

It is hence clear that there is a basic asymmetry between the positive and negative sides of the sanction aspect of the paradigm. This is that, in the cases of inducement and persuasion, alter's compliance obligates ego to "deliver" his promised positive sanction, in the former case the promised advantages, in the latter his approval of alter's "good sense" in recognizing that the decision wished for by ego and accepted as "good" by alter, in fact turns out to be good from alter's point of view. In the negative cases, on the other hand, com-

---

[1] There are complications here deriving from the fact that power is associated with *negative* sanctions and hence that, in the face of severe resistance, their effectiveness is confined to deterrence.

pliance on alter's part obligates ego, in the situational case, not to carry out his threat, in the intentional case by withholding disapproval to confirm to alter that his compliance did in fact spare him what to him, without ego's intervention, would have been the undesirable subjective consequences of his previous intentions, namely guilt over violations of his commitments.

Finally, alter's freedom of action in his decisions of compliance versus noncompliance is also a variable. This range has a lower limit at which the element of contingency disappears. That is, from ego's point of view, he may not say, if you do so and so, I will intervene, either by situational manipulations or by "arguments" in such and such a way, but he may simply perform an overt act and face alter with a *fait accompli*. In the case of inducement a gift which is an object of value and with respect to the acceptance of which alter is given no option is the limiting case. With respect to coercion, compulsion, i.e. simply imposing a disadvantageous alteration on alter's situation and then leaving it to alter to decide whether to "do something about it" is the limiting case.

The asymmetry just referred to appears here as well. As contingent it may be said that the primary meaning of negative sanctions is as means of prevention. If they are effective, no further action is required. The case of compulsion is that in which it is rendered impossible for alter to avoid the undesired action on ego's part. In the case of positive sanctions of course ego, for example in making a gift to alter, cuts himself out from benefiting from alter's performance which is presumptively advantageous to him, in the particular exchange.

Both, however, may be oriented to their effect on alter's action in future sequences of interaction. The object of compulsion may have been "taught a lesson" and hence be less disposed to noncompliance with ego's wishes in the future, as well as prevented from performance of a particular undesired act and the recipient of a gift may feel a "sense of obligation" to reciprocate in some form in the future.

So far this discussion has dealt with sanctioning acts in terms of their "intrinsic" significance both to ego and to alter. An offered inducement may thus be possession of a particular object of utility, a coercive threat, that of a particular feared loss, or other noxious experience. But just as, in the initial phase of a sequence, ego transmits his contingent intentions to alter symbolically through communication, so the sanction involved may also be symbolic, e.g. in place of possession of certain intrinsically valuable goods he may offer a sum of money. What we have called the generalized media of interaction then

may be used as types of sanctions which may be analyzed in terms of the above paradigm. The factors of generalization and of legitimation of institutionalization, however, as discussed above, introduce certain complications which we must now take up with reference to power. There is a sense in which power may be regarded as the generalized medium of coercion in the above terms, but this formula at the very least requires very careful interpretation — indeed it will turn out by itself to be inadequate.

I spoke above of the "grounding" of the value of money in the commodity value of the monetary metal, and suggested that there is a corresponding relation of the "value," i.e. the effectiveness of power, to the intrinsic effectiveness of physical force as a means of coercion and, in the limiting case, compulsion.[1]

In interpreting this formula due account must be taken of the asymmetry just discussed. The special place of gold as a monetary base rests on such properties as its durability, high value in small bulk, etc., and high probability of acceptability in exchange, i.e. as means of inducement, in a very wide variety of conditions which are not dependent on an institutionalized order. Ego's primary aim in resorting to compulsion or coercion, however, is deterrence of unwanted action on alter's part.[2] Force, therefore, is in the first instance important as the "ultimate" deterrent. It is the means which, again independent of any institutionalized system of order, can be assumed to be "intrinsically" the most effective in the context of deterrence, when means of effectiveness which *are* dependent on institutionalized order are insecure or fail. Therefore, the unit of an action system which commands control of physical force adequate to cope with any potential counter threats of force is more secure than any other in a Hobbesian state of nature.[3]

But just as a monetary system resting entirely on gold as the actual medium of exchange is a very primitive one which simply cannot mediate a complex system of market exchange, so a power system in which the only negative sanction is the threat of force is a very primitive one which cannot function to mediate a complex system of organizational coordination — it is far too "blunt" an instrument. Money cannot be only an intrinsically valuable entity if it is to serve as a generalized medium of inducement, but it must, as we have said, be institutionalized as a symbol; it must be legitimized, and must inspire "confidence" within the system — and must also within limits be deliberately managed. Similarly power cannot be only an intrinsically effective deterrent; if it is to be the generalized medium of mobilizing resources for effective collective action, and for the fulfillment of commitments made by collectivities to what we have here called their constituents; it too must be both symbolically generalized, and legitimized.

There is a direct connection between the concept of bindingness, as introduced above, and deterrence. To treat a commitment or any other form of expectation

---

[1] I owe the insight into this parallel to Professor Karl W. Deutsch of Yale University (personal discussion).

[2] "Sadistic" infliction of injury without instrumental significance to ego does not belong in this context.

[3] I have attempted to develop this line of analysis of the significance of force somewhat more fully in "Some Reflections of the Role of Force in Social Relations," in Harry Eckstein, ed. *The Problem of Internal War* (New Jersey: Princeton University Press, 1963).

as binding is to attribute a special importance to its fulfillment. Where it is not a matter simply of maintenance of an established routine, but of undertaking new actions in changed circumstances, where the commitment is thus to undertake types of action contingent on circumstances as they develop, then the risk to be minimized is that such contingent commitments will not be carried out when the circumstances in question appear. Treating the expectation or obligation as binding is almost the same thing as saying that appropriate steps on the other side must be taken to prevent nonfulfillment, if possible. Willingness to impose negative sanctions is, seen in this light, simply the carrying out of the implications of treating commitments as binding, and the agent invoking them "meaning it" or being prepared to insist.

On the other hand there are areas in interaction systems where there is a range of alternatives, choice among which is optional, in the light of the promised advantageousness, situational or "intentional," of one as compared to other choices. Positive sanctions as here conceived constitute a contingent increment of relative advantageousness, situational or intentional, of the alternative ego desires alter to choose.

If, in these latter areas, a generalized, symbolic medium is to operate in place of intrinsic advantages, there must be an element of bindingness in the institutionalization of the medium itself—e.g. the fact that the money of a society is "legal tender" which must be accepted in the settlement of debts which have the status of contractual obligations under the law. In the case of money, I suggest that, for the typical acting unit in a market system, what specific undertakings he enters into is overwhelmingly optional in the above sense, but whether the money involved in the transactions is or is not "good" is not for him to judge, but his acceptance of it is binding. Essentially the same is true of the contractual obligations, typically linking monetary and intrinsic utilities, which he undertakes.

I would now like to suggest that what is in a certain sense the obverse holds true of power. Its "intrinsic" importance lies in its capacity to ensure that obligations are "really" binding, thus if necessary can be "enforced" by negative sanctions. But for power to function as a generalized medium in a complex system, i.e. to mobilize resources effectively for collective action, it must be "legitimized" which in the present context means that in certain respects compliance, which is the common factor among our media, is not binding, to say nothing of being coerced, but is optional. The range within which there exists a continuous system of interlocking binding obligations is essentially that of the internal relations of an organized collectivity in our sense, and of the contractual obligations undertaken on its behalf at its boundaries.

The points at which the optional factors come to bear are, in the boundary relations of the collectivity, where factors of importance for collective functioning other than binding obligations are exchanged for such binding

commitments on the part of the collectivity and *vice versa*, nonbinding outputs of the collectivity for binding commitments to it. These "optional" inputs, I have suggested above, are control of productivity of the economy at one boundary, influence through the relations between leadership and the public demands at the other.[1]

This is a point at which the dissociation of the concept of polity from exclusive relation to government becomes particularly important. In a sufficiently differentiated society, the boundary-relations of the great majority of its important units of collective organization (including some boundaries of government) are boundaries where the overwhelming majority of decisions of commitment are optional in the above sense, though once made, their fulfillment is binding. This, however, is only possible effectively within the range of a sufficiently stable, institutionalized normative order so that the requisite degrees of freedom are protected, e.g. in the fields of employment and of the promotion of interest-demands and decisions about political support.

This feature of the boundary relations of a particular political unit holds even for cases of local government, in that decisions of residence, employment, or acquisition of property within a particular jurisdiction involve the optional element, since in all these respects there is a relatively free choice among local jurisdictions, even though, once having chosen, the citizen is, for example, subject to the tax policies applying within it — and of course he cannot escape being subject to any local jurisdiction, but must choose among those available.

In the case of a "national" political organization, however, its territorial boundaries ordinarily coincide with a relative break in the normative order regulating social interaction.[2] Hence across such boundaries an ambiguity becomes involved in the exercise of power in our sense. On the one hand the invoking of binding obligations operates normally without explicit use of coercion within certain ranges where the two territorial collectivity systems have institutionalized their relations. Thus travelers in friendly foreign countries can ordinarily enjoy personal security and the amenities of the principal public accommodations, exchange of their money at "going" rates, etc. Where, on the other hand, the more general relations between national collectivities are at issue, the power system is especially vulnerable to the kind of insecurity of expectations which tends to be met by the explicit resort to threats of coercive sanctions. Such threats in turn, operating on both sides of a reciprocal relationship, readily enter into a vicious circle of resort to more and more "intrinsically" effective or drastic measures of coercion, at the end of which

---

[1] Thus, if control of productivity operates through monetary funds, their possessor cannot "force" e.g. prospective employees to accept employment.

[2] This, of course, is a relative difference. Some hazards increase the moment one steps outside his own home, police protection may be better in one local community than the next, and crossing a state boundary may mean a considerable difference in legal or actual rights.

road lies physical force. In other words, the danger of war is endemic in uninstitutionalized relations between territorially organized collectivities.

There is thus an inherent relation between both the use and the control of force and the territorial basis of organization.[1] One central condition of the integration of a power system is that it should be effective within a territorial area, and a crucial condition of this effectiveness in turn is the monopoly of control of paramount force within the area. The critical point then, at which the institutional integration of power systems is most vulnerable to strain, and to degeneration into reciprocating threats of the use of force, is between territorially organized political systems. This, notoriously, is the weakest point in the normative order of human society today, as it has been almost from time immemorial.

In this connection it should be recognized that the possession, the mutual threat, and possible use of force is only in a most proximate sense the principal "cause" of war. The essential point is that the "bottleneck" of mutual regression to more and more primitive means of protecting or advancing collective interests is a "channel" into which all elements of tension between the collective units in question may flow. It is a question of the many levels at which such elements of tension may on the one hand build up, on the other be controlled, not of any simple and unequivocal conception of the "inherent" consequences of the possession and possible uses of organized force.

It should be clear that again there is a direct parallel with the economic case. A functioning market system requires integration of the monetary medium. It cannot be a system of N independent monetary units and agencies controlling them. This is the basis on which the main range of extension of a relatively integrated market system tends to coincide with the "politically organized society," as Roscoe Pound calls it, over a territorial area. International transactions require special provisions not required for domestic.

The basic "management" of the monetary system must then be integrated with the institutionalization of political power. Just as the latter depends on an effective monopoly of institutionally organized force, so monetary stability depends on an effective monopoly of basic reserves protecting the monetary unit and, as we shall see later, on centralization of control over the credit system.

The hierarchical aspect of power systems

A very critical question now arises, which may be stated in terms of a crucial difference between money

[1] *Cf.* my paper "The Principal Structures of Community," *Nomos* **2** and *Structure and Process, op. cit.*, chapter 8. See also W. L. Hurst, *Law and Social Process in the United States* (Ann Arbor: University of Michigan Law School, 1960).

[2] As already noted, in this area, I think the analysis of Chester I. Barnard, in *The Function of the Executive, op. cit.*, is so outstandingly clear and cogent that it deserves the status of a classic of political theory in my specific sense. See especially chapter X.

and power. Money is a "measure of value," as the classical economists put it, in terms of a continuous linear variable. Objects of utility valued in money are more or less valuable than each other in numerically statable terms. Similarly, as medium of exchange, amounts of money differ in the same single dimension. One acting unit in a society has more money — or assets exchangeable for money — than another, less than, or the same.

Power involves a quite different dimension which may be formulated in terms of the conception that A may have power over B. Of course in competitive bidding the holder of superior financial assets has an advantage in that, as economists say, the "marginal utility of money" is less to him than to his competitor with smaller assets. But his "bid" is no more binding on the potential exchange partner than is that of the less affluent bidder, since in "purchasing power" all dollars are "created free and equal." There may be auxiliary reasons why the purveyor may think it advisable to accept the bid of the more affluent bidder; these, however, are not strictly economic, but concern the interrelations between money and other media, and other bases of status in the system.

The connection between the value of effectiveness — as distinguished from utility — and bindingness, implies a conception in turn of the focussing of responsibility for decisions, and hence of authority for their implementation.[2] This implies a special form of inequality of power which in turn implies a priority system of commitments. The implications of having assumed binding commitments, on the fulfillment of which spokesmen for the collectivity are prepared to insist to the point of imposing serious negative sanctions for noncompliance, are of an order of seriousness such that matching the priority system in the commitments themselves there must be priorities in the matter of which decisions take precedence over others and, back of that, of which decision-making agencies have the right to make decisions at what levels. Throughout this discussion the crucial question concerns bindingness. The reference is to the collectivity, and hence the strategic significance of the various "contributions" on the performance of which the effectiveness of its action depends. Effectiveness for the collectivity as a whole is dependent on hierarchical ordering of the relative strategic importance of these contributions, and hence of the conditions governing the imposition of binding obligations on the contributors.

Hence the power of A over B is, in its legitimized form, the "right" of A, as a decision-making unit involved in collective process, to make decisions which take precedence over those of B, in the interest of the effectiveness of the collective operation as a whole.

The right to use power, or negative sanctions on a barter basis or even compulsion to assert priority of a decision over others, I shall, following Barnard, call authority. Precedence in this sense can take different forms. The most serious ambiguity here seems to derive from the assumption that authority and its attendant power may be understood as implying opposition to the wishes of "lower-order" echelons which hence includes the prerogative of coercing or compelling compliance. Though this is implicit, it may be that the higher-order authority and power may imply the prerogative is primarily significant as "defining the situation" for the performance of the lower-order echelons. The higher "authority" may then make a decision which defines terms within which other units in the collectivity will be expected to act, and this expectation is treated as binding. Thus a ruling by the Commissioner of Internal Revenue may exclude certain tax exemptions which units under his jurisdiction have thought taxpayers could claim. Such a decision need not activate an overt conflict between commissioner and taxpayer, but may rather "channel" the decisions of revenue agents and taxpayers with reference to performance of obligations.

There does not seem to be an essential theoretical difficulty involved in this "ambiguity." We can say that the primary function of superior authority is clearly to define the situation for the lower echelons of the collectivity. The problem of overcoming opposition in the form of dispositions to noncompliance then arises from the incomplete institutionalization of the power of the higher authority holder. Sources of this may well include overstepping of the bounds of his legitimate authority on the part of this agent. The concept of compliance should clearly not be limited to "obedience" by subordinates, but is just as importantly applicable to observance of the normative order by the high echelons of authority and power. The concept of constitutionalism is the critical one at this level, namely that even the highest authority is bound in the strict sense of the concept bindingness used here, by the terms of the normative order under which he operates, e.g. holds office. Hence binding obligations can clearly be "invoked" by lower-order against higher-order agencies as well as *vice versa*.

This of course implies the relatively firm institutionalization of the normative order itself. Within the framework of a highly differentiated polity it implies, in addition to constitutionalism itself, a procedural system for the granting of high political authority, even in private, to say nothing of public organizations, and a legal framework within which such authority is legitimized. This in turn includes another order of procedural institutions within which the question of the legality of actual uses of power can be tested.

Power and authority

The institutionalization of the normative order just referred to thus comes to focus in the concept of authority. Authority is essentially the institutional code within which the use of power as medium is organized and legitimized. It stands to power essentially as property, as an institution, does to money. Property is a bundle of rights of possession, including above all that of alienation, but also at various levels of control and use. In a highly differentiated institutional system, property rights are focussed on the valuation of utility, i.e. the economic significance of the objects, e.g. for consumption or as factors of production, and this factor comes to be differentiated from authority. Thus, in European feudalism the "landlord" had both property rights in the land, and political jurisdiction over persons acting on the same land. In modern legal systems these components are differentiated from each other so the landowner is no longer the landlord; this function is taken over mainly by local political authority.

Precisely with greater differentiation the focus of the institution becomes more generalized and, while specific objects of possession of course continue to be highly important, the most important object of property comes to be monetary assets, and specific objects are valued as assets, i.e., in terms of potentials of marketability. Today we can say that rights to money assets, the ways in which these can be legitimately acquired and disposed of, the ways in which the interests of other parties must be protected, have come to constitute the core of the institution of property.[1]

Authority, then, is the aspect of a status in a system of social organization, namely its collective aspect, by virtue of which the incumbent is put in a position legitimately to make decisions which are binding, not only on himself but on the collectivity as a whole and hence its other member-units, in the sense that so far as their implications impinge on their respective roles and statuses, they are bound to act in accordance with these implications. This includes the right to insist on such action though, because of the general division of labor, the holder of authority very often is not himself in a position to "enforce" his decisions, but must be dependent on specialized agencies for this.

If, then, authority be conceived as the institutional counterpart of power, the main difference lies in the fact that authority is not a circulating medium. Sometimes, speaking loosely, we suggest that someone "gives away his property." He can give away property rights in specific possessions but not the institution of property. Similarly the incumbent of an office can relinquish authority by resigning, but this is very different from abolishing the authority of the office. Property as institution is a code defining rights in objects of possession, in the first instance physical objects, then "symbolic" objects, including cultural objects such as "ideas" so far as they are valuable in monetary terms, and of course including money itself, whoever possesses them.

---

[1] Two particularly important manifestations of this monetization of property are, first the general legal understanding that executors of estates are not obligated to retain the exact physical inventory intact pending full statement, but may sell various items — their fiduciary obligation is focussed on the money value of the estate. Similarly, in the law of contract increasing option has been given to compensate with money damages in lieu of the specific "performance" originally contracted for.

Authority, similarly, is a set of rights in status in a collectivity, precisely in the collectivity as actor, including most especially right to acquire and use power in that status.

The institutional stability, which is essential to the conception of a code, then for property inheres in the institutional structure of the market. At a higher level the institution of property includes rights, not only to use and dispose of particular objects of value, but to participate in the system of market transactions.

It is then essentially the institutionalized code defining rights of participation in the power system which I should like to think of as authority. It is this conception which gives us the basis for the essential distinction between the internal and the external aspects of power relative to a particular collectivity. The collectivity is, by our conception, the definition of the range within which a system of institutionalized rights to hold and use power can be closed. This is to say, the implications of an authoritative decision made at one point in the system can be made genuinely binding at all the other relevant points through the relevant processes of feed-back.

The hierarchical priority system of authority and power, with which this discussion started can, by this criterion, only be binding within a given particular collectivity system. In this sense then a hierarchy of authority — as distinguished from the sheer differences of power of other coercive capacities — must be internal to a collectively organized system in this sense. This will include authority to bind the collectivity in its relations to its environment, to persons and to other collectivities. But bindingness, legitimized and enforced through the agency of this particular collectivity, cannot be extended beyond its boundaries. If it exists at all it must be by virtue of an institutionalized normative order which transcends the particular collectivity, through contractual arrangements with others, or through other types of mutually binding obligation.

Power, influence, equalization, and solidarity

It is on this basis that it may be held that at the boundaries of the collectivity the closed system of priorities is breached by "free" exercise, at the constituency or integrative boundary, of influence. Status in the collectivity gives authority to settle the terms on which power will be exchanged with influence over this boundary. The wielder of influence from outside, on the collectivity, is not bound in advance to any particular terms, and it is of the essence of use of power

in the "foreign relations" of the collectivity, that authority is a right, within certain limits of discretion, to spend power in exchange for influence. This in turn can, through the offer of accepting leadership responsibility in exchange for political support, replenish the expenditure of power by a corresponding input.

By this reasoning influence should be capable of altering the priority system within the collectivity. This is what I interpret policy decision as a category of the use of power as a medium to be, the process of altering priorities in such a way that the new pattern comes to be binding on the collectivity. Similarly, the franchise must be regarded as the institutionalization of a marginal, interpenetrating status, between the main collectivity and its environment of solidary groupings in the larger system. It is the institutionalization of a marginal authority, the use of which is confined to the function of selection among candidates for leadership responsibility. In the governmental case, this is the inclusion in a common collectivity system of both the operative agencies of government and the "constituencies" on which leadership is dependent, a grant not only in a given instance of power to the latter but a status of authority with respect to the one crucial function of selection of leadership and granting them the authority of office.

In interpreting this discussion it is essential to keep in mind that a society consists, from the present point of view, not in one collectivity, but in a ramified system of collectivities. Because, however, of the basic imperatives of effective collective action already discussed, these must in addition to the pluralistic cross-cutting which goes with functional differentiation, also have the aspect of a "Chinese box" relation. There must be somewhere a paramount focus of collective authority and with it of the control of power — though it is crucial that this need not be the top of the total system of normative control, which may for example be religious. This complex of territoriality and the monopoly of force are central to this, because the closed system of enforceable bindingness can always be breached by the intervention of force.[1]

The bindingness of normative orders other than those upheld by the paramount territorial collectivity must be defined within limits institutionalized in relation to it. So far as such collectivities are not "agencies" of the state, in this sense, their spheres of "jurisdiction" must be defined in terms of a normative system, a body of law, which is binding both on government and on the nongovernmental collectivity units, though in the "last analysis" it will, within an institutionalized order, either have to be enforced by government, or contrariwise, by revolutionary action against government.

Since independent control of serious, socially organized force cannot be given to "private" collectivities, their ultimate negative sanctions tend to be expulsion from membership, though many other types of sanction may be highly important.

Considerations such as these thus do not in any way

---

[1] Since this system is the territorially organized collectivity, the state with its government, these considerations underlie the critical importance of foreign relations in the sense of the relations to other territorially organized, force-controlling collectivities, since, once internal control of force is effectively institutionalized, the danger of this kind of breach comes from the outside in this specific sense of outside. The point is cogently made by Raymond Aron.

eliminate or weaken the importance of hierarchical priorities within a collective decision-system itself. The strict "line" structure of such authority is, however, greatly modified by the interpenetration of other systems with the political, notably for our purposes the importance of technical competence. The qualifications of the importance of hierarchy apply in principle at the boundaries of the particular collective system — analytically considered — rather than internally to it. These I would interpret as defining the limits of authority. There are two main contexts in which norms of equality may be expected to modify the concrete expectations of hierarchical decision-systems, namely on the one hand, the context of influence over the right to assume power, or decision-making authority and, on the other hand, the context of access to opportunity for status as a contributing unit in the specific political system in question.

It is essential here to recall that I have treated power as a circulating medium, moving back and forth over the boundaries of the polity. The "real" outputs of the political process, and the factors in its effectiveness — in the sense corresponding to the real outputs and factors of economic production — are not in my sense "forms" of power but, in the most important cases, of financial control of economic resources, and of influence, in the meaning of the category of influence, defined as a generalized mechanism of persuasion. These are very essential elements in the total political process, but it is just as important to distinguish them from power as it is to distinguish financially valuable outputs and factors of production from money itself. They may, in certain circumstances, be exchangeable for power, but this is a very different thing from being forms of power.

The circulation of power between polity and integrative system I conceive to consist in binding policy decisions on the one hand, which is a primary factor in the integrative process, and political support on the other, which is a primary output of the integrative process. Support is exchanged, by a "public" or constituency, for the assumption of leadership responsibility, through the process of persuading those in a position to give binding support that it is advisable to do so in the particular instance — through the use of influence or some less generalized means of persuasion. In the other political "market" *vis-à-vis* the integrative system, policy decisions are given in response to interest-demands in the sense of the above discussion. This is to say that interest groups, which, it is most important to note as a concept says nothing about the moral quality of the particular interest, attempt to persuade those who hold authority in the relevant collectivity, i.e. are in a position to make binding decisions, that they should indeed commit the collectivity to the policies the influence-wielders want. In our terms this is to persuade the decision makers to use and hence "spend" some of their power for the purpose in hand. The spending of power is to be thought of, just as the spending of money, as essentially consisting in the sacrifice of alternative

decisions which are precluded by the commitments undertaken under a policy. A member of the collectivity we conceive as noted to have authority to "spend" power through making binding decisions through which those outside acquire claims against the collectivity. Its authority, however, is inalienable; it can only be exercised, not "spent."

It has been suggested that policies must be hierarchically ordered in a priority system and that the power to decide among policies must have a corresponding hierarchical ordering since such decisions bind the collectivity and its constituent units. The imperative of hierarchy does not, however, apply to the other "market" of the power system in this direction, that involving the relations between leadership and political support. Here on the contrary it is a critically important fact that in the largest-scale and most highly differentiated systems, namely the leadership systems of the most "advanced" national societies, the power element has been systematically equalized through the device of the franchise, so that the universal adult franchise has been evolved in all the Western democracies.[1] Equality of the franchise which, since the consequences of its exercise are very strictly binding,[2] I classify as in fact a form of power, has been part of a larger complex of its institutionalization, which includes in addition the principle of universality — its extension to all responsible adult citizens in good standing and the secrecy of the ballot, which serves to differentiate this context of political action from other contexts of involvement, and protect it against pressures, not only from hierarchical superiors but, as Rokkan points out, from status-peers as well.

Of course the same basic principle of one member, one vote, is institutionalized in a vast number of voluntary associations, including many which are sub-associations of wider collectivities, such as faculties in a university, or boards and committees. Thus the difference between a chairman or presiding officer, and an executive head is clearly marked with respect to formal authority, whatever it may be with respect to influence, by the principle that a chairman, like any other member, has only one vote. Many collectivities are in this sense "truncated" associations, e.g. in cases where fiduciary boards are self-recruiting. Nevertheless the importance of this principle of equality of power through the franchise is so great empirically that the question of how it is grounded in the structure of social systems is a crucial one.

It derives, I think, from what I should call the universalistic component in patterns of normative order. It is the value-principle that discriminations among units of a system, must be grounded in intrinsically valued differences among them, which are, for both persons

---

[1] See, on this process, Stein Rokkan, "Mass Suffrage, Secret Voting, and Political Participation," *European Journal of Sociology* **2** (1961) 132–152.

[2] I.e., the aggregate of votes, evaluated by the electoral rules, determines the incumbency of office.

and collectivities, capacities to contribute to valued societal processes. Differences of power in decision-making which mobilizes commitments, both outward in relation to the environment of the collectivity and internally, to the assignment of tasks to its members, are ideally grounded in the intrinsic conditions of effectiveness. Similarly, differences on the basis of technical competence to fulfill essential roles are grounded in the strategic conditions of effective contribution.

These considerations do not, however, apply to the functions of the choice of leadership, where this choice has been freed from ascriptive bases of right, e.g. through kinship status or some imputed "charismatic" superiority as in such a case as "white supremacy." There is a persistent pressure of the sufficiently highly valued functions or outcomes, and under this pressure there seems to have been a continual, though uneven, process of erosion of discriminations in this critical field of the distribution of power.

It may be suggested that the principle of universalistic normative organization which is immediately super-ordinate to that of political democracy in the sense of the universal equal franchise, is the principle of equality before the law; in the case of the American Constitution, the principle of equal protection of the laws. I have emphasized that a constitutional framework is essential to advanced collective organization, given of course levels of scale and complexity which preclude purely "informal" and traditional normative regulation. The principle in effect puts the burden of proof on the side of imposing discriminations, either in access to rights or in imposition of obligations, on the side that such discriminations are to be justified only by differences in sufficiently highly valued exigencies of operation of the system.

The principle of equality both at the level of application of the law and of the political franchise, is clearly related to a conception of the status of membership. Not all living adults have equal right to influence the affairs of all collectivities everywhere in the world, nor does an American have equal rights with a citizen of a quite different society within its territory. Membership is in fact the application to the individual unit of the concept of boundary of a social system which has the property of solidarity, in Durkheim's sense. The equal

franchise is a prerogative of members, and of course the criteria of membership can be very differently institutionalized under different circumstances.

There is an important sense in which the double interchange system under consideration here, which I have called the "support" system linking the polity with the integrative aspect of the society, is precisely the system in which power is most directly controlled, both in relation to more particularized interest-elements which seek relatively particularized policies — which of course includes wanting to prevent certain potential actions — and in relation to the more general "tone" given to the directionality of collective action by the character of the leadership elements which assume responsibility and which, in exchange, are invested, in the type case by the electoral process, with authority to carry out their responsibilities. One central feature of this control is coming to terms with the hierarchical elements inherent in power systems in the aspects just discussed. Certain value systems may of course reinforce hierarchy, but it would be my view that a universalistically oriented value system inherently tends to counteract the spread of hierarchical patterns with respect to power beyond the range felt to be functionally necessary for effectiveness.[1]

There is, however, a crucial link between the equality of the franchise and the hierarchical structure of authority within collectivities, namely the all-or-none character of the electoral process. Every voter has an equal vote in electing to an office, but in most cases only one candidate is in fact elected — the authority of office is not divided among candidates in proportion to the numbers of votes they received, but is concentrated in the successful candidate, even though the margin be very narrow, as in the U.S. presidential election of 1960. There are, of course, considerable possible variations in electoral rules, but this basic principle is as central as is that of the equality of the franchise. This principle seems to be the obverse of the hierarchy of authority.

The hierarchical character of power systems has above been sharply contrasted with the linear quantitative character of wealth and monetary assets. This has in turn been related to the fundamental difference between the exigencies of effectiveness in collective action, and the exigencies of utility in providing for the requirements of satisfying the "wants" of units. In order to place the foregoing discussion of the relations between power and influence in a comparable theoretical context, it is necessary to formulate the value-standard which is paramount in regulating the integrative function which corresponds to utility and effectiveness in the economic and political functions respectively.

This is, with little doubt, the famous concept of solidarity as formulated by Durkheim.[2] The two essential points of reference for present purposes concern the two main aspects of membership, as outlined above, the first of which concerns claims on executive authority for policy decisions which integrate the total collective interest on the one hand, the "partial" interest of a sub-

[1] Of course where conditions are sufficiently simple, or where there is sufficient anxiety about the hierarchical implications of power, the egalitarian element may penetrate far into the political decision-making system itself, with, e.g., insistence that policy-decisions, both external and internal in reference, be made by majority vote of all members, or even under a unanimity rule. The respects in which such a system — which of course realistically often involves a sharply hierarchical stratification of influence — is incompatible with effectiveness in many spheres, can be said to be relatively clear, especially for *large* collectivities.

[2] It is the central concept of *The Division of Labor in Society*. For my own relatively recent understanding of its significance, see "Durkheim's Contribution to the Theory of Integration of Social Systems," in Kurt Wolff, Ed., *Émile Durkheim, 1858–1917* (Ohio: Ohio State University Press, 1960), pp. 118–153.

group on the other. The second concerns integration of rights to a "voice" in collective affairs with the exigencies of effective leadership and the corresponding responsibility.

The principle is the "grounding" of a collective system in a consensus in the sense of the above discussion, namely an "acceptance" on the part of its members of their belonging together, in the sense of sharing, over a certain range, common interests, interests which are defined both by type, and by considerations of time. Time becomes relevant because of the uncertainty factor in all human action, and hence the fact that neither benefits nor burdens can be precisely predicted and planned for in advance; hence an effective collectivity must be prepared to absorb unexpected burdens, and to balance this, to carry out some sort of just distribution of benefits which are unexpected and/or are not attributable to the earned agency of any particular subunit.

Solidarity may then be thought of as the implementation of common values by definition of the requisite collective systems in which they are to be actualized. Collective action as such we have defined as political function. The famous problem of order, however, cannot be solved without a common normative system. Solidarity is the principle by virtue of which the commitment to norms, which is "based" in turn on values, is articulated with the formation of collectivities which are capable of effective collective action. Whereas, in the economic direction, the "problem" of effective action is coping with the scarcity of available resources, including trying to facilitate their mobility, in the integrative direction it is orderly solution of competing claims, on the one hand to receive benefits — or minimize losses — deriving from memberships, on the other to influence the processes by which collective action operates. This clearly involves some institutionalization of the subordination of unit-interest to the collective in cases where the two are in conflict, actual or potential, and hence the justification of unit interests as compatible with the more extensive collective interest. A social system then possesses solidarity in proportion as its members are committed to common interests through which discrete unit interests can be integrated and the justification of conflict resolution and subordination can be defined and implemented. It defines, not the modes of implementation of these common interests through effective agency, but the standards by which such agency should be guided and the rights of various constituent elements to have a voice in the interpretation of these standards.

Power and equality of opportunity

We may now turn to the second major boundary of the polity, at which another order of modifications of the internal hierarchy of authority comes to focus. This is the boundary *vis-à-vis* the economy where the "political" interest is to secure control of productivity and services, and the economic interest lies in the collective control of fluid resources and in what we may call opportunity for effectiveness. I shall not attempt here to discuss the whole interchange complex, but will confine myself to the crucial problem of the way that here also the hierarchical structure of power can, under certain conditions, be modified in an egalitarian direction.

Productivity of the economy is in principle allocable among collective (in our sense political) claimants to its control as facilities, in linear quantitative terms. This linear quantification is achieved through the medium of money, either allocation of funds with liberty to expend them at will, or at least monetary evaluation of more specific facilities.

In a sufficiently developed system, services must be evaluated in monetary terms also, both from the point of view of rational budgeting and of the monetary cost of their employment. In terms of their utilization, however, services are "packages" of performance-capacity, which are qualitatively distinct and of unequal value as contributions to collective effectiveness. Their evaluation as facilities must hence involve an estimate of strategic significance which matches the general priority scale which has been established to regulate the internal functioning of the collectivity.

Services, however, constitute a resource to be acquired from outside the collectivity, as Weber puts it through a "formally free" contract of employment. The contracts thus made are binding on both sides, by virtue of a normative system transcending the particular collectivity, though the obligation must articulate with the internal normative order including its hierarchical aspect. But the purveyors of service are not, in advance, bound by this internal priority system and hence an exchange, which is here interpreted to operate in the first instance as between strategic significance expressed as power-potential, and the monetary value of the service, must be arrived at.

Quite clearly, when the purveyor of service has once entered into such a contract, he is bound by the aspect of its terms which articulates the service into this internal system, including the level of authority he exercises and its implications for his power position in the collectivity. If the collectivity is making in any sense a rational arrangement, this must be tailored to an estimate of the level of the value of his strategic contribution, hence his performance-capacity.

Since, however, the boundary interchange is not integral to the internal system of bindingness, the hierarchical imperatives do not apply to the opportunity aspect of this interchange on the extrapolitical side. This is to say that the same order of pressures of a higher-order universalistic normative system can operate here that we suggested operated to bring about equality in the franchise. Again the principle is that no particularistic discriminations are to be legitimized which are not grounded in essential functional exigencies of the system of reference.

In the case of the franchise there seems to be no inherent stopping place short of complete equality, qualified only by the minimum consideration of competence attached to fully responsible membership — excluding only minors, "defectives," through retardation and mental illness, and those morally disqualified through crime. In the service case, on the other hand, given commitments to optimum performance which in the present context can be taken for granted, the limit to the equating of universalism and equality lies in the concept of competence. Hence the principle arrived at is the famous one of equality of opportunity, by which there is equalization of access to opportunity for contribution, but selection on criteria of differential competence, both quantitative and qualitative.

Whereas the equalization of the franchise is a control on differential power "from above" in the hierarchy of control and operates mainly through the selection of leadership, equality of opportunity is (in the corresponding sense) a control from below, and operates to check particularistic tendencies which would tend to exclude sources of service which are qualified by competence to contribute, and/or to check tendencies to retain services which are inferior to those available in competition with them.

It is the combination of these two foci of universalization, the equalitarianism of upper rights to control through the franchise, and of rights to participate through service on the basis of competence, which account for the extent to which the "cumulative advantage,"[1] which might seem to be inherent in the hierarchical internal structure of power systems, often in fact fails either to materialize at all, or to be as strong as expected.

Long and complex as it is, the above discussion may be summed up as an attempted solution of the second of the three main problems with which this paper began, namely that of the relation between the coercive and the consensual aspects of the phenomenon of power. The answer is first premised on the conception of power as a specific but generalized medium of the functioning of social relationships in complex, differentiated systems of social interaction.

Power is secondly specifically associated with the bindingness of obligations to performance within a range of circumstances which may arise in a varying and changing situation. The obligations concerned are hence in some important degree generalized so that particularities under them are contingent on circumstances. The bindingness of obligations implies that they stand on a level of seriousness such that the invoking agent, ego, may be put in the position of asserting that, since he

"means it" that alter must comply, he is prepared to insist on compliance. Partly then as a symbolic expression of this seriousness of "meaning it" and partly as an instrument of deterrence of noncompliance,[2] this insistence is associated with command of negative situational sanctions the application of which is frequently contingent on noncompliance, and in certain cases deterrence is achieved by compulsion. We would not speak of power where situational negative sanctions or compulsion are in no circumstances attached to noncompliance in cases where a legitimate agent insists on compliance.

Thirdly, however, power is here conceived as a generalized medium of mobilizing commitments or obligation for effective collective action. As such it ordinarily does not itself possess intrinsic effectiveness, but symbolizes effectiveness and hence the bindingness of the relevant obligations to contribute to it. The operative validity of the meaningfulness of the symbolization is not a function of any one single variable but, we argue, of two primary ones. One of these is the willingness to insist upon compliance, or at least to deter noncompliance, a line of reasoning which leads to the understanding of willingness to resort to negative sanctions, the nature of which will vary, as a function of the seriousness of the question, on the dimension of their progressively more drastic nature, in the last analysis force.

The other variable concerns the collective reference and hence the justification[3] of invoking the obligations in question in the situation. This aspect concerns the dependence of power on the institutionalization of authority and hence the rights of collective agents to mobilize performances and define them as binding obligations. This justification inherently rests on some sort of consensus among the members of the collectivity of reference, if not more broadly, with respect to a system of norms under which authority and power are legitimized on a basis wider than this particular collectivity by the values of the system. More specifically, authority is the institutionalized code within which the "language of power" is meaningful and, therefore, its use will be accepted in the requisite community, which is in the first instance the community of collective organization in our sense.

Seen in this light the threat of coercive measures, or of compulsion, without legitimation or justification, should not properly be called the use of power at all, but is the limiting case where power, losing its symbolic character, merges into an intrinsic instrumentality of securing compliance with wishes, rather than obligations. The monetary parallel is the use of a monetary metal as an instrument of barter where as a commodity it ceases to be an institutionalized medium of exchange at all.

In the history of thought there has been a very close connection between emphasis on the coercive element in power systems and on the hierarchical aspect of the structure of systems of authority and power. The above

---

[1] *Cf.* C. Wright Mills, *The Power Elite* (New York: Oxford University Press, 1956) and my commentary in *Structure and Process in Modern Societies, op. cit.,* chapter 6.

[2] *Cf.* Durkheim's famous essay, "Deux lois de l'évolution pénale," *L'Année Sociologique* 4 (1899–1900): 65–95.

[3] *Cf.* my paper "On the Concept of Influence," *op. cit.,* for a discussion of the concept of justification and its distinction from legitimation.

discussion has, I hope, helped to dissociate them by showing that this hierarchical aspect, important as it is, is only part of the structure of power systems. The view advanced is that it is an inherent aspect of the internal structure of collectivities. No collectivity, even the nation, however, stands alone as a total society since it is integrated with norms and values; subcollectivities can even less be claimed to be societies. The collectivity aspect of total social structure may in a particular case be dominant over others, but always in principle it impinges on at least two sorts of boundary-problems, namely that involved in its "support" system and that involved in the mobilization of services as sources of contribution to its functioning.

In both these cases, we have argued, quite different principles are operative from that of the hierarchy of authority, namely the equality of franchise on the one hand, equality of opportunity on the other. In both cases I envisage an interchange of power, though not of authority, over the boundary of the polity, and in neither case can the principle governing the allocation of power through this interchange be considered to be hierarchical in the line authority sense. The empirical problems here are, as elsewhere, formidable, but I definitely argue that it is illegitimate to hold that, from serious consideration of the role of power as a generalized medium, it can be inferred that there is a general trend to hierarchization in the total empirical social systems involved.[1]

The zero-sum problem

We are now in a position to take up the last of the three main problems with which the discussion started, namely whether power is a zero-sum phenomenon in the sense that, in a system, a gain in power by a unit A is in the nature of the case the cause of a corresponding loss of power by other units, B, C, D. . . . The parallel with money on which we have been insisting throughout should give us clues to the answer, which clearly is, under certain circumstances yes, but by no means under all circumstances.

In the monetary case it is obvious that in budgeting the use of a fixed income, allocation to one use must be at the expense of alternative uses. The question is whether parallel limitations apply to an economy conceived as a total system. For long this seemed to many economists to be the case; this was the main burden of the old "quantity theory of money." The most obvious political parallel is that of the hierarchy of authority within a particular collectivity. It would seem to be obvious that, if A, who has occupied a position of substantial power, is demoted, and B takes his place, A loses power and B gains it, the total in the system remaining the same. Many political theorists like Lasswell and C. Wright Mills, generalized this to political systems as a whole.[2]

The most important and obvious point at which the zero-sum doctrine breaks down for money is that of credit-creation through commercial banking. This case is so important as a model that a brief discussion here is in order. Depositors, that is, entrust their money funds to a bank, not only for safe keeping, but as available to the bank for lending. In so doing, however, they do not relinquish any property rights in these funds. The funds are repayable by the bank in full on demand, the only normal restrictions being with respect to banking hours. The bank, however, uses part of the balances on deposit with it to make loans at interest, pursuant to which it not only makes the money available to the borrower, but in most cases assumes binding obligations not to demand repayment except on agreed terms, which in general leave the borrower undisturbed control for a stipulated period — or obligates him to specified installments of amortization. In other words, the same dollars come to do "double duty," to be treated as possessions by the depositors, who retain their property rights, and also by the banker who preempts the rights to loan them, as if they were "his." In any case there is a corresponding net addition to the circulating medium, measured by the quantity of new bank deposits created by the loans outstanding.[3]

Perhaps the best way to describe what happens is to say that there has occurred a differentiation in the functions of money and hence there are two ways of using it in the place of one. The ordinary deposit is a reserve for meeting current expenses, whether "private" or "business," which is mainly important with respect to the time element of the degrees of freedom mentioned above. From the point of view of the depositor the bank is a convenience, giving him safekeeping, the privilege of writing checks rather than using cash, etc., at a cost which is low because the bank earns interest through its loaning operations. From the point of view of the borrower, on the other hand, the bank is a source of otherwise unavailable funds, ideally in the economist's sense, for investment, for financing operations promising future increments of economic productivity, which would not otherwise have been feasible.

The possibility of this "miracle of loaves and fishes" of course rests on an empirical uniformity, namely that depositors do in fact, under normal circumstances, keep sufficient balances on hand — though they are not required to — so that it is safe for the bank to have substantial amounts out on loan at any given time. Underlying this basic uniformity is the fact that an individual bank will ordinarily also have access to "reserves," e.g. assets which, though earning interest,

---

[1] Failure to see this seems to me to be a major source of the utopian strain in Marxist theory, expressed above all by the expectation of the "withering away of the state." There is perhaps a parallel to the confusion connected for many centuries with the Aristotelian doctrine of the "sterility" of money.

[2] H. D. Lasswell and A. Kaplan, *Power and Society* (New Haven, Yale University Press, 1950) and Mills, *The Power Elite*, *op. cit.*

[3] Whether this be interpreted as net addition to the medium or as increase in the velocity of circulation of the "slow" deposit funds, is indifferent, because its economic effects are the same.

are sufficiently liquid to be realized on short notice, and in the last analysis such resources as those of a federal reserve system. The individual bank, and with it its depositors, is thus ordinarily relatively secure.

We all know, however, that this is true only so long as the system operates smoothly. A particular bank can meet unusual demands for withdrawal of deposits, but if this unusual demand spreads to a whole banking system, the result may be a crisis, which only collective action can solve. Quite clearly the expectation that all depositors should be paid, all at once, in "real" money, e.g. even "cash" to say nothing of monetary metal, cannot be fulfilled. Any monetary system in which bank credit plays an important part is in the nature of the case normally "insolvent" by that standard.

Back of these considerations, it may be said, lies an important relation between bindingness and "confidence" which is in certain respects parallel to that between coercion and consensus in relation to power, indeed one which, through the element of bindingness, involves a direct articulation between money and power. How is this parallel to be defined and how does the articulation operate?

First the banking operation depends on mutual confidence or trust in that depositors entrust their funds to the bank, knowing, if they stop to think about it, that the bank will have a volume of loans outstanding which makes it impossible to repay all deposits at once. It is well known with what hesitation, historically, many classes have been brought to trust banks at all in this simple sense — the classical case of the French peasant's insistence on putting his saving in cash under the mattress is sufficient illustration. The other side of the coin, however, is the bank's trust that its depositors will not panic to the point of in fact demanding the complete fulfillment of their legal rights.

The banker here assumes binding obligations in two directions, the honoring of both of which depends on this trust. On the one hand he has loaned money on contract which he cannot recover on demand, on the other he is legally bound to repay deposits on demand. But by making loans on binding contractual terms he is enabled to create money, which is purchasing power in the literal sense that, as noted above, the status of the monetary unit is politically guaranteed — e.g. through its position as "legal tender" — and hence the newly created dollars are "as good as" any other dollars. Hence I suggest that what makes them good in this sense is the input of power in the form of the bindingness of the contractual obligation assumed by the banker — I should classify this as opportunity for effectiveness. The bank, as collectivity, thus enjoys a "power position" by virtue of which it can give its borrowers effective control of certain types of opportunity.

It is, however, critically important that in general this grant of power is not unconditional. First it is power in

[1] Joseph Schumpeter, *The Theory of Economic Development* (Cambridge, Harvard University Press, 1955), translated by Redvers Opie.

its form of direct convertibility with money, and second, within that framework, the condition is that, per unit of time, there should be a surplus of money generated, the borrower can and must return more money than he received, the difference being "interest." Money, however, is a measure of productivity, and hence we may say that increasing the quantity of money in circulation is economically "functional" only if it leads after a sequence of operations over a period of time to a corresponding increase in productivity — if it does not the consequence is inflationary. The process is known as investment, and the standard of a good investment is the expected increment of productivity which, measured in money terms, is profitability. The organizational question of allocation of responsibility for decisions and payments should of course not be too directly identified with the present level of analytical argument.

It may help round out this picture if the concept of investment is related to that of "circular flow" in Schumpeter's sense.[1] The conception is that the routine functioning of economic processes is organized about the relation between producing and consuming units, we may say firms and households. So long as a series of parametric constants such as the state of demand and the coefficients of cost of production hold, this is a process in equilibrium through which money mediates the requisite decisions oriented to fixed reference points. This is precisely the case to which the zero-sum concept applies. On the one hand a fixed quantity and "velocity of circulation" of the monetary medium is an essential condition of the stability of this equilibrium, whereas on the other hand, there is no place for banking operations which, through credit expansion, would change the parametric conditions.

These decisions are governed by the standard of solvency, in the sense that both producing and consuming units are normally expected to recoup their monetary expenditures, on the one hand for factors of production, on the other for consumers' goods, from monetary proceeds, on the producing side, sale of output, on the consuming, sale of factors of production, notably labor. Solvency then is a balance between monetary cost and receipts. Investment is also governed by the standard of solvency, but over a longer time period, long enough to carry out the operations necessary to bring about an increase of productivity matching the monetary obligations assumed.

There is here a crucial relation between the time-extension of the investment process and use of power to make loan contracts binding. Only if the extension of control of resources through loans creates obligations can the recipients of the loans in turn assume further obligations and expect others to assume them.

The essential principle here is that, in the sense of the hierarchy of control, a higher-order medium is used as a source of leverage to break into the "circle" of the Schumpeterian flow, giving the recipients of this power effective control of a share of fluid resources in order to divert them from the established routine channels to new uses. It is difficult to see how this could work systematically if the element of bindingness were absent either from loan contracts or from the acceptance-status of the monetary medium.

One further element of the monetary complex needs to be mentioned here. In the case of investment there is the element of time, and hence the uncertainty that projected operations aiming at increase in productivity will in fact produce either this increase or financial proceeds sufficient to repay loans plus interest in accordance with contract. In the case of the particular borrower-lender relationship this can be handled on an individual contract-solvency basis with a legally determined basis of sharing profits and/or losses. For the system, however, it creates the possibility of inflation, namely that the net effect of credit-extension may not be increase in productivity but decline in the value of the monetary unit. Furthermore, once a system involves an important component of credit, the opposite disturbance, namely deflation with a rearrangement of the meaning of the whole network of financial and credit expectations and relationships, is also a possibility. This suggests that there is, in a ramified credit economy, a set of mechanisms which, independently of particular circular flow, and credit-extension and repayment transactions regulates the total volume of credit, rates of interest, and price-level relations in the economy.

Zero-sum: the case of power

Let us now attempt to work out the parallel, and articulating, analysis for power systems. There is, I suggest, a circular flow operating between polity and economy in the interchange between factors in political effectiveness — in this case a share in control of the productivity of the economy — and an output to the economy in the form of the kind of control of resources which a loan for investment provides — though of course there are various other forms. This circular flow is controlled by the medium of power in the sense that the output of binding obligations, in particular through the commitment to perform services, broadly balances the offer of opportunity for effective performance.

The suggestion is that it is a condition of the stability of this circulation system that the inputs and outputs of power on each side should balance. This is another way of saying that it is ideally formulated as a zero-sum system, so far as power is concerned, though because it includes the investment process, the same is not true for the involvement of monetary funds in the interchanges. The political circular flow system then is conceived as the locus of the "routine" mobilization of performance expectations either through invoking obligations under old contractual — and in some cases, e.g. citizenship, ascriptive — relations, or through a stable rate of assumption of new contractual obligations, which is balanced by the liquidation, typically through fulfillment, of old

ones. The balance applies to the system, of course, not to particular units.

Corresponding to utility as the value-pattern governing economic function I have put forward effectiveness as that governing political function. If it is important to distinguish utility, as the category of value to which increments are made by the combinatorial process of economic production, from solvency as the standard of satisfactory performance in handling money as the medium of economic process, then we need to distinguish effectiveness as the political value category, from a corresponding standard for the satisfactory handling of power. The best available term for this standard seems to be the success of collective goal-attainment. Where the polity is sufficiently differentiated so that power has become genuinely a generalized medium we can say that collective units are expected to be successful in the sense that the binding obligations they undertake in order to maintain and create opportunities for effectiveness, is balanced by the input of equally binding commitments to perform service, either within the collectivity in some status of employment, or for the collectivity on a contractual basis.

The unit of productive decision-making, however, is, in a sense corresponding to that applying to the household for the economic case, also expected to be successful in the sense that its expenditure of power through not only the output of services but their commitment to utilization by particular collectivities, is balanced by an input of opportunity which is dependent on collective organization, that is a unit in a position to undertake to provide opportunities which are binding on the unit.

In the light of this discussion it becomes clear that the business firm is in its aspect as collectivity in our technical sense, the case where the two standards of success and solvency coincide. The firm uses its power income primarily to maintain or increase its productivity and, as a measure of this, its money income. A surplus of power will therefore in general be exchanged for enhancement of its control of economic productivity. For a collectivity specialized in political function the primary criterion of success would be given in its power position, relative that is to other collectivities. Here there is the special problem of the meaning of the term power position. I interpret it here as relative to other collectivities in a competitive system, not as a position in an internal hierarchy of power. This distinction is of course particularly important for a pluralistic power system where government is a functionally specialized sub-system of the collectivity structure, not an approximation to the totality of that structure.[1] In somewhat corresponding fashion a collectivity specialized in integrative function would measure its success in terms of its "level of influence" — for example, as a political interest-group in the usual sense, its capacity to influence public policy decisions. A consequence of this reasoning

[1] If very carefully interpreted, perhaps the old term "sovereignty" could be used to designate this standard somewhat more definitely than success.

is that such an influence group would be disposed to "give away" power, in the sense of trading it for an increment of influence. This could take the form of assuring political support, without barter-like conditions, to leadership elements which seemed to be likely to be able to exercise the kind of influence in question.

Is there then a political equivalent of the banking phenomenon, a way in which the circular flow of power comes to be broken through so as to bring about net additions to the amount of power in the system? The trend of the analytical argument indicates that there must be, and that its focus lies in the support system, that is the area of interchange between power and influence, between polity and integrative system.

First I suggest that, particularly conspicuous in the case of democratic electoral systems, political support should be conceived as a generalized grant of power which, if it leads to electoral success, puts elected leadership in a position analogous to that of the banker. The "deposits" of power made by constituents are revocable, if not at will, at the next election — a condition analogous to regularity of banking hours. In some cases election is tied to barter-like conditions of expectation of carrying out certain specific measures favored by the strategically crucial voters and only these. But particularly in a system which is pluralistic not only with reference to the composition of political support, but also to issues, such a leadership element acquires freedom to make certain types of binding decision, binding in the nature of the case on elements of the collectivity other than those whose "interest" is directly served. This freedom may be conceived to be confined to the circular flow level, which would be to say that the input of power through the channel of political support should be exactly balanced by the output through policy decisions, to interest groups which have specifically demanded these decisions.

There is, however, another component of the freedom of elected leadership which is crucial here. This is the freedom to use influence — for example through the "prestige" of office as distinguished from its specified powers — to embark on new ventures in the "equation" of power and influence. This is to use influence to create additions to the total supply of power. How can this be conceived to work?

One important point is that the relation between the media involved with respect to positive and negative sanctions is the obverse of the case of creating money through banking. There it was the use of power embodied in the binding character of loan contracts which "made the difference." Here it is the optional capacity to exert influence through persuasion. This process seems to operate through the function of leadership which, by way of the involvements it possesses with

various aspects of the constituency structure of the collectivity, generates and structures new "demands" in the specific sense of demands for policy decision.

Such demands then may be conceived, in the case of the deciders, to justify an increased output of power. This in turn is made possible by the generality of the mandate of political support, the fact that it is not given on a barter basis in exchange for specific policy decisions, but once the "equation" of power and influence has been established through election, it is a mandate to do, within constitutional limits, what seems best, in the governmental case "in the public interest." Collective leadership may then be conceived as the bankers or "brokers" who can mobilize the binding commitments of their constituents in such a way that the totality of commitments made by the collectivity as a whole can be enhanced. This enhancement must, however, be justified through the mobilization of influence; it must, that is, both be felt to be in accordance with valid norms and apply to situations which "call for" handling at the level of binding collective commitments.

The critical problem of justification is, in one direction, that of consensus, of its bearing on the value-principle of solidarity as we have outlined this above. The standard therefore which corresponds to the value principle of solidarity is consensus in the sense in which that concept has been used above.

The problem then is that of a basis for breaking through the circular stability of a zero-sum power system. The crucial point is that this can only happen if the collectivity and its members are ready to assume new binding obligations over and above those previously in force. The crucial need is to justify this extension and to transform the "sentiment" that something ought to be done into a commitment to implement the sentiment by positive action, including coercive sanctions if necessary. The crucial agency of this process seems to be leadership, precisely conceived as possessing a component analytically independent of the routine power position of office, which defines the leader as the mobilizer of justifications for policies which would not be undertaken under the circular flow assumptions.

It may be suggested that the parallel to credit creation holds with respect to time-extension as well as in other respects. The increments of effectiveness which are necessary to implement new binding policies which constitute an addition to the total burden on the collectivity cannot simply be willed into being; they require organizational changes through recombinations of the factors of effectiveness, development of new agencies, procurement of personnel, new norms, and even changes in bases of legitimation. Hence leadership cannot justifiably be held responsible for effective implementation immediately, and conversely, the sources of political support must be willing to trust their leadership in the sense of not demanding immediate — by the time of the next election — "pay-off" of the power-value of their votes in their decisions dictated by their own interests.[1]

---

[1] Perhaps this is an unusually clear case of the relativity of the formal legal sense of the bindingness of commitments. Thus the populistic component in democratic government often ties both executive and legislative branches rather rigidly in what they can formally promise. However, there are many

It is perhaps legitimate to call the responsibility assumed in this connection specifically leadership responsibility and distinguish it in these terms from administrative responsibility which focuses on the routine functions. In any case I should like to conceive this process of power-enhancement as strictly parallel to economic investment, in the further sense that the pay-off should be an increment to the level of collective success in the sense outlined above, i.e. enhanced effectiveness of collective action in valued areas which could not have been expected without risk-taking on the part of leadership in a sense parallel to entrepreneurial investment.

The operation of both governmental and non-governmental collectivities is full of illustrations of the kind of phenomenon I have in mind, though because this type of formal analysis is somewhat unfamiliar, it is difficult to pin them down exactly. It has, for example, often been pointed out that the relation of executive responsibility to constituency-interests is very different in domestic and in foreign affairs. I suggest that the element of "political banking" in the field of foreign affairs is particularly large and that the sanction of approval of policy decisions, where it occurs, cannot infallibly be translated into votes, certainly not in the short run. Similar considerations are very frequently involved in what may be called "developmental" ventures, which cannot be expected to be "backed" by currently well-structured interests in the same sense as maintenance of current functions. The case of support of research and training is a good one since the "community of scholars" is not a very strong "pressure group" in the sense of capacity directly to influence large blocks of votes.

It would follow from these considerations that there is, in developed polities, a relatively "free-floating" element in the power system which is analogous to a credit-system. Such an element should then be subject to fluctuations on a dimension of inflation-deflation, and be in need of controls for the system as a whole, at a level above that of the activities of particular units.

The analogue of inflation seems to me to touch the credibility of the assertion of the bindingness of obligations assumed. Power, as a symbolic medium, is like money in that it is itself "worthless," but is accepted in the expectation that it can later be "cashed in," this time in the activation of binding obligations. If, however, "power-credit" has been extended too far, without the necessary organizational basis for fulfillment of expectations having been laid, then attempting to invoke the obligations will result in less than a full level of performance, inhibited by various sorts of resistance. In a collectivity undergoing disintegration the same formal office may be "worth less" than it otherwise would have been because of attrition of its basis of effectiveness. The same considerations hold when it is a case of over-extension of new power-expectations without adequate provision for making them effective.

It goes without saying that a power-system in which

this creditlike element is prominent is in a state analogous to the "insolvency" of a monetary system which includes an important element of actual credit, namely its commitments cannot be fulfilled all at once, even if those to whom they have been made have formally valid rights to such fulfillment. Only a strict zero-sum power system could fulfill this condition of "liquidity." Perhaps the conservatism of political ideologies makes it even more difficult to accept the legitimacy of such a situation — it is all too easy to define it as "dishonest" — than in the corresponding economic case.

There is, however, a fine line between solid, responsible and constructive political leadership which in fact commits the collectivity beyond its capacities for instantaneous fulfillment of all obligations, and reckless overextendedness, just as there is a fine line between responsible banking and "wild-catting."

Furthermore, under unusual pressures, even highly responsible leadership can be put in situations where a "deflationary" spiral sets in, in a pattern analogous to that of a financial panic. I interpret, for instance McCarthyism as such a deflationary spiral in the political field. The focus of the commitments in which the widest extension had taken place was in the international field — the United States had very rapidly come into the position of bearing the largest share of responsibility for maintenance of world political order against an expansionist Communist movement. The "loss of China" was in certain quarters a particularly traumatic experience, and the Korean war a highly charged symbol of the costs of the new stewardship.

A pluralistic political system like the American always has a large body of latent claims on the loyalty of its citizens to their government, not only for the "right sentiments" but for "sacrifices," but equally these are expected to be invoked only in genuine emergencies. The McCarthy definition of the situation was, however, that virtually anyone in a position of significant responsibility should not only recognize the "in case" priority — not necessarily by our basic values the highest — of national loyalty, but should explicitly renounce all other loyalties which might conceivably compete with that to the nation, including those to kith and kin. This was in effect a demand to liquidate all other commitments in favor of the national, a demand which in the nature of the case could not be met without disastrous consequences in many different directions. It tended to "deflate" the power system by undermining the essential basis of trust on which the influence of many elements bearing formal and informal leadership responsibilities, and which in turn sustained "power-credit," necessarily rested. Perhaps the most striking case was the allegation

de facto obligations assumed by government which are very nearly binding. Thus legally Congress could withdraw the totality of funds recently granted to universities for the support of scientific research and training, the formal appropriations being made year by year. Universities, however, plan very much in the expectation of maintenance of these funds, and this maintenance is certainly something like a de facto obligation of Congress.

of communist infiltration and hence widespread "disloyalty" in the army, which was exploited to try to force the army leadership to put the commitments of all associated personnel, including e.g. research scientists, in completely "liquid" form. Two features of the McCarthy movement particularly mark it as a deflationary spiral, first the vicious circle of spreading involvement with the casting of suspicion on wider and wider circles of otherwise presumptively loyal elements in the society and secondly the surprisingly abrupt end of the spiral once the "bubble was pricked" and "confidence restored," events associated particularly with the public reaction to McCarthy's performance in the televised army hearings, and to Senator Flanders' protest on the floor of the Senate.[1]

The focus of the McCarthy disturbance may be said to have been in the influence system, in the relation between integrative and pattern-maintenance functions in the society. The primary deflationary effect was on the "credit" elements of pluralistic loyalties. This in turn would make leadership elements, not only in government but private groups, much less willing to take risks in claiming loyalties which might compete with those to government. Since, however, in the hierarchy of control the influence system is superordinate to the power system, deflation in the former is necessarily propagated to the latter. This takes in the first instance the form of a rush to withdraw political support — which it will be remembered is here treated as a form of power — from leadership elements which could in any sense be suspected of "disloyalty." The extreme perhaps was the slogan propagated by McCarthy and played with by more responsible Republican leaders like Thomas E. Dewey, of "twenty years of treason" which impugned the loyalty of the Democratic Party as a whole. The effect was, by depriving opposition leadership of influence, to make it unsafe even to consider granting them power.

The breaking through of the zero-sum limitations of more elementary power systems opens the way to altogether new levels of collective effectiveness, but also, in the nature of the case, involves new levels of risk and uncertainty. I have already dealt briefly with this problem at the level of the particular collectivity and its extension of commitments. The problem of course is compounded for a system of collectivities because of the risk not only of particular failures, but of generalized inflationary and deflationary disturbances. There are, as we have noted, mechanisms of control which operate to regulate investment, and similarly extension of the commitments of particular collectivities, both of which have to do with the attempt to ensure responsibility, on the one hand for solvency over the long run, on the other for success of the larger "strategy" of extension. It is reasonable to suppose that beyond these, there must be mechanisms operating at the level of the system as a whole in both contexts.

In the monetary case it was the complex of central banking, credit management and their relations to governmental finance which has been seen to be the focus of these highest-level controls. In the case of power it is of course the first crucial point that there was to be some relatively paramount apex of control of the power and authority system, which we think of as in some sense the "sovereign" state.[2] This has mainly to do with the relations between what we have called justification and legitimacy, in relation to government as the highest-order tightly integrated collectivity structure — so far. This is the central focus of Weber's famous analysis of authority, but his analysis is in need of considerable extension in our sense. It seems, among other things, that he posed an unduly sharp alternative between charismatic and "routine" cases, particularly the rational-legal version of the latter. In particular it would be my view that very substantial possibilities of regulated extension of power-commitments exist within the framework of certain types of "legal" authority, especially where they are aspects of a political system which is pluralistic in general terms. These problems, however, cannot further be explored at the end of what is already a very long paper.

Conclusion

This paper has been designed as a general theoretical attack on the ancient problem of the nature of political power and its place, not only in political systems, narrowly conceived, but in the structure and processes of societies generally. The main point of reference for the attack has been the conception that the discussion of the problem in the main traditions of political thought have not been couched at a sufficiently rigorously analytical level, but have tended to treat the nation, the state, or the lower-level collectively organized "group," as the empirical object of reference, and to attempt to analyze its functioning without further basic analytical breakdown. The most conspicuous manifestation of this tendency has been the treatment of power.

The present paper takes a radically different position, cutting across the traditional lines. It takes its departure from the position of economic theory and, by inference, the asymmetry between it and the traditional political

[1] I have dealt with some aspects of the McCarthy episode in "Social Strains in America," *Structure and Process, op. cit.*, chapter 7, pp. 226–249. The inherent impossibility of the demand for "absolute security" in a pluralistic system is very cogently shown by Edward Shils in *The Torment of Secrecy* (New York: The Free Press of Glencoe, 1956), especially in chapter VI.

[2] In saying this I am very far from maintaining that "absolute" sovereignty is an essential condition of the minimal integration of political systems. On the contrary, first it is far from absolute internally, precisely because of the pluralistic character of most modern political systems and because of the openness of their boundaries in the integrative economic and other directions. Externally the relation of the territorial unit to norms and values transcending it is crucial, and steadily becoming more so. See my paper "Polarization of the World and International Order" in Quincy Wright, William M. Evan and Morton Deutsch, eds., *Preventing World War III* (New York: Simon and Schuster, 1962), pp. 310–331.

theory,[1] which has treated one as the theory of an analytically defined functional system of society — the economy — and the other as a concrete substructure, usually identified with government. Gradually the possibility has opened out both the extension of the analytical model of economic theory to the political field and the direct articulation of political with economic theory within the logical framework of the theory of the social system as a whole, so that the *polity* could be conceived as a functional subsystem of the society in all its theoretical fundamentals parallel to the economy.

This perspective necessarily concentrated attention on the place of money in the conception of the economy. More than that, it became increasingly clear that money was essentially a "symbolic" phenomenon and hence that its analysis required a frame of reference closer to that of linguistics than of technology, i.e. it is not the intrinsic properties of gold which account for the value of money under a gold standard any more than it is the intrinsic properties of the sounds symbolized as "book" which account for the valuation of physically fixed dissertations in linguistic form. This is the perspective from which the conception of power as a *generalized symbolic medium* operating in the processes of social interaction has been set forth.

This paper has not included a survey of the empirical evidence bearing on its ramified field of problems, but my strong conviction is not only that the line of analysis adopted is consistent with the broad lines of the available empirical evidence, but that it has already shown that it can illuminate a range of empirical problems which were not well understood in terms of the more conventional theoretical positions — e.g. the reasons for the general egalitarian pressure in the evolution of the political franchise, or the nature of McCarthyism as a process of political deflationary spiral.

It does not seem necessary here to recapitulate the main outline of the argument. I may conclude with the three main points with which I began. I submit, first, that the analytical path entered upon here makes it possible to treat power in conceptually specific and precise terms and thus gets away from the theoretical diffuseness called to attention, in terms of which it has been necessary to include such a very wide variety of problematical phenomena as "forms" of power. Secondly, I think it can advance a valid claim to present a resolution of the old dilemma as to whether (in the older terms) power is "essentially" a phenomenon of coercion or of consensus. It is both, precisely because it is a phenomenon which integrates a plurality of factors and outputs of political effectiveness and is not to be identified with any one of them. Finally, light has been thrown on the famous zero-sum problem, and a definite position taken that, though under certain specific assumptions the zero-sum condition holds, these are not constitutive of power systems in general, but under different conditions systematic "extension" of power

spheres without sacrifice of the power of other units is just as important a case.

These claims are put forward in full awareness that on one level there is an inherent arbitrariness in them, namely that I have defined power and a number of related concepts in my own way, which is different from many if not most of the definitions current in political theory. If theory were a matter only of the arbitrary choice of definitions and assumptions and reasoning from there, it might be permissible to leave the question at that and say simply, this is only one more personal "point of view." Any claim that it is more than that rests on the conception that the scientific understanding of societies is arrived at through a gradually developing organon of theoretical analysis and empirical interpretation and verification. My most important contention is that the line of analysis presented here is a further development of a main line of theoretical analysis of the social system as a whole, and of verified interpretation of the empirical evidence presented to that body of theory. This body of theory must ultimately be judged by its outcomes both in theoretical generality and consistency, over the whole range of social system theory, and by its empirical validity, again on levels which include not only conventionally "political" references, but their empirical interrelations with all other aspects of the modern complex society looked at as a whole.

Technical note

The above analysis has been presented in wholly discursive terms. Many decisions about categorization and detailed steps of analysis were, however, referred to a formalized paradigm of the principal structural components and process categories and relations of a society considered as a social system. For the benefit of readers with more technical interests in social system theory it has seemed advisable to present a very brief outline of the most directly relevant parts of the general paradigm here, with a brief elucidation of its relevance to the above discussion.[2]

The structural reference points are essentially two, namely first that at a sufficiently high level of differentiation of a society, economy, polity and integrative system become empirically distinct in terms of the primacy of function of structural units e.g. there is an

[1] I myself once accepted this. *Cf. The Social System* (New York: The Free Press of Glencoe, 1951), chapter V, pp. 161–163.

[2] The paradigm itself is still incomplete, and even in its present state has not been published as a whole. The first beginning statement dealing with process was made by Parsons and Smelser in *Economy and Society*, esp. Chapter II, and has been further developed in certain respects in Smelser's two subsequent independent books (*Social Change in the Industrial Revolution* and *Theory of Collective Behavior*). In my own case certain aspects, which now need further revision, were published in the article "Pattern Variables Revisited" (*American Sociological Review*, August, 1960). Early and partial versions of application to political subject matter are found in my contributions to Roland Young, ed., *Approaches to the Study of Politics*, and Burdick and Brodbeck, eds., *American Voting Behavior*.

important structural difference between a private business firm, an administrative agency of government and a court of law. Secondly every such unit is involved in plural interchange relations with other units with respect to most of its functional requirements from its situation — i.e., for factor inputs — and the conditions of making its contributions to other units in the "division of labor" — i.e., disposal of "product" outputs. This order of differentiation requires *double* interchanges between all the structural components belonging to each category-pair, e.g. firms and households, firms and political agencies (not necessarily governmental, it should be remembered) etc. The double interchange situation precludes mediation of processes in terms either of ascriptive expectations or barter arrangements, or a combination of the two. It necessitates the development of generalized symbolic media, of which we have treated money, power, and influence as cases.

At a sufficiently high level of generalized development

FIGURE 1

FORMAT OF THE SOCIETAL INTERCHANGE SYSTEM

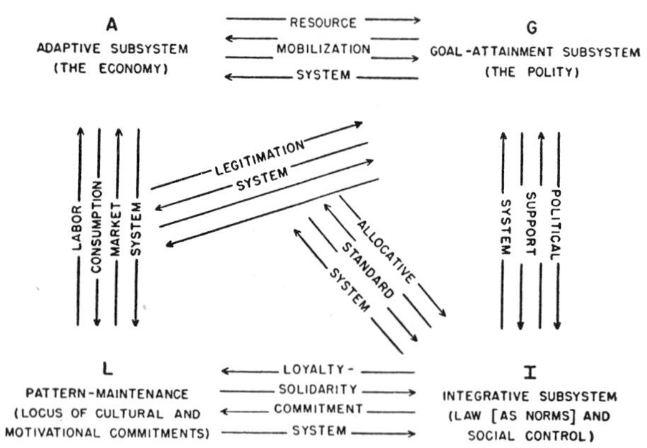

A
ADAPTIVE SUBSYSTEM
(THE ECONOMY)

RESOURCE
MOBILIZATION
SYSTEM

G
GOAL-ATTAINMENT SUBSYSTEM
(THE POLITY)

LABOR CONSUMPTION MARKET SYSTEM

LEGITIMATION SYSTEM

ALLOCATIVE STANDARD SYSTEM

POLITICAL SUPPORT SYSTEM

L
PATTERN-MAINTENANCE
(LOCUS OF CULTURAL AND
MOTIVATIONAL COMMITMENTS)

LOYALTY -
SOLIDARITY
COMMITMENT
SYSTEM

I
INTEGRATIVE SUBSYSTEM
(LAW [AS NORMS] AND
SOCIAL CONTROL)

the "governing" interchanges (in the sense of cybernetic hierarchy) take place between the media which are anchored in the various functional subsystems — as power is anchored in the polity. These media in turn serve as instrumentalities of gaining control of "lower-order" resources which are necessary for fulfillment of expectations. Thus the expenditure of money for "goods" is not, at the system or "aggregate" level (as analyzed by Keynes), acquisition of the possession of particular commodities, but consists in the generalized expectation of availability of goods on "satisfactory" market terms. This is the primary output of the economy to consumers. Similarly, when we speak of control of productivity as a factor of effectiveness, it is not managerial control of particular plants which is meant, but

---

[1] There is a very crucial problem area which concerns the nature of the interchanges between a society as a system in our sense and its environment. This set of problems unfortunately cannot be entered into here.

control of a share of general productivity of the economy through market mechanisms, without specification of particulars.

The paradigm of interchange between general media of communication is presented in figures 1 and 2. Figure 1 simply designates the format in which this part of the paradigm is conceived. The assumptions of this format are three, none of which can be grounded or justified within the limits of the present exposition. These are *1)* that the patterns of differentiation of a social system can be analyzed in terms of four primary functional categories, each of which is the focus of a primary functional subsystem of the society. As noted in the body of the essay, economy and polity are conceived to be such subsystems; *2)* The primary interchange processes through which these subsystems are integrated with each other operate through generalized symbolic media of the type which I have assumed money and power to be,[1] and *3)* at the level of differentiation of interest here, each interchange system is a double interchange, implying both the "alienation" of resources and products from their system of origin and the transcending of the barter level of exchange. Under these assumptions all figure 1 does is to portray a system of six double interchanges operating between each logically given pair among the four primary functional subsystems of a society. For convenience tentative names are given to each of these six double interchange systems.

Figure 2, then, places each of the six interchange systems on a horizontal axis, simply because they are easier to read that way. It adds to figure 1 only by introducing names of categories, directions of flow and designations as to medium (money, power, etc.) for each of the four places in each of the six interchange systems, thus presenting twenty-four categories, each of the four basic media appearing in four "forms."

Among the six interchange sets, power as a medium is involved, by our analysis, in only three, namely the interchanges of the polity (G) with each of the other three. These are the system of "resource mobilization," *vis-à-vis* the economy, the support system which involves the input of political support and the output of decisions (*vis-à-vis* the integrative system) and the system of legitimation, as I have called it, *vis-à-vis* the value aspect of the pattern-maintenance system. The last of these three is a special case which does not involve power as a medium, but rather the structure of the code governing authority as defining the institutionalized uses of power, hence the legitimation of authority. Primary attention can thus be given to the other two.

The categories included in the *A-G* (economy-polity, or resource mobilization) interchange can be described as "forms" of power and of money (or wealth) respectively. They will be seen to be the categories which have been used in the appropriate parts of the discursive exposition of the body of the paper. The double interchange here, as in the classic economy — or labor-consumption case, involves first one factor-interchange, namely control of productivity as factor of effectiveness exchanged for opportunity for effectiveness (in the particular case of capital, as a factor of production). Productivity is a monetary factor because it is a pool of resources controlled through monetary funds — which of course in turn can be exchanged for the particular facilities needed, notably goods and services. Oppor-

budgeted funds, though often generalization does not extend as high as this. Thus fluid resources in the ideal type case take the form of money funds.[1]

The second primary interchange system, which for convenience I shall call the support system, is that between polity and integrative system (*G-I*), which latter involves the associational aspect of group structure

FIGURE 2

THE CATEGORIES OF SOCIETAL INTERCHANGE

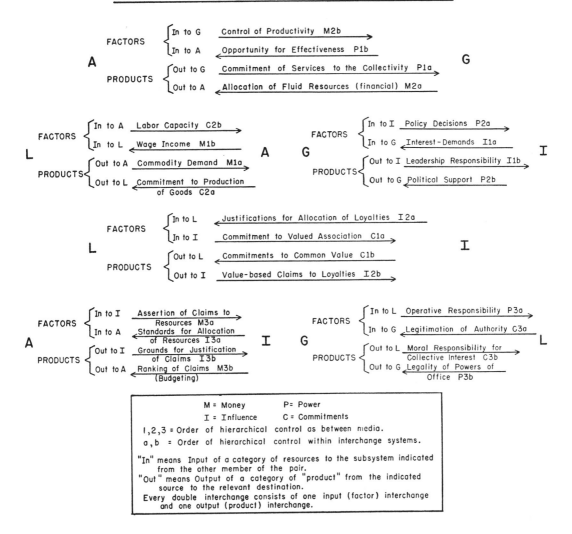

tunity, however, is a form of power in the sense discussed.

The second part of the double interchange is one of "product" outputs. This takes place between commitment of services to organization — typically through employment — which I have interpreted to be a form of power, and the allocation of fluid resources to the purveyors of service as facilities essential to the performance of their obligations — typically the control of

[1] The process of investment, which I conceive to be one very important special case of the operation of this interchange system, seems to work in such a way that the power component of a loan is a grant of opportunity, through which an increment of otherwise unavailable control of productivity is gained. The recipient of this "grant" is then, through committing (individual or collective) services, in a position to utilize these resources for increasing future economic productivity in some way. This is a special case because the resources might be used in some other way, e.g. for relieving distress or for scientific research.

and solidarity in relation to the system of norms (legal and informal) — as distinguished from values. The basic difference lies in the fact that power here is interchanged not with money but with influence, and that whereas *vis-à-vis* money it was the "controlling" medium, *vis-à-vis* influence it is controlled. This difference is symbolized by the placing of the power categories here in the outside positions whereas in the *A-G* case they were placed inside (as the monetary categories were in *L-A*).

The relevant factor interchange here is between policy decisions as a "factor of solidarity" and interest-demands as a factor of effectiveness, in the senses in which these concepts were used above. Essentially we may say that interest-demands "define the situation" for political decision-making — which of course is by no means to say that demands in their initial form are or should be simply "granted" without modification. Like other factors they are typically transformed in the

message components, and the position of the latter as sanctions controlling on the one hand factors essential to the various functional subsystems, on the other hand product outputs from these subsystems. The rows are arranged from top to bottom in terms of the familiar hierarchy of control — each row designating one of the four media. The columns, on the other hand, designate components into which each medium needs to be broken down if some of the basic conditions of its operation in mediating interaction are to be understood.

In the body of the paper I have discussed the reasons for which it seems necessary to distinguish two components in the code aspect of each medium, namely what have been called the relevant value principle on the one hand, the "coordinative standard" on the other. The most familiar example concerns the paradigmatic economic case. Here the famous concept of utility seems to be the relevant value principle whereas that of

FIGURE 3
THE MEDIA AS SANCTIONS

COMPONENTS OF MEDIA AND INTERCHANGE RECIPROCALS / MEDIA IN HIERARCHY OF CONTROL	CODES		MESSAGES (SANCTIONS)		TYPES OF SANCTION AND OF EFFECT
	VALUE-PRINCIPLE	COORDINATION STANDARD	FACTORS CONTROLLED (SOURCE)	PRODUCTS CONTROLLED (DESTINATION)	
L COMMITMENTS	INTEGRITY	PATTERN-CONSISTENCY	WAGES A / JUSTIFICATION OF LOYALTIES I	CONSUMERS' DEMAND A / CLAIMS TO LOYALTIES I	NEGATIVE-INTENTIONAL (ACTIVATION OF COMMITMENTS)
I INFLUENCE	SOLIDARITY	CONSENSUS	COMMITMENTS TO VALUED ASSOCIATION L / POLICY DECISIONS G	COMMITMENT TO COMMON VALUES L / POLITICAL SUPPORT G	POSITIVE-INTENTIONAL (PERSUASION)
G POWER	EFFECTIVENESS	SUCCESS	INTEREST DEMANDS I / CONTROL OF PRODUCTIVITY A	LEADERSHIP RESPONSIBILITY I / CONTROL OF FLUID RESOURCES A	NEGATIVE-SITUATIONAL (SECURING COMPLIANCE)
A MONEY	UTILITY	SOLVENCY	CAPITAL G / LABOR L	COMMITMENT OF SERVICES G / EXPECTATION OF GOODS L	POSITIVE-SITUATIONAL (INDUCEMENT)

course of the political process. Correspondingly policy decisions are a factor in solidarity in that they constitute commitments for collective action on which "interested parties" within limits can count.

The interchange of "product" outputs then consists of leadership responsibility as output of the polity (a form of influence, note, *not* of power), and political support as an output of the "associational" system — in the governmental case e.g. the electorate, which is a source of the political "income" of power. It will of course be noted that the units involved in any particular case of these two interchanges typically are not the same — thus party leaders may bid for support whereas administrative officials make certain policy decisions. This type of "split" (carried out to varying degrees) is characteristic of any highly differentiated system.

Figure 3 attempts to look at the generalized media from the point of view not only of their hierarchical ordering, but of the relation between the code and

solvency is the coordinative standard. Utility is the basic "measure" of value in the economic sense, whereas the imperative to maintain solvency is a category of norm for the guidance of units in economic action. For the political case I have adopted the concept of effectiveness in Barnard's sense as the parallel to the economist's utility. Success, for the unit in question, notably the collective ease, seems to be the best available term for the corresponding coordinative standard. (Possibly, used with proper qualifications, the term sovereignty might be still more appropriate for this standard.)

At the other most important direct boundary of the polity, solidarity in Durkheim's sense seems to be the value-principle of integration which is parallel to utility and effectiveness, whereas the very important (to political theory) concept of *consensus* seems adequately to formulate the relevant integrative coordinative standard. Since they are not directly involved in the interchange systems of immediate concern here, I merely call attention to the designation of the value-principle of the pattern-maintenance system as *integrity* and the corresponding coordinative standard as *pattern-consistency*.

The *A* and *G* columns of figure 3 then designate contexts of operation of each of the four media as sanctions, but arranged not by interchange system as in figure 2, but by control of factor inputs and product outputs respectively. Thus money though not itself a factor of production, "controls," i.e. buys, labor and capital as the primary factors, in the *A-L* and the *A-G* interchange systems respectively, whereas for "consuming" systems money buys outputs of the economy, namely goods (in *A-L*) and services (in *A-G*) respectively.

The involvement of power is conceived to be parallel. On the one hand it "commands" the two primary mobile factors of effectiveness, namely control of productivity (in *G-A*) and interest-demands (in *G-I*) (as justified in terms of appeal to norms). On the other hand the "consumers" or beneficiaries of the outputs from the process can use power to command these outputs in the form of fluid resources (e.g. through budget allocation in *G-A*) and of leadership responsibility for valued goals (in *G-I*).

It will be noted that in figure 3 negative and positive sanction types alternate in the hierarchy of control. Power, as the medium depending on negative situational sanctions is "sandwiched" between money (below it) with its positive situational sanctions and influence (above it) with its positive intentional sanctions.

Returning to figure 2, power is also involved in the legitimation system (*L-G*), but this time as code, as aspect of authority. This may be conceived as a mechanism for linking the principles and standards in the *L* and *G* rows. What is called the assumption of operative responsibility (*P3a*), which is treated as a "factor of integrity" is responsibility for *success* in the implementation of the value-principles, not only of collective effectiveness, but of integrity of the paramount societal value-pattern. It may be said that the legitimation of authority (*C3a*) "imposes" the responsibility to attempt such success. Legality of the powers of office on the other hand (*P3c*), as a category of output to the polity, is an application of the standard of pattern-consistency. At the various relevant levels action may and should be taken consistent with the value-commitments. In exchange for legal authorization to take such action, the responsible office-holder must accept moral responsibility for his use of power and his decisions of interpretation (*C3b*).

PATTERNS OF STATUS

"Who's Who in America" and "The Social Register"

ELITE AND UPPER CLASS INDEXES IN METROPOLITAN AMERICA
E. Digby Baltzell

IN THE NINETEEN THIRTIES and forties, the sociological literature in America was enriched by a wealth of monographs in which social stratification was the central theme.[1] With staffs trained in interviewing techniques, the filling out of schedules, and the operation of "IBM" machines, sociologists made numerous painstaking investigations of stratification in the small community. Such terms as "upper-upper," "lower-upper," and "lower-lower" were added to the language of social thought, and, even in America, aristocracy was found cohabiting with democracy.

Of the multitude of monographs describing the small community in America, the contrasting conceptual approaches of the Lynds on the one hand, and W. Lloyd Warner and his disciples on the other, represent the two divergent emphases in class analysis.[2] The Lynds, who begin both their *Middletown* volumes with a chapter on "Getting a Living," emphasize the dynamics of the economic class system and the differential distribution of power in a *changing* society. On the other hand, Warner, an anthropologist who had recently returned from a study of pre-literate cultures in Australia when he began the *Yankee City* study, categorically rejects an economic interpretation of stratification and emphasizes the differences in ritual and style of life as between sub-cultural class levels in a comparatively *static* and traditional New England community.[3] Whereas Warner defines a class system in *subjective* terms as "two or more orders of people who are believed to be, and are accordingly ranked by members of the community, in socially superior and inferior positions," the Lynds employ an *objective* definition which differentiates

[1] For an excellent recent review of the literature, see Milton M. Gordon, "Social Class in American Sociology," *The American Journal of Sociology*, vol. LV, no. 3 (Nov. 1949), pp. 262–268.

[2] See Robert S. Lynd and Helen Merrell Lynd, *Middletown* (New York: Harcourt, Brace and Company, 1929); Robert S. Lynd and Helen Merrell Lynd, *Middletown in Transition* (New York: Harcourt, Brace and Company, 1937); and W. Lloyd Warner and Paul S. Lunt, *The Social Life of a Modern Community* (New Haven: Yale University Press, 1941).

[3] Warner, *op. cit.*, p. 81.

This is an original article prepared for the first edition of the reader.

between the "business" and "working" classes.[1] While the members of the "upper-upper" class in *Yankee City*, a majority of whom are *women*, are emulated and exercise a measure of social control because of their "lineage," their "good-breeding," and the fact that they "know how to act," in *Middletown* in the nineteen-thirties, the "passage of first generation wealth into second generation power" had created a newly-self-conscious upper class whose *male* members tended to dominate the business and financial life of the city.[2]

At the present stage in the development of American sociology, the conceptual approach of the "Warner School" represents the dominant trend in stratification analysis. As perhaps the current emphasis on the subjective aspects of class is an over-reaction on the part of American social scientists to the admittedly incomplete Marxian emphasis on the objective economic indexes of class position, a more balanced approach may be achieved by utilizing *both* the subjective and the objective class concepts as differentially related variables in various social situations.[3] It is not a question of whether the objective class concept is more, or less, "real" than the subjective class concept; rather, both concepts are abstractions from concrete reality, and the failure to treat them as such may lead to reification or a sterile circular reasoning. In other words, the behavior patterns, values, and attitudes of groups of people differentially situated in any class system are presumably conditioned both by their position in the productive process (occupational rank or income) and by their subjective class position (social access, family position, and so forth). Generals who are aristocrats may be expected to behave differently than generals who are not aristocrats.

Separating out the subjective and the objective aspects of class position for purposes of analysis, in this paper, the *elite* concept refers to those *individuals* who are the most successful and stand at the top of the functional (objective) class hierarchy. These individuals are leaders in their chosen occupations or professions; they are the final-decision-makers in the political, economic, or military spheres as well as leaders in such professions as law, engineering, medicine, education, religion, and the arts. On the other hand, in any comparatively stable social structure, over the years, certain elite members and their families will tend to associate with one another in various primary group situations and gradually develop a consciousness of kind and a distinctive style of life. The *upper class* concept, then, refers to a group of *families*, descendants of successful individuals (elite members) one, two, three, or more generations ago, who are at the top of the social (subjective) class hierarchy. As Dixon Wecter puts it:

A group of families with a common background and racial origin becomes cohesive, and fortifies itself by the joint sharing of sports and social activities, by friendships and intermarriage. Rough and piratical grandfathers had seized their real estate, laid out their railroads, and provided for its trust funds. The second

and third generation, relieved from the counting-house and shop, now begin to travel, buy books and pictures, learn about horses and wine, and cultivate the art of charm.[4]

While the numerous sociological studies of small American communities have unquestionably contributed valuable knowledge about the ways of human behavior and the nature of social organization, it is perhaps fair to say that the large metropolitan area is more representative of American life in the middle twentieth century. In order to gain some insight into the nature of stratification in metropolitan America, *Who's Who in America*, a listing of individuals of high functional class position (achieved status), and the *Social Register*, a listing of families of high social class position (ascribed status), may be useful indexes of a metropolitan elite and upper class respectively.[5] The limited task of this paper is to show how, in the last part of the nineteenth century, the *Social Register* became a metropolitan upper class index, and how, in certain large cities in 1940, this upper class was related to the elite, those listed in *Who's Who in America*.

The Social Register — an index of a new upper class in selected large metropolitan areas in America

For those who see history as a record of man's creative efforts to choose between alternatives in an endless chain of historical situations and not only as a series of reactions to various abstract causes, geographic, climatic, racial, or economic, which more or less determine his destiny, human society is an historical process

---

[1] See Warner, *op. cit.*, p. 82, and Lynd, *Middletown*, p. 22.

It has been observed that, "in general, the leading exponents of the subjective (distributive) theories of class are oriented towards an examination of the forces of tradition, while the leading exponents of the objective (production) theories of class are more concerned with social change," Seymour M. Lipset and Reinhard Bendix, "Social Status and Social Structure: A Re-examination of Data and Interpretation: I." *The British Journal of Sociology*, vol. II, no. 2 (June 1951), p. 150.

[2] See Warner, *op. cit.*, p. 83, and Lynd, *Middletown in Transition*, p. 100.

[3] For example, while in *Yankee City*, a small and traditional New England community, subjective social class position may have been the independent variable in the class situation, in rapidly changing *Middletown*, on the other hand, position in the dynamic productive process may have been the independent variable. An analysis of the changing relationships between these two variables in different communities raises the mere descriptive study of stratification to the level of scientific analysis.

[4] Dixon Wecter, *The Saga of American Society* (New York: Charles Scribner's Sons, 1937), p. 6.

[5] *Who's Who in America* (Chicago: The A. N. Marquis Company, 1940), volume 21.

Social Register (New York: The Social Register Association, 1940). Separate volumes for New York, Philadephia, Boston, Baltimore, Chicago, St. Louis, Buffalo, Pittsburgh, San Francisco, Cleveland, Cincinnati-Dayton, and Washington, D. C. are issued yearly in November.

wherein each generation sifts to the top particular individual types, warriors, prophets, priests, merchants, bankers, or bureaucrats, whose talents are needed in any given period; these individuals, in turn, and within limits, make the decisions which shape the course of history. Thus Brooks Adams saw the history of England as partly reflected in the circulation of elites, wherein the feudal warrior, whose power lay in men and spears, was replaced during the Reformation by the large landowners who ruled England from the time of Henry VIII to 1688, when the rising merchant adventurer or bourgeois elites finally won their rights, only to be followed by the manufacturing men such as Watt and Boulton whose talents led them to power after the Industrial Revolution; and finally, from the time of the defeat of that symbol of martial power on the hill at Waterloo, the manufacturing and landowning elites were dominated by, and often in debt to, the money power of Lombard Street.[1] The English upper class, often called an aristocracy, centers in a group of families who are descendants of these successful individuals of the remote and recent past and of course alloyed with, and having an influence on, those with a talent for power in the modern bureaucratic period.

As in England, America has witnessed a procession of successful men who have risen to positions of wealth and power, and whose children and grandchildren have been brought up and lived in more or less socially isolated subcultural worlds. As the Beards say:

> On the eve of the Civil War there had been many "seasoned clans" on the Eastern seaboard, some of them dating their origins back a hundred years or more, and boasting of ancestors who had served as preachers, judges, warriors, and statesmen in colonial times, in the heroic epoch of the Revolution, and in the momentous age of the new Republic. Able to hold their own socially, if not politically, these select families had absorbed with facility the seepage of rising fortunes that gradually oozed into their ranks — until the flood of the new plutocracy descended upon them.[2]

All families are equally old; "old families" are those whose ancestors rose to positions of affluence in an earlier period than the so-called "new families."[3] As late as the eighteen seventies or eighties in America, "Society" in the older Eastern seaboard cities was a rather well-defined, primary group of families who knew one another well and knew "who" belonged in "polite society." Even in the middle of the twentieth century in these cities, the "old families," the "Proper" Bostonians, Philadelphians, or New Yorkers, are those whose fortunes were made in the pre-Civil War period; late nineteenth century wealth is still considered new. As Cleveland Amory says of Boston:

> All through Boston history, when a family loses its financial stability, it has a way of beginning to disappear. After the Revolution, or better still, after the War of 1812 and lasting roughly through the Civil War, in the great Family-founding days of the nineteenth century, somewhere along the line there must be a merchant prince, the real Family-founder.[4]

As with so much else in American life, the eighteen eighties mark a turning point in upper class history; the local familistic-communal upper classes were absorbed in a new upper class which was increasingly extra-communal and associationally defined.[5] After the "Second American Revolution" in which the industrial North brought the planter aristocracy to its knees, new fortunes of undreamed-of proportions were created;[6] as transportation and communication improved, from all parts of the great American continent, barons of dry goods, utilities, coal, oil, and railroads moved their families to New York, built ostentatious Victorian piles, entertained, and, where possible, moved into "Society." By the eighteen eighties, New York was the center of social life in the United States.[7]

There was the usual resistance at first but "by one process or another amalgamation was affected and new varnish softened by the must of age. As the landed gentlemen of England had on various occasions saved their houses from decay by discreet jointures with

[1] Brooks Adams, *The Law of Civilization and Decay* (New York: The Macmillan Company, 1896), pp. 186ff.

[2] Charles A. Beard and Mary R. Beard, *The Rise of American Civilization* (New York: The Macmillan Company, 1937), vol. II, p. 387.

[3] One of the reasons why W. Lloyd Warner discards an economic interpretation of stratification in *Yankee City* was that "old family" or "lineage" placed people in the "upper-upper" category although they often were less wealthy than "lower-upper", or "new family" people. While this undoubtedly vitiates any *static* economic interpretation, historically the "old families" became so largely because some ancestor had made money. Presumably, the "Riverbrook" families were just as *old* as those on "Hill Street." See Warner and Lunt, *op. cit.*, p. 81.

The "old families" on the Eastern seaboard are not Mayflower Descendants but the descendants of late eighteenth and early nineteenth century merchants or manufacturers. Hence the large number of "Proper" Bostonians, and even some Philadelphians and New Yorkers, who trace their lines back to "Salem Shippers." See S. E. Morison, *Maritime History of Massachusetts, 1783–1860* (Boston: Houghton, Mifflin, 1921).

[4] Cleveland Amory, *The Proper Bostonians* (New York: E. P. Dutton and Co., Inc., 1947), pp. 39–40.

[5] The novelist, Edith Wharton, interprets this transitional period in the history of the New York upper class in three novels — *The Age of Innocence, The House of Mirth*, and *The Custom of the Country*. The first novel opens "On a January evening in the early seventies," and portrays a small and formal "society" which is soon to disappear before the assault of the parvenu which she describes in the other two novels.

[6] "Statisticians could only roughly estimate the strength of the spreading plutocracy and the size of its share gathered from the golden flood, but, according to one guess, there were only three millionaires in the United States in 1861 and at least thirty-eight hundred at the lapse of thirty-six years." Charles A. Beard and Mary R. Beard, *op. cit.*, vol. II, p. 388.

[7] For a description of "Society" in this age of transition see Frederick Townsend Martin, *The Passing of the Idle Rich* (New York: Doubleday, 1911).

mercantile families, so many of the established families in Boston, New York, Philadelphia, and Baltimore escaped the humiliation of poverty by judicious selections from the onrushing plutocracy."[1] Amidst this incredible "Gilded Age," in the year 1887, the *Social Register* was copyrighted by the Social Register Association and the first volume appeared for New York City in 1888. There were less than two thousand families listed in this "record of society, comprising an accurate and careful list of its members, with their addresses, many of the maiden names of the married women, the club addresses of the men, officers of the leading clubs and social organizations, opera box holders, and other useful social information."[2] As Dixon Wecter put it in his *Saga of American Society:*

> Here at last, unencumbered with advertisements of dress-makers and wine merchants, enhanced by large, clear type and a pleasant binding of orange and black — which if anything, suggested the colors of America's most elegant university — was a convenient listing of one's friends and potential friends. It was an immediate triumph.[3]

The New York *Social Register* was soon followed by volumes for Boston and Philadelphia in 1890, Baltimore in 1892, Chicago in 1893, Washington, D. C. in 1900, St. Louis and Buffalo in 1903, Pittsburgh in 1904, San Francisco in 1906, and Cleveland and Cincinnati-Dayton in 1910. Volumes for all these twelve cities have been issued yearly down to the present and in substantially the same form as the original New York *Social Register*. Other volumes were issued for Providence, R. I. (1905–1926), Minneapolis-St. Paul (1907–1927), Seattle-Portland (1914–1921), Pasadena-Los Angeles (1914–1926), Detroit (1918–1927), and Richmond-Charleston-Savannah-Atlanta (1906–1927) but were discontinued because of lack of interest.[4]

It is interesting that the *Social Register* is privately owned and lists social status, as it were, for a profit. The register is issued yearly in November and is sent to all families who are listed within its pages. The yearly charge for a subscription ranges from five to ten dollars per city volume. Potential members must make application themselves and include written references from present members (see below); the only exceptions to this rule are to be found in Washington, D. C., where the President, the Vice-President, the Supreme Court, the cabinet, various members of the diplomatic corps, and all United States Senators (not Representatives) are listed automatically.[5] This last point reflects the nature of stratification in a bureaucratic social structure where, like the military services, social class position follows functional position, and the Senator, like the naval officer, is automatically a "gentleman."[6]

What evidence is there which would indicate that the *Social Register* is an index of families who are descended more or less from elite members in the past? What is the relationship between the families listed in the contemporary *Social Registers* (1940) and the captains of

industry and finance who came to power in the "Gilded Age"? In the first place, Frederick Lewis Allen takes ten "Lords of Creation" as ideal typical examples of the American financial elite at the turn of the century and shows how they — and their sons and grandsons — alloyed their gold with an American upper class.[7] Of interest here is the fact that, of these ten men — J. Pierpont Morgan, George Fales Baker, James Stillman, Edward H. Harriman, John D. Rockefeller, William Rockefeller, Henry Huddlestone Rogers, William K. Vanderbilt, James R. Keene, and Jacob H. Schiff — all but the last named were listed in the *Social Register* as of 1905;[8] Allen notes that the exclusion of Schiff was "presumably due to the fact that he was a Jew, and the Jews constituted a group somewhat apart; the fashionable clubs were almost exclusively gentile; and the 'Social Register' was virtually a gentile register."[9] As it illustrates the dynamics of upper class formation in America, it is of interest to observe that Jacob Schiff's grandson, who married George Fales Baker's granddaughter, is listed in both the *Social Register* and *Who's Who* as of 1940.

Ferdinand Lundberg's *America's 60 Families* is a study of America's wealthiest families, the majority of whose fortunes were made between the Civil War and World War I.[10] Of these sixty consanguine family units, over three-fourths have traceable descendants (the same given and surnames as the family founder) who are listed in the 1940 *Social Register*; these descendants are intermarried one with another and with others of less spectacular wealth but of higher social standing.[11]

Finally, the rather ponderous *History of the Great American Fortunes* by Gustavus Myers is another useful volume for validating the *Social Register* as an American upper class index.[12] This well known book is an exhaustive study of the men who have amassed the greatest fortunes in America from colonial times to the present

[1] Charles A. Beard and Mary R. Beard, *op. cit.,* vol. II, p. 388.

[2] Quoted from the first *Social Register* (New York: The Social Register Association, 1888).

[3] Dixon Wecter: *The Saga of American Society* (New York: Charles Scribner's Sons, 1937), p. 232.

[4] This information was obtained by checking the volumes of the *Social Register* in the Library of Congress.

[5] See Wecter, *op. cit.,* pp. 232–236.

[6] Herbert Spencer saw "progress" in terms of the movement of society from the *militant* to the *industrial* type of social structure. In the modern state where social and functional classes merge in one all-inclusive bureaucratic hierarchy, Spencer's ideal typical *militant* social structure may well be a cogent description of the "Brave New World." See Herbert Spencer, *The Principles of Sociology* (New York: D. Appleton and Company, 1896), vol. II, Chap. XVIII.

[7] Frederick Lewis Allen, *The Lords of Creation* (New York: Harper and Brothers, 1935), Chapter 3.

[8] *Ibid.,* p. 98.

[9] *Ibid.,* pp. 98–99.

[10] Ferdinand Lundberg: *America's 60 Families* (New York: Vanguard Press, 1937).

[11] At one time or another for example, "old families" such as Biddle, Peabody, Roosevelt, and so forth have absorbed, or been absorbed by Drexels, Du Ponts, Fields, and Dukes.

[12] Gustavus Myers, *History of the Great American Fortunes* (New York: The Modern Library, 1937).

TABLE I. *Deceased Elite Individuals in American Economic Life with Descendants Who Are Listed in the 1940 Social Register; the Names Are Taken from the Index of History of the Great American Fortunes, by Gustavus Myers*

Deceased elite individual	Period when wealth was acquired*	Occupation : or the way in which wealth was acquired†
(Elite individuals with descendants listed in the Philadelphia *Social Register* in 1940)		
Baer, George F.	Late 19th century	Railroads
Biddle, Nicholas	18th–19th century	Finance
Cassatt, A. J.	Late 19th century	Railroads
Cope, Thomas Pym	18th–19th century	Merchant
Dolan, Thomas	Late 19th century	Utilities
Drexel, Anthony	Late 19th century	Finance
Du Pont, Coleman	20th century	Chemistry
Elkins, William L.	Late 19th century	Utilities
Hopkins, Johns	Early 19th century	Railroads
Knox, Philander	Late 19th century	Law
Penrose, Boies	20th century	Politics
Ridgeway, Jacob	18th–19th century	Merchant
Scott, Thomas	Late 19th century	Railroads
Wanamaker, John	Late 19th century	Merchant
Widener, P. A. B.	Late 19th century	Utilities
(Elite individuals with descendants listed in the Boston *Social Register* in 1940)		
Adams, Charles F.	Late 19th century‡	Railroads
Aldrich, Nelson	Late 19th century	Finance
Ames, Oakes	Late 19th century	Railroads
Brooks, Peter C.	18th–19th century	Merchant
Cabot, George	18th–19th century	Merchant
Derby, Elias	18th–19th century	Merchant
Peabody, Joseph	18th–19th century	Merchant
Perkins, Thomas	18th–19th century	Merchant
Thorndike, Israel	18th–19th century	Merchant
(Elite individuals with descendants listed in the New York *Social Register* in 1940)		
Astor, J. J.	Early 19th century	Furs, land
Baker, George F.	Late 19th century	Finance
Beekman, Henry	18th–19th century	Land
Belmont, August	Late 19th century	Finance, utilities
Blair, John I.	Late 19th century	Railroads
Brevoort, Henry	18th–19th century	Land
Brown, Alexander	Late 19th century	Finance
Carnegie, Andrew	Late 19th century	Manufacturing
Choate, Joseph	Late 19th century	Law
Clews, Henry	Late 19th century	Finance
Cravath, Paul	Late 19th century	Law
Cromwell, W. Nelson	Late 19th century	Law
Dodge, Cleveland	Late 19th century	Copper
Duke, James B.	20th century	Cigarettes
Flagler, H. M.	Late 19th century	Oil
Ford, Henry	20th century	Automobiles
Goelet, Peter	18th century	Land
Gould, Jay	Late 19th century	Railroads
Griswold family	18th–19th century	Merchants
Harriman, E. H.	Late 19th century	Railroads
Havemeyer, H. O.	Late 19th century	Sugar
Hill, J. J.	Late 19th century	Railroads
James, D. Willis	Late 19th century	Copper
Ledyard, L. Cass	Late 19th century	Law
Lee, Ivy	20th century	Public relations
Livingston, Robert	18th century	Land
Lorillard, Pierre	Early 19th century	Snuff, land
Morgan, J. P.	Late 19th century	Finance
Payne, O. H.	Late 19th century	Oil
Perkins, George	Late 19th century	Finance, insurance
Phelps, John T.	Late 19th century	Copper
Phillips, Adolphus	18th–19th century	Merchant
Rhinelander, William C.	18th–19th century	Land
Rockefeller, John D.	Late 19th century	Oil
Rogers, H. H.	Late 19th century	Oil, finance
Roosevelt, James	18th–19th century	Land
Ryan, T. Fortune	Late 19th century	Utilities
Schermerhorn, Peter	18th century	Land
Schiff, Jacob	Late 19th century	Finance
Schley, Grant B.	Late 19th century	Finance
Schuyler, Peter	18th–19th century	Land
Stettinius, Edward R.	Late 19th century	Matches, finance
Stillman, James	Late 19th century	Finance
Stokes, Thomas	Late 19th century	Copper
Taylor, Moses	Early 19th century	Railroads
Vanderbilt, Cornelius	Early 19th century	Shipping, railroads
Van Rensselaer, K.	18th century	Land
Villard, Henry	Late 19th century	Railroads
Whitney, William C.	Late 19th century	Utilities
(Elite individuals with descendants listed in the Chicago *Social Register* in 1940)		
Armour, J. Ogden	Late 19th century	Manufacturing
Field, Marshall	Late 19th century	Merchant
Leiter, Levi	Late 19th century	Merchant
McCormick, Cyrus	Late 19th century	Manufacturing
Palmer, Potter	Late 19th century	Merchant
Patterson, Joseph M.	Late 19th century	Publisher
(Elite individuals with descendants listed in the Baltimore, Cincinnati, Pittsburgh, San Francisco, St. Louis, or Washington *Social Register* in 1940)		
Crocker, Charles	Early 19th century	Railroads
Elkins, Stephen B.	Late 19th century	Land
Frick, Henry Clay	Late 19th century	Manufacturing
Garrett, John W.	Early 19th century	Railroads
Longworth, Nicholas	18th–19th century	Land
Mellon, Andrew	20th century	Finance, mfg.
Mills, D. O.	Early 19th century	Finance
Pulitzer, Joseph	Late 19th century	Publisher

* The Family-Founders in America can be conveniently divided into three periods. First, there were the romantic merchant capitalists of the late eighteenth and early nineteenth centuries. The descendants of these men are the "Proper" Philadelphians, Bostonians, Baltimorians, or New Yorkers of the present day. Second, there were the industrial, railroad, utility, and financial capitalists who made their money in the period between the Civil War and World War I. Finally, there are the twentieth century, manufacturing, Family-Founders.

† The occupations listed are of necessity limited to the principal field of endeavor. There is much overlapping. While "land" is listed for only a few individuals, almost all of the great fortunes in this country (and in England) have profited from the ownership of urban real estate. Finally, several lawyers and politicians are listed because these men were prominent in their day and were listed in the index of Myers' book.

‡ While Charles Francis Adams (Jr.) was a prominent railroad executive, he was a man of inherited wealth. When Charles Francis Adams I, the father of Henry, Charles, and Brooks, married the daughter of Peter Charndon Brooks, one of Boston's first millionaire merchants, the Adams family became wealthy for the first time.

(1936). The names of these wealthy family-founders (taken from the index of Myers' book) have been carefully checked against the names of the families listed in the twelve 1940 *Social Registers*. The family-founders whose descendants are listed in the 1940 *Social Registers* of these cities are shown in Table 1.

The distinguished historian, Samuel Morison, once facetiously remarked that he attached great significance to the fact that the founding of the Brookline Country Club in 1882 coincided with the closing of the frontier in America. Certainly the closing of the frontier (1890), the Sherman Anti-Trust Act (1890), the formation of the United States Steel Company (1901), the founding of Groton School (1884), the opening of the new "million-aires' country club" at Tuxedo Park, New York (1885), the rule of Mrs. Astor and Ward McAlister (1880's and 1890's), the Bradley Martin ball (at the cost of 369,200 dollars in 1897), and the first issue of the *Social Register* (1888) were important variables in a social situation which pointed to a centralized America in the middle twentieth century. As wealth centered in New York and the financial elite became dominant, the *Social Register* became an index of a new upper class in America. For the first time, subcultural socializing agencies other than the family operated on almost a national scale in the form of the New England boarding school and the fashionable Eastern university. The elder Morgan and his contemporaries were on the boards of trustees and gave their money to these privately run institutions where they, in turn, sent their sons to be educated together. Groton School, for example, which opened its doors in 1884 with the elder Morgan as an original trustee, was founded by Endicott Peabody, a descendant of Joseph Peabody (see Table 1) who "in the days when Salem was at its greatest, was the greatest merchant in Salem."[1] Of the 87 men listed in Table 1, no less than 53 had one or more descendants who had attended either Groton or St. Paul's schools in the period between 1890 and 1940. In other words, these exclusive boarding schools, and universities like Harvard, Yale, and Princeton, serve to create and preserve an upper class, inter-city solidarity. The school, or college club, "tie" or "hatband" are status symbols among this new upper class in *all* cities. The available evidence at least suggests that the *Social Register* is an index of this inter-city upper class in 1940.

Who's Who in America — an elite index

As a group, an upper class is intimately connected with history as long as the family remains as the institution which introduces each generation into the culture. Thus the validity of the *Social Register* as an upper class index depends on the relationship between its members and past elites. On the other hand, an elite has no group history — only the individual members have a past; elite members are making history and some of their heirs may become part of a future upper class.

Who's Who in America is a nationally recognized listing of brief biographies of the leading men and women in contemporary American life. As such, it is a perfectly democratic index of high functional class position and has wide prestige. In response to a standard form sent to all those persons chosen to be included in the current issue, each completed biography in *Who's Who* lists the following information: name, occupation, date and place of birth, full name of both parents, education and degrees received, marital status — including name of spouse, date of marriage, and the full names of any children, occupational career, military experience, directorships and trusteeships, honorary society and associational memberships, fraternal organizations, religious and political affiliations, club memberships, publications, and finally, home and business addresses.

The following aims of the publishers of *Who's Who*, are indicative of the nature of this elite index.

The present edition contains down-to-date "Who's Who" biographies of 31,752 outstanding contemporary men and women.

The names in *Who's Who in America* are selected not as the best but as an attempt to choose the best known men and women in the country in all lines of *reputable achievements* — names much in the public eye, not locally, but nationally.

The standards of admission divide the eligibles into two classes: *1)* those who are selected on account of special prominence in creditable lines of effort, making them the subject of extensive interest, inquiry, or discussion in this country; and *2)* those who are arbitrarily included on account of official position — civil, military, naval, religious, or educational.[2]

No index is perfect, nor any sociological classification as homogeneous as might be desired. We are aware of the inadequacies of *Who's Who* as an index of an American elite. In the first place, it is too heavily weighted with educators and churchmen relative to the organizing elites of business, government, and labor. Secondly, in the distribution of power in any large community, especially urban America, one must always remain aware of the social power exercised by those persons, such as the political "boss," who are not strictly of the respectable world. *Who's Who* gives no clue to the extent of this power in America. Finally, we are well aware of the fact that certain persons are included in *Who's Who* more because of their prestige or prominence than because of any real achievement in a functional sense.

On the other hand, whatever its inadequacies, *Who's Who* is a universally recognized index of an American elite and as such, contains accurate information about a class of persons which the social scientist would be unable to secure on his own; people in this category, as

[1] Frank D. Ashburn, *Peabody of Groton* (New York: Coward McCann, Inc., 1944), p. 5.
[2] *Who's Who in America* (Chicago: The A. N. Marquis Company, 1940), pp. 1–2.

a rule, do not have either the time or the inclination to supply such data solely for the purposes of sociological analysis. Finally, and of utmost importance, *Who's Who* is a useful elite index because it is felt that one must be able to make comparisons between social structure if one is to go beyond mere anecdotal description to generalization from a systematic analysis of empirical evidence; this index may be used to compare various types of communities as well as the same community at two different periods.

One of the important differences between *Who's Who* and the *Social Register*, and very indicative of the difference between an upper class and an elite, is the way in which new members are added from time to time. On the one hand, new families are added to the *Social Register* as a result of their making a formal application to the Social Register Association in New York. In other words, a family having personal and more or less intimate social relations (in business, church, school, club, or neighborhood activities) with the various members of certain families who are members of the upper class and listed in the *Social Register* reaches a point where inclusion within the Register seems expedient; someone listed in the *Social Register*, presumably a friend of the "new" family, obtains an application blank which in turn is filled out by the new family (usually by the wife) and returned to the Social Register Association in New York along with several endorsements by present upper class members as to the social acceptability of the new family; after payment of a nominal fee, the next issue of the *Social Register*, including all pertinent information on the new family, will arrive the following November. The new family might be listed in the Philadelphia *Social Register*, for example, somewhat as follows:[1]

Van Glick, Mr. & Mrs. J. Furness III (Mary D. Bradford)   R,RC,ME,Y'15
    Miss Mary Bradford — at Vassar
Juniors Mr. John F. IV — at Yale   Phone 123
    Miss Sarah — at Foxcroft   "Boxwood"
    Mr. Bradford — at St. Paul's   Bryn Mawr, Pa.

[1] Insight into the structure and values of the upper class in America may be obtained by a perusal of the family listings in any contemporary volume of the *Social Register*. The ideal typical Mr. Van Glick, for example, belongs to three clubs in Philadelphia, the *Rittenhouse* and *Racquet* clubs in the city, and the *Merion Cricket* club along the Main Line; he is a graduate of Yale University in the class of 1915; he is educating his children at very acceptable educational institutions, and lives in a very fashionable neighborhood along the Main Line. The familistic values of this upper class are indicated by the frequent retention of family given names (J. Furness, Mary Bradford, or Bradford, the son) and the use of "III" and "IV" as symbols of family continuity. The maiden name of the wife is always given and serves a useful genealogical function. The patriarchal nature of this family is shown by the fact that the college attended, if any, by the wife is never listed. In other words, family, club membership, education, and neighborhood all perform the status-ascribing function within this upper class.
[2] *Who's Who in America*, p. 2.

In contrast to the *Social Register*, persons are listed in *Who's Who*, not on the basis of personal friendships or recommendations by present members, but rather on the objective basis of personal achievement or prominence; one does not apply for membership in this index nor is there even a nominal charge for being included; "not a single sketch in this book has been paid for — and none can be paid for."[2]

The Upper Class and the Elite in Metropolitan America. The history of Western civilization has been, in many ways, the story of the rise and fall of great metropolitan centers; Athens and Rome in the ancient world, Constantinople in the age of transition, Paris, along with Naples, Venice, and Milan in the Renaissance, London in the eighteenth and nineteenth centuries, and finally New York in the twentieth, each in its day, marked the center of pomp and power in the Western world over a span of twenty-five centuries. And in each city, at the zenith of its power, an aristocracy of wealth or an upper class has emerged; thus the last years of the Republic in Rome where the Senate was an aristocracy of wealth, and the "Gilded Age" in America when the Senate was known as the "Millionaires' Club" may be similar sociological periods.

In the same vein, American history is partly reflected in the rise of different cities to position of affluence and power. Salem and Newport rose to prominence along with the merchant shipper of the eighteenth century. Atlanta, Charleston, Richmond, New Orleans, and Mobile were centers of affluence in the days when the planter aristocracy sent their leading men to the United States Senate which they tended to dominate until just before the Civil War. Within the last few decades, Los Angeles and Detroit manifest a modern opulence as they supply the demands of a mass culture for movement and entertainment. Not the least indication of the trend of our times is the growth of the national capital as a result of the shift in power from Wall Street to the government bureaucracy.

In any complex civilization, social power tends to gravitate towards the large metropolitan areas and especially is this the case in modern bureaucratic society. Ultimately, the pattern of stratification in any social structure is reflected in the distribution of social power as between various functional and social class levels; thus, in terms of social power in America, any significant study of social stratification must inevitably be done in the large metropolis. An attempt has been made in the first part of this paper to show that, if there is an upper class in America, the *Social Register* is a useful index of its membership in twelve large cities. How is this upper class related to the contemporary elites in these cities?

The twelve metropolitan areas in the United States which had *Social Registers* in 1940 are shown in Table 2. In Table 2, column 1 shows the number of conjugal family units listed in the *Social Register* in each city, and column 2 shows the proportion of these listed in *Who's Who* in each city who are also listed in the *Social Register*.

The concentration of power and talent in these cities is indicated by the fact that, while they make up only approximately 20% of the total population of the United States, 40% of all those listed in *Who's Who* in the country reside in these twelve metropolitan areas. Furthermore, it is certainly plausible to assume that the elite members in these cities have a more pervasive influence on the American social structure as a whole than the 60% who are listed in *Who's Who* from the rest of the country.

In 1940, there were approximately 38,000 conjugal family units listed in the *Social Register* (Table 2); in that year, the estimated number of families in the country as a whole was 34,948,666.[1] Thus about one tenth of one per cent of the families in the country were members of this upper class which, in turn, contributed no less

see Table 1). Presumably, the age and size of a social structure together with the rate of social change are important variables in determining the nature of the class system. For example, Chicago, a young and rapidly changing middle western metropolis, has twice as many individuals listed in *Who's Who*, and less than half as many families listed in the *Social Register*, as Philadelphia, an old and conservative eastern seaboard city. The upper class in Chicago, in turn, has less influence on the elite than the upper class in Philadelphia (Table 2 — Chicago 11% and Philadelphia 29% of the elite are also in the upper class).

Although a more detailed analysis of the relationship between the elite and the upper class in Philadelphia will be treated in a forthcoming monograph, it is of interest here to observe that, of the Philadelphians listed in

TABLE 2. *The Number of Conjugal Family Units Listed in the Social Registers of Twelve Large Metropolitan Areas in America, and the Proportion of Those Listed in* Who's Who *in These Cities Who Are Also Listed in the* Social Register

Metropolitan Areas	CONJUGAL FAMILIES IN THE SOCIAL REGISTER IN 1940	INDIVIDUALS LISTED IN WHO'S WHO AND ARE			
		In the Social Register		Not in the Social Register	
	No.	No.	%	No.	%
New York	13,200	1,040	20	4,085	80
Philadelphia	5,150*	226	29	544	71
Boston	3,675	240	28	608	72
Washington, D.C.	3,530	715	30	1,670	70
Chicago	2,130	151	11	1,194	89
Baltimore	1,935	87	26	243	74
St. Louis	1,925	77	24	239	76
San Francisco	1,775	87	23	297	77
Pittsburgh	1,635	76	22	277	78
Cincinnati	1,305†	61	29	151	71
Dayton		11	17	51	83
Buffalo	1,125	43	37	72	63
Cleveland	1,065	65	20	260	80
All cities	38,450	2,879	23	9,651	77

* Upper class families in Wilmington, Delaware, including forty-five Du Pont conjugal family units, are listed in the Philadelphia *Social Register.*
† One volume of the *Social Register* includes families from both Cincinnati and Dayton.

than nine per cent of all those listed in *Who's Who* in that year (31,752 individuals listed in *Who's Who*, 2,879 of whom were also listed in the *Social Register*). More important, of the 12,530 residents of these twelve metropolitan areas who were listed in *Who's Who*, 2,879 or 23% were also listed in the *Social Register* (Table 2).

Of the eighteen metropolitan areas in the United States which had populations of over half a million in 1940, the twelve listed in Table 2 are the oldest social structures (they were the twelve largest in the country as of the 1900 Census). Detroit and Los Angeles, on the other hand, have grown to their present size largely in the twentieth century. The automobile and motion picture elites being relatively "new," there is apparently no coherent upper class in these cities (Henry Ford II and his family are listed in the New York *Social Register* —

Who's Who in 1940, the members of some occupational categories were more likely to be listed in the *Social Register* than those in other categories. One of the functions of upper class solidarity is the retention, within a primary group of families, of the final-decision-making positions within the social structure. As of the first half of the twentieth century in America, the final-decisions affecting the goals of the social structure have been made primarily by members of the financial and business community. Thus the contemporary upper class in Philadelphia is a business and financial aristocracy. In Table 3, the bankers, lawyers, engineers, and businessmen — the business elite — are more likely to be drawn from the upper class than those persons in other occupational categories. While Table 3 shows that 75 per cent

[1] *Statistical Abstract of the United States* (Washington: U. S. Government Printing Office, 1947), p. 47.

of the members of the banking elite in Philadelphia are upper class members, the presidents, and over 80 per cent of the directors, of the six largest banking establishments in the city are upper class members. Moreover, of the 532 directorships in industrial and financial institutions reported by *all* the Philadelphians listed in *Who's Who*, no less than 60 per cent are reported by individuals also listed in the *Social Register*. Finally, while 51 per cent of the lawyers listed in Table 3 are upper class members, over 80 per cent of the partners of the six leading law firms in the city are upper class members.

While the final-decision-making positions within the functional class hierarchy may be passed on from generation to generation, this is not the case, to the same extent, where technical or intellectual skill is a primary requirement for elite status. A Ford II, for example, may

a long tradition of good physicians and architects among its membership. Among other things, this may be due to the fact that inherited wealth is undoubtedly helpful in meeting the costs of education, and, in addition, the paying clients in these professions have traditionally been upper class members. Finally, it is characteristic of changing social structures that *new* or potentially powerful elites are under-represented in any contemporary upper class. The opinion and political (public officials) elites, *new* and as yet subservient to the money power, do not draw many members from the upper class in Philadelphia. On the other hand, it is interesting to observe that, as these words are being written, Philadelphians, led by Joseph Sill Clark, Jr. and Richardson Dilworth, have elected their first Democratic mayor in the twentieth century. As both these men are upper class

TABLE 3. *Philadelphians in* Who's Who *in 1940 — Occupation as Related to Social Class*

| | SOCIAL CLASS | | | | | | |
| | Social Register | | Non Social Register | | Who's Who total | | Per cent of each occupation in Social Register |
Occupation	No.	%	No.	%	No.	%	
Bankers	24	11	8	1	32	4	75
Lawyers	20	9	19	4	39	5	51
Engineers	10	4	12	2	22	3	45
Businessmen	53	24	72	13	125	16	42
Architects	10	4	14	3	24	3	42
Physicians	16	7	27	5	43	6	37
Museum officials	5	2	9	2	14	2	35
Authors	14	6	30	6	44	6	32
Graphic artists	8	4	31	6	39	5	21
Public officials	7	3	26	5	33	4	21
Educators	31	14	147	27	178	23	16
Opinion*	7	3	46	8	53	7	13
Musical artists	2	1	14	3	16	2	12
Church officials	8	4	72	13	80	10	10
Retired capitalists	3		0		3		
Philanthropists	1		2		3		
Social workers	2	4	2	2	4	4	39
Librarians	0		5		5		
Others	5		8		13		
Total	226	100	544	100	770	100	29

* Public relations, advertising, radio, editors.

inherit a functional class position where an Einstein II may not. Thus two large occupational categories within the elite in Philadelphia, the educators and the church officials, draw relatively few members from the upper class. On the other hand, the upper class in the city has

[1] It was in the 1880's that New York Society with a capital S was dominated by Mrs. Astor and guided by Ward McAlister. The latter coined the term, "Four Hundred" in this period and finally gave his official list to the New York *Times* "on the occasion of Mrs. Astor's great ball, February 1, 1892," Dixon Wecter, *op. cit.*, p. 216.

[2] These clubs are the means of upper class exclusiveness at these universities. At Harvard, *Porcellian* and *A.D.*, the most exclusive, are followed by *Fly*, *Spee*, *Delphic*, and *Owl*. The narrow top drawer at Yale includes *Fence*, *Delta Kappa Epsilon*, *Zeta Psi*, and *St. Anthony*, while at Princeton, the more socially circumspect clubs on Prospect Street include *Ivy*, *Cap and Gown*, and *Colonial*. It is of passing interest to observe that Harvard's newest final club, the *Delphic*, was founded by J. P. Morgan in 1889.

Philadelphians, this may well be a clue to the changing power structure in America.

In metropolitan America in the last two decades of the nineteenth century, local aristocracies of birth and breeding (old money) merged with that new and more conspicuously colorful world known as "Society."[1] As millionaires multiplied and had to be accepted, as one lost track of "who" people were and had to recognize "what" they were worth, the *Social Register* became an index of a new upper class in metropolitan America. In an age which marked the centralization of economic power under the control of finance capitalism, the gentlemen bankers and lawyers on Wall Street, Walnut Street, State Street, and La Salle Street sent their sons to Groton, St. Paul's, or St. Mark's and afterwards to Harvard, Yale, or Princeton where they joined exclusive clubs such as *Porcellian*, *Fence*, or *Ivy*.[2] These young men from many cities, educated together, got to know one another's sisters at debutante parties and fashionable weddings in Old Westbury, Tuxedo, or Far Hills, on the Main Line or in Chestnut Hill, in Dedham, Milton, or Brookline, and in Lake Forest. After marriage, almost invariably within this select circle, they lived in these same suburbs and commuted to the city where they lunched with their peers and their fathers at the *Union, Philadelphia, Somerset,* or *Chicago* clubs. Several generations repeat the cycle, and a centralized business nobility thus becomes a reality in America.

First published in New York in 1888, the current *Social Register* lists families of high social prestige in New York, Chicago, Boston, Philadelphia, Baltimore, San Francisco, St. Louis, Buffalo, Pittsburgh, Cleveland, Cincinnati-Dayton, and Washington, D. C. In 1940, approximately one-fourth of the residents of these twelve metropolitan areas who were listed in *Who's Who* in that year were also listed in the *Social Register*. In 1940, the upper class in Philadelphia was a business and especially a financial aristocracy. While 29 per cent of the Philadelphians listed in *Who's Who* were also listed in the *Social Register*, the upper class contributed more than its share of leaders within the business community.

The Middle Classes in Middle-Sized Cities
C. Wright Mills

THE PROBLEMS which the middle classes pose for the social scientist are typically metropolitan in character and nation-wide in scope. White-collar workers in particular, are thought of in connection with big cities, and most recent discussions of the middle classes as a whole focus either upon the nation or upon the metropolis. The sociology and politics of these strata in middle-sized[1] cities may nevertheless be worthy of study.

Such cities are convenient units for empirical analyses; they offer a point of contrast for information and theory dealing with nations or with big cities, and despite the fact that many large problems may be more sharply posed in national and metropolitan areas, some of the issues of politics and social structure take on fresh meaning and reality when translated into the concrete terms of smaller and more readily understood units.

If one keeps in mind the "place" of the middle-sized city in the nation and in relation to various city-size groups, it is a convenient point of anchorage for more extensive analysis of stratification, politics, and ideology. The position of the U. S. middle classes cannot be fully determined without attention to those living among the 15 million people who in 1940 resided in the 320 middle-sized cities.

A city's population may be stratified *a*) objectively in terms of such bases as property or occupation or the amount of income received from either or both sources. Information about these bases may be confined to the present, or may include *b*) the extractions, inter-marriages, and job histories of members of given strata. Such "depth stratification" adds a time dimension to the contemporary objective bases of stratification. Subjectively, strata may be constructed according to who does the rating: *c*) each individual may be asked to assign himself a position, *d*) the interviewer may "intuitively" rate each individual, or *e*) each individual may be asked to stratify the population and then to give his image of the people on each level.[2]

Properly designed studies in stratification will use both objective and subjective criteria: indeed, one of the key problems of stratification theory is to account for such discrepancies as may thus appear.

[1] Middle-sized cities include those between 25,000 and 100,000 population. Middle classes include the smaller business and the white-collar people. The small business stratum includes retail, service, wholesale, and industrial proprietors employing less than 100 workers. (In the present data from Central City, the small business men employ far fewer, on the average 2 to 4). The white-collar strata include families in the salaried professions and minor managerial positions, clerks and stenographers and bookkeepers, salesmen in and out of stores, and foremen in industry.

Materials used in this paper were gathered, in connection with studies having quite other purposes, for the Office of Reports, Smaller War Plants Corporation (6 cities extensively covered), and the Bureau of Applied Social Research, Columbia University (one city intensively covered). This is publication number A-70 of the latter institution. My colleague, Miss Helen Schneider, has been most helpful in her criticism of this manuscript.

[2] In the present paper, we are not concerned with the intuitive ratings of interviewers, and space will not permit us to utilize fully the quantitative data available.

Reprinted from *The American Sociological Review*, Vol. 11 (December, 1946), pp. 520–529, by permission of the publisher.
(Copyright, 1946, by The American Sociological Society.)

The general problem of stratification and political mentality has to do with the extent to which the members of an objectively defined strata are homogeneous in their political alertness, outlook and allegiances, and with the degree to which their political mentalities and actions are in line with the interests demanded by the juxtaposition of their objective position and their accepted values.

Irrational discrepancies between the objectively defined bases of a stratum, the subjectively held policies of its members and their commonly accepted values do not necessarily point to problems of method. They may indicate the "false consciousness" of the stratum we are examining.[1] Lack of structural unity and of political direction are symptoms of the many problems covered by this term that have as yet only been touched by modern empirical research.

Political mentalities may or may not be closely in line with objectively defined strata, but a lack of correspondence is a problem to be explained — in terms of the homogeneity of the situation of the stratum, the social relations between its members, the reach and content of the mass media and of the informal networks of communication that lie along each stratum, etc.

In examining the stratification and politics of the white collar and small business strata in middle-sized cities, we are concerned with whether or not each of them is a homogeneous stratum, with the degree and the content of political consciousness that they display, and with whether they reveal any independence of policy, or are politically dependent upon the initiative and ideologies of other strata.

The objective stratification of the U. S. middle-sized city has fallen into a rather standardized pattern. It will naturally vary from one city to another in accordance with the degree and type of industrialization and the extent to which one or two very large firms dominate the city's labor market. But the over-all pattern is now fairly set:

When the occupations of a cross section of married men in Central City[2] are coded in 24 groups and ranked according to average family income, five strata are crystallized out: between each of them there is a "natural" break in average income whereas the average income of the occupations making up each income stratum are relatively homogeneous. These strata, with their average weekly income (August 1945), are as follows:

1)	Big Business and Executives	$137.00
2)	Small Business and Free Professionals	102.00
3)	Higher White-collar[3]	83.00
4)	Lower White-collar[4]	72.00
5)	Wage Workers[5]	59.00

These strata fall objectively into the "old" (*1* and *2*) and the "new" middle classes (*3* and *4*). Both these classes, however, are definitely split by income, and this split, as we shall see, is also true of other variables.

There is one point on which both objective and subjective methods of strata construction give similar results: Of all the strata in the middle-sized city, the small businessmen and the white-collar workers occupy the most ambiguous and least clearly defined social position: *a)* The images which observers on their objective levels of the city ascribe to these occupational groups seem to vary the most widely and to be the least precise; *b)* Correspondingly, in terms of a great many attributes and opinions, the white-collar people and, to a lesser degree, the smaller businessmen are the least homogeneous strata. Both in the subjective images held of various strata and in their objective attributes, the city is polarized; the small businessmen and the white-collar workers make up the vaguer and "somewhere in-between" strata.

I. The small-business stratum

When we ask people in the several objectively defined strata to discuss the position and rank of the small businessman, a fundamental difference occurs between the ranking given him by upper-class and that given him by lower-class observers.[6]

To the lower-class observer, little businessmen are very often the most apparent element among "the higher-ups" and no distinctions are readily made between them and the "business" or "upper class" in general. Upper-class observers, on the other hand, place the little businessmen — especially the retailers — much lower in the scale than they place the larger businessmen — especially the industrialists. Both the size and the type of business influences their judgment.

In fact, two general images are held of small businessmen by upper-class people. They correspond to two elements of the upper class: *a)* The socially new, larger, industrial entrepreneurs rank small business rather low because of the *local* nature of these little businessmen's activities. Such upper-class people gauge prestige to a great extent by the scope of a business and the social and business "connections" with members of nationally

---

[1] "False consciousness," the lack of awareness of and identification with one's objective interests, may be statistically defined as the deviant cases, that is, those which run counter to the main correlations in a table: for example, the rich who vote Socialist, the poor who vote Republican. "Objective interests" refer to those *allegiances and actions* which would have to be followed if the *accepted values* and desires of the people *involved in given strata situations* are to be realized.

[2] A mid-western city of 60,000 population selected as "the most typical" on the basis of 36 statistical indicators gathered on all mid-western cities of 50,000–80,000 population. On the over-all index for all cities of 100, Central City was 99.

[3] Salaried professional and semi-professional, salesmen, government officials, minor managerial employees: income range: $80.00 to $87.00.

[4] Government protection and service, clerks, stenographers and bookkeepers, foremen; income range: $71.00 to $76.00.

[5] Due to wartime "up-grading" there are in this sample very few "manual laborers"; these make about $14.00 less than the skilled and semi-skilled average.

[6] These remarks are based on 45 open-ended interviews in Central City, a baby sample within the parent sample; and some 60 random interviews in 6 other middle-sized cities.

known firms. These criteria are opposite to the status-by-old-family-residence frequently used by the second upper-class element: *b*) The old family rentier ranks the smaller businessmen low because of his feeling about their background and education, "the way he lives." And, as we shall see, the smaller businessmen cannot often qualify with these standards.

Both upper-class elements tend to stress a Jewish element among the smaller business stratum (although there are very few Jewish families among the smaller businessmen in Central City) and both more or less agree with the blend of "ethical" and "economic" sentiment expressed by an old-family banker: "The independent ones are local operators; they do a nice business, but not nationally. Business ethics are higher, more broadminded, more stable among industrialists, as over against retailers. We all know that."

But wage-worker families do not know all that. They ascribe power and prestige to the small businessman without really seeing the position he holds within the upper strata. "Shopkeepers," says a lower-class woman, "they go in the higher brackets. Because they are on the higher level. They don't humble themselves to the poor."

a) The social composition and *b*) the actual power position of the small business stratum help us to understand these ambiguous images.

a) Since they earn about the same average income as the free professionals, the small businessmen are in the Number Two income bracket of the city. But they are not at all similar to the other high income groups in occupational, intermarriage and job histories. In these respects, the free professionals are similar to the big business owners and executives, whereas the smaller businessmen crystallize out as a distinct stratum different from any other in the population.[1]

Almost three-fourths of the small businessmen are derived from the upper half of the occupational-income hierarchy. Yet this relative lack of mobility is not the only, nor necessarily the most relevant point at hand: when we compare small business with other occupations of similar income level, we notice that they contain the greatest proportion of ascending individuals now in the higher income brackets: 18% of those who are urban-derived had wage-worker fathers and 9% had low-income white-collar fathers. Thus 27% come from the lower groups. The free professional and big business-men, on the other hand, do not include any individuals who derive from wage-worker or low-income white-collar.

Slightly more than half of these small businessmen have married girls whose fathers were in the upper half of the income-occupation ranks. About 40% of them married daughters of wage workers; the remaining married into the lower-income white-collar stratum. This 40% cross with wage workers is well over three times greater than for any other of the occupational groups in the higher income brackets.

The job histories of these little businessmen reveal the same basic pattern. Only one out of five of them were in a job as high as small business at the time of their marriage (their average age is now around 48) whereas almost half of them were working for wages at that time. Well over half (57%) did wage work for their first full-time job.

In contrast, all the free professionals were professionals by the time they married, and three-fourths of the salaried professionals — who make on the average $13.00 a month less than the small businessmen — were in their present jobs when married. At the bottom of the society we find the same type of rigidity: 9 out of 10 of all grades of labor were wage workers at their time of marriage.

There is rigidity at the bottom and at the top — except among small businessmen who, relative to comparable income groups, have done a great deal of moving up the line.

Almost twice as high a proportion of the big business and free professional men have graduated from high school as is the case for small businessmen, despite the fact that the small businessmen are slightly younger. Moreover, the wives of small businessmen rank fourth in education, just above laborers' wives, in our five-fold occupation-income strata; over half of their wives never finished high school, as compared with only one-fourth of the wives of men in comparable income groups.

The small businessmen are of the generally upper ranks only in income; in terms of occupational origin, intermarriage, job history, and education, more of them than of any other occupational group of such high income are "lower class." A good proportion of them have rather close biographical connections with the wage worker strata. These findings help us explain the difference between the images held of them by members of the upper and of the lower strata. The upper class judges more on status and "background"; the lower more by income and the appearances to which it readily leads.

b) The ambiguous prestige of small business people has to do with power as well as with "background": the small businessmen, especially in cities dominated by a few large industrial firms, are quite often "fronts" for the larger business powers. They are, civically, out in front busily accomplishing all sorts of minor projects and taking a lot of praise and blame from the rank and file citizenry. Among those in the lower classes who, for one reason or another, are "anti-business," the small business front is often the target of aggression and blame; but for the lower-class individual who is "pro-business" or "neutral," the small businessmen get top esteem because "they are doing a lot for this city."

The prestige often imputed to small business by lower-

[1] The figures on small businessmen which are given below are quite small; in an area sample of 882 homes we caught 37 small businessmen. No per cents from such a small base are given unless they are significant according to critical ratios. Nevertheless, the results should be taken with a grain of salt, and caution exercised in any further use made of them: in reality, we are here dealing with qualitative materials.

class members is based largely on ascribed power, but neither this prestige nor this ascribed power is always claimed, and certainly it is not often cashed in among the upper classes by small businessmen. The upper-class businessman knows the actual power setup; if he and his clique are using small businessmen for some project, he may shower public prestige on them, but he does not "accept" them and he allows them only such "power" as he can retain in his control.

The centers of organizational life for the top are the Chamber of Commerce and the service clubs, and for the bottom, the several trade unions. There are vast differences in their scope, energy and alertness to chances to play the larger civic role. The Chamber of Commerce is more compact and disciplined in its supporting strata and more widely influential in its infiltration and attempted manipulations of other voluntary associations. It is, in many towns, a common denominator of other voluntary organizations. Its hands, either openly *via* "committees," or covertly *via* "contacts," are in all "community" affairs of any political consequence. But the trade unions do not typically reach out beyond themselves, except when their leaders are included in projects sponsored by the Chamber of Commerce.

If both CIO and AFL unions operate in a city, the Chamber of Commerce can very often play them off against one another; usually the old AFL men are quite flattered by being included in Chamber of Commerce committees which thus build them up before the citizenry as representing "labor" in this town. The younger CIO men are confronted with the choice of following this older route of compromised inclusion or of playing the lone wolf, in which case they rest their civil chances entirely upon their strictly union success.

The organization of the Small Business Front is quite often in the hands of the Chamber of Commerce; and many of the hidden wires behind the scene are manipulated by the local bank setup, which is usually able to keep The Front in line whenever this is considered necessary by large industrial firms. The political and economic composition of a well-run Chamber of Commerce enables the organization to borrow the prestige and power of the top strata; its committee includes the "leaders" of practically every voluntary association, including labor unions; within its organizations and through its contacts, it is able virtually to monopolize the organizing and publicity talent of the city. It can thus identify its program with the unifying myth of "the community interest."

This well-known constellation of power underpins the ambiguity of prestige enjoyed by small businessmen, and provides the content of their ideology and political efforts.

The ideology of small businessmen rests upon their identification with business as such. They are well organized, but "their" organizations are pretty well under the thumb of larger businesses and the banks. The

[1] See, e.g., *Hearings*, Senate Small Business Committee, S. Res. 298 (76th Congress), Part 6.

power of big business is exercised by means of threats "to leave town," by simply refraining from participation in various organizations, by control of credit sources, and by the setting up and using of small businessmen as fronts. The small businessmen, nevertheless, cling to the identity: "business is business." They do not typically see, nor try to act upon, such differences as may exist between the interests of big and little business. The benefits derived from "good relations" with the higher-ups of the local business world, and the prestige striving, oriented towards the big men, tend to strengthen this identification, which is organized and promoted by their associations.

One of the best contemporary sources of information on small business ideology is provided by the field hearings of the SWPC.[1] These are "gripe sessions" usually held in local hotels in the presence of a congressman or his delegate. A rough content analysis of these discussions, occurring during the late war, reveals that the bull's-eyes of the small businessman's aggression are labor and government. The attitude toward "labor" magnifies its power: "We know that labor, at the present time, has the upper hand. They tell us what to do." And the resentment is quite personalized: "Think of the tremendous wages being paid to laboring men . . . all out of proportion to what they should be paid . . . a number of them have spoken to me, saying they are ashamed to be taking the wages." And another one says: "I had a young man cash a check at the store on Monday evening for $95.00. . . . Another case . . . made a total of $200.00 for 30 days. . . . We would not class him as half as good as our clerks in our store. . . . Naturally to hire men today to do this common labor we are going to have to compete with (war factories)." "A man has to run short-handed or do the work himself."

Toward government, the attitude is resentment at its regulations and at the same time many pleas for economic aid and political comfort. The only noticeable talk against big business is in such governmental statements, by staff members of Senate committees, as: the definition of a small businessman is one who "hasn't got an office or a representative in Washington." The independent little businessman believes: "We are victims of circumstances. My only hope is in Senator Murray, who, I feel sure, will do all in his power to keep the little businessman who, he knows, has been the foundation of the country [etc.] . . . We all know no business can survive selling . . . at a loss, which is my case today, on the new cost of green coffee."

"Small business . . . what is it?" asks the manager of a small business trade association. "It is American Business . . . it is the reason we have an American Way." Such phrases as "the little businessman who has built up, by sweat, tears and smiles, a business . . ." underline the importance placed by this stratum on its own virtue. The ideology of and for small business thus carries self-idealization to the point of making it the content of nationalism.

The attitude towards "government" is blended with

a self-estimate of virtue: the criterion of man is success on Main Street: "Another thing that I resent very much is the fact that most of these organizations are headed by men who are not able to make a success in private life and have squeezed into WPA [sic] and gotten over us and are telling us what to do, and it is to me very resentful. And all these men here know of people who head these organizations, who were not able to make a living on Main Street before."

This ideology apparently rests to some extent upon a sense of insecurity. For example, in Central City, the wives of low income businessmen worry about "how the postwar situation will affect you and your family" more than any other strata, although they are followed closely by the lower white-collar people. Sixty per cent of the low income business people worry a great deal, as against 45% of those of higher income. The small business families are apparently aware that they make up the margins of free private enterprise. And — in view of their ascent — perhaps they remember that everything that goes up can come down.

It is also of interest to notice that the wives of smaller businessmen are not nearly so sure as one might expect that "any young man with thrift, ability and ambition has the opportunity to rise in the world, own his own home, and earn $5,000 a year." In Central City[1] only 40% of them believe it, as against 68% of the higher income business people. They are still, however, a good deal more optimistic than the low-income white-collar people (26%) who are the most pessimistic stratum in the city. About 37% of the wage workers' wives, regardless of income, are optimistic of the climb.

II. The white-collar strata

The lower classes sometimes use the term, "white-collar," to refer to everybody above themselves. Their attitude varies from the power-class criterion: they are "pencil pushers" who "sit around and don't work and figure out ways of keeping wages cheap," to the social-pragmatic criterion: "The clerks are very essential. They are the ones who keep the ball rolling for the other guy. We would be lost if we didn't have the clerks." This latter attitude may be slightly more frequent among those workers whose children have become clerks.

The upper classes, on the other hand, never acknowledge the white-collar people as of the top and sometimes place them with laborers. An old upper-class man, for instance, says: "Next after retailers, I would put the policemen, firemen, the average factory worker and the white-collar clerks." Interviewer: "You would put the white-collar people in with the workers?" "Well, I think so. I've lived in this town all my life and come to the bank every day but Sunday, and I can't name five clerks downtown I know."

The white-collar people are split down the middle by income, extraction, intermarriage, job history, and education. Of the men in the higher of the two white-collar income classes, 61% are derived from the upper half of the extraction-income hierarchy, as compared with 49% of the lower white-collar men who are from the upper half by extraction.[2]

The *urban* origins of the several occupations of the higher white-collar stratum are homogeneous as regards extraction; but the lower white-collar stratum of urban origin contains occupations of quite different extraction which cancel out into a misleading average: the clerks are closer in origin to the higher white-collar as a whole, about 50% being from the upper half, whereas the foremen are quite like labor,[3] only 25% being from the upper half.

In intermarriage, job mobility and education similar situations exist: members of the higher white-collar bracket are homogeneous in intermarriage: about half of them have married women whose fathers were in the upper half of the hierarchy. The lower white-collar stratum is split: the women whom clerks marry are similar in background to the wives of the upper white-collar. Foremen, on the other hand, show a tendency to marry more along the lines that the labor strata follow; yet they marry small businessmen's daughters in about the same proportion (27%) as clerks, minor managerials and salaried professionals, thus forging another link between small businessmen and the laboring class.

The salesmen and the salaried professionals have not experienced much job mobility: 6 out of 10 of them were in higher white-collar at the time of their marriage. In the lower white-collar, again foremen stand out as exceptions: 67% of them were wage workers at their time of marriage and 75% worked for wages in their first full-time job.

Whereas the formal education of the clerks is similar to that of higher white-collar (only 5 to 11% of high white-collar and clerks never going beyond grade school), 40% of the foremen have never gone beyond grade school; this places them educationally only a little above skilled workers.

The lower white-collar is thus not a homogeneous stratum by extraction, intermarriage or job history: some of the occupations in it are sociologically affiliated with labor and some with the occupations we have ranked by income as higher white-collar.

The white-collar people are, as we have seen, split by income. But the images held of them as a whole seem to be drawn from the occupations belonging to the lower half of the white-collar income level. The upper white-collar people, especially the salesmen, tend to merge with the sponge term, "business," and are thought of as "businessmen" by many members of the

---

[1] We first asked this ascent question in general; then we followed it up with: "Could he do it in (Central City)?" The optimism of all strata dropped greatly when the question was brought closer home to them.

[2] There are 117 families in our higher white-collar group, and 92 in the lower. In the general origin table, farm owners are put with upper half, farm tenants and laborers with the lower half.

[3] The cases of government protection and service were too few to permit a reliable calculation.

upper class. Most upper-class people derive their images of the white-collar people largely from stereotypes of "the clerk."

The ambiguous rank of the small businessman is explained by his social origin and by the "power" which is ascribed to him by the lower but denied to him by the upper. The ambiguous position of the white-collar worker, on the other hand, rests less upon *complications* in, and pressures on his power position than upon his absence of power. They have no leaders active in civic efforts; they are not, as a stratum, represented in the councils; they have no autonomous organizations through which to strive for such political and civic ends as they may envision; they are seldom, if ever, in the publicity spotlight as a group. No articulate leaders in these cities appeal directly and mainly to white-collar people or draw their strength from white-collar support.

The few organizations in which white-collar employees predominate — the Business and Professional Women's Clubs, the Junior Chamber of Commerce, and the YWCA — are so tied in with business groups as such, that they have little or no autonomy. Socially, the lower white-collar is largely on "the Elk level" and the higher white-collar usually is in the No. 2 or 3 social clubs; in both these situations they form part of a "middle-class mingling" pattern. They are "led," if at all, by salesmen and other such "contact people" who are themselves identified with "business."

The organized power of the middle-sized city does not include any autonomous white-collar unit. Which way the unorganized white-collar people will swing politically and which of the two civic fronts they will support seems to depend almost entirely upon the strength and prestige of autonomous labor organizations within the city, a point to which we shall return.

The ideology of the white-collar people rises rather directly out of their occupations and the requirements for them. They are not a well defined group in any other readily apparent sense. This ideology is not overtly political, yet by political default, it is generally "conservative" and by virtue of the aspects of occupation which it stresses, it sets up "social" distinctions between white-collar and labor and makes the most of them.

Those white-collar people in middle-sized cities, for example, who "contact the public" exhibit the psychology of people working a small and personally known market from within small and moderate-sized firms. In this respect, they are the typological opposites of salesgirls in metropolitan department stores who work a

¹ Twelve were small business operators: two thirds are women; about one half of the total have finished high school. The implicit contrast with metropolitan salesgirls is anchored on quotational materials gathered over several years by Mr. James Gale, "Types of Macy Salesgirls," seminar paper, University of Maryland, Graduate School.

² There are of course other reasons, besides status claims and occupational ideologies for the difficulties of unionizing white-collar workers; see C. Wright Mills, "The White Collar Unions: A Statistical Portrait and an Outline of Their Social Psychology" (forthcoming).

mass public of strangers. Fifty-three small merchants and salespeople in Central City¹ almost unanimously knew personally the people they served and were very "happy" about their work. Their attitude towards this work is seldom material. It rests upon a communalization between buyer and seller: 63% spontaneously mentioned enjoyment at contacting their public, which is twice as high as for any other single reason for liking their work.

This general ideology has four discernible contents: *a)* the idea that they are *learning about human nature,* which is mentioned by about one-fourth of them; *b)* the feeling that they *borrow prestige* from their customers; sometimes the prestige source includes the merchandise itself or the store, but its center is normally the customer; *c)* the opposite of prestige borrowing: the feeling of *power in manipulating the customer's appearance and home;* this is more apparent, of course, among cosmetic and clothing sellers; *d)* The idea of *rendering service:* about one-fourth speak explicitly in terms of an ideology of service, which is interwoven in various ways with the other contents.

These key elements in the occupational ideology of salespeople in medium-sized cities, *1)* rest upon the facts of a small and personally known market; *2)* in emphasizing just this contact aspect of their work, the white-collar people seize upon precisely an occupational experience which wage workers do not and cannot have; they make a fetish of "contacts"; and *3)* the ideology, as a whole and in its parts, is either neutral or pro-business in orientation.

Similar ideological analysis of other occupations making up our two white-collar strata reveal similar tendencies. Nothing in the direct occupational experience of the white-collar people in middle-sized cities propels them towards an autonomous organization for political or civic power purposes. The social springs for such movements, should they occur, will be elsewhere.

The direct appeal to higher wages, through collective action, which the trade unions hold out, is in tension with these occupational ideologies.

"I can't understand why they don't organize," says a business agent for an old-line union. "They got a high school education or more. Looks to me like they'd be the ones to organize, not the man in the ditch with fourth grade education. But it seems to work out just the other way. . . . The solution is to come down to earth and realize that the prestige of this would-be manager and assistant manager is camouflage for cheap wages. The glory of the idea of the name takes the place of wages . . . that's all I can figure out."²

Such a contrast between status and class interest, which is rather typically known by alert trade union men, leads us to expect that only if labor gets civic power and prestige will the white-collar people in these cities string along. So long as their occupational ideology and status claims remain as they are, they will not make a "class fight," although they will try to share in the results, if those who make it for them win out.

In the general polarization of the middle-sized city's stratification, the top and the bottom are becoming more rigid: 73% of the upper half of the income-occupation scale is descended from the upper half. There is also a rather distinct polarization in organization life, in ideological loyalty, and in political tendency.

There are no available symbols which are in any way distinctly of the white-collar strata. Contrary to many expectations, these middle groups show no signs of developing a policy of their own. Neither in income nor mentality are they unified. The high white-collar are 40% more Republican than their lower white-collar colleagues.

They do not feel any sharp crisis specific to their stratum. They drift into acceptance of and integration with a business-run society punctuated by "labor troubles." In these cities, it may be pretentious to speak of "political tendencies" among white-collar workers. And such problems as the relations of party, trade union, and class cannot even be posed: The white-collar people are not a homogeneous class; they are not in trade unions; neither major party caters specifically to them, and there is no thought of their forming an independent party.

Insofar as political and civic strength rests upon organized economic power, the white-collar workers can only derive such strength from "business" or from "labor." Within the whole structure of power, they are dependent variables. They have no self-starting motor moving them to form organizations with which to increase their power in the civic constellation. Estimates of their political tendencies in the middle-sized cities, therefore, must rest upon larger predictions of the manner and outcome of the civic struggles of business and labor.

Only when "labor" has rather obviously "won out" in a city, if then, will the lower white-collar people go in for unions. If the leaders of labor are included in compromise committees, stemming from Chamber of Commerce circles, then such white-collar groups as exist will be even more so.

Lenin's remark that the political consciousness of a stratum cannot be aroused within "the sphere of relations between workers and employers" holds doubly true for white-collar employees in these cities. Their occupational ideology is politically passive. They are not engaged in any economic struggle, except in the most scattered and fragmentary way. It is, therefore, not odd that they lack even a rudimentary awareness of their economic and political interests. Insofar as they are at all politically available, they form the rear guard either of "business" or of "labor"; but in either case, they are very much rear guard.

Theories of the rise to power of white-collar people are generally inferred from the facts of their numerical growth and their indispensability in the bureaucratic and distributive operations of mass society. But only if one assumes a pure and automatic democracy of numbers does the mere growth of a stratum mean increased power for it. And only if one assumes a magic leap from occupational function to political power does technical indispensability mean power for a stratum.

When one translates such larger questions into the terms of the middle-sized American city, one sees very clearly that the steps from growth and function to increased political power include, at a minimum, political awareness and political organization. The white-collar workers in these cities do not have either to any appreciable extent.

Local Industrial Structures, Economic Power, and Community Welfare[1]

Irving A. Fowler

An old ideological conflict over who should control economic activity and to what ends reappeared in postwar America. Most conservatives were alarmed by the growth of economic and political power of farmers, organized workers, and centralized federal agencies. Most liberals, on the other hand, were equally alarmed by the persistent presence of vast concentrations of private economic power, despite fifty years of vigorous antitrust agitation. Both political camps were apprehensive over the American economy's stability. The continuous inflationary spiral and its generation of acrimonious strife between labor and management inflamed the ideological clash further.

The deepest root of this ideological conflict rests in the cultural ideology of liberal capitalism, a system of beliefs about what the structure, control, and performance of the economy should be like. Shorn of considerable detail, the ideology prescribes an economic structure composed of many small, locally-centered economic units, controlled primarily by open and freely competitive market forces. The presumed result is a maximum of economic welfare and a social environment responsive to the "needs of the people." The opposite structure, composed of a few large, absentee-centered economic units, administering prices in monopolistic markets, is proscribed, because it is presumed to result in a minimum of welfare and in a social environment exploitative of the people. The ideology also contends, implicitly or explicitly, that social and political pluralism will result, that this pluralism is a valuable corollary of economic competition, and that the competition of men for political power will somehow serve the society in the same way as competition does in the economic sphere. More detailed examinations of the ideology are available in Galbraith (9, pp.

11–34), Moore (16, pp. 417–454), Williams (26, pp. 138–140), and Sutton (24, entire volume).

Ten years ago, Mills and Ulmer published a study of small-business versus big-business cities (15) confirming the ideological "theory". Their study tentatively concluded that big-business tends to depress while small-business tends to raise the level of local "civic" welfare, as measured by the Thorndike G score. Their more detailed findings were that small-business cities had more "balanced" economies with larger proportions of independent entrepreneurs who showed greater concern for local civic affairs.

Publication of this and another study by the Senate Small Business Committee (10) created a furor over the respective contributions of small- versus big-business to societal and to local community well-being. The furor was another indication that the ideological issues were still very much alive in the behavior of many Americans.

Some social scientists are still as much victims of the ideology as other Americans. The ideology's prescriptions are implicit in the work of some community organization people. A few sociology texts still quote the Mills-Ulmer findings uncritically. (3, 5) Some economists continue to exhort public policy-makers to legislate the ideology's prescriptions into law. (11, 17, 21) With so many Americans, lay and scientific, still basing their behavior on the cultural biases of the ideology of liberal capitalism, it is little wonder that empirical analysis of all types of social power have been impeded for so long.

The fact that the current American economy differs widely from that prescribed by the ideological "theory" needs little documentation here. Many studies show conclusively that oligopolistic markets are typical. (2, 9, 23) Big-business managers share much economic control over these markets with leaders of large farm, labor, retail, and governmental organizations. Yet there is no evidence that the ubiquitous private "concentration of economic power" has had adverse effects on the *entire society's* social welfare. (4, 13, 25) A review of evidence on small- versus big-business dominance *in industrial cities* discloses, upon careful examination, highly variable

[1] A major portion of this article was presented at the Eastern Sociological Society meetings in New York City, April 14, 1957. Acknowledgements are gratefully made to Robert Hardt for his critical review of an earlier draft. (Editor's Note: This article logically belongs in the previous section on Patterns of Power. However, since it is an obvious complement to the preceding article by Mills, it has been placed together with it.)

Reprinted from *Social Problems*, Summer 1958, pp. 41–51. This article won the 4th Annual De Roy award of the Society for the Study of Social Problems.

effects. (8) The question of the differential effects of diverse kinds of local industrial structures and local power structures on local well-being remained problematical enough to suggest that continuous study is required.

Purpose of paper

This paper presents the results of a recent empirical test of three hypotheses involving the relationship between the characteristics of local economies, local power structures, and community welfare. (8) The first hypothesis, derived from the ideology's implications and from one of the Mills-Ulmer study conclusions, asserts that:

small-business industrial structures will produce higher levels of welfare than big-business structures, other relevant factors remaining relatively constant.

The second hypothesis, again derived from the ideology and from Mills and Ulmer's interpretation of their other findings, asserts that:

local pluralistic power structures will produce higher levels of welfare than local monolithic power structures.

The third hypothesis asserts that:

the "type of industry" variable has an equal, if not greater, effect on welfare as do other industrial structure variables, other relevant factors remaining constant.

Although Mills and Ulmer were unable to include "type of industry" in their classification of structures, a review of the evidence suggested that such an inclusion would be essential for more adequate classifications of local industrial structures. The factors to be held constant in the tests of the first and third hypotheses were geographical location, similarity of terrain, climate, size, and character of population. No factors were held constant in the test of the second hypothesis.

Method

The hypothetical tests were accomplished through partial[1] replication and extension of the Mills-Ulmer design: the *ex post facto* experiment. Thirty small New York State cities (10,000 to 80,000 in size in 1946) were selected in a fashion following the Mills-Ulmer procedure. Their general economic and demographic structures were analyzed prior to classifying their industrial and power structures for hypothetical tests. Small- versus big-business industrial structures were operationally defined in terms of the following two criteria and data:

a) *the degree of concentration of employment*, based on per cent of total industrial employment employed by large establishments, defined as those with 500 or more wage earners, arbitrarily defined at the 30 city median of 62.2 per cent, 1950; and

b) *the degree of local- versus absentee-ownership*, based on per cent of total industrial employment employed by absentee-owned establishments, arbitrarily dichotomized at the 30 city median of 65.1 per cent, 1950.

Since institutionalized power relations inevitably involve the evaluation of the worth and distribution of goods and services (economic values), the prestige of others (stratification values), and the control of others' behavior in a territorial area (political power values), pluralistic versus monolithic local power structures were operationally defined in terms of the following five criteria and data:

a) *the degree of concentration of employment*, described above;

b) *the degree of industrial unionism*, based on the estimated per cent of all industrial workers organized in all types of legitimate industrial unions, arbitrarily dichotomized at the 30 city median of 80 per cent, 1947–1949;

c) *the degree of presence of the "old" middle class*, based on the per cent of total employed civilian labor force "self-employed," arbitrarily dichotomized at the 30 city median of 10.0 per cent, 1947;

d) *the degree of conformity to the social characteristics (nativity, ethnicity, and religion) of the American society's majority*, based on the estimated per cent of the total population native-born, white, Protestant, arbitrarily dichotomized at the 30 city estimated median, 1940; and

e) *the degree of political conservatism*, based on the per cent of total party enrollment registered in the Republican party, arbitrarily dichotomized at the 30 city median of 59.6 per cent, 1947.

The hypothesis assumes that a "pluralistic" power structure exists when a) there are diverse sources of social power, b) exercised by numerous persons over smaller numbers of others, c) in many separated spheres of social life. Contrariwise, a "monolithic" power structure exists when a small group of persons, deriving power from a few sources, hold power over numerous others in many spheres of their social life.

The light-dispersed versus heavy-concentrated industrial structures were operationally defined in terms of the following two criteria and data:

a) *the degree of concentration of employment*, described above; and

b) *the degree of light- versus heavy-industry*, based on annual average value-added by manufacturing per industrial wage earner, arbitrarily dichotomized at the 30 city median of 52.24 per cent, 1947.

---

[1] Partially replicatory for two reasons: a) limited research resources confined city selection to one state and to smaller size cities; and b) the latter necessitated the creation of a new index of welfare, since the Thorndike G score was available for cities of 25,000 or over only.

Local welfare was also operationally defined and measured in terms of a new composite index called the General Social Welfare (GSW) score, replacing the Thorndike G score used by Mills and Ulmer.[1] The GSW score was derived from a total of 48 individual variables,[2] ranked in terms of whether more or less of the item would be regarded as indicative of "high" welfare and the rank "one" always designated the "highest" value. These 48 rankings were combined into the following eleven major welfare subcomposites:

1) Income
2) Income security
3) Consumer purchasing power
4) Home ownership
5) Housing adequacy
6) Health needs
7) Health facilities
8) Literacy
9) Adequacy of educational provision
10) Political expression
11) Municipal wealth and service

Mean ranks of these subcomposites were re-ranked and then totalled to derive the GSW scores. Lower values of the GSW scores denoted higher welfare levels. Arithmetically, the thirty cities' GSW scores would range from 11 to 330; the actual scores ranged from 89 to 277.

Controlled comparisons of cities were made with relevant variables held constant except the presumed independent variable: the prescribed and proscribed types of industrial structures.

A combination of two methods was used to equate the sample pairs of cities; *frequency distribution control* and *precision control*. The presumed dependent variables, the various levels of local welfare, were then compared to see if they confirmed or denied the predictions of the specific hypotheses.

Results

Table 1 presents seven pairs of cities for evidence to test the first hypothesis. The first five pairs compare well on five control variables (metropolitan status, population size, per cent foreign-born white, per cent non-white, and degree of dependence on manufacturing); the last two pairs compare well on three or four of these control variables. In each case of pairs, the top city is small-business with the least concentration of employment and the least absentee-ownership; the bottom

city is big-business with the greatest concentration of employment and the most absentee-ownership.

The table shows that in only three out of seven pairs of cities are the results consistent with ideological predictions, that is, small-business structures having higher levels of general social welfare than big-business structures. In a series of less rigorous hypotheses tests, the same inconclusive results were found.

Table 2 presents a typology of local power structures based on dichotomized values of five of the listed criteria: degree of concentration of employment, industrial unionism, "old" middle-class, social heterogeneity, and political conservatism. On the assumption that each indexed criterion is of equal weight, there are six possible combinations of highs and lows, ranging from five highs and no lows (the most pluralistic end of the continuum) to five lows and no highs (the monolithic, or least pluralistic end of the continuum).

The findings from Table 2 are sharply opposite to the ideological expectations. Local pluralistic power structures in greatest conformity with the five attributes prescribed by the ideology were negatively associated with high levels of welfare. The monolithic (or least pluralistic) power structures, in which there existed the greatest likelihood of coalesced social, economic, and political elites, and the least likelihood of social challenge to these cities from diverse socio-economic groups with their own socio-economic interests to pursue, were positively associated with higher levels of welfare. Equally interesting is the apparent linearity of the negative association in this sample of thirty cities — the higher the degree of local pluralism (socially, economically, and politically), the lower the local welfare score.

The third hypothesis asserted that the exclusion of the "type of industry" variable or criterion from any classification of industrial structures makes the latter inadequate. To make this test, structures with light-industry and dispersed employment were compared with structures having heavy-industry and concentrated employment. Table 3 presents five pairs of contrasted cities with appropriate data on the control, independent, and dependent variables.

Analysis shows that in five out of five cases one type of structure is consistently and positively associated with higher welfare levels. The hypothesis that "type of industry" has an important determinant effect on welfare can thus be accepted as tenable. In the paired cases studied, a specific general "type of industry" (heavy, producer goods industry, coupled with concentration of employment) had a consistently positive association with higher welfare levels.

The major findings of the study this paper reports were therefore as follows:

a) local "concentrations of economic power" *do not* have invariant "adverse" effects on local welfare levels;
b) the *type of industry* found in a local industrial structure has an important determinant effect on local welfare levels;

---

[1] Thorndike G scores were available for only 17 of the 30 selected cities. Despite dissimilarity in data, time period, and weighting, a rank order correlation of the 17 G scores with their corresponding GSW scores produced a coefficient of .69, significant at the .01 level. This finding supported the assumption that local welfare levels were fairly stable functions of underlying socio-economic structures.

[2] A complete list of these 48 items will be provided upon request.

TABLE I. *Small- Versus Big-Business City Industrial Structures Contrasted in Ownership and Employment, by GSW Scores; 1930–48 (The Top City in Each Pair is Small-Business)*

Paired cities	CONTROL VARIABLES[1]		INDEPENDENT VARIABLES[3]		DEPENDENT VARIABLE
	Popul. 1940	Mfg. ratio[2] 1940	Per cent absentee establ. 1950	Employed by large establ. 1950	GSW scores[4] 1930–48
SB	28,589	48	47.2	14.7	203.5
BB	21,506	46	72.9	65.9	124.5
SB	18,836	47	38.4	41.1	94.5
BB	15,555	54	65.1	62.4	110.5
SB	23,329	71	15.5	0.0	167.5
BB	24,379	68	75.0	65.4	94.5
SB	12,572	74	48.8	21.9	173.5
BB	17,713	71	85.0	87.4	228.0
SB	10,666	78	3.5	0.0	204.0
BB	11,328	58	95.6	95.6	198.7
SB	42,638	62	13.2	47.0	150.5
BB	34,214	68	78.1	81.0	209.0
SB	10,291	42	29.4	0.0	139.5
BB	45,106	48	66.0	79.6	136.5

[1] All cities have independent metropolitan status. Two control variables, per cent foreign born white and non-white, have been excluded for lack of table space.

[2] The higher the ratio, the higher the degree of dependence on manufacturing. This ratio is based on the per cent of employees employed in industry, computed as a per cent of "aggregate employment" in four types of economic activity: industry, retail trade, wholesale trade, and service trade.

[3] The data for these indices were gathered in personal surveys of the selected cities. "Large" establishments were defined as those with 500 or more industrial employees.

[4] The lower the GSW score, the higher the local community welfare.

TABLE 2. *Thirty Local Power Structures, by Degree of Pluralism and by Mean GSW Scores (Each Criterion Dichotomized into High and Low Values and Equally Weighted)*

No. of criteria on which cities are high[1]	EACH TYPE		COMBINE TYPES	
	No. cities	Mean GSW scores[2]	No, cities	Mean GSW scores
Pluralistic pole:				
A. Five highs*	1	237.0	8	212.2[3]
B. Four highs	7	208.7		
C. Three highs	7	158.2	15	164.2
D. Two highs	8	169.4		
E. One high	5	130.6	7	119.5
F. No highs**	2	91.9		
Monolithic pole:				
No. of cities	30		30	

* Low concentration of employment, high industrial unionism, large "old" middle-class, high social heterogeneity of population, and high political liberalism.

** High concentration of employment, low industrial unionism, small "old" middle-class, high social homogeneity of population, and high political conservativism.

[1] The following cities fall into the listed types: A) Hudson; B) Cohoes, Gloversville, Little Falls, Middletown, Oswego, Rome, Troy; C) Amsterdam, Auburn, Geneva, Glens Falls, Johnstown, Massena, Poughkeepsie; D) Beacon, Cortland, Dunkirk, Kingston, Olean, Oneida, Watertown, Waterliet; E) Binghamton, Corning, Elmira, Endicott, Jamestown, and F) Johnson City and Lockport.

[2] The lower the GSW scores, the higher the local community welfare.

[3] The differences between these mean scores are statistically significant. An *H* equal to 12.84 was computed with a probability of .01 being due to chance.

c) in the 30 cities studied, the industrial structures in *least* conformity with the ideological model (those with higher absentee-ownership, higher concentrations of employment, more heavy industry) tended to have slightly higher welfare levels than structures with the opposite characteristics; and

d) in the 30 cities studied, the local power structures in *least* conformity with the ideological model (those with higher concentrations of employment, low degrees of industrial unionism, low proportion of the "old" middle-class, low degrees of political liberalism, and low degree of social heterogeneity) tended to have substantially higher welfare levels than the structures with the opposite characteristics.

Interpretation

The findings were obviously at sharp variance with

demands larger numbers of more highly skilled and higher paid personnel. Being part of large national industrial organizations, with a greater degree of control over particular markets, such local establishments can more readily absorb such higher personnel costs. Second, their local establishment, usually the result of careful site selection and a long-range capital commitment, increases the local assessed valuation of industrial, and, indirectly, personal property, thus making more tax revenue potentially available for public services for longer periods of time.

Third, this relatively long-range commitment to site, this attraction of higher skilled personnel, plus the demand for specific supply relations, stimulates the growth of ancillary industries with similar characteristics. Finally, local consumers, like all consumers, benefit from the big-business establishment's contribution to the firm's and industry's constant increments to tech-

TABLE 3. *Light-Dispersed Employment Versus Heavy-Concentrated City Industrial Structures by GSW Scores: 1930–48 (The Top City is Light-Industry with Dispersed Employment)*

Paired cities	CONTROL[1]		INDEPENDENT		DEPENDENT
	Popul. 1940	Mfg. ratio 1940	An av. value added by mfg. per wage earner: 1946	Per cent empl. by large est. 1950	GSW scores 1930–48[2]
A	10,666	78	$3858	0.0	204.0[3]
B	11,328	58	9512	95.6	198.7
C	23,329	71	4037	0.0	167.5
D	24,379	68	6612	65.4	94.5
E	22,062	55	4944	32.2	223.0
F	21,506	46	7249	65.9	124.5
G	12,572	74	4624	21.9	173.5
H	15,881	66	6009	62.5	145.5
I	28,589	48	3745	14.7	203.5
J	45,106	48	5530	79.6	136.5

[1] See footnotes in Table 1.
[2] The lower the GSW score, the higher the local community welfare.
[3] Applying the *H* test, and *H* = 260.8 results with a *P* less than .001.

the Mills-Ulmer study and ideological implications. The discordance of this study's finding with past evidence, which partially confirmed the ideology, requires a complex interpretation of related levels of socio-economic phenomena. But because the evidence is confined to just one level (local), this paper's interpretation can only suggest connections between the empirical findings and the conditions and processes in the larger economy.

The sample cities with big-business structures tended to have higher welfare levels for four reasons related to the technically advanced nature of modern industry. First, their more advanced technical mode of production

[1] A large number of diverse variables were found associated with city welfare levels, the most important of which were: a) the extent and availability of raw resources, b) costs of assembling materials, and c) costs of marketing finished products.

nically advanced productive methods and products. Thus, these and numerous other factors intimately related to the nature of the industry,[1] whether intensely competitive or monopolistically competitive, have as determinant an effect on community welfare as the nature of industrial organization of either.

All the above local benefits were contingent, however, on the specific industry's stage of development in the locality or region, and on deeper market forces in the entire economy. If the industrial units were newly located or in earlier developmental stages, these welfare benefits would be observable locally for some time, precluding of course, severe deflationary conditions. If, on the other hand, the local units were obsolescent and the entire industry's geographical center was shifting, such benefits could be subject to dramatic reversals. Thus, the expansion of new industries and the contraction of old has entailed highly dynamic geographical shifts of local centers of production. And, while the entire economy may benefit from locational as well as technological competition, these benefits will not and cannot fall evenly on the local populations involved. (14)

With the implication that local economic and political elites were coalesced, why did not the more monolithic local power structures depress local welfare in the manner that Mills and Ulmer described? (15, pp. 22–31) The answer is simply that in both studies the coalesced power of big-business structures was more apparent than real. Mills and Ulmer abstracted from their data only that which permitted the construction of the malevolent picture that adherents of the ideology would be expected to present.

Such a picture could not take into consideration the following types of socio-economic phenomena: a) the immensely complex, historical growth pattern of modern industries and how their periodic "abuse" of economic power has provoked defensive-protective reactions of specific buyers and sellers; and b) how these developing bargaining relations intersected in different structural locations. (9) All of which shows how historically in Western democracies the exercise of coalesced economic and political power and its consequences have been highly limited *to specific issues, groups or organizations, or areas.* Nor does their picture indicate how frequently big-business executives are disinclined to "exploit" local social elements. Angell, for instance, reports that big-business executives were either disinterested in local affairs, or, if involved, had a baneful influence on local affairs, not because of any abuse of power, but because they were inept and unrepresentative leaders. (1, p. 105)

Most evidence presented here would suggest that the actions of local economic and political elites were determined by larger forces over which neither they nor those exposed to their power have much control. Furthermore, little sociological attention is given to the local community dependence on extra-community organization and to the frequent relinquishing of local authority to the broader social structure as Sjoberg points out. (22)

Important factors in the modern situation would thus seem to have made it increasingly difficult to "abuse" economic power in the local community. Among such factors, the following appear to be highly significant: a) the growth pattern of modern industry and defensive-protective adjustments of related economic groups and organizations; b) the growth of public power to protect "public welfare"; c) the growth of personal resistance to unlimited exercise of all types of social power; d) the changing occupational structure, with its "professionalization" of labor (7); and e) the solvent of increasing wealth. In short, the paradoxical finding that *local* monolithic power was not abusive economically can only be explained by the growing restraints upon it coming from the increasingly pluralistic power in the general social structure.

Social problem implications

It appears obvious that these findings provide no calm harbor for those who hope ideological conflict over the respective contributions of small- versus big-business to local welfare will evaporate. So long as the "insecurity of illusion" (9) of the cultural ideology of liberal capitalism persists, tensions between important economic and political actors in the American scene will continue.

The tensions will provide fertile soil for the continuance of still other types of social problems, only a few of which can be mentioned here. There is some evidence, for instance, that irresponsible scape-goating of big-business executives had turned modern management's attentions to the labyrinths of "human relations" to such an extent that it has lost sight of its primary economic role: production. (6, 26) A frequent problem is the mass manipulation of ideological symbols to obscure issues in the political struggle for control of governments (State and Federal) and their power to intervene in private economic affairs in the name of "public welfare." Less frequently cited, but widespread, is the following type of abuse by *inaction of locally centered* private economic and political power holders: powerful local proponents of the ideology blaming extra-local forces or persons for their own inability to act constructively on the local scene, despite the availability of numerous "enabling" resources provided by extra-local organizations in the health, welfare, civil rights problem areas. Both of the latter are so frequently observable that they require no documentation here.

Social scientists have only recently begun to contribute solutions to those problems by systematic conceptual clarification and empirical analysis of significant power problem areas. Galbraith's differentiation between "original" and "countervailing" economic power and their dynamic development (9), Parsons' clarification of economic and political power (18, p. 121), Williams' analysis of the interpenetration of American economic and political institutions (26), Rosenberg's application of Reisman's concept of "veto" groups to the desegregation issue (20, 19), and Sutton's detailed examination of the social functions of the American Business Creed (24) herald a significant "break-through" the cultural biases against investigating power problems. A sociology of knowledge inquiry into the sources, supports, and consequences of these cultural biases would be a worthy additional contribution, and provide, at the same time, a greater historical understanding of past and future power struggles in democratic societies. At any rate, sociologists and economists appear ready to produce something like Lasswell's and Kaplan's treatise on power (12) in the field of the sociology of economic organizations and institutions.

Summary

This paper presented the results of an empirical test of three hypotheses derived from ideology of liberal capitalism and from a previous study of the presumed effects of small- versus big-business on local "welfare."

Small-business cities were found to have no higher levels of welfare than big-business cities; to the contrary, small-business cities tended to have lower levels of welfare. The "type of industry" was found to be an important criterion for more adequate classification of industrial structures. In the cases studied, heavier durable-goods industry and concentrated employment were associated with higher welfare levels. The major conclusion was, therefore, that "concentrations of economic power" *do not have invariably adverse* effects on community welfare.

In a less rigorous test of the local power structure hypothesis, similar results were found. The least pluralistic power structures (concentrated employment, low industrial unionism, small "old" middle-class, low political "liberalism," and low population heterogeneity) were associated with higher welfare levels.

These findings were obviously at sharp variance with the Mills-Ulmer study and with ideological expectations. A complex interpretation of related levels of socioeconomic phenomena, tying the empirical findings of this paper to other observations on conditions and processes in the larger political economy, was required.

In the cases studied, big-business cities had higher welfare for reasons related to its monopolistically competitive and technically advanced nature. They paid higher wages, enhanced local property and tax revenues, stimulated the growth of ancillary industries, and, being forced to bargain with massive retail organizations, contributed indirectly to greater consumer satisfaction. All of these benefits, however, were dependent on whether the general economy was stable or deflationary.

Interpretation of the findings is facilitated, if conceptual distinctions are made between "original" and "countervailing" economic power, between "economic" and "political" power, and between intra-local and extra-local levels of organization. It is furthermore suggested that certain social problems will persist unless these distinctions are broadly disseminated among the people.

American social scientists have only recently broken through these biases. It would not be remiss to say that the American people and their democratic values would benefit immensely, if this "break-through" is consolidated by further intensive study.

REFERENCES

1. Angell, Robert C., "The Moral Integration of American Cities," Supplement to the *American Journal of Sociology*, 57 (July, 1951).

2. Blair, John M., *et al.*, *Economic Concentration and World War II*, Report of the Smaller War Plant Corporation to the Special Committee to Study Problems of American Small Business, U.S. Senate, 79th Cong., 2nd Sess., Doc. No. 206 (Wash: USGOP, 1946).

3. Broom, Leonard, and Philip Selznick, *Sociology* (Evanston, Ill.: Row, Peterson and Co., 1955), pp. 420–424.

4. Clark, Colin, *The Conditions of Economic Progress* (London: Macmillan Co., 1940), pp. 148–149.

5. Cuber, John F., *Sociology: A Synopsis of Principles* (N.Y.: Appleton-Century-Crofts, Inc., 1955 edit.), pp. 413–418.

6. Drucher, Peter F., *The New Society* (New York: Harper and Bros., 1950).

7. Foote, Nelson N., and Paul K. Hatt, "Social Mobility and Economic Advancement," *American Economic Review*, 43 (May, 1953), 364–378.

8. Fowler, Irving A., *Local Industrial Structures, Economic Power, and Community Welfare: Thirty Small New York State Cities 1930–1950* (unpublished Ph.D. dissertation, Cornell University, September, 1954).

9. Galbraith, John K., *American Capitalism: The Concept of Countervailing Power* (New York: Houghton, Mifflin Co., 1952).

10. Goldschmid, Walter R., *Small Business and the Community: A Study in Central Valley of California on Effects of Scale of Farm Operations*, Report of the Special Committee to Study Problems of American Small Business, U.S. Senate, 79th Cong., 2nd Sess., No. 13 (Wash.: USGOP, 1946).

11. Hayek, Frederick A., *The Road to Serfdom* (Chicago: The University of Chicago Press, 1944).

12. Lasswell, Harold D., and A. D. H. Kaplan, *Power and Society: A Framework for Political Inquiry* (New Haven: Yale Univ. Press, 1950).

13. Leven, Maurice, Harold G. Moulton, and Clark Warburton, *America's Capacity to Consume* (Washington: Brookings Institution, 1934).

14. McLaughlin, Glenn E., *Growth of American Manufacturing Areas* (Pittsburgh: Bureau of Business Research, University of Pittsburgh, 1938).

15. Mills, C. Wright, and Melville J. Ulmer, *Small Business and Civic Welfare*, Report of the Special Committee to Study Problems of American Small Business, U.S. Senate, 79th, Cong., 2nd Sess., No. 135 (Wash: USGOP, 1946).

16. Moore, Wilbert E., *Industrial Relations and the Social Order* (New York: Macmillan Co., revised edit., 1951), pp. 417–454.

17. Mund, Vernon A., *Government and Business* (New York: Harper and Bros., 1956).

18. Parsons, Talcott, *The Social System* (Glencoe: The Free Press, 1951).

19. Riesman, David, *The Lonely Crowd* (New Haven: Yale Univ. Press, 1950).

20. Rosenburg, Morris, "Power and Desegregation", *Social Problems*, 3 (April, 1956), 215–223.

21. Simons, Henry, *Economic Policy for A Free Society* (Chicago: University of Chicago Press, 1948).

22. Sjoberg, Gideon, "Urban Community Theory and Research: A Partial Evaluation", *American Journal of Economics and Sociology*, 14 (Jan., 1955), 199–206.

23. Stocking, George W., and Myron W. Watkins, *Monopoly and Free Enterprise* (New York: The Twentieth Century Fund, 1951).

24. Sutton, Francis X., *et al.*, *The American Business Creed* (Cambridge: Harvard University Press, 1956).

25. Woytinsky, *et al.*, *Employment and Wages in the United States* (New York: Twentieth Century Fund, 1953), pp. 49–53.

26. Williams, Robin M., Jr., *American Society: A Sociological Interpretation* (New York: Alfred A. Knopf, Inc. 1951).

The Disreputable Poor

David Matza

SHIFTING TERMS to designate the same entity is a familiar phenomenon in social science. The terms used to refer to backward nations are a notorious example. What used to be called savage societies came to be called primitive, then backward, then preliterate, then nonliterate, then underdeveloped or "so-called under-developed" and now, in an optimistic reversion to evolutionary theory, the emerging and even expectant nations. A similar process of word-substitution has occurred with reference to backward and immobilized enclaves within advanced and mobilized societies. I refer to the portion of society currently termed "hard-to-reach."

Though there is no great harm in such an exercise, the names we apply to things do, after all, matter. To say that a rose by any other name is just as sweet is to reckon without the findings of modern social psychology. Calling a rose an onion would under certain very special conditions provoke tears instead of delight. But this startling reversal does not mean that a rose is an onion; it only means that the perceiver can be deceived. Accordingly, word-substitution is consequential, not because the referents of concepts are thereby transformed, but because it is a deception of self and others.

The intellectual price we pay for this deception is more apparent perhaps than the social harm. When terms referring to essentially the same entity shift rapidly, and with so great a sense of orthodoxy, intellectuals and researchers, and the practitioners who depend on them for ideas, remain largely unaware of the historical continuity of the referent to which these shifty concepts apply. Moreover, word-substitution obscures and ultimately suppresses the underlying theories, especially in value-laden or offensive names.

The historical continuity of disreputable poverty has been obscured by the obsessive shifting of terms. One predictable consequence has been the continual re-discovery of the poor — an example of what Sorokin called the Columbus complex. The poor, it seems, are perennially hidden, and the brave explorers of each decade reiterate their previous invisibility and regularly proclaim the distinctive and special qualities of the "new poor." Dr. John Griscom, commenting on the wretchedness of slum life in the 1840's, said,

"One-half of the world does not know how the other half lives."[1] Griscom's language and viewpoint were echoed almost a half-century later by Jacob Riis, and now, more than another half-century later, Michael Harrington again rediscovers a heretofore invisible class of submerged poor and again stresses the novelty of their predicament.

Disreputable poverty has gone under many names in the past two centuries. The major thrust and purpose of word-substitution has been to reduce and remove the stigma, and perhaps one reason for its obsessiveness is that the effort is fruitless. The stigma inheres mostly in the referent and not the concept. In five years or so, if not already, the term *hard-to-reach* will be considered stigmatizing and relegated to the dead file of offensive labels. The culmination of this process is not hard to predict since it has already occurred in a discipline even more addicted to word-substitution and mystification than ours — the field of education. There is little doubt that we shall eventually refer to the disreputable poor as "exceptional families."

In referring to the disreputable poor, I mean disreputable in the distinguishing rather than the descriptive sense. Though there is considerable variation, at any given time only a portion of those who can reasonably be considered poor are disreputable. In the term *disreputable* I mean to introduce no personal judgment, but to reckon without the judgments made by other members of society, to ignore the stigma that adheres to this special kind of poverty is to miss one of its key aspects.

The disreputable poor are the people who remain unemployed, or casually and irregularly employed, even during periods approaching full employment and prosperity; for that reason, and others, they live in disrepute. They do not include the majority of those who are unemployed or irregularly employed during a period of mass unemployment such as we are currently experiencing in a relatively mild way. To locate the section of the able-bodied poor that remains unemployed or casually employed during periods of full employment is a difficult task, particularly in the American

[1] Robert H. Bremner, *From the Depths*, New York: New York University Press, 1956, pp. 5–6.

This paper was presented at the Conference on Social Structure and Social Mobility in Economic Development, January, 1964. It will appear in Neil J. Smelser and Seymour Martin Lipset, eds., *Social Structure and Social Mobility in Economic Growth* (Chicago: Aldine Press, forthcoming, 1966).

setting where the number unemployed is subject to frequent and relatively drastic fluctuations. The economist Stanley Lebergott finds that, "No decade [in the twentieth century] has passed without severe unemployment (over 7 percent of the labor force) occurring at least once. And none, except for that of the 1930's, has passed without seeing at least one year of what we may call minimal unemployment (3 percent or less)."[1] Consequently, the line between those who are unemployed only during periods of depression or recession and those who are permanently unoccupied is especially difficult to draw in America.

Despite the difficulties in identifying and locating it, however, one may plausibly assert the existence of a small but persistent section of the poor who differ in a variety of ways from those who are deemed deserving. These disreputable poor cannot be easily reformed or rehabilitated through the simple provision of employment, training or guidance. They are resistant and recalcitrant — from the perspective of the welfare establishment, they are "hard-to-reach."

Conceptions of disreputable poverty

Concepts are both instructive and limiting. Each conception of disreputable poverty harbors some measure of wisdom and thus illuminates the referent; each makes us one-eyed and thus obscures it. Thus a sample of conceptions of disreputable poverty may serve to introduce a consideration of its persistent features.

The current conception, "hard-to-reach," considers and defines the disreputable poor from an administrative vantage point. Implicit in the concept is a view of the disreputable poor as human material that can be worked on, helped and hopefully transformed.[2] Reasonably enough, this conception implies that one crucial difficulty is that the material cannot even be got hold of. It is hard-to-reach, at least without great expenditures of time and effort. Only a short step is required to transform the concept from one rooted in administrative perspective to one suggesting an important insight. Surely, they are not hard-to-reach only because the welfare establishment is deficient. Rather, the elusiveness resides at least partially in the stratum itself. The disreputable poor are disaffiliated; they exist in the crevices or at the margins of modern society. Thus, the empirical wisdom inherent in the concept "hard-to-reach," represents a considerable insight. The disreputable poor are probably the only authentic outsiders, for modern democratic industrial life, contrary to romantic opinion, has had a remarkable capacity for integrating increasingly larger proportions of society. For this reason, perhaps, they

have been consistently romanticized, glamorized and misunderstood by intellectuals, especially radicals and bohemians who frequently aspire to be outsiders but never quite make it.

Beyond this, the concept "hard-to-reach" tells us little. We should not be discouraged, however, since one insight per concept is doing well. Many concepts are completely nondescript, being the bland and neutral labels best exemplified in the usage of British and American sociologists when they refer as they do to Class 5 or Class E. There is nothing wrong with this. Indeed, from the viewpoint of science it is meritorious. Strictly speaking, concepts should not contain implicit theories since this permits one to smuggle in hypotheses better left to empirical investigation. But concepts that imply specific theories are a boon, providing the theory is empirically sound rather than romantic foolishness. The theory implicit, for instance, in a concept of the "happy poor" is mostly romantic foolishness.

Almost nondescript, but not quite, is the phrase initiated by Warner and still fashionable among sociologists — the lower-lower class. In repeating the term *lower* and in distinguishing it from the upper-lower class, the concept is suggestive. Since Warner's categories were ostensibly supplied by members of the community, it implies that from *their* perspective, the distinction between two sections of the lower class is meaningful. The difference between lower-lowers and upper-lowers above all pertains to reputation — the one disreputable, the other reputable.

More suggestive is the British term, "problem family." Implicit in this concept are two points. First, to refer to problem families is to observe with typical English understatement that the disreputable poor are a bit of a pain in the neck. They are bothersome, they are disproportionately costly in terms of the amount of care, welfare and policing they elicit. Second, and more important, the term suggests that these families collect problems. They contribute far more than their share to the relief recipients, to crime and delinquency rates, to rates of alcoholism, to the list of unmarried mothers and thus illegitimate children, to divorces, desertions, and to the mentally ill. The idea of plural problems, reinforcing and nurturing each other in the manner of a vicious circle was well stated and developed in the English notion, but the American adaptation, "multiproblem" family, unnecessarily reiterates. Moreover, the American term loses the *double-entendre* implicit in the British formulation.

The remaining concepts, unlike those already discussed, were not attempts to reduce stigma, but, on the contrary, are decidedly offensive terms developed outside the circle of sociologists, social workers and psychiatrists. The first term, *lumpenproletariat*, which despite its wide usage among Marxists was never really clarified or developed systematically, refers to the dirt or scum that inhabits the lower orders, nearby, but not of the working class. The *lumpenproletariat*, according to Bukharin, was one of the "categories of persons outside

[1] Stanley Lebergott, "Economic Crises in the United States," in Special Committee on Unemployment Problems, *Readings in Unemployment* (Washington: U.S. Government Printing Office, 1960), pp. 86–87.

[2] For a brief discussion of the administrative-welfare perspective, see Thomas Gladwin, "The Anthropologist's View of Poverty," in *The Social Welfare Forum* (New York: Columbia University Press, 1961), pp. 73–74.

the outlines of social labor" and barred from being a revolutionary class "chiefly by the circumstance that it performs no productive work."[1] For the Marxist, this stratum was fundamentally reactionary, and in the revolutionary situation, it would either remain apathetic or become mercenaries in the service of the bourgeoisie. Bukharin maintains that in the *lumpenproletariat* we find, "shiftlessness, lack of discipline, hatred of the old, but impotence to construct or organize anything new, an individualistic declassed 'personality,' whose actions are based only on foolish caprices."[2]

Frequently, *lumpenproletariat* was used as a derogatory term in the struggles for power among various revolutionaries. If an opponent could be associated with the *lumpenproletariat*, his stature might be lessened. Despite frequent abuse, the term maintained some distinctive meaning. It continued to refer to the disreputable poor, and implicit in the Marxian conception are a number of suggestive insights regarding their character, background and destiny. The description given by Victor Chernov, a Russian social revolutionary, is typical since it is garbed in highly evaluative language and since he uses the designation to attack an opponent, Lenin.

Besides the proletarian *"demos"* there exists in all capitalist countries a proletarian *"ochlos,"* the enormous mass of *declasses*, chronic paupers, *Lumpenproletariat*, what may be termed the "capitalistically superfluous industrial reserve army." Like the proletariat, it is a product of capitalist civilization, but it reflects the destructive, not the constructive aspects of capitalism. Exploited and down-trodden, it is full of bitterness and despair, but has none of the traditions and none of the potentialities of organization, of a new consciousness, a new law, and a new culture, which distinguish the genuine "hereditary" proletariat. In Russia the growth of capitalism has been strongest in its destructive, predatory aspects, while its constructive achievements have lagged. It was accompanied by a catastrophic growth of the *"ochlos,"* a tremendous mass of uprooted, drifting humanity. Wrongly idealized at times, as in Gorky's early works, this mob supplied the contingents for those sporadic mass outbursts, pogroms, anti-Jewish and others, for which old Russia was famous. During the war, "the personnel of industry had . . . been completely transformed. . . . The ranks of factory workers, severely depleted by indiscriminate mobilizations, were filled with whatever human material came to hand: peasants, small shopkeepers, clerks, janitors, porters, people of indeterminate trade. . . . The genuine proletariat was submerged in a motley crowd of Lumpenproletarians and Lumpenbourgeois."[3]

What may we infer from this description? First, the *lumpenproletariat* differs in economic function from the proletariat. It is not an industrial working class; instead, it consists of a heterogeneous mass of casual and irregular laborers, farmworkers, artisans, tradesmen, service workers and petty thieves. They work in traditional and increasingly obsolete jobs rather than, in the Marxian phrase, in the technologically advanced sectors of the economy. They are not of stable working-class stock, but include declassed persons of every stratum. Because of its background and character, the *lumpenproletariat* is not easily amenable to organization for political and economic protest. It is apathetic. It has been "hard-to-reach" for agitators as well as for social workers, or at least so thought the Marxists. In point of fact, it has frequently been amenable to political organization, but as soon as it was organized it was no longer *lumpenproletariat*, at least not by Marxian standards.

Another concept worth exploring is one suggested by Thorstein Veblen: the notion of a spurious leisure class. It too was never fully developed. Veblen intimated that at the very bottom of the class system, as at the very top, there developed a stratum that lived in leisure and was given to predatory sentiments and behavior.[4] The resemblance between the genuine and spurious leisure class was also noted by George Dowling in 1893. He wrote in *Scribners*, "The opulent who are not rich by the results of their own industry . . . suffer atrophy of virile and moral powers, and like paupers, live on the world's surplus without adding to it or giving any fair equivalent for their maintenance."[5] The spurious leisure class, like Veblen's pecuniary masters of society, lived in industrial society but temperamentally and functionally were not of it. Because they were not dedicated to the spirit of industrial workmanship, they never evinced the matter-of-fact, mechanistic and sober frame of mind so admired by Veblen. Instead, this class, like the genuine leisure class, was parasitic and useless, barbaric and military-minded, and given to wasteful display and frequent excess. The major difference was that its leisure was spurious, bolstered by neither aristocratic right nor financial wherewithal.[6] A spurious leisure class, then, must be peculiarly embittered and resentful. It is dedicated to luxury without the necessary finances, and thus its members are given to pose, pretense and bluster. Veblen's caricature is as harsh as anything he had to say about the pecuniary captains of society. Though there is a ring of truth in Veblen's caricature, there is just as surely distortion.

A final conception pertaining to disreputable poverty was that of pauper. The distinction between paupers and the poor, maintained during the 19th and early 20th

[1] Nikolai Bukharin, *Historical Materialism* (New York: International, 1925), pp. 284 and 290.

[2] *Ibid.*, p. 290.

[3] Victor Chernev, *The Great Russian Revolution* (New Haven: Yale University, 1936), pp. 414-415.

[4] Thorstein Veblen, *The Theory of the Leisure Class* (New York: Huebsch, 1919), Ch. 10.

[5] Bremner, *op. cit.*, p. 22.

[6] In like manner, Boulding has referred to "poor aristocrats" who pass easily into the criminal and purely exploitative subcultures which survive on "transfer of commodities and . . . produce very little." See Kenneth Boulding, "Reflections on Poverty," *The Social Welfare Forum* (New York: Columbia University Press, 1961), p. 52.

centuries, is a useful one, and its demise was one of the major casualties of obsessive word-substitution. Harriet Martineau, commenting on England in the early 19th century, observed that "Except for the distinction between sovereign and subject, there is no social difference . . . so wide as that between independent labor and the pauper."[1] Paupers as distinguished from the poor were often characterized as apathetic regarding their condition. While they were not romantically deemed happy, they were considered less miserable or unhappy than the poor. They had adapted to their poverty, and that was their distinctive feature. Robert Hunter said:

> Paupers are not, as a rule, unhappy. They are not ashamed; they are not keen to become independent; they are not bitter or discontented. They have passed over the line which separates poverty from pauperism . . . This distinction between the poor and paupers may be seen everywhere. They are in all large cities in America and abroad, streets and courts and alleys where a class of people live who have lost all self-respect and ambition, who rarely, if ever, work, who are aimless and drifting, who like drink, who have no thought for their children, and who live more or less contentedly on rubbish and alms. Such districts are . . . in all cities everywhere. The lowest level of humanity is reached in these districts . . . This is pauperism. There is no mental agony here; they do not work sore; there is no dread; they live miserably, but they do not care.[2]

Of all the conceptions reviewed, pauperism comes closest to what I wish to convey in the term, disreputable poverty. Though there are differences,[3] many of the features of disreputable poverty are implicit in the conception of pauperism. The concept of pauperism harbored the ideas of disaffiliation and immobilization which, taken together, indicate the outcasting from modern society suggested by Thomas and Znaniecki. Pauperism, like vice, "declasses a man definitely, puts him outside both the old and new hierarchy. Beggars, tramps, criminals, prostitutes, have no place in the class hierarchy."[4]

Among laymen, the common conception of disreputable poverty has persisted in relatively stable fashion, despite the shifting conceptions held by intellectuals,

social scientists and practitioners. This persistence is implicit in a lay conception of pauperism which throughout has insisted on a distinction, radical or measured, between the deserving and undeserving poor. Ordinary members of society still maintain the views expressed in 1851 by Robert Harley, the founder of the New York Association for Improving the Condition of the Poor. The debased poor, he said, "love to clan together in some out-of-the-way place, are content to live in filth and disorder with a bare subsistence, provided they can drink, and smoke, and gossip, and enjoy their balls, and wakes, and frolics, without molestation."[5] One need not concur with Harley's sentiment, still pervasive today, that the debased poor do not deserve sympathy, to concur with the wisdom in the common understanding of the differences between pauper and independent laborer. A distinction between the two, measured instead of radical, refined rather than obtuse, is a preface to understanding the working classes and especially the unemployed among them.

The situation of disreputable poverty

Disreputable poverty has been conceived in many ways. Each conception is illuminating, but also obscuring, since each stresses certain elements of disreputable poverty at the expense of others. To understand disreputable poverty, and to appreciate its complexity, one must distinguish among the various components that constitute its milieu. Disreputable poverty and the tradition it sustains are a compote, blending together the distinctive contribution of each ingredient.

DREGS

The core of disreputable poverty consists of dregs — persons spawned in poverty and belonging to families who have been left behind by otherwise mobile ethnic populations. In these families there is at least the beginning of some tradition of disreputable poverty.[6] In America, the primary examples include immobile descendants of Italian and Polish immigrants and of the remnants of even earlier arrivals — Germans, Irish, and Yankees — and Negroes who have already become habituated to the regions in which disreputable poverty flourishes. The situation of dregs is well described in a Russell Sage Foundation report on Hell's Kitchen in New York shortly before the First World War.

> The district is like a spider's web. Of those who come to it very few, either by their own efforts or through outside agency, ever leave it. Usually those who come to live here find at first . . . that they cannot get out, and presently that they do not want to . . . It is not [just] that conditions throughout the district are economically extreme, although greater misery and worse poverty cannot be found in other parts of New York. But there is something of the dullness of these West Side streets and the traditional apathy of their tenants that crushes the wish for

[1] Cited in Karl Polanyi, *The Great Transformation* (New York: Rinehart, 1944), p. 100.

[2] Robert Hunter, *Poverty* (New York: Macmillan, 1912), pp. 3–4.

[3] For instance, a pauper strictly speaking depends on public or private charity for sustenance while in my conception the disreputable poor are sometimes recipients of welfare. They also work casually or irregularly, and occasionally engage in petty crime.

[4] William I. Thomas and Florian Znaniecki, *The Polish Peasant in America* (New York: Dover, reissued 1958), p. 136.

[5] Bremner, *op. cit.*, p. 5.

[6] Boulding suggests that there is perhaps some cause for alarm when "the dependent children who have been aided ask for aid for *their* dependent children," i.e., when a sort of tradition is formed. See Boulding, *op. cit.*

anything better and kills the hope of change. It is as though decades of lawlessness and neglect have formed an atmospheric monster, beyond the power and understanding of its creators, overwhelming German and Irish alike.[1]

The above statement refers to the dregs of the mid-19th century Irish and German migrations: to those who did not advance along with their ethnic brethren. Only a small proportion of the Irish and Germans living in New York at the time were trapped in the "spider's web" of Hell's Kitchen. Putting Hell's Kitchen in its proper context, Handlin says:

> From 1870 onward the Irish and Germans were dynamically moving groups . . . [However] Some remained unskilled laborers. They stayed either downtown or in the middle West Side, beyond Eighth Avenue and between 23rd and 59th streets, where the other shanty towns were transformed into Hell's Kitchen, a teeming neighborhood that housed laborers from the docks and from the nearby . . . factories, and also a good portion of the city's vice and crime.[2]

Rural immigrants to urban areas in the United States and other nations usually entered the system at the very bottom, but in the course of a few generations — depending on the availability of new ethnic or regional replacements and numerous other factors — their descendants achieved conventional, reputable positions in society. But some proportion of each cohort, the majority of which advances to the reputable working class or the lower rungs of the middle class, remains behind. Each experience of ethnic mobility leaves a sediment which appears to be trapped in slum life, whether as a result of insistence on maintaining traditional peasant values, family disorganization, relatively lower intelligence, more emotional problems, or just plain misfortune. These are the dregs who settle into the milieu of disreputable poverty and maintain and perpetuate its distinctive style. Neighborhoods in which this style flourishes possess diversified populations which, like the layers of a geological specimen, reflect its dim history. Handlin describes a single tenement in such an area.

> The poor and the unsuccessful [of each ethnic group] were generally lost in the characterless enclaves scattered throughout the city, in part of the West Side, in Greenwich Village, in Brooklyn, and later in Queens where they were surrounded by communities of the foreign-born. The very poorest were left behind, immobilized by their failure, and swamped by successive waves of immigrants. In the notorious "Big Flat" tenement on Mott Street, for instance, lived 478 residents, of whom 368 were Jews and 31 Italians, who were just entering the neighborhood. But there were also 31 Irish, 30 Germans, and 4 natives, a kind of sediment left behind when their groups departed.[3]

Dregs are the key component of the milieu of disreputable poverty, because they link new cohorts entering the lowest level of society and the old cohorts leaving it. In the conflict between new and old ethnic arrivals, the unseemly traditions of disreputable poverty are transmitted. These traditions are manifested in a style of life distinctive to disreputable poverty, and apparently similar in different parts of the world. What are the main features of this style?

Income in this stratum is obviously low, but "more important even than the size of income is its regularity."[4] Unemployment and underemployment are common. When work can be found it is typically unskilled or at best semi-skilled. Job duration is relatively short; hiring is frequently on a day-to-day basis. Child labor lingers on,[5] and in many of these families, the wage earner, if there is one, suffers from frequent ill health resulting in intermittent employment. Savings even over a very short time are virtually unknown and as a result, small quantities of food may be bought many times a day, as the need arises. Also evident is "the pawning of personal possessions, borrowing from local money lenders at usurious rates, and the use of second-hand clothing and furniture."[6] The Brock Committee in England indignantly observed that "an important feature of this group is misspending." "Misspending," the committee asserts, "is the visible expression of thriftlessness and improvidence." The Brock Committee was impressed with the frequency with which "money is squandered on gambling, drinking, cigarettes, and unnecessary household luxuries when bare necessities are lacking."[7] Available resources are frequently mismanaged. "Rent is typically in arrears . . . and similar irresponsibility is shown towards bills and debts."[8]

To British investigators, the most obvious common feature of these families is the disorder of family life.[9] People frequently resort to violence training children and in settling quarrels; wifebeating, early initiation into sex and free unions or consensual marriage are common, and the incidence of abandoned mothers and children is high.[10] "The children play outside until late in the evening . . . and are sent to bed, all ages at the same time, when the parents are tired . . ." In many of these homes there is no clock, and "one may visit at ten in the morning to find the entire household asleep."[11]

[1] *West Side Studies*, Vol. 1 (New York: Russell Sage Foundation, 1914), pp. 8–9; also see Richard O'Connor, *Hell's Kitchen* (Philadelphia Lippincott, 1958), p. 176.
[2] Oscar Handlin, *The Newcomers* (Cambridge: Harvard University Press), 1959, p. 31.
[3] Handlin, *op. cit.*, p. 29.
[4] Tom Stephens (ed.), *Problem Families* (London: Victor Gollancz, 1946), p. 3.
[5] Oscar Lewis, *The Children of Sanchez* (New York: Random House, 1961), p. xxvi.
[6] *Ibid.*
[7] Cited in C. P. Blacker, ed., *Problem Families: Five Inquiries* (London: Eugenics Society, 1952), p. 3.
[8] Stephens, *op. cit.*, p. 3.
[9] *Ibid.*, p. 4.
[10] Lewis, *op. cit.*, p. xxvi.
[11] Stephens, *op. cit.*, p. 4.

Relations between parents are often characterized by constant dissension and an absence of affection and mutual trust.[1] As a result, family dissolution is frequent and there is a distinct pressure towards a mother-centered family — a rather disorganized version of what anthropologists call serial monogamy with a female-based household.[2] Though family solidarity is emphasized, it is an ideal that is rarely even approximated.[3] The disposition to paternal authoritarianism is strong, but since paternal authority is frequently challenged, its implementing frequently requires a show of power or force. The discipline of children has been described "as a mixture of spoiling affection and impatient chastisement or mental and physical cruelty."[4] Moreover, the household is extremely complex. It may contain "in addition to the joint off-spring, . . . children of diverse parentage. There may be children from previous marriages, illegitimate children, and children of near-relatives and friends who have deserted, died, or been imprisoned."[5] Thus, the normal manifestations of sibling rivalry are perhaps heightened.

The disreputable poor are "the least educated group in the population and the least interested in education."[6] Returning to the Brock Committee, we learn that this group suffers from "an intractable ineducability which expresses itself in a refusal, or else an incapacity to make effective use of the technical advice available."[7] To the uncritical and the indignant these families seem content with squalor,[8] a misunderstanding that obviously arises from failure to distinguish between satisfaction and apathy.

The disreputable poor "react to their economic situation and to their degradation in the eyes of respectable people by becoming fatalistic; they feel that they are down and out, and that there is no point in trying to improve . . ."[9] Their life is provincial and locally oriented. "Its members are only partly integrated into national institutions and are a marginal people even when they live in the heart of a great city."[10] Typically, they neither belong to trade unions nor support any political party.[11] They are immobilized in that they do not participate in the two responses to discontent characteristic of Western working classes — collective mobilization culminating in trade unions, ethnic federations or political action, and familial mobilization culminating in individual mobility. Members of this group are attracted episodically to revolutionary incidents[12] or at the individual level to criminal behavior in the form of a quick score or hustle.[13] Both are best viewed as forms of quasi-protest, however, since they contemplate quick and easy remedy without recognizing the onerous necessities of sustained and conscientious effort. Except for episodic manifestations of quasi-protest, the characteristic response of the disreputable poor, especially the dregs, is apathy.

Thus, the style of disreputable poverty apparently transcends national boundaries. Transmission of this style from one cohort to the next is a major contribution of dregs, but it is not the only mark they make on the texture of disreputable poverty. Just as important, perhaps, is the unmistakable tone of embittered resentment emanating from their immobility. Dregs are immobile within a context of considerable mobility in their ethnic reference groups, consequently, they are apt to see the good fortunes of ethnic brethren as desertion and obsequious ambition. Their view of those who have been successfully mobile is likely to be jaundiced and defensive. How else explain their own failure? What the reputable applaud as sobriety and effort must seem to those left behind an implicit, if not explicit, rejection of their way of life, and thus a rejection of themselves as persons.

From their resentful assessment of successful ethnic brethren, and also from the peculiarly seamy view of law enforcement agencies afforded slum denizens, another distinctive element emerges. A cynical sense of superiority appears, based on the partially accurate belief that they are privy to guilty knowledge shared only with influential insiders. In a word, they are "hip," free of the delusions regarding ethics and propriety that guide the "square" citizenry. Thus, for instance, "hip" slum-dwellers in New York knew or claimed to know of the incidents underlying the famous basketball scandals years before the public was shocked by exposés, just as "hip" slum-dwellers in Chicago knew or claimed to know of the incidents underlying the police scandals there a few years ago.

NEWCOMERS

Recent arrival is the second component of disreputable poverty. Not all newcomers gravitate to these regions — mostly those without marketable skills or financial resources. Irish newcomers escaping to America even before the great famine settled in neighborhoods already infamous and in disrepute. Ernst describes one of the most notorious of these neighborhoods in New York.

To live in the lower wards required some money.

[1] *Ibid.*, p. 5.
[2] Some, like Walter Miller, are so taken by the durability of this style that, straight-faced, they hold the adjective "disorganized" to be an unwarranted ethnocentric imputation. See *Delinquent Behavior: Culture and the Individual* (Washington: National Education Association, 1959), pp. 94–97.
[3] Lewis, *op. cit.*, p. xxvi.
[4] Stephens, *op. cit.*, p. 5.
[5] Blacker, *op. cit.*, p. 32, and for a perceptive documentation, Lewis, *op. cit.*, in its entirety.
[6] Joseph A. Kahl, *The American Class Structure*, New York: Rhinehart, 1953, p. 211.
[7] Blacker, *op. cit.*, p. 16.
[8] Hunter, *op. cit.*, pp. 3–4.
[9] Kahl, *op. cit.*, p. 211.
[10] Lewis, *op. cit.*, p. xxvi.
[11] Genevieve Knupfer, "Portrait of the Underdog," *Public Opinion Quarterly*, Spring 1947, pp. 103–114.
[12] E. J. Hobsbawm, *Social Bandits and Primitive Rebels*, New York: Free Press, 1960.
[13] Walter Miller, "Lower Class Culture as a Generating Milieu of Gang Delinquency," *Journal of Social Issues*, 14 (1958), pp. 5–19.

The penniless stranger, wholly without means, could not afford the relative luxury of a boardinghouse. His search for shelter led him to the sparsely populated sections north of the settled part of town. In the twenties and thirties Irish immigrants clustered around the "five points," a depressed and unhealthy area on the site of the filled-in Collect swamp in the old Sixth ward. Here, at little or no cost, the poorest of the Irish occupied dilapidated old dwellings and built flimsy shanties. . . . In the heart of the Five Points was the old brewery, erected in 1792. . . . Transformed into a dwelling in 1837, the Old Brewery came to house several hundred men, women and children, almost equally divided between Irish and Negroes, including an assortment of "thieves, murderers, pickpockets, beggars, harlots, and degenerates of every type" . . . As early as 1830 the Sixth ward, and the Five Points in particular, had become notorious as a center of crime. . . . The criminality of the area was usually overemphasized, but poverty was widespread, and thousands of law-abiding inhabitants led wretched lives in cellars and garrets.[1]

Numerically, newcomers are probably the largest component of the disreputable poor, but it is important to recall that except for a small proportion their collective destiny is eventually to enter reputable society. Thus, the new ethnics do not fully exhibit the features of disreputable poverty described above nor do they manifest the embittered sense of defeat and resignation characteristic of dregs. They are more apt to express a sort of naïve optimism, especially since their new urban standard of life is, if anything, higher than standards previously experienced.

Newcomers contribute an exotic element, whether they are European, Latin American, or indigenously American as in the case of southern Negroes and whites. Typically backward peoples, they season the streets of the metropolis with peasant traditions. It is this element of exotic and strange customs that has excited the imagination of bohemians and other intellectuals and led to the persistent romanticizing of life among the disreputable poor. Unfortunately, however, this exotic quality is double-edged, and one of the edges is considerably sharper than the other. Admiration from intellectuals was of little consequence for newly-arrived ethnics, especially compared with their persistent humiliation and degradation by resident ethnics.

The style of disreputable poverty was transmitted in the context of humiliation and victimization. The newcomers are, in the folklore of slum traditions and, to a considerable degree in reality, untutored in the ways of slum sophistication. "Greenhorns," "banana-boaters," whatever they were called, they learn the style of disreputable poverty primarily through being victims of it. They learn not by doing but, initially, by being had. This traditional pattern is neatly summarized in an older description of the environment of newcomers in American slums, a description refreshingly free of the contrived relativism that currently misleads some anthropologists and sociologists.

The moral surroundings are . . . bad for them. In tenement districts the unsophisticated Italian peasants or the quiet, inoffensive Hebrew is thrown into contact with the degenerate remnants of former immigrant populations, who bring influence to bear to rob, persecute, and corrupt the newcomers.[2]

Transmission of the style of disreputable poverty in the context of humiliation and victimization helped to dampen the optimism with which newcomers frequently arrived, and thus facilitated its adoption by a segment of them. Optimism and other cultural resistances were never completely obliterated, however, and only a small though variable proportion succumbed to the temptations of disreputable poverty. Ethnic groups entering America and other nations have varied considerably in their vulnerability,[3] but in each one at least a few families became dregs.

Why have the newly arrived ethnics been so persistently humiliated and degraded by the old ethnic remnants? At one level, the answer seems simple. Despite all their failings, those who were left behind could lord it over the new arrivals for they at least were Americanized, though not sufficiently Americanized to be confident. Embittered and resentful on the one hand, and anxious and uncertain about their Americanism on the other, the ethnic dregs suffered from the classic conditions under which groups seek out scapegoats.

SKIDDERS

Skidders are a third component in the milieu of disreputable poverty. These are men and women who have fallen from higher social standing. They include alcoholics, addicts, perverts and otherwise disturbed individuals who come, after a long history of skidding, to live in the run-down sections of the metropolis. To a slight extent low-cost public housing has concealed skidders from immediate view, but it still serves only a small proportion of the poor, and at any rate tends to be reserved for the deserving poor. Among the disreputable poor, the visibility of skidders remains high.

Occasionally, with the skidders, one finds some especially hardy bohemians who take their ideology seriously enough to live among their folk. But it is the skidders rather than bohemians who contribute importantly to the culture of disreputable poverty. Even when they live in sections of this sort, bohemians tend to be insulated partially by their clannishness but primarily because they are ungratefully rejected by the authentic outsiders they romanticize.

[1] Robert Ernst, *Immigrant Life in New York City, 1825–1863*, New York: King's Crown Press, 1949, p. 39.

[2] *United States Industrial Commission on Immigration*, Volume XV of the Commission's Report, Washington: Government Printing Office, 1901, p. xlvii.

[3] The reasons for this variability are complicated; some of them will be suggested in the final section on "The Process of Pauperization."

Skidders contribute a tone of neuroticism and flagrant degradation. They are pathetic and dramatic symbols of the ultimate in disreputable poverty. Perhaps more important, they are visible evidence of the flimsy foundations of success and standing in society and as such furnish yet another argument against sustained and conscientious effort. These are the fallen; they have achieved success and found it somehow lacking in worth. Skidders are important not because they are very numerous among the disreputable poor but rather because they dramatically exemplify the worthlessness of effort. While their degradation may sometimes goad others, particularly the new ethnics, to conscientious efforts to escape a similar fate, the old ethnic dregs take the skidder's fall as additional evidence of the meanness of social life, and the whimsy of destiny.

THE INFIRM

The infirm are the final element in the milieu of disreputable poverty. Before age, injury or illness made them infirm, these people belonged to other strata — especially in the reputable sections of the working class. Their downward shift may take the form of physically moving from a reputable to a disreputable neighborhood, but more frequently, perhaps, the infirm stay put and the neighborhood moves out from under them. Frequently, they belong to old ethnic groups, but not to the dregs since they have achieved or maintained reputable status. They slip because of some misfortune, aging being the most common. Their contribution is in part similar to the skidders', but without the blatant elements of neuroticism and degradation. Like the skidders, they testify to the flimsy foundations of respectability, the worthlessness of sustained effort, and the whimsical nature of fate or destiny. Like the skidders — even more so because they have done less to provoke their fate — they symbolize the beat (and not in the sense of beatific) aspects of life among the disreputable poor.

But the infirm have a distinctive contribution of their own to make. In a completely ineffective way, the infirm oppose the tradition of disreputable poverty. Their cantankerous complaints and what is surely perceived as their nosy interference frequently precipitate a flagrant and vengeful show of license and sin; the infirm become a captive and powerless audience before whom the flaunting and mischievous youth who inhabit this world can perform. Intruders in this world because they are of different stock, because they claim reputability, or both, they are simultaneously powerless and rejected. Those who claim reputability in a disreputable milieu inevitably give the appearance of taking on airs, and are thus vulnerable to ridicule and sarcasm — the typical sanctions for that minor vice. Furthermore, their opposition is weakened because before long the law enforcement agencies begin viewing them as pests, for the police cannot, after all, bother with their complaints if they are to attend to the serious violations that abound in these areas. The infirm are

the one indigenous source of opposition but their marginal status makes them powerless to effect change. Thus, their distinctive contribution is to demonstrate the pettiness of character and the incredible impotence of those who oppose disreputable poverty.

In the situation of disreputable poverty, the various elements that coincidentally inhabit its regions conspire to perpetuate immobilization. Thus, part of the explanation for its anachronistic persistence lies in the relations among its components. But at best this is a partial explanation only; at worst it begs the more basic questions. To understand how disreputable poverty is produced and maintained, we must turn to the process of pauperization.

The process of pauperization

Although disreputable poverty has always existed, we do not yet know how the ranks of the disreputable poor are periodically replenished, on something approximating a mass basis, or how fractions of newcomers are selected to join them. These two related questions make up the topic of pauperization. My answers are intended only to illustrate certain facets of the process, not to present a general theory of pauperization.

Pauperization is the process that results in disreputable poverty. That aspect of it by which the population is periodically replenished may be termed *massive generation;* that by which newcomers pass into the ranks of disreputable poverty may be termed *fractional selection.*

MASSIVE GENERATION

Let us begin cautiously by guarding against two antithetical beliefs, both common — one connected with that hardy variety of humanitarian conservatism we now call "liberalism," the other associated with that harsh variety of economic liberalism we now call "conservatism." The first view all but denies the possibility of pauperization, claiming that the very category of disreputable poverty is a prejudice with no substantive foundation and that pauperization is merely an unwarranted imputation. The second view makes rather different assumptions, claiming that pauperization occurs whenever the compulsion to work is relieved. According to this latter view, the poor are readily susceptible to the immobilization and demoralization implicit in disreputable poverty and will succumb whenever they are given the slightest opportunity. My own view is intermediate, pauperization, in the form of massive generation, is always a possibility, and occasionally occurs, but it requires extreme and special conditions. Pauperizing a significant part of a population is possible, but relatively difficult to accomplish. It must be worked at conscientiously even if unwittingly.

The circumstances attending the early phases of industrialization in England offer a classic illustration of massive pauperization. As far as can be told, mass pauperization is not, and never has been, a necessary or even a normal feature or by-product of industrialization or, more specifically, of primitive accumulation. Instead, it was probably an unanticipated consequence of purposive social action regarding the poor during the early phases of English industrialization. Mass pauperization was implicit in the sequence of Poor Laws by which the harsh reform of 1834 was built on the indulgent and slovenly base provided by Speenhamland. Neither the reform of Izy nor Speenhamland alone, I suggest, was sufficient to accomplish a massive generation of disreputable poverty. But together, they achieved a major replenishing.

The principal consequence of Speenhamland was to enlarge the ranks of the potential disreputable poor. This was accomplished through the moral confusion associated with a policy which in essence violated normal expectations regarding the relation between conscientious effort and economic reward.[1] Under Elizabethan law, which prevailed before Speenhamland, "the poor were forced to work at whatever wages they could get and only those who could obtain no work were entitled to relief."[2] In the 1790's, England experienced a series of bad harvests. Combined with a rise in prices connected with the war with France, in the wider context of enclosures, this caused distress and led to a number of disturbances, "an alarming combination in view of the horror with which the revolutionary aims of the French were regarded."[3] The reaction to this potential crisis was Speenhamland. Maurice Bruce describes the conditions attending the adoption of this plan:

Numerous were the remedies proposed, though any increase of wages was keenly deprecated lest it should prove impossible to lower them when prices fell again . . . The influential and operative remedy, the spontaneous reaction to England's first wartime inflation, was the decision of the Berkshire Justices at Speenhamland in 1795 to supplement wages from the (poor) rates on a sliding scale in accordance with the price of bread and the size of families concerned. This historic "Speenhamland system" was given legislative sanction in the following year.[4]

Thus, one major aspect of Speenhamland was a peculiar system of outdoor relief in which "aid-in-wages" was regularly endorsed in such a way as to make indistinguishable independent laborers and paupers. The wages of the former were depressed,[5] while the lot of the latter was obviously improved. "The poor-rate had become public spoil . . . To obtain their share the brutal bullied the administrators, the profligate exhibited their bastards which must be fed, the idle folded their arms and waited till they got it; ignorant boys and girls married upon it; poachers, thieves and prostitutes extorted it by intimidation; country justices lavished it for popularity and Guardians for convenience. This was the way the fund went."[6]

Consequently, Speenhamland enlarged the ranks of potential disreputable poverty by obscuring the time-honored distinction between the independent laborer and the pauper. As Harriet Martineau observed, "Except for the distinction between sovereign and subject there is no social difference in England so wide as that between independent laborer and the pauper; and it is equally ignorant, immoral and impolitic to confound the two."[7] Describing some of the ways in which this confounding occurred, Karl Polanyi has suggested the effect of this confounding on the productivity of the labor force so indiscriminately subsidized:

Under Speenhamland . . . a man was relieved even if he was in employment, as long as his wages amounted to less than the family income granted him by the scale. Hence, no laborer had any material interest in satisfying his employer, his income being the same whatever wages he earned . . . The employer could obtain labor at almost any wages; however little he paid, the subsidy from the rates brought the worker's income up to scale. Within a few years the productivity of labor began to sink to that of pauper labor, thus providing an added reason for employers not to raise wages above the scale. For once the intensity of labor, the care and efficiency with which it was performed, dropped below a definite level, it became indistinguishable from "boondoggling," or the semblance of work maintained for the sake of appearance.[8]

Though boondoggling and other forms of demotivation were implicit in Speenhamland's peculiarly indiscriminate system of outdoor relief, that in itself was probably not sufficient for the massive generation of paupers. Pauperization implies more than demotivation of effort; it also implies a more general demoralization, the emergence of a view in which work is taken as punishment or penalty. These features of pauperization both appeared in substantial, though obviously limited, sections of the amorphous mass in which laborers and paupers were confounded, and both may perhaps be traced to an institution which was already apparent under Speenhamland but came to full fruition in the subsequent policies enacted in the Poor Law reforms of 1834. Pauperization awaited an institution in which persistent poverty was *penalized*, and in which the form taken by penalization was *coerced labor* administered on an *indoor* basis.

Under Speenhamland, the penalizing of poverty in the workhouse was a minor appendage to its major

---

[1] This interpretation is based on, but departs somewhat from that suggested in Polanyi, *op. cit.*

[2] *Ibid.*, p. 79.

[3] Maurice Bruce, *The Coming of the Welfare State*, London: Batsford, 1961, pp. 41–42.

[4] *Ibid.*

[5] Polanyi, *op. cit.*, p. 280.

[6] *Ibid.*, p. 99.

[7] Cited in *ibid.*, p. 100.

[8] *Ibid.*, p. 79; also see Marcus Lee Hansen, *The Atlantic Migration, 1607–1860*, Cambridge: Harvard University, 1940, p. 128.

feature, indiscriminate outdoor relief. Under the reform of 1834 poverty was penalized on an indoor basis as the major governmental policy in regulating the poor. Since this policy of penalization was pursued, first side by side with, and subsequently in the wake of a policy that confounded laborers with paupers, it was well suited to realize the enormous potential for massive pauperization implicit in that confounding. Penalizing poverty through the workhouse reinforced and established, inadvertently but effectively, whatever mere propensities resulted from the indiscriminate use of outdoor relief under Speenhamland. The indolence and boondoggling occasioned by Speenhamland created the propensity for mass pauperization, but to be transformed into true paupers, those exhibiting indolence had to be stigmatized or defamed, work had to be reconstituted as penal sanction, and demoralization centralized under the roof of a facilitating institution. All of this was accomplished by the workhouse system.

Under Speenhamland, a man and his family would be put in the poorhouse if they had been on the rates for an extended period of time.[1] Once there, suggests Polanyi, "the decencies and self-respect of centuries of settled life wore off quickly in the promiscuity of the poorhouse where a man had to be cautious not to be thought better off than his neighbor, lest he be forced to start out on the hunt for work, instead of boon-doggling in the familiar fold."[2] In the poorhouse the ancient culture of paupers could now be disseminated to those who had been thrown together with them, and the potential for massive generation of disreputable poverty could be realized. Moreover, the confusion regarding the moral value of work could be compounded and finally resolved by the unmistakable lesson of the workhouse — work is a penalty, to be avoided and viewed with resentment.[3]

Collecting the indolents in an indoor setting was important for another reason. Persons receiving poor relief during Speenhamland were not yet overwhelmingly concentrated in the urban slums we have come to associate with a tradition of disreputable poverty. Most were still distributed over chiefly agricultural areas.[4] Thus, the concentration that facilitates the formation of a subculture was aided by the poorhouse system. The poorhouses and workhouses served the same function for the disreputable poor that Marx assigned the factories in the development of an industrial proletariat and the same function assigned by criminologists to prisons in disseminating the standards and techniques of criminal-

ity. Each is a center for the collection of traits which can then be conveniently disseminated.

The defamation of character implicit in commitment to a workhouse is clearest after the Poor Law Reform of 1834. This reform was a direct reaction to Speenhamland. It was calculated to avoid the indulgence of indolence apparent in the previous system. The Webbs summarize the reformers' motives:

> The decisive element [in the Poor Law Reform amendments of 1834] was undoubtedly a recognition of the bad behavior induced alike among employers and employed by the various devices for maintaining the able-bodied, wholly or partially, out of the Poor Rate. When, under the allowance system, the farmers and manufacturers became aware that they could reduce wages indefinitely, and the manual workers felt secure of subsistence without the need for exerting themselves to retain any particular employment, the standard of skill and conduct of all concerned rapidly declined. To single out the full-whitted employer and the lazy workman for special grants out of public funds, to the detriment of the keen organizer and the zealous worker, was obviously bad psychology as well as bad economics. When adding to the number of children automatically increased the family income, young persons hastened to get married, as it was, indeed, intended they should do by the Justices of the Peace who adopted the Speenhamland Scale . . . The Elizabethan Poor Law had become, by the beginning of the nineteenth century, a systematic provision, not so much for the unfortunate as for the less competent and the less provident, whom the humanity or carelessness of the Justices and the Overseers had combined specially to endow out of public funds.[5]

The reform of 1834 was an extreme reaction to Speenhamland, but instead of undoing the effects of Speenhamland, it compounded them, for penalizing poverty completed the historic process of pauperization begun by the moral confusion occasioned by Speenhamland. The abolition of Speenhamland was in some respects, as Polanyi suggests, "the true birthday of the modern working-classes" because it forced them to mobilize on their own behalf. But just as surely, the same abolition and the same enactment of the Reform Act was the "true birthday of the modern disreputable poor," for it signalled the last phase of the pauperization process. If "Speenhamland was an automaton for demolishing the standards on which any kind of society could be based," then the reform was an instrument for institutionalizing the standards which replaced those "on which any kind of society could be based."

The reform of 1834 was designed in the hope that the poor would be severely discouraged from going on the rates by the stigma now attached to the workhouse and the conditions characterizing it.

> The new law provided that in the future no outdoor relief should be given . . . Aid-in-wages was . . .

---

[1] Polanyi, *op. cit.*, p. 99.

[2] *Ibid.*

[3] The moral confusion regarding the status of work occasioned by this dual aspect of Speenhamland is discussed by Reinhard Bendix, *Work and Authority in Industry*, New York: Harper Torchbooks, 1963, pp. 40–42.

[4] Neil J. Smelser, *Social Change in the Industrial Revolution*, Chicago: University of Chicago Press, 1959, p. 350.

[5] Sidney and Beatrice Webb, *English Poor Law History*, Vol. 8 of *English Local Government*, London: Longmans, Green, 1929, pp. 14–15.

discontinued . . . It was now left to the applicant to decide whether he was so utterly destitute of all means that he would voluntarily repair to a shelter which was deliberately made a place of horror. The workhouse was invested with a stigma; and staying in it was made a psychological and moral torture . . . The very burial of a pauper was made an act by which his fellow men renounced solidarity with him even in death.[1]

Surely, this was to reinstitute the distinction between independent laborer and pauper, but only after forty years of confounding precisely that issue. Together the two policies comprise the classic way to generate a mass population of paupers.

Doubtless, pauperization is easier to accomplish when the population in question is a subjugated national or ethnic group rather than an indigenous group of subjects or citizens. Subjugated people are regarded as moral inferiors to begin with, capable of a variety of vices which typically include indolence and immorality. Pauperizing an indigenous population is more difficult in the measure that national affinities limit, though without necessarily precluding, the possibilities of imputing subhuman stature. The English case is classic precisely because pauperizing some parts of an indigenous population is difficult, but in that case too, the extent of indigenous pauperization is easily exaggerated, for many who were caught in the curious combination of Speenhamland indulgence and Reform penalization were in fact not English but Irish. Some of the Irish in England were pauperized by the same circumstances that affected indigenous Englishmen, but many more were pauperized by a separate process, one that illustrates the pattern of extreme subjugation by which the poor among captive or conquered peoples are commonly pauperized. This second pattern of massive pauperization is of paramount importance in the United States because it perhaps produced the two major ethnic contributors to the tradition of disreputable poverty — the Irish and the Negro.[2]

The great Irish famine was only the culmination of a long period of subjugated poverty which drove the Irish eastward across the channel to England and westward to America. Both before and during the famine it is very likely that England rather than America received the most profoundly pauperized sections of the Irish poor,[3] if only because migration to nearby England was economically more feasible.[4] Ireland was an impoverished colony, before, during, and after its great famine, and perhaps, as travelers during the period suggested, impoverished to an extent unrivaled in the rest of Europe.[5] Impoverishment, however, is not the same as pauperization. In the Irish experience, extreme economic impoverishment was combined with profound political subjugation. Just as penalization pauperizes an indigenous population, political subjugation of a captive or colonized people may transform the merely poor into paupers through the agency of oppression and degradation. The political subjugation experienced by the Irish was tantamount to the penalization of the entire island.

Beginning in 1695, the Irish were subjected to the infamous Penal Laws which Edmund Burke aptly described as "a machine of wise and elaborate contrivance, and as well fitted for the oppression, impoverishment and degradation of a people and the debasement in them of human nature itself, as ever proceeded from the perverted ingenuity of man." The Penal Laws were long, elaborate and developed over a number of generations.[6] Their character is perhaps conveyed by the fact that on two occasions it is stated that the law "does not suppose any such person to exist as a Roman Catholic."[7] Some provisions were potentially subversive of family life: "If the eldest son of a landholder apostatized and renounced the Catholic religion, he became sole owner of the property and immediately his father was inhibited from placing impediments on it . . . The son could disinherit the father,"[8] and in the process dispossess all of his younger brothers, who were otherwise entitled to an equal share.

The effects of the Penal Laws are suggested by Woodham-Smith. She says:

> The material damage suffered through the Penal Laws was great; ruin was widespread, old families disappeared and old estates were broken up; but the most disastrous effects were moral. The Penal Laws brought lawlessness, dissimilation and revenge in their train, and the Irish character, above all the character of the peasantry did become, in Burke's words degraded and debased. The upper classes were able to leave the country and many middle-class merchants contrived with guile, to survive, but the poor Catholic peasant bore the full hardship. His religion made him an outlaw; in the Irish House of Commons he was described as "the common enemy," and whatever was inflicted on him, he must bear, for

---

[1] Polanyi, *op. cit.*, pp. 101–102.

[2] For a general sense in which Irish and Negroes were at least somewhat different from other immigrant groups in America, see Nathan Glazer and Daniel P. Moynihan, *Beyond the Melting Pot*, Cambridge: The M.I.T. Press and Harvard University Press, 1963.

[3] John A. Jackson, *The Irish in Britain*, London: Routledge and Kegan Paul, 1963, p. 9; also see Cecil Woodham-Smith, *The Great Hunger*, London: Hamish Hamilton, 1962, p. 270.

[4] One cannot help observing that there was a certain poetic justice in this preference for nearby England. The paupers came home to roost, sponging, as it were, on the very regime that had so ingeniously pauperized them. There is no evidence that the Irish paupers were prompted by so frivolous a motive, however; only the gypsies among the disreputable poor are regularly guided by such considerations. For a discussion of the peculiar gypsy version of disreputable povery see my "Gypsies: Deviant Exemplars," in *Deviant Phenomena*, Prentice-Hall, forthcoming.

[5] Woodham-Smith, *op. cit.*, pp. 19–20.

[6] For a brief summary of the Penal Laws, see George Potter, *To the Golden Door*, Boston: Little, Brown 1960, pp. 26–28.

[7] *Ibid.*

[8] *Ibid.*

where could he look for redress? To his landlord? Almost invariably an alien conqueror. To the law? Not when every person connected with the law, from the jailer to the judge, was a Protestant who regarded him as "the common enemy."[1]

The lingering effects of the Penal Laws were instrumental in creating the two traditions for which the Irish later became noted, terrorist rebellion and disreputable poverty.

The pauperization of the Irish peasantry was not simply a consequence of the Penal Laws. It was also facilitated by the Irish system of land tenure headed by absentee landlords and managed largely by local agents. Under the policy of surrender and regrant of land, most Irish farmers had become rent-paying tenants.[2] Moreover, the land system, and especially the institution of "cant," seemed almost calculated to punish conscientious effort and reward slovenliness.

> The most calloused abuse by the landlord of his ownership was the practice of putting up farms for "cant" [or public auction] when leases expired. No matter how faithfully a tenant paid his rent, how dutifully he had observed regulations, or how well he had improved the property by his own labors, he was in constant danger of being outbid for his farm by the "grabber" upon the expiration of the lease . . . Moreover, in the Catholic parts of Ireland . . . the tenant was not entitled to compensation for improvements brought by himself . . . Hard experience had taught the tenant the penalties of improving the property he leased or hired and the self-interest of slovenliness. If he improved the property, his rent was raised! . . . Progress and improvement, instead of being encouraged by the landlord for his own interests, were penalized. This upside-down system withered the character, destroyed the initiative, and squelched the ambition of the Irish tenant.[3]

A key factor in pauperization, as in the English Poor Law policy, was the negative association of work with sanction. In one instance, conscientious effort was punished, whereas in the other it was used as a punishment. Either form of association of work with a negative sanction facilitates pauperization. Mere indolence is converted to an active antagonism to work. By the time the Irish began to emigrate to America, the policy of political subjugation along with the economic impoverishment of the island had had its effect. A substantial proportion of the population had been pauperized though, almost certainly, it was nothing approaching a

majority. So difficult is the process of pauperization that no more than a substantial minority are likely to succumb to it. Counteracting the forces for degradation and demoralization are always the stabilizing and moralizing forces of family, religion, and primary group solidarity; these are weakened but never obliterated. Beaumont, a French observer, put the practical effects of pauperization nicely: "All the faculties of his soul that despotism has touched are blighted; the wounds there are large and deep. All this part of him is vice, whether it be cowardice, indolence, knavery or cruelty; half of the Irishman is a slave."

In the years just before the famine and great emigration, the Irish poor were subjected to the workhouse system, which was instituted in the English parliament as part of the Irish Poor Law act of 1838. Thus, in Ireland, the penalizing of poverty in a workhouse system came in the wake of the political subjugation epitomized by the Penal Laws, whereas in the English case, the penalizing of poverty follows the indulgence of Speenhamland.

By the 1820's the poor rates in England had reached unprecedented heights. Whereas the total rate in 1696 was 400,000 pounds, in 1776 it was about one and a half million, in 1796 it passed two million, in 1802 it had risen to four and a quarter million, by 1818 close to eight million and still in 1832 seven million.[4] This represented only a small part of the national income, "probably no more than two percent," but "it amounted to one-fifth of the national expenditure and to people who had no means of assessing the national income it loomed appallingly large and seemed to threaten the economic foundations of society."[5] The rate seemed especially high since a large number of able-bodied workers were being supported by it. Not surprisingly, many of the English rate-payers "blamed the Irish paupers in England and demanded a Poor Law for Ireland."[6] Irish emigration to England and Scotland was heavy, throughout the 18th and earth 19th centuries, first as seasonal agricultural labor and increasingly as more or less settled industrial workers. "By 1841, shortly before the great famine, fully 419,256 Irish-born persons were living permanently in England and Scotland."[7] Given the English knowledge of the pauperized state of the Irish, it was to be expected that the Irish would be blamed for what were conceived as staggeringly high poor rates. The enactment by the English of an Irish Poor Law in 1838 was prompted by the desire to make Irish property responsible for its own poverty, and thus to slow the emigration of the Irish poor to England. But Irish landlords were simply not up to the task, and the major effect of the Act was to spur "Assisted Emigration" from Ireland, mostly to America via Quebec. Under the Irish Poor Law of 1838 the workhouse became an intermediate step — a halfway house between eviction from the land and emigration to America. The law taxed Irish landlords so highly that they showed "a sudden zeal to promote emigration. The new law integrated emigration with evictions by

---

[1] Woodham-Smith, 27–28.

[2] Ernst, *op. cit.*, p. 5.

[3] Potter, *op. cit.*, p. 44.

[4] These figures are from Bruce, *op. cit.*, pp. 76–77, and Polanyi, *op. cit.*, p. 110.

[5] Bruce, *op. cit.*, pp. 76–77.

[6] Ernst, *op. cit.*, p. 5.

[7] *Ibid.*

setting up workhouses for the dispossessed, and since the same act provided for assisted emigration, the workhouse became the intermediate step between eviction and departure from Ireland."[1] This sequence of eviction, sentence to the poorhouse and assisted emigration achieved special importance with the onset of the Irish famine in 1845.

The penalization of poverty was the last phase in a long history of the English pauperization of the Irish poor. By coincidence, it occurred shortly before the great emigration to America. Thus, a substantial proportion of emigrants to America had experienced *both* the punishing of conscientious effort, as a result of the cant system, and the use of conscientious effort as punishment in the workhouse, along with political subjugation under the English. The disreputable poverty of the Irish immigrant in America is best understood in the context of this dubious legacy, and the subsequent tradition of disreputable poverty in urban America is best understood by stressing that our first massive immigration of the very poor was that of already pauperized Irish fleeing in "assisted" fashion from the great famine.[2]

In America, the Irish were almost immediately considered worthless paupers. This stigma was applied not only to those who were already truly pauperized but also to those who had somehow remained simply poor. Since the worthy poor too were frequently out of work, they were lumped together with their more disreputable brethren. Potter summarizes their predicament:

> The "indolent Irish" had been a characterization fixed on the race by the English in Ireland that America inherited. Superficial observation gave it currency in America for two major reasons. One was the frequent spells of unemployment the Irishman suffered from the nature of his manual work — inclement weather, cyclical depressions, and job competition. On this score the description was unjust because of the elements beyond the individual Irishman's control. The other [reason] was the shiftlessness of a ragtag and bobtail minority, noisy, dissolute, troublesome, gravitating to public relief, which unfairly settled a distorted reputation on the race in the minds of people often initially prejudiced.[3]

Given the disreputability of the Irish, they probably encountered greater discrimination than other minorities in America. "Potential employers disliked and even feared their religion, shuddered at 'Irish impulsiveness' and turbulence, and were disgusted and morally shocked at the Irish propensity for strong drink." In all likelihood, "no other immigrant nationality was proscribed as the Catholic Irish were."[4]

FRACTIONAL SELECTION

Fractional selection is the process whereby some fraction of newcomers pass into the ranks of disreputable poverty. It is the more normal, less dramatic, process of pauperization, depending on existing traditions of disreputable poverty, which are only occasionally replenished on a massive scale by newly generated cohorts. Given the relative absence of massive generation, the process of fractional selection is the major hindrance to the gradual attrition of disreputable poverty. The conversion of newcomers to dregs provides for the partial replacement of the pauperized individuals who somehow transcend their circumstance, and pass into the reputable sections of society. Consequently, the survival of disreputable poverty has partly depended on barring newcomers from the normal routes of social mobility. Thus, the general conditions underlying fractional selection into the ranks of disreputable poverty are for the most part simply the reverse of those favoring social mobility. These general conditions need no special restatement. Instead, I want to stress the temporal context of the circumstances favoring mobility.

Strong family organization, a cultural heritage stressing achievement, an expanding economy, an upgraded labor force, a facilitating demographic context and other conditions generally favoring mobility, have their effect within a temporal context. Once a period, the length of which will be suggested, is over, these general circumstances favoring advancement are hampered by demoralization, first in the form of being severe discouragement or immobilization, and subsequently in the form of relaxed moral standards. Demoralization signals the culmination of the process by which some proportion of newcomers are selected for disreputable poverty.

The period during which newcomers enjoy relatively high morale is the temporal context within which the general factors favoring social mobility flourish. Its length varies, but the limits may be suggested. Demoralization may be avoided until newcomers are reduced to dregs, and the reduction of newcomers to dregs occurs when the steady desertion of mobile ethnic brethren is dramatically climaxed by an ecological invasion of new bands of ethnic or regional newcomers. When newcomers to the milieu of disreputable poverty predominate as neighbors and workmates, the remnants of earlier cohorts resentfully begin to notice what they have finally come to. They must now live and work with "them," and suddenly the previously obscure relation between their lot and that of their more fortunate or successful brethren from the original cohort is clear. They have become dregs, reduced to actually living and working with "niggers," or other newcomers in the milieu of disreputable poverty. Pauperization through fractional selection occurs, then, when newcomers take

---

[1] *Ibid.*
[2] The other important stream feeding this tradition in America, and massively replenishing the population of the disreputable poor, will be discussed in a later publication. It consists, of course, of Negroes, many of whom were pauperized as a result of enslavement and continued political subjugation after formal emancipation.
[3] Potter, *op. cit.*, pp. 84–85.
[4] Ernst, *op. cit.*, pp. 66–67.

over the neighborhood and workplace. This kind of pauperization becomes more pronounced when the newcomers who have overtaken the dregs are themselves replaced by yet another cohort of newcomers. Thus, the milieu of disreputable poverty is temporally stratified; the older the vintage, the more thorough the pauperization.

The spiteful and condescending clucking of the now reputable segments of the original ethnic cohort is the main agency in demoralizing those who still live in a disreputable milieu. The attitudes of the reputable are illustrated by the comments of upper-lower class Irish, reported by Warner and Srole:[1]

> 'Maybe we haven't made a million dollars, but our house is paid for and out of honest wages, too,' said Tim.
> 'Still, Tim, we haven't done so bad. The Flanagans came here when we did and what's happened to them? None of them is any good. Not one of them has moved out of the clam flats.'
> 'You're right, Annie, we are a lot better than some. Old Pat Flanagan, what is he? He is worse than the clam diggers themselves. He has got ten or twelve kids — some of them born in wedlock and with the blessings of the church, but some of them are from those women in the clam flats. He has no shame.'
> 'His children,' said Annie, 'are growing into heathens. Two of them are in the reform school, and that oldest girl of his has had two or three babies without nobody admitting he was the father.'

When they are forced to live and work with newcomers, the remnants need no longer overhear the disparaging comments of the reputable members of their ethnic cohort. They disparage themselves. They know what they have come to, for they share the wider social view that the newcomers are profoundly inferior

and detestable. The irony here is that the demoralization of old ethnics and their subsequent transformation to dregs results from the provincialism that simultaneously maintains ethnic identity long after it has been partially obscured in other parts of society, and manifests itself in pervasive prejudices perhaps unmatched elsewhere.[2] Thus, the measure in which the old cohorts are reduced to dregs depends partly on the extent to which they themselves denigrate newcomers. For now they become in the eyes of significant others, and in that measure to themselves, "just like them."[3]

I have suggested that the general conditions facilitating social mobility, and, thus, the departure of newcomers from the milieu of disreputable poverty, are rendered ineffective by the demoralizing encounter with a new contingent of ethnic or regional poor. Thereafter, though the conditions normally favoring social mobility persist, they are dampened by the pauperization of the remnant ethnic stock.

Conclusion

The disreputable poor are an immobilized segment of society located at a point in the social structure where poverty intersects with illicit pursuits. They are, in the evocative words of Charles Brace, "the dangerous classes" who live in "regions of squalid want and wicked woe."[4] This stratum is replenished only rarely through massive generation, and there is little evidence that anything in the current American political economy fosters this sort of pauperization. Still, the tradition of disreputable poverty persists, partly because the legacy of the pauperized Irish immigrants has been continued in some measure by the fractional selection of subsequent immigrants, and partly because the internal situation of disreputable poverty conspires toward that end. Additionally, however, it persists for a reason that I have hardly touched in this essay: it persists because the other main carrier of the tradition of disreputable poverty in America has only now begun to mobilize, and, thus, to undo the effects of its enduring pauperization. When the Negro mobilization has run its course, and if no other massive pauperization occurs, the tradition of disreputable poverty will have used up its main capital and be reduced to squandering the interest drawn from fractional selection and its own internal situation — a fitting fate for so improvident a tradition.

[1] W. Lloyd Warner and Leo Srole, *The Social Systems of American Ethnic Groups*, New Haven: Yale University Press, 1945, pp. 12–13.
[2] See S. M. Lipset, "Working-Class Authoritarianism," in *Political Man*, Garden City, N.Y.: Doubleday, 1960, Ch. 4.
[3] The viciousness and bigotry with which the previous ethnic cohort treats newcomers is not just a consequence of their higher levels of provincialism and prejudice; what we regard as residential and occupational desegregation is to ethnic remnants a visible social indication of pauperization.
[4] Bremner, *op. cit.*, p. 6.

The Degree of Status Incongruence and its Effects

Andrzej Malewski

Problems

IN HIS LAST BOOK Homans defines the status of an individual as the complex set of stimuli which it presents to others (and to himself) and which are evaluated by others as better or worse, higher or lower.[1] The particular kinds of such stimuli are defined by him as status factors.[2] According to Homans, status congruence is realized when all the stimuli presented by a man rank better or higher than the corresponding stimuli presented by another, or when all the stimuli presented by both rank as equal.[3]

According to such a definition, the status of the same individual may be congruent in relation to certain people and incongruent in relation to others. The incongruence of status factors is thus treated here as the characteristic of a relationship and not of an individual. Secondly, it should be agreed that in every relationship in which one of the partners is evaluated as better in certain respects and worse in others, both partners are characterized by an incongruence of status factors.

The utility of concepts depends on the aims which they are supposed to serve. The concept "incongruence of status factors" can be useful for at least two purposes. First, it may be serviceable in an analysis of society as a system, and in an enquiry concerning — for example — the problem of relationships between the congruence of status factors in particular strata on the one hand, and the sharpness of social divisions, the isolation of certain strata from others and the formation of class-consciousness on the other. Secondly, the term may be useful in the analysis of differences in the behaviour of different categories of individuals and differences in relations between people depending on the degree of congruence of the status factors.

The present article deals exclusively with the second group of problems. I shall attempt to show that the integration of the regularities which appear in this domain demands a modification of the concept of "status incongruence." Thus in the present article I shall try first of all to define the meaning of the basic terms which it will be necessary to use, and then to formulate some pertinent propositions.

The concept of "status" and "status incongruence"

I shall use here the definition of "status" and "status factors" introduced by Homans.

According to these definitions everything which distinguishes an individual from others may become a status factor; first of all there are various characteristics of the individual himself, such as skin colour, age, education, religion, sex, income, property, home, way of dressing, skills, achievements, personal appearance, abilities, different kinds of behaviour, name, etc. Secondly there are characteristics connected with the relationship of the given individual to other individuals, groups, organizations or communities, e.g. duration of membership, seniority at work, authority, degree of independence, social origin, marital status, circle of acquaintances, etc. And thirdly, there are the characteristics which are the result of the attitude of other people to the given individual, e.g. the approval or esteem he enjoys. All of the above mentioned characteristics and many others are status factors if they are perceived by others and if they are evaluated as higher or lower, better or worse.

The idea of status as a complex set of different factors involves the problem of relationships between those factors. As a result of experience people learn that certain status factors appear linked to others, and respond with normative expectations; they expect a man who is a university professor, for instance, to be a man of learning and a company director to have a good education and presence and to be of the proper age. If, having learned this, they meet someone who is a university professor and knows very little, or who is a company director at 20 odd years old and has only a primary education, they will experience some incongruence. Generally speaking, the greater the divergence between the complex of status factors presented by a given individual and the normative expectations which

[1] G. C. Homans, *Social Behavior*. New York, Harcourt, 1961, p. 149.
[2] *Op. cit.*, p. 248.
[3] *Loc. cit.*

Reprinted from *The Polish Sociological Bulletin*, No. 1 (7), 1963, by permission of the author and the publisher.

have been formed in those with whom that individual is in contact, the more incongruent is the status of that individual.

One should pay attention to the two consequences of such a definition. In order to establish the incongruence of status it is not sufficient to point out, as is commonly done, that some status factors of an individual rank much higher than others. One should also show reasons for maintaining that those differences are inconsistent with the normative expectations of the environment in which the given individual moves. This throws a new light on the dispute between W. F. Kenkel[1] and G. Lenski.[2] Kenkel in his polemic with Lenski tried to show that not every concurrence of high and low status factors will cause such consequences as the rise of social radicalism. Lenski accepted this criticism and commented to the effect that status incongruence influences the behaviour and views of an individual only if it concerns the most basic components of status. This answer, however, involves further questions. Namely, which status factors are most basic and what should be one's guide when evaluating the importance of status factors. The world champion in the 10,000 meters race who has not completed his primary education will present one very high status factor, namely athletic talent, but his other status factor, education, will be very low. Such a complex of status factors, however, may not have any undesirable consequences for him; not because great athletic ability or education are of no importance, but because the connection between championship medals and low educational attainments may be consistent with normative expectations.

If incongruence of status depends on normative expectations which have been formed in other men, such expectations may not be the same in all cases. It has been noted many times that in the United States the status of a Negro doctor is incongruent.[3] As a medical man he is a representative of a profession that is very highly evaluated. As a Negro he represents an ethnic group which is held in very low esteem by many whites. Consequently if such a doctor were to practise in a district inhabited by white people, he would often meet reactions due to his ethnic group and not to his profession and would frequently be humiliated. This is the traditional approach to the problem and is no doubt right. But the definition given above draws attention to facts which hitherto have been generally neglected.

[1] W. F. Kenkel, "The Relationship Between Status Consistency and Politico-Economic Attitudes," *American Sociological Review*, Vol. 21, 1956, No. 1, pp. 365–368.

[2] G. Lenski, "Comment on Kenkel's Communication," *American Sociological Review*, Vol. 21, 1956, No. 2, pp. 368–369; See also: L. Broom, "Social Differentiation and Stratification," in: R. Merton, L. Broom and L. S. Cottrell (ed.), *Sociology Today*, New York, Basic Books, 1960, p. 431.

[3] E. C. Hughes, "Dilemmas and Contradictions of Status," *American Journal of Sociology*, 1945, No. 3, pp. 353–359.

[4] I. W. Goffman, "Status Consistency and Preference for Change in Power Distribution", *American Sociology Review*, Vol. 22, 1957, No. 3, pp. 275–281.

[5] Cf. proposition 3, p. 305.

The status of a Negro doctor will not be incongruent in every situation, because not even in American society is the fact of being a Negro doctor incongruent with the normative expectations in every environment. One may suppose that it is not inconsistent with the expectations of progressive white people, nor inconsistent with the expectations of the majority of the Negro community. Thus if such a doctor were to live and practise exclusively in a Negro district and to have no contacts with white patients or white doctors (especially with white doctors of conservative views) he would not show any incongruence of status factors, if congruence is to be interpreted according to the definition given above. This is not only a question of terminology. It means in fact that the propositions regarding the consequences of status incongruence may not be true as applied to him.

A Negro doctor practising exclusively in a Negro district may enjoy high esteem as a physician. As a Negro he may not meet any humiliation because all the people he meets are also Negroes. One may treat analogously the position of a worker whose personal contacts are limited to a working class group and whose skills, education or income are higher than those of his fellow workers. It is worthwhile quoting here the results obtained by I. Goffman.[4] He showed that the preference for change in the distribution of power was most strongly related to incongruences of income, education and occupational status among the upper strata, and almost unrelated to the incongruence of those three status factors among the lower strata. This apparent irregularity could be partly explained if one assumes that a large proportion of people from the lower strata classified as belonging to the category of people with incongruent status factors, did not in fact belong to this category according to the definition given above. Some other factors are discussed hereinafter.[5]

Thus far I have introduced the definition of "status incongruence." One may of course suggest many different definitions. The criterion that enables one to reject some of them and to accept others can only be their utility for formulating general propositions. I should now like to go on to present propositions concerning the consequences of status incongruence, as understood in accordance with the definition suggested here.

Incongruent status and behaviour

The incongruence of status implies that the individual presents some contradictory stimuli to others. This is only so, however, when the incongruent status factors are perceived by the same people.

This condition is not always fulfilled. Let us suppose that in a society (e.g. in pre-war Poland or in the United States today) the possession of a squalid little room in a poor quarter of the town is strikingly different from the expectations as to the home of a higher executive of an important organization. A high executive living in this way would, in that situation, meet our definition of the incongruence of status factors. However, if his home and work environment are isolated from each other, if his colleagues never see the room and his neighbours never see him at his place of work, neither of these two groups of persons would perceive the inconsistent stimuli. In other words, if the incongruence of status is to give inconsistent stimuli, the incongruent status factors should be perceived by the same people.

The stimuli presented by the individual to others affect their reactions towards that individual. If the individual simultaneously presents two conflicting stimuli, of which the first causes respect and the second contempt, other people may react to the second type of stimuli and show their contempt for the individual, although this is not justified in the light of the higher status factors. This line of reasoning leads to the formulation of the following two propositions.

1) The greater the incongruence of simultaneously perceived status factors of the given individual, the more insecure is his status. This means that others are likely to react to that individual as if he had a lower status, than the one he really enjoys.

2) The incongruence of status factors simultaneously perceived by other people brings punishments and the elimination of that incongruence is a source of reward.

From proposition *2* one should not conclude that people will always avoid an incongruence of status factors. Status incongruence is a source of punishments and its elimination a source of rewards, but it is not the only kind of punishment and reward. A sharpening of the incongruence of status factors may at the same time raise the general status of the individual. A very young man who becomes a professor at one of the European universities may increase the incongruence between certain factors of his status because of the conviction, widely held in Europe, that a university professor is a man of advanced age. But at the same time he can substantially increase his status and this increase of status may greatly surpass the costs of status incongruence. Even in a case of this kind, however, the incongruence of status brings certain punishments and evokes consequent attempts to get rid of them. If this is so, it must bring forth some consequences in the form of tendencies to decrease those punishments.

3) If an individual shows several incongruent status factors, some of which are evaluated as much lower than others, and if he perceives the possibility of changing the lower factors, he will tend to raise such status factors which are evaluated as lower.

For example, the *nouveau riche* in the upper class will often obliterate signs of their parvenu background: they will marry into respected families, buy family estates, demonstrate their knowledge of a foreign language widely used among the old aristocracy, fake pedigrees, boast of their friendly relations with persons of importance and emulate the older members of the elite in conformity to the norms of their new environment. Similarly, religious converts will show greater fervour for their new faith than those who have professed it from childhood.

Systematic results backing proposition *3* are furnished by the investigation made by J. Coleman, E. Katz and H. Menzel.[1] Interviews were carried out with eighty-five per cent of the general practitioners, internists and pediatricians practising in four selected American cities. In the interviews the doctors were asked, among other things, which of three widely used drugs they prescribed most often and when had they started to apply the newest of the three drugs, which appeared on the market one after the other. An examination of prescriptions from local pharmacies made out by the same doctors over fifteen months revealed what they had actually prescribed. The comparison of these two sets of data showed some striking differences. Two-thirds of the doctors who, according to the prescription record, had mostly used the oldest drug, stated that they mostly used one of the two newer ones. Sixty per cent of those who had mainly prescribed the drug introduced second, stated that they mostly used the third, i.e. the newest drug. Half the total number of physicians stated that they had begun to apply the newest drug at an earlier date and often many months earlier than actually appeared to be the case from the analysis of the prescriptions. From these results it may be concluded that keeping up with the latest discoveries in pharmacology was highly approved by the doctors interviewed, while lagging behind was disapproved.

One of the status factors of a physician is his professional competence. One would assume that the status of a doctor who is treated as little competent is incongruent. The possession of a doctor's diploma and the right to practise is incongruent with a lack of real medical skill. In order to establish how the competence of each doctor was perceived by his colleagues, the interviewers asked: "When you need information or advice about questions of therapy, [. . .] on whom are you most likely to call?" When opinions regarding a given doctor were compared with the other data already collected, it appeared that those doctors seldom or never named as potential counsellors had most often tried to appear in interviews as more up-to-date than their prescription record showed. This was rarest in the case of those doctors who were mentioned as potential advisers by three or more colleagues. In other words, doctors who showed the most striking incongruence between the two status factors — their medical title and their professional competence as perceived by their colleagues — most often tried to present themselves in a better light.

However, the tendency to eliminate status incongruence by raising those status factors which are evaluated as much lower than others does not always give the desired effects. Different status factors may have different degrees of stability. Some of them cannot be changed,

1 See: H. Menzel, "Public and Private Conformity under Different Conditions of Acceptance in the Group," *Journal of Abnormal and Social Psychology*, Vol. 55, 1957, No. 3, pp. 398–402.

e.g. skin colour or sex. The change of others demands a long span of time (e.g. age) or very great efforts (e.g. education). Others may be changed quite easily (e.g. one's way of dressing). These differences are linked with the difference between ascribed status and achieved status, which has often been stressed. But as in the case of the notion of status, it also seems useful here to generalize about the differences observed. In fact we need to have not two categories of status — ascribed and achieved — but a whole continuum of status factors from those most to those least changeable. Such a distinction enables us to formulate the next proposition.

4) If an individual has several incongruent status factors, some of which are evaluated as much lower than others, and when this individual cannot raise the lower factors, he will show a tendency to avoid those people who react to them.

Proposition *4* is backed by the results of the investigation made by G. Lenski.[1] Four status factors — income, education, prestige of occupation and ethnic prestige — were chosen for investigation. The category of a high degree of status congruence and the category of a low degree of status congruence were compared regarding frequency of and motives for contacts with other people. It turned out that respondents in a low congruence category far more frequently than respondents in a high congruency category:

a) did not maintain any lively contacts with their neighbours or fellow-workers outside business hours and did not belong to voluntary associations for any long period of time;

b) in the case of membership in voluntary associations they did not attend meetings and were not active in the organization;

c) indicated nonsociable motives for being members of an association, i.e. motives other than a desire for pleasurable interaction with others.

All these results seem to support proposition *4* concerning the relationship between status incongruence and the tendency to avoid other people. In the light of previous reasoning, one might expect the differences to be still more striking if one could eliminate the factor of membership in an organization or interaction with people who did not share the common American pejorative evaluation of certain status factors. For example, where members of ethnic minorities were concerned, we did not take into consideration contacts with other members of those minorities. One might expect still more striking differences if those who presented status factors consistent with the expectations of their environment were eliminated from the category of low status congruence.[2]

Our next proposition will concern another type of defence against humiliations connected with status incongruence.

5) If an individual of incongruent status cannot raise the lower factors of his status, he will tend to reject the system of evaluation which justifies his humiliations and to join those who are opposed to that system. If these others represent a tendency towards changing the existing order, the above individual mentioned will be particularly inclined to accept their total program.

This proposition is supported by many different pieces of research. Lipset, in his study of the Co-operative Commonwealth Federation, the Socialist party of the Canadian province of Saskatchewan, discovered that the majority of businessmen and professional people who were members of that party belonged to minority groups such as Ukrainians, Poles, Russians and others, whereas only a few businessmen of Anglo-Saxon origin belonged to the party.[3] Many authors have noticed that Jews from the middle and upper classes have very often been members of Socialist and Communist parties.[4] Lenski established that, in the Detroit area, individuals with high incomes, high occupational or educational status and low ethnic status, or with high occupational and low educational status more often supported Democratic or Progressive candidates and were more liberal than individuals with a higher degree of status congruence.[5] Goffman reported that incongruent respondents expressed a stronger preference for changes in the distribution of power between the State government, large scale industry, the trade unions, medium industry and the federal government than congruent respondents.[6] Studies of voting behaviour have proved that in America, where differences in speech and manners between the middle and the lower classes are small and not very obvious, people who have been promoted from the lower to the middle class more often voted for the Republican party than the stable members of the middle class. In Germany, Finland, Norway and Sweden, where the differences in behaviour between the lower and middle classes seem to be much more visible, people who have been promoted to the middle class more often voted for the Social Democratic and Communist parties, probably because of their visible status incongruence.

Such results have induced many authors to accept the proposition that status incongruence always, or at least in cases where it cannot be reduced by improving the lower status factors, results in a tendency to accept

[1] G. Lenski, "Social Participation and Status Crystallization," *American Sociological Review*, Vol. 21, 1956, No. 4, pp. 458–464.

[2] A more detailed analysis should also control the factor of vertical mobility. Those who constantly move upwards in the social hierarchy will tend to break all old links and will have some difficulties in establishing new ones. See: E. Eilis, "Social Psychological Correlates of Upward Social Mobility among Unmarried Career Women," *American Sociological Review*, Vol. 17, 1952, No. 2, pp. 558–563. See also: Broom *op. cit.*, p. 432.

[3] S. M. Lipset, *Agrarian Socialism*, Berkeley, University of California Press, 1950, pp. 190–193.

[4] See: R. Michels, *Political Parties*, Glencoe, Free Press, 1949, pp. 260–261; see also: L. E. Hubbard, *Soviet Labour and Industry*, London, Macmillan, 1942, pp. 272–279; S. M. Lipset and R. Bendix, "Social Status and Social Structure," *The British Journal of Sociology*, part II, September 1951; p. 243.

[5] G. Lenski, "Status Crystallization: A Non-Vertical Dimension of Social Status," *American Sociological Review*, Vol. 19, 1954, No. 3, pp. 405–413.

[6] Goffman, *op. cit.*

leftist programs.[1] In the light of our considerations such a tendency is a particular application of a more general law, appearing in some specific conditions. If the only group rejecting the system of values justifying the humiliations felt by people with incongruent status is the radical social Left, those people will be particularly ready to accept the program of reforms launched by the Left. If, however, there are other groups, e.g. extremely Rightist ones, whose program rouses hopes for changes bringing about the increase of lower status factors, incongruent individuals can also show great readiness to accept extremely Rightist programs. This is not a purely theoretical possibility. Such a tendency has in fact been discovered, e.g., by B. Ringer and D. Sills in their study of political extremists in Iran.[2]

In the above mentioned proposition 5 the tendency to reject evaluations justifying the humiliations inflicted on people with incongruent status factors, was made dependent on the absence of any real chances of improving the lower status factors. But this proposition is only approximately true. It implicitly assumes that the real absence of opportunity for improvement is adequately perceived. It is well known, however, that perception of reality is not always adequate. In a situation in which there is an objective lack of opportunity for improving some status factor, certain people may be deluded as to the existence of such a possibility. If the situation itself is unambiguous and clear and if the given individual has no motivation for distorting reality, his perception of the situation will be adequate.[3]

These conditions, however, are not always fulfilled. People who suffer humiliations because of their origin or skin colour may see rare individuals who, although they share these features, have attained the very top of the social hierarchy. This may bolster up vain hopes of overcoming these disadvantageous status factors. This will be the easier, the more firmly the given individual has internalized the values of the privileged groups, and the stronger are his aspirations towards sharing in these values. Therefore, although skin colour is one of the least changeable status characteristics, some middle class Negroes do their best to imitate white members of the middle class in their views as well as in their behaviour.

Until now I have dealt mainly with status incongruence and various defensive responses aimed at minimizing this incongruence. Now I should like to make some comments on the behaviour of those whose status is undeniably high and stable. Status can be considered as stable as possible if an individual has a great many congruent status factors. In that situation particular behaviours in discordance with the high status will not be able to throw it in doubt. A university professor whose deep knowledge and creative talents are obvious, may openly tell his students that he does not know something, or that he has no ready answer and must stop to consider the given problem. A professor whose knowledge and abilities seem very poor to others of his circle would pay a big price for such frankness.

Similarly in the United States a prosperous member of the upper class may safely drive a cheap old car or work in his garden in his old overalls, for this would in no way shake his undoubted status as a member of the upper class. The same behaviour of someone who has only recently been promoted to the upper class would only emphasize his dubious status. This line of reasoning leads to the following proposition:

6) People whose status is very high and stable pay less attention to behaviour as the visible symbol of their higher status.

Some findings reported by H. Menzel in the paper summarized above support proposition 6. Menzel found that the doctors whose recognized professional competence was high, more often reported less up-to-date behaviour during an interview than those doctors whose professional competence was more doubtful.[4] The author could not explain this phenomenon. He discussed many hypotheses which seemed to him improbable. In the light of our discussion it seems that the result was completely in accordance with what was to be expected on the basis of proposition 6. The doctors considered by others as highly competent and who in fact followed the progress of modern medicine carefully, thought it least important to show themselves to the interviewer in the best possible light. They did not feel compelled to convince everyone they met that they were up-to-date in their medical practice. They really were up-to-date and this was well known to those whose opinion was important to them. Therefore, if they did not remember exactly when they had begun to apply the new drug for the first time, they tended to give a later rather than an earlier date. They considered it not only unnecessary but also unpleasant to present themselves in a falsely flattering light. This would have wounded their own self-esteem.

Status incongruence of group members and the system of relations in a group

Until now we have been discussing individuals or categories of individuals who differed from each other as to their degree of status congruence.

Now I should like to discuss what would be the effect of status incongruence among group members on the system of relationships within the group. A familiar example of the situation discussed here may be: *a)* an institution or an enterprise in which the director has

[1] See: S. M. Lipset and J. Linz, *The Social Basis of Political Diversity*, Centre for Advanced Study in the Behavioral Sciences, Palo Alto, 1956 (unpublished), Chapter VIII, p. 16; S. M. Lipset and R. Bendix, *Social Mobility in Industrial Society*, Berkeley, University of California Press, 1959, p. 68.

[2] B. Ringer and D. Sills, "Political Extremists in Iran, A Secondary Analysis of Communications Data," *Public Opinion Quarterly*, 1952, No. 2, pp. 668–701.

[3] See: A. Malewski, *Generality Levels of Theories Concerning Human Behaviour*, paper presented at the section devoted to Models and Theory Formation, International Congress of Sociology, Washington, 1962.

[4] See: Menzel, *op. cit.*, p. 402.

less competence or a lower education than at least some of his subordinates; *b)* a working team in which those who work poorly and are less prepared for effort have higher salaries or a higher formal position than the others; *c)* a married couple where, contrary to the normative expectations of each partner, the wife holds a much higher position and has a much higher income than her husband. In groups of this kind there will be a feeling of injustice[1] and some group members will frequently react to others in a way to cause them humiliation, and thus elicit rejection or an unfriendly response.

7) The higher the degree of status incongruence among group members the lower will be the degree of mutual friendship.

This proposition is partly supported by the results of the study made by Stuart Adams on bomber crews.[2] He took into consideration nine different status factors of crew members, i.e. age, education, length of service, length of time spent in the air, combat time, rank, function in the crew, conviction of others as to the abilities of the given airman and popularity among others. These scores were used for constructing the status congruence score of each subject. The scores of status congruence of individual crew members enabled Stuart Adams to measure the average status congruence of each crew. The subjects answered two questionnaires: *a)* on the degree of confidence which the different members of the crews felt in others, and *b)* on the degree of friendship with others.

It was found that the lower the average status congruence of the crew the lower was the average degree of mutual trust and friendship. This result is in full accordance with the implications of proposition 7.

Another more indirect piece of evidence for this proposition is furnished by the results of the study carried out by J. V. Clark.[3] He investigated the workers of eight large supermarkets, and in particular two categories of employees working in direct co-operation with each other: bundlers and cashiers. The cashiers

occupied posts superior in relation to those of the bundlers. The most comprehensive and most immediate data concerned two supermarkets: No. 6 and No. 58. The degree of status congruence of bundlers and cashiers in the first of these supermarkets was much lower than in the other. During the time of the study numerous workers left store No. 6. This fact indirectly confirms proposition 7. The mobility of personnel depends on the attractiveness of the group in which the individual works, at least when there are alternative job opportunities, and status incongruence helps to decrease that attractiveness.

In the two above mentioned studies attention was also paid to the problem of the interdependence of the degree of status congruence among crew or personnel, and their productivity. When considering this problem Homans put forward the assumption that "when they [people] are working together as a team, we expect that the degree to which they are congruent will make a difference to their effectiveness. If they are highly congruent at least one factor that might otherwise have disturbed their co-operation has been removed."[4] Some findings, particularly those reported by Clark, provide confirmation for this conclusion. In my opinion, however, there are no grounds for expecting any general relationship here. The degree of average status congruence among a given group is one of the factors increasing the attractiveness of that group to its members. The attractiveness of the group has an effect on the degree of conformity to the norms accepted in that group. If these norms require an increase in productivity we should expect such an increase; if, however, they require a decrease in productivity, this too is to be expected. It is not surprising therefore that Adams has stated that there was no direct relationship between the average status congruence of bomber crews and their effectiveness, as measured by the number of fulfilled combat operations. The propositions discussed above described merely a fraction of the relationships emerging in connection with the incongruence of status factors. Reactions of individuals to status incongruence, differing from those discussed above, require further investigation. The problem of the link between the average status incongruence of a group and the functioning of **that** group still awaits a more comprehensive analysis. The same holds true of the problem of the relationship between the degree of status congruence within various strata and the formation of class consciousness.[5] Finally, all the propositions presented in this paper will need further modification as the result of new research. It seems to me this is a field for research which deserves particular attention.

[1] M. Patchen, "A Conceptual Framework and Some Empirical Data Regarding Comparisons of Social Rewards," *Sociometry*, 1960, No. 1.

[2] S. N. Adams, "Status Congruency as a Variable in Small Group Performance," *Social Forces*, Vol. 32, 1953–54, pp. 16–22.

[3] J. V. Clark, *A Preliminary Investigation of Some Unconscious Assumptions Affecting Labor Efficiency in Eight Supermarkets*, Harvard Graduate School of Business Administration, 1958, unpublished. Quoted after Homans, *Social Behavior, op cit.*, pp. 255–262.

[4] Homans, *op. cit.*, p. 255.

[5] Problem discussed more comprehensively by Broom, *op. cit.*, pp. 433–439.

A Comparative Study of Occupational Prestige[1]

Robert W. Hodge, Donald J. Treiman, and Peter H. Rossi

As THE MAJOR ROLES through which rewards are distributed and power exercised, occupations are central to any study of social stratification. Despite local variations, the major activities of most occupations are sufficiently comparable from society to society to sustain intersocietal comparisons of occupational structures. Here we investigate the hierarchy imposed upon occupational systems by popular evaluation, studying the prestige accorded to "samples" of occupations obtained from more than a score of nations. The countries studied vary widely in cultural base, in political and economic diversity, and in the way in which major institutional complexes are articulated with each other. The basic data used in this report are prestige scores for comparable titles, all generated by empirical studies of the evaluation of occupations.

Although comparisons had been made between pairs of countries as early as 1927,[2] the first systematic national comparisons using studies based on large (although not necessarily good) samples of general populations in a number of countries were made a decade ago by Inkeles and Rossi.[3] The present paper can be regarded in large measure as an extension of their work, although we shall undertake a somewhat different mode of analysis. Because the general explanation advanced by Inkeles and Rossi for similarities and dissimilarities in occupational-prestige ratings has implications for our present investigation, it is worthwhile to recapitulate their argument.

Comparing the prestige positions accorded to occupations in six countries (all that were available at the time) Inkeles and Rossi found impressive agreement among countries in their orderings of occupations. Coefficients of determination ranged between 0.94 and

[1] This paper summarizes research ancillary to a larger project supported by a National Science Foundation Grant (NSF-#G85, "Occupations and Social Stratification") aimed at providing definitive prestige scores for a more representative sample of occupations in the United States. Review of background materials relevant to the larger, primary investigation has resulted in a number of unanticipated supporting studies. The research herein reports preliminary findings from one of the supporting investigations; the materials will be more fully analyzed in the second author's doctoral dissertation, a comparative investigation of occupational structures. We are indebted to C. Arnold Anderson for making available to us his extensive bibliography of occupational-prestige studies, and to Alex Inkeles for his careful and incisive criticism of an earlier version of this paper.
[2] Jerome Davis, "Testing the Social Attitudes of Children in the Government Schools in Russia,"*American Journal of Sociology*, 32 (May, 1927), pp. 947–952.
[3] Alex Inkeles and Peter H. Rossi, "National Comparisons of Occupational Prestige," *American Journal of Sociology*, 61 (January, 1956), pp. 329–339.

Published here for the first time by permission of the authors.

0.55 with an average of 0.83.[1] Because the nations involved (Germany, Great Britain, Japan, New Zealand, the U.S.S.R., and the United States) were all quite advanced in extent of industrialization, Rossi and Inkeles postulated that in accounting for these high correlations "a great deal of weight must be given to the cross-national similarities in social structure which arise from the industrial system and from other common structural features, such as the national state."[2] By and large Inkeles and Rossi found little evidence to favor the "culturalist" position that "within each country or culture the distinctive local value system would result in substantial — and, indeed, sometimes extreme — differences in the evaluation of particular jobs in the standardized modern occupational system" and much to support the "structuralist" contention that "there is a relatively invariable hierarchy of prestige associated with the industrial system, even when it is placed in the context of larger social systems which are otherwise differentiated in important respects. In addition, the fact that the countries compared also have in common the national state and certain needs and values, such as interest in health, apparently also contributes to the observed regularity of the ratings, since both professional and political occupations are foci of agreement. Perhaps the most striking finding is the extent to which the different classes of occupation have been woven together into a single relatively unified occupational structure, more or less common to the six countries."[3]

The explanation originally propounded by Inkeles and Rossi stresses the contribution of industrialization to the standardization of occupational-prestige hierarchies while, at the same time, *pointing to other social structural elements which complex societies have in common.* Inkeles and Rossi made no specific prediction concerning how the occupational-prestige hierarchies in relatively underdeveloped nations would compare either with each other or with industrialized countries, although the stress placed in their interpretation on the industrial

system has been interpreted to mean that underdeveloped nations should show prestige hierarchies which were more idiosyncratic than those of industrialized nations. A literal explication of the Inkeles–Rossi position, however, finds their statement rather ambiguous on this score.

The extension of the study of occupational prestige to "underdeveloped nations" has provided evidence that many such nations have occupational-prestige hierarchies which are very similar to those of more advanced nations.[4] The evidence from such studies contradicts a very heavy stress on the industrial system as the major or predominant factor in producing similarities in the occupational-prestige hierarchies of different countries. The data so far suggest that occupations stand roughly in the same order of popular evaluation across a wide variety of nations of varying levels of industrialization and varying cultural backgrounds. This new evidence requires an explanation which stresses social-structural features that all societies, whether industrialized or not, have in common.

The same evidence also speaks out strongly against a relativistic "culturalist position" which has been posed as the polar alternative to a "structuralist" hypothesis. Whatever variations local cultural traditions generate in the prestige standings of occupations must be of such a minor order that they tend to be obscured in the national comparisons which have been made.

The above comments strongly suggest the need for a theory of occupational prestige which will account for the gross similarity in the evaluations of occupations in all societies. A major step in this direction was taken by Inkeles and Rossi, and the main feature of the structuralist position laid out below is a modification of their position stressing more heavily the many structural features which national societies of any degree of complexity share. Specialized institutions to carry out political, religious, and economic functions, and to provide for the health, education, and welfare of the population exist in one form or another in all national societies. Considering the importance of these functions to the maintenance of complex social systems, it is not surprising that occupations at the top of these institutional structures should be highly regarded. Moreover, these are the very occupations which require the greatest training and skill to which the greatest material rewards accrue. Thus, any major prestige inversion would produce a great deal of inconsistency in the stratification system, canceling out rather than reinforcing status differences created by the unequal distribution of income and degree of training required for occupational entrée. By extension, this interpretation holds for comparisons of occupations located at all points in the prestige hierarchy, enough so that one can expect to find positive correlations between prestige hierarchies of different countries just from the constraints placed on evaluation by the structure of work, the system of rewards for work, and the need to maintain at least a gross consistency in the distribution of different kinds of rewards.[5]

[1] Note that the correlation coefficients reported by Inkeles and Rossi have been squared wherever they are mentioned in this paper in order to make them comparable to the coefficients of determination which we utilize in the body of our analysis.

[2] Inkeles and Rossi, *op. cit.*, p. 339.

[3] *Ibid.*

[4] For example, a rank correlation of 0.96 has been found between the prestige accorded to occupations in the United States and the Philippines and a rank correlation of 0.94 between measures of occupational prestige for Indonesia and the United States. For the Philippines, see Edward A. Tiryakian, "The Prestige Evaluation of Occupations in an Underdeveloped Country: The Philippines," *American Journal of Sociology,* 63 (January, 1958), pp. 390–399, and for Indonesia see E. Murray Thomas, "Reinspecting a Structural Position on Occupational Prestige," *American Journal of Sociology,* 67 (March, 1962), pp. 561–565.

[5] Much of the discussion presented here is in the form of assumptions which are at least theoretically subject to empirical test, the major limitation on such tests being the adequacy of foreign census materials. For example, we have argued that a strain toward consistency is an inherent aspect of all stratification systems and has the consequence of bringing different criteria of status into line with one another. If this is true, we

Furthermore, those occupations which are common to societies of divergent levels of industrial development (and these are the only occupations that enter into comparisons between countries) tend to be the very occupations that are characteristic of *any* society with a relatively developed division of labor. All such societies have positions equivalent to our medical personnel, clergy, teachers, policemen, merchants, craftsmen, agricultural laborers, etc. It is the very existence of these specialized positions that helps to define a society as "complex." Thus, the mere presence of such occupations constitutes one of the fundamental structural uniformities of all national societies. Moreover, the requisites and perquisites of these positions tend to be defined in similar terms from society to society. Thus, it is not surprising that when occupations are compared across societies which are diverse in their economic base, *those*

The foregoing structural explanation of prestige similarities clearly holds not only for comparisons between developed and underdeveloped countries, but for comparisons between industrialized societies as well. However, because there are larger numbers of comparable occupations common to pairs of such countries, we can also anticipate increased opportunities for divergences in evaluation, albeit over a very narrow range. Thus, for example, cultural variation from society to society may cause inversions in the relative positions of physician and college professor, although in every society these two occupations are among the most highly regarded.

An important implication of this interpretation is that the "culturalist" position, in a modified form, is also consistent with high gross similarities in occupational-prestige hierarchies from country to country. Cultural

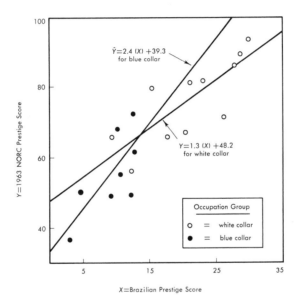

FIG. I. Scattergram and regression of 1963 NORC prestige
scores on prestige scores derived from Brazilian study

occupations which can be compared stand roughly in the same position *vis-à-vis* each other.

It is quite possible, however, that much genuine diversity in occupational-prestige systems not captured by our analysis is reflected in the relative placement of occupations that are not comparable across societies, or even across subsectors of any given society. In Tiryakian's study of the Philippines, for example, only a small number of occupations could be found about which it was sensible to ask both peasants in remote villages and the residents of Manila. One could not ask about the pro-liferated occupations of a highly developed industrial system in the remote peasant communities because knowledge about such occupations (e.g., physicist or even machinist) simply would not exist among such respondents.

variation may act to produce inversions among occupations within a narrow range of prestige positions. Thus, disagreement in the relative ratings accorded to such functionaries as priests, high government officials, scientists, and businessmen, as well as inversions among particular service and blue-collar occupations, may be

should expect substantial consistency between the amount of training required for a job, its prestige position, and its return in the form of income. A test of this central tenet of stratification theory would involve the correlation over occupations of prestige, median income, and median educational attainment (or some other appropriate measure of central tendency) for a large number of countries, much as Duncan has done for the United States. Cf. Otis Dudley Duncan, "A Socio-economic Index for All Occupations," in Albert J. Reiss, Jr., and others, *Occupations and Social Status* (New York: The Free Press, 1961), pp. 114–128. Analyses along these lines will be reported in future publications.

the major consequence of cultural differences from country to country.[1] But we can hardly expect that cultural traditions will produce inversions of the relative positions of dominant functionaries and blue-collar workers, for the reasons adduced above.[2] Once again we are led to the same conclusion: *Gross similarities in occupational-prestige hierarchies can be accounted for on the basis of gross uniformities in social structure across societies, whatever the particulars of different societies may be.* In view of the fact that we are led to expect fairly high prestige correlations between countries just by the generic character of occupational systems, such differences as can be found would seem to assume increased importance for our understanding of the relationship between occupational prestige and other aspects of social structure.

Some methodological considerations

Before beginning a substantive review and analysis of existing national prestige studies, we turn briefly to some methodological considerations. It is important to note that the cross-national prestige comparisons used here are based on data which were not designed to support such comparisons, and which are far from ideal. No single study of occupational prestige is based on a sample of occupations that is representative of the universe of occupations extant in the country where the study was conducted. For example, of the ninety occupational titles rated in the 1947 NORC survey, thirty-one fell in the census major occupation group "professional, technical, and kindred workers" and another sixteen fell into either "laborers, except farm and mine" or "service workers, except private

[1] In their analysis of cross-national prestige comparisons, Inkeles and Rossi do not rely solely on correlational techniques, but compare the relative prestige of particular occupations in different countries. At least implicitly, they recognize that inversions of this kind may be attributed to cultural variation, although they do not explicitly state that these are perhaps the only kind of inversions contemplated in a cultural formulation.

[2] The further development of the "modified" culturalist position hinted at here would require some specification of *what* cultural divergencies can be expected to lead to inversions in the relative standing of *which* occupations. Without such specification the modified culturalist position stands as too vaguely stated to be capable of being tested against empirical findings.

[3] For a discussion of this and related points bearing on the representativeness of the occupations rated in the NORC-North-Hatt study of occupational prestige, see Albert J. Reiss, Jr., *op. cit.*, pp. 61–81.

[4] The United States and Brazilian data used in Figure 1 are taken, respectively, from Robert W. Hodge, Paul M. Siegel, and Peter H. Rossi, "Occupational Prestige in the United States, 1925–63," *American Journal of Sociology*, 70 (November, 1964), Table 1, pp. 290–292, and Bertram Hutchinson, "The Social Grading of Occupations in Brazil," *British Journal of Sociology*, 8 (June, 1957), Table 2, p. 179.

[5] This hypothesis requires that the slope of the regression line relating U.S. prestige scores to foreign scores over blue-collar occupations (b_B) be larger than the slope of the regression line over white-collar occupations (b_W). Consequently, we expect the ratio (b_B)/(b_W) to be larger than unity. For seventeen countries for which both white-collar and blue-collar regression lines were established (see Table 2 following), we find that the mean

household," far exceeding the proportions of all occupational titles in these categories.[3] By and large, prestige studies tend to over-represent the extremes of the occupational hierarchy and under-represent the middle sector of the occupational ladder. Hence, comparisons among countries may produce high correlations simply because the extremes of the occupational hierarchy are over-represented and the middle, where disagreement seems most likely to occur, is poorly represented.

This difficulty is concretely illustrated in Figure 1, which shows for selected matching occupations the regression of 1963 NORC prestige scores on prestige indicators derived from a Brazilian study.[4] The regressions shown in Figure 1 are specific to white-collar and to blue-collar occupations and differ noticeably. The coefficient of determination ($= r^2$) over the matching white-collar occupations is 0.61, while that over the matching blue-collar titles is 0.58. These coefficients are not large by standards of extant international comparisons. However, the coefficient of determination for all occupations combined is, despite the demonstrably different regression lines within the white-collar and blue-collar groups, larger (0.76) than either of the within-group coefficients of determination. The drop of about 15 per cent in common variance between the United States and Brazilian prestige scores when one goes from the comparison of scores over all occupations to comparisons within white-collar and blue-collar groupings reflects the appreciable correlation between extremes which is introduced when the two groups are combined.

Comparison of the regressions plotted in Figure 1 may also be used to gain additional information about national differences in occupational-prestige structures. These lines were obtained from a multiple regression equation:

$$\hat{Y} + 2.4(X) + 16.2(Z) - 1.1(XZ) + 32.0,$$

where Y = 1963 NORC prestige scores, X = derived prestige scores for matching Brazilian titles, and Z is a dummy variable which takes on the value 1 if the occupation is white-collar and takes on the value 0 if the occupation is blue-collar. This equation implies, of course, that $\hat{Y} = 1.3(X)48.+2$ for white-collar occupations (since $Z = 1$) and that $\hat{Y} = 2.4(X) + 32.0$ for blue-collar occupations (since $Z = 0$). The interaction term XZ in the multiple regression is significantly less than zero ($p < 0.07$, with a one-tailed test) and thus we conclude that the two within-group regressions are different.

Thus, because the regression slope is steeper for blue-collar than for white-collar occupations, one can infer that, relative to white-collar occupations, blue-collar occupations are more differentiated in the United States than in Brazil. An interpretation of this finding may point to increased differentiation of blue-collar occupations accompanying advanced industrialization as unskilled, semiskilled and skilled occupations become explicitly differentiated within the factory system.[5] However, differences in regression slopes relating different pairs of countries are not strictly comparable, owing to differences in the methods of obtaining prestige ratings from country to country. Hence in the remainder of this paper, we will give primary attention to coefficients of determination rather than to the regression slopes.

Data and methods

Over the past decade more than a score of studies of occupational prestige have been conducted in as many nations. Table 1 presents short descriptions of twenty-four such studies.[1] These studies are quite heterogeneous: some are based on unsystematic samples of students and peasants, others on well designed area probability samples of whole countries; the number of occupations rated ranges from as few as thirteen to as many as ninety; the techniques of rating vary from minor alterations of the NORC procedure of having respondents judge occupations as "excellent," "good", "average," "somewhat below average," or "poor" according to "your own personal opinion of the general standing that such a job has"[2] to the task of ranking occupations according to the extent they are "looked up to."[3] The numerical measures of prestige or social standing derived from these investigations are no less diverse: average ratings, weighted scores, mean and median rankings, and even such simple order statistics as rankings of aggregate scores derived by one of the foregoing procedures.

In Table 1, it will be observed that for several countries — Germany, India, and Japan — more than one study is reported. To combine these studies and thereby retain as much information as possible about each country, it was necessary to place these several within-country studies on a common metric. This task was accomplished by establishing the linear regression over occupations common to the studies conducted within a single country. The regression equation thus derived was then used to transform the scores of the unmatched titles in one study to the metric of the other. This procedure relies, of course, upon the adequacy of the linear-regression equation as a transformation between studies, but does yield a set of roughly comparable scores for more occupations than are available from any single individual study within the nations for which several studies have been reported.[4]

In view of the great heterogeneity of these studies and the problems incurred in matching occupational titles, there may be some question about the wisdom of comparing them at all. However, there are characteristics peculiar to data of this kind which suggest that comparisons may be valid despite the obvious technical defects of these studies.

First of all, published analyses of existing studies have failed to uncover any large systematic differences in the prestige ratings accorded occupations by different subgroups of the population, and hence representativeness of the samples involved is not a very important issue. Ratings from a few respondents, however chosen,

[1] The sources of data used in this report are as follows: for *Australia*, Ronald Taft, "The Social Grading of Occupations in Australia," *British Journal of Sociology*, 4 (June, 1953), pp. 181–187; for the *Belgian Congo*, N. Xydias, "Prestige of Occupations," in C. Daryl Forde, editor, *Social Implications of Industrialization and Urbanization in Africa South of the Sahara* (Paris: UNESCO, Tension and Technology Series, 1956), pp. 489–499; for *Brazil*, Hutchinson, *op. cit*; for *Canada*, Jacob Tuckman, "Social Status of Occupations in Canada," *Canadian Journal of Psychology*, 1 (June, 1947), pp. 71–74; for *Chile*, Roy E. Carter, Jr., and Orlando Sepulveda, "Occupational Prestige in Santiago, Chile," *American Behavioral Scientist*, 8 (September, 1964), pp. 20–24; for *Denmark*, Kaare Svalastoga, *Prestige, Class, and Mobility* (Copenhagen: Glydendal, 1959), pp. 80ff; for *Germany* (1), G. Mackenroth and K. M. Bolte, "Bericht uber das Forschungsvorhaben 'Wandlungen der deutschen Sozialstruktur (am Beispiel des Landes Schleswig-Holstein),'" in *Transactions of the Second World Congress of Sociology*, Vol. II (London: International Sociological Association, 1954), pp. 91–102; for *Germany* (2), Gerhard Wurzbacher, et al., *Das Dorf im Spannungsfeld Industrieller Entwicklung* (Stuttgart: Ferdinand Enke Verlag, 1954), pp. 29–73; for *Ghana*, unpublished data from the Education in Transitional Societies Project, Comparative Education Center, University of Chicago; for *Great Britain*, John Hall and D. Caradog Jones, "Social Grading of Occupations," *British Journal of Sociology*, 1 (January, 1950), pp. 31–55; for *Guam*, James G. Cooper, et al., "The Social Status of Occupations in Micronesia," *Personnel and Guidance Journal*, 41 (November, 1962), pp. 267–269; for *India* (1), B. Krishnan, "Social Prestige of Occupations," *Journal of Vocational and Educational Guidance*, Baroda, India, 3 (August, 1956), pp. 18–22; for *India* (2), B. Krishnan, "Regional Influence on Occupational Preferences," *Psychological Studies*, Mysore, India, 6 (July, 1961), pp. 66–70; for *India* (3), David R. Cook, "Prestige of Occupations in India," *Psychological Studies*, Mysore, India, 7 (January, 1962), pp. 31–37; for *Indonesia*, R. Murray Thomas and Soeparman, "Occupational Prestige: Indonesia, and America," *Personnel and Guidance Journal*, 41 (January, 1963), pp. 430–434; for *Ivory Coast*, unpublished data from the Education in Transitional Societies Project, Comparative Education Center, University of Chicago; for *Japan* (1), Research Committee of Japan Sociological Society, "Social Stratification and Mobility in Six Large Cities of Japan," in *Transactions of the Second World Congress of Sociology*, Vol. II (London: International Sociological Association, 1954), pp. 414–431; for *Japan* (2), Charles E. Ramsey and Robert J. Smith, "Japanese and American Perceptions of Occupations," *American Journal of Sociology*, 65 (March, 1960), pp. 475–482; for the *Netherlands*, F. Van Heek, et al., *Sociale Stijging en Daling in Nederland*, Vol. I (Leyden: H. E. Stenfert Kroese N.V., 1958), pp. 25–26; for *New Zealand*, A. A. Congalton, "Social Grading of Occupations in New Zealand," *British Journal of Sociology*, 4 (March, 1953), pp. 45–59; for *Northern Rhodesia*, J. Clyde Mitchell and A. L. Epstein, "Occupational Prestige and Social Status Among Urban Africans in Northern Rhodesia," *Africa*, 29 (January, 1959), pp. 22–40; for *Norway*, William Simenson and Gilbert Geis, "A Cross-cultural Study of University Students," *Journal of Higher Education*, 26 (January, 1955), pp. 21–24 and 56–57; for the *Philippines*, Tiryakian, *op. cit.*; for *Poland*, Adam Sarapata and Wlodzimierz Wesolowski, "The Evaluation of Occupations by Warsaw Inhabitants," *American Journal of Sociology*, 66 (May, 1961), pp. 581–591; for *Sweden*,

footnotes continued on p. 316.

ratio $(b_B)/(b_W)$ is equal to 1.38. Since all of these countries are less developed than in United States, the observed mean value of the ratio is in accord with the hypothesis. However, and perhaps more importantly, variation from country to country in the value of the ratio $(b_B)/(b_W)$ is not correlated with variation in economic development. Thus, the hypothesis in question must stand as a plausible suggestion worthy of further investigation as precisely comparable national prestige studies become available.

TABLE I. *Summary of Sample and Technical Characteristics of National Prestige Studies*

Country	Year completed	Sample size and characteristics	Prestige rating procedure	Prestige measure used in this study*	No. of occupations rated
Australia	1953	Six samples of students and adults involved in adult education; 277 respondents	"Social standing" of occupations rated on 5-point scale	Mean score	20
Belgian Congo	1956	Upper-form students in African secondary and technical schools in Stanleyville; 72 respondents	Occupations ranked "in order of the social standing which most people granted them"	Mean rank	30
Brazil	1955	Representative sample of first-year students at the University of São Paulo; 500 respondents	Occupations rated on 6-point scale according to "general social standing," then ranked within groups	Mean of median ranks for 15 sex-SES-IQ subgroups	30
Canada	1947	Three hundred seventy-nine college students and 40 job applicants at Jewish vocational service; 410 respondents in all	Occupations ranked according to extent they are "looked up to"	Rank order (procedure by which derived unclear)	25
Chile	1963	Area probability sample of residents of Santiago, Chile; 230 respondents	"Level of prestige" of occupations rated on 5-point scale	Mean score, multiplied by 20	16
Denmark	1953	Stratified national probability sample of adults; 3,128 respondents	Respondent handed card with occupational title, amount of education incumbent normally has, and number of people supervised, and asked to rate "prestige" of occupation on 5-point scale	Mean score	75
Germany (1)	1952	Approximately 1,500 individuals, including university, trade, and commercial school students and adults from a number of towns in Schleswig-Holstein. Only responses from adult males are used here; unfortunately the size of this sub-sample was not reported	Occupations ranked in order of their "social standing"	Rank order, derived from mean rank	38
Germany (2)	1950	"Informed citizens" — members of business and professional organiza-tions, associations, etc., in a small West German town; 156 respondents	Occupations ranked in order of their "prestige"	Mean rank	17
Ghana	1961	Fifth-form males in 23 secondary institutions (average age 19.2 years). The sample constituted 45 per cent of all fifth-form male students in Ghana's secondary schools at the time; 775 respondents	"Prestige" of occupations rated on 5-point scale	Mean score	25
Great Britain	1949	Questionnaires distributed through adult education and other organiza-tions; male reponses (N = 749) used here	"Social standing" of occupations rated on 5-point scale, then ranked within categories	Mean of median ranks for 20 age-SES subgroups	30
Guam	1962	Guamanian high-school seniors in Guam's largest high school; 144 respondents	Occupations ranked according to their "social status"	Rank order; (procedure by which derived unclear)	22
India (1)	1954	Male college students in Mysore, India, from four high-status castes. Results reported separately for each subgroup; 234 respondents in all	Occupations ranked in order of their prestige	Weighted average of median ranks over subgroups	25
India (2)	1960	Individuals from 5 districts in Mysore State and from neighboring Madras State. Results reported separately for each subgroup; 381 respondents in all	Occupations ranked in order of their prestige	Weighted average of median ranks over subgroups	25

Country	Year completed	Sample size and characteristics	Prestige rating procedure	Prestige measure used in this study*	No. of occupations rated
India (3)	1962	School children (N = 120), graduate students (N = 60), and illiterate village males (N = 30); 210 respondents in all	Occupations ranked "in the order in which you admire the occupation"	Rank order; (procedure by which derived unclear)	22
Indonesia	1961	Students from 6 Bandung, Java, high schools; 939 respondents	Occupations ranked "according to their prestige"	Rank order; (procedure by which derived unclear)	30
Ivory Coast	1963	Two hundred fifty-nine male students in 8 secondary schools preparing for the first part of the *Baccalaureat* examination (average age 20.3 years). The sample constituted 82 percent of all students at this level in the Ivory Coast	"Prestige" of occupations rated on 5-point scale	Mean score	25
Japan (1)	1952	Stratified probability sample of males age 20–69 in the six largest cities in Japan; 899 respondents	Occupations ranked according to "social status and prestige"	Mean rank	30
Japan (2)	1958	High school seniors in two Tokyo and two small-town (20,000 population) high schools; 536 respondents	"Prestige" of occupations rated on 5-point scale	Mean score	23
Netherlands	1952	Stratified national probability sample of adults; 500 respondents	Occupations ranked according to prestige	Mean rank	57
New Zealand	1952	Questionnaires mailed to residents of town of 4,000 (11 per cent return); interviews conducted with other small town residents, some students; 1,033 respondents in all	Occupations rated on 5-point scale according to "social standing," then ranked within groups	Median rank	30
Northern Rhodesia	1959	Male students at academic, trade, and teachers' training schools near Lusaka (median age 22.5 years); 653 respondents	Occupations rated on 5-point scale in terms of the "respect they have in the eyes of African people in towns"	Mean score	31
Norway	1955	Random sample of University of Oslo students: 145 respondents	Occupations ranked "in order of social prestige"	Rank order (procedure by which derived unclear)	14
Philippines	1954	Quota samples of residents of a Manila suburb and four rural communities; 606 respondents in all	Occupations ranked "in order of social standing"	Rank order, derived from mean rank	30
Poland	1958	Stratified quota sample of Warsaw residents; 763 respondents	"Social prestige" of occupations rated on 5-point scale	Mean score	29
Sweden	1958	Stratified national probability sample of approximately 1,700 divided into two subsamples, each rating half the titles	Occupations rated on 5-point scale in terms of desirability for one's son	Mean score	26
Turkey	1955	Students from rural, town, and city high school; 310 respondents	Occupations rated on 7-point scale in terms of the "honor or importance" accorded them	Mean score, multiplied by 14.2	63
U.S.S.R.	1950	Former Soviet citizens who were in displaced person camps in Germany or who had recently emigrated to the east coast of the United States; 2,146 respondents	Occupations rated on 5-point scale (0–4) according to their "general desirability"	Mean score, multiplied by 25	13
United States	1963	Stratified national quota sample of 651	Occupations rated on 5-point scale in terms of "your own personal opinion of the general social standing that such a job has"	Mean score, multiplied by 20	90

Sources: See footnote on pages 313 and 316.
* Where necessary, prestige measures used were inverted so that for all countries the higher the prestige of an occupation, the higher its score.

[1] High correlations between occupational-prestige ratings derived from raters in different occupational groups are reported for the United States and Denmark, respectively, by Albert J. Reiss, Jr., *op. cit.*, pp. 187–190, and Kaare Svalastoga, *op. cit.*, pp. 107–108. For the Philippines, a matrix of rank correlations between the ratings obtained from each of ten occupational groups contains no entry less than 0.9. See Edward A. Tiryakian, *op. cit.*, Table 4, p. 396. Some evidence suggesting subgroup variation in prestige ratings among adolescent Japanese boys living in different types of communities is provided in David M. Lewis and Archibald O. Haller, "Rural–Urban Differences in Pre-Industrial and Industrial Evaluations of Occupations by Japanese Adolescent Boys," *Rural Sociology*, 29 (September, 1964), pp. 324–329. There is also some indication in some of the studies utilized in this report that rural–urban differences in prestige ratings accorded to occupations are magnified in underdeveloped nations. However, neither this evidence nor that of Lewis and Haller is very impressive beside the detailed documentation found in Tiryakian's investigation.

[2] This claim is based largely upon unpublished comparisons between a plethora of American studies. Here, one example may suffice to illustrate the point. One investigator requested respondents to sort seventy occupations in the NORC list into groups of *similar* occupations. The respondent was then asked to order the groups of similar occupations he had formed into social levels. Nevertheless, a rank-order correlation of 0.97 was found between the scores derived from this study and those observed in the 1947 NORC-North-Hatt study. See John D. Campbell, "Subjective Aspects of Occupational Status," unpublished Ph.D. dissertation, Harvard University, 1952, Chapter II.

[3] For a discussion of this point see Reiss, *op. cit.*, pp. 47–48.

[4] A complete listing of the titles matched between each pair of countries for purposes of this study will be published elsewhere, together with a conversion of the scores used in each

---

footnotes continued from p. 313.

Gösta Carlsson, *Social Mobility and Class Structure* (Lund: C. W. K. Gleerup, 1958), pp. 145–155; for *Turkey*, George Helling, "Changing Attitudes Toward Occupational Status and Prestige in Turkey," unpublished paper, University of Omaha, n.d.; for *U.S.S.R.*, Peter H. Rossi and Alex Inkeles, "Multidimensional Ratings of Occupations," *Sociometry*, 20 (September, 1957), pp. 234–251; for the *United States*, Robert W. Hodge, Paul M. Siegel, and Peter H. Rossi, *op. cit.*

In addition to the studies utilized in this report, we are aware of or have received studies for Argentina, Ceylon, Costa Rica, Spain, and Yugoslavia. Also, we have uncovered additional studies for New Zealand, Poland, and Japan. These studies were, however, received too late for inclusion in this initial report; we will be grateful if readers inform us of any studies known to them which are not *explicitly* identified in this paper.

Our gratitude is heartily extended to Messrs. Philip Foster, Remi Clignet, and George Helling for making available to us their unpublished data for Ghana, Ivory Coast, and Turkey, respectively.

[2] For a discussion of the NORC rating procedure see Reiss, *op. cit.*, pp. 18–23.

[3] See, for example, Tuckman, *op. cit.*, p. 71.

[4] To illustrate the procedures, we may note that the Japanese study in the six largest cities (J_1) contained fifteen titles in common with the study of high school seniors (J_2). For these fifteen matching titles we find a correlation of 0.91 between the two studies. The regression of the scores obtained from the first study on those obtained in the second is given by $\hat{J}_1 = 7.67$ (J_2) -7.65. This regression equation was then used to convert the eight titles in the second study which did not have matching titles in the first study to the metric employed in the first study. Similar procedures were used to combine the two German and the three Indian studies, choosing as a benchmark the study deemed best with respect to the representativeness of the sample, the method of soliciting ratings, and the reported summary measure of the ratings.

---

duplicate very well those obtained from larger and more representative samples. Evidence bearing on this appreciable consensus among subgroups of raters comes, however, largely from industrialized countries and there may be greater disagreement among raters in less developed places.[1]

Secondly, within a single country there appears to be a very high order of agreement between prestige scores collected by different methods and/or summarized by different statistics.[2] Consequently, there is little reason to believe that international comparisons are invalidated by formal differences in rating tasks and procedures.

Finally, there is evidence that slight changes in the title of an occupation are unlikely to affect the rating of the stimulus in any appreciable way.[3] Thus, cross-national comparisons are not apt to be invalidated by matching occupational titles referring to slightly different jobs. This is especially true if some care is taken to avoid gross mismatches and to retain only the titles most nearly comparable.[4]

The preceding evidence indicates that no gross errors should arise from incomparability in the several studies to be compared, although care should be taken not to interpret any small differences in the rating of particular occupations. Until such time as carefully executed studies are conducted in a number of countries, utilizing occupational titles which are comparable across countries and which are at the same time more representative of all occupations in the labor forces of each country, we will have to deal with the fragile data presently at hand. The results reported in this paper, therefore, should be regarded as exploratory, rather than definitive, as a prolegomenon to carefully designed comparative studies in social stratification.

Similarities in occupational-prestige hierarchies

There are obviously many issues which may be taken up in the analysis of the relationships among the prestige hierarchies of the twenty-four nations for which we have found empirical occupational-prestige studies. As a first step we have chosen to compare each of the twenty-three foreign nations with the United States, reserving for later publication, analyses of the 253 other possible pairs of comparisons. There were two reasons for choosing this mode of analysis: first of all, the 1963 American study[5] provides the greatest amount of overlap with other studies because its coverage of occupational titles is greatest. Secondly, because the United States is one of the most industrially advanced nations, comparisons between it and other countries can be used to investigate the effects of industrialization on similarities in prestige hierarchies.

To compute indices of similarity between the occupational-prestige order of each foreign country and that of the United States, we matched wherever possible the occupations in each of the foreign studies with those included in the 1963 NORC study. In Table 2 we present the linear regression and associated correlations between the twenty-three sets of matched pairs of occupations, using the regression of the 1963 NORC scores on the prestige measures available for each foreign country.[1] These regressions were computed for all nonfarm titles, and, whenever possible, for blue-collar and white-collar titles separately.[2]

The coefficients of association presented in Table 2 are coefficients of determination ($= r^2$), a measure with the advantage of having specific interpretation as the proportion of the total variance which two variables share in common.

Comparisons are presented separately for blue-collar and white-collar occupations. These within-group correlations attenuate the range of variation between occupations and enable one to detect total correlations over all occupations which are spuriously high owing to the correlation of extremes. Also, it was considered instructive to examine patterns of intersocietal prestige correlations for subsets of occupations located in different sectors of the prestige hierarchy, and the blue- and white-collar distinction was one that could easily be made in each set of comparisons. Although it would be desirable to compute correlations over even more restricted occupational categories, the number of titles matching between the United States and other countries is typically too small to permit such an analysis. Because agricultural occupations are extremely difficult to match — the term farmer can mean anything from the operator of a mechanized farm like those of the American plains area to the tiller of a subsistence plot — the correlations shown in Table 2 include only nonfarm occupations.[3]

Inspecting first the coefficients of determination for all nonfarm occupations combined (in the second column of Table 2), we can observe an impressive amount of agreement between the occupational prestige hierarchy of the United States and those of twenty-three other countries. The average coefficient of determination is 0.83, not much different from the average of 0.88 observed between the United States and five other countries by Inkeles and Rossi.[4] Thus, the gross similarity between occupational-prestige hierarchies in the United States and elsewhere is not substantially altered by inclusion of less industrialized nations. These averages conceal, however, considerable variation from country to country observed in the present study. The coefficients of determination range from a low of 0.62 between the United States and Poland to a high of 0.95 between the United States and New Zealand, whereas the range observed in the earlier report of Inkeles and Rossi was only from 0.81 to 0.94, for the five associations involving comparisons with the United States.

The utility of considering white- and blue-collar occupations separately is amply seen by examination of the regression slopes and intercepts which are also shown in Table 2. For some countries, as for example, Canada, the regression slopes and intercepts are virtually identi-cal for blue-collar and white-collar occupations, as well as for all occupations combined. In these cases, the major gain to be derived from considering white- and blue-collar occupations separately is simply the reduction of the correlation between extremes as revealed in the

[1] Here we may comment on the use of *ranks* in linear regressions and correlations, an expedient utilized when continuous type measures of prestige were not available. In doing this, we did not re-rank the occupations in a study after deleting titles which did not have matching lines in the NORC-North-Hatt list. Thus, if the occupation ranked second did not have a matching title, the rank "2" does not appear in the data used in deriving the correlation with the United States. All regressions, whether involving ranked data or not, were inspected for linearity and no appreciable departures were observed when blue-collar and white-collar occupations were considered separately. Other investigators might well have preferred to rank the data independently for each comparison and compute Spearman rank order correlations between countries. However, to our way of thinking, such a procedure throws away too much information and, in any case, employing non-parametric procedures can just as easily lead one astray as the alternative employed here. There is one impressive piece of evidence, moreover, that the procedures used here do not in fact result in any gross errors. When the ninety occupations in the NORC-North-Hatt list are ranked from high to low, we find a product-moment correlation of 0.99 between these ranks and the NORC scores. Ranking occupations always amounts to making a monotonic transformation of some (real or hypothetical) continuous measure and it appears that such a transformation can change observed correlations but slightly. However, in subsequent reports, we will evaluate these procedures more fully, comparing parametric results with non-parametric ones and estimating product-moment correlations with rank-order ones.

[2] At least five matching white-collar or blue-collar titles were required before the correlation within these groups was computed separately.

[3] Although the organization of agriculture varies widely from country to country, a case could be made for including agricultural occupations on the ground that studying the effects of this variation on the prestige of agricultural occupations is one objective of comparative studies of occupational prestige. However, since the tasks of agriculturalists vary so widely from country to country, one can never be sure whether the relative ratings of agricultural titles across countries are the result of differential evaluation of similar occupational tasks or of common evaluation of different occupational tasks. We know, for example, that in the United States the prestige of "farm owner and operator," "tenant farmer," and "sharecropper" are quite different. (See Hodge, Siegel, and Rossi, *op. cit.*, Table 1, pp. 290–292.) Differential evaluation of a generic title like "farmer" in different countries could merely be a reflection of the prestige gradient of different kinds of farmers within the same country, since the typical "farmer" is not doing the same kind of work in different countries. These considerations apply, of course, to other titles as well; they strike us, however, as especially relevant in the case of farmers.

[4] Inkeles and Rossi, *op. cit.*, p. 332, Table 2. As indicated above, the correlations represented in that table were squared before their average was computed, in order to make them comparable to those reported in the present study. Even so, the Inkeles, Rossi coefficients are not precisely comparable to the present ones because the occupations on which they are based include farm titles which were excluded from our analysis.

foreign study to the metric employed in the NORC-North-Hatt study.

[5] No appreciable difference in the analysis is introduced by the use of the 1963 NORC study as compared to the 1947 NORC study since the correlation between the two studies = 0.99; correlations over subsets of the ninety occupations yield correlations of the same order of magnitude.

coefficients of determination. However, in other countries, such as Sweden, the regression slopes and intercepts are quite different within blue-collar and white-collar occupations. In these cases, the total linear-regression line demonstrably fails to capture the relationship between the prestige scores observed in the United States and those reported for the country in question: there are subsets of occupations whose ratings in the two nations are linked by different least-squares linear regressions. Thus, in those cases where the white-collar and blue-collar regression lines differ appreciably, the coefficient of determination may still be too high owing to the correlation of extremes, but may also be

there is somewhat less agreement over blue-collar than over white-collar occupations. The modified structural interpretation of prestige similarities discussed above is borne out in these findings. Major institutional complexes serving central societal needs which exist in all societies, and the common bureaucratic hierarchy imposed by the nation state, act to insure (despite vast differences in level of economic development) similarity between nations in the white-collar prestige hierarchy of doctors, scientists, teachers, public officials, and clerks, but these factors cannot be expected to induce a corresponding degree of prestige similarity at the blue-collar level. However, the fundamental conclusion that wide differ-

TABLE 2. *Correlation and Regression of 1963 NORC Scores on Prestige Scores of Matching Nonfarm Titles for Selected Foreign Countries*

CORRELATION AND REGRESSION WITH NORC SCORES OVER

	ALL NONFARM OCCUPATIONS				ALL WHITE-COLLAR OCCUPATIONS				ALL BLUE-COLLAR OCCUPATIONS				
			REGRESSION EQUATION				REGRESSION EQUATION				REGRESSION EQUATION		GNP per capita
Country	N*	r^2	Intercept	Slope	N*	r^2	Intercept	Slope	N*	r^2	Intercept	Slope	
Australia	16	.89	18.5	16.3	8	.89	20.4	15.6	8	.86	11.2	19.5	1,215
Belgian Congo	12	.63	50.0	1.1	—	—	—	—	9	.57	52.9	0.8	98
Brazil	19	.76	40.3	1.7	11	.62	48.2	1.3	8	.57	32.0	2.4	262
Canada	19	.93	46.8	1.8	9	.90	45.2	1.8	10	.85	46.3	1.9	1,667
Chile	12	.84	25.8	0.7	10	.63	15.4	0.8	—	—	—	—	180
Denmark	35	.86	35.1	13.9	22	.86	43.1	11.6	13	.65	20.7	21.7	913
Germany	22	.81	48.5	1.0	13	.85	49.0	1.1	9	.42	52.0	0.7	762
Ghana	13	.83	28.3	13.3	8	.79	31.3	12.6	5	.62	25.8	14.2	135
Great Britain	20	.83	41.4	1.7	11	.82	39.2	1.8	9	.54	41.6	1.7	998
Guam	16	.90	51.6	1.8	8	.59	57.1	1.8	8	.83	52.2	1.7	
India	25	.75	59.8	1.8	13	.78	44.9	2.0	12	.51	49.6	1.2	72
Indonesia	20	.81	56.1	1.2	14	.76	59.4	1.1	6	.68	45.4	4.0	127
Ivory Coast	15	.83	31.2	13.0	8	.76	47.2	9.2	7	.78	18.4	17.7	58
Japan	26	.84	39.2	2.0	16	.76	43.1	1.8	10	.72	26.6	3.4	240
Netherlands	28	.86	45.6	0.9	20	.90	52.3	0.7	8	.79	34.5	1.5	708
New Zealand	20	.95	39.9	1.9	11	.94	39.4	1.9	9	.92	37.8	2.2	1,249
N. Rhodesia	13	.86	24.9	12.3	—	—	—	—	9	.89	24.7	12.4	134
Norway	10	.90	63.8	2.1	7	.81	63.6	1.9	—	—	—	—	969
Philippines	20	.90	47.3	1.5	10	.95	54.7	1.6	10	.48	49.7	1.2	201
Poland	17	.62	31.5	12.9	15	.65	29.3	13.4	—	—	—	—	468
Sweden	14	.74	0.6	19.6	7	.81	13.1	17.2	7	.66	17.2	16.1	1,165
Turkey	28	.91	37.9	0.6	20	.84	47.4	0.5	8	.73	39.3	0.5	276
U.S.S.R.	7	.79	29.1	0.8	6	.75	51.1	0.5	—	—	—	—	682
Average	—	.83	—	—	—	.79	—	—	—	.69	—	—	—

Sources: See footnotes pp. 313 and 316.
* Number of matching titles.

too low since a single linear-regression equation does not adequately describe the relationship of the two sets of scores.

While the different regression lines over white-collar and blue-collar occupations indicate a *methodological* advantage gained from introducing the distinction, inspection of the coefficients of determination over white- and blue-collar occupations reveals some findings of *substantive* interest. First, one can ascertain that the average coefficient of determination over white-collar occupations is 0.79, only slightly less than that observed for all occupations combined. Second, the average coefficient of determination over blue-collar occupations falls to 0.69, a value which indicates that

ences in cultural traditions, institutional forms, and levels of living are insufficient to produce major inversions in the occupational-prestige hierarchy is not altered by these findings, since even the lower average within blue-collar titles is still sizeable.

Within the context of this gross similarity and with due respect for variations attributable to the utilization of different matching sets of occupations, there appear to be some variations from country to country in prestige similarity to the United States. Whether or not this variation is systematic is a question to which we now turn.

Let T_i = the *total* coefficient of determination over all nonfarm occupations of the prestige scores for the *i*th country with the 1963 NORC scores, W_i = the coefficient of determination over *white-collar* occupations of prestige scores for the *i*th country with the 1963 NORC score, and B_i = the similarly defined coefficient of determination over *blue-collar* occupations. The white-collar coefficients (W) bear a modest association ($r_{TW} = 0.52$) over countries with the total coefficients over all nonfarm occupations (T). Similarly, T and B have a modest positive association ($r_{TB} = 0.57$). In contrast, however, W and B are for all practical purposes orthogonal since the correlation between them (r_{WB}) is only 0.06. If the association between W and B should, in the light of better and more nearly comparable studies, remain near zero, then theories more complex than those posed thus far will have to be developed. For if similarities in prestige hierarchies at the blue-collar level are in fact uncorrelated with similarities in prestige hierarchies at the white-collar level, then any factor

The effects of industrialization

Although general societal processes such as economic development are unlikely to explain fully patterns of congruence between societies in prestige evaluations, it still is instructive to examine the pattern of association between gross national product per capita,[2] taken as a crude measure of the extent to which a nation has modernized its industrial structure, and the degree of similarity to the United States in occupational-prestige evaluations. Figure 2 presents the scatterplot of gross national product per capita (GNP) against our measure of prestige similarity to the United States for the twenty-two nations for which data are available. (Note that GNP is given in the rightmost column of Table 2 to facilitate any other comparisons the reader may wish to make.)

Of these twenty-two countries, eleven fall among the

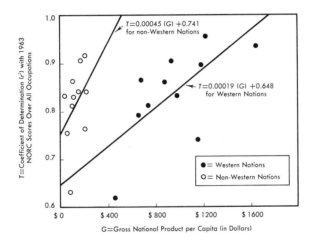

FIG. 2. Scattergram of coefficient of determination (r^2) with NORC scores over all occupations on gross national product per capita, for selected countries

highly correlated with observed similarity among manual occupations will be uncorrelated with observed similarity among nonmanual occupations. One needs under these conditions a theory which predicates convergence in the evaluation of white-collar occupations on different grounds than convergence in evaluation of blue-collar ones. It does not, however, seem worthwhile to proceed along these lines until the sets of blue-collar and white-collar occupational titles being compared are standardized from country to country. Indeed, such theoretical developments might also be postponed until comparisons can be based on a greater number of titles, enabling one to replace the relatively crude manual–nonmanual contrast with the examination of regressions within finer groups of occupations.[1] However, here we can attempt to show that variation in prestige similarity to the United States is systematic by exploring its connection to economic development.

nations generally regarded as "Western" in culture pattern: Australia, Canada, Denmark, Germany, Great

[1] Inkeles and Rossi, *op. cit.*, p. 335, attempted an analysis along these lines by classifying occupations according to major institutional contexts and showing the proportion of times there was disagreement between pairs of countries in the evaluation of the particular occupations falling in each context. The validity of such an approach depends on whether the assumption of linearity holds, an assumption fairly well fulfilled in most of the comparisons made by Inkeles and Rossi. In the present materials, the variation in the regression coefficients over white-collar and blue-collar occupations does not *prima facie* support the assumption of linearity.

[2] This measure was taken from Norton Ginsburg, *Atlas of Economic Development* (Chicago, Ill.: The University of Chicago Press, 1961), p. 18, Table 3. Data for Guam are not available. The value of gross-national product per capita employed for Poland in fact refers to net national product per capita. Inspection of the regression plots indicates that relationships discussed herein would be obscured somewhat if an adequate measure for Poland had been available.

Britain, the Netherlands, New Zealand, Norway, Poland, Sweden, and the U.S.S.R. These are indicated in the figure by solid points. The remaining countries — the Belgian Congo, Brazil, Chile, Ghana, India, Indonesia, the Ivory Coast, Japan, Northern Rhodesia, the Philippines, and Turkey — all retain important "non-Western," indigenous populations and cultures, although they are obviously differentiated in their degree of contact with and acceptance of Western European traditions. Non-Western nations are indicated in Figure 2 by open circles.

Lest the distinction between Western and non-Western countries seem arbitrary, it can be observed from the diagram that there is a radical disjunction in the level of GNP between the two groups of countries. No non-Western nation has a level of GNP higher than $300, while for Western countries GNP is never less than $450. The point biserial correlation of the Western–non-Western grouping with GNP is 0.87.

Despite their divergence in level of GNP, the two groups of countries do not differ significantly in their similarity to the United States in prestige evaluations. The mean coefficient of determination for Western countries is 0.84 while for non-Western countries it is 0.82. This finding is of considerable importance for our understanding of any relationship between industrialization and prestige similarity, as will be indicated below.

Inspection of the scatter-diagram suggests that the relationship between GNP and prestige similarity to the United States is rather different for Western and for non-Western countries. Looking only at the points for Western countries, GNP and prestige similarity appear to have a modest positive correlation: $r = 0.67$. Moreover, the regression of prestige similarity on GNP, given by $T_W = 0.00019(G) + 0.648$, implies that countries which are reasonably close to the United States in GNP will manifest almost perfect agreement with the United States in the prestige they accord occupations. (GNP for the U.S. is $2,343 while a prestige correlation of unity would be predicted from a GNP of $1,853. This is higher than the actual GNP of any country in the world at the present time, except the U.S.)[1] In contrast, inspection of the points for non-Western countries indicates that they tend to lie on a line more nearly perpendicular to the horizontal axis of the diagram. Relative to Western countries, they vary considerably more in prestige similarity than they do in GNP. Although a correlation exists between GNP and prestige similarity ($r = 0.44$), it is clear that most of these countries have prestige correlations with the United States that are much higher than could be expected from their level of GNP, taking the regression over Western countries as a standard.

Our confidence in the pattern exhibited in the figure under consideration is strengthened by the fact that inspection of comparable scatterplots (not shown here) utilizing white-collar and blue-collar prestige similarity

[1] Norton Ginsburg, *loc. cit.*

independently lead one to the same conclusion. (The reader will recall that T, B, and W are not highly inter-correlated, so in theory the three figures could show quite different clusters with respect to Western and non-Western countries.)

These findings suggest that it is impossible to argue, at least for newly developing countries, that similarities in levels of industrialization induced similarities in the hierarchical evaluation of occupations, since without any substantial progress toward industrialization, many "new nations" have achieved a structure of occupational evaluations quite similar to that observed in the United States.

Thus, level of economic development is apparently of little account in understanding the variation in prestige similarity to the United States among non-Western nations. Several alternative explanations come to mind, although their *ad hoc* character does not enhance their plausibility. For example, because the samples for the underdeveloped countries often consist mainly of students in Western-type schools (e.g., Turkey, Northern Rhodesia, Ghana, and the Ivory Coast), one may surmise that the correlations are high relative to those which would obtain had prestige scores been derived from a sample of the general population. Or, one may posit that Western patterns of occupational evaluation have been diffused through colonial bureaucracies and technical-aid programs. Following this interpretation, it is not unduly surprising, for example, that two African nations, Northern Rhodesia and the Belgian Congo, roughly similar in their level of economic development but differing greatly in the character of their colonial administrations, should manifest substantially different degrees of similarity to the U.S. in prestige evaluations. Northern Rhodesia, which enjoyed a reasonably enlightened colonial administration, exhibits a coefficient of determination of 0.86, while the coefficient of determination for the Belgian Congo is but 0.63.

Putting our doubts about the data aside for the moment, the findings do suggest that for newly developing nations there may be an important causal link in the direction opposite to that usually posited: structural similarities may in part be the product of similarities in occupational evaluation. Development hinges in part upon the recruitment and training of persons for the skilled, clerical, managerial, and professional positions necessary to support an industrial economy. Thus, acquisition of a "modern" system of occupational evaluation would seem to be a necessary precondition to rapid industrialization, insofar as such an evaluation of occupations insures that resources and personnel in sufficient numbers and of sufficient quality are allocated to those occupational positions most crucial to the industrial development of a nation. In one important regard, then, adoption of an occupational-prestige hierarchy similar to that of industrial nations may be a prerequisite for development, notwithstanding the fact that increased development may in turn induce further similarities in occupational prestige evaluations.

One could well argue that for Western countries the latter process is the primary one operating at present. In contrast to the non-Western countries, most Western nations are not currently undergoing radical social change. Increases in gross national product are largely the result of secular trends toward greater concentration of the labor force in the industrial sector which produce concomitant changes in occupational requirements. Thus, it is not surprising that for these countries differences in GNP should quite accurately reflect differences in the details of occupational structure which give rise to the differential evaluation of occupations.

Summary and conclusions

Commenting on the cross-national prestige comparisons undertaken by Inkeles and Rossi, James S. Coleman recently has stated that the observed correlations "show the striking uniformity of occupational prestige from country to country," and that as such they "constitute a regularity to be explained."[1] It is our hope that this essay has contributed something toward the understanding of the gross similarity of prestige evaluations of occupations from country to country, by reference to the essential structural similarity shared by all nations of any degree of complexity.

Moreover, we hope we have clearly demonstrated that while there is gross similarity in prestige structures from country to country, it is not perfect and shows more variation than observed between the United States and the five other nations studied by Inkeles and Rossi. Invoking even so gross a distinction as the manual–nonmanual dichotomy reveals divergences between national prestige structures which are concealed by the total correlation over all occupations. The evidence mustered above not only points to dissimilarities from country to country in occupational-prestige structures, but also suggests that this variation is intertwined with economic development in a way which is not fully captured by a simple "structuralist" or a simple "culturalist" expectation of prestige differences. We find in our data a suggestion that occupational evaluations of the appropriate kind may well lead to economic expansion, providing a necessary though not sufficient condition for development rather than being a simple consequence of it. Thus the data suggest reconsideration of existing formulations of the causal links between patterns of occupational evaluation and other aspects of occupational structure.

It should be emphasized that the above comments are to be treated as *plausible speculations* about *possible* relationships between occupational prestige and economic development which are at best *not inconsistent* with the data at hand. It is clear that these relationships are extraordinarily complex, and not easy to unravel considering the paucity of adequate data.[2]

Whatever modifications of extant empirical generalizations and theoretical formulations seem required by the findings presented above, the major contribution of this paper must be the impetus it gives toward collection of a set of truly comparable national prestige scores. The conclusions of this paper must be tentative ones, but we can now support both the expectation of gross similarities in prestige structures around the world and the expectation that such dissimilarities as can be observed may prove systematically related to patterns of economic development perhaps intertwined with diffusion through colonial contacts and the path toward modernization. Precision about the exact degree of these associations requires detailed, *comparable* investigations in several countries.

[1] James S. Coleman, *Introduction to Mathematical Sociology* (New York: The Free Press, 1964), p. 27.

[3] We have explored the data reported in this paper with a variety of multiple regressions between GNP per capita, a measure of urbanization, and the percentage of the labor force engaged in agriculture. These results, while consistent with the discussion herein, lend an air of precision which is wholly unjustified by the quality of the data, and thus are not reported.

Occupational Prestige in the United States: 1925–1963[1]

Robert W. Hodge, Paul M. Siegel, and Peter H. Rossi

THE RESEARCH reported in this paper represents an attempt to add historical depth to the study of the prestige of occupations in the United States. It reports mainly on a replication conducted in 1963 of the National Opinion Research Center's well-known 1947 study of the prestige positions accorded to ninety occupations by a national sample of the American adult population.[2] We also deal with several fragmentary earlier studies which together with the two main NORC studies provide a time series of sorts going back to 1925. Since the two NORC studies were not replications of the earlier ones, we shall dwell mainly on change and stability in the prestige of occupations during the period 1947 to 1963.

The prestige hierarchy of occupations is perhaps the best studied aspect of the stratification systems of modern societies. Extensive empirical studies have been undertaken in a variety of nations, socialist and capitalist, developed and underdeveloped. Intensive analyses have been undertaken of results of particular studies searching for the existence of disparate prestige hierarchies held by subgroups within nations.[3] Despite rather extensive searches conducted by a variety of techniques, it appears that occupational prestige hierarchies are similar from country to country and from subgroup to subgroup within a country. This stability reflects the fundamental, but gross similarities among the occupational systems of modern nations. Furthermore, knowledge about occupations and relatively strong consensus on the relative positions of occupations are widely diffused throughout the populations involved.

The consensus within and among populations on the prestige positions of occupations leads one to expect that there will be considerable stability over time in the positions of particular occupations. Industrialization has proceeded to different points in the several countries whose prestige hierarchies have been studied without seriously affecting the relative positions of occupations in the countries involved. Cross-sectional comparisons between countries at different stages of industrial evolution suggest that it would be erroneous to expect any considerable change in the *prestige* structure of a single country over time, even though that country might experience appreciable changes in *occupational* structure. Within one country we can only expect to observe changes over time as large as the differences we have previously observed between two nations at different stages of economic development.

On the other hand, there are cogent reasons for expecting that changes in occupational structure will be reflected, at least ultimately, in corresponding changes in the prestige positions of occupations. The prestige position of an occupation is apparently a characteristic of that occupation, generated by the way in which it is articulated into the division of labor, by the amount of power and influence implied in the activities of the occupation, by the characteristics of incumbents, and by the amount of resources society places at the disposal of incumbents. (Other factors are undoubtedly at work but these are the most obvious and the most massively observable.) Hence as occupations shift in these respects over time, corresponding adjustive shifts in prestige positions can be anticipated.

[1] A shortened version of this paper appeared under the same title in the *American Journal of Sociology*, 70 (November, 1964), pp. 286–302.

[2] The replication was undertaken as the first stage of a larger project supported by National Science Foundation Grant (NSF-#GS85, "Occupations and Social Stratification") aimed at providing definitive prestige scores for a more representative sample of occupations and at uncovering some of the characteristics of occupations that generate their prestige scores. The replication was undertaken as the first step in the research program in order to determine whether appreciable shifts had occurred in prestige scores in the time period 1947–1963 so that the effects of improvements in technical procedures could be distinguished from effects of historical changes in any comparisons that would be undertaken between the 1947 study and the more definitive researches presently underway.

[3] See, for example, Kaare Svalastoga, *Prestige, Class and Mobility*, Copenhagen: Gyldendal, 1959, pp. 43–131; C. A. Moser and J. R. Hall, "The Social Grading of Occupations," in D. V. Glass, ed., *Social Mobility in Britain*, London: Routledge and Kegan Paul Ltd., 1954, pp. 29–50; and Albert J. Reiss, Jr., and others, *Occupations and Social Status*, N.Y.: The Free Press of Glencoe, 1961. The last-mentioned volume contains the major analyses of the 1947 North-Hatt-NORC study of occupational prestige.

Published here for the first time by permission of the authors.

The occupational structure and labor force of the United States have undergone considerable change since 1947. The long-term trend in the growth of professional and scientific occupations persisted and was even accelerated during this period. Governmental and popular concern over the numbers and quality of our professional and technical manpower was expressed in a great expansion of our universities as well as in more attention being given lower levels of schooling. The proportion of the labor force devoted to agricultural pursuits declined along with the unskilled and heavy labor components. This was also the period during which automation continued to expand, raising a serious question as to whether the American labor force could absorb both workers freed from jobs eliminated by technological progress and the large cohorts of postwar births now beginning to enter the labor force. Mention must be made of the stepped-up drive for equality on the part of Negroes, although we cannot tarry here to examine it. The question at issue is whether changes in the occupational structure have been reflected in shifts in the prestige of occupations between the two points in time.

On the basis of our empirical knowledge concerning the stability under a variety of conditions of the hierarchy of occupational prestige, we can support an expectation that there will be relatively few changes in the positions of occupations as we proceed from the earlier 1947 to the later 1963 studies. On the basis of what seems to be a reasonable model of how these prestige positions have been generated, we expect somewhat more in the way of changes. Neither point of view produces very precise expectations for we need to know what is an acceptable level of stability (or change) either to conform with or negate each expectation.

Methods and procedures

A small scale replication of the 1947 study was undertaken in the spring of 1963. In order properly to compare the replication with the original, free of confounding factors, it was necessary to replicate the study using procedures as identical as possible with those of the earlier study. The same question was used to elicit ratings and the ninety job titles were rated in the same orders (using rotated blocks) in the same way. Most of the items (with the exception of those which were historically obsolete) were repeated. Even the sample was selected according to the outmoded quota sampling methods employed in 1947. The few new items included in the restudy were placed in the questionnaire after the occupational ratings.

Because of the stability of prestige positions of occupations from subgroup to subgroup in the 1947 study, it was felt that a relatively small national sample would be sufficient for the replication. In all a total of 651 interviews were collected according to quota

sampling methods from a national sample of adults.[1]

As in the 1947 study, occupational ratings were elicited by asking respondents to judge an occupation as having *excellent, good, average, somewhat below average,* or *poor* standing (along with a "don't know" option) in response to the item: "For each job mentioned, please pick out the statement that best gives *your own personal opinion* of the *general standing* that such a job has."

One indicator of prestige position is the proportion of respondents (among those rating an occupation) giving either an "excellent" or a "good" response. Another measure which can be derived from a matrix of ratings by occupation requires weighting the various responses with arbitrary numerical values: We can assign an excellent rating a numerical value of 100, a good rating the value of 80, an average rating the value of 60, a somewhat below average rating the value 40, and a poor rating the value 20. Calculating the numerical average of these arbitrarily assigned values over all respondents rating the occupation yields the NORC prestige score. This latter measure has received rather widespread use despite arbitrariness in the numerical weights assigned to the five possible ratings.[2]

The distribution of ratings

The ratings and derived scores for each of the ninety occupations obtained in 1947 and in 1963 are shown in Table 1. We present the findings in such detail because of their intrinsic interest. However, the bulk of the analysis contained in this paper is more concerned with characteristics of the distributions of these ratings than with the positions of particular occupations.

As shown in Table 2, in both 1947 and 1963, the poorly educated were rather more charitable in their granting of "excellent" or "good" ratings than the

[1] Justification for our claim that 651 cases suffice to give a reliable intertemporal comparison can be derived from an examination of sampling error estimates based on the assumption of a random sample. Such estimates indicate that confidence limits at the .10 level for p = .50 and N = 651 are .47 and .53. For N = 60 (smaller than any subgroup used in this paper) the corresponding error estimates are .39 and .61. Thus for even relatively small subgroups any dramatic changes are likely to be detected, although it must be clearly understood that error estimates for quota sampling are only approximated by assuming that formulas for random samples apply.

[2] The reader will observe that the correlation between the two ways of ordering occupations need not be unity. Of the two measures mentioned above, the proportion of excellent or good ratings enjoys some advantages over the NORC prestige scores. Its range and variance are somewhat larger than the NORC prestige scores which tend to obscure differences between occupations at the extremes of the prestige hierarchy. However, the two measures are, in fact, highly intercorrelated (r = .98) and the advantages of the proportion excellent or good ratings over the NORC prestige scores are largely statistical in nature. Throughout this paper, the bulk of our analysis employs the NORC prestige scores — a decision based largely on the wide use and popularity of the prestige scores derived from the original 1947 study.

TABLE I. *Distributions of Prestige Ratings, United States, 1947 and 1963*

Occupation	MARCH, 1947								JUNE, 1963							
	Excellent[a] %	Good %	Average %	Below avg. %	Poor %	Don't know[b] %	NORC score	Rank	Excellent[c] %	Good %	Average %	Below avg. %	Poor %	Don't know[d] %	NORC score	Rank
U.S. Supreme Ct. Justice	83	15	2	*	*	3	96	1	77	18	4	1	1	1	94	1
Physician	67	30	3	*	*	1	93	2.5	71	25	4	*	*	1	93	2
Nuclear physicist	48	39	11	1	1	51	86	18	70	23	5	1	1	10	92	3.5
Scientist	53	38	8	1	*	7	89	8	68	27	5	*	*	2	92	3.5
Government scientist	51	41	7	1	*	6	88	10.5	64	30	5	*	1	2	91	5.5
State governor	71	25	4	*	*	1	93	2.5	64	30	5	*	1	1	91	5.5
Cabinet member in the Federal Government	66	28	5	1	*	6	92	4.5	61	32	6	1	1	2	90	8
College professor	53	40	7	*	*	1	89	8	59	35	5	*	*	1	90	8
U.S. Representative in Congress	57	35	6	1	1	4	89	8	58	33	6	2	*	2	90	8
Chemist	42	48	9	1	*	7	86	18	54	38	8	*	*	3	89	11
Lawyer	44	45	9	1	1	1	86	18	53	38	8	*	*	*	89	11
Diplomat in the U.S. Foreign Service	70	24	4	1	1	9	92	4.5	57	34	7	1	1	3	89	11
Dentist	42	48	9	1	*	*	86	18	47	47	6	*	*	*	88	14
Architect	42	48	9	1	*	6	86	18	47	45	6	*	*	2	88	14
County judge	47	43	9	1	*	1	87	13	50	40	8	1	*	1	88	14
Psychologist	38	49	12	1	*	15	85	22	49	41	8	1	*	6	87	17.5
Minister	52	35	11	1	1	1	87	13	53	33	13	1	1	1	87	17.5
Member of the board of directors of a large corporation	42	47	10	1	*	5	86	18	42	51	6	1	*	1	87	17.5
Mayor of a large city	57	36	6	1	*	1	90	6	46	44	9	1	1	*	87	17.5
Priest	51	34	11	2	2	6	86	18	52	33	12	2	1	6	86	21.5
Head of a dept. in a state government	47	44	8	*	1	3	87	13	44	48	6	1	1	1	86	21.5
Civil engineer	33	55	11	1	*	5	84	23	40	52	8	*	*	2	86	21.5
Airline pilot	35	48	15	1	1	3	83	24.5	41	48	11	1	*	1	86	21.5
Banker	49	43	8	*	*	1	88	10.5	39	51	10	1	*	*	85	24.5
Biologist	29	51	18	1	1	16	81	29	38	50	11	*	*	6	85	24.5
Sociologist	31	51	16	1	1	23	82	26.5	35	48	15	1	1	10	83	26
Instructor in public schools	28	45	24	2	1	1	79	34	30	53	16	1	*	*	82	27.5
Captain in the regular army	28	49	19	2	2	2	80	31.5	28	55	16	1	*	1	82	27.5
Accountant for a large business	25	57	17	1	*	3	81	29	27	55	17	1	*	*	81	29.5
Public school teacher	26	45	24	3	2	*	78	36	31	46	22	1	*	*	81	29.5
Owner of a factory that employs about 100 people	30	51	17	1	1	2	82	26.5	28	49	19	2	1	1	80	31.5
Building contractor	21	55	23	1	*	1	79	34	22	56	20	1	*	*	80	31.5
Artist who paints pictures that are exhibited in galleries	40	40	15	3	2	6	83	24.5	28	45	20	5	2	4	78	34.5
Musician in a symphony orchestra	31	46	19	3	1	5	81	29	25	45	25	3	1	3	78	34.5
Author of novels	32	44	19	3	2	9	80	31.5	26	46	22	4	2	5	78	34.5
Economist	25	48	24	2	1	22	79	34	20	53	24	2	1	12	78	34.5
Official of an international labor union	26	42	20	5	7	11	75	40.5	21	53	18	5	3	5	77	37
Railroad engineer	22	45	30	3	*	1	77	37.5	19	47	30	3	1	1	76	39
Electrician	15	38	43	4	*	1	73	45	18	45	34	2	*	*	76	39
County agricultural agent	17	53	28	2	*	5	77	37.5	13	54	30	2	1	4	76	39
Owner-operator of a printing shop	13	48	36	3	*	2	74	42.5	13	51	34	2	*	2	75	41.5
Trained machinist	14	43	38	5	*	2	73	45	15	50	32	4	*	*	75	41.5
Farm owner and operator	19	46	31	3	1	1	76	39	16	45	33	5	*	1	74	44
Undertaker	14	43	36	5	2	2	72	47	16	46	33	3	2	3	74	44
Welfare worker for a city government	16	43	35	4	2	4	73	45	17	44	32	5	2	2	74	44
Newspaper columnist	13	51	32	3	1	5	74	42.5	10	49	38	3	1	1	73	46
Policeman	11	30	46	11	2	1	67	55	16	38	37	6	2	*	72	47
Reporter on a daily newspaper	9	43	43	4	1	2	71	48	7	45	44	3	1	1	71	48
Radio announcer	17	45	35	3	*	2	75	40.5	9	42	44	5	1	1	70	49.5
Bookkeeper	8	31	55	6	*	1	68	51.5	9	40	45	5	1	*	70	49.5
Tenant farmer — one who owns livestock and machinery and manages the farm	10	37	40	11	2	1	68	51.5	11	37	42	8	3	1	69	51.5
Insurance agent	7	34	53	4	2	2	68	51.5	6	40	47	5	2	*	69	51.5
Carpenter	5	28	56	10	1	*	65	58	7	36	49	8	1	*	68	53
Manager of a small store in a city	5	40	50	4	1	1	69	49	3	40	48	7	2	*	67	54.5
A local official of a labor union	7	29	41	14	9	11	62	62	8	36	42	9	5	4	67	54.5

Occupation	MARCH, 1947								JUNE, 1963							
	Excellent[a] %	Good %	Average %	Below avg. %	Poor %	Don't know[b] %	NORC score	Rank	Excellent[c] %	Good %	Average %	Below avg. %	Poor %	Don't know[d] %	NORC score	Rank
Mail carrier	8	26	54	10	2	*	66	57	7	29	53	10	1	*	66	57
Railroad conductor	8	30	52	9	1	1	67	55	6	33	48	10	3	*	66	57
Traveling salesman for a wholesale concern	6	35	53	5	1	2	68	51.5	4	33	54	7	3	2	66	57
Plumber	5	24	55	14	2	1	63	59.5	6	29	54	9	2	*	65	59
Automobile repairman	5	21	58	14	2	*	63	59.5	5	25	56	12	2	*	64	60
Playground director	7	33	48	10	2	4	67	55	6	29	46	15	4	3	63	62.5
Barber	3	17	56	20	4	1	59	66	4	25	56	13	2	1	63	62.5
Machine operator in a factory	4	20	53	20	3	2	60	64.5	6	24	51	15	4	1	63	62.5
Owner-operator of a lunch stand	4	24	55	14	3	1	62	62	4	25	57	11	3	1	63	62.5
Corporal in the regular army	5	21	48	20	6	3	60	64.5	6	25	47	15	6	2	62	65.5
Garage mechanic	4	21	57	17	1	*	62	62	4	22	56	15	3	*	62	65.5
Truck driver	2	11	49	29	9	*	54	71	3	18	54	19	5	*	59	67
Fisherman who owns his own boat	3	20	48	21	8	7	58	68	3	19	51	19	8	4	58	68
Clerk in a store	2	14	61	20	3	*	58	68	1	14	56	22	6	*	56	70
Milk route man	2	10	52	29	7	1	54	71	3	12	55	23	7	1	56	70
Streetcar motorman	3	16	55	21	5	2	58	68	3	16	46	27	8	2	56	70
Lumberjack	2	11	48	29	10	8	53	73	2	16	46	29	7	3	55	72.5
Restaurant cook	3	13	44	29	11	1	54	71	4	15	44	26	11	*	55	72.5
Singer in a nightclub	3	13	43	23	18	6	52	74.5	3	16	43	24	14	3	54	74
Filling station attendant	1	9	48	34	8	1	52	74.5	2	11	41	34	11	*	51	75
Dockworker	2	7	34	37	20	8	47	81.5	2	9	43	33	14	3	50	77.5
Railroad section hand	2	9	35	33	21	3	48	79.5	3	10	39	29	18	2	50	77.5
Night watchman	3	8	33	35	21	1	47	81.5	3	10	39	32	17	1	50	77.5
Coal miner	4	11	33	31	21	2	49	77.5	3	13	34	31	19	2	50	77.5
Restaurant waiter	2	8	37	36	17	1	48	79.5	2	8	42	32	16	*	49	80.5
Taxi driver	2	8	38	35	17	1	49	77.5	2	8	39	31	18	1	49	80.5
Farm hand	3	12	35	31	19	1	50	76	3	12	31	32	22	*	48	83
Janitor	1	7	30	37	25	1	44	85.5	1	9	35	35	19	1	48	83
Bartender	1	6	32	32	29	4	44	85.5	1	7	42	28	21	2	48	83
Clothes presser in a laundry	2	6	35	36	21	2	46	83	2	7	31	38	22	1	45	85
Soda fountain clerk	1	5	34	40	20	2	45	84	*	5	30	44	20	1	44	86
Share-cropper — one who owns no livestock or equipment and does not manage farm	1	6	24	28	41	3	40	87	1	8	26	28	37	2	42	87
Garbage collector	1	4	16	26	53	2	35	88	2	5	21	32	41	1	39	88
Street sweeper	1	3	14	29	53	1	34	89	1	4	17	31	46	1	36	89
Shoe shiner	1	2	13	28	56	2	33	90	*	3	15	30	51	2	34	90
AVERAGE	22%	31%	30%	11%	7%	4%	70		22%	32%	29%	11%	6%	2%	71	

* Less than one-half on one percent.
[a] Bases for the 1947 occupational ratings are 2,920 less "don't know" and not answered for each occupational title.
[b] Base is 2,920 in all cases.
[c] Bases for the 1963 occupational ratings are 651 less "don't know" and not answered for each occupational title.
[d] Base is 651 in all cases.

Source of 1947 distributions: Albert J. Reiss, Jr., and others, *Occupations and Social Status* (New York: Free Press of Glencoe, 1961), Table ii–9.

better educated. It can also be seen that the spread between the three educational groups was slightly reduced between the two time periods, indicative of slightly greater consensus between educational groups.

Table 2, which gives the distribution of ratings by educational attainment of respondents, shows that for each of the three educational groups, slightly more excellent or good ratings were given in 1963 than in 1947.[1] The reader will also note that in both time periods education was inversely — albeit slightly — related to the proportion of excellent or good ratings given.

What is the meaning of the gross upward shift in the proportion of excellent or good ratings? One interpretation is that in the aggregate the ninety occupations had more prestige in 1963 than in 1947. Although this may well be the case in view of the large number of professional occupations included in the list, *there is no*

conceivable way of answering the question with the present data. If prestige is regarded as a "commodity" which behaves like the payoff in a "zero-sum" game, then, to be sure, what one set of occupations gains another must lose. Perhaps the NORC occupations receive more excellent or good ratings in 1963 than in 1947 because there is all told a greater *amount* of prestige in the system. If the latter is the case, the ninety NORC occupations may get more excellent or good ratings and, at the same time, a smaller share of all prestige.[2]

[1] The educational controls were used to take into account changes in "socioeconomic" composition over the period 1947 to 1963.

[2] This point is perhaps more clearly illustrated with a more familiar commodity: money income in dollars. It is fairly easy to see how a group could receive a smaller proportion of all income over time, but at the same time have greater income because there is more income to spread between groups.

The above remarks are perhaps sufficient to alert the reader to the ambiguities that characterize the study of occupational prestige. Indeterminacies encountered in the study of a set of occupations are, of course, duplicated when the focus is upon a single occupation. It is for this reason that our focus is largely on the ordering of ninety NORC occupations in two time periods and not upon changes in the prestige of particular occupations. All indications of changes in occupational prestige revealed here are of necessity relative to the set of ninety occupations under consideration. These occupations exhaust our universe and changes in the NORC prestige scores are *assumed* to indicate restructuring of the relative prestige of the occupations under consideration.[1]

occupations, as in Table 3, we can see that the regression lines within the three groups are quite similar.[3]

The very slight effect of grouping occupations is shown again in Figure 1, where the three within group regression lines are plotted over the range of the 1947 NORC scores contained within each group. The three lines nearly coincide over the observed range of the NORC scores and do not appreciably depart from the line Y = X (where the 1963 and 1947 scores are equal).

The gross similarity between the 1947 and 1963 NORC scores tends to overshadow some interesting small changes which are revealed by the data. Thus, in Figure 1 the regression line for blue-collar occupations lies above (and, in fact, parallels) the line Y = X. Con-

TABLE 2. *Distribution of Prestige Ratings and Mean NORC Prestige Score by Educational Attainment of Respondents Aged 20 and over, 1947 and 1963*

Education	PER CENT OF RATINGS, EXCLUDING DK'S,[a] WHICH WERE:						Per cent DK of all ratings[a]	Mean NORC score[b]	Number of respondents[c]
	Excellent	Good	Average	Below average	Poor	Total			
1963									
Attended college	22%	30%	29%	13%	6%	100%	1%	70	157
Attended high school	22	33	30	10	5	100	1	71	272
Eighth grade or less	23	34	28	8	7	100	4	71	144
1947									
Attended college	19%	28%	29%	15%	9%	100%	1%	67	537
Attended high school	22	31	30	11	6	100	3	70	1,125
Eighth grade or less	23	33	29	10	6	101	8	71	861

[a] DK = Don't know.
[b] Computed by taking the average of the scores for each occupation by each education group. The figures that can be derived from the distributions of all ratings will be slightly different owing to occupational variation in the proportion "Don't know."
[c] The number of ratings, including "dont' know's" is just ninety (the number of occupations rated) times the number of respondents. The number of respondents differs from the total sample size in the two periods largely because those under age twenty are excluded, the number not reporting on educational attainment being negligible.

Congruities in occupational prestige: 1947–1963

The major result of the 1963 restudy is dramatically summarized in the product-moment correlation coefficient of .99 between the scores in 1947 and the scores in 1963. The linear regression of the 1963 on the 1947 scores is given by

$$\hat{Y} = .97X + 2.98,$$

a result that indicates there is very little regression toward the mean and a slight gross upward shift in scores.[2]

The high overall correlation in the total set of occupations is matched by high correlations within subsets of occupations. If we group occupations into professional occupations, other nonmanual occupations and manual

sequently, one infers that all blue-collar occupations had slightly higher scores in 1963. For professionals and other white-collar workers, however, the picture is more complex, since the within group regression lines for these two broad groupings cross the line Y = X.

TABLE 3. *Regressions within Subsets of Occupations*

Occupation group	Regression coefficient	Regression constant	Correlation
Total, all occupations (n = 90)	.97	2.98	.99
Professional, including one title duplicated for validation purposes (n = 33)	1.05	−3.61	.96
Other nonmanual occupations (n = 21)	.92	5.85	.98
All manual occupations, including one craft occupation duplicated for validation purposes and two military titles (n = 32)	1.00	2.00	.99
Farm occupations (n = 4); not computed	. . .	. . .	. . .

[1] It should be noted that mean shifts of the kind noted above do not affect *correlation* techniques, but alter only the constant associated with the regression slope.

[2] When the NORC scores are ranked, we find a Spearman rank order correlation of .98 between the 1947 and 1963 ranks.

[3] The hypothesis that a common regression line fits all groups may be rejected at the .07 level of confidence, as indicated by the F-ratio resulting from an analysis of covariance.

Consequently, in the case of professionals, those particular occupations with the highest prestige scores in 1947 (largely scientific and free professional occupations) slightly increased their scores, whereas those professional occupations with relatively low prestige in 1947 (marginal professional occupations such as "singer in a nightclub") receive somewhat lower scores. Among "other white-collar occupations" the situation is reversed. That is, from the within group regression line we see that the other white-collar occupations with highest prestige in 1947 (largely managerial and political occupations) tended on the average to decline slightly, whereas lower white-collar occupations slightly increased their prestige.[1]

One other point is brought out sharply by Figure 1

similarity between the structure of the 1947 and the 1963 NORC scores. While we shall subsequently document a number of systematic shifts in the prestige of specific occupational groups, it is abundantly clear that these shifts were small and did not produce any substantial reordering of the relative prestige of the ninety occupations under consideration.

There are several good reasons for this observed stability. First, the educational requirements, monetary rewards, and even the nebulous "functional importance" of an occupation are not subject to rapid change in an industrial society.[3] Second, any dramatic shifts in the prestige structure of occupations would upset the dependency that is presumed to hold between the social evaluation of a job, its educational prerequisites, its

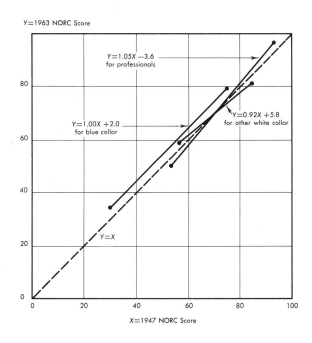

FIG. 1. Regressions of 1963 NORC score on 1947 NORC score
within occupational groups

and deserves mention before passing to other matters. Since the within occupational group regression lines are plotted only for the range of 1947 scores observed for each group, one can easily see the appreciable overlap in scores between professional, other white-collar, and blue-collar occupations. Although these divisions are often employed by social scientists as though they represented fundamental class barriers,[2] Figure 1 makes clear that no such barrier can be detected on the basis of occupational prestige. The cleavage between white-collar, blue-collar, and farm occupations — if it exists at all — is based not so much upon matters of societal evaluation as perhaps upon the character of dress and work in the three groups.

All in all the preceding results indicate a striking

[1] There is a slight increase in the ability of the within group regression lines to predict the direction of changes in scores between 1947 and 1963, as compared with the regression line for the total set. Correct predictions about the directions of change can be made by the overall regression in 60.5 percent of the cases and by the within group regression lines in 62.8 percent of them, an increase of efficiency of 5.9 per cent.

[2] This is, for example, the major distinction employed in a recent comparative study of occupational mobility. See Seymour Martin Lipset and Reinhard Bendix, *Social Mobility in Industrial Society*, Berkeley: University of California Press, 1959.

[3] For a discussion of this point see Otis Dudley Duncan, "Properties and Characteristics of the Socio-economic Index," in Albert J. Reiss, Jr., and others, *op. cit.*, pp. 152–153. A correlation of .94 was found between an aggregate measure of the income of an occupation in 1940 and a similar indicator in 1950; a correlation of .97 was found between the proportion of high school graduates in an occupation in 1940 and the same measure in 1950.

rewards, and its importance to society. Finally, instabilities would further ambiguities or status inconsistencies if the prestige structure were subject to marked and rapid change. Indeed, the meaning of achievement, career, seniority, and occupational mobility would be fundamentally altered if occupational prestige was subject to large-scale changes. No small amount of intragenerational mobility between prestige classes would, for example, be induced solely by the changing structure of occupational prestige *even though individuals did not change their occupations over time.*

Knowledge about occupations and occupational ratings

Occupations vary in their visibility to wide segments of the members of a society. To capture the extent to which such knowledge is distributed throughout the American population, one of the options on the NORC rating scales was "I don't know where to place that one." "Don't know" responses of this sort may indicate ignorance about an occupation and/or ambivalence about its location in the hierarchy of prestige. Given the pattern of heavier proportions of "don't know" responses for the more esoteric occupations (see Table 1) it would appear that such responses indicate primarily lack of knowledge rather than ambivalence.

Knowledge about occupations has increased markedly over the period 1947 to 1963. The correlation between proportions "don't know" for the two periods is .85, with the linear regression of 1963 proportions on 1947 proportions represented by

$$\hat{Y} = .29X + 0.62.$$

The "don't know" percentages were considerably less in 1963 as compared with 1947, and for only two occupations did the percentages increase during the period.

Since the correlation between percentage "don't know" for the two periods was very high, occupations receiving high proportions of "don't knows" in 1947 also received high proportions in 1963, even though the average proportion "don't know" for the entire group of occupations dropped.

Inspection of the scattergram of the 1963 and 1947 percentages "don't know" for the ninety occupations reveals the results reported above are strongly affected by the inclusion of "nuclear physicist" which elicited a very large proportion of "don't know" responses in 1947. Omitting "nuclear physicist," the regression of the 1963 percentage "don't know" on the 1947 percentage "don't know" over the remaining 89 occupations becomes $\hat{Y} = .44X + 0.26$ and r increases to .91. While these results lead to much the same interpretation as those reported above, they do call attention to the remarkable change in knowledge about the prestige rating of "nuclear physicist." In 1947, 51 percent of all respondents did not know where to place "nuclear physicist," but by 1963 this figure had dropped to 10 percent.

Insights into the quality of information about occupation held by respondents can be gained from responses to a supplementary question included in both the 1963 and 1947 studies. Respondents were asked, "A good many people don't know exactly what a *nuclear physicist* does, but what is your *general* idea of what he does?" In 1947 only 3 percent of all respondents supplied a "correct" answer by indicating that a nuclear physicist "investigates the properties of the nucleus of the atom, breaks down nuclear or atomic energy, studies the innermost part of the atom, works on nuclear fission" or some similar description of the subject matter of nuclear physics. In 1963, only 2 percent of respondents provided a correct answer of the kind indicated above. In response to this item in 1947, 55 percent of the respondents claimed they "did not know" what a nuclear physicist was, while in 1963 this figure had dropped to 25 percent. Thus, while there is no indication that more persons "knew" in a precise way what a nuclear physicist does, there were considerably more persons in 1963 who were willing not only to rate "nuclear physicist" but to provide indications — such as "works with atomic bomb," "runs Cape Canaveral," "is a laboratory worker," or "does atomic research" — of their impression of what a "nuclear physicist" does. Many of these indications are vague and erroneous, but they apparently provide a sufficient basis for respondents to draw inferences about the general standing of nuclear physicists. Thus, it appears that respondents are willing to evaluate occupations without a clear and well-defined idea of the duties involved in their performance.

The situation of the nuclear physicist suggests an hypothesis to which we will pay some attention. As it turned out the 1947 NORC score for "nuclear physicist" was 86, while the 1963 score was 92. Thus, an increase in the standing of "nuclear physicist" accompanied a remarkable increase in the proportion of respondents willing to rate the occupation. One may presume that the frequent mention of nuclear physicists in the press between 1947 and 1963 contributed to the increased willingness of respondents to give their impressions of the occupation. The particular hypothesis which concerns us is whether publicity enhances prestige. The case of nuclear physicist and several other occupations (subsequently discussed) suggests there may be some truth to this hypothesis. Here we can examine whether changes in the ability to rate occupations (as indicated by the proportion of "don't know" responses), which should be a consequence of publicity, affect occupational standings.

Most of the 90 NORC occupations were already well known in 1947, so that little if any change in the ability of respondents to rate them could be expected. We consider, therefore, only those 25 NORC occupations which 5 or more percent of respondents refused to rate in 1947. The correlation between changes in percentages "don't know" between 1947 and 1963 with changes in prestige scores for this subset of occupations is .48.[1] Thus, for this subset of occupations for which there was some room for the diffusion of knowledge, the expected positive relationship between decreases in the percentage "don't know" and score increases apparently holds.[2]

Occupational prestige since 1925

Since the appearance of George S. Counts' pioneering 1925 study of occupational prestige, a number of readings have been taken on the distribution of occupational prestige. These studies have utilized a variety of different measurement techniques with different types of samples of raters, college students being quite popular. However, there is evidence that the overall structure of prestige is invariant under quite drastic changes in technique.[3] Furthermore, one of the major findings of the original 1947 NORC survey was the demonstration that *all* segments of the population share essentially the same view of the prestige hierarchy and rate occupations in much the same way.[4] With these findings in mind, we may utilize selected prestige studies conducted since 1925 to ascertain if any substantial changes in the prestige structure of occupations have occurred since that date.

A pre-World War II and post-Depression benchmark is provided by the investigations of Mapheus Smith, who provides the mean ratings of 100 occupations as rated by college and high-school students in the academic years 1938–1939, 1939–1940, and 1940–1941. The rating technique by Smith differs considerably from that employed in the NORC study. Respondents were originally required to *rank* occupations according to how far an average incumbent would be seated from the guest of honor at a dinner honoring a celebrity and then to *rate* the occupations on a 100-point scale of prestige (according to the rater's personal estimation).[5]

A pre-Depression benchmark of occupational prestige is provided by Counts' study, which provides rankings of 45 occupations according to their "social standing." The data were collected from high-school students, high-school teachers and college students.[6] Unlike the NORC and Smith studies, rankings rather than ratings were obtained by Counts. Counts provides rankings by six different groups of respondents and a continuous variable can be derived by taking the average rank of an occupation over the six groups, weighting for the number of respondents in each group.

These studies, together with the two NORC surveys, provide an opportunity to examine occupational prestige since 1925. A fairly large number of titles are shared in common between each pair of studies, so that the number of titles utilized in any given comparison is larger than the total number of titles that have been rated in many prestige studies.[7]

Product moment correlations between the prestige of occupations common to each pair of studies are presented in Table 4, together with the number of matching titles. It is evident from the data presented in Table 4 that *there have been no substantial changes in occupational prestige in the United States since 1925.* The lowest correlation observed is .934, and this occurs between the 1963 NORC scores and the mean ranks derived from the 1925 study of Counts. In view of the high correlation between the 1947 and 1963 NORC scores, it is not particularly surprising that high correlations are found between any pair of studies from adjacent points in time. That no substantial changes are observed over a span of approximately forty years is a bit more surprising and is further evidence of constraints toward the stability of prestige hierarchies.

Slight though the variation in correlations in Table 4 may be, it is noteworthy that the observed variation is apparently a function of elapsed time. The longer the elapsed time between any two studies, the smaller tends to be the correlation between them. Although this point is readily apparent on inspection of Table 4, we can provide a convenient quantitative summary by correlating the squares of the correlations between scores obtained at times *i* and *j* and the elapsed times between the *i*th and *j*th measurements, yielding a coefficient of −.85, a value significantly different from zero at the .025 level despite the fact that only six observations are involved.

Small changes in occupational prestige can be obscured by the very high degree of intertemporal stability.

[1] The regression of change in prestige score on change in the percentage "don't know" is given by $\hat{Y} = .16X - 0.11$.

[2] However, "nuclear physicist" which shows the most dramatic change in "don't knows" falls among these 25 occupations. Upon exclusion of this occupation, we find that for the remaining 24 occupations r falls to .33. On the other hand, the regression slope is two-thirds again as large since for the 24 occupations under consideration, $\hat{Y} = .27X - 0.61$. Thus, whether elimination of "nuclear physicist" upsets the observed relationship between decreases in the proportion "don't know" and score changes, depends on whether you take the point of view of regression or of correlation. On the one hand, the inclusion of "nuclear physicist" increases the variance around the regression line, but on the other hand, score changes increase more rapidly with decreases in the percentage "don't know". In any case, for the 24 occupations, we have found some evidence, albeit slight, in support of the predicted positive association between score changes and shifts in public knowledge of occupational standings.

[3] For example, one study requested respondents to sort seventy of the occupations in the NORC list into groups of *similar* occupations. The respondent was then asked to order the groups of similar occupations he had formed into social levels. Nevertheless, a rank order correlation of .97 was found between scores derived from this study and scores obtained from the 1947 NORC study. See John D. Campbell, "Subjective Aspects of Occupational Status," unpublished Ph.D. thesis, Harvard University, 1952, Chapter II.

[4] Reiss, *op. cit.*, pp. 189–190.

[5] Mapheus Smith, "An Empirical Scale of Prestige Status of Occupations," *American Sociological Review*, 8 (April, 1943), pp. 185–192.

[6] George S. Counts, "The Social Status of Occupations: A Problem in Vocational Guidance," *The School Review*, 33 (January, 1925), pp. 16–27.

[7] See, for example, the national studies cited by Alex Inkeles and Peter H. Rossi, "National Comparisons of Occupational Prestige," *American Journal of Sociology*, 61 (January, 1956), pp. 329–339.

Although the techniques used in the studies by NORC, Smith, and Counts make direct comparisons impossible, regression analysis permits us to follow changes in the prestige of nineteen occupations common to all studies over the span 1925–1963. Let C = the mean rankings derived from Counts' 1925 study; S = the mean ratings taken from Smith (circa 1940); X = the 1947 NORC scores; and Y = the 1963 NORC scores.

TABLE 4. *Correlations between Occupational Prestige Ratings at Selected Time Periods, 1925–1963*

Correlations Placed Above Diagonal in Figure 1; Number of Matching Titles Placed Below Diagonal

Study and time period	C	S	X	Y
C = Counts' mean ranks, 1925	—	.968	.955	.934
S = Smith's mean ratings, c. 1940	23	—	.982	.971
X = NORC scores, 1947	29	38	—	.990
Y = NORC scores, 1963	29	38	90	—

Sources: George S. Counts, "The Social Status of Occupations: A Problem in Vocational Guidance," *The School Review*, 33 (January, 1925), Table I, pp. 20–21; Mapheus Smith, "An Empirical Scale of Prestige Status of Occupations,' *American Sociological Review*, 8 (April, 1943), Table I, pp. 187–188; National Opinion Research Center, "Jobs and Occupations: A Popular Evaluation," *Opinion News*, IX (September 1, 1947), pp. 3–13. See text for details.

Three regression equations relating these studies are as follows:

$$\hat{S} = 1.62(C) + 15.47,$$
$$\hat{X} = 0.60(S) + 37.04,$$
$$\hat{Y} = 0.97(X) + 2.98,$$

all computed over the total number of matching occupations between the studies involved. We can consider the residuals from these regressions, $S-\hat{S}$, $X-\hat{X}$, $Y-\hat{Y}$ as indicators of change. Thus, for example, the values of $S-\hat{S}$ are indicators of change over the period 1925–1940.

Are the changes in one period systematically related to changes in the next or later periods? To answer this question the correlations between the three sets of residuals were computed.

In the linear regression model which underlies the three regression equations presented in the preceding paragraph, $S-\hat{S}$, $X-\hat{X}$, and $Y-\hat{Y}$, are assumed to be random errors and should, therefore, be uncorrelated.

[1] Note the use of *changes* rather than *trends*; because of the fact that the prestige scales have a ceiling and a floor, one might argue that $S-\hat{S}$ will be negatively correlated with $X-\hat{X}$ which will in turn be negatively correlated with $Y-\hat{Y}$, but that $S-\hat{S}$ will be positively related to $Y-\hat{Y}$. Reference to secular changes rather than secular trends is used advisedly since it seems unlikely that *most* occupations increasing or decreasing in prestige in one period would continue to do so in the next time period, owing to the presence of a floor and ceiling to the prestige scale.

If, to the contrary, they prove correlated, then we will have adduced some evidence of the presence of long run secular *changes* in prestige.[1]

None of the correlations involving the three sets of residuals are significantly different from zero: $r_{(S-\hat{S})(X-\hat{X})} = -.24$ and $r_{(S-\hat{S})(Y-\hat{Y})} = +.23$, over the 19 occupations matching between the studies of Counts, Smith, and NORC, while $r_{(X-\hat{X})(Y-\hat{Y})} = +.10$, over the 38 occupations matching between the Smith and NORC studies. Thus there is little evidence of any particular pattern to the small changes in prestige observed between the studies and no evidence whatsoever of any substantial changes in the overall structure of prestige.

The residuals from the three regression equations linking the four studies in a time sequence can be examined in another way. If $S-\hat{S}$ is positive, then we conclude that the prestige of the occupation in question increased between 1925 and 1940, since the observed value of S exceeds the value of Counts' study expected on the basis of Counts' study. Thus, we might examine fluctuations in the prestige of a given occupation by scoring the values of $S-\hat{S}$, $X-\hat{X}$, and $Y-\hat{Y}$ either "+" or "−" according to whether they are positive or negative,

TABLE 5. *Summary of Prestige Changes in Selected Occupations, 1925–1963**

Occupations — given by matching NORC titles	PERIOD OF CHANGE		
	1925–1940	1940–1947	1947–1963
Physician	+	+	−
Banker	+	−	−
Minister	−	+	+
Lawyer	+	+	+
Public school teacher	−	+	+
Railroad engineer	−	+	−
Farm owner and operator	−	+	−
Electrician	+	+	+
Manager of a small store in a city	−	−	−
Bookkeeper	−	+	+
Policeman	+	−	+
Railroad conductor	+	+	−
Carpenter	−	+	+
Machine operator in a factory	−	+	+
Barber	+	+	+
Clerk in a store	−	−	−
Coal miner	−	−	+
Restaurant waiter	+	−	+
Janitor	−	−	+

* Occupations are those common to the studies of Counts, Smith, and NORC. A "+" indicates that the regression estimate based on the prestige at the beginning of the period was less than the prestige observed at the end of the period, while "−" indicates the regression estimate exceeded the observed prestige at the end of the period. See text for details.

respectively. The 19 occupational titles common to the four studies are scored in Table 5. If an occupation is marked with "+" for the period 1940–1947 in Table 5, this means that the residual from the regression of the 1947 NORC scores on the Smith ratings (c. 1940) was greater than zero for the occupation in question. Conversely, "−" would indicate that the residual was less than zero.

All of the changes shown in Table 5 are quite small and many would lie within a 5 percent confidence band which might be drawn about the regression lines from which they are calculated. The values of the residuals for the last time period do not necessarily have the same sign as the differences Y−X which might also be taken as a plausible measure of change between the two NORC studies, which are exactly comparable.

Table 5 shows patterns of change that do not lend themselves easily to an overall interpretation. However, a number of *ad hoc* interpretations may be constructed. For example, it might be argued that the great strides made in medical technology between 1925 and 1947 would account for slight increases in that period in the prestige of physicians, while the profession's attitude toward Medicare and other public medical plans in the past few years has offset these gains by slightly reducing their prestige. Such *ad hoc* interpretations, however, have nothing but plausibility to support them.

The major finding in Table 5 is that the prestige of occupations shifted in an irregular fashion over the period 1925 to 1963. For example, only five of the nineteen occupations either increased or decreased their prestige continuously over the entire period, 1925–1963.

Table 5 also illustrates two contrasting approaches to the explanation of such changes. Earlier in this paper, we considered the relationship between 1947–1963 prestige changes and changes in the proportion "don't know." We were thus adducing an *ubiquitous* element in the movement of prestige, or, at least, one common to all occupations considered. In contrast, the *ad hoc* explanation advanced to account for the movement in the prestige of physicians over the period 1925–1963 relied on factors *unique* to physicians, but not necessarily applicable to other occupations. Both approaches to the study of changes in occupational prestige would necessarily have to be used, were a truly comparable and extensive time series pertaining to the prestige of selected occupations available.

Changes in occupational prestige, 1947–1963

Owing to the sample size of the 1963 replication of the 1947 study, small changes in the prestige of particular occupations are apt to be unreliable. However, changes in the prestige of occupational *groups* may be more reliably inferred. This is the strategy we have adopted for summarizing the small changes that were observed between 1947 and 1963.

To illustrate that overall changes in prestige were not random, we can look at changes in ratings by different subgroups: those with some college experience, those with only high school education, and those with an eighth grade education or less. Changes between 1947 and 1963 as derived from the three groups were then intercorrelated in order to determine the consistency of changes. A correlation of +.76 was found between changes observed for those with some college and

changes observed for those with some high school. Changes observed for those with no more than a grade school education were correlated +.56 and +.64 with the corresponding changes observed for those with some college and some high school, respectively. These coefficients indicate an appreciable consistency in the score changes observed within the three educational groups. In addition, it is interesting to note that the lowest correlation occurs between the best educated and poorest educated groups, suggesting that some of the differences between the changes observed in the three groups are attributable to the dissimilarity between them.[1]

In Table 6 the NORC occupations are allocated to the major occupation groups employed by the U.S. Bureau of the Census. The results shown in Table 6 are quite clear: among all blue-collar groups there was

TABLE 6. *Selected Measures of Prestige Change, 1947–1963, by Major Occupation Group*

Major occupation group	Number of NORC titles	Average score difference	Average percent change
Total, all occupations	90	+0.8	+1.4
White collar	*54*	*+0.3*	*+0.4*
Professional	33	+0.7	+0.8
Managerial	16	−0.4	−0.3
Clerical and sales	5	−0.2	−0.4
Blue collar[a]	*32*	*+1.8*	*+3.4*
Craftsmen[a]	9	+1.6	+2.3
Operatives	8	+0.9	+1.6
Service	9	+2.4	+4.9
Laborers	6	+2.2	+5.3
All farm	*4*	*−0.2*	*−0.0*

[a] Contains two military titles in NORC list which are not classified by the U.S. Bureau of the Census into major occupation groups, since they are non-civilian pursuits.

a net upward shift in prestige which exceeded the mean shift experienced by all occupations; although professional titles in the NORC list remained roughly the same, the two remaining white-collar groups experienced a net downward drift in prestige; and, finally, farming pursuits — which represent a declining proportion of the experienced civilian labor force — likewise lost slightly in prestige. As one could detect in the regression equation relating the 1947 and 1963 scores, the pattern of change by major occupation group reveals an attenuation between 1947 and 1963 in the range of the NORC scores. In part, this pattern represents regression toward the mean, but since *all* blue-collar groups shifted upward and professionals remained much the same, it also appears likely that some further obscuring of the white-collar–blue-collar distinction was underway.

[1] Results of this kind strongly suggest that the observed changes were not random and that had the 1947 and 1963 samples been randomly split into two subgroups, nearly identical changes would have been observed in the two groups.

Table 6 also contains by major occupation group another measure of change, viz., the percent change in 1947 score. As the reader can easily see these changes are in every case quite small, even at the lower levels of prestige where the scores were initially low. The percent change in score is, of course, patterned in the same way as the score differences.[1]

The major occupation groups of the U.S. Bureau of the Census are far from homogeneous and the allocation of NORC titles to these groups tends to obscure a number of important differences in the patterns of change observed within various occupational situses. Indeed, we find that the correlation ratio, *eta*, of the score differences on the major occupation groups is only .29, while a correlation ratio of .42 is found between the percent change in score and the classification of titles into major occupation groups.[2] Thus, despite the fairly clear pattern that emerges upon consideration of the major occupation groups, a considerable portion of the variance in the score differences and percent change is obscured by the classification.

In order to surmount this difficulty and to highlight some of the systematic, if small, prestige changes that were taking place, a classification of NORC titles was expressly designed to illuminate the changes; its chief virtue is the economy of presentation it facilitates. The groups used in the classification are given in the stub of Table 7 and the specific NORC titles allocated to each group are shown at the bottom of the table. Some titles are dubiously classified and the classification clearly employs several dimensions of occupational structure ranging from class of worker to the kinds of interpersonal contact most frequently encountered on the job.

Several important points emerge on consideration of the classification of NORC titles into occupational situses, which had been obscured in the previous classification by major occupation group. First, it is clear that the lack of change among the professions in Table 6 stems not from an absence of change, but from an averaging out of contradictory ones. The free professions, including occupations like physician and civil engineer, increased in prestige, while cultural or communication oriented professions such as "musician

---

[1] The correlation between the percent change in score and the scores in the initial period, 194 percent turns out to be −.37, illustrating one of the dangers in interpreting the percent change in score. Since a score of a single point represents a larger percentage of change for an occupation of low prestige than for one of high prestige, the negative correlation of the percent change in score with the initial score is to be expected and one is faced with the problem of comparing percentage changes based on quite different initial points of departure. The correlation also reflects to a lesser extent the problem of regression toward the mean which also plagues the analysis of change.

[2] The correlation ratios reported here and those reported below have been adjusted for the number of degrees of freedom utilized in computing the coefficient. For the correction formula see, Mordecai Ezekial and Karl A. Fox, *Methods of Correlation and Regression Analysis*, third edition, N.Y.: John Wiley and Sons, 1959, p. 301.

TABLE 7. *Selected Measures of Prestige Change, 1947–1963, by Occupational Situs*

Occupational situs	Number of NORC titles	Average score difference	Average percent change
Total, all occupations	90	+0.8	+1.4
Free professionals	13	+1.5	+1.8
Cultural/communication oriented professions	7	−2.0	−2.4
Scientific professions	8	+2.6	+3.1
Political/government occupations	10	−0.7	−0.6
Big businessmen	4	−0.8	−0.8
Customer-oriented occupations	11	+0.1	+0.4
Artisans	8	+1.6	+2.4
Outdoor-oriented occupations	10	+1.7	+3.2
Dead end occupations	5	+2.8	+7.2
All farm	4	−0.2	−0.0
Other	10	+1.0	+1.5

NORC titles are classified into occupational situses as follows:

Free professions: physician, college professor, minister, architect, dentist, lawyer, priest, civil engineer, accountant for a large business, instructor in the public schools, public school teacher, undertaker, welfare worker for a city government.

Cultural/communication oriented professions: artist who paints pictures that are exhibited in galleries, musician in a symphony orchestra, author of novels, radio announcer, newspaper columnist, reporter on a daily newspaper, singer in a nightclub.

Scientific occupations: scientist, government scientist, chemist, nuclear physicist, psychologist, sociologist, biologist, economist.

Political/government occupations: U.S. Supreme Court Justice, state governor, cabinet member in the federal government, diplomat in the U.S. Foreign Service, mayor of a large city, United States Representative in Congress, county judge, head of a department in a state government, county agricultural agent, policeman.

Big businessmen: banker, member of the board of directors of a large corporation, owner of a factory that employs about 100 people, building contractor.

Customer-oriented occupations: which require face to face contact with the public in the ordinary course of a day's work: manager of a small store in a city, railroad conductor, owner-operator of a lunch stand, barber, clerk in a store, streetcar motorman, taxi driver, restaurant waiter, soda fountain clerk, bartender, filling station attendant.

Artisans: owner-operator of a printing shop, electrician, trained machinist, carpenter, automobile repairman, plumber, garage mechanic, restaurant cook.

Outdoor-oriented occupations: in which an ordinary day's work is typically performed either outside or in an out-of-doors setting: airline pilot, mail carrier, railroad engineer, fisherman who owns his own boat, milk route man, truck driver, lumberjack, coal miner, railroad section hand, dock worker.

Dead end occupations: which have no future possibilities of advancement: night watchman, janitor, garbage collector, street sweeper, shoe shiner.

All farm: farm owner and operator, tenant farmer (one who owns livestock and machinery and manages the farm), farm hand, share cropper (one who owns no livestock or equipment and does not manage farm).

Other: captain in the regular army, official of an international labor union, bookkeeper, insurance agent, traveling salesman for a wholesale concern, playground director, local official of a labor union, corporal in the regular army, machine operator in a factory, clothes presser in a laundry.

Some of the titles in the "other" category might be reclassified into the remaining categories at some expense in homogeneity; such a reclassification does not affect the results presented in this table.

in a symphony orchestra" and "radio announcer" declined in standing. Perhaps the most dramatic change is among the scientific occupations, which with the single exception of "economist" enjoyed positive score differences. A second change obscured by previous analysis was the slight decrease in prestige experienced by political and governmental occupations. One major exception to the rule for other governmental titles was "policeman" which experienced an upswing in prestige. However, such a change is difficult to interpret since there are no other governmental titles of fairly low prestige. Whether it represents regression toward the mean or a genuine increment in respect for law enforcing officers is difficult to say. The remaining situses in Table 7 are more loosely identified and we are loath to place any interpretation upon the directions of change observed in them (with the exception of "artisans" which are largely craft occupations). They may, however, provide useful guidelines for other researchers seeking to classify the NORC titles into more meaningful categories than those currently available. Taken as a whole, however, the classification is more closely related to the score differences and the percent change in score than are the major occupation groups. Correlation ratios of .50 and .51 were found between the classification and, respectively, the score differences and percent changes in scores.

A few other changes not previously noted and still obscured by the classification of NORC titles into occupational situses should be mentioned. Among the more important of these are the increases in scores observed for "a local official of a labor union" and "official of an international labor union." That these titles should experience increasing prestige, despite the sensational government investigations into the conduct of labor officials during the past decade, is perhaps indicative of the extent to which unions have been assimilated by and have themselves adopted a more accommodating attitude toward the established order.

The two military titles in the NORC list, "captain in the regular army" and "corporal in the regular army," remained much the same in the two time periods. Similarly, the two occupations rated twice under slightly different titles for reliability purposes, "public school teacher" (instructor in the public schools) and "automobile repairman" (garage mechanic), received nearly identical ratings under both stimulus titles in the replication, as had been the case in 1947. The results for these duplicated titles are as follows:

Occupational titles	NORC SCORE	
	In 1947	*In 1963*
Public school teacher	78	81
Instructor in the public schools	79	82
Automobile repairman	63	64
Garage mechanic	62	62

The reader will notice that one- and two-point differences in NORC scores can be produced by simply rating the same occupation under slightly different titles. It seems likely, therefore, that changes of one or two points in the NORC score of an occupation could hardly be adequate for establishing a real change in prestige or even the direction of change in prestige (if any). The results for the duplicated titles indicate, therefore, that many of the observed changes in prestige scores discussed above are quite negligible and might possibly have been reversed if a slightly different phrasing of the occupational title had been employed.

One other point is worthy of mention before turning to a summary. Duncan has recently used regression techniques to extend the 1947 NORC scores to all occupations in the detailed classification of the U.S. Bureau of the Census. In the course of presenting his results, Duncan had occasion to discuss the temporal stability of his index and the implication that changes in occupational socioeconomic status might have for the validity of his results. On the basis of comparisons between aggregate education and income of occupations as observed in the 1940 and 1950 censuses, Duncan suggested that "changes — albeit minor ones for the most part — were indeed occurring in the socioeconomic status of occupations during the decade 1940–50," adding that "such evidence as we have suggests a rather high temporal stability of occupational prestige ratings, although the time periods concerned have not been lengthy ones."[1] Surely, there is nothing in the present study to alter these conclusions (which, indeed, provide a fair summary of the results of this paper). As the 1960 census data become available for detailed occupations it will, of course, be possible to revise Duncan's index on the basis of the present replication, but barring any dramatic shifts in the aggregate income and education of occupations over the period 1950–1960, there is no reason to believe such a revision would alter in any appreciable way the socioeconomic scores that Duncan assigned to occupations on the basis of the 1947 NORC study and 1950 census data.

Conclusions

The theme of this paper has been accurately captured by an eminent pathologist who remarked of biochemical phenomena, "Universal instability of constituents seems to be compatible with a stability and even monotony of organized life."[2] Such is the picture one gleans of occupational structure from the present endeavor. Between 1947 and 1963 we are fully aware that many *individual* changes in occupation were under way as men advanced in their career lines, retired, or entered the labor force. Yet, despite the turnover of incumbents, occupational morphology, at least insofar as prestige is concerned, remained remarkably stable. To be sure, systematic patterns of change could be detected, but one would miss the import of this paper if one failed to recognize that these changes were minor relative to the overall stability. The view developed here is that a

[1] Duncan, *op. cit.*, pp. 152–153.
[2] René Dubos, *The Dreams of Reason: Science and Utopias*, N.Y.: Columbia University Press, 1961, p. 124.

stable system of occupational prestige provides a necessary foundation to which individuals may anchor their careers.

System maintenance is, however, only part of the story. Small, but nevertheless systematic, changes can be detected between 1947 and 1963. In some cases these changes appear to be attributable to increasing public knowledge of occupations, but it was suggested that any complete understanding of prestige shifts and their causes would require a time series pertaining to the standing of particular occupations. The present study is a step in that direction. Our purposes will be adequately accomplished if others are stimulated to make periodic readings of, as it were, the occupational weather.

Residential Segregation of Social Classes and Aspirations of High School Boys

Alan B. Wilson

CONSISTENT AND STRONG EVIDENCE has been accumulated showing that members of different socio-economic strata, as groups, adhere to differing values which reinforce their respective statuses.[1] Members of the working class tend to devalue education and to aspire to modest but secure occupations and income levels. Through familial socialization and divergent perceptions of their opportunities these aspirations are transmitted to the younger generation. The social inheritance of such values and attitudes tends to inhibit social mobility.

Many investigations have shown the relevance of individual personality characteristics to aspirations. These aspects of personality have been linked in turn to such variations in the familial socialization of children as direct exhortation and positive valuation of education and status, early independence training, the level of adult-child contact indicated by the size of family or the child's position in the order of siblings, and matriarchal *versus* patriarchal authority structure within the family.[2] Since the familial characteristics which are conducive to a high level of aspirations are more typical of the middle class than of the working class, these variates can be viewed, at least in part, as intervening between the parent's social class and his children's aspirations.

While the association between youths' educational and occupational aspirations and their parents' class position is strong, regardless of what dimension of social stratification is employed, there is considerable variation in aspirations among youths within a single class. This study is concerned with a related matter: the derivation of values from the immediate social milieu — the climate of the school society.

A variety of experimental and descriptive investigations have demonstrated the influence of social context upon judgments, attitudes, and aspirations.[3] Berenda, using the technique developed by Solomon Asch, found that when a child is confronted with classmates giving

[1] See, e.g. H. H. Hyman, "The Value Systems of Different Classes: a Social Psychological Contribution to the Analysis of Stratification," R. Bendix and S. M. Lipset, editors, *Class, Status and Power,* Glencoe, Ill.: Free Press, 1953, pp. 426–442; J. A. Kahl, "Educational and Occupational Aspirations of 'Common Man' Boys," *Harvard Educational Review,* 23 (Summer, 1953), pp. 186–203; W. H. Sewell, A. O. Haller, and M. A. Straus, "Social Status and Educational and Occupational Aspiration," *American Sociological Review,* 22 (February, 1957), pp. 67–73.

[2] See especially, S. M. Lipset and R. Bendix, *Social Mobility and Industrial Society,* Berkeley: University of California Press, 1959, Chapter 9.

[3] See, e.g., R. K. Merton, *Social Theory and Social Structure,* Glencoe, Ill.: Free Press, 1957, Chapters 8 and 9; E. Katz and P. F. Lazarsfeld, *Personal Influence,* Glencoe, Ill.: Free Press, 1955, *passim.*

Reprinted from the *American Sociological Review,* V. 24 (1959), pp. 836–845, by permission of the author and the publisher.

unanimous, incorrect judgments, only seven per cent of the younger children (ages 7 to 10) and 20 per cent of the older children (ages 10 to 13) remained independent.[1] A series of studies have shown the homogenization of certain social and political attitudes at college.[2] Herbert Hyman also has suggested that a current reference group, such as one's current co-workers, may provide a systematic factor accounting for differences in values among individuals with common class-origins.[3]

Because of the sifting of like social types into specific zones within an urbanized area, school districting tends to segregate youths of different social strata. Consequently school populations have modally different

aspirations of the sons of professionals more modest if they attend a predominantly working-class school?

Procedure

The data for this study are provided by a survey of students' interests as related to their success in school and their decisions about educational and occupational specialization. This survey gathered information on students in thirteen high schools in and around the San Francisco-Oakland Bay area.[4] Five of these schools, located in cities and places outside the urbanized area, are excluded from the present analysis; and the study is

TABLE 1. *Census and Sample Distributions of Educational and Occupational Variates by Schools*

| | 1950 CENSUS | | | HIGH SCHOOL SAMPLE | | | |
| | | | | COLLEGE GRADUATES | | FATHERS' OCCUPATION | |
Schools	Median years of schooling	Professional	Laborers	Fathers	Mothers	Professional	Manual
Group A: Upper white collar							
1) Private boys' school	*	*	*	65%	53%	30%	6%
2) Residential	13.3	26%	2%	51	35	22	2
3) Sub-urban	12.3	13	8	28	23	14	22
Group B: Lower white collar							
4) Metropolitan	12.0	13	5	27	21	8	32
5) Metropolitan	11.1	11	9	21	17	13	38
Group C: Industrial							
6) Predominantly Catholic	10.7	5	10	11	5	1	53
7) Heterogeneous	9.6	4	12	2	2	4	56
8) Predominantly Negro	8.7	2	32	9	7	6	72

* The private school's population is drawn from scattered tracts.

attitudes toward educational achievement and aspirations for a college education. The proposition that the aspirations of the bulk of the students in a high school district provide a significant normative reference influencing the educational aspirations of boys from varying strata is investigated in this paper by comparing the aspirations of students with similar social origins who attend schools characterized by different climates of aspiration. Concretely, are the sons of manual workers more likely to adhere to middle-class values and have high educational aspirations if they attend a predominantly middle-class school, and, conversely, are the

[1] R. W. Berenda, *The Influence of the Group on the Judgment of Peers*, New York: King's Crown, 1950; the technique is presented in S. E. Asch, *Social Psychology*, New York: Prentice-Hall, 1952, pp. 450–501.

[2] T. M. Newcomb, "Attitude Development as a Function of Reference Groups: the Bennington Study," in E. E. Maccoby, T. M. Newcomb, and E. L. Hartley, editors, *Readings in Social Psychology*, New York: Henry Holt, 1958, pp. 265–275. Several studies are summarized by P. E. Jacob, *Changing Values in College*, New Haven: Hazen Foundation, 1957.

[3] Hyman, *op. cit.*, pp. 441–442.

[4] The schools were selected purposively from those accessible which had been stratified on the basis of census data. Confidence in the findings depends upon their internal consistency and their congruence with the body of parallel research and relevant theory. Ultimately, the generalizability of the study must depend upon replication with other populations rather than statistical inference to a population of schools which, necessarily, would also be arbitrarily limited by their accessibility.

confined to boys, since the educational and occupational aspirations of girls are more homogeneous and are conditioned by different factors.

A high degree of concordance ($W = .92$) is found

TABLE 2. *Distributions of Selected Variates by School Groups*

| Variate | SCHOOL GROUP | | |
Category	A	B	C
Fathers' occupation			
Professional	22%	8%	2%
White collar	42	29	25
Self employed	17	20	8
Manual	10	30	49
Not available	9	12	15
Fathers' education			
Some college or more	65	35	14
High school graduate	20	29	26
Some high school or less	14	32	54
Not available	2	3	6
Mothers' education			
Some college or more	56	31	12
High school graduate	34	41	39
Some high school or less	9	25	45
Not available	1	3	4
Residence in California			
Over 25 years	58	48	32
Race			
White	98	78	66
Religion			
Catholic	21	27	38
Number of cases	(418)	(480)	(457)

among the several rank orders of occupational and educational stratification obtained from the census data describing the populations from which the student bodies were recruited, and the data from the observed sample of students at the seven public schools.[1] The entire population of a private boys' school, the students of which are not recruited from continuous tracts, was sampled. The sample distributions obtained clearly place this school in the first rank (group *A*) in Table 1. The schools are grouped, for this study, on the basis of these rank orders, as well as congruent distinctions not reflected in the statistics — impressions of the school "atmospheres" obtained while observing students in the classrooms, halls, and playgrounds. Because of the high concordance between the various dimensions of stratification, the grouping would be the same whichever combination one might choose to emphasize.[2]

Detailed contrasts between the three groups of schools

TABLE 3. *Percentages Aspiring to Go to College by School Groups and Fathers' Occupations*

Fathers' occupation	SCHOOL GROUP		
	A	B	C
Professional	93%	77%	64%
	(92)	(39)	(11)
White collar	79	59	46
	(174)	(138)	(111)
Self employed	79	66	35
	(68)	(90)	(37)
Manual	59	44	33
	(39)	(140)	(221)
Weighted mean of per cents	80	57	38
Total	(373)*	(407)*	(380)*

* The total number of cases on which these percentages are based is less than the totals shown in Table 2 because cases for which data were unavailable for either the control or dependent variates are not shown. Variation in the total number of cases in the succeeding tables is for the same reason unless otherwise noted.

(designated *A*, *B*, and *C*, respectively) in the distribution of several dimensions of stratification are shown in Table 2. The distributions show the gross correlation between these various dimensions of stratification, and reflect the extent of segregation between strata due to school districting along lines of social concentration. While only 10 per cent of the students in the group *A* schools are children of manual workers, one-half of the boys in the group *C* schools are manual workers' sons; and while 65 per cent of the fathers in the group *A* schools have at least some college education, only 14 per cent of the fathers of students at the group *C* schools have any college training. Other comparisons show similar contrasts. (It is interesting to note that the families of the students in the group *A* schools have resided in California longer than those in the group *C* schools. This reflects the predominantly working-class origins of the recent large-scale immigration into

California and the upward mobility of the established urban residents.)

Findings

It was found, as anticipated, that there is a great divergence between the schools in the proportions of students aspiring to a college education.[3] Eighty per cent of the students in the *A* schools, 57 per cent in the *B* schools, and only 38 per cent in the *C* schools want to go to college. (See the bottom row of Table 3.) This difference is due to a great extent, of course, to attributes of the parents who serve as reference individuals for the

[1] The census data use different classifications, based upon a wider population (not limited to the parents of high school boys), and were gathered at an earlier date than the sample data. The concordance of ranks rather than the correlation of actual percentages is all that is pertinent, in any event, to confirm the appropriateness of the ordering and grouping of schools.

[2] The grouping of schools on the basis of occupational and educational dimensions of stratification, and the subsequent pooling of a predominantly Catholic with a predominantly Negro school as working-class schools might be unjustified if religion and race were independently associated with the dependent variable, i.e., educational aspirations. Altogether, 58 per cent of the Protestants and only 47 per cent of the Catholics in the sample aspire to go to college. But within educational and occupational strata the difference between Protestants and Catholics is small and unsystematic, while within each religious group the differences between occupational and educational strata are large. For example, among the children of professionals with at least some college education, 87 per cent of both Protestants and Catholics wish to go to college; among the children of manual workers who are high school graduates, 44 per cent of the Protestants and 46 per cent of the Catholics so wish; 34 per cent of the Protestants and 28 per cent of the Catholics whose fathers are manual workers who have not finished high school, want to go to college.

Similarly, the overall differences in educational aspirations between Negroes and whites are "explained" by the predominantly working-class and low educational status of the Negroes.

[3] Educational aspirations were inferred from the following question:

After I graduate from high school (and, if necessary, serve in the military forces) —

1) .... I plan to get a job right away
2) .... I plan to be a housewife
3) .... I plan to go to a technical or trade school
4) .... I plan to go to a junior college
5) .... I plan to go first to a junior college, and then to a four-year college or university
6) .... I plan to go directly to a four-year college or university
7) .... I have other plans

....

(What are they?)

Responses 5 and 6 were considered as indicating an aspiration to go to college. Since there are several free junior colleges in the area which are open to all high school graduates regardless of past scholarship, poor students can and often do use them as a means of remedying their academic deficiencies. Any student who *wants* to go to college can *plan* to do so, unless, of course, he does not believe he is capable of improving and, therefore, has no intention of trying. A student might value higher education without aspiring to attain a higher education. However, differences in school achievement do not account for the differences between schools in aspirations. (See Tables 11 and 12.)

students. This is seen by making vertical comparisons in Table 3: many more children of professionals have collegiate aspirations than children of manual workers in each school group. But *within* occupational strata, reading across the table, we see that attributes of the reference group — the norms of the school society — symmetrically modify attitudes: while 93 per cent of the sons of professionals in the group *A* schools want to go to college, less than two-thirds of the sons of professionals in the group *C* schools wish to do so; whereas only one-third of the sons of manual workers wish to go to college if they attend a predominantly working-class school, more than one-half of such sons so wish in the middle-class schools. This isotropic relationship provides *prima facie* confirmation of the cumulative effects of the primary and contextual variates — the boys' own class origins and the dominant class character of the high schools' student body.

It is possible, however, that these differences between

TABLE 4. *Percentages within each Occupational Category with High Status Jobs and High Education by School Groups*

Occupational stratum Sub-stratum and education	SCHOOL GROUP		
	A	B	C
Professional			
"Free" (self employed)	59%	55%	27%
Some college or more	96	98	73
Number of cases	(92)	(40)	(11)
White collar			
"Executive"	42	14	3
Some college or more	65	47	20
Number of cases	(177)	(141)	(113)
Self employed			
Merchants (e.g., retail)	51	41	30
Some college or more	62	36	14
Number of cases	(71)	(95)	(38)
Manual			
Skilled	60	52	43
Some college or more	21	14	9
Number of cases	(40)	(144)	(225)

schools reflect uncontrolled systematic variation in the attributes of the parents. Within each of these broad occupational strata there is considerable variation of occupational status, income, education, habits of consumption, and the like, each of which makes a cumulative impact upon values. The more successful and better educated professionals tend to move to more exclusive residential areas, send their children to private schools, or both; among the "white collar" occupations more prosperous executives reside in the group *A* school districts, clerks in the group *C* districts, and so on. Differences of this kind between schools within roughly defined occupational strata are shown in Table 4.

If the apparent effects of the school climate were in fact due to such uncontrolled variation along several dimensions of familial status, then one would expect the

---

[1] The largest irregularities — the sons of merchants at the group *C* schools, and the sons of semi- and unskilled manual workers at the group *A* schools — are based upon very few cases.

differences between the aspirations of the students at the different schools to diminish as the control categories are progressively refined — that is, as the students are compared within more homogeneous background categories. The refinement of any one or a few dimensions of stratification will result in groups which one

TABLE 5. *Percentages within Occupational Substrata Aspiring to Go to College by School Groups*

Fathers' occupation	SCHOOL GROUP		
	A	B	C
"Free" professional	94%	67%	...
	(54)	(21)	(3)
Salaried professional	92	89	...
	(38)	(18)	(8)
Executive	88	79	...
	(75)	(19)	(3)
Upper white collar	79	59	55
	(68)	(64)	(40)
Lower white collar	55	53	40
	(31)	(55)	(68)
Self employed: merchants	88	77	18
	(33)	(35)	(11)
Self employed: artisans	73	60	44
	(33)	(53)	(25)
Manual: skilled	75	46	40
	(24)	(74)	(93)
Manual: semi- and unskilled	33	42	29
	(15)	(66)	(128)

may reasonably assume are also somewhat more homogeneous with respect to uncontrolled correlated dimensions.

This question is considered in Table 5, which is designed to show the impact of school norms upon students from more homogeneous occupational strata. This table is not, of course, "independent" of Table 3, which can be reproduced by recombining the sub-strata shown

TABLE 6. *Percentages Aspiring to Go to College by School Groups and Fathers' Education*

Fathers' education	SCHOOL GROUP		
	A	B	C
College graduate	88%	73%	73%
	(207)	(109)	(30)
Some college	79	68	58
	(61)	(56)	(33)
High school graduate	74	51	35
	(81)	(138)	(115)
Some high school	63	39	30
	(32)	(74)	(109)
Grammar school or less	32	29	33
	(22)	(76)	(131)

in Table 5. But it indicates that the refinement — the homogenization, so to speak — of the control categories, does not systematically modify the effect of the school society upon aspirations. For example, three-fourths of the children of self-employed artisans and skilled manual workers aspire to go to college at the group *A* schools, while considerably fewer than one-half of them do so at the group *C* schools.[1]

The education of the parents is likewise known to have a strong independent effect upon students' aspirations. Fathers' and mothers' educations are controlled in Tables 6 and 7, respectively. The effect of the school society upon aspirations is still found to be operative and strong when holding constant the influence of either parent's education. A comparison of these two tables does not substantiate the notion that the mother's

TABLE 7. *Percentages Aspiring to Go to College by School Groups and Mothers' Education*

	SCHOOL GROUP		
Mothers' education	A	B	C
College graduate	87%	77%	67%
	(64)	(88)	(24)
Some college	87	54	53
	(67)	(57)	(30)
High school graduate	74	54	35
	(140)	(191)	(170)
Some high school	50	35	39
	(20)	(69)	(120)
Grammar school or less	44	34	24
	(16)	(47)	(83)

education is more influential than the father's upon the high school boy's educational aspirations. Hyman suggests the importance of the woman's role in the transmission of educational values on the basis of the fact that youths and adult women both *recommended* college more frequently than adult men.[1] Perhaps women directly exhort educational values more frequently, independently of their own educational background. But these data do not suggest that the mother's

TABLE 8. *Percentages Aspiring to Go to College by Fathers' and Mothers' Education*

	MOTHERS' EDUCATION			
Fathers' education	Col.	H.S.	Less than H.S.	Total*
Some college or more	85%	72%	53%	79%
	(309)	(149)	(36)	(495)
High school graduate	71	50	37	51
	(65)	(191)	(75)	(334)
Some high school or less	40	38	31	35
	(50)	(154)	(239)	(445)
Total*	77	53	35	56
	(430)	(501)	(355)	(1311)

* Marginal totals include those cases for which information is unavailable on the respective control variates.

role is more significant than the father's with respect to the more subtle and indirect effects of the parents' own education.

Looking more closely at the effect on educational aspirations of the interaction between the education of the two parents, it can be seen, in Table 8, that each makes an independent and cumulative impact of about the same degree. The only asymmetrical effect lies in the extreme combinations: if the father has not com-

pleted high school it makes little difference whether the mother has gone to college or not, but it makes considerable difference whether or not the father has gone to college even though the mother has not completed high school. Since these extreme combinations are the rarest, however, their effects are the least reliable.

The possibilities of holding several variates constant simultaneously are limited in tabular analysis, due to the rapid reduction of the number of cases which can be matched. The homogenization of categories is carried as far as is feasible within the limitations of the size of our sample in Table 9. In this table the educational and occupational attributes of the parents are simultaneously held constant while comparisons are made between the educational aspirations of students in different groups of schools. While the reduced numbers of cases makes these percentages less reliable, of the nine comparisons available,[2] seven clearly substantiate the hypothesis, while the two reversals are small. The average percentile differences between adjacent schools are as great within these homogeneous groups as in the coarser groupings of Tables 3, 6, and 7, where the fathers' occupations and parents' education are controlled separately. The only comparison available for all three school groups is among the sons of manual workers both of whose parents have a high school education. Among these boys, 60 per cent in the *A* schools, 54 per cent in the *B* schools, and 32 per cent in the *C* schools seek to go to college.

Achievement and educational values

Educational values and achievement interact and reinforce one another. On the one hand, those who devalue education are poorly motivated to achieve; on the other, those who have been poor achievers will defensively devalue education, and perhaps realistically, modify their educational aspirations. A much higher proportion of students in the middle-class schools obtain "A's" and "B's" than do those in the working-class schools. In addition to the influence of the family and school norms upon achievement, with which hitherto we have been concerned, there is the possibility that teachers grade more liberally at the middle-class schools — either for entirely extraneous reasons or, more plausibly, because the parents' expectations and the students' aspirations place pressure on them to raise the grading curve.

If the latter interpretation is sound, then the students who are high achievers at the group *C* schools will be higher achievers, on an absolute basis, than those at the group *A* schools. But, holding grades constant and reading across the rows in Table 11, we see that even under these conditions more students receiving the same

[1] Hyman, *op. cit.*, pp. 431–432.
[2] Percentages are shown in Table 9 for each classification where there are ten or more cases in two school groups on which to base a comparison. The empty cells and categories not shown have fewer than ten cases.

TABLE 9. *Percentages Aspiring to Go to College by School Groups within Educational and Occupational Strata*

	MOTHERS' EDUCATION						
	COLLEGE GRADUATE		HIGH SCHOOL GRADUATE			LESS THAN HIGH SCHOOL	
Fathers' education	SCHOOL GROUP		SCHOOL GROUP			SCHOOL GROUP	
Fathers' occupation	*A*	*B*	*A*	*B*	*C*	*B*	*C*
College graduate							
Professional	92% (52)	78% (18)	—	—	—	—	—
Upper white collar	86 (57)	94 (17)	83% (24)	62% (13)	—	—	—
High school graduate							
Upper white collar	—	—	85 (20)	65 (20)	—	—	—
Lower white collar	—	—	—	50 (10)	20% (15)	—	—
Manual	—	—	60 (10)	54 (26)	32 (25)	32% (25)	35% (48)
Less than high school							
Lower white collar	—	—	—	60 (10)	27 (15)	—	—
Manual	—	—	—	—	—	36 (45)	26 (86)

grade in the middle-class schools want to go to college.[1] Virtually all of those who receive "A's" at the group *A* schools want to go to college, but only three-fourths of the "A" students at the group *C* schools want to go to college.[2]

TABLE 10. *Percentages Attaining High ("A" or "B") Median Grades by School Groups and Fathers' Occupations*

	SCHOOL GROUP		
Fathers' occupation	*A*	*B*	*C*
Professional	66% (91)	50% (40)	18% (11)
White collar	50 (176)	28 (138)	18 (111)
Self employed	51 (71)	35 (95)	11 (37)
Manual	35 (40)	13 (141)	11 (221)
Weighted mean of per cents	52 (378)	27 (414)	13 (380)

Using IQ scores as an index of achievement which is standardized across school lines, and thus eliminating the possibility of systematic differences between school grading policies, we see in Table 12 that high achievers are less likely to wish to go to college if they attend a working-class school and, conversely, that low achievers are more apt to want to go to college if they attend a middle-class school.[3] Almost all of the students with

TABLE 11. *Percentages Aspiring to Go to College by School Groups and Grades*

	SCHOOL GROUP		
Median academic grade	*A*	*B*	*C*
"A"	98% (60)	96% (24)	78% (9)
"B"	90 (152)	89 (90)	72 (46)
"C"	72 (145)	55 (207)	41 (184)
"D"	43 (47)	21 (120)	25 (169)

IQ scores over 120 at the group *A* schools hope to go to college, whereas only one third of those with such scores at the group *C* schools want to do so. Those who adhere to the interpretation of intelligence test scores as more or less valid measures of innate capacity will see the "waste" of talent implicit in the horizontal contrasts

TABLE 12. *Percentages Aspiring to Go to College by School Groups and IQ Scores*

	SCHOOL GROUP		
IQ score	*A*	*B*	*C*
120+	96% (100)	83% (81)	33% (18)
110–119	93 (128)	72 (108)	51 (53)
100–109	76 (87)	52 (89)	41 (82)
90–99	47 (30)	24 (63)	35 (68)
89–	25 (12)	29 (69)	25 (111)

[1] The number of cases on which these percentages are based reflects the fact, shown in Table 10, that far fewer students do receive "A's" at the group *C* schools.

[2] Note that the aspirations of the students who receive high grades at the group *B* schools resemble those of the students of the group *A* schools, while those who get low grades have aspirations similar to those students at the group *C* schools. This suggests the possibility of two dominant norms in the intermediate schools providing alternative normative references.

[3] This relationship disappears among those with IQ's below 89 — that is, those for whom collegiate aspirations are unrealistic.

in Table 12, from the stance of the prevalent concern with the conservation of talent.

Comparing the effect of the school climate upon grades and upon educational aspirations in Tables 10 and 3, we can see that the devaluation of education in the working-class schools affects academic achievement as much as it is reflected in educational aspirations. In fact, it adversely affects the achievement of the sons of professional and white-collar workers more than it does their aspirations.

Tangential confirmation

The imputation of the variation in educational aspirations and behavior between schools to the "moral force" of the normative values within the school society is of course inferential.[1] This interpretation has been argued, up to this point, by holding constant other factors known to affect educational attitudes and attributing the residual difference to the hypothetical factor. The hypothesis, moreover, is theoretically congruent with a considerable accumulation of research on small groups, studies of peer-group influences, and of the differential effects of contrasting community structures: it has been shown that the perception of the opportunity for upward mobility by lower-strata youth is facilitated by the economic and occupational heterogeneity of the community.[2] Yet, if Occam's razor is to be scrupulously applied against the contextual hypothesis, it might be argued that, however homogeneous the students' familial backgrounds may be in terms of all available external indices, those working-class families living in predominantly middle-class districts are showing "anticipatory socialization" in their values and are inculcating them in their children.

TABLE 13. *Distribution of Peer-Group Offices among Occupational Strata by Schools*

	SCHOOL GROUP		
Fathers' occupation	A	B	C
Professional	25%	9%	3%
White collar	49	38	40
Self employed	18	29	7
Manual	8	24	50
Number of cases*	154	160	92

* Percentages are based on the number of students who have held some peer-group office — either within the school, such as team captain, student council member or class president, or outside of school, as an officer of "De Molay," "Teen-age Club," or similar group.

While the latter interpretation is reasonable, it is not so persuasive to argue the corollary that middle-class families would act to depress the aspirations of their children if they live in a predominantly working-class neighborhood. "... inherent in the very existence of a stratification order, of higher and lower valuations of social positions, is the motivation to move up in the social structure if one's position is low, or to retain one's position if it is high."[3] It is plausible to assume that middle-class youth, even when living in a predominantly working-class neighborhood, will be stimulated by their families toward educational diligence and to aspire to high-status occupations. The fact that the aspiration of these children is depressed when they attend a working-class school is more compelling evidence for the effect of the school milieu and peer-group norms than is the fact of the upward mobility of working-class youths in middle-class schools.

It has been reported frequently that students from middle-class families are generally over-selected for peer-group leadership positions. But "in order to become a *leader* . . . one must share prevailing opinions and attitudes."[4] This view has led to a presumption of the universality of upward aspirations. It was found in the present study, however, that one-half of those who had held peer-group offices in the group *C* schools were children of manual workers, while only eight per cent of those in the group *A* schools were the sons of manual workers (see Table 13). The distribution of peer-group offices among occupational strata is very close to that of the student bodies at large at each school group (as can be seen by comparing Table 13 with the first distribution in Table 2). But, consequently, the leaders who reflect, express, and mold the attitudes of the school society reinforce and extend the pre-existing differences in group characteristics.

The impact of school norms upon other values

Sociologists concerned with inter-generational mobility and the formation of social attitudes might well direct more attention to the investigation of contextual variables — attributes of membership groups which serve as references during the adolescent period of socialization — particularly to the society of the school. While the importance of both the family and the peer-group in the development of the economic and political values of the adolescent have been pointed out, most investigations have concentrated upon the influence of the family.[5] That the influence of the school climate is not confined to educational aspirations is shown by brief explorations, presented in Tables 14 and 15, into the differences between schools in occupational aspirations and in political preferences. These tables provide *prima*

[1] This requires no apology — the step from data to a theoretical proposition is always inferential. One does not *see* a cause.

[2] Lipset and Bendix, *Social Mobility* . . . , *op. cit.*, pp. 220–224.

[3] *Ibid.*, p. 203.

[4] Katz and Lazarsfeld, *op. cit.*, p. 52.

[5] Richard Centers, "Children of the New Deal: Social Stratification and Adolescent Attitudes," in *Class, Status and Power, op. cit.*, pp. 359–370; S. M. Lipset *et al.*, "The Psychology of Voting: An Analysis of Political Behavior," in G. Lindzey, editor, *Handbook of Social Psychology*, Cambridge: Addison-Wesley, Vol. II, pp. 1124–1175.

facie evidence, comparable to that of Table 3, suggesting that the dominant climate of opinion within a school makes a significant impact upon students' occupational goals and their political party preferences.

Conclusion

Whether the modification of attitudes by the normative climate of the school society persists or a reversion toward familial norms in later life takes place cannot be determined on the basis of static comparisons.

TABLE 14. *Percentages Aspiring to Professional Occupations by School Groups and Fathers' Occupations*

Fathers' occupation	SCHOOL GROUP		
	A	B	C
Professional	78%	60%	60%
	(81)	(35)	(10)
White collar	61	37	35
	(160)	(120)	(31)
Self employed	44	47	23
	(62)	(79)	(106)
Manual	44	31	27
	(36)	(121)	(198)
Weighted mean of per cents	60	39	30
	(339)	(355)	(345)

But certainly the student's high school achievement and his decision for or against college entrance have irreversible consequences in channeling him into the stream of economic and social life, and in biasing the probability

of future intimate contact with countervailing reference groups.

The Supreme Court has found that, even though the "tangible" provisions of schools are the same, schools segregated along racial lines are inherently unequal. The "sense of inferiority affects the motivation of the child

TABLE 15. *Percentages Expressing Preference for the Republican Party by School Groups and Fathers' Occupations*

Fathers' occupation	SCHOOL GROUP		
	A	B	C
Professional	81%	71%	33%
	(73)	(31)	(9)
White collar	72	64	36
	(120)	(98)	(72)
Self employed	80	62	39
	(56)	(68)	(23)
Manual	50	32	24
	(26)	(107)	(161)
Weighted mean of per cents	74	53	29
	(275)*	(304)*	(265)*

* Percentages are based on the number of students expressing preference for the Republican or Democratic party, omitting those who indicated "other," "none," or failed to respond.

to learn." The *de facto* segregation brought about by concentrations of social classes in cities results in schools with unequal moral climates which likewise affect the motivation of the child, not necessarily by inculcating a sense of inferiority, but rather by providing a different ethos in which to perceive values.

The Position of the Jews in English Society[1]
Howard Brotz

I. The civil status of English Jews

THE CIVIL STATUS of the Jews in England, both in theory and in practice, is similar to, if not identical with, that of the Jews in the United States. There are no important sore spots as far as civil rights are concerned.

[1] This study is part of a longer report prepared for the Library of Jewish Information (American Jewish Committee). I should like to thank the Library for its generous support. I am particularly indebted to Mr. Milton Himmelfarb for his able assistance in planning the inquiry.

The Jewish community, when it was re-established in England in the seventeenth century, was a tightly-knit, enclosed society which exerted a great deal of control over its members, not only in religion but also with respect to those things done by Jews which might provoke anti-Jewish feeling and action. The community was not, however, a ghetto on the model of those existing in the continental absolute monarchies of the time, that is, involved in a net of legal and customary arrangements that would require a major political

Reprinted from *The Jewish Journal of Sociology*, V. 1 (April, 1959) pp. 94–113, by permission of the author and the publisher.

upheaval to undo. Its status, by contrast, was vague, an ambiguous mixture of medieval and modern practice. This made it possible for the Jews to acquire civic equality through *ad hoc* judicial decisions or acts of legislation.[1] Still, this process, which was by no means a continuous and even development, took about two hundred years. Full civic emancipation was preceded by the gradual rise of modern political philosophy, a change in the aspirations of the Jews themselves (which, of course, was largely a result of the former), and the development of social relationships between Jews and Gentiles in high places. What is crucial in all this is that once the goal was attained, the opposition surrendered completely. There has never been since then a responsible proposal to deprive the Jews of their civic rights.[2]

From the point of view of personal security there is the same legal protection as in the United States and a similar quality of enforcement of the law. Illegal or extra-legal violence or defamation, particularly from hooligans, may, in fact, be somewhat greater in the United States. (For example, there is probably more desecration of Jewish graveyards in America than in England.) In any event, this is under control in England.[3] The British police act with dispatch and efficiency in such cases.

Further, there is no danger from organized political groups with anti-Jewish views. Before the war the government, by a single act of legislation, effectively prevented the transformation of the British fascists into the kind of private army which wrecked the Weimar Republic in Germany. The Public Order Act of 1936 forbade the carrying of offensive weapons and empowered the Home Secretary to forbid political processions and to close provocative meetings. When, shortly after the war, the British fascists had a brief resurgence and began a series of processions into the heart of Jewish districts in London, with considerable disorder, the Home Secretary revoked their permit to march.[4] Thus, in England, which is by no means an unfree society, the concern for civil liberties has never become the doctrinaire obsession which has been so paralysing to some modern democracies. The Jewish community, for its part, enjoys excellent relations with the police in the surveillance and control of fascism. Partly because of the support which it gets from the society at large, partly because of relative freedom from the "it can't happen here" delusion, the Jewish community has never been frightened into abject cowardice. In short, the security of Jews, individually and as a community, is in no danger.[5]

What is more, Anglo-Jewish society maintains itself in a benign and altogether decent atmosphere. The Jewish community, as an organized entity, is treated with respect; and the non-Jewish society is prepared to accommodate itself in a variety of ways to the requirements of religious practice where careless collision might otherwise take place. During the war, for example, Jews who desired to observe kashruth were given special ration arrangements. (So were vegetarians.) At a few of the public schools there are provisions for kosher food. And, in general, blatant anti-Jewishness would not be regarded as "good form". Further, yet, the entry into leading political and social positions of Jews who are identified as Jews and who are under no pressure to convert is relatively greater and altogether a much more normal phenomenon than in the United States. The proportion of Jewish Members of Parliament is more than five times as high as the proportion of Jews in the population. And, it must be borne in mind, there is no Jewish vote.[6] Since 1886, when Rothschild was created the first Jewish peer, Jews have been regularly elevated to the House of Lords; and for some time before that they had already been granted the distinctions of baronet and knight. A Jew, Lord Samuel, is the leader of the Liberal Party in the House of Lords; there are Jews who are heads of Oxford and Cambridge colleges; a Jew has been elected to the board of governors of Eton; Jews, though in small number, are present at all the great public schools, which are crucial institutions in the social class system of England; Jews are members of leading London clubs.

In fact, though discrimination exists, the attitude of "no Jews admitted" is more characteristic of the middle class (such as in the suburban golf and tennis clubs) than of the upper class. Their entry into the upper stratum of English social life, small though it may be, is still significant enough to make the situation of English Jews considerably different from that of American Jews.

II. The nature of English society and culture

England is a country which combines the spirit of aristocracy with the political forms of democracy.[7]

---

[1] Native-born Jews, for example, were not assured of their right to own land until 1718, when this was settled by a decision of the Attorney General: Albert Hyamson, *A History of the Jews in England*, London, 1908, p. 262.

[2] For further details of the history of the community from the Resettlement to the Emancipation period see Hyamson, op. cit., Cecil Roth, *A History of the Jews in England*, Oxford, 1949, and James Parkes, "History of the Anglo-Jewish Community", in M. Freedman, ed., *A Minority in Britain*, London, 1955.

[3] A few years back there was a sign in the London buses which was chronically written over by hooligans so as to become offensive to Jews. Complaints to the London Transport brought about a change in wording which eliminated this provocation.

[4] This was done, in fact, by a ban on *all* processions. Mr. Sidney Salomon in his pamphlet *Anti-Semitism and Fascism in Post-War Britain*, London, 1950, is of the opinion that the Act could be so interpreted as to be restricted to a provocative type of procession.

[5] Cf. Salomon, op. cit., which sums up the security situation very well.

[6] The significance of this observation must be slightly qualified. In England Jews are proportionally more numerous in national politics than in the United States; but American Jews would appear to be more active in local political affairs, which are much more important in the United States than in England.

[7] A. de Staël-Holstein, *Letters on England*, 2nd ed., London, 1830, pp. 115-139.

Besides such visible marks of aristocracy as the cult of the horse, aristocratic conceptions pervade the heart of the educational system. These embrace not only a belief in unequal capacities but also a respect for standards of excellence which extends throughout the entire nation. A rigorous classical education and the apprentice system fit together in the same society. But what is most significant in this discussion is that the aristocracy in England is still, to a great extent, a ruling class. Not only does politics have great dignity and importance for the members of the titled and landed classes themselves. Aristocracy, in addition, has provided a model for the whole of the civil service and, in general, for the democratic elements in English political life. In fact, if one examines the direction of the egalitarian changes which have been taking place in England in recent times, one finds that the attack upon the position of the landed classes, in so far as it has been these and not the capitalist system as such that have come under attack, has been aimed less against aristocracy as such than against caste — to use Tocqueville's distinction — and against those gross forms of privilege that derive from inordinate wealth.[1] The gentleman, which is the aristocratic conception separable from caste, is still regarded as the ideal type of man in this society. He is expected to, and does, find the natural outlet for his leadership in holding political office.

The United States presents a wholly different set of facts. The absence of a powerful landed gentry, particularly in the new areas opened up by pioneers, enabled the triumph of democracy to be much more complete than in England and to penetrate far beyond mere outward forms. Aristocracy, which increasingly came to mean plutocracy in America, was eclipsed in politics, which it subsequently came to despise and seek to control only from behind the scenes. Authority, in other words, split into its two components of power and honour, which then became separate elements in the society. Deprived of the natural outlet for leadership, namely, the open exercise of political authority, the vanity of those who consider themselves to be the leading men is by this very fact inflamed. In so far as they resign themselves to the political situation, their vanity is thus led to find a refuge in social things — for example, an obsession with ancestry or social exclusiveness. In America it is in this social sphere that the aristocracy has taken its revenge upon the democracy. Having been

forced to retreat to a sector which by its very nature can only be peripheral to the centre of gravity of the political community, they have invested it with an importance out of all proportion to good taste, let alone political reality. In England, by contrast, the question of dignities and honours is settled. The regulation of ranks and distinctions by the monarchy assures widespread respect for them (though it is of course possible for a monarch deliberately to cheapen the value of a title by distributing it almost *en masse*). Thus, in England, the desire for recognition and status does not have to create its own, essentially private symbols of distinction, but can aim at honours that are universally acknowledged.[2]

It is no accident that in a democracy snobbishness can be far more vicious than in an aristocracy. Lacking that natural confirmation of superiority which political authority alone can give, the rich, and particularly the new rich, feel threatened by mere contact with their inferiors.[3] This tendency perhaps reached its apogee in the late nineteenth century in Tuxedo Park, a select residential community composed of wealthy New York businessmen, which, not content merely to surround itself with a wire fence, posted a sentry at the gate to keep non-members out.[4] Nothing could be more fantastic than this to an English lord living in the country in the midst, not of other peers, but of his tenants. His position is such that he is at ease in the presence of members of lower classes and in associating with them in recreation. It is this "democratic" attitude which, in the first instance, makes for an openness to social relations with Jews. One cannot be declassed, so to speak, by play activities.

Furthermore, the English aristocracy, having never been displaced from power by a violent revolution, and having thus had a long experience of responsible administration, have all the characteristics of political maturity: reasonableness, good sense, and freedom from romantic reaction. Prepared to bow gracefully to their gradual eclipse, and themselves in large measure the very agents of the alteration of the class structure, they neither feel threatened by democratization nor would be predisposed to react to these changes by harbouring desires and plans for revenge. Hence they are not the logical carriers of an anti-Jewish political programme. (This freedom from reaction is, one might add, a distinguishing feature of British politics in general.)

But what is perhaps the most important fact about the stratification of English society is that its upper class is a stratum of gentlemen. Now in speaking of a gentleman, one must consider the natural marks as well as those conventional marks of social status, such as accent, which vary from one society to another. The first would include such things as pride and a sense of dignity, freedom from pettiness, courteousness towards inferiors, a responsible concern for the public life, etc. Though by no means every member of the English upper class is a gentleman in this precise sense — one has only to think of the international set — such qualities are sufficiently present in this class to distinguish it from

---

[1] A. de Tocqueville, *L'Ancien Régime*, tr. M. W. Patterson, Oxford, 1947, p. 88; 'Wherever the feudal system established itself on the continent of Europe it ended in caste; in England alone it returned to aristocracy.'

[2] H. L. Mencken has an interesting description of the misuse of English honours and titles in the United States during the nineteenth century in his *American Language*, 4th ed., New York, 1946, pp. 271–284.

[3] A historical account of social pretension in the United States is to be found in Dixon Wecter, *The Saga of American Society*, London, 1937. See also Cleveland Amory, *The Proper Bostonians*, New York, 1947, and *The Last Resorts*, New York, 1952.

[4] Amory, *Last Resorts*, pp. 98–99.

almost all continental aristocracies. These qualities are, of course, developed by a specific type of training and education — non-technical and non-co-educational — such as the public and the grammar schools provide. To be sure, these schools are intertwined with the conventional usages of the upper class. These are, of course, if not indispensable, at least convenient places for learning the style of life, the cultural habits, and what Hobbes called the "small morals" of the peculiarly English gentleman. But what is in fact more important to emphasize is that these schools, and the wider social fabric of which they are a natural part, have a great deal to do with the formation of those qualities that compose a gentlemanly character. They do not always succeed, but this is, by and large, their explicit goal.

As I have said above, the gentleman is a conception that is separable from caste. What relationship is there, then, between family background and this ideal and the class structure in general? This is the age-old question of birth versus breeding that has occupied the writers of manuals on the gentleman at least since the Renaissance. Observation shows that wise men can beget fools, which is enough to dispel the absolute pretensions of heredity. But awareness of great descent can act upon one as an obligatory standard, just as awareness of inferior descent can make one ashamed, nervous, and too anxious to impress. In so far as it affects one's pride and ease, not to mention the chances for education and leisure, family background evidently limits the individuality of the gentlemanly ideal. Then, also, it would be beyond reason to expect that in a society with a family system, caste-like snobbery would be altogether abolished. None the less, the English upper class is the most open aristocracy in the world, free of that obsession with blood and quarterings which marks the continental aristocracies (with whom, to be fair, the English could hardly compete in this respect).

These characteristics of the English aristocracy taken together — their established position, their adherence to the gentlemanly ideal, and their political maturity as peers amongst a free tenantry who are not peasants, let alone serfs — explain a number of facts, including the case, in contradistinction to all European aristocracies, with which the English aristocracy has been able to assimilate the bourgeoisie in general. On the one hand it has been prepared to trade social acceptance for the right to govern and mould a society whose wealth is, in fact, commercial.[1] On the other hand it has had the good sense to be willing to form family alliances with the business class to replenish fortunes and even to send its younger sons into commerce.[2] The aristocracy has never had that thoroughgoing contempt for commerce which might have permanently sundered aristocracy and bourgeoisie. Unthreatened, provided the bourgeoisie were willing to surrender themselves at least potentially to the aristocratic ideal, the aristocracy have not only looked with amusement upon the ambitions of those who would buy social position but have also openly engaged in the selling of the prerequisites.[3] It has been

much easier to buy one's way into society (including titles) in England than in the United States.[4] If "first-generation peer" is a term of derision, it at least suggests future possibilities.

All this was true in the heyday of the aristocracy. Today members of the gentry enter business (though typically managerial positions in large corporations) as a matter of course. And even though the security that great wealth could confer is rapidly disappearing with the attrition of inherited fortunes, one thing remains to fix the social pre-eminence of the aristocracy: the monarchy and the activities of the court around it.

Respect for the rights of the Jewish community as a corporate entity and fair treatment for Jews by government officials are logical consequences of rule by gentlemen. The malice of the German and Austrian civil servants, who gave the Jews absurd surnames, is lacking in their English counterparts. Even where a civil servant might privately have anti-Jewish sentiments, he would not allow these so to obtrude upon the conduct of his administration as to make him deviate from the impartiality required of his office.

Finally, the position and outlook of the aristocracy explain their willingness to associate as social equals with Jews who have acquired the specific cultural traits of the gentry. These are signs by which one gentleman recognizes another.

Altogether one may say that in a society like the English, with a relatively firm aristocratic structure, it is paradoxically easier to move up the social ladder than in a democracy like the American. In the United States there has been no lack of opportunity to get rich, as the achievements of poor immigrants have impressively shown. But is this not as much a testimony to the wealth of the country as it is to political and social equality? In England, at any rate, provided one has brains, one can be *selected*, by virtue of the scholarship system at both public schools and the ancient universities, for admission to those institutions. And with the fixed place that they occupy in English society, anyone who has attended them is at once granted the standing of a gentleman as well as endowed with a skein of connexions — for jobs, clubs, political life, social life, etc. — that serve to solidify his social position for the rest of his life. Furthermore, once one has this standing it is not

[1] Tocqueville, op. cit., p. 91: "The English aristocracy . . . was prepared to stoop to conquer."

[2] Staël-Holstein, op. cit., p. 125: "The younger sons of peers daily engage in trade without any idea of derogation entering into their minds."

[3] This deference to the aristocracy has sometimes been regarded as a source of weakness for English capitalism (as compared with the United States). There is at least one enclave, the City of London banking families, which has not been willing to surrender and which is disliked by the aristocracy.

[4] James Bryce, *The American Commonwealth*, London, 1889, vol. ii, p. 620: "In England great wealth can, by using the appropriate methods, practically buy rank from those who bestow it; or by obliging persons whose position enables them to command fashionable society, can induce them to stand sponsors for the upstart, and force him into society, a thing which no person in America has the power of doing."

easily lost, as it does not depend exclusively on wealth. Thus, where there is a fixed class structure, provided it does not freeze altogether into a caste system, there can be great opportunity for personal talent.

Thus a Jew who goes to one of the leading public schools has a wide entry into high places in English society. This entry may also be won, but with less certainty, through attendance at one of the ancient universities, Oxford and Cambridge. These are larger and socially more heterogeneous than the public schools; and associations formed there are obviously not of the same character as those that develop between adolescents. It is the extraordinary durability of the relationships between boys away from their families which makes the public school such an important social institution in English life. But it is well to recall that the gentry, by the most mannered application of class distinctions, can appear extremely cruel to "pushers" lacking in the subtle qualifications of the class to which they aspire.[1]

The Jews on the whole did not play a direct part in the classic industrial revolution. Wealthy Jews before this century were merchants, brokers or bankers. They were thus outside the strife which emerged, for example, between miner and mine-owner in times of depression. The trade unions, for their part, have been motivated in their demands less by ideological considerations (such as characterized, for example, Nazism or Marxism) than by a haunting fear of unemployment. Their objectives have been concerned with matters like wages, hours, and production quotas. Their conservatism in this respect, one might add, is a serious problem for the efficiency of British technology.

In so far as Jews became manufacturers in the textile and furniture trades, they were until this century owners of small-scale shops, whose workmen, besides, were overwhelmingly Jewish. It is only recently that Jewish ownership — for example, in industry and department stores — has faced a really sizeable body of non-Jewish employees. There is no problem of anti-Jewish feeling in this sphere. In fact, a firm which has perhaps the most benign policy of labour relations in England is not merely Jewish but is distinctively known as such.

What about the business class itself? The Jews had the good fortune to be supported in England by political men like Cromwell who, themselves not businessmen, regarded commercial activity as a source of national strength. It was they who not only were in favour of the resettlement of a Jewish community of traders but also were prepared to grant them increasing freedom from civil disabilities. From the beginning, however, these political men had to cope with and placate the intransigent anti-Jewish opinion of the Corporation of the City of London, who feared the Jews as competitors. Until 1831 the City, which jealously guarded its prerogatives, excluded Jews from the right to engage in retail trade within its boundaries and opposed every effort to grant

the Jews full civic rights.[2] It seems reasonable to conclude that if the City had dominated the government, the Jews would not have been readmitted to England as early as they were.

Whatever light this throws upon the mentality of the business class, it must be borne in mind that the guild organization of the City merchants, with their ability to speak politically as a corporate group, was distinctive in the modern commercial scene. (Perhaps the nearest equivalent is the trade union, the voice of which has been effective in influencing immigration policy.) Nowhere else, including the area adjacent to the City walls, did the Jews encounter effective opposition to the right to do business. It is also true that after 1831 the City's opposition to further Jewish emancipation dwindled quickly; the first Jewish M.P., Baron Lionel de Rothschild, was in fact elected from the City of London. And the acquisition of civic rights gave the Jews the means for protecting themselves against a resurgence of the selfishness of the City or any other special-interest group.

The Jews won all their civil rights during a period when British power and prestige were reaching their zenith. What would happen if Britain were to experience a profound collapse would be difficult to predict. The one blot on an exemplary record in the treatment of Jews occurred during the early part of the last war, when the German Jewish refugees, who by and large had not yet acquired British citizenship, were interned as enemy aliens. In Australia, where many of them were transported, it is said that they would have been interned in the same cantonment with German non-Jews if native-born Australian Jews had not protested vigorously. But this blemish in the English record may have been a result of momentary panic; it does not indicate how the government would behave with people who felt themselves fully possessed of the rights of Englishmen.

In summary, English society is marked by the absence of any powerful group that either is actually threatened by Jewish success or would be predisposed to use Jews as a scapegoat. There is a remarkable wholeness to the fabric of the society, which has its most visible manifestation in the public order which prevails. The police, as everyone knows, are unarmed in the ordinary course of their duties. Underlying this fact is the great public trust which exists. There is no general fear of internal subversion, and this in turn rests upon the high level of public life and upon an absence of deep class conflicts, or of narrow and rigid selfishness, or of corruption generally. It is therefore readily understandable why the elements with anti-Jewish propensities are politically a fringe group.

III. Manners and traditions: the character of the people

RELIGION

The outstanding fact about Christianity in England is that it is weakest in the decisive respect, belief, and

---

[1] Compare the stories and novels of Saki.
[2] Hyamson, op. cit., pp. 259 f., 274.

strongest and most attractive essentially in its ceremonial. To exaggerate only somewhat for purposes of clarification, one may say that throughout the whole range of English society religion is for marriages, funerals, and coronations. Anglicanism, more nearly than any other modern branch of Christianity, would seem to approximate the status which paganism had for the educated classes in antiquity. The upper classes are simply bored by doctrinal controversy, and the workers' abandonment of the church is the obverse side of Orwell's observation that a key change in the England of this century is the passing of the general belief in immortality. Hence the possibilities of an anti-Jewish outlook or programme grounded on Christian doctrine are limited to tiny coteries of intellectuals amongst converted Catholics and Anglo-Catholics. The anti-Jewishness of such people is probably greater than that of any other group in England. Although they seem to take religion seriously, no one, of course, can tell exactly in what way. It is plausible, however, and even suggested by their own statements, that their attraction to a hierarchical and ritually elaborate religion rests upon an ultimately utilitarian consideration: religion is a prop for a romantic conservative outlook hostile to commerce and democracy. The Jews, from this point of view, are not so much the enemies of Christ as the purveyors of mass-produced vulgarity. This, of course, is hardly the stuff out of which a mass movement is made. Nor would these individuals (at least in the Anglo-Saxon world) lend their support to palpable enemies of civilization.

In so far as Christian belief was a living force in the English past, as for example during the seventeenth century, it was imbued with a Puritanism based on the Old Testament that made for a strange kind of philo-Hebraism.[1] (To this day Hebraic scholarship is highly esteemed in English academic life and is of a high calibre.) The same philo-Hebraism was true of Presbyterianism, the established religion in Scotland, and of all the Non-conformist sects. The resettlement of the modern Jewish community under Cromwell was made possible in part by the sympathy which the Puritans of the time gave to Menasseh ben Israel's religious petition. From that time to this many Englishmen have seen the Jews as the wondrous people of the Biblical drama.[2] This may still be so in Scotland.[3] There has also been an interesting kinship between Unitarianism and Reform Judaism.

POLITENESS AND FAIRNESS

Throughout the whole of English society there is a diffusion of the gentlemanly ideal and the political habits it embraces. As Max Weber noted, the gentleman, amongst the variety of types of men which societies regard as ideal, and in sharp contrast to the standards of the Prussian Junker, is intrinsically capable of being imitated.[4] This must be slightly qualified. The gentleman is essentially an aristocratic, unegalitarian conception which embraces a sense of pride and dignity that is in practice incompatible with the performance of many

degrading activities that have to be performed in every society. If there is, however, this natural limit to *successful* imitation of the gentlemanly ideal, the things that are ordinarily understood today by the terms politeness and courtesy are capable of vast democratization.[5] It is with respect to these that the essentially *civil* ideal of the gentleman has so widely penetrated the manners of the English.

Then too, like those of the Dutch, English manners have been sweetened by several centuries of commerce. The English lack great warmth and are rather distant from one another, but they are polite. In fact, below the upper class and particularly in the lower middle class, it is very common to see an almost servile sort of over-politeness: what the upper class derides as "refaynment". The crucial precipitate of all this, in more specifically political terms than the word polite nowadays connotes, is reasonableness. In this the English have attained a style. One can explain one's point of view to an Englishman. One does not have to cringe before a civil servant.

This reasonableness coalesces, furthermore, with the ideal of fair play, that canon of a liberal society, which is buttressed by the English passion for sports. It is extraordinarily easy for anyone to assert and obtain his rights under this code. I have seen this countless times in such public situation as queues, where someone — probably inadvertently — got ahead of his proper place, was asked to "play the game, old boy", and became terribly embarrassed and conceded without further ado.

INDIVIDUALISM

English liberty, with its emphasis on rights, has produced a heightened sense of what is one's own private business. The respect for privacy is further buttressed by the Englishman's attitude towards his home. To invade this improperly is very offensive indeed. In addition, the English conduct themselves with fantastic restraint and reserve; and it would be as much a violation of the standards which this imposes to do things which are casually done in the public square in Latin countries — one hardly ever, for example, sees a child slapped in public — as it would be to stare. Altogether, as a German

---

[1] Hyamson, op. cit., pp. 164–166. Fantastic Judaizing proposals emanated from such Puritanism, e.g. a suggestion to adopt Hebrew as the national language.

[2] Cecil Roth, *Anglo-Jewish Letters*, London, 1938, pp. 49–51, Letter of Henry Oldenburgh to Menasseh ben Israel.

[3] David Daiches has a vivid account in *Two Worlds: An Edinburgh Jewish Childhood*, New York, 1956, of what it was like to grow up as a Jew in Edinburgh. When he was absent for Jewish holidays, the Christian schoolchildren would ask him whether it was "a feast or a fast".

[4] Max Weber, "National Character and the Junkers", in Gerth and Mills, eds., *Essays from Max Weber*, New York, 1946, p. 391. Tocqueville also, op. cit., p. 90, discusses the democratization of the word gentleman, but shows that in the process it changes its meaning.

[5] It is in this somewhat vulgarized sense that the term gentleman is ordinarily understood in the United States outside of the South.

Jewish refugee put it, "The English are a decent people. They leave you alone."

In the upper classes in particular the eccentric is not merely tolerated, he is admired. When John Stuart Mill wrote his famous essay *On Liberty*, he feared that social pressure emanating from the rising middle classes would extinguish the open display of any deviation from prevailing custom. Though there is pressure towards conformity in England as in America, the full measure of Mill's fear has not been realized. Either he underestimated the number of cranks which English life produces so prolifically, or else he failed to see the possibilities of protection for individuality which an admirable sense of humour confers. If the British perceive something as "dotty", it is safe.

When the Jews first began holding public services in the seventeenth century, the synagogue was frequented by visitors.[1] It is my impression that Judaism in England to this day derives protection from being viewed in the light of something exotically interesting.

HUMANITARIANISM

The humanitarianism of Victorian England seems to have been a blend of political ideas and a religious impulse. Into the democratic theory and ideology of the Enlightenment was infused the enthusiasm of the Non-conformist sects, in particular, for salvation. Tempered by all the virtues of English politics, humanitarianism never seriously approached revolutionary dimensions. The result was the spirit of reform: a sense of sympathy for oppression and suffering, and a determination to correct abuse by public action.

Much must be made of the part that women began to play in this society, for it was in essence a woman's conscience that attacked the slave trade and the brutal criminal code. This spirit gradually prevailed to such a degree that agitation about impersonal causes and voluntary organization in their behalf became a normal political phenomenon. It can, of course, reach cranky proportions. There have probably been more bequests to cats in England than in any other civilized society and there was an organization of ladies called the M.A.B.Y.S. — the Metropolitan Association for the Betterment of Young Servant Girls. A most solid achievement, however, lay in the quality to which the standards of public life were raised. This was the period that witnessed the formation of the most humane and efficient civil service in the world, the disappearance of corruption from English politics, and the transformation of the raw oligarch of the eighteenth century into an educated, public-spirited gentleman.

The abolition of all civil disabilities for Jews, Dissenters, and Catholics, which occurred long after the

real religious issues had been settled and which was spearheaded by the Liberals, drew for its success upon the support of this educated, humanitarian opinion. Sir Moses Montefiore's personal action in alleviating the distress of foreign Jewries had not only the sympathy but also the semi-official support of the British Government.[2]

UNTHEORETICAL INCONSISTENCY

The English are a curious blend of gentleness and toughness. On the one hand, the anti-vivisection society is strong enough to be a perpetual nuisance to biologists; on the other hand, corporal punishment is more prevalent in English schools than anywhere else. One aspect of this toughness is a kind of bluntness in the very way in which Englishmen speak of Jews, and of other minorities as well. The "dumb" Englishman does not have any of the restraint his American equivalent might have in publicly referring to a Jew as a Jew, a restraint imposed in America by the necessity felt in a democratic and ethnically heterogeneous environment to play down minority labels. This bluntness, even where it reaches vulgar forms, must not be uncritically identified as Jew-hatred. (A Jewish army officer overheard one of his men saying to another, "The b—— Jew is all right.") Bluntness of this kind is not seated in deep emotional involvements. Nor, what is more important, is it part of a theoretical stance that seeks perfect consistency.

The English, who pride themselves on their practical wisdom and good sense, properly despise the intrusion of theory into the domain of politics; they boast about the fact that their constitution is unwritten and have a low opinion of intellectuals altogether. As practical men their main concern, in resolving political differences, is to find an area of agreement in which compromise is possible, and they would be reluctant to press discussion to those intellectually clear-cut extremes where irreconcilable conflict is explicitly spelled out and from which retreat is difficult. They would therefore hardly be disturbed by the inconsistencies to which we are necessarily impelled by genuine political life. Though this practical, gentlemanly point of view has grave consequences for the quality of theoretical reflection, it protects them within the sphere of practice from the disastrous effects of ideology.

The intellectual anti-Semite is not at home in this milieu. Jewish "theoreticians," for example, have only just ceased worrying about the accusation of "dual loyalty" which, they felt, unqualified support of Israel must necessarily bring about, taking pains to define Jewry, as a "religious, not national" group. Their fears were simply beside the point. Most Englishmen would be amazed (as well as amused) to learn of their very existence.

A corollary of this attitude is the absence of ideological support for Jewish-Gentile harmony or good relations. Groups working for these ends exist. But the English, in general, regard such talk as cant; and, as in America, it has little effect on actual social relations.

[1] Roth, op. cit., p. 55: John Greenhalgh, curious about all the sects of the time, approached a Jew in the street, who arranged for him to visit a service. This he describes in his letter.
[2] For details about the Damascus affair, see Hyamson, op. cit., pp. 335–336.

IV. The general character of the Jewish community

Anglo-Jewry altogether is relatively smaller than American Jewry. To take London alone, which is roughly equal to New York in population, the 250,000 Jews of London are only one-eighth as many as the Jews of New York. Though there are large enough concentrations to give a Jewish cast to certain districts of London (as well as to one or two resort cities and districts of some provincial cities), Jews do not make a visible impact at the centre of things. Then, too, because of both the small size of the Jewish community and the more restrictive, "party manners" atmosphere of England, English Jews, even among intellectuals, would not, for example, feel as free to use Yiddish expressions in the presence of non-Jews as American Jews would in comparable circles here. The degree to which comedians in America freely use occasional Yiddish words, which surely must account in great measure for the penetration of several such words into the general vocabulary, is not equalled in England. (English, Scottish, Welsh, and Irish dialects, of course, are very much a part of the British comedian's stock in trade.) Absent from the English radio are those minority-group family serials, such as the "Rise of the Goldbergs," which make their appearance on the American radio and television partly as a matter of right.

This is related to certain underlying political facts. Jews are neither a political bloc nor one of a number of minority blocs with whom they are roughly equated in the public eye. Minority-group politics does not exist in England. Though Jewish M.P.s may speak in behalf of Jewish interests, they do not control a Jewish vote. Both the small size of the community and the centralized party structure make it impossible for Jews to control strategic levers in the electoral machine. The government is therefore not responsive to Jewish opinion or interests as a force that must be placated. The recent shift in British policy towards Israel was wholly independent of calculation about Jewish interests in these terms.

Thus Jews entering politics are more or less forced to transcend the boundaries not only of the Jewish community but also of the minority group as such. In fact, the significant aspects under which the Jewish community is treated as a corporate entity is in its character of a religious group — for the most part on ceremonial occasions. The Chief Rabbi from time to time is commanded to have an audience of the sovereign and would be invited to coronations.

All this very much suited the old Anglo-Jewish leadership, who deliberately avoided the publicity of parliamentary procedures. Following in the path of the traditional *shtadlan*, they preferred to act quietly, out of the public eye, in their dealings with government officials with whom they had patiently established personal connexions of long standing.[1] In the split which occurred within the Jewish community over Zionism, the Zionist mass came to depreciate this preference as cowardly and wrested control of the chief representative institution, the Board of Deputies, away from the old leadership. The public resolution then began to be an instrument of the Board's activities. In part the disdain for the old quietness had a demagogic character, heightened by the first flush of a great enthusiasm, but more fundamentally a difference about aims rather than method caused the breach. With the establishment of the State of Israel this whole issue has expired; and in any case personal relations between *shtadlanim* (who are coming more and more to be salaried officials of the Jewish community) and governmental officials have remained and will remain a characteristic feature of minority life.

In general, English Jews in high places, throughout the history of the modern settlement, have avoided becoming controversial public figures. There is no English equivalent of the hatred which Léon Blum aroused in certain French quarters.

All this points to what cannot be a too flattering observation. This is that Anglo-Jewry has slumbered beneath the visible surface of English life. With the one exception of Disraeli, who is altogether atypical, the Anglo-Jewish community has not dazzled, to cause either admiration or resentment in the non-Jewish world. It has not made a mark upon this world. Its inner life, too, exhibits a similar lack of brilliance. What accounts for this?

First and foremost, there is the character of the leadership of Anglo-Jewry, the men who set the tone of the comunity's outlook and way of life.[2] From the days of the resettlement (and earlier in Holland, as well), there was a marked change from the standards of what we may loosely call the traditional Jewish community. Authority passed from the learned rabbi to the businessman. Early in their history the London Jews had acquired the reputation of being interested only in business.[3] This is not quite correct. They also wanted to be gentlemen. It is the hybrid ideal of the gentleman and the businessman that defined the spirit of the Anglo-Jewish community and which can be summed up in one word: respectability.

Absorbed in commerce, which was just beginning to enjoy the prestige it has in the modern world, English Jews could in full propriety look down not merely upon heroism (as did their non-Jewish counterparts) but also upon the impractical matter of Jewish scholarship as well. As gentlemen, too, they disdained the passionate immersion in study that constituted the way of the Jewish scholar. The sphere of religion proper thus

[1] This was particularly true in foreign affairs. There has been no lack of out-spokenness in openly combating domestic fascism.

[2] I have dealt with this in further detail in "The Outlines of Jewish Society in London", in Freedman, ed., *A Minority in Britain*, pp. 153–159.

[3] Roth, op. cit., p. 180. In a letter to his brother in Frankfort, the eighteenth-century Chief Rabbi Tevele Schiff complains: "I have no colleagues nor pupils to study with, and no one even to whom I can talk on these [learned] matters. . . . "

became restricted to the practice of formal, unfanatical piety. As gentlemen, they had to take themselves seriously; the gentleman does not mock the conventions of his society. And so they lost that Jewish sense of comedy which is derived from a transcendence, if not of all conventions, at least of those concerned with pomp and circumstance.

Their sphere of public life was the Jewish community, in the administration of which they conducted themselves like gentlemen. Though later accused by immigrants from the Russian ghetto of being cold and of looking at matters from a businessman's point of view, they were, none the less, charitable, humane, efficient, loyal. Son followed father in a family tradition of voluntary communal work. In their business activities and in their conduct generally they sought to comply with a high standard of integrity to protect the good name of Anglo-Jewry. This led to inevitable collision with Jews coming from Eastern Europe, whose outlook was in many ways wholly at variance with that of the long-established English Jews. But if as a result community leaders indulged themselves in the snobbery of Anglo-Jewish ancestor worship, they never developed the kind of contempt which the German Jews had for the East European Jews. Apart from the charity they extended to the immigrant Jewish poor, their reaction to these aliens in their midst was to help them become "anglicized" or "established". The Jews' Free School and the many youth clubs in East London, which were founded and directed by individuals from old Anglo-Jewish families, owe their origin to this beneficent impulse.[1]

Besides the character of the leadership, other factors influenced the nature of the minority life. Chief among these is that the English Jews were never under the despotic control of a master. To be sure, the Jews before full civil emancipation had to seek protection in high places — both from Cromwell and from Charles II[2] — but they were far removed from the *servi camerae* of the Middle Ages. Brought over to increase the wealth of the nation by trade,[3] they did not achieve a degree of economic power that would make a monarch dependent upon them, and, because gratitude can be painful, dangerous to them. They were thus not attached to the society in one singular respect as were the medieval moneylenders, who were displaced when Christians developed their skills.

Then, the English Jews, modelling themselves on their hosts, were not intellectuals but businessmen, bent on living well, who avoided coming into open collision with prevailing opinion. It is also plausible that a high rate of intermarriage can provoke the enmity of non-Jews when, from the point of view of the non-Jews, it may appear that the Jews are marrying the most desirable spouses. In this respect the situation in England has never been comparable to that in Germany or urban Hungary, where the rate of intermarriage was very high. Nor has Jewish criminality in England ever exceeded those limits within which it could be successfully repudiated and even suppressed by the responsible members of the community. Perhaps the one occupational sore spot was the moneylender; aristocrats who gambled and borrowed were said to be "in the hands of the Jews". But this hardly had serious effects.

All told, the Anglo-Jewish community has been obscure and dull, but, in a manner of speaking, it saved itself by this very obscurity and dullness. Its historians have noted with evident pride how, in contrast to the situation on the continent, its most assimilated (or anglicized) members did not desert the community.[4] Although the Reform movement in English Judaism was begun and led by individuals from old Anglo-Jewish families (for example, Claude Montefiore), it is a striking fact that the community is at its heart Orthodox in religious practice and is led by families which are both anglicized *and* Orthodox.

But if the more benign atmosphere of England has permitted them to combine both worlds, to combine in other words the gentleman and the Jew, this has not been possible without some restriction of what are, perhaps, the highest human potentialities. It has not been an atmosphere to sustain the pinnacle of Jewish life, namely great Jewish scholarship. Nor has English Jewry lived in an atmosphere like that which prevailed in Catholic and aristocratic Vienna before the First World War, where the educated, assimilated middle-class Jew, having deserted the synagogue but not being accepted socially by the non-Jews, lived in a kind of *demi-monde* with other Jews of his type. Living in this *demi-monde* may not have permitted them to go unnoticed as Jews, but the compensation was that their thought was uncontrolled, particularly by such social demands as a gentlemanly code. They were free to develop not only psychoanalysis but other lines of thought and art as well.

V. Concluding remarks

Anglo-Jewry is a minority and is thus, in some more or less tangible respects, a separate group within English society.[5] There are no barriers to assimilation; and if the members of the community had wished to do so they could have gradually fused with the general population, like the Huguenots. That they wished to remain distinct, which means not only for the practice of Judaism but also for the maintenance of a somewhat autonomous communal life, is manifest by the very survival of the community to this date. That they wish to do so in the future accords with the sentiments not only of the mass of Jews, who lead a highly enclosed social life, but also of those anglicized Jews who enjoy

[1] V. D. Lipman, *Social History of the Jews in England, 1850–1950*, London, 1954, pp. 30–31.

[2] Hyamson, op. cit., p. 218.

[3] Ibid., p. 176. The part which Marrano merchants were playing in the commercial rise of Holland was very much in the forefront of Cromwell's mind.

[4] Cecil Roth, "The Collapse of Anglo-Jewry", *Jewish Monthly*, July 1947.

[5] See Brotz, op. cit., pp. 165–197.

a much greater degree of intimacy with non-Jewish society but who remain linked with the Jewish community, and are in this fundamental respect honest with themselves.

To compare briefly the position of Catholics and Jews, the former may almost be said to have something of the status of political traitors, people who have lapsed. If one looks at the extreme expression of this attitude, as it exists in Ulster, Catholics are regarded with a mistrust and even hatred far beyond anything that Jews normally would experience. Upper-class Englishmen have recalled that in their school days what seemed to matter was not whether a person was a Jew but whether he was a Catholic.

This relative blindness permits the Jew a great deal of freedom pleasantly to penetrate English social life and to feel accepted as an individual. But the fact cannot be gainsaid that the Jew as such is something of a stranger. The non-Jew will take note of this fact, if only to avoid the very use of the word Jew in the presence of Jews in that casual way which connotes distance or difference — e.g. the term "Jew-tailor". This distance, which is the result of group consciousness, must be distinguished from two things which may be included in it but which are not intrinsic to it. The first is Jew-hatred, which is to be encountered in England, but which is not so great or so organized as to be a danger to the community; the Jewish community, as Mr. Salomon has noted, is properly vigilant about the growth of anti-Jewish sentiment but would agree with the contention made here. The second thing is the distance which is the result of different tastes. There are some Jews who would never be at home in certain non-Jewish environments, and *vice versa*.

But wholly apart from the last two phenomena, so long as Jews are a separated group there will be a limitation upon the degree to which Jews will be accepted in a society. This limitation is quantitative rather than qualitative. As Lessing indicated in *Nathan the Wise*, love and friendship, let alone the idea of humanity, freely cross religious lines. Furthermore, there is no discernible limit upon the height to which a Jew, openly professing Judaism, could rise, short of the monarchy itself, the subordinate world of the Court, and, obviously, the leadership of the Church. If the fact that Disraeli was baptized is cited against this contention, it can be replied that there have been few of his calibre, Jew or Gentile, since his time.

The quantitative restriction is another matter. This refers to a numerical preponderance of Jews in *leading* positions of a society: politics, the professions and social life. Psychoanalysis in England is crowded not merely with Jews but with German Jewish refugees, who are objects of the not inconsiderable xenophobia that exists in England above and beyond anti-Jewish sentiment; but because psychoanalysis does not have high standing in England, the concentration of Jews does not cause resentment. The same can be said for trade generally and for those particular lines of business which Jews dominate. They are below the pinnacle of the society and therefore do not enter into conflict with any powerful interest. Placed against this fact, the significance of propaganda attacking the Jews for being in trade is small.

For the leading positions, however, it is fair to say that by and large a tacit *numerus clausus* exists in England. But because, with certain exceptions, its limits have not been approached, it has never become explicit; and this makes for a genuinely pleasant atmosphere. There are four reasons for this state of affairs: first, the relatively small size of the Jewish community; second, the tenacity of English life and social institutions, particularly amongst the upper class, which makes it possible for one to accept a Jew without even conceiving of the possibility of being "invaded" by the Jewish community; third, the stratification of English society, which overlaps with that within the Jewish community, and which makes possible the development of genuine bonds between all who have had a gentlemanly education; and fourth, the proclivities and preferences of the Jews themselves, most of whom do not regard a separate Jewish social life as any kind of hardship.

Certainly, the situation of the Jews in England is desirable in many ways. A number of the minor irritations that befall an American Jew — as, for example, in taking a vacation — are absent in England. Denied in many typical instances the possibility of anonymity by the larger society, an American Jew sometimes finds it hard to avoid having to associate with people not congenial to him — vulgar people, for instance — merely because they too are Jews. It is possible but he must check beforehand. Though vulgarity of the *nouveau riche* sort — an almost complete renunciation of the traditional Jewish virtues — exists within Anglo-Jewry, yet the few older Anglo-Jewish families, who have had several generations of inherited wealth and English manners, are still a force in setting a tone of propriety for the community. Just as vulgarity is less dominant and brash in England than in America altogether, so does Anglo-Jewry have more polish than American Jewry.

But what choice is available to those English Jews to whom the life of the spirit is almost life itself? It seems to be, mainly, a choice between vulgarity or pedestrian decency, wrapped up in the administration of communal affairs which, though necessary, are nonetheless pedestrian and dull. It is no wonder that such people have few to talk to. The really vulgar can evoke nothing but distaste (or, perhaps, a benign amusement); and in so far as the Anglo-Jewish upper class are interested in intellectual activities, it is typically in Anglo-Jewish history, the gentleman's hobby, and without passion.

The American community, by contrast, has much more intellectual vigour. In part this difference is due to the greater size of American Jewish communities. But of greater importance is the fact that American Jewry can turn more freely and naturally within itself, into its own intellectual tradition, without a concern that by so doing it is violating the canons of good taste.

What is at issue here is the age-old question of assimilation. Certainly the Anglo-Jewish leadership were not crude assimilationists and prided themselves precisely on the fact that while achieving a balance between the two worlds, they remained fully loyal Jews. It is the quality of this balance, which rested essentially upon an opposition of the gentleman ideal to the ghetto, that one must question. In so far as they set themselves against the narrowness of the ghetto — uncritical contempt or fear of the non-Jewish world and an illiberality of spirit in relations even with other Jews — they were only opposing the best of one mode of life to the worst of another. But to go further and to deride the very fullness of what it means to be a Jew as the narrowness of the ghetto is a mistake, for this fullness is not narrowness. Every people, to have pride, dignity, inner freedom and, hence, contentment, must have an attachment to a tradition that is something of its own. And is the Jewish tradition, with its answer to the question of how man should live, merely just another tradition? The alternative is an obsessional concern with the approval of the non-Jewish world, with all the emptiness of life in a glasshouse.

In this respect immersion in communal work and even piety itself are only parts. In attachment to the gentleman ideal they have been capable — though not necessarily — of precluding that genuine respect for, not to say devotion to, the Jewish intellectual tradition which is the source of the fullness I have mentioned. This may have flourished in the ghetto, but to regard it as something that could be produced only there is to commit a grave historical error.

Perhaps those Jews of England who wished to be Jewish gentlemen went further than they had to even to capture the virtues of the gentlemen, let alone to save the community.

Four

Differential Class Behavior

POPULATION

Trends in Class Fertility in Western Nations[1]
Dennis H. Wrong

ALTHOUGH THE BIRTH-RATE has declined in all Western nations since the middle of the nineteenth century, the decline has not been equal among the various groups that compose their population. Measures of fertility for national units conceal differences in the fertility of the many distinct groups in urban-industrial societies. Changes in the pattern of these differences are of particular significance in the later stages of the demographic transition from high to low birth-rates and death-rates which the Western world has undergone in the past century. Changes in the birth-rate rather than in the death-rate are the main determinants of growth in societies where mortality has been brought under control by modern medicine and public health practices.

Demographers have often treated differential fertility as a special, virtually autonomous subject instead of viewing it in the broad historical context of the Western demographic transition. In fact, as J. W. Innes has pointed out, few studies have been made of *trends* in differential fertility by comparison with the numerous studies which simply establish the existence of group differences in fertility at a single point in time.[2] The present paper is concerned with class differences — probably the most pervasive of all group differences in advanced societies. The attempt is made to gather together by historical period the available data on trends in class differences in fertility for several Western countries in order to present

a systematic picture of the way in which these differences have evolved in modern times.

The problem of dividing a population into socio-economic classes that are genuinely distinct from one another in a sociologically meaningful sense has been widely discussed by sociologists. Demographers, however, usually work with official data which provide only limited information on the characteristics of populations. They are, therefore, unable to employ the more refined indices of class developed by sociologists and are forced to use as indices such relatively simple objective attributes as income, occupation, or education. Censuses provide data on the occupational distribution of the population and their ready-made categories can easily be combined to form broad stratified groups. Occupation is by no means a perfect index of class, for within an occupation there is a good deal of variation in income and education, and neither of these attributes can be ignored in arriving at an adequate, objective measure of class. Nevertheless, most contemporary sociologists agree that, if defined with sufficient specificity, occupation

[1] This paper is the concluding chapter, somewhat revised, of a larger study in which statistics on socio-economic fertility-differences in Western nations are intensively analysed. I am indebted to Kingsley Davis for valuable advice and to the Canadian Social Science Research Council for financial assistance.

[2] J. W. Innes, *Class Fertility Trends in England and Wales, 1876–1934* (Princeton: 1938), v.

Reprinted from *The Canadian Journal of Economics and Political Science*, V. XXIV, No. 2 (May, 1958), pp. 216–229, by permission of the author and the publisher.

is probably the best *single* index which it is feasible to use in large-scale statistical inquiries.

Since different nations use different systems of occupational classification, precise international comparisons are usually impossible. The systems vary widely both with respect to the number of groups distinguished and the criteria on the basis of which the classification is constructed. Moreover, few nations use systems of classification that correspond with classes or with a socio-economic scale of status. Frequently only broad industrial groups are distinguished or the labour force is subdivided solely according to work status — that is, into employers, self-employed, salaried employees, and wage-workers. For all these reasons, changes that may have been taking place are sometimes obscured.

What is true of measures of class is also true of measures of fertility. Current fertility-rates, both crude and refined, fertility-ratios, and cumulative birth-rates based on retrospective reporting of births in response to census questions asking the numbers of children ever born to women in specified categories of the population — all these familiar but different measures have been used in studies of differential fertility. The present study makes greatest use of cumulative rates,[1] particularly for women whose years of childbearing are over. Such rates are especially useful to the student of trends for they permit comparisons of the childbearing performance of successive groups or cohorts of women who were born or married at different dates.

The nations included in the survey have been selected primarily because they possessed the most adequate data on trends in class differences in fertility. Both primary and secondary sources have been used for Great Britain, the United States, Norway, Sweden, France, and Australia. Germany, Switzerland, Denmark, and Canada have been treated more cursorily, reliance being placed largely on secondary sources. The trend and pattern of class differences in fertility are reviewed for each of the three broad periods into which the data have been grouped, and the agencies — delayed marriage, birth control, and so on — that apparently account for group differences in fertility are briefly discussed.

[1] Cumulative birth-rates are the total numbers of births before a specified age or date per 1,000 women surviving to that age or date.

[2] The conclusions for this period are based on the following sources. Innes, *Class Fertility Trends in England and Wales*. Great Britain, Census of England and Wales, 1911, XIII, *Fertility of Marriage* (London, 1917). United States Bureau of the Census, Sixteenth Census of the United States (1940), *Population: Differential Fertility, 1940 and 1910* (5 vols., Washington, D.C., 1943–47). Edgar Sydenstricker and Frank W. Notestein, "Differential Fertility According to Social Class," *Journal of the American Statistical Association*, XXV, no. 30, March, 1930. France, Bureau de la Statistique Générale, *Statistique des familles en 1906* (Paris, 1912); *Statistique des familles en 1911* (Paris, 1918). Joseph J. Spengler, *France Faces Depopulation* (Durham, N.C., 1938). *Census of the Commonwealth of Australia*, 1911, II, Part X (Melbourne, 1921). Jacques Bertillon, "La Natalité selon le degré d'aisance," *Bulletin de l'Institut Internationale de Statistique*, XI, 1899.

First period: from the beginning of the decline in the birth-rate to 1910[2]

Before the general decline in the birth-rate, fertility in Western Europe and the United States varied among classes and tended to be inversely correlated with class, but the relative stability of the differences paralleled the stability of national levels of the fertility. Fertility began to decline sharply in most Western countries in the 1870's or 1880's and the general trend of class differences from this period until about the First World War is well defined.

As national birth-rates turned downward, class fertility-differentials increased greatly. The inverse association between fertility and socio-economic status which before the downturn of the birth-rate was clear-cut only for groups at the upper and lower ends of the socio-economic scale — the higher non-manual urban occupations on the one hand, and agricultural and unskilled industrial workers on the other — became deeper and more consistent as groups occupying intermediate positions in the class structure began to conform to it as well. Rural–urban and agricultural–non-agricultural differentials also widened in most countries. While all occupational and economic groups were affected by the general decline in fertility, the evidence that the groups of highest socio-economic status were the leaders of the decline is altogether decisive, though the reduced fertility of the more numerous agricultural population and urban lower classes had a greater quantitative effect on the drop in national fertility.

There is very little evidence that the rate of increase in class differentials in England, the United States, or the many European cities for which data on the birth-rates of residential areas are available, or even in France, was slowing down before the First World War, which in this as in so many other features of modern life seems to mark a crucial watershed of historical transition. There is some evidence to suggest that in Australia class fertility-differentials did not begin to increase until the first two decades of the twentieth century rather than in the final decades of the nineteenth, but the evidence is far from conclusive.

The inverse correlation of fertility and socio-economic status was probably more marked in the period considered in this section of the paper than it has ever been before or since in Western civilization. Yet even as the more rapid decline in fertility of the less fertile upper classes enhanced the relation, exceptions to it emerged. Data on the cumulative fertility of women born and married before 1910 in the United States are tabulated by the most detailed socio-economic categories used in studies made during this period; they show that within the infertile, higher occupations, the group composed of clerical, sales, and kindred workers was somewhat less fertile than either the group of professionals and semi-professionals or the group composed of proprietors, managers, and officials, though both these last two groups were generally higher in status than the white-collar employees of the first group.

Differences in income within broad groups of non-manual occupations may have been to some degree positively correlated with fertility. The lower fertility of wage-earners and salaried employees as compared with employers in Australia, and of salaried employees as compared with proprietors in France, suggests this possibility. Unfortunately, adequate data on differences in fertility by income are not widely available for this period, although data for later periods have indicated that the familiar inverse pattern is, in urban populations, more marked for income groups than for occupational classes. A 1906 study of differences in fertility by income among French salaried employees in the public service showed that above a certain level of income, family size and income were positively correlated,[1] but it is not known whether this same pattern existed in the general population or in other countries at that time. Since fertility began to decline earlier in France than in other Western nations, French differential fertility may have deviated from the inverse pattern before the First World War, resembling the pattern that developed at a later date in other Western countries.

British textile workers, American service workers, Australians engaged in domestic service, and French domestic servants are other occupational groups whose fertility was lower than that of groups of equal or higher socio-economic status. The reason may probably be found in the special circumstances associated with the environment of these occupations — the British textile industry employed large numbers of women, and personal and domestic service necessitates frequent contacts with people of higher status.

A partially positive relation between fertility and status also existed in the farm populations of several Western countries. The American South, Australia, and probably rural French Canada, which as late as 1941 did not exhibit the usual inverse pattern, showed a direct relation between fertility and class within their farm or rural populations before 1910. In all these areas the direct pattern was associated with relatively high levels of fertility. A direct relation between fertility and status has often been observed in the agricultural areas of under-developed countries such as India and China,[2] so good grounds exist for concluding that it is to some degree characteristic of economically backward and semi-industrialized rural populations. Its presence fifty years ago in the American South, rural Australia, and French Canada, therefore, is not surprising.

Differences in age at marriage by class continued to contribute to socio-economic fertility-differentials after the beginning of the general decline in the birth-rate. The average age at marriage in the upper classes was higher than in the lower classes, as it evidently had been for a long time in Western history, and a direct relation between age at marriage and socio-economic status held from the top to the bottom of the social scale.[3] Yet the trend and pattern of class differences in fertility were not substantially altered when cumulative birth-rates were standardized for age at marriage in England and Wales

and for duration of marriage in the United States; class differences in the fertility of marriage were evidently the major immediate cause of class differences in average family size. The spread of family limitation throughout the population during this period is strongly indicated, for by the turn of the century all socio-economic groups were declining in fertility in the nations for which data are available. It was, of course, in the last decades of the nineteenth century that public opinion became more receptive to family limitation throughout the Western world.[4]

Class differences in the incidence of celibacy undoubtedly created greater class differences in *total* as distinct from *marital* fertility. A later age at marriage is usually associated with a lower proportion of ultimate marriages,[5] so low-status groups must have exceeded high-status groups in total fertility by an even larger amount than in marital fertility.

Second period: from 1910 to 1940[6]

Data on class fertility-differentials reveal trends and patterns that are by no means as uniform after 1910, either within or between nations, as in the decades

[1] France, Bureau de la Statistique Générale, *Statistique des familles en 1906*, 46.

[2] Kingsley Davis, *The Population of India and Pakistan* (Princeton, 1950), 76–79; Herbert D. Lamson, "Differential Reproduction in China." *Quarterly Review of Biology*, X, no. 3, Sept., 1935; Frank W. Notestein, "A Demographic Study of 38,256 Families in China," *Milbank Memorial Fund Quarterly*, XVI, no. 1, Jan., 1938, 68–70; Ta Chen, *Population in Modern China* (Chicago, 1946), pp. 30–31 and Table 19, p. 93.

[3] Frank W. Notestein, "Differential Age at Marriage According to Social Class," *American Journal of Sociology*, XXXVII, no. 1, July, 1931.

[4] A. M. Carr-Saunders, *World Population* (Oxford, 1936), chaps. VIII, IX; D. V. Glass, *Population Policies and Movements* (Oxford, 1940), chap. I; James A. Field, *Essays on Population and Other Papers* (Chicago, 1931), chaps. VI, XII.

[5] Kingsley Davis, "Statistical Perspective on Marriage and Divorce," *Annals of the American Academy of Political and Social Science*, CCLXXII, Nov., 1950, 9–17.

[6] The conclusions for this period are based on the following sources. Innes, *Class Fertility Trends in England and Wales*. D. V. Glass and E. Grebenik, *The Trend and Pattern of Fertility in Great Britain*, Part I, Papers of the Royal Commission on Population, VI (London, 1954). Great Britain, Census, 1951, *One Per Cent Sample Tables*, Part 2 (London, 1953). U.S. Bureau of the Census, Sixteenth Census, *Population: Differential Fertility, 1940 and 1910*. Frank W. Notestein, "Differential Fertility in the East North Central States," *Milbank Memorial Fund Quarterly*, XVI, no. 2, April, 1938. Clyde V. Kiser, *Group Differences in Urban Fertility* (Baltimore, 1942). Paul H. Jacobson, "The Trend of the Birth Rate among Persons on Different Economic Levels, City of New York, 1929–1942," *Milbank Memorial Fund Quarterly*, XXIII, no. 2, April, 1944. Bernard D. Karpinos and Clyde V. Kiser, "The Differential Fertility and Potential Rates of Growth of Various Income and Education Classes of Urban Populations in the United States," *Milbank Memorial Fund Quarterly*, XVII, no. 4, Oct., 1939. Evelyn M. Kitagawa, "Differential Fertility in Chicago, 1920–1940," *American Journal of Sociology*, LIII, no. 5, March, 1953. France, Bureau de la Statistique Générale, *Statistique des familles en 1926* (Paris, 1932); *Statistique des familles en 1936* (Paris, 1946); Resultats statistiques de recensement général de la population, effectué le 10 mars 1946, IV, *Familles* (Paris, 1954). Spengler, *France*

immediately following the downturn of national birth-rates. No doubt this appearance of greater diversity is in part merely a result of the fact that vastly more data are available for the more recent period. The findings of later studies also reflect improvements in the techniques of demographic measurement as well as actual changes in the conditions observed by earlier investigators. More careful control of the demographic variables that influence fertility-rates, the use of a greater number of indices of socio-economic status, and the development of more sociologically meaningful indices, were the chief methodological improvements. Yet certain general features can be discerned which broadly differentiate trends and patterns in the period under consideration from trends and patterns in the earlier period.

Some contraction of the relative differences in fertility among socio-economic groups occurred. This contrasts with the progressive increase in differentials during the latter part of the nineteenth century. The fertility-levels of non-manual groups in Great Britain, the United States, France, and Norway converged. In Great Britain the fertility-differential between manual and non-manual groups remained remarkably stable from the beginning of the century until the 1930's, when it narrowed slightly but unmistakably. The differential also ceased to widen in the United States, although it did not contract to any appreciable degree. It was also fairly stable in France from 1906 to 1946.

Before 1910, the upper classes everywhere led the decline in fertility, but after 1910 intermediate groups assumed the lead. In Great Britain all groups declined more slowly after the turn of the century, but the non-manual groups of low status declined most rapidly. Small business men, farmers and farm managers, and salaried employees were the leaders from 1890 to 1925. After 1925, non-manual wage-earners and manual wage-earners — the manual group of highest status — exhibited higher rates of decline than the high-status non-manual groups and the low-status manual groups. In the United States between 1910 and 1940, proprietors, managers, and officials showed the greatest decline, but wage-workers of all degrees of skill declined slightly more rapidly than the other non-manual groups and agriculturalists. In Norway, three white-collar salaried groups, factory workers, and small business men showed the greatest relative declines in cumulative fertility between 1920 and 1930. In Sweden, where no direct data on trends exist, comparison of the fertility of marriages of different durations indicates that leadership

in the decline in fertility had passed by the 1930's to salaried employees and to the middle-income groups. In France, a stabilization of average family size in the upper socio-economic strata was apparently reached as early as 1911; the fertility of people engaged in industrial occupations declined most rapidly from 1911 to 1926, and from 1926 to 1936 average family size in all groups except the most fertile (fishermen) remained fairly stable. Australia alone may have been an exception to the general trend; there is no clear evidence that the least fertile occupational groups were declining less rapidly than the more fertile groups from 1911 to 1921. Australian employers, however, declined more rapidly than wage- and salary-earners, although they continued to have larger families.

It can be concluded, then, that leadership in rate of decline tended to pass in this period to the low-status non-manual workers, urban wage-workers, and the middle-income groups. Of those in the non-manual occupations who had previously led the decline, only white-collar workers and small business men — those with the lowest socio-economic status in the non-manual group — continued to take the lead in several nations. The relatively rapid decline shown by small business men in both Great Britain and Norway suggests that small business men in the American "proprietors, managers, and officials" group may have been responsible for that group's leadership in rate of decline in the United States.

The fertility of an occupational class continued on the whole to be inversely correlated with its socio-economic status, but by 1940 a larger number of exceptions to this relation existed than in the late nineteenth and early twentieth centuries. In Great Britain, salaried employees had smaller families than large employers in all marriage cohorts after 1890, and in the 1910–14 cohort they fell below members of the professions in average size of family to become the least fertile class in British society. In the United States, clerical and sales workers continued to be the least fertile occupational group. In Norway in 1930, white-collar clerks in business and commerce had smaller families than factory owners and merchants, and factory workers had smaller families than artisans. In Sweden in 1936, employers and entrepreneurs in non-agricultural occupations had larger families than salaried employees and officials. In France, where the census classifications fail to differentiate occupations by socio-economic status, people engaged in personal-service occupations had smaller families than those in the liberal professions in 1926 and 1936, proprietors had by 1936 increased the margin by which their average family size exceeded that of both salaried employees and wage-workers in 1911, and in 1946 white-collar employees in commerce and public service were less fertile than a combined high-status group of large employers, the liberal professions, and high officials. In Denmark, salaried employees in manufacturing, construction, and commerce were less fertile in 1940 than proprietors in these occupations.

Faces Depopulation. Folketellingen i Norge, 1. desember 1930, Niende hefte, *Barnetallet i norske ekteskap* (Oslo, 1935), Statistika Centralbyran, Sarskilda Folkrakningen 1935/1936, VI, Partiella Folkrakningen Mars 1936, *Barnantal och Doda Barn i Aktenskapen* (Stockholm, 1939), Karl A. Edin and Edward P. Hutchinson, *Studies of Differential Fertility in Sweden* (London, 1935). *Census of the Commonwealth of Australia,* 1921, Part XXVIII (Melbourne, 1927); *Census of the Commonwealth of Australia,* 1947, Part XI (Canberra, 1952). Danmarks Statistik, *Statistik Arbog 1952* (Copenhagen, 1952). Enid Charles, *The Changing Size of the Family in Canada,* Eighth Census of Canada (1942), Census Monograph, no. 1 (Ottawa, 1948).

Agricultural workers, miners, fishermen, and unskilled labourers were the most fertile occupational groups in all countries. In Great Britain and France, miners were more fertile than farmers and agricultural workers, but in all the other countries agricultural owners and labourers were more fertile than any of the non-agricultural groups. In the United States in particular, the differential between agricultural and non-agricultural workers was wide and continued to increase from 1910 to 1940.

Clearly the degree to which fertility was inversely correlated with social class diminished between 1900 and 1940. In general, clerical and sales workers, subordinate officials in both government and business, and small business men were the least fertile groups in the Western world and constituted the major exceptions to the inverse pattern of fertility and status. Their exceptionally low fertility, which was already evident in some nations shortly after the beginning of the decline in the Western birth-rate, became more conspicuous in the present century. Only in Canada, where a third of the total population is composed of French-speaking Catholics, traditionally highly fertile, was there no evidence of any break in the inverse pattern. In Australia, on the other hand, the inverse pattern may not yet have fully developed: occupational classes seemed in general to conform to it, but employers and workers on their own account had larger families than wage- and salary-earners within most of the occupational groups.

Studies of differences in the birth-rates of urban areas classified by various indices of economic status also showed a reduction of the inverse relation in the 1920's and 1930's. In New York, London, Paris, Edinburgh, Glasgow, Hamburg, and Vienna the differences in birth-rates between upper-class and lower-class city districts diminished, while in Dresden, Königsberg, Stockholm, and Oslo the differences had disappeared by the late 1920's. In Berlin, Bremen, and Zürich lower-class districts still had the highest crude birth-rates in the 1930's, but upper-class districts had higher birth-rates than middle-class districts.[1]

When we examine variations in family size by income rather than by occupation, several variant patterns of differential fertility can be identified.

a) The most common pattern was for family size to decrease as income increased, until a fairly high income was reached, and then family size increased slightly. French public-service employees conformed to this reverse J-shaped pattern in 1906. In the 1930's it was observed in numerous cities and urban areas of the United States, and (using average monthly rental as an index of income), in the urban population of the entire nation in 1940.[2] Most of the American studies showed that only the highest or the two or three highest income groups, amounting to a relatively small percentage of the total population, deviated from the usual inverse pattern. This pattern was also observed in Melbourne, Australia, in 1942, in urban Sweden in 1936 among all occupations and among employers and entrepreneurs

not in agriculture for marriages of from fifteen to thirty-five years duration; and in Canada in 1941 in several high educational groups and two urban occupational groups of English-speaking Canadians.[3]

b) In several countries deviation from the inverse correlation of family size to income had developed somewhat further. Among marriages of ten years duration in Greater Oslo in 1930, the highest income group equalled the lowest in average family size.[4] The smallest families were located in the middle of the income range. The distribution of family size by income conformed to a U-shaped curve, suggesting that this pattern represented a later stage of development of the reverse J-shaped curve which was observed in countries and cities where fertility had not yet fallen to the uniformly low level of the Norwegian capital. A somewhat similar pattern also characterized families of less than fifteen years duration in urban Sweden among employers and entrepreneurs not in agriculture, and among salaried employees and officials, although the older marriages in these groups conformed more closely to the reverse J-shaped pattern. Among salaried employees and officials, however, an exceptionally infertile group in most Western countries, there was in Sweden no well-defined relation between average family size and income for the majority of both the older and the younger marriages, and group differences were very slight. They had almost vanished in the two groups of shortest marriage-duration and their disappearance may possibly have indicated the completion of a process of transition to a final stage in which differential fertility ceases to exist.

c) However, the studies of Stockholm by Edin and Hutchinson showed that there was a direct relation in

[1] For New York, see Jacobson, "The Trend of the Birth Rate, City of New York, 1929–1942." For London, see Innes, *Class Fertility Trends in England and Wales*, chaps. IV, V; Glass, *Population Policies and Movements*, 76–82; Frank Lorimer and Frederick Osborn, *Dynamics of Population* (New York, 1934), 79–82; K. Mitra, "Fertility and Its Relation to Social Conditions," *Journal of Hygiene*, XXXVII, no. 1, Jan., 1937. For Paris, see Spengler, *France Faces Depopulation*, 98–100; Adolphe Landry, *Traité de démographie* (Paris, 1945), 307. For Edinburgh, Glasgow, Hamburg, Dresden, Königsberg, and Berlin, see Roderich von Ungern-Sternberg, *The Causes of the Decline of the Birth Rate within The European Sphere of Civilization* (Cold Spring Harbor, N.Y., 1931), 115–116. For Vienna, see Alexander Stevenson, "Some Aspects of Fertility and Population Growth in Vienna," *American Sociological Review*, VII, no. 4, Aug., 1942. For Stockholm, see Edin and Hutchinson, *Studies of Differential Fertility in Sweden*. For Oslo, see Folketellingen i Norge, *Barnetallet i norske ekteskap*. For Bremen, see A. Grotjahn, "Differential Birth Rate in Germany" in Margaret Sanger, ed., *Proceedings of the World Population Conference* (London, 1927), 153–154. For Zürich, see Kurt B. Mayer, *The Population of Switzerland* (New York, 1952), 109–110.

[2] U.S. Bureau of the Census, Sixteenth Census, *Population: Differential Fertility 1940 and 1910: Women by Number of Children Ever Born* (1945), Tables 57–62, pp. 173–206.

[3] For Melbourne, see W. D. Borrie, *Population Trends and Policies* (Sydney, 1948), 120. For urban Sweden, see Statistika Centralbyran, *Barnantal och Doda Barn i Aktenskapen*. For Canada, see Charles, *The Changing Size of the Family in Canada*, 112.

[4] Folketellingen i Norge, *Barnetallet i norske ekteskap*, Tabel 9.

the 1920's between family size and income for marriages of incomplete fertility. Moberg also found a direct relation between family size and income among students taking the Swedish matriculation examinations in 1910, 1920, and 1930.[1] Several American studies of differences in fertility by income within highly educated groups have also reported a direct pattern.[2]

Possibly these three different types of relation between fertility and income represent different stages in a process of transition from the inverse pattern. The "straight line" inverse pattern yields first to a reverse J-shaped curve which is then succeeded by a U-shaped pattern. A final equilibrium, characterized either by the complete disappearance of group fertility-differentials or by the emergence of a positive correlation between fertility and status, may ultimately be attained in relatively stationary populations with uniformly low birth- and death-rates. However, there are not enough data on differences in fertility by income and occupation combined to justify a conclusion that class differentials in the Western world as a whole are following such a process of evolution. The possibility that such a trend is occurring may be regarded as a major hypothesis for future investigation arising out of the present study.

The trends and patterns described above are indirect evidence strongly supporting the view that the practice of family limitation has gradually diffused from the upper to the lower socio-economic strata. Indeed, descriptive studies of differential fertility provided the initial empirical support for this view before there was much direct evidence pertaining to class differences in the use of birth-control. Alternative explanations can hardly account for the divergence of class fertility-rates followed by their convergence, the low fertility in

occupations such as clerical and sales work and minor government employment, which are characterized by a combination of "bourgeois" standards of living with incomes lower than those of professional people, employers, and even some groups of manual workers, and the greater modification of the inverse pattern in the countries of lowest over-all fertility. The study of Indianapolis by Whelpton and Kiser and Lewis-Fanings' study of the contraceptive practices of English wives supplied the first massive direct evidence that family planning was both more frequent and more effective in the groups at the upper end of the socio-economic scale, and had been adopted earliest by these groups.[3] Whelpton's and Kiser's demonstration that socio-economic fertility-differentials are greatly reduced and the inverse pattern modified and partly reversed when only successful users of birth-control in the different classes are compared, strikingly confirms the class-diffusion-gradient theory of the causation of differential fertility.[4]

It is quite apparent, however, that the process of diffusion was not yet complete in the United States by the 1940's or even in Norway and Sweden by the 1930's. It remains uncertain whether its final result will be the disappearance of group fertility-differentials, the persistence of differentials varying in an almost random manner with socio-economic status in a context of universally low fertility, or, as many demographers contend,[5] the emergence of a direct relation completely reversing the former inverse relation. Whatever group differentials do survive will clearly not be as great in populations of uniformly low fertility where all groups successfully limit the size of their families as they were during the period of transition from high to low fertility.

Discussions of the future of differential fertility often overlook the fact that most of the available data deal only with differences in marital fertility. The few studies which take into account group differences in proportions of marriages show larger fertility-differentials and a more consistent inverse correlation of fertility to socio-economic status. In countries such as Norway and Sweden where the rate of illegitimacy is high, the greater frequency of births out of wedlock in the lower classes may help perpetuate the older pattern of differential fertility with respect to differences in total fertility. Later marriage in the upper classes is also likely to persist in view of the time needed for higher education and the later achievement of peak earning-power in high-status occupations. The report on the 1946 family census of Great Britain, however, demonstrates more fully than earlier family censuses that class differences in average age at marriage make only a minor contribution to differences in marital fertility.[6]

[1] Sven Moberg, "Marital Status and Family Size among Matriculated Persons in Sweden," *Population Studies*, IV, no. 1, June, 1950.

[2] John C. Phillips, "Success and the Birth Rate," *Harvard Graduates Magazine*, XXXV, no. 160, June, 1927; John J. Osborn, "Fertility Differentials among Princeton Alumni," *Journal of Heredity*, XXX, no. 12, Dec., 1939; Ernest Havemann and Patricia Salter West, *They Went to College* (New York, 1952), 46; Frederick Osborn, *Preface to Eugenics* (New York, 1952), 175–176.

[3] P. K. Whelpton and Clyde V. Kiser, *Social and Psychological Factors Affecting Fertility* (3 vols., New York, 1946, 1950, 1953); E. Lewis-Faning, *Family Limitation and Its Influence on Human Fertility During the Past Fifty Years*, Papers of the Royal Commission on Population, I (London, 1949).

[4] Whelpton and Kiser, *Social and Psychological Factors Affecting Fertility*, II, Part IX.

[5] See, e.g., Rudolph Heberle, "Social Factors in Birth Control," *American Sociological Review*, VI, no. 5, Oct., 1941, 800; Margaret Jarman Hagood, "Changing Fertility Differentials among Farm-Operator Families in Relation to Economic Size of Farm," *Rural Sociology*, XIII, no. 4, Dec., 1948, 373; Charles F. Westoff, "Differential Fertility in the United States: 1900 to 1952," *American Sociological Review*, XIX, no. 5, Oct., 1954, 561.

[6] Glass and Grebenik, *The Trend and Pattern of Fertility in Great Britain*, 113–128.

[7] The conclusions for this period are based on the following sources: Glass and Grebenik, *The Trend and Pattern of Fertility in Great Britain*; Great Britain, Census, 1951, *One Per Cent*

Third period: the baby boom after 1940[7]

The main difference between trends in differential fertility before and after 1940 arises from the fact that after 1940 the decline in the birth-rate which had continued since the second half of the nineteenth century was reversed in most of the Western world. Increases in the proportions of marriages, a decline in the average age at marriage, a reduction in the numbers of women remaining childless, and a slight increase in the average size of completed families appear to have been the major demographic trends underlying the general rise in indices of current fertility.[1] The rise has occurred too recently to permit definitive conclusions about its long-range significance. It remains to be seen whether the cohorts who contributed to the wartime and post-war baby boom will have given birth to more children by the time they reach the end of the reproductive period than the cohorts who preceded them. Forecasts made in the 1930's that fertility would continue to decline and that ultimately there would be actual decreases in the populations of Western countries were clearly mistaken, but few demographers today are of the opinion that recent increases in current fertility represent a long-term renewal of rapid growth in the West.

The long-run effects on differential fertility of the rise in birth-rates that occurred after 1940 are even more debatable. Apparently spectacular reversals of earlier trends may turn out to be of transitory significance when rates of cumulative complete fertility for baby-boom mothers are finally available.

Data for Great Britain and the United States indicate that the narrowing of class fertility-differentials already evident in the 1930's was accelerated by the baby boom. Differential rates of increase in fertility replaced the differential rates of decline of the previous period. There is, of course, no reason in principle why different socio-economic groups might not exhibit opposite trends — some increasing in fertility, others declining. But national societies seem to have responded as wholes to new conditions influencing childbearing and this is as true of the period after the Second World War as it was of the previous long period of declining fertility. Just as all intra-national groups participated in the decline, so did all groups contribute to the increase in the 1940's.

In both Great Britain and the United States, the less fertile high-status groups increased their fertility by greater amounts after 1940 than the more fertile low-status groups. The converging of socio-economic fertility-differentials was thus accelerated. In Great Britain non-manual and manual groups were already converging somewhat in the 1940's when fertility was still declining, and Evelyn Kitagawa observes that trends in differential fertility in the city of Chicago point to "the conclusion that the so-called 'post-war' developments in earlier age at marriage and the convergence of fertility differentials may have started about two decades ago. . . ."[2]

Rates of current fertility and of cumulative incomplete fertility for non-manual workers showed a greater increase in the United States than in Great Britain. Moreover, in Great Britain the earlier pattern of greater increases among non-manual workers was reversed

towards the end of the 1940's when manual workers showed greater increases at low marriage-durations.

Greater participation of the less fertile high-status groups in the baby boom has clearly increased the deviation from the inverse relation of fertility to status. In Great Britain non-manual workers remain less fertile than manual workers, but within these broad groups a direct relation between fertility and social class partially replaced the inverse pattern among marriages of less than fifteen years duration in 1951. Data on cohorts by socio-economic group are not yet available for the United States, but fertility-ratios for married women indicate sharp reversals of the inverse relation; the non-manual occupational groups of highest status show higher ratios than some manual groups.

In the past, planned families have invariably been smaller than unplanned families and continuously declining fertility has been associated with the spread of family planning. No inherent reason exists, however, why social and economic conditions favourable to childbearing might not induce married couples to decide to have slightly larger families. Certainly the capacity to "move ahead" one's reproductive schedule is a consequence of planning and has played a large part in the recent rise of current fertility-rates for high-status groups and in cumulative rates for cohorts of incomplete fertility. Changes in the scheduling of births may lead to changes in the ultimate size of family desired. Slightly larger families in the middle classes may be a consequence of the baby boom which has been incorporated into the middle-class concept of the standard of living.

The narrowing of class fertility-differentials since 1940 has also been effected by a relatively greater increase in the rate of marriage among the less fertile, later-marrying, upper classes. Greater lowering of the average age at marriage and of the proportions married at given ages in the high-status groups have undoubtedly resulted in as marked a narrowing of socio-economic differences in total fertility as in marital fertility.

The future of class fertility-differences

The view that the trend of class fertility-differences reflects the gradual spread of family limitation to all

[1] John Hajnal, "The Analysis of Birth Statistics in the Light of the Recent International Recovery of the Birth Rate," *Population Studies*, I, no. 2, Sept., 1947; Clyde V. Kiser, "Fertility Trends and Differentials in the United States"; P. K. Whelpton, "Future Fertility of American Women," *Eugenics Quarterly*, I, no. 1, March, 1954.

[2] Kitagawa, "Differential Fertility in Chicago, 1920–1940," 493.

Sample Tables; Kiser, "Fertility Trends and Differentials in the United States"; Westoff, "Differential Fertility in the United States, 1900 to 1952"; U.S. Bureau of the Census, *Current Population Characteristics*, Series P-20, no. 46 (Washington, D.C., Dec. 31, 1953); John Hajnal, "Differential Changes in Marriage Patterns," *American Sociological Review*, XIX, no. 2, April, 1954, and "Analysis of Changes in the Marriage Pattern by Economic Groups," *ibid.*, no. 3, July, 1954.

intra-national population groups does not go much beyond the descriptive level of statement. Some strata exhibit greater susceptibility to family limitation than others, and the studies by Whelpton and Kiser and Lewis-Faning demonstrate the need for more intensive inquiries into the motivational and ideological predispositions towards family limitation and into their class distribution.

American sociologists have given considerable attention to the relative "openness" of class structures, conducting numerous studies of social-mobility rates and of the complex of attitudes associated with mobility aspirations. Demographers since Arsène Dumont have often suggested that the exceptionally low fertility of mobile persons may account for the persistence in Western societies of the inverse correlation of fertility and status. Westoff, for example, has advanced the hypothesis that "social class differences in fertility planning and differential fertility itself are related to the differential frequency of socio-economic ambitions and social mobility within and between class levels — the middle classes exhibiting the clearest manifestations of this type of 'atmosphere' and having the lowest fertility."[1] An increase in the frequency of mobility aspirations in low-status groups would, on this assumption, lead to an increase in the practice of family limitation and accelerate the contraction of class fertility-differentials.

Whether or not an actual increase in the amount of upward social mobility in Western urban-industrial societies has taken place in the past two decades is subject to dispute.[2] Certainly, increases in agricultural and industrial productivity have changed the occupational composition of the labour force and reduced the number of low-status occupations in proportion to those of high status.[3] On the other hand, the narrowing of both absolute and relative class fertility-differences restricts upward mobility by reducing the population "surpluses" of the lower classes and rural areas.[4] The recent increases in the fertility of high-status groups enable them to supply a larger number of candidates for high-status occupations than formerly.

Trends in social mobility, however, are not the only

or necessarily the most important feature of the class system related to differential fertility. If mobility and mobility aspirations are associated with low fertility, they can hardly be invoked to explain the *increases* in fertility shown by all socio-economic groups since 1940. Changes in mobility between occupational classes on the one hand, and the upgrading of entire classes as a result both of a redistribution of incomes and of a general rise in the standard of living on the other, are two distinct social processes which may affect fertility in different ways.

Significantly, before the baby boom of the 1940's, the contraction of class fertility-differences had proceeded furthest in the Scandinavian countries. They were the first Western nations where trade unions and co-operatives became powerful pressure groups favouring reduction of the economic inequalities of unregulated capitalism and succeeded in electing to power reformist socialist governments by secure majorities. Since 1940 a marked levelling of incomes has taken place in most Western countries, the result of a sustained period of prosperity during which the lower strata have benefited from increases in productivity, steep progressive taxation of income, and the social policies associated with the rise of the welfare state.

What is of crucial importance so far as the effects of these changes on fertility is concerned, is that "middle-class" standards of living have been brought within the reach of the least privileged strata and made popular by the new mass media. Accordingly, it is not surprising to find that class fertility-differences have diminished in the past thirty years or that, since 1940, all intra-national groups have responded similarly to conditions favourable to higher rates of childbearing.

It is the writer's belief that class fertility-differences are destined to disappear as a feature of the demographic structure of Western populations. This seems a more probable outcome of present trends than the emergence of the positive correlation of fertility to status predicted by several demographers. Yet within the general context of a growing uniformity of behaviour on the part of all classes and groups, some significant differences in standards of living and styles of life are likely to persist, and it is possible that a positive correlation of family size to income will develop within homogeneous occupational and educational groups which are small enough to serve as psychological reference groups for their members.[5] Indeed, studies of differential fertility within high-status groups in the United States and Sweden indicate that this development has already taken place.

Much research and analysis remains to be done before we shall fully understand the changes in fertility that are now taking place. The most useful type of inquiry into the underlying causes of trends in differential fertility must address itself primarily to the relation between fertility-trends and secular economic growth in Western industrial society, or, more accurately, to the changes in class structure and in the styles of life of

[1] Charles F. Westoff, "The Changing Focus of Differential Fertility Research: The Social Mobility Hypothesis," *Milbank Memorial Fund Quarterly*, XXXI, no. 1, Jan., 1953, 31.

[2] William Petersen, "Is America Still the Land of Opportunity?" *Commentary*, XVI, no. 5, Nov., 1953; S. M. Lipset and Natalie Rogoff, "Class and Opportunity in Europe and the U.S." *Commentary*, XVIII, no. 6, Dec., 1954; Ely Chinoy, "Social Mobility Trends in the United States," *American Journal of Sociology*, XX, no. 2, April, 1955; Herbert Luethy, "Social Mobility Again — And Elites," *Commentary*, XX, no. 3, Sept., 1955.

[3] Nelson Foote and Paul K. Hatt, "Social Mobility and Economic Advancement," *American Economic Review*, XLIII, May, 1953.

[4] Elbridge Sibley, "Some Demographic Clues to Stratification," *American Sociological Review*, VII, no 3, June, 1942.

[5] A similar hypothesis has been advanced by Albert Mayer and Carol Klapprodt, "Fertility Differentials in Detroit: 1920–1950," *Population Studies*, IX, no. 2, Nov., 1955, 15.

the various classes that are a consequence of rapid and sustained economic expansion.[6] Inquiries into the individual psychological attributes associated with high or low fertility, such as the Indianapolis study by Whelpton and Kiser are of undoubted value, but they are supplementary to analysis of the effects on fertility of the historical transformations which have so pro-foundly altered the class structures and cultural outlooks of Western populations in the past half-century.

[6] Heberle ("Social Factors in Birth Control," 805) makes a similar general point, although, writing in 1941, he forecast a continuing decline in fertility to levels below replacement requirements — a trend he regarded as an inevitable result of structural changes in the economic system in the era of "late capitalism."

FAMILY

Socialization and Social Class Through Time and Space[1]

Urie Bronfenbrenner

I. Background and resources

DURING THE PAST dozen years, a class struggle has been taking place in American social psychology — a struggle, fortunately, not *between* but *about* social classes. In the best social revolutionary tradition the issue was joined with a manifesto challenging the

assumed superiority of the upper and middle classes and extolling the neglected virtues of the working class. There followed a successful revolution with an overthrow of the established order in favor of the victorious proletariat, which then reigned supreme — at least for a time. These dramatic changes had, as always, their prophets and precursors, but they reached a climax in 1946 with the publication of Davis and Havighurst's influential paper on "Social Class and Color Differences in Child Rearing."[2] The paper cited impressive statistical evidence in support of the thesis that middle-class parents "place their children under a stricter regimen, with more frustration of their impulses than do lower-class parents." For the next eight years, the Davis-Havighurst conclusion was taken as the definitive statement of class differences in socialization. Then, in 1954, came the counter revolution; Maccoby and Gibbs published the first report[3] of a study of child-rearing practices in the Boston area which, by and large, contradicted the Chicago findings: in general, middle-class parents were found to be "more permissive" than those in the lower class.

In response, one year later, Havighurst and Davis[4] presented a reanalysis of their data for a subsample more comparable in age to the subjects of the Boston

[1] This article was made possible only by the work of others; for, in effect, it is a synthesis of the contribution of a score of investigators over a score of years. The author is particularly grateful to Nancy Bayley, Melvin L. Kohn, Richard A. Littman, Daniel R. Miller, Fred L. Strodtbeck, Guy E. Swanson, and Martha S. White, who made available copies of their research reports prior to publication. For their invaluable suggestions, he is also indebted to John E. Anderson, Wesley Allinsmith, Alfred L. Baldwin, John A. Clausen, Robert J. Havighurst, Harry Levin, Eleanor E. Maccoby, and Theodore M. Newcomb.

[2] A. Davis and R. J. Havighurst, "Social Class and Color Differences in Child Rearing." *Am. Sociol. Rev.*, 1948, XI, 698–710.

[3] E. E. Maccoby, P. K. Gibbs, and the staff of the Laboratory of Human Development at Harvard University, "Methods of Child Rearing in Two Social Classes," in W. E. Martin and C. B. Standler (eds.), *Readings in Child Development* (New York: Harcourt, Brace & Co., 1954).

[4] Havighurst and Davis, "A Comparison of the Chicago and Harvard Studies of Social Class Differences in Child Rearing," *Am. Sociol. Rev.*, 1955, XX, 438–442.

Reprinted from E. E. Maccoby, T. M. Newcomb, and E. L. Hartley (eds.), *Readings in Social Psychology* (New York: Henry Holt and Co., 1958, 3rd edition), pp. 400–425, by permission of the author, editors, and the publisher.

study. On the basis of a careful comparison of the two sets of results, they concluded that "the disagreements between the findings of the two studies are substantial and large" and speculated that these differences might be attributable either to genuine changes in child-rearing practices over time or to technical difficulties of sampling and item equivalence.

A somewhat different view, however, was taken by Sears, Maccoby, and Levin[1] in their final report of the Boston study. They argued that Davis and Havighurst's interpretation of the Chicago data as reflecting greater permissiveness for the working-class parent was unwarranted on two counts. First, they cited the somewhat contrasting results of still another research — that of Klatskin[2] in support of the view that class differences in feeding, weaning, scheduling, and toilet training "are not very stable or customary." Second, they contended that the Chicago findings of greater freedom of movement for the lower-class child were more properly interpreted not as "permissiveness" but as "a reflection of rejection, a pushing of the child out of the way." Such considerations led the Boston investigators to conclude:

This re-examination of the Chicago findings suggests quite clearly the same conclusion that must be reached from Klatskin's study and from our own: the middle-class mothers were generally more permissive and less punitive toward their young children than were working-class mothers. Unfortunately, the opposite interpretation, as presented by Davis and Havighurst, has been widely accepted in education circles during the past decade. This notion of working-class permissiveness has been attractive for various reasons. It has provided an easy explanation of why working-class children have lower academic achievement motivation than do middle-class children — their mothers place less restrictive pressure on them. It has also provided a kind of compensatory comfort for those educators who have been working hard toward the goal of improving educational experiences for the noncollege-oriented part of the school population. In effect, one could say, lower-class children may lack the so highly desirable academic motivation, but the lack stems from a "good" reason — the children were permissively reared.[3]

It would appear that there are a number of unresolved issues between the protagonists of the principal points of view — issues both as to the facts and their interpretation. At such times it is not unusual for some third party to attempt a reappraisal of events in a broader historical perspective with the aid of documents and information previously not available. It is this which the present writer hopes to do. He is fortunate in having at his disposal materials not only from the past and present, but also seven manuscripts unpublished at the time of this writing, which report class differences in child-rearing practices at four different places and five points

in time. To begin with, Bayley and Schaefer[4] have reanalyzed data from the Berkeley Growth Study to provide information on class differences in maternal-behavior ratings made from 1928 to 1932, when the children in the study were under three years old, and again from 1939 to 1942, when most of them were about ten years old. Information on maternal behavior in this same locale as of 1953 comes from a recent report by Martha Sturm White[5] of class differences in child-rearing practices for a sample of preschoolers in Palo Alto and environs. Miller and Swanson have made available relevant data from their two comprehensive studies of families in Detroit, one based on a stratified sample of families with children up to 19 years of age,[6] the other a specially selected sample of boys, ages 12 to 14 years.[7] Limited information on another sample of adolescent boys comes from Strodtbeck's investigation of "Family Interaction, Values, and Achievement".[8] Also Littman, Moore, and Pierce-Jones[9] have recently completed a survey of child-rearing practices in Eugene, Oregon for a random sample of parents with children from two weeks to 14 years of age. Finally, Kohn[10] reports a comparison of child-training values among working and middle-class mothers in Washington, D.C.

The writer has made use of nine additional published researches.[11] In some instances — notably for the monu-

[1] R. R. Sears, E. Maccoby, and H. Levin, *Patterns of Child Rearing* (Evanston, Ill.: Row, Peterson & Co., 1957).

[2] E. H. Klatskin, "Shifts in Child Care Practices in Three Social Classes under an Infant Care Program of Flexible Methodology," *Am. J. Orthopsychiat.*, 1952, XXII, 52–61.

[3] Sears, Maccoby, and Levin, *op. cit.*, pp. 446–447.

[4] N. Bayley and E. S. Schaefer, "Relationships between Socioeconomic Variables and the Behavior of Mothers towards Young Children," unpublished manuscript, 1957.

[5] M. S. White, "Social Class, Child Rearing Practices, and Child Behavior," *Am. Sociol. Rev.* 1957, XXII, 704–712.

[6] D. R. Miller and G. E. Swanson, *The Changing American Parent* (New York: John Wiley & Sons, Inc., 1958).

[7] Miller and Swanson, *Inner Conflict and Defense* (New York: Henry Holt & Co., Inc., 1960).

[8] F. L. Strodtbeck, "Family Interaction, Values, and Achievement," in A. L. Baldwin, Bronfenbrenner, D. C. McClelland, and F. L. Strodtbeck, *Talent and Society* (Princeton, N.J.: D. Van Nostrand Co., 1958).

[9] R. A. Littman, R. A. Moore, and J. Pierce-Jones, "Social Class Differences in Child Rearing: A Third Community for Comparison with Chicago and Newton, Massachusetts," *Am. Sociol. Rev.*, 1957, XXII, 694–704.

[10] M. L. Kohn, "Social Class and Parental Values," paper read at the Annual Meeting of the American Sociological Society, Washington, D.C., August, 27–29, 1957.

[11] H. E. Anderson (Chrmn.), *The Young Child in the Home*, report of the Committee on the Infant and Preschool Child, White House Conference on Child Health and Protection (New York: D. Appleton-Century, 1936); A. L. Baldwin, J. Kalhorn, and F. H. Breese, *Patterns of Parent Behavior*, Psychol. Monogr., 1945, LVIII, No. 3 (Whole No. 268): W. E. Boek, E. D. Lawson, A. Yankhauer, and M. B. Sussman, *Social Class, Maternal Health, and Child Care* (Albany: New York State Department of Health, 1957); Davis and Havighurst, *op. cit.*; E. M. Duvall, "Conceptions of Parenthood," *Am. J. Sociol.*, 1946–1947, LII, 190–192; Klatskin, *op. cit.*; E. E. Maccoby and P. K. Gibbs, *op. cit.*; D. C. McClelland, A. Rindlisbacher and R. DeCharms, "Religious and Other Sources of Parental

[*footnote continued on p. 365*

TABLE I. *Description of Samples*

Sample	Principal investigator source	Date of field work	Age	NO. OF CASES			Description of sample
				Total	Middle class	Working class	
National cross section,* I, II, III, IV	Anderson	1932	0–1 1–5 6–12 1–12	494 2420 865 3285	217 1131 391 1522	277 1289 474 1763	National sample of white families "having child between 1 and 5 years of age" and "representing each major geographic area, each size of community and socioeconomic class in the United States." About equal number of males and females. SES (seven classes) based on Minnesota Scale for Occupational Classification.
Berkeley, Cal., I–II	Bayley and Schaefer	1928–32 1939–42	1–3 9–11	31 31	Information not available		Subjects of both sexes from Berkeley Growth Study, "primarily middle class but range from unskilled laborer, relief, and three-years education to professional, $10,000 income and doctoral degrees." SES measures include education, occupation (Taussig Scale), income, home and neighborhood rating, and composite scale.
Yellow Springs, Ohio	Baldwin	1940	3–12	124	Information not available		Families enrolled in Fels Research Institute Home Visiting Program. "Above average" in socioeconomic status but include "a number of uneducated parents and from the lower economic levels." No SES index computed but graphs show relationships by education and income.
Chicago, I *	Davis and Havighurst	1943	5 (approx.)	100	48	32	Middle-class sample "mainly" from mothers of nursery-school children; lower class from "areas of poor housing." All mothers native born. Two-level classification SES following Warner based on occupation, education, residential area, type of home, etc.
Chicago, II	Duvall	1943–44	5 (approx.)	433	230	203	Negro and white (Jewish and non-Jewish) mothers. Data collected at "regular meetings of mothers' groups." SES classification (four levels) following Warner.
New Haven, Conn., I *	Klatskin	1949–50	1 (approx.)	222	114	108	Mothers in Yale Rooming-in Project returning for evaluation of baby at one year of age. SES classification (three levels) by Hollingshead, following Warner.
Boston, Mass.*	Sears, et al.	1951–52	4e6	372	198	174	Kindergarten children in two suburbs. Parents American born, living together. Twins, adoptions, handicapped children, and other special cases eliminated. Two-level SES classification follows Warner.
New Haven, Conn., II	Strodtbeck	1951–53	14–17	48	24	24	Third-generation Jewish and Italian boys representing extremes of under- and over-achievement in school. Classified into three SES levels on basis of occupation.
Detroit, Mich., I *	Miller and Swanson	1953	12–14	112	59	53	Boys in grades 7–8 above borderline intelligence within one year of age for grade, all at least third-generation Americans, Christian, from unbroken, nonmobile families of Northwest European stock. SES (four levels) assigned on basis of education and occupation.
Detroit, Mich., II *	Miller and Swanson	1953	0–18	479	Information not available		Random sample of white mothers with child under 19 and living with husband. Step-children and adoptions eliminated. SES (four levels) based primarily on U.S. census occupation categories.
Palo Alto, Cal.,*	White	1953	2½–5½	74	36	38	Native-born mothers of only one child, the majority expecting another. Unbroken homes in suburban area SES (two levels) rated on Warner scale.
Urban Connecticut	McClelland et al.	1953–54	6–18	152	Information not available		Parents between 30–60 having at least one child between six and eighteen and representing four religious groups. "Rough check on class status" obtained from educational level achieved by parent.
Upstate New York	Boek, et al.	1955–56	3–7 months	1432	595	837	Representative sample of N.Y. state mothers of new-born children, exclusive of unmarried mothers. SES classification (five levels) as given on Warner scale.
Eugene, Oregon *	Littman, et al.	1955–56	0–14	206	86	120	Random sample of children from preschool classes and school rolls. Two SES levels assigned on same basis as in Boston study.
Washington, D.C.	Kohn and Clausen	1956–57	10–11	339	174	165	Representative samples of working- and middle-class mothers classified by Hollingshead's index of social position.

* Denotes studies used as principal bases for the analysis.

mental and regrettably neglected Anderson report — data were reanalyzed and significance tests computed in order to permit closer comparison with the results of other investigations. A full list and summary description of all the studies utilized in the present review appear in Table 1. Starred items designate the researches which, because they contain reasonably comparable data, are used as the principal bases for analysis.

II. Establishing comparable social-class groupings

Although in most of the studies under consideration the investigators have based their classification of socioeconomic status (SES) explicitly or implicitly on the criteria proposed by Warner,[1] there was considerable variation in the number of social class categories employed. Thus, in the Anderson report data were analyzed in terms of seven SES levels, the New York survey distinguished five, the second Chicago and the two Detroit studies each had four, and Klatskin used three. The majority, however, following the precedent of Havighurst and Davis, differentiated two levels only — middle vs. lower or working class. Moreover, all of these last studies have been reanalyzed or deliberately designed to facilitate comparison with each other. We have already mentioned Havighurst and Davis' efforts in this regard, to which the Boston group contributed by recalculating their data in terms of medians rather than means.[2] Both White and Littman *et al.* were interested in clarifying the contradictions posed by the Chicago and Boston studies and hence have employed many of the same indices. As a result, both necessity and wisdom call for dropping to the lowest common denominator and reanalyzing the results of the remaining researches in terms of a two-level classification of socioeconomic status.

In most instances, the delicate question of where to establish the cutting point was readily resolved. The crux of the distinction between middle and working class in all four of the studies employing this dichotomous break lies in the separation between white- and blue-collar workers. Fortunately, this same differentiation was made at some point along the scale in each of the other researches included in the basic analysis. Thus, for the several studies[3] using four levels of classification (upper and lower middle, upper and lower lower), the split occurred, as might be expected, between the two middle categories. For the New York State sample an examination of the occupations occurring at each of the five class levels used pointed to a cutting point between Classes III and IV. Klatskin, in comparing the social-class groupings of the New Haven study with the middle and lower classes of the original Chicago research, proposed a division between the first and second of her three SES levels, and we have followed her recommendation. Finally, for the seven-step scale of the Anderson report, the break was made between Classes III and IV, placing major clerical

workers, skilled mechanics and retail business men in the middle class, and farmers, minor clerical positions, and semiskilled occupations in the working class.

In all of the above instances it was, of course, necessary to compute anew percentages and average scores for the two class levels and to calculate tests of significance (almost invariably χ^2, two-tailed test, with Fisher-Yates correction for continuity). These computations, the results of which appear in the tables to follow, were performed for the following samples: National I–IV, New Haven I, Detroit I and II, and Upstate New York. All other figures and significance tests cited are taken from the original reports.

The effort to make the division between middle and working class at similar points for the basic samples, however successful it may have been, does not eliminate many other important sources of difference among the several researches. We now turn briefly to a consideration of these.

III. Problems of comparability

The difficulties involved in comparing the results of more than a dozen studies conducted at different times and places for somewhat different purposes are at once formidable, delicate, and perilous. First of all, even when similar areas are explored in the interview, there is the problem of variation in the wording of questions. Indeed, however marked the changes may be in child-rearing practices over time, they are not likely to be any more dramatic than the contrasts in the content and, above all, connotation of the queries put to mothers by social scientists from one decade to the next. Thus, the comprehensive report from the first White House Conference, which covered the gamut from the number of children having rattles and changing their underwear to the number of toothbrushes by age, and the times the child was frightened by storms (analyzed by seven SES levels), says not a murmur about masturbation or sex play. Ten years later, in Chicago, six questions were devoted to this topic, including such items as: "How did you frighten them out of the habit?" and "What physical methods did you use (such as tight diaper, whipping them, tying their hands, and so forth)?" In the next decade the interviewer in the Boston study (perhaps only a proper Bostonian) was more restrained, or simply less interested. He asked only two questions: first, whether the mother noticed the child playing with himself, then, "How important do you feel it is to prevent this in a child?" Nor is the difficulty completely eliminated in those

---

[1] W. L. Warner, M. Meeker, and others, *Social Class in America* (Chicago: Science Research Associates, 1949).

[2] Sears, Maccoby, and Levin, *op. cit.*, p. 427.

[3] Duvall, *op. cit.*, Miller and Swanson, *Inner Conflict and Defense* and *The Changing American Parent, op. cit.*

[footnote continued from p. 363
Attitudes toward Independence Training," in McClelland (ed.), *Studies in Motivation* (New York: Appleton-Century-Crofts, Inc., 1955); Sears, Maccoby, and Levin, *op. cit.*

all-too-few instances when a similar wording is employed in two or more studies, for there is the very real possibility that in different contexts the same words have different meanings.

Serious problems arise from the lack of comparability not only in the questions asked but also in the character of the samples employed. Havighurst and Davis, for example, point out that the Chicago and Boston samples had different proportions of cases in the two bottom categories of the Warner scale of occupations. According to the investigators' reports, the Palo Alto and Eugene studies deviated even further in both directions, with the former containing few families from the lowest occupational categories, and the Oregon group exceeding previous studies in representation from these same bottom levels. The authors of several studies also call attention to the potential importance of existing differences in ethnicity, religious background, suburban vs. urban residence, and strength of mobility strivings.

A source of variation perhaps not sufficiently emphasized in these and other reports is the manner in which cases were selected. As Davis and Havighurst properly pointed out in their original publication, their sample was subject to possible bias "in the direction of getting a middle-class group which had been subjected to the kind of teaching about child rearing which is prevalent among the middle-class people who send their children to nursery schools." Equally important may be the relatively high proportion in the Chicago lower-class sample of mothers coming from East European and Irish background, or the four-year discrepancy in the average ages of the mothers at the two-class levels. The first New Haven sample consisted entirely of mothers enrolled in the Yale Rooming-in Project who were sufficiently interested to bring the baby back for a check-up a year after mother and child had left the hospital. As Klatskin recognized, this selectivity probably resulted in a "sample composed of the families most sympathetic to rooming-in ideology," a fact which, as she noted, was reflected in her research results. White's Palo Alto group consisted solely of mothers of only one child, most of whom were expecting a second offspring; cases were recruited from a variety of sources including friends, neighbors, personnel managers, nursery school teachers, Public Health nurses, and maternal prenatal exercises classes. In short, virtually every sample had its special eccentricities. For some of these, one could guess at the extent and direction of bias; in others, the importance or effect of the selective features remains a mystery. Our difficulties, then, derive as much from ignorance as from knowledge — a fact which is underscored by the absence, for many of the samples, of such basic demographic information as the distribution of subjects by age and sex.

[1] It is true that because of the rising birth rate after World War II the sample probably included more younger than older children, but without knowledge of the actual distribution by age we have hesitated to make further speculative adjustments.

It is clear that many factors, some known and many more unknown, may operate to produce differences in results from one sample to the next. It is hardly likely, however, that these manifold influences will operate in a consistent direction over time or space. The possibility of obtaining interpretable findings, therefore, rests on the long chance that major trends, if they exist, will be sufficiently marked to override the effects of bias arising from variations in sampling and method. This is a rash and optimistic hope, but — somewhat to our own surprise — it seems to have been realized, at least in part, in the analyses that follow.

IV. Social class differences in infant care, 1930–1955

In interpreting reports of child-rearing practices it is essential to distinguish between the date at which the information was obtained and the actual period to which the information refers. This caution is particularly relevant in dealing with descriptions of infant care for children who (as in the Eugene or Detroit studies) may be as old as 12, 14, or 18 at the time of the interview. In such instances it is possible only to guess at the probable time at which the practice occurred by making due allowances for the age of the child. The problem is further complicated by the fact that none of the studies reports SES differences by age. The best one can do, therefore, is to estimate the median age of the group and from this approximate the period at which the practice may have taken place. For example, the second Detroit sample, which ranged in age from birth to 18 years, would have a median age of about nine. Since the field work was done in 1953, we estimate the date of feeding and weaning practices as about 1944.[1] It should be recognized, however, that the practices reported range over a considerable period extending from as far back as 1935 to the time of the interview in 1953. Any marked variation in child-rearing practices over this period could produce an average figure which would in point of fact be atypical for the middle year 1944. We shall have occasion to point to the possible operation of this effect in some of the data to follow.

If dates of practices are estimated by the method outlined above, we find that the available data describe social-class differences in feeding, weaning, and toilet training for a period from about 1930 to 1955. The relevant information appears in Tables 2 through 4.

It is reasonable to suppose that a mother's reports of whether or not she employed a particular practice would be somewhat more reliable than her estimate of when she began or discontinued that practice. This expectation is borne out by the larger number of statistically significant differences in tables presenting data on prevalence (Tables 2 and 3) rather than on the timing of a particular practice (Tables 4-6). On the plausible assumption that the former data are more reliable, we shall begin our discussion by considering

TABLE 2. *Frequency of Breast Feeding*

1	2	NO. OF CASES REPORTING			PERCENTAGE BREAST FED			
		3	4	5	6	7	8	9
Sample	Approx. date of practice	Total sample	Middle class	Working class	Total sample	Middle class	Working class	Difference *
National I	1930	1856	842	1014	80	78	82	−4†
National II	1932	445	201	244	40	29	49	−20†
Chicago I	1939	100	48	52	83	83	83	0
Detroit I	1941	112	59	53	62	54	70	−16
Detroit II	1944	200	70	130	Percentages not given			+
Eugene	1946–47	206	84	122	46	40	50	−10
Boston	1947–48	372	198	174	40	43	37	+6
New Haven I	1949–50	222	114	108	80	85	74	+11†
Palo Alto	1950	74	36	38	66	70	63	+7
Upstate New York	1955	1432	594	838	24	27	21	+6†

* Minus sign denotes lower incidence for middle class than for working class.
† Denotes difference significant at 5-percent level of confidence or better.

TABLE 3. *Scheduled versus Self-demand Feeding*

1	2	NO. OF CASES REPORTING			PERCENTAGE FED ON DEMAND			
		3	4	5	6	7	8	9
Sample	Approx. date of practice	Total sample	Middle class	Working class	Total sample	Middle class	Working class	Difference *
National I	1932	470	208	262	16	7	23	−16†
Chicago I	1939	100	48	52	25	4	44	−40†
Detroit I	1941	297	52	45	21	12	53	−41†
Detroit II	1944	205	73	132	55	51	58	−7
Boston	1947–48	372	198	174	Percentages not given			−
New Haven I	1949–50	191	117	74	65	71	54	+17
Palo Alto	1950	74	36	38	59	64	55	+9

* Minus sign denotes lower incidence of self-demand feeding in middle class.
† Denotes difference significant at 5-percent level of confidence or better.

TABLE 4. *Duration of Breast Feeding (for those Breast Fed)*

Sample	Approx. date of practice	NO. OF CASES ††			MEDIAN DURATION IN MONTHS			
		Total sample	Middle class	Working class	Total sample	Middle class	Working class	Difference **
National II*	1930	1488	654	834	6.6	6.2	7.5	−1.3†
Chicago I	1939	83	40	43	3.5	3.4	3.5	−.1
Detroit I*	1941	69	32	37	3.3	2.8	5.3	−2.5
Eugene	1946–47	95	34	61	3.4	3.2	3.5	−.3
Boston	1947–48	149	85	64	2.3	2.4	2.1	+.3
New Haven I*	1949–50	177	97	80	3.6	4.3	3.0	+1.3
Upstate New York	1955	299	145	154	1.2	1.3	1.2	+.1

* Medians not given in original report but estimated from data cited.
† Denotes difference significant at 5-percent level of confidence or better.
** Minus sign denotes shorter duration for middle class than for working class.
†† Number of cases for Chicago, Eugene, Boston, and Upstate New York estimated from percentages cited.

TABLE 5. *Age at Completion of Weaning (either Breast or Bottle)*

Sample	Approx. date of practice	NO. OF CASES			MEDIAN AGE IN MONTHS			
		Total sample	Middle class	Working class	Total group	Middle class	Working class	Difference*
Chicago I	1940	100	48	52	11.3	10.3	12.3	−2.0†
Detroit I	1942	69	32	37	11.2	10.6	12.0	−1.4†
Detroit II	1945	190	62	128	— Under 12 months —			−
Eugene	1947–48	206	85	121	13.6	13.2	14.1	−.9
Boston	1948–49	372	198	174	12.3	12.0	12.6	−.6
New Haven I	1949–50	222	114	108	— Over 12 months —			−
Palo Alto	1951	68	32	36	13.1	14.4	12.6	+1.8

* Minus sign denotes earlier weaning for middle than for working class.
† Denotes difference significant at 5-percent level of confidence or better.

TABLE 6. *Toilet Training*

Sample	Approximate date practice begun	NO. OF CASES		DIRECTION OF RELATIONSHIP			
		Bowel training	Bladder training	Beginning bowel training	End bowel training	Beginning bladder training	End bladder training
National II	1931	2375	2375		−†		−*
National I	1932	494	494		−		−
Chicago I	1940	100	220†	−†	−	−†**	+†
Detroit I	1942	110	102	−	−	+	−
Detroit II	1945	216	200	+†	−	−	
Eugene	1947–48	206	206	+	−	+	+
Boston	1948–49	372		−	+†		
New Haven I	1950–51	214		+†			
Palo Alto	1951	73		+†			

* Minus sign indicates that middle class began or completed training earlier than lower class.
† Denotes difference significant at 5-percent level of confidence or better.
** Based on data from 1946 report.

the results on frequency of breast feeding and scheduled feeding, which appear in Tables 2 and 3.

General trends   We may begin by looking at general trends over time irrespective of social-class level. These appear in column 6 of Tables 2 and 3. The data for breast feeding are highly irregular, but there is some suggestion of decrease in this practice over the years.[1] In contrast, self-demand feeding is becoming more common. In both instances the trend is more marked (column 8) in the middle class; in other words, it is they especially who are doing the changing. This fact is reflected even more sharply in column 9 which highlights a noteworthy shift. Here we see that in the earlier period — roughly before the end of World War II — both breast feeding and demand feeding were less common among the middle class than among the working class. In the later period, however, the direction is reversed; it is now the middle-class mother who more often gives her child the breast and feeds him on demand.

The data on duration of breast feeding (Table 4) and on the timing of weaning and bowel training (Tables 5 and 6) simply confirm, somewhat less reliably, all of the above trends. There is a general tendency in both social classes to wean the child earlier from the breast but, apparently, to allow him to suck from a bottle till a somewhat later age. Since no uniform reference points were used for securing information on toilet training in the several studies (i.e., some investi-gators report percentage training at six months, others at ten months, still others at 12 or 18 months), Table 6 shows only the direction of the difference between the two social classes. All these figures on timing point to the same generalization. In the earlier period, middle-class mothers were exerting more pressure; they weaned their children from the breast and bottle and carried out bowel and bladder training before their working-class counterparts. But in the last ten years the trend has been reversed — it is now the middle-class mother who trains later.

These consistent trends take on richer significance in the light of Wolfenstein's impressive analysis[2] of the content of successive editions of the United States Children's Bureau bulletin on *Infant Care*. She describes the period 1929–38 (which corresponds to the earlier time span covered by our data) as characterized by

---

[1] As indicated below, we believe that these irregularities are largely attributable to the highly selective character of a number of the samples (notably, New Haven I and Palo Alto) and that the downward trend in frequency and duration of breast feeding is probably more reliable than is reflected in the data of Tables 2 and 4.

[2] M. Wolfenstein, "Trends in Infant Care," *Am. J. Orthopsychiat.*, 1953, XXIII, 120–130. Similar conclusions were drawn in an earlier report by Stendler surveying 60 years of child-training practices as advocated in three popular women's magazines. *Cf.* C. B. Stendler, "Sixty Years of Child Training Practices," *J. Pediatrics*, 1950, XXXVI, 122–134.

...a pervasive emphasis on regularity, doing everything by the clock. Weaning and introduction of solid foods are to be accomplished with great firmness, never yielding for a moment to the baby's resistance...bowel training...must be carried out with great determination as early as possible... The main danger which the baby presented at this time was that of dominating the parents. Successful child training meant winning out against the child in the struggle for domination.

In the succeeding period, however,

...all this was changed. The child became remarkably harmless... His main active aim was to explore his world... When not engaged in exploratory undertakings, the baby needs care and attention; and giving these when he demands them, far from making him a tyrant, will make him less demanding later on. At this time mildness is advocated in all areas: thumbsucking and masturbation are not to be interfered with; weaning and toilet training are to be accomplished later and more gently.[1]

The parallelism between preachment and practice is apparent also in the use of breast feeding. Up until 1945, "breast feeding was emphatically recommended," with "warnings against early weaning." By 1951, "the long-term intransigence about breast feeding is relaxed." States the bulletin edition of that year: "Mothers who find bottle feeding easier should feel comfortable about doing it that way."

One more link in the chain of information completes the story. There is ample evidence that, both in the early and the later period, middle-class mothers were much more likely than working-class mothers to be exposed to current information on child care. Thus Anderson cites table after table showing that parents from higher SES levels read more books, pamphlets, and magazines, and listen to more radio talks on child care and related subjects. This in 1932. Similarly, in the last five years, White, in California, and Bock, in New York, report that middle-class mothers are much more likely than those in the working class to read Spock's best-seller, *Baby and Child Care*[2] and similar publications.

Our analysis suggests that the mothers not only read these books but take them seriously, and that their treatment of the child is affected accordingly. Moreover, middle-class mothers not only read more but are also more responsive; they alter their behavior earlier and faster than their working-class counterparts.

In view of the remarkably close parallelism in changes over time revealed by Wolfenstein's analysis and our own, we should perhaps not overlook a more recent trend clearly indicated in Wolfenstein's report and vaguely discernible as well in the data we have assembled. Wolfenstein asserts that, since 1950, a conservative note has crept into the child-training literature; "there

is an attempt to continue...mildness, but not without some conflicts and misgivings...May not continued gratification lead to addiction and increasingly intensified demands?"[3] In this connection it is perhaps no mere coincidence that the differences in the last column of Tables 2 to 4 show a slight drop after about 1950; the middle class is still more "relaxed" than the working class, but the differences are not so large as earlier. Once again, practice may be following preachment — in the direction of introducing more limits and demands — still within a permissive framework. We shall return to a consideration of this possibility in our discussion of class differences in the training of children beyond two years of age.

Taken as a whole, the correspondence between Wolfenstein's data and our own suggests a general hypothesis extending beyond the confines of social class as such: *child-rearing practices are likely to change most quickly in those segments of society which have closest access and are most receptive to the agencies or agents of change (e.g., public media, clinics, physicians, and counselors).* From this point of view, one additional trend suggested by the available data is worthy of note: rural families appear to "lag behind the times" somewhat in their practices of infant care. For example, in Anderson's beautifully detailed report, there is evidence that in 1932 farm families (Class IV in his sample) were still breast feeding their children more frequently but being less flexible in scheduling and toilet training than nonfarm families of roughly comparable socioeconomic status. Similarly, there are indications from Miller and Swanson's second Detroit study that, with SES held constant, mothers with parents of rural background adhere to more rigid techniques of socialization than their urban counterparts. Finally, the two samples in our data most likely to contain a relatively high proportion of rural families — Eugene, Oregon and Upstate New York — are also the ones which are slightly out of line in showing smaller differences in favor of middle-class permissiveness.

The above observations call attention to the fact that the major time trends discerned in our data, while impressive, are by no means uniform. There are several marked exceptions to the rule. True, some of these can be "explained" in terms of special features of the samples employed. A case in point is the New Haven study, which — in keeping with the rooming-in ideology and all that this implies — shows the highest frequency and duration of breast feeding for the postwar period, as well as the greatest prevalence of feeding on demand reported in all the surveys examined. Other discrepancies may be accounted for, at least in part, by variations in time span encompassed by the data (National 1930 *vs.* 1932), the demonstrated differential rate in breast feeding for first *vs.* later children (Palo Alto *vs.* National

[1] Wolfenstein, *op. cit.*, p. 121.
[2] Benjamin Spock, *Baby and Child Care* (New York: Pocket Books, Inc., 1957).
[3] Wolfenstein, *op. cit.*, p. 121.

1930 or Boston), ethnic differences (Boston *vs.* Chicago), contrasting ages of mothers in middle- *vs.* working-class samples (Chicago), etc. All of these explanations, however, are "after the fact" and must therefore be viewed with suspicion.

Summary   Despite our inability to account with any confidence for all departures from the general trend, we feel reasonably secure in our inferences about the nature of this trend. To recapitulate, over the last 25 years, even though breast feeding appears to have become less popular, American mothers — especially in the middle class — are becoming increasingly permissive in their feeding and toilet-training practices during the first two years of the child's life. The question remains whether this tendency is equally apparent in the training of the child as he becomes older. We turn next to a consideration of this issue.

V. Class differences in the training of children beyond the age of two

Once we leave the stage of infancy, data from different studies of child training become even more difficult to compare. There are still greater variations in the questions asked from one research to the next, and results are reported in different types of units (e.g., relating scales with varying numbers of steps diversely defined). In some instances (as in the Chicago, Detroit II, and, apparently, Eugene surveys) the questions referred not to past or current practices but to the mother's judgment about what she would do at some later period when her child would be older. Also, when the samples include children of widely varying ages, it is often difficult to determine at what period the behavior described by the mother actually took place. Sometimes a particular age was specified in the interviewer's question and when this occurred, we have made use of that fact in estimating the approximate date of the practice. More often, however, such information was lacking. Accordingly, our time estimates must be regarded as subject to considerable error. Finally, even though we deal with substantially the same researches considered in the analysis of infant care, the total period encompassed by the data is appreciably shorter. This is so because the mothers are no longer being asked to recall how they handled their child in infancy; instead they are reporting behavior which is contemporary, or at least not far removed, from the time of the interview.

All of these considerations combine to restrict severely our ability to identify changes in practices over time. Accordingly, the absence of evidence for such changes in some of the data is perhaps more properly attributed to the limitations of our measures than to the actual course of events.

Permissiveness and restriction on freedom of movement The areas of impulse expression documented in Table 7 reflect a continuity in treatment from babyhood into early childhood. With only one minor, statistically in-

significant exception, the results depict the middle-class parent as more permissive in all four spheres of activity: oral behavior, toilet accidents, sex and aggression. There is no suggestion of a shift over the somewhat truncated time span. The now-familiar trend reappears, however, in the data on restriction of freedom of movement shown in Table 8.

In Table 8 we see a gradual shift over time with the middle class being more restrictive in the 1930's and early 1940's but becoming more permissive during the last decade.

Training for independence and achievement Thus far, the trends that have appeared point predominantly in one direction — increasing leniency on the part of middle-class parents. At the same time, careful consideration of the nature of these data reveals that they are, in a sense, one-sided: they have been concerned almost entirely with the parents' response to the expressed needs and wishes of the child. What about the child's response to the needs and wishes of the parent, and the nature of these parental demands? The results presented in Table 9 are of especial interest since they shed light on all three aspects of the problem. What is more, they signal a dramatic departure from the hitherto unchallenged trend toward permissiveness.

Three types of questions have been asked with respect to independence training. The first is of the kind we have been dealing with thus far; for example, the Boston investigators inquired about the mother's reaction to the child's expression of dependence (hanging on to the mother's skirt, demanding attention, etc.). The results for this sort of query, shown in column 6 of Table 9, are consistent with previous findings for the postwar period; middle-class mothers are more tolerant of the child's expressed needs than are working-class mothers. The second type of question deals with the child's progress in taking care of himself and assuming responsibility (column 7). Here no clear trend is apparent, although there is some suggestion of greater solicitousness on the part of the middle-class mother. For example, in the 1932 material the middle-class child excelled in dressing and feeding himself only "partially," not "completely." In the 1935 Palo Alto study, the middle-class mother viewed her child as more dependent even though he was rated less so by the outside observer. It would appear that middle-class mothers may be on the alert for signs of dependency and anxious lest they push too fast.

Yet, as the data of column 8 clearly indicate, they push nevertheless. By and large, the middle-class mother expects more of her child than her working-class counterpart. All five of the statistically significant differences support this tendency and most of the remaining results point in the same direction. The conclusion is further underscored by the findings on class differences in parental aspirations for the child's academic progress, shown in column 9. The only exception to the highly reliable trend is in itself noteworthy. In the Boston study, more middle-class mothers

TABLE 7. *Permissiveness toward Impulse Expression*

| Sample | Approx. date of practice | No. of cases reported | DIRECTION OF TREND FOR MIDDLE CLASS | | | |
			Oral behavior	Toilet accidents	Sex	Aggression
National I	1932	470			More infants allowed to play on bed unclothed.*	
Chicago	1943	100		Treated by ignoring,* reasoning or talking, rather than slapping,* scolding, or showing disgust.*		More children allowed to "fight so long as they don't hurt each other badly."*
Detroit II	1946	70–88	Less often disciplined for thumb sucking.		Less often disciplined for touching sex organs.	
New Haven	1949–50	216	Less often disapproved for thumb sucking, eating habits, mannerisms, etc.*			
Eugene	1950	206		Less often treated by spanking or scolding.	More permissive toward child's sexual behavior.*	Fewer children allowed "to fight so long as they don't hurt each other badly." More permissiveness toward general aggression.
Boston	1951–52	372	Less restriction on use of fingers for eating.*	Less severe toilet training.*	Higher sex permissiveness (general index).*	More permissive of aggression toward parents,* children† and siblings. Less punishment of aggression toward parents.*
Palo Alto	1953	73		Less severe toilet training.*		More permissive of aggression toward parents.* Less severe punishment of aggression toward parents.

* Indicates difference between classes significant at the 5-percent level or better.
† The difference between percentages is not significant but the difference between ratings is significant at the 5-percent level or better.

TABLE 8. *Restriction on Freedom of Movement*

Sample	Approx. date of practice	No. of cases reported	Age	Item	Direction of relationship*
National II	1932	2289	1–5	Play restricted to home yard	−
				Play restricted to block	+
				Play restricted to neighborhood	+†
				No restriction on place of play	+†
National III	1932	669	6–12	Child goes to movie with parents	+
				Child goes to movie with other children	+
National IV	1932	2414	1–12	Child goes to bed earlier	+
Chicago	1943	100	5	Age at which child is allowed to go to movie alone or with other children	+†
				Age at which child is allowed to go downtown	−†
				Time at which children are expected in at night	+†
New Haven I	1949–50	211	1	Definite bed time	−†
Boston	1951–52	372	5	Restriction on how far child may go from home	−
				Frequency of checking on child's whereabouts	−**
				Strictness about bed time	−†
				Amount of care taken by persons other than parents	−†
Detroit II	1953	136	0–18	Child supervised closely after 12 years of age	−†
Palo Alto	1953	74	2½–5½	Extent of keeping track of child	0

* Plus sign denotes greater restriction for middle class.
† Denotes difference significant at 5-percent level or better.
** The difference between percentages is not significant but the difference between mean ratings is significant at the 5-percent level or better.

expected their children to go to college, but they were less likely to say that it was important for their child to do well in school. Are these mothers merely giving what they consider to be the socially acceptable response, or do they really, as Sears and his colleagues suggest, have less cause for concern because their children are living up to expectations?

The preceding question raises an even broader and more significant issue. Our data indicate that middle-class parents are becoming increasingly permissive in response to the child's expressed needs and desires. Yet, these same parents have not relaxed their high levels of

[1] R. Benedict, "Continuities and Discontinuities in Cultural Conditioning," *Psychiat*, 1938, I, 161–167.

expectations for ultimate performance. Do we have here a typical instance of Benedict's "discontinuity in cultural conditioning,"[1] with the child first being encouraged in one pattern of response and then expected to perform in a very different fashion? If so, there are days of disappointment ahead for middle-class fathers and mothers. Or, are there other elements in the parent-child relationship of the middle-class family which impel the child to effort despite, or, perhaps, even because of, his early experiences of relatively uninhibited gratification? The data on class differences in techniques of discipline shed some light on this question.

Techniques of discipline   The most consistent finding documented in Table 10 is the more frequent use of

TABLE 9. *Training for Independence and Academic Achievement*

					DIRECTION OF RELATIONSHIP			
1	2	3	4	5	6	7	8	9
Sample	Approx. date of practice	No. of cases reported	Age	Item	Parents' response to child's dependency	Child's behavior*	Parental demands and expectations	Academic aspirations for child*
National II	1932	2380	1–5	Dress self not at all		+		
				Dress self partially		+		
				Dress self completely		−		
		2391		Feed self not at all		−		
				Feed self partially		+		
				Feed self completely		−		
		2301		Children read to by parents				+
National III	1932	865	6–12	Runs errands	0			
				Earns money				
				Receive outside lessons in music, art, etc.	−			+†
National IV	1932	2695	1–12	Books in the home				+†
Chicago I	1943	100	5	Age child expected to dress self			0	
				Expected to help at home by age 5			+†	
				Expected to help with younger children			+†	
				Girls expected to begin to cook			+	
				Girls expected to help with dishes			+	
				Child expected to finish high school only				+†
				Child expected to finish college				+†
				Father teaches and reads to children				+†
Detroit II	1946		0–18	All right to leave three-year-old with sitter			0	
	1947	128		Expected to pick up own toys			+	
	1948	127		Expected to dress self by age 5			+	
	1948	126		Expected to put away clothes by age 5			+†	
				Children requested to run errands at age 7			0	
				Agree child should be on his own as early as possible			+	
Urban Connecticut	1950	152	6–18	Age of expected mastery (Winterbottom scale)			+†	
Eugene	1950	206	0–18	Household rules and chores expected of children			+	
Boston	1951–52	372	5	Parent permissive of child dependency	−†			
				Punishment, irritation for dependency	−†			
				Parents give child regular job around house			0	
				Importance of child's doing well at school				−†
				Expected to go to college				+†
New Haven II	1951–53	48	14–17	Father subscribes to values of independence and mastery			+†	
		1151**	14–17	Expected to go to college				+†
				Family checks over homework				+†
Palo Alto	1953	74	2½–5½	M's report of child's dependency		−		
				Amount of attention child wants		+		
				Child objects to separation		−		
				Judge's rating of dependency		+		
Upstate New York	1955	1433	0–1	Mother's educational aspirations for child				+†

 * Plus sign denotes greater independence or achievement required for middle-class child.
 † Difference between classes significant at the 5-percent level or better.
 ** This is the entire high-school sample which Strodtbeck surveyed in order to select his experimental and control group.

TABLE 10. *Techniques of Discipline*

Sample	Approx. date of practice	No. of cases reporting	Age	DIRECTION OF RELATIONSHIP*				Nature of love-oriented technique	Other significant trends for middle class
				Physical punishment	Reasoning	Isolation	Love-oriented technique		
National II	1932	1947	1–5	−†					
National III	1932	839	6–12			+†			
National IV	1932	3130	1–12		+†				Infractions more often ignored† / More children deprived of pleasure as punishment
Chicago I	1943	100	5	+		−	+†	Praise for good behavior	Soiling child more often ignored,† rather than spanked† or shown disgust
Detroit I	1950	115	12–14	−†			+†	Mother expresses disappointment or appeals to guilt	
Detroit II	1950	222	0–19	−			+	Mother uses symbolic rather than direct rewards and punishments	
Eugene	1950	206	0–18	−		0	+†		
Boston	1951–52	372	5	−†	+	+	0	No difference in overall use of praise or withdrawal of love	Less use of ridicule,† deprivation of privileges** or praise for no trouble at the table†

* Plus sign indicates practice was more common in middle class than in working class.
† Denotes difference between classes significant at 5-percent level or better.
** The difference between percentages is not significant but the difference between mean ratings is significant at the 5-percent level or better.

physical punishment by working-class parents. The middle class, in contrast, resort to reasoning, isolation, and what Sears and his colleagues have referred to as "love-oriented" discipline techniques.[1] These are methods which rely for their effect on the child's fear of loss of love. Miller and Swanson referred to substantially the same class of phenomena by the term "psychological discipline," which for them covers such parental behaviors as appeals to guilt, expressions of disappointment, and the use of symbolic rather than direct rewards and punishments. Table 10 shows all available data on class differences in the use of corporal punishment, reasoning, isolation, and "love-oriented" techniques. Also, in order to avoid the risks, however small, involved in wearing theoretical blinders, we have listed in the last column of the table all other significant class differences in techniques of discipline reported in the studies we have examined.

From one point of view, these results highlight once again the more lenient policies and practices of middle-class families. Such parents are, in the first place, more likely to overlook offenses, and when they do punish, they are less likely to ridicule or inflict physical pain. Instead, they reason with the youngster, isolate him, appeal to guilt, show disappointment, — in short, convey in a variety of ways, on the one hand, the kind of behavior that is expected of the child; on the other, the realization that transgression means the interruption of a mutually valued relationship.

These consistent class differences take on added significance in the light of the finding, arrived at independently both by the Boston and Detroit investiga-

tors, that "love-oriented" or "psychological" techniques are more effective than other methods for bringing about desired behavior. Indeed, both groups of researchers concluded on the basis of their data that physical punishment for aggression tends to increase rather than decrease aggressive behavior. From the point of view of our interest, these findings mean that middle-class parents, though in one sense more lenient in their discipline techniques, are using methods that are actually more compelling. Moreover, the compelling power of these practices, rather than being reduced, is probably enhanced by the more permissive treatment accorded to middle-class children in the early years of life. The successful use of withdrawal of love as a discipline technique implies the prior existence of a gratifying relationship; the more love present in the first instance, the greater the threat implied in its withdrawal.

In sum, to return to the issue posed in the preceding section, our analysis suggests that middle-class parents are in fact using techniques of discipline which are likely to be effective in evoking the behavior desired in the child. Whether the high levels of expectation held by such parents are actually achieved is another matter. At least, there would seem to be some measure of functional continuity in the way in which middle-class parents currently treat their children from infancy through childhood.

Before we leave consideration of the data of Table

[1] These investigators also classify "isolation" as a love-oriented technique, but since this specific method is reported on in several other studies as well, we have tabulated the results separately to facilitate comparison.

10, one additional feature of the results deserves comment. In the most recent study reported, the Boston research, there were three departures from the earlier general trend. First, no class difference was found in the over-all use of praise. Second, working-class parents actually exceeded those of the middle class in praising good behavior at the table. Third, in contrast to earlier findings, the working-class mother more frequently punished by withdrawing privileges. Although Sears *et al.* did not classify "withdrawal of privileges" as a love-oriented technique, the shift does represent a change in the direction of what was previously a method characteristic of the middle-class parent. Finally, there is no clear trend in the differential use of love-oriented techniques by the two social classes. If we view the Boston study as reflecting the most recent trends in methods of discipline, then either middle-class mothers are beginning to make less use of techniques they previously relied upon, or the working class is starting to adopt them. We are inclined toward the latter hypothesis in the belief that the working class, as a function of increasing income and education, is gradually reducing its "cultural lag." Evidence from subsequent studies, of course, would be necessary to confirm this speculative interpretation, since the results cited may merely be a function of features peculiar to the Boston study and not typical of the general trend.

Over-all character of the parent-child relationship   The material considered so far has focused on specific practices employed by the parent. A number of researches document class differences as well in variables of a more molar sort — for example, the emotional quality of the parent-child relationship as a whole. These investigations have the additional advantage of reaching somewhat further back in time, but they also have their shortcomings. First of all, the results are not usually reported in the conventional form of percentages or means for specific social-class levels. In some studies the findings are given in terms of correlation coefficients. In others, social status can only be estimated from educational level. In others still, the data are presented in the form of graphs from which no significance tests can be computed. Partly to compensate for this lack of precision and comparability, partly to complete the picture of available data on class-differences in child rearing, we cite in Table 11 not only the results from these additional studies of molar variables but also all other statistically significant findings from researches considered previously which might have bearing on the problem at hand. In this way, we hope as well to avoid the bias which occasionally arises from looking only at those variables in which one has a direct theoretical interest.

The data of Table 11 are noteworthy in a number of respects. First, we have clear confirmation that, over the entire 25-year period, middle-class parents have had a more acceptant, equalitarian relationship with their children. In many ways, the contrast is epitomized in

¹ Kohn, *op. cit.*

Duvall's distinction between the "developmental" and "traditional" conceptions of mother and child. Duvall asked the mothers in her sample to list the "five things that a good mother does" and the "five things that a good child does." Middle-class mothers tended to emphasize such themes as "guiding and understanding," "relating herself lovingly to the child," and making sure that he "is happy and contented," "shares and cooperates with others," and "is eager to learn." In contrast, working-class mothers stressed the importance of keeping house and child "neat and clean", "training the child to regularity," and getting the child "to obey and respect adults."

What is more, this polarity in the value orientation of the two social classes appears to have endured. In data secured as recently as 1957, Kohn[1] reports that working-class mothers differ from those of the middle class in their choice of characteristics most desired in a child; the former emphasize "neatness, cleanliness, and obedience," while the latter stress "happiness, considerateness, and self-control."

Yet, once again, it would be a mistake to conclude that the middle-class parent is exerting less pressure on his children. As the data of Table 11 also show, a higher percentage of middle-class children are punished in some manner, and there is more "necessary" discipline to prevent injury or danger. In addition, though the middle-class father typically has a warmer relationship with the child, he is also likely to have more authority and status in family affairs.

Although shifts over time are difficult to appraise when the data are so variable in specific content, one trend is sufficiently salient to deserve comment. In the early Berkeley data the working-class parent is more expressive of affection than his middle-class counterpart. But in the follow-up study of the same children eight years later the trend is reversed. Perhaps the same mothers behave differently toward younger and older children. Still, the item "Baby picked up when cries" yields a significant difference in favor of the working-class mother in 1932 and a reliable shift in the opposite direction in 1953. *Sic transit gloria Watsoniensis!*

Especially with terms as heavily value laden as those which appear in Table 11, one must be concerned with the possibility that the data in the studies examined document primarily not actual behavior but the middle-class mother's superior knowledge of the socially acceptable response. Undoubtedly, this factor operates to inflate the reported relationships. But there are several reassuring considerations. First, although the items investigated vary widely in the intensity of their value connotations, all show substantially the same trends. Second, four of the studies reported in Table 11 (Berkeley I and II, Yellow Springs, and New Haven II) are based not on the mother's responses to an interview but on observation of actual interaction among family members. It seems highly unlikely, therefore, that the conclusions we have reached apply only to professed opinions and not to real behavior as well.

TABLE 11. *Overall Character of Parent-child Relationship*

Sample	Approx. date of practice	No. of cases reported	Age	Middle-class trend	Working-class trend
Berkeley I	1928–32	31	1–3	Grants autonomy Cooperative Equalitarian	Expresses affection Excessive contact Intrusive Irritable Punitive Ignores child
National I	1932	494	0–1		Baby picked up when cries†
National IV	1932	3239	1–12	Higher percentage of children punished†	Nothing done to allay child's fears†
Yellow Springs, Ohio	1940	124	3–12	Acceptant-democratic	Indulgent Active-rejectant
Berkeley II	1939–42	31	9–11	Grants autonomy Cooperative Equalitarian Expresses affection	Excessive contact Intrusive Irritable Punitive Ignores child
Chicago I	1943	100	5		Father plays with child more†
Chicago II	1943–44	433	1–5	"Developmental" conception of "good mother" and "good child."†	"Traditional" conception of "good mother" and "good child."†
New Haven I	1949–50	219	1	More necessary discipline to prevent injury or danger†	More prohibitive discipline beyond risk of danger or injury
Boston	1951–52	372	5	Mother warmer toward child† Father warmer toward child* Father exercises more authority* Mother has higher esteem for father† Mother delighted about pregnancy† Both parents more often share authority*	Father demands instant obedience† Child ridiculed† Greater rejection of child† Emphasis on neatness, cleanliness, and order† Parents disagree more on child-rearing policy*
New Haven II	1951–53	48	14–17	Fathers have more power in family decisions† Parents agree in value orientations†	
Palo Alto	1953	73	2½–5½	Baby picked up when cries†	Mother carries through demands rather than dropping the subject††
Eugene	1955–56	206	0–18	Better relationship between father and child†	
Washington, D.C.	1956–57	400	10–11	Desirable qualities are happiness,* considerateness,* curiosity,* self-control*	Desirable qualities are neatness, cleanliness,* obedience*

* Trend significant at 5-percent level or better.
† The difference between percentages is not significant but the difference between mean ratings is significant at the 5-percent level or better.

VI. Retrospect and prospect

It is interesting to compare the results of our analysis with the traditional view of the differences between the middle- and lower-class styles of life, as documented in the classic descriptions of Warner,[1] Davis,[2] Dollard,[3] and the more recent accounts of Spinley,[4] Clausen,[5] and Miller and Swanson.[6] In all these sources the working class is typically characterized as impulsive and uninhibited, the middle class as more rational, controlled and guided by a broader perspective in time. Thus Clausen writes:

> The lower class pattern of life ... puts a high premium on physical gratification, on free expression of aggression, on spending and sharing. Cleanliness, respect for property, sexual control, educational achievement — all are highly valued by middle class Americans — are of less importance to the lower class family or are phrased differently.[7]

To the extent that our data even approach this picture, it is for the period before World War II rather than for the present day. The modern middle class has, if any-thing, extended its time perspective so that the tasks of child training are now accomplished on a more leisurely schedule. As for the lower class the fit is far better for the actual behavior of parents rather than for the values they seek to instill in their children. As reflected in the data of Tables 10 and 11, the lower-class parent — though he demands compliance and control in his child — is himself more aggressive, expressive, and impulsive than his middle-class counterpart. Even so, the picture is a far cry from the traditional image of the casual and carefree lower class. Perhaps

[1] W. L. Warner and P. S. Lunt, *The Social Life of a Modern Community* (New Haven: Yale University Press, 1942); Warner, Meeker, and others, *op. cit.*
[2] A. Davis, B. Gardner, and M. R. Gardner, *Deep South* (Chicago: University of Chicago Press, 1941).
[3] J. Dollard, *Caste and Class in a Southern Town* (New Haven: Yale University Press, 1937).
[4] B. M. Spinley, *The Deprived and the Privileged: Personality Development in English Society* (London: Routledge & Kegan Paul, Ltd., 1953).
[5] J. A. Clausen, "Social and Psychological Factors in Narcotics Addiction," *Law and Contemporary Problems*, 1957, XXII, 34–51.
[6] Miller and Swanson, *The Changing American Parent, op. cit.*
[7] Clausen, *op. cit.*, p. 42.

the classic portrait is yet to be seen along the skid rows and Tobacco Roads of the nation, but these do not lie along the well-trodden paths of the survey researcher. He is busy ringing doorbells, no less, in the main section of the lower-class district, where most of the husbands have steady jobs and, what is more important, the wife is willing to answer the door and the interviewer's questions. In this modern working-class world there may be greater freedom of emotional expression, but there is no laxity or vagueness with respect to goals of child training. Consistently over the past 25 years, the parent in this group has emphasized what are usually regarded as the traditional middle-class virtues of cleanliness, conformity, and control, and although his methods are not so effective as those of his middle-class neighbors, they are perhaps more desperate.

Perhaps this very desperation, enhanced by early exposure to impulse and aggression, leads working-class parents to pursue new goals with old techniques of discipline. While accepting middle-class levels of aspiration he has not yet internalized sufficiently the modes of response which make these standards readily achievable for himself or his children. He has still to learn to wait, to explain, and to give and withhold his affection as the reward and price of performance.

As of 1957, there are suggestions that the cultural gap may be narrowing. Spock has joined the Bible on the working-class shelf. If we wish to see the shape of the future, we can perhaps do no better than to look at the pages of the newly revised edition of this ubiquitous guidebook. Here is a typical example of the new look — a passage not found in the earlier version:

> If the parent can determine in which respects she may be too permissive and can firm up her discipline, she may, if she is on the right track, be delighted to find that her child becomes not only better behaved but much happier. Then she can really love him better, and he in turn responds to this.[1]

Apparently "love" and "limits" are both watchwords for the coming generation of parents. As Mrs. Johnson, down in the flats, puts away the hairbrush and decides to have a talk with her unruly youngster "like the book says," Mrs. Thomas, on the hill, is dutifully striving to overcome her guilt at the thought of giving John the punishment she now admits he deserves. If both ladies are successful, the social scientist may eventually have to look elsewhere in his search for everlarger *F*'s and *t*'s.

Such speculations carry us beyond the territory yet surveyed by the social scientist. Perhaps the most important implication for the future from our present analysis lies in the sphere of method rather than substance. Our attempt to compare the work of a score of investigators over a score of years will have been worth the labor if it but convinces future researchers of the wastefulness of such uncoordinated efforts.

[1] Spock, *op. cit.*, p. 326.

Our best hope for an understanding of the differences in child rearing in various segments of our society and the effects of these differences on personality formation lies in the development of a systematic long-range plan for gathering comparable data at regular intervals on large samples of families at different positions in the social structure. We now have survey organizations with the scientific competence and adequate technical facilities to perform the task. With such hopes in mind, the author looks ahead to the day when the present analysis becomes obsolete, in method as well as substance.

VII. Recapitulation and coda

A comparative analysis of the results of studies of social-class differences in child rearing over a 25-year period points to the following conclusions.

A. TRENDS IN INFANT CARE

1) Over the past quarter of a century, American mothers at all social-class levels have become more flexible with respect to infant feeding and weaning. Although fewer infants may be breast fed, especially over long periods of time, mothers are increasingly more likely to feed their children on demand and to wean them later from the bottle.

2) Class differences in feeding, weaning, and toilet training show a clear and consistent trend. From about 1930 till the end of World War II, working-class mothers were uniformly more permissive than those of the middle class. They were more likely to breast feed, to follow a self-demand schedule, to wean the child later both from breast and bottle, and to begin and complete both bowel and bladder training at a later age. After World War II, however, there has been a definite reversal in direction; now it is the middle-class mother who is the more permissive in each of the above areas.

3) Shifts in the pattern of infant care — especially on the part of middle-class mothers — show a striking correspondence to the changes in practices advocated in successive editions of U.S. Children's Bureau bulletins and similar sources of expert opinion.

4) In addition to varying with social-class level, methods of infant care appear to differ as a function of cultural background, urban vs. rural upbringing, and exposure to particular ideologies of child rearing.

5) Taken together, the findings on changes in infant care lead to the generalization that socialization practices are most likely to be altered in those segments of society which have most ready access to the agencies or agents of change (e.g., books, pamphlets, physicians, and counselors).

B. TRENDS IN CHILD TRAINING

6) The data on the training of the young child show middle-class mothers, especially in the postwar period, to be consistently more permissive toward the child's expressed needs and wishes. The generalization applies in such diverse areas as oral behavior, toilet accidents, dependency, sex, aggressiveness, and freedom of movement outside the home.

7) Though more tolerant of expressed impulses and desires, the middle-class parent, throughout the period covered by this survey, has higher expectations for the child. The middle-class youngster is expected to learn to take care of himself earlier, to accept more responsibilities about the home, and — above all — to progress further in school.

8) In matters of discipline, working-class parents are consistently more likely to employ physical punishment, while middle-class families rely more on reasoning, isolation, appeals to guilt, and other methods involving the threat of loss of love. At least two independent lines of evidence suggest that the techniques preferred by middle-class parents are more likely to bring about the development of internalized values and controls. Moreover, the effectiveness of such methods should, at least on theoretical grounds, be enhanced by the more acceptant atmosphere experienced by middle-class children in their early years.

9) Over the entire 25-year period studied, parent-child relationships in the middle class are consistently reported as more acceptant and equalitarian, while those in the working class are oriented toward maintaining order and obedience. Within this context, the middle class has shown a shift away from emotional control toward freer expression of affection and greater tolerance of the child's impulses and desires.

In the past few years, there have been indications that the gap between the social classes may be narrowing. Whatever trend the future holds in store, let us hope that the social scientist will no longer be content to look at them piece-meal but will utilize all the technical resources now at his command to obtain a systematic picture of the changes, through still more extended space and time, in the way in which humanity brings up its children.

Marital Satisfaction and Instability

A CROSS-CULTURAL CLASS ANALYSIS OF DIVORCE RATES
William J. Goode

BECAUSE FAMILY EXPERIENCES arouse so much emotion and social philosophers continue to believe that the family is a major element in the social structure, the field has for over two millennia attracted more ideologists than theorists and has been the object of much speculation but little rigorous research. Personal acquaintance with a family system has usually been confused with valid knowledge, and journalistic descriptions of the past have been the main source of information for the analysis of family changes.

The past two decades have witnessed important changes in this situation. We have come to agree that theory is not opposed to fact but is a structure of inter-related empirical propositions.[1] Good theory not only orders known facts; it also leads to new ones. In this sense, good theoretical work on the family has been rare,[2] and the younger generation of theorists does not

[1] See the clear statement of this position by Robert K. Merton, "The Bearing of Sociological Theory on Empirical Research", in: *Social Theory and Social Structure*, 2nd edition, Glencoe, Ill., The Free Press, 1957, pp. 85-101.

[2] Three serious monograph attempts may be noted here: George P. Murdock, *Social Structure*, New York, Macmillan, 1949; Claude Levi-Strauss, *Les Structures Elémentaires de la Parenté*, Paris, Presses Universitaires de France, 1949; and William J. Goode, *After Divorce*, Glencoe, Ill., The Free Press, 1956. Various reviews of the research over the past decade are now available: Robert F. Winch, "Marriage and the Family", in: Joseph B. Gittler (ed.), *Review of Sociology*, 1945-55, New York, John Wiley, 1957; Reuben Hill and Richard L. Simpson, "Marriage and Family Sociology, 1945-55", in: Hans L. Zetterberg (ed.), *Sociology in the United States*, Paris, Unesco, 1956, pp. 93-101; and Nelson Foote and Leonard S. Cottrell, *Identity and Interpersonal Competence*, Chicago, University of Chicago Press, 1955. See also William J. Goode, "Horizons in Family Theory", in: Robert K. Merton, Leonard Broom and Leonard S. Cottrell (eds.), *Sociology Today*, New York, Basic Books, 1959.

Reprinted from *International Social Science Journal*, V. XIV (1962), pp. 507-526, by permission of the author and the publisher.

enter the field.[1] However, we have at least come to understand the necessity of adequate theory even in this field. In addition, anthropologists — whose work is all too often neglected by sociologists — are no longer content to report that a tribe prefers some type of cross-cousin marriage but attempt to find out how frequently such marriages occur.[2] Moreover, the ideologist who sermonizes for or against some family behaviour, such as egalitarianism for women, is no less free to pursue his taste, but we no longer believe that his value-laden expositions should be given the same respect we pay to responsible research.

These changes do not imply that we should ignore ideological writings about the family. On the contrary, they are phenomena — like political or economic changes or public attitudes about morality — that affect family behaviour, and therefore must be taken seriously without being regarded at all as scientific reports. Moreover, an ideological position may determine a man's choice of the scientific problem he investigates. Nevertheless, we must keep clearly in mind that the ideological bases from which a scientific problem is chosen are essentially irrelevant to the truth of the research findings. We are properly suspicious when the author's aim seems to be to persuade us of his ideology, rather than to demonstrate, by a precise exposition of his methods, the accuracy of his data. On the other hand, the work itself is to be judged, not the motives of the researcher. We evaluate the importance of the research by its fruitfulness, and its validity and reliability by methodological canons; if it is adequately done, it is a contribution to science even if we deplore its policy sources and implications.

Finally, it is obvious that ideological positions can sometimes point to good research problems. For example, egalitarianism is certainly one motive for

investigating how culture determines sex roles.[3] In general, however, ideology is a poorer compass than good theory for discovering important facts, and is at times successful only because it may happen (in the social sciences at least) that what is at the centre of ideological debate is also a key to understanding how a social pattern operates.

In any event, we are now better able to distinguish what is from what ought to be, and even the ideologist may gradually understand that without good science, policy is inevitably misguided.

MARITAL ADJUSTMENT AND HAPPINESS

Salon sociologists have talked and written much about the modern "right to marital happiness", but it is not clear that spouses even in the United States really accept such a norm. Society does not seek to create the conditions which would assure its achievement, or punish anyone who fails to make others happy. On the other hand, all societies recognize the desirability of marital contentment and the intimate misery of marital discontent. The scientific problem of studies in marital adjustment was to try to predict whether certain types of couples were more or less likely to be content in their marriages. The ideological impulse was simply, as in the field of medicine, that it would be good to advise couples beforehand not to marry if they seemed ill-suited to one another. The pragmatic basis was simply that the wisdom of elders, who have in all societies made such predictions, might be systematized, standardized, and made more precise. The first published predictive instrument in this country was developed by Jessie Bernard,[4] but at that time Burgess and Cottrell had already begun (1931) their larger study, growing out of Burgess' creation of an instrument for parole prediction. The psychologist Lewis M. Terman utilized some of their findings in a similar study, but the Burgess-Cottrell work remained the most sophisticated attempt at developing a marital prediction instrument until the Burgess-Wallin study in 1953. Locke tested its discriminative power, and various men have tried the instrument in one form or another on other populations (Chinese, Swedes, Southern Negroes).[5]

Unfortunately, this line of research seems to have come to a dead end. Widely used by marital counsellors in this country, the instrument has not improved so as to achieve greater predictive power and its power was never great. Successive studies have confirmed the relevance of only a few items: for example, most show that if the couple's parents' marriages were happy, if the couple have been acquainted for a long time, and if the engagement was long, there is greater chance for marital success; but most other items are not confirmed by various researches. Most of the variance is not accounted for by the items that have been singled out as important.[6] In short, no new, and only few corroborating, findings have emerged in recent years.

[1] Theorists of the rank of Talcott Parsons, Kingsley Davis, Robert K. Merton, and George C. Homans have all written theoretical papers on the family, however.

[2] See Meyer Fortes, "Kinship and Marriage among the Ashanti", in: A. R. Radcliffe-Brown and Daryll Forde (eds.), *African Systems of Kinship and Marriage*, London: Oxford University Press, 1956, p. 282.

[3] See Margaret Mead, *Sex and Temperament*, in: *From The South Seas*, New York, Morrow, 1939.

[4] "An Instrument for Measurement of Success in Marriage", *Publications of the American Sociological Society*, No. 27, 1933, pp. 94–106.

[5] The major publications noted here are Ernest W. Burgess and Leonard S. Cottrell, *Predicting Success or Failure in Marriage*, New York, Prentice-Hall, 1939; Lewis M. Terman *et al.*, *Psychological Factors in Marital Happiness*, New York, McGraw-Hill, 1939; Harvey J. Locke, *Predicting Adjustment in Marriage*, New York, Henry Holt, 1951; Ernest W. Burgess and Paul W. Wallin, *Engagement and Marriage*; and Georg Karlsson, *Adaptability and Communication in Marriage*, Uppsala, Sweden, Almqvist & Wiksells, 1951. For a convenient summary of the meaning of various parts of the instrument, see Ernest W. Burgess and Harvey J. Locke, *The Family*, 2nd edition, New York, American, 1953, Chapters 14, 15.

[6] For a summary of the main findings, see: ibid., pp. 408–429, and Clifford Kirkpatrick, *What Science says About Happiness in Marriage*, Minneapolis, Burgess Publishing Co., 1947.

THE THEORY OF COMPLEMENTARITY

The primary key to this sterility can be found in the picture of the contented couple which emerges from these studies: it is the conventional bourgeois couple, meeting for the first time under respectable auspices, coming from non-divorcing families, not venturing far toward intimacy during acquaintanceship, holding steady jobs, enjoying a relatively higher education, and so on. Since, to a perhaps increasing degree, modern couples do not always come from such backgrounds, the instrument cannot estimate their future success relative to one another. To a considerable extent, the instrument in its various forms merely discriminates the old-fashioned from the modern couple, but does not discriminate from within the population of modern couples those who will be more or less successful.

One line of theory has emerged which might be helpful in gauging which men and women might live in harmony with one another, after granting that "modern" couples are less prone to be happy in marriage. The "Theory of Complementarity" was developed by Robert F. Winch to explain why, within a given pool of marital eligibles (leading to homogamy), certain people fall in love with one another and marry.[1] No one, unfortunately, has attempted either to verify this theory on a substantial random population, or even to extend it to other areas of courtship and marriage.[2]

This theory, developed with considerable rigour, accepts the wide range of findings which show that couples who marry are usually of the same religion, ethnic group, occupational background, education, and so on. However, the specific attraction between socially homogamous couples[3] is the heterogamy of their basic psychological needs.[4] For example, those who need to show deference are attracted by those who wish to achieve; those who seek abasement by those who seek dominance, and so on. Whether X falls in love with Y seems a trivial enough scientific issue, but precisely because this is a theory, it has further implications, pragmatic, sociological and psychological. It suggests, for example, why some divorcees continue to marry precisely the kind of spouses who will make them unhappy. It points to the structurally determined misperceptions of others in the courtship situation — the Western male should, for example, exhibit a relatively dominant personality, seeking achievement and autonomy, but the woman who is attracted to him may find later that he is quite different in his real needs. Winch himself denies that the theory applies to marital happiness,[5] but such an application seems worthwhile. Essentially, it is the pleasure that the young man and woman give to one another by the mutual satisfaction of their basic personality needs which determines their serious emotional involvement and commitment. To the extent that this need-satisfaction continues after marriage, the union should have greater stability and happiness (other things being equal). That is, if need-satisfaction continues, then so should the attraction between spouses. A further implication is that the new situational elements of marriage may be very different from those of courtship, and thus frustrate (or perhaps enhance) the satisfaction of each other's needs. In addition, it is of psychological importance to ask, with reference to both courtship and marriage, just how much need-satisfaction of what kind (abasement, autonomy, deference, achievement, etc.) may outweigh a failure to get satisfaction of other needs. Next, one or the other spouse may eventually obtain some of these satisfactions outside marriage, e.g., in his or her work, thus posing a new set of questions to be answered.[6] Finally, the theory seems to elucidate to some extent the attraction between very close friends.

MARITAL INSTABILITY

I have suggested elsewhere that happiness is probably not a strategic variable in the analysis of marital institutions. Marital strain and instability, however, or the stability of the family as a boundary-maintaining social unit, may well be because at such points the individual has an option and must decide among several sets of consequences (mostly difficult for him to predict) on the basis of a complex set of value and situational elements. By contrast, there can be no problem of moral choice as between happiness and unhappiness, or "happiness and duty". Happiness would always win. Moreover, happiness cannot be built into the structure of any marriage and kinship system as a statistical likelihood or a moral norm. Again by contrast, the stability of the family unit can be, and often is.

As fruitful as the view that marital instability is the failure of boundary-maintaining forces, is the view that the family is made up of role relations. Then instability can be defined as the failure of one or more individuals to perform their role obligations. The major forms of instability or disorganization could thereby be classified as follows:[7]

[1] Robert F. Winch, *Mate Selection*, New York, Harper, 1958.

[2] Several studies claim to have tested it, but they have not used the same measures for each important factor, or an appropriate population.

[3] Burgess and Locke, op. cit., p. 369, note that over one hundred studies exist to show that married couples are homogamous with respect to a wide variety of traits.

[4] Winch developed his categories from the work of Henry A. Murray, *Explorations in Personality*, New York, Oxford University Press, 1938.

[5] Personal communication, 22 July 1961.

[6] Winch has commented on this point in *Mate Selection*, op. cit., pp. 202–210, 300–303. For some of the consequences of such actions in general terms, see the author's two related papers, "Norm Commitment and Conformity to Role-Status Obligations", *American Journal of Sociology*, No. 65, November, 1960, pp. 246–258; and "A Theory of Role Strain", *American Sociological Review*, No. 25, August 1960, pp. 483–496, as well as the use of this theory in "Illegitimacy in the Caribbean Social Structure", *American Sociological Review*, No. 25, February 1960, pp. 21–30.

[7] This classification is developed and applied in my article, "Family Disorganization", in: Robert K. Merton and Robert

1) The uncompleted family unit: illegitimacy. Here, the family unit did not come into existence. However, the missing individual obviously fails in his "father-husband" role-obligations as defined by society, mother, or child. Moreover, a major indirect cause of the illegitimacy is likely to be the role-failure of both mother and father.

2) Instability when one spouse wilfully departs: annulment, separation, divorce, and desertion. Instances of "job desertion" might also be included here, when the individual stays away from home for a long period of time on the excuse of a distant job.

3) The "empty-shell" family: in which individuals interact instrumentally, but fail essentially in the role-obligation to give emotional support to one another. Here, of course, there is no public dissolution or instability but the unit is in effect dissolved.

4) The crisis and strain caused by "external" events such as the temporary or permanent unwilled absence of one of the spouses because of death, imprisonment, or some impersonal catastrophe such as flood, war or depression.

5) Internal crises which create "unwilled" major role-failures: mental, emotional, or physical pathologies; severe mental retardation of a child, psychoses, chronic and incurable physical conditions.

Such a conception poses nearly impossible problems of data collection under present conditions, but does offer one way of conceptualizing the strains and options in certain kinds of marital instability. Indeed, precisely because at the present time we have no way of knowing, in any country, how many families fall into one or another of these categories at a given time, I shall in a moment limit my perspective somewhat and consider only certain problems of divorce rates.

For the moment, however, it is at least useful to keep in mind certain distinctions in this area of analysis. A primary distinction is that between the instability of the family unit and the instability of the family system in a given society. Both of these in turn must be distinguished from social change in the family system, as well as from disorganization. With respect to the first distinction, it is evident that all families do end, but this need not affect the family system. It is likely that high divorce rates have been common in Arab countries for many generations, as they are now, but there is no evidence that this has been until recently a changing family system. That is, the Arab family system creates — and, within limits, copes with — the problems of a high divorce rate and its essential structure remains unchanged. As we shall note in a moment, this may be also said of the Japanese Tokugawa family

[1] George P. Murdoch notes that among the Crow a man might be ridiculed if he stayed too long with one woman ("Family Stability in Non-European Cultures", in: *Annals*, No. 272, November 1950, p. 198).

___

A. Nisbet (eds.), *Contemporary Social Problems*, New York, Harcourt Brace, 1961, pp. 390ff.

system. With respect to change, it is evident that if the rates of occurrence of major family happenings, such as the percentage eventually marrying, percentage married at certain ages, divorce rates, fertility, patterns and so on, are changing, then it may be that the family system is also changing and that at least some parts of it are dissolving or undergoing disorganization. On the other hand, some of these changes may actually reduce the rates of occurrence of some phenomena classically called "disorganization", such as divorce, separation, illegitimacy or desertion. Thus, for example, the rate of desertion has been dropping in the United States. In Latin American countries in process of industrialization, with all its predictable *anomie*, the rate of illegitimacy has been dropping. Japan's family system has been undergoing great changes over the past generation and thus by definition certain parts of it must have been "dissolving", but the divorce rate has steadily dropped. Finally, even though the old family patterns may be dissolving, they may be replaced by new ones which control as determinately as the old.

Returning for the moment to a publicly recognized form of marital instability, divorce, we ought at least to ask the ideological question of whether a high divorce rate is "good" or "bad". Doubtless, there is more marital disharmony in a period of great social change than in periods of stability (assuming one can find such periods). However, marital disharmony is probably ubiquitous, and one may ask the sociological question, what are the institutional patterns that cope with that potential or real strain? All family systems include some mechanisms for keeping the hostilities between spouses within limits. A primary pattern is, of course, to lower expectations of emotional performance on both sides, so that neither side expects great happiness or love but does expect a minimal set of behavioural performances. A second obvious pattern noted by many is to place the greatest social value on the kin network and to reduce the importance of the husband-wife relation. As a consequence the tensions between the two are less likely to build to an intolerable level. Thirdly, all groups have patterns of avoiding marital tensions, by suppression, by defining certain types of disagreements as unimportant, and by seeing to it that husbands and wives have similar social backgrounds so that the areas of disagreement will be fewer.

Nevertheless, despite such mechanisms of prevention, disharmony is bound to arise. Societies differ, however, as to how much strain should be tolerated, just as they also differ in their solutions of problems when the level of tension seems intolerable.

Of course, divorce is one of the major solutions for an intense degree of marital disharmony and is to be found in most societies and nations. Yet I know of no contemporary society, primitive or industrialized, in which divorce is actually valued.[1] Divorce has its consequences for the society, the kin networks, and the individual; and these are tedious when not awkward, and burdensome when not destructive. On the other hand, we cannot say as yet why one society develops the pattern of divorce rather than separation or taking on an additional wife or concubine. Its primary difference is that it permits both partners to remarry. In societies without divorce, it is ordinarily only the man who is permitted to enter a new union. Thus in Western nations such as Brazil, Italy, Spain, and Portugal, the public attitudes opposing a wife's entering an unsanctioned public union are very strong while the husband is usually permitted to have a mistress outside his household. Viewing these alternatives, it seems false to speak of divorce as a "more extreme" solution than other patterns. We do not know at present whether the introduction of a concubine into a Japanese or Chinese household created more unhappiness than a divorce might have done. And whatever the answer might be, the judgement as to its desirability would still remain a matter of personal or social evaluation.

The objective and ideological evaluation of marital instability

One's ideological position primarily determines the evaluation of marital instability, and evidently the "rising tide" of divorce in Western nations arouses dismay even among objective social scientists — the dismay arising mainly from the peculiar historical place of divorce in Church dogma. Adequate assessment of the costs of marital instability, by any ideological standards, is hampered by the lack of a good measure of "total marital instability" in even the most statistically sophisticated countries, if we are to include in such a rate all the five major types of instability listed above. In fact, we know neither the total rate nor the psychological or social costs of any one of the five types.

We do not even know the effects of divorce although more analysts have busied themselves with this than with any other form of marital instability.[1] Moreover, such costs must always be assessed by reference to the genuine alternatives open to the participants. For example, children of divorce suffer many disadvantages compared to those who live in a happy home. But the divorcing couple cannot choose between creating a happy home and getting a divorce. They can will a divorce or not; they cannot will (and achieve) marital harmony. And, unfortunately, at least in the United States, the best opinion and data insist that children of discord or separation suffer greater disadvantages than those whose parents actually divorce.[2]

Divorce differentials

Lacking a total rate of marital instability, I should like to explore further a question which I dealt with some years ago and which seems to relate the family in several interesting ways to the larger social structure: class differentials in the divorce rate. A fuller inquiry would be introduced by an analysis, which I am attempting elsewhere, of the broader social-structural con-

comitants of divorce rates. At present, we have no good study of the problem. Instead, current writers seem to be guided by the clichés, partly wrong in important theoretical and empirical respects, that urbanization and industrialization necessarily increase the divorce rates and that low divorce rates are only to be found in pious, peasant, patriarchical family systems. In addition, a good inference from anthropological data may be noted, that matrilineal societies are prone to a high divorce rate.[3]

Class differentials: United States

Postponing such a necessarily extended discussion of the structural conditions creating high divorce rates, let us confine ourselves instead to class differentials in the divorce rate, beginning with the United States which seems to foreshadow so many of the changes which later take place in other countries.

Prior to the first world war, social analyses had guessed that the social relations of certain occupations created a greater proneness to divorce: the travelling salesman because he lived much of the time away from the social control of his neighbours; the bartender and entertainers because of the temptations to which their lives exposed them; the physician because of the emotional responses ("transference phenomenon" in the modern psychodynamic vocabulary) he aroused; and so on. Occupational data were indeed collected at that time although registration procedures were poor.[4] Most American textbooks that dealt with the topic in succeeding decades repeated these findings in one form or another. But though predictions could be made from a few specific occupations, (clergymen, physicians, teachers, dancers) our knowledge of most occupations permitted no prediction at all, and occupation was soon dropped from most records.

By contrast, it seems likely that class position, with its concomitant patterning of social relations and styles of life, might affect divorce rates in at least a rough

[1] For example, I have been unable to locate in any Western country a monograph study comparable to my own *After Divorce*, dealing with the consequences of divorce in the lives of 425 young urban mothers.

[2] See Sheldon and Eleanor Glueck, *Unraveling Juvenile Delinquency*, Cambridge, Mass., Harvard University Press, 1950, Table VIII–19, p. 91; Paul H. Landis, *The Broken Home in Teenage Adjustment*, Pullman, Washington, Institute of Agricultural Sciences, State College of Washington, 1953, p. 10 (*Rural Sociology Theories on The Family*, No. 4); and Raymond Ilsey and Barbara Thompson, "Women from Broken Homes", *Sociol. Rev.*, No. 9, March 1961, pp. 27–53.

[3] Although in earlier drafts he does not deal systematically with the problem of divorce, David L. Schneider in his excellent analysis of matriliny shows some of the inherent strains in such a system. See "The Distinctive Features of Matrilineal Descent Groups", Chapter 1 of his larger book, *Matrilineal Descent Groups*, Palo Alto, Center for Advanced Study in the Social Sciences, 1959, mimeographed. See also his "A Note on Bridewealth and the Stability of Marriage", in: *Man*, April 1953, No. 75.

[4] *Marriage and Divorce, 1867–1906*, Washington, Bureau of the Census, 1909. See my critique of these items in *After Divorce*, pp. 52ff.

fashion. Popular belief, and to some extent that of social scientists, supposed until recently that United States divorce rates were higher among the upper strata and lower among the lower strata, where desertion was and is a common occurrence. However, a summary of the available data extending over half a century, together with new calculations from national surveys and censuses, shows that in fact there was an inverse correlation between class position and divorce rates. These findings may be summarized briefly:

1) The findings do not negate the hypothesis that specific occupations in any class position may have high or low divorce rates. Thus clergymen and professors will have relatively low rates, while psychiatrists, surgeons, and perhaps general practitioners may have higher rates.

2) Negroes have a higher divorce rate than whites.

3) When occupation is used as an indicator of class, roughly following the Alba Edwards system used by the Census Bureau, the upper occupational groups have lower rates of divorce.

4) When income is used as an indicator, the upper income groups have lower rates of divorce.

5) When education is used as an indicator, the upper groups have lower rates of divorce.

6) However, the relationship between the education of non-whites and divorce rates is positive: the higher the education, the higher the proneness to divorce.

Class and a model of divorce decision

If we avoid the pitfall of attempting to analyse divorce through so-called "cause" and focus instead on rates, a simple model of divorce decision clarifies the inverse correlation between class and divorce. We would need at least these items:

1) Predispositions in the economic and social stratum in favour of or against divorce: values and attitudes.

2) Internal strains in, or satisfactions from, the marriage.

3) Alternatives outside marriage.

4) Supporting or dissolving pressures on the part of relevant social networks. It seems likely that ideologically the upper strata in the United States are more tolerant of divorce than the lower strata. However, the following factors would seem to create a somewhat lesser propensity to divorce toward the upper socio-economic strata:

1) The network of social relations and of kin relations is more extended, more tightly organized, and exercises greater control over the individual.

2) The income differentials between the wife and husband in the upper strata are greater than in the lower strata; consequently the wife has more reason to maintain the marriage if she can.

3) Toward the upper strata, far more of the husband's income is committed to long-term expenditures, from which he cannot easily withdraw to support an independent existence.

4) The husband in the lower strata can more easily escape the child-support payments and other post-divorce expenditures because his life is more anonymous and legal controls are less effective.

5) The strains internal to the marriage are greater toward the lower strata: marital satisfaction scores are lower, romantic attachment between spouses is less common, the husband is less willing to share household tasks when the wife is working, and so on.

Class differentials in other societies: phases of development

The relationship between social structure and divorce seems general enough to apply to other societies. Let us explore the matter. Where there is a well-developed stratification system it would seem likely that the lower class does not count on the stability of the marriage, that the marriage itself costs less, less is invested in it than in the upper strata, the kin ties are less important and therefore the ambiguity created by divorce would not be taken so seriously as in the upper strata.

In the past, on the other hand, without any questions the divorce rate (as distinguished from the general rate of instability) was higher in the upper strata of the United States. In some states' jurisdictions, an act of the legislature was necessary to obtain a divorce and generally divorce was costly. Consequently at some unknown point in American history, the lower strata began to surpass the upper strata in the divorce rate, just as happened with respect to the Negro-White divorce differential. Thus a fuller exploration must at some point introduce the notion of phase in these considerations. In other words, the lower strata may generally have a higher rate of marital instability, but their divorce rate may not always be higher until some stage of development in the marriage and divorce system occurs.

This general theory of the relationship between the larger social structure and class divorce rates may correctly apply to the Western culture complex where Church dogma with respect to the family was translated into State laws in every nation, and where the administration of these restrictive laws was until recently in the hands of the *élite*. However, those laws have been altered greatly over the past half-century in most Western States. Moreover, if the theory is to be generalized, it must be modified to fit those cultures such as China, India, Japan and Arab Islam where marriage and divorce were not generally under the jurisdiction of State officials (except for extreme cases) and where marriage was not primarily a sacred affair (Japan, China).

Finally, the use of occupation as a class index, perhaps the best in view of the necessarily crude data available for cross-national comparisons, may at times introduce a new variable into the analysis, the peculiar style of life of certain occupations. For example, clergymen and teachers (in the West) will have low divorce rates but physicians and artists will have high ones — yet in most national tabulations of divorce these will all be classified together. In the West, farmers have lower divorce rates, but in Japan a special pattern of "trial marriage" creates high divorce rates among agriculturists — though many of these are never recorded.

If these necessary modifications are integrated, several inferences can be tested. *a)* In the pre-industrial or early industrialization period of Western nations the upper classes will have higher divorce rates. Indeed, there may be almost no lower class divorces. *b)* As a Western nation industrializes, its divorce procedures are gradually made available to all classes. Since family strain toward the lower strata is greater, the proportion of lower strata divorces will increase, and eventually there should be an inverse relation between class and divorce rate, as in the United States. *c)* In China, India, Japan and Arab Islam, where the power to divorce remained in the hands of the groom's family, no such set of phases will occur. Indeed — though very likely precise data do not exist — I hypothesize that the relation between class and divorce rate moves in the opposite direction: that is though the lower strata will continue to furnish more than their "share" of the divorces, the class differential will narrow somewhat as the upper strata begin to divorce more. *d)* Finally (though here again the data will very likely never become available) since the dominant pattern of respectability was set by the urban *élite*, and the rural marriage and divorce patterns seem to have been looser, it is likely that in China, Japan, India and Arab Islam any modern changes would be toward a decline in the divorce rate of agriculturists.

Let us look at the data that bear on the first of these three hypotheses.

New Zealand The ratio of divorced to married by income distribution shows clearly that toward the lower strata the divorce rate is higher.

Ratio of Percentage of Divorced to Percentage of Married, within Income Groups

Income group	Ratio*	Income group	Ratio*
Under £100	1.78	£400–£449	.67
£100–£149	1.84	£450–£549	.58
£150–£199	1.86	£550–£649	.56
£200–£249	1.50	£650–£749	.48
£250–£299	1.10	£750 and over	.34
£300–£349	.96	Not specified	2.01
£350–£399	.87		

* Figures higher than 1.00 indicate that the income group concerned contributes more than its numerical "share" to the total number of divorces.
Source: A. J. Dixon, *Divorce in New Zealand*, Auckland, Auckland University College Bulletin No. 46, 1954, p. 42 (Sociology Series No. 1).

The same relationship shows by occupation; the ratio of comparative frequency of divorce to numbers in each of various occupational groups being:

Proneness to Divorce by Occupation, New Zealand

Occupation	Ratio*	Occupation	Ratio*
Architect, dentist, lawyer, lecturer, doctor	.07	Mechanic	.96
Engineer	.72	Railway employee	.80
Farmer	.17	Clerk	.55
Manager (not company)	.32	Salesman	1.17
Carpenter	.78	Barman	4.73
Butcher	1.05	Labourer	2.30

* Figures higher than 1.00 indicate that the occupation concerned contributes more divorces than its numerically proportionate "share" within all occupations.
Source: ibid.

United States Although an extensive summary of the relevant data is available for the United States,[1] it may be relevant to note that a more recent summary has corroborated these findings, and from one of these the following table has been taken.

Ratio of Divorced to 1,000 of Ever-Married Men by Occupation of Civilian Labour Force, 14 Years and Over, 1950 United States Census

Occupations	Number divorced per 1,000 ever-married men
Professional technical and kindred workers	18.49
Managers, officials and proprietors (excluding farm)	16.59
Clerical and kindred workers	25.70
Craftsmen, foremen and kindred workers	24.15
Operatives and kindred workers	26.18
Farm labourers and foremen	40.76

Source: Karen G. Hillman, *Marital Instability and Its Relation to Education, Income and Occupation: An Analysis Based on Census Data*, Evanston, Illinois, Northwestern University, 1961, p. 19, mimeographed.

Australia In Australia, too, the relationship holds:

Ratio of Divorced to 1,000 Married Males by Occupational Class, 1947 Census of Australia*

Occupational level	Number divorced per 1,000 married males
Employer	9
Self-employed	9
Employee (on wage)	15
Helper (not on wage)	23

* Calculated from: *Census of the Commonwealth of Australia, 30 June 1947. Statistician's Report*, Canberra, 1952, p. 268.

Sweden A similar ratio may be found in the 1950 Swedish census.

[1] *After Divorce*, op. cit., pp. 52ff. *et passim*.

Ratio of Divorced per 1,000 Married Men, by Occupational Category

Category	Number divorced per 1,000 married men
Employers	12
Salaried employees	21
Wage-earners	28

* Calculated from: Personal correspondence, Central Bureau of Statistics, Sweden. Statistiska Centralbyran, Folkräkningen, Den 31 December 1950, V, VI, Totala Räkningen, Folkmängden Efter Yrke. Hushall. Utrikes Födda Och Utlänningar: Tab. 8.,"Förvärvsarbetande befolkning efter naringsgren (huvudoch undergrupper) och yrkesstallning i kombination med kön, alter och civilstand den 31 december 1950" (Economically active population by industry (divisions and major groups) and occupational status, and by sex, age and marital status), pp. 162–163 (Males only).

Belgium   In the following table calculated from the 1947 Belgian census, a similar relation appears, although here the differences are very small.

Ratio of Divorced per 1,000 Married Men, by Occupational Category (excluding Agriculture, Farming and Fishing)*

Category	Number divorced per 1,000 married men
Employers	13
Salaried workers	14
Skilled and unskilled workers	15
Auxiliary personnel	31

* Calculated from: Institut national de Statistique, *Recensement Général de la Population, de l'Industrie et du Commerce au 31 Decembre 1941. Vol. 8: Répartition de la Population d'aprés l'Activité et la Profession.* Tableau 18 — Répartition de la population active masculine de nationalité belge d'aprés l'État Civil, l'État Social et les Sections d'Activité, pp. 34–35.

France   The relationship also holds here.

Ratio of Divorced per 1,000 Married Men, by Occupational Category*

Category	Number divorced per 1,000 married men
Liberal professions and senior cadres	17
Intermediate cadres	20
Salaried workers	21
Skilled and unskilled workers	24
Domestic servants	78

* Calculated from: *Résultats du sondage au 1/20ᵉ, Institut National de la Statistique et des Études économiques,* Presses Universitaires de France, 1960 (Recensement général de la Population de Mai 1954), p. 61, p. 62, p. 63.

[1] See the table on divorce and occupation in *Egskeiding in Suid-Afrika* by Hendrik Johannes Piek, Pretoria Ph.D., 1959, p. 262.

England   A special study of the occupational structure of the divorcing and the "continued married relations population" in England and Wales in 1951 reveals that the proportions of the divorcing population in the selected occupational categories were almost exactly those of the proportions in the continued married population. Thus the "professional and managerial class" accounted for 13.5 per cent of the divorcing sample and 13.9 per cent of the continuing married.

Much more instructive, however, and strongly confirming our second hypothesis is the change in the distribution of the husband's occupation at divorce. Such a comparison is presented below, showing how the "gentry, professional and managerial workers" dropped from 41.4 per cent of the total divorcing population, to 11.4 per cent between 1871 and 1951. During the same period, the proportion furnished by the manual workers increased from 16.8 to 58.5 per cent.

Husband's Occupation at Divorce, 1871 and 1951, England and Wales*

Year	Gentry, professional and managerial workers %	Farmers and shopkeepers %	Black-coated workers %	Manual %	Unknown occupations %	Total of occupation
1871	41.4	12.7	6.3	16.8	22.8	285
1951	11.4	6.7	7.6	58.5	15.8	1,813

* Calculated from: Griselda Rowntree and Norman H. Carrier, "The Resort to Divorce in England and Wales, 1858–1957," in: *Population Studies,* No. 11, March 1958, p. 222.

South Africa   Up to the time of writing, I have been unable to make a similar comparison for South Africa because the categories used for occupation and divorce do not correspond to one another in the sources available to me.[1]

Netherlands   The data from the Netherlands do not fit the hypothesis because of the extremely high divorce

Ratio of Divorce per 1,000 Married Male Heads of Households, Netherlands 1955–57 (excluding Agriculture)*

Categories	Number of divorces per 1,000 male household heads
Heads of enterprises	18
Free professions	50
Civil Service and office employees	21
Teaching	15
Other bureaucrats	37
Manual workers	30

* Calculated from: Number of households taken as of 30 June 1956; divorces as of 1955–57.
Source: Echtscheidingen in Nederland, 1900–57, Central Bureau Voor De Statistiek, Zeist, W. de Haan, 1958, Appendix II, Table D, p. 63.

ratio among the free professions, which include both the established professions of medicine and law, and such occupations as musician, artist, writer and so on. Teaching is separate and of course has a low ratio. Unfortunately, skilled workers seem to be classified with manual labourers. Thus, although the extreme categories in the Netherlands do fit our thesis, the "free professions" do not fit.

Yugoslavia Yugoslavia has recently begun to industrialize, and our hypothesis would suggest that the divorce ratio would be higher towards the upper strata. If education is used as an index, this appears to be so as of 1959.

Ratio of Divorce to 1,000 Married Males, by Education

School achievement of husband	Number of divorced per 1,000 married
Without school	124
Primary school	124
Secondary school (incomplete)	144
Secondary school (completed)	148
Faculty, high and higher school	144

Source: Statistical Yearbook of the Federal People's Republic of Yugoslavia, Federal People's Republic of Yugoslavia Federal Statistical Institute, Belgrade, August 1961. Calculated from: Table 202-23 — Contracted Marriages by School Qualifications of Bridegroom and Bride in 1959 (preliminary data), p. 83; Table 202-27 — Divorces by School Qualifications of Husband and Wife in 1959 (preliminary data), p. 85.

However, the ratios by occupation are puzzling. Here the technical problem of the ratio itself is important: if the ratio used is actual divorces and marriages in one given year, the result may be an anomaly: e.g., a high divorce-marriage ratio among pensioners because they do experience some divorces, but very few marriages on account of their age. However, this result is a function of age level rather than of a high propensity to divorce.

In any event, with this warning, the following table presents data comparable in part to the previous tables.

Ratio of Divorces to Marriages by Occupation of Husband*

Occupation of husband	Number of divorces per 1,000 marriages
Unskilled	144
Workers in manufacturing industries, arts, crafts	140
Administrative and managing personnel	256
Professional and technical occupations and artists	132

* Calculated from: Statistical Yearbook of the Federal People's Republic of Yugoslavia, Federal Statistical Institute, Belgrade, August 1961. Data calculated from: Table 202-21 — Contracted Marriages by Occupation of Bridegroom and Bride in 1959 (preliminary data), p. 83; Table 202-28 — Divorces by Occupation of Husband and Wife in 1959 (preliminary data), p. 85.

These figures are also somewhat different from those which Milic has calculated, apparently from the same sources.[1]

Egypt Egyptian data on such a matter raises the problem, common to all countries in which divorce has been a limited concern of the State, of how adequate the coverage of divorces is, and whether the more literate or better educated couples who divorce are more likely to record their divorces. As can be seen in the succeeding table, the divorce/married ratio predicted holds good primarily for the distinction between employers on the one hand and all other occupations on the other.

Ratio of Divorces to Marriages by Occupation of Husband (excluding Agriculture, Fishing and Hunting)*

Categories	Number of divorces per 1,000 marriages
Employers	9
On own account	18
Directors and sub-directors	12
Employees	11
Labourers and artisans	18
Unemployed	117

* Calculated from: Population Census of Egypt, 1947, General Tables, Ministry of Finance and Economy, Statistical and Census Department, Government Press, Cairo, 1954. Table XXIX (concluded) — Working Status for Persons engaged in Industries by Sex, Age Group and Civil Status (excluding children below 5 years). Table refers to males and excludes occupations in agriculture, fishing, and hunting, pp. 362–363.

However, one comparison of illiteracy and divorce shows no difference in the literacy of bridegrooms and divorced males in 1956 (47 and 45 per cent).[2]

Ratios calculated for those engaged in agriculture, fishing and hunting in Egypt follow the pattern presented above for occupations outside these categories.[3]

Jordan Corresponding data do not exist for Jordan, but it is at least possible to calculate that in 1959 75 per cent of the males who married were literate, but only 59 per cent of those who divorced; and 25 per cent of the females who married were literate, but only 5 per cent of the divorcees.[4] Therefore we can conclude

---

[1] Vojin Milič, 'Sklapanje I Razvod Braka Prema Zanimanju', in: *Statisticka Revija*, No. 7, March 1957, pp. 19–44, especially p. 38.

[2] United Arab Republic (Egypt), Presidency of the Republic, Statistics and Census Department, *Vital Statistics, 1956*, Vol. II, Table XXIII, p. 340 — Classification of Divorced Males by Locality according to Literacy for year 1956; Table VI, pp. 274–275 — Classification of Bridegrooms by Locality according to Literacy (and Marital Condition) for the year 1956. Perhaps the literate are more likely to record their divorces officially.

[3] Population Census of Egypt, 1947, General Tables, op. cit., Table XXIX, — Working Status for Persons engaged in Industries by Sex, Age Group and Civil Status (excluding children under 5 years). This table refers to those engaged in agriculture, fishing and hunting only.

[4] *Statistical Yearbook, 1959*, Hashemite Kingdom of Jordan, Jerusalem, pp. 45–50.

that the better educated divorced less than the less educated. This general conclusion also emerges from many non-quantitative analyses of divorce in Arabic Islam. Specifically, it is sometimes asserted that divorce and remarriage are the "poor man's polygyny".[1]

Finland   Allardt found that in 1947 the divorce rate per 100,000 of the main supporters of the family was higher toward the upper strata, which would fit our first hypothesis. Using these three classes, labouring, middle, and upper, he found rates of 527, 543, and 1022.

However, most of the *élite* are to be found in Helsinki, where the divorce rates are higher than elsewhere in Finland and a comparison of the divorce applications in different classes in 1945–46 showed no statistically significant differences among them, i.e., in the more industrialized areas, the older class pattern had already changed. Allardt notes that the differences among the classes were greater at the beginning of the century but that there is now very little difference (second hypothesis).[2]

Hungary   As a newly industrializing nation, Hungary would be expected to have a somewhat lower divorce rate toward the lower strata. Our data suggest caution but do conform.

Ratio of Divorces to Marriages, 1958

Occupation	Number of divorces	Number of marriages	Number of divorces per 1,000
Agricultural workers	1 827	25 154	72
Manual workers	9 133	51 017	179
Intellectuals	3 481	15 156	223

Source: *Statisztikai Evkonyv, 1958*, Kozponti Statisztikai Hivatal, Budapest, 1960. Table 20 — Marriages by the Professional Status of Husband and Wife, p. 20; Table 26 — Divorces by Professional Status of Husband and Wife, p. 22.

India   The Indian pattern is, of course, very well known though no quantitative data exist. Divorce has been impossible for Brahmans until very recently (1955). On the other hand, the lower castes and the outcasts, as well as tribal groups, have long permitted divorce. As a consequence there is no doubt that the general relationship presented earlier fits at least the observed differences among the strata — though in this

instance it is perhaps not possible to make a strong case for differential strain.[3]

China   The case of China is similar to that of Japan. Though China has permitted divorce from at least the T'ang period, divorce has not been a respectable step in Chinese culture and thus would tend to be more common towards the lower strata. Indeed among the *élite*, other solutions were open to the dissatisfied husband.[4]

Japan   The divorce rate in Japan has been dropping over the past half century, though at the same time divorce has been much more completely recorded than formerly. Again, our hypothesis is confirmed.

The Ratio of Divorce per 1,000 Married Male Workers 15 Years and Over, Japan, July 1957*

Occupation	Number divorced per 1,000 male workers
Technicians and engineers	7
Professors and teachers	3
Medical and public health technicians	5
Managers and officials	4
Clerical and related workers	8
Farmers, lumbermen, fishermen and related workers	10
Workers in mining and quarrying	18
Craftsmen, production process workers, and labourers not elsewhere included	18
Domestic	238

* Calculated from: Japan, Bureau of Statistics, Office of the Prime Minister, *1955 Population Census of Japan*, Vol. II: *One Percent Sample Tabulation*, Part III, "Occupation, July 1957", Table 3 — Occupation (Intermediate Group) of Employed Persons 15 Years Old and Over by Marital Status and Sex, for all Japan, all *Shi* and all *Gun*, pp. 136–137 (Males only).

The "easy divorce" phase: further inferences

Fully to resolve all of these irregularities would require an institutional analysis of each country. Our earlier analysis seems to be correct, that there is likely to be more marital instability towards the lower strata than towards the upper. But whether this set of forces is exhibited in actual divorce proceedings depends on the extent to which divorce itself has become easy, that is, has come to "cost" little — these costs being calculated necessarily by reference to the available resources of the family, and including both monetary and social costs. We also noted that in a country with "easy" divorce (Japan, Arab Islam), industrialization would reduce the divorce rate of the lower strata relative to the upper. In a country moving toward the easy divorce phase, the upper strata begin to furnish a smaller proportion of total divorces. Let us consider the further implications of these notions.

First, where divorce costs little, there will be a high divorce rate. This is a reciprocal and reinforcing relationship. Easy divorce means in effect that there are fewer strong factors to maintain the boundaries of the family

[1] Lester Mboria, *La Population de l'Égypte*, University of Paris Faculty of Law Thesis, Cairo, Procaccia, 1938, p. 63.

[2] Erik Allardt, *The Influence of Different Systems of Social Norms on Divorce Rates in Finland*, Columbia University, 1954, mimeographed. These data are taken from Allardt's *Miljö-betingade differenser i skilsmässofrekvensen i Finland 1891–1950*, Helsingfors, Finska Vetenskaps-Societeten, 1953.

[3] See *India: Sociological Background*, HRAF-44 Cornell 8, Vol. I (M. Opler, ed.) New Haven, Yale University Press, 1958, p. 25; P. V. Kane, *Hindu Custom and Modern Law*, Bombay, University of Bombay Press, 1950, p. 82; Mohindar Singh, *The Depressed Classes*, Bombay, Hind Kitebs, 1947, p. 168.

[4] A good historical analysis of divorce in China is Wang Tse-Tsiu, *Le Divorce en Chine*, Paris, Lovitow, 1930.

unit. Moreover, in that type of situation, the peers of any individual are likely to have had similar experiences, that is, divorce, and therefore have less basis on which to chide or deprecate anyone who gets a divorce. And the ubiquitous strains in all marriage systems will ensure a high number of individuals who seek this way out and who are also available as potential mates.

Where divorce is difficult and costly, it is primarily an upper-class privilege. There are rarely special laws for the lower classes, other than those which prevent the lower classes from attacking the privileges of the *élite*. On the other hand, if and when there are upper-class family difficulties that have to be solved in a social structure posing barriers against divorce, there must be at least a few mechanisms for handling them, such as annulment and migratory divorce. The property stakes and problems of lineage are too important to permit the merely informal solutions which the lower classes may enjoy.

In a family system permitting easy divorce and thus having a high divorce rate, there will also be a very high rate of remarriage.[1] In the United States, this rate of eventual remarriage among divorcees is roughly as high as that for the unmarried population, about nine in ten. No such figures exist for Arab Islam, but the few data available, including observations made in specific studies, suggest that there is an extremely high rate of marital turnover. The percentage married in the upper age groups in Japan has been over 95 per cent for decades, while the divorce rate was extremely high, thus showing that the rate of remarriage was high. Irene Taeuber has in addition used demographic techniques to show that the divorced as well as the widowed "disappear" in successive age groups.[2] In such a high-divorce system, divorce creates no social stigma, there are many available divorcees to marry, and divorce is no longer likely to be a deviant in many psychological or social respects.

Indeed the divorce system then becomes in effect part of the courtship and marriage system: that is, it is part of the "sifting out" process, analogous to the adolescent dating pattern. Individuals marry, but there is a free market both in getting a first spouse, and in getting a second spouse should the individual not be able to create a harmonious life with the first one. Indeed, to the extent that marriage becomes a personal bond between husband and wife, and they marry after they are formed psychologically, there would seem to be at least some ideological arguments for their being free to shift about in order to find someone who fits better.

Finally, as such a system becomes established, heavy investments in bride-price or dowry will decline. These are never individual investments in any family system, but represent the commitment of an extended family network to the marriage. Where the likelihood is great that the marriage will be unstable, and undoing it expensive, then neither side is likely to be willing to make a large, long-term investment in it.

Some but not all of these hypotheses can be tested by available data, and in some of my current research I am attempting to assemble such materials from many countries — a formidable task! The present paper has aimed at presenting a small theoretical perspective, developing hypotheses from that theoretical position and then testing them.

[1] Jesse Bernard, *Remarriage*, New York, Dryden, 1956, Chapters 2, 3.
[2] Irene Taeuber, *The Population of Japan*, Princeton, Princeton University Press, 1958, pp. 226ff.

RELIGION

Social Class, Religious Affiliation, and Styles of Religious Involvement

N. J. Demerath III

Social Class and American Religion

TWO HALLMARKS of American religion are its susceptibility to non-religious factors and its resulting variety. In the absence of any state church, religion is particularly vulnerable to influences such as social class. This has been a central theme in observations of American society since the beginning of the nineteenth century. In 1832, Alexis de Tocqueville[1] commented that the denominational competition in American religion lent it a unique vitality. Only a few years later, Harriet Martineau[2] witnessed the same competition but saw it as contributing more hypocrisy than vitality, and she pointed an especially accusing finger at an unscrupulously tyrannical clergy. Contemporary observers have also agreed on the perception of diversity while disagreeing over its effects. On the one hand, Talcott Parsons[3] has urged that denominationalism provides an adaptable religious system to meet the needs of a variegated society. On the other hand, H. Richard Niebuhr[4] deplored denominationalism as a fragmentation of the true religious spirit.

While denominationalism is not our concern, it reflects the influence of social class, and this is very much to the point. It is no secret that class has had more than passing effect on American religion. Not only is this a theme among foreign journalists, social theorists, and theologians, but it has also commanded the attention of empirical analysts. By now, it is almost *de rigueur*, and certainly a commonplace, to begin studies of American religious variation with a table showing the relation between social class and denominational affiliation. This study is no different, and Table 1 is drawn from data that originally appeared in the National Council of Churches' Information Service.

Based on a national sample, the table orders the major United States religious groups by decreasing status. At the high-status extreme, nearly one-fourth of the Christian Scientists, Episcopalians, and Congregationalists are from the upper class; fewer than one-half

[1] Alexis de Tocqueville, *Democracy in America* (New York: Vintage Books, 1954), Vol. II.

[2] Harriet Martineau, *Society in America*, ed. S. M. Lipset (Garden City, N.Y.: Doubleday Anchor Books, 1962), especially pp. 332–355.

[3] Talcott Parsons, *Structure and Process in Modern Societies* (Glencoe, Ill.: The Free Press, 1960), Ch. X.

[4] H. Richard Niebuhr, *The Social Sources of Denominationalism* (New York: Henry Holt & Company, 1929).

Abstracted from Chapters 1 and 2 of the author's *Social Class in American Protestantism* (Chicago: Rand McNally & Co., 1965). This volume explores these and other issues empirically and in depth. It explores different facets of stratification ranging from status consistency to status as a contextual variable. In addition to examining the social psychological causes of differential involvement, it explores the organizational consequences, seeking to generalize beyond religion and the church to institutions generally.

are from the lower class. At the other end, fewer than one-tenth of the Roman Catholics, Baptists, and Mormons are from the upper class; roughly two-thirds are from the lower class.

Although the particulars of the relationship will vary over time and between different areas of the country,[1] Table I is generally representative of myriad studies of local communities as well as of large national samples. There are, however, two important caveats which bear upon the present study. First, even though denominations can be ranked by status, there is no justification for converting relative rankings into absolute categorizations. Episcopalians may be *relatively* upper class, but more than 40 percent are from the lower class. Baptists may be *relatively* lower class, but they claim their Rockefellers as well. Thus, status heterogeneity

TABLE I. *Social Class Profiles of American Religious Groups*

| Denomination | CLASS | | | |
	Upper	Middle	Lower	N
Christian Scientist	24.8%	36.5%	38.7%	(137)
Episcopal	24.1	33.7	42.2	(590)
Congregational	23.9	42.6	33.5	(376)
Presbyterian	21.9	40.0	38.1	(961)
Jewish	21.8	32.0	46.2	(537)
Reformed	19.1	31.3	49.6	(131)
Methodist	12.7	35.6	51.7	(2100)
Lutheran	10.9	36.1	53.0	(723)
Christian	10.0	35.4	54.6	(370)
Protestant (small bodies)	10.0	27.3	62.7	(888)
Roman Catholic	8.7	24.7	66.6	(2390)
Baptist	8.0	24.0	68.0	(1381)
Mormon	5.1	28.6	66.3	(175)
No preference	13.3	26.0	60.7	(466)
Protestant (undesignated)	12.4	24.1	63.5	(460)
Atheist, Agnostic	33.3	46.7	20.0	(15)
No Answer or Don't Know	11.0	29.5	59.5	(319)

From Herbert Schneider, *Religion in 20th Century America* (Cambridge, Mass.: Harvard University Press, 1952), Appendix, p. 228.

within denominations may be almost as important as the status differences between them.

A second qualification concerns the difference between religious *affiliation* and religious *involvement*. These are not identical, and it is possible that their relations to social class may be dissimilar. Thus, lower-class Episcopalians may be more religiously involved than their more heralded upper-class co-members. Although Baptists are generally lower class, the upper-class adherents may control the church organization.

But if research on actual religious involvement is more important, it is also less common and less precise compared to studies of affiliation. Perhaps because of its relative sparseness, its neglect of denominational distinctions, its oversight of the differences between various kinds of involvement, and its general quality as a research "aside," research on involvement has harbored an unexposed contradiction. The majority[2] of

studies find those of high status[3] more religiously involved. Yet an important minority[4] reports the reverse in noting that those of low status are more involved.

William James once suggested that wherever one finds a contradiction there is a latent distinction begging to become manifest. Put another way, the present contradiction indicates a profound confusion of the whole with its parts. While focusing on only one aspect of religious involvement such as attendance, parish activity, belief, or prayer, studies have made assumptions about the whole. But, like the fabled blind men of India, different studies may describe different parts of the same religious elephant. While relating social class to the *degree of involvement*, research has

[1] Temporal variation in status composition is a theme as old as the sociology of religion itself. Religious groups frequently begin as lower-class splinter movements, but undergo upward mobility in the quest for stability and community influence. As one example of geographical variation, note the contrast between the lower-class Methodism of Warner's Catholic-dominated Yankee City (Newburyport, Massachusetts) and the middle-class Methodism in the South. In fact, a number of southern Methodists are concerned about their "exclusiveness" as a high-status church. While they may be guilty of a bit of status up-grading, a meeting of Methodists in Richmond, Virginia, recently recommended increased attention toward the lower classes. "Methodists Told Church in Danger of 'Class' Label," *Richmond Times Dispatch*, July 14, 1960.

[2] See, for example, Robert and Helen Lynd, *Middletown* (New York: Harcourt, Brace, & Co., 1929), W. Lloyd Warner and Paul S. Lunt, *The Social System of a Modern Community* (Yale University Yankee City Series; Vol. 1; New Haven: Yale University Press, 1941); Louis Bultena, "Church Membership and Church Attendance in Madison, Wisconsin," *American Sociological Review*, XIV (1949), 384–389; August Hollingshead, *Elmtown's Youth* (New Haven: Yale University Press, 1949); Lee G. Burchinal, "Some Social Status Criteria and Church Membership and Church Attendance," *Journal of Social Psychology*, XLIX (1959), 53–64; Paul M. Harrison, *Authority and Power in the Free Church Tradition* (Princeton: Princeton University Press, 1959); Gerhard Lenski, *The Religious Factor* (Garden City: Doubleday and Co., 1961).

[3] Note that there is a minor contradiction within this group of studies alone. Some report a linear relation with the upper classes most involved of all; others find a curvilinear relation in which involvement is highest among the middle classes and declines among the upper class. Here much of the explanation concerns the population studied. Studies reporting curvilinearity examined highly urban contexts where the upper class often insulated from the rest of the community by choice as well as by structure. Studies reporting linearity examined small towns in which the upper classes have little opportunity to retreat and are much more entangled in community affairs, including the affairs of the churches.

[4] See, for example, Charles Y. Glock and Benjamin B. Ringer, *Society, the Church, and its Parishioners* (Book in preparation, Survey Research Center, University of California, Berkeley); Yoshio Fukuyama, "The Major Dimensions of Church Membership," *Review of Religious Research*, II (1961), 154–161; Clyde Z. Nunn, "Child-Control Through a 'Coalition With God,'" *Child Development*, XXXV (1964), 417–432; Gerald Gurin, Joseph Veroff, and Sheila Feld, *Americans View Their Mental Health* (New York: Basic Books, 1960), pp. 372–376; Gerhard Lenski, "Social Correlates of Religious Interest," *American Sociological Review*, XVIII (1953), 533–544.

generally ignored differences in the *kind of involvement* at issue.

To emphasize these distinctions in kind, consider two hypothetical individuals with contrasting religious styles. The first has inherited his church membership as a family legacy. Although the congregation is across town from his present home and none of his closest friends are members, he remains loyal to the church and reserves Sundays for dispensing his obligations to it. His attendance record is virtually unblemished. As a banker, he is chairman of the parish's financial committee. But while a sincere participant in the congregation's weekly prayers of thanks, he is not given to spontaneous devotion. A modernist, religious doctrine is neither very urgent nor very clear to him. The church provides a point of stability and reinforces his views on business ethics, yet his religious experience is rarely emotional. For all of this, he is esteemed within the church and within the community as an eminently religious man with unassailable integrity and a sense of Christian service.

By contrast, the second person is not a formal church member at all. However, he does have a denominational preference and feels nominally affiliated with the denomination's neighborhood parish. While he attends church infrequently and participates in no responsibilities, the congregation provides a local symbol of the traditional doctrine that he accepts and applies. Further, most of his close friends are also affiliated with the parish. This affords a religious fellowship that is more meaningful than his contacts on the job, and independent of the church's formal structure. Peaks and depressions in his everyday affairs often lead to private prayer. He and his wife are mindful of an afterlife and have fostered in their children a similar regard. In general, religion transcends and uplifts his life, though it is the source of no prestige and is more a feeling than an activity.

Now who is to say which of these is the more religious? Both are involved in different kinds of religion; neither is *hypocritical*. The first is a mainstay of the church as an institution. Without him, the parish would founder and, in return, the church offers him support for his position in society. This is not only a matter of social standing. It is also justification for his values and way of life. It was this type that Alexis de Tocqueville had in mind when he commented of an earlier day that:

> Not only do Americans follow religion from interest but they place in this world the interest which makes them follow it. In the middle ages the clergy spoke of nothing but the future state. They hardly

cared to prove that Christians may be happy here below. But American preachers are constantly referring to the earth. . . . To touch their congregations they always show them how favorable religious opinion is to freedom and public tranquility; and it is often difficult to ascertain from their discourses whether the principal object of religion is to obtain eternal felicity or prosperity in this world.[1]

De Tocqueville, of course, spoke from the skeptical perspective of a European Catholic among American Protestants. Nevertheless, his description is apt, if not his denigration.

The second person is equally important to religion, and, indeed, religion is equally important to him. Yet, his is a less formal, more internal religiosity. It may be that he retreats from the organized church precisely because of its effort to relate to the religious needs of the first type. It is as if he were responding to the advice of a contemporary of de Tocqueville's, Soren Kierkegaard.

> Though plain man! . . . one thing I adjure thee, for the sake of God in heaven and all that is holy, shun the priests, shun them, those abominable men whose livelihood it is to prevent thee from so much as becoming aware of what Christianity is, and who thereby would transform thee, befuddled by galimatias and optical illusion, into what they understand by a true Christian, a paid member of the State Church, or the National Church, or whatever they prefer to call it. Shun them. But take heed to pay them willingly and promptly what money they should have. . . . No, pay them double, in order that thy disagreement with them does not concern thee at all, namely, money; and, on the contrary, that what does not concern them concerns thee infinitely, namely Christianity.[2]

Kierkegaard's distinction between religion and the church remains relevant. Hyperbole and the clergy aside, it seems that the plain men have, in fact, withdrawn from the church as a formal institution. And yet this is not to equate withdrawal with total alienation. The second type is also involved in the organized church but to a lesser degree and in a different way.

The point of all this is that one cannot assess the degree of religiosity without also evaluating the different kinds of involvement that are possible. If one were to measure only membership, attendance, and parish activity, the first individual would put the second to statistical shame. If one looked only at personal devotion, traditional beliefs, and the quality of the church as an informal community, the first would pale beside the second. Both errors can be found in past research. In order to avoid them in the future, it is necessary to see the issue of involvement in a broader perspective. Such a perspective is the heralded church-

---

[1] Alexis de Tocqueville, *Democracy in America* (New York: Vintage Books, 1954), II, 127.
[2] Soren Kierkegaard, *Attack upon "Christendom,"* trans. by Walter Lowrie (Boston: Beacon Press, 1960), p. 288. Copyright 1944 by Princeton University Press.

sect distinction as it may be applied to individuals rather than organizations.

Church–sect theory in general review

No field is more indebted to its predecessors than the sociology of religion, and none of its legacies is more enduring than the church–sect dichotomy. The dichotomy has cut a wide swath through religious scholarship. Its various facets should illuminate the problem of social class and individual religiosity, while relating this to other areas. Before applying the distinction to individual involvement, it is worth reviewing the theory as it has been traditionally applied to religious organizations.

The concepts of "church" and "sect" are not wholly anchored in reality. Intended as ideal types, no actual religious group is expected to satisfy all of the criteria for one type or the other. Rather groups can be compared on the extent to which they approximate either of the ideal extremes. The extremes differ along two principal axes; first, their internal characteristics, and second, their relation to the external world at large.

INTERNALLY

Internally, the church has a professional leadership, a relatively impersonal fellowship, and lax criteria for membership. It stresses the sacraments and ritualistic religion. In sharp contrast, the sect's leadership is charismatic and non-professional. Its founder is typically a religious eccentric in the eyes of the church, and his successors in authority are drawn from the ranks of the congregation. Further, the sect's membership standards are stringent and include conversion and signs of salvation. The fellowship is an exclusive moral community and charged with intimacy. Spontaneity replaces ritual; personal testimony is valued more highly than any sacrament.

EXTERNALLY

Externally, the church accommodates the secular order. Its posture is one of adaptive compromise, and this leads to organizational stability and a large following. But a compromise carries its own imperatives. Traditional doctrine is deemphasized if it is willing to share its adherents with a number of secular institutions. Again in contrast, the sect is either aloof or antagonistic toward the secular society. Animated by a distinctive doctrine, the sect is unwilling and unable to capitulate. Its members have only secondary allegiances to secular groups and their contaminating ideologies.

In all of this, Max Weber[1] is credited with the original formulation, although the distinction was applied more extensively by his student, Ernst Troeltsch.[2] The latter's *The Social Teachings of the Christian Churches* is a compendium of examples of both churches and sects. It is a lengthy account of their historical anta-

gonisms, with the church emerging as the ultimate winner in a pyrrhic victory that sacrificed many of the original Christian ideals.

Unlike the previous concepts, "church" and "sect" were related to social class differences from the start. Weber comments upon the low status of American sects compared with the "genteel" constituency of the churches. Troeltsch makes the point more generally:

The fully developed Church, however, utilizes the State and the ruling classes, and weaves these elements into her own life; she then becomes an integral part of the existing social order; from this standpoint, then, the Church both stabilizes and determines the social order; in so doing, however, she becomes dependent upon the upper classes, and upon their development. The sects, on the other hand, are connected with the lower classes, or at least with those elements in Society which are opposed to the State and to Society; they work upwards from below, not downwards from above.[3]

Theoretically, then, church and sect form a division of labor among religious organizations. This is reflected in the status of their members as well as in their programs.

The church–sect dichotomy and individual religiosity

There is, of course a reason why the church–sect distinction has not been applied among individuals within the same denomination or congregation. One of the criteria of the ideal church and the ideal sect is that the members of each will be similar. But there is an important sense in which any ideal type is intended for contamination. As a methodological device, it is meant to provide a model against which the departures of reality can be charted systematically. This is hardly possible if the ideal becomes so unreal as to be irrelevant. Hence there must be continual refinements, and this is a part of the goal in using it as a framework for individual religiosity. Not only may the distinction aid

[1] Max Weber, *The Protestant Ethic and the Spirit of Capitalism* (New York: Charles Scribner's Sons, 1958), especially pp. 145–154.

[2] Ernst Troeltsch, *The Social Teachings of the Christian Churches* (New York: The Macmillan Company, 1932), especially I, 331–382. In contemporary usage sects are generally thought of as splinter movements that retreat to a more conservative and more extreme religious position when compared to the "church" that spawned them. This, however, is not necessarily the case. Troeltsch points out that many of the early Catholic sects were movements of liberalization. Subsequent theorists have suggested that the terms "church" and "sect" are independent of theology and should be restricted to purely organizational matters. Others argue the reverse and seek to relate church and sect primarily to theology. The debate persists and may outlive the distinction.

[3] Ibid., I, p. 331.

the research, but the research may further clarify the distinction.

Now we have already seen in Table 1 that even the most churchly and aristocratic denominations have more members from the lower class than from any other status group. On the other hand, established sects such as the Mormons, the Quakers, and especially the Christian Scientists have a considerable following among the middle and upper classes. These are all "cross-pressured" situations, to borrow a metaphor from the students of voting. Both the lower-class church member and the high-status sect member have status influences at odds with their religious affiliation. It would seem that their religious needs are inevitably frustrated. But one release from this frustration is the individual's control over his mode of involvement. The higher-status sect member may have a churchlike orientation to the sect. The low-status church member may have a sectlike orientation to the church. Actually the latter may have the best of both worlds. His style of religiosity fits his current illness. Yet, in belonging to a church, he is not insulated from the community at large, and church contacts may make upward mobility more likely.

Yet the hypothesis that religious organizations host two divergent forms of involvement in the sectlike and the churchlike may seem radical and without justification. Actually it is neither. There is already evidence on the point, ranging from the historical to the statistical. Troeltsch himself discussed the coexistence of churchlike and sectlike tendencies within the typical Christian church. While much of his argument concerned organizational and ideological characteristics,

he also makes the point with reference to heterogeneity in class composition. Thus, his remarks on the "primitive church" of the first century were meant to rebut the Marxian view of Christianity as a proletarian movement. It included a substantial number of upper-class members who saw to the financial and organizational exigencies, while the more sectarian lower-class members attended to doctrine and the purities of the spirit.[1] The Marxists may reply that this is all part of the proletariat model. Nevertheless, Troeltsch gives succor to the present argument.

Nor was he alone. Moving from the primitive to the monolithic, a number of authors have noted a similar coexistence in the Catholicism of the Middle Ages and the Renaissance. Huizinga[2] contrasts the skeptical ecclesiasticism of the upper and middle classes with the gullible devotionalism and anti-clericalism of the peasantry. Burckhardt sees the gulf widening during the Renaissance as a pre-condition for the Reformation.[3] He describes the churchlike religiosity of the upper classes as "compounded of a deep and contemptuous aversion" to spirituality and doctrinal disputes, but an "acquiescence in the outward ecclesiastical customs" and a "sense of dependence on ceremonies and sacraments."[4] By contrast, the lower classes were more fervent and, in some senses, less obedient. They were played upon by itinerant preachers and given to intense emotionalism. Yet this was more revivalistic than ecclesiastical and their allegiance was to a different aspect of Catholicism. Alfred von Martin's *Sociology of the Renaissance* makes a similar point.[5] He goes further, however, to contrast lower-class Catholicism as an end in itself with middle-class Catholicism as a means to more political and economic goals.

Moving on to the Reformation and the first flowering of Protestantism, we again find coexisting religious styles within the same religious house. It is true that Max Weber's celebrated but controversial treatment[6] has a way of assuming equal and total involvement among all Protestants. But R. H. Tawney goes to some pains to indicate the error.[7] He suggests that much of the development of Calvinism and Puritanism was due to a warring of social doctrines within the movement itself. He contrasts the religious, political and economic views of several groups within the early Protestant folds. It is true, of course, that lower-class movements like the Levellers and the Diggers give clear indication that Protestantism was dominated by the middle classes who pushed their inferiors to rebellion. And yet part of the problem was that the middle-class religiosity was more churchlike than Weber indicates. According to Tawney, and more recently to Kurt Samuelson,[8] we again find the middle classes using the church as a means to an end rather than an end in itself. Tawney describes middle-class religious involvement as secondary to economic pursuits and conditional upon a favorable ruling for those pursuits.

Or consider Protestantism in nineteenth-century America. Here too there was a coexistence of social

[1] Troeltsch, op. cit., I, pp. 42–43.

[2] J. Huizinga, *The Waning of the Middle Ages* (Garden City, N.Y.: Doubleday Anchor Books, n.d.), especially pp. 165–181. It is fair to point out, however, that my own interpretation violates much of the spirit of Huizinga's analysis. Although he mentions such distinctions he prefers to explain the variety in styles of religiosity in terms of the "marvelous complexity of the human soul" rather than any similar complexity of the social structure. Huizinga is primarily concerned with the deterioration and excesses in religious symbolism, however, and this leads him to a more psychological analysis.

[3] Jacob Burckhardt, *The Civilization of the Renaissance in Italy* (New York: The Modern Library, 1954), pp. 341–369. Burckhardt suggests paradoxically that it was the Reformation that came to the ultimate rescue of Catholicism. In order to combat the new force and prevent any further fragmentation, Catholicism regrouped its forces and sought to provide more of a home for all classes rather than restrict its organizational appeal to the middle and upper classes. Without the Reformation, Catholicism might have deteriorated to a point where it was beyond recovery as a religious, rather than specifically political, institution.

[4] Ibid., pp. 342–343.

[5] Alfred von Martin, *Sociology of the Renaissance* (New York: Harper Torchbooks 1963), p. 90.

[6] Weber, *The Protestant Ethic and the Spirit of Capitalism*, op. cit.

[7] R. H. Tawney, *Religion and the Rise of Capitalism* (Baltimore, Md.: Penguin Books, Inc., 1947), especially p. 262 fn.

[8] Kurt Samuelson, *Religion and Economic Action: A Critique of Max Weber* (New York: Harper Torchbooks, 1961), especially pp. 27–79.

classes and religious styles. Here too the middle-class churchlike religiosity dominated. In fact, many of the lower-class sectlike congregants were forced into a marginal position in the church as their cause was spurned by a middle-class leadership. Issues like the right to strike, socialism, and, indeed, poverty itself, were divisive influences that made class distinctions especially salient. Who can wonder that the lower classes should have retreated from Protestant services when the prominent minister Henry Ward Beecher advised workers to rest content on a dollar a day for a family of eight since "water costs nothing; and a man who cannot live on bread is not fit to live."[1] At the same time, the *Congregationalist* of 1878 described the migrant workers of the day as "profane, licentious, filthy, vermin-swarming thieves" and suggested that "the long obsolete whipping-post" might be brought back into use for discipline. Yet even so there remained a substantial proportion of lower-class members in these denominations. These people did not leave the church, but they did leave churchlike involvement for a more private, more traditional, and more comforting sectarian allegiance. It is true that the Social Gospel helped to stem a total alienation, though its policies were hardly radical and it was a disappointment to many and a sop to others. But the important thing about the Social Gospel was the groundwork it laid for Protestantism in the 1930's and the change in tone that finally took root after the Great Depression.

More recently, two authors have dealt with contemporary instances of coexistence, using the same terminology and framework that I have adopted above. After observing the membership of several Protestant churches in southwestern Germany, Peter Berger[2] distinguishes between a congregation's "elite" and the mass of its parishioners. He urges that the former are more sectarian because of their greater devotion to the congregation and their greater influence within it. He labels the latter as more churchlike because of their less intense allegiances to the organization. Although I would reverse the labels and call the elite more churchlike, precisely because of their greater involvement in the organizational and administrative aspects of the parish, the semantic differences are less important than the common perception.

Finally, Russell Dynes[3] has not only used the same terms but applied them as they are used in this study. Dynes provides the first statistical support, although his study deals with hypothetical religious preferences rather than actual religious involvement. To study the preferences of an adult sample in Columbus, Ohio, Dyne's questionnaire included twenty-four items for which there were five possible responses ranging from "strongly agree" to "strongly disagree." The items were largely based upon Liston Pope's list of characteristics that distinguish the ideal sect from the ideal church.[4] They include statements such as "I think a minister should preach without expecting to get paid for it," . . . "I feel that a congregation should encourage

the minister during his sermon by saying 'amen'" . . . "I think success in one's job is one mark of a good Christian," and "I think it is more important to live a good life now than to bother about a life after death." The first two of these examples are clearly more sectlike; the last two are more churchlike.

Dynes assigned the respondents scores on a church–sect scale. A high mean score on all the items represents an over-all churchlike preference. A low mean score signifies an over-all propensity for sectlike religiosity. Table 2 presents the relation between these scores and social class. In this case, class is measured by the North–Hatt scale of occupational prestige in which a high score represents high prestige. The prestige ranks run down the left-hand column. For each prestige level, the respondent's church–sect scores were averaged, and there is a strong relationship. In general, the mean score decreases with declining occupational prestige or class standing. Thus, sectlike preferences wax, while churchlike propensities wane.

TABLE 2. *Church–Sect Scale of Religious Preferences by Occupational Prestige*

Occupational prestige	Mean church–sect scale score
80 and above	80.5
75–79	77.0
70–74	78.2
65–69	69.9
60–64	62.2
Under 60	56.8

From Russell R. Dynes, "The Church–Sect Typology and Socio-Economic Status," *American Sociological Review*, XX (1955), 559. By permission of the author and The American Sociological Association.

Dynes found in addition that this relationship obtains even among those who gave verbal allegiance to the same denomination. Among Methodists, for example, the high-status score was 78.0 on the church–sect scale compared with a low-status score of 67.1. Among

[1] Henry F. May, *Protestant Churches in Industrial America* (New York: Harper and Brothers, 1949), p. 96. See also Martin E. Marty, *The Infidel: Freethought and American Religion* (New York: Meridian Books, 1961).

[2] Peter L. Berger, "Sectarianism and Religious Sociation," *American Journal of Sociology*, LXIV (1958), pp. 41–44.

[3] Russell R. Dynes, "The Church–Sect Typology and Socio-Economic Status," *American Sociological Review*, XX (1955), pp. 555–560. Note that the term "typology" is technically inappropriate, however common here. It implies that all of the distinguishing dimensions are made explicit and that all of their combinations have been taken into account. Lamentably, this is not yet the case with church–sect theory. In fact, the failure to isolate its dimensions and their multiple combinations has been a considerable disadvantage in its use and development.

[4] Liston Pope, *Millhands and Preachers*, with a new Introduction by Richard A. Peterson and N. J. Demerath III. (New Haven: Yale University Press, 5th printing, 1965), pp. 122–124.

Presbyterians, the comparable scores are 78.4 and 71.1. Apparently, then, churchlike and sectlike orientations

[1] For further data on actual religious involvement as opposed to hypothetical religious preferences see Demerath, *Social Class in American Protestantism*, op. cit.

do coexist within the same religious institution.[1] Research on social class and religion has come a long way from the initial distinction between church and sect as wholly separate organizations and from the initial research on the individual's surface religious affiliation.

Roman Catholic Sainthood and Social Status
Katherine George and Charles H. George

To the student of religions, saints have a peculiar fascination: they are the key to any proper appreciation of the genius of a particular religion in that they afford unique opportunities for observation of religious idealism in its concrete human manifestations. What the saint is, we may assume, represents the highest human realization of the religious profession in question. This interest in saints can also serve as the starting point for investigations of matters other than the core idealism of a faith. Almost any of the humanistic or social disciplines can find in the cult of the saints basic materials for understanding the cultural components of past or present eras — so all-embracing a phenomenon is religion, so central to religion is the saint.

For any such investigation the saints of Roman Catholicism are a convenient group, numerous and clearly designated as they are. Stimulated by this rich resource, the authors of this study set out to discover some of the salient social circumstances involved in the choice and making of Roman Catholic saints. It had come to our attention, moreover, in a previous analysis of the writings of St. Thomas Aquinas that the structure of human nature and the course of human destiny were so formulated by this most orthodox of Roman Catholic theologians and philosophers that the fixed hierarchy of eternity might well be expected to match to a significant degree the transient hierarchies of earth.[1] The question arose naturally therefore whether the facts

to be found in a roster of saints would contradict or substantiate the suggestions of Thomistic theory. What indeed had been the status in the City of Man of these saints who had come to be recognized as first citizens in the City of God?

The principal source of data for this inquiry was *The Lives of the Saints* by Alban Butler, the product of thirty years of work by an English Catholic priest and first published in the mid-eighteenth century. The work has become a classic in its field and has been issued in many editions and translations. The edition upon which this study focuses was that which appeared in a series of twelve volumes published between 1926 and 1936 (with a supplementary volume being issued in 1949).[2] Using this source for the list of saints and *beati* (between whom we made no distinction; indeed a small number of venerables are included as well), we proceeded then to obtain from it and from other sources[3] as much information as possible concerning the class or status in society into which the saint was born. We accepted the orthodox tripartite division of society into upper, middle, and lower classes which we translated into the terms of an aristocratic or estate society with a topmost stratum composed of a landed nobility; a middle stratum composed of merchants, industrialists, professionals and free farmers; and a lower stratum composed of all those others who, whether enslaved, enserfed, or free, have depended for their livelihood on barter or sale of their basic labor power.

Our statistics pretend to no absolute precision. The accounts in Butler's *Lives* were, for the most part, the only data we had to work with; there was little possibility of checking the reliability of these accounts by recourse to original source material. Often the accounts themselves were brief and especially grudging in information about the early lives of the saints. In view of the additional fact that there are always borderlines of

[1] See Katherine Archibald (George), "The Concept of Social Hierarchy in the Writings of St. Thomas Aquinas," *Historian* XII, 1949), 50.

[2] Herbert Thurston *et al.* (eds.), *Butler's Lives of the Saints* (rev. ed.; 12 vols.; New York: P. J. Kennedy & Sons, 1926–1938).

[3] E.g., F. G. Holweck, *A Biographical Dictionary of the Saints* (St. Louis, 1924); *The Book of Saints*, compiled by the Benedictine monks of St. Augustine's Abbey in England (New York, 1944).

This article, which originally appeared in the *Journal of Religion*, V. 33–35, (1953–5), was revised for this book by Katherine George. Reprinted by permission of the authors and the publisher.

transition and uncertainty between each of the three class categories, errors in the placement of particular saints have no doubt been made. Minor imprecision is of no great consequence in this study, however, because the mass of data is great and the trends are very clear.

The overall results of our survey of the social status of saints are quickly stated. We obtained a total listing of 2,489 saints whom we were able to catalogue by the century in which they died and by the social class or status into which they were born. Of this total, 1,938, or 78 percent, were members of the upper class; 430, or 17 percent, were members of the middle class; and 121, or 5 percent, were members of the lower class. The full significance of these figures is realized only when account is taken of the proportion of the population which these classes constituted. One might simply reverse the figures given above for the percentages of saints and arrive at an approximate average for the almost two millennia of Christian history. Or perhaps a more accurate estimate for the aristocratic societies principally characteristic of Western Christendom would be 5 percent for the upper class at most, 10-15 percent for the middle class, and 80-85 percent for the lower class.[1]

The century variations in the percentages of saints belonging to the three class categories are clearly and succinctly presented in Table 1. In this table it is apparent at a glance that the only striking departures from the monotonous monopoly of the catalogue of saints by individuals of the aristocratic class are to be found in the first century of the Christian era and then again in the eighteenth and, above all, the nineteenth and twentieth centuries. These breaks from the norm are in themselves challenging and worthy of study and explanation, but the rule must be dealt with first before the exceptions can be analyzed.

The dominance of the roster of Roman Catholic sanctity by representatives of the elite and powerful of the world demands analysis the more emphatically because of the marked social abasement of the origins of Christianity, a faith unique among the religions of the world in this regard. Christ himself, short of being born a slave, could hardly have found a humbler entrance into the world of Roman hegemony and hierarchies. The great majority of his followers, during his lifetime and for the decades which grew into centuries thereafter, shared his low place or were even more degraded in that they indeed were slaves. "For ye see your calling, brethren," writes Paul to his Corinthians, "how that not many wise men after the flesh, not many mighty, not many noble, are called. But God hath chosen the foolish things of the world to confound the wise ... And base things of the world, and things which are despised, hath God chosen ..."[2] Among these followers, moreover, there were no distinctions of sanctity. The Christian was by virtue of his faith alone, assuming its true-heartedness, a saint, a certain future member of the Kingdom of God. All Christians in this early Christianity were equally saints.[3]

There is evidence, nonetheless, in the very earliest writings of the Christian movement of a desire on the part of the leadership of the new faith to reach beyond the obscure circle of its beginnings and to impress, persuade, and, if possible, convert the highly placed. The emphasis on the Davidian descent of Joseph in the Gospels and the infrequent reference to the actual carpenter's occupation of the foster father of Christ exemplify this hope and purpose. An associated custom of thought and writing is to display unusual gratifica-

TABLE 1. *Variations by Century in Number and Percentage of Saints in Three Class Categories*

Century	UPPER CLASS		MIDDLE CLASS		LOWER CLASS	
	No.	Percentage	No.	Percentage	No.	Percentage
First	39	47	34	41	10	12
Second	56	74	11	14	9	12
Third	127	60	70	33	15	7
Fourth	211	66	89	28	18	6
Fifth	141	84	21	13	5	3
Sixth	207	94	11	5	2	1
Seventh	242	96	8	3	3	1
Eighth	125	97	4	3	0	0
Ninth	94	94	5	5	1	1
Tenth	56	97	2	3	0	0
Eleventh	93	94	4	4	2	2
Twelfth	120	90	12	8	2	2
Thirteenth	118	80	25	17	5	3
Fourteenth	85	72	20	17	12	11
Fifteenth	72	81	15	17	3	2
Sixteenth	59	63	23	25	11	12
Seventeenth	69	68	26	25	7	7
Eighteenth	13	39	16	48	4	13
Nineteenth	17	29	31	53	11	18
Twentieth	0	0	3	75	1	25
Total	1,938	78	430	17	121	5

[1] The heavy representation by individuals of superior status by birth and the very small representation by individuals of truly humble status by birth among the listings of Roman Catholic saints have been cited in other studies and sources. G. G. Coulton in Appendix 32 to his book *Medieval Village, Manor, and Monastery*, employing a random sample of saints from an unspecified edition of Butler's *Lives*, gives for the group of saints he studies a percentage of 6% for saints of lowly origin. The statistical results of Pitirim Sorokin's analysis of this same material, *Altruistic Love: A Study of American "Good Neighbors" and Christian Saints* (Boston, 1950), also closely coincide with our findings.

[2] First Corinthians 1: 26-28.

[3] The presumption of the essential sanctity of all true believers is a quality of Christian sectarianism wherever it is found. Protestantism, furthermore, even in its magisterial and church-building forms, shakes off the Roman Catholic cult of saints in good part because of its similar insistence that all members of the invisible church, which is encased within the visible, are saints. They are expected to be unknown to or unacknowledged by the world, but they are certainly known to God and probably to themselves and possibly even to each other. They do not need to be institutionally designated or set apart. Protestant saints also, at least theoretically, may be found at any social level and in any occupation. The broadening-out in Protestantism of the doctrine of the calling, beyond the Roman Catholic emphasis on religious and ecclesiastical vocation, is intimately related to this concept that for the Christian who lives his life in the spirit of his faith any and all actions are sanctified and holy.

tion and to be especially generous with praise when an individual from an exalted station in life is sympathetic with Christianity or becomes a convert to it.[1]

Likewise of significance in this regard is the apologetic interest of early Christian writers, already to some extent apparent in the Gospels and clearly defined in Acts, which expressed itself as an effort to conciliate Roman authority, the real source of power in the Christian world of the first centuries, and to dissociate the religion from the suspect and unpopular Jewish group which gave it birth. All this is understandable ambition, but it does lead to a disproportionate emphasis on the deeds and virtues of those relatively few Christians in the infant years of the faith who were of good birth or high station. These names are noted, remembered, and recorded, whereas the names of the large number of typically humble believers who sacrificed equally for their faith tend more often to be lost in anonymity.

The Christians were undoubtedly pushed farther along this line of policy by the taunts of cultivated pagans regarding the menial origins of the troublesome religion and the lowly character of most of its followers. The claim of the adversaries of Christianity that the new sect was almost entirely composed of the dregs of the populace, of artisans and slaves and beggars, was met by such challenging rebuttals as that of Tertullian, who, in a time of persecution, assured the proconsul of Africa that, if he persisted in his probes and condemnations, he would find among the guilty many persons of his own rank, senators and matrons of noblest extraction.[2] It was met also, no doubt, by a tendency to name and emphasize among the martyrs those whose social status was aristocratic.

We are dealing here, of course, simply with one

aspect of the fairly rapid progress of Christianity from the stable to the palace. In the context of this drive to social advancement and the conquest of the world, it is perhaps not altogether surprising that, even during the centuries of persecution and martyrdom, the third and fourth, when still the great majority of the membership of the new sect was being drawn from the poor of Roman cities, 60 and 66 percent of the saints, respectively, are listed as being upper-class by birth.

Another factor must be considered here, however, which, operative perhaps to some degree throughout much of the span of our study, undoubtedly strongly affects in these first three centuries the percentages of aristocratic saints presented in the accounts. This is the tendency for later hagiographers, on the basis of their own aristocratic prejudices, to upgrade the status of saints where actual information is scanty or ambiguous. Accounts of saints' lives are by their very nature particularly subject to embellishment over time; accretions of edifying and glorifying legend are readily added to whatever slim core of fact there is. In dealing with the biographies of saints, we are dealing not only with the fact of status but also with the legend.

In the instance of only one body of saints, the saints of the New Testament, was investigation of the force of this distorting factor possible, and, comparing status as given in the accounts with status as defined on the basis of the Gospel record, we found indeed some sharp discrepancies. It is possible to debate and disagree as to whether the precise social status of Jesus, his earthly family, and most of his disciples was in a vague way proletarian and lower-class or more properly middle-class. We chose to define it as proletarian in order to allow for the social distinction existing between such disciples as Simon Peter or James the Great, both fishermen, on one hand, and Matthew, the tax-gatherer, or Paul, the Roman citizen, on the other. But though the Gospels themselves exhibit a certain amount of ambivalence regarding the matter and, as we have previously noted, give far more space to the presumably royal genealogy of Joseph than to his workingman's occupation, it is not a realistic estimate of the data available to assign an aristocratic status to any saint named in the New Testament, except perhaps to St. Joseph of Arimathea, who provided for Christ's burial and is reported to have been both wealthy and a member of the Sanhedrin.

And yet, either in the original eighteenth-century collection of saints' lives by Alban Butler or in the modern revised edition, and usually in both, fourteen saints in the immediate entourage of Jesus, two of whom are not even mentioned in the New Testament,[3] are declared to be of upper-class status. When we include the three unnamed astrologers or wise men who figure in Matthew's version of the Nativity story as visitors to the newborn Savior, and who, in succeeding centuries, acquire names and become kings, the total rises to seventeen, which is more than half of all the New Testament saints on our listing.[4] If the percentages of

---

[1] There is something of this viewpoint in the anecdote in the Gospels of Luke and Matthew regarding the Roman captain who recognizes the wisdom and the power of Jesus (Luke 7: 2–10; Matt. 8: 5–13) and also in the prideful account in Acts of the conquest by the missionary Philip, of the eunuch who was chief treasurer in the court of the queen of Ethiopia (Acts 8: 27–40).

[2] See Edward Gibbon, *The Decline and Fall of the Roman Empire* (6 vols.; London, 1910), I, 496.

[3] These are St. Joachim and St. Anne, the parents, according to tradition, of the Blessed Virgin Mary. In the 1926–1938 edition of Butler's *Lives* they are not only included among the saints but are also credited with being "exceedingly rich." In the biography of the Blessed Virgin's life contained in the same edition of Butler it is stated that she is of the royal house of David, and this fact, coupled with the "exceeding richness" of her parents, makes all three of these personages members of the upper class.

[4] By far the most dramatic and intriguing instance of the exaltation of the rank of a New Testament saint in later legend is embodied in the person and story of St. Mary Magdalen. This saint is named in the Gospels as a woman from whom seven devils were exorcised by Christ and who, becoming one of his followers, stood with the two other Marys at the foot of the Cross and was the first or at least among the first to receive the news of his resurrection and to see the risen Lord. This is all that is known of her, but tradition has added to her legend the anecdote in the Gospel according to Luke concerning the unnamed penitent woman sinner, who in Simon's house anointed the feet of Christ, and has further identified her with

class representation among the saints of the first century are reconstructed in terms of this New Testament record, the following figures are obtained; upper class, 28 percent (as compared with the 47 percent established on the basis of the unedited account of saints' lives); middle class, 48 percent (as compared with 41 percent); and lower class, 24 percent (as compared with 12 percent).

The bulk of this distortion and uncertainty in the hagiographers' accounts is swept away, however, with the firm foundation of the Christian church on a basis of institutional respectability in the fourth and fifth centuries. An intimate and now undoubted linkage was established between secular dignities and the society of saints. In the fifth century 84 percent of the saints are upper-class in origin and for seven centuries thereafter the percentage never falls below 90. These eight centuries — the fifth through the twelfth — are, then, the centuries in which the problem of this paper is peculiarly centered. The virtual monopoly of the official catalogue of new entrants into the Kingdom of Heaven held during these centuries by those already born to high place in the kingdoms of the world is all the more interesting because the period in question, or at least the latter part of it, has been widely viewed as being uniquely Christian in its motivations and outlook.

The church in this time was far more, of course, than a spiritual and intellectual influence. It was an institution which possessed great economic and political power. With the disintegration of the established patterns of political hegemony in western Europe in the fifth and sixth centuries, ecclesiastical leadership was to some extent compelled to substitute for nonexistent or inefficient secular activity, but it soon became the kind of leadership which did not choose to abandon such functions readily even when other powers were available and eager to care for them. The great task of the Middle Ages, after all, was to absorb into the routines of civilization a vast group and a vast area which had heretofore been primitive, and military conquest, political and economic organization, and conversion to Christianity were all intimately interworking parts of an enormous project in acculturation. Strict division of labor between secular and ecclesiastical agencies was not possible.

It is little to be wondered at therefore that the ecclesiastical officialdom, who were the agents of the church's efforts to organize the disorganized society of Europe, should come for the most part from the same social milieu, the same families even, which produced the military and political leadership of the time. And service to the institutional interests of the church and leadership within the church are the particular marks of the saint in this epoch. Hence we come to this further factor which tends to tie saintly status to exalted status in the world. For throughout most of the history of the church as an institution, and most markedly in the Middle Ages, high birth and wealth have been aids, even essential prerequisites, to the attainment of high

office in the church;[1] and high office in the church has been, on the basis of the statistical evidence, an undoubted aid to the acquisition of acknowledged sanctity. Beginning in the fifth century and continuing through the twelfth, 50 percent and over of the saints in our listing are drawn from the area of ecclesiastical authority; they were, that is, at some time in their lives popes, bishops, abbots, or abbesses.

Service to the church, service to God, and service to God's children and one's fellow-men, are, in the view of the church, never incompatible; and one service, indeed, is equivalent to another. Upon this threefold service, which has its worldly rooting, however, always in service to the church, the edifice of Roman Catholic sanctity is constructed. It is easy to see how nobility of birth and relative abundance of possessions would contribute to such service both in the secular and in the ecclesiastical fields and would make it more feasible. It is even easier to see the obverse: how impossible would be accomplishments of a conspicuously meritorious sort to the low-born, the totally uneducated, the absolutely powerless — the common people of a disturbed and force-ridden age.

"Now that is signal virtue," St. Thomas Aquinas writes in his *De regimine principum*, "by which a man can guide not himself alone, but others, and the more persons he rules the greater is his virtue." The degree of heavenly reward, the Angelic Doctor argues further, is proportionate to the degree of earthly virtue, and he completes his discussion with the statement that "a king is worthy of a greater reward if he governs his subjects well than any of his subjects who lives well

[1] There has been to our knowledge no particular analysis of the extent of inter-linkage in lineage terms between the secular and the ecclesiastical hierarchies of medieval Western Europe, but the fact of inter-linkage is generally assumed in historical analysis. Our own figures, furthermore, support this assumption of a strong positive correlation. Medieval society must not be viewed, of course, as wholly static or closed in any area. Opportunities for social mobility varied from time to time and place to place, no doubt, but social mobility of some amount there always was, probably as much in the military and secular-administrative as in the churchly sphere. (See Section 2, "Serjeants and Serf-Knights," in ch. XXV, "Class Distinctions Within the Nobility," in Marc Bloch, *Feudal Society*.)

Mary, the sister of Lazarus and Martha. In Jacobus de Voragine's thirteenth-century collection of the biographies of saints, the *Golden Legend*, however, Mary Magdalen is said to have come of "royal lineage" and her name is derived from a certain town of Magdala, which was presumably part of her inheritance. Much the same tale is told in the thirteenth-century *Early South English Legendary* and in the fourteenth-century *Legendys of Hooly Wummen*. Though Butler in the eighteenth century has become somewhat hesitant about the whole story of Mary Magdalen, his own account still contains traces of the earlier tradition, and he does not scruple to designate Martha, the presumed sister of Mary Magdalen, as a person of "rank and riches." The 1926–1938 edition of Butler's *Lives* strips this account still further of its glamor and reduces Mary Magdalen to a "middle-class" status in which she may be placed on the basis of the prosperity supposedly gained by her from her presumed profession.

under his king."[1] For members of royal and noble families, in fact, becoming a saint during the Middle Ages appears often to have been distressingly routine. The combating of paganism and heresy by force of arms, the endowing of churches and monasteries, and the guidance of subjects in the ways of Christian orthodoxy were ready roads to sainthood for such. Charlemagne, for instance, despite the notorious lapses in his personal morality, has been numbered since his own time among the *beati* of the church. Here, to be sure, was a man of remarkable political achievement. Again and again, however, the member of a royal or noble house won a place in the catalogue of saints through nothing more remarkable than serving as abbot or abbess of a family-endowed foundation, or, choosing instead to remain in the world, through a greater than average generosity to the church and the poor and then, ideally, through pursuit in the last years of old age of the austerities of monastic life.

A further noteworthy aspect of the connection which existed between noble or royal birth and sanctity is the frequency with which family relationships are to be found among the saints of the period. The tendency is not limited to the centuries of the Middle Ages, of course, since the saints of early Christianity are likewise sometimes linked by bonds of blood as well as by bonds of faith. The fullest development of the pattern in question, however, occurs in those very centuries when the roster of saints is most decisively monopolized by representatives of the upper class. A typical example is that of the family of St. Adalbald, a seventh-century lord attached to the court of Dagobert I and listed as a saint and martyr because, after living the life of the ideal Christian noble, he was killed in a family feud. His mother or grandmother was St. Gertrude, who founded the monastery of Hamage. His wife, by whom he had four children, who ultimately became an abbess, was St. Rictrudes. And, finally, all of his four children are venerated among the saints, namely: St. Mauront, abbot of Breuil; St. Clotisenda, abbess of Marchiennes; St. Eusebia, abbess of Hamay; and St. Adalsenda, a nun at Hamay. A still more remarkable instance of the maintenance of a family tradition for sanctity involves Brychan, a fifth-century Welsh chieftain, thirteen of whose sons and daughters and seven of whose less immediate descendants are to be found in our listing of saints. The family of Cunedda, a Welsh chieftain of the twelfth century, however, is said to have produced no less than fifty saints.

Up to this point the services — the good works — upon which sanctity has been based have been defined primarily in the concrete terms of gifts and actions directly advantageous to the church and its interests, and it has been apparent that a number of factors have tended to associate birth in a position of power and prestige with a special facility in the performance of such church-building and administrative services. It is a mistake to think of the genius of the Roman Catholic Church as passive, contemplative, or primarily ascetic. The great majority of her saints are activist in the most practical and bureaucratic sense of the term. Even her martyrs can be seen as being essentially church-builders. The ascetic strain is present too, of course, and all saints are expected to exhibit to some degree the self-denial and self-mortification which constitute asceticism. That an individual practiced various austerities from his earliest years is an item frequently to be found in the accounts of the lives of even the most modern saints. But of the classic saints of asceticism, the hermits, the walled-in recluses, the body-torturing penitents, who appear to the outside observer to do little else than to endure their self-inflicted suffering and to pray, there are not many in our list.

At first glance it would seem that in so far as this avenue of sanctity was available, however narrow it might be, it would at least be open to any one of any class or station. And indeed with respect to the late fourth and early fifth centuries when such practices were particularly in vogue (as a substitute, it has often been suggested, for the martyrdom no longer possible), our listing does include some members of the lower and middle classes who engaged in fantastic ascetic exercises and became saints thereby. The pillar-sitting St. Simeon Stylites, for example, is of lower-class birth. But even here among these hermits and recluses, as among the bishops and abbots on our roster, by far the majority were born to upper-class status, and it was this birthright background of comfort and security which made the suffering of their sanctity particularly dramatic and noteworthy.

An anecdote as told in an early edition of Butler's *Lives* beautifully illustrates the point. The tale concerns the fourth century St. Arsenius, who in secular life was of senatorial rank and had been tutor to the children of the emperor Theodosius. In his middle years he left his position of dignity and joined a society of ascetics in the Egyptian desert. His austerities were so extreme that he became ill, and a priest of the area caused him to be carried to an enclosed place and laid upon a little bed. "One of the monks coming to see him," Butler continues, "was much scandalized at his lying so easy, and said, 'Is this the Abbot Arsenius?' The priest took him aside, and asked him what his employment had been in the village before he was a monk. The old man answered, 'I was a shepherd, and lived with much pains and difficulty.' Then the priest said, 'Do you see this abbot Arsenius? When he was in the world he was the father of the emperors: he had a thousand slaves clothed in silk, with bracelets and girdles of gold, and he slept on the softest and richest of beds. You who were a shepherd, did not find in the world the ease you now enjoy.' The old man, moved by these words, fell down and said, 'Pardon me, father, I have sinned; he is in the true way of humiliation;' and he went away exceedingly edified."[2]

[1] St. Thomas Aquinas, *De regimine principum* (Toronto, 1935), Bk. I, ch. 9.
[2] Rev. Alban Butler, *Lives of the Saints* (4 vols.; Baltimore, 1854), III, 107–111.

Voluntary poverty, an aspect of asceticism, is, to one degree or another, characteristic of great numbers of the saints in our catalogue. The large majority of them were clerics at some stage of their lives, and limitation on the possession and enjoyment of personal property has always been a rule of the clerical vocation in Roman Catholicism, particularly in its regular form. The saints, of course, tended to go well beyond the rule in this regard. But here again we meet a situation — and there is in this instance a special element of the paradoxical — where those born poor to begin with are less capable of achieving the standards of sanctity than the rich. The man born poor is poor of necessity. Only the rich man, by abandoning his goods for the sake of his faith, can offer altogether convincing proof that he is indeed voluntarily poor.

Thus the typical saint, according to these accounts, is one who has heeded the Gospel warning that "it is easier for a camel to pass through the needle's eye than for a rich man to enter into the Kingdom of God" and has taken Christ's counsel to the young man seeking holiness to sell "all that thou hast" as a guide for himself, and, being born wealthy, has given his wealth, or most of it, to the church and the poor and has contemned the preferred honors of the world. He is the fifth-century saint, Paulinus, bishop of Nola, who, having come of "a long line of illustrious senators" and being both enormously wealthy and extremely well-educated, determined to renounce his estates and to turn to the life of the church. "The saint," Butler declares of him, "had, indeed, for the sake of virtue forsaken all that the world could give. . . . Courted in the world by all that would be thought men of genius and caressed by all that valued themselves upon a true taste, he had courage to renounce those flattering advantages; and with honors and riches he made a sacrifice also of his learning and great attainments that he might consecrate himself to the divine service."[1]

The dominance of the catalogue of saints by persons belonging by birth to the aristocratic elite of society by no means suddenly ceased with the movement of western Europe into the late Middle Ages and the early modern period. As a glance at Table 1 will indicate, members of this upper class continued for five centuries yet after the twelfth century to compose well over a majority of our century groupings of saints. One is tempted to generalize the results of this study and merely to say that, with the exception of the data from the first three or four centuries, when Christianity was not yet part of the establishment, the statistics regarding class affiliations of Roman Catholic saints indicate little more than a faithful mirroring in the church's choice of saints of the power relationships in society at large. Just as such a generalization would lead one to expect, it is the middle class which is by far the principal beneficiary of such decline in prominence among the saints as the upper class undergoes after the twelfth century.

In the thirteenth, fourteenth, and fifteenth centuries the mendicant orders emerge to provide the living fire within the crusted institutionalism of the church and incidentally to enlarge the citizenry of heaven with many saints; these orders have a far more intimate involvement with the life of the growing towns and cities than did the monastic organizations of the past and hence with the class derivative from the towns, the bourgeoisie. St. Francis of Assisi, indeed, founder of one of the most important of the mendicant orders is best categorized as a member of this middle class.

The trend to the occurrence of a larger number of individuals of middle-class status among the saints, which was established in the thirteenth, fourteenth, and fifteenth centuries, is continued and strengthened in the sixteenth and seventeenth centuries. These last are the centuries, it should be remembered, of embattled Catholicism; when the church marshaled its resources against the threat of spreading heresy. In one area in particular, in England, they were centuries of defeated and persecuted Catholicism, and there were many martyrs, the saintly quality of whose martyrdom was not officially acknowledged until the nineteenth and twentieth centuries, but who come close to dominating the roster of sixteenth and seventeenth-century saints in recent editions of Butler's *Lives*. These English martyrs are for the most part relatively little people, incidentally. There are very few titles among them or impressive fortunes. The socially successful, after all, found themselves more comfortable and more likely to continue prospering on the other side. Many of the martyrs, to be sure, were from families of the gentry and are still included thus in our upper-class listings. One may reasonably argue, however, about the proper class position of the gentry in sixteenth and seventeenth-century England; it was certainly a transitional and shifting category. Another relatively small contingent of these English martyrs were of yeoman-farmers or even urban middle-class derivation. To a large group we could give no status at all, however, since all we knew of them was that they had been educated at Oxford or Cambridge, information which was sufficient to place them above the common mass but not to make clear whether their origins were the upper or middle class.

Many of the English martyrs, participants in the formally organized English Mission as they were, were members of the Jesuit Order. The Jesuit Order was a force to be reckoned with in the world of sanctity in the sixteenth and seventeenth centuries. Though its founder was Spanish and an aristocrat and it made no effort either to serve or attract representatives of the peasantry or urban proletariat, both its educational work and its membership do have a significantly middle-class reach and inclusiveness. The saints of this enormously activist Order are fully as likely to be of middle-class as of aristocratic lineage.

Another element enters into the seventeenth-century

---

[1] *Op. cit.*, II, 423-428.

situation which serves to increase middle-class opportunities for achievement of sainthood in the life of religion. For this is the century when the first efforts were made to deal with the problems of urban poverty by means of religious orders specifically devoted to social service. And though these orders found support and an occasional recruit among the nobility, they drew most of their working force from the less squeamish members of the middle class. One of the most noted of the saints of the seventeenth century, St. Vincent de Paul, founded such an order for work among the poor and was himself of middle-class status.

The real emergence of the middle class into commanding prominence in the catalogue of saints does not come until the eighteenth and nineteenth centuries, however, when the proportion of saints of this social status rises to 48 percent in the first of the two centuries and 53 percent in the second. (In a volume of a 1956 edition of Butler's *Lives*, which is specifically devoted to recently canonized saints and which includes some saints or *beati* not found on our original listing, the proportion of middle-class saints in the nineteenth century grouping is 60 percent.)[1]

At the same time that there is this marked increase in the number of middle-class saints there is an increase too in the frequency with which the work of the saints comes to consist primarily of activities of social service in the secular sense, such as the teaching of the children of the poor or the tending of the sick in hospitals or the providing of rescue havens for the destitute and abandoned. In Catholic, as in non-Catholic, western Europe the eighteenth and nineteenth centuries witness the first massive developments of programs for popular education. In Catholic areas, notably in France and Italy, this movement provided the basis for the founding of many new orders and the ultimate beatification or canonization of their founders or, very frequently, their foundresses,[2] who, in either case, were almost always derived from middle-class stock.

The old ways of the saints, to be sure, continue likewise to be followed. Bishops remarkable for their administrative capacities are still to be found among the saints of the eighteenth and nineteenth centuries as well as preachers famous for the fire of their sermons and their success in saving souls and here and there an occasional religious pilgrim or pure contemplative.

[1] Rev. Bernard Kelly (ed.), *Butler's Lives of the Saints* (rev. ed.; 5 vols.; Chicago: Catholic Press, 1956), Vol. V, *More Recently Canonized Saints*.

[2] As might be expected from the institutional and activist orientation of Roman Catholic sanctity, the number of men among the saints greatly exceeds the number of women. The total number of saints in our basic list (including both those for whom status was definable and those for whom it was not) is 3347. Of these only 633 or 19% are women. The only marked departure from this overall tendency occurs in the nineteenth and twentieth centuries. When nineteenth-century saints of European origin only are considered (not the Asiatic and African martyrs), 42% of these saints are found to be women, and three of the four individuals from the twentieth century who have been canonized to this point are women likewise.

The French Revolution even supplies its very extensive list of martyrs. But whatever the nature of the religious activity, the saint who participates in it is far more likely to be of middle-class status than in the past.

The twentieth century marks the ultimate triumph of the middle class in the realm of achievement currently in question. Of the four individuals who alone are listed for this century but all of whom have been canonized, three, or 75 percent, are of middle-class birth, and the remaining one is the poor Italian peasant child, Maria Goretti, who died more than half a century ago as a martyr to chastity.

We are confronted in this situation with statistical differences which are sufficiently large to indicate that a basic change is at work. Of what does this change consist? It appears to us that it is a change in the structure and functioning of society which is fundamentally involved. By the eighteenth and nineteenth centuries, even in Catholic Europe, or at least in Italy and France, which are the nations of birth for almost all of the saints of the period, the middle class, with its spearhead, the bourgeoisie, has achieved a position of unprecedented prominence and power. In the nineteenth century, in fact, one might safely say that it dominates the political and economic scene and, except for certain preserves of social prestige, has altogether displaced the landed aristocracy in the seats of leadership. And though the Catholic church itself tended to cling to the shadow of dying institutions and vigorously combated the spirit of liberalism which was abroad in these centuries, it nevertheless responded to the movement of events to this extent: more than half of its saints now came from the class with which political and social liberalism was identified.

In analyzing the numbers of individuals of lower-class status among the saints, the first and most striking fact to be noted is that participation by this group in the eminence of sainthood is exceedingly meager. Such saints comprise only 5 percent of our total. In two centuries, the eighth and tenth, there is no single individual from the lower class upon our list, while in eight other centuries the proportion is 3 percent or less. In addition to the first two centuries of the Christian era, in both of which 12 percent of the saints are catalogued as members of the lower class, the few other centuries in which 10 percent or over of the saints are of this lowly status are the fourteenth, the sixteenth, the eighteenth, the nineteenth, and the twentieth. It is difficult to consider the twentieth century statistically because of the small number of saints — only four — who lived into this century and who are included in the collections of saints' lives which we have used, but, as we have already noted, one of these four, Maria Goretti, was lower class in an almost dramatic sense. The nineteenth-century figure of 18 percent is based on a wider sampling, of course, and manifests a real advance over the minuscule percentages of earlier eras. (In terms of the list established on the basis of the previously cited last volume of a 1956 edition of Butler's *Lives*, which is devoted to recently canonized saints, lower-class saints in the nineteenth century constitute a full 20 percent of the total.)[1] But when one remembers that, even in nineteenth-century Europe, at least three-quarters of the population were, by our definition, of lower-class status, it is apparent that an 18 or 20 percent representation among the saints does not amount to the triumph of equalitarianism in this area of public honor.

The reasons for this niggardly scattering of ones and fives and tens of lower-class individuals among the thronging hundreds of the saints have been for the most part made already evident, as implications at least, in previous analysis. The factors which in the Middle Ages in particular tended to open out the religious sphere of opportunity to members of the aristocracy, tended reciprocally to close it for the poor, the powerless, the great mass of peasant laborers who were, after all, not technically free in large part to do anything else with their lives than to spend them in basic toil. In addition, it is questionable how deeply medieval Christianity penetrated the populace of Europe. For centuries considerable pockets of paganism persisted, and such adherence to the church as existed was often highly nominal and routine.[2] No doubt most medieval peasants were, what quantities of their clerical critics declared them to be, ignorant, superstitious, gross in their manners and their morals, more subjects for damnation, from the Christian standpoint, than for sainthood.[3] How, under the circumstances and in a cruel age hardly noted for delicacies at any level (save in the fantasies of chivalric love), could they have been otherwise?

The broad historical process we have been observing with regard to the selection of the prototype Christian heroes by the institution of Roman Catholicism should neither surprise nor dismay us, therefore. Some modern Roman Catholic apologists may well be disturbed by statistics which run counter to their own presentation of Roman Catholic sainthood as the essence of spiritual democracy in action,[4] but for the rest of us this study will prove merely another illustration of the sound view that social and ideological history are all of a piece; that, when Christianity became a part of the historical process, it thereby became subject to the same potent social influences and tendencies which the historian of ideas is increasingly obliged to recognize as crucial. Hence it is really not unaccountable that, as the data we have been considering demonstrate, the practice of Christian virtue, in any public and institutionally recognized form, should have been, like most other rewards and distinctions in life, largely reserved to the social elites of European culture. The value systems of stratified societies, particularly in their more extreme and exacting aspects, are typically encapsulated in and radiated by privileged and ruling groups. It is to be expected that individual members of these groups will be the ones most frequently and most adequately to embody and express these values in their lives.

[1] One might conceivably include 22 of these recently canonized saints (canonized October 18, 1964) to enlarge still further the nineteenth-century percentage of lower-class saints. The 22 saints in question are the Negro martyrs from the Banda tribe of Uganda, Christian converts who were killed by fellow tribesmen because of their adherence to the alien faith. We chose not to include these saints in our analysis, however, because they stand apart from European society and its hierarchies. There are other native martyrs who have been similarly honored by the church, notably a group of Japanese converts who gave their lives for their faith in the seventeenth century and of Korean converts who were martyred in the nineteenth century.

[2] Stephen Neill, *The Christian Society* (London: Nisbet & Co. Ltd., 1952), pp. 101–102; M. A. Murray, *The Witch-Cult in Western Europe* (Oxford: Clarendon Press, 1962), pp. 20–24; Kenneth Scott Latourette, *The Thousand Years of Uncertainty: A.D. 500–A.D. 1500* (London: Eyre and Spottiswoode, 1938), pp. 32–33, 91, 412–413.

[3] G. G. Coulton, *Medieval Village, Manor, and Monastery*, ch. XVIII, "Church Estimates of the Peasant."

[4] It should be noted that the Catholic church makes no claim to a knowledge of all of God's saints who have lived on the earth. Its only claim to infallibility in this regard, through the infallibility of the Pope, who since the seventeenth century has presided over all beatifications and canonizations, is that those who have been officially designated as saints are saints indeed and are so recognized by God as well as by the church of God. Beatification and canonization are nothing more than the exterior marks with which the church honors such individuals as have become known to it for outstanding holiness of life, a selection only from among the possibly many more who have found their way to God. A special holy day, November 1, has long been set aside for the honor of all saints in general but especially of those who may have been slighted and forgotten in the commemorations of the previous year or who have left no visible trace in human recollection and the historical record.

FASHION

A Note on the "Trickle Effect"

Lloyd A. Fallers

MUCH HAS BEEN WRITTEN—and much more spoken in informal social scientific shop talk—about the so-called "trickle effect"—the tendency in U. S. society (and perhaps to a lesser extent in Western societies generally) for new styles or fashions in consumption goods to be introduced via the socio-economic elite and then to pass down through the status hierarchy, often in the form of inexpensive, mass-produced copies.

In a recent paper, Barber and Lobel have analyzed this phenomenon in the field of women's clothes.[1] They point out that women's dress fashions are not simply irrational shifts in taste, but that they have definite functions in the U. S. status system. Most Americans, they say, are oriented toward status mobility. Goods and services consumed are symbolic of social status. In the family division of labor, the husband and father "achieves" in the occupational system and thus provides the family with monetary income. Women, as wives

and daughters, have the task of allocating this income so as to maximize its status-symbolic value. Since women's clothing permits much subtlety of expression in selection and display, it becomes of great significance as a status-mobility symbol.[2] The ideology of the "open class" system, however, stresses broad "equality" as well as differential status. The tendency of women's dress fashions to "trickle down" fairly rapidly via inexpensive reproductions of originals created at fashion centers helps to resolve this seeming inconsistency by preventing the development of rigid status distinctions.[3]

In the widest sense, of course, the "trickle effect" applies not only to women's dress but also to consumption goods of many other kinds. Most similar to women's dress fashions are styles in household furnishings. A colleague has pointed out to me that venetian blinds have had a similar status career—being introduced at relatively high levels in the status hierarchy and within a few years passing down to relatively low levels. Like women's dress styles, styles in household furnishings are to a substantial degree matters of taste and their adoption a matter of "learning" by lower status persons that they are status relevant. The trickling down of other types of consumption goods is to a greater degree influenced by long-term increases in purchasing power at lower socio-economic levels. Such consumers' durables as refrigerators and automobiles, being products of heavy industry and hence highly standardized over relatively long periods and throughout the

[1] Bernard Barber and Lyle S. Lobel, " 'Fashion' in Women's Clothes and the American Social System," *Social Forces*, Vol. 31, pp. 124–131. Reprinted in Reinhard Bendix and S. M. Lipset, *Class, Status and Power: A Reader in Social Stratification*, Glencoe: The Free Press, 1953, pp. 323–332.

[2] It is not suggested that women are *solely* in charge of status-symbolic expenditure, merely that they play perhaps this major role in this respect. See also: Talcott Parsons, *Essays in Sociological Theory*, Glencoe: The Free Press, 1949, p. 225.

[3] Our thinking concerning the status–symbolic role of consumption patterns owes a great debt, of course, to Veblen's notion of "conspicuous consumption" and more recently to the work of W. L. Warner and his colleagues.

Reprinted from *Public Opinion Quarterly*, V. 18 (1954), pp. 314–321, by permission of the author and the publisher.

industries which produce them, are much less subject to considerations of taste. They do, however, trickle down over the long term and their possession is clearly status-relevant.

The dominant tendency among social scientists has been to regard the trickle effect mainly as a "battle of wits" between upper-status persons who attempt to guard their symbolic treasure and lower-status persons (in league with mass-production industries) who attempt to devalue the status-symbolic currency. There is much truth in this view. Latterly we have observed a drama of this sort being played out in the automotive field. Sheer ownership of an automobile is no longer symbolic of high status and neither is frequent trading-in. Not even the "big car" manufacturers can keep their products out of the hands of middle- and lower-status persons "on the make." High-status persons have therefore turned to ancient or foreign sports-cars.

It seems possible, however, that the trickle effect has other and perhaps more far-reaching functions for the society as a whole. Western (and particularly U. S.) society, with its stress upon the value of success through individual achievement, poses a major motivational problem: The occupational system is primarily organized about the norm of technical efficiency. Technical efficiency is promoted by recruiting and rewarding persons on the basis of their objective competence and performance in occupational roles. The field of opportunity for advancement, however, is pyramidal in shape; the number of available positions decreases as differential rewards increase. But for the few most competent to be chosen, the many must be "called," that is, motivated to strive for competence and hence success. This, of course, involves relative failure by the many, hence the problem: How is the widespread motivation to strive maintained in the face of the patent likelihood of failure for all but the few? In a widely-quoted paper, Merton has recognized that this situation is a serious focus of strain in the social system and has pointed to some structured types of deviant reaction to it.[1] I should like to suggest the hypothesis that the *trickle effect is a mechanism for maintaining the motivation to strive for success, and hence for maintaining efficiency of performance in occupational roles, in a system in which differential success is possible for only a few.* Status-symbolic consumption goods trickle down, thus giving the "illusion" of success to those who fail to achieve *differential* success in the opportunity and status pyramid. From this point of view, the trickle effect becomes a "treadmill."

There are, of course, other hypotheses to account for the maintenance of motivation to strive against very unfavorable odds. Perhaps the most common is the notion that the "myth of success," perhaps maintained by the mass-communications media under the control of the "vested interests," deceives people into believing that their chances for success are greater than is in fact the case. Merton seems to accept this explanation in part while denying that the ruse is entirely effective.[2]

Somewhat similar is another common explanation, put forward, for example, by Schumpeter, that though the chances for success are not great, the rewards are so glittering as to make the struggle attractive.[3] Undoubtedly both the "success myth" theory and the "gambling" theory contain elements of truth. Individual achievement certainly *is* a major value in the society and dominates much of its ideology, while risk-taking is clearly institutionalized, at any rate in the business segment of the occupational system. Taken by themselves, however, these explanations do not seem sufficient to account for the situation. At any rate, if it is possible to show that the system *does* "pay off" for the many in the form of "trickle-down" status-symbolic consumption goods, one need not lean so heavily upon such arguments.

It seems a sound principle of sociological analysis to assume "irrationality" as a motivation for human action only where exhaustive analysis fails to reveal a "realistic" pay-off for the observed behavior. To be sure, the explanation put forward here also assumes "irrationality," but in a different sense. The individual who is rewarded for his striving by the trickling-down of status-symbolic consumption goods has the *illusion*, and not the *fact*, of status mobility among his fellows. But in terms of his life history, he nevertheless *has* been rewarded with things which are valued and to this degree his striving is quite "realistic."[4] Though his status position *vis-à-vis* his fellows has not changed, he can look back upon his own life history and say to himself (perhaps not explicitly since the whole status-mobility motivational complex is probably quite often wholly or in part unconscious): "I (or my family) have succeeded. I now have things which five (or ten or twenty) years ago I could not have had, things which were then possessed only by persons of higher status." To the degree that status is *defined* in terms of consumption of goods and services one should perhaps say, not that such an individual has only the *illusion* of mobility, but rather that the entire population has been upwardly mobile. From this point of view, status-symbolic goods and services do not "trickle-down" but rather remain in fixed positions; the population moves up through the hierarchy of status-symbolic consumption patterns.

The accompanying diagram illustrates the various possibilities in terms of the life-histories of individuals.

[1] R. K. Merton, "Social Structure and Anomie," reprinted as Chapter IV, *Social Theory and Social Structure*, Glencoe: The Free Press, 1949.

[2] Ibid.

[3] J. A. Schumpeter, *Capitalism, Socialism and Democracy*, New York: Harpers, 1947, pp. 73-74.

[4] By "irrationality" is meant here irrationality *within the framework of a given value system.* Values themselves, of course, are neither "rational" nor "irrational" but "non-rational." The value of individual achievement is non-rational. Action directed toward achievement may be termed rational to the degree that, in terms of the information available to the actor, it is likely to result in achievement; it is irrational to the degree that this is not so.

The two half-pyramids represent the status hierarchy at two points in time (X and Y). A, B, C and D are individuals occupying different levels in the status hierarchy. Roman numerals I through V represent the hierarchy of status-symbolic consumption patterns. Between time periods X and Y, a new high-status consumption pattern has developed and has been taken over by the elite. All status levels have "moved up" to "higher" consumption patterns. During the elapsed time, individual C has "succeeded"; in the sense of having become able to consume goods and services which were unavailable to him before, though he has remained in the same relative status level. Individual B

Hierarchy of Consumption Patterns	Status Hierarchy: Time X	Status Hierarchy: Time Y
V		A
IV	D	C
III	C	B
II	B	D
I	A	

has been downwardly mobile in the status hierarchy, but this blow has been softened for him because the level into which he has dropped has in the meantime taken over consumption patterns previously available only to persons in the higher level in which B began. Individual D has been sufficiently downwardly mobile so that he has also lost ground in the hierarchy of consumption patterns. Finally, individual A, who has been a spectacular success, has risen to the very top of the status hierarchy where he is able to consume goods and services which were unavailable even to the elite at an earlier time period. Needless to say, this diagram is not meant to represent the actual status levels, the proportions of persons in each level or the frequencies of upward and downward mobility in the U. S. social

[1] Merton, *op. cit.*
[2] W. Balfour, "Productivity and the Worker," *British Journal of Sociology*, Vol. IV, No. 3, 1953, pp. 257–265.

system. It is simply meant to illustrate diagrammatically the tendency of the system, in terms of status-symbolic consumption goods, to reward even those who are not status mobile and to provide a "cushion" for those who are slightly downward mobile.

Undoubtedly this view of the system misrepresents "the facts" in one way as much as the notion of status-symbolic goods and services "trickling down" through a stable status hierarchy does in another. Consumption patterns do not retain the same status-symbolic value as they become available to more people. Certainly to some degree the "currency becomes inflated". A more adequate diagram would show both consumption patterns trickling down and the status hierarchy moving up. Nonetheless, I would suggest that *to some degree* particular consumption goods have "absolute" value in terms of the individual's life history and his motivation to succeed. To the degree that this is so, the system pays off even for the person who is not status-mobile.

This pay-off, of course, is entirely dependent upon constant innovation and expansion in the industrial system. New goods and services must be developed and existing ones must become more widely available through mass-production. Average "real income" must constantly rise. If status-symbolic consumption patterns remained stationary both in kind and in degree of availability, the system would pay off only for the status-mobile and the achievement motive would indeed be unrealistic for most individuals. Were the productive system to shrink, the pay-off would become negative for most and the unrealism of the motivation to achieve would be compounded. Under such circumstances, the motivational complex of striving-achievement-occupational efficiency would be placed under great strain. Indeed, Merton seems to have had such circumstances in mind when he described "innovation," "ritualism," "rebellion," and "passive withdrawal" as common patterned deviations from the norm.[1]

This suggests a "vicious circle" relationship between achievement motivation and industrial productivity. It seems reasonable to suppose that a high level of achievement motivation is both a cause and a result of efficiency in occupational role performance. Such an assumption underlies much of our thinking about the modern Western occupational system and indeed is perhaps little more than common sense. One British sociologist, commenting upon the reports of the British "Productive Teams" which have recently been visiting American factories, is impressed by American workers' desire for status-symbolic consumption, partly the result of pressure upon husbands by their wives, as a factor in the greater "per man hour" productivity of American industry.[2] Greater productivity, of course, means more and cheaper consumption goods and hence a greater pay-off for the worker. Conversely, low achievement motivation and inefficiency in occupational role performance would seem to stimulate one another. The worker has less to work for, works less efficiently, and in turn receives still less reward. Presumably these relationships would tend to hold, though in some cases less directly, throughout the occupational system and not only in the sphere of the industrial worker.

To the degree that the relationships suggested here between motivation to status-symbolic consumption, occupational role performance, and expanding productivity actually exist, they should be matters of some importance to the theory of business cycles. Although they say nothing about the genesis of up-turns and down-turns in business activity, they do suggest some social structural reasons why upward or downward movements, once started might tend to continue. It is not suggested, of course, that these are the only, or even the most important, reasons. More generally, they exemplify the striking degree to which the stability of modern industrial society often depends upon the maintenance of delicate equilibria.

The hypotheses suggested here are, it seems to me, amenable to research by a number of techniques. It would be most useful to discover more precisely just which types of status-symbolic consumption goods follow the classical trickle-down pattern and which do not. Television sets, introduced in a period of relative prosperity, seem to have followed a different pattern, spreading laterally across the middle-income groups rather than trickling down from above. This example suggests another. Some upper-income groups appear to have shunned television on the grounds of its "vulgarity" — a valuation shared by many academics. To what degree are preferences for other goods and services introduced, not at the upper income levels, but by the "intelligentsia," who appear at times to have greater pattern-setting potential than their relatively low economic position might lead one to believe? Finally, which consumption items spread rapidly and which more slowly? Such questions might be answered by the standard techniques of polling and market analysis.

More difficult to research are hypotheses concerning the motivational significance of consumption goods. I have suggested that the significance for the individual of the trickling down of consumption patterns must be seen in terms of his life-history and not merely in terms of short-term situations. It seems likely that two general patterns may be distinguished. On the one hand, individuals for whom success means primarily rising above their fellows may be more sensitive to those types of goods and services which must be chosen and consumed according to relatively subtle and rapidly changing standards of taste current at any one time at higher levels. Such persons must deal successfully with the more rapid devaluations of status-symbolic currency which go on among those actively battling for dominance. Such persons it may be who are responsible for the more short-term fluctuations in consumption patterns. On the other hand, if my hypothesis is correct, the great mass of the labor force may be oriented more to long-term success in terms of their own life-histories — success in the sense of achieving a "better standard of living" without particular regard to *differential* status. Interviews centered upon the role of consumption patterns in individuals' life aspirations should reveal such differences if they exist, while differences in perception of symbols of taste might be tested by psychological techniques.

Most difficult of all would be the testing of the circular relationship between motivation and productivity. Major fluctuations in the economy are relatively long term and could be studied only through research planned on an equally long-term basis. Relatively short-term and localized fluctuations, however, do occur at more frequent intervals and would provide possibilities for research. One would require an index of occupational performance which could be related to real income and the relationship between these elements should ideally be traced through periods of both rising and falling real income.

Social Class and the Experience of Ill Health
Charles Kadushin

MALTHUS IN HIS FAMOUS *Essay on Population*, written in 1798, was not the first to say it, but he was the most eloquent.[1] In his view, "misery and vice" adjusted the size of a human population to match the available food supply.

The positive check to population by which I mean the check that represses an increase which is already begun, is confined chiefly, though not perhaps solely, to the lowest orders of society. This check is not so obvious to common view as the other I have mentioned [restraint upon marriage], and to prove distinctly the force and extent of its operation would require, perhaps, more data than we are in possession of. But I believe that it has been very generally remarked by those who have attended to bills of mortality that of the number of children who die annually, much too great a proportion belongs to those who may be supposed unable to give their offspring proper food and attention, exposed as they are occasionally to severe distress and confined, perhaps, to unwholesome habitations and hard labour. . . . Indeed, it seems difficult to suppose that

[1] T. R. Malthus, *Population: The First Essay*, Ann Arbor: The University of Michigan Press, 1959, Chapter V.
[2] *Ibid.*, Chapter VII.

a labourer's wife who has six children, and who is sometimes in absolute want of bread, should be able always to give them the food and attention necessary to support life.

All the elements which have gone into modern public health and sickness surveys are present in this early statement. Illness and early death are more frequent in the lower classes. The causes for this unhappy state are poor nutrition, bad housing, overwork, and lack of attention. Elsewhere Malthus notes that overcrowding and lack of cleanliness explain plagues, sickly seasons, and epidemics.[2] He even hints at the need for survey research data to verify these propositions.

This paper reviews the evidence collected since Malthus and concludes that in recent years in North America there is very little association between becoming ill and social class, although the lower classes still *feel* more sick. Nevertheless, social scientists and public health experts have consistently refused to recognize that the world is changing. For example, one expert in a review article written in 1946 began by reminding us that "the earliest studies of morbidity indicated a negative correlation of illness with economic status; the lowest income group had the highest morbidity rate and the higher income groups had lower rates of illness. More recent studies have con-

A revised version of a paper presented to the ASA, Los Angeles, 1963. This is Columbia University Bureau of Applied Social Research publication No. A-387.

Reprinted from *Sociological Inquiry*, Volume XXXIV (Winter 1964) Number 1, pp. 67–80, by permission of the authors and the publisher.

firmed and added to these facts."[1] But on the very next page she asserts that the United States National Health Survey, conducted during the height of the depression, shows that "except for the lowest income groups, there seems to be little association between all chronic illness and family income." The "more recent studies" she mentioned all show similar "associations," or lack of them. Moreover, her view of public health is shared by almost everyone in the field.[2]

What seems to be the matter here? It is doubtful whether any of the scientists are even aware of their possible misrepresentation of the facts. Rather, the difficulties are four-fold. First, there is the problem of conceptualizing morbidity and illness. Current terminology often conceals the difference between disease and feeling sick. Second, because illness is poorly conceptualized, the variables intervening between social class and illness are almost forgotten. Third, when one is standing in the midst of a newborn trend, it is very difficult to realize that change has taken place. Fourth, sociologists and public health researchers may have a vested interest in the traditional class variables.

Illness, disease, and feedback

It is well known that there is a difference between contracting a disease and the illness which may then ensue. Trussel and Elinson in introducing their study of chronic illness,

> take note of a major deficiency in . . . virtually all household or family interview studies of "morbidity" . . . The failure adequately to conceptualize, make clear, and take account of the distinction between disease and illness. . . . Disease is *abnormal structure or functioning*. Illness is the feeling of discomfort which arises out of disease.[3]

Although this distinction is clear in principle and in clinical practice, the usage of "abnormal" probably begs the question in epidemiological application. For example, although only 5 per thousand per year die in England of coronary heart disease, population samplings show that 500 per thousand have much or moderate coronary atheroma.[4] Similar statistics have shocked students of mental health. Nevertheless, the difference between illness and disease is important since it forces one to ask whether a given statistic or measurement is closer to indicating disease or suggesting illness.

Reaction to disease is determined not only biologically and psychologically. Among social classes demonstrated differences in their rates of suicide, crime, or juvenile delinquency, for example, may be caused by "feedback" between the institution which is supposed to deal with the particular behavior and the observed occurrence of the behavior. High rates of crime and juvenile delinquency among lower classes may be a function of police tendencies to arrest lower class persons. This relationship is caused by "spurious feedback,"

that is, an association between social categories and deviance which is caused by the way the controlling agency measures deviancy. Similarly, if middle class psychiatrists do not like lower class patients, and accordingly call them schizophrenic, then a relationship between social class and schizophrenia may simply be a case of spurious feedback. It is believed that high death rates for laborers but low ones for craftsmen may reflect a habit of hospital personnel of calling all working class men laborers.[5]

The very structure of an institution may also cause systematic differentials in observed rates of actions which come under its jurisdiction. These differences are not spurious but a part of the social structure. Some of the class differentials in death rates from specific diseases can be explained on the basis of the fact that lower class persons are less likely to go to doctors, and that only the more serious of their illnesses are the ones to be properly diagnosed. High lower class death rates may also reflect less adequate treatment of disease.

These problems of feedback between the institution of medicine and rates of illness have to do with reactions to disease, rather than mere exposure to it. But there are also factors within social classes completely unrelated to medical institutions which influence reactions to illness. The oft-quoted Zborowski study suggests that there are differences between ethnic groups in their reactions to pain.[6] Later, systematic class differences in how sick a person feels he is will be shown.

Finally, when it comes to actual exposure to disease and the subsequent contracting of it the traditional Malthusian factors such as filth, overcrowding, and the like are important class related variables.

The differences between contracting a disease or condition and reacting to it, and the different roles of variables intervening between class and illness, mean that great care must be exercised in the choice of indicators of illness. Reports by doctors or by lay respondents of the prevalence of "conditions" are more akin to measurement of disease, but reports of "disability," days sick in bed, days lost from work, not to mention self-estimates of good or poor health, are much more akin to reaction to illness. Further, in view of the feedback between medicine and rates of illness, the best estimates of prevalence are those based on sample surveys

[1] J. Downes, "Social and Environmental Factors in Illness," *Milbank Memorial Fund Quarterly*, 26 (1948), pp. 366–385.
[2] K. B. Laughton, *et al.*, "Socioeconomic Status and Illness," *Milbank Memorial Fund Quarterly*, 36 (1958), pp. 46–57; M. E. Patno, "Mortality and Economic Level in an Urban Area," *Public Health Reports*, 27 (1960), pp. 841–851.
[3] R. E. Trussel and J. Elinson, *Chronic Illness in a Rural Area*, Cambridge: Harvard University Press, 1959, p. 55.
[4] J. N. Morris, *The Uses of Epidemiology*, London: E. & S. Livingstone, 1957, p. 45.
[5] J. M. Stamler, *et al.*, "Epidemiological Studies of Cardiovascular Renal Diseases," *Journal of Chronic Diseases*, 12 (1960), pp. 440–475.
[6] M. Zborowski, "Cultural Components in Response to Pain," in E. G. Jaco (ed.), *Patients, Physicians and Illness*, Glencoe: The Free Press, 1958.

rather than on cases brought to doctors. Death rates compound error, for they reflect referral patterns, the quality of care, and the accuracy of diagnosis. Death rates tell us more about medicine than they do about illness and disease. Malthus' estimate of lower class misery systematically confuses the getting of a disease with the outcome of an illness, but there is no need to continue his mistake.

Malthus implicitly takes a sociological view of illness, however. He speaks not of specific diseases but of the total impact of illness and disease upon the lower classes. Recently, Hinkle and Wolff found that " 'illness' is a state of the total organism."[1] Since the present interest is in the total impact of social systems on the experience of disease and illness, most of the data to be presented deals with the total number of diseases or conditions reported by respondents in home interviews. While this position makes little sense for the biological scientist interested in tracing the causes of a particular disease, it makes excellent sense for the scientist of human action. Further, detailed sample survey prevalence rates for specific illnesses among the various social classes are generally not available.

When it comes to a consideration of the independent variable, social class, it may be noted that one of the best ways of initiating controversy among sociologists is to discuss the relative utility of various indicators of social class. Is income, occupation, education, location of residence or the style of one's furniture the best way of measuring social class? Perhaps some combination of indicators is best? Or perhaps it makes no difference at all how one measures class? These arguments are in part an academic exercise when it comes to relating illness to social class, because in this review one has to take the data the way they were published – which means that some data will be reported in terms of income, other data in terms of occupation and some ranked by education. There are considerable differences in the meaning of these indicators, however, and problems pertaining to this will be pointed out.

Social class and illness

Every social survey conducted before 1940 in Malthus' home territory, Great Britain, has indeed shown negative correlations between illness and social class.[2] All these studies pointed to a gloomy picture of lower class life corresponding to Malthus' informal observations. The first systematic national study of

[1] L. E. Hinkle, Jr., and H. G. Wolff, "Health and the Social Environment," in A. H. Leighton, *et al.* (eds.), *Explorations in Social Psychiatry*, New York: Basic Books, 1957.
[2] W. P. D. Logan, and E. Brooke, *The Survey of Sickness*, 1943–1952, London: Her Majesty's Stationery Office, 1957.
[3] *Loc. cit.*
[4] F. J. W. Miller, *et al.*, *Growing Up in Newcastle upon Tyne*, London: Oxford University Press, 1960.
[5] P. S. Lawrence, "Chronic Illness and Socio-Economic Status," in Jaco, *op. cit.*; S. D. Collins, "A Review and Study of Illness and Medical Care with Special Reference to Long-Time Trends," *Public Health Service Publication* 544, 1957.

Great Britain, however, is the Survey of Sickness undertaken between 1942 and 1952.[3] Table 1, taken from this study, shows that the lowest two of five income groups have higher proportions of sick people, but that the rate flattens out for the other groups. It is true that the same survey shows a steeper

TABLE 1. *Number of Persons Ill per Month per 100 Men and Women in Great Britain According to the Weekly Income of the Head of Household (1951)*

Weekly income (pounds)	SEX	
	Men	Women
Under 3	77	82
3–5	71	76
5–7.10	65	73
7.10–10	63	71
10 or more	63	71

Source: W. P. D. Logan and E. Brooke, *The Survey of Sickness, 1943–1952*, London: Her Majesty's Stationery Office, 1957, p. 57.

relationship between the sheer *number* of illnesses and income, but these data are more sensitive to *1)* the fact that illnesses cause a drop in income; *2)* older persons are poorer and have more illnesses; *3)* the sheer number of illnesses a given person reports are in part an indication of his reactions to disease, as the notion of hypochondriasis suggests.

In England, a five year follow-up of all children born in Newcastle upon Tyne in 1947, shows that the overwhelming majority of diseases, including tuberculosis, were *not* related to the social class of parents.[4]

So it is by no means clear that in Great Britain of today there is a linear relationship between social class and the chance of becoming ill.

Recent data from Japan suggest what Great Britain must have looked like a number of years ago. Table 2 shows a much steeper relationship between the proportion of ill persons and the income of wage earners. Even here, however, the rates flatten out in the upper income levels.

Malthus had always suspected that North America was different in the occurrence of "positive checks" to the growth of population. Recent data seem to bear him out. The first household sample survey of illness in the United States using techniques that have since become standard was made in Hagerstown, Maryland in 1923.[5] Here, there was a linear relationship between social class, as rated by interviewers (largely on the basis of economic factors), and the prevalence of chronic illness. But the differential for the same families in 1943 was considerably reduced. And an ingenious analysis by Lawrence shows that illness was more likely to cause a decline in a person's rated social class than was low social class likely to cause an increase in illness.[1]

TABLE 2. *Number of Persons Ill at Time of Interview per 1000 Wage Earners in Japan (1956), According to Household Income*

Household income (yen per month)	TYPE OF ILLNESS		
	All diseases	T.B.	Other diseases
Under 2,000	73.7	20.4	53.3
2,000–4,000	71.8	21.0	50.8
4,000–6,000	61.8	15.7	46.1
6,000–8,000	51.0	13.6	37.4
8,000–10,000	40.2	10.3	29.9
10,000–15,000	34.4	8.3	26.1
15,000–20,000	26.5	6.7	19.8
20,000–25,000	25.1	7.0	18.1
30,000–40,000	28.2	7.9	20.3
40,000 or more	29.1	5.1	24.0

Source: T. Soda, "Main Findings Obtained in Sickness Surveys of Japan," in *International Population Conference, Wien, 1959*, Wien: Louis Henry-Wilhelm Winkler, 1959, pp. 519–534.

The first U.S. National Health Survey was conducted during 1935 and 1936.[2] The data shown in Table 3 were earlier described as showing little association between all chronic (and we might add, acute) illnesses and family income, except for the two lowest income groups.[3] These data are strikingly similar to the British rates collected ten years later.

TABLE 3. *Annual Frequency per 1000 in the United States of Acute and Chronic Illnesses Disabling for One Week or Longer (1935–1936), According to Annual Family Income and Relief Status*

Annual family income (in dollars)	NATURE OF ILLNESS		
	All illnesses	Acute	Chronic
Relief	232	160	72
Non relief			
Under 1,000	176	120	56
1,000–1,500	155	117	38
1,500–2,000	146	111	35
2,000–3,000	145	110	36
3,000–5,000	145	109	36
5,000 or more	146	107	39

Source: R. H. Britten, et al., "The National Health Survey: Some General Findings as to Disease, Accidents, and Impairments in Urban Areas." *Public Health Reports*, 55 (1940), pp. 444–470.

Since illness can make for a reduced income, a measure of social class based on one's usual occupation is more suited to our purposes. Table 4, also from the depression National Health Survey, shows the relationship between illness and occupational rank. When occupational injuries are excluded and unemployment controlled, there is practically no difference between types of occupations in the proportion of those ill at the time of the survey. The possible exception is the high rate among Female "Others" — largely service workers. Saxon Graham, also using an occupation based measure of social class found no variation in chronic illnesses in Butler County, Pennsylvania.[4] Thus, illness which seems strictly attributable to the general environment is not especially related to social class. Incidentally, this is not meant to upset the time honored study of occupational medicine. All studies do show that manual workers have more on the job injuries than non manual workers, and that certain occupations have definite health hazards.[5] What is discussed here is a different matter, namely social rank which, although related to one's specific occupation, is not coterminous with occupational situs.

TABLE 4. *Proportion* of Male and Female Workers in the United States Disabled on the Day of the Interview (1935–1936), Excluding Illnesses from Puerperal and Female Genital Causes, and from Occupational Injuries, According to Class of Occupational Employment Status*

Own occupation	EMPLOYMENT STATUS			
	EMPLOYED		UNEMPLOYED	
	Male	Female	Male	Female
Business and professional	1.39	2.33	3.65	4.82
Clerical	1.32	2.20	3.32	4.38
Industrial	1.41	2.32	3.38	4.74
Other	1.49	2.59	3.84	6.36

* Age adjusted.
Source: D. E. Hailman, "The Prevalence of Disabling Illness Among Male and Female Workers and Housewives," *Public Health Bulletin 260* (1941).

Finally, there are the most recent surveys of the United States, Canada, California, and New York City.[6] With proper controls for age and other such

[1] Lawrence, *op. cit.*

[2] G. T. Perrott, *et al.*, "The National Health Survey, 1935–36," *Public Health Reports*, 54 (1940), pp. 1663–1687.

[3] Downes, *op. cit.*

[4] S. Graham, "Socio-Economic Status, Illness, and the Use of Medical Services," in Jaco, *op. cit.*

[5] R. H. Britten, *et al.*, "The National Health Survey: Some General Findings as to Disease, Accidents, and Impairments in Urban Areas," *Public Health Reports*, 55 (1940), pp. 444–470; D. E. Hailman, "The Prevalence of Disabling Illness Among Male and Female Workers and Housewives," *Public Health Bulletin 260* (1941); and U.S. National Health Service, "Persons Injured While at Work, United States, July 1959–June 1960," *Public Health Service Publication 534*, Service B, No. 41, 1963.

[6] California Department of Public Health, "Health in California," California Health Survey, 1957; Department of National Health and Welfare, "Illness and Health Care in Canada, 1950–51," E. A. Suchman, "Sociocultural Variations in Illness and Medical Care," New York City Department of Health, 1963, processed.

disturbing factors, none of these data show a relationship between social class and the prevalence of illness except, perhaps, among the elderly. Table 5 shows the story for the United States in 1957 and 1958. For persons under 45, whose incomes are not likely to be severely affected by illness, there is even a slightly positive relationship between income and the prevalence of chronic illness.

TABLE 5. *Per cent of Persons in the United States with One or More Chronic Illness According to Income and Age (1957–1958)*

FAMILY INCOME PER YEAR IN DOLLARS

Age in years	Under 2,000	2,000–4,000	4,000–7,000	7,000 or more
Under 15	14.0	15.1	18.3	20.6
15–44	39.1	40.2	44.8	43.6
45–64	68.7	63.6	58.3	57.6

Source: U.S. National Health Service, "Limitation on Activity and Mobility Due to Chronic Conditions, U.S., July, 1957–June, 1958," *Public Health Service Publication 584, Series B, No. 11,* 1959, Table 5.

All the pertinent studies have not been reviewed here but there is every indication that in modern Western countries, the relationship between social class and the prevalence of illness is certainly decreasing and most probably no longer even exists.[1]

Not even Malthus attributed the greater rate of diseases among the lower classes to something inherent in class itself. Rather, he called attention to some specific intervening variables such as malnutrition and lack of proper attention. As countries advance in their standard of living, as public sanitation improves, as mass immunization proceeds and as Dr. Spock becomes even more widely read, the gross factors which intervene between social class and the exposure to disease will become more and more equal for all social classes.

Social class and the prevalence of illness are associated only in those countries whose lower classes have serious subsistence problems which are not sufficiently alleviated by public assistance. Certainly this is the picture revealed by the data just presented. Japan has the steepest increase in illness with lowered social class. The United States during the depression had a less pronounced difference, Great Britain of 12 years ago still less (before the full impact of the National Health Service), and finally contemporary United States shows little or no social class differences in the prevalence of illness. It may be

[1] For a similar view see C. U. Willie, "A Research Note on the Changing Association Between Infant Mortality and Socioeconomic Status," *Social Forces,* 37 (1958–1959), pp. 221–227.

[2] D. M. Wilner, *et al., The Housing Environment and Family Life,* Baltimore: The Johns Hopkins Press, 1962.

[3] Morris, *op. cit.,* p. 20, 39.

assumed that had comparable data been available for an earlier era or for less developed nations, much stronger relationships between social class and illness would have been demonstrated.

Proof of the changing association between social class and illness is found in the effect of housing upon illness. Factors associated with poor housing were once related to high rates of illness. But our mode of living has so changed and the quality of public health measures so improved, that a recent experiment in Baltimore showed that good housing had a negligible effect on reducing illness.[2] It is interesting to note that the tables presented and not the text itself make this point abundantly clear. The authors themselves are reluctant to admit that the equation of bad housing with poor health no longer holds true.

TABLE 6. *Number of Days Away from Work or Confined to House* per Month per 100 Men and Women in Great Britain, According to the Weekly Income of the Head of Household (1951)*

Weekly income (in pounds)	SEX	
	Men	Women
Under 3	198	139
3–5	179	133
5–7.10	112	100
7.10–10	76	97
10 or more	72	91

* For housewives.
Source: Same as Table 1.

Finally, the specific diseases most prevalent in the population have changed. Mass immunization, better sanitation, and more immediate medical attention have drastically cut down the prevalence of diseases such as typhoid, rheumatic heart, and bronchitis, that were once the scourge of the lower classes. Large scale epidemics are controlled. Mortality from the "new" diseases such as coronary heart condition, cancer of the bronchus and duodenal ulcers are said by J. N. Morris not to be related to social class but to "personal habits."[3] These may be interpreted to mean social factors other than class. For example, the intervening variables such as adequacy of parental care and social dependence in the Newcastle study of child illnesses previously mentioned are much stronger in their effects than social class. And in the case of tuberculosis, lack of parental care but not social class is associated with the illness.

Social class and feeling sick

Getting a disease, as indicated by rates of illness reported in sample surveys, has been discussed. The reaction to illness is a different matter altogether. Earlier, it was suggested that one reason public health experts have by and large missed this trend toward reduced social class differences in disease is that lower classes continue to *feel* sicker than persons of higher rank. There is a fairly linear trend between income and days away from work for both the United States and Great Britain. Persons of lower income who have a chronic condition are more likely to say they are limited in their activity as a result of their condition. There is a linear relationship (not shown) between income and the average number of days persons in the United States spend in bed each year because of illness.[1] Observe that the relationships shown are fairly strong.

These indicators of illness are much more sensitive to "how much does it hurt" than the mere reporting of conditions. Indeed Woolsey, who has studied the relationship between medical examinations and home

TABLE 7. *Number of Days Away from Work per Year per Currently Employed Men and Women in the United States, According to Family Income (1959–1960)*

Yearly income (in dollars)	SEX	
	Men	Women
Under 2,000	9.8	6.5
2,000–4,000	6.4	6.6
4,000–7,000	4.5	5.4
7,000 or more	4.9	4.9

Source: U.S. National Health Service, "Currently Employed Persons, Illness and Work Loss Days, July 1959–June 1960," *Public Health Service Publication 584, Series C, No. 7*, 1962.

TABLE 8. *Percent of Persons in the United States Who Have One or More Chronic Conditions Who Are Limited in Their Activity, According to Income and Age (1957–1958)*

Age in years	FAMILY INCOME PER YEAR IN DOLLARS			
	Under 2,000	2,000– 4,000	4,000– 7,000	7,000 or more
Under 15	13.0	9.2	7.1	7.0
15–44	24.3	17.0	13.6	11.5
45–64	41.2	31.4	23.0	18.9

Source: Same as Table 5 (percentages recalculated to the base of the number of persons with one or more conditions).

interviews believes that "the measurement of illness . . . has some of the characteristics of the measurement of attitudes."[2] And when it comes to actual attitudes, such as requests of respondents to state whether they are

in good or poor health, there is a strong, almost linear relationship, between social class indicators and responses of "poor health."[3] A recent study which both asked subjective questions about health and checked for chronic conditions shows no relationship between occupation and number of conditions, but even with number of conditions held constant, there is a strong relationship between manual occupations and reports of ill health.[4]

The contention of the present author is that lower class persons do not have more diseases or conditions. They are, however, more concerned about illness. Using a number of appropriate controls, including the adequacy of local medical facilities, Levine shows that lower class persons are more fearful of serious diseases.[5] What is more, home survey respondents of lower income or education in various studies are either *more* likely or hardly less likely than higher class persons to match a physician's report of conditions.[6] Since one expects lower class persons to be less knowledgeable about medicine, and hence less reliable in their reports, these incredible findings cannot be understood unless one assumes that lower class respondents are also more concerned about their illnesses, and hence pay more attention to their symptoms. These findings show that the lack of relationship between the presence of a condition and lower class membership previously shown is not a spurious relationship caused by poor lower class reporting.

To what extent is lower class concern with the experience of ill health a matter of cultural attitude and to what extent is it a product of social circumstances? There is a good deal of theory and some supporting evidence to indicate that lower class persons in the United States are more prone to think in physical terms and more likely to express their emotional anxieties in physical forms.[7] But there is also considerable reason to

---

[1] U.S. National Health Service, "Disability Days, United States, July 1959–June 1960," *Public Health Service Publication 485, Series B, No. 29*, 1961.

[2] T. D. Woolsey, "The Health Interview, the Respondent and the Interviewer in the U.S. National Health Survey," 1959 AAPOR Conference, processed.

[3] G. Gurin, *et al.*, *Americans View Their Mental Health*, New York: Basic Books, 1960, Chapter 7. L. F. Schnore, and J. D. Cowhig, "Some Correlates of Reported Health in Metropolitan Areas," *Social Problems*, 3 (1959–1960), pp. 218–226.

[4] National Opinion Research Center, Study No. 383, as analyzed by Ursula Dibble.

[5] G. N. Levine, "Anxiety About Illness: Psychological and Social Bases," *Journal of Health and Human Behavior*, 3 (1962), pp. 30–34.

[6] Trussel, *op. cit.*, p. 365; U.S. National Health Survey, "Reporting of Hospitalization in the Health Survey Interview," *Public Health Service Publication 584, Series D, No. 4*, 1961; U.S. National Health Survey, "Health Interview Responses Compared with Medical Records," *Public Health Service Publication 584, Series D, No. 5*, 1961; U.S. National Health Service, "Comparisons of Hospitalization Reporting in Three Survey Procedures," *Public Health Service Publication 584, Series D, No. 8*, 1963.

[7] D. R. Miller and G. E. Swanson, *Inner Conflict and Defense*, New York: Henry Holt, 1960.

believe that objective factors also influence lower class concern with ill health.

First, the effects of institutional feedback are quite strong. For any given condition, lower class persons are more reluctant to consult a doctor.[1] The expense involved must be a major factor, for in the United States lower class persons visit doctors less often.[2] This is not true in Great Britain with its National Health Service or in New York City with its widespread clinic facilities.[3]

Second, precisely because of their reluctance or inability to use physicians lower class persons may be more fearful of disease. As Levine puts it,

> The better educated . . . are less apt to tremble in the face of unforeseen . . . events. . . . For them, the onset of grave illness demands clear-cut steps: the very best doctors are to be summoned, the newest remedies and machinery of medical science are to be marshalled. The less educated are, as well, less in control of their world; less confident of their ability to cope successfully with serious illness, they are more unnerved when confronted with its possibility.[4]

Objectively, this situation may result in longer and more "serious" illnesses and a higher death rate for lower class persons even though their rate of exposure to disease is about the same as for higher classes.

As rates of absenteeism caused by illness indicate, sickness may have different consequences for the manual laborer than for white collar persons.[5] This paper could be written if the author had a broken leg. He

could not drive a truck in that condition, however. And absenteeism means loss of pay for wage earners, something to be anxious about. It may also be true, however, that working class persons are less motivated to go to work when barriers such as illness are present. The interaction between attitudes to work, anxiety about supporting one's family and barriers to performing one's job remains to be studied.

Conclusion

The fact is that the lower classes are not more likely than the middle class to have a disease or condition but they do react more violently to it and are more concerned about it. Nonetheless, neither sociologists nor public health researchers have for the most part taken proper note of the split between getting sick and reacting to it.[6] For example, in a recent general review of chronic illness the author does not even mention his own study which shows no relationship between class and the prevalence of illness.[7] Rather, he shows that some few chronic illnesses diagnosed in hospitals are related to living in lower class neighborhoods. Yet, he avoids making an overall statement about chronic illness and social class.

There are obviously some problems here in the sociology of sociology. First, there is a serious problem in the interpretation of tables which is caused by a lack of satisfactory non-parametric measures of association and analyses of variance. Second, we have fallen prey to the fallacy of forgetting why we thought social class was related to illness in the first place. "Vice and misery" were responsible, not class *per se*. The importance of specifying the meaning of all the variables in the low-social-class-equals-illness equation cannot be overstressed, for it is only through clarity that we can avoid falling prey to our own preconceptions. Finally, we should not be afraid of the consequences of our findings. Policy makers probably will not cease to support medical care for lower class persons because we say that they are not especially sick. Public housing will continue to be built even if it no longer directly affects disease. Research money may yet be obtained even if social class is not related to the prevalence of illness. The present paper concludes that social factors are important in the experience of ill health, although not in the gross fashion that had been imagined.

[1] E. L. Koos, *The Health of Regionville*, New York: Columbia University Press, 1954, p. 30; National Opinion Research Center, Survey No. 367.

[2] U.S. National Health Survey, "Volume of Physician Visits, United States, July 1957–June 1959," *Public Health Service Publication 584*, Series B, No. 19, 1960.

[3] Logan, *op. cit.*; Suchman, *op. cit.*

[4] *Op. cit.*, p. 30.

[5] Britten, *op. cit.*; Logan, *op. cit.*; U.S. National Health Service, *Public Health Publication 584*, Series C, No. 7, *op. cit.*

[6] For an exception, see G. S. Goldstein and P. F. Wehrle, "The Influence of Socioeconomic Factors on the Distribution of Hepatitis in Syracuse, New York," *American Journal of Public Health*, 49 (1959), pp. 473–480.

[7] S. Graham, "Social Factors in Relation to Chronic Illnesses," in H. E. Freeman, *et al.* (eds.), *Handbook of Medical Sociology*, Englewood: Prentice Hall, 1963.

Elections: The Expression of the Democratic Class Struggle

Seymour Martin Lipset

IN EVERY MODERN democracy, conflict among different groups is expressed through political parties which basically represent a "democratic translation of the class struggle."[1] Even though many parties renounce the principle of class conflict or loyalty, an analysis of their appeals and their support suggests that they do represent the interests of different classes. On a world scale, the principal generalization which can be made is that parties are primarily based on either the lower classes or the middle and upper classes. This generalization even holds true for the American parties, which have traditionally been considered an exception to the class-cleavage pattern of Europe. The Democrats from the beginning of their history have drawn more support from the lower strata of the society, while the Federalist, Whig, and Republican parties have held the loyalties of the more privileged groups.[2]

There have been important exceptions to these generalizations, of course, and class is only one of the structural divisions in society which is related to party support. The fact that many interests and groups which are not social classes take part in the party struggle does not vitiate the thesis that "the rationale of the party-system depends on the alignment of opinion from right to left," as the sociologist and political philosopher Robert MacIver has pointed out. "The right is always·the party sector associated with the interests of the upper or dominant classes, the left the sector expressive of the lower economic or social classes, and the center that of the middle classes. Historically this criterion seems acceptable. The conservative right has defended entrenched prerogatives, privileges and powers; the left has attacked them. The right has been more favorable to the aristocratic position, to the hierarchy of birth or of wealth; the left has fought for the equalization of advantage or of opportunity, for the claims of the less advantaged. Defense and attack have met, under democratic conditions, not in the name of class but in the name of principle; but the opposing principles have broadly corresponded to the interests of the different classes."[3]

[1] This apt phrase was taken from the title of the book by Dewey Anderson and Percy Davidson, *Ballots and the Democratic Class Struggle* (Stanford: Stanford University Press, 1943). This book and the earlier one by the sociologist Stuart A. Rice, *Quantitative Methods in Politics* (New York: Alfred A. Knopf, 1928) deserve to stand as the first American classics of the political-behavior field. Rice did the first panel (repeat interview) study in 1924, made the first statistical studies of the sources of voting behavior by legislators, and correlated changes in party support over periods of time with changes in the business cycle. Anderson and Davidson also analyzed who among voters changed their party in the early 1930s.

[2] See my "Classes and Parties in American Politics," *Political Man*, 303-331, for a more detailed analysis of American politics.

[3] Robert M. MacIver, *The Web of Government* (New York: Macmillan, 1947), pp. 216, 315. It is interesting to note that Talcott Parsons, whose sociology has often been criticized for

Reprinted from *Political Man* (N.Y.: Doubleday and Co., Anchor Edition, 1963), pp. 230-278, by permission of the publisher.

Such terms as "left," "liberal", and "progressive," and their opposites, "right," "conservative," and "reactionary," have been defined on the basis of many different issues — political democracy versus monarchy, the free market system versus traditional economic restrictions, secularism versus clericalism, agrarian reform versus landlordism and urban exploitation of

[1] M. Duverger, *Political Parties* (London: Methuen and Co., 1954), pp. 215–216, 228–239; M. Duverger, "Public Opinion and Political Parties in France," *American Political Science Review*, 46 (1952), pp. 1069–1078. Of course, this groups together parties which have quite different approaches to social change and which may in practice be bitterly hostile toward one another. It ignores the question of the finer degrees of "left" and "right" and neglects other issues which at times cut completely across the left-right dimension as defined here, such as regional autonomy vs. centralism, national self-determination vs. imperialism, and, most recently, political democracy vs. totalitarianism.

[2] See also Edward Shils, "Authoritarianism: 'Right' and 'Left'," in R. Christie and M. Jahoda, eds., *Studies in the Scope and Method of "The Authoritarian Personality"* (Glencoe: The Free Press, 1954), pp. 24–49.

deprecating problems of conflict and overemphasizing the degree of cohesion in society, has stressed the need to analyze American political history and voting contests in terms of an enduring conflict between the left and the right: those oriented to the lower strata and change, and those more concerned with stability and the needs of the more well to do. See his "Voting and the Equilibrium of the American Political System," in E. Burdick and A. Brodbeck, eds., *American Voting Behavior* (Glencoe: The Free Press, 1959), p. 88.

the countryside, social reform versus *laissez-faire*, socialism versus capitalism. The parties and social groups which have been "left" on one of these issues have by no means always been "left" on another, and the "center" has emerged to oppose both left and right parties. Nevertheless, at any given period and place it is usually possible to locate parties on a left to right continuum.[1]

The issue of equality and social change has been a dominant one in most countries over the last two or three generations, and overlaps the older left-right issues like democracy versus monarchy and clericalism versus secularism. The most significant issue cutting across the left-right dimension today is political democracy versus totalitarianism which was discussed earlier.[2] In some countries the great majority of the traditional leftist vote goes to totalitarian Communist parties, while in others the traditional centrist and rightist vote has gone to various forms of "fascism." But even in such cases the economic and stratification left-right issues are probably much in the minds of the rank-and-file voters. More than anything else the party struggle is a conflict among classes, and the most impressive single fact about political party support is that in virtually every economically developed country the lower-income groups vote mainly for parties of the left, while the higher-income groups vote mainly for parties of the right.

T A B L E I . *Support of Political Parties in France among Different Occupational Groups*

1956*

	Industrial workers	Agric. workers	White collar	Civil servants and teachers	Merchant	Farm owner	Professional
Communist	39%	37%	16%	14%	7%	5%	11%
Socialist	31	19	33	48	21	17	23
Radical	11	13	7	21	12	13	20
M.R.P. (Catholic)	8	9	21	9	17	14	13
Independent	3	17	11	3	21	45	20
U.R.A.S. (De Gaulle)	4	—	10	5	3	4	8
Poujade	4	4	2	—	19	2	5
Total	100%	99%	100%	100%	100%	100%	100%
(N)	(169)	(67)	(61)	(58)	(81)	(180)	(64)

* Computed by author from cards of a national opinion survey conducted in May 1956 by the Institut national d'études démographiques. I am indebted to Alain Girard for use of the data.

1954†

Occupation	INDUSTRIAL WORKERS			FARMERS			
Economic level	B Above average	C	D	A	B Above average	C	D
	Above average	Average	Poor	Wealthy	Above average	Average	Poor
Party choice							
Communist	18%	40%	45%	4%	9%	27%	43%
Socialist	41	27	22	12	28	14	10
Radical	4	7	5	9	12	24	10
M.R.P.	17	7	10	12	12	10	10
Independent	18	15	18	60	30	23	26
R.P.F. (De Gaulle)	2	5	—	3	8	1	—
Total	100%	101%	100%	100%	99%	99%	99%

† Recomputed from J. Stoetzel, "Voting Behavior in France," *British Journal of Sociology*, 4 (1955), pp. 118–119.

TABLE 2. *Occupation and Party Choice in Italy**
(*1953 — Males Only*)

OCCUPATION

	Employers professionals	FARM				Artisan	White collar	WORKERS (SOCIOECONOMIC LEVELS)		
		Large owner	Small owner	Share tenant	Farm labor			Middle	Upper-lower	Lower
Communist	—%	5%	4%	33%	58%	7%	5%	24%	31%	53%
Nenni Left Socialist	6	5	4	10	11	17	3	16	32	25
Saragat Right Socialist	11	5	15	3	2	15	26	12	13	3
Republican	2	5	—	—	—	4	—	4	1	—
Christian Democrat	41	29	41	33	17	23	42	36	10	9
Liberal	22	29	10	2	—	4	—	4	—	3
Monarchist	6	14	10	8	—	15	13	—	5	3
Neo-Fascist (M.S.I.)	11	9	15	11	12	15	11	4	8	3
Total per cent	99%	101%	99%	100%	100%	100%	100%	100%	100%	100%
(N)	(46)	(21)	(71)	(61)	(64)	(53)	(38)	(25)	(78)	(32)

* Computed by author from cards of a national opinion survey conducted by International Public Opinion Research for the M.I.T. Center for International Studies.

The differences in political preference between lower- and upper-income groups which are typical of many countries are illustrated in Tables 1 and 2 which report on the support of French and Italian parties. In both countries the industrial and agricultural workers give strong support to the Communists, and in Italy to the left (Nenni) socialists as well, and the middle and upper classes back the parties of the center and the right.

Though this broad pattern holds, there is a great amount of variation within income groups. In the middle-income groups white-collar workers and teachers give strong support to the moderate socialists in France and the Saragat (right-wing) socialists in Italy. The considerable variation within lower-income groups in the two countries is also shown in these tables. The lower the economic level of the worker, the more likely he is to vote Communist. The higher-income workers prefer the moderate socialist parties or the center parties.

The same pattern holds in countries with stable two-party systems. As Table 3 shows, in Great Britain the higher one goes in the social structure, the smaller the support for the Labor party, until among top business-men and higher-level professionals the party is supported by less than 10 per cent of the class. Almost identical patterns differentiate the backing of the Democrats and Republicans in the United States.

Further striking evidence of the pervasiveness of the effect of class position on political attitudes comes from a country in which real party competition does not exist: Communist Poland. In 1957 the young Polish sociologist Andrzej Malewski conducted a public opinion survey on attitudes concerning the proper level of differences in income for different occupations — an issue which in capitalist countries is strongly linked to leftist or conservative views. As in the capitalist countries he found "that there is a strong correlation between the incomes of people and their views concerning a maximum scale of income differences. . . . The poll

shows that factory workers, technicians, and certain groups of the intelligentsia with low salaries (teachers, post office workers, social service officials, etc.) are in favour of egalitarianism. On the other hand, an unfavourable attitude prevails among people of whom many have possibilities of high incomes." At the extremes, 54 per cent of the Polish workers interviewed

TABLE 3. *Estimated Percentages of Persons in Different Occupations Voting Labor or Conservative, Great Britain, 1951**

	Conservative (%)	Labor (%)
Business group		
Top business	80	8
Middle business	73	10
Small business	64	15
Managerial	65	19
Professional group		
Higher professional	78	6
Lower professional	52	24
White collar group		
Higher office	63	13
Lower office	48	29
Intermediate group	41	39
Manual workers	28	51
Whole adult population	40	41

* John Bonham, *The Middle Class Vote* (London: Faber & Faber, 1954), pp. 129 and 173. The figures for the manual workers were compiled from a graph on p. 173. All figures were estimated from survey data from the British Institute of Public Opinion. The difference between the per cent secured by the two main parties and 100 per cent is accounted for by nonvoters and third-party voters.

favored "relatively equal incomes" as contrasted with 20 per cent of the executives. Fifty-five per cent of the latter were strongly against sharply narrowing the income gap, as compared with only 8 per cent of the manual workers. So in a Communist country, too, the struggle between the more and the less privileged is reflected in attitudes comparable to those voiced by similarly placed strata in the West. The one major difference is that in a Communist country "both those in favor of the limitation of income scale span and those opposing it often use the traditional slogans of the left."[1]

The simplest explanation for this widespread pattern is simple economic self-interest. The leftist parties represent themselves as instruments of social change in the direction of equality; the lower-income groups support them in order to become economically better off, while the higher-income groups oppose them in order to maintain their economic advantages. The statistical facts can then be taken as evidence of the importance of class factors in political behavior.

This relationship between class position (as measured by education, income, status, power, occupation, or property status) and political opinions or party choice is far from consistent, however. Many poor people vote conservative and some wealthy ones are socialists or Communists. Part of the explanation of these deviations has already been pointed out: other characteristics and group affiliations such as religious belief are more salient in particular situations than high or low social and economic position. But the deviations are also a consequence of the complexity of the stratification system itself. In modern society, men are subjected to a variety of experiences and pressures which have conflicting political consequences because men have disparate positions in the class structure. Men may hold power, like some civil servants, but have a low income or status; they may enjoy high occupational prestige, like many intellectuals, but receive low income; they may enjoy a relatively high income, but have low social status like members of some ethnic minorities or *nouveaux riches* businessmen, and so forth. Some of their social positions may predispose them to be conservative, while others favor a more leftist political outlook. When faced with such conflicting social pressures, some men will respond more to one than to another, and therefore appear to deviate from the pattern of class voting.

These conflicting and overlapping social positions probably injure the leftist lower-class-based parties more than they do the conservative right. Men are constantly struggling to see themselves favorably, and some of their status-attributes will produce a favorable self-evaluation, others a negative one. It seems logical to assume that men will arrange their

impressions of their environment and themselves so as to maximize their sense of being superior to others. Thus the white-collar worker will stress the identification of white-collar work with middle-class status (a point to be discussed further later); the low-income white worker will regard himself as superior to the Negro, and so forth. A variety of evidence gathered in the course of research on social mobility indicates that those who are occupationally upwardly mobile seek to get rid of the characteristics which still link them to their past status. The man who succeeds will in fact often change his neighborhood, seek to find new, higher-status friends, perhaps leave his church for one whose members are higher in status, and also vote more conservatively. The more conservative parties have the advantage of being identified with the more prestigeful classes in the population, an asset which helps to overcome the left's appeal to the economic interests of the lower strata.

Although it is not always possible to predict whether a right or a left political direction will result from specific status-discrepancies, the concept itself points up sources of change in political values flowing from the tensions of contradictory social positions. A discrepancy in status may even lead an old but declining upper class to be more liberal in its political orientation. For example, most observers of British politics have suggested that the emergence of Tory socialism, the willingness of British nineteenth-century conservatism to enact reforms which benefited the working class, was a consequence of the felt hostility of the old English landed aristocracy to the rising business class, which was threatening its status and power. Some of the sources of comparable American upper-class liberalism are discussed in more detail in *Political Man*.

But although variations in the political behavior of the more privileged strata constitute one of the more fascinating problems of political analysis, the available reliable evidence which permits us to specify why people differ in their political allegiances is largely limited to the largest segments of the population, particularly workers and farmers. Public opinion surveys and studies of the voting patterns of different rural districts can deal statistically with different types of workers and farmers in ways that cannot as yet be done on a comparative international level for most sections of the urban middle and upper classes. This chapter focuses, therefore, on the politics of the lower and more numerous strata.

Table 4 presents a summary of the social characteristics that are related to these variations within the lower-income group, i.e., those whose standard of living ranges from poor to just adequate by local middle-class standards — most workers, working farmers, lower white-collar workers, etc. In comparing international political behavior, it is difficult to make a more precise classification.

These generalizations are made on the basis of having examined public opinion or survey data from a large

---

[1] The quotations and the statistics are from an apparently as yet unpublished report by Andrzej Malewski which is translated in part in Leopold Lebedz, *Sociology and Communism 1957–1958* (London: Soviet Survey, 1959), p. 10. A more extensive report of this study may be found in Zeigniew Socha, "Postawy wobec egalitaryzmu," (Attitudes toward egalitarianism), *Przeglad Kulturalny*, No. 3 (333), Warsaw, January 15, 1959. In Denmark, "the Social Democratic Party increases monotonically in relative popularity with decreasing social status, while exactly the opposite regularity applies to the Conservatives," K. Svalastoga, *Prestige, Class and Mobility* (Copenhagen: Scandinavian Universities Press, 1959), pp. 264–265.

number of countries including the United States, Argentina, Chile, Brazil, Canada, Australia, Japan, India, Finland, Norway, Sweden, Denmark, Germany, the Netherlands, Belgium, France, Austria, Italy, Great Britain, and Hungary.[1]

TABLE 4. *Social Characteristics Correlated with Variations in Leftist Voting in the Lower-Income Groups within Different Countries**

Higher leftist vote	Lower leftist vote
Larger cities	Smaller towns, country
Larger plants	Smaller plants
Groups with high unemployment rates	Groups with low unemployment rates
Minority ethnic or religious groups	Majority ethnic or religious groups
Men	Women
Economically advanced regions	Economically backward regions
Manual workers	White-collar workers
Specific occupations:	Specific occupations:
Miners	Servants, service workers
Fishermen	Peasant, subsistence farmers
Commercial farmers	
Sailors, longshoremen	
Forestry workers	
Less skilled workers	More skilled workers

* The major exceptions to some of these patterns are discussed below.

Left voting: a response to group needs

Leftist voting is generally interpreted as an expression of discontent, an indication that needs are not being met. Students of voting behavior have suggested the following needs as central:

1) The need for security of income. This is quite closely related to the desire for higher income as such; however, the effect of periodic unemployment or a collapse of produce prices, for example, seems to be important in itself.

2) The need for satisfying work — work which provides the opportunity for self-control and self-expression and which is free from arbitrary authority.

3) The need for status, for social recognition of one's value and freedom from degrading discrimination in social relations.

In terms of this list, let us see how various groups vote.

INSECURITY OF INCOME

Certain occupational groups in the lower-income category suffer from extreme insecurity of income — one-crop farmers, fishermen, miners, and lumbermen — and these groups have histories of high rates of leftist voting.

The prototype of a "boom-and-bust" agricultural economy is the North American wheat area. Depression or drought, or both, have hit the wheat belt in every generation since it was settled. Many studies of the

political behavior of this region have been made, and all agree that the wheat farmers are the most leftist of all farmers in times of economic crisis. They have formed the core of the great agrarian radical movements — the Greenbackers, Populists, and Non-Partisan League in the United States, and in Canada the Progressives, Social Credit, and the Cooperative Commonwealth Federation.[2] The only socialist government in North America above the local level is the Cooperative Commonwealth Federation provincial government of Saskatchewan, a one-crop wheat area.

Studies of one-crop commercial farmers in other parts of the world show that they too tend to support periodic protest movements which are often (as we have seen earlier) authoritarian in character.[3] In contrast, farmers whose crops are diversified, who depend on local rather than world markets, and even very poor subsistence farmers whose level of income is steady and reliable tend to support conservative parties.

Fishermen selling to national or international markets are in much the same position as the wheat farmers, and commercial fishermen vote left around the world. In Norway, the first labor representatives in the Storting were elected from a fishing district.[4] In Iceland, the fishermen support the second strongest Communist party in Scandinavia.[5] André Siegfried in his pioneer study of voting statistics in western France in 1913

[1] Many of the statements made in this chapter are based on as yet unpublished results of analyses of studies made by academic or commercial survey research organizations who have either turned over duplicate copies of their IBM cards to me, or have made new computations at my request. There are a number of good compendia of such data from various countries. These include J. J. de Jong, *Overheid en Onderdaan* (Wageningen: N. V. Gebr, Zomer and Keunings Uitgeversmij, 1956), esp. pp. 75–121, *passim*; Michael P. Fogarty, *Christian Democracy in Western Europe* (London: Routledge and Kegan Paul, 1957), esp. pp. 352–376; Hadley Cantril, ed., *Public Opinion, 1935–1946* (Princeton: Princeton University Press, 1951), esp. pp. 602, 623, 627, and 630 for the United States; p. 197 for Great Britain.

[2] S. M. Lipset, *Agrarian Socialism* (Berkeley: University of California Press, 1950); J. D. Hicks, *The Populist Revolt* (Minneapolis: University of Minnesota Press, 1931); S. A. Rice, *Farmers and Workers in American Politics* (New York: Columbia University Press, 1924), Chap. II; V. O. Key, Jr., *Politics, Parties, and Pressure Groups* (New York: Crowell, 4th ed., 1952), Chap. II; C. B. MacPherson, *Democracy in Alberta* (Toronto: University of Toronto Press, 1953).

[3] A. Siegfried, *Tableau politique de la France de l'ouest sous la troisième république* (Paris: Librairie Armand Colin, 1913), Chap. 44; R. Heberle, *From Democracy to Nazism* (Baton Rouge: Louisiana State University Press, 1943), Chap. III; Charles P. Loomis and J. Allen Beegle, "The Spread of German Nazism in Rural Areas," *American Sociological Review*, 2 (1946), pp. 724–734; S. S. Nilson, *Histoire et sciences politiques* (Bergen: Chr. Michelsens Institut, 1950); S. S. Nilson, "Aspects de la vie politique en Norvege," *Revue française de science politique*, 3 (1953), pp. 556–579.

[4] E. Bull, *Arbeiderklassen i Norsk Historie* (Oslo: Tilden Norsk Forlag, 1948).

[5] S. S. Nilson, "Le Communisme dans les pays du nord — les élections depuis 1945," *Revue française de science politique*, 1 (1951), pp. 167–180. Rudolf Heberle reports on the success of the leftist parties among the fishermen in Schleswig-Holstein in *From Democracy to Nazism, op. cit.*, p. 104.

found the fishermen to be a strong leftist group.[1] The fishermen of British Columbia are a strong source of support for the leftist unions.[2] In the United States the West Coast fishermen are traditionally militant and have been organized in a Communist-dominated union, even though they are mostly owners or part owners of their own boats. Great Lakes fishermen have been disproportionately Democratic. And in Great Britain fishing districts are Labor party strongholds.[3]

Miners are among the working-class groups most exposed to unemployment, and the fact that they are one of the strongest leftist groups throughout the world has already been noted. In the British elections of 1950, the thirty-seven Labor party candidates, sponsored by the National Union of Mineworkers, were elected with a median vote of 73 per cent.[4] In Canada, the only eastern district which has elected a socialist on different occasions is a coal-mining area in Nova Scotia; the only Quebec constituency ever to elect a socialist to the provincial legislature was a metal-mining area. Studies in the United States show that coal miners are among the most consistent supports of the Democractic party.[5]

In France, where workers in nationalized industries elect representatives to Works Councils, the under-ground workers in coal mines gave the Communist-controlled C.G.T. 80 per cent of their votes — a higher figure than that for any other group, including railroad, rapid transit, public utility, shipyard, aircraft, and automobile workers. Data from Germany indicate that in pre-1933 elections as well as in elections to Works Councils in the 1950s, mining areas gave heavy support to the Communists.[6] An ecological analysis of voting in Chile in 1947 showed that the small Communist party had its greatest strength in mining areas. In the coal, copper, and other mineral mining areas the Communists received from 60 to 80 per cent of the votes as compared to only 10 per cent in the country as a whole.[7]

Lumber workers are also subject to severe cyclical fluctuations. In Sweden lumbering areas give the Communists a higher vote than do the large industrial centers.[8] Analysis of the results of an Austrian provincial election in 1952 showed that 85 per cent of the forestry workers voted for the Socialist party.[9] California and Michigan data indicate that lumber areas give more support to leftist candidates than do other areas.[10] and lumber workers were prominent in the old Industrial Workers of the World (I.W.W.).

An occupation which in many respects resembles lumbering both in economic insecurity and social isolation is sheepshearing, especially in Australia. Australia has tremendous sheep stations which are usually located far from population centers. The sheepshearers live in camps somewhat like lumber camps, and stay at a station for some time cutting the wool from the sheep. The workers are migratory, moving from one sheep station to another. They are reported to have strong group-consciousness and solidarity. Though there are no voting data reported which have separated out the votes of the sheep station workers, reports on their union behavior suggest that they are militant and radical.[11]

A general depression makes economic insecurity widespread, and in the elections of 1932 and 1936 the counties in the U.S. which were hardest hit by the Depression were the most strongly pro-Roosevelt. Survey data pinpoint the fact that in 1936 and 1940, of all low-income people, those on relief were the most strongly Democratic — over 80 per cent.[12] A study of political attitudes in 1944 found that among American manual workers who had never been unemployed, 43 per cent were "conservative" as compared with only 14 per cent conservative among those who had experienced more than a year of unemployment.[13]

Comparable findings are reported from Great Britain — the higher the unemployment in an area, the stronger the Labor vote. Moreover, the extent of unemployment in the 1930s was still affecting voting during the full-employment year of 1950 — the districts that showed the least decline in Labor vote between 1945 and 1950 were those with the most depression-time unemployment.[14] Similarly in Finland, areas with the most depression-time unemployment gave highest support to the Communist

[1] See also B. Leger, *Les opinions politiques des provinces françaises*, 2nd ed. (Paris: Recuiel Sirey, 1936), pp. 49–50.

[2] S. Jamieson and P. Gladstone, "Unionism in the Fishing Industry in British Columbia," *Canadian Journal of Economics and Political Science*, 16 (1950), pp. 1–11 and 146–171.

[3] J. K. Pollock and S. J. Eldersveld, *Michigan Politics in Transition* (Ann Arbor: University of Michigan Press, Michigan Governmental Studies, No. 10, 1942), p. 54. For the behavior of British fishermen see *The Economist* (Aug. 15, 1959), p. 435.

[4] H. G. Nicholas, *The British General Election of 1950* (London: Macmillan, 1951), pp. 42, 61. See also J. F. S. Ross, *Parliamentary Representation* (New Haven: Yale University Press, 1944), pp. 58–77.

[5] H. F. Gosnell, *Grass Roots Politics: National Voting Behavior of Typical States* (Washington: America Council on Public Affairs, 1942), pp. 31–32; see also Malcolm Moos, *Politics, Presidents, and Coattails* (Baltimore: The Johns Hopkins Press, 1952), pp. 47–48.

[6] O. K. Flechtheim, *Die Kommunistische Partei Deutschlands in der Weimarer Republik* (Offenbach am Main: Bollwerk-Verlag Karl Drott, 1948), p. 211, for pre-1933 data; for statistics on Works Councils elections in the 1950s see Michael Fogarty, *op. cit.*, p. 213.

[7] Ricardo Cruz Coke, *Geografia electoral de Chile* (Santiago de Chile: Editorial del Pacifico, S.A., 1952), pp. 53, 81–82.

[8] S. S. Nilson, "Le Communisme dans les pays du nord — les élections depuis 1945," *op. cit.*, pp. 167–180.

[9] Walter B. Simon, *The Political Parties of Austria* (Ph.D. thesis, Department of Sociology, Columbia University, 1957, Microfilm 57-2894 University Microfilms, Ann Arbor, Michigan), p. 263.

[10] H. F. Gosnell, *op. cit.*, p. 77, and J. K. Pollock and S. J. Eldersveld, *op. cit.*, p. 54.

[11] See T. C. Truman, *The Pressure Groups, Parties and Politics of the Australian Labor Movement* (unpublished M.A. thesis, University of Queensland, 1953), Chap. IV, pp. 70–72.

[12] H. F. Gosnell, *op. cit.*, pp. 3, 32, 37, 90.

[13] R. Centers, *The Psychology of Social Classes* (Princeton: Princeton University Press, 1949), pp. 177–179.

[14] H. G. Nicholas, *op. cit.*, pp. 297–298; Wilma George, "Social Conditions and the Labor Vote in the County Boroughs of England and Wales," *British Journal of Sociology*, 2 (1951), pp. 255–259.

party in 1951–54.[1] In Germany, the extent of unemployment was directly related to the size of the Communist vote in the 1932 elections. A French public opinion poll of 1956 states that 62 per cent of the members of the Communist trade-union movement, the C.G.T., report having been unemployed at some time in the past, as compared to 43 per cent of the members of the socialist *Force Ouvrière*, and 33 per cent of the members of the Catholic C.F.T.C.[2]

The relative conservatism of white-collar workers in the United States may be due to their greater job security during the Depression. Only about 4 per cent of the white-collar workers were unemployed in 1930, as compared to 13 per cent of urban unskilled workers. In 1937, 11 per cent of the former and a quarter of the latter were out of work.[3] In Germany this middle-class group was much more affected by the postwar economic crisis than in the United States. The German white-collar workers tended to turn to the fascist movement rather than to the leftist parties with their doctrinaire emphasis on the proletariat.[4]

UNSATISFYING WORK

Students of working-class movements have often suggested that the nature of the work situation itself, aside from wages and security, is an important factor in creating satisfaction or dissatisfaction. The factory worker spends his days under the control of others, often subject to arbitrary discipline. And workers in mass-production industries with minutely segmented, routine tasks have little opportunity to interest themselves in their work and to exercise creative abilities.[5]

From this it should follow that the more arbitrary the managerial authority and the more monotonous the work, the more discontented the workers would be and the more likely to support political movements aiming at social change. And there is evidence that the larger the industrial plant (and therefore, usually, the more segmented the work) the more leftist the workers. A study of voting in large German cities before 1933 found that the higher the proportion of workers in large plants the higher the Communist vote.[6] A study of the American printing industry has likewise found a relation between political leftism and size of shop.[7]

In general, the more skilled are almost everywhere the more conservative among manual workers. Whether job satisfaction and creativity contribute independently to political behavior over and beyond differences in status and economic conditions is still, however, not proved.

STATUS

Feelings of deprivation and consequent political radicalism on the part of those in lowly occupations are not solely due to the objective economic situation. All societies are stratified by status (prestige) as well as by economic rewards, and while status and income tend to be related, they are far from identical. Status involves invidious distinctions — men and groups defined as superior or inferior to others — and it does not follow from what we know about human behavior that men will accept a low social evaluation with equanimity. Wherever the possibility exists, therefore, people will try either to improve their prestige position through individual efforts (social mobility) or to improve the position of their group through collective action of some sort. And if self-interest describes the motivation flowing from the desire to improve the material conditions of existence, then *resentment* decribes the feelings of lowly placed persons toward the social system and those who are high in prestiges.[8]

The lack of respect with which workers are treated by office personnel, salespeople, clerks, minor officials, etc., and the general failure of middle-class society to recognize the workers' economic contributions and personal abilities undoubtedly contribute to dissatisfaction with the *status quo* and to political leftism.

While low prestige plus low income and high prestige plus high income join together to reinforce leftist or conservative political motivation, situations in which one factor places the individual much higher or lower on relative ranking scales help, as has been already noted, to account for seemingly deviant patterns of behavior. In all societies for which we have data, white-collar workers receive more prestige than manual workers, and identify in many ways (dress, speech, family patterns) with those higher in the system, even when their income is not higher than that of skilled manual workers.[9] And many studies show that the white-collar workers in different countries are much more likely to vote for the more conservative parties than are manual workers — in general, taking a position midway between that of the higher business strata and

[1] Erik Allardt, *Social Struktur och Politisk Aktivitet* (Helsingfors, Söderstrom and Co., 1956), p. 84.

[2] *Réalités*, No. 65, April 1956.

[3] C. W. Mills, *White Collar* (New York, Oxford University Press, 1951), p. 281.

[4] T. Geiger, *Die Soziale Schichtung des Deutschen Volkes* (Stuttgart: Ferdinand Enke, 1932), pp. 109–122; Samuel Pratt, *The Social Basis of Nazism and Communism in Urban Germany* (unpublished M.A. thesis, Department of Sociology, Michigan State University, 1948), Chap. 8.

[5] The difference in job satisfaction between such jobs and those allowing more creativity are documented, with a review of the literature, in R. Blauner, "Attitudes Toward Work," in W. Galenson and S. M. Lipset, eds., *Readings in the Economics and Sociology of Trade Unions* (New York: John Wiley & Sons, 1960).

[6] S. Pratt, *loc. cit.*

[7] Unpublished data from a study of the International Typographical Union. For other details of this study see S. M. Lipset, M. Trow, and J. Coleman, *Union Democracy* (Glencoe: The Free Press, 1956), esp. pp. 150–197, which discuss the differences in environments in small and large shops.

[8] For a more detailed discussion of the reactions to position in the status structure see S. M. Lipset and Hans Zetterberg, "Social Mobility in Industrial Societies," in S. M. Lipset and R. Bendix, *Social Mobility in Industrial Society* (Berkeley: University of California Press, 1959), pp. 60–64.

[9] For a detailed summary of evidence bearing on this point from many countries, see *ibid.*, pp. 14–17.

the manual workers on the left-right continuum.[1] This greater conservatism is not due solely to higher income. A study of voting in the 1949 Norwegian election showed that the vote for leftist parties (Communist and socialist) was almost twice as high among manual workers as it was for white-collar workers on each income level (see Table 5.) A survey study of political affiliation in Germany gave similar results.[2]

TABLE 5. *Percentage Voting for Labor and Communist Parties by Occupational Group and Income in Norway — 1949**

Yearly income in Kroner	Industrial workers	White-collar workers
Under 4,000	56	35
4,000–7,000	70	28
7,000–12,000	69	24
Over 12,000	—†	13

* A. H. Barton, *Sociological and Psychological Implications of Economic Planning in Norway* (unpublished Ph.D. thesis, Department of Sociology, Columbia University, 1954), p. 327.
† Too few cases.

Direct evidence of the importance of the status motive in white-collar political behavior is provided by a study of "class identification" in the United States where 61 per cent of white-collar workers called themselves "middle-class," as against only 19 per cent of manual workers. Among the white-collar workers this self-labeling made a great difference in political attitudes — 65 per cent of those who considered themselves "middle-class" had conservative attitudes, compared with 38 per cent of the "working-class" white-collar workers. Among manual workers, subjective class identification made much less difference in attitudes — 37 per cent of "middle-class" manual workers had conservative attitudes, compared with 25 per cent of the "working-class" workers.[3]

The political role of the white-collar workers was studied intensively in Germany, but unfortunately before the days of sampling survey.[4] Studies using available area voting statistics suggest that the white-collar vote swung from the centrist parties to the Nazis under the impact of the Depression of 1929.[5] A strong correlation existed between the proportion of the unemployed among the white-collar workers in German cities and the Nazi vote.[6] The usual explanation offered by Germans for this is that the Nazis represented a hope for solving the economic crisis and at the same time for maintaining the status position of the white-collar workers, while the Marxist parties offered them economic gains only at the cost of "proletarianization."[7]

Some of the variations in the way workers vote in different countries may possibly be explained by differences in the rigidity of the status-hierarchy. The data on political party choices of Australian, British, American, French, and Italian workers all suggest that the lower the socioeconomic position of a worker, the more likely he is to vote for a party of the left. On the other hand, in Germany and Sweden the lowest stratum of workers is most likely to back the nonlabor oriented parties. In these countries the higher strata within the working class are more prone to support left parties.[8] For each level of skill in a sample of workers in Germany, the workers earning over 250 marks per month were more likely to support left (Socialist and Communist) parties than workers earning less than that amount. Nearly half of the workers in every group supported these parties, but the lowest support was found in the unskilled, low-income group (45 per cent going to those parties) and the highest (65 per cent) in the skilled, better-paid group (see Table 6).

In absence of more detailed investigations of the varying situation of workers in these two countries as compared with others, it would be foolhardy to attempt to explain these striking differences. The one hypothesis which some people more familiar with life in different parts of Europe than I am have suggested is that there is more frustration among the upper levels of the working class in Germany and perhaps Sweden precisely because these nations remain among the most status-differentiated countries in the Western world. The nobility retained power and influence in these countries until well into the twentieth century, and interpersonal relations still reflect a considerable explicit emphasis on status. Superiority and inferiority in status position are expressed in many formal and informal ways. Conversely, Australia,

[1] G. Gallup, *The Gallup Political Almanac for 1948* (Princeton: American Institute of Public Opinion, 1948), p. 9; R. Centers, *op. cit.*, p. 38; E. G. Benson and Evelyn Wicoff, "Voters Pick Their Party," *Public Opinion Quarterly*, 8 (1944), pp. 165–174; L. Harris, *Is There a Republican Majority?* (New York: Harper & Bros., 1954); H. Cantril, *op. cit.*

[2] Institut für Marktforschung und Meinungsforschung, E.M.N.I.D., *Zur Resonanz der Parteien bei Männer und Frauen in den Soziologischen Gruppen* (Bielefeld: mimeographed, no date), pp. 5, 7, 9.

[3] R. Centers, *op. cit.*, pp. 130–132.

[4] T. Geiger, *op. cit.*, pp. 109–122.

[5] W. Dittmann, *Das Politische Deutschland vor Hitler* (Zurich: Europa Verlag, 1945); A. Dix, *Die Deutschen Reichstagswahlen, 1871–1930, und die Wandlungen der Volksgliederung* (Tübingen: J. B. C. Mohr, Paul Siebeck, 1930); W. Stephan, "Zur Soziologie der Nationalsozialistischen Deutschen Arbeiterpartei," *Zeitschrift für Politik*, 20 (1931), pp. 293–300.

[6] S. Pratt, *op. cit.*, Chap. 8.

[7] T. Geiger, *op. cit.*, p. 114.

[8] Similar German findings are also reported in Institut für Marktforschung und Meinungsforschung, E.M.N.I.D., *op. cit.*, and in Divo Institut, *Umfragen 1957* (Frankfurt: Europaiische Verlag-anstalt, 1958), p. 53. Thus three different research institutes report that the more skilled in Germany are more radical than the less skilled. The Divo Institut found these results in both its surveys of the 1953 and 1957 elections. In the latter year 62 per cent of the skilled workers who voted were for the Social Democrats as contrasted with 43 per cent among the semiskilled and unskilled, p. 5. For Sweden see Elis Hastad, *et al.*, eds., *"Gallup" och den Svenska Valjarkaren* (Uppsala: Hugo Gebers Forlag, 1950), pp. 157–170.

Britain, America, and France are nations in which these status differences have declined in importance, given the decline or absence of aristocracy. And an emphasis on status differentiation should affect the more skilled and better-paid workers more than their less privileged class brethren. While the more skilled are better off than other workers, their very economic success makes more obvious to them their rejection by the middle classes. They are in a sense like successful Negroes or Jews in societies which discriminate socially against members of these groups. The more successful among them are more likely to be aware of, and consequently resentful of, their status inferiority. The lower group of workers, Negroes, or Jews, will be less likely to feel deprived of status.

TABLE 6. *Proportion of Male Workers Supporting the Social Democratic and Communist Parties in Germany — 1953**

Skill level and income			
All skilled workers		61%	(230)
Over 250 marks per month	65		(140)
Under 250 marks per month	55		(94)
All semiskilled		58	(209)
Over 250 marks per month	65		(113)
Under 250 marks per month	50		(96)
All unskilled		51	(97)
Over 250 marks per month	59		(42)
Under 250 marks per month	45		(55)

* Computations made for the purposes of this study from IBM cards kindly supplied by the UNESCO Institute, Cologne, Germany, from their survey of the 1953 German population.

Thus the tentative hypothesis may be offered that the more open the status-linked social relations of a given society, the more likely well-paid workers are to become conservatives politically. In an "open" society, relative economic deprivation will differentiate among the workers as it has traditionally done in the United States and Australia. In a more "closed" society, the upper level of the workers will feel deprived and hence support left-wing parties. Whether these hypotheses correspond to the actual facts is a moot question. It is a fact, however, that these differences in political behavior exist. We need more research to account for their sources.

A second prestige hierarchy is based on religious or ethnic differences. Minority religions, nationalities, and races are usually subjected to various forms of social discrimination, and the low-income member of a minority group consequently faces additional obstacles to economic and social achievement. The poor majority group member, on the other hand, may find substitute gratifications in his ethnic or religious "superiority." High-income members of a low-status ethnic or religious group are therefore, as we have noted, in a situation comparable to the upper level of the working class in those countries with "closed" status systems.

In the English-speaking countries, studies show that among the various Christian denominations, the more well-to-do the *average* socioeconomic status of the church members, the more likely the lower-status members are to vote for the more conservative party. In Britain, Australia, Canada, and the United States, workers belonging to the more well-to-do churches like the Anglican (Episcopal in the U.S.) are more likely to back the more conservative party than workers belonging to poorer churches.

Similarly, middle-class voters who belong to a relatively less well-to-do church like the Catholic or the Baptist are more prone to be Laborites or Democrats than their class peers in other denominations. One British study reports that among industrial workers voting in the 1951 elections, the percentage backing the Labor party was 73 among Catholics, 64 among Nonconformists, and 43 among Anglicans. "The proportion of Anglicans who voted Conservative is almost exactly twice as great as the proportion of non-Anglicans who did so; and three-fifths of all the industrial workers who voted Conservative were Anglicans."[1]

In Australia in 1951 and 1955, Gallup Poll data indicate that approximately 50 per cent of the Catholics in urban nonmanual jobs backed the Labor party, as contrasted with less than 30 per cent of the Anglicans in comparable positions. Similarly, among manual workers, Australian Catholics have been more heavily Laborite than any other denomination.[2]

In all of the above countries, Jews, although relatively well-to-do, are politically the least conservative denomination, a pattern which holds as well in many non-English-speaking Western nations. Electoral data in Austria show that the Jewish districts of Vienna, although middle class, were disproportionately Socialist in many elections before 1933.[3] A study of voting in Amsterdam, the Netherlands, also indicated that the predominantly Jewish district of that city was a strong

[1] A. H. Birch, *Small-Town Politics* (London: Oxford University Press, 1959), p. 112; for national data on British voting see H. J. Eysenck, *The Psychology of Politics* (London: Routledge and Kegan Paul, 1954), p. 21, and M. Benney, A. P. Gray, and R. H. Pear, *How People Vote: A Study of Electoral Behavior in Greenwich* (London: Routledge and Kegan Paul, 1956), p. 111; for data dealing with Britain and the United States see Michael Argyle, *Religious Behavior* (Glencoe: The Free Press, 1959), pp. 81–83; for a more detailed discussion of religion and politics in the United States together with further bibliographic references see Chap. 9, pp. 307–308; for published Australian data see Louise Overacker, *The Australian Party System* (New Haven: Yale University Press, 1952), pp. 166–170, 298, 305–306, and Leicester Webb, *Communism and Democracy in Australia* (Melbourne: F. W. Cheshire, 1954), pp. 91–100. The Australian Gallup Poll has made available considerable data which show the relationship between political affiliation and religion. The references to Canada are based on an inspection of unpublished data collected by the Canadian Gallup Poll.

[2] All the Australian Labor parties are considered as Labor for the purposes of this analysis, although the dissident right-wing Labor parties are largely based on the Catholics.

[3] Walter B. Simon, *op. cit.*, pp. 335, 338–341.

Social Democratic center.[1] The leftist voting patterns of the Jews have been explained as flowing from their inferior status position (social discrimination) rather than from elements inherent in their religious creed.[2]

The differential impact of religious affiliation on political allegiances does not flow solely from the current status position of the different denominations. In a number of countries churches which have been established, protected by the state, and linked to the landed aristocracy often provide the base for a religious political party which seeks to defend or restore religious rights and influence against the attacks of more left-wing and anticlerical political movements. Thus in Catholic Europe working-class Catholics have disproportionately voted for the more conservative and Catholic parties, while middle-class Protestants, Jews, and free-thinkers have been more leftist, even to the point of backing Marxist parties.[3]

The close link between political behavior patterns and religious practice in two European countries, France and the Netherlands, may be seen in Table 7. The sharp differences in party choice between those who attend church and those who do not are apparent from the tables. In France, for example, 68 per cent of the practicing Catholics supported either the M.R.P. or the Independent party, both conservative, but 56 per cent of the nonpracticing and 63 per cent of the "indifferent" Catholics supported either the Communists or the Socialists. There were not enough Protestants in the sample to differentiate between degrees of religious practice, but among these members of a formerly persecuted minority, 39 per cent supported the leftist parties, and another 34 per cent backed the Radical party, the liberal anti-clerical party. Among those with no religion 79 per cent supported the Marxist parties.

[1] J. P. Kruijt, *De Onkerkelikheid in Nederland* (Groningen: P. Noordhoff, N. V., 1933), pp. 265, 267.

[2] See Robert Michels, *Political Parties* (Glencoe: The Free Press, 1949), pp. 261–262, for an analysis of the sources of Jewish radicalism in Willhelmine Germany that still seems applicable to other countries.

[3] See Stuart R. Schram, *Protestantism and Politics in France* (Alençon, France: Corbiere and Jugain, 1954), pp. 183–186. For example, 55.5 per cent of the registered voters in the Protestant communes (in the *Gard*) voted Communist or Socialist in 1951, as against only 35.1 per cent in the Catholic communes. On the whole, the Protestant communes are more well-to-do than the Catholic ones. For the best discussion of the characteristics of Catholic and other religious political parties in Europe, see Michael Fogarty, *op. cit.*, Chap. 22.

[4] The full extent of the unity of the religious and political cleavage in the Netherlands is clear from the numbers of persons who do not practice their religion. Whereas in France the number of nonpracticing Catholics was almost as great as those practicing, in the Netherlands they formed only one tenth of the total of Catholics, and the nonpracticing Calvinists were only one sixth of the total of Calvinists. The number of nonpracticing moderate Protestants was almost twice as many as those practicing, but the differences in voting behavior were equally plain. These polls were taken on the basis of random samples of the entire population, so that it is legitimate to infer that the proportion of those practicing their religion is representative.

In the Netherlands information was available on church attendance for the three major religious groups, and here again, striking differences are evident in the voting choices of the different denominations.[4] Fully 94 per cent of the practicing Catholics supported the Catholic party, but only 52 per cent of those nonpracticing did, with 30 per cent of their choices going

TABLE 7. *Religion and Party Choice by Church Attendance*

France — 1956*

	Catholics			Pro-testants	No religion
	Practicing	Non-practicing	In-different		
Communist	2%	17%	18%	5%	49%
Socialist	9	39	45	34	30
Radical	10	17	17	34	8
M.R.P.	34	4	2	7	1
Independent	34	14	12	10	4
R.P.F.	6	3	2	2	1
Poujade	5	6	4	7	6
Total	100%	100%	100%	99%	99%
(N)	(609)	(507)	(168)	(41)	(144)

The Netherlands — 1956†

Party choice	Catholic		Moderate Protestant		Calvinist		No religion
			Church attendance				
	Yes	No	Yes	No	Yes	No	No
Catholic	94%	52%	—%	—%	—%	—%	1%
Socialist	3	30	22	51	2	27	75
Antirevolu-tionary (Calvinist)	—	6	17	6	90	63	—
Christian Historical (Moderate Protestant)	—	—	45	19	3	—	—
Liberal	—	9	7	18	—	—	11
Communist	—	—	—	—	—	—	7
Calvinist Splinter	—	—	5	3	1	5	—
Other	2	3	4	3	4	5	6
Total	99%	100%	100%	100%	100%	100%	100%
(N)	(329)	(33)	(134)	(236)	(101)	(22)	(218)

* Computed by author from the IBM cards of a national opinion survey conducted in May 1956 by the Institut national d'études demographiques.

† Computed by author from the IBM cards of a Netherlands Institute of Public Opinion survey conducted in May 1956.

to the Socialists. Ninety per cent of the practicing Calvinists supported the Calvinist Antirevolutionary party, as compared with 63 per cent of the nonchurch-going. The difference is far less significant among the moderate Protestant practicing members, whose religious patterns are more nearly like those of American Protestants and who are therefore under less social pressure to vote for their party. The Christian Historical party commanded 45 per cent of the practicing church members' allegiances, and 19 per cent among those nonpracticing.

In West Germany Catholics and Protestants are

linked to direct political action through one religious party, the Christian Democrats. And there also, the more involved a man is in church activity, the more likely he is to back a religious party.[1]

Although we have ignored other factors in reporting the impact of religion in these countries, it is important to note that class factors continued to operate within each denomination. Among French Catholics, as among Dutch and German Protestants and Catholics, those who voted for the leftist parties were predominantly manual workers. The available evidence suggests that workers in these countries are much more subject to tensions flowing from the conflict between their religious and class positions than members of the middle strata. While most religious workers resolve this tension, at least as far as voting is concerned, by backing the religious party, a significant minority, particularly among the less faithful church attenders, backs the Socialists. It may be that this tension leads some workers into the ranks of the free-thinkers.

Many ethnic and religious minorities suffering social or economic discrimination support the more left parties in different countries, although this pattern is most commonly found in the Jews. In the United States, the Negro minority tends to be more Democratic than whites on a given income level; indeed, within the Negro group economic status makes little difference in voting.[2] Other examples can be found in Asia. In India the Andhras, a large linguistic minority, have been among the strongest supporters of the Communist party,[3] while in Ceylon the Communists are disproportionally strong among the Indian minority. In Japan the Korean minority gives considerable support to the Communists.[4] In Israel the Arab minority and in Syria the Christian minority have been relatively pro-Communist.[5]

Social conditions affecting left voting

Granted that a group of people is suffering from some deprivation under the existing socioeconomic system, it does not automatically follow that they will support political parties aiming at social change. Three conditions facilitate such a response: effective channels of communication, low belief in the possibility of individual social mobility, and the absence of traditionalist ties to a conservative party.

CHANNELS OF COMMUNICATION

Perhaps the most important condition is the presence of good communications among people who have a common problem. Close personal contacts between such people further awareness of a community of interests and of the possibilities of collective action, including political action, to solve the common problems. When informal contacts are supplemented by formal organization in trade-unions, farm groups, or class political movements, with all their machinery of organizers, speakers, newspapers, and so forth, political awareness will be intensified still more.

For example, Paul Lazarsfeld has shown that membership in social or other organizations reinforces the tendency to vote Republican among upper- and middle-class people. Similarly, among the lower socioeconomic groups "only 31 per cent of those who were union members, but 53 per cent of those who were not union members voted Republican."[6] The greater political interest and more leftist vote of trade-union members has been documented by studies in a number of countries.[7]

We have already discussed several occupational groups which suffer from severe insecurity of income and which vote strongly leftist in different countries — one-crop farmers, fishermen, miners, sheepshearers, and lumbermen. In each of these groups, there was not

---

[1] In Germany, 60 per cent of the male Catholic churchgoers support either the C.D.U. or the *Zentrum*, while only 33 per cent of the nonchurchgoing Catholics support these parties. See Juan Linz, *The Social Bases of German Politics* (unpublished Ph.D. thesis, Department of Sociology, Columbia University, 1958), p. 700. See J. J. de Jong, *op. cit.*, pp. 179–187, for further data on Holland. This book also presents a survey of voting patterns in different European countries for different occupations, age groups, and other aspects of social structure.

[2] J. A. Morsell, *The Political Behavior of Negroes in New York City* (Ph.D. thesis, Department of Sociology, Columbia University, 1951).

[3] S. S. Harrison, "Caste and the Andhra Communists," *American Political Science Review*, 50 (1956), pp. 378–404.

[4] R. Swearingen and P. Langer, *Red Flag in Japan: International Communism in Action, 1919–1951* (Cambridge: Harvard University Press, 1952), pp. 181–184.

[5] Bureau of Applied Social Research, *Syrian Attitudes Toward America and Russia* (New York: Columbia University, 1952), mimeographed.

[6] P. F. Lazarsfeld, B. Berelson, and H. Gaudet, *The People's Choice* (New York: Duell, Sloan & Pearce, 1944), pp. 146–147.

[7] Other studies in the United States are A. Campbell, G. Gurin, and W. E. Miller, *op. cit.*, p. 73. B. Berelson, P. F. Lazarsfeld, and W. N. McPhee show that the more involved in union activities the members are the more likely they are to vote Democratic, *op. cit.*, pp. 49–52. This study also shows the reinforcing effect of organization membership upon Republican votes among the middle and upper classes. Ruth Kornhauser has demonstrated that the relationship between Democratic vote and union membership holds in all sizes of community, though more strongly in the larger cities. "Some Determinants of Union Membership," (mimeographed, Institute of Industrial Relations, Berkeley, 1959).

In Britain, 66 per cent of trade-union members in Droylsden, England, in 1951 voted Labor as against 53 per cent of other employees, P. Campbell, D. Donnison, and A. Potter, "Voting Behavior in Droylsden in October 1951," *Journal of the Manchester School of Economics and Social Studies*, 20 (1952), p. 63. R. S. Milne and H. C. Mackenzie found an even stronger relationship between union membership and Labor vote, *Straight Fight; A Study of Voting in the Constituency of Bristol North-East at the General Election of 1951* (London: The Hansard Society, 1954), pp. 62–64; see also M. Benney, A. P. Gray, and R. H. Pear, *op. cit.*, p. 112. Data supplied by the Canadian Institute of Public Opinion Research indicate that union members give greater support to the C.C.F. (socialists) and the Communists than do nonunionized workers. In Germany union members are twice as likely to support the Socialist party as those workers who do not belong to any voluntary associations, Juan Linz, *op. cit.*, pp. 215, 828–830.

only a strong reason for social discontent but also, as has been pointed out in detail earlier, a social structure favorable to intragroup communications and unfavorable to cross-class communications, an "occupational community."

In contrast to such groups the service industries generally are composed of small units scattered among the well-to-do populations they serve, and their workers tend to be not only less politically active but also more conservative. The white-collar workers' well-known lack of organization and class consciousness may also be partly due to the small units in which they work and to their scattering among higher-level managerial personnel.[1]

Two general social factors that correlate with leftist voting are size of industrial plants and size of city. We have already noted that there was a correlation between size of plant and leftist vote in German elections before 1933, a finding which was reiterated in a 1953 German survey (see Table 8). Among workers the combined Socialist and Communist vote increased with size of the plants. Twenty-eight per cent of the workers in plants with under ten workers voted left; as contrasted with 57 per cent of those in establishments of over a thousand. Similarly, the vote for the Christian Democrats and the conservative parties was smaller

for each larger category of plant size. Interestingly enough, the percentage of workers preferring no party also decreased with increasing plant size, indicating both social pressure to vote left, and simply pressure to vote. The earlier study also found a relation between over-all city size and leftist vote.[2]

A later German study (1955) showed that among men the leftist vote increased with size of city in every occupational group except that of people with independent means. But the increase was greatest among manual workers (see Table 8).[3] Similar results are indicated by an analysis of the election returns for Works Councils in Italy in 1954 and 1955. The larger the city and the larger the factory, the more votes received by the Communist-controlled C.G.I.L. (General Confederation of Italian Labor) in elections to Works Councils. The Communist union federation secured 60 per cent of the vote in cities with less than 40,000 population and 75 per cent in cities with over a million people. The same pattern held up when comparing union strength by size of factory for the entire country, and even within most specific industries. For example, in the textile industry, the Communist-controlled union secured 29 per cent of the vote in plants employing 50–100 people (the smallest size reported for this industry) and 79 per cent in plants employing over 2,000.[4]

---

[1] C. Dreyfuss, "Prestige Grading: A Mechanism of Control," in R. K. Merton, *et al.*, eds., *Reader in Bureaucracy* (Glencoe: The Free Press, 1952), pp. 258–264.

[2] S. Pratt, *op. cit.*, Chap. 3.

[3] See also Juan Linz, *op. cit.*, pp. 347 ff. Both men and women and male workers at each skill level were more leftist in larger cities.

[4] For detailed statistical breakdowns of specific cities and plants see *L'Avanzata della C.I.S.L. nolle commissioni interne* (Rome: Confederazione Italiana Sindacati Lavoratori, 1955), pp. 46–95. This report was prepared by an anti-Communist labor federation. The categories in which data are given for size of factories for each industry vary from industry to industry so that it was impossible to add the data to get an over-all statistic. However, the differences are consistent, and the report in any case does not give all the returns for the entire country. A number of British factory studies by the Acton Society Trust have reported a "clear relationship . . . between size and sick-leave; between size and the number of accidents . . . " and various other indices of worker morale. See Acton Society Trust, *Size and Morale* (London: 1953); *The Worker's Point of View* (London: 1953); and *Size and Morale, II* (London: 1957). Somewhat comparable American findings are reported in Sherrill Cleland, *The Influence of Plant Size on Industrial Relations* (Princeton: Princeton University Press, 1955).

[5] R. Centers, *op. cit.*, pp. 58, 185–190; P. Ennis, "Contextual Factors in Voting Decisions," in W. N. McPhee, ed., *Progress Report of the 1950 Congressional Voting Study* (New York: Bureau of Applied Social Research, Columbia University, 1952), mimeographed. Leon Epstein demonstrates that in Wisconsin gubernatorial elections, the Democratic vote increased consistently with size of city, "Size of Place and the Division of the Two-Party Vote in Wisconsin," *Western Political Quarterly*, 9 (1956), p. 141. N. A. Masters and D. S. Wright show that though workers are distinctly less inclined to vote Democratic in small cities than in large ones, people in the managerial group tend to vote Republican in the same degree regardless of the size of the city they live in. "Trends and Variations in the Two-Party Vote: The Case of Michigan," *American Political Science Review*, 52 (1958), p. 1088.

TABLE 8. *Percentage of Male Workers Voting for Different Parties, by Size of City and Size of Plant*

Germany — 1955*

Size of city	Percentage of Socialist and Communist votes	(N)
Less than 2,000	43%	(453)
2,000–10,000	46	(587)
10,000–100,000	51	(526)
More than 100,000	54	(862)

Germany — 1953†

	SIZE OF PLANT				
Party choice	Under 10 workers	10–49 workers	50–299 workers	300–999 workers	Over 1,000 workers
Socialist and Communist‡	28%	40%	45%	45%	57%
Christian Democrat	22	20	18	22	15
Bourgeois parties	21	16	13	7	5
No party	26	22	23	22	15
Total	97%	98%	99%	96%	92%
(N)	(134)	(116)	(163)	(124)	(130)

* E.M.N.I.D., *Zur Resonanz der Parteien bei Männer und Frauen in den Soziologischen Gruppen* (Bielefeld: mimeographed, no date), p. 4.
† Computed by author from cards supplied by the UNESCO Institute at Cologne, Germany.
‡ Less than 2 per cent Communist.

The same relationship between size of community and party choice is to be found in France, Australia, and the United States.[5] The Australian Gallup Poll isolates the responses of those living in mining communities from those living in other smaller communities and finds, as should be anticipated, that the "isolated" miners are less likely to back middle-class-based parties than are manual workers in large cities (see Table 9). These Australian data further show that, although the skilled workers were less likely to vote Labor than the semi- and unskilled workers, both groups voted Labor more heavily in the large cities than in the small ones.

TABLE 9. *Size of Community and Workers' Party Preference in Australia – 1955**

COMMUNITY SIZE

Party choice	LARGE CITIES		SMALL CITIES		MINING COMMUNITIES†	
	Skilled workers	Semi- and unskilled workers	Skilled workers	Semi- and unskilled workers	Skilled workers	Semi- and unskilled workers
Liberal	35%	19%	44%	29%	15%	17%
Labor	64	81	56	71	77	83
Total (N)	99% (333)	100% (241)	100% (96)	100% (107)	92%‡ (13)	100% (6)

* Computed from IBM cards of a 1955 election survey conducted by the Australian Gallup Poll and kindly supplied to the author for further analysis.
† The number of cases is, of course, too small to justify any inferences from one sample, but previous surveys show comparable results. For example, a survey of the 1951 electorate indicates that 12 out of 13 manual workers living in mining towns were Labor voters.
‡ One respondent preferred one of the minor parties.

In all these cases the communications factor may be involved. A large plant makes for a higher degree of intraclass communication and less personal contact with people on higher economic levels. In large cities social interaction is also more likely to be within economic classes. In certain cases the working-class districts of large cities have been so thoroughly organized by working-class political movements that the workers live in a virtual world of their own, and it is in these centers that the workers are the most solidly behind leftist candidates, and, as we have already seen, vote most heavily.

BELIEF IN OPPORTUNITIES FOR INDIVIDUAL MOBILITY

Instead of taking political action, some discontented individuals attempt to better their lot within the existing economic system by working their way up the ladder of success. If such a possibility seems to exist, there will be a corresponding reduction in collective efforts at social change, such as the support of unions and leftist parties.

This has long been the major explanation offered for the fact that American workers tend to vote for mildly reformist parties, while European workers normally vote socialist or communist. Supposedly living in an open-class society, with a developing economy which

continually creates new jobs above the manual-labor level, the American worker is presumably more likely to believe in individual opportunity. His European counterpart, accepting the image of a closed-class society which does not even pretend to offer the worker a chance to rise, is impelled to act collectively for social change. While these stereotypes of the relative degree of social mobility in Europe and America do not correspond to reality, their acceptance may well affect voting.[1]

Unfortunately, it is not easy to give precise statistical validation for this explanation, since there are so many other ways in which European and American society differ. In America the working class as a whole has risen, through a large long-term increase in real wages, to a position which in other countries would be termed "middle class." There is a good deal of evidence that American workers believe in individual opportunity; various surveys show about half the workers saying that they have "a good chance for personal advancement in the years ahead."[2] A study in Chicago in 1937 during the Great Depression found that no less than 85 to 90 per cent of every economic group believed that their *children* had a good chance to be better off economically.[3] The most recent data indicate that *actual* social mobility in Europe is as high as it is in the United States but the *belief* in mobility differs. A relatively high rate of actual social mobility appears to be characteristic of all industrial societies.

Two factors are involved in the differential *belief* in mobility: the differences between the United States and Western Europe in total national income and its distribution and, second, the different value systems of the American and European upper classes. As I have put it elsewhere: "Income, in every class, is so much greater in America, and the gap between the living styles of the different social classes so much narrower, that in effect the egalitarian society envisaged by the proponents of high social mobility is much more closely approximated here than in Europe. While Europeans rise in the occupational scale as often as we [Americans] do, the marked contrast between the ways of life of the different classes continues to exist. Thus, in the United States workers and middle-class people have

---

[1] A recent survey of the literature and research relating to mobility in many different countries found that the total vertical mobility (movement from lower- or working-class occupations to nonmanual or higher-prestige occupations) in the United States was not substantially different (30 per cent of the population) than in most other relatively developed countries. Other rates were Germany, 31 per cent; Sweden, 29 per cent; Japan, 27 per cent; France, 27 per cent; Denmark, 31 per cent; Great Britain, 29 per cent. Slightly lower was Switzerland, 23 per cent, and the lowest country in Western Europe was Italy at 16 per cent. These studies are fully reported in S. M. Lipset and R. Bendix, *op. cit.*, Chap. II.
[2] E. Roper, "Fortune Survey: A Self-Portrait of the American People," *Fortune*, 35 (1947), pp. 5–16.
[3] A. W. Kornhauser, "Analysis of Class Structure of Contemporary American Society," in G. W. Hartmann and T. M. Newcomb, eds., *Industrial Conflict* (New York: The Cordon Co., 1939), pp. 199–264.

cars, while in Europe only the middle class can own an automobile."[1]

But divergent value systems also play a role here, since the American and European upper classes differ sharply in their conceptions of egalitarianism. The rags-to-riches myth is proudly propagated by the successful American businessman. Actual differences in rank and authority are justified as rewards for demonstrated ability. In Europe aristocratic values and patterns of inherited privilege and position are still upheld by many of the upper class, and therefore the European conservative wishes to minimize the extent of social mobility.

Given the much wider discrepancy in consumption styles between the European and American middle and working class, one would expect the upwardly mobile European of working-class origin to have somewhat greater difficulties in adjusting to his higher status, and to feel more discriminated against than his American counterpart, much like the successfully upwardly mobile Negro or other minority ethnic member in America comparing himself with a native-born Protestant white. The comparative materials bearing on the effect of mobility on party choice are, in fact, consistent with the hypothesis that Europeans remain more dissatisfied or retain more ties with their previous status. Surveys in five European nations — Sweden, Finland, Germany, Norway, and Britain — find that upward-mobile Europeans are more likely to vote for left parties than are their fellow countrymen who were born into the middle class, while in the United States, three different survey studies report that the upward mobile

are more conservative (Republican) than those who grew up in middle-class families.[2] Some indication that the propensity to adjust to the cultural style of the class into which one moves is associated with political views is suggested by Swedish data which indicate that men in nonmanual occupations who have risen from the working class will continue to vote for the left party unless they change their consumption styles (symbolized in Table 10 by the automobile). Conversely, among those still in the class in which they grew up, variations in consumption style seem to have no relationship to voting choice.

The American version of this difference in "consumption styles" may be the move to the suburb, and several studies have shown the differences in the political behavior of lower-status persons who make such a move. A re-analysis of the 1952 survey conducted by the Survey Research Center at Michigan (and analyzed generally in *The Voter Decides*) along lines of suburban–urban differences found that there were indeed shifts in party loyalties which could not be explained simply as the movement of already conservative people to the suburbs. Both hypotheses suggested by the authors of this study are consistent with the thesis suggested

TABLE 10. *Relationship between Social Origin, Consumption Patterns, and Voting Behavior among Men in Sweden*

	MANUAL FROM MANUAL HOMES		NONMANUAL FROM MANUAL HOMES		NONMANUAL FROM NONMANUAL HOMES	
	Without car	With car	Without car	With car	Without car	With car
Non-Socialist	15%	14%	38%	74%	79%	83%
Socialist	85	86	63	26	21	17
(N)	(221)	(72)	(78)	(55)	(170)	(145)

* H. L. Zetterberg, "Overages Erlander," *Vecko-Journalen*, 48 (1957), pp. 18, 36. Reproduced in S. M. Lipset and Reinhard Bendix, *Social Mobility in Industrial Society*, p. 68.

[1] S. M. Lipset and Natalie Rogoff, "Class and Opportunity in Europe and the United States," *Commentary*, 18 (1954), pp. 562–568.

[2] See S. M. Lipset and Hans Zetterberg, *op. cit.*, pp. 64–72, for a detailed report on the political consequences of social mobility. Data which indicate that the relationship between upward mobility and vote choice in England is like that in other European countries rather than the United States may be found in R. S. Milne and H. C. Mackenzie, *op. cit.*, p. 58.

[3] See Fred I. Greenstein and Raymond E. Wolfinger, "The Suburbs and Shifting Party Loyalties," *Public Opinion Quarterly*, 22 (1958), pp. 473–483. Another study which dealt with one city rather than the whole country found little political change in the suburb of Kalamazoo, Michigan, and its authors concluded that the effect of the suburb has been overestimated. Yet, as their data show, the suburb from which they drew their interpretation was far from typical of the tract-type, relatively low-priced suburb which attracts the low-income buyer with aspirations to better himself and his family's future. Most of the homes were high priced for the area, 83 per cent of the respondents voted for Eisenhower in 1956, and 85 per cent were Protestants. It is not surprising that in an area like this, in which almost everyone was already a Republican, the effects of mobility upon political choice were not to be seen. For a report of this study see Jerome G. Manis and Leo C. Stine, "Suburban Residence and Political Behavior," *Public Opinion Quarterly*, 22 (1958), pp. 483–490.

[4] Samuel Lubell, *The Revolt of the Moderates* (New York: Harper & Bros., 1956) and William H. Whyte, *The Organization Man* (New York: Simon and Schuster, 1956) discuss the political impact of suburbia. Lubell also sees a rising Republican trend in the cities, as part of general social trends not confined to the suburbs.

here of the impact of social mobility upon lower-class people. Whether self-selection is the crucial factor (implying that the new suburbanites are upwardly mobile and anxious to become socialized into a higher environment, which means voting Republican) or whether the effects of being exposed to a more Republican environment — friends and neighbors — accounts for greater conservative voting, the data show that mobility of this kind produces higher Republican voting on the part of previously Democratic voters.[3] When occupation was held constant, in both "medium" and "high" status occupations there was considerably more Republican voting in the suburbs.[4]

While most discussions of the impact of mobility on the political and social systems emphasize the supposed consequences of different rates of upward mobility, considerable evidence indicates that there is a substantial degree of downward movement from one generation to another in every modern industrial society — a father's high position is no guarantee of a similar position for his children. And the most recent American data do in fact indicate that about one third of the sons of professionals, semi-professionals, proprietors, managers, and officials — the most privileged occupations — are in manual employment.[1] Similarly, there is extensive movement from rural to urban areas in most societies, much of which helps to fill the ranks of the manual workers.

These rather extensive movements into the industrial proletariat are one of the major sources of conservative politics within that class. In every country for which data are available — Germany, Finland, Britain, Sweden, Norway, and the United States — workers of middle-class parentage are much more likely to vote for the conservative parties than are workers whose fathers are of the same class. Those of rural background are also relatively more conservative. The difference is even more accentuated when variations in background over three generations are compared. In Germany a 1953 survey found that 75 per cent of the workers whose grandparents were workers voted for the Socialists or the Communists, but only 24 per cent of the workers with a middle-class father did.[2] In Finland, a similar study in 1948 showed that 82 per cent of the workers whose father and paternal grandfathers were workers voted for left parties as compared with 67 per cent of those with a rural background, and 42 per cent of those of middle-class parents.

Given the fact of extensive social mobility in all industrial societies, perhaps the most important effect of mobility on politics which should be noted is that the bulk of the socially mobile, whether their direction be upward or downward, vote for the more conservative parties. In Germany, where over three quarters of the manual workers of middle-class parentage voted for the nonsocialist parties in 1953, almost 70 per cent of those in nonmanual positions of working-class family background also opted for the "middle-class" parties. Similarly in Finland, two thirds of the workers of middle-class origin remained loyal to nonleftist parties, while less than a quarter of those who had risen into middle-class occupations from working-class family background voted for the Socialists or Communists.[3] These findings illustrate the pervasive influence of contact with superior status on attitudes and behavior. Those subject to a cross-pressure between the political values congruent with a higher and a lower status as a result of having been in both positions are much more likely to resolve the conflict in favor of the former.

The effort to account for the variations in the electoral behavior of different groups by pointing up different aspects of the class structure in various societies has involved a discussion of several factors, many of which operate simultaneously. It is obvious that an explanation

[1] S. M. Lipset and R. Bendix, *op. cit.*, pp. 87–91.
[2] Data computed from materials supplied by the UNESCO Institute in Cologne, Germany.
[3] Data supplied by Dr. Erik Allardt of the University of Helsinki, and based on two surveys conducted by the Finnish Gallup Poll. Both German and Finnish studies are reported in more detail in Lipset and Bendix, *op. cit.*, pp. 69–71.

TABLE II. *Explanatory Factors Related to Original Statistical Regularities in Voting within the Lower-Income Groups*

	TYPES OF DEPRIVATION			FACILITATING CONDITIONS			
	Insecurity of income	Unsatisfying work	Low prestige status	Good intra-class communications	Low expectation of mobility	Lack of traditionalism	Left vote
Workers in:							
Large plants	+	+	+	+	+	+	Higher
Small plants	+	−	+	−		−	Lower
Workers in:							
Large cities				+		+	Higher
Small towns				−		−	Lower
Workers in:							
Europe				+	+		Higher
United States				−	−		Lower
Manual workers			+	+			Higher
White-collar			−	−			Lower
Minority group			+				Higher
Majority			−				Lower
Commercial farmers, fishermen	+	−		+		+	Higher
Local market, subsistence farmers	−	−				−	Lower
Miners, lumbermen	+	+	+	+	+	+	Higher
Servants, service workers				−		−	Lower
Economically advanced areas	+					+	Higher
Backward areas	−					−	Lower
Men				+		+	Higher
Women				−		−	Lower

Note. — Plus signs indicate factors favoring leftist voting in lower classes.

of the behavior of any one group involves treating a whole pattern, and in discussing each factor separately, it is perhaps difficult to see all the variables at work on any one group, like the miners whose behavior has been cited a number of times to illustrate the operation of different factors. Table 11 indicates some of the ways in which different sets of variables combine to form a pattern in the separate groups.

Although it seems evident that most of the structural factors which determine party choice in modern society can be viewed as aspects of the stratification system, there are clearly many other social variables which interact with class and politics. The next chapter continues the discussion of the conditions of the democratic order by analyzing one such major determinant of electoral behavior — variations in the experiences of different generations — and by treating the related issue of historical change in voting patterns.

The Appeal of Communism to the Peoples of Underdeveloped Areas

Morris Watnick

IF TIME IS A POWER dimension in any political strategy, the odds facing the West in the underdeveloped areas of the world today are heavily weighted against it. The effort to capture the imagination and loyalties of the populations of these areas did not begin with the West in President Truman's plea for a "bold new program" of technical aid to backward areas. It began more than a generation earlier when the Communist International at its second world congress in 1920, flung out the challenge of revolution to the people of colonial and dependent countries, and proceeded to chart a course of action calculated to hasten the end of Western overlordship. We thus start with an initial time handicap, and it is a moot question whether we can overcome the disadvantage by acquiring the radically new appreciation of the human stakes involved necessary to meet the challenge of the Communist appeal to the peoples of these areas.

Fortunately, there is no need to trace out the tortuous course of the careers of the various Communist parties in the backward areas of the world in order to gain some appreciation of the extent and intensity of their indigenous appeal. For purposes of this discussion we can confine ourselves to China, India and the area of southeast Asia where they have had their greatest successes to date. Despite the blunders and ineptitudes which marked their initial grand play in China in 1924–27, ending in almost complete disaster for their most promising single party organization in these areas, they have emerged today as a political magnitude of the first order, boasting a seasoned leadership, a core of trained cadres and a mass following recruited mainly from the peasant masses of the region. It is the purpose of this paper to indicate the nature of the Communist appeal to the peoples of these areas and to suggest some of the sociological factors which have made that appeal so effective.

It was once the wont of certain continental writers, preoccupied with the problem of imperialism, to refer to the peoples who form the subject of our deliberations as the *history-less* peoples. Better than the Europacentric term, "underdeveloped peoples," it delineates in bold relief all the distinctive features which went to make up the scheme of their social existence; their parochial isolation, the fixity of their social structure, their tradition-bound resistance to change, their static, subsistence economies and the essential repetitiveness and uneventfulness of their self-contained cycle of collective activities. With a prescience which has not always received its due, these theorists of imperialism also called the right tune in predicting that the isolated careers of these archaic societies would rapidly draw to a close under the impact of economic and social forces set in motion by industrial capitalism, and that these *history-less* peoples would before long be thrust onto the arena of world politics, impelled by a nascent nationalism born of contact with the West and nurtured by a

This is the revised text of a paper given before the Norman Wait Harris Foundation proceedings at the University of Chicago in June 1951.

Reprinted from "The Appeal of Communism to the Peoples of Underdeveloped Areas," *Economic Development and Cultural Change* (1952), pp. 22–36 by permission of the author and the University of Chicago Press. (Copyright, 1952, by The University of Chicago Press.)

swelling resentment against the exactions of its imperialism.[1]

The final result of this process is unfolding today with a disconcerting force and speed in almost all the backward regions of the world. We can see its culmination most clearly among the classic examplaries of *historyless* peoples in China, India and the regions of south Asia where the political and economic predominance of western Europe is being successfully challenged by forces unmistakably traceable to the forced absorption of these societies into the stream of world history. Their internal cohesiveness, largely centered on self-sufficient village economies, has been disrupted by enforced contact with the West, giving way to a network of commercialized money transactions in which the strategic incidence of economic activity has shifted from subsistence agriculture to plantation production of raw materials and foodstuffs for the world market. Their economies thus took on a distorted character which rendered the material well-being of the native populations peculiarly subject to the cyclical fluctuations of the world market. All this, coupled with rapid population increases which the existing state of primitive technique, available area of cultivation and customary allocation of soil could not adjust to the requirements of maximum output, have conspired to create wide-spread rural indebtedness, abuses of plantation and tenant labor and other excrescences traditionally associated with the prevalence of a raw commercial and financial capitalism super-imposed on a predominantly agricultural economy.[2]

Given the fact that the new economic dispensation in these regions was fashioned under the aegis, if not active encouragement, of the Western imperialisms, it should occasion no surprise that these regions, particularly southeast Asia, have seen the efflorescence of a distinctive type of nationalism, especially after the debacle of western rule during the second World War, differing in many crucial respects from the historical evolution of nationalism as experienced by western Europe. Indeed, the employment of a term like "nationalism" with all its peculiarly western connotations to describe what is going on in south Asia today is in a sense deceptive precisely because it diverts our attention from some of the distinctive attributes of native sentiment which set it apart from the nineteenth century manifestations of nationalism in Europe. It is moreover a particularly inappropriate characterization because it inhibits a full appreciation of the potency of the Communist appeal among the populations of these regions. Historically, nationalism in western Europe has flourished with the burgeoning of an industrial technology, the urbanization of the population, the growth of a self-conscious middle class and an industrial proletariat, the spread of literacy and the multiplication of media of mass communication. Now it is one of the distinctive features of the movements of revolt in southeast Asia today that they lack any of these marks of Western nationalism. The indigenous "nationalism" of southeast Asia today lacking any of these props, nevertheless derives its peculiar potency from a universal reaction of personalized resentment against the economic exploitation of foreign powers. Whether all the economic and social dislocations of this region are directly attributable, in refined analytic terms, to Western rule is quite beside the point. The simple and crucial datum which we must take as the point of orientation in our thinking is that to the mind of masses of indigenous peoples they do stem from this common source. The Indochinese intellectual debarred from a higher post in the government service, the Burmese stevedore underpaid by the *maistry* system of contract labor all tend to attribute the source of their grievances to the systems of government and economy imposed on them from without. The distinctive and novel aspect of the native movements of southeast Asia, then, is that they represent a mass collective gesture of rejection of a system of imposed economic and social controls which is compelled by historic circumstances to take the form of a nationalist movement of liberation from foreign rule.[3]

It is this distinctive coalescence of two sources of resentment which offers Communist parties the opportunities they lack elsewhere to any comparable degree. The two-dimensional direction of native resentment lends itself ideally to Communist appeal and manipulation for the simple reason that Communists can successfully portray Soviet Russia both as a symbol of resistance to political imperialism imposed from without as well as a model of self-directed and rapid industrialization undertaken from within.[4] This twin appeal gains added strength from the multi-national composition of the USSR which enables indigenous Communists of south Asia to confront their audience with the glaring disparity between the possibilities of ethnic equality and the actualities of western arrogance and discrimination. Communist propaganda has accordingly exploited this theme in almost all important policy pronouncements directed to the people of Asia.[5]

[1] For typical discussions, see Otto Bauer, *Die Nationalitätenfrage und die Sozialdemokratie*, Vienna, 1907, pp. 494–497 *et passim*; Rudolf Hilferding, *Das Finanzkapital* (originally published in Vienna, 1910), Berlin, 1947, p. 441.

[2] For an excellent analysis of the economic impact of the West on the rural economies of southeast Asia where the results are most clearly apparent today, see Erich Jacoby, *Agrarian Unrest in Southeast Asia*, New York, 1949.

[3] O. Bauer, *op. cit.*, esp. pp. 262–263, has given the classic formulation of this relationship in his analysis of the problem of national conflicts in the old Austro-Hungarian Empire which showed some formal resemblance to the situation in the backward regions today. The resemblance was superficial, however, since the lines of conflict were far less clearly drawn in Austria-Hungary, especially as regards professional and intellectual groups.

[4] It is noteworthy that variations of both types of Communist propaganda have also been attempted in western Europe in the last three years. The Marshall Plan, for example, has been presented to Europeans as an attempt on the part of the U.S. to impose its political rule over the continent and to throttle its industries, without however carrying the conviction it enjoys in Asia.

[5] See report by L. Soloviev at Congress of Asian and

With the victory of the Chinese Communists, the incidence of these appeals has perceptibly shifted the symbolism of successful resistance and internal reconstruction from Russia to China which is now being held up as a model for emulation by the other areas of southeast Asia.[1] The shift is not without its tactical and propaganda value since the adjacent region of southeast Asia is now regarded as the "main battle-front of the world democratic camp against the forces of reaction and imperialism."[2] Success in this case carries its own rewards beyond the frontiers of China itself for it is altogether probable that Mao Tse-tung will take his place alongside Lenin and Stalin as a fount of revolutionary sagacity for these movements in India and southeast Asia.[3]

Unfortunately, recent discussions of the Communist movement in Asia have done more to obscure than to clarify the nature and direction of its appeal to the indigenous populations. All too frequently, the tendency has been to fall back on the blanket formula that Communists have sought to identify themselves with local nationalism and demands for agrarian reform. We have already seen that their identification with nascent nationalism, if such it must be called, derives its peculiar strength from certain of its unique qualities. It is no less important to an appreciation of the problem to recognize that the Communist appeal does not by mere virtue of this process of identification, acquire the same uniform access to all sectors of the population. Indeed, the most striking and disconcerting feature of much of the propaganda appeal emanating both from Moscow, Peking, and other centers is that it is not, and in the nature of the case, cannot be designed for peasant or worker consumption. The appeal of Communism as such in these areas is first and foremost an appeal which finds lodgment with indigenous professional and intellectual groups. Its identification with native nationalism and demands for land reform turns out to be, when carefully scrutinized, not so much a direct appeal to specific peasant grievances, powerful though its actual results may be, as it is an identification with the more generalized, highly conscious and sharply oriented outlook of the native intelligentsia.[4]

Given the entire range of sociological and economic forces at work in these areas, the very logic and terms of the Communist appeal must of necessity filter through to the peasant masses by first becoming the stock-in-trade of the intellectual and professional groups. To revert to the terminology suggested at the outset of this paper, we may say that by and large, it is the old *history-less* style of social existence which still claims the loyalty and outlook of the bulk of the indigenous populations. It is still the old village community which serves as the center of peasant and worker aspirations, and if they have taken to arms it is because European rule has destroyed the old securities and values without replacing them by new ones.[5] Without leadership and organization their unrest would be without direction and certainly without much chance for success, quickly dissipating itself in spontaneous outbursts against individual land-owners and achieving no lasting goals. Whatever else it may be that we are facing in southeast Asia today, it certainly does not resemble the classic uprisings of peasant *jacquerie*, but a highly organized and well-integrated movement, with a leadership that has transcended the immediate urgencies of its mass following and can plan ahead in terms of long range perspectives.

That leadership is supplied by the new indigenous intelligentsia. It is from this group that native Communist and non-Communist movements alike recruit their top leadership as well as the intermediate layers of cadres for, of all the groups which make up the populations of these areas, it is the intelligentsia alone (taking the term in its broadest sense) that boasts an ideological horizon which transcends the *history-less* values of the

---

[1] "Mighty Advance of National Liberation Movements in Colonial and Dependent Countries," *For a Lasting Peace, For a People's Democracy!* (organ of the Cominform), Jan. 27, 1950, cf. speech by Liu Shao-chi at the Trade Union Conference of Asian and Australasian countries, Peking, *World Trade Union Movement*, No. 8, Dec. 1949, pp. 12–15.

[2] R. Palme Dutte, "Right Wing Social Democrats in the Service of Imperialism," *For a Lasting Peace, For a People's Democracy!*, Nov. 1, 1948, p. 6.

[3] See statement of Ho Chi Minh's newly constituted Laodong Party which "pledges itself to follow the heroic example of the Communist Party of China, to learn the Mao Tse-tung concept which has been leading the peoples of China and Asia on the road to independence and democracy." Vietnam News Agency, English Morse to Southeast Asia, March 21, 1951. Likewise, the ruling body of the Indian Communist Party fell into line with the general trend by declaring its adherence to Mao's strategy. *Crossroads*, Bombay, March 10, 1950.

[4] Failure to appreciate the true direction of the Communist appeal in these areas frequently causes some observers to commit the mistake of minimizing its effectiveness. Thus, Mr. Richard Deverall, the A. F. of L. representative in these areas and an otherwise very perceptive student of the subject, ventures the opinion that Communist propaganda in these areas is mere "rubbish" because it is for the most part couched in terms which hold no interest for the masses, having meaning only for intellectuals. See his "Helping Asia's Workers" in *American Federationist*, Sept. 1951, p. 16. Mr. Deverall's account of the nature of Communist propaganda is quite accurate, but if the thesis presented above is a valid estimate of the current situation in Asia, he has not drawn the conclusion which follows from the evidence.

[5] In most backward areas, the tie to the countryside is still apparent in the tendency of laborers engaged in industry and mining periodically to drift back to the village. W. E. Moore, "Primitives and Peasants in Industry," *Social Research*, Vol. XV, No. 1, March 1948, pp. 49–63. See also observations of S. Sjahrir in his *Out of Exile* (tr. C. Wolf), New York, 1949, pp. 74–75, concerning the mental outlook of the masses in these regions. This fact was not lost on the leaders of the Communist movement. In the 1928 resolution on colonial strategy, the Sixth Comintern Congress noted that the proletariat "still have one foot in the village" a fact which it recognized as a barrier to the development of proletarian class consciousness. See *International Press Correspondence* (Vienna), Vol. VIII, No. 88, Dec. 12, 1928, p. 1670.

Australasian Trade Unions at Peking, Nov. 19, 1949, in *World Trade Union Movement* (organ of the WFTU), No. 8, Dec. 1949, pp. 25–27. Also cf. Manifesto to All Working People of Asia and Australasia, *ibid.*, pp. 43–46.

bulk of the population and makes it the logical recruiting ground for the leadership of political movements. For this, it can thank the formal schooling and intellectual stimulus provided by the West, which not only brought such a group into existence but also — and this is crucial — condemned large sections of that intelligentsia to a form of *déclassé* existence from the very beginnings of its career. The new intelligentsia was in large measure consigned by the imperial system to hover uneasily between a native social base which could not find accommodation for its skills and ambitions, and the superimposed imperial structure which reserved the best places for aliens. There were, of course, considerable variations and differences in the various areas of south Asia — India, for example, did succeed in absorbing a good many of its professionally trained native sons — but by and large, the picture is one of a rootless intellectual proletariat possessing no real economic base in an independent native middle class. The tendency in all these areas, moreover, has been to train technicians, lawyers, and other groups of professional workers in numbers far out of proportion to the absorptive capacity of the social structures of the home areas, even if more of the higher posts in industry and administration were thrown open to native talent. In any case, those who did find such employment were frozen in minor posts, the most coveted positions going to Europeans.[1]

But if these groups could not be integrated into the social structure of these dependent areas, the same does not hold true of their acclimatization to the cross currents of political doctrine. Western education exposed many of them to the various schools of social thought contending for influence in Europe, and from these they distilled the lessons which seemed to offer the best hope for their native communities. Western capitalism was necessarily excluded from their range of choices if for no other reason than that its linkage with imperialist rule over their own societies debarred it from their hierarchy of values. The anti-capitalist animus is common to the intellectual spokesmen of these areas, whatever their specific political allegiance or orientation may be.[2] Nor does it appear that any populist variety of Gandhism, with its strong attachment to the values of a static subsistence economy, has won any considerable following among these intellectual groups, Soeten Sjahrir voiced a common sentiment when he wrote:

> We intellectuals here are much closer to Europe or America than we are to the Boroboedoer or Mahabrata or to the primitive Islamic culture of Java or Sumatra.... For me, the West signifies forceful, dynamic and active life. I admire, and am convinced that only by a utilization of this dynamism of the West can the East be released from its slavery and subjugation.[3]

The sole possibility, then, which appeared acceptable to

them was one or another of the forms of state-sponsored reconstruction and industrialization, for which liberation from the rule of European states was naturally considered to be a prerequisite. Liberation and internal reconstruction thus came to be two inseparable operations, intimately tied together as they seldom have been before.

We can now appreciate the enormous initial advantage which was thus offered the Communist movements in these backward areas. The Russian Revolution of 1917 and the subsequent course of planned industrialization could not fail but to impress native intellectuals as offering a model pattern of action by which they could retrieve their communities from precapitalist isolation and backwardness without repaying the price of continued foreign exploitation. There is doubtless a large measure of self-revelation in Mao's reaction to the Russian experience in his statement that:

> There is much in common or similar between the situation in China and pre-revolutionary Russia. Feudal oppression was the same. Economic and cultural backwardness was common to both countries. Both were backward. China more so than Russia. The progressives waged a bitter struggle in search of revolutionary truth so as to attain national rehabilitation; this was common to both countries. ... The October Revolution helped the progressive elements of the world, and of China as well, to apply the proletarian world outlook in determining the fate of the country.... The conclusion was reached that we must advance along the path taken by the Russians.[4]

It should also be noted, in passing, that the Comintern lost no time in launching a large number of international front organizations such as the Red International of Trade Unions, International League Against Imperialism, International of Seamen and Dockers, International Red Aid, etc., all of which provided the necessary

[1] Some interesting data on this score for Indonesia is offered by J. M. van der Kroef's "Economic Origin of Indonesian Nationalism" in *South Asia in the World Today*, ed. by P. Talbot, Chicago, 1950, pp. 188–193, and his article "Social Conflicts and Minority Aspirations in Indonesia," *American Journal of Sociology*, March 1950, pp. 453–456. Cf. L. Mills (ed.) *New World of Southeast Asia*, Minneapolis, 1949, pp. 293–295.

[2] For a typical rejection of the capitalist solution coming from anti-Communist sources see D. R. Gadgil, "Economic Prospect for India" in *Pacific Affairs*, Vol. 22, June, 1949, pp. 115–129; S. Sjahrir, *op. cit.*, pp. 161–162, and the remarks of H. Shastri, of the Indian Trade Union Congress at the Asian Regional Conference of the ILO, Ceylon, Jan. 16–27, 1950, *Record of Proceedings* (Geneva 1951), p. 112. Cf. J. M. van der Kroef's article in the *American Journal of Sociology* cited above, pp. 455–456 and J. F. Normano, *Asia Between Two World Wars*, New York, 1944, pp. 83–87.

[3] S. Sjahrir, *op. cit.*, pp. 67, 144.

[4] Mao Tse-tung, *On People's Democratic Rule*, New York (New Century Publishers), 1950, pp. 2–4. For the same reaction of M. N. Roy, one of the earlier leaders of the Indian Communists who later broke with the Comintern, see his *Revolution and Counter-Revolution in China*, Calcutta, 1946, p. 522.

organizational scaffolding and support for facilitating the dissemination of propaganda. Finally, as will be noted presently, the Comintern provided a rallying point for their aspirations by outlining a program of revolutionary action in the colonies and dependent areas which was ideally calculated to provide them with a mass peasant following.

The result, though viewed with some misgivings by the leadership of the Comintern, was merely what might have been expected under the circumstances. The Communist parties of these underdeveloped areas of Asia were from their very beginnings, initiated, led by, and predominantly recruited from (prior to their conversion into mass organizations as has been the case in China after 1949) native intellectual groups. Though this vital sociological clue to the nature of the Communist appeal in the colonial areas has not received the recognition it deserves, amidst the general pre-occupation with the theme of Communist appeals to the peasantry, its implication was perfectly plain to the leaders of the Comintern. One of the most revealing (and to date largely unnoticed) admissions on this score is contained in the Sixth Comintern Congress in 1928 in its resolution on strategic policy in the colonies and semi-colonies in which the point is very clearly made that:

> Experience has shown that, in the majority of colonial and semi-colonial countries, an important if not a predominant part of the Party ranks in the first stage of the movement is recruited from the petty bourgeoisie, and in particular, from the re-volutionary inclined intelligentsia, very frequently students. It not uncommonly happens that these elements enter the Party because they see in it the most decisive enemy of imperialism, at the same time not sufficiently understanding that the Com-munist Party is not only the Party of struggle against imperialist exploitation ... but struggle against all kinds of exploitation and expropriation. Many of these adherents of the Party, in the course of the revolutionary struggle will reach a proletarian class point of view; another part will find it more difficult to free themselves to the end, from the moods,

waverings and half-hearted ideology of the petty bourgeoisie. . . .[1]

The fact that this did not accord with the idée fixe of this and all other Comintern pronouncements that leadership of colonial revolutionary movements is properly a function of the industrial urban workers should in no way blind us to the fact which Comintern leadership was realistic enough to acknowledge, namely that membership of these Communist Parties is heavily weighted in favor of the intelligentsia. One may, in fact, go one step further and say that in accepting the predominance of the "colonial" intelligentsia, the Comintern was closer to the *genus* of Leninist doctrine than were any of its endorsements of the leadership role of the urban proletariat. No other group in these areas but the intelligentsia could be expected to under-take the transformation of the social structure under forced drafts and in a pre-determined direction and thus fulfill the main self-assigned historical mission of Leninism.[2]

If we bear this key factor in mind, it throws a new light on the nature of the grip which Communists exercise on the political movements of these areas. The usual formulation of the character of these movements is that they stem from mass discontent with the pre-vailing system of land distribution, with the labor practices in force, with the overt or indirect political control of these areas by foreign governments, etc. These are perfectly valid empirical descriptions of the neces-sary conditions for the rise of liberation movements in these areas. But they obviously fail to take notice of the specific social groups that give these movements their *élan*, direction and whatever measure of success they have had thus far. As matters stand today, the intellec-tuals are the sole group in these areas which can infuse these raw social materials of agrarian discontent, etc., with the necessary organization and leadership necessary for their success. And it is largely this group which has acted as the marriage broker between the inter-national Communist movement and the manifestations of indigenous revolt.

Enough empirical material exists to warrant the conclusion that the "colonial" Communist parties of Asia today, as in the 1920's, are the handiwork of native intellectuals. Since 1940, they have, of course, greatly expanded their mass following and membership, but their leadership is still drawn overwhelmingly from the intelligentsia. As regards China, this elite character of Communist party leadership was expressly recognized by Mao Tse-tung in 1939[3] and the entire history of the party from its founding by Li Ta-chao and Ch'en Tu-hsu to Mao Tse-tung and Liu Shao-sh'i is virtually an unbroken record of a party controlled by intellec-tuals.[4] India illustrates the same trend. Its earliest Com-munist leadership is exemplified in M. N. Roy (who later broke with the movement), a high-caste Brahmin of considerable intellectual attainments. Also indicative of the predominance of intellectuals in the leadership

[1] "The Revolutionary Movement in the Colonies; Resolution of the Sixth World Congress of the Communist International," adopted Sept. 1, 1928, *International Press Correspondence*, Vol. VIII, No. 88, Dec. 12, 1928, p. 1670.

[2] Though cognizant of the role of the intellectual in the Chinese party, Benjamin Schwartz's illuminating study, *Chinese Communism and the Rise of Mao*, Cambridge, 1951, falls short of an appreciation of its significance by focusing attention on a purely strategic problem — Mao's peasant-oriented movement — and concluding from this that Mao's ideology represents a radical break with classical Leninism.

[3] Mao Tse-tung, *The Chinese Revolution and the Communist Party of China* (Committee For a Democratic Far Eastern Policy), New York, undated translation, pp. 13–14.

[4] Mao Tse-tung's excursion into an instrumentalist approach to Marxian philosophy is one manifestation; see his "On Practice" in *Political Affairs* (organ of the U.S. Communist Party), Bombay, June 13, 1943.

of the Indian Communist Party is the fact that at its first All-Indian Congress in 1943, eighty-six of a total attendance of 139 delegates were members of professional and intellectual groups.[1] And in the post-war period, the leading position of this social group in the affairs of the Indian Communist Party finds expression in men like Joshi, Ranadive and Dange.[2] The same pattern also holds good for the Communist parties of Indo-China, Thailand, Burma, Malaya and Indonesia, all of which show a heavy preponderance of journalists, lawyers and teachers among the top leadership.[3] The Burmese Communists afford an especially pointed illustration in this respect since the parent organization, the Thakens, originated among university students in the early 1930's who today comprise the leadership of both rival Communist factions.[4] If any doubt exists as to the extent to which the leadership of these movements is dominated by intellectual groups, it is quickly dispelled by an examination of the top echelons of trade unions, as instanced, for example, by the names of those attending the WFTU-sponsored Congress of Asian and Australasian Unions in Peking in 1949. Here, at least, we can appreciate the full impact of the trend by noting that while European trade union leadership (in contrast to the leadership of parties) has been largely recruited from within membership ranks, the reverse is true in south Asia. The trade union movement in that region is largely a new-born, post-war phenomenon and the various bodies (whether Communist-dominated or controlled by other political groups) have been fashioned and directed by professionals with no direct experience in the occupations concerned.[5]

This, in its larger perspectives, is the structure of leadership both for the Communist and non-Communist groups in the entire region. More detailed research might serve to throw some light on the sociological factors which determine the distribution of these professional groups among Communist and anti-Communist movements. But even if a completely detailed analysis is still lacking, enough is already known of the larger trends to indicate that these sections of the native populations constitute the key operational factor in the Communist appeal. It is they who spearhead the propaganda drive, organize the unions, youth groups and other organizations, and plan the tactics of their parties, etc.

As matters stand, then, the organization and leadership of Communist parties in colonial areas do not accord with their accepted doctrinal precepts. For over a generation now it has been a standard item of doctrine, reiterated again and again, that the leadership of these parties must rest with the industrial working class.[6] The realities of the situation in these areas have not been very obliging to this formula though it still occupies its customary niche in all their pronouncements. From the standpoint of their own strategic imperatives and long-term objective however, the Communist parties of these areas have not hesitated to draw the necessary practical conclusions. They have acquiesced in the

primacy of the intellectuals in the movement because the acceptance of any alternative leadership coming from the ranks of the peasantry of the industrial workers (assuming the possibility of such leadership), would entail the sacrifice of the prime objectives of the party — viz., the seizure of power and the launching of a long-range plan for internal planning and reconstruction. Gradual and piecemeal reforms and certainly basic reforms designed to bring immediate relief to the masses (for instance in the credit structure of an area) undertaken by non-Communist regimes would be welcomed by the mass of the peasantry because they are in accord with their immediate and most pressing interests.[7] A program of seizing political power followed by prolonged industrialization, economic planning, recasting of the social structure, re-alignment of a country's international position in favor of the USSR — these are considerations of the type which can attract intellectuals only.[8]

Accordingly, if the main appeal of Communism *per se*, in underdeveloped areas, has been to the native intelligentsia, a transgression has apparently been committed against an expendable item of party dogma, but the fundamental spirit of the Leninist position with regard to the relation between leadership and the masses, has actually been preserved in its pristine form. There is no need to labor this point since there is enough evidence to indicate that the leadership of Communist parties in underdeveloped areas is acutely aware of the conflict between its own long-range objectives and the "interests" of its mass following, as well as of the conclusions to be drawn for the practical guidance of their parties' activities. Thus a recent party document issued by the Malaya Communist Party to cope with

[1] *People's War* (organ of the CPI), Bombay, June 13, 1943.

[2] See a review of the latter's "India, from Primitive Communism to Slavery," Bombay, 1949, in *The Communist* (organ of the CPI), Bombay, Vol. III, No. 4, October–November 1950, pp. 78–91. Cf. M. R. Masani, "The Communist Party in India" in *Pacific Affairs*, March 1951, pp. 31–33.

[3] See for example, biographic data in V. Thompson and R. Adloff, *The Left Wing in South East Asia* (New York), 1950, pp. 231–286.

[4] *Ibid.*, pp. 80–82.

[5] *New York Times*, May 21, 1950; see also Institute of Pacific Relations, *Problems of Labor and Social Welfare in South and Southeast Asia*, Secretariat Paper No. 1 prepared by members of the ILO, New York, 1950, p. 20. Cf. statements of delegates from India and Ceylon to Asian Regional Conference of the ILO in Ceylon, Jan. 16–27, 1950, *op. cit.*, pp. 98, 113.

[6] See for example, Resolution on the Revolutionary Movement in Colonial and Semi-Colonies, Sixth Congress of Comintern, Sept. 1, 1928, *op. cit.*, pp. 1670–1672, *et passim*, and Mao's pamphlet, cited above, pp. 15–16.

[7] This is all the more true of large sections of southeast Asia where the land problem is not identical with the structure of ownership distribution and where no direct correlation prevails between tenancy and poverty. In large sections of this region, the problem arises largely from the primitive credit and marketing facilities rather than from concentration of land titles.

[8] Communist leaders are not loath to recognize that this cleavage exists between the immediate interests of the masses and the party's long-range perspectives. See Liu Shao-chi, "On the Party," *Political Affairs*, October 1950, p. 88.

internal criticism of its leadership and policies contains this cogent passage:

> Regarding these masses, our responsibility is not to lower the Party's policy and to accede to the selfish demands of small sections of the backward elements, but to bring out a proper plan to unite and direct them courageously to carry out the various forms of struggle against the British. If this course is not followed we will retard the progress of the national revolutionary war, and will lose the support of the masses. The proper masses route is not only to mix up with them [mingle with them?] but to resolutely and systematically lead them to march forward to execute the Party's policy and programme. By overlooking the latter point, we will not be able to discharge the historical duty of a revolutionary Party.[1]

If we discern the central driving force of Communism in the underdeveloped areas to be its appeal to a considerable number of the indigenous intelligentsia, we are also in a position to reassess the meaning and changes of its mass appeal, most notably its program of land redistribution. To no inconsiderable extent, much of the confusion which attends thinking and discourse on the subject in this country can be traced to a widespread impression, still current, that the Communist movement in underdeveloped areas owes its success to the fact that it is finely attuned to the most urgent and insistent "land hunger" of millions of the poorest peasants living on a submarginal level of existence. There is just enough historical truth in this impression to make it a plausible explanation of Communist strength. It is unquestionably true that the mass base of the Communist parties in south Asia can be accounted for by the almost universal prevalence of local agrarian unrest which thus constitutes the necessary precondition for the activities of the Communists. But if — as is not infrequently done — this is offered as the crucially strategic element in the

complex of circumstances which have served the cause of the Communist parties, we are once again confronted with the old confusion of necessary with sufficient causes.[2] For there is no intrinsic reason which compels the groundswell of agrarian discontent to favor the fortunes of the Communist parties — unless that discontent can be channelled and directed in predetermined fashion by the intervention of a native social group capable of giving organized shape to its various amorphous and diffused manifestations. If the foregoing analysis has any merit, the balance of the sociological picture in these areas will have to be redressed in our thinking to give greater weight to the Communist-oriented intelligentsia, and to its role as the prime mover of the native Communist movements.

A more balanced picture of the sociological roots of the Communist movement in the underdeveloped areas would also serve to throw some light on the shift which has recently taken place in their agrarian reform program and therefore too in the direction of their appeal.

In its original form, the agrarian program of the Comintern was an outright bid for the support of the poorest, and therefore the numerically preponderant sections, of the peasantry. At the second Congress of the Comintern in 1920, Lenin placed the question of agrarian reform at the very center of the Communist appeal and dismissed as Utopian any notion that a Communist movement in these areas was even conceivable without an appeal to the masses of peasantry.[3] The resolution adopted by that Congress repudiated any attempt to solve the agrarian problem along Communist lines, and instead accepted the inevitable fact that in its initial stages, the agrarian revolution in these areas would have to be achieved by a "petty bourgeois" program of land distribution, directed "against the landlords, against large landownership, against all survivals of feudalism . . ."[4] Eight years later the Sixth Congress of the Comintern was more specific. Its resolution on the strategy of the Communist movement in colonial areas called attention to the presence of a "hierarchy of many stages, consisting of landlords and sublandlords, parasitic intermediate links between the laboring cultivator and the big landowner or the state" who were destroying the basis of the peasant's livelihood. More particularly, ". . . . the peasantry . . . no longer represents a homogeneous mass. In the villages of China and India . . . it is already possible to find exploiting elements derived from the peasantry who exploit the peasants and village laborers through usury, trade, employment of hired labor, the sale or letting out of land . . ." While the Comintern was willing to collaborate with the entire peasantry during the first period of the liberation movement, the upper strata of the peasantry was expected to turn counter-revolutionary as the movement gained momentum. When the chips were down, therefore, the program would have to shift to "a revolutionary settlement of the agrarian question."[5]

[1] The document from which this passage is taken is contained in a Malaya Communist Party publication titled "How to Look After the Interests of the Masses," *Emancipation Series No. 5*, published secretly by the Freedom Press in Malaya, Dec. 15, 1949 and made public after its seizure by the local authorities. Another document titled "Resolution to Strengthen Party Character" reaffirms the doctrine of democratic centralism against the more "extremist democratic" demands of some of the members. For an expression of the same standpoint regarding the relation between the party and the masses from a Chinese source, see Liu-Shao-chi, "On the Party," *Political Affairs*, Oct. 1950, p. 78.

[2] An otherwise excellent discussion by Miss Barbara Ward verges on this error, especially in its opening remarks. See her article in the *New York Times*, March 25, 1951.

[3] For the text of Lenin's remarks, see *Selected Works*, Vol. X, pp. 239–240.

[4] "Theses on National and Colonial Questions," *ibid.*, pp. 231–238. See also the speech of Zinoviev at the Congress of Eastern Peoples held in Baku, 1920. *I S'zed Narodov Vostoka September 1–8, 1920, Bauk, Stenograficheskii Otchety*, Petrograd, 1920.

[5] "The Revolutionary Movement in the Colonies and Semi-

The "revolutionary settlement of the agrarian question" was never accomplished, save in the case of Korea. Wherever the Communists have achieved power in these areas, the program of agrarian revolution, stipulated in the resolution of the Sixth Comintern Congress, soon became a dead letter. Except for Northern Korea where its application was dictated by the previous expropriation of native lands in favor of the Japanese, its place was taken by a series of moderate reforms designed to mollify the poorer sections of the peasantry without alienating the "parasitic intermediate links" or impairing the productive capacity of agriculture. During the period when the Chinese Communists held sway in the border regions, for example, steps were taken to alleviate the lot of the poorer peasantry in such matters as rentals and interest rates, but wholesale confiscation and redistribution were not attempted to any great extent.[1] Similarly, under the present regime in China, the revolutionary formula has been virtually dismissed as a propaganda appeal, once useful for enlisting the support of the poorer peasantry in the period before the Communist accession to power, but having no relevance to the problem of agriculture today. In fact, the propaganda appeal is now designed to reconcile the middle and wealthier sections of the Chinese peasantry to the new regime in political terms, and to promote increased output and land improvements as prerequisites to a program of industrialization.[2] Without the active intervention of a Communist-oriented intelligentsia, a large scale peasant movement in China as well as in the region of south Asia, if successful, would not go beyond agrarian reform pure and simple. The end goal would be Sun Yat Sen's and Stambulisky's rather than Lenin's, given the essentially static and conservative temper of the bulk of the peasant populations. As matters stand now, however, the schedule of agrarian reform under Communist sponsorship has definitely been subordinated to the long-range perspectives of industrialization with a program of collectivization in store for the future when conditions are more favorable to its success.[3] Accordingly, the imperatives of the "New Democracy" require a shift in the main incidence of Communist appeal to secure for the regime a base of support more in accord with its long-range plans.

The shift is equally apparent in the industrial field where attempts are being made to enlist the support of the "national bourgeoisie" during an indefinite transition period pending the introduction of "genuine" socialism. The present program envisions a form of limited, state sponsored and regulated capitalist enterprise to promote the process of industrialization[4] and the attractions now being employed to enlist entrepreneurial cooperation are strangely reminiscent of the "infant industry" argument so familiar in "imperialist" countries.[5]

An identical transposition of appeal may also be detected in the program of Ho Chi-minh's newly organized Laodong (Worker's) Party in Vietnam.[6]

Its program proclaims it the leader of a national united front comprising *all* classes, parties and races, and its leading motif is the need to oust the French oppressors who are charged not only with exploiting Vietnamese workers, but also native landlords and capitalists who must pay a tribute to the French in the form of high prices for imports and the sale of their own products at depressed prices.[7] The socialist regime is indefinitely postponed until such time as the country is ready for it and in the meantime:

> The national bourgeoisie must be encouraged, assisted and guided in their undertakings, so as to contribute to the development of the national economy. The right of the patriotic landlords to collect rent in accordance with the law must be guaranteed.
>
> Our agrarian policy mainly aims at present in carrying out the reduction of land rent and interest ... regulation of the leasehold system, provisional allocation of land formerly owned by imperialists to poorer peasants, redistribution of communal lands, rational use of land belonging to absentee landlords....[8]

To say, then, that the Communist program in the underdeveloped areas of Asia is designed purely and simply as an appeal to the poorest and landless sections of the peasant population is to indulge in an oversimplification of the facts. The Communist appeal is rather a

[1] Except in Kiangsi and Fukien in the late 1920's and later discontinued. Similarly, the radical confiscatory program of 1946–1949 was abandoned with the Communists' final accession to power.

[2] Liu Shao-chi, "On Agrarian Reform in China" in *For a Lasting Peace, for a People's Democracy!*, July 21, 1950, pp. 3–4; see also Teh Kao, "Peasants in the New China," *ibid.*, Oct. 13, 1950, p. 2. For a summary of the history of the Communist agrarian program, see F. C. Lee, "Land Redistribution in Communist China," *Pacific Affairs*, March 1948, pp. 20–32.

[3] Mao Tse-tung, *On the Present Situation and Our Tasks* (East China Liberation Publishers), 1946; see also remarks of Kiu Shao-ch'i in *People's China*, July 16, 1950.

[4] See for example, Mao Tse-tung, *On People's Democratic Rule*, New York (New Century Publishers), 1950, p. 12 and the text of the "Common Program of the People's Political Consultative Conference of 1949" included as an appendix to Mao's speech, esp. p. 19.

[5] Wu Min, "Industry of People's China Grows," in *For a Lasting Peace, for a People's Democracy!*, Nov. 17, 1950, p. 4. This outright nationalistic appeal to the interests of domestic business groups is also plainly apparent in the latest draft program of the Indian Communist Party. See *For a Lasting Peace, for a People's Democracy!*, May 11, 1951, p. 3.

[6] Actually a revival of the Communist Party dissolved in 1945.

[7] Vietnam News Agency in English Morse to Southeast Asia, April 12, 1951.

[8] Vietnam News Agency in English Morse to Southeast Asia, March 18 and April 10, 1951.

Colonies," Resolution adopted by Sixth Congress of the Communist International, Sept. 1, 1928, *International Press Correspondence*, Vol. VIII, No. 88, Dec. 12, 1928, pp. 1663–1667.

complicated function of the total interplay of political forces in these areas, and has therefore tended to shift both in direction and content with the degree of influence and political power exercised by the Communist parties. The only constant element among all these changes has been the abiding appeal of the Communist system to certain sections of the intelligentsia. Whether the new dispensation of the appeal can be expected to evoke the same degree of sympathetic response from the "national bourgeoisie" and the more prosperous peasantry as the discarded slogan of outright land confiscation had for the impoverished peasants is open to considerable doubt. The avowed transitional character of the program of the "People's Democracy" is alone sufficient to rob these appeals of any sustained response. It does not require any high degree of political sophistication on the part of the "national bourgeoisie," for example, to realize that a full measure of cooperation with a Communist-controlled regime would only serve to hasten its own extinction. How seriously such a withdrawal of support would affect the fortunes of a Communist regime would depend to a crucial extent on the speed with which it could find a substitute support in newly evolved social groups with a vested stake in its continued existence. Some indication of how the problem is visualized by the leaders of the Communist regime in China may be gleaned from the following remarks made by Li Shao-chi in a speech to Chinese businessmen last year:

> As Communists we consider that you are exploiting

[1] Quoted by M. Lindsay in *New China*, ed. O. van der Sprenkel, London, 1950, p. 139.

your workers; but we realize that, at the present stage of China's economic development, such exploitation is unavoidable and even socially useful. What we want is for you to go ahead and develop production as fast as possible and we will do what we can to help you. You may be afraid of what will happen to you and your families when we develop from New Democracy to Socialism. But you need not really be afraid. If you do a really good job in developing your business, and train your children to be first-class technical experts, you will be the obvious people to put in charge of the nationalized enterprise and you may find that you earn more as managers of a socialized enterprise than as owners.[1]

For the time being the challenge which confronts the West in its efforts to deny the underdeveloped areas of south Asia to the Communist appeal is therefore of two distinct elements. The more obvious of these is, of course, the problem of depriving the Communists of their actual and potential "mass base" by an adequate program of technical aid and economic reform designed to remove the blight of poverty and exploitation from the scheme of things heretofore in force in these areas. The other and more imponderable aspect of this twofold challenge requires the development of an ethos and system of values which can compete successfully with the attraction exercised by Communism for those sections of the native intelligentsia which have been the source and mainstay of its leadership. To date, there is little evidence that the West is prepared to meet either of these challenges on terms commensurate with its gravity.

The Second Transformation of American Secondary Education

Martin Trow

THE PAST FEW YEARS have seen a very large amount of public controversy over education in America. The controversy has touched on every aspect and level of education, from nursery school to graduate education, and the spokesmen have represented many different interests and points of view. But the focus of the controversy has been the public high school, its organization and curriculum, and the philosophy of education that governs it. On one side, with many individual exceptions and variations in views, stand the professional educators and their organizations. As the creators and administrators of the existing system, American educators not surprisingly by and large defend it, and while accepting and even initiating specific reforms, tend to justify existing practices, institutional arrangements, and dominant philosophies of education. On the other side, a more heterogeneous body of laymen, college and university professors, politicians and military men have attacked fundamental aspects of secondary education in America. The disputes extend over a broad range of educational issues, but at the heart of the argument is the charge by the critics that the *quality* of American secondary education is poor, that the time and energies of teachers and students are scattered and dispersed over a great variety of activities and subjects, and that there ought to be far greater emphasis on intellectual training, academic subject matter, and the acquisition of traditional skills and knowledge.[1] Very often, the call for reform is coupled

with attacks on the policies and philosophies of professional educators; the critics claim that a watered-down progressive education, doctrines of "life adjustment," the "child-centered school" and the "education of the whole person" have provided the rationale for an indifference to the acquisition of knowledge and the development of clarity of thought and expression which students gain when held to high standards of achievement in course work centering on the traditional "solid" subject matters of English, history, mathematics and the natural sciences.

The public debate has largely restricted itself to issues internal to education – to the curriculum, to teacher training and certification, and the like. But the forces that most heavily affect developments within education largely lie outside it, and are often not reflected in the debates about it. It may be useful to consider some of the historical forces which give rise to the current controversies over secondary education.

The transformation of America

The Civil War is the great watershed of American

[1] For discussion and analysis of the controversy, and references to representative books and articles about the issues, see Paul Woodring. *A Fourth of a Nation* (New York: McGraw Hill, 1957), Chapters I–III. For a very different view of the controversy and the issues, see Myron Lieberman, *The Future of Public Education* (Chicago: The University of Chicago Press, 1960), Chapters i and ii.

Reprinted from *The International Journal of Comparative Sociology*, by permission of the author and the publisher.

history. It stands midway between the Revolution and ourselves, and symbolically, but not just symbolically, separates the agrarian society of small farmers and small businessmen of the first half of the nineteenth century from the urbanized industrial society with its salaried employees that followed. And the mass public secondary-school system as we know it has its roots in the transformation of the economy and society that took place after the Civil War.

In 1820, at least seven out of every ten Americans in the labor force were farmers or farm laborers. In 1870, farmers still comprised about half the labor force. By 1960, that figure was below 10 percent. At the same time, the proportion of salaried white-collar workers rose from less than 10 percent in 1870 to nearly 40 percent today.[1] The proportion of nonfarm manual workers in the labor force rose until 1920, leveled off at about 40 percent since then and has shown signs of falling over the past decade. Thus, there has been a large and rapid growth of a new salaried middle class, paralleled by a large and rapid decline in the proportion of the labor force in agriculture, with the proportions of manual workers rising till about 1920 but relatively constant over the past forty years.

These changes in the occupational structure have reflected tremendous changes in the economy and organization of work. Since the Civil War, and especially in the past fifty years, an economy based on thousands of small farms and businesses has been transformed into one based on large bureaucratized organizations characterized by centralized decision-making and administration carried out through coordinated managerial and clerical staffs.

When small organizations grow large, papers replace verbal orders; papers replace rule-of-thumb calculations of price and profit; papers carry records of work flow and inventory that in a small operation can be seen at a glance on the shop floor and materials shed. And as organizations grew, people had to be trained to handle those papers — to prepare them, to type them, to file them, to process them, to assess and use them. The growth of the secondary-school system after 1870 was in large part a response to the pull of the economy for a mass of white-collar employees with more than an elementary school education.

The first transformation of American secondary education

In 1870 there were roughly 80,000 students enrolled in high schools of all kinds in this country, and the bulk of these were in tuition academies. Public high schools were just beginning to grow in numbers — there were perhaps no more than 500 in the whole country, concentrated in the Northeast, and still greatly outnumbered by the tuition academies.[2] The 16,000 high-school graduates in that year comprised only about 2 percent of the seventeen-year-olds in the country.[3] Moreover, a very large proportion of those who went to secondary school went on to college.[4]

The American secondary school system of 1870 offered a classical liberal education to a small number of middle- and upper-middle-class boys.[5] Very few students went to secondary school, most who went graduated, and many who graduated went on to college. By 1910, there were over 1,100,000 high-school students, nearly 90 percent of them enrolled in the over 10,000 public high schools, and they comprised about 15 percent of the 14–17 year age group.[6] But for the bulk of these students, high school was as far as they were going. By 1957, 90 percent of the 14–17 year age group were in school, while 62 percent of the 17-year-old cohort were gaining high-school diplomas. Before 1870, the small secondary-school system offered a curriculum and maintained standards of scholarship geared to the admissions requirements of the colleges.[7] After 1870, the growing mass secondary system was largely terminal, providing a useful and increasingly vocational education for the new body of white-collar workers.

The evidence for the connection between education and occupation that developed after the Civil War is embedded in the census reports. In 1950, at the end of the fifty-year period that might be called "the age of the terminal high school" the median years of schooling completed by men and women 25 years and older in various occupational groups were as follows.[8]

[1] Sources: U.S. Bureau of the Census, *Statistical Abstract of the United States: 1960* (Eighty-first edition, Washington, D.C.: 1960), Table 279, p. 216. Donald J. Bogue, *The Population of the United States* (Glencoe, Illinois: The Free Press, 1959). Kurt Mayer, "Recent Changes in the Class Structure of the United States," *Transactions of the Third World Congress of Sociology* (Amsterdam: 1956), III, pp. 66–80.

[2] Ellwood P. Cubberley, *Public Education in the United States* (Boston: Houghton-Mifflin Co., 1934), pp. 255, 627.

[3] U.S. Bureau of the Census, *Historical Statistics of the United States, Colonial Times to 1957* (Washington, D.C.: 1960), p. 207.

[4] Compare the annual output of the secondary schools in 1870 (16,000 graduates) with the total college enrollment of 52,000 in that year. *Ibid.*

[5] On the academies in the nineteenth century, see E. E. Brown, *The Making of Our Middle Schools* (New York: Longmans, Green and Co., 1903). While the early academies were not intended as preparatory schools, "the idea of liberal culture [was] the dominant note of both academy and college education in the nineteenth century." (*Ibid.*, p. 229.)

[6] U.S. Department of Health, Education, and Welfare, *Progress of Public Education in the United States, 1959–60* (Washington, D.C.: 1960), Table 2, p. 11. *Historical Statistics of the United States, Colonial Times to 1957*, p. 207.

[7] Brown, *op. cit.*, p. 231.

[8] Bogue, *op. cit.*, Table 17–11, p. 510. For over sixty years, the dominant stereotype of social class in America, based on solid reality but enshrined in folk-lore and mass fiction, has been that white-collar people have been to high school, while manual workers by and large have not. These educational and class cleavages in America have also roughly coincided with religious and ethnic cleavages — between the older Protestant immigration from Northern and Western Europe and the later Catholic immigration from Southern and Eastern Europe. But the educational dimension of this cleavage is now changing. See footnote 2, p. 444.

Professionals:	16+
Managers, officials, and proprietors:	11.3
Clerical and kindred:	11.4
Sales workers:	11.2
Craftsmen, foremen, and kindred:	8.3
Operatives and kindred:	7.7
Laborers, except mine and farm:	7.0
Service workers:	7.8

Of course, changes in the occupational structure do not provide the whole explanation of the extraordinary growth of secondary and higher education in the United States. The changes in the occupational structure have raised the educational aspirations of large parts of the American population, and the educational system has been responsive to these higher aspirations. The role of public education in American thought and popular sentiment, and its perceived connection both with the national welfare and individual achievement, have, at least until recently, been greater in America than in any other country. Other countries, Great Britain to name one, have had comparable revolutions in their economic structure without comparable educational transformations. The commitment of America to equality of opportunity, the immense importance attached to education throughout American history, the very great role of education as an avenue of mobility in a society where status ascribed at birth is felt to be an illegitimate barrier to advancement — all of these historical and social psychological forces are involved in the extraordinary American commitment to mass secondary and higher education. Moreover, there were forces involved in the growth of the high school — such as large-scale immigration and urbanization, and the movement to abolish child labor[1] — which are not present in the growth of mass higher education, whereas transformations of the occupational structure are common to both educational movements.

Now, the creation of a system of mass secondary education that accompanied the growth of mass organizations after 1870 could not be simply the extension of the old elite secondary system; it would be different in function (terminal rather than preparatory) and in organization (public and locally controlled, rather than private tuition and endowed schools). Moreover, it needed its own curriculum and its own teacher-training programs and institutions. It needed its own teacher-training programs first because the sheer number of secondary teachers required by mass secondary education was far beyond the capacities of the traditional colleges to supply, as they had supplied the older tuition academies.[2] In the old academies, the principals and masters were products of the colleges, and often went on to teach in the colleges; there was no sharp break between the academies and the colleges since they taught roughly the same subjects to the same kinds of students.[3] This was no longer possible with the new terminal public high school; the students were different, the curriculum was not preparation for college, by and large, and new Departments of Education and

State Teachers Colleges were created at least in part to train the staffs of these new high schools.[4] These centers of professional education were not identified with the older, elite traditions of higher education, but created their own traditions of education for life, for citizenship, for useful tasks, the traditions, that is, of the mass democratic terminal secondary system that came to full flower between 1910 and 1940.[5]

By 1935, an observer sympathetic to these developments could write:

> The twentieth century so far has witnessed a steady shifting of . . . control [over secondary education] by college presidents and faculties to people more immediately concerned with the operation or professional study of secondary education . . . Not only are national committees dealing with the general aspects of secondary education becoming exclusively manned by secondary school leaders and specialists, but the whole process of curriculum making for high schools within states and within local school systems is rapidly becoming assumed by these professional categories. High school courses of study are less and less often handed down by college authorities even in the old academic fields. Secondary textbooks are more and more written by public school superintendents, high school principals, supervisors, teachers, and students of educational methods.

[1] Although "the raising of the school-leaving age in many states followed the change in the pattern of school attendance of a majority of the youth." James Conant, *The Child, The Parent and The State* (Cambridge, Mass.: Harvard University Press, 1959), p. 95.

[2] The number of public high-school teachers increased from about 20,000 in 1900 to over 200,000 in 1930. U.S. Office of Education, *Biennial Survey of Education, 1928–1930*, Bulletin, No. 20, Vol. II (1931), pp. 8, 222.

[3] "In 1872, 70 percent of the students entering the eastern colleges were graduates of the academies." Cubberley, *op. cit.*, p. 260, footnote 1.

[4] On the upgrading of Normal Schools to the status of four-year State Teachers Colleges, and the establishment of departments of education in other colleges and universities in the decades before 1920, see Benjamin W. Frazier, "History of the Professional Education of Teachers in the United States," and E. S. Evenden *et al.*, "Summary and Interpretations," U.S. Office of Education, *National Survey of Education, Bulletin 1933*, No. 10, Vols. V and VI (1935).

[5] "During the first half of the present century, while many liberal arts colleges turned their backs on the problems of teacher education, legal requirements for certification were established in nearly all states. . . . [W]hile the liberal arts colleges were preoccupied with other things, while they ignored the problems of teacher education, a like-minded group of school administrators and other professional educators came to agreement among themselves on the necessity for professional preparation for teachers and transmitted their convictions into law. It was during this same period that the educators became imbued with a new philosophy of education, one far removed from the academic traditions of the liberal arts colleges." Paul Woodring, *New Directions in Teacher Education* (New York: The Fund for the Advancement of Education, 1957), p. 23. See also Merle L. Borrowman, *The Liberal and Technical in Teacher Education* (New York: Teachers College, Columbia University, 1956).

A further evidence of this general trend is the continuing introduction of new subjects and courses. Whereas in the past most new subjects appeared in the secondary school as reflections of the growing differentiation of the academic disciplines, most of the new subjects now appearing represent hitherto neglected aspects of social existence. As illustrations may be cited innumerable vocational courses, health courses, citizenship courses, and character courses.[1]

In the fifty years between 1880 and 1930, the numbers of students in public high schools in the United States roughly doubled every decade, rising from 110,000 to nearly four and a half million. And the new secondary education was shaped both by the enormous increase in numbers of students, and by their social characteristics. Many of the new students were in school unwillingly, in obedience to the new or more stringent state compulsory education laws; many came from poor, culturally impoverished homes and had modest vocational goals; many of these were the sons and daughters of recent immigrants, and seemed to observers very much in need of "Americanization."[2] These new students posed new problems for secondary education; and these

problems, and the answers which they engendered, transformed public secondary education, its philosophy and its curriculum. Commenting on the influential National Education Association Report of 1918 entitled *Cardinal Principles of Secondary Education*, a report strongly influenced by the writings of John Dewey, and responsive to the new demands of mass secondary education, James Conant observes:

> Confronted with a "heterogeneous high school population destined to enter all sorts of occupations," high school teachers and administrators and professors of education needed some justification for a complete overhauling of a high school curriculum originally designed for a homogeneous student body. The progressives with their emphasis on the child, "on learning by doing," on democracy and citizenship, and with their attack on the arguments used to support a classical curriculum were bringing up just the sort of *new* ideas that were sorely needed. After closing John Dewey's volume, *Democracy and Education*, I had the feeling that, like the Austro-Hungarian Empire of the nineteenth century, if John Dewey hadn't existed he would have had to be invented. In a sense perhaps he was, or at least his doctrines were shaped by school people with whom he talked and worked.[3]

The creation of a mass terminal system, with functions and orientations quite different from that of the traditional college-preparatory system it succeeded, forced not merely certain changes in the curriculum, but a drastic shift in the basic assumptions underlying secondary education. Speaking of the writings of G. Stanley Hall in support of the "child-centered school," Lawrence Cremin notes that they

> paved the way for a fundamental shift in the meaning of equal opportunity at the secondary level. Formerly, when the content and purpose of the secondary school had been fairly well defined, equal opportunity meant the right of all who might profit from secondary education as so defined to enjoy its benefits. Now, the "given" of the equation was no longer the school with its content and purposes, but the children with their background and needs. Equal opportunity now meant simply the right of all who came to be offered something of value, and it was the school's obligation to offer it. The magnitude of this shift cannot be overestimated; it was truly Copernican in character. And tied as it was to the fortunes of the child-study movement, it gained vast popularity during the first decade of the twentieth century.[4]

The popularity of these new ideas and assumptions, and their impact on secondary education in the succeeding decades, suggests how educational doctrines are influenced by social trends.[5] With schools full of

---

[1] Matthew H. Willing, "Recent Trends in American Secondary Education," in William S. Gray, ed., *The Academic and Professional Preparation of Secondary-School Teachers* (Chicago: The University of Chicago Press, 1935), pp. 8–9, 12. See also, Alfred L. Hall-Quest, *Professional Secondary Education in the Teachers Colleges*, "Contributions to Education," No. 169 (New York: Teachers College, Columbia University, 1925), pp. 20–27.

[2] During the twelve years immediately preceding World War I, an average of almost one million new immigrants a year arrived in America; they were predominantly from Southern and Eastern Europe, and settled chiefly in the big cities of the Midwest and the Eastern seaboard.

[3] Conant, *op. cit*, pp. 93–94.

[4] Lawrence A. Cremin, "The Revolution in American Secondary Education, 1893–1918," *Teachers College Record*, Vol. LVI (1955), No. 6, p. 303.

[5] For a detailed account of the transformation of secondary education in Muncie, Indiana, during the twenties and early thirties, see Robert S. and Helen Merrell Lynd, *Middletown* (New York: Harcourt, Brace and Co., 1929), and *Middletown in Transition* (New York: Harcourt, Brace and Co., 1937). The Lynds make clear that in the middle twenties the Muncie high school offered a terminal, primarily vocational education, although the formal curriculum was still predominantly composed of the traditional academic courses. As the president of the School Board of Muncie said to them: "For a long time all boys were trained to be President. Then for a while we trained them all to be professional men. Now we are training boys to get jobs." (*Middletown*, p. 194). The hollowness of the traditional course work under those circumstances is reflected in the remark of one high school English teacher: "Thank goodness, we've finished Chaucer's *Prologue*! I am thankful and the children are, too. They think of it almost as if it were in a foreign language, and they *hate* it." (*Ibid.*, p. 193). These sentiments, shared by both teachers and students in Muncie, were reflected in the quality of the academic preparation given those students who did go on to college; as the Lynds report, most of them dropped out or did poorly. (*Ibid.*, p. 195). By 1930 the new "scientific" educational philosophy had found expression in Muncie in a new curriculum "devoted to the principle that the schools should fit the needs of the indivi-

children for whom the traditional content and purpose of the secondary-school curriculum were irrelevant, educators needed some rationale and justification for what they were doing. And what they were doing was trying to teach something that promised to be of some use for these terminal students, in ways that would hold, at least fleetingly, the interest of indifferent students whose basic interests lay outside the classroom. It was precisely the interest and motivation that one could no longer assume in the student, but had to engender in the school, that lay at the heart of W. H. Kilpatrick's influential *The Project Method*,[1] and before that, underlay the importance of motivation in Dewey's writings.

The growth of mass higher education in America

During the decades when the institutions, the curriculum, and the philosophies of mass terminal education were being created, the college population was rising very slowly.[2] As recently as 1940 the total number of students enrolled in college comprised only 15 percent of the college age group (the 18- to 21-year-olds). By 1954, that proportion was up to 30 percent, and by 1960 it was around 37½ percent. Over both the longer twenty-year period between 1940 and 1960 and the recent six-year period, 1954–1960, the rate of increase in college enrollments as a proportion of the college age group has been about 1.3 percent a year. If that rate of increase is maintained, and that is a conservative forecast, then by 1970 college enrollments will comprise about half of the college age group.[3] The rapid rate of increase since 1940 is in marked contrast with the average rate of increase of only .35 percent per annum between 1920, when college enrollments comprised 8 percent of the college age group, and 1940, when that figure had risen to 15 percent.

Figure 1 shows the phases in the parallel development of American secondary and higher education graphically. If we take, somewhat arbitrarily, an enrollment of 15 percent of the age-grade as the beginning of the mass phase of an educational system, then secondary education passed this line around 1910, and higher education in 1940. The period 1870–1980 with which we are dealing falls naturally then into three phases. In Phase I secondary and higher education were by and large offering an academic education to an elite minority. Phase II, between roughly 1910 and 1940, saw the rapid growth of mass terminal secondary education, with higher education still offered to a small but slowly growing minority.[4] Since 1940, or more precisely, since World War II, we are (in Phase III) seeing the rapid growth of mass higher education. With enrollments in higher education continuing to grow, and with secondary-school enrollments (as a proportion of the 14-17-year-old population) near saturation, the transformation of the terminal secondary system into a mass preparatory system is well under way.

It is interesting to compare rates of increase in college attendance during the first two decades of Phase III with the rate of increase in high-school enrollments during the decades 1909–1939 (Phase II), the years of growth of the mass secondary system. In the last twenty years of Phase I, 1889–1909, the high-school population (as a proportion of the 14–17-year-olds) rose from 6.7 percent to 15.4 percent, an annual rate of increase of about .44 percent. Over the next three decades (Phase II), the rate increased from 15.4 percent to 73.3 percent,

---

[1] *Teachers College Record*, Vol. XIX (1918), No. 4. Kilpatrick describes the "project" as "the hearty purposeful act" wherein the student pursues his own purposes wholeheartedly and with enthusiasm. And as "the purposeful act is . . . the typical unit of the worthy life in a democratic society, so also should it be made the typical unit of school procedure." (p. 323.) The aim of this education would be "the man who is master of his fate, who with deliberate regard for a total situation forms clear and far-reaching purposes, who plans and executes with nice care the purposes so formed." (*Ibid.*, p. 322.) This is, of course, the ideal citizen of liberal democratic theory, a kind of man America had produced in larger numbers during the eighteenth and nineteenth centuries than any other society in history, and without benefit of the "project method." It was the decline of this liberal society, under the impact of industrialization and large organization, that led Kilpatrick and others to seek to achieve in and through education what one could no longer assume could be achieved through the economic and political life of the society.

The new philosophy of education was a response not merely to a new kind of student but also to a new kind of society. An emphasis on the new students in the schools led to a new curriculum keyed to their vocational interests; an emphasis on the new society led to calls for the radical reconstruction of society through education. It was the first emphasis that found a response in Muncie and had by far the greater impact on the schools there and elsewhere.

[2] Data on enrollments in both high school and college drawn from *Historical Statistics of the United States, Colonial Times to 1957*; *Progress of Public Education in the United States, 1959–60*; Bogue, *op. cit.*; American Council on Education, *Fact Book on Higher Education* (Washington, D.C.: n.d.).

[3] Indeed, projections of the college age population of the United States reported in the *Fact Book* (*op. cit.*) coupled with U.S. Bureau of the Census estimates of college enrollments in 1970 (reported in Bogue, *op. cit.*, Table 26–10, p. 778), give a figure of 55 percent of the 18–21 age group. And a recent Roper study of parental expectations regarding their children's education suggests that even this figure may be considerably low. (See "Why College Enrollments May Triple by 1970", *College Board Review*, No. 40 (Winter, 1960), pp. 18–19.)

[4] But the social composition of this minority was changing during this phase. Already in 1920, when college enrollments comprised only 8 per cent of the 18–21 year old population, some 40 percent of the college population, by one estimate, came from lower-middle and working-class backgrounds. By 1940, at the end of Phase II, 60 percent of college students came out of those classes. (R. J. Havighurst, *American Higher Education in the 1960s* (Columbus: Ohio State University Press, 1960), Table 7, p. 34).

---

dual pupil instead of forcing the child to fit himself to the standard curriculum, as has been the practice in the past." (*Middletown in Transition*, p. 221). "With the high school and even the college no longer serving as a screen sifting out the 'scholars' from the 'non-scholars' even as roughly as they did before the World War, and with secondary education becoming a mass experience, the feeling has grown that education must not only be good but must be good for something — to the individual and to society." (*Ibid.*, p. 222.)

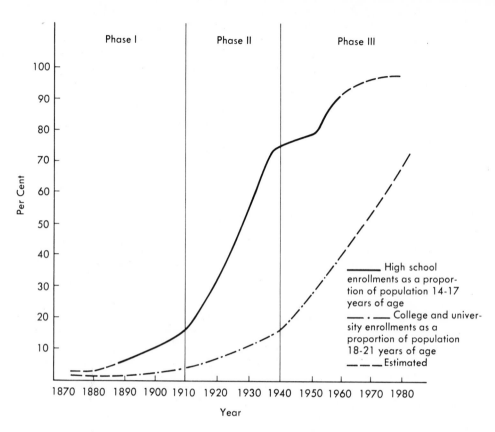

an annual rate of increase of about 1.9 percent. While this is somewhat higher than the rate of increase of about 1.3 percent annually in college attendance (as a proportion of the 18–21-year-olds) thus far in Phase III, there is in both cases a marked increase in the rate of growth over the previous period. In the case of both secondary and higher education, the rate of increase has been about four times as great in the period of rapid growth as compared with the immediately preceding periods of slow growth. The fact that these rates of growth are comparable suggests that the forces behind them are also comparable. In both cases we see the rapid transformation of an education for a relatively small elite into a system of mass education. This process is about completed for the secondary education (in 1958 the high-school population com-

[1] Compare the recent Roper study done in 1959 (*Parents' College Plans Study*, The Ford Foundation, New York: mimeographed, n.d.), which shows that nearly 70 percent of children under 12 are expected by their parents to go to college, with the Roper study of a decade earlier (*Higher Education*, a supplement to *Fortune*, September, 1949). The hopes of the earlier decade have become the expectations of today, and will probably be the enrollments of tomorrow. Of the latest Roper study, one observer noted that "it demonstrated that a college education has come to be widely regarded as the *sine qua non* of personal success, just as the high school diploma did earlier." (Philip Coombs, *College Board Review*, No. 40 (1960), p. 18.)

prised nearly 90 percent of the high-school age group), while we are in the middle of the expansion of opportunities for higher education. And as with secondary education, there is no reason to believe that the United States will stop short of providing opportunities and facilities for nearly universal experience of some kind in higher education.

The immediate force behind these trends in both secondary and higher education are changes in public sentiment — in people's ideas of what they want and expect for their children in the way of formal education. Where most Americans have come to see a high-school education as the ordinary, expected thing for their children, they are now coming to think of at least some time in college in the same way.[1] Behind these changes in sentiment are other social forces, not least among which is another change in our occupational structure, parallel to the massive growth in the white-collar population which underlay the growth of the public secondary-school system. The current change is the immense growth of demand for more highly trained and educated people of all kinds. Between 1940 and 1950, the number of engineers in the country doubled; the number of research workers increased by 50 percent. Even more striking, between 1950 and 1960 the total labor force increased by only 8 percent; but the number of professional, technical, and kindred workers grew by 68 percent[1] — and these, of course, are the occupations that call for at least some part of a college education. Moreover, it is estimated that the period 1957–1970 will see an increase of a further 60 percent in this category of highly educated workers.[2] Where in the decades 1900–1930, clerical and kindred workers were the fastest growing occupational classification and by far, in the period 1950–1970 it has been and will be the professional and technical occupations.[3]

The second transformation of American secondary education

There are two major points to be made in summary here. First, much the same forces which made for the development of the mass secondary system in this country are now at work creating a system of mass higher education. And second, this development is rapidly changing the function of the secondary system. Secondary education in the United States began as an elite preparatory system; during its great years of growth it became a mass terminal system; and it is now having to make a second painful transition on its way to becoming a mass preparatory system. But this transition is a good deal more difficult than the first, because while the first involved the *creation* of the necessary institutions, the second is requiring *transformation* of a huge existing institutional complex. It is almost always easier to create new institutions to perform a new function than it is to transform existing institutions to meet new functions. And as a further complication, during these long decades of transition, the secondary schools are going to have to continue to perform the old terminal-education functions for very large if decreasing proportions of students who are not equipped, motivated, or oriented toward college. In the earlier transition, the old college-preparatory schools continued to exist and to perform their preparatory functions, with much the same curriculum and kinds of personnel, thus permitting a rough division of function between the older and the newer schools. And where this was not possible, the number of preparatory students was shortly so small as compared with the terminal students that the schools did not have quite the same sense of equal but conflicting functions that secondary people are now coming to feel.[4] And in some parts of the country that proportion is very much higher.[5]

By contrast, now and for the foreseeable future, both the preparatory and terminal functions will have to be performed by the same institutions and the same personnel. Of course, that has always been true to some extent — there have always been college-oriented students in our high schools, and provisions have been made for them. But by and large, they have been a minority in an institution created for the great mass of terminal students. The dominant philosophies and structure of the high school could be determined by its central function of providing a terminal secondary education for the mass of American youth. As pre-

paratory students become an increasingly large proportion of all high-school youth, and in more and more places a majority, they provide by their existence not just a demand for special provision, but a challenge to the basic structure and philosophy of the school. And this is the challenge that underlies the criticism of secondary education that flows from many sources.

The rough equality of the terminal and preparatory functions today may account for why the critics and the defenders of the schools largely talk past one another. The critics, who are often university professors, say, in effect, "We need not merely better provision for the preparatory student, but rather, a different guiding educational philosophy for a preparatory secondary system."[6] And the defenders, who are often professional educators, since it is they who created the educational system now under attack, reply, "We cannot ignore the needs and requirements of the great numbers of students who are not going on to college."[7] And when the numbers going on and the numbers not going on are approximately equal, as they are now in many places, neither side can point to numbers as simple justification for its argument.

The high school and its changing public

In the coming decades the high schools will be dealing not only with a different kind of student, but also with a different kind of parent. During the forma-

[1] *Statistical Abstract of the United States, 1960*, p. 216.

[2] Bureau of Labor Statistics estimates, reported in Newell Brown, "The Manpower Outlook for the 1960's: Its Implications for Higher Education," Office of Education, U.S. Department of Education, *Higher Education* (December, 1959), pp. 3–6. It is also estimated that the number of engineers will double during this period.

[3] Bogue, *op. cit.*, Table 17–2, p. 475 and *Fact Book, op. cit.*, p. 146.

[4] For example, of those students entering high school in 1938, only 1 in 5 went on to college four years later, and only 2 in 5 of the high-school graduates of 1932 went on to college. But in the coming decades the numbers of terminal and preparatory students in the high schools will be nearly equal. A third of the students entering high school in 1954 went on to college, and by 1958 half of the high-school graduates in the United States were going on to some kind of higher education. (Computed from data in *Progress of Public Education, op. cit.*, Figure 1, p. 13.)

[5] These transformations can be shown in another way. In 1880, there were roughly the same number of students in American colleges and universities as in our public high schools. By 1940 there were nearly five times as many students in the public high schools as in institutions of higher education. But by 1960, the ratio of high school to college students had fallen to about three to one. (*Historical Statistics, op. cit.*, pp. 207 and 209, and for 1960, *Fact Book, op. cit.*, pp. 10 and 237.)

[6] See for example the *Report of the San Francisco Curriculum Survey Committee* (April, 1960), prepared for the Board of Education, San Francisco Unified School District, by a committee of faculty members from various academic departments of the University of California, Berkeley, and Stanford University.

[7] See *Judging and Improving the Schools: Current Issues*, California Teachers Association, 1960, prepared in answer to the San Francisco Curriculum Survey Committee Report cited above.

tive years of the mass terminal secondary system in the United States, the teachers and educators who were building the system were dealing by and large with parents who themselves had gone no further than grade school. These people, many of them immigrants or of rural origins, whose children were going no further than high school, had neither the competence nor the motivation to be greatly concerned with the high-school curriculum. And the debates about secondary education were carried on largely over the heads of these parents, among the professionals themselves, and between the educators and sections of the academic community. But increasingly, secondary school people are dealing with educated parents of preparatory students, who possess both the competence and the direct motivation to be concerned with the character of their children's secondary education. As recently as 1940, three American adults in five had never been to high school, and only one in four had completed high school.[1] By 1960 three in five had been to high school,

[1] *Bogue*, Table 13–8, p. 343.

[2] Between 1940 and 1959, the average educational level of the whole adult population rose from 8.4 to 11.0 years of schooling completed (U.S. Bureau of the Census, *Current Population Reports*, Series P-20, No. 99 (1959), p. 5). Moreover, recent increases in educational opportunity are closing the historic gap in education between white-collar people and manual workers. In 1940, at the end of Phase II, the broad white-collar categories had on the average completed high school, while manual workers had on the average no more than an elementary schooling. (*Mayer*, Table 5, p. 76). By 1950, young men between 25 and 29 who were skilled workers and foremen already had an average of nearly 12 years of schooling — less than a year of schooling separated them as a group from young white-collar people. Even the semiskilled and service workers among these young men had completed two or three years of high school on the average. (*Ibid.*) By 1959, semiskilled and service workers of all ages had completed an average of two years of high school.

[3] *Bogue*, Table 26–11, p. 779.

[4] The relation of professional educators to their public resembles that of the organized medical profession, whose position on medical insurance is under widespread public criticism, more than it does that of the individual physician or hospital staff.

[5] The extensive studies done with national samples by the Educational Testing Service and others show that students who major in Education score lowest, on comprehensive tests of verbal and mathematical competence, as compared with majors in almost every other field. (Henry Chauncey, "The Use of the Selective Service College Qualification Test of the Deferment of College Students," *Science*, Vol. 116, No. 3301 (July 4, 1952), p. 75.) See also Dael Wolfle and Toby Oxtoby, "Distribution of Ability of Students Specializing in Different Fields," *Science* (September 26, 1952), pp. 311–14), and Dael Wolfle, Director, *America's Resources of Specialized Talent*, The Report of the Commission on Human Resources and Advanced Training (New York: Harper and Brothers, 1934), pp. 189–208. This finding is supported by a recent study on the campus of the University of California at Berkeley, which shows that the men who take the education courses had, on the average, poorer grades and less knowledge about public affairs than did men in other majors. They were also, as a group, both less informed and more illiberal on matters of political tolerance and academic freedom than were the men on the same campus in other areas of specialization. (H. C. Selvin and Warren O. Hagstrom, "Determinants of Support for Civil Liberties," *The British Journal of Sociology*, Vol. XI (March, 1960), pp. 51–73.)

and over 40 percent were high-school graduates.[2] By 1970 over 50 percent will be high-school graduates, and by 1980 it is estimated that figure will reach 60 percent.[3] Parents who have themselves been through high school, and many of them through some years of college as well, feel themselves more competent to pass judgment on the secondary education of their children, and are less likely to accept passively and on faith the professional recommendations of school administrators, educators and counsellors. It is this rapidly growing group of educated parents whose children are going on to college which provides both the audience and the support for the "academic" critics of the secondary school and its curriculum. There is every reason to believe that their interest will grow as their numbers increase, and as competition among their children for the better college places becomes sharper.

This development places a strain on the professional autonomy of educators, who paradoxically find that their professional expertise and judgment is increasingly challenged even while their professional standards and organizations are strengthened, and as the body of knowledge and theory on which their professional status rests is steadily enlarged. This paradox inevitably creates bewilderment and resentment among the professional educators. But it may be that as educators recognize that the very success of their efforts to extend educational opportunities through high school and beyond creates a large body of parents who take a detailed and active interest in the education of their children, they may find some solace in what is probably a permanent condition of external scrutiny and criticism. Moreover, wistful and wholly misleading parallels with the enviable autonomy of doctors and lawyers only sharpen their bewilderment and resentment; they will neither reduce the volume of lay criticism nor account for its existence.[4] Professional educators in America will have to resign themselves to the fact that mass public education, especially at the secondary level, involves conflicts of values and interests which are independent of professional skills and knowledge, and which are increasingly less likely to be left solely to professional decision. And foremost among these is the relative weight and importance placed in each school and district on college preparation as over against a terminal "education for life."

Teachers for mass preparatory secondary education

The difficulties of strengthening secondary education for college preparatory students in public high schools are complicated by what is clearly a pattern of negative selection to teaching below the college level. And this pattern is especially marked for the recruitment of men, who comprise about half of all high-school teachers.[5] Moreover, a recent nationwide study of beginning teachers conducted by the U.S. Office of Education shows that 70 percent of the men and over 80 percent of the women did not expect to continue teaching until retirement.[1] The bulk of the women said, as might be expected, that they hoped to leave teaching for homemaking. More significant for the college-preparatory programs in high schools, over half of the men in the sample expected to leave teaching for some other job in education, chiefly administration, while fully 20 percent were already planning to leave education entirely. And the evidence suggests that the men who remain in the classroom are by and large less able than those who move on to administration or out of education altogether.[2]

The much lower incomes of teachers, as compared with school administrators, with men who leave education, and with most other occupations requiring a comparable amount of education, account for much of this unfortunate pattern of recruitment and retention of male teachers.[3] Moreover, the relatively low status of teaching below the college level, which is both a cause and a consequence of the low salaries, also helps explain why teaching attracts and holds too few of the most able men.[4] And while teachers' salaries are rising, it is unlikely that the gross differentials in pay and prestige between high-school teaching and other occupations requiring a college education are likely to be significantly narrowed in the near future. On the contrary, there is reason to fear they may be widened. The continued extension of opportunities for higher education to able students — through public and private scholarships, the expansion of public higher education, and the like — is offering to able young college men a wider range of occupational alternatives, many of which carry greater prestige and higher incomes than does secondary teaching. In the past a career in teaching was often the only intellectual occupation (aside from the ministry) open to serious young boys from farms and small towns; and the local normal schools or state teachers' college were often the only educational avenues of mobility open to such boys. There are proportionately fewer boys from farms and small towns today, and wider opportunities for them, as for the great mass of urban youth, in higher education, This, together with the continued growth of the "intellectual occupations", is almost certain to make the competition for able men sharper in the years to come. Our society's demands for scientists, engineers, technically trained people of all kinds appears insatiable, and the rewards for work in these fields are usually considerably more generous than for high-school teaching. Of even greater importance, the very rapid expansion of higher education currently underway in this country, and the enormous demands for college teachers that it creates, constitutes perhaps the strongest set of competitive opportunities open to young men who want to teach.[5]

Substantial increases in pay for public-school teachers may ameliorate, but are not likely to reverse, the pattern of recruitment of academically less able men to high-school teaching.[6] And men comprise roughly half the population of American high-school teachers.[7]

Thus, no matter how teacher education, secondary-school curricula, and school organization are reformed to strengthen the college-preparatory function of high schools, a substantial part of the actual teaching itself will be carried on by relatively poorly paid, low status, and often academically less able people. These things may not have mattered so much when secondary education was largely terminal; at least it can be argued that qualities other than academic ability — for example, a deep interest in young people and skills in working with them — are more important for teachers of students whose interests are not academic or intel-

[1] W. S. Mason, R. J. Dressel, and R. K. Bain, "Sex Role and Career Orientations of Beginning Teachers," *Harvard Educational Review*, Vol. 29, No. 4 (Fall, 1959), pp. 370–384. A study done of men who entered education below the college level after World War II showed that by 1955 fewer than half of them (48 percent) were still in the classroom, 23 percent had become educational administrators, and 29 percent had left education entirely. R. L. Thorndike and Elizabeth Hagen, *Characteristics of Men Who Remained in and Left Teaching* (Teachers College, Columbia University, n.d.) Table 3, p. 19.

[2] The study by Thorndike and Hagen (*op. cit.*) of a group of men who were aviation cadet candidates in World War II shows that of all those who went into public school teaching after World War II, "those who were academically more capable and talented tended to drop out of teaching and that those who remained as classroom teachers in the elementary and secondary schools were the less intellectually able members of the original group." (p. 10.) Both the men who remained in education as administrators, and those who had left education completely, showed more academic ability on the Air Force tests than did those who stayed in the classrooms.

[3] In the study by Thorndike and Hagen (*op. cit.*), fewer than one in ten of the men still in classroom teaching were earning more than $600 a month, while over half of both the school administrators and the men who had left education were earning more than that. The median earnings of the administrators and the ex-teachers exceeded that of the teachers by over 25 percent. Two-thirds of the ex-teachers in this study mentioned "low pay" as one of the major reasons for their having left teaching.

[4] In addition, teaching in primary and secondary schools, by contrast both with school administration and with college teaching, is widely perceived as a woman's occupation. And "female occupations" are generally less well paid and give less status to the men in them than do comparable "male occupations."

[5] See M. A. Trow, "Reflections on Recruitment to College Teaching," in Halsey, Floud and Anderson, eds., *Education, Economy and Society* (Glencoe, Illinois: The Free Press, 1961). Junior colleges, in particular, draw a substantial proportion of their faculties directly from the high schools, and in all likelihood the more academically oriented teachers at that. The continued expansion of the junior colleges cannot help but impoverish the teaching staffs of the high schools.

[6] Over the four years between 1955-56 and 1959-60, the average salaries of all public school teachers, principals, and supervisors, rose by nearly a quarter. But during the same period, the salaries of college teachers in all ranks rose by about as much, and in most categories of institutions, by more. From data in *Fact Book*, pp. 105, 106, 239.

[7] Women who enter high-school teaching probably compare more favorably with women in other occupations requiring equivalent amounts of education; among other things, the alternative opportunities are not as broad or attractive for them as for the men. But women are almost as eager to leave the classroom as are men, though for different reasons. Nor, in light of their interests and preparation, can we count on women to carry the burden of teaching the advanced courses in the college preparatory subjects.

lectual. But that can hardly be claimed for teachers of college-bound youngsters, whose success in college will rest very heavily on the knowledge and intellectual habits they acquire in secondary school.

Pressures for reform of the curriculum

The character and quality of high-school teachers are especially important in view of the recent efforts to strengthen the academic and preparatory aspects of the high-school curriculum which are predicated on the existence of large numbers of teachers in the schools able to put the new curriculum into effect. The pressures for reform of the curriculum have been strongest in the areas of science and mathematics. The enormous expansion during and since World War II of scientific research and development, both in government and industry, has created a continuing demand for large numbers of highly trained technicians, and at the same time has generated very strong pressures for the reform of what was a manifestly inadequate curriculum in high-school science and mathematics. And this in turn has involved many more academic scientists in efforts to reform the secondary school curriculum.[1] Largely on the initiative of the university scientists, a number of studies and programs have been initiated expressly to develop new secondary-school courses in the sciences and mathematics, and to prepare textbooks and other materials for use in them. The first of these was the

[1] Bentley Glass, "The Academic Scientist, 1940–1960," *AAUP Bulletin*, June, 1960, p. 153.

[2] See Richard Pearson, "Advanced Placement Programs: Opportunities Ahead," *College Board Review*, No. 39, Fall, 1959, pp. 24–27.

[3] For example, a recent study by the U.S. Office of Education shows that 39 percent of the teachers in the study who were teaching one or more courses in high school mathematics had not had the calculus or a more advanced course in mathematics, while 7 percent had had no college mathematics at all. (K. E. Brown and E. S. Obourn, *Qualifications and Teaching Loads of Mathematics and Science Teachers in Maryland, New Jersey, and Virginia*, U.S. Department of Health, Education, and Welfare, Office of Education, Circular 575 (1959), Tables 20 and 22, p. 46). Similarly, a recent report of the National Council of Teachers of English observes that half of the nation's high-school English teachers do not have a college major in English, and that because of deficiencies in preparation, 70 percent of American colleges and universities must offer remedial work in English. (Reported in *Phi Delta Kappan*, XLII, 6 (March, 1961), p. 271.)

[4] For example, the National Science Foundation through its Summer Institute Program during 1961 supported the attendance of about 20,000 high-school and college teachers of science, mathematics, and engineering at some 400 Institutes around the country.

[5] See I. L. Kandel, *The Dilemma of Democracy* (Cambridge: Harvard University Press, 1934).

[6] But this will almost certainly continue to be the comprehensive high school. The resistance of most American educators to selective schools which "segregate" students of academic ability and interests is very great, despite the reputation and accomplishments of such academically "segregated" high schools as New York's High School of Music and Art, the Bronx High School of Science, and the late Townsend Harris High School. See I. L. Kandel, "Current Issues in Expanding Secondary Education," *International Review of Education*, Vol. 2 (1959), pp. 155–165.

Physical Science Study Committee, begun at the Massachusetts Institute of Technology in 1956, followed closely by the School Mathematics Study Group (1958), the Biological Sciences Curriculum Study (1958), the Chemical Education Material Study (1959), and many others. There are movements afoot to extend these programs and studies aiming at the reform of the secondary-school curriculum to the social studies and the humanities. Moreover, the Advanced Placement Program has introduced college-level work directly into the high school by allowing students who have taken college-level work in high school and who pass standard achievement tests in those fields to be admitted to a large number of colleges with advanced standing. This program is growing rapidly, as more and more able students, most with graduate and professional schools in mind, try for advanced placement both to improve their chances for admission to the better colleges and also as a way of saving time in the early stages of a lengthy higher education.[2]

All of these efforts to reform and strengthen the preparatory work offered by the high schools require teachers with both academic ability and training. The lack of preparation of many teachers in academic fields is real though reparable.[3] Extensive programs of summer training sessions and workshops, supported in large part by Federal funds, are now organized on a continuing basis to strengthen the high-school teachers' own skills in the subjects they teach, and to introduce them to more recent developments in their subjects.[4] A more serious question raised by the evidence cited earlier is that of the academic aptitudes and abilities of high-school teachers; this question conditions every proposal for the reform of the curriculum. Of course, efforts can and should be made to recruit and retain highly competent teachers. Meanwhile, the reform of the curriculum calls for new ways to make the best use of the most able teachers already in the schools.

It may be that the matching of academically oriented and able teachers and students which already takes place informally will be encouraged and even formalized. But it is precisely such invidious distinctions that American public schools try hard to avoid. It is in the schools that the American value of equality is most deeply rooted, and it is in the doctrines of democratic education that we find the most determined equation and encouragement of all kinds of talents and abilities, with academic abilities only one kind among many. When college-preparatory students were only a small minority of all students in high schools, they could be dealt with as "exceptions" without challenging the basic equalitarian ethos of the school which equated all students and all activities and interests.[5] But the transformation of the secondary schools into predominantly preparatory institutions profoundly challenges this ethos; the criteria of academic ability and achievement which are so much more important in higher education are increasingly relevant to and applied within the walls of the high school.[6]

Under pressures such as these, it is likely that both the philosophy and organization of American secondary education will change in the decades ahead. And the nature of these changes will in turn affect the kinds of people drawn to high-school teaching, how they are trained,[1] and how they are used in the schools. The more emphasis placed on academic subject matter in the high-school curriculum, and in the training and employment of teachers, the more likely people with academic interests will be attracted to teaching. This is certainly the direction of change in public secondary education's Phase III. But where does this leave the high school's remaining responsibility for terminal education?

The impact of the transformation on terminal education

The expansion of the college-going population fills the high schools with college-preparatory students, and generates the pressure for a strengthening of the preparatory function that we have spoken of. But this development also affects the character of the terminal students, and of terminal education in high school, as well. When few students went on to college, there was no disgrace in not doing so; moreover, except for the professions, it was not so clear that occupational success was closely linked to academic achievement. The Horatio Alger myth, and the American folklore celebrating the successes of the self-made (and self-educated) man, served to define school achievement as only one among several legitimate avenues to success. But the rationalization of industry, and the increased importance of higher education for advancement beyond the lowest levels of the occupational structure, make educational achievement objectively more important for later success; the increased numbers of college-going students make this importance visible to high-school students. The consequence of all this is to change the character of the students who do not go on to college when increasing majorities of students do so. Already in some localities, and increasingly in coming decades, the students not going on to college are being reduced to a hard core composed of two groups: children from ethnic and racial groups which do not place strong emphasis on high educational and occupational aspirations — for example, Negroes and Mexicans; and children of low intelligence who simply cannot handle college-preparatory work.

The transformation of "not going to college" into "failure" has both social and psychological consequences. Among those who want to succeed in school but cannot, the effects of failure may be a loss of self-respect, with widespread if not highly visible and dramatic consequences for the social behaviors of those so affected. One English observer suggests that:

As a result of the close relationship between education and occupation a situation may soon be reached

when the educational institutions legitimize social inequality by individualizing failure. Democratization of the means of education together with the internalizing of the achievement ethic by members of the working-class strata may lead to an individualizing of their failure, to a loss of self-respect which in turn modifies an individual's attitude both to his group and to the demands made upon him by his society.[2]

This problem of the motivated student of low ability may be more severe in England, and in other Western countries in the earlier stages of the democratization of education, than in the United States, where among our nearly 2,000 institutions of higher education there is a college somewhere for everybody.[3] Moreover, the elaborate student-counselling programs in our mass public institutions are designed explicitly to help students of low academic ability accept their limitations, and direct their energies toward attainable educational and occupational goals without a sense of personal failure and resentment toward society.[4]

But while the emerging American educational system promises to make some provision for all those who accept its values, regardless of their academic ability, it is not so clear what it can do for those who deeply reject its values and purposes, along with many of the values and purposes of the larger society. The increasing extent and violence of juvenile delinquency in the United States may be closely linked to the extension of educational opportunities to the conforming majority. Where educational achievement (in terms at least of years completed) becomes more widespread and thus more visible, and more important to even modest success in the occupational world, then educational failure *pari passu* becomes more devastating to one's hopes of achieving the advertised "good life" through legitimate channels. Failure in school for many is part of a familiar vicious cycle. Absence of encouragement

[1] We cannot here discuss the controversies over teacher training, certification, and the like, except to suggest that they also reflect the deep cleavage between the terminal and preparatory functions of secondary education. In most other advanced countries, which have rather distinct terminal and preparatory school systems, the patterns of social recruitment and training of teachers for these systems also differ: Teachers in the terminal systems usually get their training in teacher training institutes, while teachers in the preparatory systems are educated in the universities for which they are preparing the best of their students. It is probably neither possible nor desirable to reintroduce this pattern into American education. Yet pressures for a reform in teacher education rise, in response to the changing function of the schools. For example, a bill introduced in the California legislature in 1961 would eliminate the "education major" in college by requiring all teachers to have a degree in some academic discipline.

[2] Basil Bernstein, "Some Sociological Determinants of Perception: An Enquiry Into Sub-cultural Differences," *The British Journal of Sociology*, I, 2 (June, 1958), p. 173.

[3] See T. R. McConnell and Paul Heist, "The Diverse College Student Population," in N. Sanford, ed., *The American College* (New York: John Wiley and Sons, forthcoming).

[4] See Burton R. Clark, "The Cooling-Out Function in Higher Education," *American Journal of Sociology*, LXV, 6 (May, 1960).

or concern with school performance in the home (especially marked in certain ethnic and racial groups) leads to failure to acquire basic skills, such as reading, in the early grades, which ensures academic failure in higher grades. These repeated failures make school seem a punishing prison, from which the boy escapes as early as the law allows. But lacking education or training, it is unlikely that he can get any but the poorest jobs. And the habits and resentments generated at home, on the street, and in school make it unlikely that such a boy can move into better jobs. After repeated failures in school and a succession of poorly paid odd jobs, the rewards of membership in a gang, and of participation in its delinquent subculture are considerable. And the more the high school is organized around the college preparatory programs, the more it stresses academic achievement, the more punishing it will be for the nonachievers.[1] The delinquent subculture is a way of dealing with deprivations of status, very largely experienced in the schools, and as a response to these deprivations, "the gang offers an heroic rather than an economic [or intellectual] basis of self-respect."[2]

Special school programs may help meet the complex problems of low aspirations and juvenile delinquency, though children growing up in disorganized families, or in cultures cut off from the dominant American value system, or exposed to the corrosive effects of racial prejudice, present problems that cannot be wholly dealt with in and by the schools. The point here is that the growth of educational opportunity threatens to make the greater part of terminal education in high schools coincidental with the social problems of juvenile delinquency. This is not to say that every classroom full of non-college-going students is or will be a "blackboard jungle." It does mean that the hostility toward the school characteristic of the juvenile gangs, but much more widespread than their membership, will be an increasing part of the educational problem faced by schools and teachers dealing with terminal students. The cluster of values which characterize juvenile delinquency – "the search for kicks, the disdain of work . . . and the acceptance of aggressive toughness as proof of masculinity"[3] – is incompatible with disciplined school work, either academic *or* vocational. Moreover, much of the serious vocational training the high schools has offered in the past is being increasingly shifted to higher education, especially to the junior colleges.[4]

The terminal education of the future will not simply be the terminal education of the past offered to a decreasing proportion of students. The growth of the college-going population changes the character of the remaining terminal students, it changes the meaning of their terminal work, and it will force changes in the organization and curriculum of terminal secondary education. It may also call for teachers with special skills and training in dealing with the problems of the minority or "hard core" of terminal students. But if the increasingly important preparatory programs claim the best resources of secondary education and command the most able teachers, then terminal education will indeed be a second-class program for second-class students. And they will know it, and that knowledge will feed their bitterness and resentment. Neither the old terminal education for life, nor the strengthened academic programs will meet their needs. If the terminal education of the future is not to be an educational slum, it will demand large resources and much intelligence. But these are always in short supply, and terminal education will be competing for both with the more attractive programs of preparatory education.

Conclusion

Universal secondary education in the United States was achieved through a system of comprehensive high schools, devoted primarily to the education of the great mass of its students for work and life, and secondarily to the preparation of a small minority for higher education. The present concern with the reform of the high-school curriculum and teacher training reflects the rapid growth of the college-going population, and the increased importance of the preparatory function.

Nevertheless, it may have been possible to combine terminal education for a majority and preparatory education for a minority more successfully than it will be to combine preparatory education for a majority and terminal education for a minority under one roof. Moreover, the shortage of highly qualified and motivated teachers of academic subjects may require that they be used where their talents and interests are most productive — that is, in teaching the academically most talented fraction of the student body. Secondary education in America may have to accept a higher measure of division of labor and differentiation of function than it has in the past. As a terminal system,

[1] Speaking of this group "for whom adaptation to educational expectations at *any* level is difficult," Parsons notes: "As the acceptable minimum of educational qualifications rises, persons near and below the margin will tend to be pushed into an attitude of repudiation of these expectations. Truancy and delinquency are ways of expressing this repudiation. Thus the very *improvement* of educational standards in the society at large may well be a major factor in the failure of the educational process for a growing number at the lower end of the status and ability distribution." (Talcott Parsons, "The Social Class as a Social System: Some of its Functions in American Society," *Harvard Educational Review*, IV, 4 (Fall, 1959), p. 313.

[2] Jackson Toby, "Hoodlum or Business Man: An American Dilemma," in Marshall Sklare, *The Jews* (Glencoe, Illinois: The Free Press, 1958), p. 546. See also, R. K. Merton, *Social Theory and Social Structure* (revised ed.; Glencoe, Illinois: The Free Press, 1957), Chapter iv, "Social Structure and Anomie"; and Albert K. Cohen, *Delinquent Boys: The Culture of the Gang* (Glencoe: The Free Press, 1955), especially Chapter v, "A Delinquent Solution."

[3] David Matza and Gresham Sykes, "Juvenile Delinquency and Subterranean Values," *American Sociological Review* (forthcoming).

[4] See Burton R. Clark, *The Open Door College* (New York: McGraw-Hill Book Co., Inc., 1960).

it could in its comprehensiveness and emphasis on "education for life" simply carry further the basic education of the elementary school of which it was an outgrowth. As it becomes increasingly a preparatory system, it may be forced to take on some of the characteristics of higher education for which it is preparing, and place greater emphasis on differences among both teachers and students in academic ability and intellectual and occupational interests.

American higher education deals with the diversity of student abilities and talents largely through the great diversity of institutions which compose it, institutions which vary greatly in their selectivity, and in the academic abilities of their students.[1] American comprehensive high schools contain all this diversity within themselves, providing different streams or tracks for students with different educational or vocational intentions, or, as Conant has urged, grouping by ability, subject by subject.[2] But these arrangements ignore the effects of the students on one another, and of the student "mix" on the intellectual climate of the school. In a school where the academically-motivated students are in a minority, they cannot help but be affected by the predominantly anti-intellectual values (and behaviors) of the majority;[3] similarly, where the low-achieving terminal students are in the minority, it is hard for them not to be defined as second-class students by other students and teachers, with the effects on them discussed earlier. It may be that the period we are entering will call for a critical evaluation of the comprehensive high school, the institution created by and for mass terminal secondary education.[4]

The current controversies in and about secondary education in America are a natural and healthy response to the transformation of the secondary education in this country. It can be expected that the discussion will grow in volume and scope as this transformation proceeds in the decades ahead. It can also be expected that the discussion ahead will be carried on largely between critics located outside the schools, and professional educators inside them. On one side there is a detached perspective but without first-hand knowledge of the schools; on the other, defensiveness, but also intimate experience with the problems under discussion. If the critics and the professional educators can sharpen and clarify the issues in the course of their discussion, and go on to learn from one another about the inconvenient facts that their respective positions do not adequately take into account, then the controversy may become a dialogue, and perhaps a fruitful one for American secondary education.

[1] McConnell and Heist, *op. cit.*

[2] See his remarks on "ability grouping" in *The American High School Today* (New York: McGraw-Hill Book Co., Inc., 1959), pp. 49–50.

[3] See James S. Coleman, "Academic Achievement and the Structure of Competition," *Harvard Educational Review*, XXIX, 4 (Fall, 1959), pp. 330–352. See also Alan B. Wilson, "Residential Segregation of Social Classes and Aspirations of High School Boys," *American Sociological Review*, Vol. XXIV, No. 6 (December 1959), pp. 836–845.

[4] One possibility, in the best experimental tradition of American education, would be to organize one or two academically selective high schools in each major city, where some of the gains and losses of institutional differentiation can be observed, and where experimental programs can be developed for later application in the comprehensive schools. The "hard-core" terminal students present a more difficult problem.

Modes of Social Ascent through Education

SPONSORED AND CONTEST MOBILITY[1]

Ralph H. Turner

THE OBJECT of this paper is to suggest a framework for relating certain differences between American and English systems of education to the prevailing norms of upward mobility in each country. Others have noted the tendency for educational systems to support prevailing schemes of stratification, but this statement will dwell specifically on the manner in which the *accepted mode of upward mobility* shapes the school system directly and indirectly through its effects on the values

[1] This is an expanded version of a paper presented at the Fourth World Congress of Sociology, 1959, and abstracted in the *Transactions* of the Congress. A special indebtedness should be expressed to Jean Floud and Hilde Himmelweit for helping to acquaint the author with the English school system.

Reprinted from the *American Sociological Review*, Vol. XXV (1960), pp. 121–139, by permission of the author and the publisher.

that implement social control. The task will be carried out by describing two ideal-typical normative patterns of upward mobility and suggesting their logical ramifications in the general character of stratification and social control. In addition to showing relationships among a number of differences between American and English schooling, the ideal-types have broader implications than those developed in this paper. First, they suggest a major dimension of stratification, which might profitably be incorporated into a variety of studies on social class. Second, they can be readily applied in further comparisons, between countries other than the United States and England.

The nature of organizing norms

Many investigators have concerned themselves with rates of upward mobility in specific countries or internationally,[1] and with the manner in which school systems facilitate or impede such mobility.[2] Preoccupation with *extent* of mobility has precluded equal attention to the predominant *mode* of mobility in each country. The central assumption underlying this paper is that within a formally open class system providing mass education the organizing folk norm that defines the accepted mode of upward mobility is a crucial factor in shaping the school system, and may be even more crucial than is the extent of upward mobility. In England and the United States there appear to be different organizing folk norms, which may be labelled *sponsored mobility* and *contest mobility* respectively. *Contest* mobility is a system in which elite[3] status is the prize in an open contest and is taken by the aspirants' own efforts. While the "contest" is governed by some

rules of fair play, the contestants have wide latitude in the strategies they may employ. Since the "prize" of successful upward mobility is not in the hands of the established elite to give out, the latter are not in a position to determine who shall attain it and who shall not. Under *sponsored* mobility, elite recruits are chosen by the established elite or their agents, and elite status is *given* on the basis of some criterion of supposed merit and cannot be *taken* by any amount of effort or strategy. Upward mobility is like entry into a private club, where each candidate must be "sponsored" by one or more of the members. Ultimately, the members grant or deny upward mobility on the basis of whether they judge the candidate to have the qualities that they wish to see in fellow members.

Before elaborating this distinction, we must note that these systems of mobility are ideal types, designed to clarify observed differences in the predominantly similar English and American systems of stratification and education. As organizing norms, these principles are assumed to be present at least implicitly in people's thinking, guiding their judgments of what is appropriate and inappropriate on many specific matters. Such organizing norms do not correspond perfectly with the objective characteristics of the societies in which they exist, nor are they completely independent of them. Out of the complex interplay of social and economic conditions and ideologies, the people in a society come to develop a highly simplified conception of the way in which events take place. This conception of the "natural" as contrasted with the unnatural is translated into a norm — the "natural" becomes what "ought" to be — and in turn imposes a strain toward consistency upon relevant aspects of the society. Thus, the norm reacts upon the objective conditions to which it refers and has ramifying effects upon directly and indirectly related features of the society.[4]

Four statements will briefly outline the conception of an ideal-typical organizing norm. *1)* The ideal types are not fully exemplified in practice since they are normative systems, and no normative system can be devised so as to cope with all empirical exigencies. *2)* Predominant norms usually compete with less ascendant norms engendered by changes and inconsistencies in the underlying social structure. *3)* Although not fully explicit, organizing folk norms are reflected in specific value judgments. Those judgments, regarded as having a convincing ring to them irrespective of the logic expressed, or seeming to require no extended argumentation, may be presumed to reflect the prevailing folk norms. *4)* The predominant organizing norms in one segment of society will be functionally related to those in other segments.

Two final qualifications to the scope of this paper must be made. First, the organizing folk norm of upward mobility affects the school system because the school has as one of its functions the facilitation of mobility. Since fostering mobility is only one among several social functions of the school, and not the most

---

[1] A comprehensive summary of such studies appears in Seymour M. Lipset and Reinhard Bendix, *Social Mobility in Industrial Society* (Berkeley and Los Angeles: University of California Press, 1959).

[2] *Cf.* C. A. Anderson, "The Social Status of University Students in Relation to Type of Economy: An International Comparison," *Transactions of the Third World Congress of Sociology*, V, 51–63; J. E. Floud, A. H. Halsey, and F. M. Martin, *Social Class and Educational Opportunity* (London: Heinemann, 1956); W. L. Warner, R. J. Havighurst, and M. B. Loeb, *Who Shall be Educated?* (New York: Harper and Bros., 1944).

[3] Reference will be made throughout the paper to "elite" and "masses." The generalizations presented are, however, intended to apply throughout the stratification continuum to relations between members of a given class or classes above it. Statements about mobility are intended in general to apply to mobility from manual to middle-class levels, lower-middle to upper-middle class, etc., as well as into the strictly elite groups. The simplified manner of expression avoids the repeated use of cumbersome and involved statements that might otherwise be required.

[4] The normative element in an organizing norm goes beyond Max Weber's *ideal type*, conveying more of the sense of Emile Durkheim's *collective representation*. *Cf.* R. H. Turner, "The Normative Coherence of Folk Concepts," *Research Studies of the State College of Washington*, XXV (1957), 127–136. Charles Wagley has developed a similar concept, which he calls "ideal pattern" in his as yet unpublished work on Brazilian kinship. *Cf.* also Howard Becker, "Constructive Typology in the Social Sciences," *American Sociological Review*, V (February, 1940), 40–55.

important function in the societies under examination, we can give only a very partial accounting of the whole set of forces making for similarities and differences in the school systems of United States and England. Only those differences directly or indirectly reflecting the performance of the mobility function can be noted here. Second, the concern of this paper is with the current dynamics of the situation in the two countries rather than their historical development. No effort will be made to explain how the systems became what they are. The concern will be solely with what keeps them operating as they do.

Major distinctions between the two norms

Contest mobility is like a sporting event in which many compete for a few recognized prizes. The contest is judged to be fair only if all the players compete on an equal footing. Victory must be won solely by one's own efforts. The most satisfactory outcome is not necessarily a victory of the most able, but of the most deserving. The tortoise who defeats the hare is a folk prototype of the deserving sportsman. Enterprise, initiative, perseverance, and craft are admirable qualities if they allow the person initially at a disadvantage to triumph. Even clever manipulation of the rules may be admired if it helps the contestant who is smaller or less muscular or less rapid to win. Applied to mobility, the contest norm means that victory by a person of moderate intelligence accomplished through the use of common sense, craft, enterprise, daring, and successful risk-taking[1] is more appreciated than victory of the most intelligent or the best-educated.

Sponsored mobility, on the other hand, rejects the pattern of the contest and substitutes a controlled selection process. In this process the elite or their agents, who are best qualified to judge merit, *call* those individuals to elite status who have the appropriate qualities. Individuals do not win or seize elite status, but mobility is rather a process of sponsored induction into the elite following selection.

Pareto had this sort of mobility in mind when he suggested that the governing class might dispose of persons potentially dangerous to it by admitting them to elite membership, provided the recruits change character by adopting elite attitudes and interests.[2] Danger to the ruling class would seldom be the major criterion for choice of elite recruits. But Pareto's assumption was that the established elite would select whom they wished to enter their ranks and would train the recruits to the attitudes and interests of the established elite.

The governing objective of contest mobility is to give elite status to those who earn it, while the goal of sponsored mobility is to make the best use of the talents in society by sorting each person into his proper niche. In different societies the conditions of competitive struggle may reward quite different attributes, and sponsored mobility may select on the basis of such diverse qualities as intelligence or visionary capability, but the difference in principle remains the same.[3]

Under the contest system, society at large establishes and interprets the criteria of elite status. If one wishes to have his high status recognized he must display certain credentials that identify his class to those about him. The credentials must be highly visible and require no special skill for their assessment, since credentials are presented to the masses. Material possession and mass popularity are perfect credentials in this respect, and any special skill that produces a tangible product easily assessed by the untrained will do. The nature of sponsored mobility precludes this type of operation but assigns to credentials instead the function of identifying the elite to one another.[4] Accordingly, the ideal credentials are special skills requiring the trained discrimination of the elite for their recognition. Intellectual, literary, or artistic excellences, which can only be appraised by those trained to appreciate them, are perfect credentials in this respect. Concentration on such skills lessens the likelihood that an interloper will succeed in claiming the right to elite membership on grounds of the popular evaluation of his competence.

In the sporting event there is special admiration for the slow starter who makes a dramatic finish, and many of the rules are designed to insure that the game should not be declared over until it has run its full course. Contest mobility incorporates this fear of premature judgments and of anything that would give special advantage to those who are ahead at any point in the race. Under sponsored mobility, fairly early selection of only the number of persons necessary to fill the anticipated vacancies in the elite is desirable. Early selection allows time to prepare the recruits for their elite position. Aptitudes, inherent capacities, and spiritual gifts can be assessed fairly early in life, by techniques ranging from divination to the most sophisticated psychological

---

[1] Geoffrey Gorer remarks on the favorable evaluation of the successful gamble in American culture. "Gambling is also a respected and important component in many business ventures. Conspicuous improvement in a man's financial position is generally attributed to a lucky combination of industry, skill, and gambling, though the successful gambler prefers to refer to his gambling as 'vision.'" *The American People* (New York: W. W. Norton, 1948), p. 178.

[2] Vilfredo Pareto, *The Mind and Society* (New York: Harcourt, Brace & Co., 1935), IV, 1796.

[3] Many writers have noted that different kinds of society facilitate the rise of different kinds of personalities, either in the stratification hierarchy or in other ways. *Cf.* Jessie Bernard, *American Community Behavior* (New York: Dryden, 1949), p. 205. A particularly interesting statement in Martindale's exploration of "favored personality" types in sacred and secular societies. *Cf.*, Don Martindale and Elio Monachesi, *Elements of Sociology* (New York: Harper and Bros., 1951), pp. 312–378.

[4] At one time in the United States, a good many owners of expensive British Jaguar automobiles carried large signs on the cars identifying the make. Such a display would have been unthinkable under a sponsored mobility system, since the Jaguar owner would not care for the esteem of the uninformed masses who could not tell a Jaguar from a less prestigious automobile.

test, and the more naive the subject at the time of selection, the less likely his talents are to be blurred by differential learning or conspiracy to defeat the test. Since the elite will take the initiative in training the recruit, they are more interested in his capabilities than in what he will do with them on his own, and they are concerned that no one else should first have an opportunity to train the recruit's talents in the wrong direction. Contest mobility tends to delay the final award as long as practicable, to permit a fair race; sponsored mobility tends to place the selection point as early in life as practicable, to insure control over selection and training.

A system of sponsored mobility develops most readily in a society with but a single elite or with a recognized elite hierarchy. When multiple elites compete among themselves, the mobility process tends to take the contest pattern, since no group is able to command control of recruitment. Sponsored mobility further depends upon a societal structure fostering monopoly of elite credentials. Lack of such monopoly undercuts sponsorship and control of the recruitment process. Monopoly of elite credentials is in turn typically a product of a society with a well-entrenched traditional aristocracy, employing such intrinsically monopolizable credentials as family line and bestowable title, or of a society organized along large-scale bureaucratic lines, permitting centralized control of movement up the hierarchy of success.

English society has been described as the juxtaposition of two systems of stratification, the urban-industrial class system and the surviving aristocratic system. While the sponsored-mobility pattern reflects the logic of the latter, our impression is that it pervades popular thinking rather than merely coexisting with the logic of industrial stratification. Students of cultural change note that patterns imported into an established culture tend to be reshaped into coherence with the established culture as they are assimilated. Thus, it may be that the changes in stratification attendant upon industrialization have led to many alterations in the rates, the specific means, and the rules of mobility, but that these changes have taken place within the unchallenged organizing norm of sponsored mobility.

Social control and the two norms

Every society must cope with the problem of maintaining loyalty to its social system, and every society does so in part through norms and values, some of which vary by class position and some of which are relatively uniform through the social strata. Norms and values prevalent within each class must direct behavior into channels that support the total system,

while the values that transcend strata must support the general class differential. The way in which upward mobility takes place determines in part the kinds of norms and values that will serve the indicated purposes of social control in each class and throughout the society.

The most conspicuous control problem is that of ensuring loyalty in the disadvantaged classes toward a system under which they receive less than a proportional share of society's goods. Under a system of contest mobility, this is accomplished by a combination of future orientation, the universal norm of ambition, and a general sense of fellow-feeling with the elite. Every individual is encouraged to think of himself as competing for an elite position, so that in preparation he cultivates loyalty to the system and conventional attitudes. It is essential that this future orientation be kept alive by delaying any sense of final irreparable failure to reach elite position until attitudes are well established. Likewise, by thinking of himself in the successful future, the elite aspirant forms considerable identification with the elite, and any evidence that they are just ordinary human beings like himself helps to reinforce this identification as well as to keep alive the conviction that he himself may someday succeed in like manner. To forestall rebellion among the disadvantaged majority, then, a contest system must avoid any absolute points of selection for mobility and immobility and must delay clear recognition of the realities of the situation until the individual is too committed to the system to change radically. The future orientation cannot, of course, be inculcated successfully in all members of lower strata, but sufficient training to a norm of ambition tends to leave the unambitious as individual deviants and forestalls their forming a genuine subcultural group able to offer collective threat to the established system. Where this kind of control system operates rather effectively, it is notable that such organized or gang deviancy as does develop is more likely to take the form of an attack upon the conventional or moral order rather than on the class system itself. Thus, the United States has its "beatniks,"[1] who repudiate ambition and worldly values altogether, and its delinquent and criminal gangs, who try to evade the limitations imposed by conventional means,[2] but very little in the way of active revolutionaries who challenge the class system itself.

The system of sponsorship makes the foregoing control system inappropriate, since the elite recruits are chosen from above. The principal threat to the system would lie in the existence of a strong group who sought to *take* elite positions themselves. Control under this system is by training the masses to regard themselves as relatively incompetent to manage society, by restricting access to the skills and manners of the elite, and by cultivating belief in the superior competence of the elite. The earlier that selection of the elite recruits can be made, the sooner the masses can be taught to accept their inferiority and to make "realistic" rather than phantasy plans. Early selection prevents

[1] Lawrence Lipton, *Holy Barbarians* (New York: Messner, 1959).
[2] *Cf.*, Albert K. Cohen, *Delinquent Boys: The Culture of the Gang* (Glencoe, Ill.: Free Press, 1955).

raising the hopes of large numbers of people who might otherwise become the discontented leaders of a class challenging the sovereignty of the established elite. If we assume that the difference in competence between masses and elite is seldom so great as to support the usual differences in advantage accruing to each,[1] then the differences must be artificially augmented by discouraging acquisition of elite skills by the masses. Likewise, a sense of mystery about the elite is a common device for supporting in the masses an illusion of a much greater hiatus of competence than in fact exists.

While the elite are unlikely to reject a system that benefits them, they must still be restrained from taking such advantage of their favorable situation as to jeopardize the entire elite. Under the sponsorship system, the elite recruits, who are selected early, freed from the strain of competitive struggle, and kept under close elite supervision, may be thoroughly indoctrinated in elite culture. A norm of paternalism toward inferiors may be inculcated; a heightened sensitivity of the good opinions of fellow-elite and elite recruits may be cultivated; and the appreciation of the more complex forms of aesthetic, literary, intellectual, and sporting activities may be taught. A norm of courtesy and altruism can well be maintained under sponsorship, since the elite recruits are not required to compete for their standing and since the elite may deny high standing to any who strive for position by unseemly methods. The system of sponsorship provides an almost perfect setting for the development of an elite culture characterized by a sense of responsibility for inferiors and for preservation of the "finer things" of life.

Elite control under the contest system is more difficult since there is no controlled induction and apprenticeship. The principal control seems to lie in the insecurity of elite position. In a sense, there is no final arrival under contest mobility, since each person may be displaced by newcomers throughout his life. The limited control of high standing from above prevents the clear delimitation of levels in the class system, so that success itself becomes relative. Rather than constituting primarily an accomplishment, each success serves to qualify the participant for competition at the next higher level.[2] The restraints upon the behavior of a person of high standing, therefore, are principally those applicable to a contestant who must not risk having the other contestants "gang up" on him, and who must pay some attention to the masses, who are frequently in a position to impose penalties upon him. However, any special norm of paternalism is hard to establish, since there is no dependable procedure for examining the means by which a man achieves elite credentials. While mass esteem is an effective brake upon overexploitation of position, it does not so much reward scrupulously ethical and altruistic behavior as it rewards evidence of fellow-feeling with the masses.

Under both systems, unscrupulous or disreputable persons may become or remain members of the elite, but for different reasons. In contest mobility, popular tolerance of a little "craft" in the successful combined with the fact that the newcomer does not have to undergo the close scrutiny of the old elite leaves considerable leeway for unscrupulous success. In sponsored mobility, the unpromising recruit reflects unfavorably on the judgment of his sponsors and threatens the myth of elite omniscience. Consequently, he may be tolerated, and others may "cover up" for his deficiencies in order to protect the unified front of the elite to the outer world.

Certain of the general values and norms of any society incorporate emulation of elite values by the masses. Under sponsored mobility, a good deal of the protective attitudes and interest in classical subjects percolates to the masses. Under contest mobility, however, there is not the same apparent homogeneity of moral, aesthetic, and intellectual values to be emulated, so that the conspicuous attribute of the elite is their superior level of material consumption. Consequently, emulation follows this course. There is neither effective incentive nor punishment for the elite individual who fails to interest himself in promoting the arts or literary excellence, or who continues to maintain the vulgar manners and mode of speech of his class origin. The elite have relatively less power and the masses relatively more power to punish or reward a man for his adoption or disregard of any special elite culture. The extreme importance of accent and of grammatical excellence to the attainment of high status in England, as contrasted with the "twangs" and "drawls" and grammatical ineptitude among American elites, is the most striking example of this difference. The strength of the class system is therefore not geared into support of the *quality* of aesthetic, literary, and intellectual activities in a contest system. Only those well versed in such activities are qualified to distinguish authentic products from cheap imitations. Unless those who claim superiority in those areas are forced to submit their credentials to the elite for evaluation, poor quality will often be honored equally with high quality, and class prestige will not serve to maintain an effective norm of high quality.

The foregoing is not to imply that there will be no groups in such a society devoted to protection and fostering of high standards in art, music, literature, and intellectual pursuits, but that such standards will lack the support of the class system, which is frequently found when sponsored mobility prevails. The selection, by official welcoming committees in California, of a torch singer to entertain a visiting king and queen and "can can" dancers to entertain Mr. Krushchev illustrates how little American elites suppose that high prestige and popular taste cannot go together.

[1] D. V. Glass (ed.), *Social Mobility in Britain* (Glencoe, Ill.: Free Press, 1954), pp. 144–145, reports studies showing only small variations in intelligence between occupational levels.
[2] Geoffrey Gorer, *op. cit.*, pp. 172–187.

Formal education under contest and sponsorship

Returning to our conception of an organizing ideal form, we assume that to the extent to which one such norm of upward mobility is prevalent in a society there will be a constant strain to shape the educational system into conformity with that norm. These strains will operate in two fashions: directly, through blinding people to alternatives and through coloring their judgments of what are successful and unsuccessful solutions to recurring educational problems; and indirectly, through the functional interrelationships between school systems and other aspects of the class structure, systems of social control, and many features of the social structure neglected in this paper.

The most obvious application of the distinction between sponsored and contest mobility norms is to afford a partial explanation for the different policies of student selection in the English and American secondary schools. Although American high-school students take different courses of study and sometimes even attend specialized high schools, a major preoccupation has been to avoid any sharp social separation between the superior and inferior students and to keep the channels of movement between courses of study as open as possible. Even recent criticisms of the way in which superior students may be thereby held back in their development usually are qualified by insistence that these students must not, however, be withdrawn from the mainstream of student life.[1] Any such segregation offends the sense of fairness implicit in the contest norm and also arouses the fear that the elite and future elite will lose their sense of fellow-feeling with the masses. Perhaps the most important point, however, is that schooling is presented as an opportunity, and the principal burden of making use of the opportunity depends on the student's own initiative and enterprise.

The English system has undergone a succession of liberalizing changes during this century, but all of them have remained within the pattern of attempting early in the educational program to sort out the promising from the unpromising, so that the former may be segregated and given a special form of training to fit them for higher standing in their adult years. Under the Education Act of 1944, a minority of students have been selected each year by means of a battery of examinations properly known as "eleven plus," supplemented to varying degrees by grade-school record and personal interview impressions, for admission to grammar schools.[2] The remaining students attend secondary modern or technical schools, in which the opportunities to prepare for college or train for the better occupations are minimal. The grammar schools supply what, by comparative standards, is a high quality of college preparatory education. Such a scheme embodies well the logic of sponsorship, with early selection of those destined for middle-class and better occupations, and specialized training to suit each group for the class in which they are destined to hold membership. The plan facilitates considerable mobility, and recent research reveals surprisingly little bias against the child from a manual-laboring family in the selection for grammar school, when related to measured intelligence.[3] It is altogether possible that adequate comparative research would show a closer correlation of school success with measured intelligence and a lesser correlation between school success and family background in England than in the United States. While selection of superior students for mobility opportunity is probably more efficient under such a system, the obstacles to a person not so selected "making the grade" on the basis of his own initiative or enterprise are probably correspondingly greater.

That the contrasting effects of the two systems accord with the social-control pattern under the two mobility norms is indicated by research into student ambitions in the United States and England. Researches in the United States consistently show that the general level of occupational aspiration reported by high-school students is quite unrealistic in relation to the actual distribution of job opportunities. Comparative study in England shows much less in the way of "phantasy" aspiration, and, specifically, shows a reduction in aspiration among those not selected following the "eleven-plus" examination.[4] One of the by-products of the sponsorship system is the fact that students from middle-class families whose parents cannot afford to send them to a private school suffer severe personal adjustment problems when they are assigned to secondary modern schools on the basis of this selection.[5]

While this well-known difference between the early British sorting of students into grammar and modern schools and the American comprehensive high school and junior college is the clearest application of the distinction under discussion, the organizing norms penetrate more deeply into the school systems than is initially apparent. The most telling observation regarding the direct normative operation of these principles would be evidence to support the author's impression that major critics within each country do not usually

[1] *Los Angeles Times*, May 4, 1959, Part I, p. 24.

[2] The nature and operation of the "eleven plus" selection system are fully reviewed in a recent report by a committee of the British Psychological Society and a report of extensive research into the adequacy of selection methods. *Cf.*, P. E. Vernon (ed.), *Secondary School Selection: A British Psychological Inquiry* (London: Methuen and Co., Ltd., 1957); and Alfred Yates and D. A. Pidgeon, *Admission to Grammar Schools* (London: Newnes Educational Publishing Co., 1957).

[3] J. E. Floud, A. H. Halsey, and F. M. Martin, *op. cit.*

[4] Mary D. Wilson documents the reduction in aspiration characterizing students in British Secondary Modern schools and points out the contrast with American studies revealing much more "unrealistic" aspiration. *Cf.*, "The Vocational Preferences of Secondary Modern School-children," *British Journal of Educational Psychology*, XXIII (1953), 97–113. *Cf.* also R. H. Turner, "The Changing Ideology of Success," *Transactions of the Third World Congress of Sociology, 1956*, V, esp. p. 37.

[5] Pointed out by Hilde Himmelweit in private communication.

transcend the logic of their respective mobility norms in their criticisms. Thus, British critics debate the best method for getting people sorted according to ability, without proposing that elite station should be opened to whoever can take it. Although fear of "sputnik" in the United States introduced a flurry of sponsored-mobility thinking, the long-standing concern of school critics has been the failure to motivate students adequately. Preoccupation with motivation appears to be an intellectual application of the folk idea that people should *win* their station in society by personal *enterprise*.

The functional operation of a strain toward consistency with the organizing norm of upward mobility may be illustrated by reference to several other features of the school systems in the two countries. First, the value placed upon education itself is different under the two organizing norms. Under sponsored mobility, schooling is valued for its cultivation of elite culture, and those forms of schooling directed toward such cultivation are more highly valued than those which are not. Education of the non-elite is difficult to justify clearly and tends to be half-hearted, while the maximum educational resources are concentrated on "those who can benefit most from them." In practice, the latter means those who can learn the elite culture. The secondary modern schools in England have regularly suffered from less adequate financial provision and a lower teacher–student ratio, from less-well-trained teachers, and from a general lack of prestige, in comparison with the grammar schools.[1]

Under contest mobility in the United States, education is valued as a means of getting ahead, but the contents of education are not highly valued in their own right. There is even a suspicion of the educated man as one who may have gotten ahead without really earning his position. Over a century ago, De Tocqueville had commented on the absence in the United States of an hereditary class "by which the labors of the intellect are held in honor." In consequence he remarked that, "A middling standard is fixed in America for human knowledge."[2] In spite of recent criticisms of lax standards in American schools, it is in keeping with the general mobility pattern that a Gallup Poll in April, 1958, showed that school principals were much more likely to make such criticisms than parents. While 90 per cent of principals thought that ". . . our schools today demand too little work from the students," only 51 per cent of parents thought so, with 33 per cent saying the work was about right, and 6 per cent that schools demanded too much work.[3]

Second, the logic of preparation for a contest prevails in United States schools, with emphasis on keeping everyone in the running until the final stages. In primary and secondary schools, the assumption tends to be made that those who are learning satisfactorily need little special attention, while the less successful require help to be sure that they remain in the contest and may compete for the final stakes. As recently as December, 1958, a nationwide Gallup Poll gave evidence that this attitude had not been radically altered by the international situation. When asked whether teachers should devote extra time to the bright students, 26 per cent said "yes," and 67 per cent answered "no." But the responses changed to 86 per cent "yes," and only 9 per cent "no," when the question was asked concerning the "slow students."[4]

In western states, the junior college offers many students "a second chance" to qualify for university, and all state universities have some provision for sub-standard high-school students to earn admission.

The university itself is run like the true contest, standards being set competitively, students being forced to pass a series of trials each semester, and only a minority of the entrants achieving the prize of graduation. Such a pattern contrasts sharply with the English system in which selection is supposed to have been relatively complete before entry into university, and students may be subject to no testing whatsoever for the first year or more of university study. Although university completion rates have not been estimated in either country, some figures are indicative. The ratio of bachelor's and first-professional degrees in American institutions of higher learning, in 1957–58, to the number of first-time degree-credit enrollments in the fall, four years earlier, was reported to be .610 for men and .488 for women.[5] The indicated 39 and 51 per cent drop-out rates are probably underestimates, because transfers from two-year junior colleges swell the number of degrees without being included in first-time enrollments. In England, a study following up the careers of individual students, found that in University College, London, 81.9 per cent of entering students, between 1948 and 1951, eventually graduated with a degree. A similar study a few years earlier at the University of Liverpool revealed a figure of 86.9 per cent.[6] Under contest mobility, the object is to train as many as possible to the skills necessary for elite status so as to give everyone a chance and to maintain competition at the highest pitch. Under sponsored mobility, the

[1] Less adequate financial provision and a lower teacher-student ratio are mentioned as obstacles to parity of secondary modern schools with grammar schools in *The Times Educational Supplement*, Feb. 22, 1957, p. 241. On difficulties in achieving prestige comparable with grammar schools, see G. Baron, "Secondary Education in Britain: Some Present-Day Trends," *Teachers' College Record*, LVII (1956) 211–221; and O. Banks, *Parity and Prestige in English Secondary Education* (London: Routledge and Kegan Paul, 1955). *Cf.* also P. E. Vernon, *op. cit.*, pp. 19–22.

[2] Alexis de Tocqueville, *Democracy in America* (New York: Alfred Knopf, 1945), I, 52.

[3] An earlier Gallup Poll had disclosed that 62 per cent of parents opposed stiffened college entrance requirements, while only 27 per cent favored them. *Time*, April 14, 1958, p. 45.

[4] *Los Angeles Times*, December 17, 1958, Part I, p. 16.

[5] U.S. Department of Health, Education and Welfare, Office of Education, *Earned Degrees Conferred by Higher Education Institutions, 1957–58* (Washington: Government Printing Office, 1959), p. 3.

[6] Nicolas Malleson, "Student Performance at University College, London 1948–51," *Universities Quarterly*, XII (May, 1958), 288–319.

objective is to train in elite culture only those for whom the presumption is that they will enter the elite, lest there be a dangerous number of "angry young men" who have elite skills without elite station.

Third, systems of mobility precipitate different emphases regarding educational content. Induction into elite culture under sponsored mobility makes for emphasis on school *esprit de corps*, which can be employed to cultivate norms of intraclass loyalty and elite tastes and manners. Likewise, formal schooling built about highly specialized study in fields with entirely intellectual or aesthetic concern and no "practical" value serves the purpose of elite culture. Under contest mobility in the United States, in spite of faculty endorsement of "liberal education," schooling tends to be measured for its practical benefits and to become, beyond the elementary level, chiefly vocational. Education does not so much provide what is good in itself as it provides skills necessary to compete for the real prizes of life, and of these vocational skills are the most important.

An application of these points can be seen in the different national attitudes toward students being gainfully employed while in university. More students in the United States than in Britain have part-time employments, and in the United States relatively fewer of the students receive subsidies toward subsistence and living expenses. The most generous programs of state aid in the United States, apart from those applying to veterans and other special groups, do not normally cover expenses other than tuition and institutional fees. British maintenance grants are designed to cover full living expenses, taking into account parents' ability to pay.[1] Under sponsored mobility, gainful employment serves no apprentice or testing function, and is thought merely to prevent the student from gaining the full benefit of his schooling. L. J. Parry speaks of the general opposition to students working and asserts that English university authorities almost unanimously hold that ". . . if a person must work for financial reasons, he should never spend more than four weeks on such work during the whole year."[2]

Under contest mobility, success in school work is not a sufficient test of practical merit, but must be supplemented by a test in the world of practical affairs. Thus, in didactic folk tales, the professional engineer

will also prove himself a superior mechanic, the business tycoon, a superior behind-the-counter salesman. Consequently, by "working his way through school" the enterprising student "earns" his education in the fullest sense, keeps in touch with the practical world, and has an apprenticeship into vocational life. Students are often urged to seek part-time employment, even when there is no financial need, and in extreme instances schools have incorporated paid employment as a requirement toward graduation. As R. H. Eckleberry states the typical American view, a student willing to work part-time is a "better bet" than "the equally bright student who receives all of his financial support from others."[3]

Finally, social-adjustment training is peculiar to the system of contest mobility. The reason for emphasis on adjustment training is clear when its nature is understood. Adjustment training is preparation to cope with situations in which there are no rules of intercourse or in which the rules are unknown, but in which the good opinions of others cannot be wholly ignored. Under sponsored mobility, the elite recruits are inducted into a homogeneous stratum in which there is consensus regarding the rules, and in which they succeed socially by mastering these rules. Under contest mobility, the elite aspirant must relate himself both to the established elite and to the masses, who follow different rules; and the elite themselves are not sufficiently homogeneous to evolve consensual rules of intercourse. Furthermore, in the contest the rules may vary according to the background of the competitor, so that each aspirant must deal successfully with persons playing the game with slightly different sets of rules. Consequently, adjustment training becomes one of the important skills imparted by the school system.[4] That the emphasis on adjustment training in the schools has had genuine popular support is indicated by a 1945 Fortune poll, in which a national sample were asked which one of two things would be very important for a son of theirs to get out of college. Over 87 per cent chose "Ability to get along with and understand people," in answer to the question.[5] This answer was the second most frequently chosen as being the very most important thing to get out of college. In the present connection, it is possible that British education is better preparation for participation in an orderly and controlled world, while American education prepares better for a less ordered situation. The reputedly superior ability of "Yanks" to get things done seems to apply to this ability to cope with a chaotic situation.

To this point discussion has centered on the tax-supported school systems in both countries, but the different place and emphasis of the privately supported secondary schools can also be related to the framework at hand. Since private secondary schools in both countries are principally vehicles for transmitting high family status to the children, the mobility function is quite tangential. Under contest mobility, the private schools should presumably have no mobility function. On the

---

[1] See C. A. Quattlebaum, *Federal Aid to Students for Higher Education* (Washington: Government Printing Office, 1956); and "Grants to Students: University and Training Colleges," *The Times Educational Supplement*, May 6, 1955, p. 446.

[2] "Students' Expenses," *The Times Educational Supplement*, May 6, 1955, 447.

[3] "College Jobs for College Students," *Journal of Higher Education*, XXVII (1956), 174.

[4] Adjustment training is not a necessary accompaniment of contest mobility. The shift during the last half-century toward the increased importance of social acceptability as an elite credential has brought social adjustment training into correspondingly greater prominence.

[5] Hadley Cantril (ed.), *Public Opinion 1935–1946* (Princeton: Princeton University Press, 1951), p. 186.

other hand, if there is to be mobility in a sponsored system, the privately controlled school, populated largely with the children of elite parents, would be the ideal device through which to induct selected children from lower levels into elite status. By means of a scholarship program, promising members of lesser classes could be chosen early for recruitment into the top classes. The English "public" schools have, in fact, incorporated into their charters provisions to insure that a few boys from lesser classes would enter each year. Getting one's child into a "public" school, or even into one of the lesser private schools, assumes an importance in England relatively unknown in the United States. If the children cannot win scholarships the parents often make extreme financial sacrifices in order to pay the cost of this relatively exclusive education.[1]

Just how much of a place private secondary schools have played in mobility in either country is difficult to determine exactly, since American studies of social mobility regularly omit information on private or tax-supported secondary school attendance, and English studies showing the advantage of "public" school attendance generally fail to separate the mobile from the non-mobile in this respect. However, it has been observed that during the nineteenth century the English "public" schools were largely used by the new-rich manufacturing classes to enable their sons to achieve an unqualified elite state.[2] In one sense, the rise of the manufacturing classes through free enterprise represent a genuine contest mobility that threatened to destroy the traditional sponsorship system. But by accepting the "public" schools in this fashion they bowed to the legitimacy of the traditional system — an implicit acknowledgment that upward mobility was not complete until the final sponsored induction had been carried out. Dennis Brogan speaks of the nineteenth-century public schools' task as "the job of marrying the old English social order to the new."[3]

It is of interest to note the parallel between the tax-supported grammar schools and the "public" schools in England. The former have been in important respects patterned after the latter, adopting the latter's view of mobility but making it a much larger part of their total function. In a general way, the grammar schools are the vehicle for sponsored mobility throughout the middle ranges of the class system, modelled after the pattern of the "public" schools, which are the agencies for sponsored mobility into the elite.

Effects of mobility on personality

Passing note should be taken of the importance of the distinction between sponsored and contest mobility for the supposed personality-shaping effects of the upward mobility experience. Not a great deal is yet known about the distinctiveness of the mobile personality nor about the specific features of importance in the mobility experience.[4] However, three facets of the mobility experience are most frequently stressed

in discussions of the problem. First is the stress or tension involved in striving higher than others under more difficult conditions than they. Second is the complication of interpersonal relations introduced by the necessity to abandon lower-level friends in favor of an uncertain acceptance into higher-level circles. Third is the problem of working out an adequate personal value system in the face of movement between classes having somewhat variant or even contradictory value systems.[5] The impact of each of these three facets of mobility experience should be different depending upon whether the pattern is that of the contest or of sponsorship.

Under the sponsorship system, recruits to mobility are selected early, segregated from their class peers, grouped with other recruits and with youth from the class to which they are moving, and are trained specifically for the class that they are to enter. Since the selection is made early, the mobility experience should be relatively free from the strain that comes with the series of elimination tests and long-extended uncertainty of success. The school segregation and the integrated school community of the "public" school or grammar school should clarify the mobile person's social ties. It is to be noted that A. N. Oppenheim failed to discover clique formation along lines of social class in a sociometric study of a number of grammar schools.[6] The problem of a system of values should be well solved when the elite recruit is taken from his parents and peers to be placed in a boarding school, although it may be less well clarified for the grammar-school boy who returns each evening to his working-class family. Undoubtedly, this latter limitation has something to do with the observed failure of working-class boys to continue through the last years of grammar school and into the universities.[7] In general, then, the crucial factors that have been stressed as affecting personality formation among the upwardly mobile are rather specific to the contest system of mobility, such as is found in the United States, or the incompletely functioning sponsorship system.

It is often taken for granted that there is convincing evidence to show that the mobility oriented student in American secondary schools suffers from the tendency

[1] For a popular account of the place of "public" schools in the English educational system, see Dennis Brogan, *The English People* (New York: Alfred Knopf, 1943), pp. 18–56.

[2] A. H. Halsey of Birmingham University called my attention to the importance of this fact.

[3] *Op. cit.*, pp. 24–25.

[4] *Cf.* Lipset and Bendix, *op. cit.*, pp. 250 ff.

[5] *Cf.* August B. Hollingshead and Frederick C. Redlich, *Social Class and Mental Illness* (New York: Wiley and Sons, 1958); W. Lloyd Warner and James Abegglen, *Big Business Leaders in America* (New York: Harper and Bros., 1955); Warner *et al.*, *Who Shall Be Educated?*, *op. cit.*

[6] "Social Status and Clique Formation among Grammar School Boys," *British Journal of Sociology*, VI (1955), 288–45. Oppenheim's findings may be compared with A. B. Hollingshead, *Elmtown's Youth* (New York: Wiley and Sons, 1949), pp. 204–242. *Cf.* also Joseph Kahl, *The American Class Structure* (New York: Rinehart and Co., 1957), pp. 129–138.

[7] J. E. Floud *et al.*, *op. cit.*, pp. 115 ff.

for cliques to form along lines predetermined by family background. However, these tendencies are statistically quite moderate, leaving much room for individual exception. Furthermore, the mobility oriented students have not generally been examined separately to see whether they might in fact be incorporated into higher-level cliques in contrast to the general rule. Nor is it adequately demonstrated whether the purported working-class value system, which is at odds with middle-class values, is as pervasive and constraining throughout the working class as it is conspicuous in delinquent gangs. Thus, while the model of contest mobility indicates that there should be more serious and continuing strain over the uncertainty of attaining mobility, more explicit and continued preoccupation with the problem of changing friendships to fit class position, and more contradictory learning to inhibit the acquisition of a value system appropriate to class of aspiration than should be found under sponsored mobility, the ramifications of these differences depend upon further understanding of the workings of the American class system. A search for personality-forming experiences specific to a sponsorship system has yet to be made.

Conclusion

In the foregoing statement, two ideal-typical organizing norms concerning the manner in which mobility should properly take place have been outlined. On the one hand, mobility may be viewed as most appropriately a *contest* in which many contestants strive, by whatever combinations of strategy, enterprise, perseverance, and ability they can marshal, restricted only by a minimum set of rules defining fair play and minimizing special advantage to those who get ahead early in the game, to take possession of a limited number of prizes. On the other hand, it may be thought best that the upwardly mobile person be *sponsored*, like one who joins a private club upon invitation of the membership, selected because the club members feel that he has qualities desirable in a club member, and then subjected to careful training and initiation into the guiding ethic and lore of the club before being accorded full membership.

Upward mobility actually takes place to a considerable degree by both the contest pattern and the sponsorship pattern in every society. But it has been suggested that in England the sponsorship norm is ascendant and has been so for a century or more, and that in the United States the contest norm has been ascendant for a comparable period. A norm is ascendant in the sense that there is a constant "strain" to bring the relevant features of the class system, the pattern of social control, and the educational system into consistency with the norm, and that patterns consistent with the ascendant norm seem more "natural" and "right" to the articulate segments of the population.

The statement has been broadly impressionistic and speculative, reflecting more the over-all impression of an observer of both countries than a systematic exploration of data. Relevant data of a variety of sorts have been cited, but their use has been more illustrative than demonstrative. Several lines of research are suggested by the statement. One of these is an exploration of different channels of mobility in both countries to discover the extent to which mobility corresponds to each of the types. Recruitment to the Catholic priesthood, for example, probably follows a strictly sponsorship norm regardless of the dominant contest norm in the United States.

The effect of changes in the major avenues of upward mobility upon the dominant norms requires investigation. The increasing importance of promotion through corporation hierarchies and the declining importance of the entrepreneurial path to upward mobility undoubtedly compromise the ideal pattern of contest mobility. The increasing insistence upon higher education as a prerequisite to a variety of employments is a similar modification. On the other hand, there is little evidence of a tendency to follow the logic of sponsorship beyond the bureaucratic selection process. The prospect of a surplus of college-educated persons in relation to jobs requiring college education tends to restore the contest situation at a higher level, and the further fact that completion of higher education may be more determined by motivational factors than by capacity suggests that the contest pattern continues within the school.

In England, on the other hand, two developments may dull the distinctive edge of the sponsorship system. One is response to popular demand to allow more children to secure the grammar-school type of training, particularly through including such a program in the secondary modern schools. The other is introduction of the comprehensive secondary school, relatively uncommon at present but a major plank in the Labour Party's education platform. It remains to be determined whether the comprehensive school in England will take a distinctive form and serve a distinctive function that preserves the pattern of sponsorship or whether it will approximate the present American system.

Finally, the assertion that these types are embedded in genuine folk norms requires specific investigation. A combination of direct study of popular attitudes and content analysis of popular responses to crucial issues is necessary. Perhaps the most significant search would be for evidence showing what courses of action seem to require no special justification or explanation because they are altogether "natural" and "right," and which courses of action, whether approved or not, seem to require special justification and explanation. Such evidence, appropriately used, would permit study of the extent to which the patterns described are genuine folk norms rather than the mere by-product of particular structural factors in society. It would also permit determination of the extent to which acceptance of the ascendant folk norm is diffused among the varied segments of the population.

The Growth of the Professions and the Class System

Joseph Ben-David

AS HAS BEEN SHOWN elsewhere, there is no unequivocal definition of professions, but only a set of characteristics which are in different degrees present in an increasing number of occupations. Some occupations, therefore, may be considered as professions in one country, or at one time, but not in another, or at a different time. Besides, even if one decided to draw up an arbitrary list of professions, it would be most difficult to find comparable data about their growth in different countries, since historical statistics of occupations of a sufficiently detailed kind exist only for a few countries. Rather than try to measure, therefore, the growth of professions proper, we shall rely as an index on statistics of higher education, the latter being the most important element of professionalism.[1]

For a general view of the situation in a large number of countries we shall use data about *1)* the supply of people with higher educational qualifications, and *2)* the output of graduates in different countries in a selected year.[2]

While Table 1 presents the situation as it existed about 1950 as a result of past development, Table 2 refers to recent trends.[3] Comparison of the two tables shows that some countries have considerably changed their positions recently. Japan and the Philippines which are about the middle of the distribution in Table 1 are very near the top in Table 2, and Britain which is conspicuous for its low proportion of graduates in Table 1 appears among the rest of the European countries in Table 2.[4] Otherwise the pictures presented in the two tables are consistent, and in accordance with what is known about the educational systems of the different countries.

For the analysis of the present situation the data of Table 2 are also presented graphically (Diagram 1).

The countries can be divided into four or five groups. Those on the bottom left hand side of the distribution, i.e. with up to about four graduates per 10,000 population, among whom less than one is a graduate of science or technology, are, besides Spain and Portugal, all developing countries of Latin America and the Middle East. The group next to them on the diagram, with 4–9.9 graduates per 10,000 population (with the exception of Norway only) of whom (with the exception of Greece) one to four are graduates of science and technology, consists mainly of European countries with the addition of Australia, India and Israel. More difficult to classify is the heterogeneous group of countries further to the right, having more than 10 graduates for each 10,000 of the population. It includes Belgium, Canada, Czechoslovakia, Japan, the Netherlands, New Zealand, the Philippines, the United States and the U.S.S.R. In respect to the science and technology graduates, only the United States and the U.S.S.R. differ considerably from the European countries. Even though the percentages of their science and technology graduates among the total number of graduates are not very high, each have more than 5.5 graduates in these

[1] Britain is a partial exception in this respect, since there full professional status can be attained in law, engineering, and accountancy without university education. But even there a growing majority of members of these professions attend university. Cf. *Census of Great Britain, 1951 – 1% Sample*, London, H.M.S.O., 1952, Table VIII, 5 and *Census 1961, Great Britain, Scientific and Technological Qualifications*, London, H.M.S.O., 1962, Table 3. In any case this difference will have to be kept in mind in the subsequent analyses.

[2] In this latter set of figures the graduates in science and technology are shown separately, because of the different requirements involved in their training, as well as the importance usually attributed to them at the present stage of industrialization.

[3] The fact that higher education in different countries includes different fields of study as well as different levels of training is no objection to the making of comparisons, since it is the spread of professional elements in different countries to different occupations, and their penetration to different levels of the status scale which are to be described and explained.

[4] There are also discrepancies in the position of Chile and Israel in the two tables. The case of Chile, as pointed out in the footnote to Table 1, remains unexplained and is probably due to differences in the definitions of higher education in the two tables. That of Israel reflects the difference between the unusually high ratios of academically trained people among immigrants to Israel in the past and the relatively modest numbers of graduates in her new higher educational establishments. The proportion of students among Israel's population has, however, grown very rapidly during the last few years. In 1961–2 the number of graduates (first and professional degrees) was 1,742 in a population of 2,233,600, i.e. 7.8 graduates per 10,000 of the general population. Cf. *Statistical Abstract of Israel*, No. 13, Jerusalem, 1962.

Reprinted from *Current Sociology*, V. 12 (1963–4), pp. 256–277. by permission of the author and the publisher.

fields per 10,000 of the population. However, it will be shown later that the real ratio of science and technology graduates in the U.S.S.R. is probably even higher, presumably about 8–9 per 10,000, thus considerably exceeding that of the United States, while the total proportion of graduates is much higher in the United States. These two are, therefore, also distinct types. Concerning the rest of these countries, all except Canada and Czechoslovakia have only recently changed their positions, having previously possessed graduate ratios similar to those of the bulk of European countries. As far as science and technology graduates are concerned, the ratios of the countries in this group are still similar to those of Europe.[1]

By and large this clustering of countries distinguishes between three influential academic systems, the European, the American, and the Soviet, each of which produces different ratios and kinds of graduates. The positions of the other countries seem to be, at least superficially, the function of respective spheres of influence. The developing countries of the Middle East and Latin America whose academic traditions were imported from Europe, are situated close to and below the European countries, while the Philippines, which used to be an American dependency, are trailing the United States. The position of Canada and that of Japan reflect the replacement of European influence by American. Among the communist countries of Eastern and Central Europe there is a tendency to approach the U.S.S.R. They have greatly increased their ratios of graduates in general and that of their science and technology graduates in particular, as a result of the adoption of various features of the Soviet academic system.[2]

An obvious hypothesis to explain these differences would be that they are related to some aspects of economic development, since higher education can be

regarded either as consumption or investment, and more developed countries can better afford to pay for the former, as well as to absorb the latter usefully.[3] How-

TABLE I. *Population by Educational Attainment (Latest Census between 1945–57) (in ascending order of prevalence of higher education)*

Country	Census year	Age level		Number of persons (thousands)[1]	Percentage possessing higher education[2]
Paraguay	1950	25+	M.	231	0.7
			F.	265	0.1
Ecuador	1950	25+	M.	602	1.2
			F.	635	0.1
Brazil	1950	25+	M.	9,889	1.4
			F.	9,853	0.1
Argentina	1947	20+	M.	4,746	1.4
			F.	4,488	0.2
Portugal	1950	25+	M.	2,009[3]	1.6
			F.	2,372[3]	0.3
Venezuela	1950	25+	M.	988	1.7
			F.	967	0.3
U.K. — England and Wales	1951	25+	M.	10,697[4]	1.7
			F.	3,779[4]	1.3[5]
Turkey	1950	25+	M.	4,074	1.9
			F.	4,504	0.3
Scotland	1951	25+	M.	1,273[4]	2.0
			F.	412[4]	2.4[5]
Puerto Rico	1950	25+	M.	424	2.1
			F.	415	1.4
Italy	1951	25+	M.	13,223[3]	2.5
			F.	14,536[3]	0.5
Japan	1950	25+	M.	17,670	2.7
			F.	19,743	0.1
Norway	1950	25+	M.	994	2.7
			F.	1,051	0.3
Canada	1951	25+	M.	3,832	3.1
			F.	3,753	1.2
Philippines	1956	25+	M.	3,751	3.2
			F.	3,930	1.7
France	1954	25+	M.	10,965	3.3
			F.	12,921	0.7
Greece	1951	25+	M.	1,840[3]	3.4
			F.	2,067[3]	0.7
Chile	1952	25+	M.	1,212	3.4[6]
			F.	1,302	1.4[6]
Hungary	1949	25+	M.	2,490	3.5
			F.	2,866	0.6
Israel (Jews)	1954	25+	M.	395	6.1
			F.	391	2.8
Israel (Arabs)	1954	15+	M.	48	0.6
			F.	47	0.2
U.S.A.	1950	25+	M.	41,286	7.3
			F.	43,784	5.2

Sources: *Basic Facts and Figures*—International Statistics Relating to Education, Culture and Mass Communication, UNESCO, 1950, pp. 15–23, Table 3.
Cf. source for further detailed comments about the data.
[1] Excluding those whose education is unknown.
[2] In general, four years or more of higher education.
[3] Includes persons whose educational attainments are unknown.
[4] These figures refer only to the working population.
[5] These are percentages of graduates among the adult women who are in the working population. They are, therefore, not comparable to percentages in other countries.
[6] There is an unexplained discrepancy between these percentages and the figures about the current numbers of graduates which do not seem to be in excess of those of the rest of Latin American countries (cf. Table 2). It seems that "higher education" in this table includes more than "graduates of higher education".

[1] By using other indexes the rank order of the individual countries within each group may change, but not the composition and the relative place of the groups themselves, cf. for instance, A. H. Halsey (ed.), *Ability and Educational Opportunity*, O.E.C.D., 1961, pp. 192–193 for a table counting first degrees of university level only and relating them to college age population in O.E.E.C. and associated countries.
[2] The only country which had been influenced by the Russian academic model prior to its becoming a communist country is China; cf. Y. C. Wang, "Intellectuals and Society in China 1860–1949," *Comparative Studies in Society and History*, 3 (1961), pp. 395–426.
[3] One hypothesis of this kind about the existence of a relationship between Gross National Product and the supply of highly educated manpower has been recently investigated by means of a model constructed by J. Tinbergen and H. Correa. Cf. L. T. Emmerij, "Manpower Forecasts in Latin America; Problems Involved and Possible Methods," Université de Paris, Institut d'Étude du Développement Economique et Sociale, mimeographed. For an earlier attempt at classification of countries by attendance in higher educational institutions and economic development, measured by the percentage of the working population engaged in primary production and international income units per man-year in employment, cf. C. Arnold Anderson, "The Social Status of University Students in Relation to Type of Economy: an International Comparison", *Transactions of the Third World Congress of Sociology*, vol. V, pp. 51–63.

TABLE 2. *Population, Total Graduates and Science and Technology Graduates in Several Countries (Number and Rates) 1958 or Nearest Available Year (in ascending order)*

	Country	Year	1 Total number of graduates	2 Graduates in science and technology[1]	3 2 as percentage of 1	4 Population (thousands)	5 Total graduates	6 Science and technology graduates
							Per 10,000 of population	
1	Pakistan	1958	8,092	2,066	25.53	89,136	0.91	0.23
2	Iran	1958	1,936	293[2]	15.13	19,677	0.98	0.15
3	Colombia	1957	1,752	250	14.27	13,227	1.32	0.19
4	Turkey	1957	4,049	971	23.98	25,498	1.59	0.38
5	Syria	1957	745	64	8.59	4,082	1.83	0.16
6	Chile	1957	1,396	284	20.34	7,121	1.96	0.40
7	Cuba	1956	1,566	92	5.87	6,256	2.50	0.15
8	Portugal	1958	2,298	530	23.06	8,981	2.56	0.59
9	Brazil	1957	15,749	1,788	11.35	61,268	2.57	0.29
10	Norway	1957	1,038	493	47.50	3,494	2.97	1.41
11	Spain	1958	9,903	1,703	17.20	29,662	3.34	0.57
12	Argentina	1957	7,382[4]	909[4]	12.31	19,873	3.71	0.46
13	Peru	1957	3,732	322	8.63	9,923	3.76	0.32
14	Egypt	1957	9,080	1,929	21.24	24,179	3.76	0.80
15	Italy	1956	20,379	5,202	25.53	48,279	4.22	1.08
16	Austria	1957	3,058	815	26.65	6,997	4.37	1.16
17	France	1958	19,493	7,685	39.42	44,584	4.37	1.72
18	Switzerland	1958	2,298[3]	777[3]	33.81	5,185	4.43	1.50
19	Australia	1958	4,605[5]	1,411[5]	30.64	9,842	4.68	1.43
20	Israel	1957	965	571	59.17	1,937	4.98	2.95
21	Yugoslavia	1958	10,206	2,642	25.89	18,189	5.61	1.45
22	Britain[8]	1957	28,554[6]	10,879[6]	38.10	50,254	5.68	2.16
23	Greece	1957	4,882	629	12.88	8,098	6.03	0.78
24	German Fed. Rep. and West Berlin	1957	33,743[6]	17,211	51.00	54,357	6.21	3.17
25	Sweden	1958	4,715	1,263	26.79	7,415	6.36	1.70
26	Poland	1958	18,509	10,006	54.06	28,783	6.43	3.48
27	India	1955	268,566	70,842	26.38	393,826	6.82	1.80
28	Hungary	1958	7,166	2,811	39.23	9,898	7.24	2.84
29	Bulgaria	1958	5,783	2,878	49.77	7,728	7.48	3.72
30	Finland	1957	3,508	682	19.44	4,336	8.09	1.57
31	Ireland	1959	2,383	495	20.78	2,846	8.39	1.74
32	Czechoslovakia	1958	13,470	5,774	42.87	13,474	10.00	4.29
33	Netherlands	1958	11,296	2,813	24.90	11,186	10.10	2.51
34	Belgium	1957	9,182	2,267	24.69	8,989	10.21	2.52
35	Canada	1958	22,259[7]	5,609[7]	25.20	17,048	13.06	3.29
36	U.S.S.R.	1958	290,700[9]	114,600[9]	39.42	207,100(ca)	14.04	5.53
37	Philippines	1956	35,987	6,492	18.04	24,513	14.68	2.65
38	Japan	1958	160,301	27,412	17.10	91,540	17.51	2.99
39	New Zealand	1958	5,095	583	11.44	2,282	22.33	2.55
40	U.S.A.[10]	1958	438,030	96,509	22.03	174,788	25.06	5.52

Source: UNESCO, *Basic Facts and Figures, 1961*; Paris, 1962.
Demographic Yearbook 1961. United Nations, New York, 1961.
[1] Graduates of faculties of natural sciences, engineering and agriculture.
[2] Since the duration of agricultural courses had just been lengthened, there were no agricultural graduates in 1958.
[3] Our source includes a note saying that: "Diplomas awarded by Polytechnic schools of Zurich, Geneva and Lausanne were included under fine arts and were, therefore, not included with scientific and technical degrees". This, however, seems to be a mistake, since according to the *Statistisches Jahrbuch Der Schweiz, 1958*, pp. 466–470, the total number of all graduates of engineering and natural sciences, including graduates of the Zurich, Geneva and Lausanne Polytechnic schools, was 743.
[4] Not including private institutions.
[5] Figures refer to universities only.
[6] Students of architecture were included under engineering.
[7] Includes Official estimates; some scientific and technical degrees were granted in other faculties and are, therefore, not included in the scientific and technical total.
[8] Figures for Northern Ireland were not available.
[9] Including correspondence students.
[10] Includes Alaska and Hawaii; graduates under the bachelor degree level in the U.S.A. and Hawaii not counted in statistics.

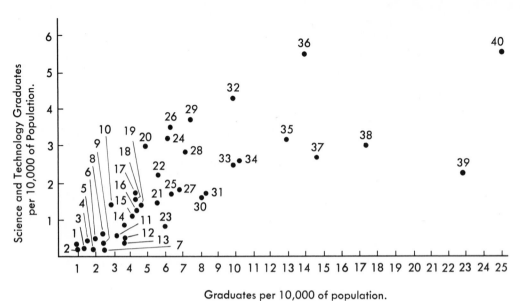

DIAGRAM 1

GRADUATES OF HIGHER EDUCATION PER 10,000 OF GENERAL POPULATION AND SCIENCE AND TECHNOLOGY GRADUATES PER
10,000 OF POPULATION IN DIFFERENT COUNTRIES, 1958 OR NEAREST AVAILABLE YEAR
Note 1. — The distance representing the unit on the vertical axis is twice as long as on the horizontal axis.
Note 2. — For the names of the countries represented by numbers next to the dots cf. Table 2.

ever, even though some such correlations can be established, there still remain obvious and glaring exceptions, such as India, the Philippines, etc. Besides, economic factors do not account for the generally high ratios of students, and particularly high ratios of scientists and technologists in the countries belonging to the Soviet sphere of influence, as compared with the economically more advanced European countries.

Finally, the diffusion of educational systems and traditions from metropolitan centers to other countries, rather than explaining something, is in itself a pheno-

¹ Enrolment, rather than graduation statistics are used because of the greater availability of the former. Some of the figures may not be strictly comparable. Most countries include foreign students in their enrolment figures, and in some cases this might have altered the figures considerably. The numbers of local and foreign students were, therefore, given separately for countries where they have formed more than 15 per cent of the total (Austria, France, Switzerland) and as far as such figures were available. There may have also occurred changes in the definition of students. Finally, the rates of attrition vary a great deal among countries, so that those with much higher student ratios than others may produce similar ratios of graduates. This consideration is particularly relevant in determining the position of Britain which has a lower rate of attrition than most other countries: about 85 per cent of those who enrol obtain degrees, as compared with about 55 in the U.S., 60 in Australia, and 66 in Canada, cf. Sir Eric Ashby, "Investment in Man", *The Listener*, LXX: 1796 (29.8.'63), p. 296. As can be seen, therefore, from a comparison of Tables 2 and 4, the rank order of this country is quite different in the statistics of graduates from those of student enrolments.

menon which needs explanation. As it has been shown time and again, diffusion of institutional characteristics is not a sufficient explanation of adoption. In our case, too, there does not exist a uniform relationship between the metropolitan and the adopting countries. Most of the latter lag behind their metropolitan models, but a minority of them has attained or even surpassed the models in proportions of students to population. There are similar examples from the recent past: the Eastern European countries, including Russia, had been until World War I or some of them even World War II, adopting countries following German and French models, yet by the twenties or the thirties they had already attained or surpassed their models at least in the quantity of their students. The same applies to the relationship at the beginning of this century between the United States on the one hand and Britain and Germany, which had served as models for its institutions of higher education, on the other.

In order to understand the causes of these differences we shall trace the changes which occurred in the past in the relative size and composition of the higher educational systems of the countries here surveyed. As we can see from Tables 3 and 4, the differences in size between the European and the United States systems have existed since the beginning of this century, while the characteristic features of the Russian system have evolved only since about 1930.¹

In the European system important changes have

taken place between the thirties and the fifties. The differences between the European countries have diminished. In the early thirties the student population ratios varied from a low of 11.3 per 10,000 of the population in Britain to about three times as much in the small Baltic countries, and the distribution of countries along this range was fairly continuous. In 1958 the student population ratio of Czechoslovakia, which is on the upper end of the distribution, is still about three times that of Britain, which is still at its lower end. But only two more European countries, Norway and Switzerland (Swiss students only), have less than 30 students for every 10,000 of the general population. Twelve out of the fifteen European countries in the distribution (not including the U.S.S.R.) have ratios of between about 30–50 per 10,000. Thus among European countries only Britain and one small country, Norway, have student population ratios considerably smaller than 30/10,000, while presumably no European

country (except the U.S.S.R.) has ratios higher than 50/10,000.

Changes occurring within such a short period of time in a relatively large number of societies cannot be without significance. Indeed, the historical antecedents of this change are well known and form a crucial part of the history of modern professions. As it has been mentioned in the previous chapter, European countries in the twenties and thirties faced a grave problem of overcrowding in the learned professions. Dividing these countries (not including the U.S.S.R.) according to a somewhat arbitrarily fixed criterion of high and low student/population ratios in 1934 and fast or slow rates of growth of these ratios between 1913–34, we obtain a clustering of countries indicative of the severity of this problem (cf. Table 5).

France and all the countries of Central and Eastern Europe which, with the exception of Switzerland (all students) and Poland, are in the upper left hand square,

TABLE 3. *Total Enrolment of Students in Institutions of Higher Learning in 1913, 1925, 1930, 1934, 1948, 1958*

	1913	1925	1930	1934	1948	1958
Australia	4,576	8,285	9,483	—	29,034	72,564
Austria	18,129	19,852	—	19,297	19,762	29,804
(Austrian students only)	—	—	—	—	—	19,974
Belgium	8,532	9,848	10,845	11,038	21,485 (1949–50)	44,724
Bulgaria	1,822 (1910)	5,905	8,037	—	49,911 (1947)	33,205
Canada	—	47,059	51,250	—	77,426 (1947)	92,560
Czechoslovakia	13,477	26,167	28,892	30,142	60,727	75,306
Denmark	2,707	4,193	5,021	5,405	7,311	14,182
Estonia	—	4,988	3,913	3,366	—	—
France	41,044 (1910)	58,507	73,601	87,152	129,035	226,173
(French students only)	34,803 (1910)	49,717	57,347	75,758	120,901	192,340
Germany	76,847	89,481	132,090	129,606 (1932)[3]	—	164,045[2]
Great Britain	27,728 (1910–1)[1]	41,606	47,826	50,638	78,507 (1947–8)	94,666
Greece	3,345	11,726	—	—	—	25,206
Holland	5,568	9,438	11,489	13,683	25,955 (1947–8)	35,131
Hungary	18,238[4]	15,229	16,229	15,659	—	31,178
India	36,284 (1912)	93,741 (1927)	100,349	—	262,605	833,450 (1957)
Italy	28,026	44,906	44,460	51,003	180,149 (1947–8)	163,945
Japan	9,527	50,727	67,555	70,162 (1933)	309,900 (1950)	636,232
Latvia	2,088	7,194	8,577	8,066	—	—
Norway	2,294	4,154	4,622	5,387	6,209 (1946–7)	7,549
Poland	—	37,125	48,155	49,599	84,680 (1946–7)	120,765
Rumania	—	29,930	40,300	39,670	—	67,849
Sweden	6,363	8,989	—	—	14,626	28,343
Switzerland	6,881[5]	8,105	8,501	10,545	17,172	18,877
(Swiss students only)	3,881[5]	6,164	6,973 (1932)	7,783	12,469	13,038
Turkey	—	3,930	4,443	7,020	20,177	49,161
U.S.A.	355,213 (1910)	822,859	1,100,737	1,055,360	2,616,262	3,236,414
U.S.S.R. (Regular students)	117,000	167,000 (1925–6)	291,000	521,800	845,100 (1950)	1,333,000
U.S.S.R. (including correspondence students)	117,000	167,000 (1925–6)	291,000	521,800	1,247,400 (1950)	2,179,000
Yugoslavia	—	10,673	14,539	15,267	60,566 (1949–50)	97,323

Sources: W. M. Kotschnig, *Unemployment in the Learned Professions*, London, Oxford University Press, Humphrey Milford, 1937, p. 13, Table 1.
World Handbook of Educational Organization and Statistics, UNESCO, 1951.
UNESCO Basic Facts and Figures, 1960, pp. 52–5, Table 7, Higher education.
U.S.S.R.: For 1913, 1925, A. G. Korol, *Soviet Education for Science and Technology*, Massachusetts Institute of Technology, 1957, pp. 131–132. For 1930, 1948, 1958, N. DeWitt, *Education and Professional Employment in the U.S.S.R.* Washington, National Science Foundation, 1961, pp. 638–639, Table IV-A-1-E.
Statistical Yearbooks of Austria, France, Germany and Switzerland.
[1] This figure is probably incomplete.
[2] German Federal Republic.
[3] Although figures for 1934 are available, 1932 figures were used because this had been the last year before Hitler's advent which was accompanied by drastic curtailments of higher education.
[4] Pre-World War I area.
[5] Estimates, based on figures from Kotschnig, p. 25 and *Statistisches Jahrbuch Der Schweiz, 1959-60*, pp. 466, 470, 472.

TABLE 4. *Frequency of Students in Total Population for 1913, 1934, 1948*
and 1958, and Change in Frequency 1913–34 and 1934–58
(in ascending order according to the frequency of students in 1934)

| Country | Number of students per 10,000 inhabitants[1] | | | | Increase in frequency[1] | |
	1913	1934	1948	1958	1913–34 (1913=100)	1934–58 (1934=100)
India	(1912) 1.2	(1932) 3.0	7.5	21.2	260	710
Japan	1.7	(1933) 10.9	(1950) 37.5	69.4	640	640
Great Britain	6.8	11.3	(1947) 16.3	18.8	165	165
Italy	7.9	12.4	(1947) 39.2	33.7	155	270
Greece	6.9	(1932) 13.1	—	30.9	190	240
Belgium	11.2	13.6	(1949) 24.9	49.5	120	365
Denmark	9.5	15.2	17.5	31.4	160	205
Poland	(1925) 12.1	(1934) 15.4	(1946) 35.3	42.0	(1925–34) 130	270
Holland	8.9	17.3	26.9	31.4	195	180
Hungary	8.5	18.1	—	31.6	215	175
Sweden	11.3	(1932) 18.4	21.3	38.2	165	210
Norway	9.3	19.1	(1946) 19.9	21.4	205	110
Germany	11.5	(1932) 19.7	—	31.4	170	160
Czechoslovakia	(1925) 18.4	21.0	(1947) 50.0	55.9	114	265
France	10.3	20.8	31.4	50.8	200	245
(French students only)	9.0	18.3	29.2	43.1	203	235
Rumania	7.6	22.0	—	37.6	290	170
Switzerland	18.2	25.3	36.3	36.2	140	143
(Swiss students only)	10.3 (approx.)	18.7	26.4	25.0	180	135
Austria[2]	10.0	29.1	28.4	42.4	290	145
Estonia	(1920) 18.7	30.1	—	—	160	—
U.S.S.R. (full-time students)	8.3	(1932–33) 31.3	(1950) 43.8	63.7	377	200
U.S.S.R. (including correspondence students)	8.3	31.3	64.6	104.3	377	335
Latvia	(1920) 13.8	42.4	—	—	310	—
U.S.A.	(1910) 38.6	83.3	178.6	185.2	215	220

Sources: As in Table 3.
[1] Figures are rounded.
[2] The figures refer to both Austrian and foreign students. In 1958 the number for Austrian students only was 28.4 per 10,000 inhabitants.

had high ratios and rapid rates of growth. At the lower right hand are Britain, Italy, Belgium and Denmark. The other two squares are relatively empty, the upper right hand one containing two Scandinavian countries and Switzerland (all students), while the lower right hand one contains Greece and, presumably, Poland.

This distribution corresponds to the prevalence of overcrowding in the learned professions in Europe. According to the already mentioned survey of Kotschnig published in 1937, there was a severe problem of unemployment and unemployability among professional people in Europe, except in Britain, Belgium and Southern Europe; the problem was most severe in the

countries appearing in our upper left hand square.[1] Yet compared to the United States and the U.S.S.R., the student/population ratios of even these most "overcrowded" countries were relatively modest. It appears, therefore, that European countries were able to absorb only much smaller proportions of professional people than the United States or the U.S.S.R.

At least one important source of this tendency to professional overcrowding and intellectual unemployability becomes apparent from a breakdown of enrolment figures by faculties.

In Europe between 1913 and 1933 the two old established faculties of law and medicine remained unchangingly the most important part of university study. Only in one small country, Belgium, were the combined percentages of students in these two faculties less than 40 per cent of the total. The percentages in

[1] Outside of Europe the problems were either non-existent or less serious. Japan seems to have been the only non-European country with a relatively serious problem; cf. Kotschnig, *op. cit.*, pp. 133–136.

five more countries, Denmark, Germany, Holland, Switzerland and Yugoslavia, ranged between 40 and 49, while in Czechoslovakia and France the percentages were 50 or more (in Britain the combined percentage of medical and arts students – the later including law – was 74). Only in Holland had there been a significant reduction in the share of these two old faculties between 1913 and 1933.[1] The percentage in France dropped from a very high 65 to a still very high 62 per cent. In all other countries – except Switzerland (Swiss students only) – the combined percentage of law and medical students had even increased, in some of them very substantially.

TABLE 5. *Students per Population and the Growth of the Ratio of Students in the Population in Several European Countries, 1913–34*

Number of students per 10,000 of population (1934)	RATES OF GROWTH (BASE 1913)	
	Rapid (171% or more)	Slow (165% or less)
17.3 or more	Austria Czechoslovakia (?) Estonia (?) France Germany Holland Hungary Latvia Rumania Switzerland (Swiss students only)	Sweden Switzerland (all students) Norway
15.4 or less	Greece Poland (?)	Belgium Britain Denmark Italy

Thus higher education in Europe during that period hardly responded either to changes which occurred in the economy or to changes in the intellectual and scientific culture. The increase in the service occupations was already taking place. There was a shortage of professionally trained manpower in some of them; in others the opportunities were largely unperceived. Yet the universities continued to train young people for medicine, law and secondary school teaching – fields which were already overcrowded. Social sciences, psychology, education as a professional field of study (as distinct from the study of scientific and humanistic disciplines taught at secondary schools), and certain new specializations in science and technology, were either unrepresented or very poorly represented at the European universities of that time. The overwhelmingly important place of the medical faculty in the universities was far from truly reflecting the place of medicine among the developing sciences. The large numbers of law students were a similar anachronism. Even taking into consideration that the law faculties usually included some social science studies, especially economics and political science, these studies were not very well developed and their combination with law was not conducive to their growth. The intellectuals and

professional people growing up in the universities in the twenties and thirties were, therefore, of essentially the same background and steeped in the same tradition as those who grew up in them before World War I. This may explain at least in part their difficulties in finding jobs and adjusting to the changing world, and their subsequent alienation from it.

Since the Second World War, especially since the early fifties, there have been signs of change in the European system of universities. The combined percentages of students in the law and medical faculties dropped everywhere to less than 35 per cent.[2] Even if we add to this the percentage of social science students which in the pre-war statistics were usually included in the law faculties (but which – as we have pointed out – were only very rudimentarily developed), we still obtain percentages of less than 45.

With few exceptions social sciences have become a substantial part of university study. In Britain and France there has been in addition a very considerable increase in the percentage of science and technology students, so that now they have about the same proportions of such students as Germany, Holland and Switzerland, though still smaller proportions than Czechoslovakia (where the exceptionally high proportion of technology students has been a long-standing feature of the system of higher education and is not an innovation of the communist regime). The changes have thus consisted of a relatively greater expansion of certain fields and the introduction of new ones in the broad categories of arts, sciences, social sciences and technology.

However, the new fields of study and specialization introduced in European universities lately have not been created there, but usually followed existing American examples. It is, therefore, difficult to assess the importance of the changes which are occurring in Europe. The phenomenon of "trained unemployability" which Schumpeter and others regarded as an endemic feature of the "intellectuals", has disappeared. But only the future can tell whether this indicates a permanent new kind of relationship between the academic systems of these countries on the one hand and their economic and political structure on the other.

In contrast to the European system the two other major systems of higher education in this century, namely the American and the Russian, have been able to expand very rapidly. Since there are no precise time

[1] The even greater reduction which occurred in Denmark was due to the fact that there were no technology students in 1913.

[2] This is undoubtedly true for Britain as well. Even though the percentage of law students is not shown separately, it is known that they formed only 11.8 per cent of the 1956-7 honors graduates. Cf. University Grants Committee, *University Development, 1952–7*, London, 1958, p. 17. The decrease in the percentage of medical students is, of course, clear. Cf. also E. E. Butler, "University Students, Staff and Recurrent Grants," *Journal of the Royal Statistical Society*, Series A (General), 125 : 1 (1962), pp. 119–123. The seemingly higher combined ratio of medicine and law students in Switzerland (Swiss students only) is due to the inclusion of social sciences in "law".

series of student enrolments in the United States for the earlier periods, we shall use the estimates of Wolfle about conferred bachelor and first professional degrees (cf. Table 7). Although graduation figures are not strictly comparable to figures of enrolment because the fraction of students who graduate varies from field to field, they still give a good idea of the changes in the relative interest in different fields.[1]

This is an entirely different picture from that in Europe. The growth in America has been more permanent and greater than elsewhere (with some setback during the War compensated for in the late forties). But the most conspicuous difference between the United States and the European systems has been the constant change in the distribution of students among the faculties. At the beginning of the century the distribution was similar to that in Europe. The health

[1] Another difficulty is the exclusion of Ph.D. students, but their inclusion would not significantly alter the distribution of students between the various disciplines, cf. Wolfle, *op. cit.*, pp. 298–299.

fields accounted for a third of the graduates — medicine and dentistry alone for 24.6 per cent; 11.2 per cent were law students; some 17 per cent studied science and technology. There were small numbers of graduates in the social sciences, education, and a variety of other fields, most of which probably appear in the European statistics under "arts" and "law". By the thirties these miscellaneous studies grew to well over a third of the total. The fields which grew most slowly were medicine and law. The slow growth of medicine is usually attributed to the reform of medical education which took place after 1910, and to the restrictive practices of the American Medical Association. Both of these certainly influenced developments but can explain only a part of the decrease in the relative share of medical students. The decline in the share of dentistry was similar to that which occurred in medicine and, as said, there was a very considerable decline in the proportion of law students. In neither of these latter fields can this be attributed to far-reaching reforms or severe restrictions on entrance. What happened was simply that the

TABLE 6. *Student Enrolment by Faculties or Subjects in Several Countries.*
1913–4; 1925–6; 1930–1; 1933–4; 1958 (Percentages)

	ALL STUDENTS		Medicine	Law	Social science	Arts[1]	Science	Tech-nology[2]	Other	No state
	Numbers	Percentages								
Belgium										
1913–4	7,784	100.3	17.1	13.4[3]	—	12.0	26.8	31.0	—	—
1925–6	8,734	100.0	22.7	10.0[3]	—	14.6	26.2	26.6	—	—
1930–1	9,029	100.1	21.4	12.8[3]	—	17.8	30.5	17.6	—	—
1933–4	10,503	100.0	25.0	12.4[3]	—	22.0	24.7	15.9	—	—
1951–2	22,777	99.8	29.2	18.1	17.6	11.3	7.5	16.1	0.01	—
1958	44,724	100.0	19.0	6.6	17.7	27.1	7.0	22.4	—	0.2
Czechoslovakia										
1913–4	12,922	100.1	14.4	24.6[3]	—	14.1		47.0	—	—
1924–5	23,147	100.2	17.3	25.4[3]	—	10.0		47.5	—	—
1929–30	28,904	100.0	18.6	29.7[3]	—	9.1		42.6	—	—
1933–4	26,265	100.2	27.1	33.1[3]	—	9.5		30.5	—	—
1958	75,306	99.9	11.6	2.4	10.1	27.9	2.1	45.8	—	—
Denmark										
1913	2,047	100.3	36.2	37.5[3]	—	19.4	7.2	—	—	—
1925	4,673	100.1	21.4	21.2[3]	—	15.5	7.2	34.8	—	—
1930	5,961	100.1	21.0	19.0[3]	—	17.5	7.1	35.6	—	—
1934	7,001	99.9	22.6	19.5[3]	—	14.0	5.6	38.2	—	—
1950–1	13,607	100.0	21.2	13.5	21.8	19.7	5.9	17.6	0.3	—
1958	20,554	99.6	15.7	5.9	15.0	42.4	5.7	14.6	—	0.3
France										
1913	38,047	100.1	21.7	44.1[3]	—	16.8	17.5		—	—
1924	47,728	100.1	23.1	35.4[3]	—	19.0	22.6		—	—
1930	66,361	100.0	24.5	29.5[3]	—	25.5	20.5		—	—
1932	77,527	100.0	32.3	29.6[3]	—	18.7	19.4		—	—
1951	142,019	100.0	26.1	27.8[3]	—	26.2	19.9		—	—
1958	226,173	99.8	18.2	16.5[3]	—	27.7	35.1		—	2.3
Germany										
1914	64,657	100.0	26.3	14.5[4]	—	21.2[4]	13.9	24.1	—	—
1925	74,418	100.0	11.8	22.0[4]	—	13.4[4]	14.4	38.4	—	—
1931	124,047	100.0	22.5	16.8[4]	—	23.4[4]	14.1	23.2	—	—
1932	114,320	100.3	27.7	16.1[4]	—	20.0[4]	13.2	23.3	—	—
1933	102,352	100.2	30.9	14.8[4]	—	18.4[4]	13.9	22.2	—	—
1934	85,036	100.0	33.0	13.2[4]	—	19.7[4]	12.5	21.6	—	—
1951	113,294	100.0	17.1	11.2	—	42.1[4]	15.5	14.1	—	—
1958	180,561	100.0	14.2	11.5	12.5	26.2	14.2	21.4	—	—
Great Britain										
1925–6	40,834	100.2	21.3	—	—	50.9[5]	18.0	10.0	—	—
1930–1	46,704	100.0	21.2	—	—	52.8[5]	16.8	9.2	—	—
1933–4	49,935	100.0	23.9	—	—	49.7[5]	17.5	8.9	—	—
1956–7	89,866	100.0	17.4	—	—	43.1[5]	22.2	17.3	—	—

| | ALL STUDENTS | | | | Social | | | Tech- | | No |
	Numbers	Percentages	Medicine	Law	science	Arts[1]	Science	nology[2]	Other	State
Holland										
1913–4	5,167	100.2	35.1	18.5[3]	—	6.8	10.0	29.8	—	—
1925–6	8,857	100.0	29.4	14.6[3]	—	21.6	15.9	18.5	—	—
1930–1	11,289	100.3	28.7	16.1[3]	—	13.6	15.8	26.1	—	—
1933–4	12,809	100.0	29.4	14.8[3]	—	13.2	16.3	26.3	—	—
1951–2	29,887	100.5	25.3	11.7	12.6	11.7	15.5	23.7	—	—
1958	35,131	99.8	18.5	7.4	17.7	19.6	13.7	22.9	—	—
Switzerland (All Students)										
1913–4[6]	5,031	100.0	22.3	18.6[3]	—	39.9		19.2	—	—
1920–1	9,372	100.0	21.7	20.2[3, 7]	—	17.1	16,8[8]	24.2[7]	—	—
1929–30	8,347	100.0	20.6	25.9[3]	—	20.1	14.5[8]	18.9	—	—
1939–40	11,011	100.0	21.5	24.1[3]	—	22.3	14.6[8]	17.5	—	—
1949–50	16,848	100.0	19.9	23.6[3]	—	19.4	16.0[8]	21.1	—	—
1958	18,877	99.9	19.2	8.8	12.8	26.5	16.9	15.5	—	0.2
Switzerland (Swiss Students only)										
1910–15	3,648	100.2	25.6	25.0[4]	—	49.6		—[5]	—	—
1920–1	7,146	100.0	21.6	21.3[3]	—	32.9		24.2	—	—
1929–30	6,049	100.0	21.6	26.2[3]	—	33.5		18.7	—	—
1939–40	9,258	100.0	21.8	25.5[3]	—	36.6		16.1	—	—
1949–50	12,441	100.0	18.8	25.9[3]	—	33.2		22.1	—	—
1958–9	12,836	100.0	16.2	22.1[3]	—	39.6		22.1	—	—
Yugoslavia										
1925	10,326	100.2	13.2	28.4[3]	—		22.6	36.0	—	—
1933	14,479	100.4	8.6	33.8[3]	—		26.0	32.0	—	—
1934	14,926	100.2	9.6	38.7[3]	—		20.6	31.3	—	—
1950	60,395	100.0	17.2	18.4	—		32.6	31.8	—	—
1958	97,323	99.8	11.7	13.0	18.6	29.0	4.5	23.0	—	—

Sources: Kotschnig, *op. cit.,* pp. 23–25.
UNESCO — World Survey of Education, 1955, UNESCO, Paris.
UNESCO — Basic Facts and Figures, 1960.
United Kingdom, University Grants Committee, *University Development, 1952–7.*
London, H.M.S.O. 1958, Cmnd. 534, p. 19.
Statistisches Jahrbuch Der Schweiz, 1959–60.
[1] Including Humanities, Education and Fine Arts.
[2] Including Engineering and Agriculture.
[3] Including Social Sciences.
[4] Including part of Social Sciences.
[5] Including Law and Social Sciences.
[6] Does not include students of the Zurich Polytechnic and of the St. Gallen School of Commerce. The number of students in Zurich Polytechnic was in 1909–10, 836 and at St. Gallen School in 1914–15, 151.
[7] The figures on which these percentages are based include University students during the academic session 1920–1, and students of the St. Gallen School of Commerce (included in the category "Law") and students of the Zurich Polytechnic (included in "Technology") during the academic session 1919–20.
[8] Including a small number of Engineering and Architecture students at the Universities of Geneva and Lausanne.

disciplines which were well established at the beginning of the century grew, compared with new fields, relatively slowly. In other words, changes of the kind which have been taking place in European university study since World War II took place in the United States starting with World War I, or even before.

The fast growing fields were those which were of negligible size at the beginning of the century. Out of the rapidly growing disciplines, only in engineering did the number of graduates during 1901–5 exceed one per cent of the total (3.3 per cent). There were one per cent in economics and less than 0.5 per cent each in psychology, sociology, political science, agriculture, home economics, business and commerce, education, architecture, journalism, library science, social work, etc. Considering that engineering consists today of many more specialities than it did in 1900 it is evident that the growth of higher education in the United States took place in an entirely different way than in Europe. In Europe, students pursued more or less the same kinds of study in the thirties, as they did in the early days of this century, and the variety is still limited.

In the United States, on the other hand, growth of higher education took place through a process of constant differentiation. Fields of intellectual and occupational interest which elsewhere remained outside the academic framework became academic subjects in the United States. This goes probably a long way in explaining the fact that, in spite of the tremendous growth of higher education and the economic depression, there did not arise in America such problems of intellectual unemployability as in Europe, nor has there emerged in the United States anything but a faint mirror image of the revolutionary intellectual. American college graduates were a much more mixed lot than the European ones, and in consequence much less likely to act as a group. Besides, their choices of study and their expectations of career seem to have been much more varied and flexible than those of their European counterparts. It was unlikely that large parts of them would be equally frustrated in their aspirations by unexpected conditions prevailing in the market for professional services. They could, therefore, adjust more easily to changing conditions than European graduates.

TABLE 7. *Bachelors' and First Professional Degrees in the U.S., and Students in Higher Educational Institutions in the U.S.S.R. in Selected Periods and Years by Fields of Specialization[1]*

U.S.A.			Period					
			1901–5	1911–15	1921–25	1931–35	1941–45	1951–3
Absolute Numbers			149,500	206,000	360,200	684,800	779,900	1,021,100
Percentage								
I.	1.	Engineering	3.3	6.0	10.3	8.0	8.8	9.6
II.	2.	Agriculture and Home Economics	0.2	2.0	5.1	4.2	6.5	5.3
III.	3.	Psychology	0.3	0.6	0.9	1.3	1.7	2.0
	4.	Social Sciences	3.8	6.4	7.9	8.9	10.1	11.2
	5.	Law	11.2	10.7	8.2	6.1	2.4	3.7
	6.	Business and Commerce	0.2	0.7	5.8	6.9	8.6	14.4
IV.	7.	Natural Sciences	13.3	14.3	12.7	10.4	10.9	9.8
	8.	Humanities and Arts	25.3	23.7	18.5	16.1	12.9	12.0
	9.	Education	0.4	1.3	7.5	20.1	22.4	19.4
V.	10.	Health Fields	33.2	23.2	12.1	7.0	7.4	6.0
	11.	Other Professions[2]	0.1	0.2	0.8	2.2	2.3	2.1
	12.	All Other	8.7	10.9	10.2	8.8	6.0	4.5

U.S.S.R.		Period				
		1928–29	1932–33	1940–41	1950–51	1955–56
Absolute Numbers[3]		166,800	459,800	585,000	845,100	1,227,900
Percentage		100.0	100.0	100.0	100.0	100.0
I.	Engineering	31.4	50.8	30.2	31.7	40.5
II.	Agriculture	16.1	13.5	7.8	10.6	12.2
III.	Socio-Economic Studies	9.9	5.3	3.8	5.1	3.9
IV.	Education (including Arts and Sciences)	27.3	20.3	39.4	39.8	31.0
V.	Health and Physical Culture	15.3	10.1	18.8	12.8	12.4

Sources: Wolfle, D., *America's Resources of Specialized Talent*, Harper & Brothers, New York, 1954, pp. 292–3, Table B; and DeWitt, N., *Education and Professional Employment in U.S.S.R.*, National Science Foundation, Washington, D.C., 1961, p. 318.

[1] The categories are not precisely comparable. A very tentative attempt at comparison is made here by combining the U.S. categories into groups approximately similar to the U.S.S.R. classification. Note that the U.S. statistics refer to degrees, the U.S.S.R. ones to enrolled students, and that the U.S. figures are given for five year periods, while those of the U.S.S.R. are for academic years.

[2] Architecture, journalism, library science, social work.

[3] Regular students only. Does not include students in party higher schools.

The situation in the Soviet Union has again been different (cf. Table 7). There, the main emphasis has been on science, in particular applied science and education. In 1928–9, when the great transformation of Soviet education began, engineering and agriculture students amounted to 47.5 per cent of the total student body, their proportion increased to nearly 55 per cent in the early thirties, then dropped considerably in the late thirties, rising again to about 50 per cent in the fifties.[1] About 15 per cent were in the medical field in 1928–9. Moreover, probably a high percentage of students in the educational fields studied natural science. The socio-economic field, including law, comprised only about 10 per cent of the students. By 1950–2 an important change had occurred in the relative percentages of education on the one hand and socio-

economic studies on the other. The former increased from 27.3 to 39.8 per cent, while the latter decreased from 9.9 to 5.1 per cent. This is all the more significant since in the twenties socio-economic disciplines has also been taught in party high schools which are not included in our statistics. Since the party high schools have been abolished in the meantime, the relative decrease in the proportion of students in the socio-economic fields has been even greater than indicated by the present figures.[2] The category of "education" comprises art as well as science students at the universities and pedagogical institutes. In 1955–6 57 per cent of the university students studied natural sciences and the percentage was probably quite high in the pedagogical institutes as well.

The distinguishing mark, therefore, of Soviet higher education has been that natural science and especially technology have developed with practically no restraint. Many aspects of this development are reminiscent of the early development of American college education: the branching out into technological specializations

[1] They formed 46 per cent of the graduates among full-time students of higher education in 1955, Korol, *op. cit.*, p. 202.

[2] Including correspondence students the percentages were somewhat higher: 5.7 per cent in 1955-6 and 7.3 per cent in 1958-9, cf. DeWitt, *op. cit.*, p. 318.

(despite successive reductions of their number, 295 specialties were taught in Soviet engineering schools in 1953–4)[1] the readiness to satisfy every industrial or agricultural demand; and finally the virtually unlimited opportunities for the realization of new ideas about the possible uses of higher education for training specialists, without paying much attention to existing academic traditions. There are certain similarities in the development of the pedagogical institutes too. They were raised to the status of higher educational institutions and expanded rapidly to satisfy specialized and varied needs of education. This was an important departure from the general European tradition of leaving the function of training secondary school teachers to the universities, which perform it more or less as a by-product of teaching academic subjects and pay relatively little attention to the professional aspects of teaching. On the other hand, unlike in American and like in the European academic institutions, education has not become much of a professional speciality and area of research in its own right. Pedagogical institutes train teachers for specific fields: mathematics, history, etc., teaching the students in considerable detail how to teach each part of the curriculum. Their special field is the methodology of teaching particular subjects, while educational theory and research, human development, diagnosis of individual differences and needs, guidance, and all the other specifically educational fields, have not been developed.

Another important difference between the United States and Soviet development has been the fact that while in the United States the differentiation of scientific and professional fields has occurred in all types of academic institutions, in the U.S.S.R. this differentiation — whether in technology, education or medicine — has occurred chiefly through the emergence of higher educational and research institutions other than universities. The latter, and the most prestigeful academies which have been apparently less subject to state interference than the various institutes, have remained more traditional in their selection of fields considered suitable for academic teaching and research.

Thus the readiness of the Russian academic system to create new professions has been more limited than that of the United States. It has been particularly flexible in catering to the needs of the military, industrial and agricultural production, and the health and educational services. Concerning, however, innovations in some of the basic sciences and humanities, a much more "European" spirit of hierarchy and traditionalism has prevailed.[2] Finally, in law and the social sciences flexibility and the tendency toward innovation have been prevented by the restrictions imposed on these fields by the authoritarian rulers.

In any case, neither in the United States nor in the U.S.S.R. has there been any basis for the emergence of a class of alienated intellectuals. The educational system of the United States has been closely interwoven with the occupational structure of the mobile middle classes. It readily responded to its changing needs, at the same time establishing within it various professions initiated by the academic system itself. In the U.S.S.R. this has been true only with regard to some academic fields. However, the large majority of students is in these fields, whereas the number of students in the more traditional fields has been relatively small. Professionally trained people have therefore a variety of educational backgrounds and the large majority of them presumably possesses the pragmatic outlook of the specialist rather than the wide ranging interests and involvements of the "intellectual".

This is how various systems of education have influenced the rates of growth and the varieties of the professions. European types of academic systems have been much less inclined to adjust to changing needs for professionally trained people than the United States, or, partly, the Soviet systems. As a result the latter have expanded more rapidly and into more fields than the former. These different degrees of flexibility or tendency to innovation of the academic systems are due to differences in the class structure of these societies. Without going into great detail, European societies used to have — and perhaps still have — relatively closed and permanent central elites.[3] Universities have been closely linked to these elites, and tended to adopt conservative policies concerning academic innovations. In the United States, where class structure has been more equalitarian and decentralized, and in the U.S.S.R., where the power of the elites other than that of the party has been drastically curtailed, much more flexible academic policies have prevailed.

All this answers the question why European universities have trained relatively fewer students than corresponding institutions in the United States and the U.S.S.R. It still remains to be seen why there has been a tendency in some — but by no means all — societies with unflexible (European type) academic systems to produce a surplus of professionally trained people. Pre-World War II German, Hungarian and French, pre-communist Russian and Chinese, present-day Indian and a great many other academic systems of this type had or have attracted and admitted students far in excess of the positions available for them as graduates. In contrast to them, Britain, Belgium, Switzerland and some other countries have always shown a fairly good adjustment between the supply of and the demand for graduates.

The process which brought about the overcrowding of the professions can be clearly observed in nineteenth-century Russia and twentieth-century India and China; it also occurred at one time or another in most European

[1] Korol, *op. cit.*, p. 163.
[2] Cf. Eric Ashby, *Scientist in Russia*, Penguin Books, London, 1947, pp. 17–40.
[3] For a more detailed description of the relationship between class system and academic organization. Cf. Joseph Ben-David and Awraham Zloczower, "Universities and Academic Systems in Modern Societies," *European Journal of Sociology*, III (1962), pp. 45–84.

countries.[1] Its broad outlines seem to have been like this: Modern high (and secondary) education arose in all these countries as a result of the initiative of small groups of "enlightened" and usually upper class people with foreign contacts. Some foreign, usually Western, country, served as a model according to which traditional native society was to be transformed. In eighteenth-century France the models were Britain and the U.S.; in Germany, France; in Russia and Eastern Europe, the "West" as a whole; and in Asia, Africa and Latin America, either Britain, France, Germany or, more recently, the U.S. and the U.S.S.R. In China and some other Asian countries Japan, too, used to be included among the model nations. Everywhere there were able young men, eager to acquire wider social and cultural horizons than those of their surroundings. Sending this youth abroad for study or importing teachers and/or curricula in order to educate it were easier things to accomplish than creating new factories or developing local agriculture. These latter had taken place in developed countries through a barely understood process of social evolution and displayed a bewildering variety of forms. Besides, it was understood,

[1] The classic statement about the alienation of intellectuals in France is that of Alexis de Tocqueville, *L'ancien regime et la revolution*, Paris, Calmann, Levyn, n.d., pp. 203–217. The general problem is dealt with in a somewhat one-sided but theoretically important way – by Joseph Schumpeter, *op. cit.*, *loc. cit.* and comparatively by Crane Brinton, *The Anatomy of Revolution*, New York, Vintage Books, 1957, pp. 41–52. For descriptions and analyses of the situation, of intellectuals in different countries at different times, cf. John E. E. D. Acton, *Lectures on the French Revolution*, London, Macmillan, 1932, pp. 1–38; Henri Brunschwig, *La Crise de L'etat prussien a la Fin du XVIIIe siecle et la genese de la mentalite romantique*. Paris, Presses Universitaire, 1947, pp. 161–186; Karl Griewank, *Deutsche Studenten und Universitäten in der Revolution von 1848*, Weimar: Hermann Boehlau's Nachfolger, 1949, Hans Kohn, *Die Europäisierung des Orients*, Berlin, Schocken, 1934, pp. 259–340; Nicolas Berdyaev, *The Origin of Russian Communism*, Geoffrey Bles, 1937; Alexander von Schelting, *Russland und Europa*, Bern, A. Franck, 1948; Richard Pipes (ed.). *The Russian Intelligentsia*, special issue of *Daedalus*, Summer, 1960; Vladimir C. Nahirny, "The Russian Intelligentzia: from Men of Ideas to Men of Convictions", *Comparative Studies in History and Society*, IV: 4 (1962), pp. 403–435; Edward Shils, *The Intellectual Between Tradition and Modernity: The Indian Situation, Comparative Studies in Society and History*, Supplement 1, Mouton & Co., Publishers, 1961; Shanti S. Tangri, "Intellectuals and Society in 19th Century India", *Comparative Studies in History and Society*, III: 4 (July) 1961, p. 368 and Y. C. Wang, *op. cit.*

[2] The term middle class is used here to describe categories of people engaged in occupations which have a wide range of career mobility. A businessman or a professional person starts his career often at the lowest levels of income, but can rise to the top without changing occupation. This cannot happen to a laborer, whose rise beyond a modest level has to be accompanied by change of occupation, nor to a person born into the upper class in societies where such classes exist, since he cannot sink below a fairly high level without changing his occupation or losing his inherited fortune. Middle class is therefore a misnomer, since it suggests a set of fixed positions situated between, and parallel to those of the upper and the lower classes. As a matter of fact, however, if there is such a stable class in the middle of the status hierarchy, it should be distinguished from the class of mobile people.

or at least quickly learnt through trial and error, that production needed markets which were non-existent in the first stages of development. There seemed, however, a virtually unlimited demand for education. After a while, though, it was recognized that the demand for education (usually to a large extent provided at the expense of the state) was not enough, and that there was also a need for a market for the services of the professionally trained people. But by that time an institutional system including schools and universities with high status, elite ideology and restricted scope, had already come into existence, continuing to serve as a center of attraction for the intellectually alert and the socially mobile.

A vicious circle was created: the able sons of small and medium shopkeepers, independent artisans, well-to-do farmers, etc., all chose advanced education as the main avenue of social advancement. To the extent, however, that this education was of the type which prevailed in European universities (or secondary schools closely geared to the needs of the university) this education channelled their aspirations towards a few narrowly defined professional and civil service careers. Thus the anyway weak and narrow trading and industrial classes became deprived of their potential elite, which further stunted their growth. In the absence of a vigorous trading and industrial class there was, of course, little demand for professional services, so that even modest numbers of professionals were unable to find suitable employment. Furthermore, it became permanently impossible for the weak commercial and industrial classes to develop a civilized way of life and attract highly educated people, since they became deprived of their intellectually most valuable members. Small and medium-sized cities became or remained, as a result, cultural backwaters where professional people could hardly bear to live. They congregated in a few large cities such as Vienna, Budapest, Moscow, Peking or Calcutta. There, if not steady employment, they could at least find an intellectually suitable environment. Dissatisfied with their lot, frustrated in their search for a positive occupational identity, and feeling cut off from the bulk of the population, but possessing at the same time a virtual monopoly of articulate self-expression, they became a problematic group, prone to political radicalism and subversion.

This typical sequence of events also explains why in the more developed countries of Western and Northern Europe and in Switzerland the overcrowding of the professions and the concomitant emergence of a class of alienated intellectuals were less severe than in the relatively less developed countries of Central and Eastern Europe. In the former group of countries there usually existed a strong and articulate middle class prior to the rise of the modern universities in the nineteenth century.[2] Apart from a high standard of living, this class had a tradition of education and culture of its own, capable of competing with the academic-professional culture. Literature, music, theater, painting and sculpture, journalism and even much of technology were all thriving non-academic pursuits practiced mainly by middle class people. The flocking of all the potential elite to the universities was thereby prevented, while the existence of a middle class widely dispersed over the country created at the same time conditions for a greater decentralization and wider absorption of professional services among the population. Thus professional people did not become a separate class, and were far from alienated. Rather they became an integral part of a prosperous and educated middle class. Higher education attracted only the exceptionally talented and/or motivated few and, in addition, those who deliberately and for good economic reasons chose a professional career. It never became the only, nor even the main channel of mobility through which one could rise from the "masses" to the "classes", so that there was no reason for people to choose this particular channel in excess of the opportunities which it realistically offered.

Britain, in addition to such a long established middle class, also possessed a non-academic type of education for the professions. Until the end of the last century and well into the present one, British universities had played only a modest role in the education for professions. Law, medicine and engineering were learned to a large extent through apprenticeship arrangements requiring previous university study only in the case of medicine. University education was a matter of luxury, part of the way of life of the upper classes. Originally the clergy was the only profession for which people were trained at universities. Higher civil service and secondary school teaching were added to this during the second part of the last century. All these professions, or important parts of them, were closely connected to the upper class, or were actually upper class callings. Professional education became an important function with the rise of the new provincial universities, but these were conceived as utilitarian institutions, not primarily conferring status, but teaching a job.

As a result, although British universities were not less open to members of the middle and lower class than European ones — as a matter of fact they were relatively more open — they did not become very important channels of mobility even for the professions prior to World War II. British universities were assimilated to the class structure, but in a different way from that on the European Continent. On the Continent an academic title was regarded as a means of conferring on its bearer privileges of status and a legitimate claim on the State for a secure income. In Britain, in contrast, an academic title was regarded as a symbol of status, somewhat like an aristocratic title, possessed by a few who either inherited it or on whom it was conferred in recognition of great personal achievement. It was not so much a means of achieving status, as a confirmation of it. Or else, it became a means of learning a useful occupation, the efficiency of which

was judged by its economic results. Higher education in Britain was, consequently, not a source of class formation. It was, rather, a direct result of the latter.

In the meantime, of course, the class structure of the European societies has changed, and the middle and lower classes have become more or less part and parcel of the political society. But even in Britain, where this development has probably gone farthest in Europe, there is still an essentially hierarchic, elitist conception of society. The flexibility of the academic system, which in all these societies is identified with the elite, is therefore limited, in comparison with such equalitarian societies as the United States and perhaps the U.S.S.R.

To sum up and recapitulate briefly the main points of this survey, it is obvious that several factors have determined the growth of higher education — and, thereby, the size of the potential professional group — in various countries. As pointed out, economic factors have certainly played an important role, both because more highly developed economies need greater numbers of highly trained people and because more higher education costs more money. These factors do not, however, explain all the variation, and in this paper we were concerned with that part of the variation which is not economically determined. This, according to the present analysis, depends on 1) the existence or absence of alternative channels of mobility besides higher education; and 2) the range of the professionalized occupational fields and specializations within fields (i.e. careers, for which higher educational institutions prepare their students). The existence of alternative channels of mobility depends, in its turn, on the size, strength and cultural development of the middle classes prior to the rise of modern universities during the nineteenth century, while the range of professionalization depends on the hierarchic versus equalitarian character of the class system.

It is not always easy to identify and account separately for the effects of these two factors. Britain has been a relatively clear case possessing a highly developed and articulated middle class before the rise of the modern universities, as well as a firmly established elite (whose composition is, however, changeable) providing undisputed leadership in all the important fields of social and cultural life. Both of these factors tended to reduce the numbers of students and graduates, relative to the level of economic development of the country.

The power and influence of ruling elites has been no less decisive in other European and most Asiatic and Latin American countries than it has been in Britain. They may have been less glorified and less generally accepted by the population at large, but they were usually more autocratic and less flexible. Thus the range of professionalization in these countries remained limited, to the same degree, or even more so than in Britain. But having less well established middle classes than Britain, these societies had more people, relative to their economies, choosing higher education as a channel of mobility. Thus, these countries have had a stronger tendency than Britain to expand their higher education beyond the narrow limits determined by the small number of professionalized occupations, causing, thereby, an overcrowding of the professions.

In some societies of this latter type, professional study became a primary factor of class formation. Intellectuals (including students and other not fully trained aspirants to professional status) became a sizeable group compared to other middle class groups. In the metropolitan centers of Central and Eastern Europe and Asia where universities were situated, they were, at times, relatively large and probably the most easily organized middle class group. Under such circumstances, students and "intellectuals" assumed increasingly important parts in the revolutionary or reformatory movements which used to be led by the *bourgeoisie* in Western countries. Whether the role was revolutionary or reformatory depended on the character of the ruling classes as well as on the educational system adopted. Foreign colonial rulers, autocratic feudal upper classes constituting an impenetrable caste or aristocracy, created a feeling that change was possible only through revolutionary transformation. Furthermore, an elite-oriented education, placing the upper class way of life as an ideal before the students, as well as restricting their range of occupational choice, produced intellectuals unable or unwilling to perform the concrete tasks necessary for the gradual transformation of their societies into modern states. Such education gave the educated no other means than political action for achieving their aims.

Expansion of higher education without the risk of overcrowding the professions existed in countries with equalitarian class systems that allowed for the professionalization of an ever broader range of occupations. The typical country in this respect has been the United States. Yet it is difficult to assess the role of the first factor, that of the existence of a strong middle class, in this case. Certainly there was such a class in the United States and it was no less strong there than in Britain. According to our hypothesis, it should have served as a check on higher educational expansion. But there is no way of knowing whether indeed this was the case, so

that in the absence of such a middle class the proportion of students in the population would have been even higher.

The most plausible explanation of the United States' case, however, seems to be that the existence of strong middle classes diminishes the tendency to attend universities only as long as the latter represent the cultural traditions of restricted upper elites. Once, however, institutions of higher education are divested of their upper class associations and transformed into pragmatic institutions of teaching and research in a growing variety of basic and practical fields, the relationship between them and the class system changes. Instead of serving as agents for the selection of the few middle or working class people destined for upper elite careers, they become auxiliary channels of mobility for a growing range of occupations, decreasing, incidentally, the social distance between elite and other callings. As such they will be used increasingly by people destined for all kinds of careers, entrance to which did not usually take place through universities in the past. Furthermore, at this stage, universities themselves may create new professions which then become part of the occupational system.

This explanation seems to fit the facts: until the 1860's American universities were traditional institutions, adhering closely to the religious and upper class values of British universities, which served as their models. As a result, they were neither very popular nor very important in the overwhelmingly equalitarian "middle class" American society. Following the reform of higher education about that time which introduced technological and professional training on the one hand and scientific research on the other, into the universities, the attitude towards them had completely changed, and there began the era of their untrammelled expansion.[1]

Of the other countries which have expanded their higher education through broadening its range, the most conspicuous are the U.S.S.R. and Japan. In both of these there had existed powerful elites, but their influence was — at least temporarily — destroyed and equalitarian systems of education introduced by decree. In addition there were no strong middle classes in either of these countries. To what extent, however, they will be able to maintain such expanding and popular systems of higher education in the long run depends on the permanent transformation of their class systems, about which too little is known yet. The same question applies to the signs of increased flexibility and expansiveness in the European systems of higher education.

---

[1] The view that at least partly these reforms were due to lack of demand for the older type of college education is expressed by Mary Jean Bowman, "The Land Grant Colleges and Universities in Human Resource Development", prepared for the annual meeting of the American Economic History Association, September 1962. University of Chicago, School of Education (mimeographed).

THE SOCIAL PSYCHOLOGY OF JOB AND CLASS

Work Satisfaction and Industrial Trends in Modern Society

Robert Blauner

IN 1880 that famous pioneer of survey research, Karl Marx, drew up a questionnaire of 101 items, 25,000 copies of which were sent to various workers' societies and socialist circles. This long schedule, which exhorts workers to describe "with full knowledge the evils which they endure," is composed entirely of questions of *objective fact* relating to size of plant, working conditions, wages, hours, strikes and trade unions. What appears strange in contrast with present-day surveys is the lack of questions concerning the *feelings* of the workers about their work, employers, and place in society.[1]

It is not that Marx believed that the subjective beliefs of workers were automatic and immediate reactions to their objective material conditions. He knew that workers might experience "false consciousness" instead of the "correct" awareness of their class position. But whereas the development of political class consciousness was problematic for Marx (in the short run, although not over the long haul), there seemed nothing problematic about the subjective reactions of the working class to the wretched conditions of factory labor in the early industrial society of the nineteenth century. Marxists assumed that the *alienation* of labor (which referred to an objective relationship between the employee and the social organization of the work process) would have as its subjective consequence the *estrangement* of the laborers from the factory system. The worker's lack of control, epitomized in his social status as a "wage slave" and his psychotechnic status as an "appendage of the machine," would result in *feelings of dissatisfaction*, which, along with the development of the more problematic consciousness of shared class interests, would be powerful enough to launch revolutionary movements and sustain them to victory.

Two recent students of Marx have stated that "the Marxian theory of why men under capitalism would revolt was based on an assumption of what prompts men to be satisfied or dissatisfied with their work."[2]

[1] One could argue that Marx was not only half a century ahead of his time in the use of the survey technique, but that he understood, even in 1880, the methodological difficulties in getting at subjective feelings. But then it might be retorted that he still had something to learn about eliminating bias in his questions: for example, item 59: "Have you noticed that the delay in paying your wages makes it necessary for you to resort frequently to the pawnbroker, paying a high rate of interest, and depriving yourself of things which you need; or to fall into debt to shopkeepers, becoming their victim because you are their debtor?" The entire questionnaire which was first published on April 20, 1880 in the *Revue Socialiste* appears in English in T. B. Bottomore and Maximilien Rubel, *Karl Marx, Selected Writings in Sociology and Social Philosophy* (London: Watts and Company, 1956), pp. 204–212. Bottomore and Rubel mention that very few workers took the trouble to return Marx' extremely long and difficult questionnaire and that no results were ever published.

[2] Reinhard Bendix and Seymour Martin Lipset, "Karl Marx' Theory of Social Classes," in R. Bendix and S. M. Lipset, *Class, Status and Power* (1st Edition, Glencoe: The Free Press, 1953), p. 32 ff.

This article was originally prepared as a research memorandum for a survey of workers' attitudes being conducted by the Fund for the Republic's Trade Union Project, in cooperation with the Institute of Industrial Relations of the University of California, Berkeley. Reprinted from Walter Galenson and Seymour Martin Lipset (eds.), *Labor and Trade Unionism: An Interdisciplinary Reader* (New York, Wiley, 1960).

And since these expected revolts of industrial workers did not occur in many Western countries, even Marxist intellectuals in recent years have begun to look more closely at workers' subjective dispositions and attitudes. While socialists and general intellectuals were writing about the proletariat in an impressionistic fashion, sometimes without direct contact with the working classes, more empirical social researchers in industry and in the academic disciplines began to question workers directly. Systematic surveys of employee attitudes, begun in the early 1920's, developed so rapidly that in the bibliography of a recent review of research and opinion on job attitudes more than 1500 items are listed.[1]

The present paper surveys research on attitudes of workers toward their work, especially those investigations commonly called job satisfaction studies. To assess the absolute level of job satisfaction in the working population is not my aim, for this is an impossible task, but rather, my purposes are, *1*) to locate differences in the incidence and intensity of work satisfaction among those in diverse occupations and work settings, and *2*) to discern the factors that, in accounting for these differences, seem to indicate the important preconditions of satisfaction in work. Further, the paper considers the implications of these findings for theories of work and workers in modern society, in the light of industrial and social trends.

Extent of satisfaction:
a review of general research

Before considering occupational differences and the factors that account for them, I shall briefly consider evidence on the general extent of job satisfaction by looking at the results of six representative sample studies. In Table 1 the figure in the extreme right-hand

column indicates the percentage of workers who gave the dissatisfied response to such a question as "Taking into consideration all the things about your job (work), how satisfied or dissatisfied are you with it?"[2]

In the 1946 issue of the *Personnel and Guidance Journal*, Robert Hoppock began summarizing the results of all published studies of job satisfaction, most of which were non-representative samples of individual companies or occupations. When, by 1958, 406 percentages of the proportion of persons dissatisfied with their jobs in these several hundred studies had been averaged out, they yielded a median percentage of 13 per cent dissatisfied.[3] This figure is quite similar to the summary percentages of dissatisfaction resulting from more representative labor force samples.

Thus the most recent American research on satisfaction attitudes seems to support the generalization that: "Even under the existing conditions, which are far from satisfactory, most workers like their jobs. Every survey of workers' attitudes which has been carried out, no matter in what industry, indicates that this is so."[4]

But a caveat should be inserted at this point. Many of these studies, which seek to determine the proportion of workers who are satisfied or dissatisfied with their jobs, fail to specify sufficiently an inherently vague concept and ignore the cultural pressures on workers to exaggerate the degree of actual satisfaction. Despite this, the evidence shows that in the numerous samples of the labor force which have been interviewed, more than 80 per cent indicate general job satisfaction.[5] Even though the methodological limitations make it hard to accept the findings of any one of these studies by itself, it is much harder to reject the weight of their cumulative evidence.

Although it is difficult, therefore, not to accept the proposition that at least the majority (and possibly a very large majority) of American workers are moderately satisfied in their work, such a finding is neither particularly surprising nor sociologically interesting. Under "normal" conditions there is a natural tendency for people to identify with, or at least to be somewhat positively oriented toward, those social arrangements in which they are implicated. Attitude surveys show that the majority of employees like their company, that the majority of members are satisfied with their unions, and undoubtedly research would show a preponderance of positive over negative attitudes toward one's own marriage, family, religion, and nation-state. It is the presence of marked occupational *differences* in work attitudes to which I turn in the next section that is of more theoretical interest.

Occupational differences
in work satisfaction

Work satisfaction varies greatly by occupation. Highest percentages of satisfied workers are usually found among professionals and businessmen. In a given

[1] Frederick Herzberg, Bernard Mausner, Richard A. Peterson, and Dora P. Capwell, *Job Attitudes: Review of Research and Opinion* (Psychological Service of Pittsburgh, 1957).

[2] This is the question used in the Morse and Weiss study.

[3] H. Alan Robinson, "Job Satisfaction Researches of 1958," *Personnel and Guidance Journal*, 37 (1959), p. 670.

[4] J. C. Brown, *The Social Psychology of Industry* (Baltimore: English Pelican Edition, 1954), pp. 190–191. He proceeds to give supporting evidence from British studies.

[5] Of course, as the industrial psychologist Arthur Kornhauser has written, "Simple summary conclusions of this kind are dangerously inadequate. Feelings of satisfaction or dissatisfaction are complicated and varied. Working people may be satisfied with many of the conditions of their employment and still be markedly dissatisfied about other features of the job or of their working lives. The number considered dissatisfied will depend in large measure upon the arbitrary method of defining what the term dissatisfaction refers to in the given case." "Psychological Studies of Employee Attitudes," in S. D. Hoslett, ed., *Human Factors in Management* (Parkville, Mo.: Park College Press, 1946), p. 304. In this extensive critique of the methodology of job satisfaction research, Kornhauser also points out that respondents may not want or even be able to answer such questions honestly. There is a certain naivete in expecting frank and simple answers to job satisfaction questions in a society where one's work is so important a part of one's self that to demean one's job is to question one's own competence.

TABLE I. *Proportion of Dissatisfied Workers in Major Job Satisfaction Studies*

Researchers	Scope of sample	Composition of study	Date	Per cent dissatisfied
Morse and Weiss*	Random national	401 employed men	1955	20
Centers†	Representative national	811 men	1949	17
Palmer‡	Norristown, Pa.	517 labor force members	1957	10
Shister and Reynolds§	New England city	800 manual workers	1949	12
				21**
Hoppock‖	New Hope, Pa.	309 labor force members	1935	15
Kornhauser¶	Detroit area	324 employed persons	1952	11

* Nancy C. Morse and Robert S. Weiss, "The Function and Meaning of Work and the Job," *American Sociological Review*, 20 (1955), pp. 191–198.

† Richard Centers, *The Psychology of Social Classes* (Princeton: Princeton University Press, 1949), p. 172.

‡ Gladys L. Palmer, "Attitudes toward Work in an Industrial Community," *American Journal of Sociology*, 63 (1957), pp. 17–26.

§ Joseph Shister and L. G. Reynolds, *Job Horizons: A Study of Job Satisfaction and Labor Mobility* (New York: Harper, 1949), p. 33.

‖ Robert Hoppock, *Job Satisfaction* (New York: Harper, 1935), p. 246.

¶ Arthur Kornhauser, *Detroit as the People See It* (Detroit: Wayne University Press, 1952), p. 54.

** Two separate samples.

plant, the proportion satisfied is higher among clerical workers than among factory workers, just as in general labor force samples it is higher among middle-class than among manual working-class occupations. Within the manual working-class, job satisfaction is highest among skilled workers, lowest among unskilled laborers and workers on assembly lines.

When a scale of relative job satisfaction is formed, based on general occupational categories, the resulting rank order is almost identical with the most commonly used occupational status classification — the Edwards scale of the Bureau of the Census. For example, the mean indexes of satisfaction in Table 2 resulted from a survey of all New Hope Pa. jobholders in 1935.

A similar rank order resulted in a national survey when the proportions of workers in each occupational group who would continue the same kind of work in the event they inherited enough money to live comfortably were computed[1] (Table 3).

TABLE 2

Occupational group	Mean index[2]	Number in sample
Professional and managerial	560	23
Semiprofessional, business and supervisory	548	32
Skilled manual and white collar	510	84
Semiskilled manual workers	483	74
Unskilled manual workers	401	55

The generally higher level of job satisfaction of white-collar over blue-collar workers is confirmed by a study of twelve different factories in 1934, in which the scores of clerical workers on job satisfaction were considerably higher than those of factory workers;[3] by the Centers national sample, which found that only 14 per cent of workers in middle-class occupations were dissatisfied with their jobs, compared to 21 per cent of those in working-class occupations;[4] and by a 1947 *Fortune* poll, which revealed that the proportion of employees who said their jobs were interesting was

92 per cent among professionals and executives, 72 per cent among salaried employees and 54 per cent among factory workers.[5] However, a study of the Detroit area population found that only among such upper white-collar employees as secretaries, draftsmen, and bookkeepers was the incidence of job satisfaction greater than among manual workers; such lower white-collar employees as clerks, typists, and retail sales-people were somewhat less satisfied than blue-collar workers.[6]

Further evidence of the relation of job satisfaction to occupational status is provided by studies of retirement plans. Although there are a number of factors which affect the retirement decision, it is plausible to argue that the more satisfying a job is to the worker, the more likely he will choose not to retire. In a study of work

[1] Morse and Weiss, *op. cit.*, p. 197.

[2] In this index, the figure 100 would indicate extreme dissatisfaction, 400 indifference, and 700 extreme satisfaction. Hoppock, *op. cit.*, p. 255. A rather similar rank order was found by Donald Super. In his study, the percentages of satisfied workers were 85.6 for professionals, 74.2 for managerial, 41.9 for commercial (lowest white collar), 55.9 for skilled manual and 47.6 for semiskilled. However, Super's study has serious weaknesses: the sample was not chosen randomly but taken from members of hobby groups, and it overrepresented workers with high education and in high status occupations. D. Super, "Occupational Level and Job Satisfaction," *Journal of Applied Psychology*, 23 (1939), pp. 547–564.

[3] R. S. Uhrbock, "Attitudes of 4430 Employees," *Journal of Social Psychology*," 5 (1934), pp. 365–377, cited in Hoppock, *op. cit.*, p. 141.

[4] Centers, *op. cit.*, p. 134.

[5] Alexander R. Heron, *Why Men Work* (Stanford: Stanford University Press, 1948), pp. 71–72. A 1948 *Fortune* poll which asked the same question of *youths* between the ages of 18 to 25 found that the proportion of those who found their work interesting or enjoyable "all the time" was 85 per cent for professionals and executives, 64 per cent for white-collar workers, 59 per cent for non-factory manual labor and 41 per cent for factory labor. Cited in Lawrence G. Thomas, *The Occupational Structure and Education* (Englewood Cliffs, N. J.: Prentice-Hall, 1956), p. 201, whose summary of studies on the extent of, and occupational differences in, job satisfaction is one of the best in the literature.

[6] Kornhauser, *Detroit . . .*, p. 55.

and retirement in six occupations it was found that the proportion of men who wanted to continue working or had actually continued working after age sixty-five was more than 67 per cent for physicians, 65 per cent for department store salesmen, 49 per cent for skilled printers, 42 per cent for coal miners, and 32 per cent for unskilled and semiskilled steel-workers.[1]

TABLE 3

Occupational group	Percent who would continue same kind of work	Number in sample
Professionals	68	28
Sales	59	22
Managers	55	22
Skilled manual	40	86
Service	33	18
Semiskilled operatives	32	80
Unskilled	16	27

As has been shown in the preceding section of this paper, the majority of workers in all occupations respond positively when asked whether or not they are satisfied with their jobs. But that does not mean they would not prefer other kinds of work. The average worker in a lower-status occupation says that he would choose another line of work if he had the chance to start his working life anew. This question then, is perhaps a more sensitive indicator of latent dissatisfactions and frustrations; the occupational differences it points to, though forming the same pattern as the other, are considerably greater. For example, when a survey of 13,000 Maryland youths was made during the depression it was found that 91 per cent of professional-technical workers preferred their own occupation to any other, compared to 45 per cent of managerial personnel and farm owners, 41 per cent of skilled manual workers, 37 per cent of domestic workers, 36 per cent of office and sales personnel, 14 per cent of unskilled, and 11 per cent of semiskilled manual workers.[2]

[1] E. A. Friedmann and R. J. Havighurst, *The Meaning of Work and Retirement* (Chicago: University of Chicago Press, 1954), p. 183.

[2] Howard M. Bell, *Youth Tell Their Story* (Washington: American Council on Education, 1938), p. 134.

[3] Theodore Caplow has pointed to the importance of this factor in his *The Sociology of Work* (Minneapolis: University of Minnesota Press, 1954), p. 133.

[4] F. H. Harbison, "Collective Bargaining and American Capitalism," in A. W. Kornhauser, Robert Dubin, and Arthur Ross, eds., *Industrial Conflict* (New York: McGraw-Hill, 1954), p. 278.

[5] Brown, *op. cit.*, pp. 98–99.

[6] A summary of the findings of the hundreds of job factor studies is found in Chapter 3 of F. Herzberg, et al., *op. cit.*, pp. 37–94. A critical discussion of the methodological problems involved in the attempt to assess the relative saliency of various factors is A. W. Kornhauser, "Psychological Studies of Employee Attitudes," *op. cit.*, pp. 305–319.

[7] Omission of other factors, such as skill, variety of operations, wages, and job security, does not suggest their lack of importance. But these are at once highly related to occupational prestige and control, and, at the same time, they do not seem as useful in explaining gross occupational differences.

More detailed data for a number of professional and manual working-class occupations strongly confirm these general findings. Note how for six different professions, the proportion of satisfied persons ranges from 82 per cent to 91 per cent, whereas for seven manual occupations it varies from 16 per cent for unskilled automobile workers to 52 per cent for skilled printers. (See Table 4.)

To some extent, these findings on occupational differences in job satisfaction reflect not only differences in the objective conditions of work for people in various jobs, *but also occupational differences in the norms with respect to work attitudes.*[3] The professional is expected to be dedicated to his profession and have an intense intrinsic interest in his area of specialized competence; the white-collar employee is expected to be "company" oriented and like his work; but the loyalty of the manual worker is never taken for granted and, more than any other occupational type, cultural norms permit him the privilege of griping. In fact, it has been asserted that "the natural state of the industrial worker . . . is one of discontent."[4] The same point has been clearly made in an analysis of the latent function of the time clock:

> The office staff does not "clock-in" — ostensibly because they are not paid by the hour, but it seems likely that at least part of the reason for this is the supposition that, unlike labourers, they do not necessarily dislike work and can be placed on their honour to be punctual. The working classes, as we have seen, are supposed to dislike work and therefore need "discipline" to keep them in order. Since "clocking-in" has been abolished in many firms, it cannot be accepted as absolutely necessary.[5]

Factors that account for occupational differences in satisfaction

The literature on work is filled with numerous attempts to list and often to estimate the relative importance of the various components, elements, or factors involved in job satisfaction. These lists do not correspond neatly with one another; they bear a large number of labels, but they all are likely to include, in one way or another, such variables as the income attached to a job, supervision, working conditions, social relations, and the variety and skill intrinsic in the work itself. The classification of these items is quite arbitrary and the number of factors considered relevant can be broken down almost indefinitely.[6]

Whereas most studies attempt to explain variations in job satisfaction among individual employees in the same company or occupation, the interest of the present paper is to explain the gross differences in work attitudes that exist among those in *different* occupations and industries. Four factors that seem useful in accounting for these differences are discussed: occupational prestige, control, integrated work groups, and occupational communities.[7]

OCCUPATIONAL PRESTIGE

Occupational prestige is the one best explanatory factor in the sense that if all occupations (for which sufficient data are available) were ranked in order of extent of typical job satisfaction, and these ranks were compared with the rank order in which they partake of public esteem, the rank-order correlations would be higher than those resulting from any other factor. This is because the prestige of any occupation depends on the level of skill the job entails, the degree of education or training necessary, the amount of control and responsibility involved in the performance of the work, the income which is typically received — to mention the most readily apparent factors. Since occupational prestige as a kind of composite index partly subsumes within itself a number of factors which contribute heavily to differences in satisfaction, it is not surprising that it should be itself the best individual measure of satisfaction.

TABLE 4. *Proportion in Various Occupations Who Would Choose Same Kind of Work if Beginning Career Again*

Professional occupations, %		Working class occupations,§ %	
Mathematicians*	91	Skilled printers	52
Physicists*	89	Paper workers	52
Biologists*	89	Skilled automobile workers	41
Chemists*	86	Skilled steelworkers	41
Lawyers†	83	Textile workers	31
Journalists‡	82	Unskilled steelworkers	21
		Unskilled automobile workers	16

Sources:

* "The Scientists: A Group Portrait," *Fortune*, October 1948, pp. 106–112.

† "The U.S. Bar," *Fortune*, May 1939, p. 176.

‡ Leo Rosten, *The Washington Correspondents* (New York: Harcourt, Brace and Company, 1938), p. 347.

§ These are unpublished data which have been computed from the IBM cards of a survey of 3,000 factory workers in 16 industries, conducted by Elmo Roper for *Fortune* magazine in 1947. A secondary analysis of this survey is being carried out by the Fund for the Republic's Trade Union Project. The general findings of the original study appeared in "The Fortune Survey," *Fortune*, May 1947, pp. 5–12, and June 1947, pp. 5–10.

In addition, jobs that have high prestige will tend to be valued for their status rewards even when "objective" aspects of the work are undesirable; similarly, low-status jobs will tend to be undervalued and disliked.

> . . . the lowliness or nastiness of a job are subjective estimates. . . . A doctor or a nurse, for example, or a sanitary inspector, have to do some things which would disgust the most unskilled casual laborer who did not see these actions in their social context. Yet the status and prestige of such people is generally high. . . . Above all, it is the prestige of his working group and his position in it which will influence the worker's attitude to such jobs.[1]

That the actual findings on differences in job satisfactions correspond quite closely to the scale of occupational prestige has been shown in the previous section. Professionals and business executives have the highest prestige in our society; they also consistently report the highest degree of work satisfaction. According to the most thorough occupational prestige study, doctors are the most esteemed major occupational group in the United States.[2] It is not surprising therefore that this public esteem is an important source of their satisfaction with their work:

> [For] physicians . . . work is a source of prestige. Some doctors stated that to be a physician meant that one belonged to an elite class. It meant that one associated with important people and was in a position of leadership in the community.[3]

Among non-professional or managerial employees, white-collar workers are generally more satisfied with their jobs than manual workers. Again status considerations play an important role. Even when white-collar work does not outrank manual jobs in income or skill, office workers are accorded higher social prestige than blue-collar personnel.[4]

Although this is so, manual work seems to be viewed with greater respect in America, with its democratic frontier traditions, than in many other nations.[5] The historic "social inferiority complex," the "sense of social subordination" of the European industrial worker, to use the words of Henri DeMan,[6] has never been well developed in the United States. We might expect, therefore, that the level of work satisfaction among manual workers would be higher in this country than in Europe.[7] With the rapidly increasing number of at-

[1] Brown, *op. cit.*, pp. 149–150. One's prestige *within* an occupation or work group is paramount for job satisfaction; I ignore it in my discussion because it explains individual rather than group differences in satisfaction.

[2] When a national sample rated 90 occupations, doctors were second only to Supreme Court justices. National Opinion Research Center, "Jobs and Occupations: A Popular Evaluation," in Bendix and Lipset, eds., *Class, Status and Power* (1st Edition, Glencoe: The Free Press, 1953), p. 412.

[3] Friedmann and Havighurst, *op. cit.*, p. 161. Thus "to be a doctor was to be doing the best of all possible jobs in the best of all possible professions." A consequence of the high satisfaction received from identifying oneself with a profession in such public esteem is that the doctor is reluctant to give up such identity: the authors found that, "except on rare occasions, physicians do not retire while they are in reasonably good physical condition."

[4] See Lipset and Bendix, *Social Mobility in Industrial Society* (Berkeley: University of California Press, 1959), pp. 14–17.

[5] Now a rather stock generalization, Werner Sombart was evidently one of the first to state it.

[6] H. DeMan, *Joy in Work* (London: George Allen and Unwin, 1929), pp. 59–60, 208–209.

[7] On the other hand when the norms of an "open society" encourage *all* to strive for upward advancement, large numbers of people who do not succeed will feel dissatisfied and frustrated, as the sociologist Robert Merton has emphasized in his "Social Structure and Anomie." See Merton, *Social Theory and Social Structure* (Glencoe: The Free Press, 1957), pp. 131–160. In

titude surveys of European workers since the war, such a comparison would be of considerable interest.

Within the world of manual work, occupational differences in satisfaction are also related to the differences in prestige that exist among various working class jobs. The higher incidence of positive work attitudes consistently found among skilled workers is not only caused by the skill factor per se; the craftsman takes pride in the fact that he is looked on with more respect

---

1 Friedmann and Havighurst found this to be true among the printers they studied, *op. cit.*, pp. 176–177. It has been noted that Chicago plumbers, who express a high level of work satisfaction, often stress their function of "protecting public sanitation" and compare their contribution to community health with that of doctors. Joel Seidman, et al., *The Worker Views His Union* (Chicago: University of Chicago Press, 1958), pp. 52–53.

2 Quotation from an interview with a coal miner in Friedmann and Havighurst, *op. cit.*, pp. 73–76. I do not intend to give the impression that the above is a representative quotation; the typical reaction seems to be an overt rejection of the anti-union media and public image. However, it seems likely that such feelings as the above might still haunt the average worker who would never express them. The role of the coal miner's "occupational community" in insulating him from these derogatory evaluations is discussed later in this paper.

3 DeMan, *op. cit.*, p. 67. "Even the worker who is free in the social sense, the peasant or the handicraftsman, feels this compulsion, were it only because while he is at work, his activities are dominated and determined by the aim of his work, by the idea of a willed or necessary creation. Work inevitably signifies subordination of the worker to remoter aims, felt to be necessary, and therefore involving a renunciation of the freedoms and enjoyments of the present for the sake of a future advantage."

4 E. C. Hughes, *Men and Their Work* (Glencoe: The Free Press, 1959), pp. 47–48. William Foote Whyte has put it in more general terms, "No normal person is happy in a situation which he cannot control to some extent." *Money and Motivation* (New York: Harper, 1955), p. 94.

5 Twenty-three per cent of the manual workers in a labor force sample in Oakland, California, had been in business at some time during their work history. Lipset and Bendix, *Social Mobility in Industrial Society*, p. 179. Cultural differences in aspirations for independence and control in work as well as differing economic opportunities are suggested in the contrast between British and American opinion poll data. Fifty-one per cent of the Americans questioned wanted to start their own businesses compared to only 33 per cent of the Britons; Americans were also considerably more likely to say they would actually do so. Hadley Cantril, *Public Opinion 1935–1946* (Princeton: Princeton University Press, 1951), p. 528.

6 See especially Ely Chinoy, *Automobile Workers and the American Dream* (Garden City: Doubleday, 1955). He quotes a machine operator: "The main thing is to be independent and give your own orders and not have to take them from anybody else. That's the reason the fellows in the shop all want to start their own business. Then the profits are all for yourself. When you're in the shop there's nothing for yourself in it. So you just do what you have to in order to get along. A fellow would rather do it for himself. If you expend the energy, it's for your own benefit then," pp. xvi–xvii.

Europe, manual workers have more distinctive class cultures and reference groups than in America; therefore they are probably much less likely to subscribe to the advancement norms of the whole society. Consideration of this factor alone would suggest *less* dissatisfaction with jobs and occupational status in Europe.

---

in the community than the factory operative or the unskilled laborer.[1] Moreover, those manual workers in occupations which are particularly looked down on will find difficulty in deriving overall positive satisfactions in their work. Interviewers of coal miners have remarked on the great pride with which they are shown various home improvements made possible by the higher wages of a period of prosperity, and on the sensitivity with which some miners react to the public image of the occupation, which has been, in part, created by the hostility of the mass media to the militancy of the union.

> I don't like to strike, because people all get mad at the miners then. I wish the people would realize that the miner has to live too, and not hate him when he tries to better conditions for himself. It bothers me the way people say bad things about the miners, and makes me ashamed of my job.[2]

An attempt has been made to illustrate the manner in which variations in work satisfaction among different occupations tend to follow variations in occupational prestige. Although this generalization is, to an impressive extent, supported by the evidence, it does not hold unfailingly. We can note occupations with relatively high prestige whose general level of satisfaction is lower than would be expected, whereas some low-status jobs seem to be highly satisfying. This suggests that in certain cases other factors play a role even more important than status. A good test of the approach applied here is to see whether the other factors which have been advanced as critical ones can indeed account for discrepancies in the generally marked association between occupational prestige and job satisfaction.

CONTROL

In a perceptive passage, the Belgian socialist Henri DeMan remarks that "all work is felt to be coercive."[3] The fact that work inherently involves a surrender of control, a "subordination of the worker to remoter aims," is probably what makes the relative degree of control in work so important an aspect of job attitudes. As Max Weber, the German sociologist, suggested long ago, "no man easily yields to another full control over the effort, and especially over the amount of physical effort he must daily exert."[4]

There seem to be significant cultural as well as individual differences in the need for control and independence in work. In America, where individual initiative has long been a cultural ideal, we would expect strong pressures in this direction. And we do find that surprising proportions of manual workers in this country have attempted to succeed in small business.[5] and that for many others the idea of running a gas station or a number of tourist cabins is a compelling dream.[6]

Lack of control over the conditions of work is most pronounced for industrial workers.

The very evidence of his daily work life brings home to the manual worker the degree to which he is directed in his behavior with only limited free choices available. From the moment of starting work by punching a time clock, through work routines that are established at fixed times, until the day ends at the same mechanical time recorder, there is impressed upon the industrial worker his narrow niche in a complex and ordered system of interdependency . . . a system over which he, as an individual, exercises little direct control.[1]

The factory worker is at the bottom of the bureaucratic hierarchy; he is a person for whom action is constantly being originated, but who himself originates little activity for others.[2]

At the same time, diverse factory jobs and working-class occupations vary greatly in the degree of control they permit over the conditions of work: it is these variations, of which workers are keenly aware, that are most interesting for the purpose of accounting for differences in satisfaction.

The notion of control in work, as I am using it, is, of course, a vague, *sensitizing* concept which covers a wide range of phenomena rather than a concept which is precisely delimited and identifiable by precise indicators. Among its most important dimensions are control over the use of one's *time* and physical *movement*, which is fundamentally control over the *pace* of the work process, control over the *environment*, both technical and social, and control as the *freedom* from *hierarchal authority*. Naturally, these dimensions are highly interrelated; a business executive high on the occupational ladder will tend to be high in each, whereas an unskilled laborer will have little control from any of these viewpoints. *It is possible to generalize on the basis of the evidence that the greater the degree of control that a worker has (either in a single dimension or as a total composite) the greater his job satisfaction.*[3]

Control over time, physical movement and pace of work. Assembly line work in the automobile industry is a good example of the almost complete absence of this aspect of control.

Its coerced rhythms, the inability to pause at will for a moment's rest, and the need for undeviating attention to simple routines made it work to be avoided if possible and to escape from if necessary. So demanding is the line that one worker, echoing others, complained: "You get the feeling, everybody gets the feeling, whenever the line jerks everybody is wishing, 'break down, baby!' "[4]

The consensus of the work literature is that assembly line work, especially in the automobile industry, is more disliked than any other major occupation, and the prime factor in dissatisfaction with the assembly line is the lack of control over the pace of production.[5] Workers in assembly line plants have strong preferences

for jobs off the line. A study of the job aspirations of 180 men on the line found that the "workers' motivations were not what might normally be expected. It was not promotion or transfer in order to improve one's economic status. Rather, it was primarily a desire 'to get away from the line.' " *Only 8 per cent* were satisfied, in the sense of not preferring to get an off-line job.[6] The difference between line and off-line jobs has been clearly stated by the sociologist Ely Chinoy who worked in an automobile plant and studied automobile workers:

Work at a machine may be just as repetitive, require as few motions and as little thought as line assembly, but men prefer it because it does not keep them tied as tightly to their tasks. "I can stop occasionally when I want to," said a machine-operator. "I couldn't do that when I was on the line." Production standards for a particular machine may be disliked and felt to be excessive, but the machine operator need only approximate his production quota each day. The line-tender must do all the work that the endless belt brings before him. . . .[7]

The greater dissatisfaction with mass production assembly line jobs is confirmed by the findings in an automobile plant that "men with highly repetitive jobs, conveyor paced, and so forth, were far more likely to take time off from work than those whose jobs did not contain such job characteristics," and that quit rates were almost twice as high among men on the assembly line as among men off the line.[8] In a study of Maryland youth during the depression, it was found that the occupation most disliked by female workers was that of operator on cannery conveyor belts. Every one of the fifty-three cannery operatives in the sample expressed a preference for different work![9] The control of these workers over the pace of production is at least as minimal as that of automobile workers, and in addition they lack even the protection of a strong union.

---

[1] Dubin, "Constructive Aspects of Industrial Conflict," in Kornhauser, Dubin and Ross, *op. cit.*, p. 43.

[2] W. F. Whyte, *op. cit.*, p. 234.

[3] Control, of course, is not independent of the other factors. The relationship between occupational status and control is particularly marked; in fact, the (status) "hierarchy is a direct reflection of freedom from control. . . ." Edward Gross, *Work and Society* (New York: Crowell, 1958), p. 428. The relationship of control to skill is intimate; in fact, skill may be conceived as a form of control over the technological process of work. Finally, control is related to integrated work teams. An important result of the pioneering research of Elton Mayo and his colleagues was the increased awareness that the informal work group, in setting and enforcing informal production standards, gives many industrial workers some control over their job situations.

[4] Chinoy, *op. cit.*, p. 71.

[5] C. R. Walker and Robert H. Guest, *Man on the Assembly Line* (Cambridge: Harvard University Press, 1952), p. 62.

[6] *Ibid.*, pp. 113, 110.

[7] Chinoy, *op. cit.*, pp. 71–72.

[8] Walker and Guest, *op. cit.*, pp. 120, 116–117.

[9] Bell, *op. cit.*, p. 135.

A machine operator may go all out in the morning to produce 100 pieces, take it easy in the afternoon, only putting out 50; at any rate, it is his own decision. In similar fashion a few assembly line workers may be able to build up a "bank" of automobile seats which they assemble to the oncoming bodies; a few try to get ahead and gain time for rest by working up the line, but for the great majority it is hopeless. Assembly line workers are "alienated," according to the researchers who have studied them. In their work they "can secure little significant experience of themselves as productive human beings." As one automobile worker put it a little wistfully:

You understand, if you get a job that you're interested in, when you work you don't pay attention to the time, you don't wait for the whistle to blow to go home, you're all wrapped up in it and don't pay attention to other things. *I don't know one single job like that.[1]*

According to David Riesman, what these wage earners are deprived of is "any chance to extend themselves, to go all-out". A stark example is the worker on the packinghouse assembly line who goes home after his day's work in order to "try to accomplish something for that day."[2] How do these workers stand it? Here is the deadly answer of a Hormel meat worker: "The time passes."

Most workers are so busily engaged in pushing the flow of work that they do not *consciously* suffer from the inherent monotony of their work. They are well adjusted, because they have reduced their level of aspirations to the rather low level of the job. They coast along, keeping busy, visiting, talking, making time go by, and getting the work done in order to get "out of there" in order to get home![3]

The great dissatisfaction with automobile assembly work is an example of a discrepancy between occupa-

tional status and job satisfaction. The status of the automobile worker is not lower than that of other semi-skilled American factory workers; in fact, the level of wages would suggest that it is higher than manual workers in many other industrial occupations, especially those in non-durable goods manufacturing. But the control of the automobile assembly line worker over the work process is considerably less than in other major industrial occupations, and this is a big factor in accounting for the prevalence of job discontent.

It is interesting to contrast automobile manufacturing with mining, an occupation which, though considered lower in prestige,[4] seems to provide marked work satisfaction. Alvin Gouldner, in his study of a gypsum plant, found that although the miners had considerably less status in the community than surface workers, they showed much greater work motivation. He attributed this high job satisfaction to the fact that miners

were not "alienated" from their machines: that is, they had an unusually high degree of control over their machine's operation. The pace at which the machines worked, the corners into which they were poked, what happened to them when they broke down, was determined mainly by the miners themselves. On the surface, though, the speed at which the machines worked and the procedures followed were prescribed by superiors.[5]

Finally, the higher job satisfaction of skilled workers (documented in the preceding sections of this paper) is related to the fact that they have a large measure of control over the pace of their work. The fact that craftsmen themselves largely determine the speed at which they work gives them a marked advantage over most factory workers.[6]

Control over the technical and social environment. In those occupations in which the physical environment or the technological work process is particularly challenging, control over it seems to be an important aspect of job satisfaction. Coalminers have "a very personal sense of being pitted against their environment" and express "feelings of accomplishment and pride at having conquered it."[7] That steel production is found fascinating is suggested by a mill worker: "It's sort of interesting. Sometimes you have a battle on your hands. You have to use your imagination and ability to figure out what move to make."[8] Similarly, it has been noted that railroad workers derive a sense of power in "the manipulation of many tons of railroad equipment." Engineers derive more pleasure in running large engines rather than small ones; switchmen and brakeman "give the signals that move fifty or so freight cars back and forth like so many toys."[9]

A further source of the dissatisfaction with automobile assembly, then, is the fact that these jobs provide so little scope for control over the technical environment; there is little that is challenging in the actual work operation. As a man on the line puts it:

[1] Chinoy, *op. cit.*, p. 70.
[2] Fred H. Blum, *Toward a Democratic Work Process* (New York: Harper, 1953), p. 96.
[3] *Ibid.*, p. 85.
[4] In the North-Hatt occupational prestige study, "Machine operator in a factory" (the category closest in social meaning to an auto worker) ranked 65th in prestige among 90 occupations, considerably higher than "coal miner" which was ranked 77th. Most people ranked machine operator in a factory as "average" in general standing, and coal miners as "somewhat below average" or "poor."
[5] Alvin W. Gouldner, *Patterns of Industrial Bureaucracy* (Glencoe: The Free Press, 1954), pp. 140–141.
[6] Seidman, et al., *op. cit.*, p. 55.
[7] Friedmann and Havighurst, *op. cit.*, p. 176.
[8] C. R. Walker, *Steeltown* (New York: Harper, 1950), p. 61.
[9] John Spier, "Elements of Job Satisfaction in the Railroad Operating Crafts,'" unpublished paper, Berkeley, California, 1959.

There is nothing more discouraging than having a barrel beside you with 10,000 bolts in it and using them all up. Then you get a barrel with another 10,000 bolts, and you know that every one of those 10,000 bolts has to be picked up and put in exactly the same place as the last 10,000 bolts.[1]

Paralleling the control of industrial workers over the technical environment is the satisfaction derived by professional and white-collar employees from control over a social environment, namely, clients and customers. A study of salespeople concluded that "the completion of the sale, the conquering of the customer, represents the challenge or the 'meaningful life experience' of selling."[2] As one salesclerk, contemplating the import of his retirement, said: "I think to be perfectly truthful about it, the thing I miss most is being able to project myself into a sphere, conquer it, and retire with a pleased feeling because I have conquered it."[3]

Control as the freedom from direct supervision. On a slightly different level of analysis is this third dimension, which refers not to the aspects of the work process under control, but rather to the locus of control. One of the most consistent findings of work research is that industrial workers consider light, infrequent supervision, "foremen who aren't drivers," a crucial element in their high regard for particular jobs and companies.

The absence of close supervision in the mines has been considered an important determinant of the miners' high level of satisfaction.[4] And truck drivers and railroad workers, in explaining their preference for their own trades, stress the independence they experience in these jobs where the contact between employees and supervisor is so much less frequent than in factory work. As two railroad engineers put it:

I'd work anywhere except at a shop or in the factory. Just don't like a place where someone is watching you do your work all the time. That's why I like my job on the railroad now.

I wouldn't last three days working in a shop with a foreman breathing down my neck. Here I'm my own boss when I run the trains, nobody tells me what to do. . . .[5]

Such impressionistic evidence is confirmed by the more systematic comparisons of Hoppock, who found that the mean job satisfaction index of railroad employees ranked only below professional men and artists; it was higher than managers, clerical workers, small business proprietors, salesmen, and storeclerks! Although railroading is a high-status industrial occupation — railroaders have historically been part of the labor aristocracy — its occupational prestige is below most white-collar occupations. On the other hand, truck driving is a lower-status manual occupation (truck drivers are classified as semi-skilled operatives by the census, and the popular stereotypes of this occupation are somewhat derogatory), and yet in the Hoppock survey the satisfaction of truck drivers outranked all industrial occupations except railroading and was approximately the same level as that of salesmen.[6]

It is plausible that the marked discrepancy between job satisfaction and occupational status in these industries can be explained by the high degree of control, especially as reflected in freedom from supervision, which the workers enjoy.

If control in the work process is a crucial determinant of a worker's subjective feelings of well-being on the job, as I am trying to demonstrate, the question whether industrial trends are increasing or decreasing these areas of control becomes quite significant. It is interesting that Faunce's recent study of an *automated* engine plant shows that various dimensions of control may not change in the same direction. Compared to work in a non-automated, non-assembly line engine plant, automation greatly decreased the worker's direct control over his machine and pace of work, and this was felt to be a source of serious dissatisfaction. On the other hand, the increased responsibility and control over a complex technical environment of automated equipment was seen as a source of greater satisfaction and heightened status. Thus, while Faunce was able to locate the elements which made for satisfaction and those which made for dissatisfaction in these jobs (his analysis seems very congruent with the present discussion), it was rather difficult to assess the overall effect of the change on work satisfaction.[7]

INTEGRATED WORK GROUPS

A third factor that is important in explaining occupational differences in work satisfaction is the nature of on-the-job social relations. The technological structure of certain industries such as steel production and mining requires that the work be carried out by *teams* of men working closely together, whereas in industries such as automobile assembly the formation of regular work groups is virtually prohibited by the organization of production. There is much evidence to support the proposition that the greater the extent to which workers are members of integrated work teams on the job, the higher the level of job satisfaction.

In a steel mill in which 85 per cent of sixty-two workers interviewed were satisfied with their jobs,

[1] Walker and Guest, *op. cit.*, p. 54.
[2] Friedmann and Havighurst, *op. cit.*, p. 178.
[3] *Ibid.*, p. 106.
[4] Gouldner, *op. cit.*, pp. 55 ff. Seidman, et al., *op. cit.*, p. 23.
[5] Reynolds and Shister, *op. cit.*, pp. 13–14.
[6] Hoppock, *op. cit.*, pp. 225 ff. In Bell's Maryland youth survey the majority in all occupational categories except professionals preferred a different kind of job. However, the proportion of truck drivers who were so "discontented" was less than that of clerks, salespersons, farm laborers and operatives in clothing and textiles. Bell, *op. cit.*, p. 135.
[7] William A. Faunce, "Automation and the Automobile Worker," in Walter Galenson and S. M. Lipset, eds., *Labor and Trade Unionism: An Interdisciplinary Reader* (New York: John Wiley & Sons, 1960), pp. 370–379.

Charles Walker found that "the source of satisfaction most often articulated or implied was that of being part of, or having membership in, the hot mill crew." As three steel workers express it:

(A heater helper) We work for a while, it's like playing baseball. First one fellow is up and then you have your turn at bat. We can knock off every so often and take a smoke and talk. I like working with men I know and working like a team.

(A piercer plugger) The crew I am in is very good. Our foreman likes to see his men on top and he does everything to help us . . . this attitude makes a lot of people put out more steel. . . . Over here it's teamwork. . . . You can have a lot of Hank Greenbergs on the team but if you don't work together, it isn't a team at all. And we like our work because we carry on a lot of conversation with signs and the men laugh and joke and the time passes very quick.

(A piercer dragout worker) There's nothing like working here in this mill. Everybody cooperates. Every man works as a member of a team and every man tries to turn out as much steel as they possibly can. We work hard and get satisfaction out of working hard.[1]

While recognizing that close kinship ties and a small town atmosphere encouraged such cooperative spirit, Walker attributed the principal cause of the integrated work teams to the basic technological process of making steel, which requires small group operations. He compared this technology and its results with that of the automobile assembly plants in which the technological structure is such that the majority of workers perform their operations individually. There, the pattern of social interaction produced by the moving line is such that although workers will talk to the man in front of them, behind them, and across from them,

no worker will interact with exactly the same group of men as any other worker will; therefore, no stable work groups are formed. Walker considered this a major element in the greater dissatisfaction he found among automobile workers compared to steel workers.

Mining is another occupation where technological conditions seem to favor the development of closely knit work groups. Since, as one miner expressed it, "the mines are kind of a family affair," where "the quality of the sentiment is of a depth and complexity produced only by long years of intimate association," it is not surprising that many miners feel that the loss of social contacts at work is a major disadvantage of retirement. The dangerous nature of the work is another factor that knits miners together:

To be an old-timer in the mines means something more than merely knowing the technique of a particular job; it also means awareness and acceptance of the responsibility which each man has for his fellow-workers. The sense of interdependence in relation to common dangers is undoubtedly an important factor in the spirit of solidarity which has characterized miners in all countries for many generations.[2]

Within the same factory, departments and jobs vary considerably in the extent to which the work is carried out by individuals working alone or by groups; the consequences of these differences have been a major interest of the "human relations in industry" movement. A recent study of one department in a factory manufacturing rotating equipment found that the employees who were integrated members of informal work groups were, by and large, satisfied with both the intrinsic characteristics of their jobs, and such "extended characteristics" as pay, working conditions, and benefits, whereas the non-group members tended to be dissatisfied. Sixty-five per cent of "regular" group members were satisfied, compared to 43 per cent of members of groups which were deviant in accepting less fully the values of the factory community, and compared to only 28 per cent of isolated workers.[3]

The classic investigations of the functions of informal work groups in industry have been produced by the "human relations in industry" school, associated most directly with the Harvard Business School and the writings of Elton Mayo, and represented by the pioneering experiments at the Hawthorne plant of the Western Electric Company.[4] These studies have demonstrated that informal work groups establish and enforce norms which guide the production and other behavior of workers on the job, and that such management problems as absenteeism, turnover, and morale can often be dealt with through the manipulation of work groups and supervisorial behavior. But it is striking that the human relations school has concerned itself so little with the job itself, with the relation between the worker and his work, rather than the relation between the worker and his mates.[5] A typical human

[1] Walker, *op. cit.*, pp. 66–67.

[2] Friedmann and Havighurst, *op. cit.*, pp. 65, 90–91.

[3] A. Zaleznik, C. R. Christensen, and F. J. Roethlisberger, *The Motivation, Productivity and Satisfaction of Workers: A Prediction Study* (Cambridge: Harvard University, 1958), pp. 258–277. In this factory the most important thing in accounting for group membership was ethnicity: the Irish workers tended to be the integrated members of "regular groups," while the non-Irish employees were by and large isolates or in deviant groups.

[4] The most complete account of this study appears in F. J. Roethlisberger and W. J. Dickson, *Management and the Worker* (Cambridge: Harvard University Press, 1939). Other accounts of the research of the Mayo school may be found in Elton Mayo and George F. Lombard, *Teamwork and Labor Turnover in the Aircraft Industry of Southern California* (Cambridge: Harvard University Graduate School of Business Administration, 1944); Elton Mayo, *The Human Problems of an Industrial Civilization* (New York: The Macmillan Co., 1933); and *The Social Problems of an Industrial Civilization* (Cambridge: Graduate School of Business Administration, Harvard University, 1946).

[5] It is difficult to determine whether this neglect stems from an implicit assumption that work tasks are sufficiently challenging for basically "non-rational" workers, or conversely, from a view that the alienation of the worker from his work is so

relations discussion of the conditions of employee morale is likely to give all its emphasis to matters of communication, supervision, and the personality of workers and ignore almost completely intrinsic job tasks.[1] In a recent study by the Harvard Business School entitled *Worker Satisfaction and Development*, the only sources of work satisfaction discussed are those which directly concern workers' integration in work groups and cliques. Although creativity is a major concern of the author, it is the creativity of the *work group* to adapt to new circumstances, rather than the creative expression of an individual in his work, that he is interested in.[2]

In its emphasis on the importance of integrated work groups the human relations approach has made an important contribution. But "a way of seeing is a way of not seeing," and its neglect of the other factors imposes serious limitations on the usefulness of this approach, at least in providing an adequate theory of the conditions of work satisfaction.[3]

OCCUPATIONAL COMMUNITIES

The nature of the association among workers *off-the-job* is also a factor in work satisfaction. The evidence of the work literature supports the notion that levels of work satisfaction are higher in those industries and in those kinds of jobs in which workers make up an "occupational community." One such industry is mining. Not only is the actual work carried out by solidary work groups, but, in addition, miners live in a community made up largely of fellow workers. This kind of "inbreeding" produces a devotion to the occupation which is not characteristic of many other working class jobs:

> Somehow when you get into mining and you like the men you work with, you just get to the place after a while that you don't want to leave. *Once that fever gets hold of a man, he'll never be good for anything else.*
>
> A fellow may quit the mines, but when they whistle, he goes back. I've had a lot better jobs, but I've always liked to work in the mines. I can't explain it, except I like being with the gang; I never could just sit around much.[4]

Such occupational communities are likely to develop in occupations that are isolated, either spatially or on the basis of peculiar hours of work. Coal mining and textile industries characteristically have grown up in *isolated small communities*; sailors, cowboys, and long-distance truck drivers are also isolated from contact with persons in other jobs. Similarly, *off-hours shifts* favor the development of occupational communities; this is the case with printers, a large proportion of whom work nights,[5] steel-workers, who often rotate, between day, swing, and graveyard shifts, firemen, and, of course, railroad men.

The essential feature of an occupational community is that workers in their off-hours socialize more with

persons in their own line of work than with a cross section of occupational types. Printers generally go to bars, movies, and baseball games with other printers.[6] In a small town steel mill, 87 per cent of the workers had spent "in the last week," at least some time off the job with other workers in their department; almost half said they had seen many or almost all of their fellow workers.[7] However, in a large tractor plant of 20,000 people only 41 per cent of the employees said that they got together socially outside the plant with employees from their own work groups.[8] *Occupational communities rarely exist among urban factory workers.*

A second characteristic of an occupational community is that its participants "talk shop" in their off-hours. That this is true of farmers, fishermen, miners, and railroaders has been described far more by novelists

---

[1] For example, Robert N. McMurray, "Management Mentalities and Worker Reactions," in Hoslett, *op. cit.*, especially his discussion of the morale study of J. D. Houser.

[2] A. Zaleznik, *Worker Satisfaction and Development* (Cambridge: Harvard University Business School, 1956). A similar case in point is the excellent study of an Indian textile mill by A. K. Rice of the London Tavistock Institute. In his theoretical discussion, Rice gives equal weight to three dimensions of work satisfaction: psychological closure or the doing of a complete task, responsibility and control over the task, and work group integration. But in presenting his findings, Rice ignores almost completely the first two intrinsic job dimensions and concentrates on the work group factor. *Productivity and Social Organization: The Ahmedabad Experiment* (London: Tavistock Publications, 1958).

[3] For a summary of the major theoretical and ideological criticisms that have been made of the Mayo School, see Henry A. Landsberger, *Hawthorne Revisited* (Ithaca: Cornell University Press, 1958), especially Chapter III.

[4] Friedmann and Havighurst, *op. cit.*, pp. 70–71.

[5] The most thorough analysis of an occupational community is the study of the printers by S. M. Lipset, M. Trow, and J. Coleman, *Union Democracy* (Glencoe: The Free Press, 1956). This section is considerably indebted to the insights of these authors. An important discussion of occupational communities in another context is C. Kerr and A. Siegel, "The Inter-Industry Propensity to Strike," in Kornhauser, Dubin, and Ross, *op. cit.*, pp. 189–212. They argue that the fact that workers in these occupations form an "isolated mass" and are not integrated into the society as a whole encourages militant strike activity.

[6] Lipset, Trow, and Coleman, *op. cit.*

[7] Walker, *op. cit.*, pp. 111–112.

[8] Daniel Katz, "Satisfactions and Deprivations in Industrial Life," in Kornhauser, Dubin, and Ross, *op. cit.*, p. 102.

---

immutable that one must concentrate instead on engineering work groups and supervision, since these are amenable to change. From a history of ideas point of view the most important source of this neglect is probably the intellectual heritage of Elton Mayo, who was greatly influenced by Emile Durkheim's theory of the increasing atomization of modern society and the consequent growth of *anomie*. Whereas Marx saw the solution to the modern social problem in the "restoration" to the worker of control over his conditions of work, Durkheim rather saw it in the reintegration of individuals into solidary social groups which could buttress the individual from the pressures of the mass state and, in addition, provide personal equilibrium and security. Mayo, in following Durkheim rather than Marx, ignores almost completely the relation of the worker to his work and concentrates instead on his integration into small work groups as a condition of industrial harmony and social health.

than by social scientists. The significance of talking about work off the job has been well expressed by Fred Blum, who notes that the assembly line workers in the meat packing plant he studied rarely do so.

> Whether they are with their family or their friends, rare are the occasions when workers feel like talking about their work. In response to the question: "Do you talk with your friends about the work you are doing?" only a very small number indicated that they do talk with their friends — or their wife — about their work. Quite a few said that they "only" talk with their friends "if they ask me" or that they talk "sometimes" or "seldom." Some workers are outspoken in saying that they do not like to talk about their work. "If we get out of there, we are through with that to the next day." Another worker said, "When I leave down there, I am through down there. I like to talk about something else." *He adds to this with some astonishment: "Railroadmen always want to talk about their work."[1]*

Third, occupational communities are little worlds in themselves. For its members the occupation itself is the reference group; its standards of behavior, its system of status and rank, guide conduct.[2]

> Railroading is something more than an occupation. Like thieving and music, it is a world by itself, with its own literature and mythology, with an irrational system of status which is unintelligible to the outsider, and a complicated rule book for distributing responsibility and rewards.[3]

[1] Blum, *op. cit.*, pp. 96–97. My emphasis.

[2] The French sociologist Emile Durkheim felt that occupational communities which he termed "corporations" were the one agency which could provide stable norms for individuals living in an essentially normless society. See the preface to the second edition, *The Division of Labor in Society* (Glencoe: The Free Press, 1949).

[3] Caplow, *op. cit.*, p. 96.

[4] The reverse process, high job satisfaction leading to high participation in an occupational community, has been described by Lipset and his colleagues in their study of union printers. Lipset, et al., *op. cit.*, pp. 124–126.

[5] Evidence on this point is reviewed in Herzberg, et al., *op. cit.*, pp. 17–20.

[6] Marx's classic characterization is the best known: "Owing to the extensive use of machinery and to the division of labor, the work of the proletarians has lost all individual character, and consequently, all charm for the workman. He becomes an appendage of the machine, and it is only the most simple, most monotonous, and most easily acquired knack, that is required of him." But almost identical accounts abound in the writings of non-Marxist intellectuals. Compare Adriano Tilgher, *Work: What It Has Meant to Men Through the Ages* (New York: Harcourt Brace and Co., 1930), p. 151, and Henry Durant, *The Problem of Leisure* (London: George Routledge and Sons, 1938), pp. 6 ff.

[7] DeMan, *op. cit.*, p. 146. The 10 per cent estimate is from Brown, *op. cit.*, p. 24.

[8] Brown, *op. cit.*, p. 207. A leading advocate of the alienation thesis, the French industrial sociologist, Georges Friedmann, was unable to find any decline in the proportion of skilled workers in selected German, French, and English industries during the

We can suggest a number of mechanisms by means of which occupational communities increase job satisfaction.[4] First, when workers know their co-workers off the job, they will derive deeper social satisfactions on the job. In the second place, an effect of the isolation of the occupation is that workers are able to develop and maintain a pride in and devotion to their line of work; at the same time, isolation insulates them from having to come to grips with the general public's image of their status, which is likely to be considerably lower than their own. Participation in an occupational community means not only the reinforcement of the group's sense of general prestige; in such worlds one's skill and expertise in doing the actual work becomes an important basis of individual status and prestige. Finally, unlike the "alienated" assembly line worker, who is characterized by a separation of his work sphere from his non-work sphere — a separation of work from life as Mills and Blum put it — the work and leisure interests of those in occupational communities are highly integrated. If the integration of work and non-work is an important element in general psychic adjustment, as some assert, then these workers should exhibit higher job satisfaction, since satisfaction with life in general seems to be highly related to satisfaction in work.[5]

Conclusions

When we read modern accounts of what work and workers were like before the industrial revolution, we continually find that the dominant image of the worker of that period is the craftsman. Viewed as an independent producer in his home or small shop with complete control over the pace and scheduling of his work, making the whole product rather than a part of it, and taking pride in the creativity of his skilled tasks, his traits are typically contrasted with those of the alienated factory worker — the allegedly characteristic producer of modern society.[6]

It is remarkable what an enormous impact this *contrast* of the craftsman with the factory hand has had on intellectual discussions of work and workers in modern society, *notwithstanding its lack of correspondence to present and historical realities.* For, indeed, craftsmen, far from being typical workers of the past era, accounted for less than 10 per cent of the medieval labor force, and the peasant, who was actually the representative laborer, was, in the words of the Belgian socialist Henri DeMan, "practically nothing more than a working beast."[7] Furthermore, the real character of the craftsman's work has been romanticized by the prevalent tendency to idealize the past, whereas much evidence suggests that modern work does not fit the black portrait of meaningless alienation. In fact, it has been asserted "that in modern society there is far greater scope for skill and craftsmanship than in any previous society, and that far more people are in a position to use such skills."[8]

For intellectuals, it seems to be particularly difficult to grasp both the subjective and relative character of monotony and the capacity of workers to inject meaning into "objectively meaningless" work. Their strong tendency to view workers as dissatisfied suggests the idea that the alienation thesis, though a direct descendant of Marxist theory and related to a particular political posture, also reflects an intellectual perspective (in the sociology of knowledge sense) on manual work.

Surprisingly enough, business executives also tend to view manual workers as alienated. Perhaps this attitude reflects, in part, the growing influence of intellectual ideas, including neo-Marxist ones, on the more progressive business circles; perhaps, more importantly, this stems again, as in the case of the intellectual, from the middle-class businessman's separation and distance from the workaday world of his industrial employees. At any rate, such industrial spokesmen as Peter Drucker and Alexander Heron are likely to generalize much as does James Worthy of Sears Roebuck, who, in discussing "overfunctionalization," has written:

> The worker cannot see that total process, he sees only the small and uninteresting part to which he and his fellows are assigned. In a real sense, the job loses its meaning for the worker — the meaning, that is, in all terms except the pay envelope.
>
> Thus a very large number of employees in American industry today have been deprived of the sense of performing interesting, significant work. In consequence, they have little feeling of responsibility for the tasks to which they are assigned.[1]

But, *work has significant positive meanings to persons who do not find overall satisfaction in their immediate job.* A still viable consequence of the Protestant ethic in our society is that its work ethic (the notion of work as a calling, an obligation to one's family, society, and self-respect, if no longer to God), retains a powerful hold. This is most dramatically seen in the reactions of the retired and unemployed. The idea is quite common to American workers at all occupational levels that soon after a worker retires, he is likely to either "drop dead" or "go crazy" from sheer inactivity.[2] An English industrial psychiatrist states that this is actually a common calamity in British industry.[3] Similarly, the studies made in the 1930's of unemployed people show that the disruption of the work relationship often leads to the disruption of normal family relations, to political apathy, and to a lack of interest in social organizations and leisure-time activities.[4]

The studies of job satisfaction reviewed in this paper further question the prevailing thesis that most workers in modern society are alienated and estranged. There is a remarkable consistency in the findings that the vast majority of workers, in virtually all occupations and industries, are moderately or highly satisfied, rather than dissatisfied, with their jobs.

However, the marked occupational differences in work attitudes and the great significance which workers impute to being, at least to some extent, masters of their destiny in the work process, along with the fact that surrender of such control seems to be the most important condition of strong dissatisfaction are findings at least as important as the overall one of general satisfaction. Perhaps the need for autonomy and independence may be a more deep-seated human motive than is recognized by those who characterize our society in terms of crowdlike conformity and the decline of individualism.

These findings also have clear implications for industrial engineering. If industry and society have an interest in workers' experiencing satisfaction and pride in their work, a major effort must be made to increase the areas of control which employees have over the work process, especially in those industries and occupations where control is at a minimum. Charles Walker, who has written perceptively of the automobile worker's lack of control, has advocated two major solutions for humanizing repetitive assembly line work:

[1] James C. Worthy, "Organizational Structure and Employee Morale," *American Sociological Review*, 15 (1950), p. 175. Cf. Peter Drucker, *Concept of the Corporation* (John Day Co., 1946), p. 179, and Heron, *op. cit.*

[2] Morse and Weiss, *op. cit.*, p. 192; Friedmann and Havighurst, *op. cit.*, pp. 89, 162, 36 ff. Eric Hoffer notes that death rates increased among older longshoremen when a retirement plan was put into effect. A convention of general practitioners recently advised against compulsory retirement on this basis. See *SF Chronicle*, October 7, 1958. That this may be more of a stereotyped notion than a fact is suggested by the directors of the Cornell Study of Occupational Retirement who found in a panel of more than 1,000 males of the same age that those who retired were more likely to *improve* in health, while those who remained working were more likely to decline in health. Wayne E. Thompson and Gordon F. Streib, "Situational Determinants: Health and Economic Deprivation in Retirement," *Journal of Social Issues*, XIV (1958), pp. 18–34.

[3] Brown, *op. cit.*, p. 190.

[4] See E. W. Blake, *Citizens Without Work* (New Haven: Yale University Press, 1940), and *The Unemployed Man* (New York: Dutton, 1934); M. Jahoda-Lazarsfeld and H. Zeisel, *Die Arbeitslosen von Marienthal* (Leipzig: Psychologische Monographien: 1933); Mirra Komarovsky, *The Unemployed Man and His Family* (New York: Dryden Press, 1940). Daniel Bell in considering the possibilities of automation has raised the question: "Work, said Freud, was the chief means of binding an individual to reality. What will happen, then, when not only the worker but work itself is displaced by the machine?" *Work and Its Discontents* (Boston: Beacon Press, 1956), p. 56.

---

early years of the twentieth century. *Industrial Society* (Glencoe: The Free Press, 1955), p. 200. Statistics of the American labor force show that the proportion of skilled workers has risen considerably since 1940 and is expected to continue rising; the proportion of unskilled laborers has been declining consistently since 1920. Semiskilled operatives, the largest manual category, increased the fastest until 1940. The increase since then has been negligible and it is expected that this group will decline in the future. *The most striking change in occupational composition, reflecting a general upgrading in skill, is the increase in the proportions of clerical and professional workers.* U. S. Department of Labor, Bureau of Labor Statistics, Bulletin 1215, *Occupational Outlook Handbook, 1957*, pp. 34–35.

job rotation and job enlargement. Where job rotation was introduced in one section of the automobile plant he studied, job satisfaction increased without loss of efficiency or production. The idea of recombining a number of jobs into one enlarged job seems especially to appeal to the line workers: as one man said, "I'd like to do a whole fender myself from the raw material to the finished product."[1] But such radical job enlargement would be a negation of the assembly line method of production. Therefore, we must anticipate the day when the utopian solution of eliminating assembly line production entirely will be the practical alternative for a society which is affluent and concerned at the same time that its members work with pride and human dignity.

Finally, the findings of this paper indicate a need for considerable further research on industrial statistics and industrial trends. If the evidence shows that extreme dissatisfaction is concentrated among assembly line workers, it becomes terribly important, for a total assessment of the conditions of work in modern America, to know what proportion of the labor force works on assembly lines or in other job contexts involving little control over their work activities. It is startling, considering the importance of such data, that such figures do not exist. This situation helps maintain the conventional belief that the mechanized assembly line worker is today's typical industrial worker in contrast to the craftsman of the past.

An indication that the actual proportion of assembly line workers is quite small is suggested by figures of the automobile industry, the conveyor belt industry par excellence. If we consider total employment in the industrial groupings involved in the manufacture, sales, repair, and servicing of automobiles, we find that assembly line workers make up less than 5 per cent of all workers in this complex. There are approximately 120,000 automobile workers who are line assemblers, yet the number of skilled repair mechanics in all branches of the industry, a job which in many ways resembles the craft ideal, exceeds 500,000. In addition, the 120,000 assemblers are outnumbered by 400,000 managers who own or operate gas stations, garages, new and used car lots, and wrecking yards, and by 200,000 *skilled* workers in automobile plants.[2] Recent developments, especially

automation, have served further to decrease the proportion of assembly line operatives in the industry.

If the situation in the automobile industry is at all typical, research might well show that those kinds of job contexts which are associated with high work satisfaction and control over one's time and destiny, such as skilled repair work and self-employment, are more representative than is commonly believed, and are even increasing over the long run. Such a prospect should bring considerable satisfaction to all those in the diverse intellectual traditions who have been concerned with what happens to human beings in the course of their major life activity, their work. And yet, this would not necessarily mean that the problem of the lack of fulfillment in work had become less serious. For as one industrial sociologist has suggested, this problem *may become more acute*, not because work itself has become more tedious, fractionated, and meaningless, but because the ideal of pride in creative effort is shared by an increasingly large proportion of the labor force as a result of the rise of democratic education and its emphasis on individualism and occupational mobility.[3]

Note on methodological problems in job satisfaction research

By far the most common technique employed in job satisfaction studies is the poll-type questionnaire in which workers are asked directly, "How satisfied are you with your occupation?" or, "Do you like your job?" These questions have a number of advantages. They are quite straightforward and, in general, are easily understood in a common-sense fashion. Research costs are relatively economical, and what may be the guiding consideration is that the data are quantifiable and easily expressed in a form which can both indicate the total distribution of work satisfaction and dissatisfaction in a given population, and can readily locate differences among workers according to occupation, industry, educational level, sex, etc.

However, such a direct questionnaire runs certain risks which are common to all opinion polls. The respondent may not want, or may not be able, to answer honestly. In this case we suggest a cultural bias toward indicating contentment; the meaning of the question may not always be the same to the worker as it is to the interviewer; and simply the manner in which the question is phrased or asked may favor one response rather than another. For example, it has been suggested that dichotomizing responses into only "satisfied" and "dissatisfied" categories has the effect of overestimating the actual degree of satisfaction by pushing those who are in a middle category toward the satisfied alternative.[4]

There are further problems which stem from the special character of work attitudes. There is a certain naivete in expecting frank and simple answers to job satisfaction questions in a society where one's work is so

[1] Walker and Guest, *op. cit.*, p. 154.

[2] The source for the estimate of 120,000 assembly line workers is a statement on page 426 of the U. S. Department of Labor's *Occupational Outlook Handbook, 1957*, which says that assembly line workers "in mid-1956 represented approximately 15 per cent of all the automobile workers." In this context all automobile workers refers to the 800,000 employed in manufacturing, 15 per cent of which is 120,000. The total employment in automobile manufacturing, automobile sales, automobile garage and repair shops, and gasoline service stations, according to 1950 census figures, is almost 2.5 million. This total was used as the base to compute the estimate of 5 per cent as the proportion of assembly line workers among all employees in the complex of automobile industries. The other figures are from the 1950 Census.

[3] Moore, *op. cit.*, p. 231.

[4] Herzberg, et al., *op. cit.*, p. 4.

important a part of one's self that to demean one's job is to question one's very competence as a person. In addition, even if a person could be as honest in reporting about his job satisfaction as in reporting the number of children in his family, this problem is as inherently vague and nebulous as the latter question is precise. While most empirical investigators in this field operate with a common-sense notion of satisfaction, a few writers have been aware of the problem of conceptualization. In the first full-length book on job satisfaction, Hoppock wrote in 1935:

> The problem is complicated by the ephemeral and variable nature of satisfaction. Indeed, there may be no such thing as *job* satisfaction independent of the other satisfactions in one's life. Family relationships, health, relative social status in the community, and a multitude of other factors may be just as important as the job itself in determining what we tentatively choose to call job satisfaction. A person may be satisfied with one aspect of his job and dissatisfied with another. Satisfactions may be rationalized, and the degree of satisfaction may vary from day to day. A person may never be wholly satisfied.[1]

Assuming that we are able to arrive at some kind of definition or delimitation of the concept, the problem then arises as to who is to judge a person's satisfaction in work. Are people really satisfied because they say they are satisfied: since Freud this question has become standard currency. If they are honest with the interviewer, can they be honest with themselves? And if people who say they are satisfied are actually so, is this not on a superficial level, a kind of normal adjustment to reality? What about the depth of satisfaction? How many people derive profound, creative fulfillment in work? And does not the existence of general satisfaction reflect a generally low level of

aspiration; an adaptation to what Marx called an *animal*, rather than a *human*, level of living?[2]

The above considerations suggest the extent to which the study and analysis of work satisfaction is fraught with problems not only of conceptualization, but of differences in ideals and value premises. At the heart of the question is the philosophic controversy between those who uphold an objective, and those who advocate a subjective theory of values. For the latter, people are satisfied in work if they truly feel themselves satisfied. The former approach, however, organizes a set of objective standards of behavior which individuals must meet. True fulfillment involves meeting the standards of the observer (an intellectual), rather than the standards of the individuals themselves. This is the characteristic approach of the critics of mass culture who do not find reassurance in the fact that most viewers today actually like the movies and television fare.

Although the above discussion indicates the enormous difficulties involved in getting a fair estimate of the absolute level of job satisfaction, we can speak with far greater assurance about relative levels of satisfaction experienced by members of different occupational groups. It is difficult to interpret a finding that 70 per cent of factory workers report satisfaction with their jobs because we do not know how valid and reliable our measuring instrument is. But when 90 per cent of printers compared to only 40 per cent of automobile workers report satisfaction, the relative difference remains meaningful. For this reason, the present paper has concentrated on interpreting differences in work satisfaction among people in different occupations and work settings, rather than attempting to assess absolute levels of job attitudes.

[1] Hoppock, *Job Satisfaction* (New York: Harper, 1935), p. 5.
[2] See K. Marx, "On Alienated Labor," translated by Johnson, et al. (dittoed). This is the position of Fred Blum, *Toward a Democratic Work Process*.

The Value Systems of Different Classes

A SOCIAL PSYCHOLOGICAL CONTRIBUTION TO THE ANALYSIS OF STRATIFICATION

Herbert H. Hyman

Introduction

THE EXISTENCE of stratification in American society is well known. The corollary fact — that individuals from lower strata are not likely to climb far up the economic ladder is also known. However, what requires additional analysis are the factors that account for this lack of mobility. Many of these factors of an objective nature have been studied. Opportunity in the society is differential; higher education or specialized training, which might provide access to a high position, must be bought with money — the very commodity which the lower classes lack. Such objective factors help maintain the existing structure. But there are other factors of a more subtle psychological nature which have not been illuminated and which may also work to perpetuate the existing order. It is our assumption that an intervening variable mediating the relationship between low position and lack of upward mobility is a system of beliefs and values within the lower classes which in turn reduces the very *voluntary* actions which would ameliorate their low position.

The components of this value system, in our judgment, involve less emphasis upon the traditional high success goals, increased awareness of the lack of opportunity to achieve success, and less emphasis upon the achievement of goals which in turn would be instrumental for success. To put it simply the lower class individual doesn't want as much success, knows he couldn't get it even if he wanted to, and doesn't want what might help him get success. Of course, an individual's value system is only one among many factors on which his position in the social hierarchy depends. Some of these factors may be external and arbitrary, quite beyond the control of even a highly motivated

individual. However, within the bounds of the freedom available to individuals, this value system would create a *self-imposed* barrier to an improved position.

Presumably this value system arises out of a realistic appraisal of reality and in turn softens for the individual the impact of low status. Unfortunately, we have at the moment little information on its genesis. However, we aim to document in this paper the presence of these values as a contemporary factor to be considered in discussions of the larger problems of stratification and mobility.

There are implications in such an analysis that go far beyond the specific problem of understanding the lack of upward mobility. The study of the psychological correlates of the objective class structure is in itself a problem to which social psychologists have and continue to address themselves for its relevance to the larger theoretical problem of attitude formation. And the study of values specific to the economic realm contributes much to the social psychological analysis of adjustment and deviant behavior. Thus in Merton's influential paper, *Social Structure and Anomie*, deviant behavior is analyzed as a phenomenon concentrated in certain strata and emerging out of strains that differentially burden those lower in the social structure.[1] For example, one type of deviance is hypothesized as resulting from the frustration of the lower class individual's desire to achieve the cultural goal of economic success because the access to the means for such success is less available to him. "This syndrome of lofty aspirations and limited realistic opportunities . . . is precisely the pattern which invites deviant behavior." (p. 148). It is clear that Merton's analysis assumes that the cultural goal of success is in actuality internalized by lower class individuals. Perhaps it also requires that the lower class individual *recognize* that the means to success are not available to him. It is certainly true *at a given point in time* that an individual frustrated in his goal because

---

[1] R. K. Merton, Social Structure and Anomie, reprinted as Chapter IV, *Social Theory and Social Structure*, Glencoe, The Free Press, 1949.

The National Opinion Research Center, University of Chicago, kindly provided unpublished survey materials herein used. A grant-in-aid from the Behavioral Science Division of the Ford Foundation defrayed part of the analytic costs. This is an original article prepared for the first edition of *Class, Status and Power*.

488

access to means is not open to him, will experience the incident as frustrating *whether or not he realizes* that the means are beyond his grasp. But it seems also true in the larger time perspective that if he continues to think that the means for a *future* success are available to him that the frustration will be milder and that deviance might not occur.[1] Conversely, if the individual regarded his chances to achieve his goal of success as negligible, when in reality they were good, there would be a psychologically produced strain toward deviance.

What is obviously required is empirical evidence on the degree to which individuals in different strata value the culturally prescribed goal of success, believe that opportunity is available to them, and hold other values which would aid or hinder them in their attempts to move towards their goal. This paper, in a preliminary way, is thus complementary to Merton's theoretical analysis.

While there is considerable literature on the beliefs and attitudes of the different economic classes, the specific realm that concerns us seems to have been generally neglected. Kornhauser's early writings come close to our problem and we shall allude to his findings in considerable detail. While Centers gives considerable attention to such values, he concentrates much more on the problem of the politico-economic ideology of individuals in different positions in the class structure. These studies provide the only quantitative evidence predicated on representative samples of large universes. Knupfer's study, while concerned with the problem and guided by the explicit hypothesis that there are "psychological restrictions which reinforce the economic," is essentially a characterology of the lower class individual describing in qualitative terms a diversity of attitudes, behaviors, and values. Similarly, Davis, Gardner and Gardner give some evidence on the way in which the class structure is experienced by individuals in different objective positions, but the reports are qualitative and literary in character. A number of quantitative studies are relevant but are limited in scope to specialized samples. Chinoy's study deals directly with our problem but is confined to a homogeneous group of 62 industrial workers in one automobile plant. Similarly, Hollingshead provides information on one aspect of the problem, the occupational goals of youth in different classes, but the study is limited to one community of about 6000 people in the Middle West. Form presents data on occupational and educational aspirations for contrasted groups of white collar and manual workers living in the relatively homogeneous planned community of Greenbelt, Maryland. Galler also presents information on the occupational goals of children in two contrasted classes for a sample limited to Chicago.[2]

A variety of other psychological concomitants of objective class position have been explored. The political ideology of the different classes is a classic realm for research by social scientists. Aesthetic values such as tastes and preferences have been mapped for the

different classes by communication research specialists. Attitudes towards child rearing in the different classes have been studied by Allison Davis and Erickson.[3]

In seeking additional information in the realm of values, we shall avail ourselves of the accumulated findings of public opinion surveys, and use a procedure of secondary analysis. It is our belief that public opinion surveys have much rich information on many social science problems, such information often being an accidental by-product of the continuing inquiry into the characteristics of the public which opinion polls have been conducting for the past 15 years. While these inquiries often deal with applied problems of a transitory and insignificant character, from the great mass of data available much can be extracted by reanalysis which bears on problems of fundamental theoretical interest. We shall limit this analysis to the United States, but it should be noted that surveys parallel in content have been conducted in other countries, for example, Germany and England. Ultimately the analyses of these studies would permit us to examine the psychological variations between the classes as a function of the larger societal setting.

Most such inquiries also have the usual advantage of being conducted on the basis of scientific sampling of the national population, and therefore permit more precise and generalized inferences than is usually the case in academic research. By contrast, Erickson's analysis of class and child rearing practices was based on

---

[1] Farber has demonstrated that the experience of suffering as a consequence of some objective frustration is dependent on the time perspective of the individual. See M. L. Farber, Suffering and Time Perspective of the Prisoner. *Univ. Iowa Stud. Child Welf.*, 1944, 20, 155–227.

[2] See, Arthur W. Kornhauser, Analysis of "Class Structure" of Contemporary American Society — Psychological Bases of Class Divisions, in *Industrial Conflict*, G. W. Hartmann and T. Newcomb (ed.), New York: Dryden Press, 1939; A. Davis, B. B. Gardner and M. Gardner, *Deep South, A Social Anthropological Study of Caste and Class*, Chicago: U. of Chicago Press, 1941; Centers, R., *The Psychology of Social Classes*, Princeton: Princeton Univ. Press, 1949, see especially Chap. IX for a treatment of other values; also see his paper Motivational Aspects of Occupational Stratification, *J. Soc. Psychol.*, 28, 1948, pp. 196–197; Knupfer, G., Portrait of the Underdog, *Publ. Opin. Quart.*, 11, 1947, 103–114; E. Chinoy, The Tradition of Opportunity and the Aspirations of Automobile Workers, *Amer. J. Sociol.*, LVII, 1952, 453–459; A. B. Hollingshead, *Elmtown's Youth*, New York: Wiley, 1949; Wm. H. Form, Toward an Occupational Social Psychology, *J. Soc. Psychol.*, 1946, 24, 85–99; E. H. Galler, Influence of Social Class on Children's Choices of Occupations, *Elem. School J.*, LI, 1951, 439–445.

[3] For summaries of literature on attitudes as related to objective class position the reader is referred to H. Hyman, The Psychology of Status, *Arch. Psychol.*, No. 269, 1942, especially Chapter VI; for summaries of aesthetic values as related to class factors the reader is referred to J. T. Klapper, *The Effects of Mass Media*, Columbia University, Bureau of Applied Social Research, 1950 (mimeo); for studies in the child-rearing realm see, Erickson, M. C., Social Status and Child-rearing Practices, in T. Newcomb, and E. L. Hartley, *Readings in Social Psychology*, New York: Holt, 1947; Allison Davis, *Social-class Influences Upon Learning*, Cambridge: Harvard Univ. Press, 1951.

100 families in the Chicago area and the major study by Havighurst and Davis on differences in child-rearing was based on 100 white and 100 Negro families living in Chicago.[1]

Such studies while pioneering in character were limited in size by lack of resources. We are suggesting that even with minimal resources, academicians can fall heir to massive data collected at considerable expense for other purposes, and achieve greater generality in their findings.

Limitations are present, of course. The area of inquiry that interests us may have been touched only tangentially in the original survey, and possibilities for analysis may be scanty. Particularly, where the published account of the survey has to be used rather than the original data, the re-analysis is gravely limited. However, what we sacrifice in these respects is compensated for by the efficiency of the procedure and the great gain in generality. The sections to follow seek to demonstrate that secondary analyses are worthwhile, and that implicit in many surveys are data of great theoretical significance.[2]

Achievement in any realm is dependent upon two factors; the possession of both the necessary ability and the motivation to reach the goal. Ability is of course limited by *socially imposed* barriers to training and lack of channels to given types of positions. However, ability may also be retarded by lack of individual striving to obtain whatever training in turn is instrumental to economic advancement.

Consequently if we find that both motivation to advance to high positions and to obtain the training which is instrumental in achieving such positions are

[1] Ibid.

[2] The basic source for such analyses is now available in H. Cantril and M. Strunk, *Public Opinion*, 1935–1946, Princeton Press.

[3] For a summary report of this survey, the reader is referred to "*Opinion News*", Sept. 1, 1947, National Opinion Research Center, University of Chicago. The survey was conducted in conjunction with Ohio State University; Profs. Hatt and North representing that institution and Don Cahalan of the Center acting as Study Director.

[4] The numbers do not add to the total sample because farm respondents and certain other groups are excluded from the rental question.

[5] On the basis of a variety of studies, Havighurst and Rodgers confirm these findings. They remark "the motivational reasons for not going to college may be summarized as follows: Practically all of the superior youths who do not continue their education beyond high school are children of people who have had less than a high school education. These families participate in a culture which has little personal contact with higher education. They value a job and an earning career highly for their young people. . . . While these people have come to look favorably on a high school education for their children they do not regard colleges really within the reach of their aspirations or their financial means." Havighurst and Rodgers do, however, point to the interesting phenomenon of the deviant case, and note that a substantial *minority* of the working class do view higher education for their children in favorable terms. They attribute this to exposure to "upper middle class culture." See, *Who Should Go to College*, Columbia University Press, 1952, p. 162.

reduced in the lower class individual we shall have established our hypothesis. The same formula as applies to achievement, with minor modification, is relevant to Merton's theory. We need evidence here on the acceptance of success goals and on the belief in the accessibility of such goals.

THE VALUE PLACED ON FORMAL EDUCATION

Part of the ideology of American life is that important positions are not simply inherited by virtue of the wealth of one's parents, but can be achieved. Such achievement, however, requires for many types of important positions considerable formal education. One cannot, for example, become a physician or a lawyer or an engineer without advanced education. Consequently, insofar as the lower classes placed less value on higher education, this would constitute an aspect of a larger value system which would work detrimental to their advancement. That such is really the case is evidenced in data collected by the National Opinion Research Center in a nationwide survey in 1947.[3] Within the total sample of approximately 2500 adults and 500 youths about half indicated that they regarded "some college training" as their answer to the question: "About how much schooling do you think most young men need these days to get along well in the world?" That this value is not equally shared by the lower groups is clear from the data presented in Table 1 below where the value is distributed by various stratification measures.

TABLE 1. *The Differential Emphasis among Economic Classes upon College Education as an Essential to Advancement*

Interviewer's rating of economic level	Per cent recommending college education	N
Wealthy and prosperous	68	512
Middle class	52	1531
Lower class	39	856
Occupation		
Professional	74	301
Businessmen and proprietors	62	421
White collar workers	65	457
Skilled labor	53	392
Semiskilled	49	416
Domestic and personal service workers	42	194
Farmers	47	417
Non-farm laborers	35	132
Highest education achieved		
Attended college	72	564
Attended high school	55	1411
Attended grammar school	36	926
Among renters, monthly rental		
Above $60	70	327[4]
$40–60	64	666
$20–40	54	990
Below $20	37	403

It is clear that whatever measure of stratification is employed the lower groups emphasize college training much less.[5] Insofar as such training is one avenue to upward movement, this value would operate to maintain the present system.

These data emphasize the difference in the belief in the value of higher education. A related finding is available from a survey done by Roper in 1945 in which a more direct question was put to adults on their desire for their own children to go on to college. The exact question and the data are presented in Table 2.

TABLE 2. *Preference for a College Education for the Children of the Different Classes*

"After the war, if you had a son (daughter) graduating from high school would you prefer that he (she) go on to college, or would you rather have him (her) do something else, or wouldn't you care one way or the other?"

	Per cent preferring college[1]
Prosperous	91
Upper middle	91
Lower middle	83
Poor	68

In terms of the perpetuation of the present system of stratification, however, these values as measured among adults only take on relevance insofar as they would be passed on to the children.[2] As a possible contribution to a more precise treatment of the consequences of this adult value we present in Table 3, the same datum for groups varying in age and sex. Thus, if one were to hypothesize that American mothers are more important in the indoctrination of children than fathers, and that this value becomes crucial among those who would have children of college age, one could determine from the table below whether this reduced emphasis on college education impinges at the most crucial points in the developmental process. Incidental to this analysis, one can note whether or not the major finding of a differential value system by class continues to be demonstrated even when one controls factors of age and sex simultaneously.

It is clear that even when factors of age and sex composition are controlled the differential emphasis upon education persists. There is a suggestion that women, presumably the more significant group in the rearing of children than men, are more likely to vary in their values as their class position changes. While women thus appear to be more conscious of their class, it can also be noted that women emphasize the value of education more than their male counterparts *for every age and class* group in the table, i.e., women in general place greater premium on formal education. Such phenomena of sex differences *per se* can also be observed in other findings yet to be presented. Parenthetically, it might be noted in the data of both Tables 1 and 3 that the middle class groups approximate closer to the value system of the prosperous, rather than being a kind of halfway group between lower and upper.

While we cannot clearly establish any major differences within the family structure of the different classes with respect to the distribution of this value, it is clear from additional data that the children of the different classes show value systems parallel to their parents.[3] In this survey, a sample of youths between the ages of 14 and 20 were studied in addition to the regular sample of the adult population. Table 4 presents the distribution of this value for youths of the different classes. The data are presented separately for males and

TABLE 3. *The Emphasis upon the Need for College Education as Related to the Sex and Age Composition of the Classes*

	Per cent recommending college education	N
Males over 40		
Wealthy and prosperous[4]	58	147
Middle class	47	312
Lower class	29	202
Difference between wealthy and poor +29%[5]		
Females over 40		
Wealthy and prosperous	73	139
Middle class	63	330
Lower class	41	189
Difference between wealthy and poor +32%		
Males between 21-39 years of age		
Wealthy and prosperous	56	66
Middle class	54	334
Lower class	35	143
Difference between wealthy and poor +21%		
Females between 21-39 years of age		
Wealthy and prosperous	79	78
Middle class	64	327
Lower class	43	187
Difference between wealthy and poor +36%		

[1] Taken from Cantril, *op. cit.*, p. 186. The number of cases in the different classes is unfortunately not given. The measure of stratification is presumably an interviewer's rating of standard of living. A parallel question asked by the Fortune Poll in 1949 yielded essentially similar differences by class. See *Publ. Opin. Quart.*, 13, 1949, pp. 714-715. Confirmatory data are also available in Centers, Motivational Aspects, *op. cit.*, p. 202.

[2] Merton similarly calls attention to the role of parents as central to his analysis: *op. cit.*, p. 148.

[3] A variety of measures of objective class could be used in this and subsequent tables. The interviewer's rating of economic level will be used wherever possible since it is the most efficient for our purposes. However, the correlations among all these different indices are high so that the particular index chosen makes little difference. Thus the relation between interviewer's rating and monthly rental as expressed by a contingency coefficient is .74 and between the rating and education is .55.

[4] Plus sign will be used to denote the fact that the difference is in the direction of greater endorsement of the value by the upper class.

[5] In a national survey of high school youth conducted in 1942 by Elmo Roper, all students were asked "what do you expect to do when you finish high school?" "Continuing with education is the first choice of every occupational group, including the children of laboring and farming families." However, Roper reports that this choice "is . . . outranked by the idea of going to work among the poor and the Negroes." Thus, not only is there a difference in the value attached to education among the different classes, there is also a difference in the expectation or aspiration for higher education among the different classes. See *Fortune*, XXVI, No. 6, 1942, p. 9.

females. In addition to demonstrating the persistence of the difference when sex is controlled, this breakdown would permit us again to examine whether the differential value of the classes is most prominent in the very place in the social structure where it would have greatest significance. Insofar as male youth are the major future participants in economic life, the difference between upper and lower groups would have most social consequences if it were greater in males. It is interesting to note that the youth of both sexes and all classes are closer in their values to adult women than to adult men. This can be noted by comparing Tables 3 and 4 and it is suggestive of the greater influence of mothers in the transmission of values.

TABLE 4. *The Differential Emphasis upon the Need for College Education among Youths of the Different Classes*

	Per cent recommending college education	N
Males between 14-20		
Wealthy and prosperous families	74	39
Middle class	63	100
Lower class	42	62
Difference between wealthy and lower classes +32%		
Females between 14-20		
Wealthy and prosperous families	85	45
Middle class	71	128
Lower class	49	73
Difference between wealthy and lower classes +36%		

MOTIVATION TO ADVANCE IN THE ECONOMIC STRUCTURE

Achievement in any realm is as previously noted a function of motivation. Of course, *motivation* is only one of the factors leading toward success; the other being *ability* to succeed which would be dependent on degree of competence or training or barriers imposed on those of lowly position. Given the strongest motivation, a man might still be incapable of advancement if other factors reduced his ability to advance. A variety of data suggest that the lower class individual holds values of such a nature as to reduce his striving towards those ends which would result in his moving up the class structure.

In the same study where values with respect to higher education were ascertained, the respondents were asked a question which provided evidence on the

[1] Similar findings are reported by Centers. When his samples were shown a card and asked which kind of job they would choose, if they had the choice, the middle class emphasized "self-expression" and the working class emphasized "security" as the basis for choice. *Op. cit.*, pp. 151–158.

[2] In a comparison of children between the ages of 10–14 from a "lower class school" with children from an "upper middle class school" in Chicago, Galler obtained parallel findings. The reasons the lower class children gave for their choice of an occupation emphasized extrinsic rewards whereas the upper class children emphasized interest of the job, *op. cit.*

desiderata the different classes considered in choosing an occupation. The findings show that lower class individuals emphasize those factors which would lead them to strive for careers which would be less high in the economic structure. The sample was asked, "what do you think is the most important *single* thing for a young man to consider when he is choosing his life's work?" The major considerations fell into two groups, 49% of the total sample answering in terms of the congeniality of the career pattern to the individual's personality, interests, and individual qualifications, and 32% answering in terms of direct economic considerations such as security, wages or subsidiary economic benefits, the steadiness of employment, etc. It can be clearly shown that the lower classes emphasize the latter desiderata, and the upper classes the more personal aspects of the work.[1] It is our belief that this difference in what would be sought in a career would lead the lower class individuals into occupations that would be less likely to enhance their position. Such desiderata will be achieved in a "good job" but not in such positions as managerial or professional jobs. These latter careers have greater elements of risk and are the very ones that would not mesh with the desire for stability, security and immediate economic benefits, but would mesh with the goal of congeniality to the individual's interests. Admittedly, this is only inferential but it will be clear from related questions to be presented shortly that interpreting these respective orientations in the above terms is warranted. The data for adults of the different classes, separated by age and sex, are presented in Table 5 on page 493.

It can be noted that the influence of class position on the desiderata mentioned declines with age. This might appear paradoxical, in that one would expect the younger poor still to have their illusions whereas the older individuals among the poor would have confronted reality longer and any illusions they might have would have been dissipated. Therefore, one might expect among the old a greater difference among the classes. However, what seems to be the case is that with age *all* individuals regardless of class give greater emphasis to such factors as stability and security, and therefore the differences while sizeable are somewhat reduced.

Findings of a parallel nature are found for the sample of youth. The data are presented in Table 6.[2]

We have some confirmatory data on the desiderata in choice of an occupation from surveys conducted by Roper. In 1942 a national sample of high school students were asked to express their preference for one of three types of jobs: a low income but secure job, a job with good pay but with a 50–50 risk of losing it, or a job with extremely high income and great risk. Data are presented for the different classes in Table 7 on page 493.

The poor youth cannot accept the risk involved in becoming less poor. Similar data are available for adults from surveys conducted by Roper. In 1947, in answer

TABLE 5. *The Desiderata in Choosing an Occupation as Related to Class Position*

	PER CENT MENTION-ING THE FACTOR OF		Ratio of con-geniality to economic answers	N
	Congeniality to person	Economic benefit		
Males between 21-39				
Wealthy or prosperous	72	17	4.2	66
Middle class	55	20	2.7	334
Lower class	37	32	1.2	143
Difference between upper and lower classes	+35%	−15%		
Females between 21-39				
Wealthy or prosperous	72	7	10.0	78
Middle class	53	24	2.2	327
Lower class	37	30	1.2	187
Difference between upper and lower classes	+35%	−23%		
Males over 40				
Wealthy or prosperous	58	22	2.7	147
Middle class	49	21	2.3	312
Lower class	32	31	1.0	202
Difference between upper and lower classes	+26%	−9%		
Females over 40				
Wealthy or prosperous	51	14	4.3	137
Middle class	48	19	2.5	330
Lower class	32	33	1.0	189
Difference between upper and lower classes	+29%	−19%		

TABLE 6. *The Desiderata in Choosing an Occupation among Youth of the Different Classes*

	PER CENT MENTION-ING THE FACTOR OF		Ratio of con-geniality to economic answers	N
	Congeniality to person	Economic benefit		
Males between 14-20				
Wealthy or prosperous	61	15	4.1	39
Middle class	57	17	3.4	100
Lower class	42	29	1.4	62
Difference between upper and lower classes	+19%	−14%		
Females between 14-20				
Wealthy or prosperous	60	14	4.3	45
Middle class	55	19	2.9	128
Lower class	45	27	1.7	73
Difference between upper and lower classes	+15%	−13%		

TABLE 7. *Type of Occupation Chosen by Youth of the Different Classes[1]*

Among high school youth	Per cent preferring job that offers all-or-nothing opulence
Poor	14
Prosperous, upper middle	29
From laboring parents	16
From executive and professional parents	31

to the identical question, one obtains a similar pattern by class. Thus, for example, a low income but secure job is chosen by 60% of factory workers but only by 26% of professional and executive persons. In 1949,

a question presenting a similar choice situation between a secure job and a risky but promising career in one's own business yielded parallel results.[2]

TABLE 8. *Types of Occupations Recommended by the Different Classes*

	PER CENT RECOMMENDING		
	Professional occupation	Skilled manual work	N
Males between 21-39			
Wealthy and prosperous	45	5	66
Middle class	49	13	334
Lower class	38	22	143
Difference between wealthy and poor	+7%	−17%	
Females between 21-39			
Wealthy and prosperous	51	3	78
Middle class	55	7	327
Lower class	44	17	187
Difference between wealthy and poor	+7%	−14%	
Males over 40			
Wealthy and prosperous	49	9	147
Middle class	43	20	312
Lower class	27	22	202
Difference between wealthy and poor	+22%	−13%	
Females over 40			
Wealthy and prosperous	54	3	139
Middle class	49	13	330
Lower class	32	15	189
Difference between wealthy and poor	+22%	−12%	

The inference that the desideratum of economic benefit rather than congeniality of work would lead the lower class individual to prefer occupations which are lower in the hierarchy can be supported by other data from a more direct question in this same NORC survey.[3] The respondents were asked: "Suppose some outstanding young man asked your advice on what

[1] The youth data are from *Fortune, op. cit.* Unfortunately the number of cases in the different groups is not given. In 1948, the Fortune Poll repeated an almost identical question of a sample of youths aged 18–25. The stratification measure available in the published report was formal-education which correlates highly with other measures. The all-or-nothing opulent job was chosen by 33% of the college educated but only by 11% of those with grade school education. See *Publ. Opin. Quart.* 13, 1949, p. 168.

[2] *Fortune*, 1947, p. 10; *Publ. Opin. Quart.* 14, 1950, p. 182.

[3] In a study by Lipset and Bendix based on a probability sample of 1000 cases representing the city of Oakland, exclusive of highest and lowest socio-economic segments, somewhat contradictory data are reported. They note that a considerable majority of manual workers have had aspirations to own their own businesses, and that a sizeable minority have actually attempted such a career. Moreover, differences between various grades of manual workers are negligible. These data certainly do not conform to our picture of reduced aspirations among the lower groups, and increased emphasis upon desiderata such as security. However, apart from the restriction of the findings to the city of Oakland, it should also be noted, as the authors point out, that they are based on a somewhat truncated economic distribution. S. M. Lipset and R. Bendix, "Social Mobility and Occupational Career Patterns, II, Social Mobility," *Amer. J. Sociol.,* LVII, 1952, pp. 494–504. By contrast Centers found sizeable differences between various grades of workers with respect to the hope or expectation of owning one's own business. See "Motivational Aspects," *op. cit.,* pp. 199–201.

would be one of the best occupations to aim toward. What *one* occupation do you think you would advise him to aim toward?" Partial data for the different classes are presented in Table 8 above, where it can be noted that the upper classes are more likely to stress professional careers whereas the lower groups emphasize skilled manual occupations.

Parallel data are presented for youths of the different classes in Table 9 below.

TABLE 9. *Types of Occupations Recommended by Youth of the Different Classes*

	PER CENT RECOMMENDING		
	Professional occupation	Skilled manual work	N
Males between 14-20			
Wealthy or prosperous	76	5	39
Middle class	52	6	100
Lower class	21	27	62
Difference between wealthy and poor	+55%	−22%	
Females between 14-20			
Wealthy or prosperous	81	4	45
Middle class	64	5	128
Lower class	42	18	73
Difference between wealthy and poor	+39%	−14%	

That the occupational goals of the lower classes are limited is evidenced by other data in the area of personal income aspirations. In a number of different surveys, respondents have been asked to indicate the level of future income they would like to have, or expect to be earning. The exact question varies from survey to survey in terms of the time perspective involved and the level of reality emphasized. Correspondingly the measure obtained is expressive variously of an aspiration that is geared either to realistic expectations or to rather wild hopes and remote strivings. In general, these data show for the lower class a pattern of more limited expectations and/or strivings.[1] Thus, in 1942 in Roper's national survey of youth, the question was put: "How much a week do you think you should be earning about ten years from now?" The average for the entire sample was $49.81 but the children of the prosperous and middle classes gave a figure of $58.94, whereas the

children of the poor gave an average estimate of $40.26.[2]

Centers and Cantril report in 1946 on a survey conducted with a national sample of about 1200 adults. The question that was asked was: "About how much more money than that (the current income) do you think your family would need to have the things that might make your family happier or more comfortable than it is now?" As one goes up in the economic ladder, the increment of income desired decreases.

Relatively speaking the wealthier need and want less of an increase.[3] However, in terms of *absolute aspiration* level, the situation is quite different. The poor do not aspire to achieve the same dollar level as the wealthier. Thus, the absolute increase in dollars among those with a current income of less than $20 is only $16.20 on the average, whereas for those with a weekly income between $60 and $100, the absolute increase wanted is $41.60. As Centers and Cantril remark, "Individuals in the lowest income group do want a great deal more than they are now getting, but, in comparison to the sums wanted by those above them, theirs is a modest want indeed. An individual's present earnings obviously provide him with a frame of reference by means of which he sets his aspirations and judges his needs."[4]

Similar data are available from a study involving the sampling of male college students conducted by NORC in 1947.

The students were asked the weekly income they expected to be earning five years out of college. Among those students who come from families where the father is in a professional or managerial occupation, the median expectation was $119 a week whereas among those students whose fathers are in semi-skilled or skilled jobs the median figure was $103. Thus the aspirations vary with the class origins of the student. However, this particular study bears on certain interesting subtle aspects of reference group processes. The very fact that some children from lower class families entered college implies that they deviated in their behavior from the modal pattern of this class. A similar interpretation is made of this phenomenon of lower class college attendance by Havighurst and Rogers and was alluded to earlier. Consequently, one might expect such individuals to show the lower class motivational pattern but in an attenuated form. That it is somewhat attenuated is suggested by the fact that the difference between the students of different classes is not as striking in magnitude as the differences we have just reported from other studies. In an early study by Gould there is some evidence of an even more extreme form of deviant value system among lower class college students.[5] In an experimental study of levels of aspirations among 81 male college students, two groups contrasted with respect to the size of their discrepancy score on six experimental tasks were studied. The group whose aspiration far exceeded their achievement were of predominantly *lower* class backgrounds and from minority ethnic groups. This appears to contradict our

---

[1] Hollingshead presents similar findings for Elmtown. Each youth "was asked to name the occupation he would like to follow when he reached maturity." As one goes down in the class structure, the per cent choosing a profession or business declines from 77% to 7% and indecision or lower occupational choices increases. *Op. cit.*, p. 286. Galler presents similar findings for her youth group in Chicago, *op. cit.*

[2] *Fortune*, 1942, *op. cit.*

[3] Merton remarks on a study conducted by H. F. Clark which appears to contradict the Centers-Cantril finding. He states that Clark indicates a constant increment of 25% for each income level. However, it is not clear on what kind of sample or research procedure these data are based. *Op. cit.*

[4] R. Centers and H. Cantril, "Income Satisfaction and Income Aspiration," *J. Abnorm. Soc. Psychol.*, 41, 1946, pp. 64–69.

[5] See R. Gould, "Some Sociological Determinants of Goal Strivings," *J. Soc. Psychol.*, 1941, 13, pp. 461–473.

findings that lower class individuals set their goals lower than upper class groups. However, the apparent contradiction may imply the very interesting fact — that among those lower class individuals who do orient themselves to upper class patterns, i.e., enter college, their goal striving can be even more extreme.

In the NORC study of college students, one other datum suggests the attenuation of the expected pattern in the lower class college student. The students indicated those items within a list which were the three major desiderata in their choosing a job. It can be noted that this question corresponds very closely to the question previously analyzed in Table 5 for a national sample of adults. If we analyze these answers in terms of the differential emphasis upon factors of "economic benefit" vs. factors of "congeniality" for the different classes the differences by occupation of father are generally in the expected direction, but are of much smaller magnitude than those previously reported. They are presented in Table 10.

TABLE 10. *The Desiderata in Choosing an Occupation among College Students of Different Class Origins*

Per cent mentioning desideratum of:[1]	PER CENT AMONG STUDENTS WHOSE FATHERS ARE	
	Professional or managerial	Skilled or semi-skilled
Adventure — excitement	7	8
Being one's own boss	27	18
Congenial atmosphere	31	23
Intellectual challenge	55	42
Advancement	50	55
Money	26	30
Security	58	58
N =	301	106

BELIEFS IN OPPORTUNITY

This pattern of reduced personal aspirations and reduced appeal or valence of given occupations among the lower classes seems to derive from the perception of reality that the lower classes have. The goals of *all* individuals are governed to some extent by the appraisal of reality. Since a variety of data indicate that the poor are more aware of their lack of opportunity, presumably they would set their goals in the light of such beliefs.[2] In a national survey in 1947 by Roper, a series of questions dramatically demonstrate the difference in the beliefs of the lower classes about opportunity. The data are presented in Table 11.

A parallel finding is available from 1937 when Roper asked a national sample of adults the question: "Do you think that today any young man with thrift, ability, and ambition has the opportunity to rise in the world, own his own home, and earn $5000 a year?" Among the prosperous 53% indicated categorically that such an aspiration was realistic, whereas among the poor only 31% indicated their belief in this possibility.

TABLE 11. *Beliefs In Economic Opportunity Among the Different Classes[3]*

	AMONG EMPLOYEES WHO ARE	
	Professional or executives	Factory workers
Per cent believing that years ahead hold good chance for advancement over present position[4]	63	48
Per cent believing that following factor is important consideration in job advancement:[5]		
Quality of work	64	43
Energy and willingness	56	42
Getting along well with boss	12	19
Friend or relative of boss	3	8
Being a politician	6	4
Per cent believing that harder work would net them personally a promotion	58	40

Evidence from a variety of psychological studies sheds further light on the way in which the person's own expectations and striving for a goal are affected by his social position. These are all based on the analysis of

[1] The per cents add to much more than 100% since each respondent was asked to name the *three* most important desiderata.

[2] Chinoy makes the same general point on the basis of his study of automobile workers. "The aspirations of the automobile workers . . . represent a constant balancing of hope and desire against the objective circumstances in which they find themselves. . . . By and large they confine their aims to those limited alternatives which seem possible for men with their skills and resources." *Op. cit.*, p. 454. The statistical data in support of this conclusion are that: only 8 out of his 62 subjects felt they had a promising future outside of the factory; only five felt they had any real hope of becoming foremen within the factory; only 3 of the semi-skilled group felt it might be possible to move up to skilled levels. The remaining 46 subjects could see little in the way of opportunity and hence reduced their goals. However, Kornhauser in his original analysis of class differences in attitudes and values disagrees with our interpretation. He remarks that people at the lower income levels "cling devotedly to the American belief in individual opportunity." He predicates this interpretation on a number of questions asked in his survey of attitudes in Chicago in which differences were small between income groups, and in which the majority of the lowest group endorsed the view that they and their children can get ahead. Yet, in certain other questions he asked in the realm of satisfaction with the opportunities for their children and satisfaction with their own life chances, differences between income groups were large and in the direction of our hypothesis. Admittedly, the wide variety of data that exists, some of it contradictory, permits of some qualification of the conclusions we have drawn. See A. W. Kornhauser, *op. cit.*, pp. 241–242.

[3] *Fortune*, 1947. Unfortunately the size of the different groups is not reported. For the exact questions asked, the reader is referred to the original table.

[4] The identical question asked seven years before shows approximately the same pattern of findings for the different classes. See Cantril, *op. cit.*, p. 830. Parallel findings are reported by Centers. See "Motivational Aspects," *op. cit.*, pp. 196–197.

[5] Chinoy confirms this general picture in his study of automobile workers. His subjects stressed as criteria for achieving promotion such considerations as "pull," "connections," and various personal techniques for gaining favor. *Op. cit.*, p. 455. In 1948 the Fortune Poll queried a sample of youth aged 18–25 with a similar question and obtained parallel results by class.

[*footnote continued on p. 496*

levels of aspiration with respect to experimental tasks.[1] Although these tasks do not have a direct relevance to behavior in the economic sphere and constitute mere analogies, the analysis of the process of setting of goals may contribute much to our problem.

In one experimental level of aspiration study, there is a graphic demonstration of the way in which the socially defined opportunity of a group affects specific aspirations, and specific responses to past success. Adams matched groups of white and Negro subjects on a series of characteristics and compared successive aspirations in an experimental task involving dart throwing. Among the white college subjects, achievement of their aspiration on the task was followed by raising of the aspiration level on the next trial, whereas for the matched Negro college group past success on the task was less likely to result in their raising their goal on the next trial.[2]

In a series of other experiments, beginning with the work of Chapman and Volkmann individuals alter their level of aspiration on experimental tasks when informed of the achievement on that task of some other social group. When this fictitious standard represents a group ostensibly superior in standing to the individual, he reduces his estimate of his own future performance.[3] Implicitly, these findings demonstrate that the individual in lowly position sets his strivings and expectancies for success in the light of the established social hierarchy of groups and a belief in differential opportunities within the hierarchy.

Two illustrative experiments show this process graphically for groups with well defined social positions. Preston and Bayton found that an experimental group

of Negro college students reduced their aspiration levels when informed that white college students had achieved a certain level in the task more than the control group of Negro students informed that the same fictitious standard of achievement had been achieved by other Negroes. The mirror image of this experiment was conducted by MacIntosh who used white college students as subjects and presented them with the fictitious standard of performance of a Negro group. In the case of the white students, they orient themselves to the knowledge of Negro achievement by raising their estimates.[4]

ALTERED FORMS OF STRIVING FOR SUCCESS

Thus far the data presented show clearly that there is reduced striving for success among the lower classes, an awareness of lack of opportunity, and a lack of valuation of education, normally the major avenue to achievement of high status. However, there may well be subtle ways in which the lower class individual shows the effect of the cultural emphasis on success. Conceivably, our data might be interpreted to indicate that the person *really* wants to achieve the goal of great success, but that he has merely accommodated himself to his lesser opportunities and reduced his aspirations so as to guard against the experience of frustration and failure. Yet, the fact that the data for the sample of youth parallel so closely the findings on adults suggests that this explanation is not generally tenable. Such a dynamic readjustment of goals in relation to reality would be expected to come later. Youth seem to have internalized differentiated goals dependent on their class at an age too early to represent a kind of secondary re-setting of their sights.[5]

Similarly, one might argue that adults would have accommodated *themselves* to reality, but that the cultural emphasis upon success would be reflected by a vicarious aspiration for their children to achieve high success. Chinoy, for example, remarks on the existence of this pattern among his automobile workers. He notes that everyone of his 26 subjects with young children had greater hopes for them and believed in better opportunities for their children.[6] Merton notes the same process, and reports preliminary data from his housing studies. He notes that the lower the occupational level of the parent, the larger the proportion having aspirations for a professional career for their children.[7]

Yet, if such were *generally* the case, we would expect our youth sample to reflect such a pattern of indoctrination. They seem instead to show the pattern of aspirations of the adult members of their class.

Another possibility that presents itself is that the cultural emphasis upon success is reflected in the lower class groups in substitute forms. They cannot achieve occupational success, and so substitute other goals more readily achieved, and regard these symbolically as equivalents. Chinoy remarks on such a "shift in the context of advancement from the occupational to the

[1] For a discussion of the level of aspiration experiment, and a summary of the literature, the reader is referred to K. Lewin, T. Dembo, L. Festinger and P. Sears, "Level of Aspiration," Chap. X, in J. McV. Hunt, *Personality and the Behavior Disorders*, New York, Ronald Press, 1944.

[2] D. K. Adams, "Age, Race, and Responsiveness of Levels of Aspiration to Success and Failure," *Psychol. Bull.*, 1939, 36, p. 573 (abstract).

[3] K. Lewin, et al., *op. cit.*, pp. 341–342.

[4] Preston and Bayton, J., "Differential Effect of a Social Variable upon Three Levels of Aspiration," *J. Exp. Psychol.*, 1941, 29, pp. 351–369. A. MacIntosh, "Differential Effect of the Status of the Competing Group upon the Levels of Aspiration," *Amer. J. Psychol.*, 1942, 55, pp. 546–554. Minor differences in the findings in these two experiments on minimum and maximum aspirations do not concern us in this context.

[5] Yet it is conceivable that even in the case of youth the limited occupational goals of the lower class represents a re-adjustment to reality occurring at a very early age. Hollingshead notes among his lower class youth *who are already employed* that the frequency of choice of professional or business careers is less than such choices among youth of the *same classes who are still in school*. He concluded that they have adjusted their hopes, in most cases, to the reality of the work world. *Op. cit.*, pp. 382–383.

[6] Chinoy, *op. cit.*, p. 459.

[7] Merton, *op. cit.*, p. 148.

[*footnote continued from p. 495*
See *Publ. Opin. Quart.*, 13, 1949, p. 174. Also Centers reports similar findings from a national sample of adults. See *J. Soc. Psychol.*, 27, 1948, pp. 168–169.

consumption sphere."[1] We have no data on the problem unfortunately for large samples.

We have some data, however, on one substitute form of motivation for success in the economic sphere.

Deviant Occupational Goals In general, it has been shown that the lower class individual has less opportunity and less motivation to advance in the hierarchy. However, there are certain occupations in America which provide wealth and benefits to which he might have singular access. These would be occupations which the more genteel classes might regard with disdain and consequently, the lower class person would have less competition. Insofar as the lower class person would have a value system which would endorse the pursuit of such occupations, this would provide a deviant and "sheltered" avenue to success. Such occupations might, for example, exist in the entertainment realm, the realm of politics, and in certain specialized jobs which appear distasteful in character.[2]

Inferential evidence in support of such a pattern is available from a series of measures of the prestige accorded by the different classes to certain selected types of occupations.

Each individual in the sample related the prestige of a series of occupations. We shall assume that according high prestige to an occupation would so-to-speak correspond to that occupation having a strong positive valence for the individual, i.e., he would be more likely to direct his strivings toward occupations he regards as prestigious and not towards occupations he regards as non-prestigious. The hierarchy of prestige has been found in past investigations to be uniform among different occupational groups and, among groups geographically diverse, to be stable over long periods of time.[3] In the national sample studied by NORC, there was, similarly, a general uniformity to the prestige accorded to different occupations by persons in widely

different groups. However, despite this cultural norm, we note certain interesting differences in the prestige accorded by the different classes to occupations which we have labelled deviant. County Judge is used in this analysis as exemplifying a political career goal; singer in a night club as exemplifying an entertainment career goal, and undertaker as exemplifying a distasteful but lucrative occupation. It will be noted from Table 12 below that the lower classes are more likely to accord high prestige to these careers. Conceivably the judge and singer could be regarded as positions of respectability in the judiciary and cultural world or the reactions could be predicated on the intrinsic content of the work. Therefore in the table we present results for two "control" occupations, Supreme Court Justice and musician in a symphony orchestra. Insofar as the responses of the different classes were to the intrinsic contents and the respectability of the occupation, one would expect a similar pattern to the two judicial posts and the two musical positions. However, it can be noted that the classes reverse themselves for the control occupation. In other words, a judicial post of respectability is differentially favored by the upper classes; a judicial post of a *political* nature is favored by the lower classes. Similarly, a *long haired* musical post is favored

[1] Chinoy, *op. cit.*

[2] Certain kinds of professional athletics might also fall into this grouping. For evidence on the way the occupation of boxer provides such an avenue to high status to ethnic minorities and lower socio-economic individuals, see S. K. Weinberg and H. Arond, "The Occupational Culture of the Boxer," *Amer. J. Sociol.*, LVII, 1952, pp. 460–469.

[3] See G. S. Counts, "Social Status of Occupations," *School Review*, XXXIII, 1925, pp. 16–27; M. E. Deeg and D. G. Paterson, "Changes in Social Status of Occupations," *Occupations*, XXV, 1947, pp. 205–208; J. Tuckman, "Social Status of Occupations in Canada," *Canad. J. Psychol.*, 1, No. 2, 1947, pp. 71–75; "Jobs and Occupations, Soldiers' Evaluation," *Opinion News* (NORC), June 15, 1948.

TABLE 12. *The Prestige Accorded to Deviant Occupations by the Different Classes*

	PER CENT GIVING THE RATING OF EXCELLENT STANDING TO:					
	Supreme Court Justice	Musician in symphony orchestra	County judge	Singer in night club	Undertaker	N
Males between 21–39						
Wealthy or prosperous	88	31	32	0	12	66
Middle class	85	25	42	1	10	334
Lower class	82	21	44	6	16	143
Difference between upper and lower classes	+6%	+10%	−12%	−6%	−4%	
Females between 21–39						
Wealthy or prosperous	95	37	41	3	8	78
Middle class	83	31	44	1	13	327
Lower class	72	30	55	5	22	187
Difference between upper and lower classes	+23%	+7%	−14%	−2%	−14%	
Males over 40						
Wealthy or prosperous	84	25	48	0	12	147
Middle class	81	26	49	2	14	312
Lower class	79	23	52	4	17	202
Difference between upper and lower classes	+5%	+2%	−4%	−4%	−5%	
Females over 40						
Wealthy or prosperous	92	37	52	0	11	139
Middle class	81	36	55	2	18	330
Lower class	72	29	49	6	20	189
Difference between upper and lower classes	+20%	+8%	+3%	−6%	−9%	

by the upper classes, and a popular musical position by the lower classes.

It can be noted that there is one inversion in the table which violates the general hypothesis. However, among the 20 possible regressions by class in the table, this is the only inversion found.

Evidence of a more direct nature supports the conclusions just presented. In 1944, the NORC asked a national sample of 2500 cases, "If you had a son just getting out of school, would you like to see him go into

TABLE 13. *Disapproval of a Career in Politics by the Different Classes*

Economic level	Per cent disapproving[1]
Wealthy or prosperous	78
Middle class	73
Lower class	54

politics as a life work?" About two-thirds of the total sample disapproved of such a career, but the disapproval was much more characteristic of the upper classes.

REFERENCE GROUP PROCESSES AND THE DEVIANT CASE

While the evidence thus far presented provides consistent and strong evidence that lower class individuals *as a group* have a value system that reduces the likelihood of individual advancement, it is also clear from the data that there is a sizeable proportion of the lower group who do not incorporate this value system.

Similarly, there are individuals in the upper classes who do not show the modal tendency of their group. In part, such deviant instances can be accounted for in terms of the crudity of the measurements used. In part, one must recognize that the members of these classes have much heretogeneity in such other social respects as their ethnic, religious, and other memberships and have been exposed to a variety of idiosyncratic experiences.

The value systems would be correspondingly diverse. However, one systematic factor that can be shown to account for the deviant cases which confirms at *a more subtle psychological level* the influence of class factors is that of the reference group of the individual. Some of our lower class individuals may well be identifying themselves with upper groups, and absorbing the value system of another class to which they refer themselves. Some of our upper class individuals may for a variety of reasons refer themselves psychologically to other classes. That the reference group of the individual affects his value system, was suggested by data presented earlier on lower class college students and can be shown inferentially from additional data collected in the NORC survey. Evidence was available on the occupation of the parent of each respondent. If we classify each individual in a lower class occupation in terms of whether his parental background is that of a lower or higher occupation group, we presumably have a contrast between individuals of objectively identical class, but who differ in the class with which they might identify. We shall assume that those with upper class origins would not think so much in lower class terms and would continue to reflect their more prestigious origins. If we, similarly, take individuals who are now objectively in upper class occupations and divide them in terms of parental occupation we shall presumably be classifying respondents in more psychological terms. For these four groups we shall contrast their values in each of the realms previously analyzed purely by *current* objective class membership.[2] The patterning of the findings is

---

[1] Unfortunately, the number of cases in each of the economic groups was not available in the published report.

[2] Lipset and Bendix on the basis of noting the large amount of "temporary" mobility, or shifting of jobs within the careers or workers, make the basic point that such changes contribute much to reference group selection and to beliefs about mobility. Thus, they remark: "Those in the middle and upper brackets of the occupational hierarchy may continue to insist that ready

TABLE 14. *Reference Group Processes as Revealed in the Influence of the Class History of the Individual on His Values*

	AMONG RESPONDENTS WHOSE OCCUPATIONS ARE			
	PROFESSIONAL OR BUSINESS		SKILLED OR SEMI-SKILLED	
Per cent who —	*Father prof. or bus.*	*Father skilled or semi*	*Father prof. or bus.*	*Father skilled or semi*
Recommend college education	71	60	57	50
Recommend as best occupation:				
Professional work	44	29	31	25
Skilled manual work	10	29	23	44
Mention the desideratum in choosing an occupation of:				
Congeniality	65	62	52	46
Economic benefit	15	19	23	27
N	(377)	(140)	(298)	(397)

presented in Table 14 above. It can be noted that the values are a resultant of both the "class history" of the individual and his current position. Individuals of equal current position reflect the values of their parents' class. This can be noted by comparing Col. 1 with Col. 2 of the table and Col. 3 with Col. 4. It is also true, however, that individuals with the same class origins have different values depending on their current position. This requires the comparison of Col. 1 with Col. 3 and Col. 2 with Col. 4. Where the two sets of class factors combine in an additive way, the effect on the value system is maximal as seen in the comparison of

Col. 1 with Col. 4. The residues of earlier class experiences in some manner are present suggesting that reference group processes are at work.

opportunities for social and economic advancement exist, because from 40 to 80% of their numbers have at one time or another worked in the manual occupations. While this is not the place to explore the subjective aspects of mobility, we want to emphasize the importance of considering the impact of casual job experiences on the subjective appraisals of opportunities and on the presence or absence of subjective class identifications." By extension, the same theory can be generalized from mobility within the life history of the individual to mobility between generations. *Op. cit.*, p. 495.

Five

Social Mobility

STRUCTURAL TRENDS AND VALUE PREMISES IN THE UNITED STATES

The "Rags to Riches Story"

AN EPISODE OF SECULAR IDEALISM

R. Richard Wohl

> For me, I say it's saddening, if you please,
> As to men who've enjoyed great wealth and ease,
> To hear about their sudden fall, alas!
> But the contrary's great joy and solace.
> As when a man has been in poor estate
> And he climbs up and waxes fortunate,
> And there abides in all prosperity.
> Such things are gladsome, as it seems to me.
> And of such things it would be good to tell.
> — *Prologue to the Nun's Priest's Tale*
> Geoffrey Chaucer

EVERY YEAR, the American Schools and Colleges Association polls thousands of "college leaders" to select a few men for public acclaim who have risen from humble origins to great success. When the final tally discloses the names of these fortunate few, they are summoned to New York City to receive the Horatio Alger award. Great businessmen and potent industrialists interrupt their affairs to gather for the ceremony. They are tendered a banquet in the course of which each is presented with a bronze plaque testifying that he has "climbed the ladder of success through toil and diligence and responsible application of his talents to whatever tasks were his." Newspaper photographers snap their pictures, press releases are handed out, and the next day's newspapers hold up the winners as the cynosure of a nation's admiring eyes.[1]

Horatio Alger, in whose name these honors are dispensed, is himself not described in the newspaper accounts. His title to fame is casually taken for granted, although his reputation rests on a long shelf of books written for children, all forgotten, all out of print, all

[1] A sample newspaper treatment of this event, with thumbnail sketches of the winners' careers will be found in *The New York Herald Tribune*, April 9, 1953.

This is an original article prepared for the first edition of *Class, Status and Power.*

of them often and roundly condemned by literary critics and historians.[1] To the continued bafflement of these accredited intellectuals who regard the preservation of literary reputations as their special province (and who, incidentally, have been expecting Alger's reputation to exhaust itself for the past fifty years) his glory will not down.[2]

Of Alger's many works, not one survives to be widely read today. Contemporary opinion has judged them all to be dull, vulgar and trashy. Alger himself had never claimed them as works of art or great discernment but he had hoped, at least, that they would be edifying. Present day adult opinion condemns them as positively pernicious to right-thinking boys and girls.[3] The children for whom these books were intended have no opinion in the matter: they have not read Alger, could not easily obtain a copy of one of his books even if they wished to do so. When they get one, they are bored with it.[4]

These stories, even the most kindly disposed contem-

porary judgment would concede, are contrived and uninteresting to today's readers. Alger's powers of characterization were limited to painting impossibly virtuous, snow-white heroes and their opposites, wretched villains of the deepest dye; both have as much life in them as a wooden Indian. The tangle of plot wanders along, in confusion, until it is interrupted by a jarring coincidence which tries even a child's willing faith in the unlikely. Shameless, embarrassing sentimentality abounds. The dialogue (the life-blood of a juvenile) is stilted, drab, didactic. The story's moral is mercilessly drubbed into the reader on every possible occasion.

A not unfair example of the kind of transaction with which these stories teem can be drawn from *Hector's Inheritance*, a typical story. Hector, a fresh-faced, eupeptic lad, is being interviewed by a benefactor:

"Have you any taste for liquor?"

"No, sir," answered Hector promptly.

"Even if you had, do you think you would have self-control enough to avoid entering saloons and gratifying your tastes?"

"Yes, sir."

"That is well. Do you play pool?"

"No, sir," answered Hector wondering whither all these questions tended.

"I ask because playing pool in public places paves the way for intemperance, as bars are generally connected with such establishments."

At this juncture it is not difficult to imagine a modern boy flinging the book from him in disgust and unbelief if, indeed, he had successfully weathered the story so far.

Yet Alger found fifty million readers for his books in the United States, and labored all his life to keep pace with an insatiable demand for more of his novels. When he died, in 1889, he left behind him a Horatio Alger industry: New York publishers kept hacks at work turning out successful imitations of his stories as long as the market demanded them. (The last such book was copyrighted in 1904.)[5]

This, it might be thought, from the standpoint of hindsight is paradox enough for one man; but Alger's greatest glory awaited him when he had died and his works had disappeared from the nation's bookshelves. Just as he was mocked and execrated by the literary men as a trifler and bungler, another set of intellectuals elevated him to the status of philosopher and moralist.[6] As recently as 1948, Harold Laski, in analyzing American democracy, found this country's workers "living in a state of psychological coma embodied in Horatio Alger," so hypnotized by his optimistic creed that they could not properly define or adequately struggle for what was held to be their class interests. David McCord Wright, writing in 1951, selected "the Horatio Alger 'rags to riches' story" as one of the small bundle of beliefs which, he felt, formed the underlying faith of American capitalist democracy.[7] This trite plot formula, frozen into a host of clumsily written novels, has many times been picked out by shrewd observers as charac-

[1] Henry Steele Commager, *The American Mind* (New Haven 1950) gives a detailed indictment of Alger on p. 231, and says that "the values in the Alger books were vulgar," p. 31. A detailed denigration of the books is to be found in Russell Crouse (ed.), *Struggling Upward* (New York 1945), pp. i–xiv. This book reprints four of Alger's novels all of whose works, until that time, had been out of print.

[2] An anonymous feature writer in *The New York Tribune*, January 28, 1917 reported that Alger's novels were forgotten and no longer available. Eleven years earlier, an editor of a juvenile magazine in reporting his editorial requirements is quoted as saying: "We want such stories as Horatio Alger . . . used to write." Cf. C. L. Munger, "A Talk with Harry Castleman," *American Boy*, April 1906.

[3] Alger's opinion of his own works, in Herbert R. Mayes, *Alger, a Biography Without a Hero* (New York 1928), pp. 225–226. A sample condemnation of Alger's work by an authority on juvenile literature in Alice M. Jordan, *From Rollo to Tom Sawyer* (Boston 1948), p. 32. "Supposedly an educated man," Miss Jordan writes, "his writing was cheap and tawdry. . . . Alger vulgarized high ideals and stressed the aim of life to be material success; his values were false . . . his books have actually had a wide and possibly hurtful effect upon the reading tastes of countless young people."

[4] A survey in New York, covering 20,000 children between the ages of 8 and 14, revealed that 92% had never heard of him; 7% had heard his name but had never read one of his books; 1% had actually read an Alger novel. *The New York Times*, January 13, 1947. The Alger novels have been banished from the Children's Department of the New York Public Library; the librarian in charge reported that children did not find them "interesting."

[5] Fantastic estimates of Alger's audience have been made, some ranging as high as 200 million. Frank Luther Mott, in his study of best-sellers estimates that 17 million copies were sold. It is not unreasonable to infer that each copy had three readers. *Golden Multitudes* (New York, 1947), p. 159. The continued publication of Alger books after the original author's death, and the evidence for it is given in Malcolm Cowley, "The Alger Story," *The New Republic*, September 10, 1945, p. 319.

[6] Alger never had any luck with highbrow reviewers even in his own life time. Two years after he published his first juvenile his most recent production was devastatingly reviewed in *The Nation*, December 30, 1869.

[7] Harold J. Laski, *The American Democracy* (New York, 1948), p. 266, cf. also pp. 659, 622. David McCord Wright, *Capitalism* (New York, 1951), p. 66.

terizing a fundamental and crucial aspect of American culture.[1]

II

What, then, is the Alger "rags to riches" saga? Like every proper legend, recalled in nostalgia, transmitted by hearsay, and buffeted by changing circumstances it exists in two versions: its present form (much altered from the original) and its first version.

In its latter-day phrasing it is solemnly reported in textbooks as a national by-word. The Horatio Alger hero is described as[2]

A boy who was born in the slums of a great city with a very low social position, becomes a bootblack, works hard, applies himself to his studies, saves his money, and rises through sheer effort to a position of social, economic and occupational importance.

Yet a careful study of Alger's novels shows that the message of the stories he wrote, and the deeds he commemorated, do not follow this pattern at all.[3]

With few exceptions (the memory of which faded as the list of Alger's works grew longer) his heroes are not slum children. On the contrary, they are well-brought-up, comfortably nourished middle-class boys, the sons of property owners with substantial social reputation. Originally, the heroes come from farms and rural villages to the city to seek their fortunes; they are country-bred. They are rendered physically and socially mobile by personal or family misfortune. Typically, the father of the hero has died recently and the boy is devoting himself to supporting his mother. An evil, merciless "squire" holds the mortgage on the family home and threatens to foreclose and dispossess the widow. The hero, thrown on his mettle, goes off to the city to earn enough to forestall this unfortunate outcome.

While purposefully ambitious, he surrenders none of the careful middle-class socialization by which he has been reared to boyhood. He is conspicuously clean and courteous (many of the city boys he meets are dirty and rude); he speaks perfect English with irreproachable diction (he never picks up city street slang); unlike city boys, particularly unambitious city boys, he does not drink, smoke, or indulge in frivolous pastimes. He helps the weak, is as charitable as it is in his power to be, and contrives to keep his disposition sunny and winning. He is, however, strong enough to stand up to a bully; shrewd enough successfully to match wits with the sharpers and scoundrels with which the city teems.

Established in the city, the hero proves his resolution and self-reliance by finding a low-status job, with poor pay, by which he barely manages to maintain himself. Alger with a rare faithfulness to reality portrays the hero's plight with sympathy and accuracy. The boy makes enough to live on and no more; the slightest extravagance or indulgence is punished by immediate want. Alger heroes, like good middle class boys, im-

prove their minds with good books and live in clean, moral boarding houses, but they save no money; it is impossible for them to accumulate enough to form a little capital that might be pregnant with fortune, because they have no money to save.

For a time, the hero continues to work hard, keeps clean and cheerful, courteous and calm. He is firm in his belief that honesty is the best policy and ambition is sensible; but he remains poor. In Alger's world, success and redeemed ambition depend on proper sponsorship, and our hero makes no headway at all until he finds a benefactor. And, unwittingly, without planning or foresight, he is suddenly rewarded. He performs a noble deed. Down a busy street a pair of maddened runaway horses will come careening, in the carriage behind lies a terrified little girl. Our hero will rush out, drag the horses to a halt, and restore the sobbing child to her father. Or, he will leap (like *Ragged Dick*) from a ferryboat into New York harbor and save a child from drowning in the bay; or he will catch a thief (like *Frank the Bond Boy*). Alger's expedients are inexhaustible.

The noble deed accomplished the grateful parent (or the affluent merchant, often the sponsor is both) will confront the hero swearing eternal gratitude. "My brave boy," says Mr. Roswell to Ragged Dick when his daughter is restored to him, "I owe you a debt I can never repay." Trained Alger readers will immediately recognize this for the rhetorical flourish that it is. Immediate, tangible evidences of this acknowledged obligation are forthcoming. The hero will invariably get a job in his patron's business where, under his watchful and grateful eye, the reader is assured that he will progress upward and onward to fame and fortune. When the hero is in dire financial straits (most are) there may also be an outright gift of money (usually $5,000 or $10,000) which serves to lift him and his kin out of the reach of want until he can make his way to permanent prosperity. (One of the first things the hero usually does to celebrate his good fortune is to buy a nice, new suit and a watch.) In many of the stories the reader is assured in a final, editorial paragraph that the hero and the sponsor's daughter will one day marry — and presumably inherit.

Alger himself admitted the quandary into which such solutions thrust him. The moralizing, the resolute virtue, and the steady application did not bring reward (and as a good Puritan moralist, it was perhaps necessary for Alger that pay-off and virtue should be decently separated) but rather unpredictable and unearnable luck. Alger avoids the logical dilemma raised up by this turn of events by admitting it in a puzzled and bemused fashion. Frank the Bond Boy after much unrewarding and dreary work as a messenger, with a

---

[1] Robert Waithman, *Report on America* (London, 1940), p. 99.
[2] Marion B. Smith, *Survey of Social Science* (Boston, 1945), p. 134.
[3] The comments which follow are based on an analysis of some 55 Alger novels (he wrote 135 in all).

pittance for wages, captures a thief and reaps a rich reward. "Frank did not exaggerate his own merits in the matter," Alger reports. "He felt that it was largely due to luck that he had been the means of capturing the bond robber." "However," concludes Alger gravely, "it is precisely to such lucky chances that men are often indebted for their advancement."

In final contradiction to the modern version, the original form of the Alger story stops significantly when the hero has his foot on the first rung of the ladder to success. Having employed a *deus ex machina* to give his hero the needed leg up, Alger leaves room open for the continued exercise of virtue to make the initial success permanent and to justify its ultimate consummation.

III

We may now address ourselves once again to the involved paradox of Alger's literary reputation: how to account for his great, initial success with an audience of millions, the subsequent disappearance of this audience, and the puzzling phenomenon of his resurgent fame after his books had disappeared from view.

The period of Alger's greatest popularity coincided with the filling up of the nation's cities. Farm boys by the millions, seeking wider horizons and enlarged opportunity, left the farms on which they had been born to take up an urban existence. Alger became the apostle of this migration.

Alger helped define the aspirations of those boys — to make money, to get ahead, to make good — he described for them the experience which they were bracing themselves to undertake. His city (he mainly wrote about New York) was accurately described with a loving attention to authentic detail. It teems with people and traffic. It is a busy place, full of strange and various sights: colorful, noisy and knowing. His heroes may have always triumphed over the villains; but the tricksters, the criminals and confidence men, the drunkards, loafers and urchins were all truly and fully depicted. Their jargon was faithfully rendered; their follies and bad habits exactly catalogued.

His books, in addition, were full of practical and minute information about how one lived and worked in a city once one got there. One could learn from such a novel what kinds of boarding houses there were, and what was fair value in shelter; there were careful lists of the prevailing prices of food and clothing, utensils and amusement; an audience eager for just this kind of practical counsel snapped up these books as fast as they were printed.

Even if we did not know from other sources that

Alger's books were addressed to youngsters in the hinterland, we might fairly infer it from an inquiry of what city life meant to the urban boy who actually lived in a slum because he was born there, had low status, and worked as a boot-black or match boy. Even in Alger's day there were too many such boys already in the cities for even that sanguine age to promise much opportunity or hope of advancement. These city boys — the unredeemed gamins in his novels — were systematically encouraged by benevolent urban philanthropists to forsake city life, to go West and try to set up as independent farmers!

A contemporary social worker has recorded for us a parody of the Alger paradigm as rendered, with cutting sarcasm, by an Irish street-boy in New York to his irreverent and enormously amused companions.[1]

> Boys, gintlemen, chummies: Praps you'd like to hear summit about the West, the great West, you know, where so many of our friends are settled down and growing' up to be great men. . . . Do you want to be newsboys always, and shoeblacks, and timber merchants in a small way selling matches? If ye do you'll stay in New York, but if you don't you'll go out West, and begin to be farmers. . . .
>
> You haven't any idear of what ye may be yet, if you will only take a bit of my advice. How do you know but honest, good, and industrious you may get so much up in the ranks that you won't call a gineral or judge your boss. . . .

The city boy, wry, hardened and wise in the ways of the seamy side of slum life found no prophet at all in Alger. Had they been asked, they would have told Alger that his image of the city's life was already obsolete for many of those he was inspiring.

For Alger's audience at large, living away from the metropolis and not knowing the true state of affairs there, Alger's message was reinforced by some of the most potent and irreproachably respectable public opinion of the day. Protestant ministers had for decades addressed the fathers and mothers of the young people for whom Alger wrote and their message was identical with his. Sound morals in a sturdy character was the whole equipment for success in life, it was urged. The imputation of poverty or failure to social conditions or prevailing institutions was a wicked falsehood, a positive evidence of evil. So persistent was this message that, 1889, the very year in which Alger died, heard the first voices of exasperated protest against this dogma. "If you tell a single concrete workman on the Baltimore and Ohio Railroad," wrote Richard T. Ely, economist and reformer, "that he may yet be president of the company, it is not demonstrable that you have told him what is not true, although it is within bounds to say that he is far more likely to be killed by a stroke of lightning."[2]

The press, like the pulpit, echoed the same message that Alger sent out to his young folk. Popular novels,

[1] Charles Loring Brace, *The Dangerous Classes of New York* (New York, 1880). This book was first published in 1872.

[2] Henry F. May's brilliant monograph, *The Protestant Churches and Industrial America* (New York, 1949), summarizes opinion on this and related points from various Protestant standpoints. The quotation cited above appears at p. 141.

like pulpit oratory, reflecting metaphors which were fast growing obsolescent, preached the gospel of thrift, hard work, and endurance. In one such novel, representative of many, a young lady of unblemished character noted for her delicate sentiments finds occasion to say (and to be applauded for saying); "In the laboring class, property is a sign of good morals. In this country no one sinks to deep poverty except by vice, directly or indirectly." The ambiguities in the qualifying phrases for long escaped careful scrutiny.[1]

Alger's original contribution to this tired controversy was to inject it into a new dimension. While the other great juvenile writers of his day — Oliver Optic, Edward Ellis and Henry Castlemon — were producing adventure tales full of pirates, cowboys and Indians, and war heroes Alger cut down this adult theme to fit the needs and understanding of children. In doing so, he had behind him the combined efforts not only of much articulate and expounded public opinion, but he geared his tales in with the very injunctions that many parents were giving their children to fit them for life as grown men and women.

His success was founded, too, in the solid example afforded by the many men who had started with nothing and built a fair fortune by their own exertions. In Alger's native Massachusetts, a list of rich men was published in 1852 when Alger was himself a young man, which described the 1,257 men in the state who possessed property worth $50,000 or more. The origin of their wealth could be traced for some 1,092 of these rich men. No less than 775 are described as having begun poor or nearly so; 342 inherited their wealth or gained it through marriage; 140 farmers are listed of whom many were self-made but precise details are not given by the author.[2]

Alger reported a common fact from the time of his own youth to an age already markedly different from the one in which he had grown up. For many opportunity was narrowing, industrialization and wage work offered a slim base for advancement for those employed in the shops and factories, although even then much room was left for the determined and the canny. It is revealing, however, that Alger dragged in luck rather than occupational strategy, not to explain success, but to explain how an aspirant got a foothold on the upward path. Alger's patrons interestingly enough are merchants not industrialists, another obsolete element in his outlook. His boys are not child laborers in factories but street-traders, messengers, shop-clerks.

As the cities filled, and a realistic picture of urban life became more general; as the face of industrialization was discerned in unfettered, uncontrolled growth, Alger's audience fell away in disbelief. By this time, millions of his books had been sold and read: the popular magazines had scattered his stories broadcast through the land. His name, his catchy titles, the skeleton of the plot he had endlessly repeated in his novels, remained behind in the memories of those to whom he had once been an inspiration. By word of mouth they carried his fame further than even his books could reach.

The Alger saga, it has been remarked, "is almost too simple to believe, but oddly moving too."[3] It is this capacity to inspire and excite which has kept Alger's name and fame alive even after his stories have collapsed under their simplicity — their uncritical, naive optimism. Their theme has universal appeal. In all ages, the disadvantaged hero struggling against odds, bearing witness to aspiration, but finally redeemed by success is a folk figure everywhere rejoiced in. It is not surprising, therefore, that a story cognate to this universal theme survives. All that was required for it to survive in association with Alger's name was that it be edited and revised to fit new conditions. In its modern version, the snug congruity between the altered legend and the changed circumstances is achieved. The new hero is a slum boy making his way in the modern world. As the stories which Alger had written disappeared there was no canon against which revision might be measured. Modification proceeded unchecked.

The society into which the new version fell was, in very many ways, much like the older world Alger knew. It believed in comfort, ample and conspicuous consumption; it believed, albeit a little differently, in the worth of work and the test of character in achieving a dream; it believed in earning privilege and its justification by meritorious achievement. In short, it believed in success: rich, juicy, and obvious. Alger's vastly publicized name and his slogans became detached from the rationale to which he had affixed them and were transferred, as something known and esteemed, to a new explanation, a new rhetoric of persuasion.

The only effective challenge to the myth would be an attack on the underlying zeal for success. And the strain of striving, and the emptiness of the rewards once they were won, could tell against the legend and weaken its hold on the imagination. Frank Munsey, the great newspaper tycoon, was the Alger hero *par excellence*. All his life, even in death, he was dramatized as an Alger hero. But one terrible anecdote survived him which drained force from the label with which he was tagged.

A friend, calling on Munsey to keep an appointment, found him staring from his tower office window like a man hypnotized. He cleared his throat to catch Munsey's attention, and at the sound Munsey turned to face him.

"Oh, yes, yes," he said, as if apologizing. "We've a luncheon engagement." Then he turned to the window and said as if he were explaining, "Today is

---

[1] For a summary of the contexts of novels on this subject cf. Herbert Ross Brown, *The Sentimental Novel in America, 1789–1860* (Durham, North Carolina, 1940), especially pp. 358–370. The quotation cited above appears at p. 362.

[2] Abner Forbes, *The Rich Men of Massachusetts* (Boston, 1852), p. 223. Similar listings for other large cities of the time (New York, Philadelphia and others) confirm these data.

[3] *Ladies Home Journal*, July, 1951, p. 39.

my birthday. I've no family. My only relative is a sister who is older than I am. I wonder is it worthwhile."[1]

Somehow this black mood has begun to sap the vitality of the Alger saga, and its chief exponents are calling for fresh resources to refurbish it and renew its vitality. Such a straw in the wind is a prominent advertisement which recently appeared in an advertising journal. WANTED . . . A MODERN HORATIO ALGER ran the bold headline[2]

There is immediate need for an author who can popularize *today's* success stories! For, today, those who believe in the philosophy of *Strive and Succeed* are all too few. *A recent public opinion poll sets the number at less than 50%* ! And the fact that this disbelief in the faith of work runs through all age groups

[1] Cf. George Britt, *Forty Years — Forty Millions* (New York, 1935), especially chapter V, "Alger Story." The anecdote above comes from a résumé of obituaries, "Frank A. Munsey as a Horatio Alger Hero," *Literary Digest*, January 9, 1926, p. 56.

[2] *Advertising Age*, December 1, 1947, pp. 18–19. [Italics in original.]

[3] *Commonweal*, August 24, 1945; *The New Yorker*, September 1, 1945. For other attacks castigating Crouse cf. "Topics of the Times," *New York Times*, January 16, 1947, and *New York Herald Tribune*, August 17, 1945.

indicates that our author is faced with the task of writing stories that will carry the message to our youth — and their elders.

Alger, and the story imputed to him, remain a strong symbol still. In 1945, four of Alger's novels were reprinted with a sarcastic introduction by Russell Crouse. He, like many others before him, attacked Alger as an execrable literary craftsman who had committed "literary murder" in all his 135 novels. He derided Alger's lessons, mocked the success of his heroes as windfalls unearned by work or merit. Crouse reaped a prompt harvest of angry criticism. "It is a frightening thought," commented the Catholic weekly *Commonweal*, "that today *Jed, the Poorhouse Boy* has been supplanted by Dick Tracy." It was almost as if a sacred sentiment had been tampered with, and the blasphemy would not be allowed. "Mr. Crouse," remarked the usually hypercritical *New Yorker* icily, "in his introduction is amusing at times but he couldn't have done a better job of missing the importance and significance of Alger if he had tried."[3] The story was still a too simple story, but it remained "oddly moving" nonetheless, a dream to be defended from attack.

Where Do You Fit in the Income Picture?

Herman P. Miller

To START WITH, you must take my word for it that figures on income distribution are reasonably accurate.

The American people received one-third of a trillion dollars in cash income in 1959. That is a lot of money: too much for anyone to imagine comfortably. But this vast sum had to be shared by fifty-eight million families and individuals. If each one got an equal share, it would only be $5,700. There is a number with some meaning! And to many it will seem surprisingly low.

There are many reasons why the average is low. For one thing, it assumes that each family gets exactly the same amount of money. That doesn't make much sense. Some families are larger than others; they "need" more. Some people work harder than others; they "deserve" more. Some people take bigger risks than others; they gain (or lose) accordingly. But there are also other reasons for the low average.

On the following pages are figures showing the spread of income in the United States. They come from the last census. You may be interested in finding out where you fit in the income picture. Since only six different income groups are shown, these figures give an unrealistic view of the actual spread of incomes. It is really much greater than most people imagine. The noted economist Paul Samuelson has described income distribution in the following terms: "If we made an income pyramid out of a child's blocks, with each layer portraying $1,000 of income, the peak would be far higher than the Eiffel Tower, but almost all of us would be within a yard of the ground." This gives you some idea of the diversity that is compressed within these six income groupings.

The average factory worker earns about $100 a week, or more than $5,000 a year. In addition, many families have more than one worker. How then can

---

Reprinted from *Rich Man, Poor Man* (Thos. Y. Crowell Co., N.Y., 1964), pp. 1–13, by permission of the author and the publisher.

there be 25 million families and individuals — nearly one-half of the total — with incomes under $4,000? There must be a joker somewhere.

Notice that unrelated individuals (a technical term for "one-person" families who live alone or as boarders in other people's homes) have been lumped with family groups consisting of two or more persons. That makes a big difference. One person living alone has only his income and only himself to support. Where there are two or more people in a home, more

TABLE I

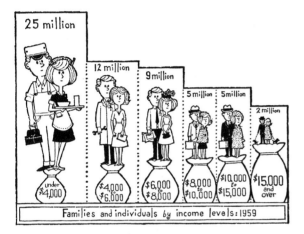

U.S. Bureau of the Census, *How Our Income Is Divided*, Graphic Pamphlet No. 2, 1963.

than one can work — but there are also more mouths to feed.

It is obvious that before any more can be said about income, the unrelated individuals must first be separated from the families.

Unrelated individuals by income levels

At the time of the last census, there were 13 million unrelated individuals in the United States. They are often overlooked in the figures because their number is so small relative to the 165 million people who live in families. But they are a special group and they deserve special attention.

9% are under 25 ⎫
34% are over 65 ⎬ Young and old
57% are 25–64 ⎭ Working age

Together, the young and the old constitute more than two-fifths of all unrelated individuals. Many in the group called unrelated individuals are widows and widowers who spent most of their lives as family members. When their mates died, they kept their own homes and did not move in with children or enter old-age homes. Their incomes are low by all standards — half received less than $1,000 in the prosperous year of 1959. It was received largely as pensions and public assistance — although many of these people work.

Younger persons are also important in the unrelated individual population; they account for about one-tenth of the total. The average income of the youngsters was also low ($1,500), largely because their lack of skill and experience prevented them from commanding high wages.

Unrelated individuals in the most productive age brackets (twenty-five to sixty-four years) make up about three-fifths of the total. Their incomes are considerably higher than those cited for the younger and older persons; but they are nevertheless quite low by most standards. One-half had incomes under $2,500. The relatively low incomes of this group can be blamed on their inability to work, failure to find work, or their concentration in low-paying jobs when they are employed.

Families by income levels

The distribution of families by income levels is considerably different from that shown for unrelated individuals. At the time of the last census there were forty-five million families in the United States and they received nearly $300 billion. If this total had been equally divided, each would have received $6,600. In 1959, about six families out of every ten received less than that amount.

Millions of families in the United States still try to get by on less than $40 a week. There were six million such families, to be exact, in 1959. They represented 13 percent of all families but they received only 2 percent of the income. Many of them lived on farms where their cash incomes were supplemented by food and lodging that did not have to be purchased. Yet, even if this income were added to the total, it would not change the results very much.

TABLE 2. *Families by Income Levels in 1959*

| Income level | Number of families | PERCENT | |
		Families	Income
All families	45 million	100%	100%
Under $2,000	6 million	13	2
Between $2,000 and $4,000	8 million	18	8
Between $4,000 and $6,000	11 million	23	18
Between $6,000 and $8,000	9 million	19	20
Between $8,000 and $10,000	5 million	12	15
Between $10,000 and $15,000	5 million	11	19
Between $15,000 and $25,000	1½ million	3	10
$25,000 and over	½ million	1	8
Median income	$5,660		

U.S. Bureau of the Census, *How Our Income Is Divided*, Graphic Pamphlet No. 2, 1963.

At the golden apex of the income pyramid there were about one-half million families with incomes over $25,000. They represented 1 percent of the total but they received 8 percent of the income.

Another way to view these figures is to examine the share of income received by each fifth of the families ranked from lowest to highest by income. In Table 3 you will see that in 1959 the poorest fifth of the families had incomes under $2,800; they received 5 percent of the total. In that same year, the highest fifth of the families had incomes over $9,000; they received 43 percent of the total.

Who sits at the top of the heap? The figures show that until you get to the very top the incomes are not so high. The top 5 percent of the families had incomes over $14,800. They received 18 percent of all the income. Families with incomes over $25,000 were in the top 1 percent and they received 8 percent of the total. Is $15,000 or $25,000 a year a very high income? To those near the base of the pyramid, it might be; but to a skilled worker with a working wife, an annual income of $15,000 may not seem like an unattainable goal. Economist Henry Wallich remarks that in America "the $25,000 family enjoys a variety of extras, but its basic form of living is not very obviously distinguishable from that of the $6,000 family."

If $25,000 a year is not a very high income, what is? Sociologist C. Wright Mills, in his book *The Power Elite*, defines the corporate rich as those with incomes of $100,000 a year or more. Relatively few American families have incomes this high. In 1959, there were only 28,000 individual income tax returns filed with adjusted gross incomes over $100,000. These returns accounted for about $5 billion or slightly more than 1 percent of the total distributed to the entire economy. These people certainly got more than their share; but the figures hardly support the view that the lower-

TABLE 3. *Share of Income Received in 1959 by each Fifth of U.S. Families and by Top 1% and 5%*

Families ranked from lowest to highest	Income range	Percent of income received
Lowest fifth	Less than $2,800	5%
Second fifth	Between $2,800 and $4,800	12
Middle fifth	Between $4,800 and $6,500	17
Fourth fifth	Between $6,500 and $9,000	23
Highest fifth	$9,000 and over	44
Top 5%	$14,800 and over	18
Top 1%	$25,000 and over	8

U.S. Bureau of the Census, *How Our Income Is Divided,* **Graphic Pamphlet No. 2, 1963.**

income groups would be much better off if these very high incomes were confiscated and spread around more evenly. The fact of the matter is that they might be worse off if the golden goal of an income this high were removed.

The top income receivers are highly concentrated in the large metropolitan areas. The hundred largest urban centers contain about one-half of the population but about four-fifths of those who pay taxes on incomes over $100,000. In 1959, the New York metropolitan area provided 6,700 tax returns reporting incomes over $100,000. Chicago and Los Angeles

followed New York with about 1,800 high-income returns each.

Are U.S. incomes too unequally distributed

There is no objective answer to this question. It all depends on how unequally you think incomes should be distributed.

Around the turn of the century, the French poet and philosopher Charles Péguy wrote: "When all men are provided with the necessities, the real necessities, with bread and books, what do we care about the distribution of luxury?" This point of view went out of style with spats and high-button shoes. There is an intense interest in the distribution of luxury in the modern world.

Since we all cannot have as many material things as we should like, many people are of the opinion that those who are more productive should get more both as a reward for past performance and as an incentive to greater output in the future. This seems like a reasonable view, consistent with the realities of the world. Lincoln said: "That some should be rich shows that others may become rich and hence is just encouragement to industry and enterprise." The fact is that all modern industrial societies, whatever their political or social philosophies, have had to resort to some forms of incentives to get the most work out of their people.

Despite its reasonableness, this view has its critics. Some have argued that a man endowed with a good mind, drive, imagination, and creativity, and blessed with a wholesome environment in which these attributes could be nurtured, has already been amply rewarded. To give him material advantages over his less fortunate fellows would only aggravate the situation. The British historian R. H. Tawney wrote in his book *Equality*: ". . . some men are inferior to others in respect to their intellectual endowments. . . . It does not, however, follow from this fact that such individuals or classes should receive less consideration than others or should be treated as inferior in respect to such matters as legal status or health, or economic arrangements, which are within the control of the community."

Since there is no objective answer to the question as it has been formulated, it may be fruitful to set it aside and turn to the comparison of income in the United States and other major countries for which such data are available.

Anyone who doubts that real incomes — purchasing power — are higher in the United States than in all other major countries just hasn't been around. But, how much higher? That is hard to say. How do you compare dollars, pounds, rubles, and francs? Official exchange rates are often very poor guides. Differences in prices, quality of goods, and living standards add to the complexity. In view of these problems, international comparisons are often made in terms of the purchasing power of wages. But even this measure has serious limitations. What constitutes a representative market basket in different countries, and how does one compare the market basket in one country with another? For example, Italians may like fish, which is relatively cheap, whereas Americans may prefer beef, which is quite expensive. How then would one compare the cost of a "typical" meal for families in the two countries? Because of this kind of problem, and many others, international comparisons of levels of living must be made with great caution. One study that casts some light on the subject was published in 1959 by the National Industrial Conference Board. It shows the amount of work it would take to buy the following meal for a family of four in several different countries. The items were selected from an annual survey of retail prices conducted by the International Labor Office:

Beef, sirloin	150 grams
Potatoes	150 grams
Cabbage	200 grams
Bread, white	50 grams
Butter	10 grams
Milk	.25 liter
Apples	150 grams

The results are shown in the pictograph (Table 4). The industrial worker in the United States had to work one hour to buy the meal above. The Canadian worker, whose level of living is not far behind that of his American cousin, had to work nine minutes more to buy the same meal. In Europe, the Danes came closest to the American standard, but even in Denmark the average worker had to toil one-half hour longer to feed his family. In West Germany and Great Britain it took more than two hours of work to buy the same meal and in Italy it took five hours. These and many other figures of a similar nature show that American workers are paid more in real terms than the workers of any other major country.

If international comparisons of levels of income are difficult, comparisons of the distribution of income are

TABLE 4

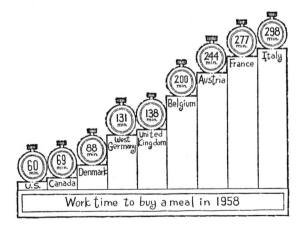

Zoe Campbell, "Food Costs in Work Time Here and Abroad," *Conference Board Business Record*, December, 1959.

virtually impossible. There are many opinions on the subject, but few of them are solidly based. Aldous Huxley, for example, believes that incomes are more unequally distributed in England than in France because "the highest government servants in England are paid forty or fifty times as much as the lowest." Following a similar line of reasoning, Max Eastman finds inequality greater in Russia than in the U.S. because the managing director of an American mining firm receives about forty times as much as one of his miners whereas a man in the same position in Russia may earn up to eighty times as much as a miner. This type of evidence might satisfy a literary man. The statistician is harder to please.

The United Nations, which has done some work in this field, cautions that "despite the intense interest in international comparisons of the degree of inequality in the distribution of income . . . surprisingly little

TABLE 5. *Percent of Income Received by Top 5% of Families in Selected Countries*

United States	(1950)	20%*
Sweden	(1948)	20
Denmark	(1952)	20
Great Britain	(1951–52)	21
Barbados	(1951–52)	22
Puerto Rico	(1953)	23
India	(1955–56)	24
West Germany	(1950)	24
Italy	(1948)	24
Netherlands	(1950)	25
Ceylon	(1952–53)	31
Guatemala	(1947–48)	35
El Salvador	(1946)	36
Mexico	(1957)	37
Colombia	(1953)	42
Northern Rhodesia	(1946)	45
Kenya	(1949)	51
Southern Rhodesia	(1946)	65

* The numbers represent total income before taxes received by families or spending units.
Simon Kuznets, "Quantitative Aspects of the Economic Growth of Nations," *Economic Development and Cultural Change*, Vol. XI, No. 2, January, 1963, Table 3.

incontrovertible evidence has been amassed. The margins of error of the available statistics . . . combined with differences in the underlying definitions . . . make it extremely hazardous to draw conclusions involving any but possibly a very few countries." No reputable scholar would deny the wisdom of these remarks. Yet judgments must be made and some figures, if they are carefully considered and properly qualified, are better than none. Even the world's leading authority on income distribution, Professor Simon Kuznets of Harvard University, agrees that international comparisons of income distribution, despite their serious limitations, have value because they are based on "a variety of data . . . rather than irresponsible notions stemming from preconceived and unchecked views on the subject."

Do the rich get a larger share of income in the

United States than they do in other countries? According to the available evidence this is not the case. The United States has about the same income distribution as Denmark, Sweden, and Great Britain and a much more equal distribution than most of the other countries for which data are shown. There is no evidence that incomes are more widely distributed in any country than they are in the United States.

The figures in Table 5 classify the top 5 percent as "rich." This is a rather low point on the income scale. In the United States it would include all families receiving more than $15,000 a year. A more interesting comparison would be the share of income received by the top 1 percent ($25,000 or more per year) or perhaps even a higher income group. Such information, however, is not available for most other countries.

A comprehensive study of international comparisons of income was made in 1960 by Professor Irving Kravis of the University of Pennsylvania. He summarized the income distribution among the countries for which data are available in the following way:

More nearly equal distribution than U.S.
Denmark
Netherlands
Israel (Jewish population only)

About the same distribution as U.S.
Great Britain
Japan
Canada

More unequal distribution than U.S.
Italy
Puerto Rico
Ceylon
El Salvador

Reference Group Theory and Social Mobility
Robert K. Merton and Alice Kitt Rossi

OTHER RESEARCHES reported in *The American Soldier*[1] which do not make explicit use of the concept of relative deprivation or kindred concepts can also be recast in terms of reference group theory. One of the more rigorous and seminal of these is the panel study of relationships between the conformity of enlisted men to official values of the Army and their subsequent promotion.

This study also illustrates the widely-known but seldom elucidated point that the same social research can be variously analyzed in at least three separate, though related, respects: its documented empirical findings, its methodology or logic of procedure, and its theoretical implications.

Since the methodology and the empirical findings of this study have been amply discussed — the one in the paper by Kendall and Lazarsfeld, the other in *The American Soldier* itself — we need not concern ourselves

with them here. Instead, we limit our discussion to some of its theoretical implications.

These implications divide into three related kinds. First, the implications for reference group theory as the empirical findings are re-examined within the context of that theory. Second, are the implications which enable us to connect reference group theory with hypotheses of functional sociology. And third, the implications which, once suitably generalized, enable us to see that this study bears, not only on the conformity-and-mobility patterns of American soldiers in World War II, but possibly also on more general and seemingly disparate patterns of behavior, such as group defection, renegadism, social climbing, and the like.

Tracing out these implications comprises a large order which can scarcely be entirely filled, not because of limitations of space but because of limitations of our own sociological knowledge. But even an approximation to achieving our purpose should help us recognize the theoretical linkages between presently separated types of social behavior.

We begin by following our now customary practice of briefly sketching out the chief findings of the study as these are set forth in *The American Soldier*.

Case No. 5 (*I, 258–275*). This research was concerned, not with *rates* of promotion which were determined by changes in the table of organization, but with the

---

[1] The references in this article are to *The American Soldier* series, volume one, *Adjustment During Army Life* (Stouffer, Suchman, Devinney, Star, and Williams) and volume two, *Combat and Its Aftermath* (Stouffer, A. Lumsdaine, M. Lumsdaine, Williams, Smith, Janis, Star, and Cottrell), Princeton, N.J.: Princeton University Press, 1949.
References to the two volumes are handled in the following way. The first and second volumes are referred to as I and II respectively. Chapter numbers are also indicated by subsequent Roman numerals; page numbers, by Arabic numerals. — Ed.

Reprinted from *Continuities in Social Research*, edited by Robert K. Merton and Paul F. Lazarsfeld, by permission of the authors and the publisher. (New York: The Free Press, 1950.)

incidence of promotion: which men were the more likely to be advanced? Since the decision of the commanding officer regarding promotions was by no means based upon objective tests of capacity or performance by enlisted men, there was much occasion for interpersonal relations and sentiments to play their part in affecting this decision. Accordingly, the Research Branch advanced the hypothesis that, "One factor which hardly would have failed to enter to some extent into the judgment of an officer in selecting a man for promotion was his conformity to the officially approved military mores." (I, 259) It is noted further, and we shall have occasion to return to this point in some detail, that "in making subjective judgments, the commanding officer necessarily laid himself wide open to charges of favoritism and particularly of succumbing to the wiles of those enlisted men most skilled at 'bucking.'" (I, 264)

A panel study of three groups of enlisted men was designed to find out whether the men who expressed attitudes in accord with the established military mores subsequently received promotions in proportions significantly higher than the others. This was consistently found to be the case. For example, "of the privates who in September 1943 said they did not think the Army's control was too strict, 19 per cent had become Pfc's by January 1944, while only 12 per cent of the other privates had become Pfc's." (I, 261-2). So, too, when men in the three samples are arranged according to their scores on a "quasi-scale of attitudes of conformity," it was uniformly found in all three groups "that the men whose attitudes were most conformist were the ones most likely to be promoted subsequently." (I, 263)[1]

THEORETICAL IMPLICATIONS

In discussing this panel study, we want to bring into the open some of the connections between reference group theory and functional sociology which have remained implicit to this point, — an objective to which this study lends itself particularly well, since the findings of the study can be readily reformulated in terms of both kinds of theory, and are then seen to bear upon a range of behavior wider than that considered in the study itself.

The value of such reformulation for social theory is perhaps best seen in connection with the independent variable of "conformity." It is clear, when one thinks about it, that the type of attitude described as conformist in this study is at the polar extreme from what is ordinarily called "social conformity." For in the vocabulary of sociology, social conformity usually denotes conformity to the norms and expectations current in the individual's *own* membership-group. But in this study, conformity refers, not to the norms of the immediate primary group constituted by enlisted men but to the quite different norms contained in the official military mores. Indeed, as data in *The American Soldier* make clear, the norms of the in-groups of associated enlisted men and the official norms of the Army and of

the stratum of officers were often at odds.[2] In the language of reference group theory, therefore, attitudes of conformity to the official mores can be described as a positive orientation to the norms of a non-membership group that is taken as a frame of reference. Such conformity to norms of an out-group is thus equivalent to what is ordinarily called nonconformity, that is, nonconformity to the norms of the in-group.[3]

This preliminary reformulation leads directly to two interrelated questions which we have until now implied rather than considered explicitly: what are the consequences, functional and dysfunctional, of positive orientation to the values of a group other than one's own? And further, which social processes initiate, sustain or curb such orientations?

FUNCTIONS OF POSITIVE ORIENTATION TO NON-MEMBERSHIP REFERENCE GROUPS

In considering, however briefly, the possible consequences of this pattern of conformity to non-membership group norms, it is advisable to distinguish between the consequences for the individuals exhibiting this behavior, the sub-group in which they find themselves, and the social system comprising both of these.

For the individual who adopts the values of a group to which he aspires but does not belong, this orientation may serve the twin functions of aiding his rise into that group and of easing his adjustment after he has become part of it. That this first function was indeed served is

[1] As the authors themselves say and as Kendall and Lazarsfeld indicate in some detail, these data do not conclusively demonstrate that conformist attitudes, rather than other correlates of these attitudes, made for significantly higher likelihood of promotion. In principle, only a completely controlled experiment, obviously not feasible in the present instance, would demonstrate this beyond all reasonable doubt. But controlled experiment aside, this panel study, holding constant the factors of age and education which had been found to be related both to attitudes and promotion, goes a long way toward demonstrating a relationship between the incidence of conformist attitudes and subsequent advancement. In this respect the study moves well beyond the point reached by the use of less rigorous data, indicating a static correlation between rank and conformist attitudes, inasmuch as it can show that those with conformist attitudes were more likely to be *subsequently* promoted. See I, 272-273.

[2] Although the absolute percentages of men endorsing a given sentiment cannot of course be taken at face value since these percentages are affected by the sheer phrasing of the sentiment, it is nevertheless suggestive that data presented earlier in this volume (*e.g.*, I, 147 ff.) find only a small minority of the samples of enlisted men in this study adhering to the officially approved attitudes. By and large, a significantly larger proportion of officers abide by these attitudes.

[3] There is nothing fixed about the boundaries separating in-groups from out-groups, membership-groups from non-membership-groups. These change with the changing situation. *Vis-à-vis* civilians or an alien group, men in the Army may regard themselves and be regarded as members of an in-group; yet, in another context, enlisted men may regard themselves and be regarded as an in-group in distinction to the out-group of officers. Since these concepts are relative to the situation, rather than absolute, there is no paradox in referring to the officers as an out-group for enlisted men in one context, and as members of the more inclusive in-group, in another context.

the gist of the finding in *The American Soldier* that those privates who accepted the official values of the Army hierarchy were more likely than others to be promoted. The hypothesis regarding the second function still remains to be tested. But it would not, in principle, be difficult to discover empirically whether those men who, through a kind of *anticipatory socialization*, take on the values of the non-membership group to which they aspire, find readier acceptance by that group and make an easier adjustment to it. This would require the development of indices of group acceptance and adjustment, and a comparison, in terms of these indices, of those newcomers to a group who had previously oriented themselves to the group's values and those who had not. More concretely, in the present instance, it would have entailed a comparative study among the privates promoted to higher rank, of the subsequent group adjustment of those who had undergone the hypothesized preparation for status shifts and those who had previously held fast to the values of their in-group of enlisted men. Indices of later adjustment could be related to indices of prior value-orientation. This would constitute a systematic empirical test of a functional hypothesis.

It appears, further, that anticipatory socialization is functional for the individual only within a relatively open social structure providing for mobility. For only in such a structure would such attitudinal and behavior preparation for status shifts be followed by actual changes of status in a substantial proportion of cases. By the same token, the same pattern of anticipatory socialization would be dysfunctional for the individual in a relatively closed social structure, where he would not find acceptance by the group to which he aspires and would probably lose acceptance, because of his out-group orientation, by the group to which he belongs. This latter type of case will be recognized as that of the marginal man, poised on the edge of several groups but fully accepted by none of them.

Thus, the often-studied case of the marginal man[1] and the case of the enlisted man who takes the official military mores as a positive frame of reference can be identified, in a functional theory of reference group behavior, as special cases of anticipatory socialization. The marginal man pattern represents the special case in a relatively closed social system, in which the members of one group take as a positive frame of reference the norms of a group from which they are excluded in principle. Within such a social structure, anticipatory socialization becomes dysfunctional for the individual who becomes the victim of aspirations he cannot achieve and hopes he cannot satisfy. But, as the panel study seems to indicate, precisely the same kind of reference group behavior within a relatively open social system

[1] Qualitative descriptions of the behavior of marginal men, as summarized, for example, by E. V. Stonequist, *The Marginal Man* (New York: Scribner's, 1937), can be analytically recast as that special and restricted case of reference group behavior in which the individual seeks to abandon one membership group for another to which he is socially forbidden access.

is functional for the individual at least to the degree of helping him to achieve the status to which he aspires. The same reference group behavior in different social structures has different consequences.

To this point, then, we find that positive orientation toward the norms of a non-membership group is precipitated by a passage between membership-groups, either in fact or in fantasy, and that the functional or dysfunctional consequences evidently depend upon the relatively open or closed character of the social structure in which this occurs. And what would, at first glance, seem entirely unrelated and disparate forms of behavior — the behavior of such marginal men as the Cape Coloured or the Eurasian, and of enlisted men adopting the values of military strata other than their own — are seen, after appropriate conceptualization, as special cases of reference group behavior.

Although anticipatory socialization may be functional for the *individual* in an open social system, it is apparently dysfunctional for the solidarity of the *group* or *stratum* to which it belongs. For allegiance to the contrasting mores of another group means defection from the mores of the in-group. And accordingly, as we shall presently see, the in-group responds by putting all manner of social restraints upon such positive orientations to certain out-group norms.

From the standpoint of the larger social system, the Army as a whole, positive orientation toward the official mores would appear to be functional in supporting the legitimacy of the structure and in keeping the structure of authority intact. (This is presumably what is meant when the text of *The American Soldier* refers to these conformist attitudes as "favorable from the Army's point of view.") But manifestly, much research needs to be done before one can say that this is indeed the case. It is possible, for example, that the secondary effects of such orientations may be so deleterious to the solidarity of the primary groups of enlisted men that their morale sags. A concrete research question might help clarify the problem: are outfits with relatively large minorities of men positively oriented to the official Army values more likely to exhibit signs of anomie and personal disorganization (*e.g.* non-battle casualties)? In such situations, does the personal "success" of conformists (promotion) only serve to depress the morale of the others by rewarding those who depart from the in-group mores?

In this panel study, as well as in several of the others we have reviewed here — for example, the study of soldiers' evaluations of the justification for their induction into the Army — reference group behavior is evidently related to the legitimacy ascribed to institutional arrangements. Thus, the older married soldier is less likely to think it "fair" that he was inducted; most enlisted men think it "unfair" that promotions are presumably based on "who you know, not what you know"; and so on. In part, this apparent emphasis on legitimacy is of course an artifact of the research: many of the questions put to soldiers had to do with their conception of the legitimate or illegitimate character of their situation or of prevailing institutional arrangements. But the researchers' own focus of interest was in turn the result of their having observed that soldiers were, to a significant degree, actually concerned with such issues of institutional legitimacy, as the spontaneous comments of enlisted men often indicate.[1]

This bears notice because imputations of legitimacy to social arrangements seem functional related to reference group behavior. They apparently affect *the range of the inter-group or inter-individual comparisons* that will typically be made. If the structure of a rigid system of stratification, for example, is generally defined as legitimate, if the rights, perquisites and obligations of each stratum are generally held to be morally right, then the individuals within each stratum will be the less likely to take the situation of the other strata as a context for appraisal of their own lot. They will, presumably, tend to confine their comparisons to other members of their own or neighboring social stratum. If, however, the system of stratification is under wide dispute, then members of some strata are more likely to contrast their own situation with that of others, and shape their self-appraisals accordingly. This variation in the structure of systems and in the degree of legitimacy imputed to the rules of the game may help account for the often-noticed fact that the degree of dissatisfaction with their lot is often less among the people in severely depressed social strata in a relatively rigid social system, than among those strata who are apparently "better off" in a more mobile social system. At any rate, the *range of groups* taken as effective bases of comparison in different social systems may well turn out to be closely connected with the degree to which legitimacy is ascribed to the prevailing social structure.

Though much remains to be said, this is perhaps enough to suggest that the pattern of anticipatory socialization may have diverse consequences for the individuals manifesting it, the groups to which they belong, and the more inclusive social structure. And through such re-examination of this panel study on the personal rewards of conformity, it becomes possible to specify some additional types of problems involved in a more comprehensive functional analysis of such reference group behavior. For example:

1) Since only a fraction of the in-group orient themselves positively toward the values of a non-membership group, it is necessary to discover the social position and personality types of those most likely to do so. For instance, are isolates in the group particularly ready to take up these alien values?

2) Much attention has been paid to the processes making for positive orientation to the norms of one's own group. But what are the processes making for such orientations to other groups or strata? Do relatively high rates of mobility serve to reinforce these latter orientations? (It will be remembered that *The American Soldier* provides data tangential to this point in the discussion of rates of promotion and assessment of promotion chances.) Suitably adapted, such data on actual rates of mobility, aspirations, and anticipatory socialization to the norms of a higher social stratum would extend a functional theory of conformist and deviant behavior.

3) What connections, if any, subsist between varying rates of mobility and acceptance of the legitimacy of the system of stratification by individuals diversely located in that system? Since it appears that systems with very low rates of mobility may achieve wide acceptance, what other interpretative variables need be included to account for the relationship between rates of mobility and imputations of legitimacy?

4) In civilian or military life, are the mobile individuals who are most ready to reaffirm the values of a power-holding or prestige-holding group the sooner accepted by that group? Does this operate effectively primarily as a latent function, in which the mobile individuals adopt these values because they experience them as superior, rather than deliberately adopting them only to gain acceptance? If such orientations are definitely motivated by the wish to belong, do they then become self-defeating, with the mobile individuals being characterized as strainers, strivers (or, in the Army, as brown-nosers bucking for promotion)?

SOCIAL PROCESSES SUSTAINING AND CURBING POSITIVE ORIENTATIONS TO NON-MEMBERSHIP GROUPS

In the course of considering the functions of anticipatory socialization, we have made passing allusion to social processes which sustain or curb this pattern of behavior. Since it is precisely the data concerning such processes which are not easily caught up in the type of survey materials on attitudes primarily utilized in *The American Soldier*, and since these processes are central to any theory of reference group behavior, they merit further consideration.

As we have seen, what is anticipatory socialization from the standpoint of the individual is construed as defection and nonconformity by the group of which he is a member. To the degree that the individual identifies himself with another group, he alienates himself from his own group. Yet although the field of sociology has for generations been concerned with the determinants and consequences of group cohesion, it has given little *systematic* attention to the complementary subject of group alienation. When considered at all, it has been

[1] For example, in response to the question, "If you could talk with the President of the United States, what are the three most important questions you would want to ask him about war and your part in it?", a substantial proportion of both Negro and white troops evidently raised questions regarding the legitimacy of current practices and arrangements in the Army. The Negro troops of course centered on unjust practices of race discrimination, but 31 per cent of the white troops also introduced "questions and criticisms of Army life." (I, 504, *et passim*.)

confined to such special cases as second-generation immigrants, conflict of loyalties between gang and family, *etc.* In large measure, the subject has been left to the literary observer, who could detect the drama inherent in the situation of the renegade, the traitor, the deserter. The value-laden connotations of these terms used to describe identification with groups other than one's own definitely suggest that these patterns of behavior have been typically regarded from the standpoint of the membership group. (Yet one group's renegade may be another group's convert.) Since the assumption that its members will be loyal is found in every group, else it would have no group character, no dependability of action, transfer of loyalty to another group (particularly a group operating in the same sphere of politics or economy), is regarded primarily in affective terms of sentiment rather than in detached terms of analysis. The renegade or traitor or climber — whatever the folkphrase may be — more often becomes an object of vilification than an object for sociological study.

The framework of reference group theory, detached from the language of sentiment, enables the sociologist to identify and to locate renegadism, treason, the assimilation of immigrants, class mobility, social climbing, *etc.* as so many special forms of identification with what is at the time a non-membership group. In doing so, it affords the possibility of studying these, not as *wholly* particular and unconnected forms of behavior, but as different expressions of similar processes under significantly different conditions. The transfer of allegiance of upper class individuals from their own to a lower class — whether this be in the pre-revolutionary period of 18th century France or of 20th century Russia — belongs to the same family of sociological problems as the more familiar identification of lower class individuals with a higher class, a subject which has lately begun to absorb the attention of sociologists in a society where upward social mobility is an established value. Our cultural emphases notwithstanding, the phenomenon of topdogs adopting the values of the underdog is as much a reference group phenomenon lending itself to further inquiry as the underdogs seeking to become topdogs.

In such defections from the in-group, it may turn out, as has often been suggested, that it is the isolate, nominally in a group but only slightly incorporated in its network of social relations, who is most likely to become positively oriented toward non-membership groups. But, even if generally true, this is a static correlation and, therefore, only partly illuminating. What needs to be uncovered is the process through

which this correlation comes to hold. Judging from some of the qualitative data in *The American Soldier* and from other studies of group defection, there is continued and cumulative interplay between a deterioration of *social relations* within the membership group and positive *attitudes* toward the norms of a non-membership group.

What the individual experiences as estrangement from a group of which he is a member tends to be experienced by his associates as repudiation of the group, and this ordinarily evokes a hostile response. As social relations between the individual and the rest of the group deteriorate, the norms of the group become less binding for him. For since he is progressively seceding from the group and being penalized by it, he is the less likely to experience rewards for adherence to the group's norms. Once initiated, this process seems to move toward a cumulative detachment from the group, in terms of attitudes and values as well as in terms of social relations. And to the degree that he orients himself toward out-group values, perhaps affirming them verbally and expressing them in action, he only widens the gap and reinforces the hostility between himself and his in-group associates. Through the interplay of dissociation and progressive alienation from the group values, he may become doubly motivated to orient himself toward the values of another group and to affiliate himself with it. There then remains the distinct question of the objective possibility of affiliating himself with his reference group. If the possibility is negligible or absent, then the alienated individual becomes socially rootless. But if the social system realistically allows for such change in group affiliations, then the individual estranged from the one group has all the more motivation to belong to the other.

This hypothetical account of dissociation and alienation, which of course only touches upon the processes which call for research in the field of reference group behavior, seems roughly in accord with qualitative data in *The American Soldier* on what was variously called brown-nosing, bucking for promotion, and sucking up. Excerpts from the diary of an enlisted man illustrate the interplay between dissociation and alienation: the outward-oriented man is too sedulous in abiding by the official mores — "But you're *supposed* to [work over there]. The lieutenant said you were supposed to," — this evokes group hostility expressed in epithets and ridicule—"Everybody is making sucking, kissing noises at K and S now" — followed by increasing dissociation within the group — "Ostracism was visible, but mild . . . few were friendly toward them . . . occasions arose where people avoided their company" — and more frequent association with men representing the non-membership reference group — "W, S, and K sucked all afternoon; hung around lieutenants and asked bright questions." In this briefly summarized account, one sees the mechanisms of the in-group operating to curb positive orientation to the official mores[1] as well as the process through which this orienta-

---

[1] An official War Department pamphlet given to new recruits attempted to give "bucking" a blessing: " 'Bucking' implies all the things a soldier can honestly do to gain attention and promotion. The Army encourages individuals to put extra effort into drill, extra "spit and polish" into personal appearance. At times this may make things uncomfortable for others who prefer to take things easier, but it stimulates a spirit of competition and improvement which makes ours a better Army." I. 264.

tion develops among those who take these mores as their major frame of reference, considering their ties with the in-group as of only secondary importance.

Judging from implications of this panel research on conformity-and-mobility, then, there is room for study of the consequences of reference group behavior patterns as well as for study of their determinants. Moreover, the consequences pertinent for sociology are not merely those for the individuals engaging in this behavior, but for the groups of which they are a part.

There develops also the possibility that the extent to which legitimacy is accorded the structure of these groups and the status of their members may affect the range of groups or strata which they ordinarily take as a frame of reference in assessing their own situation. And finally, this panel research calls attention to the need for close study of those processes in group life which sustain or curb positive orientations to non-membership groups, thus perhaps leading to a linking of reference group theory and current theories of social organization.

Social Stratification and Mobility in the Soviet Union[1]

Alex Inkeles[2]

IN INTRODUCING the new Soviet Constitution in 1936 Stalin stated that the Soviet population was divided into two major classes, the working class and the peasantry, and a third group, the intelligentsia, which as a genuflection in the direction of Marxian orthodoxy he called a *stratum*. The members of all groups were defined as being "equal in rights" within Soviet society, and Stalin further asserted that under Soviet conditions the amount of social distance and the political and economic contradictions between the groups was diminishing and indeed was being obliter-

ated.[3] Even as he made these declarations, however, the actual relations between and within the major social groups were moving in a very different direction under the impact of social forces which Stalin had himself largely set in motion in 1931.

For in that year, faced by severe problems in relation to the productivity of labor and an extraordinarily high rate of labor turnover under the First Five Year Plan,[4] Stalin launched an attack against "equality-mongering" and wage equalization and began a movement for personal incentive based on differential rewards. No working class in history had managed without its own intelligentsia, he asserted, and there were "no grounds for believing that the working class of the U.S.S.R. can manage without its own industrial and technical intelligentsia." There were in every shop and factory, furthermore, certain "leading groups" of skilled workers who are "the chief link in production." In consideration of these facts he called for an end to the "baiting of specialists" and its replacement by a new policy "of showing them greater attention and solicitude, displaying more boldness in enlisting their cooperation . . . (and) creating suitable conditions for them to work in, without stinting money for this purpose." In regard to the skilled workers, he ordered that they be treated to

---

[1] Expanded version of paper read at the annual meeting of the American Sociological Society held in New York, December 28–30, 1949.

[2] The author is indebted to the Russian Research Center of Harvard University, of which he is a Research Associate, for making available research assistance in the persons of Arnold Horelick and Hans Rogger.

[3] Joseph Stalin, *Voprosy Leninizma*, 11th ed., Moscow: Ogiz, 1940, pp. 510–512, 516.

[4] In 1930, for example, the average number of workers engaged was 174 per cent and the average number who left jobs was 152 per cent of the total average in employment during the year. See Alexander Baykov, *The Development of Soviet Economic System*, New York: Macmillan Company, 1947, p. 215. See also Maurice Dobb, *Soviet Economic Development Since 1917*, New York: International Publishers, 1948, pp. 239–243.

Reprinted from "Social Stratification and Mobility in the Soviet Union: 1940–1950," *American Sociological Review* (1950), pp. 465–479, by permission of the editor and the author. (Copyright, 1950, by American Sociological Review.)

promotion to higher positions and to payment of higher levels of wages, to a "a system of payment which gives each worker his due according to his qualifications." The unskilled workers were to be given a similar "stimulus and the prospect of advancement" by this pattern of wage payments. And, Stalin affirmed, "the more boldly we do this the better."[1]

Rapidly implemented in the succeeding years, Stalin's campaign produced a series of new institutions for differential economic reward and strengthened those which existed only in rudimentary form: on the collective farms, the labor-day and the piecework system of payment; in industry, more precise gradings between the various skill categories, increasingly great spreads between the wages of the least skilled and the most skilled workers, and the extreme extension of the progressive piece-rate system; and in the case of managers and technicians, pay scales separate and distinct from those for workers, special "personal salaries," and bonuses taken out of the enterprises' profits.

As a result of these and related economic and political measures the Soviet Union possessed by 1940 an elaborately and precisely stratified status system within which at least ten major social-class groups could be distinguished for purposes of sociological analysis. Unfortunately, limits of space permit neither full description of each of the groups nor a detailed statement of the method by which they were delineated, and we must restrict ourselves here merely to enumerating them.[2]

The intelligentsia was actually divided into at least four sub-units:

1) The ruling élite, a small group consisting of high Party, government, economic, and military officials, prominent scientists, and selected artists and writers.

2) The superior intelligentsia, composed of the intermediary ranks of the categories mentioned above, plus certain important technical specialists.

3) The general intelligentsia, incorporating most of the professional groups, the middle ranks of the bureaucracy, managers of small enterprises, junior military officers, technicians, etc.

4) The white collar group, largely synonymous with the Soviet term for employees, which ranges from petty-bureaucrats through accountants and bookkeepers down to the level of ordinary clerks and office workers.

The working class was also markedly differentiated, incorporating:

1) The working class "aristocracy," this is, the most highly skilled and productive workers, in particular large numbers of the so-called Stakhanovites.

2) The rank and file workers, those in one of the lesser skill grades earning slightly above or below the average wage for all workers.

3) The disadvantaged workers, estimated to include as many as one-fourth of the labor force, whose low level of skill and lack of productivity or initiative kept them close to the minimum wage level.

The peasantry, although relatively homogeneous, also was divided into distinguishable subgroups:

1) The well-to-do peasants, consisting of those particularly advantaged by virtue of the location, fertility, or crop raised by their collective farms — i.e., those living on the so-called "millionaire" farms — and those whose trade, skill, or productivity pushes them into the higher income brackets even on the less prosperous farms.

2) The average peasant, shading off into the least productive or poor peasant groups.

There was, in addition, a residual group of those in forced labor camps who are really outside the formal class structure, although available reports indicate that these camps have an internal class structure of their own which derives its main lines from the class structure of the society as a whole.

The sequence in which the subgroups are listed above may be taken as reflecting their rank order within each of the three major categories, but this does not apply to the list as a whole. The rank order within the structure as a whole appears to be as follows: ruling élite (1); superior intelligentsia (2); general intelligentsia (3); working class aristocracy (4); white collar (5.5); well-to-do peasants (5.5); average workers (7); average peasants (8.5); disadvantaged workers (8.5); forced labor (10). It must be recognized, however, that the complexity of the structure and the degree of variation within each of the subgroups was such as to make any such rank ordering a very rough approximation. In addition, this type of rank ordering does not reflect the actual degree of social distance between strata.

Membership in any one of these major social-class groups[3] was predominantly determined on the basis of a complex of conditions, of which occupation, income, and the possession of power and authority were the main elements. Thus, the system was essentially based on differences in the functions performed by individuals in the productive process, the administrative apparatus, and the power structure rather than on either hereditary

---

[1] See his speeches of February 4 and June 23, 1931 addressed to Soviet economic managers in J. Stalin, *Selected Writings*, New York: International Publishers, 1942, pp. 194–202 and 203–221.

[2] The class structure of the Soviet Union has not yet been given adequate extended treatment in the sociological literature. Some brief general treatments of varying quality are available. See David Dallin, *The Real Soviet Russia*, New Haven: Yale University Press, 1947, pp. 108–226; Rudolph Schlesinger, *The Spirit of Post-War Russia*, London: Dennis Dobson, Ltd., 1947, pp. 21–47; Nicholas S. Timasheff, *The Great Retreat*, New York: E. P. Dutton, 1946, pp. 293–331; Julian Towster, *Political Power in the U.S.S.R., 1917–1947*, New York: Oxford University Press, 1948, pp. 313–343; A. Yugow, *Russia's Economic Front for War and Peace*, New York: Harper Brothers, 1942, pp. 220–243, 256–259.

[3] The term "social-class group" as used here represents a composite, based on the criteria used by Max Weber to distinguish "economic class" and "social status groups." See *From Max Weber: Essays in Sociology*, H. H. Gerth and C. W. Mills, eds., New York: Oxford University Press, 1946, pp. 180–195; *The Theory of Social and Economic Organization*, A. M. Henderson and Talcott Parsons, eds., New York: Oxford University Press, 1947, pp. 424–429.

and semi-hereditary factors, which were primary in defining social position in Tsarist Russia, or on ideological considerations, which predominantly determined the stratification patterns during the earlier years of the Soviet regime.

Yet while these divisions were essentially economic and functional, the valuation of the different occupations was markedly affected by cultural factors, such as the traditional tendency to rate brain work above physical labor. The strength of such tendencies, inadvertently strengthened by the regime itself,[1] is strikingly reflected in the following criticism directed at Soviet parents:

> Many of us are to blame for spoiling our children, asking them when they are still in rompers, "What do you want to be when you grow up?" and falling into raptures at their answers — an academician, a ballerina, or something else of that sort. And now these same children are called upon to be steel smelters, rolling mill operators, forge hands — dirty, hot, and hard jobs.[2]

Furthermore, despite the fact that the range of income and special privilege available to each of the major groups was fairly distinct, there was a significant degree of overlapping. Thus, an appreciable number of workers and peasants had incomes on the average higher than those of large segments of the white collar group

and in some cases equaling the incomes of many individuals in the general and even in the superior intelligentsia.[3] Highly skilled workers, particularly the Stakhanovites, were also granted greater privileges in the access to scarce goods and services — especially under rationing — and were awarded more formal prestige and status by the regime than most ordinary employees. Finally, the major groupings based on income and power had begun to develop fairly definitive styles of life, to elaborate differential patterns of association, and to manifest varying degrees of group-consciousness.

As a result of these conditions the component social-class groups were enmeshed in a complicated system of inter-relationships producing a pattern of social stratification which was certainly not as simple as Stalin's description of it. Neither did it conform to some of the descriptions of it in Western literature on the U.S.S.R. in which the error was frequently made of placing all Party members — regardless of income, power, or prestige — at the head of the social hierarchy, or of assuming that the divisions between the *occupational* groups were so sharp and distinct that all employees ranked above all workers, and all workers above all peasants.

Although a relatively precise system of social stratification had been elaborated by 1940, this system was the product of a recent and enormous shifting of population into the newly developed positions opened up as a result of the expansion of the national economy under the industrialization and collectivization programs from 1928 on. It is to be noted that while the total number of workers and employees more than doubled in roughly the first decade of the Plans,[4] the size of the intelligentsia increased at the striking rate of 3.8 times between 1926 and 1937. In the same period the number of responsible managers of large and small scale enterprises increased by 4.6 times, and other categories showed even more marked expansion — the number of engineers and architects being 7.9 times, and the number of scientific workers (including professors) being 5.9 times greater in 1937 than in 1926. In the case of agriculture alone some 580,000 positions, almost all newly created, were filled by collective farm chairmen and their deputies.[5]

Comparable opportunities for advancement became available at other levels as the changes in the socio-economic and political structure created a demand for enormous numbers of lower managerial personnel, semi-professionals, and skilled workers. During 1938, for example, the program for giving initial and refresher training for those in industry and allied fields encompassed 6,580,500 people outside of the universities and secondary schools. The great bulk (5,418,000) were enrolled in "courses" designed to impart rudimentary industrial skills, but almost 300,000 were training to be foremen and Stakhanovites. Similarly in the field of agriculture, 1,211,387 persons completed brief training courses during 1937 and 1938 to qualify for positions

---

[1] Both because of its desire to capitalize on the promise of social mobility for all strata of the population, and because of the extreme need for technically competent personnel created by the expansion of the economy, Soviet propaganda in the 'thirties glorified the status of the professionally trained. The consequences of such emphasis were apparently far from fully foreseen by the leaders. Note the comment of the late President Kalinin: "Formerly we educated people to become intellectuals and not persons doing physical labor. I personally consider this incorrect, since in our state the majority of the population is, after all, occupied in physical labor." Quoted in *Oktyabr*, No. 10, 1944, p. 119.

[2] A. Loginov, "Young Complements of the Working Class," *Oktyabr*, No. 10, 1944, pp. 120–121, quoted in Philip R. Lever, the "State Labor Reserves System of the Soviet Union," unpublished M.A. thesis, Columbia University, 1948.

[3] See Abram Bergson, *The Structure of Soviet Wages*, Cambridge: Harvard University Press, 1946, *passim*, and William Schumer, "Incomes of Selected Professions in the U.S.S.R." unpublished M.A. thesis, Columbia University, 1948. Unfortunately, both of these works deal only with the period up to the mid-thirties, after which the dispersion of incomes within and between particular occupations generally increased. For comments on later developments see: Gregory Bienstock, S. M. Schwarz, and A. Yugow, *Management in Russian Industry and Agriculture*, Oxford University Press, 1944, pp. 91–95, 163–169; Baykov, *op. cit.*, pp. 339–350; Dobb, *op. cit.*, pp. 424–429; Naum Jasny, *The Socialized Agriculture of the U.S.S.R.*, Stanford University Press, 1949, pp. 688–705.

[4] *Sotsialisticheskoe Stroitel'stvo Soyuza SSR, 1933–1938*, Moscow: Gosplanizdat, 1939, p. 20.

[5] K. Seleznev, "On the New Soviet Intelligentsia," *Partiinoe Stroitel'stvo*, No. 13, 1939, p. 40. *XVIII S'ezd Vsesoyusznoi Kommunisticheskoi Partii*, Stenographic Report, Moscow: Ogiz, 1939, pp. 309–310.

as combine operators, mechanics, veterinary assistants, field brigade leaders, etc.[1]

A description of mobility in this period must, finally, give attention to the marked changes in the position of women in the Soviet Union. The proportion which women constituted of the total labor force increased from 28 per cent in 1928 to 38 per cent in 1938,[2] which meant that the absolute number of women workers and employees was more than doubled. Throughout this period women comprised a large part, in some cases over half, of the students at industrial training schools, and as a result they came to represent a significant proportion of the skilled workers in Soviet industry.[3] Their advance in fields requiring higher training was even more impressive. Between 1928 and 1938 the proportion of women in the universities increased from 28 per cent to 43 per cent, and from 37 per cent to 51 per cent in the specialized secondary schools.[4] The effect of this upward movement was reflected in the fact that they constituted about 40 per cent of all specialists in the Soviet Union before the war.[5] The shifts in the rural regions were no less striking, as large numbers of women assumed positions of responsibility and skill on the collective farms.[6]

Thus it may be said that on the eve of the war decade the Soviet Union possessed virtually a completely open class system, characterized by a high degree of mobility. This mobility was created predominantly by the tremendous expansion of the national economy, but was given additional impetus by the high rate of natural attrition accompanying the revolutionary process, by the declassing — and in part physical elimination — of major portions of the former upper and middle classes, and by a political system which periodically removed large numbers of people from responsible positions by means of the *chistka* or purge.

The war decade must be recognized as having provided an extreme test of the stability and solidity of the system of stratification existing in 1940. For on the two former occasions when the Soviet Union had experienced extensive social upheaval and strain there had been a marked tendency for the society to move away from stratification towards social equalization and the elimination of economic class differences.[7] This tendency was most evident in the period of War Communism from 1918 to 1921, and was perhaps best reflected in the fact that in the later year the wages of the most skilled workers were only 102 per cent of those of the least skilled workers, that is, they were in effect equal.[8] A similar tendency, although less marked, was manifested during the early turbulent years of the First Plan. In industry this took most concrete form in the tendencies towards wage equalization which Stalin later fought. And in agriculture it was apparent in the tremendous levelling effect of the forced collectivization, which swept away the entire stratum of rich peasants or *kulaks* along with many of the middle peasants, and reduced the remainder to the common, and initially relatively impoverished, status of collective farm members.

In sharp contrast, during the war years the system of stratification was in no major respect subjected by the Communist leaders to measures designed to press equalization and to erase the lines of stratification. On the contrary, almost all of the war-time measures respected the major pre-war lines of demarcation. This applied in the realm of monetary rewards; in the structure and operation of the rationing system, particularly through the use of "closed stores" open only to specified segments of the population; in the application of differential patterns for evacuating populations from threatened areas, and so on.

Not only did the system of stratification demonstrate its durability during the war years, but there was an intensification of the process of lending greater precision to the lines of division and of more fully formalizing and institutionalizing the differences between the major social-class groups. This was most strikingly indicated, indeed it was symbolized, by the regulations established to govern the award of the most important military decorations created during the war. For the first time in Soviet history it was provided by law that certain awards such as the Order of Victory, formally defined

---

[1] *Kul'turnoe Stroitel'stvo SSSR*, Moscow: Gosplanizdat, 1940, pp. 136, 138.

[2] *Planovoe Khozyaistvo*, No. 10, 1939, p. 114. This increase was not bought cheaply. Women worked very largely because of the need to supplement family income. Despite considerable strides in the provision of creches, kindergartens, and communal services, the available resources were far from enabling women to work without extreme hardships arising from their continuing responsibilities as wives and mothers.

[3] In 1941, for example, women constituted 32 per cent of the electricians in electrical sub-stations, 29 per cent of the machine molders, and 27 per cent of the compressor operators. It is important to note that they were represented as well in occupations most unsuited for women, being 17 per cent of the stevedores and 6 per cent of the steamboiler stokers. N. Voznesensky, *The Economy of the U.S.S.R. During World War II*, Washington: Public Affairs Press, 1948, p. 66.

[4] *Kul'turnoe Stroitel'stvo*, p. 113.

[5] By 1949 women constituted 44 per cent of all specialists in the Soviet Union. The pre-war percentage was, of course, somewhat lower. *Izvestiya*, March 8, 1949.

[6] In addition to providing concrete opportunities for training and advancement, the collective farm introduced a more general and far-reaching change in the position of women. For under the labor-day system of payment each woman is paid directly for her work, rather than having the rewards for her labor go into the general family funds through the person of her husband or father. Sir John Maynard regarded this change as having produced one of the fundamental social sources of support for the regime, by putting the village women "on the side of the Soviets." *Russia in Flux*, New York: The Macmillan Co., 1948, pp. 399–400.

[7] This applied, of course, only in regard to those segments of the population considered eligible for membership in the new society, especially workers and poor peasants. The policy in regard to the former so-called "possessing classes" was not merely to equalize but to eliminate them. The old technical and administrative intelligentsia were associated with the possessing classes in this respect; but since they could not be destroyed without irreparable loss to the society, the initial goal in their case was the more limited one of declassing them and bringing them to the same or even a lower status level than workers or peasants.

[8] Baykov, *op. cit.*, p. 43.

as the highest Soviet military decoration, was to be granted only to commanding personnel of highest rank, and so on through the hierarchy of military command down to such medals as the Orders of Glory, which were awarded only to junior officers and enlisted personnel.[1] This was in marked contrast to the conditions for granting the military awards in existence before the war, such as the Order of the Red Banner, granted without distinction to the rank and file, officers, and high commanding personnel alike.[2]

Thus, the Soviet regime has adopted the principle that recognition and reward are to be determined not only by the *extent* of a man's contribution beyond the call of duty, but also by the *status* he held when he made this contribution. A comparable development occurred with the creation in 1939 of special "Stalin Prizes" for outstanding contributions in the arts, sciences, and industry. The prizes are awarded annually to as many as a thousand persons, and range from 50,000 to 300,000 rubles in cash.[3] Ordinary citizens, of course, have very slight chances of qualifying for awards in the arts and sciences, but even in the case of prizes granted for inventions and fundamental improvements in production methods there is almost no representation of the rank and file worker or even of the lower ranks of industrial management such as foremen.[4]

Perhaps even more striking has been the recent practice of providing large cash grants and substantial annuities for the widows and heirs of prominent Soviet officials, scientists, and artists. To choose some examples more or less at random: the wife of Peoples' Artist of the U.S.S.R., A. V. Aleksandrov, was given

50,000 rubles and a personal pension of 750 rubles per month, and his son Yuri a pension of 750 rubles per month until completion of his higher education; the widow of Lt. General of Engineering Troops D. M. Karbyshev was granted a pension of 1,000 rubles a month, and his daughter and son each 700 rubles per month until the completion of their education.[5] No instances are known to this writer of comparable grants made to persons of lesser social rank who made outstanding contributions at the level of *their* occupational skill.

A second major development which tended further to formalize the distinctions between the major social groupings was the adoption of a series of laws which placed several millions of Soviet citizens in civilian uniforms. At the present time all officials and responsible personnel, and in some cases rank and file employees and workers, in the railway and river transport systems, in the coal and iron ore industries, in the Ministry of Foreign Affairs and the Procuracy, as well as students in State Labor Reserves Schools, must wear either uniforms — which vary in quality, color, and style according to the status of the wearer — or distinctive insignia of rank in the form of collar tabs and sleeve markings similar to the insignia worn by military personnel.[6] The main reason stated for this innovation was its importance for improving discipline and increasing the authority of those in positions of responsibility,[7] which is itself significant. But this was not simply a wartime emergency measure since in the majority of cases the decision to adopt this system came near the end or after the formal cessation of hostilities, and there has been no indication that a shift in policy is forthcoming.

The fact that large numbers of Soviet citizens now wear insignia of rank formally designating their position in the hierarchy of income, power, and prestige, must be recognized as giving the most direct, formal, and official sanction to a precise system of social stratification. Thus, in effect, the Bolshevik leaders have restored to the Soviet Union the system of *chiny*, a formal civil service ranks, which was a central aspect of the Tsarist system of social differentiation and had traditionally been treated by the Bolsheviks as one of the paramount symbols of class exploitation and stratification.[8] In addition, the insignia of rank will probably serve as a focus around which informal patterns for demanding and giving social deference will develop, and this in turn may be expected to go far in institutionalizing the existing system of stratification.

A third major development was the removal of several economic restrictions which formerly tended to exert an equalizing influence. Among the more striking measures was the abolition of the inheritance tax, in force since 1926, which had provided for taxes graded progressively according to the size of an estate up to 90 per cent of its total value. Under the new law only a governmental registration fee is collected and this fee may not exceed more than 10 per cent of the estate's valuation.[9]

---

[1] For a description of the major decorations created during the war (up to 1944) and the conditions for their award, see *Sbornik Zakonov SSSR: Ukazov Prezidiuma Verkhovnogo Soveta SSSR 1938–1944*, Moscow: 1945, pp. 260–286.

[2] *Malaya Sovetskaya Entsiklopediya*, Moscow: Ogiz, 1938, Vol. 7, p. 767.

[3] For the decree which initially established the Prizes, then limited to 100,000 rubles, see *Pravda*, December 21, 1939.

[4] Of 121 awards made in 1948 for inventions and fundamental improvements in production methods, only 4 went to persons with the rank of foreman and below — to a shepherd, a chief drill master, two foremen, and in one case "the workers of the plant." In each instance, the prize was given *jointly* to these persons and to a man of higher rank — engineer, director of the plant, senior scientist, etc. Based on the notice of awards published in *Pravda*, July 3, 1948.

[5] *Pravda*, August 17, 1946.

[6] For examples see *Vedomosti Verkhovnogo Soveta*, 1943, Nos. 22, 32, 39; *Pravda*, September 5, 12, 24, 1947.

[7] See, for example, the quotation from the 1945 text on *Soviet Administrative Law* cited by V. Gsovski, *Soviet Civil Law*, Ann Arbor: University of Michigan Law School, 2 Vols., Vol. I, p. 144. Also see the *Information Bulletin*, Embassy of the U.S.S.R., Washington, D. C., Nov. 7, 1943, pp. 33–37.

[8] The first major shift in Soviet policy in this respect came with the restoration of regular military ranks in the Soviet armed forces in 1935. See Gsovski, *op. cit.*, pp. 142–143. Special significance, however, attaches to the extension of this practice to status groups in civil life, and particularly to restoration of the term *chin*.

[9] *Vedomosti Verkhovnogo Soveta SSSR*, 1943, No. 3. See V. Gsovski, "Family and Inheritance in Soviet Law," *The Russian Review*, 1947, Vol. 7, No. 1.

This new inheritance law must be seen in the context of the Soviet personal income tax structure. Under the scale established in 1943 progressive rates are applied only up to the level of 1,000 rubles of income per month, with a single rate of 13 per cent for all earnings beyond that point. Thus, a man earning 6,000 rubles per year would pay 5.2 per cent of that sum as income tax, whereas a man earning 60,000 rubles, or ten times the approximate average annual wage in industry, would pay only 12 per cent of his earnings.[1] Incomes of 60,000 rubles per year are by now common in certain segments of the population, and are frequently greatly exceeded. It is significant, for example, that the income tax law of 1940 included provisions for a special tax on incomes in excess of 300,000 rubles made by writers, actors, and other artists.[2] Finally, it must be noted that the large special awards such as the Stalin Prizes are tax free, as is the total income of those who hold such awards as Hero of the Soviet Union and Hero of Socialist Labor,[3] categories which include many of the country's high income earners.

Since only certain groups — such as the ruling élite, the superior intelligentsia, the highly skilled workers, and some *kolkhoz* members[4] — are capable of accumulating large sums of money, these laws act further to reinforce the stratification system. They do so by protecting large income differentials during the life of the earners,[5] and by providing families with the means to maintain their socio-economic position for protracted periods after the death of the head of the household.

As a fourth point here, brief notice must be given to shifts in the relations to the power structure of the various social-class groups. The 18th Communist Party Congress in 1939 placed members of the intelligentsia on an equal footing with workers and peasants seeking to enter the Party, and in fact since that time the Party has given first priority to the enrollment of intellectuals.[6] This shift in the value system and in the practice of the Communist leaders was also reflected more subtly in the manner in which they evaluated the contribution to the war effort of each of the major social groups. The intelligentsia were at all times given full credit for at least an equal share in the victory, and indeed were at times assigned a foremost role.

Just as the system of social stratification emerged essentially intact from this period so did the fact of high social mobility. Indeed, severe wartime personnel losses vacated many positions and thus created new opportunities for advancement. In addition, the restoration of the devastated economy and the further program of expansion undertaken in the Fourth Five-Year Plan have encouraged relatively rapid mobility. It is perhaps sufficient to indicate that by 1946 the number of students in higher educational institutions had reached the pre-war levels, after having fallen to about a third of the former enrollment during the early part of the war, and a large expansion beyond that point has been undertaken.

Yet, it must also be stated that during the war decade forces were set in motion which may in time act seriously to restrict social mobility and to transform the present pattern of stratification into a much more closed class system. There are at least five such developments which deserve mention here.

1) Restrictions on access to education opportunities: On October 2, 1940 the Soviet government simultaneously introduced a labor draft of up to one million youths per year between the ages of fourteen and seventeen for training as industrial workers,[7] and tuition fees at higher schools and for the last three years of secondary education.[8] Both laws continue in effect and appear to be intended for extended operation.

[1] A. K. Suchkova (ed.) *Dokhody Gosudarstvennogo Byudzheta SSSR*, Moscow: Gosfinizdat, 1945, pp. 133–136; K. N. Plotnikov, *Byudzhet Sotsialisticheskogo Gosudarstva*, Leningrad: Gosfinizdat, 1948, pp. 278–282. The new tax law of 1943, in comparison with the previous law, actually provided slight tax relief for those in the lower brackets and a slight increase in the rates for the upper brackets. The striking fact about the law was that it continued in force a tax system involving only the most modest progression in rates for higher income brackets. This pattern was set in the early thirties at a time when there were relatively few incomes over 600 rubles per month, and the general income spread was relatively slight.

[2] V. P. D'yachenko (ed.), *Finansy i Kredit SSSR*, Moscow: Gosfinizdat, 1940, p. 321.

[3] Plotnikov, *op. cit.*, p. 281.

[4] Special income tax provisions (and inheritance laws) govern peasants on the collective farms. Major segments of the peasantry accumulated very large sums of cash holdings during the recent war through the sale of extremely scarce food products. It was largely to prevent this money from flooding the consumers goods market that the monetary reform of 1947 was carried out. See B. Alexandrov, "The Soviet Currency Reform," *The Russian Review*, Jan., 1949, Vol. 8, No. 1, pp. 56–61.

[5] Probably of even greater significance than the modest direct income tax in protecting existing income differentials is the Soviet system of indirect taxation. The turnover tax — not seen by the consumer since it is included in the price — is levelled primarily on consumption goods, about 85 per cent of the collections in 1940 being derived from food and textile products. The importance of this tax is clear when it is recognized that it regularly accounts for about 60 per cent of the total budget receipts of the government and that this budget, unlike those in most countries, includes almost all of the nation's allocations for new industrial capital investment in the coming year. Its impact on personal income is highlighted by the fact that it represents from 50 to 80 per cent of the selling price of most mass consumption items. It appears to be, in its social effect, a regressive tax. Yugow, *op. cit.*, pp. 125–138. For an opposing view see Dobb, *op. cit.*, pp. 360–374.

[6] See B. Moore, Jr., "The Communist Party of the Soviet Union: 1928–1944," *American Sociological Review*, IX (June, 1944), 267–268; Merle Fainsod, "Postwar Role of the Communist Party." *The Annals of the American Academy of Political and Social Science*, 263 (May, 1944), 20–32.

[7] *Vedomosti Verkhovnogo Soveta SSSR*, 1940, No. 37. The initial decree provided for the drafting of boys only, but a later decree of June 19, 1947 provided as well for the drafting of girls in the 15–18 age group, and extended the age of eligible males up to and including 19 years.

[8] The following fees were established: for the eighth through the tenth grades of regular secondary and specialized (*tekhnikum*) secondary schools — 200 rubles per year in Moscow, Leningrad, and capital cities of union republics, 150 rubles elsewhere; for higher educational institutions — 400 rubles per year in Moscow, Leningrad, etc., 300 rubles elsewhere. Students at higher schools for the study of art, music, and the theater must pay 500 rubles.

[*footnote continued on p. 522*

In terms of human freedom, the state labor-reserves draft serves to restrict the right of millions of Soviet youths to choose their occupation and place of work,[1] and the fee system was certainly a departure from standard Soviet practice and ideology — the original decree being in violation of the explicit provisions of the Constitution, since amended to eliminate the discrepancy.[2] But specification of the implications of these

[1] For a description of the structure and functioning of the system see Philip R. Lever, *op. cit., passim.*

[2] Article 121 of the 1936 (Stalin) Constitution had provided for "free education, including higher education." (*Konstitutsiya Soyuza Sovetskikh Sotsialisticheskikh Respublik*, Moscow, 1938, p. 87). It was amended by the Supreme Soviet on Feb. 25, 1947, to read: "free education, up to and including the seventh grade. . . ." *Constitution of the Union of Soviet Socialist Republics*, Moscow, 1947 (in English).

[3] For relevant citations and discussion see Lever, *op. cit.,* pp. 39–45.

[4] *Bolshevik*, Nos. 7–8, April, 1943, p. 21, cited by Lever, *op. cit.,* p. 59.

[5] Order No. 1, Chief Administration of Labor Reserves under the Council of Peoples' Commissars, Article 17, provided that one-third of the funds received for goods and services produced by the schools should be paid to the students. *Izvestiya*, October 5, 1940.

[6] Decree of the Central Committee of the All-Union Communist Party (Bolshevik) and the Council of Peoples' Commissars of the U.S.S.R., of July 11, 1940, No. 1228; Instruction of the Ministry of Higher Education of the U.S.S.R. of February 25, 1947. *Vysshaya Shkola*, Moscow, 1948, pp. 81–86.

[7] Since September 1, 1948, stipends are granted only to students who have either excellent or good grades, with the exception of those in certain important schools, such as those for mining and metallurgy, in which all passing students receive stipends. In 1946 S. Kaftanov, Minister of Higher Education, reported that more than 78 per cent of the students had passed all their courses with grades of "good" or better. Previously, with the exception of the war years, 1940–43, stipends had been granted on a more liberal basis, being given to all with "passing grades." This change has meant some reduction in the number receiving stipends, since in 1939 90.6 per cent of all students in higher schools received them. *Byulleten' Ministerstva Vysshego Obrazovaniya SSSR*, No. 10, October, 1948, p. 7; *Vestnik Vysshei Shkoli*, No. 11–12, 1946, p. 2; *Vysshaya Shkola*, p. 496; *Kul'turnoe Stroitel'stvo*, p. 115.

[8] Students in most secondary schools receive from 80 rubles per month in the first year to 140 in the fourth. In particularly important transport and industrial *tekhnikums* the rates are from 125 to 200 rubles per month. In most higher schools the basic rates range from 140 rubles for the first year to 210 in the fifth, whereas the rates at the most important industrial and transport higher training institutes range from 210 to 315 rubles per month. *Vysshaya Shkola*, pp. 496–497.

[9] For the relevant decisions of the Council of Peoples' Commissars see *Vysshaya Shkola*, pp. 554–555.

[10] Decision of the Committee on Higher Schools under the Council of Peoples' Commissars, October 12, 1940, No. 857, *Vysshaya Shkola*, p. 548.

[11] Plotnikov, *op. cit.*, p. 281. This applies on amounts up to and including 210 rubles per month.

[12] Dormitory fees (including bedding) are 7 rubles per month for students at secondary schools, and 15 rubles per month for those at higher educational institutions. In 1938 the proportion of all students living in dormitories at higher schools and

[*footnote continued from p. 521*
Students studying through correspondence courses pay half fees, as do those studying at comparable night schools. *Sobranie Postanovlenii i Rasporyazhenii Pravitel'stva SSSR*, 1940, No. 27, Sect. 637; 1940, No. 29, Sect. 698.

measures for social mobility must be approached with caution, and certainly the evidence does not support sweeping assertions, such as have been made, that these measures introduce hereditary social status into the Soviet system.

The labor draft, for example, places prime emphasis on those not attending school, and is in part designed to get rural youths off the farms into industry.[3] Although most of these youths undoubtedly come from families low in the social-class hierarchy, there is no reason to believe that they would have been upward mobile even if not drafted as industrial laborers. Indeed, the training they receive may increase their opportunities for mobility. Graduates of the six-month factory training schools, for example, are given a skill rating in the third or fourth category, and those from the two-year craft and railway schools are placed in the relatively high fourth to sixth skill categories.[4] Thus, the graduates of these schools are placed at a distinct advantage over unskilled workers entering Soviet industry without training. They are, in addition, trained free of charge, provided with room, board, and clothing, and may receive some small cash payment for the value of the goods produced during their training.[5]

As for the tuition fees, it must be recognized that admittance to higher educational institutions remains on the basis of uniform, nation-wide competitive examinations. The law specifies that those with the highest grades among the examinees shall be selected for admission, and that those not accepted in the field in which they took their examination may be admitted to fill vacancies in higher schools in related fields. Students with grades of distinction in their secondary school work are admitted without examination. Persons who served in the recent war are admitted directly, i.e., on a non-competitive basis, so long as they receive a passing grade on the examinations.[6]

Students in higher and specialized secondary schools who earn "good" grades, and this apparently includes almost 80 per cent of the total,[7] are granted stipends by the government. The stipends are graded according to the type of institution attended and the student's year of study, with a bonus of 25 per cent for those with excellent grades in all subjects. Thus, students receiving the smallest sums, e.g., those in the first year of a secondary school for teacher training, can pay the cost of the full year's tuition with two of their monthly stipend payments; a senior in a major university, such as one for training transport engineers, can cover the full cost of a year's tuition with one monthly payment of his stipend if he makes excellent grades.[8] In addition, students from many of the national minority groups in several of the union-republics are exempt from tuition payments,[9] as are those students with good or excellent grades who can prove that they are "needy."[10] The stipends, furthermore, are not subject to income tax.[11] Finally, legal provision is made for low cost rooms and meals.[12] As a result, the stipends should enable many students to cover a very large part of the costs of their education independent of their parents' financial resources.

These reservations being made, however, it still seems justified to conclude that the fee system and the labor draft act to a significant degree to restrict the mobility of some and to facilitate maintenance of status of others. The labor draft, for example, is conducted on a very large scale involving a significant proportion of the eligible youths. Nine hundred thousand boys and girls were to graduate annually from the labor-reserves schools during the years of the post-war Fourth Five-Year Plan, and they were expected to account for two-thirds of the anticipated increase in the labor force during the Plan years. The youths called up are regarded as "mobilized," and are subject to penalties of up to a year of forced labor for desertion from the school or gross violation of labor discipline while in training. And upon graduation they must work for a period of four years at an enterprise designated by the state.[1]

Undoubtedly some segment of this group which might otherwise have gone on to further schooling will find its chance for upward mobility seriously reduced, if not effectively cut off because of the accident of the draft. This remains true despite the fact that a special system of schools for working youths was developed after 1943 to permit those whose education was interrupted by the war, and of course those drafted into the State Labor Reserves, to complete their secondary education. Instruction in these schools is apparently free. There are forty-four weeks in the school year, with sixteen hours of class instruction and four hours of consultation in each week. Similar schools are established for working peasant youths. Students at the end of the seventh year (incomplete secondary) and those at the end of the tenth year (complete secondary) classes may obtain fifteen and twenty days of leave with pay, respectively, in which to prepare for the nationwide matriculation examinations. If they perform successfully their certificate has equal weight with the diploma from regular secondary schools. These students are at an obvious disadvantage, however, since their instruction is very limited in time, and since they must continue to carry virtually a full time job in production while attending school.[2] And the youths so affected are most likely to be from families of lower social-class standing because of the operation of the fee system, the labor draft, and other factors not touched on in this paper.

Similarly, there is no doubt that the fee system will place some segment of the eligible youth at a disadvantage in obtaining a higher education in competition with other youths of only equal or even inferior aptitude whose parents can spare the loss of their earning power, support them, and provide them with the money to pay the fees. It is significant that of the students who dropped out of higher schools in the Russian Republic (R.S.F.S.R.) between the school year 1940-41, during which the fees were introduced, and 1942-43, some 20

per cent left due to "the sifting out in connection with the introduction of fees for tuition and the changes in the methods of allotting stipends."[3] Although the system for allocating stipends was liberalized once again after 1943,[4] and although the magnitude of the percentage of withdrawals given above was undoubtedly affected by wartime financial strains,[5] there is no mistaking the initial impact of the introduction of the fee system.

But beyond this direct effect, the tuition fees act more subtly to permit a class influence on that type of social mobility which is based on the acquisition of higher education. Although the tuition fees are the same for regular (academic) and technical or specialized secondary schools, no stipends are granted to students in the academic secondary schools.[6] Under Soviet law graduates of academic secondary schools are permitted to enter higher schools directly if they qualify. But only 5 per cent of the graduates of the technical and specialized secondary schools are permitted to do so, the remainder being obliged to spend three years "in production" as technicians, teachers, etc., according to their specialty.[7] Thus of those entering higher schools in 1938, 58.8 per cent came from regular secondary schools, 12.9 per cent from technical, and 22.9 per cent from the *rabjak* (workers' faculty), i.e., special schools for preparing working and peasant youths and adults whose education had been interrupted for admission to higher educational establishments.[8] The *rabjak* appears to have gone out of existence during the war, and has apparently been replaced by special secondary schools for working urban and peasant youths described above. Students from the less well-to-do homes are obviously

---

[1] See Lever, *op. cit., passim.*

[2] *Narodnoe Obrazovanie* (compiled by A. M. Danev), Moscow: Uchpedgiz, 1948, pp. 247-265.

[3] *Narodnoe Obrazovanie v RSFSR v 1943 gody* (Otchet Narodnogo Komissariata Prosveshcheniya RSFSR), Moscow, 1944, p. 42.

[4] In October, 1940, it was provided that only students making excellent progress should receive stipends. In 1943 the pre-war system of granting the stipends to all students who made passing grades was restored. See fn. 7, p. 522. *Pravda*, October 3, 1940, *Vyssmaya Shkola*, p. 496.

[5] In the first war year in the Russian Republic 130,000 students, almost half of the enrollment in higher schools and teachers' institutes in the R.S.F.S.R., withdrew for various reasons. In the school year 1943-44, as judged by a small sample of the schools, 26 per cent of the enrollment, then much reduced, left the schools. Of these only 2.5 per cent were dismissed for non-payment of fees or left for reasons of their "material conditions," and 11.3 per cent because of family obligations other than illness in the family. *Narodnoe Obrazovania v RSFSR v 1943 gody*, p. 42. *Narodnoe Obrazovanie v RSFSR v 1944 gody*, p. 72.

[6] *Vysshaya Shkola*, pp. 496-497.

[7] Those who have served three years on active military duty may substitute such service for the requirement. *Vysshaya Shkola*, p. 83.

[8] *Kul'turnoe Stroitel'stvo*, p. 127.

---

tekhnikums for training specialists (industrial, transport, and agricultural) ranged from 56 to 80 per cent. See *Vysshaya Shkola*, p. 537; *Kul'turnoe Stroitel'stvo*, p. 127.

more likely to gravitate toward the technical and specialized secondary schools to become eligible for the stipends.[1] In 1938 for example the social composition of the students in technical and specialized secondary schools was as follows: workers and their children 27.1 per cent; employees, specialists and their children, 16.1 per cent; collective farmers and their children, 49.8 per cent; and others, 7 per cent. A comparable distribution for the regular secondary schools is unfortunately not available, but these figures will be seen to differ sharply from the social composition of the student body in higher educational establishments as given below.[2] It would appear, therefore, that there is a much higher probability that students from less well-to-do homes will find their attendance at a higher school long postponed, if not put off indefinitely, while their age mates from richer homes are pursuing their higher education.[3]

2) Changes in the inheritance taxes: The new in-

[1] There is, of course, a "cultural" factor operating here as well. Students of parents in the intelligentsia are more likely to be oriented in childhood toward the academic secondary schools, and are more likely to be better qualified to pursue such courses.

[2] *Kul'turnoe Stroitel'stvo*, p. 114.

[3] It appears that of those graduating from the regular or academic schools about 75 of 100 graduates succeed in entering higher schools, but of the graduates of the specialized secondary schools only 13 of 100 are able to go on. Estimates based on data given in *Kul'turnoe Stroitel'stvo*, pp. 109, 111–112, 127.

[4] In 1935, the last year on which adequate data has been published by the Soviet government, 64 per cent of all depositors had savings accounts of below 25 rubles, and these represented less than 6 per cent of the value of all deposits; in contrast, less than .3 per cent of all depositors had accounts of more than 1,000 rubles, but these represented almost 43 per cent of the value of all deposits. This pattern apparently still prevailed in 1940, with a very large percentage of the total deposits in accounts of over 3,000 rubles. *Sotsialisticheskoe Stroitel'stvo SSSR*, Moscow, Tsunkhy, 1936, 668–669, Plotnikov, *op. cit.*, p. 201.

[5] The currency reform of 1947 served, however, as a progressive tax on these savings accounts, since savings of up to 3,000 rubles were refunded on a 1–1 basis, those from 3,000–10,000 on the basis of 2 new rubles for 3 old, and sums above 10,000 on the basis of 1 new for 2 old rubles. See B. Alexandrov, *op. cit.*

[6] Use of such houses for income purposes through rental is of course sharply circumscribed by the legal proscriptions against "speculation."

[7] See Gsovski, *Soviet Civil Law*, Vol. I, p. 147, citing *Krasnaya Zvezda*, August 22 and December 1, 1943.

[8] Article 4, Order No. 1, October 4, 1940, Chief Administration of Labor Reserves under the Council of Peoples' Commissars. (*Izvestiya*, Oct. 5, 1940). Up to 1943, of course, provisions of this type were used to keep children of the disfranchised former "ruling" classes from obtaining a higher education.

[9] For a description of the development of Soviet policy on this question see Solomon M. Schwarz's analysis in *Management in Soviet Industry and Agriculture*, pp. 104-124. Mr. Schwarz's conclusions go beyond what is warranted by the available data, and should therefore be used with caution.

[10] See the address of Malenkov to 18th Party Conference and the Resolutions of the Conference, *Izvestiya*, February 16 and 19, 1942; also see *Planovoe Khozyaistvo*, No. 7, 1940, p. 19. This ruling should not be misunderstood, however, as being designed to inhibit the mobility of skilled workers. Its intent — as against its effect — was to secure persons of a higher technical skill at

heritance and income tax laws, mentioned above, when combined with the fact that some members of Soviet society now earn cash incomes of up to 100,000 rubles — quite apart from the valuable services they may obtain free, such as assignment to a desirable apartment or the use of an automobile — make it possible for some families to have large sums of cash savings.[4] Such savings receive interest at the rate of 3 per cent, or 5 per cent if deposited for fixed terms, and this interest is not treated as income for tax purposes.[5] In addition, families may accumulate significant quantities of physical property in the form of houses,[6] and household and personal goods, easily convertible to liquid assets because of the Soviet goods scarcity. Although this fact does not necessarily restrict the upward mobility of other individuals, it does to some degree prevent or forestall the downward mobility of some individuals whose earning power would reduce them to a much lower standard of living if they were dependent on it alone.

3) The tendency to make access to certain desirable statuses dependent at least in part on birth: For example, it appears that in admitting boys to the recently created military cadet (*Suvorov* and *Nakhimov*) schools for training the Soviet equivalent of "an officer and a gentleman," preference was given to the children of high officers.[7] At a lower point in the social scale the regulations governing admittance to the State Labor Reserves Schools for training railroad workers provide that preference shall be given to children whose parents are railway workers. Thus a provision which makes access to an occupational status partially dependent on kinship has now been made a part of Soviet law.[8] Such provisions by no means freeze anyone in the social-class position into which he is born. But by restricting access to desirable training opportunities on the basis of kinship they give preferential advantage to some in maintaining the class position of their family, and by thus reducing the number of training opportunities open to all they indirectly restrict the mobility of others who might seek to acquire that training.

4) The tendency to draw individuals for important managerial posts predominantly from the ranks of those trained in the regular programs of secondary and higher technical education:[9] During the first decade of Soviet rule, and particularly during the first years of the Five Year Plan, large numbers of adults who were regarded as politically reliable were rapidly trained and then advanced to high managerial positions. In the last decade the personnel newly entering into the ranks of management in Soviet industry have tended to come almost exclusively from among the graduates of Soviet higher schools. The Party ruled in 1941, for example, that the position of foreman, lowest rung in the administrative hierarchy, should be filled predominantly by persons possessing specialized technical training — skilled workers being utilized only when engineers and technicians are not available.[10]

Insofar as political and social conditions permit it to do this, the regime is of course acting logically and rationally. But the fact does remain that movement from the status of worker to high managerial positions within the *same* generation, the Soviet equivalent of the American dream of rags to riches, is now becoming less usual whereas it was commonplace, if not the standard practice, in an earlier period. In this sense and to that degree social mobility has decreased in the Soviet Union in the last decade.

5) The strengthening of the family: The Soviet regime has sought to rehabilitate and strengthen the family through a series of measures inaugurated in 1936 and considerably extended during the wartime decade.[1] If we accept the proposition that strong emphasis on kinship ties in any social system acts to inhibit social mobility, then the measures adopted warrant at least the presumption that as the family is strengthened in the Soviet Union kin relations will play an increasingly important role in determining Soviet youth's opportunities for mobility. It should be noted that stories about persons in responsible positions exerting influence to favor their kin have appeared with considerable frequency in recent years, both in the Soviet press and in the reports of first-hand observers.

It would appear that the Communist regime has not been highly successful in preventing the stratification of society into social-class groups, and is certainly a long way from having eliminated them. In contrasting these facts with the relevant doctrines of Soviet ideology, however, it must be recognized that Lenin was very explicit in stating that inequality of reward would persist — *and be protected by the state* — for a protracted period after the revolution transferred ownership of the means of production to the workers.[2] But Lenin certainly did not envision anything like the present *pattern* of stratification, nor did he imagine that the differentiation would be nearly as intensive as that currently manifested in the Soviet Union. He assumed, for example, that all persons in administrative positions would receive the same salary as an average worker.[3]

It seems relevant to state, therefore, that Lenin seriously underestimated the degree to which strong tendencies towards social differentiation inhere in the organization of modern industry and mechanized agriculture. Indeed Lenin assumed that the development of this complex organization of production, with its attendant rationalization and routinization of function provided the necessary basis for social equalization.[4] Actually, Soviet experience indicates that the very fact of modern large-scale production — involving extreme division of labor, precise differentiation of function, emphasis on technical competence, and elaborate hierarchies of authority and responsibility — provides a natural basis for the development of distinct social groups.[5]

Such differences in the relations of individuals to the productive process tend to yield inequalities in economic reward because of the differential position of certain persons in the labor market. This was particularly marked in the Soviet case, where the initial economic backwardness of the country combined with the exceptionally rapid tempo of industrialization to produce an extreme scarcity of skilled labor and technically trained personnel. The occupational structure, furthermore, is so important a focus in contemporary large-scale social systems that occupational status can serve very largely to determine the *general* social status of individuals. It requires only the appearance of distinctive patterns of speech, manners, and dress, differential patterns of association, and social group consciousness, to lay the foundation of a system of stratification based on social-class groupings. Once established, such stratification, as Max Weber indicated, "goes hand in hand with a monopolization of ideal and material goods or opportunities in a manner we have come to know as typical."[6] Thus, in the Soviet case, as stratification has become institutionalized there has been a noticeable tendency for social mobility to decline and for the system to become less an open class structure.

These facts must in part be attributed to the decreasing opportunities made available by the economic system as it passed beyond its initial period of enormous growth and approached a more modest and stable rate of development. Soviet university officials, for example, report that the number of applicants for each vacancy in the higher schools grows greater every year. Full weight must also be given, however, to the fact that there is now a large group of people who have achieved high status by means legitimate within the existing social system, and who wish to pass some of their benefits and privileges on to their children. This creates strong pressures for the establishment of conditions which make it easier for children from this group to maintain or improve their position and simultaneously constitute obstacles to effective competition from the children born into families lower in the scale of stratification. It is certainly not accidental that since 1938 the Soviet Union has not published statistics on the social composition of the student body in higher educational institutions, since at that time — even

---

[1] See Alex Inkeles, "Family and Church in the Post-war USSR," *The Annals of the American Academy of Political and Social Science*, 263 (May, 1949), 33–44.

[2] Vladimir I. Lenin, *State and Revolution*, New York: International Publishers, 1935, pp. 75–78.

[3] *Ibid.*, p. 92.

[4] *Ibid.*, p. 83.

[5] For a fuller discussion of this point see Barrington Moore, Jr., *Soviet Politics — The Dilemma of Power: The Role of Ideas in Social Change*, Cambridge: Harvard University Press, (1950).

[6] Gerth and Mills (eds.), *op. cit.*, p 190.

---

the working level, to get the technically trained out of offices and down to the production level, and to give recently graduated engineers first-hand practical experience. It should also be noted that in 1940 of the "directors of shops" in industry, a position far above that of foreman, only 22 per cent were specialists with higher education. But 32 per cent of the *assistant* shop directors had higher education, indicating the nature of the trend.

before the introduction of school fees and the labor draft — it was already true that children of the intelligentsia and employees constituted 47 per cent of the student body although the group made up only some 17 per cent of the total population.[1]

None of this is meant to imply that there are any absolute reasons why stratification could not have been kept at a minimum and mobility at a maximum in the Soviet Union. However much the "objective" conditions which existed may have structured the situation in favor of the course adopted, it was nevertheless a choice among alternatives. For even granting that the speed of industrialization severely limited the supply of consumers goods and the simple necessities of life,[2] this merely posed in more acute form, but did not answer, the question: "Who will get what share?" The decision made under Stalin's guidance was in the direction of maximizing the rewards of the relative few whom Stalin defined as crucial to the productive process, and who were in tremendous demand because of the shortage of skilled hands. But there was always the alternative of spreading the available resources in a relatively uniform, albeit thin, manner.

Yet the Soviet leaders today remain formally committed to the goal of attaining a classless society. What then is the prognosis for the future development of the present structure of stratification? An unequivocal answer appears warranted. The present system of stratification seems to be not merely stable, but is of such an order that it would probably require a new social and political revolution to restore the kind of dynamism necessary to create even an approximation of a classless society as defined in classical Marxist terms.

To state that the system is highly stable is by no means to indicate that the particular individuals in the intelligentsia and other favored groups have absolute secu-

rity in their positions. For the ruling political élite at the head of the Party recognizes the ever-present possibility that group-consciousness might develop in these favored strata with the implied threat of a challenge to the authority of the present leaders. This possibility is met in part by the incorporation and absorption of groups like the intelligentsia, foremen, and Stakhanovites into the Party,[3] where their members can be indoctrinated, subordinated to the Party's discipline and purposes, and carefully watched. It is also met by maintaining what appears to be an almost calculated degree of relatively constant instability — by means of rapid and sudden turnover in personnel, by intensive criticism, purging, and at times police action, and by consistent bidding up of the lower strata. But although these measures introduce an additional element of dynamism, and aid the top leaders in controlling some of the potential consequences of their policy, they do not represent in any sense an attack on the system of stratification *as a system*.

The reasons for this inhere in the very structure of contemporary Soviet society. For the social classes which are currently most highly rewarded in income, status, and power are precisely those social groups on which the present regime relies most heavily as its basis of social support. A new program aimed at social equalization could, therefore, be accomplished only at the expense, and hence with the alienation, of those groups on whose support the regime rests. Any such effort would consequently subject the whole system to real jeopardy. The interest of the ruling élite in social stability as a foundation for its programs of internal and foreign expansion is such that it seems most unlikely that it would undertake a program designed to effect one phase of its ideological goals at the expense of the stability of the system as a whole. It may in fact be said that despite recurrent affirmations of the aim of achieving a classless society, this goal can no longer be realistically regarded as one towards which the present leadership is actively and effectively oriented. Indeed, there is no absolute reason to assume that the present rate of social mobility, which probably equals that in the United States and possibly surpasses it, will be maintained. But if it is not, major consequences for the structure and functioning of Soviet society as now "traditionally" constituted may be expected.

---

[1] *Kul'turnoe Stroitel'stvo SSSR*, p. 114.

[2] The decision to industrialize at so rapid a tempo was itself not inevitable. Industrialization based on a significantly lower rate of investment, particularly if combined with greater emphasis on consumers goods industries, would have had a profound effect on Soviet internal conditions. In particular, it would have made it possible to have much less intensive economic stratification, since the striking aspect of the Soviet system in this respect is not the absolute level of luxury at which the richer groups live but rather the relatively low level at which the population as a whole finds itself.

[3] See fn. 6, page 521.

Toward the Classless Society?

Robert A. Feldmesser

Agreat deal has been written on the emergence of gross inequalities of wealth, privilege, and official honor in Soviet society. The process, fully described and documented, may be said to have begun with a famous speech by Stalin in 1931, in which he denounced "equality-mongering" in the wage structure and called for a new attitude of "solicitude" toward the intelligentsia; it manifested itself in highly differentiated incomes, in a change in the composition of the Communist Party, in the establishment of tuition fees and other more subtle obstacles to higher education, in elegant uniforms and elaborate titles, and in a host of other ways. By the end of World War II, and particularly during the last years of Stalin's life, the trend was clear: the Soviet Union was well advanced along a seemingly irreversible course toward a rigid system of social stratification, in which the upper classes would remain upper, the lower classes lower, and the twain would rarely meet.

Yet the irreversible has now been reversed. With that breathtaking facility which so often startles us, the Soviet leadership has launched a series of measures calculated to reduce the degree and rigidity of differentiation in Soviet society to a very considerable extent. Many observers have not yet fully apprehended this turn of events, if only because all its component parts had not been assembled in one place; to do so is one objective of the present study. But partly, too, the lack of comprehension is due to a reluctance to credit Soviet leaders with the desire or ability to achieve so "virtuous" an aim as social equality — rather, it is due to a failure to appreciate the *meaning* of equality in the Soviet system. A second objective here is to define that meaning.

The "revival of democracy"

[He] began to trample crudely on the methods of collectivity in leadership ... to order people around and push aside the personnel of Soviet and economic organizations ... [He] decided questions great and small by himself, completely ignoring the opinions of others.

[He] flattered himself with the belief that all [improvements] were due only to his own merits.

The more successfully things went, the more conceited he became, the more airs he gave himself.

... you get the impression that everything other people do is bad, and only the things [he] does are good.

These scathing remarks could well have been taken from Khrushchev's secret speech to the 20th Congress of the CPSU exposing the incredible extremes to which Stalin's method of one-man rule had gone. A common reaction to this speech abroad was to see in it a confirmation of the trend toward inequality. The intelligentsia, or the "state bourgeoisie,"[1] despite their privileges *vis-à-vis* other elements of the population, had long resented the Stalinist tyranny. Now, as a result of their increasing power in an industrialized and militarized state, they had reached the point where they could force Khrushchev to confess that they had been unjustly treated, to promise them the freedom of decision-making, and to guarantee the security of their status.

Subsequent comments in the Soviet press have belied this interpretation. The quotations do not come from the secret speech; they are attacks on, respectively, a *raion* party secretary, the chairman of a city soviet executive committee, and a factory director.[2] For, as it now appears, the secret speech was directed not only at the one big Stalin, but also at all the other little Stalins who had grown up in his image. It has been followed up not with praise for Soviet administrators, but with denunciations of "*administrirovanie*" — the high-handed, arrogant ways of officials who have exercised "petty tutelage" over their subordinates; who have glossed over shortcomings, suppressed criticism, and persecuted their critics; who have been "inattentive to the workers and their needs"; who have, in short, violated the letter of Soviet law and the spirit of "Communist morality."

Denunciations of this sort are not, of course, a new phenomenon; but what is interesting today is not only

[1] The term is Hugh Seton-Watson's, in an article presenting this interpretation: "The Soviet Ruling Class," *Problems of Communism*, No. 3 (May–June), 1956.

[2] Respectively, in *Pravda*, Nov. 23, 1957, and *Izvestia*, Jan. 16, 1958, and June 13, 1959. These are samples from a plethora of similar articles.

Reprinted from "Equality and Inequality Under Khrushchev," *Problems of Communism*, a publication of the United States Information Agency, Vol. 9 (1960), pp. 31–39, by permission of the author and the publisher.

the frequency and vehemence of such attacks but the implicit admission that the inspiration for bad administrative habits came from very high up. Accordingly, Khrushchev's own behavior, so sharply at variance with Stalin's, has been held up as an example for others to follow: Soviet officials have been urged to get closer to the people, to pay more attention to them, and not to rely exclusively on existing channels of authority. Sessions of local soviets are being held more frequently; there have been occasional reports of ministers and department heads being subjected to questioning by deputies; in some instances, agendas of meetings have been posted and public hearings held on the items under discussion. The number of deputies in local soviets has been increased by 1,800,000, and unpaid activists have been taking on tasks formerly performed by the executive staff — as if housewives were indeed to run the state.[1] Along the same lines, there has been a large-scale effort to reinvigorate the system of worker and peasant correspondents, to protect them from reprisals by the targets of their criticism, and to have them do more of the newspapers' work in place of the professional journalistic staff.[2] A party journal has told *raion* newspapers that they were not limited to criticizing "only rank-and-file workers and 'second-rank' officials of *raion* organizations."[3]

The appeal for "popular participation" to reform the deeply ingrained bureaucratic habits of Soviet officialdom has even been extended to the party-controlled trade unions, which have been urged to shake off their submissiveness to factory executives and to offer vigorous opposition when necessary.[4] Instances of rambunctious local trade-union committees have been held up for emulation, and workers enjoined to criticize "without being afraid that it will upset some director or other," and without having their remarks "prepared" or "cleared" by higher authorities.[5]

Another indication of the new spirit antedating the 20th Congress, has been the abolishment of the uniforms, insignia of rank, and titles which had been authorized for many civilian occupations during and after the war.[6] There has been an appeal for more

informal relations and less social distance between those of high rank and those of low, and for an end to such practices in the armed forces as separate dining rooms for the several ranks.[7]

In general, the party seems to have been going out of its way to assert its respect for "ordinary" workers and peasants, a development reminiscent, as are many aspects of this campaign, of the attitude prevailing during the first decade after the October Revolution. Reversing a trend of more than 20 years' duration, the party has made a deliberate attempt to recruit more workers and peasants into its ranks: so much so, that Khrushchev was able to report at the 21st Congress that two-thirds of current admissions were in those categories, a figure which he accurately called a "considerable increase."[8] In addition, the Soviet press has published numerous editorials, articles, and letters passionately proclaiming the honor and worth of manual labor in a socialist society, filled with glowing words about citizens who are not afraid of soiling their hands, who are "creating material values for the people," rather than "sitting in offices and filing papers." This is not a new line, either, though it had lain dormant for some time. In recent speeches and articles, the third member has often been missing from the traditional trinity of "workers, collective farm peasants, and intelligentsia."

The rights and privileges mentioned thus far may seem to be only honorific. To be sure, they do not signify any real diffusion of the locus of power in Soviet society. Nevertheless, their importance should not be underrated; they do, after all, attempt to raise the ordinary worker's self-respect, and to imbue him with the consciousness — denied to him under Stalin — of his own contribution to the country's industrial progress. Having for years been exposed to harassment, incessant exhortations, and an attitude on the part of the authorities bordering on contempt, he is not likely to scorn even this — however mild — token of recognition and respect.

Adjustments in the income structure

In any event, more tangible rewards have also resulted from the new policy. Although we need not take too literally all of the promises made by Khrushchev — and by Malenkov before him — to increase the output of consumers' goods, there is every indication that the lowest-paid Soviet workers and peasants have been placed in a better competitive position to buy whatever is available.

On the one hand, minimum wages were raised in 1956, and two more increases scheduled in the current plan will bring the wage floor up to 500–600 rubles a month by 1965 — hardly a level of luxury, but approximately twice what it is now; raises have also been promised to "medium-paid workers and employees."[9] Old-age and disability pensions have been increased, too. Income taxes have been revised in favor of the lowest income brackets.[10]

[1] See especially the editorial in *Sovetskoe Gosudarstvo i Pravo*, No. 3 (May), 1956, pp. 3–14; *Izvestia*, May 22 and 23, Oct. 12, and Nov. 24, 1957; Aug. 1, 1958; and May 24, 1959.

[2] *Pravda*, June 3, 1959, and many earlier sources. This matter as well as the treatment of readers' letters were the subjects of Central Committee resolutions: *Pravda*, Aug. 26, 1958, and *Izvestia*, Oct. 11, 1958.

[3] *Partiinaia Zhizn*, No. 14 (July), 1959, p. 55.

[4] Report to the 20th Congress, *Pravda*, Feb. 15, 1956.

[5] *Pravda*, July 11, 1959; see also *Izvestia*, June 25, 1957.

[6] Decree of July 12, 1954, in *Sbornik Zakonov SSSR i Ukazov Prezidiuma Verkhovnovo Soveta SSSR*, Moscow, 1959, pp. 411–413.

[7] *Krasnaia Zvezda*, Aug. 21, 1957.

[8] *Pravda*, Jan. 28, 1959. See also T. H. Rigby, "Social Orientation of Recruitment and Distribution of Membership in the Communist Party of the Soviet Union," *American Slavic and East European Review*, No. 3 (October), 1957.

[9] *Pravda*, Sept. 9, 1956, and Nov. 14, 1958.

[10] *Sbornik Zakonov . . .*, pp. 505–506.

On the other hand, there has been a good deal of talk, and some action, aimed at reducing the incomes of managerial and scientific personnel. In particular, the awarding of lavish bonuses to administrative, party, and other officials has been repeatedly attacked; and it is almost certain that the worst abuses are being corrected, "voluntarily" if not otherwise. A decree of the Council of Ministers has warned against excessive expense accounts on *komandirovki* (business trips) — another common source of added income for economic staffs.[1] Sputniks notwithstanding, the scientists have come in for their share of criticism, too, for holding multiple jobs and for receiving high incomes "merely" because they have higher degrees.[2]

The range of differentiation is being contracted not only between manual and non-manual workers, but within the manual group as well. Wages in a number of industries have been sporadically revised over the past five years, the guiding principle being "a rise in the proportion of basic wage rates in workers' earnings." Although the primary motives seemed to be economic and bookkeeping concerns — to restrain inflationary forces and restore simplicity to the wage structure — it was implied that many of the premiums and increments which had permitted the rise of an inner aristocracy among the workers would be curtailed or eliminated. It has now been authoritatively stated that greater equality of wages is a deliberate intention. A. Volkov, who succeeded Kaganovich as head of the Committee on Labor and Wages, has declared that, "with the aim of decreasing the gap between maximum and minimum wage rates," such measures as these are to be undertaken: a reduction in the number of skill categories and in the ratio between the highest and lowest rates to "no more than" two to one; a "sharp" decrease in the use of progressive piece-work rates; and a replacement of individual bonuses by collective bonuses, spreading the benefits of a single worker's accomplishment to his whole work team.[3]

Rural remedies

Even more striking have been the changes in the agricultural sector. Adjustments in crop-purchase prices and agricultural taxes and other steps taken since 1953 have raised the income of collective farmers in general while diminishing the range of earnings among and within the collectives.[4] On several occasions, Khrushchev has referred to the "excessively high incomes" of some collective farms (as he has to the "unjustifiably high incomes" of some workers). One remedy, analogous to the industrial wage reform, has been the establishment of a uniform pricing system for agricultural purchases, without bonuses for exceeding the purchase plan, with the result, according to Khrushchev, that "many collective farms will undoubtedly get more, while the leading collective farms will receive . . . somewhat less than now. And this," he added, "will be entirely fair."[5] Especially interesting is his implicit

denial of the principle laid down by Stalin in 1931: that wide income differentials were needed as incentives to raise production. Khrushchev, on the contrary, has asserted that the farms with low income due to poor production are discouraged from increasing their output:

> . . . collected farms that did not achieve the planned harvest . . . were penalized, as it were. . . . This, of course, did not spur them on. . . . The goal here must be a more correct determination of pay . . . in order to provide incentive not only to the leading but to all collective farms.[6]

In connection with the shift, now apparently under way, from payment by workdays to guaranteed cash payments, the whole problem of income differentiation in agriculture was recently discussed in three articles in the Soviet Union's leading economic journal. Among situations they cited as "unjustifiable" are: income differentials among collective farms due to varying locations, soil fertility, or crops; those between peasants and farm executives, due to the closer linking of peasant earnings to the volume of output; and those among the peasants themselves, due to too many pay-rate categories with too steep increases, and to inequitable discrepancies in output norms. The remedies are fairly obvious, and cases are cited in which they are already being applied.[7]

Reform in education

The school system initiated in the 1930's was one of the major props of social differentiation. Its salient features, for present purposes, were these: seven years of education were nominally compulsory, although it has been revealed that as late as 1958 only 80 per cent of the young people were completing the course.[8] After the seven-year school, a youngster might: *1)* go to work in a job requiring little or no skill; *2)* be drafted into a labor-reserves school, providing training of up to two years for occupations of moderate skill; *3)* enter a *tekhnikum*, a three- or four-year school for

---

[1] *Izvestia*, April 4 and June 6, 1959.

[2] *Kosomolskaia Pravda*, March 20 and April 6, 1956; *Pravda*, July 2, 1959.

[3] *Pravda*, Nov. 25, 1958. At the 21st Congress, Khrushchev remarked that it was also time to eliminate the differential paid for work in remote places: *Pravda*, Feb. 1, 1959. Premiums evidently will be preserved for hot or underground jobs and hard physical labor.

[4] Lazar Volin, "Reform in Agriculture," *Problems of Communism*, No. 1 (Jan.–Feb.), 1959.

[5] *Pravda*, June 21, 1958.

[6] *Ibid.*

[7] *Voprosy Ekonomiki*, No. 2 (Feb.), 1959, pp. 80–88, 113–122, 143–149. In addition, see *Izvestia*, Nov. 30, 1958, in which a collective farm chairman reports that his own earnings now vary according to the volume of output, but are not to exceed 1500 rubles a month.

[8] *Literaturnaia Gazeta*, July 3, 1958. Khrushchev has used this figure on several occasions.

highly-skilled manual and some nonmanual occupations; or *4)* proceed to the upper grades of a ten-year school for essentially "academic" training, preparatory in almost all cases to matriculation at a higher educational institution (*vuz*). Tuition fees were charged in the *vuzes*, ten-year schools and *tekhnikums*. Scholarships were available at *tekhnikums*, while room, board, and uniforms were free in the labor-reserves schools, but no such aids were offered to pupils of the ten-year school. For both material and "cultural" reasons, therefore, the tendency was for children from lower-status families to attend the vocational schools and enter the same sort of occupations already held by their parents, while children of the "elite" were more likely to take the academic sequence preparing them for professional and administrative positions. The greater informal influence which highly-placed parents could exercise on those responsible for *vuz* admission strengthened this tendency. The schools thus contributed to the cleavage between manual and nonmanual groups.

The decision, adopted at the 19th Congress and reaffirmed at the 20th, to implement universal ten-year education wreaked havoc with this arrangement. Since ten-year schooling was to be compulsory, tuition fees made little sense, and they were accordingly abolished.[1] On the other hand *vuz* enrollments were not expanded; most of the ten-year graduates were expected to go directly to work, or into *tekhnikums* or other vocational schools.[2] This meant, in turn, a revision of the ten-year-school curriculum: physical education, music, art, mechanical drawing and other "practical studies," were increased at the expense of academic courses, and the latter were simplified in content, with fewer examinations and less homework. The effect of these changes — again in part intended — was to make school more accessible and more comfortable for the children of workers and peasants, improving their chances for scholastic success; and to blur the distinction between education for the manual worker and education for his occupational and social superior.

NEW PROBLEMS AND A NEW PROGRAM

But the reform proved unsatisfactory in important respects. In particular, graduates of the ten-year schools clung to the idea that they were entitled to a higher education. Many of them resented going either to work

[1] *Izvestia*, June 10, 1956.
[2] Nicholas DeWitt, "Upheaval in Education," *Problems of Communism*, No. 1 (Jan.-Feb.), 1959.
[3] Memorandum to the Central Committee, *Pravda*, Sept. 21, 1958.
[4] Khrushchev estimated an annual increment of 2 to 3.5 million youths in the labor force two years earlier than under the old program (*ibid.*); this gain is exclusive of the part-time work to be performed by pupils in most grades.
[5] It should be pointed out that the eight-year school is not a condensation of the ten-year curriculum but an expansion of the seven-year school — again indicative of the relaxation of academic rigor.
[6] See especially Khrushchev's speech to the 13th Congress of the Komsomol, *Pravda*, April 19, 1958, and his memorandum to the Central Committee, *ibid.* Sept. 21, 1958.

or to a vocational school, preferring to wait until they could gain admission to a *vuz* — and this in the face of an imminent labor shortage caused by the birth deficiencies of the war years. One attempt at solving this problem was the campaign, referred to above, stressing anew the dignity of manual labor; but it proved futile. Khrushchev then struck boldly: rejecting the ten-year principle, he declared that eight years of education were all that was necessary, and that such training should be "close to life" — i.e., primarily vocational. He proclaimed a "sacred slogan": "All students must prepare for useful work" and take a full-time job upon completion of the eighth grade.

> This ... will be democratic since more equal conditions will be created for all citizens: neither the position nor the pleas of parents will exempt anyone, whoever he may be, from productive labor. . . .[3]

This program met two related goals: a labor force would be trained, in a minimum amount of time, for the kind of work that would be the lot of most,[4] and the notion of an automatic transition from secondary school to higher education would be dispelled. The purpose and atmosphere of the new type of school are suggested by the fact that pupils will combine their studies with productive work and with such chores as cleaning classrooms, tending shrubbery, and preparing and serving lunches. After the educational overhaul is completed, in three to five years, all students who wish to receive full secondary schooling (now to be of eleven years' duration)[5] will do so by correspondence or in evening or off-season schools, without taking time away from their jobs. Although there was much discussion of schools for the "gifted", which would not require students to work while studying, it is significant that no provision was made for them (except in the areas of music and dance) in the reform as it was finally enacted. The labor-reserves system as such now seems to be a dead letter, though it might be more accurate to say that in effect it has been extended to embrace all schools and all young people.

Regulation of vuz *admissions* At the same time, changes have been effected to improve the chances of workers' and peasants' children competing for entrance to higher educational institutions. Khrushchev and others had repeatedly deplored the handicaps faced by children of lower-status families, scoring in particular the fact that the "competition of parents" with influence was as important in determining *vuz* admissions as was the competition in entrance examinations.[6] In Moscow's higher schools, said Khrushchev, children of workers and collective farmers made up only 30 to 40 per cent of the enrollment. The abolition of tuition fees in the *vuzes*, along with those in the secondary schools, was one move calculated to alter this situation. It is particularly revealing that this step was taken at a time when pressure for admission to higher education from the growing ranks of ten-year graduates was reaching its peak — that is, when selectivity in admissions was becoming most necessary. If there were truth in the hypothesis of growing class stratification under pressure from a powerful "state bourgeoisie," just the opposite might have been expected — i.e., a rise in the tuition fees as a convenient way of shutting out low-income applicants.

Very different rules of competition were instead set up. A rising proportion (currently, 80 per cent) of *vuz* admissions was reserved for applicants with at least two years of work experience or military service;[1] presumably, this will become a universal requirement when the secondary-school reform is complete. Meanwhile, honor graduates of the ten-year schools and the *tekhnikums* are now obliged to compete in entrance examinations along with everybody else — and, for the sake of "objectivity," the written part of the examinations is turned in under a pseudonym.[2] In most fields, the first two or three years of higher education are to be combined with full-time work, in order both to weed out the less serious students and to impress the future *vuz* graduates with the "glorious traditions of our working class and collective-farm peasantry" — i.e., to blunt the forces making for social separateness.[3] The method of awarding scholarships has been revised to take more account of the material needs of the student, and somewhat less of his grades; special courses are being organized to help *vuz* applicants who have not completed secondary education, or who have been out of school for a while; and all applicants must present recommendations from places of work and also from party, Komsomol, or trade-union organizations, whose representatives in addition sit on admissions boards[4] — all of which recall the days when the official aim was to "proletarianize" the higher schools. Given the recent Soviet willingness to publish more figures (so long as they "look good"), it may be predicted that we shall soon have, for the first time since 1938, comprehensive data on the social origins of students in higher education.[5]

The subject of educational reform cannot be passed over without taking notice of the boarding schools. When Khrushchev first broached the topic at the 20th Congress, observers assumed (as in the case of the secret speech) that his proposal demonstrated the influence of the elite and that the new schools — despite his protestation to the contrary — would be exclusive institutions for the privileged.

The reality of the boarding school has been a far cry from these suppositions. Priority in admission has gone — as, after all, Khrushchev said it should — to children from large or low-income families, and to others from disadvantaged environments. Fees are charged, but they have been waived for those who could not' afford them — again in accord with Khrushchev's original suggestion. Moreover, the curriculum has been strictly polytechnical, providing training for such occupations as lathe operators, electricians, farm machine operators, stenographers, typists, etc. — hardly pursuits becoming to an aristocratic caste.[6]

Is the classless society coming?

The scope and force of the trend away from extreme differentiation are unmistakable. There are many clues other than those which have already been cited: criticism of the practice of assigning chauffeured cars to officials; a pervasive, if still partial, change in the method of awarding medals and orders; a demand that the Soviet fashion journal concern itself less with evening gowns and furs and more with "everyday" clothes. To dismiss all this evidence as mere window-dressing, as ritual obeisance to an ideology, explains nothing: for why is it happening *now*? Why should Khrushchev feel compelled to renew rituals that Stalin had long neglected, rituals that offend the sensibilities of the "elite"? What, then, does account for the change? Is one facet of the "transition to communism" to be the end of class distinctions?

Stalin, it seems clear, had felt that a high degree of differentiation was necessary to achieve his overriding goal — a very rapid process of industrialization subject to his absolute control. This meant, in the first place, that a group of loyal and competent administrators and other brain-workers had to be created, and quickly. It also meant that large segments of the population would have to be deprived, at least "temporarily," of material returns from their labor, in order that greater proportions of production could be applied to the expansion of industrial capacity. The consequently depressed condition of the workers and peasants Stalin sought to turn to good purpose, by offering them great rewards for joining the administrative and technical corps — hence the wealth, privilege, and prestige which

[1] *Ibid.*, June 4, 1958.

[2] *Ibid.*, June 4 and Nov. 12, 1958; *Izvestia*, April 4, 1959. Since honor graduates formerly were admitted without entrance examinations, high-status parents (according to Khrushchev) often put pressure on secondary-school teachers to give their children good grades (*Pravda*, Sept. 21, 1958).

[3] See Khrushchev's memorandum, *Pravda*, Sept. 21, 1958, and the Central Committee resolution on school reform, *ibid.*, Nov. 14, 1958; also Minister of Higher Education Yelyutin's discussions of the problem, *ibid.*, Sept. 17, 1958, and *Izvestia*, Dec. 24, 1958.

[4] See *Komsomolskaia Pravda*, Aug. 16, 1956; *Vestnik Vysshei Shkoly*, No. 9 (Sept.), 1957, pp. 3–5; *Pravda*, June 4, 1958; and *Izvestia*, Dec. 24, 1958, and April 4, 1959.

[5] Another prediction which might be ventured is the resurrection of intelligence and aptitude tests, abolished in the 1930's on the grounds that they emphasized inherited rather than acquired traits and discriminated against children of workers and peasants. In effect, the criteria of "ability" became instead school examinations, grades, and *vuz* entrance examinations, which actually discriminate more heavily against low-status students in terms of the motivational or "cultural" influences in their lives. Intelligence-test scores are now considered less immutable than was once thought to be the case, and Khrushchev may "discover" that IQ tests are a more "objective" (i.e., less class-biased) measure of ability than achievement tests.

[6] On the schools, see *Pravda*, Feb. 15 and July 1, 1956; *Uchitelskaia Gazeta*, June 27, 1956; *Trud*, July 27, 1956; *Pravda*, Oct. 9, 1958. It might be noted that many, if not most, of the boarding schools have been converted from former seven- or ten-year schools, probably due to insufficient construction funds.

came to define the upper end of the occupational hierarchy. The need for upward mobility to escape a life of privation would induce people to strive for educational training and vocational achievement, and would encourage obedience to Stalin's dictates, while the chance for upward mobility would serve as a substitute for the more prosaic benefits of a slow and moderate rise in the general standard of living.

The gap thus generated between the higher statuses and the lower ably served Stalin's purposes in some respects. Those in high position came to live a different kind of life, free from the material anxieties of those over whom they stood. They became, in short, "insulated" from the less fortunate: blind or indifferent to the needs and wishes of the masses. For they learned that success was to be had by winning the favor not of those below them but of those above them, which was exactly what Stalin wanted them to learn. Now that the policy has come under fire, the attitude which it engendered has been amply described in the Soviet press, for example in this criticism of the "self-willed" official as a type:

> Tell such an official that he has disturbed his subordinate's state of mind, and he will probably be amazed: "His state of mind? Brother, we're having trouble meeting our plan here, and I have no time to look into all sorts of cases of melancholia."[1]

The problems of Stalinist policy

Nevertheless, extreme social differentiation had its less desirable aspects, too. For one thing, it "over-motivated" the population: anything less than a higher education, and the higher occupation it brought, was regarded as a disgrace for an upper-status child and as a sad fate for a lower-status child — hence, the intense pressure exerted on the educational institutions, the reluctance of youths to commit themselves to factory jobs. For another and more important thing, it interfered with the operation of the impersonal selection system necessary to an efficient economy and to the reward-function of upward mobility. Those in higher and better-paid positions were able to use their influence and their money to assure similar places for their children, at the expense of potentially more capable or more loyal children from less-favored families. Perhaps even worse, some children from well-to-do families neither studied nor worked, but lived off their parents' income — an idle existence which not only meant a loss to the labor force but also, if the Soviet press is to be believed, led in many cases to alcoholism, crime, or even to the acceptance of "bourgeois ideology."[2]

This excessive measure of status security perverted

adults as well as children. Once a man was granted local power, he was able to suppress or punish, if not ignore, criticism from his inferiors, and he cooperated with his colleagues to evade the regime's cross-checks on him. This had been intermittently acknowledged in the Soviet Union under the label of *semeistvennost* ("family-ness"), but the full dimensions of the problem are only now being revealed. Among many instances, one may be cited concerning the chairman of a city soviet executive committee who "forbade his assistants and the heads of the city executive committee departments to appeal to party organs without his consent."[3] Thus, higher authorities were precluded from receiving the information they needed to keep tabs on their own subordinates. Or, if the party did manage to find out about and remove some incompetent or dishonest official, he often reappeared in another responsible position — partly, at least, as the result of friendships formed and mutual obligations exacted. Indeed, an integral part of the pattern has been the concern of officials to find places in the *apparat* for friends and relatives who could reciprocally provide a haven if necessary.

All of this was simply the obverse side of the arbitrary power delegated to local officials, for the sake of allowing them to carry out their instructions from above without interference from below. But it was ironically self-defeating: by being freed of criticism from below, administrators were able to free themselves of supervision from above. This threatened to contravene the cardinal dogma of the Soviet system, which has come to be known as Stalinism though it could as well be called Leninism or Khrushchevism: that ultimate power belongs exclusively to the party — or more accurately, to the head of the party. Whenever any group jeopardizes that principle, it must be struck down, and that is what Khrushchev is doing. Stalin, in other words, forgot his Stalinism; and Khrushchev is not repudiating Stalinism, he is, if anything, reinstating it.

Khrushchev's two-sided task

No doubt, the Soviet press, in characteristic fashion, has exaggerated the threat. Stalin was not a complete fool, and when all is said and done, he does seem to have kept things pretty well under control. If the group whose growth he fostered was an "elite," then surely no elite has ever proved so utterly helpless in preventing actions which, like those at present, so adversely affect it. The danger was a distant cloud — but a good Bolshevik tries not to wait until the storm has swept away his fortifications. Khrushchev's task, then, is to rid the "state bourgeoisie" of its cockiness, to disabuse it of the notion that it is safe whatever it does, to infuse into it fresh blood, personnel more responsive to orders. Just because of the kinds of positions these people occupy, the task will not be easy, and the plan may be "underfulfilled." But given the Soviet political structure, the odds are on Khrushchev's side.

The nature of the targets at which Khrushchev has

[1] *Izvestia*, Jan. 18, 1958.

[2] Mark G. Field, "Drink and Delinquency in the U.S.S.R.," *Problems of Communism*, No. 3 (May–June), 1955; Allen Kassof, "Youth vs. the Regime: Conflict in Values," *ibid.*, No. 3 (May–June), 1957.

[3] *Izvestia*, Jan. 16, 1958.

taken aim makes his crusade sound like an echo of earlier revolutionary periods; but in actuality, the development does not connote a return to the situation that prevailed in the early 1920's, for Khrushchev has learned something from Soviet history. The extremes of high and low incomes are to be moderated — but "equality-mongering" is still wrong. Mass participation and criticism from below are to be permitted — but not "violations of state discipline" or "slander of the party and its leaders." Executives should be more humble, more attentive to their subordinates — but the principle of "one-man management" is to be preserved. "The struggle against the cult of the individual does not at all mean a belittling of the significance of leadership and leaders. . . . The party does not advocate the denial of authorities."[1] Moreover, Khrushchev has expressly defended the nonmanual pursuits — "those who work in offices are not at all bureaucrats, they are the creative people who originate that which is new . . ." — and he has strongly implied that, even under communism, there will still be the bosses and the bossed; communist society will be "highly organized."[2] Complete equality is not just around the corner, nor even being contemplated.

"Classlessness" defined

Nevertheless, Khrushchev *is* seeking a classless society, in the proper sense of the term. If an "upper class," for example, means anything, it means a group of people who share fairly distinctive values and advantages which they are able to hold on to for some length of time, even against the resistance of others. Yet in the totalitarian scheme of things, it is essential to the preservation of party supremacy that no group become so entrenched in positions of strength as to become insulated against further demands from the party. An "upper class," or any other "class," is no more admissible than an autonomous trade union or ethnic group. Hence the party must insist — in the long run — that every man be individually and continuously on trial, that status and rewards remain contingent and ephemeral. The greatest threat to the party is the development of a sense of identification or solidarity within a group — or class — and this is precisely what was happening to the Soviet elite. Khrushchev's war against the bourgeoisie is, in fact, only an extension of the battle with the bureaucrats which has long been a part of Soviet policy, even if it was sometimes muted. In short, "classlessness" is essentially a corollary of Stalinism.

Khrushchev, however, believes himself to be in a better position to attain it than Stalin ever was. The creation of a substantial industrial base has relieved him

of the urgency which Stalin so acutely felt. Automation, as he has frequently pointed out, really has diminished the differences between mental workers and manual. The spread of education has freed him from dependence on a relatively small group as the only source of administrative and intellectual personnel; workers and peasants can now be brought into the *vuzes* with less risk of lowering the quality of education (as happened in the 1920's). Finally, he evidently presumes that a long period of enforced political homogeneity has led to the withering away of deviant values among Soviet citizens. Criticism from below would thus be less dangerous, since it is more likely to accord with what the party wants. The only agency left which has enabled Soviet man to maintain and transmit both "hostile" values and favored positions, with even a small degree of success, is the family — whence the significance of the boarding schools (and other attempts to loosen family bonds). For the boarding schools are destined to be not elite institutions, but universal ones: the instrument by which the regime hopes finally to achieve control over the last remaining semi-autonomous activity, the rearing of children.[3] This, too, is an objective which will be familiar to students of Soviet history, but unlike the situation earlier, Soviet leaders may well feel that they now have, or can produce, the material facilities with which to realize it.

Yet it is unlikely that the regime has solved, once and for all, the problem of inequality. Power corrupts — even delegated power. Workers and peasants, no less than intelligentsia, will sooner or later try to put their privileges to uses which, so far as the party is concerned, are "selfish." They may, for example, try to develop a monopoly of their own on higher education, or act "prematurely" to increase the production of consumers' goods or raise wages, in a kind of latter-day "workers' opposition." Or, once terror is removed, they may turn out not to have lost all their hostile values, after all. When that happens, they will once more be put back in the inferior position they knew up to Stalin's death. No end is in sight to this ancient practice of paying one off against the other, this alternate granting of status privilege within a basically classless framework, as the Soviet system struggles with its perennial and fundamental problem: the need to control the controllers.

[1] *Partiinaia Zhizn*, No. 7 (April), 1956, p. 5.
[2] *Pravda*, July 2, 1959; also Khrushchev's report to the 21st Congress, *Pravda*, Jan. 28, 1959.
[3] "The sooner we provide nurseries, kindergartens, and boarding schools for all children, the sooner and the more successfully will the task of the Communist upbringing of the growing generation be accomplished": Khrushchev's theses on the Seven-Year Plan, *Pravda*, Nov. 14, 1958. See also the decree on the boarding schools in *Pravda*, May 26, 1959.

Economic Growth, Social Structure, Élite Formation
THE CASE OF POLAND

Zygmunt Bauman

THE CONCEPT of two crucial technological revolutions – the neolithic and the industrial – defining two basic turning points in the sociological history of mankind has already gained relatively broad acknowledgement among historians and anthropologists. It is noted that, since the neolithic era, when the art of producing and storing the surplus of goods was discovered, until the industrial revolution, when the machine and big productive organization were introduced, no single new plant or new animal was domesticated, no basically new tools added to the human industrial equipment, no basic changes made in the social relations pattern and in the fundamental set of economic, political and cultural institutions of society. Naturally, no significant changes in the mood of scholarly thinking emerged (according to Levi-Strauss, this period was dominated by one of the two known variations of scientific thinking – the knowledge of the singular and particular, born in neolithic times and sharply different from typically modern knowledge of the general). Both in social reality and in human minds, pre-industrial history had no time dimension; it was "flat", deprived of "depth". Forms of social organization initiated in epochs quite remote from each other co-existed: Plato and Descartes, Aristotle and Bacon addressed each other as if they were contemporaries. The time factor in the modern image of pre-industrial society is a kind of retrospective mental projection of the much later experience of a rapidly expanding and changing society; it was hardly part of the cultural reality of pre-industrial times themselves.

I believe the basic stability and "flatness" (in terms of time dimension) of pre-industrial society was a product of the well developed re-equilibrating negative feedback institutions (the only deviation from this predominant model were some parts of the ancient world with relatively vigorous market relations which were, for this reason, fairly close to the threshold of an industrial pattern). These institutions are in turn typical of a society with weak market relations; for a society organized on the basis of the local community satisfying the basic needs of its members by commonly regulated, homogeneous and integral activity comprises all discriminated functions later divided up between family, households, productive, distributive and trade organizations, and many other specialized agencies. The main features of the predominant type of pre-industrial social fabric is the convergence and coalescence of objective, supra-psychical social dependencies and the psychically embraceable sphere of conscious social bonds – so sharply cut off from each other in the industrial type of society with its particularization and segmentation of the need-satisfaction process, and the corresponding dispersion of the human personality into a set of relatively autonomous roles and behavior patterns.

There was nothing about pre-industrial society which made its development into an industrial one in any sense inevitable. On the contrary, given efficient re-equilibrating and stabilizing institutions and the basic self-sufficiency of self-sustained local communities, the likelihood of any particular society evolving towards industrialization by the sheer logic of inner change alone was very meagre indeed. The industrial revolution required the convergence of many factors, accidental from the point of view of the inner, self-perpetuating societal process. It occurred once in history and in one relatively small part of the globe. But this particular and almost improbable convergence did happen, and it moulded into the self-invigorating and self-expanding process of industrialization and urbanization the factors of accumulated wealth, an accumulated propertyless mass of the population, a broad and unsatiated market for industrial goods, and the relevant ideology favouring the increase of income by means of the rational organization of the production of market goods. It occurred, let us repeat, just once in time, in striking contrast, for example, to the feudal type of pre-industrial society (in the economic and the political sense of the term as understood by Marx, Fustel de Coulanges, F. Seebohm or G. B. Adams, and not by Rushton Coulborn, Marc

Reprinted from the *International Social Science Journal*, V, XVI (1964), pp. 203–216, by permission of the author and the publisher.

Bloch, F. Lot, F. L. Ganshof or C. Stephenson) which emerged spontaneously literally everywhere as a product of the decomposition of tribal or slave society. But by creating new types of social relations and introducing new cultural values in one region only, the industrial revolution rapidly contaminated the rest of the world, introducing everywhere the market type of need satisfaction and the corresponding cultural matrix. As far as this "rest of the world" is concerned, the industrial pattern of economic growth as a cultural value was born before the appropriate changes in the social institutions were accomplished. It was introduced primarily as a political postulate, the new pattern of economic activity being its result rather than its premise. The industrial pattern of societal organization becoming a conscious political postulate, the basic social pre-conditions to industrial growth were transferred automatically from the economic and cultural to the political sphere. Adequately organized political forces, achieving their fullest form in centralized economic initiative, now became the chief social pre-requisite to economic growth. The higher the stage of growth already achieved by the industrialized part of the world, the greater and more decisive the role of central political forces in initiating the industrial type of development. This is why it would be rather misleading to analyse the social pre-requisites problem in the modern world by examining exclusively the features of the elemental cultural patterns and the structure of basic economic units, while neglecting politically organized social forces.

These preliminary remarks seem necessary to explain the approach I have taken to describe the Polish case of economic growth. Most of what is described in this article results from the conscious efforts of the organized centres of political and economic decision; and it must be so in the modern world, where the spontaneous birth of an industrial pattern — always in history an event of a very low probability — has become almost logically impossible, but where the same industrial pattern emerging as the result of organized and planned action is practically inevitable.

I

Pre-war Poland could not be classified as a "classical" underdeveloped country in the generally accepted meaning of the term. The total national product as well as the yearly output of some goods often used as reliable indices to measure economic growth were evidently much lower than in the highly industrialized societies, but above the level of many other countries (in 1937 Polish output of electric power was three times higher than Hungarian, Rumanian, Danish, etc.; the output of steel was much higher than in Sweden, Australia, Hungary, Spain, etc.). But in general, particularly from the sociological point of view, pre-war Poland shared many characteristic features with societies usually chosen as examples of pre-industrial economic system.

First of all, Poland was a country based on a predominantly rural economy, two-thirds of its population living in village-type communities and deriving their only incomes from agriculture. Hardly 8 per cent of the population was employed in the non-agricultural occupations. The family enterprise was the most usual and popular unit of the productive system; kinship ties interfered greatly with traditional economic activity thus accounting for the unusual strength of traditionalism, patterned by the institutions sanctioned and controlled by the local community. The traditional mentality was solidly entrenched in and nourished by the system of social relations almost unmodified for many generations and continuously re-created, since inheritance almost exclusively determined social status. The preservation of the traditional set of social relations by all-pervading community control was facilitated by the universal character of the social bonds located in the community. This was the initial stage in the long process of ramification of the social ties leading gradually to the institutionalization of particular aspects of human activity in specialized formal organizations.

Poland was not a feudal country; on the contrary, it was well advanced on the road to capitalist development. But an inert and non-expansive economy strengthened the domination of the typically feudal hierarchy of values with its main discriminating features: "orientation to the past" which emphasized the inherited ingredients in the individual's status and seriously weakened the stimuli to personal achievement; the relatively backward economy which provided little scope for many candidates to ascend the social ladder. To these factors must be added one further important obstacle — the lofty scorn for hard work deeply ingrained in the traditional gentry culture. The contempt for hard work, especially manual, was something like the first commandment in the decalogue of the dominating culture. Making one's living at this kind of work was sufficient to exclude one from well-bred society. The other side of the medal of the same cultural system was the extremely high prestige ascribed to all kinds of "clean" jobs, "cleanness" being a value in itself, independent of any estimate of the social utility, rationality, and appropriateness of the job and its role in increasing wealth. Pre-war Poland was a country with a considerable surplus of professionals and intellectuals, particularly those with the kind of skills which are irrelevant to industrial activity. There was one more important element in the cultural bequest of gentry rule: attachment to individual sovereignty and independence, called liberty. This particular concept of liberty was rooted historically in the long struggle of the Polish gentry against the rule of the aristocracy. The equality of social and political rights of the gentry won in this struggle was based on land ownership; it was the equality of landowners. The enormous attachment to one's scrap of land or workshop, even the most miserable one constituting no base for success-ful economic activity, was the direct result of this historically conditioned understanding of "liberty". The permanent unemployment of a great part of the population in the few industrial centres offered addi-tional arguments to those who preferred the most pitiful but "independent" existence to the position of an actual or potential employee and thus clung frantically to artisan or peasant ways of life. According to the pro-minent Polish economist, Ludwik Landau, the number of artisans in pre-war Poland was equal to those em-ployed in the entire Polish industry. That industry was concentrated in a few big towns meant that nearly all local communities lived under continuous and almost unchallenged pressure of the small ownership culture, and that this culture shaped the dominating goals and patterns of success.

The view of the order of the human world as some-thing unchangeable and almost eternal flourished under the weight of inertia. There were neither bourgeois nor political or industrial revolutions in the Polish past — nothing that could reveal the fundamental flexibility of the framework of human existence and emphasize the secular potential of social readjustment. The rate of economic growth was too small and slow to be easily observed; in fact there were long periods of recession. In 1929 there were 2.4 million people employed outside agriculture; in 1938 their number hardly reached 2 million.

Much has been reported already on pre-war Poland's semi-colonial position as a market ruthlessly exploited by foreign capital. Heavy pressure exercised by big land-owning interests on the economic policy of the ruling Polish élite and the subordination of native Polish business circles to foreign financial and industrial companies, are also quite well known. Here perhaps the basic causes of Polish economic backwardness are to be found. But the point I would like to stress parti-cularly is that the result of all these intertwining factors, and at the same time the direct cause of the absence of anything we may reasonably call economic growth, was the lack of a reliable social force capable of leading and organizing the effort to set the country moving along the path of industrial development. This force being absent, or in any event deprived of political power, Poland was not able to free itself from the bonds of a stagnant economy nourishing the pre- and anti-indus-trial mentality and the pre-industrial culture which reinforced economic inertia.

II

Such a force appeared in 1945, when the social structure of the country was not very different to the one described. The nature of this force was political and its appearance was the result of a political upheaval. The adherents of central economic planning based on centralization of ownership of basic means of pro-duction were brought to power. Enormous resources accumulated through the sheer act of nationalization provided the initial basis for rapid economic growth and intensive capital investment. The policy of strict thrift which was possible solely under conditions of centralized ownership and, perhaps, centralized political power since it slackened the rise of living standards, also contributed to the accelerated rate of economic growth. Social changes often singled out as the necessary conditions for an industrial revolution (and what has happened in Poland during the last seven-teen years surely deserves the name) were delayed, but they emerged mainly as the result and not as the cause of economic action.

As we are interested in the change in the social struc-ture of Polish society, two measures organized "from above" by forces holding political power must be of primary importance. The first is the nationalization of big business, the second, agrarian reform. During 1945-49, 814,000 new peasant farms were created and the area of many others considerably increased thus providing healthy conditions for normal agricultural activity in formerly declining farms. Altogether, well above 6 million hectares of land were divided among 1,068,000 peasant farms. Thanks to the abolition of large landed property, the so-called rural proletariat, the most mercilessly exploited section of the pre-war Polish population, disappeared entirely. But agrarian reform influenced not only the social position of those who benefited from it directly: the whole socio-economic stigma on the rural population as the sinister spectre of over-population was removed and thus the bargaining position of the poor peasantry fundamentally improved.

The real social consequences of agrarian reform cannot, however, be correctly appreciated if they are analysed in isolation. Agrarian reform was carried out simultaneously with the beginning of an unprecedented expansion of Polish industry (during the post-war years the number of people employed outside agri-culture increased fourfold, the total volume of output eightfold. Agrarian reform by itself was inadequate to cope with the social problems of the Polish village; only in conjunction with the nationalization of big industry and finance which opened the road to rapid economic growth could it bring a real and lasting social change.

Incessant industrial expansion created broad and smoothly functioning channels of social mobility link-ing the previously overpopulated rural communities and small semi-rural towns with the new industrial centres. It offered the owners of economically senseless and irrelevant tiny shops and workshops an attractive alternative of stable and secure employment in industry or the many auxiliary services. This great exodus of peasants and artisans towards industry which took place in Poland in the middle of the twentieth century differed in many crucial respects from the apparently similar process in Britain since the beginning of the nineteenth century. English, Welsh and Scottish peasants and artisans, thrown forcibly out of their farms and workshops and turned into homeless vagabonds and paupers perceived this change as a real social decline from their former conditions. These, seen and felt by them as decent and relatively "human" were replaced by the melting-pot of the first factories; they lost their cherished independence and were submitted instead to the greedy pioneers of industrialization and the semi-feudal practices of foremen. The majority of former peasants and artisans in Poland perceived the change in their social status as a real advancement; they exchanged a shabby and shaky living in an apparently independent, but in fact severely exploited "enterprise" — the kind of living already defined culturally as abhorrent — for a stable and safe existence in civilized and attractive urban conditions. At least by the young people leaving the land of their forefathers and becoming factory workers, this was undoubtedly considered as upward mobility.

One of the foremost results of rapid industrial expansion was the general increase in the number of social positions of relatively high rank available to those from the "lower strata" (this process as a universal feature of industrialization has been pointed out by Lipset and Bendix in their studies on social mobility in industrial society) and thus the substantial extension of upward social mobility. In Poland, this result was very marked indeed; social mobility of an unprecedented intensity literally turned the traditional social structure upside down. Roughly half of the present Polish population now lives on incomes drawn from non-agricultural activity. The notorious "over-production" of intellectuals appeared to be merely "under-consumption"; there are no unemployed members of the "intelligentsia" nowadays, although the number of students in technical and engineering schools has increased seven times, the total number of students in institutions of higher education being three times greater than before the war.

The intense social mobility heavily influenced the place of the family in the class structure, a phenomenon already mentioned by G. D. H. Cole in his studies of British class structure, but beyond doubt much more advanced under present Polish conditions owing to the extreme rapidity and scope of social change. The family no longer plays the traditional role as the elementary unit of social class: at the birthday table in a peasant's house an engineer and a miner, a junior or senior executive and an army officer, a peasant and a physician sit together. Instead of being a rough brick in the construction of one particular class, the family becomes often the exchange market for multifarious class and class-like subcultures and behaviour patterns. As a result, the traditionally sharp differences in the way of life of the social classes previously isolated from each other are visibly blurring, though their force is not yet spent and they ought not to be considered as finally blotted out.

Neither differences, nor barriers dividing social classes have disappeared in present Polish society. The tradition of relative separation of the socially differentiated milieu, long established and deeply rooted in the national culture, still heavily influences the dominating customs, style of living, the whole class subcultures. With regard to the structure of the family budget consumption patterns, cherished life goals and the general mode of life there still persist sharp differences between individuals socialized in intellectual, working-class or peasant environments. Though a manual worker and a white-collar worker may earn the same amount of money, this does not mean that their behaviour patterns conform. Serious differences in selection and perception of cultural goods, in educational expectancies and — partly because of this — in the scope of opportunities are still in full force. In respect to opportunities, we face the problem of persistent barriers between classes: the actual equality of educational and thus of status achievement opportunities, the necessary condition for the real abolishment of these barriers, demands not only equality of formal rights, but equality of cultural standards, too. As research done by Stanislaw Widerszpil showed, among schoolboys of working-class origin only 7 per cent, and among schoolgirls of the same origin only 17 per cent, aspire to a university education; at the same time the percentage of brain-workers' children wishing to enter universities is 30 for boys and 60 for girls. The number of manual workers' children who do not seek any kind of higher education at all is twice as high as the corresponding number among the children of brain-workers. Widerszpil investigated the distribution of aspirations and turning to the degree of fulfilment of aspirations the discrepancy was found to be even greater. This is an important constraint on social mobility as a destroyer of the class barriers. As education becomes the chief ladder between social classes and the most important tool of individual achievement and advancement, the persistence of differences in educational opportunities reinforces the natural tendency of each social class to perpetuate itself in the next generations — and so to reproduce the whole class structure of society.

III

The concepts of "higher" and "lower" constitute the principal indicators of social stratification. The image of stratification depicts society as consisting of layers; as a hierarchy of aggregated individuals classified together because they possess certain common features. The choice of these, and not of other features, is always justified, and can only be justified, by their being accepted and highly esteemed values in the cultural system of the society under analysis. Thus any stratification is the product of evaluation. The high degree of universality which exemplifies social acceptance of the chosen values is a *sine qua non* for strata discrimination, if it is to be something more than the mere product of the scientist's research operations and logical divisions.

This very important trait of social stratification is

often overlooked; in the United States of America, where the theoretical and empirical studies in this field originated and developed, acceptance of dominant cultural standards is so deep and universal (owing to social continuity in American history) that they can easily and reasonably be taken for granted. The crucial question whether there exist some generally accepted value standards constituting the real foundation of the stratification system can be disregarded. As far as the United States of America is concerned, no false conclusions follow from this omission. Without going too far into the problem of universality of cultural standards, one can be certain that the stratification analysed is a real thing, a part of social reality.

But in certain other societies the problem is not so simple. We can speak sensibly of social stratification in relatively stable societies only, where the same class has dominated in social, political and economic spheres for many generations, the same class shaping for many decades the uniform cultural framework for the processes of socializing individuals. Step by step their values, which are functional to the existing social system and therefore supported by all means the dominating class can utilize, become an integral part of the common culture; they are internalized during and through the process of societally organized education; general consensus concerning the inequality of social positions occupied by the various milieux on the social ladder is an outcome of this process. This general consensus leads to fairly real and "material" divisions in society: individuals placed on the same level of the social hierarchy maintain reciprocal social relations, socially accept each other, marry their children to each other, enter the same clubs and social circles, live in the same neighbourhoods, wear similar clothes, fill their dwellings with the same kind of furniture, share similar viewpoints, likewise abstain from intimacy with people from "below" and are filled with reverence toward those from "above". In short, they gradually form a fairly cohesive social group. Thus the final result of the evaluation of social structure is the emergence of large self-accepting and self-perpetuating groups, having an attitude of superiority towards some, and of inferiority towards others.

If there are no sufficiently universal value standards, the question whether social stratification exists at all has to be answered before we pose the next question of how it is constructed. That is the case of Poland (and I suppose of all countries experiencing rapid social and economic change). Ogburn's "cultural lag" here supplies the main argument: the image of the social structure and its manifestations in human folkways is in general much more conservative than the structure itself and tends to outlive its changes. All available theoretical and empirical data show that the upheavals in Polish class structure undermined the old system of social stratification but the construction of the new system did not keep pace with the rapid metamorphosis in the composition of social classes and in the web of their mutual relations. I doubt if we are at all justified in

speaking of social stratification in present-day Poland. Manifold value standards intertwine here in highly unexpected ways. In such conditions any coherent image of social stratification can only be the product of statistical operations and does not correspond to real attitudes and behavioural manifestations of hierarchical appraisal. Two traditional values which had formerly been the main thread in the texture of social stratification – the values of "money" and "noble birth" – still compete with the new values, partly popularized by official propaganda and partly gaining acceptance as a result of their great instrumental significance, such as "social utility" or "participation in power". There is no unique and monopolistic value on which a coherent and stable social stratification, based on the consensus of all parts of the nation, could be built.

Investigations of this extremely intricate problem were conducted by Sarapata and Wesolowski, two Polish sociologists. Let us not forget that the image of social stratification emerging from this kind of research owes its apparent focus to statistical method and not to the actual divisions of the reality investigated. Nevertheless, we can discern from the accumulated data the main trends in the process of societal restratifications, and the kind of positional criterion that becomes preponderant in the mixture of cultural influences. Such a cautious interpretation allows us to select level of skill and education as the value most often used to rank an individual on the social ladder. Men of science and teachers, engineers, professionals, and politicians of high rank were most often placed at the top of the social hierarchy. If these different groups have anything in common, it is the very high degree of skill and education they are generally expected to possess. This value considerably outstripped other values, such as income, or the "clean" character of work. Clerks and other auxiliary office workers were ranked well below the position ascribed to skilled manual workers; it is not enough to do "brain work" to be endowed with great social prestige; one must also perform a function to which an image of high skill and educational achievements is attached.

As Robert Presthus has already demonstrated in his study of Middle-Eastern bureaucratic systems, the pattern of prestige distributions in bureaucracies superimposed somewhat artificially on a generally traditional society differs in many respects from the Weberian ideal-type model. Making management rational and efficient (which is according to Weber the primary task and function of modern bureaucracy) demands the meticulous observance of particular institutional and behavioural norms, such as conformity of the level of skill attached to a given position with the actual skill possessed by the individual appointed to this position, and conformity of the prestige with which the person is actually endowed with the amount of prestige attached to the bureaucratic function this person performs. When other criteria of prestige distribution compete with this functional criterion – the only one permissible and acceptable in an ideal bureaucracy — the model of perfect management is distorted, the performance of bureaucratic tasks is in danger, the role of bureaucracy as the tool of rational management cannot be played successfully. Thus the distance between the actual prestige distribution and the ideal one may be considered as a valuable index for the measurement of the level of maturity of particular societal institutions of the industrial type of development (also, the opposite, when the degree of pre-industrial traditionality of societal institutions is the object of measurement). Discrepancy between the ideal type and the actual bureaucratic framework should be considered one of the most important obstacles to be overcome on the way to an industrial pattern of society. Scrutinizing previously presented research data from this angle we can conclude that, changes in the relative strength of values being the basis of stratification, this should be understood as a manifestation of the growing adaptation of Polish society to the requirements functional to the industrial pattern.

IV

A comprehensive study of the Polish power élite still awaits its author. Owing to lack of reliable investigations, detailed data on its composition, internal stratification, prevailing type of career, sources and levels of recruitment, behavioural patterns, degree of inner cohesion and uniformity of attitudes, etc. are not available. The accessible data on the top level of the power élite are particularly meagre; somewhat better known are certain problems of the middle level of power — élites of local communities and of the managerial level of the social system (according to Parsons' conceptualization). Thus we are not yet able to sketch a complete picture of power élite dynamics; nevertheless, some conclusions important to our purpose can be drawn, as the élite of the middle level more readily reflects general social change in its composition and behavioural patterns than does the top level of power, which is obviously much more conservative.

Let us first examine the changes which took place in the élite at the managerial level. The Sociological Research Bureau of the Higher School of Social Sciences in Warsaw investigated the composition of the party "activists" and party executives in all great industrial enterprises in Poland. This investigation showed a very remarkable trend: the composition of both party "activists" and executives changes consistently and continuously, the main characteristics of the change being *a)* considerable increase in the number of persons with relatively higher educational achievements; *b)* considerable increase in the number of people with relatively greater vocational skill, in particular engineers and technicians (graduates of technical colleges).

We need to explain here why we consider the members of the party executive as representative of the managerial level of the power élite. The power relations in a Polish factory cannot be analysed relevantly without taking into account the role of the party organization and of those who derive their political power from their official functions in the party structure. The party executive is an important element of factory management; party "activists" are an influential link in the chain of power control over the working personnel and over management itself. No major decision concerning factory problems is conceivable without the participation and perhaps support of the party organization. We cannot here go too deeply into this very intricate problem, but what has been said is probably sufficient to justify our looking upon the party "activist" as a crucial part of the power élite at the managerial level.

Returning to the trend we have noted already, we would like to support it by some statistical proofs. According to the research results we have obtained, the percentage of party members among factory staff with higher education is thrice that of those with primary education only. This disproportion is further increasing due to the even greater prevalence of the highly educated among those recently recruited. "Higher education" means here principally training as technical experts and managers. Engineers and technicians constituted 6.82 per cent of the factory staffs investigated, but 13.24 per cent of the party members among these staffs. The relative number of engineers and technicians among party "activists" is even higher and amounts to roughly 24 per cent. This means that among all employed engineers and technicians one in every fifteen actively belongs to the party, the corresponding index among the manual workers being much lower — one in 75 for skilled workers and one in 198 for the unskilled. At the level of the party executive the proportions are still further in favour of increasing participation of engineers, managers and experts.

Important changes were found also in the institutional and behavioural standards prevailing in the factory party organizations; we can reasonably relate these changes to the trends just presented. By this I mean, first of all, a remarkable shift from predominantly ideological to mainly technical and managerial preoccupations; the party meetings come gradually to resemble consultative assemblies; the content of individual and collective tasks confided to people in their capacity as party members is, in much greater proportion than before, connected directly with the purely industrial life of the factory. Meetings and everyday activities of party members and especially the party executives take on a more and more "expert" character; speeches and conversations are full of technical terms. Political merit and ideological virtues are no longer a sufficient qualification for the performance of party functions: one must possess vocational education and professional skill to deal with technical and administrative problems at a table with specialists of the highest rank. In this respect the metamorphosis now taking place in the party function of the managerial power élite is no more than a somewhat belated reflection of a similar change which had already taken place in the managerial staff itself. Directors and experts who had advanced rapidly from the ranks on the strength of their political merit alone, a phenomenon very often encountered in the early period of the socialist revolution in Poland, either became themselves graduates of various colleges or gave way to the younger generation of duly educated engineers and technicians.

In our investigation of the power élite in the local communities, carried out in ten small towns in Poland, we have come to identical conclusions. We have found two different types of the local élite, one being replaced gradually by the other, this succession being connected directly with general economic growth in general and, in particular, industrial development. The élite of the first type holds power so long as the community remains outside the general economic development of the country and does not itself experience economic expansion. A decision to locate the construction of an industrial or mining enterprise in a given community usually means the end of this élite, at the same time it means the beginning of a new type of rule, which demands also a new type of person. New men come to the commanding posts in the local hierarchy of power; very often they arrive from outside the community and consider their present position as an episode in their career, their relevant frame of reference being the general hierarchy of power in the country as a whole.

The two types of local élite are made up of two different types of personalities. The first is composed predominantly of persons whose career in politics is based on their skill as propagandists and on their ideological virtues. They were members of the Communist organizations from the clandestine period onward, soldiers or partisan (guerilla) units during the German occupation, pioneers of reconstruction in the times immediately following the war. Most of them never attended secondary schools and were not trained in handling administrative and organizational problems. What they do know, they owe to their own predispositions and to hard experience. Placed in positions of considerable power and influence, some of them became bureaucrats in the behavioural meaning of the word; still they prefer ideological values when defining and estimating situations which demand decisions involving a choice and candidly use broad humanitarian principles in describing and justifying their behaviour. During our interviews we asked members of the local élite what they would do if there were only one unoccupied dwelling left and two families asking to be accommodated in it: a poor widow with two small children and a young engineer who will not want to stay and work in the town if the opportunity to bring his wife is not soon guaranteed. Most of the older type of élite members decided in favour of the widow, while representatives of the new echelons voted for the engineer (several of them commented: "the engineer will build a house for the widow"). Having gradually adapted themselves

to the requirements of their power function, members of the old élite achieved a certain level of organizational and administrative skill, quite sufficient in the conditions of a stable and traditional, non-expansive local community; this amount of skill appeared, however, quite inadequate when adaptation to the conditions of a rapidly expanding industrial community became the immediate necessity for all who wished to keep or acquire power positions. The members of the old élite awakened one day to find themselves "morally worn out" and replaced by relatively young men. Accustomed to command, feeling their vitality by no means exhausted, they felt themselves suddenly pushed from the mainstream, the job they loved and were used to, the only job they were still able to do. This explains why many of them behaved in the new situations according to typical frustration patterns, often plotted against newcomers, manifested strongly unco-operative attitudes toward new-style executive power, grudgingly opposed the imminent change, tried to organize "old inhabitants" or "old, local activists" against the newcomers and the politics they symbolized. Thus conflict was inevitable. In some instances it was actually open and manifest, in other cases it took rather a latent form and withered away by itself, no strong measures having been applied.

The type of personality predominant in the new echelons of local power élites may be described by the simple conversion of the former characteristics. Members of the new local élite have in general no picturesque political past; they are highly educated men with formal diplomas and rather high expert skill in technical subjects and economics, trained systematically, often at special courses, in the art of administration and management. They think rationally in terms of expediency and utility, eagerly seek reliable means to prescribed goals, are ready to devote all their energy to the tasks they are entrusted to fulfil. They are expedient, efficient, industrious, full of initiative, and rather ruthless in pushing forward what is to be done. They are able to guarantee conditions indispensable to organizing rapid economic growth; they appear in the local community, not coincidentally, when command to start economic growth has been given.

Thus both our investigations lead to similar conclusions. There is a clear trend in the dynamics of middle-level élite composition, a tendency away from political-minded, traditional and past-oriented people to managerial, rational and achievement-oriented men. Surely this second kind of élite suits the conditions of economic growth much better. The first type was indispensable to set society moving, to construct the necessary political and ideological basis for the immense industrial revolution of the future. This important task being now fulfilled, the first type had to be replaced by the second type, as administrative and managerial issues took precedence over the tasks of propaganda. The change in the composition of the local power élite is another important index to the growing adaptation of the country to conditions of economic growth.

STRUCTURAL TRENDS AND VALUE PREMISES IN ASIAN COUNTRIES

The Middle Classes in Japan
Kunio Odaka

I. Introduction

DURING the last few years there has been much controversy centering around the nature and future prospects of the middle classes in Japan. This may in part be accounted for by the rise in the national standard of living, and particularly in that of the working classes, since the boom which started in 1956. The days of poverty and starvation which immediately followed World War II are now a thing of the past. During recent years people's clothes have improved, and many homes have been equipped with such consumer durables as a TV set, a washing machine and a refrigerator. Even working-class people have recently begun to spend a good deal of money on household equipment and recreation.

A more direct cause of the recent middle-class controversy, however, may be found in the campaigns started by both the conservative and the progressive parties, under such slogans as "Making everyone middle class". Whether these slogans were seriously conceived, as basic political programs, or were mere propaganda to attract votes for the forthcoming general election, there is no doubt that they have stimulated the middle-class controversy.

It should also be pointed out that the "new middle" or "white-collar" classes — clerical as well as technical workers and lesser administrative staff employed in private enterprises, public service workers, school teachers, etc. — have in Japan grown as in other highly industrialized countries. The census data clearly indicate, for example, that in 1955 the population identified as "white-collar" amounted to a little over 14% of the entire employed population, as against only 8% in 1930. Moreover, recent technological innovations adopted by many large-scale enterprises are gradually converting a majority of manual or "blue-collar" into "white-collar" workers, in terms of both job and life styles.

These changes have become fairly clear to the general public, so that talk of the "spread of the new middle strata" or of the "increase of the middle classes" has attracted their attention. We also cannot overlook the fact that empirical studies on class structure and inter-class mobility, undertaken since World War II, have now reached the stage at which their results are beginning to be popularized. The national surveys on social stratification and social mobility conducted in 1952 and 1955 by the Research Committee of the Japan Sociological Society (which will be hereafter abbreviated to "Stratification and Mobility Surveys"), and a similar survey with special reference to the middle classes in the Tokyo district undertaken in 1960 by the Institute

Originally appeared in Japanese in the *Nihon Rodo Kyokai Zasshi* (Monthly Journal of the Japan Institute of Labor), Vol. 3, No. 1, January 1961. Its English version was contributed to the First International Symposium on Social Stratification and Social Mobility in East Asian Countries held in Tokyo, April 5–9, 1964. The present version omits the detailed methodological discussion which was contained in the above article.

541

of Statistical Mathematics (hereafter abbreviated to "Middle Classes Survey") may be regarded as representative studies on this subject.[1] Although such surveys are not themselves known to the general public, a number of books have recently employed these findings in an attempt to describe changes in the class structure, and the life and psychology of people who struggle for status and success. There are a few books of this sort on the Japanese situation,[2] while many of the same *genre* appearing in the United States and England[3] are now available in Japanese translation, and have a fairly large circle of readers. These various sources have provided a background for Japanese interest in the middle classes.

II. Conflicting views on the middle classes

Despite the recent controversy about the middle classes — or perhaps because of it — there has been no clear answer to such questions as: What are the middle classes? Of what kind of people are they composed? What are their major characteristics? What is their role in the total class structure of modern Japanese society? We never have succeeded in framing a clear and common definition of the middle classes. It is not surprising, therefore, if we find a number of conflicting views on such questions as: In what direction are these classes moving? Is the proportion of the population in these classes increasing or decreasing? Will their social importance and political influence rise or fall?

There are those who follow the Marxist view in arguing that the population of a capitalist society will in the end be polarized into two main contending classes: capitalist and worker. They emphasize that white-collar personnel are essentially working class in nature,

and that the relative status of the new middle strata is actually declining. On the other hand, those who look to the establishment of a welfare state and gradual social reform stress the fact that: *1)* the middle strata are gradually expanding; *2)* the socio-economic status of the working class has been much improved since the early period of capitalism; and *3)* the whole society is becoming more "middle class". Unfortunately, we can find plenty of data to support both views. Nor is this situation limited to Japan; similar divergences, and difficulties with data, are as evident in England and the United States. In addition, there are still considerable gaps in level between Japan and the more advanced countries of the West, which must be taken into consideration in dealing with these problems.

III. The superficial homogeneity of modern Japanese society

Perhaps one of the reasons why the concept of the "middle classes" remains vague is the fact that external differences among people are not today as discernible as they were in Japan's past. During the depression of the early 1930's, and again right after World War II — to say nothing of during the feudal period, when there were sharp institutionalized class distinctions among "military, agricultural, industrial and mercantile" classes — one could easily differentiate among people by external criteria. Variations in the type of clothes and belongings, in food, in style of housing, in the quality and quantity of furniture, decorations and other domestic utensils, in the type of recreation and amusement favored, etc., were sufficient to distinguish an executive from a general employee, a university professor from an insurance agent, or a white-collar from a blue-collar worker. Along with the recent development of mass production systems and a "revolution" in the consumption habits of the general public, however, such distinctions are rapidly fading out of modern Japanese society.

Distinctions are being blurred not only in external appearances, but in more subjective matters as well — in people's information, views, judgments and values. With the development of mass communication, information and judgments are being transmitted in a homogeneous form to vast numbers at one time, and people are rapidly being "homogenized," regardless of their academic backgrounds, occupations, or incomes.

These tendencies are of course appearing elsewhere than in Japan. More or less similar processes, obscuring class attributes, can be observed in other advanced countries, wherever industrialization has made great progress and the characteristics of a mass society are conspicuous. Such tendencies become more pronounced as industry flourishes, as economic growth becomes more rapid, and as people's social life grows more stable. Thus, for example, in the United States recent propaganda has it — with no doubt some exaggeration — that the whole nation has been turned into "one great

[1] See Research Committee, Japan Sociological Society, *Report of a Sample Survey of Social Stratification and Mobility in the Six Large Cities of Japan*, Tokyo, 1952 (mimeographed); ditto, "Social Stratification and Mobility in the Six Large Cities of Japan", International Sociological Association, Transactions of the Second World Congress of Sociology, Vol. 2, London, 1954, pp. 414–431; ditto, *Social Mobility in Japan: An Interim Report on the 1955 Survey of Social Stratification and Social Mobility in Japan*, Tokyo, 1956 (mimeographed); and ditto, *Modern Japanese Society: Its Class Structure* (in Japanese), Tokyo: Yuhikaku, 1958. As to the Middle Classes Survey, see Kunio Odaka, "How Has the Japanese Class Structure Changed?" (in Japanese), *Jiyu* (Freedom), No. 7, June 1960, pp. 131–154; Chikio Hayashi, "Where are the Japanese Middle Classes?" (in Japanese), *ibid.*, pp. 156–170; Shigeki Nishihira, "Consciousness of the Japanese Middle Classes" (in Japanese), *ibid.*, pp. 170–180.

[2] See e.g., Kunio Odaka, ed., *Occupation and Social Stratification* (in Japanese), Tokyo: Mainichi Shinbun Sha, 1958.

[3] Cf. Roy Lewis and Angus Maud, *The English Middle Classes*, London: Phoenix House, 1950; David Riesman, *The Lonely Crowd: A Study of the Changing American Character*, New Haven: Yale University Press, 1950; C. Wright Mills, *White Collar: The American Middle Classes*, New York: Oxford University Press, 1953; Vance Packard, *The Status Seekers: An Exploration of Class Behavior in America*, New York: David McKay Co., 1959; Andrew Grant, *Socialism and the Middle Classes*, London: Lawrence & Wishart, 1958, pp. 11 ff., 46 ff.; G. D. H. Cole, *Studies in Class Structure*, London: Routledge and Kegan Paul, 1955, pp. 78 ff.

middle class" or "the most genuine classless society in history."

The appearance of change here is perhaps stronger than its reality. If we examine a society in detail, it will become evident that there are many sorts of discrimination between classes, and various differences and inequalities even within a single class. Moreover, such countertendencies themselves spread with economic growth and the prosperity of national life. Nevertheless, it seems true that the ordinary citizen's most dominant impression of daily life is that class discriminations are gradually diminishing. And this no doubt in turn leads to a gradual benumbing of the consciousness of rivalry or of antagonism among classes, a factor which is relevant to class discrimination. This is perhaps one of the reasons why the Marxist theory of polarization into the two classes, capitalist and worker, is losing its persuasive power.

In such a situation, it becomes difficult readily to discern distinctions among classes, and to assign individuals securely among them. A class is gradually losing any character as a spontaneously formed grouping, distinct from other similar aggregates, but instead becomes a label for that part of a continuous population which an outside student wishes to set off. If the subject of study is caste society in India or feudal society in Japan, the student would be able to discern rather easily the natural distinctions among classes — in these cases, of course, castes or ranks. Each of such classes is a separate group, constituted by members who have "consciousness of kind", and each person who belongs to it has a definite appearance and way of living by which his class membership can be easily ascertained. If the subject is a contemporary large city, on the other hand, it is far more difficult to find any natural distinctions among classes, and the observer's difficulties multiply. Even if we take income as an index of class, we will find that it varies more or less continuously and gradually between the minimum and maximum values, so that the decision as to the points at which differences significant for class are to be recognized is one in a sense arbitrarily made by the student. Any discussion of the class structure of a contemporary society thus tends to lack a common, empirical basis, and is thereby made more complex.

IV. Overlapping indicators of status: property, prestige and stratum

So far, some of the difficulties in the way of an objective analysis of class structure and of class distinctions have been described. There is, however, another factor that makes any discussion of the middle classes confusing. That is the muddle in terminology.

In English, only the term *middle class* is in common usage. In German, besides *Mittelklasse* there are the terms *Mittelstand*, in which the idea of "rank" or "occupation" is emphasized, and *Mittelschicht*, in which the sense of "stratum" is strong. In French,

"middle class" is expressed by *bourgeoisie* as well as by *classe moyenne*. In Japanese, there are at least three kinds of terms — "middle economic class" (*chusan kaikyu*), "middle prestige class" (*churyu kaikyu*) and "middle stratum" (*chukan kaiso*) — and these are used freely and interchangeably in the recent arguments about the middle classes in this country.

More important, each of these three Japanese terms fits into a quite different set of complementary terms — "middle economic" between "capitalist" and "worker", "middle prestige" between "upper" and "lower" prestige categories, etc. — and each set conveys a different image to a listener's mind. It seems a reasonable observation that the man in the street thinks of property or income when confronted with the term "middle economic class"; he will think of persons so labelled as people with considerable property and a large revenue, who can afford a high consumption standard. He will think, in other words, of a class pyramid based on economic power. On the other hand, the term "middle prestige class" will bring to his mind a picture of relative social status occupied, a measure of social esteem and prestige enjoyed. The factor most relevant here will not be one's crude economic power, but rather one's birth, circle of acquaintances, educational background, or, even more commonly, one's occupation and post. Therefore also, an ordinary "salaried man", for example, regarding himself as economically worse off than a small enterpriser or a skilled worker, but as superior to them in terms of education, culture and staff rank in a modern occupational structure, will identify himself as of "middle prestige". In our three surveys of class structure already cited (1952, 1955 and 1960), the percentage of those who evaluated themselves as of "middle prestige" was always much higher than of those who said they were of "middle economic" rank.

The term "middle stratum", on the other hand, seems to elicit the negative aspect of being in the "middle" — the sense of ambiguity, of fluidity, of not having succeeded better. Such being the case, it is perhaps not surprising that the survey findings show that those who identified themselves as being of "middle stratum" — even though it is the academically most widely used term — were fewer than those who put themselves in the middle on more explicit criteria.

In order to make these points more concrete, Table 1 shows data from the Stratification and Mobility Survey of 1955 and the Middle Classes Survey of 1960. Because of space, we shall omit any explanation of the subjects of the surveys and the methods adopted.[1] It may be pointed out, however, that in all of these surveys not only was the respondent's class judged by objective indices, such as income and occupation, but also

---

[1] As for the methods used in these surveys, see Section VI (A Methodology for Distinguishing Social Classes) of this paper. See also Research Committee, Japan Sociological Society, *Modern Japanese Society: Its Class Structure* (in Japanese), Tokyo: Yuhikaku, pp. 7–35.

subjectively, by asking him to place himself. Subjects were questioned so as to obtain a self-evaluation in terms of each of three separate scales: A) as "capitalist class, middle economic class, working class"; B) as "upper, upper-middle, lower-middle, upper-lower, and lower-lower" in prestige; and C) as "leader stratum, managerial stratum, intermediate stratum, working stratum".

As can be seen in Table 1, males (all over 20 years of age) on both occasions evaluated themselves as of "middle prestige" (B) more frequently than they saw themselves to be "middle economic" (A) or "intermediate" (C), the latter being least frequent. Moreover, the differences are great; in 1960, whereas 56% gave the answer "middle prestige", 29% thought themselves "middle economic", and only 19% "intermediate". If we were to recombine the categories of measure B so that upper and upper-middle became a single class of "upper prestige", lower-middle and upper-lower were

their economic circumstances. For example, an ordinary "salaried man" may think that he is at least intermediate in terms of educational background and occupation. At the same time, however, he would hesitate to profess himself to be economically middle class, preferring to see himself as "worker", on account of the small size of his income (perhaps around ¥30,000 a month), the small amount of property he owns, and his consequent austerity as a consumer. On the other hand, the small size of the "middle stratum" group may be explained by the detestation of the Japanese mind for ambiguity and uncertainty, its preference for the clear distinctions of black or white.

These conjectures receive some substantiation, moreover, in the 1960 Survey (males only). Only 42% of the entire middle prestige category saw themselves as being also of "middle economic" grouping. And only 26% of the latter category identified themselves as being also of the "middle stratum". By contrast, self-evaluation as

TABLE 1. *Class Self-Identification* (%)*

		A	Capitalist	Middle Economic	Worker	Others and Unknown	Total (No.)
1955		Tokyo (male)	2	23	74	1	100 (500)
		Japan (male)	1	23	74	2	100 (2,000)
1960		Tokyo (male)	3	29	62	5	100 (356)
		Tokyo (female)	3	34	51	12	100 (381)
		B	Upper	Middle Prestige	Lower	Others and Unknown	Total (No.)
1955		Tokyo (male)	1	51	47	1	100 (500)
		Japan (male)	—	42	56	2	100 (2,000)
1960		Tokyo (male)	—	56	42	2	100 (356)
		Tokyo (female)	1	59	38	2	100 (381)
		C	Leader and Managerial	Intermediate	Working	Others and Unknown	Total (No.)
1960		Tokyo (male)	18	19	57	6	100 (356)
		Tokyo (female)	10	26	43	20	100 (381)

* Data for 1955 are taken from the Stratification and Mobility Survey; those for 1960 from the Middle Classes Survey.

to be a single "middle prestige" grouping, etc., the proportion of the respondents who put themselves in the middle rises to 80% in the 1960 males and 76% in the 1955 Tokyo males (not shown in Table 1). Such an alteration can in fact be defended if we consider the following points: that there were hardly any cases of self-evaluation as "upper"; that the respondents tended to a lower ranking of themselves than would seem objectively warranted; and that the objective data show a definite difference between those who ranked themselves as of "upper-middle" and of "lower-middle" classes in income and property.

Why should there be these differences in self-evaluation? We may conjecture that in general, many Japanese who regard themselves as of around middle prestige, in terms of social status or role, would be reluctant to classify themselves as "middle" when they think about

[1] Cf. Research Committee, Japan Sociological Society, *op. cit.*, pp. 92–94.

"working class" or "working stratum" is, in both surveys, exceedingly common. As indicated in Table 1, males in 1960 put themselves in these two categories in 62% and 57% of cases, respectively. This tendency was even stronger in 1955, when 74%, both in Tokyo and in all Japan, so classified themselves; in other words, three-quarters of the total thought themselves to be of working class. There is no other economically-advanced country in which so many people regard themselves in this light. Although similar surveys, employing the same methods, have been carried out in England, the United States, France, and West Germany,[1] the proportion who identify themselves as "workers" is only around 50% in each of these four countries. The proportion for Japan is 20% more in 1955, and 10% more even in 1960, than the average of these four.

In the same vein, those who identify themselves as middle economic in class are fewer than in the other countries. In contrast to 49% in England, 43% in the

United States, 42% in West Germany and 40% in France, only 23% in either Tokyo or the whole of Japan in 1955 so classified themselves. If we change the question, and ask it in terms of "prestige", however, the proportion who see themselves in the middle becomes larger — in the case of Tokyo in 1960, over 10% more than those in these foreign countries.[1]

Thus, it is plain that these three terms — "middle economic", "middle prestige", and "middle stratum" — are understood by ordinary Japanese as having clearly different meanings. However, these three terms are used interchangeably by scholars in their arguments about the middle classes. Recently, moreover, the terms "new intermediate stratum" and "old intermediate stratum" have been employed, intensifying the terminological confusion. And naturally, discussions of the middle classes have become entangled by such words. It is by no means rare to find one debater arguing about the middle prestige class and another writing about the new and old intermediate strata, though both employ the term "middle economic class". There are even more extreme cases, as when, for example, people in non-manual occupations — professional, administrative, clerical, sales, and services — are counted as "middle economic class". On this basis, the middle economic class increases from below 30% (Table 1) to around 60% of the employed male population in Tokyo. This conclusion, however, will be inaccurate and even misleading in at least two respects: first, the definition excludes such centrally economic factors as income and property; and secondly, it completely neglects the ordinary person's image of the middle economic class.

V. Working-class consciousness in Japan

We have already seen that the proportion of the population which identifies itself as of "working" class is large in Japan. It may be useful here to suggest some interpretations of this fact.

The consciousness of belonging to the working class may have in it any of several elements. They are: *1)* A positive satisfaction and pride in being a worker; *2)* a spirit of "resistance", born of dissatisfaction with their present condition and of the force for reform that the working class itself represents; *3)* a simple "working-stratum" consciousness, mixed with neither pride nor antagonism; and *4)* an inferiority complex, or sense of being resigned to the fact that they are after all underdogs and the bottom layer of society, a position from which it is difficult to escape, at least within the foreseeable future.

Of these four, perhaps 2 and 3 are the main elements in the Japanese working-class consciousness. It has often been pointed out that the working classes of England and West Germany have a strong pride in being workers; in them, that is, the first element is strong. Indeed, English people in general are said to have a relatively strong status consciousness, so that a policeman, a gate-keeper, an engine-driver or a coalminer is positively proud of his occupation and does not desire a higher one for his children. However common a similar view may once have been among the Japanese, it is no longer characteristic. The so-called "American Creed", i.e., the belief that a person of any social origin can rise in the social hierarchy according to his own efforts and ability, the belief in the principle of equal opportunity, is now perhaps more common in Japan than in Western Europe. In any event, people with this "American" aspiration are by no means few. This holds as much for the working class as for other Japanese. And if this is the case, it is clear that the first element cited above contributes very little to the Japanese consciousness about the working class.

Likewise, there are fewer people with an inferiority complex in Japan today than there were some years ago. Of course, the number of people who are in real want is still large even today, as is made clear in the situation of such groups as households protected under the Daily Life Security Law, day-laborers, temporary factory hands, and outside workers. However, according to the findings of the 1960 Middle Classes Survey,[2] 42% of those who saw themselves as working class also identified themselves as of "lower-middle", and 41% as "upper-lower", in prestige class. If these two categories together comprise the middle class proper, as was argued in the previous chapter, 83% of those who see themselves as workers would also claim to belong to a middle class. It seems, in other words, that the "workers" do not at all put themselves at the bottom or underdog position in society. Furthermore, we must take into consideration the fact that, with the development of the trade union movement, the word "worker" has a much happier connotation in postwar, than it had in prewar, Japan.

We may conclude, therefore, that the spirit of resistance and a simple working-stratum consciousness constitute the major elements operative in the minds of working-class Japanese. The latter may in fact, in some unexplained way, become directly transmitted into a middle-class consciousness. The spirit of resistance, on the other hand, has as its background a feeling of discontent, derived from the fact that life is not easy in spite of being middle class. The consciousness of belonging to the working class will take various forms according to the ways in which these two elements are combined.

What does it signify that the number of people with a working-class consciousness is conspicuously large in Japan, a country that must be counted among the great industrial nations of the world today? Of the entire

[1] More detailed explanations of the international comparison can be found in Kunio Odaka, ed., *Occupation and Social Stratification* (in Japanese), Tokyo: Mainichi Shinbun Sha, 1958, pp. 73–80. See also Shigeki Nishihira, "Cross-National Comparative Study on Social Stratification and Social Mobility", *Annals of the Institute of Statistical Mathematics*, Vol. VIII, No. 3, 1957, pp. 181–191.
[2] Data from the Survey given here are all on Tokyo males. Likewise, when we employ the findings of the 1955 Stratification and Mobility Survey here, we are concerned with Tokyo males only.

category of "middle prestige", those who also have a "worker" consciousness composed 57% in 1955 and 51% in 1960, while those who also saw themselves as being "middle economic" were only 39% and 42%, respectively. Conversely, of the "worker" category those who also gave themselves "middle prestige" were 39% in 1955 and 46% in 1960 — less than those who classified themselves as being "workers" and of "lower prestige" (59% and 52% respectively), yet still relatively large. It seems reasonable to conclude from these facts that more people in Japan, than in the other countries considered, feel themselves to be of middle class in terms of social status, but nonetheless to be poorly rewarded workers economically.

This point will be further clarified if we correlate these two indices of self-evaluation with occupational category, as in Table 2. From this examination it appears that only in Stratum I, and among small enterprisers A of Stratum II, is "middle prestige" selected more often than "lower prestige", while those of "middle economic" class are more numerous than "workers". These

status is high in terms of education and general occupational rank, so that they naturally feel themselves to be of the middle prestige class. If their income, or their influence in the work place, is proportionately high enough, they will no doubt gain psychological stability and tend to be satisfied with a peaceful life as *petite-bourgeoisie*. In reality, however, both their economic power and their influence are small, disproportionate to their other class attributes, and about the same as, or even lower than, those of blue-collar workers, whom they evaluate as in these other attributes lower than themselves. As Minobe and Matsushita[1] have pointed out, the real income indices of 1958 (taking the pre-war real income as 100) are: 111.2 for farmers; 122.2 for blue-collar workers; 176.7 for private enterprisers; but only 67.3 for 8-year-service white-collar and 68.4 for 15-year-service white-collar staff workers. Or, if we judge influence in the work place by the balance between the ratios of orders which a person receives and those which he gives, according to the findings of the Middle Classes Survey,[2] only administrators and small enter-

TABLE 2. *Class Self-Identification by Occupational Category* (%)*

	Upper Prestige	Capitalist	Middle Prestige	Middle Economic	Lower Prestige	Worker
Stratum I						
Professional	—	8	88	54	13	33
Administrative	—	6	77	65	12	29
Stratum II						
Clerical	—	2	63	26	37	71
Small Enterpriser A[1]	3	6	71	47	24	38
Small Enterpriser B[2]	—	9	46	34	49	49
Stratum III						
Shop-assistant	—	—	36	21	64	79
Factory Worker	—	1	36	10	63	89
Simple Laborer[3]	—	—	43	7	57	86

* Based on the 1960 Middle Classes Survey (Tokyo, males).
[1] Owner of a small enterprise with non-family employees.
[2] Owner of a small enterprise employing family members only.
[3] Includes odd-job man, janitor, day-laborer, etc.

people tend to see themselves as "middle" in terms both of prestige *and* economic structure. On the other hand, in three occupational categories (shop-assistant, factory worker, and simple laborer) of Stratum III, the "lower-prestige *and* worker" consciousness appears. Small enterprisers B of Stratum II are similar. The exception is the white-collar, i.e., the clerical worker, the nucleus of the new middle class; in this group, those of "middle prestige" are almost twice as numerous as those of "lower prestige", but those who see themselves to be "workers" are almost three times the number of those who claim to be of "middle economic" class. In other words, this group insists upon a contradiction; it is both "middle prestige *and* worker".

Among white-collar workers, the spirit of resistance would seem to be particularly dominant. Their social

[1] Ryokichi Minobe and Keiichi Matsushita, "Can the Middle Classes Grow?" (in Japanese), *Asahi Journal*, January 24, 1960, p. 11.

[2] For more details on this point, refer to Kunio Odaka, "How Has the Japanese Class Structure Changed?" (in Japanese). *Jiyu*, No. 7, June 1960, pp. 146 f.

prisers A have a plus balance (+71 and +56 respectively), while white-collar as well as blue-collar workers have a minus balance (both −41). If such an imbalance exists between economic power and influence, on the one hand, and other attributes of prestige, it is only to be expected that frustration will give rise to a spirit of resistance in such people.

Those who are conscious of being working class are of course not limited to white-collar workers. They should also be found among professionals, including teaching and technical staff, such administrators as assistant managers and middle public officials, and university students. According to the results of the Middle Classes Survey, as shown in Table 2, 33% of the entire professional category and 29% of the entire administrative category have a working–class consciousness, and of university students, 39% regard themselves as of working class. If we consider the social status and educational level of these people, it can easily be conjectured that a spirit of resistance runs through this consciousness, just as in the case of white-collar workers.

These arguments can, therefore, be summarized as follows: *1)* there are many people in Japan who see themselves to be of the working class from a spirit of "resistance" and desire for reform; *2)* there are of course many blue-collar workers to whom this characterization applies, but the point to regard here is that in Japan such persons are found in some numbers among white-collar workers, intellectuals, and students — i.e., would-be white-collar workers or intellectuals — who experience a serious imbalance between their social status and their economic power or influence; and *3)* white-collar workers and intellectuals have in recent years been increasing rapidly. It is from these considerations that we can explain the fact that there are more in Japan who have a working-class consciousness than there are in other advanced countries.[1]

VI. A methodology for distinguishing social classes

It has been pointed out that one of the difficulties in the way of understanding the Japanese middle classes is the differing meanings of the Japanese terms "middle economic", "middle prestige", and "middle stratum". A more crucial cause of confusion, however, is perhaps the diversity of methods by which scholars discriminate classes and assign individuals to them. Research methods and techniques of measurement have progressed since World War II, but attempts to unify or integrate them have been inadequate.

Methods generally employed in the social sciences today can be classified into three categories: *1)* the subjective method; *2)* the objective method; and *3)* a combination of these two.

The subjective method, originally derived from public opinion research, is one in which the research subject is asked to which class he thinks he belongs.[2] In the use of this approach in our surveys, we ask for self-evaluations in terms of each of three classification systems, i.e., *a)* "working, middle economic, capitalist"; *b)* "upper, upper-middle, lower-middle, upper-lower, lower-lower"; and *c)* "leader, managerial, intermediate, working".

The objective method is of course more complex to handle. Ordinarily the procedure for doing so comprises four steps, as follows: *1)* a researcher must choose objective factors which are crucial in distinguishing classes; *2)* he must then set up a quantitative rank order for each factor; *3)* he must further grade and classify each social unit to be ranked (individual or household) on this scale; and *4)* finally, he cuts the rank order continuum at several points, and counts the number of social units included between any two points. The most commonly used objective criteria of class are occupation, education, income, property, and consumption level.

It goes without saying that each of the various methods for distinguishing social class which are used has a certain merit. The difficulty is that the pictures that

emerge from the use of any two approaches will not necessarily be identical. The profile drawn by the subjective technique represents only one aspect of the total picture, and so does that produced by any of the

TABLE 3. *Class Structure Based on Income (%)**

	High-Income Stratum (monthly income over ¥70,000)	Middle-Income Stratum (¥30,000–¥60,000)	Low-Income Stratum (below ¥30,000)	Total (No.)
1955 Tokyo (male)	2	7	91	100 (462)
1960 Tokyo (male)	3	27	70	100 (344)

* Excluding "Unknown". In 1955, annual — including incidental — income was asked, and those with ¥500,000–¥1,000,000 are counted here as belonging to Middle Stratum. The two surveys, of course, are not strictly comparable, since average incomes may have risen since 1955, and respondents might have defined "middle" income differently then, if they had been asked.

objective approaches through occupational status, economic position or other attributes.

To delineate the class structure of our society in all its richness, we have in fact to superimpose the results obtained from these several ways of studying the

TABLE 4. *Class Structure Based on Occupation (%)**

	Stratum I (Professional and Administrative)	Stratum II (Clerical, Small Enterpriser, Artisan, Owner Farmer, etc.)	Stratum III (Shop-assistant, Factory Worker, Simple Laborer, etc.)	Total (No.)
1955 Tokyo (male)	21	63	16	100 (491)
1960 Tokyo (male)	13	67	20	100 (313)

* Excluding "No Occupation", "Others", and "Unknown".

problem one upon another. Only thus can we ascertain, at least to some extent, the total role of the middle classes. A combination of the subjective and objective approaches is, in other words, indicated.

Unfortunately, we failed to include income measures

---

[1] "Consciousness of belonging to the working class" is not, of course, identical with "class consciousness of the worker" in the Marxist theory. The former is one form of consciousness of class membership only, while the latter is what should be called "consciousness of class antagonism". I regard that which includes both as "class consciousness" in a wider sense. Concerning this argument, see Kunio Odaka, *ibid.*, pp. 132 f.

[2] Richard Centers was the first social scientist to employ this method systematically, and it was on this basis that he developed his theory concerning the psychology of social classes. He divides social classes into four — "upper, middle, working, and lower" — and determines the people belonging to each and the class ratio by the subjects' own self-identification. Cf. Richard Centers, *The Psychology of Social Classes: A Study of Class Consciousness*, Princeton: Princeton University Press, 1949.

in the combined method of our 1955 Stratification and Mobility Survey. In the following, therefore, I shall attempt to draw a more complex outline of the total class structure, and to analyze the role and characteristics of the middle classes within it, using the results of our 1960 Middle Classes Survey.

To begin with, let us compare four different profiles of the class structure — those obtained from the objective method based on   *1)* income (Table 3) and   *2)* occupational status (Table 4), and those based upon the respondent's identification of himself on the scales, *3)* "capitalist-middle-worker" (hereinafter abbreviated to "Self-identification A") and   *4)* "upper-middle-lower class" (hereinafter "Self-identification B"). Table 5 shows the result. It will be seen that there is a considerable correspondence between the structure by income and that by Self-identification A. There also is a certain similarity between the profile based upon occupation and that by Self-identification B-II (in which the categories are: upper combined with upper-middle,

investigated. In the second approach, the procedure is almost the reverse. The proportion of people to be categorized as "middle class" is to be determined upon the basis of their self-identification, after which the fit of this with the picture resulting from the objective status indices is to be examined.

The first of these approaches has recently been used by Chikio Hayashi, of the Institute of Statistical Mathematics, in a study of the data of the 1960 Middle Classes Survey.[1] In his analysis, however, the distinction between the middle economic class and the middle stratum is rather ambiguous. It is also conceivable that certain modifications should be made to the six classes that he discriminates, shown in Table 6. According to him, the most "middle class like" are the first and second categories (Classes 1 and 2), and 40% of the total sample belonging to these two classes should be especially set off to represent the "real" middle class. The sub-categories "a" of both Classes 1 and 2 represent what he calls the "core of the middle classes", their propor-

TABLE 5. *Comparison of Four Class Structures (%)**

	Upper	Middle	Lower	Others and Unknown	Total
Objective Method					
Class Structure by Income (High, Middle, Low)	3	27	70	—	100
Class Structure by Occupation (Stratum I, II, III)	13	67	20	—	100
Subjective Method					
Class Structure by Self-Identification A (Capitalist, Middle, Worker)	3	29	62	5	100
Class Structure by Self-Identification B-I (Upper, Middle, Lower)	—	56	42	2	100
Class Structure by Self-Identification B-II (Upper, Middle, Lower)	9	80	9	2	100

* 1960 Tokyo males only. The categories in Self-Identification B-I consist of upper, upper- and lower-middle, and upper- and lower-lower, while those in Self-Identification B-II, upper combined with upper-middle, lower-middle with upper-lower, and lower-lower.

lower-middle with upper-lower, and lower-lower). On the other hand, there are considerable discrepancies between the structures by Self-identification A and B, and between those in terms of income and occupation. In order to ascertain the character of the middle classes, therefore, it is necessary to find out the internal relationships among these four profiles of class, and to analyze how the middle class on one measure may correspond to the same class on another.

Two different approaches to this task are conceivable. In the first,   *1)* a combined class measure based upon the objective indices is to be established, by combining occupation, income, and standard of living, the latter to be indicated by the amount of consumer durables, securities, and real estate owned by respondents;   *2)* a certain portion of the class structure thus delineated is then to be considered "middle" in character; and   *3)* the extent to which the respondents belonging to this category have a middle-class consciousness is to be

[1] Chikio Hayashi, "Where are the Japanese Middle Classes?" (in Japanese), *Jiyu*, No. 7, June 1960, pp. 156 ff.

tions of the total sample being 11% and 10% respectively. These sub-categories include, however, only about 3% of the total of respondents with income of ¥70,000 or more a month. As to self-identification, 46% of those belonging to Classes 1 and 2 identify themselves as middle economic class, as against only 14%, 22%, 20%, and 9% who so labelled themselves in Classes 3, 4, 5 and 6, respectively.

There is no doubt that the picture he gives approaches the sort of total representation of the class structure we have been seeking. Moreover, the techniques he has used have the advantage that they can be applied successfully to a national sample. My question is whether it is appropriate to call his Classes 1 and 2 the "middle class"; they represent, after all, the uppermost part of a pyramid. Likewise, it may well be misleading to call the sub-categories "a" of these two classes the "core of the middle classes". I should like to suggest, therefore, the following modification of Hayashi's analysis.   *1)* People falling into his Classes 1 and 2 (40% of the total sample) are to be divided into three different categories, i.e., Class I — the highest income class (a monthly income of ¥70,000 or more, about 3% of the total male respondents in Tokyo), Class II — the remainder of what he calls the "core of the middle classes" (18%), and Class III — the remainder of the total of Classes I and II (19%). These three groups are referred to here as Uppermost Class (I), Upper-Middle Class (II), and Lower-Middle Class (III), respectively. 2) Hayashi's remaining three classes — i.e., his Class 3, roughly representing the labor aristocracy; Class 4, lower-order white-collar workers and intellectuals; and

"Class V, or Lower Class", numbering about 28% of the sample. The class structure that results from this re-arrangement is shown in Table 8.

It will be clear that the three classes to which I append the term "middle" — Classes II, III, and IV of Table 7 — display quite different characteristics. In the first place, about half the people belonging to my Classes II and III are conscious of being middle class, whereas only about 20% of Class IV exhibit this point of view. Again, Classes II and III consist mainly of people having a monthly income of ¥30,000 or more, or at least a

TABLE 6. *Class Structure Based on Occupation, Income and Property* *

Class		Occupation	Income	Consumer Durables	Property	%
1	a)	White Collar	Over ¥30,000	3 or more	Yes	23.3
	b)	"	"	"	No	
	c)	"	"	Less than 2	Yes or no	
	d)	"	Below ¥30,000	3 or more	Yes	
2	a)	Small Enterpriser	Over ¥30,000	3 or more	Yes	16.7
	b)	"	"	"	No	
	c)	"	"	Less than 2	Yes or no	
	d)	"	Below ¥30,000	3 or more	Yes	
3	a)	Blue Collar	Over ¥30,000	3 or more	Yes	7.3
	b)	"	"	"	No	
	c)	"	"	Less than 2	Yes or no	
	d)	"	Below ¥30,000	3 or more	Yes	
4	a)	White Collar	Below ¥30,000	3 or more	No	19.3
	b)	"	"	Less than 2	Yes or no	
5	a)	Small Enterpriser	Below ¥30,000	3 or more	No	5.0
	b)	"	"	Less than 2	Yes or no	
6	a)	Blue Collar	Below ¥30,000	3 or more	No	28.4
	b)	"	"	Less than 2	Yes or no	
Total						100.0
(No.)						(301)

* * 1960 Tokyo males only. Excluding "No Occupation". White Collar includes Professional, Administrative and Clerical in Table 2; Small Enterpriser includes Small Enterprisers A and B; Blue Collar includes Shop-assistant, Factory Worker and Simple Laborer. The figures in Consumer Durables indicate the number of home electric equipments (television, washing machine, etc.) owned by respondents; "Yes" or "No" in Property indicate whether or not respondents have stocks, securities, real estate, etc. Chikio Hayashi, "Where are the Japanese Middle Classes?", Tables 9 and 12.*

Class 5, who constitute petty entrepreneurs — are put together to compose Class IV in our definition. This fourth class might better be termed "Intermediate Class" than "middle class". Approximately 32% of the sample belongs here. 3) Finally, Hayashi's sixth and lowest class, consisting of blue-collar workers, we call

TABLE 7. *Total Class Structure Based on Approach I* *

Class Category	%	Class Category by Hayashi	%	Degree of Middle-Class Consciousness (%)[1]
I Uppermost Class	3	1 & 2	3	46
II Upper-Middle Class	18	1 & 2	18	46
III Lower-Middle Class	19	1 & 2	19	46
		3	7.3	14
IV Intermediate Class	32	4	19.3	22
		5	5.0	20
V Lower Class	28	6	28.4	9
Total	100		100.0	29

* * 1960 Tokyo males only.*
* [1] As indicated by percentage for each class of those who identified themselves as "middle economic class".*

comparable level of property or expenditure, while in Class IV a majority belong to a low-income stratum, with a monthly income of less than this amount. Similarly, members of my Classes II and III are for the most part engaged in professional or administrative occupations, or are well-to-do small industrialists, while Class IV is made up mainly of the labor aristocracy, white-collar workers, and petty enterprisers.

Moreover, there is a clear difference among these three classes with regard to their influence in their work place. Members of Classes II and III in general have more subordinates than superiors apiece. The reverse is true of those in Class IV, and particularly of the white-collar worker component. They have very little voice in their work place, even when compared with blue-collar workers.

What are, then, the political leanings of these classes? In the following, I shall deal only with support of the Liberal-Democratic (Conservative) and the Socialist Parties, excluding that of the Democratic-Socialist Party. Our data show that an overwhelming majority of

Uppermost Class (Class I) supports the Liberal-Democratic Party, rather than the Socialist Party (82% versus 9%), and that the greater part of the small enterprisers have the same political leaning, whether they belong to Middle Class (Class II or III) or Intermediate Stratum (Class IV) (56% versus 16%, and 53% versus 7%, respectively). Even when such small enterprisers are excluded from the computations, support of the Liberal-Democratic Party is still larger than that of the Socialist Party in Classes II and III. On the whole, therefore, it may be said that the middle classes tend to support the conservative party, a phenomenon which is commonly to be seen in advanced countries.

With the exception of petty industrialists, on the other hand, more people belonging to Classes IV and V supported the Socialist Party. Among the labor aristocracy (Hayashi's Class 3), 36% as against 27% were of this persuasion, among lower-class blue-collar workers (Class V), 36% as against 24%. In this connection, it should be noted that support of the Socialist Party was even stronger among white-collar workers (Hayashi's Class 4) (40% versus 24%) than among the blue-collar ranks.

Much the same conclusion is to be reached through the second type of approach mentioned above – i.e., where the middle classes are first distinguished by respondents' own identifications. The procedure used here is roughly as follows. 1) Persons who consider themselves to be of the middle prestige class are divided into those who identify with the upper-middle (9% of the total sample) and with the lower-middle (47%); and 2) the objective status attributes of these people – i.e., income, property, consumption level, power in the work place, political party support, etc. – are compared.

In this way we can discern a sharp distinction between these two sub-categories. As to income, for example, about 10% of the upper-middle also belong to the high-income class, with a monthly revenue of ¥70,000 or more, whereas only 3% of the lower-middle are in this category. When the quantity of consumer durables owned is taken as an index of consumption level, 48% of the former, and only 18% of the latter, possess four or more kinds of electric equipment. Again, the upper-middle grouping has a much larger voice in its work places, whereas the lower-middle has a considerable minus score in this regard. Finally, 52% of the former category support the Liberal-Democratic Party, whereas only 35% of the latter do so, as against 50% who are behind the Socialists or Democratic Socialists.

When we turn to an analysis in terms of middle economic (rather than middle prestige) class consciousness, we find that persons so identifying themselves can be placed closer to those who see themselves to be of upper-middle prestige class, in terms of income, property, consumption level, as well as of their power in the work place.[1]

[1] For more details on the second type of approach, see Kunio Odaka, "How Has the Japanese Class Structure Changed?" (in Japanese), *ibid.*, pp. 150–152.

From the self-identification approach, therefore, we can, at least tentatively, set up the following four class categories. 1) The first category, which corresponds to Class I of Table 8, consists of those who have a monthly income of ¥70,000 or more. 2) The second grouping is composed of – in addition to those who identify themselves as of upper and upper-middle classes – middle-income class people with a monthly salary of between ¥30,000 and ¥60,000, who see themselves to be only lower-middle or upper-lower in prestige. It will be clear that this grouping roughly corresponds to Classes II and III of Table 8. 3) The third, which corresponds to Class IV of Table 8, is composed of those low-income earners who identify themselves as of lower-middle prestige. 4) Finally, the remainder, including those belonging to Class V of Table 8, comprise those low-income earners who see themselves to be upper- and lower-lower in prestige.

When this second set of class categories was applied to the data of the 1960 Middle Class Survey, Table 8 resulted. In comparing this with Table 8, it appears that the percentages belonging to roughly similar categories in each table are much closer than might have been

TABLE 8. *Comparison of Two Total Class Structures (%)**

Class Category	Approach I	Approach II
I Uppermost Class	3	3
II Upper-Middle Class	18	32
III Lower-Middle Class	19	32
IV Intermediate Class	32	28
V Lower Class	28	37
Total	100	100

* 1960 Tokyo males only.

expected. The only difference of much significance is that the percentage falling into Lower Class is a good deal larger when the second, rather than the first, approach is used.

VII. Conclusion – what are the Japanese middle classes

We may conclude, at least insofar as the data drawn from the Middle Classes Survey is concerned, as follows:

1) There are two different classes within the total class structure of present-day Japanese society to which the term "middle" can with some justice be applied. They are different not only in their place in the total structure but also in the attributes and consciousness of people who belong to them. To avoid confusion, we suggest that one of them be called "middle class (*chusan kaikyu*)" – within which we distinguish an upper and a lower sub-classes – and the other "intermediate class (*chukan kaikyu*)".

2) The upper-middle class includes only about 18% of the total sample, while the middle class as a whole reaches about 35%. The middle class forms the upper

part of the total class structure only next to the upper-most class, which consists of only 3% of the total sample. The intermediate stratum, on the other hand, is literally intermediate and contains a considerable proportion, about 30%, of the total sample.

3) The class structure of the society in which we live cannot be described graphically after the model of a pyramid, as has commonly been done. When a figure is drawn proportional to the sample size belonging to each class, an awkward-looking structure resembling a

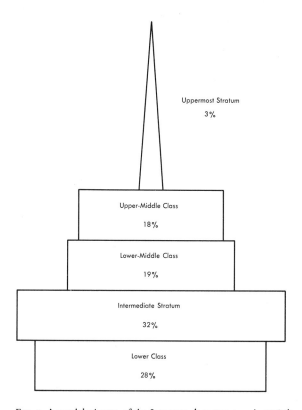

Uppermost Stratum

3%

Upper-Middle Class

18%

Lower-Middle Class

19%

Intermediate Stratum

32%

Lower Class

28%

FIG. 1. A model picture of the Japanese class structure in 1960*

* Based upon the class distinctions and percentages shown in Table 8.

thin-steepled four story church results (cf. Fig. 1). And as the Japanese economy has become more prosperous in recent years, the steeple seems to grow thinner and taller, and at the same time the gap between the two top floors (representing the upper- and lower-middle classes) and the two bottom floors (the intermediate class and the lower class) seems to be widening. There is little doubt that such a change has been the result of increasing differences in economic power.

The last point can be substantiated by comparing

occupational and income data drawn from the 1955 Stratification and Mobility Survey with those of the 1960 Middle Classes Survey. In the case of people in the administrative occupations, for example, those who belong to the high-income category increased by some 15% or so during these years, whereas those in the low-income brackets have declined to one-tenth of the total number in 1955. A similar tendency can be found among small industrialists. A sharp rise in income has also occurred among a portion of professionals, the greater majority of whom five years previously belonged in the low-income ranks.

In contrast with the above change, the economic position of white-collar and industrial workers who belong to the intermediate stratum has undergone very little improvement during these years, despite the general prosperity. As far as the research data go, they suggest that none of those workers who belonged to the low-income category in 1955 had succeeded in attaining a high income five years later. Moreover, the economic position of common laborers belonging to the lower class is in fact declining. When asked about their hopes for a future rise on the class ladder, people belonging to this category seemed to have no expectations at all, whereas five years previously there was at least a certain proportion who expressed hope.

Vance Packard, in *The Status Seekers* (1959), points out that the popular view that America has recently come nearer the ideal of a classless society is a matter of appearance only, and that the gaps between various classes have actually been expanding. According to him, moreover, the direction of the separation opening out is today between the two upper classes (which he calls the "real upper class" and "semi-upper class") and the three lower classes which cannot expect success, rather than between white-collar and blue-collar workers, or between manual and non-manual workers, as was the case up to the 1930's.[1] Doubtless the five Japanese classes delineated are not identical with the five that Packard describes. So far as its position relative to the other classes is concerned, however, there seems to be a growing similarity between the Japanese middle class and the "semi-upper class" in Packard's definition. In Japan too, the line between white- and blue-collar workers has become obscure, while the intermediate class (including mostly white-collar workers) has now fallen into the situation that Packard calls the "limited-success class."

Present-day Japanese society, having experienced unprecedented prosperity since 1956, seems to be trending in a direction similar to that of American society, not only in a widening of the gaps between different classes, but also very likely in an increase in social tensions and insecurity.

[1] Vance Packard, *op. cit.*, chapters 2 and 3.

A Note on Sanskritization and Westernization

M. N. Srinivas

THE CONCEPT of "Sanskritization" was found useful by me in the analysis of the social and religious life of the Coorgs of South India. A few other anthropologists who are making studies of tribal and village communities in various parts of India seem to find the concept helpful in the analysis of their material, and this fact induces me to attempt a re-examination of it here.

The first use of the term Sanskritization in this sense occurs in my book, *Religion and Society among the Coorgs of South India* (Oxford, 1952), p. 30:

> The caste system is far from a rigid system in which the position of each component caste is fixed for all time. Movement has always been possible, and especially so in the middle regions of the hierarchy. A low caste was able, in a generation or two, to rise to a higher position in the hierarchy by adopting vegetarianism and teetotalism, and by Sanskritizing its ritual and pantheon. In short, it took over, as far as possible, the customs, rites, and beliefs of the Brahmans, and the adoption of the Brahmanic way of life by a low caste seems to have been frequent, though theoretically forbidden. This process has been called "Sanskritization" in this book, in preference to "Brahmanization," as certain Vedic rites are confined to the Brahmans and the two other "twice-born" castes.

Sanskritization is no doubt an awkward term, but it was preferred to Brahmanization for several reasons: Brahmanization is subsumed in the wider process of Sanskritization though at some points Brahmanization and Sanskritization are at variance with each other. For instance, the Brahmans of the Vedic period drank *soma*, an alcoholic drink,[1] ate beef, and offered blood sacrifices. Both were given up in post-Vedic times. It has been suggested that this was the result of Jain and Buddhist influence. Today, Brahmans are, by and large, vegetarians; only the Saraswat, Kashmiri, and Bengali Brahmans eat non-vegetarian food. All these Brahmans are, however, traditionally teetotallers. In brief, the customs and habits of the Brahmans changed after they had settled in India. Had the term Brahmanization been used, it would have been necessary to specify which particular Brahman group was meant, and at which period of its recorded history.

Again, the agents of Sanskritization were (and are) not always Brahmans. In fact, the non-twice-born castes were prohibited from following the customs and rites of the Brahmans, and it is not unreasonable to suppose that Brahmans were responsible for this prohibition as they were a privileged group entrusted with the authority to declare the laws. But the existence of such a prohibition did not prevent the Sanskritization of the customs and rites of the lower castes. The Lingayats of South India have been a powerful force for the Sanskritization of the customs and rites of many low castes of the Karnāṭak. The Lingayat movement was founded by a Brahman named Basavā in the twelfth century, and another Brahman, Ekāntada Rāmayya, played an important part in it. But it was a popular movement in the true sense of the term, attracting followers from all castes, especially the low castes, and it was anti-Brahmanical in tone and spirit.[2] The Lingayats of Mysore claim equality with Brahmans, and the more orthodox Lingayats do not eat food cooked or handled by Brahmans. The Smiths of South India are another interesting example: they call themselves Vishwakarma Brahmans, wear the sacred thread, and have Sanskritized their ritual. But some of them still eat meat and drink alcoholic liquor. This does not, however, explain why they are considered to belong to the Left-hand division of the castes, and no caste belonging to the Right-hand division, including the Holeyas (Untouchables), will eat food or drink water touched by them. Until recently they suffered from a number of disabilities: they were allowed to celebrate their weddings only in villages in which there was a temple to their caste-deity Kāḷi. Their wedding procession was not allowed to go along streets in which the Right-hand castes lived. And there were also other disabilities. Normally Sanskritization enables a caste to obtain a higher position in the hierarchy. But in the case of the Smiths it seems to have resulted only in their drawing upon themselves the wrath of all the other castes. The reasons for this are not known.

The usefulness of Sanskritization as a tool in the analysis of Indian society is greatly limited by the

[1] See "Soma" in the *Encyclopaedia of Religion and Ethics*, XI, 685–686.

[2] See E. Thurston, *Castes and Tribes of Southern India* (Madras, 1909), V. 237 f; see also *Encyclopaedia Britannica*, 14th ed., XIV, 162.

Reprinted from *The Far Eastern Quarterly*, V. 15 (Nov. 1955–Aug. 1956), pp. 492–496, by permission of the author and the publisher.

complexity of the concept as well as its looseness. An attempt will be made here to analyze further the conceptual whole which is Sanskritization.

II

The structural basis of Hindu society is caste, and it is not possible to understand Sanskritization without reference to the structural framework in which it occurs. Speaking generally, the castes occupying the top positions in the hierarchy are more Sanskritized than castes in the lower and middle regions of the hierarchy, and this has been responsible for the Sanskritization of the lower castes as well as the outlying tribes. The lower castes always seem to have tried to take over the customs and way of life of the higher castes. The theoretical existence of a ban on their adoption of Brahmanical customs and rites was not very effective, and this is clear when we consider the fact that many non-Brahmanical castes practice many Brahmanical customs and rites. A more effective barrier to the lower castes' taking over of the customs and rites of the higher castes was the hostile attitude of the locally dominant caste, or of the king of the region. In their case there was physical force which could be used to keep the lower groups in check.

The point which is really interesting to note is that in spite of the existence of certain obstacles, Brahmanical customs and way of life did manage to spread not only among all Hindus but also among some outlying tribes. This is to some extent due to the fact that Hindu society is a stratified one, in which there are innumerable small groups which try to pass for a higher group. And the best way of staking a claim to a higher position is to adopt the custom and way of life of a higher caste. As this process was common to all the castes except the highest, it meant that the Brahmanical customs and way of life spread among all Hindus. It is possible that the very ban on the lower castes' adoption of the Brahmanical way of life had an exactly opposite effect.

Though, over a long period of time, Brahmanical rites and customs spread among the lower castes, in the short run the locally dominant caste was imitated by the rest. And the locally dominant caste was frequently not Brahman. It could be said that in the case of the numerous castes occupying the lowest levels, Brahmanical customs reached them in a chain reaction. That is, each group took from the one higher to it, and in turn gave to the group below. Sometimes, however, as in the case of the Smiths of South India, a caste tried to jump over all its structural neighbors, and claimed equality with the Brahmans. The hostility which the Smiths have attracted is perhaps due to their collective social megalomania.

Occasionally we find castes which enjoyed political and economic power but were not rated high in ritual ranking. That is, there was a hiatus between their ritual and politico-economic positions. In such cases Sanskritization occurred sooner or later, because without it the claim to a higher position was not fully effective. The three main axes of power in the caste system are the ritual, the economic, and the political ones, and the possession of power in any one sphere usually leads to the acquisition of power in the other two. This does not mean, however, that inconsistencies do not occur — occasionally, a wealthy caste has a low ritual position, and contrariwise, a caste having a high ritual position is poor.

III

The idea of hierarchy is omnipresent in the caste system; not only do the various castes form a hierarchy, but the occupations practiced by them, the various items of their diet, and the customs they observe, all form separate hierarchies. Thus practicing an occupation like butchery, tanning, herding swine, or handling toddy, puts a caste in a low position. Eating pork or beef is more degrading than eating fish or mutton. Castes which offer blood-sacrifices to deities are lower than castes making only offerings of fruit and flowers. The entire way of life of the top castes seeps down the hierarchy. And as mentioned earlier, the language, cooking, clothing, jewelry, and way of life of the Brahmans spreads eventually to the entire society.

Two "legal fictions" seem to have helped the spread of Sanskritization among the low castes. Firstly, the ban against the non-twice-born castes performing Vedic ritual was circumvented by restricting the ban only to the chanting of mantras from the Vedas. That is, the ritual acts were separated from the accompanying mantras and this separation facilitated the spread of Brahmanic ritual among all the castes of Hindus, frequently including Untouchables. Thus several Vedic rites, including the rite of the gift of the virgin (*kanyādān*), are performed at the marriage of many non-Brahmanical castes in Mysore State. And secondly, a Brahman priest officiates at these weddings. He does not chant Vedic mantras, however, but instead, the *mangalāṣṭaka stōtras* which are post-Vedic verses in Sanskrit. The substitution of these verses for Vedic mantras is the second "legal fiction."

IV

The non-Brahmanical castes adopt not only Brahmanical ritual, but also certain Brahmanical institutions and values. I shall illustrate what I mean by reference to marriage, women, and kinship. I should add here that throughout this essay I have drawn on my experience of conditions in Mysore State, except when I have stated otherwise.

Until recently, Brahmans used to marry their girls before puberty, and parents who had not succeeded in finding husbands for daughters past the age of puberty were regarded as guilty of a great sin. Brahman marriage is in theory indissoluble, and a Brahman widow, even if she be a child widow, is required to shave her head, shed all jewelry and ostentation in clothes. She was (and still is, to some extent) regarded as inauspicious. Sex life is denied her. Among Hindus generally, there is a preference for virginity in brides, chastity in wives, and continence in widows, and this is specially marked among the highest castes.

The institutions of the "low" castes are more liberal in the spheres of marriage and sex than those of the Brahmans. Post-puberty marriages do occur among them, widows do not have to shave their heads, and divorce and widow marriage are both permitted and practiced. In general, their sex code is not as harsh towards women as that of the top castes, especially Brahmans. But as a caste rises in the hierarchy and its ways become more Sanskritized, it adopts the sex and marriage code of the Brahmans. Sanskritization results in harshness towards women.

Sanskritization has significant effects on conjugal relations. Among Brahmans for instance, a wife is enjoined to treat her husband as a deity. It is very unusual for a wife to take her meal before the husband has his, and in orthodox families, the wife still eats on the dining leaf on which her husband has eaten. Normally, such a leaf may not be touched as it would render impure the hand touching it. Usually the woman who removes the dining leaf purifies the spot where the leaf had rested with a solution of cowdung, after which she washes her hands. There is no pollution, however, in eating on the leaf on which the husband has eaten.

Orthodox Brahman women perform a number of *vratas* or religious vows, the aim of some of which is to secure a long life for the husband. A woman's hope is to predecease her husband and thus avoid becoming a widow. Women who predecease their husbands are considered lucky as well as good, while widowhood is attributed to sins committed in a previous incarnation. A wife who shows utter devotion to her husband is held up as an ideal, as a *pativratā*, i.e., one who regards the devoted service of her husband as her greatest duty. There are myths describing the devotion and loyalty of some sainted women to their husbands. These women are reverenced on certain occasions.

While polygyny is permitted, monogamy is held up as an ideal. Rāma, the hero of the epic Ramayana, is dedicated to the ideal of having only one wife (*ekapat-nīvrata*). The conjugal state is regarded as a holy state, and the husband and wife must perform several rites together. A bachelor has a lower religious status than a married man, and is not allowed to perform certain important rites such as offering *piṇḍa* or balls of rice to the manes. Marriage is a religious duty. When bathing in a sacred river like the Ganges, the husband and wife have the ends of their garments tied together. A wife is entitled to half the religious merit earned by her husband by fasting, prayer, and penance.

[1] See M. Monier-Williams, *A Sanskrit-English Dictionary,* 2nd ed. (Oxford, 1899), p. 632: "*put* or *pud* (a word invented to explain *putra* or *put-tra,* see Mn. ix, 138, and cf. Nir. ii, 11) hell or a partic. hell (to which the childless are condemned)"; and "*putrá,* m. (etym. doubtful ... traditionally said to be a comp. *put-tra* 'preserving from the hell called Put,' Mn. ix, 138) a son, child ..."

In the sphere of kinship, Sanskritization stresses the importance of the *vaṃśa*, which is the patrilineal lineage of the Brahmans. The dead ancestors are apotheosized, and offerings of food and drink have to be made to them periodically by their male descendants. Absence of these offerings will confine the manes to a hell called *put.* The Sanskrit word for son is *putra,* which by folk etymology is considered to mean one who frees the manes from the hell called *put.*[1] In short, Sanskritization results in increasing the importance of sons by making them a religious necessity. At the same time it has the effect of lowering the value of daughters because, as said earlier, parents are required to get them married before they come of age to a suitable man from the same subcaste. It is often difficult to find such a man, and in recent years, the difficulty has increased enormously owing to the institution of dowry.

Among the non-Brahmans of Mysore, however, though a son is preferred, a daughter is not unwelcome. Actually, girls are in demand among them. And there is no religious duty to get a girl married before puberty. The code under which a woman has to live is not as harsh among them as among the Brahmans. But the theory of the religious and moral unity of husband and wife is not as explicit among them. The non-Brahmans are also patrilineal, and the patrilineal lineage is well developed among them. The dead ancestors are occasionally offered food and drink. But it could be said that in the lineage of the non-Brahmans the religious element is less prominent than among the Brahmans.

V

Sanskritization means not only the adoption of new customs and habits, but also exposure to new ideas and values which have found frequent expression in the vast body of Sanskrit literature, sacred as well as secular. Karma, dharma, *pāpa, puṇya, māyā, saṃsāra* and *mokṣa* are examples of some of the most common Sanskritic theological ideas, and when a people become Sanskritized these words occur frequently in their talk. These ideas reach the common people through Sanskritic myths and stories. The institution of *harikathā* helps in spreading Sanskrit stories and ideas among the illiterate. In a *harikathā* the priest reads and explains a religious story to his audience. Each story takes a few weeks to complete, the audience meeting for a few hours every evening in a temple. *Harikathās* may be held at any time, but festivals such as Dasara, Rāmanavamī, Shivarātri, and Ganesh Chaturthī are considered especially suitable for listening to *harikathās.* The faithful believe that such listening leads to the acquisition of spiritual merit. It is one of the traditionally approved ways of spending one's time.

The spread of Sanskrit theological ideas increased under British rule. The development of communications carried Sanskritization to areas previously inaccessible, and the spread of literacy carried it to groups very low in the caste hierarchy. Western technology — railways, the internal combustion engine, press, radio, and plane — has aided the spread of Sanskritization. For instance, the popularity of *harikathā* has increased in the last few years in Mysore City, the narrator usually using a microphone to reach a much larger audience than before. Indian films are popularizing stories and incidents borrowed from the epics and puranas. Films have been made about the lives of saints such as Nandanār, Pōtana, Tukārām, Chaitanya, Mīrā, and Tulasīdās. Cheap and popular editions in the various vernaculars of the epics, puranas, and other religious and semi-religious books are available nowadays.

The introduction by the British of a Western political institution like parliamentary democracy also contributed to the increased Sanskritization of the country. Prohibition, a Sanskritic value, has been written into the Constitution of the Republic of India, and the Congress Governments in various states have introduced it wholly or partly.

In some places like Mysore State, the local Congress party is busy conducting a campaign against offering blood-sacrifices to village deities. The Congress in the South is dominated by non-Brahmanical castes, the vast majority of which periodically sacrifice animals to their deities. In spite of this, the leaders of the Congress are advocating the substitution of offerings of fruit and flowers for animals. This is again a triumph for Sanskritic, though post-Vedic, values against the values of the bulk of the population.

So far, I have mentioned only the ways in which the westernization of India has helped its Sanskritization. In another sense, however, there is a conflict between Sanskritic and Western values. One aspect of the conflict which to my mind appears to be very important is the conflict, real or apparent, between the world view disclosed by the systematic application of scientific method to the various spheres of knowledge and the world view of the traditional religions.

No analysis of modern Indian social life would be complete without a consideration of westernization and the interaction between it and Sanskritization. In the nineteenth century, the British found in India institutions such as slavery, human sacrifice, suttee, thuggery, and in certain parts of the country, female infanticide. They used all the power at their disposal to fight these institutions which they considered to be barbarous. There were also many other institutions which they did not approve of, but which, for various reasons, they did not try to abolish directly.

The fact that the country was overrun by aliens who looked down upon many features of the life of the natives, some of which they regarded as plainly barbarous, threw the leaders of the native society on the defensive. Reformist movements such as the Brahmā Samāj were aimed at ridding Hinduism of its numerous "evils."[1] The present was so bleak that the past became golden. The Ārya Samāj, another reformist movement within Hinduism, emphasized a wish to return to Vedic Hinduism, which was unlike contemporary Hinduism.

The discovery of Sanskrit by western scholars, and the systematic piecing together of India's past by western or western-inspired scholarship, gave Indians a much-needed confidence in their relations with the West. Tributes to the greatness of ancient Indian culture by western scholars such as Max Müller were gratefully received by Indian leaders (see, for instance, appendices to Mahatma Gandhi's *Hind Swaraj*).[2] It was not uncommon for educated Indians to make extravagant claims for their own culture, and to run down the West as materialistic and unspiritual.

The caste and class from which Indian leaders came were also relevant in this connection. The upper castes had a literary tradition and were opposed to blood-sacrifices, but in certain other customs and habits they were further removed from the British than the lower castes. The latter ate meat, some of them ate even pork and beef, and drank alcoholic liquor; women enjoyed greater freedom among them, and divorce and widow marriage were not prohibited. The Indian leaders were thus caught in a dilemma. They found that certain customs and habits which until then they had looked down upon obtained also among their masters. The British who ate beef and pork and drank liquor, possessed political and economic power, a new technology, scientific knowledge, and a great literature. Hence the westernized upper castes began acquiring customs and habits which were not dissimilar from those they had looked down upon. Another result was that the evils of upper caste Hindu society came to be regarded as evils of the entire society.

The form and pace of westernization of India, too, varied from one region to another, and from one section of the population to another. For instance, one group of people became westernized in their dress, diet, manners, speech, sports, and in the gadgets they used, while another absorbed Western science, knowledge, and literature while remaining relatively free from westernization in externals. It is clear that such a distinction cannot be a hard and fast one, but one of relative emphasis. It has to be made, however, in order to distinguish different types of westernization which obtained among the different groups in the country.

In Mysore State, for instance, the Brahmans led the other castes in westernization. This was only natural as the Brahmans possessed a literary tradition, and, in addition, a good many of them stood at the top of the rural economic hierarchy as landowners. (In a good many cases land had been given as a gift to Brahmans in return for their services as priest, or as an act of charity by a king.) They sensed the new opportunities which came into existence with the establishment of British rule over India, and left their natal villages for

[1] See "Brahmā Samāj" in the *Encyclopaedia of Religion and Ethics*, II, 813–814.

[2] (Ahmedabad, 1946) See the Appendices which contain "testimonies by eminent men" to the greatness of Indian culture. Among the eminent men are Max Müller, J. Seymour Keay, M.P., Victor Cousin, Col. Thomas Munro, and the Abbé Dubois.

cities such as Bangalore and Mysore in order to have the benefit of English education, an indispensable passport to employment under the new dispensation.

Though the scholarly tradition of the Brahmans placed them in a favorable position for obtaining the new knowledge, in certain other matters they were the most handicapped in the race for westernization. This was especially so in the South where the large majority of them were vegetarians and abstained from alcoholic liquor. Also, the fear of being polluted prevented them from eating cooked food touched by others, and from taking up occupations considered defiling. To orthodox Brahmans the Englishman who ate pork and beef, drank whisky, and smoked a pipe, was the living embodiment of ritual impurity. On the other hand, the Englishman had political and economic power, for which he was feared, admired, respected, and disliked.

The net result of the westernization of the Brahmans was that they interposed themselves between the British and the rest of the native population. The result was a new and secular caste system superimposed on the traditional system, in which the British, the New Kshatriyas, stood at the top, while the Brahmans occupied the second position, and the others stood at the base of the pyramid. The Brahmans looked up to the British, and the rest of the people looked up to both the Brahmans and the British. The fact that some of the values and customs of the British were opposed to some Brahmanical values made the situation confusing. However, such a contradiction was always implicit, though not in such a pronounced manner, in the caste system. Kshatriya and Brahmanical values have always been opposed to some extent, and in spite of the theoretical superiority of the Brahman to all the other castes, the Kshatriya, by virtue of the political (and through it the economic) power at his disposal, has throughout exercised a dominant position. The super-imposition of the British on the caste system only sharpened the contrast.

The position of the Brahman in the new hierarchy was crucial. He became the filter through which westernization reached the rest of Hindu society in Mysore. This probably helped westernization as the other castes were used to imitating the ways of the Brahmans. But while the westernization of the Brahmans enabled the entire Hindu society to westernize, the Brahmans themselves found some aspects of westernization, such as the British diet, dress, and freedom from pollution, difficult to accept. (Perhaps another caste would not have found them so difficult. The Coorgs, for instance, took quite easily to British diet and dress, and certain activities like dancing, hunting, and sports.)

The Brahmans of Mysore are divided into *vaidikas* or priests, and *laukikas* or the laity, and a similar distinction seems to obtain among the Brahmans in other parts of India. It is only the *vaidikas* who follow the priestly vocation while the *laukikas* follow other and secular occupations. Ritually, the priests are higher than the laity, but the fact that the latter frequently enjoyed economic and political power gave them a superior position in secular contexts. British rule widened further the gulf between the two, for it provided the laity with numerous opportunities to acquire wealth and power. And one of the long-term effects of British rule was to increase the secularization of Indian life. The secularization as well as the widening of the economic horizon pushed the priests into a lower position than before. Also traditional Sanskrit learning did not have either the prestige, or yield the dividends, which Western education did. The priests began by being aggressive towards the westernized laity, but gradually, as the number of the latter increased, they were thrown more and more on the defensive. Worse was to follow when the priests themselves started becoming westernized. They wanted electric lights, radios, and taps in their houses. They began riding cycles. The leather seat of the cycle was considered defiling, and so it was at first covered with the pure and sacred deerskin. In course of time the deerskin was discarded and the "naked" leather seat was used. Tap water was objected to at first as the water had to pass through a leather washer, but in time even this objection was set aside. Finally, the priests started sending their sons to Western-type schools, and this frequently meant that there was none in the family to continue the father's occupation.

There is, however, another tendency in modern India which is buttressing the position and authority of the priests. Educated and westernized Indians are showing some interest in Sanskrit and in ancient Indian culture, and in the country at large, politicians are frequently heard stressing the importance of Sanskritic learning. Pandit Nehru's *Discovery of India* has started many a young man on a similar journey into the country's past. Also, many Westerners have suddenly begun discovering new virtues in India, Indians, and Indian culture, and this has resulted in more Indians wanting to seek a better acquaintance with their culture.

The westernization of the Brahmans of Mysore brought about a number of changes in their life. I will mention only a few here. There was a change in their appearance and dress. The tuft gave way to cropped hair and the traditional dress gave place at least partially, to western-type dress and shoes. The change in dress marked a gradual weakening of ideas regarding ritual purity. For instance, formerly eating was a ritual act, and a Brahman had to wear ritually pure robes while eating or serving a meal. This meant wearing either a freshly washed cotton dhoti, or a silk dhoti, and a pure upper cloth. Wearing a shirt was taboo. But as Western clothes became more popular Brahman men sat to dinner with their shirts on. And today dining at a table is becoming common among the rich.

Formerly, the morning meal was offered to the domestic deity before being served to the members of the family, and all the male members who had donned the sacred thread performed a few ritual acts before beginning the meal. Nowadays, however, many Brahmans have discarded the sacred thread, though the *upanayana* ceremony at which the thread is donned still continues to be performed. And it is only at formal dinners where the orthodox are present that certain ritual acts are performed before eating. Where people eat at a table, purification with a solution of cowdung is no longer done.

The Brahman dietary has been enlarged to include certain vegetables which were formerly forbidden such as onion, potato, carrot, radish, and beetroot. Many eat raw eggs for health reasons and consume medicines which they know to be made from various organs of animals. But meat eating is even now rare, while the consumption of western alcoholic liquor is not as rare. Cigarettes are common among the educated.

The Brahmans have also taken to new occupations. Even in the thirties, the Brahmans showed a reluctance to take up a trade or any occupation involving manual work. But they were driven by the prevalent economic depression to take up new jobs, and World War II completed this process. Many Brahmans enlisted in the Army and this effected a great change in their habits and outlook. Before World War II, young men who wanted to go to Bombay, Calcutta, or Delhi in search of jobs had to be prepared for the opposition of their elders. But the postwar years found young men not only in all parts of India, but outside too. There was a sudden expansion in the geographical and social space of the Brahmans. Formerly the Brahmans objected to becoming doctors as the profession involved handling men from all castes, including Untouchables, and corpses. This is now a thing of the past. A few educated Brahmans now own farms where they raise poultry. One of them even wants to have a piggery.

Over seventy years ago, the institution of bride-price seems to have prevailed among some sections of Mysore Brahmans. But with westernization, and the demand it created for educated boys who had good jobs, dowry became popular. The better educated a boy, the larger the dowry his parents demanded for him. The age at which girls married shot up. Over twenty-five years ago it was customary for Brahmans to marry their girls before puberty. Nowadays, urban and middle class Brahmans are rarely able to get their girls married before they are eighteen, and there are many girls above twenty who are unmarried. Child widows are rare, and shaving the heads of widows is practically a thing of the past.

There has been a general secularization of Hindu life in the last one hundred and fifty years, and this has especially affected the Brahmans whose life was permeated with ritual. The life of no other caste among Hindus was equally ritualized. One of the many interesting contradictions of modern Hindu social life is that while the Brahmans are becoming more and more westernized, the other castes are becoming more and more Sanskritized. In the lower reaches of the hierarchy, castes are taking up customs which the Brahmans are busy discarding. As far as these castes are concerned, it looks as though Sanskritization is an essential preliminary to westernization.

To describe the social changes occurring in modern India in terms of Sanskritization and westernization is to describe it primarily in cultural and not structural terms. An analysis in terms of structure is much more difficult than an analysis in terms of culture. The increase in the social space of the Brahmans, and its implications for them and for the caste system as a whole, needs to be studied in detail. The consequences of the existence of the dual, and occasionally conflicting, pressures of Sanskritization and westernization provide an interesting field for systematic sociological analysis.

A NOTE TO THE ABOVE[1]

The British conquest of India set free a number of forces, political, economic, social, and technological. These forces affected this country's social and cultural life profoundly and at every point. The withdrawal of the British from India not only did not mean the cessation of these forces, but meant, on the contrary, their intensification. For instance, the economic revolution which the British began with the gradual introduction of a new technology under a capitalist and laissez-faire ideology has given place to a vast and planned effort to develop the country as quickly as possible under a socialist and democratic ideology. The idea of Five-Year Plans may be described as the culmination of the slow and unplanned attempts of the British to transform the country industrially and economically. The political integration which the British began is also being carried further, though here the division of the country into the two states of India and Pakistan is a step away from the integration of the sub-continent. But this does not mean that forces inherent in Indian society have been destroyed by the British impact; they have only undergone modification and, in some cases, have been even strengthened. Pre-British economy was a stationary one in which money was relatively scarce, and barter obtained extensively in the rural areas. Relations between individuals were unspecialized, multiplex, and largely determined by status. The British gradually brought in a growing and monetary economy, participation in which was not banned to any group or individual on the ground of birth in a particular caste. For instance, the abolition of slavery by the British enabled the Untouchable castes in Coorg to desert their Coorg masters and to work as laborers on the coffee plantations started by Europeans.[2] But for the emancipating legislation they could not have participated in the

---

[1] It is nearly a year since the preceding essay was written, and in the meantime I have given some more thought to the subject. The result is the present Note in which I have made a few additional observations on the twin processes of Sanskritization and westernization. In this connection I must thank Dr. F. G. Bailey of the School of Oriental and African Studies, London, for taking the trouble to criticize my paper in detail in his letters to me. I must also thank Dr. McKim Marriott of the University of California, and the delegates of the Conference of Anthropologists and Sociologists held at Madras on Oct. 5–7, 1955, for criticisms which followed the reading of the paper.

[2] See *Religion and Society among the Coorgs of South India*, p. 19.

new economy. This should serve to remind us that British rule also brought in a new set of values and world view.

I have elsewhere tried to argue[1] that the traditional and pre-British caste system permitted a certain amount of group mobility. Only the extremities of the system were relatively fixed while there was movement in between. This was made possible by a certain vagueness regarding mutual rank which obtained in the middle regions of the caste hierarchy. Vagueness as to mutual rank is of the essence in the caste system in operation as distinct from the system in popular conception.[2] And mobility increased a great deal after the advent of the British. Groups which in the pre-British days had had no chance of aspiring to anything more than a bare subsistence came by opportunities for making money, and having made money, they wanted to stake a claim for higher status. Some of them did achieve higher status. The social circulation which was sluggish in pre-British times speeded up considerably in the British period. But the change was only a quantitative one.

Economic betterment thus seems to lead to the Sanskritization of the customs and way of life of a group. Sometimes a group may start by acquiring political power and this may lead to economic betterment and Sanskritization. This does not mean, however, that economic betterment must necessarily lead to Sanskritization. What is important is the collective desire to rise high in the esteem of friends and neighbors, and this should be followed by the adoption of the methods by which the status of a group is raised. It is a fact that such a desire is usually preceded by the acquisition of wealth; I am unable, however, to assert that economic betterment is a necessary precondition to Sanskritization. For instance, the Untouchables of Rampura village in Mysore State are getting increasingly Sanskritized and this seems to be due to their present leadership and to the fact that the younger men are more in contact with the outside world than their parents. Also, if the reports which one hears from some local men are to be believed, Rampura Untouchables are being egged on by Untouchable leaders from outside to change their way of life. Whether the economic position of Untouchables has improved during the last seventy years or so is not easy to determine, though it is likely that they also have benefited from the greater prosperity which resulted when the area under irrigation increased nearly eighty years ago. In brief, while we have no evidence to assert that all cases of Sanskritization are preceded by the acquisition of wealth, the available evidence is not definite enough to state that Sanskritization can occur without any reference whatever to the economic betterment of a group. Economic betterment, the acquisition of political power, education, leadership, and a desire to move up in the hierarchy, are all relevant factors in Sanskritization, and each case of Sanskritiza-

tion may show all or some of these factors mixed up in different measures.

It is necessary, however, to stress that Sanskritization does not automatically result in the achievement of a higher status for the group. The group concerned must clearly put forward a claim to belong to a particular varna, Vaishya, Kshatriya, or Brahman. They must alter their customs, diet, and way of life suitably, and if there are any inconsistencies in their claim, they must try to "explain" them by inventing an appropriate myth. In addition, the group must be content to wait an indefinite period, and during this period it must maintain a continuous pressure regarding its claims. A generation or two must pass usually before a claim begins to be accepted; this is due to the fact that the people who first hear the claim know that the caste in question is trying to pass for something other than what it really is, and the claim has a better chance with their children and grandchildren. In certain cases, a caste or tribal group may make a claim for a long time without it being accepted. I have in view only acceptance by other castes and I am not considering individual sceptics who will always be present.

It is even possible that a caste may overreach in its claims, with the result that instead of moving up it may incur the disapproval of the others. This has probably happened with the Smiths of South India though nothing definite can be said about them except after a thorough study of their history. It is also not unlikely that a claim which may succeed in a particular area or period of time will not succeed in another. A developed historical sense would be inimical to such claims but it is as yet not forthcoming among our people.

Group mobility is a characteristic of the caste system, whereas in a class system it is the individual and his family which moves up or down. One of the implications of group mobility is that either the group is large enough to constitute an endogamous unit by itself, or it recruits girls in marriage from the original group while it does not give girls in return. This implies that the original group is impressed with the fact that the splinter group is superior to it for otherwise it would not consent to such a one-sided and inferior role. A larger number of people are needed in North India than in the South to constitute an endogamous group, for marriage with near kin is prohibited in the North, and there is in addition an insistence on village exogamy. In the South, on the other hand, cross-cousin and uncle-niece marriages are preferred, and the village is not an exogamous unit. But I am straying from my main theme; what I wish to stress here is that Sanskritization is a source of fission in the caste system, and does occasionally bring about hypergamous relations between the splinter group and the original caste from which it has fissioned off. It both precedes as well as sets the seal on social mobility. It thereby brings the caste system of any region closer to the existing politico-economic situation. But for it the caste system would have been subjected to great strain. It has provided a traditional

---

[1] See my essay, "Varna and Caste," in A. R. Wadia, *Essays in Philosophy Presented in his Honour* (Bangalore, 1954).

[2] *Ibid.*, p. 362.

medium of expression for change within that system, and the medium has held good in spite of the vast increase in the quantum of change which has occurred in British and post-British India. It has canalized the change in such a way that all-Indian values are asserted and the homogeneity of the entire Hindu society increases. The continued Sanskritization of castes will probably mean the eventual introduction of major cultural and structural changes in Hindu society as a whole. But Sanskritization does not always result in higher status for the Sanskritized caste, and this is clearly exemplified by the Untouchables. However thorough-going the Sanskritization of an Untouchable group may be, it is unable to cross the barrier of untouchability. It is indeed an anachronism that while groups which were originally outside Hinduism such as tribal groups or alien ethnic groups have succeeded in entering the Hindu fold, and occasionally at a high level, an Untouchable caste is always forced to remain untouchable. Their only chance of moving up is to go so far away from their natal village that nothing is known about them in the new area. But spatial mobility was very difficult in pre-British India; it meant losing such security as they had and probably going into an enemy chiefdom and facing all the dangers there. Movement was near impossible when we remember that Untouchables were generally attached as agrestic serfs to caste Hindu landlords.[1]

The fact that Sanskritization does not help the Untouchables to move up does not, however, make Sanskritization any the less popular. All over India there are discernible movements more or less strong, among Untouchables, to discard the consumption of carcass beef, domestic pork, and toddy, and to adopt Sanskritic customs, beliefs, and deities. It is very likely that in the next twenty or thirty years the culture of Untouchables all over the country will have undergone profound changes. Some of them may become even more Sanskritized than many Shudra castes. The Constitution has abolished untouchability and practical steps are being taken to implement the legal abolition. One naturally wonders what position Untouchables will have in the Hindu society of the future.

I have been asked by more than one student of Indian anthropology whether I regard Sanskritization as only a one-way process, and whether the local culture is always a recipient. The answer is clear: it is a two-way process though the local cultures seem to have received more than they have given. In this connection, it should be remembered that throughout Indian history local elements have entered into the main body of Sanskritic belief, myth, and custom, and in their travel throughout the length and breadth of India, elements of Sanskritic culture have undergone different changes in the different culture areas. Festivals such as the Dasara, Deepavali, and Holi have no doubt certain common features all over the country, but they have also important regional peculiarities. In the case of some festivals only the name is common all over India and everything else is different — the same name connotes different things to people in different regions. Similarly each region has its own body of folklore about the heroes of the Ramayana and Mahabharata, and not infrequently, epic incidents and characters are related to outstanding features of local geography. And in every part of India are to be found Brahmans who worship the local deities which preside over epidemics, cattle, children's lives, and crops, besides the great gods of all-India Hinduism. It is not unknown for a Brahman to make a blood-sacrifice to one of these deities through the medium of non-Brahman friend. Throughout Indian history Sanskritic Hinduism has absorbed local and folk elements and their presence makes easier the further absorption of similar elements. The absorption is done in such a way that there is a continuity between the folk and the theological or philosophical levels, and this makes possible both the gradual transformation of the folk layer as well as the "vulgarization" of the theological layer.

In the foregoing essay I have stated that it looks as though for the non-Brahman castes of Mysore, Sanskritization is an essential preliminary to westernization. I wish to stress here that this is a matter of empirical observation only, and does not refer to any logical necessity for Sanskritization occurring prior to westernization. It is possible that westernization may occur without an intermediary process of Sanskritization. This may happen to groups and individuals living in the cities as well as to rural and tribal folk; it is especially likely to happen under the swift industrialization contemplated by the Five-Year Plans. Increasing westernization will also mean the greater secularization of the outlook of the people and this, together with the movement towards a "classless and casteless society" which is the professed aim of the present government, might mean the disappearance of Hinduism altogether. To the question of whether the threat to religion from westernization is not common to all countries in the world and not something peculiar to Hinduism, the answer is that Christianity and Islam are probably better equipped to withstand westernization because they have a strong organization whereas Hinduism lacks all organization, excluding the caste system. If and when caste disappears, Hinduism will also disappear, and it is hardly necessary to point out that the present climate of influential opinion in the country is extremely hostile to caste. Even those who are extremely skeptical of the effectiveness of the measures advocated to do away with caste consider industrialization and urbanization to be effective solvents of caste in the long run. The question is how long is the run going to be? A warning must however be uttered against the facile assumption that caste is going to melt like butter before westernization. The student of caste is impressed with its great strength and resilience, and its capacity to adjust itself to

---

[1] Dr. Adrian Mayer, however, states that the Balais (Untouchables) in the Mālwa village which he is studying are trying to move into the Shūdra *varṇa*. It would be interesting to see if they succeed in their efforts. I thank Dr. Mayer for allowing me to read his unpublished paper "Caste and Hierarchy."

new circumstances. It is salutary to remember that during the last hundred years or more, caste became stronger in some respects. Westernization has also in some ways favored Sanskritization. The assumption of a simple and direct opposition between the two and of the ultimate triumph of westernization, I find too simple a hypothesis, considering the strength of caste as an institution and the great complexity of the processes involved.

It is necessary to underline the fact that Sanskritization is an extremely complex and heterogeneous concept. It is even possible that it would be more profitable to treat it as a bundle of concepts than as a single concept. The important thing to remember is that it is only a name for a widespread social and cultural process, and our main task is to understand the nature of these processes. The moment it is discovered that the term is more a hindrance than a help in analysis, it should be discarded quickly and without regret.

Apropos of the heterogeneity of the concept of Sanskritization, it may be remarked that it subsumes several mutually antagonistic values, perhaps even as westernization does. The concept of varna, for instance, subsumes values which are ideally complementary but, as a matter of actual and historical fact, have been competitive if not conflicting. In this connection it is necessary to add that the grading of the four varnas which is found in the famous *Purushasukta* verse and subsequent writings, probably does not reflect the social order as it existed everywhere and at all times. Historians of caste have recorded a conflict between Brahmans and Kshatriyas during Vedic times, and Professor G. S. Ghurye has postulated that the Jain and Buddhist movements were in part a revolt of the Kshatriyas and Vaishyas against the supremacy of the Brahmans.[1]

Today we find different castes dominating in different parts of India, and frequently, in one and the same region, more than one caste dominates. In Coorg, for instance, Coorgs, Lingayats, and Brahmans all dominate. The Coorgs are the landed aristocracy and they have certain martial institutions and qualities, and a good

[1] See *Caste and Class in India* (Bombay, 1952), p. 65.

many low castes have tried to imitate them. But the Coorgs themselves have imitated the Lingayats and Brahmans. The Brahmans have not wielded political power, and it could be said that some of the qualities traditionally associated with that caste are not respected by the Coorgs, to say the least. Still they have exercised a hold over the Coorgs, as the writings of European missionaries testify. The imitation of the Lingayats by the Coorgs was facilitated by the fact that Coorg was ruled by Lingayat Rajas for nearly two centuries.

But I am digressing; what I wish to emphasize is that in the study of Sanskritization it is important to know the kind of caste which dominates in a particular region. If they are Brahmans, or a caste like the Lingayats, then Sanskritization will probably be quicker and Brahmanical values will spread, whereas if the dominating caste is a local Kshatriya or Vaishya caste, Sanskritization will be slower, and the values will not be Brahmanical. The non-Brahmanical castes are generally less Sanskritized than the Brahmans, and where they dominate, non-Sanskritic customs may get circulated among the people. It is not inconceivable that occasionally they may even mean the de-Sanskritization of the imitating castes.

One way of breaking down Sanskritization into simpler and more homogeneous concepts would be to write a history of Sanskritic culture taking care to point out the different value-systems subsumed in it and to delineate the regional variations. The task would be a stupendous one even if the period beginning with the British rule was excluded. Such a study is not likely to be forthcoming in the near future and anthropologists would be well advised to continue studying Sanskritization as they are doing at present: study each field-instance of Sanskritization in relation to the locally dominant caste and other factors. The next task would be to compare different instances of Sanskritization in the same culture-area, and the third task would be to extend the scope of comparative studies to include the whole of India. Such an approach might also enable us to translate historical problems into spatial problems. It will not, however, satisfy perfectionists, but perfectionism is often a camouflage for sterility.

A Theory of Social Mobility[1]

Seymour Martin Lipset and Hans L. Zetterberg

THE LION'S SHARE of the studies of social mobility to date are descriptive. Most researchers have been preoccupied primarily with the construction of measures and with the establishing of rates of mobility,[2] or, they have been concerned with the background of members in certain élite groups.[3] It is our contention that enough descriptive material has now been collected to suggest a shift in the emphasis of future research. While we still have to answer many further questions of the type "*how much* mobility?" we might now also begin to ask such questions as "*what causes* account for this rate of mobility?" and "*what consequences* follow from this rate of mobility?" more consciously and systematically than has been done in the past.

To contribute to this shift from descriptive to verificational studies we would like to offer a simple theory of social mobility. We shall present *1)* a few definitions delineating different kinds of mobility, and *2)* a few hypotheses about factors affecting *a)* the extent of mobility, and *b)* the political or ideological consequences of various kinds of mobility. These hypotheses will be illuminated with some data already available, but for the main part, they require a great deal of additional empirical support.

1. Some dimensions of mobility

Max Weber has indicated how useful it is to conceive of stratification along many dimensions.[4] More recently Parsons has suggested that one way of viewing stratification is to conceive of it as "the ranking of units in a social system in accordance with the standards of the common value system."[5] This approach also affords a multitude of cross-cutting stratifications. Of this multi-

[1] The preparation of this paper was facilitated by funds made available by the Bureau of Applied Social Research, Columbia University, from a grant by the Ford Foundation for an inventory of political research, and a grant from the Ida K. Loeb Fund. We are also indebted to the Center for Advanced Study in the Behavioral Sciences for assistance. We would like to acknowledge the advice of Professor Leo Lowenthal, Dr. Natalie Rogoff, Mr. Juan Linz, and Mr. Yorke Lucci. None of these institutions or individuals have any responsibility for the statements made in this article.

[2] Among the best studies analyzing mobility in large populations are Theodore Geiger, *Soziale Umschichtungen in einer dänischen Mittelstadt* (Aahrus Universitet, 1951), Natalie Rogoff, *Recent Trends in Occupational Mobility* (Glencoe: The Free Press, 1953), and David V. Glass, ed., *Social Mobility in Britain* (London: Routledge and Kegan Paul, 1954).

[3] References to various élite studies will be found in Donald R. Matthews, *The Social Background of Political Decision Makers* (Garden City: Doubleday & Co., 1954), S. M. Lipset and Reinhard Bendix, "Ideological Equalitarianism and Social Mobility in the United States," in *Transactions of the Second World Congress of Sociology*, II (London: International Sociological Association, 1954), pp. 53-54.

[4] Max Weber, *The Theory of Social and Economic Organization* (New York: Oxford University Press, 1947), p. 425, see also pp. 424-429, and Max Weber, *Essays in Sociology* (New York: Oxford University Press, 1946), pp. 180-195.

[5] Talcott Parsons, *Essays in Sociological Theory* (Glencoe: The Free Press, 1954), p. 388.

Reprinted from *Transactions of the Third World Congress of Sociology*, V. 2 (1956), pp. 155-177, by permission of the authors and the publisher.

tude we would like to single out a few for discussion. They deal with the ranking of occupational and economic statuses, and with the ranking of certain properties of role relationships such as intimacy and power.

(1) OCCUPATIONAL RANKINGS

From Plato to the present, occupation has been the most common indicator of stratification. Observers of social life — from novelists to pollsters — have found that occupational class is one of the major factors which differentiate people's beliefs, values, norms, customs and occasionally some of their emotional expressions.

We now have good measures of the prestige ranks of various occupations that can be used as bases for computation of occupational mobility. Occupations are differentially esteemed and studies show a remarkable agreement as to how they rank in esteem. In a well-known survey ninety occupations ranging from "Supreme Court Justice" and "Physician" to "Street Sweeper" and "Shoe Shiner" were ranked by a national sample of the United States.[1] On the whole, there is substantial agreement among the rates from different areas of the country, different sizes of home towns, different age groups, different economic levels, and different sexes. Lenski reports that occupations not mentioned in the survey can be fitted into the original rank order with high reliability.[2] Thus it appears that we have available a technique which makes the notion of occupational rank quite feasible for the researcher. Occupations receiving approximately the same rank will be called an *occupational class*. There appears to be a great deal of international consensus about occupational prestige classes. A recent analysis by Inkeles and Rossi compares the relative position of occupational categories as judged by samples of Americans, Australians, Britons, Japanese, Germans, and Russian defectors.[3] They report a very high degree of agreement among the people of these six countries. The fact, however, that these studies were for the most part conducted separately, and that the analysis could only deal with published results, did not make possible any basic study of the variations in occupational prestige, or in the relative desirability of different occupations as occupational goals in different countries. Popular as well as academic consensus (which,

of course, cannot be trusted as a substitute for actual measurement) suggest that civil service occupations have higher prestige in much of Europe than they do in America. Similarly, most American intellectuals believe that intellectual positions have lower prestige in the United States than they do in Europe. (The aforementioned study of the prestige of occupations in the United States, incidentally, throws doubt upon the common belief of American intellectuals that business men are overly appreciated as compared with themselves; a college professor ranks higher than an owner of a factory that employs one hundred people.) New cross-national research might want to focus on such presumed difference in the prestige of occupations.

The above approach to occupational classes in the form of ranking of different occupational titles is theoretically neat and operationally easy. However, one must be aware that it sometimes obscures significant shifts such as those involved in movements from a skilled manual occupation to a low-level white-collar position, or from either of these to a modest self-employment. All these occupations might at times fall in the same prestige class. The difficulties inherent in relying solely on this method of classification can be observed most vividly in the fact that many changes in social position which are a consequence of industrialization would *not* be considered as social mobility since they most frequently involve shifts from a low rural to a low urban position. This points to the need of recording not only occupational class but also *occupational setting*, that is, the kind of social system in which the occupation is found. Changes between occupational settings may also be important: white-collar workers behave differently in specified ways from small businessmen or skilled workers although the prestige of their occupational titles may not differ greatly. For example, most researchers in the United States place small business ownership higher than white-collar employment, and the latter, in turn, higher than the blue-collar enclave of the same corporation. When estimating their own social status level, white-collar workers and small businessmen are much more likely to report themselves as members of the "middle class" than are manual workers who may earn more than they do.[4] Studies of occupational aspirations indicate that many manual workers would like to become small businessmen.[5] Political studies suggest that at the same income level, manual workers are more inclined to support leftist parties which appeal to the interests of the lower classes, than are white-collar workers or self-employed individuals.[6]

(2) CONSUMPTION RANKINGS

It is theoretically and empirically useful to separate occupational and economic statuses. For example, economists have for good reasons differentiated between their subjects in their status as "producers" in the occupational structure, and in their status as "consumers." Both statuses might be ranked but it is not necessarily true that those who receive a high rating in

[1] National Opinion Research Center, "Jobs and Occupations: A Popular Evaluation," *Opinion News*, September 1, 1947, pp. 3-13.

[2] G. H. Lenski, "Status Crystallization: A Non-vertical Dimension of Social Status," *American Sociological Review*, 19 (1954), pp. 405-413.

[3] Alex Inkeles and Peter Rossi, "Cross National Comparisons of Occupational Ratings," *American Journal of Sociology*, 61, January, 1956, pp. 329-339.

[4] Richard Centers, *The Psychology of Social Class* (Princeton: Princeton University Press, 1949), p. 86.

[5] Nancy C. Morse and Robert S. Weiss, "The Function and Meaning of Work and the Job," *American Sociological Review*, 20 (1955), pp. 191-198.

[6] S. M. Lipset, *et al.*, "The Psychology of Voting: An Analysis of Political Behaviour," in G. Lindzey, ed., *Handbook of Social Psychology* (Cambridge: Addison-Wesley, 1954), p. 1139.

their producing capacity would also receive a high consumption rating.

The ranking of consumer status is difficult. Yet it is plain that styles of life differ and that some are considered more "stylish" than others. Those whose style of life carries approximately the same prestige might be said to constitute a *consumption class*. Changes in consumption class may or may not be concomitant with changes along other stratification dimensions.

At the same occupational income level, men will vary in the extent to which they are oriented toward acting out the behaviour pattern common to different social classes. For example, highly-paid workers may choose to live either in working-class districts or in middle-class suburbs. This decision both reflects and determines the extent to which workers adopt middle-class behaviour patterns in other areas of life. A study of San Francisco longshoremen has indicated that longshoremen who moved away from the docks area after the income of the occupation improved tended to be much more conservative politically than those who remained in the docks area.[1] A British Labour Party canvasser has suggested that one can differentiate between Labour Party and Conservative voters within the working class by their consumption patterns. The Tory workers are much more likely to imitate middle-class styles.

The changes which have occurred in many Western countries in recent years in the income of different occupational groups point up the necessity to consider consumption class as a distinct stratification category. In countries such as the United States, Sweden, and Great Britain, the lower classes have sharply improved their economic position, while the proportion of the national income going to the upper fifth of the population has declined.[2] An interesting result in many countries having a long-term full employment economy combined with a reduced working-class birth rate is that a large number of families headed by men in low prestige occupations receive higher incomes than many middle-class families in which the wife does not work, and the children receive a prolonged education. A vivid illustration of this may be seen in the fact that over 100,000 families in the United States, whose principal breadwinner is a "laborer," have an income of over $10,000 a year.[3] (This income is, of course, in most cases a consequence of having more than one wage-earner in the family.)

It is plain that as an index to consumption class, total income is inadequate, although it obviously sets the ultimate limit for a person's consumption class. It is the way income is spent rather than the total amount, that determines a man's consumption class. The best operational index to consumption class is, therefore, not total income, but amount of income spent on prestigious or cultural pursuits. The fact, however, that lower prestige occupations now often have incomes at the level of white-collar occupations is likely to affect both the style of life and the political outlook of manual workers in a high income bracket and of salaried members of the white-collar class in a relatively lower income

position. A comparison of these two groups in terms of their consumption patterns or styles of life is thought to be of particular importance in forecasting future political behaviour, as well as crucial for an understanding of the factors related to other types of mobility in different societies.

It is, of course, difficult to measure the extent of the shift up or down in consumption class. In part, this might be done by comparing the consumption pattern of families at the same income level whose occupational class or income has changed over some particular period of time. Perhaps the best, although most expensive way of dealing with the problem, is to employ a "generational" panel. That is, to interview the parents of a portion of the original random sample, and to compare income in father's and son's family, and their scores on a consumption scale.

(3) SOCIAL CLASS

Much of the research in stratification in America has been concerned with *social class*. This term, as used by American sociologists, refers to roles of intimate association with others. Essentially, other classes in this sense denote strata of society composed of individuals who accept each other as equals and qualified for intimate association. For example, the Social Register Association of American cities only considers candidates for membership after three or more individuals already belonging to the Social Register certify that they accept the candidate as a person with whom they associate regularly and intimately. Men may change their occupational class by changing their job, but they may improve their social class position only if they are admitted to intimate relationships by those who already possess the criteria for higher rank.

One method of studying social class mobility would be a comparison of the occupational or economic class position of husbands and wives before marriage, or of the respective in-laws.[4] Another index of social class might be obtained by asking respondents in a survey to name the occupational status of their best friends. These latter methods would give us some measure of the extent to which upward or downward mobility in the occupational structure is paralleled by upward or downward movement in the social class structure. Such research would be best done in the context of a study which used a "generational" panel.

(4) POWER RANKINGS

Certain role-relationships are also authority or power

[1] Unpublished study of Joseph Aymes, former graduate student in the Department of Psychology, University of California at Berkeley.

[2] Selma Goldsmith, *et al.*, "Size Distribution of Income Since the Mid-thirties," *The Review of Economics and Statistics*, 36 (1954), p. 26.

[3] Fortune Magazine, *The Changing American Market* (Garden City, New York, Hanover House, 1955).

[4] See S. M. Lipset and Natalie Rogoff, "Class and Opportunity in Europe and America," *Commentary*, 19 (1954), pp. 562–568; and David V. Glass, ed., *op. cit.*, pp. 321–338, 344–349.

relationships, that is, they involve subordination on one part and superordination on the other. The extent to which a person's role-relationship affords the means to impose his version of order upon the social system might be ranked as his power, and persons having approximately the same power might be said to constitute a *power class*. It is plain that power classes may be, in part at least, independent of other classes. A labour leader may have a low occupational status and yet wield considerable political influence. A civil servant or parliamentarian whose office is vested with a great deal of political power may enjoy a high occupational and social class, but not be able to meet the consumption standards of these classes. Power as a vehicle for other kinds of social mobility has so far been a neglected area of research.

The most feasible way of using information about improvements in power status is to analyse its effects on economic and occupational position and political orientation. The findings of a recent British study are suggestive in this regard. On the basis of a study of participation in community affairs in Wales we learn that "the adult sons of [low-level unpaid] local union leaders ... achieved middle-class occupational status much more frequently than others of their generation."[1] In a study of members of the Typographical Union in New York City it was found that men holding the equivalent of shop steward's positions in the union were much more likely to say that they would try to get a nonmanual occupation if beginning their work career over again, than were men who did not hold these offices.[2] When one considers that at least 10 per cent. of the members of the trade union movement hold some unpaid union office, and that many more have held one in the past, it is probable that this avenue to power mobility plays an important role in the dynamics of social mobility. Of course, politics, itself, may be even more important (than trade unions) in providing opportunity for power-mobility. Various students of American politics have pointed out the way in which different ethnic groups, in particular the Irish, have been able to improve their position through the medium of politics. In Europe, the Labour and Socialist parties undoubtedly give many lower-class individuals an opportunity to secure power and status far above their economic position. Robert Michels, among others, has suggested that the children of socialist leaders of working-class origin, often secure higher education and leave the working-class.[3]

An operational index to power class is difficult to construct. The public debate in Western societies seems rather shy when it comes to matters of power. While there is a fairly freely admitted consensus about the desirability of high occupational consumption and social status, there is less consensus about the loci of power, and less admittance that power might be desirable. Perhaps the best one can do at present is to ask a panel of informed social scientists to list the various types of power positions available to individuals at different class levels. Among workers in the United States, for example, these might include positions in political parties, trade unions, veterans' organizations, and ethnic groups. After collecting the data on all positions held by members of a sample, it should be possible to rank the relative importance of different posts.

The complexity of this problem is of such a magnitude that one cannot anticipate more than fragmental findings on *individual* changes of power class position. The relative power position of various *groups*, however, may change over time, as witnessed, for example, by the return to power of the industrialists in Germany, the decline of the gentry in England, and throughout the Western world the manifest increase in the power of organized labour. It is plain that individuals change in their power class to the extent that they belong to these groups. Such membership (easy to ascertain by survey methods) may reflect itself in different feelings of political involvement and influence; for example, a study of two cities in Sweden by Segerstedt and Lundquist indicates that workers have these feelings to a greater extent than the white-collar class.[4] Likewise, the British worker may experience himself and his class as politically less impotent than, say, the American worker.

This concludes the discussion of the dimensions of social stratification which seem to us theoretically most rewarding and which are accessible by available research techniques. Previous studies of class mobility have, for the most part, ignored the possibility that a society may have a higher rate of mobility on one of these dimensions and a lower one on others. Similarly, an individual may rank high along one dimension while occupying a lower rank along another. We would like to draw attention to the possibility that such a multi-dimensional approach makes it possible to draw more qualified and accurate conclusions about comparative mobility and stratification systems, and above all, might enable us to deal with many interesting problems of intra-society dynamics, particularly in the realm of politics.

A METHODOLOGICAL NOTE

A basic difficulty inherent in most discussions of social mobility has been the absence of a comparative frame of reference. That is, when faced with a table showing that a given per cent. of males in certain occupations are of lower class origins, one does not know whether this proportion is relatively high or low. The conception of high or low mobility, after all, assumes a comparison with something else which is higher or lower. Basically, there are three types of comparison which can be made. The first is a comparison with the past, i.e., is there more

[1] T. Brennan, "Class Behaviour in Local Politics and Social Affairs," in *Transactions of the Second World Congress of Sociology*, II, *op. cit.*, pp. 291–292.

[2] S. M. Lipset, Martin Trow and J. S. Coleman, *Union Democracy* (Glencoe: The Free Press, 1956).

[3] Robert Michels, *Political Parties* (Glencoe: The Free Press, 1949), pp. 280–281.

[4] Torgny Segerstedt and Agne Lundquist, *Människan i industrisamhället II: Fritidsliv samhällsliv* (Stockholm: Studieförbundet Näringsliv och Samhälle, 1955), pp. 287–280.

or less social mobility today than in the past. The second comparison is with other areas or countries; is the U.S. a more mobile society than Germany or Great Britain. Efforts at such comparisons lead into the third type, comparison with a model expressing equal opportunity. How nearly does a given country approach the utopian concern for complete equality? Thinking of mobility in terms of equality rather than absolute rates leads us to recognise that there may be more mobility in country A than in country B, and yet less equality of opportunity. For example, if a country is 90 per cent. peasant, even with completely equal opportunity, most children of peasants must remain peasants. Even if every non-peasant position is filled by a peasant's son, only about eleven per cent. of them could change their occupation. On the other hand, if a country undergoes rapid economic transformation and the proportion of non-manual positions increases to, say, one half of all positions, then 50 per cent. of the children of manual workers would have to secure nonmanual work in order to meet the criterion of equality.[1]

A word should be said about the conventional operational method of ascertaining mobility in comparing a father's position with that of his son. If one asks in a survey "what is your occupation?" and "what is your father's occupation?" most of the time we obtain the father's position at the peak of his career while the information for the son refers to a period prior to his peak occupation. It is, therefore, wise to record also the occupation of the father at an earlier time, for example, by asking "what was your father's occupation when he was at your age?" Also, one should not overlook the possibility of measuring intragenerational mobility, that is advancement from the first position held to the present. It might well be that the length of the leap along the rank ladder might be substantially greater in one country than in another although the same proportion of the population can obtain a better position than their parents in both countries.

2. Some causes of social mobility

Much of the discussion about the degree of openness of a given society is confused by the failure to distinguish between two different processes, both of which are described and experienced as social mobility. These are:

1) The supply of vacant statuses The number of statuses in a given stratum is not always or even usually constant. For example, the expansion in the proportion of professional, official, managerial, and white-collar positions, and the decline in the number of unskilled labour positions require a surge of upward mobility, providing that these positions retain their relative social standing and income. Demographic factors also operate to facilitate mobility, when the higher classes do not reproduce themselves and hence create a "demographic vacuum."[2]

2) The interchange of ranks Any mobility which occurs in a given social system, which is not a consequence of a change in the supply of statuses and actors must necessarily result from an interchange. Consequently, if we think of a simple model, for every move up there must be a move down. Interchange mobility will be determined in large part by the extent to which a given society gives members of the lower strata the means with which to compete with those who enter the social structure on a higher level. Thus the less emphasis which a culture places on family background

as a criterion for marriage, the more class mobility that can occur, both up and down, through marriage. The more occupational success is related to educational achievements, which are open to all, the greater the occupational mobility.

The description of these processes does not, of course, account for *motivational* factors in mobility. If mobility is to occur, individuals need to be motivated to aspire to secure higher positions. The obvious common sense starting point for a discussion of mobility motivation is the observation that people do not like to be downwardly mobile: they prefer to keep their rank or to improve it.

An insightful motivation theory which accounts for men's desire to improve themselves, as well as to avoid falling in social position may be found in Veblen's analysis of the factors underlying consumption mobility.

Those members of the community who fall short of [a] somewhat indefinite, normal degree of prowess or of property suffer in the esteem of their fellow-men; and consequently they suffer also in their own esteem, since the usual basis for self-respect is the respect accorded by one's neighbours. Only individuals with an aberrant temperament can in the long run retain their self-esteem in the face of the dis-esteem of their fellows.

So as soon as the possession of property becomes the basis of popular esteem, therefore, it becomes also a requisite to that complacency which we call self-respect. In any community where goods are held in severality, it is necessary, in order to ensure his own peace of mind, that an individual should possess as large a portion of goods as others with whom he is accustomed to class himself; and it is extremely gratifying to possess something more than others. But as fast as a person makes new acquisitions, and becomes accustomed to the resulting new standard of wealth, the new standard forthwith ceases to afford appreciably greater satisfaction than the earlier standard did. The tendency in any case is constantly to make the present pecuniary standard the point of departure for a fresh increase of wealth; and this in turn gives rise to a new standard of sufficiency and a new pecuniary classification of one's self as compared with one's neighbours. So far as concerns the present question, the end sought by accumulation is to rank high in comparison with the rest of the community in point of pecuniary strength. So long as the compari-

[1] For statistical techniques developed to handle this problem, see Donald Marvin, "Occupational Propinquity as a Factor in Marriage Selection," *Publications of the American Statistical Association,* 16, 1918, pp. 131–150; Natalie Rogoff, *op. cit.,* pp. 29–33; David V. Glass, ed., *op. cit.,* pp. 218–259; see also Federico Chessa, *La Trasmissione Ereditaria delle Professioni* Torino: Fratelli Bocca, 1912), for early presentation of the logic of this approach.
[2] See P. Sorokin, *Social Mobility* (New York: Harper Brothers, 1927), pp. 346–377; and Eldridge Sibley, "Some Demographic Clues to Stratification," *American Sociological Review,* 7, 1942, pp. 322–330.

son is distinctly unfavourable to himself, the normal, average individual will live in chronic dissatisfaction with his present lot; and when he has reached what may be called the normal pecuniary standard of the community, or of his class in the community, this chronic dissatisfaction will give place to a restless straining to place a wider and ever-widening pecuniary interval between himself and this average standard. The invidious comparison can never become so favourable to the individual making it that he would not gladly rate himself still higher relatively to his competitors in the struggle for pecuniary reputability.[1]

Implicit in this passage seem to be the following hypotheses:

1) The evaluation (rank, class) a person receives from his society determines in large measure his self-evaluation.
2) A person's actions are guided, in part at least, by an insatiable desire to maximize a favourable self-evaluation.

Hence, if the society evaluates a high consumption standard favourably, the individual will try to maximize his consumption level, since he thereby maximizes his self-evaluation. This theory can easily be generalized to any other dimension of class. Since any ranking is an evaluation by the society, it will be reflected in a person's self-evaluation; since any person tries to maximize his self-evaluation, he tries to maximize his rank. This would go for all the rankings we discussed earlier, that is, occupational consumption, social and perhaps also power classes. The basic idea is that persons like to protect their class positions in order to protect their egos and improve their class positions in order to enhance their egos. For example, societies with a more visible occupational stratification — such as Western Europe — are likely to produce stronger ego-needs favouring occupational mobility. Societies which place less emphasis on visible signs of occupational class and stress themes of equality — for example, the United States — are likely to produce less strong ego-needs favouring mobility.

We cannot discuss here all the qualifications that modern research must impose on the Veblen theory of motivation for mobility. However the theory is interesting from the point of view that it does not assume that mobility occurs only as a result of specific social norms, pressuring people to be mobile; instead the motivations for mobility are placed in the realm of more or less universal ego-needs operating within stratified societies. This is not to say that the presence of

norms to the effect that people should be mobile, are without enough authority to be a general law of social psychology that those who follow them out are rewarded by more favourable sentiments from their environment.[2] Motivation arising from norms pressuring for mobility might supplement the motivations to rise derived from ego-needs. It is perhaps precisely in societies where these ego-needs are weakest due to cultural themes of equality that mobility norms are most necessary. Thus, the intriguing paradox arises that the United States because of the emphasis on equality must emphasize also mobility norms in order to furnish the motivation necessary to fill higher positions.

This theory, stressing supply of actors and statuses, interchange of rank, and universal ego-needs, goes a long way to explain one of the most intriguing findings that seems to emerge from comparative mobility research. Popular and academic consensus have long held that occupational mobility in the United States is higher than in Western Europe. Examination of available evidence suggests that this is perhaps not the case.[3] It is now possible to expand the empirical basis for this conclusion. It has been possible to locate data from ten countries which have been collected by survey methods on national samples. The studies comprise Denmark, Finland, Germany (two studies), Great Britain, Italy, Soviet Russia (post-war emigrés), Sweden (two studies), and the United States (three studies). The studies afford only very crude international comparisons, largely using the three categories of manual, nonmanual, and farm occupations. In presenting these materials in Table 1 we make the assumption that a move from manual to nonmanual employment constitutes upward mobility among *males.* This assumption may be defended primarily on the grounds that most male nonmanual occupations receive higher prestige than most manual occupations, even skilled ones. It is true, of course, that many white-collar positions are lower in income and prestige than the higher levels of skilled manual work. Most of the less rewarded white-collar positions, however, are held by women. The men who hold them are often able to secure higher level supervisory posts. Consequently, we believe that using the division between manual and nonmanual occupations as indicators of low and high occupational status is justified as an approximate dichotomous break of urban male occupations. It is important to recognize, however, that like all single item indicators of complex phenomena, this one will necessarily result in some errors.

When examining the results of these studies, especially the ones for the United States, France, Switzerland, and Germany (which are most comparable), there can be little doubt that the advanced European societies for which we have data have "high" rates of social mobility, if by a high rate we mean one which is similar to that of the United States. In each country, a large minority is able to rise above the occupational position of their fathers, while a smaller but still substantial minority falls in occupational status. A British research group,

[1] Thorstein Veblen, *The Theory of the Leisure Class* (New York: The Modern Library, 1934), pp. 30–32.
[2] H. W. Riecken and G. C. Homans, "Psychological Aspects of Social Structure," in G. Lindzey, ed., *op. cit.,* pp. 787–789.
[3] See Lipset and Rogoff, *op. cit.*

under the direction of David Glass, attempted a quantitative comparison of their data with the findings from the French, Italian and the third American study. Glass and his associates concluded that Britain, the U.S. and France had similar rates of mobility.[1] The Italian and Finnish findings, however, indicate a lower rate of social mobility than in the other countries. It is difficult to make any clear judgment concerning the Finnish data, since the father's occupation in the Finnish study is based on the reply to "what class do you consider your father belongs(ed): white-collar, working-class, or farmer?" while the sons are grouped according to their objective occupation.[2] The British, Danish, Italian and second Swedish studies combine urban and rural occupations in the same classes. This has the consequence of increasing downward mobility since many sons of farmers who are middle class become urban workers. It also reduces upward mobility since children of farm laborers are less likely to move up than the offspring of manual workers.

The data from these studies tend to challenge the popular conception that America is a land of wide-open occupational mobility as compared to Europe, where family background is alleged to play a much more important role in determining the position of sons. It is important to note, however, that the available data should not be treated as if they were a set of quantitatively comparable censuses of mobility in different countries. All that we can say from the existing survey studies is that they do not validate the traditional assumptions. Considerable mobility occurs in every country for which we have data. Furthermore, available historical material tends to indicate that much of Europe had occupational mobility rates from 1900 to 1940 which are similar to the present, and which did not lag behind the American one.[3] Whether there are significant differences among these countries can only be decided after the completion of an integrated comparative research project, which employs the same methods of collecting, classifying, and processing the data. Thus far, no such study exists.

According to our theory, the explanation of these findings has to be sought in structural and motivational factors which are similar on both continents. Both Europe and America have experienced differential fertility, that is, the tendency of those in upper classes to have fewer children, a condition that leaves room for the lower classes to rise. Both have seen an expansion in the number of white-collar positions at the expense of manual workers, thus creating a surge of upward occupational mobility to the extent that new industrial labour is drawn from farm areas. Bendix has compared the ratio of administrative (white-collar) and production (manual) workers over the last half-century in the United States, the United Kingdom and in Sweden, and finds the parallel in trends very great. Thus, in the United States in 1899 there were 8 administrative employees per 100 production workers while in 1947 there were 22 administrative employees per 100 pro-

duction workers. The corresponding rise in Britain between 1907 and 1948 is from 9 to 20 administrative employees per 100 production workers, and in Sweden the figures jump from 7 in 1915 to 21 administrative employees per 100 production workers in 1950.[4]

Likewise, the United States and Western Europe have experienced a parallel process in interchange of ranks. On both continents the majority of nonmanual and high-status positions are no longer in the category of self-employment. A bureaucrat father unlike a businessman cannot give his job to his son. Many non-self-employed middle-class parents have little to give their children except a better opportunity to secure a good education and the motivation to attempt to obtain a high-class position. If for any reason, such as the early death of the father or family instability, a middle-class child does not complete a higher education, he is in a

[1] David V. Glass, ed., *op. cit.*, pp. 260–265.

[2] The findings indicating considerable fluidity in the occupational class structure outside of America are buttressed by the results of studies of mobility in individual cities in different countries. A study based on a random sample of the Tokyo population indicates that about one-third of the sons of fathers employed in manual occupations were in nonmanual jobs when interviewed, while about thirty per cent of the sons of men in nonmanual occupations had become manual workers. (A. G. Ibi, "Occupational Stratification and Mobility in the Large Urban Community: A Report of Research on Social Stratification and Mobility in Tokyo, II," *Japanese Sociological Review*, 4 (1954), pp. 135–149. We describe the results of this study in general terms since close to twenty per cent. of the men were in occupational categories, which we could not fit into the conventional manual–nonmanual farm groups without more knowledge about Japanese occupational titles.) A study of mobility among a group of young residents of Stockholm indicates that over half of the sons of manual workers who grew up in Stockholm were in nonmanual occupations at the age of twenty-four (Gunnar Boalt, "Social Mobility in Stockholm: A Pilot Investigation," in *Transactions of the Second World Congress of Sociology*, II, *op. cit.*, pp. 67–73). Two excellent studies of social mobility in a Danish (Geiger, *op. cit.*) and an American (Rogoff, *op. cit.*) provincial city permit an even more detailed comparison of mobility between Europe and America, which is presented in Lipset and Rogoff, *op. cit.* It is clear that there is no substantial difference in the patterns of social mobility in Aarhus and Indianapolis.

[3] For example, a study which secured questionnaire data from over 90,000 German workers in the late 1920's reported that almost one-quarter of the males in this group came from manual working-class families (Gewerkschaftsbund der Angestellten, *Die wirtschaftliche und soziale Lage der Angestellten* (Berlin, 1931), p. 43; see also Hans Speier, *The Salaried Employee in German Society*, Vol. I (New York: Department of Social Science, Columbia University, 1939), pp. 86–98). An early British survey of the social origins of the owners, directors and managers in the cotton industry found that over two-thirds of this group had begun their occupational careers either as manual workers or in low-status clerical positions. (S. J. Chapman and F. J. Marquis, "The Recruiting of the Employing Classes from the Ranks of Wage Earners in the Cotton Industry," *Journal of the Royal Statistical Society*, February, 1912, pp. 293–306). Pitirim Sorokin (*op. cit.*) who made an extensive analysis of social mobility research around the world before 1927 also concluded that the assumption that the United States was a more open society in terms of occupational mobility than the industrial sections of Europe was not valid. For early data on mobility in the city of Rome, see Chessa, *op. cit.*

[4] Reinhard Bendix, *Work and Authority in Industry* (New York: John Wiley and Sons, 1956).

TABLE 1. *Social Mobility in Ten Populations*[1]

Father's occupation

Respondent's occupation	France (a) Nonman.	Man.	Farm	Germany (b) Nonman.	Man.	Farm	Germany (c) Nonman.	Man.	Farm	Russian emigrés (d) Nonman.	Man.	Farm
Nonmanual	73%	35%	16%	58%	27%	19%	80%	30%	12%	90%	28%	20%
Manual	18	55	13	38	68	28	20	60	19	10	68	36
Farm	9	10	71	4	5	54	—	10	70	—	3	44
N	(1109)	(625)	(1289)	(579)	(406)	(321)	(236)	(210)	(139)	(265)	(376)	(541)

Respondent's occupation	Switzerland (e) Nonman.	Man.	Farm	U.S. (f) Nonman.	Man.	Farm	U.S. (g) Nonman.	Man. and farm lab.	Farm	U.S. (h) Nonman.	Man.	Farm
Nonmanual	84%	44%	27%	71%	35%	23%	64%	31%	24%	81%	30%	—
Manual	13	54	19	25	61	39	34	67	46	19	70	—
Farm	3	3	54	4	4	38	1	2	30	—	—	—
N	(582)	(239)	(303)	(319)	(430)	(404)	(180)	(291)	(323)	(259)	(399)	(—)

Respondent's occupation	Finland (i) "White-collar class"	"Working class"	"Farmer"
Nonmanual	64%	11%	9%
Manual	24	56	21
Farm	12	33	70
N	(590)	(1868)	(2302)

	Great Britain (j) High levels of nonman. and farm owners	Routine nonman. and farm workers
Higher levels of nonman. and farm owners	51%	20%
Routine nonman., man. and farm workers	49	80
N	(1144)	(2358)

	Denmark (k) High levels of nonman. and farm owners	Routine nonman. and farm workers
High levels of nonman. and farm owners	56%	22%
	44	78
	(796)	(1174)

Italy (l)	Nonman. and well-to-do peasants	Manual, farm labor and poor peasants
Nonman. and well-to-do peasants	66%	8%
Manual, farm labor and poor peasants	34	92
N	(224)	(472)

Sweden (m) Sons, aged 22–28	Nonmanual	Manual	Farm
Nonmanual	67%	59%	44%
Manual	32	39	44
Farm	1	2	12
N	(57)	(101)	(73)

Sweden (n)

Father's occupation	Respondent's occupation Better situated	Middle class	Worker
Better situated	54%	5%	—
Middle class	39	72	35
Worker	7	23	65

(N's are not given)

[1] While these studies, viewed comparatively, constitute a significant addition to our knowledge of international variations in stratification and mobility, they present many difficulties to anyone who is interested in making any systematic generalizations. Only a few of the sets of data were collected for stratification or social mobility studies. For example, six of the national surveys which collected mobility data did so in the context of research focusing on other problems. The German, and one set of American data have never been published, since they were unrelated to the major problem of the research. These were obtained through private correspondence. But more important than this is the fact that most of the data were gathered without any reference to the need for international or even national comparisons. For example, the three American studies are not comparable with one another. One reports only the relationship between the occupation of fathers and sons who are urban dwellers. The other two report mobility patterns for the entire population, but one secured the information about father's principal occupation while the other asked for the occupation while "you were growing up." The Italian study used a third method, by asking for the father's occupation when he was the respondent's age, while the Danish study contrasts occupations of father and son at age 30. It is possible to argue that each form of the question is worthwhile, but clearly, using different versions makes comparison difficult if not impossible.

An even more serious problem is inherent in the system of classification of the occupational or social status of respondents and their fathers. Most of the studies employed noncomparable systems of classification. Thus, the Danish, British, Italian, and second Swedish studies differ from the others in classifying rural occupations in the same categories as urban occupations of presumed comparable status. Farm owners are grouped with high level nonmanual occupations, while farm labourers are placed in the same category as semi- and unskilled urban workers. All other studies differentiate between urban and rural occupational strata. The British and Danish study, in addition, does not differentiate between manual and nonmanual occupations. Lower levels of nonmanual employment are classified with skilled workers, while all other studies keep manual and clerical occupations separate. Some of the European studies classify "artisans," i.e., self-employed workers such as carpenters, together with manual workers, while other studies group them with independent business men. We have reclassified for consistency and placed artisans in the same category as other nonmanual jobs. Some studies differentiate between salaried and free professionals, the first group being classified as "officials," while others use the category "professional" for both groups. The Finnish study differed from all the others in using a different system of classification for fathers and sons. All the studies except the second Swedish one are given in terms of their relationship between fathers' and sons' occupations. The latter does not allow us to present it in comparable terms since the number of cases in each cell is not given. It should also be noted that all the tables, except the Finnish and Swedish, deal with fathers' and sons' occupations. The latter ones include women among the respondents.

(a) M. Bresard, "Mobilité sociale et dimension de la famille," *Population*, Vol. V, No. 3, pp. 533–67.

(b) This table was computed from the data kindly supplied by the U.N.E.S.C.O. Institute at Cologne, Germany, which were secured in their study of German attitudes in 1953.

(c) This table was computed from data kindly supplied by the Institut für Demoskopies, at Allensbach, Germany, from one of their national surveys of West German opinion.

(d) Robert A. Feldmesser, "Observations on Trends in Social Mobility in the Soviet Union and Their Implications," in A. Kassof *et al.* "Stratification and Mobility in the Soviet Union: A Study of Social Class Cleavages in the U.S.S.R." (Cambridge, Harvard Russian Research Centre, mimeo, 1954), p. 8.

(e) Recalculated from data kindly supplied by Professor Roger Girod from his paper in this volume.

(f) This table was derived by Natalie Rogoff from data published by the National Opinion Research Centre. See N.O.R.C., "Jobs and Occupations," *Opinion News*, September 1, 1947, pp. 3–13.

(g) This table was computed from data kindly supplied by the Survey Research Centre, which were secured in their study of the 1952 presidential election.

(h) Richard Centers, *The Psychology of Social Classes*. (Princeton, University Press, 1949), p. 181.

(i) Tauno Hellevuo, "Poimintatutkimus Säätykerrosta" (A Sampling Study of Social Mobility), *Suomalainen Suomi*, No. 2, 1952, pp. 93–96.

(j) This table was adapted from material in David V. Glass, ed. *Social Mobility in Britain*. (London: Routledge and Kegan Paul, 1954.)

(k) We are indebted to Professor K. Svalastoga, University of Copenhagen, Denmark, for these data based on a probability sample.

(l) L. Livi, "Sur la mesure de la mobilité sociale," *Population*, January–March, 1950, pp. 65–76.

(m) This table was computed from data kindly supplied by Svenska Institutet för Opinionsunder sökningar, Stockholm, Sweden, from a probability sample of youth.

(n) Elis Håstad, "Gallup" Och Den Svenska Väljarkåren. Uppsala: Hugo Gebers Förlag, 1950), p. 271.

worse position in terms of prospective employment than the son of a manual worker who completes college, lycee, or gymnasium. Clearly, some proportion of the children of the middle class are so handicapped, and many of them fall in socioeconomic status. In addition, some simply do not have the abilities to complete higher education or to get along in a bureaucratic hierarchy, and fall by the wayside. Thus, whatever the reason that some persons of middle-class origin move downward, they leave room for others of lower-class background to rise.

Given these structural prerequisites for mobility, it seems to make little difference that Americans are exposed to stronger norms and more vivid models encouraging mobility. The more visible occupational class distinctions in Europe actually may make for stronger ego-needs pressuring for upward mobility. Thus the resulting motivation to move upward appears approximately equal on both continents. There is, unfortunately, little available data on the aspiration level of men in the same class in different countries.

The more pronounced presence of mobility norms in the American "open class" value system might, however, make for more "planned" mobility in the United States, while mobility in Europe would be more "unplanned." That is, the emphasis placed on mobility in the value system of the United States should lead more Americans than Europeans to make conscious plans to secure the skills necessary to be upwardly mobile. On the other hand, the age of marriage and the age of parents at the arrival of the first child in Northern and Western Europe is somewhat higher than in the United States. Consequently, a European will have a longer period without family responsibilities to take risk or advance his skills. In this sense, "unplanned" mobility may be facilitated in Europe and restricted in America.

The norms dictating class behaviour in a social class oriented society may actually serve to open the occupational ladder for lower strata individuals since they sometimes operate to inhibit the sons of higher strata families from securing the type of education which will enable them to obtain a high position in the economic structure. The fact that in some European countries engineering and other high level industrial positions appear to have less prestige in the eyes of the upper classes than high posts in the civil service, or the military, has the effect of eliminating from competition for industrial posts some men who could secure them if they so desired. This

means that room is left for individuals of lower social origins to secure these high positions.

3. Some political consequences of mobility

Earlier, we called attention to the fact that most studies of social mobility have been descriptive in character and have not attempted to relate findings concerning mobility to other aspects of the society. In this concluding section, we shall discuss the relevance of mobility theory and research to political analysis. Our guiding general assumption is that *many of the major political problems facing contemporary society are, in part, a consequence of the conflict and tensions resulting from the contradictions inherent in the need for both aristocracy and equality.*[1]

Much of the writing in the general area of social stratification has been concerned with the problem of equality. Writers from the time of the Greek civilization on have pointed to the need for tenure in high status positions and the inheritance of social position as requirements for the stability of complex societies. These theorists have suggested that the division of labour requires differential rewards in prestige and privilege as the means of motivating individuals to carry out the more difficult leadership or other positions requiring a great deal of intelligence and training. Also, given a system of differential rewards, the particularistic values which are a necessary part of family organization require high-statused individuals to attempt to pass their gratifications to their children. The simplest way to assure these rewards for their children is to pass their privileged positions on to them. Thus, a strain towards aristocracy, or the inheritance of rank, is, as Plato indicated, a necessary concomitant of a stratified society.

The legitimation of inherited rank immediately gives rise to another problem, that is the problem of reconciling the legitimation of inherited privilege with the social need to encourage some men born into lower status positions to aspire to and attain higher positions. Thus all economically expanding societies such as the United States, most of Western Europe, India, the Soviet Union, South Africa, and many others, must encourage individuals to aspire to higher or at least different occupational positions from those held by their parents. The dilemma confronting a society in doing this may best be seen in the problems faced by the Soviet Union. Soviet writers have complained that most Russian schoolchildren only desire important bureaucratic and military positions. They have castigated the school system for failing in its obligation of making the children of workers and peasants proud of their fathers' occupations.[2] Yet, while the new ruling class of the Soviet Union attempts on the one hand to reduce the ambitions of lower-class youth, its goal of an expanding industrial society forces it to recruit constantly from the ranks of the lower classes.

[1] See Talcott Parsons, "A Revised Analytical Approach to the Theory of Stratification," in R. Bendix and S. M. Lipset, eds., *Class, Status and Power* (1st Edition, Glencoe: The Free Press, 1953), p. 117; and K. Davis and W. E. Moore, "Some Principles of Stratification," *American Sociological Review*, 10, 1945, pp. 242–249. For a critique of this position and an answer to it, see M. M. Tumin, "Some Principles of Stratification: a Critical Analysis," *American Sociological Review*, 18, 1953, pp. 387–394; K. Davis, "Reply to Tumin," *ibid.*, pp. 394–397.

[2] Alex Inkeles, "Social Stratification and Mobility in the Soviet Union: 1940–1950," in R. Bendix and S. M. Lipset, eds., *op. cit.*, pp. 611–621.

However, social mobility is not only an issue for the politicians, it is also a force generating political and ideological pressures. There can be little doubt that a system of differential rewards and inherited privilege entails internal strains which make for instability. Such a system requires a large proportion of the population to accept a lower conception of its own worth as compared with others (this follows from the first hypothesis we derived from Veblen). This barrier to the possibility of enhancement of the self may in some cases lead to a rejection of self, described as "self-hatred" in the analyses of the personalities of lower-status minority group members. Such a rejection, however, is necessarily difficult to maintain, and in all stratified societies, some men have tended to reject the dominant valuation placed on the upper classes. Sometimes this rejection takes the form of lower-class religious values which deny the moral worth of wealth or power; at other times it may take the form of rebellious "Robin Hood" bands, or formal revolutionary or social reform movements; often it may lead to individual efforts to improve one's status through legitimate or illegitimate means.

It is entirely conceivable that the political consequences of class deprivation might be different depending on what dimension of class is challenged. Some recent analysts of the development of rightist extremism in the United States have suggested that this movement is, in part, a response to insecurity about social class position.[1] Essentially, these analyses assume that when the occupational and consumption aspects of stratification are salient, the ideological debate and the political measures will be concerned with the issues of job security, redistribution of property, and income. Political movements with this motivation are most common in times of depression when many see their economic position decline. On the other hand, when the social class dimension is challenged or confused, the ideological debate will contain endless discussions of traditional values of ascription, often with elements of irrationality and scape-goating. Political movements with this motivation are likely to occur in times of high occupational and consumption mobility when the old upper class feels itself threatened by *nouveaux arrivées*, and when the latter feel frustrated in not being accepted socially by those who already hold high social position.

The political themes related to threats to social class position, or to frustrations in achieving higher position in the social class structure are likely to be more irrational than those related to the desire for economic security or achievement. Franz Neumann has suggested that the adoption of a conspiracy theory of politics, placing the blame for social evils on a secret group of evil-doers is related to social class insecurity.[2] Groups in this position account for the actual or potential decline which they desire to avert by blaming a conspiracy rather than themselves or their basic social institutions. In doing so, they can continue to believe in the ongoing social structure which accords them their status, while at the same time feel that they are taking action to eliminate the threat to their social status.

It might be interjected at this point that the above is not untestable speculation. We already know how to measure the kinds of mobility which are the independent variables of the hypotheses. The dependent variables — the political themes — can also be measured by the conventional kind of public opinion poll questions. In fact, many already existing questions presumed to measure along a conservatism-liberalism continuum would tap some of the themes, and for the others equally simple items can be constructed. It is also easy to ascertain by survey methods memberships in groups or associations known to embrace any of the above political themes.

Short of having survey data, it is possible to present some impressionistic evidence for the hypothesis that strains introduced by mobility aspirations or anxieties will predispose individuals towards accepting more extreme political views. Political literature knows several suggestions that class discrepancies, e.g. high social class and lower economic position, has this effect. Such hypotheses about rank discrepancies are not strictly hypotheses about social mobility. However, it is plain that whenever social mobility occurs, rank discrepancies are likely to occur, since it is extremely rare that a person would rise or decline at the same rate along all dimensions of class. For example, this hypothesis has been suggested in explaining political behaviour in contemporary Canada. In the province of Saskatchewan, governed since 1944 by a socialist party, it was found that the leaders of the socialist party who were either businessmen or professionals, were largely of non-Anglo-Saxon origin, that is, of low social class. On the other hand, the big majority, over 90 per cent. of the middle-class leaders of the Liberal and Conservative Parties, were Anglo-Saxons.

> Socially, the businessmen of the ethnic minority are part of the lower class group of the Saskatchewan population. They are not exploited economically, but they are deprived socially of many of the privileges that usually go with business status. The cleavage between them and the Anglo-Saxon "upper class" is often as great as the split between the farmers and the business community. Subject to the cross pressures of contradictory statuses, many members of minority groups have seen fit to identify themselves with the political party which is opposed by the "upper class" and which promises to strike at the community power of these dominant groups.[3]

Robert Michels, in his analysis of European socialism before World War I made a similar hypothesis explicit:

[1] See the various essays reprinted in Daniel Bell, ed., *The New American Right* (New York: Criterion Books, 1955); and Richard Hofstadter, *The Age of Reform* (New York: Alfred A. Knopf, 1955), esp. pp. 131–172.
[2] Franz Neumann, "Anxiety in Politics," *Dissent*, Spring 1955, pp. 135–141.
[3] S. M. Lipset, *Agrarian Socialism* (Berkeley: University of California Press, 1950), p. 191.

The origin of this predominant position [of the Jews in the European socialist movement] is to be found, as far at least as concerns Germany and the countries of eastern Europe, in the peculiar position which the Jews have occupied and in many respects still ocupy. The legal emancipation of the Jews has not been followed by their social and moral emancipation. . . . Even when they are rich, the Jews constitute, at least in eastern Europe, a category of persons who are excluded from the social advantages which the prevailing political, economic, and intellectual

So far, we have reported hypotheses which have predicted a political orientation to the left when a group's social class position is lower than its occupational or economic position, in spite of the fact that the latter normally would predispose a conservative outlook. It has also been suggested, however, that a rightist orientation also occurs among people in such positions. It has been argued, for example, that *nouveaux riches* are sometimes even more conservative than the old rich, because some of them seek to move up in the social class structure by adapting to the value and behaviour

TABLE 2. *Left Vote of Finnish, German and American Middle-Class Men Related to their Social Origins**

Father's occupation	Per cent. both Left parties	Finland—1949 Per cent. Social-Democratic	Per cent. Communist	Germany—1953 Per cent. Social-Democratic	U.S. 1952 Per cent. Democratic	U.S. 1948
Manual	23	20	3 (157)	32 (200)	22 (67)	35 (72)
Nonmanual	6	5	1 (356)	20 (142)	30 (79)	39 (83)
Farm	10	10	— (183)	22 (58)	34 (59)	49 (61)

* The data from which these tables were constructed were furnished by the Finnish Gallup Poll, the UNESCO Institute of Social Science and the Survey Research Center. We would like to express our thanks to them. Non-voters and persons not expressing a party choice are eliminated from this table.

system ensures for the corresponding portion of the Gentile population: Society in the narrower sense of the term is distrustful of them, and public opinion is unfavourable to them.[1]

Evidence derived from analysis of electoral behaviour, or the composition of the membership or leadership of political parties in different countries, indicates that Jews still react in the same way in more recent times. In the United States the bulk of the Jewish middle class supports the more liberal or left-wing parties, even

patterns which they believe are common in the class above them, or more simply, perhaps because they have not developed patterns of *noblesse oblige*, characteristic of established upper classes. Riesman and Glazer have argued that the economically successful upwardly mobile Irish in America have become more conservative as a concomitant of their search for higher status.[3]

• The political orientation of a group whose social class position is higher than their occupational-economic class should be also affected by this discrepancy in class positions. We have already reported hypotheses which

TABLE 3. *Left Vote of Finnish, German and American Workers Related to Their Social Origins*

Father's occupation	Per cent. both Left parties	Finland—1949 Per cent. Social-Democratic	Per cent. Communist	Germany—1953 Per cent. Social-Democratic	U.S. 1952 Per cent. Democratic	U.S. 1948
Manual	81	53	28 (1017)	64 (357)	62 (119)	82 (101)
Nonmanual	42	34	8 (50)	52 (58)	54 (37)	64 (36)
Farm	67	56	11 (378)	38 (75)	58 (87)	89 (64)

though their occupational and economic position would seem to suggest a more conservative outlook.[2] It would be interesting to see how well this would hold in countries with relatively little anti-Semitism, for example, Scandinavia. In such countries where presumably Jews are achieving a higher social class position we would not expect them to have the same extent of leftist political orientation.

[1] Robert Michels, *op. cit.*, pp. 260–261.
[2] Lawrence A. Fuchs, "American Jews and the Presidential Vote," *American Political Science Review*, 49 (1955), pp. 385–401.
[3] David Riesman and Nathan Glazer, "The Intellectuals and the Discontented Class," in D. Bell, ed., *op cit.*, pp. 66–67.

indicate that this may result in rightist political behaviour. On the other hand, however, are suggestions that a discrepancy in status may lead an old but declining upper class to be more liberal in its political orientation. For example, most observers of British politics have suggested that the emergence of Tory Socialism, the willingness to enact reforms which benefited the working class, was a consequence of the hostility of the old English landed aristocracy toward the rising business class, which was threatening its status and power. W. L. Warner reports a situation in which members of old families in an American city characterized by a high degree of emphasis on ascriptive social class supported the efforts of a radical trade union to organize the plants, which were owned by newly wealthy Jews.[1]

Unfortunately, there is no empirical research and little speculation on the conditions which are related to such varying reactions. Much of the speculation and evidence presented above suggests alternative reactions to seemingly similar social pressures. That is, both rightist and leftist political behaviour has been explained as a reaction to discrepancies in status. Three studies of electoral choice offer a similar dilemma. These studies were made by the Survey Research Center of the University of Michigan in 1952, by the UNESCO Institute of Social Science in Cologne, Germany, in 1953, and by the Finnish Gallup Poll in 1949. The Finnish and German studies suggest that middle-class individuals of working-class origin are more likely to vote for the more liberal or left-wing party, than are those who are in the same class position as their fathers. The American data, on the other hand, indicate that successfully upward mobile sons of workers are even more conservative in their party choice than those middle-class individuals whose fathers held occupations comparable to their own[2] (Table 2).

It would be easy to construct some *ex post facto* interpretations for the variations in the consequences of upward social mobility in Finland, Germany and the United States. Rather than do so at this point, we prefer to simply present these results as another illustration of both the complexities and potential rewards inherent in cross-national comparisons.

While the political consequences of upward mobility vary among Germany, Finland and the United States, downward mobility seems to have the same result in the three countries. The working-class sons of middle-class fathers are less likely to back the left parties than are the sons of workers (Table 3).

It is clear from these data that the more consistent the class position of a worker and his father, the more likely he is to accept the dominant political pattern of his class.[3] Also, there can be little doubt that the facts of downward social mobility go at least a part of the way in accounting for conservatives among the working class.

These two studies, like the qualitative and more speculative political analyses reported earlier, only begin to open up the area of the impact of stratification dynamics on political behaviour. The consequences of social mobility, and the determinants of political behaviour are, of course, much more complex than has been hinted above. There is obviously a need for

further exploratory research in order to suggest hypotheses that are better than random guesses. From this point of view, it would be gratifying if public opinion surveys concerning political matters see fit to include, in the future, mobility information as a standard category.

[1] W. L. Warner and J. O. Low, *The Social System of the Modern Factory* (New Haven: Yale University Press, 1947); see also S. M. Lipset and R. Bendix, *op. cit.*, pp. 230–233.

[2] Two other American studies suggest similar conclusions. Maccoby found that upward mobile youth in Cambridge were more Republican than nonmobiles in the class to which the upward mobile moved. Eleanor E. Maccoby, "Youth and Political Choice," *Public Opinion Quarterly*, Spring 1954, p. 35. The M.I.T. Center for International Studies interviewed a random sample of 1,000 American business executives in 1955. These data show that only 5 per cent. of the children of manual workers are Democrats as compared with 10 per cent. Democratic among the executive sons of middle- or upper-class fathers. Hans Speier in his study of white-collar workers in pre-Hitler Germany estimated that 50 per cent. of the members of the Socialist white-collar union were the sons of workers, while less than 25 per cent. of the members of the two conservative white-collar unions were sons of workers. This finding is similar to the pattern in contemporary Germany, see Speier, *op. cit.*, pp. 92–93.

Hence three American studies agree that the upward-mobile are more conservative that the stationary middle-class, while two German and one Finnish study find that the upward-mobile in these countries are more radical than the stationary nonmanual workers.

[3] Similar patterns are suggested in other American studies. Richard Centers reported that workers who have middle-class fathers are more likely to give conservative responses on questions designed to measure liberalism-conservatism, while the successfully upward mobile sons of manual workers do not differ from those in nonmanual occupations whose fathers held similar posts. Centers, *op. cit.*, p. 180. A study of the United Automobile Workers Union found that 78 per cent. of the sons of workers were Democrats in 1952 as compared to 60 per cent. of the off-spring of middle-class fathers. Arthur Kornhauser, *When Labor Votes — A Study of Auto Workers* (New Hyde Park, N.Y.: University Books, 1956). Two studies of trade union membership indicate that mobile individuals are less likely to belong to, or be active in, trade unions. S. M. Lipset and Joan Gordon, "Mobility and Trade Union Membership," in R. Bendix and S. M. Lipset, eds., *op. cit.*, pp. 491–500 and Arnold Tannenbaum, *Participation in Local Unions* (Ann Arbor: University of Michigan Survey Research Center, Mimeo, 1954), p. 292. It is interesting to note that one study based on survey materials, which attempted to relate social mobility to ethnic prejudice in an American city found that both upward and downward mobile persons were more prejudiced than individuals who were in the same social position as their fathers. This result suggests that the socially mobile, whether upward or downward, are more insecure in their dealings with others than those who are stationary in the class structure. It is congruent with our findings that the socially mobile in America are more conservative than the nonmobile at the same level. See Joseph Greenblum and Leonard I. Pearlin, "Vertical Mobility and Prejudice: A Socio-Psychological Analysis," in R. Bendix and S. M. Lipset, eds., *op. cit.*, pp. 480–491.

Intra-Country Variations

OCCUPATIONAL STRATIFICATION AND MOBILITY[1]

Thomas Fox and S. M. Miller

The study of social mobility

THE SOCIOLOGICAL STUDY of social mobility is almost exclusively concerned with occupational mobility. Changes in the distribution of citizenship rights or in social acceptance are not likely to be in the forefront of study of social mobility. Within the investigation of occupational social mobility, primary emphasis is on ranking occupations by prestige levels rather than by indicators of skill, income, or span of control. Occupational prestige indicators, based on surveys of attitudes of a national cross section, are assumed to be adequate summaries of the other dimensions of job positions. The emphasis in present day studies is still chiefly on intergenerational mobility (the relation of son's occupation to father's) rather than on intragenerational mobility (the course of job movement in one individual's career) or of stratum mobility (the movement of one stratum relative to other strata along the relevant dimensions). Thus, the definition of social mobility and the indicators employed to measure it provide only a limited slice of the phenomena commonly regarded as social mobility by other social scientists.[2]

In making comparisons among nations, a leap of courage must be made. Many of the difficulties of individual studies are compounded in comparative perspective. Some national studies are of poor technical quality, but we have no choice of substitutes if we wish to include a particular nation in a comparison. Time periods differ in various studies; occupational titles and ratings are not fully comparable. Consequently, it is important to recognize that *any comparisons are at best only approximations.*

The usual comparison in mobility studies is the movement of sons of manual families into nonmanual occupations.[3] The concern is with vertical mobility, though downward mobility from nonmanual strata into manual strata has been widely neglected. Cross-national studies of manual–nonmanual mobility make the heroic assumption that the manual–nonmanual divide has equal importance in all nations at all times. This assumption is obviously untrue but it is difficult to make comparisons without it. The manual–nonmanual comparison also suffers from a neglect of intra-stratum mobility, e.g., the movement from unskilled to skilled; from the lower levels of the middle class to elite positions. This kind of movement can be substantial and important but is not caught when the manual–nonmanual divide is the focus of attention.

A number of technical problems intrude in international comparisons. The number of strata employed in a study affects the amount of mobility: the more strata, the more mobility. Therefore, for comparative purposes it is necessary to compress categories into a similar number of groupings. This technical need encourages the utilization of manual–nonmanual compressions. Another difficulty is that while we speak of a sons' generation and of a fathers' generation, we do not in actuality have such pure categories. There are fathers and sons in each occupational category but we treat our data as though each could be factored out.

A number of different types of comparisons are possible with the same data. Movement can be viewed from different perspectives and it is easy to become dizzy with perspectives and over-produce results. In the standard mobility matrix, the rows represent the outflow: "What is the occupational distribution of sons born of fathers in a given stratum?" This type of analysis is the usual one. But we can look across the principal diagonal of the matrix and note the degree of inheritance by sons of fathers' occupations. The columns provide inflow data: "What are the social origins of individuals presently in a given occupational stratum?". Now, the same sons are involved in outflow and inflow analyses; the difference is in what base they are related to in computing rates or percentages. For example, an outflow analysis can show that of 1,000 nonmanual sons 250, or 25 percent, move into manual strata. From the point of view of manual strata which are larger than the nonmanual strata say, 2,500 sons, the extent of inflow is only 10 percent. The same movement can have different implications from varying perspectives.

Despite myriad difficulties, comparative studies of

---

[1] This study has been supported by Project 6-25-124 of the National Science Foundation.

[2] *Cf.* S. M. Miller, "Comparative Social Mobility: A Trend Report," *Current Sociology*, Vol. IX, No. 1, 1960, pp. 1–5.

[3] We are interchangeably and loosely using terms like stratum, occupations, and categories.

This article is published here for the first time by permission of the authors. Presented at an International Conference on the Use of Quantitative Political, Social and Cultural Data in Cross-National Comparison.

social mobility have endured. Sorokin, in his classical study of *Social Mobility* in 1927 amassed a great deal of data but it was not subjected to careful, systematic analysis. Yet, his work was prescient in many ways. For almost two decades comparatively little work was done that referred to nations as a whole. David Glass and Theodore Geiger, in their own work and in the work they fostered in the Research Sub-Committee on Social Stratification and Social Mobility, emphasized in the fifties national studies executed with similar concerns and well-developed methodologies. As a result, we now have many more studies of national rates of social mobility. Seymour Martin Lipset and his collaborators, Reinhard Bendix, Hans Zetterberg and Natalie Rogoff Ramsoy, attempted to make sense out of the array of national mobility data by suggesting a basic similarity in the rates of advanced industrial nations. Miller, in his appraisal of the data, emphasized the neglect of downward mobility in most generalizations about mobility, the varied contours of mobility, (e.g., knowledge of manual–nonmanual movement is not revealing about manual–elite movement), and the value of developing typologies of mobility. The work of Peter Blau and Otis Dudley Duncan in making a careful analysis of mobility patterns in the United States based on fresh data in a comparative perspective, may have great significance. At the moment, though, there seems to be a standstill in developing international comparisons of mobility.

The present paper illustrates a few of the various ways of utilizing mobility data. It does not question the international comparability of the data but attempts to improve comparability by restricting analysis to four nations. The concern is with both outflow and inflow. Its particular contribution is that it introduces a new measure which facilitates statements comparing the degree of equality and inequality of mobility among nations.

The manual–nonmanual dichotomy

The conventional profile of social mobility is projected by the manual–nonmanual dichotomy. Table 1 presents profiles for the four nations by way of passage into (inflow mobility) and away from (outflow mobility) the manual and nonmanual strata. Our analysis encompasses both upward and downward mobility in contrast to the more frequent solitary emphasis on upward mobility.[1] Manual inflow and nonmanual outflow illustrate *downward* mobility for sons of nonmanual origins from two points of views — the manual stratum and the nonmanual stratum. Conversely, manual outflow and nonmanual inflow record the *upward* mobility of sons of manual origin into the nonmanual stratum. The importance of qualifying statements about mobility rates by specifying a particular point of reference (inflow or outflow for a particular stratum) is exemplified by studying Table 1.

Beginning with the data on outflow mobility we see that in Great Britain the rate of outflow is greater for the

nonmanual stratum than for the manual. Downward movement is greater than upward movement: this description also applies to Japan and the Netherlands but not the United States where upward mobility predominates.

A comparison of the nations on the outflow indicators shows that the United States has the highest rate of upward movement, i.e., manual to nonmanual. It also has the lowest rate of downward movement from the nonmanual stratum. Great Britain has the most downward movement and is second in terms of upward mobility.

Downward mobility may be more indicative of social fluidity than upward mobility. To illustrate, we

TABLE 1. *Comparative Manual and Nonmanual Inflow and Outflow Mobility (in percentages)*

Nation	MANUAL MOBILITY		NONMANUAL MOBILITY	
	Inflow	Outflow	Inflow	Outflow
Great Britain	24.83	24.73	42.01	42.14
Japan	12.43	23.70	48.00	29.66
Netherlands	18.73	19.77	44.84	43.20
United States	18.06	30.38	32.49	19.55

Source: Data sources for computations are D. V. Glass, *et. al.*, *Social Mobility in Britain* (London: Routledge and Kegan Paul, Inc., 1954), p. 183; Special tabulations of Johannes van Tulder based on the Survey of the Institute for Social Research in the Netherlands; Sigeki Nishihira, "Cross-National Comparative Study on Social Stratification and Social Mobility," (Japan), *Annals of the Institute of Statistical Mathematics*, Vol. VIII, No. 3, 1957, p. 187; Richard Centers, "Occupational Mobility of Urban Occupational Strata," *American Sociological Review*, Vol. XIII, No. 2, April, 1948, p. 138 (limited to sons of urban whites). These social mobility matrices are given in appendix of S. M. Miller, "Comparative Social Mobility," *Current Sociology*, Vol. IX, No. 1, 1960, pp. 1 ff. (Note: in Center's data for the U.S. as cited by Miller above, categories VIII [farm owners or managers] and IX [farm tenant or laborers] which appear only in the sons' generation have been omitted.)

are well aware that the process of industrialization has been associated with a decline in the size of the manual stratum, relative to the nonmanual — a phenomenon contributing to upward intergenerational mobility. Downward movement on the other hand may be evidence that sons are not always entitled to their fathers' social position as heir apparent but must be able in their own right or suffer displacement by more capable individuals from lower social strata.[2] If this argument is valid, then the social structures of Great

[1] Cf. Seymour M. Lipset and Reinhard Bendix, *Social Mobility in Industrial Society* (Berkeley: University of California Press, 1959).

[2] But the possibility of downward mobility by choice can not be denied. In this case the son simply prefers an occupation and "way-of-life" that differs from that of his "origin."

Britain and the Netherlands are less congealed in some respects than in the United States and Japan — contrary to popular opinion.

The inflow patterns pertain to mobility into a stratum. All four nations are characterized by more heterogeneity of social origins in the nonmanual stratum than in the manual. Heterogeneity is measured by the extent to which sons born into another stratum become members of a given stratum. With Herrington C. Bryce, we have elsewhere dealt in depth with the concepts of heterogeneity–homogeneity that are used here.[1] Britain has the highest heterogeneity in the manual stratum as we would expect from its nonmanual pattern of outflow. But the Netherlands with a similar percentage of nonmanual outflow has less heterogeneity in the manual stratum. Even though nonmanual outflow is high in the Netherlands, its compositional effect on Dutch manual inflow is less than in Great Britain because of the relatively larger proportion of manual sons in the Netherlands.

Japan and the United States are similar in their manual occupations. The corresponding Dutch occupational interchange is about 19 percent. The inference is that a virtual exchange of social position occurred between the manual sons moving up and an equal *absolute* number of nonmanual sons moving down.

As we have seen, the nonmanual strata are characterized by higher rates of both inflow and outflow mobility than the manual strata in these countries. Interestingly without a deep-seated change in the occupational distributions among generations, Great Britain and the Netherlands have considerable interchange among social strata. For Japan and the United States, the relative growth of the nonmanual stratum (see Table 2) can account for much of the observed upward mobility. But in Britain and the Netherlands with relatively constant occupational distributions, technological or demand induced mobility fails to explain the fluidity of their respective social structures.

The lower portion of Table 2 pictures changes in occupational structures between generations in greater detail. The elite and middle class were formerly sub-

TABLE 2. *Percentage Distribution of Strata by Fathers' Generation and Sons' Generation*

	GREAT BRITAIN		JAPAN		NETHERLANDS		UNITED STATES	
	Fathers'	*Sons'*	*Fathers'*	*Sons'*	*Fathers'*	*Sons'*	*Fathers'*	*Sons'*
Nonmanual	37.11	37.02	26.74	36.17	29.98	30.87	43.97	52.40
Manual	62.89	62.98	73.26	63.82	70.02	69.13	56.03	47.60
Total	100.00	100.00	100.00	99.99	100.00	100.00	100.00	100.00
Elite	7.98	7.49	11.15	11.74	7.18	11.08	8.92	16.86
Middle class	29.13	29.53	15.59	24.45	22.80	19.79	35.04	35.54
Skilled	38.74	33.91	8.52	12.06	32.65	34.22	29.59	19.50
Semiskilled	13.09	16.95	4.02	7.50	26.41	27.39	20.16	20.33
Unskilled	11.06	12.12	60.72	44.26	10.96	7.52	6.28	7.77
Total	100.00	100.00	100.00	100.01	100.00	100.00	99.99	100.00

Source: See Table 1.

changing occupational patterns. Japan has a lower rate of movement out of the manual stratum than the United States but an even higher degree of nonmanual heterogeneity: almost half the nonmanual workers originated in manual families. The United States has an expanding nonmanual stratum which absorbs many from manual homes and, as the nonmanual outflow figure (19 percent) shows, has the highest level of inheritance of the nonmanual strata.

The data for Great Britain and the Netherlands show little change in the contours of the occupational structure between generations: a contour map which *only approximates* reality is presented in Table 2. In the British manual stratum (Table 1), about 25 percent are of nonmanual backgrounds, "replacing" the 25 percent born in manual families who have moved up into non-

[1] Herrington J. Bryce, S. M. Miller, and Thomas Fox, "The Heterogeneity of Social Classes in Industrial Societies: A Study in Social Mobility," paper presented at the Spring meetings of the Eastern Sociological Associations, New York City, April, 1963.

sumed under the nonmanual category; the skilled, semiskilled, and unskilled collectively composed the manual stratum.

In Great Britain, little change is evident in the sizes of either the elite or middle-class groups — little mobility can be attributed to variations in the relative number of positions within the nonmanual stratum. However the structure within the manual category has altered between generations. The data suggest a decrease in the level of manual skills: the relative size of the skilled substratum has diminished while the semiskilled and unskilled groups have expanded in the sons' generation.

Japan shows little change in the relative size of elites between generations, but a large increase in the middle class. The quality of the manual stratum has shifted upward; the proportion of unskilled declined while both the skilled and semiskilled proportions have increased. Use of the manual classification blankets considerable intra-stratum mobility due to structural changes over time.

The compositional change within the Dutch nonmanual stratum is unusual. Here we note that the relative size of the elite increases, but accompanied by a shrinking middle class. (The other countries portray, at minimum, a moderate middle-class expansion.) Within the manual category, the qualitative trend parallels that in Japan; the unskilled proportion diminishes while that of the skilled and semiskilled increases.

The trend for the elite in the United States shows a large increase, but little change for the middle class. A sharp decline is evident for the skilled group. The semiskilled and unskilled substrata have moderate increments in proportions in the sons' generation. Over half the sons are in the nonmanual stratum, which, as in Japan, is characterized by a large increase in the relative number of nonmanual positions between generations.

Skilled, semiskilled and unskilled outflow into the nonmanual stratum

Table 3 breaks down the manual stratum into integral parts, skilled, semiskilled, and unskilled, for a closer look at the sources of upward mobility into the nonmanual category.

TABLE 3. *Outflow of Sons of Skilled, Semiskilled and Unskilled Origins into the Nonmanual Stratum (in percentages)*

Social origin	Great Britain	Japan	Netherlands	United States
Skilled	29.08	30.19	26.92	38.55
Semiskilled	18.78	29.33	14.79	21.31
Unskilled	16.54	22.42	10.47	21.05

Source: See Table 1.

In Great Britain, the chances of sons of skilled workers entering the nonmanual stratum are less than two times that of semiskilled sons. Unskilled sons have the greatest disadvantage for such movement but not strikingly less than the semiskilled. The data for the Netherlands and the United States roughly parallels that of the British case: all three nations are characterized by a large gap between the skilled and semiskilled components of the manual stratum with a relatively smaller gap between the semiskilled and unskilled substrata.

In Japan there is little difference between the skilled and semiskilled movement into nonmanual occupations although intuitively one would expect the skilled to enjoy a relative advantage over the unskilled for upward mobility; both have considerably better opportunities than the unskilled.

Great Britain, the Netherlands and Japan have quite similar percentages of skilled sons entering the nonmanual stratum, but considerably less than in the United States. Inter-country similarities are less pronounced as we turn to the semiskilled and unskilled groups. Semiskilled outflow in Japan is greater than skilled outflow in the Netherlands and has an 8-percentage-point edge on United States semiskilled outflow,

which in turn is less than 3 points greater than Great Britain and almost 7 points over the Netherlands. Unskilled outflow is similar in Japan and the United States, followed at some distance by Great Britain, and at a much larger interval by the Netherlands.

This table demonstrates the importance of compositional effects. Despite the highest rate of overall manual movement into the nonmanual stratum, the United States ranks but second in terms of semiskilled and unskilled movement into the top stratum. The United States overall manual rank as highest is primarily due to a considerably larger degree of skilled outflow than that observed in the other nations, and to the numerical importance of the skilled component within the manual stratum.

Sources of nonmanual heterogeneity

Table 4 shows the contribution of skilled, semiskilled and unskilled mobility to the composition of the nonmanual stratum. We are now looking at the sources of heterogeneity in social origins among the nonmanual occupations.

TABLE 4. *Sources of Nonmanual Heterogeneity (in percentages)*

Social origin	Great Britain	Japan	Netherlands	United States
Skilled	30.42	7.11	28.47	21.77
Semiskilled	6.64	3.26	12.65	8.20
Unskilled	4.94	37.63	3.71	2.52
Total nonmanual inflow	42.00	48.00	44.83	32.49

Source: See Table 1.

In Great Britain, almost three-quarters of the heterogeneity of the nonmanual stratum is due to the mobility of sons of skilled workers. The semiskilled contribution to nonmanual heterogeneity is slightly higher than the unskilled, but considerably less than the skilled. In the Netherlands, the entry of skilled sons accounts for somewhat less than two-thirds of the nonmanual heterogeneity; the semiskilled sons are decidedly more important than the unskilled. Two-thirds of United States nonmanual heterogeneity is due to the movement of skilled sons; semiskilled sons are three times as numerous in the nonmanual stratum as are unskilled. Japan is an anomaly: unskilled sons are the predominant source of nonmanual heterogeneity. This is largely but not fully due to the high percentage of the Japanese labor force which is classified as unskilled. Except for Japan, the skilled category is the greatest contributor to nonmanual heterogeneity. Movement of the semiskilled is greatest in the Netherlands and the United States.

Elite and middle-class movement into the manual stratum

A breakdown of the nonmanual stratum into the

elite and middle class permits a closer look at the sources of manual heterogeneity. Taking the outflow mobility dimension first, Table 5 gives the percentages of *downward* elite and middle-class mobility.

TABLE 5. *Outflow of Sons of Elite and Middle-Class Origins into the Manual Stratum (in percentages)*

Social origin	Great Britain	Japan	Nether- lands	United States
Elite	17.92	26.92	24.26	14.81
Middle Class	47.62	31.62	49.16	20.75

Source: See Table 1.

The United States and Great Britain have low rates of elite outflow. The low figure for the United States was anticipated from prior observations where we noted nonmanual inheritance to be high. Given the extremely high rate of nonmanual outflow in Great Britain (42.1 percent), a much greater rate of elite outflow would be expected if this substratum is almost as congealed as in the United States. Elite inheritance is lowest in Japan and is similar to the Netherlands in terms of elite outflow.

Middle-class outflow in Great Britain and the Netherlands are similar and high, 50 percent higher than in Japan and more than double that of the United States. The difference between elite and middle-class outflow rates into the manual stratum is greatest in Great Britain, lowest in Japan.

TABLE 6. *Sources of Manual Heterogeneity (in percentages)*

Social origin	Great Britain	Japan	Nether- lands	United States
Elite	2.27	4.70	2.52	2.78
Middle class	22.56	15.28	16.22	15.28
Total manual inflow	24.83	18.06	18.74	18.06

Source: See Table 1.

Table 6 shows the impact on manual heterogeneity by the *downwardly* mobile sons of elite and middle-class origins. For all countries the elite contribution to the composition of the manual stratum is relatively small, less than 5 percent (less than 3 percent if Japan is excepted.) Most of the heterogeneity results from the downward movement of the middle-class origins. Middle-class origins in the manual stratum account for over 20 percent of the sons in this category in Great Britain and over 15 percent for the other countries. The four nations each have a noticeable middle-class origin effect on the composition of the manual stratum but elite representation is almost nil.

[1] Robert A. Feldmesser, *Aspects of Social Mobility in the Soviet Union* (unpublished Ph.D. thesis, Harvard University, 1955), pp. 223–225.

Intra-country equality of mobility opportunity

Within each country, the distribution of opportunities of sons of other social origins entering any given stratum can be studied with the aid of Feldmesser's index of equality of opportunity.[1] This index takes the proportion of sons remaining in their stratum of origin (e.g., nonmanual sons of nonmanual fathers) in each country as 100. The proportions of sons of other origins

TABLE 7. *Indices of Equality of Opportunity for Entry into Elite, Middle Class, Skilled, Semiskilled, and Unskilled Strata*

Equality of opportunity for:	Great Britain	Japan	Nether- lands	United States
Elite				
Elite	100	100	100	100
Middle class	19	39	22	37
Skilled	7	21	20	22
Semiskilled	3	17	6	6
Unskilled	2	18	5	9
$\bar{x}$	26.2	39.0	30.6	34.8
Middle class				
Middle class	100	100	100	100
Elite	88	65	57	51
Skilled	61	41	41	45
Semiskilled	39	43	29	31
Unskilled	36	29	20	27
$\bar{x}$	64.8	55.6	49.4	50.8
Skilled				
Skilled	100	100	100	100
Semiskilled	84	53	64	70
Unskilled	80	18	62	56
Middle class	76	20	68	28
Elite	29	20	39	27
$\bar{x}$	73.8	42.2	66.6	56.2
Semiskilled				
Semiskilled	100	100	100	100
Unskilled	75	23	89	47
Skilled	54	50	46	47
Middle class	36	29	31	21
Elite	16	25	13	8
$\bar{x}$	56.2	45.4	55.8	44.6
Unskilled				
Unskilled	100	100	100	100
Semiskilled	57	33	48	27
Skilled	48	19	28	18
Middle class	23	24	18	6
Elite	7	18	3	5
$\bar{x}$	47.0	38.8	39.4	31.2

entering the given stratum are expressed as ratios to 100. If the proportions or frequencies of sons of all social origins entering any given stratum are equal, all ratios will have the value of 100. In other words, this index examines the proportional representation of all social strata in any given stratum. The further any ratio is from 100, the less opportunity that group has for entering any given stratum than do the sons who inherit the status.

Table 7 presents the indices of intra-country equality of opportunity for the elite, middle class, skilled, semiskilled, and unskilled strata for each of the four nations.

Equality of opportunity in entering the elite and middle-class strata

In Great Britain, sons of middle-class fathers enjoy a distinct advantage over sons of skilled, semiskilled and unskilled in securing membership in the elite stratum. The middle-class sons have almost three times the opportunities of the semiskilled sons (19/7) of entering the elite, six times the opportunities of the semiskilled (19/3), and nine times the chances of the unskilled (19/2). But the son of an elite father has the best opportunity to become an elite himself — his chances are five times greater than for the son of a middle-class father (100/19) and fifty times that for the son of an unskilled father (100/2). Thus equality of opportunity for movement into the elite category appears extremely limited in Great Britain.

The son of a middle-class father in Japan enjoys almost twice the opportunity of a skilled son (39/21) for gaining admission to elite status, and only slightly more than twice the advantages of the semiskilled and unskilled (respectively, 39/17 and 39/18). Japanese sons of middle-class origins are more than one-third of the way toward achieving elite entry equality with the sons of elite fathers (100/39).

In the Netherlands, sons of middle-class origins have very little advantage over the sons of skilled origins in securing elite status, their chances are almost equal (22/20). But skilled and middle-class sons have considerably better chances of entering the elite than the semiskilled or unskilled sons. The close proximity of the opportunities of the middle-class and skilled for elite entry suggest, as a possibility, that these groups are more closely related to each other than to the elite category.

Turning now to the United States, we find that here, as in Japan, the sons of middle-class fathers have traveled more than a third of the route leading to equality of opportunity with sons of elite fathers (100/37). Middle-class advantage over offspring of the skilled exists but is less than double the chances of the latter (37/22). The son of a skilled father has almost four times the opportunity of a semiskilled to reach the elite stratum (22/6). (Although the index for equality of opportunity for entry into the elite in the United States is greater for the unskilled than for the semiskilled, its validity may be questioned and perhaps attributed to weaknesses in the original study.)

An average value for the index is given below the last stratum for equality of opportunity of movement into the elite (and for each strata below) but can only be compared within countries, not between them. The data in Table 7 then, do not say that equality of opportunity is greatest in Japan and least in Great Britain.

Equality of opportunity in entering the skilled, semiskilled, and unskilled strata

One of the most striking findings, with the exception of Japan, is that the averages of the indices of equality of opportunity are largest within each country for entry into the skilled stratum, not the middle class, which might be expected. Lloyd Reynolds has recently argued (with respect to the manual stratum) that there is a tendency for the skilled category to become more of a closed group, with the opportunities of movement from unskilled and semiskilled occupations into the skilled stratum declining.[1] Although our data are not appropriate for directly questioning this hypothesis, our calculations for Great Britain, Netherlands and the United States show that the skilled stratum is *the group* in which equality of opportunity is the greatest.

Turning to the other end of the social spectrum from the elites — the unskilled — we find an interesting pattern in the USA. The USA shows a relatively lower degree of equality of access to this occupational substratum than do the other nations. At this end of the occupational ladder, low access has different implications than it does at the other end. At the high end, it shows the inability of those below the elite to overcome the barriers. For at the low end, it represents the pooling of the unskilled, their low ability to leave and the relative invulnerability of the higher strata to such drastic falls in position.[2]

Inter-country equality of opportunity

Feldmesser's index of equality of opportunity for each of the four nations can be made directly comparable by selecting the proportion of occupational inheritance within any given country as the base of the index for each stratum. This measure, developed by Fox, gives the inter-country equality of opportunity indices for all countries, relative to the nation selected as the base. Great Britain has been used as the base nation for this paper. If the index for, say, elite inheritance is above 100 in the United States, occupational inheritance would be greater in the United States than in Great Britain with the difference between the respective index values indicating how much greater. (The values of the comparative indices for the base-country Great Britain in Table 8 are the same as in Table 7.)

Elite stratum comparisons

Table 8 clearly shows that the ability of sons of elite fathers to inherit their fathers' socioeconomic status is greatest in the United States, 24 percent greater than in Great Britain. The proportion of elite inheritance is second greatest in the Netherlands — least in Japan. Middle-class and skilled sons in the United States also have better chances of becoming elites than their counterparts in the other three nations. The USA has high inheritance and high accessibility. The middle class in Japan has almost double the opportunity of the

[1] Lloyd G. Reynolds, "Economics of Labor", p. 277 in Howard S. Ellis, ed., *A Survey of Contemporary Economics* (Philadelphia: American Economic-Assoc., Blakiston Co., 1948), pp. 255–287.
[2] *Cf.* Lipset and Bendix, *op. cit.*, pp. 57–58 and 64–68.

British middle class of gaining elite membership and 30 percent better than the Netherlands middle class. Skilled opportunity for elite entry in the Netherlands is about three and one-half that of the skilled in Great Britain — one and one-fourth that in Japan. The Japanese semiskilled and unskilled have the advantage over their contemporaries in Great Britain, the Netherlands, and the United States in terms of their chances of becoming elites — almost the opportunities of the middle class in Great Britain.

TABLE 8. *Comparative Indices of Equality of Opportunity for Entry into Elite, Middle Class, Skilled, Semiskilled and Unskilled Strata (Base = Great Britain)*

Equality of opportunity for:

Elite	Great Britain	Japan	Nether-lands	United States
Elite	100	86	119	124
Middle class	19	34	26	46
Skilled	7	18	24	27
Semiskilled	3	15	7	7
Unskilled	2	15	6	12
$\bar{X}$	26.2	33.6	36.4	43.2
Middle class				
Middle class	100	143	92	137
Elite	88	93	53	70
Skilled	61	59	38	62
Semiskilled	39	61	27	42
Unskilled	36	42	18	37
$\bar{X}$	64.8	79.6	45.6	69.6
Skilled				
Skilled	100	111	112	81
Semiskilled	84	59	72	56
Unskilled	80	19	69	45
Middle class	76	22	77	22
Elite	29	22	43	23
$\bar{X}$	73.8	46.6	74.6	45.4
Semiskilled				
Semiskilled	100	81	148	144
Unskilled	75	19	132	67
Skilled	54	40	69	68
Middle class	36	23	45	30
Elite	16	20	19	12
$\bar{X}$	56.2	36.6	82.6	64.2
Unskilled				
Unskilled	100	233	74	144
Semiskilled	57	78	35	39
Skilled	48	44	21	26
Middle class	23	56	14	9
Elite	7	42	2	7
$\bar{X}$	47.0	90.6	29.2	45.0

Strikingly, the averages of the indices for elite entry show opportunity to be greatest in the United States (more than one and a half that in Great Britain), followed at some distance by the Netherlands, then Japan and Great Britain. When we examined the intra-country equality of opportunity in Table 7 (within countries), Japan had the highest rate of intra-country elite equality, followed by the United States. This means that in Japan, there is less difference between the proportions of various strata entering the elite and the proportion of elite inheritance. But in the United States (with its expanding elite) the *actual* proportions of the different strata entering the elite are greater than those in Japan. In other words, relatively larger proportions of non-elite and elite origin sons tend to become members of the elite stratum in the United States than in Japan.

Middle class comparisons

Middle-class stratum inheritance is proportionally highest in Japan, then the United States, both with a degree of middle-class inheritance at least 35 percent greater than in Great Britain. The Netherlands has the lowest proportion of inheritance. Sons of elite fathers have the highest relative chance of falling into the middle class in Japan and England. This might be expected since elite inheritance was lowest in Japan and England, therefore, relatively more sons of elites experience downward mobility of one step to the middle class.

Strikingly, although United States elite inheritance was the highest, then closely followed by the Netherlands, United States sons of elite fathers have considerably greater relative likelihood of entering the middle class than in the Netherlands.

There is little difference between the proportion of skilled entering the middle class in the United States and Great Britain, with Japan in close proximity. But much less opportunity for skilled movement into the middle class exists in the Netherlands.

Semiskilled and unskilled opportunity for middle-class movement is greatest in Japan and the United States, then Great Britain. The opportunity for unskilled entry into the middle class in Japan is about two and a half times as great as in the Netherlands.

Skilled comparisons

When the focus of attention shifts to comparison of equality of opportunity for entry into the skilled category, the United States loses much of its former prominence, showing considerably less skilled inheritance than the base-country Great Britain and the other two nations. Dutch skilled inheritance is slightly greater than Japan; both are about 10 percent greater than in Great Britain. The proportion of semiskilled entering the skilled category is highest in Great Britain, strangely enough, with this holding also for sons of unskilled origins. In the Netherlands, the opportunity of semi-skilled and unskilled movement into the skilled stratum is considerably less than in Great Britain but well above that in the United States and Japan. Japanese sons of semiskilled fathers have but a slight advantage over those in the United States. The Japanese unskilled are the most disadvantaged, having but about one-half the chances of the United States unskilled to enter the skilled stratum and one-third the Dutch unskilled chances. The unskilled in Great Britain have four times the proportion of sons in the skilled categories as in Japan.

Overall, averages of the indices show the chance to become a member of the skilled stratum is highest in the Netherlands and Great Britain, with both countries ranking well above Japan and the United States.

Semiskilled comparisons

The Netherlands and the United States have considerably greater semiskilled inheritance than Great Britain. In turn, Japan has about 20 percent less than Great Britain. The proportion of unskilled entering the semiskilled stratum in the Netherlands is double that in the United States, less than twice that in Great Britain. Skilled and unskilled chances for semiskilled stratum entry are about equal in the United States. The middle classes and elites are less represented in the semiskilled stratum.

Unskilled comparisons

Unskilled socioeconomic inheritance in Japan is two and one-third that in Great Britain — significantly greater than in the United States, the second highest nation on unskilled inheritance. Dutch unskilled inheritance is but about one-half that in the United States. Japanese unskilled inheritance of such astronomical proportions is in part explained by the tremendous size of this group in the Japanese social structure. But the most astounding index value for the unskilled stratum occurs for the elite chance in Japan of becoming a member of the unskilled. Elite entry into the unskilled in Japan is six times greater than in the United States and Great Britain, twenty times that in the Netherlands. The unskilled entry values in Japan for skilled, middle-class and elite movement are similar within a limited range, whereas the spread between these social strata is considerably greater for the other three countries. In the case of Great Britain, we find, however, that the proportion of the skilled entering the unskilled is somewhat greater than in Japan, but around twice that in the United States and Netherlands.

CONCLUSIONS?

We wish that we could offer a concise and parsimonious explanation of the variations in the rates of social mobility both within and between the countries. But we cannot. The following fragmentary observations are substitutes for all-encompassing empirical generalizations or explanatory theorems.

There are a host of different ways of measuring mobility. And mobility has many varied contours. Mobility statements, as we have said elsewhere,[1] must be specific — indicative of a particular frame of reference, e.g., only manual into nonmanual; or the degree of heterogeneity of the elite substratum. As a corollary, patterns of mobility seem to differ in different parts of the class structure. A statement of accessibility to elite status is inadequate for describing (let alone understanding) accessibility to the unskilled stratum. Inheritance and accessibility are different dimensions of similar phenomena.

Aware of the pitfalls inherent in mobility analysis, we still find it a fruitful area of research. We think it can be further extended, as we plan to do, attempting to see under what conditions of social mobility, political stability is greatest. If political scientists and others would give us indicators of political stability, it would be helpful.

Mobility analysis is not an "open sesame" to understanding everything — studies of fertility have shown this. We think American sociologists have a dreadful predilection to explain *everything* in terms of status panic or reward, instability or stability. This status concern may be more revealing about sociologists than about societies! But we believe that the study of social mobility, especially if broadly conceived, gives us a picture, though not complete, of changes taking place in socio-occupational patterns. And it gives snapshots of different periods of time, which if used judiciously, should be illuminating.

[1] Miller, *op. cit.*, p. 5; Bryce, Miller, and Fox, *loc. cit.*

Family and Mobility

William J. Goode

FAR MORE IMPORTANT than the political revolutions that shed blood and topple governments here and there in every major region of the world is the social revolution of our time, that spares no nation. If we focus unduly on the swift change in the political constitution of a nation, or the sudden appearance of factories, we may fail to see that both of these alterations, which do set in motion a train of significant consequences, are themselves created by subtle but massive social forces.

Machines and factories are built by men, and first appear as *ideas*. Moreover, they are successful only if men's social habits, expectations, and aspirations come to judge that industrialization is worthwhile. In so complex a network of causation, it is nearly meaningless to speak of a single cause, such as "industrialization" or "urbanization," but certainly the first alterations occur in men's inner life, in their ideas, in the family influences that mould the child who as an adult will become an innovator.

Perhaps one of the prime alterations, both as a massive social event and an individual aspiration, is that everywhere people seek to change the stratification system, the pattern of economic, social, and power rankings of families in their society. That keen student of eighteenth century arrangements of power and privilege, Jacques Casanova, remarked that no people who were permitted to bear arms ever tolerated for long an unjust, severe burden of taxation. Whether a high level of education leads to democracy is open to question, but clearly when the lower social strata obtain power, they demand the right to education as well. In every new nation, whatever its political position, the surge and sweep of power is partly directed against the family inheritance of class advantages. In almost all nations, however tyrannical and dictatorial their political past, the voices of the lower strata are increasingly listened to, and they demand at least the chance to rise.

To inquire into the confusing web of relations between family and stratification is therefore to seek an understanding of the core processes of any society and its changes, at once of prime importance and difficulty. The family is the keystone of the stratification system, and this in turn is made up of the rewards granted by the society for filling its posts. How rigidly the family system enforces its rules determines how rigidly people are kept in the positions ascribed to them at birth.

When, in the modern world, more men and women rebel against the older regulations about mate choice, consulting their elders in personal and occupational decisions, or how to rear their children, they are also trying to free themselves from the shackles that prevent free ascent up the social ladder, or mobility in space. By altering the rules of inheritance, they change both the structure of the family and a stratification system which rests on property. In so doing, they cause family dissension and fission as well as personal tragedy, while perhaps allowing more effective men to move into positions of importance.

Stratification systems place *families* rather than individuals in various social positions high and low, because the family is the social unit, because all members of the conjugal family are socially defined as being at the same social level, and because children are given the rank of their families. But this is only a static view, yielding some sort of social pyramid, made up of the many family units of the society, with all their more or less common traits at any given level. In most modern societies, most people are at the bottom of the pyramid, and few at the top. In a society with rigidly defined castes, the barriers between the layers of the pyramid will be rigid and supposedly impenetrable. In societies with different ethnic groups, each such group will have its own internal class system, which fits into the larger pyramid rather imperfectly. Some would claim that the modern industrial society does not have a pyramidal form; rather, it is diamond-shaped, with a large middle class and a small lower class.

But even this static view only presents the characteristics of families at various social strata. We have no clear understanding of *how* they came to be there, or how they acquired those traits. Perhaps families as such contribute *nothing* to that process, and merely serve as conduits, as channels, passing the cultural traits of one generation to the next, moved by political and economic forces upward or downward, a merely passive system.

Whether family systems and behavior affect class systems or vice versa, as participants in both we wish to understand how they operate. Whichever direction the causal influences run, we seek to trace them out, but to

This is an abbreviated version of a report, *Family and Mobility*, written under a grant from the Institute of Life Insurance, N.Y., 1964.

do so, we shall have to abandon a simple listing of family traits as they appear in different strata. Instead, we shall make the strategically more difficult but fruitful step of looking for connections between family and social *mobility*. By focusing on movement and change, we can see more clearly the *processes* by which families are later placed in one or another social position. Both families and social mobility systems change, and we should see in which ways they alter together, if indeed they correlate at all.

To see some of the problems in such a step, and as an aid in clarifying a research program, let us consider in brief form some of the notable correlations between class position and various traits. Here are a few, drawn from a wide range of inquiries.

Toward the higher social strata, people are taller, healthier, heavier, and have higher I.Q.'s.

Divorce rates and rates of juvenile delinquency are lower toward the upper strata.

The birth rate is lower toward the upper strata in most countries; but the differences between the bottom and the top strata are becoming smaller in industrialized societies; within any *given* social stratum, the wealthier families have more children; and in some countries the upper strata may have had a higher birth rate.

The age at marriage is higher toward the upper social strata; but in the past in most countries the nobility married *earlier*.

In the U.S., middle-class adolescents are more likely than lower-class adolescents to engage in petting; but the latter are more likely to engage in sexual intercourse.

The better educated wives in the U.S. are more likely than the less educated to experience orgasm in sexual intercourse; but generally toward the upper social strata, the frequency of marital sexual intercourse is lower.

Middle- and upper-class husbands have greater authority over their wives and children than do lower-class husbands; in Western countries, nevertheless, the ideology and values of middle- and upper-class husbands are more likely to be permissive and egalitarian.

Upper- and middle-class families control more fully the social, dating, and courtship behavior of their children.

Toward the upper social strata, men and women travel greater distances on the average to obtain spouses.

Toward the lower social strata, a higher percentage of total social activity takes place within the kin network, but the upper social strata interact with a larger number of kin.

These items, as we shall see, by no means exhaust the findings of research, because almost *any* social characteristic of individuals or families is associated in some way — negatively or positively — with class position.[1] However, these items vary greatly in significance for mobility processes, and perhaps most could be under-

stood better if we sought those processes directly, rather than trying to unravel each of such individual traits, to see what it might contribute to mobility.

Moreover, some of these traits (like intelligence) may be a *causal* factor in moving or maintaining the individual and his family at a higher or lower social rank; while others may be a resultant of having *been* socially mobile — for example, the breaking of family ties when some members of a family rise in social rank far above the rest.

We would, then, make a division of the problem, looking separately for a) factors that *facilitate* upward *or* downward movement of families and individuals, and b) the *consequences* for family structure when families do rise or fall. Specifically, looking at many societies, are certain types of family structures and systems more likely to be found in socioeconomic systems of high mobility? Most contemporary experts believe, for example, that an industrial system generates high rates of social mobility, and is also associated with a certain type of family system, the small conjugal family made up of a married couple with their children and with few strong kin ties with an extended network of relatives. On the other hand, the classical Chinese society exhibited considerable mobility, and yet its family system was a patriarchal, patrilineal pattern with great kin extension (called "clans" in the literature).

For this type of problem, time data are necessary but rarely available. A cross section of families at one time may not, for example, tell us accurately just what the time trends are. For example, it is difficult to ascertain how much social mobility is occurring over the span of a generation, from the knowledge that, say, 40 percent of the elite in one generation came from non-elite families. It is possible that a high percentage of brothers of the present elite with elite parents *lost* their elite positions; or, the number of high positions may have risen greatly (as has happened in Western industrial countries) so that the "new men" did not displace many of the older elite. In classical China, a high proportion of the official elite at any given time were "new men," but these made up few of the total number in the working force. Just how much *total* mobility there was, we cannot ever know.

This technical problem suggests another, related gap in our knowledge. Most attempts to measure social mobility begin with a sample of successful men — taken from *Who's Who*, *American Men of Science*, or similar compilations. From questionnaire data, we find out, as noted above, what percentage of them came from which socioeconomic strata. For example, we know that about 78 percent of all saints had upper-class origins, that most Nobel Prize winners came from families distinguished in the professions, government, and science.

[1] For a brief but relatively systematic statement of how these variables interact, see my *The Family*, N.Y.: Prentice-Hall, 1964, chs. 3, 4, 8; see also Seymour M. Lipset and Reinhard Bendix, *Social Mobility in Industrial Society*, Berkeley: University of California Press, 1959, chs. 9, 10.

However, we do *not* learn about two equally import-and groups: *a*) The men at similar levels who did not rise to eminence; and   *b*) the men who began with substantial advantages but moved downward in the social scale. We would like to know, for example, what happened to the brothers of a large sample of upper-class men. Or, in pragmatic terms, it is a measure of how open the mobility system is in a given society, when we can say how much energy, intelligence, and training are required for a family to maintain its social position for more than one generation. Or, if two young people are equal in their competence, and dedication, how much easier is it for an upper-class boy to remain in that position through adulthood, than for a lower-class boy to rise to such a position?

For over two thousand years, social philosophers have devoted some attention to the processes and problems in social mobility. Several implicit principles are discernible in these discussions. One of these is that a society will operate better if its best talent is given adequate training and placed in the higher positions of the nation, where skills can be fully utilized.

Second, philosophers have generally suggested that the amount of mobility is not *enough*. Plato makes the suggestion, for example, that since families retard individual improvement and full opportunity for personal development, we must abolish the family system. So radical a solution has not been common, but almost every thinker who has imagined a utopia has made several suggestions as to how the talented might be discovered among the lower social strata, and then given the training that would maximize their growth and thus yield the fullest return to the society.

Another principle is somewhat less common, and perhaps less explicit, the criticism that the wrong *criteria* have been used for placing people in their various social positions. Specifically, it has been understood that for the most part people were *born* into their social positions, thus assuming the rank of their families, but social position, it is often asserted, *ought* to be based upon intellectual and moral qualities — while inferior people in fact can be found at the upper levels, just as superior ones may be born in the lower levels.

It is only since World War II that a substantial amount of information about the *amount* of ability has been developed. A goodly number of international comparisons have been made, and though not all the technical problems noted above have been solved, available data have become more precise and more comparable. These findings are too complex to sum-marize here, but a few highlights are relevant for our subsequent analysis. They also cast some doubt on commonly held assumptions about social mobility.

These assumptions deserve brief mention here. The most important is really a pair of contradictory assump-tions, often held by the same person at different times. These are   *1*) almost any young man with ambition

and talent can rise to the top in this country — this is a version of the "rags to riches" ideology; and   *2*) that class barriers are fairly strong, so that the chances of such a man rising far are rather low. As might be expected, the former belief is more widely held among the successful strata in the population.

Another assumption is that the opportunities for upward social mobility in the United States have declined somewhat over the past generation, and especi-ally since the closing of the frontier at the end of the nineteenth century. A third assumption, related to it, is that nevertheless America is the land of opportunity, and that the chances of rising from the lower social strata to the upper are much greater here than in even the technologically advanced European countries.

Related to this is the further assumption that wide-spread opportunity was fairly uncommon in all parts of the world until recently, and that mobility was very low in the old traditional societies both in Europe and in Asia. Thus the stereotype of Japan, India, and China is that everyone remained at the social level of the family in which he was born. The rigidity of class lines is described in many historical discussions as well as in accounts of the great Eastern civilizations.

It is necessary now to cast doubt on all of these assumptions though not all of them can be fully contradicted.

The vast amount of research on social mobility since World War I now permits us to make comparisons among a wide range of nations with respect to both upward mobility and downward mobility. In assessing these data it should be kept in mind that the use of only two large categories (manual and nonmanual) under-states the total amount of mobility. Thus if an individual moves from a lower white-collar position to a managerial position, this is recorded as no change at all; similarly if a man moves from agricultural or unskilled factory work to a skilled trade, this is recorded as no change. Thus, these categories do some injustice to the amount of mobility, but they do permit a rough comparison to be made.[1]

Several findings emerge from these studies. The first is partly a matter of perspective. In the following tables, we learn how much upward and downward mobility there is in a wide variety of countries: What percentage of men moved into white-collar jobs, after having been born in a family whose head was a manual laborer; or what percentage of men made the downward trek in the generation between father and son.

Before commenting on these tables, in which about one-fourth to one-third of the men in the working force cross the line between white-collar and manual jobs, let us also look at more detailed figures from several countries. As can be seen, when the *number* of categories is larger, the amount of apparent mobility is greater, since the distance traveled is less. A very high proportion of all men do *not* remain in exactly the same occupational category as their father.

As Evelyn Waugh has commented, the less advantaged

---

[1] Tables from data in S. M. Miller, "Comparative Social Mobility," *Current Sociology*, IX (Number 1, 1960), pp. 34–36.

TABLE I. *Nonmanual Sons of Manual and Working-class Fathers (in percentages)*

	(1) Manual into nonmanual	(2) Working classes into nonmanual
I. National data		
Denmark	24.1	*
Finland	11	*
France I	30.1	34.9
France II	29.6	32.9
Great Britain	24.8	*
Hungary	14.5	21.8
Italy	8.5	*
Japan	23.7	*
Netherlands	19.6	*
Norway	23.2	25.8
Puerto Rico	14.3	18.7
Sweden	25.5	29.3
USA I	28.8	*
USA II	28.7	*
West Germany	20.0	21.2
II. Urban data		
Australia (Melbourne)	24.1	*
Belgium I (St-Martens-Latem)	5.7	6.4
Belgium II (Mont-Saint-Guibert)	30.9	*
Brazil (Sao Paulo)	29.4	*
India (Poona)	27.3	*
III. Special data		
USSR (emigrés)	*	34.9

* Unavailable.

TABLE Ia. *Manual Working-class Sons of Nonmanual Fathers (in percentages)*

	(1) Nonmanual into manual	(2) Nonmanual into working classes
I. National data		
Denmark	36.8	*
Finland	24.0	*
France I	20.5	18.2
France II	26.9	25.9
Great Britain	42.1	*
Hungary	27.5	25.8
Italy	34.4	*
Japan	29.7	*
Netherlands	43.2	*
Norway	28.6	27.9
Puerto Rico	42.7	35.6
Sweden	27.7	25.7
USA I	19.7	18.6
USA II	22.6	*
West Germany	29.0	28.2
II. Urban data		
Australia (Melbourne)	37.1	*
Belgium I (St-Martens-Latem)	8.9	7.1
Belgium II (Mont-Saint-Guibert)	3.4	*
Brazil (Sao Paulo)	18.5	*
India (Poona)	26.9	*
III. Special data		
USSR (emigrés)	15.0	12.8

* Unavailable.

TABLE Ib. *Inequality of Opportunity*

	(1) Nonmanual into nonmanual (stability)	(2) Manual into nonmanual	(3) Index of inequality $\frac{(1)}{(2)}$
	%	%	
Australia (Melbourne)	62.9	24.1	261
Belgium I (St-Martens-Latem)	91.1	5.7	398
Belgium II (Mont-Saint-Guibert)	96.6	30.9	313
Brazil (Sao Paulo)	81.5	29.4	277
Denmark	63.2	24.1	262
Finland	76.0	11.0	691
France I	79.5	30.1	164
France II	73.1	29.6	247
Great Britain	57.9	24.8	134
Hungary	72.5	14.5	500
India (Poona)	73.1	27.3	268
Italy	63.5	8.5	747
Japan	70.3	23.7	297
Netherlands	56.8	19.6	290
Norway	71.4	23.2	308
Puerto Rico	57.3	14.3	401
Sweden	72.3	25.5	284
USA I	80.3	28.8	279
USA II	77.4	28.7	270
USSR (emigrés)	85.0	34.9	244
West Germany	71.0	20.0	355

social strata commonly complain that the barriers to mobility are great, that the Establishment takes great pains to keep out the talented men who wish to rise. However, by contrast, the elite feel that they are being flooded by the newly arrived men who have risen from the lower strata. He suggests that this is a matter of perspective, and that both are correct. The men toward the lower strata see only a small percentage of their peers rising. The men in the upper strata, who are few in number, may feel pressed by the newly arrived men and their families, simply because their *percentage* of the total in this small stratum appears to be large. We noted this point earlier with respect to the technical problem of measuring the amount of mobility. Note too, that if the top-most stratum constitutes only about 1 or 2 percent of the national population, but a substantial percentage of that stratum is recruited from the lower social levels (for example in Imperial China, 30 percent to 45 percent), then in fact the chances of movement from a lower level to a high level may be extremely low, simply because the numerical proportions are so disparate.

Thus, if in most industrial nations most sons of white-collar fathers hold that rank, or most people move one step in a seven-step pyramid, whether we decide this is a large amount of stability or immobility will depend upon our judgment as to how much there *ought to be*. If one-third to one-fourth white-collar sons have moved downward, shall we consider this a large or a small amount?

Thus even when we limit ourselves to the gross movement from white-collar to laboring classes or vice versa, a substantial amount of movement seems to take place. Moreover, in a majority of nations for which data are available *downward* mobility equals or exceeds

TABLE 2. *Occupational Inheritance and Mobility in a Representative National Sample of the American Population, 1947*[1]

| | Father's occupation (in percentages) | | | | | | | | |
Son's occupation	Professional	Business	White-collar	Skilled	Semiskilled	Service	Farmer	Nonfarm labor	Don't know
Professional	23	24	10	13	5	5	17	2	1
Business	4	31	9	18	8	3	25	2	0
White-collar	9	23	15	21	10	3	16	3	0
Skilled	3	7	4	30	14	5	29	7	1
Semiskilled	2	11	6	19	19	3	32	7	1
Domestic and personal service	4	6	3	20	12	8	28	12	7
Farmer	2	2	2	3	4	0	84	3	0
Nonfarm labor	3	12	0	9	17	1	32	19	7

TABLE 2a. *Occupational Inheritance and Mobility in a Representative Sample of the Urban American Population, 1945*

| | Sons in various occupations (in percentages) | | | | | | | | |
Occupation of father	Large-business owners and managers	Professional	Small-business owners and managers	White-collar	Farm owners and managers	Skilled	Semiskilled	Farm tenant or laborer	Unskilled
Large-business owners and managers	50	19	6	25	0	0	0	0	0
Professional	15	32	17	10	5	12	5	2	2
Small-business owners and managers	10	11	32	24	3	8	10	1	1
White-collar	8	9	10	45	6	9	7	1	5
Skilled	6	6	8	17	4	31	20	1	7
Semiskilled	1	2	6	11	4	22	43	1	10
Unskilled	0	6	5	10	4	17	20	1	37

TABLE 2b. *Australia (Melbourne)*

Fathers	I		II		III		IV		Totals	
I. Employer and self-employed	35.6		24.4		24.4		15.6		100%	
		16		11		11		7		45
II. White collar	22.7		45.4		13.6		18.2		100	
		5		10		3		4		22
III. Skilled	10.0		10.0		50.0		30.0		100	
		2		2		10		6		20
IV. Semiskilled	0.0		26.5		20.6		52.9		100	
		0		9		7		18		34
	19.0		26.4		25.6		28.9		100	
Totals		23		32		31		35		121

Time: 1949–50(?).
Unit: Males in Melbourne, Australia.
Comment: Nonmanual (I) Employer and self-employed.
　　　　　　　　(II) White-collar.
　　　　　Manual (III) Skilled labor.
　　　　　　　　(IV) Semiskilled labor.

[1] Data in Tables 2–2h reported in S. M. Miller, "Comparative Social Mobility: A Trend Report and Bibliography," *Current Sociology*, IX (No. 1, 1960).

TABLE 2c. *Belgium II (Mont-Saint-Guibert)*

	Fathers	I	II	III	Sons IV	V	VI	Totals
I.	Merchants and artisans	30.4	7.1	35.7	14.3	12.5	—	100%
		17	4	20	8	7	—	56
II.	Officials	—	35.8	28.6	21.4	7.1	7.1	100
		—	5	4	3	1	1	14
III.	White-collar employees	14.7	9.8	58.5	12.2	4.8	—	100
		6	4	24	5	2	—	41
IV.	Skilled workers	9.4	—	21.3	38.7	30.6	—	100
		7	—	16	29	23	—	75
V.	Semiskilled, unskilled workers and farm labor	11.6	—	19.5	36.4	32.5	—	100
		9	—	15	28	25	—	77
VI.	Independent farmers	6.1	12.1	18.2	21.2	27.3	15.1	100
		2	4	6	7	9	5	33
	Totals	13.8	5.8	28.8	27.0	22.6	2.0	100
		41	17	85	80	67	6	296

Time: 1953.
Unit: Male heads of households in Mont-Saint-Guibert, Belgium.
Comments: Nonmanual (I) Merchants and artisans.
                     (II) Officials.
                     (III) White-collar employees.
            Manual (IV) Skilled workers.
                     (V) Semiskilled and unskilled workers and farm labor.
      Agricultural (VI) Independent farmers

upward mobility. Indeed, it can be ascertained from the data now available that in some nations there is high downward *and* high upward mobility; some have high downward and low upward mobility; almost as many have low downward mobility and high upward mobility; and at least two samples have been drawn that suggest that there may be both low downward and low upward mobility.

Current research has attempted to ascertain what are the socioeconomic conditions which generate these very great differences in the mobility patterns. As yet, data on these conditions do not explain the movement, and we must consider further the competitive process that is intrinsic to the static picture of stratification at any given time.

Ultimately, any stratification system is based upon some pattern of *evaluation*. In the early Middle Ages, class position was placed in part upon property ownership and in part upon religious learning and even saintliness. In the period just prior to that, perhaps from the ninth to the twelfth centuries, family histories are short: Courage and skill in war played a very great part in establishing a family in high place or toppling it from that place. In Imperial China, movement upward was based upon a knowledge of the classics, calligraphy, philosophy, and general humanistic learning, tested by successive examinations that were set by the Imperial bureaucracy.

However, no matter what the basis for the stratification — skill, honor, courage and success in war, technical

TABLE 2d. *Brazil (Sao Paulo)*

	Fathers	I	II	III	Sons IV	V	VI	Totals
I.	Professional and high administrative	56.9	20.7	17.2	5.2	0.0	0.0	100%
		33	12	10	3	—	—	58
II.	Managerial and executive	23.3	41.7	26.7	5.0	3.3	0.0	100
		14	25	16	3	2	—	60
III.	Inspectional, supervisory and other nonmanual high grades	9.6	11.8	50.4	15.6	11.8	0.7	100
		13	16	68	21	16	1	135
IV.	Inspectional, supervisory and routine grades of nonmanual lower grades	2.8	13.8	13.4	34.1	28.1	3.2	100
		6	30	39	74	61	7	217
V.	Skilled manual	2.0	5.6	7.6	18.1	53.2	9.8	100
		5	16	26	45	132	24	248
VI.	Semiskilled and unskilled manual	0.3	2.7	8.6	12.1	42.0	31.2	100
		1	9	29	41	142	116	338
	Totals	6.8	10.2	17.8	17.7	33.4	14.0	100
		72	108	188	187	353	148	1056

Unit: Males in Sao Paulo, Brazil.
Comments: Elite I (I) Professional and high administrative.
           Elite II (II) Managerial and executive.
  Middle classes (III) Higher grades of inspectional, supervisory and other nonmanual.
                   (IV) Lower grade of inspectional, supervisory and routine grades of nonmanual.
          Manual (V) Skilled manual.
                   (VI) Semiskilled and unskilled manual.

TABLE 2e. *India (Poona)*

Fathers	I	II	III	IV	V	Sons VI	VII	VIII	IX	X	Totals
I. Owners of factories	73.1	3.9	7.8	—	3.9	3.9	—	—	7.8	—	100%
	19	1	2	—	1	1	—	—	2	—	26
II. Higher professional, business and administrative	3.2	31.9	5.3	28.7	16.0	7.6	1.1	2.1	2.1	2.1	100
	3	30	5	27	15	7	1	2	2	2	94
III. Medium merchants	9.0	2.6	43.5	7.5	7.5	10.9	6.4	2.3	6.0	4.5	100
	24	7	116	20	20	29	17	6	16	12	267
IV. Intermediate professional, business and administrative	0.9	10.6	2.7	25.7	26.1	16.0	4.0	5.3	3.1	5.8	100
	2	24	6	58	59	36	9	12	7	13	226
V. Clerks and shop assistants	—	6.1	1.8	14.5	42.4	14.6	3.6	7.3	3.7	6.1	100
	—	10	3	24	70	24	6	12	6	10	165
VI. Highly skilled and supervisory	—	1.0	2.7	4.2	7.3	63.5	3.9	5.4	6.6	5.8	100
	—	2	7	11	19	165	10	14	17	15	260
VII. Small business	2.4	1.1	13.8	2.1	9.8	8.8	40.1	5.0	8.0	9.0	100
	9	4	52	8	37	33	151	19	30	34	377
VIII. Lower professional, administrative positions	0.5	2.1	3.5	10.0	14.6	17.5	5.4	26.2	8.7	11.6	100
	2	9	15	42	62	74	23	111	37	49	424
IX. Skilled manual workers	0.1	0.2	1.5	1.1	4.7	11.6	4.2	5.9	55.4	15.0	100
	3	1	10	7	31	77	28	39	367	99	662
X. Unskilled manual workers	0.8	1.0	3.5	3.2	5.0	10.4	6.4	10.8	15.7	43.2	100
	16	19	71	64	101	208	128	217	315	865	2004
Totals	1.7	2.4	6.4	5.8	9.2	14.5	8.3	9.6	17.7	24.3	100
	78	107	287	261	415	654	373	432	799	1096	4505

Unit: Males (?), Poona, India.

Comments: *Elite I*   (I) Owners of factories.
             Elite II   (II) Higher professional, business and administrative.
             Middle classes (III) Medium merchants.
                            (IV) Intermediate professional, business and administrative.
                            (V) Clerks and shop assistants.
                            (VII) Small business.
                            (VIII) Lower professional and administrative.
             Nonmanual   (I) Owners of factories.
                            (II) Higher professional, business and administrative.
                            (III) Medium merchants.
                            (IV) Intermediate professional, business and administrative.
                            (V) Clerks and shop assistants.
                            (VII) Small business.
                            (VIII) Lower professional and administrative.
             Manual   (VI) Highly skilled and supervisory.
                            (IX) Skilled manual.
                            (X) Unskilled manual.

TABLE 2f. *Italy*

Fathers	I	II	III	Sons IV	V	VI	Totals
I. Owners and managers of large enterprises, etc.	33.3	8.3	25.0	8.3	16.7	8.3	100%
	4	1	3	1	2	1	12
II. Owners and managers of smaller enterprises, etc.	1.1	22.8	23.9	14.1	32.6	5.4	100
	1	21	22	13	30	5	92
III. Lower-level officials, etc.	0.0	11.8	23.5	58.8	5.9	0.0	100
	—	2	4	10	1	—	17
IV. Lower white-collar employees	1.0	5.8	7.8	48.5	22.3	14.6	100
	1	6	8	50	23	15	103
V. Service workers, artisans	0.0	0.8	0.6	7.6	68.3	22.9	100
	—	2	1	20	179	60	262
VI. Unskilled labor and agricultural workers	0.0	2.7	2.7	2.7	28.0	64.0	100
	—	4	4	4	42	96	150
Totals	0.9	5.7	6.6	15.4	43.6	27.8	100
	6	36	42	98	277	177	636

Comments: *Elite I*   (I) Proprietors and managers of large industrial, commercial and financial enterprises, high civil servants, high officials.
             Elite II   (II) Proprietors of large and medium-size agricultural enterprises, proprietors and managers of middle-sized enterprises, independent professionals.
             Middle classes (III) Other employees of responsibility in first category, rentiers and students of well-to-do families.
                            (IV) Ordinary white-collar workers, students, supervisory artisans.
             Manual   (V) Service personnel, agricultural foremen, nonsupervisory artisans.
                            (VI) Agricultural workers, unskilled workers.

TABLE 2g. *Japan*

Fathers	I	II	III	Sons IV	V	VI	VII	Totals
I. Professional	43.9	4.9	17.1	8.5	9.8	2.4	13.4	100%
	36	4	14	7	8	2	11	82
II. Administration	15.9	15.9	21.4	19.1	8.7	8.7	10.3	100
	20	20	27	24	11	11	13	126
III. Clerical	10.8	7.2	27.7	14.5	10.8	6.0	22.9	100
	9	6	23	12	9	5	19	83
IV. Commercial	7.2	6.7	18.8	38.9	8.2	7.7	12.5	100
	15	14	39	81	17	16	26	208
V. Skilled	3.8	4.4	13.8	8.2	45.3	12.6	12.0	100
	6	7	22	13	72	20	19	159
VI. Semiskilled	4.0	2.7	6.7	16.0	24.0	25.3	21.3	100
	3	2	5	12	18	19	16	75
VII. Unskilled	3.9	2.9	7.6	8.0	7.9	5.9	63.7	100
	44	33	86	91	90	67	722	1133
Totals	7.1	4.6	11.6	12.9	12.1	7.5	44.3	100
	133	86	216	240	225	140	826	1866

Time: 1955.
Unit: Males.
Comments: *Elite I*   (I) Professional.
          Elite II   (II) Administrative.
          Middle classes (III) Clerical.
                    (IV) Commercial.
          Manual   (V) Skilled.
                    (VI) Semiskilled.
                    (VII) Unskilled.

and scientific knowledge, etc. — by definition the upper social strata have more of it than do the lower. That is indeed how one defines lower and upper classes.

Moreover, in spite of the repeated revolts and perhaps continuing resentment on the part of the lower strata about their position, societies in general do share common values about why certain positions and families must be given a high rank, and others a low rank.

To the degree that most people in the society share these evaluations, there are always some families and individuals who seek to have more of whatever this society offers; that is, more of its honor, its material comforts, its power and so on. All the data that are available show that talent is not distributed in the same way as these honors and rewards. The talents of most people center around a common average, while in

TABLE 2h. *West Germany*

Fathers	I	II	III	Respondents IV	V	VI	VII	Totals
I. Upper middle	50.6	27.1	9.4	4.7	2.4	—	5.8	100%
	43	23	8	4	2	—	5	85
II. Lower middle	8.3	55.6	12.0	17.6	2.0	0.9	3.6	100
	70	470	101	149	17	8	30	845
III. Upper lower	3.6	32.9	31.5	21.5	3.1	1.7	5.7	100
	15	138	132	90	13	7	24	420
IV. Lower lower	0.7	14.5	12.4	61.5	2.6	3.6	4.7	100
	8	154	132	655	28	38	50	1065
V. Farm owner	2.1	17.3	7.9	25.1	39.3	3.9	4.4	100
	16	129	59	188	294	29	33	747
VI. Farm worker	0.6	8.3	10.2	43.4	4.4	25.5	7.6	100
	1	13	16	69	7	40	12	158
VII. Unclassified	3.0	20.9	14.9	37.3	1.5	7.5	14.9	100
	2	14	10	24	1	5	10	65
Totals	4.6	27.8	13.6	35.2	10.7	3.7	4.8	100
	155	941	458	1181	361	125	164	3385

Unit: Heads of households.
Time: 1955.
Comments: *Elite I and II*   (I) Upper middle, professionals, managers and proprietors of larger
                                  establishments and upper civil servants.
          Middle classes   (II) Lower middle, minor officials, clerical and sales persons, small
                                  businessmen, and independent artisans.
          Working classes (III) Upper lower, skilled workers and employed artisans.
                              (IV) Lower lower, semiskilled and unskilled workers.
          Agricultural   (V) Farm owners.
                              (VI) Farm workers.
          Manual   (III) Skilled workers.
                              (IV) Semiskilled and unskilled workers.
                              (VI) Farm workers.

nearly all societies the mass of people are clustered toward the bottom of the stratification pyramid: clearly, position is not determined by talent alone.

Aside from this source of pressure, the fact is that families cannot even remain at the top of the class system without considerable training, discipline, and even devotion to duty. Where skill in arms is essential, the sons of the upper strata must learn to handle their horses, swords, and lances, and must also learn to command men. Where the humanities and classics are central, then the sons of the upper strata must work at memorizing huge quantities of material, at learning the appropriate languages. Competition is rife, whether *between* strata or within strata. Powerful families vie with one another for place and position, and the losers sometimes fall to lower strata. Thus, even the effort to maintain their *own* stratum intact, their own class position, means that the ensuing competition will shoulder aside some families that fail in developing a new generation of sons who are equal to others at the same level.

All this is true, even where a stratification system explicitly attempts to keep every person in his place, where the ideology of the system asserts that people must remain where they are born. The individual family may *attempt* to protect their inept sons, but in so doing, they hand over their place and power to younger men who cannot maintain them.

One consequence of this is that upper-class families actually have more to lose than do lower-class families, and must spend much more energy on training their young, and on controlling their adults by group pressures. They must maintain greater group cohesion in order to keep from falling in class position. At the same time, of course, they have more *resources* with which to control the young who might marry wrongly, or behave so foolishly as to lose the power, the influence, and the control of courts and law that the upper-stratum families enjoy. The upper-class young have typically far more to lose by failing to conform to family dictates (such as marrying outside the elite circle) and they have more to gain by helping their kin maintain their positions.

Consequently, when we look at social mobility over many generations, few upper-class families hold their positions intact. Examples are many, but perhaps one of the more striking cases may be taken from Sweden. A study of the genealogical records of the houses of nobility showed that of the 1547 noble families that

were registered in 1626 when the *Riddarhus* was established, 84 per cent had been wiped out by the third generation, or they continued only through the marriages of daughters. Only two of these families lasted for nine generations by succession from father to son.[1]

Of course, many of these were killed in the many battles of the seventeenth century. A similar turnover occurred in the two-hundred-year period between the seventeenth and nineteenth centuries in England.[2]

The data on individual families of the upper strata in China are especially voluminous. Hsu has shown, on the basis of regional histories, that one-third to four-fifths of the higher bureaucratic positions went to "new men," that is, men without high-class background. Only about 20 percent of the total number of families managed to maintain their upper-class positions for more than three generations.[3] A recent study has ascertained the social composition of the men who held the highest degree in China, which gave them nearly automatically a place in the middle stratum of the imperial bureaucracy. Over the total period from 1371 until the beginning of the twentieth century, about 30 percent of these men came from families of no distinction, that is, their families had not produced a single holder of the elementary degree. In the earliest period, the Ming Dynasty, nearly half of these men came from families that had not produced a degree holder.[4]

In a careful analysis of Danish mobility, Svalastoga has calculated that if we compare the class position of the great grandsons of working-class people, and those of upper-class people, the difference will be small; indeed, by the later generation, social position is only 5 percent removed from complete equality of change – perhaps demonstrating the truth of the Danish adage, "In one hundred years everything is forgotten."[5]

Numerical data are not available for India except for the large city of Poona but – again contrary to common expectation – the amount of mobility is comparable to that of many industrial countries in the West, having high upward and downward mobility. It should be emphasized that this movement does not represent as yet a serious breakdown in the rigid caste system of India. Caste ascription remains the rule in that country. But in fact castes have always competed among themselves for prestige and power, so that there was always some mobility among the thousands of sub-castes in India. In addition, however, within almost all castes a wide range of occupations could be followed, so that families from lower castes could rise over time in the economic system.[6]

Such data, crude as they are, suggest that in most countries in the past and present time there has been a substantial amount of upward and downward mobility. We do not know as yet the extent to which these figures would vary over time. Moreover, and perhaps more important, we do not know the *specific* amounts of mobility from one class level to another. We can suppose that in a nation undergoing great social change, as

[1] Bernard Barber, *Social Stratification*, New York: Harcourt, Brace and Co., 1957, p. 425.

[2] See for example A. S. Turberville, *The House of Lords in the Eighteenth Century*, Oxford: Clarendon Press, 1927.

[3] Barber, *op. cit.*, p. 426.

[4] Ping-Ti Ho, *The Ladder of Success in Imperial China*, New York: Columbia University Press, 1962, p. 112.

[5] Kaare Svalastoga, *Class Prestige and Mobility*, Copenhagen, Gyldendal, 1959, p. 354.

[6] For an excellent summary of mobility trends in India see, Bernard Barber, *Social Mobility in Hindu India*, Barnard College, Columbia University (unpublished MS.).

during a revolution or a protracted war, there will be much class mobility. When a nation engages many of its men in colonial ventures, doubtless mobility is high. Nevertheless we do not have adequate quantitative measures of these changes as yet.

Yet it is clear that changes of mobility from the *lowest* to the highest levels in one generation are rare even in highly industrialized societies, where presumably opportunities are greatest. In most countries, from about 1 to 4 percent of the elite come from the working class. In this respect, nations differ rather substantially. In the recent past few men of the working class in Great Britain rose to the top professions and positions. In the latter part of the nineteenth century, about one-third of the Cambridge students who were sons of doctors became doctors themselves; and a further 40 percent entered the professions of the church, the law, or teaching. At Aberdeen and Glasgow Universities well over four-fifths of the students who were sons of doctors entered their father's profession of medicine. In the mid-1930's at Cambridge, this figure was well over one-half for medicine and about one-half for law.[1]

However, we should keep in mind that these are all elite occupations that require a university education, which in turn has been confined until recently in Great Britain and on the continent to sons and daughters of middle-class families. However, recruitment into other occupations has generally not required a university education, so that many studies of the social origin of high-level occupations have suggested a relatively high rate of mobility from lower positions, whether these were white-collar or manual jobs.

For example, a study in 1912 showed that some two-thirds of the managers, directors, and owners in the cotton industry of Great Britain had begun their working lives in lower-level occupations, whether clerical or manual.[2] In a more recent study, it was ascertained that 65 percent of the staff of an English rolling mill, and 36 percent of the top management came from manual social origins.[3] Studies of business elites in Great Britain, the Netherlands, the United States, and Sweden have shown that about 60 percent had fathers who were businessmen, but about 15 percent of these were small businessmen, and some 10 to 15 percent of all of these elites came from either manual working-class origins or lower white-collar strata. Contrary to popular mythology, in fact the American businessmen typically has more education than his European counterpart.

Nevertheless in all industrial countries, some form of university education is increasingly becoming a basis for recruitment into the top levels of business, while at the same time democratic forces have been pressing toward the opening of the university to all social strata on a more equal basis.

It is not necessary here to state in detail the complex relationships between family position and education, and between education and later occupation. A few of the relevant points may be summarized as follows:

1) Although in general there is an association between I.Q. level and class position, the relationship is very modest. For example, in one English study unskilled manual workers' sons had an average I.Q. of 95, as against 113 for sons of professionals and managerial personnel. The overlap is extremely great, and the range *within* each social class is much wider than the range *between* averages of each stratum. Consequently it must be concluded, from a vast body of information, that a substantial proportion of each class has at least the initial capacity to achieve high position.

2) One of the best predictors of attendance at college is class position. It is true that the ablest students are more likely to go to college, but even when we control for level of ability, the socioeconomic position of the family remains strong. For example, in one study based on a national sample, some three-fourths of the children from professional or managerial families planned to attend college, and the percentage drops successively to one-fourth in the lowest social educational status categories. At the top level of ability *and* family position, 83 percent plan to go to college and in this same status group over half of the children with *lowest* ability *still* plan to go to college. By contrast at the lowest socioeconomic levels, only 43 percent of the students with top abilities plan to go to college, and this percent drops steadily through the levels of ability to the lowest, where it is only 18 percent.[4]

No matter which index of socioeconomic position is used, the same relationship holds. School grades follow a similar pattern. Although in the earliest years of school in the United States, there is a very high relationship between I.Q. and grades, the social position of the family seems to have little effect. By junior high school and high school, the pupil of higher social position makes higher grades, even when I.Q. is held constant. This suggests of course that family elements in motivation play a substantial role in the education and training that eventually leads to social mobility.

Nevertheless we should keep in mind that, except for specific professions requiring education, it is not clear how much access to education affects total mobility. Fairly substantial percentages of sons of good education fall in social position relative to the position of their family of origin. In a reanalysis of social mobility data from Great Britain, C. Arnold Anderson has noted that, "half of the sons moving into the top stratum were in the two poorest categories of schooling. Moreover half

[1] R. K. Kelsall, "Self-Recruitment in Four Professions," in D. V. Glass (ed.), *Social Mobility in Great Britain*, Glencoe, Ill.: The Free Press, 1954, p. 310.

[2] S. M. Lipset and Reinhard Bendix, *Social Mobility in Industrial Society*, (Berkeley: University of California Press, 1959), p. 35.

[3] *Ibid.*, p. 36. The study is by W. H. Scott, et al., *Technical Change and Industrial Relations*, Liverpool: Liverpool University Press, 1956.

[4] Natalie Rogoff, "Local Social Structure and Educational Selection," in *Education, Economy, and Society*, ed. A. H. Halsey, Jean Floud, and C. Arnold Anderson, Glencoe, Illinois: The Free Press, 1962, p. 246.

of these poorly educated sons moving into the top level originated in the two lowest strata."[1]

About half of the most able 5 percent of American high-school graduates do not graduate from college, but it would be erroneous to suppose that all of these pupils fail to achieve positions commensurate with their abilities. It is at least clear that at the *same* level of completed education, a wide variation in the amount of *achievement* is exhibited.

We may also speculate that perhaps the relationship between education and mobility is highly dependent on the socioeconomic structure of *opportunities* within a given nation. Until World War II, the few poor boys who attended good universities in Great Britain were almost invariably extremely brilliant, or talented young men who entered on scholarships. It seems likely that most of these men were thereby guaranteed high-level positions after graduation. At the same time, their talents and drive might have given them a similar position had they entered the ranks of business.

On the other hand, in the United States almost everyone who achieves high position has had some college education. This education, however, does not typically prepare the graduate for any occupation whatsoever. It is primarily humanistic, and is not professional. A college education has become a prerequisite for managerial posts in business, but mainly as a social necessity, having nothing to do with the individual's talent or later achievement. At most, it is a certificate stating that the individual ought to have a white-collar job. Thus, it guarantees nothing at all beyond that. Perhaps all this is another way of saying that where the university system is highly selective, it secures to the very talented poor some measure of mobility. On the other hand where the university experience is nearly guaranteed by ascribed, high social position, as has been the situation in Great Britain until recently, it serves as no guarantee at all that that position can be *maintained*.

The foregoing comments hint at the importance and complexity of the relations between family and social mobility. It is in the family setting that the individual's motivation to achieve is developed, as well as the social and intellectual skills that may hinder or help him in the first steps along that road.

The social *values* of aspiration as well as the psychological drive to succeed seem to be related to family variables. Moreover, from the beginning the child is given the social rank of his own family, and in turn the family that he founds will be given his own rank, modified in part by his own social origins. Individuals who move upward or downward are concerned not only about the consequences of such a move for them personally, but more profoundly about the consequences for their families. It is clear that in order for a family to maintain its position over time, it must not only reproduce biologically a next generation, but it must also achieve a successful socialization of its children, so that

[1] "A Skeptical Note of Education and Mobility", in *ibid.*, p. 171.

they will have the training and capacity for maintaining that social position.

It seems useful then at this time to sketch some of the central structural points at which family variables seem to affect the mobility process in general, or the specific rise and fall of individuals. Sufficient data are not available to prove some of them, and some effort is being made now to remedy that gap. In others the theoretical problems seem as great as the sheer factual ones.

In the following sections, we shall explore several of these structural nexuses between family and mobility. Omitted from the present exposition is an analysis of the dynamics *internal* to the family, specifically the relations among family, achievement motivation, and mobility.

Unigeniture versus equal division of property

All families' systems have two conflicting aims, *1)* to maintain intact the family property as it descends from one generation to the next; and   *2)* to provide for all its children adequately. Since property is limited, a division of property in each generation will mean that the children in the first generation will very likely not have as much individually as the parents have enjoyed together — and of course in successive generations the property is dissipated into holdings that become financially trivial. On the other hand, to give all the property to one child only, whether the first child or the last child, means that the others will not be properly provided for. Even where there is only one son, it is likely that the dowry system will require a substantial amount of family property to leave with the daughter who marries. Some evidence now suggests that the single-heir or unigeniture system of inheritance may affect economic and social mobility patterns. Since the data remain fragmentary, as yet, it seems useful merely to offer the following speculations.

First, with regard to population growth itself, where a single heir inherited all the property, this landowner himself had little reason to limit the number of his children, but his own brothers and sisters often could not marry at all, or had to remain unmarried for many years. Where there was an equal division of property, almost everyone could marry, even at a low level of subsistence, but in turn the lower level of subsistence may have motivated some to limit the number of their own offspring. It seems likely that the regions of equal division of property had in general a higher rate of population growth.

With respect to geographical and social mobility, two types of processes are visible. In all the agricultural regions of Europe in the nineteenth century, there was considerable short-term or seasonal geographical mobility, in which the basic occupation did not change. An individual might have a small landholding from which he worked with his kinsmen, but during the harvest season he might move a short distance in order to earn wages.[1]

As for geographic mobility over a greater distance, permanent migration, and change of occupation, it seems likely that the single-heir system facilitated all three far more than the equal division of property. This system created more unmarried males, who at best were given some small financial settlement, but no hope of any substantial amount of family property. The system of equal inheritance gave little to each individual, but each person thereby had some stake in keeping his own holding, and supplementing his small income with wages for hired labor in the locality.

This last factor created another difference. Since people in the regions of equal division were somewhat more tied to their locality, if industry was to develop at all it had to come to the population, and this would happen only if the region possess some advantage in natural resource. However, in regions of countries of single-heir inheritance, the population could go to the area in which industry was being established, usually in areas where natural resources facilitated its development. By contrast, in equal-division areas, small local industries could develop. Thus the theoretical speculation seems warranted, that at least one factor in the industrial development of both England and Germany was a relatively greater preponderance of single-heir inheritance, which also thrust more of the sons of any given generation into new occupations some distance from home.

Heterogamy and homogamy

As more than one analyst has noted, marriage and courtship systems may be viewed as market systems. In some societies it is the elders who do the haggling, while in Western countries generally it is the young people themselves who select one another, but in either case, the most common result is that people at any given social level usually marry others at that same level. In a free market system such as our own, where the woman does not typically rise in social position through her occupation, she must seek a mobile husband if she wishes to be mobile herself. Because a man loses esteem in our society if he does not work for a living, very few men can solve their personal problem of support by marrying a woman with sufficient wealth, but this fact must not disguise the possibility that he may be helped in his upward movement by marrying into a family that will afford him additional opportunities.

Although the pattern of homogamy — "like marries like" — is found in all societies, it is more than an expression of preference for a mate similar to oneself or one's family. It is the resultant of a market process in which either elders or courting young people attempt to locate the most desirable mate, just as a seller attempts to obtain the very best price for his commodities. However, since others in marriageable ages are doing precisely the same thing, the net result is that in general

those who marry will actually be able to choose a spouse who has roughly the same market value. Even in the romance-laden system of the United States, young people are highly aware of the potential advantages that this or that possible spouse might offer, and peers are quick to point out to an individual that he "can do better than that."

Homogamy, then, is not merely ethnocentrism. It is also the blind result of many individuals who in seeking the very best possible spouse for their children or for themselves, and by virtue of the types of offers made or rejections received, come to find a spouse at their own social and economic level.

This process however opens the possibility, again universally found in all societies, of exchanging desirable characteristics *other* than those of simple social rank, and of making a bargain in which there is rough equality of exchange, but very different things are exchanged. Perhaps at all times in the history of the world it has been possible for some women to exchange their beauty for a man's social rank or power. Many men whom years have carried beyond youth and beauty must throw into the scales some of their achievements in the market place or in family lineage, in order to obtain the charm and loveliness of a young woman as wife. Women of social position may also exchange it for *potential achievement;* that is, a talented young man may, even without much income, obtain a wife above him in the social scale, simply because his future worth is worth a good deal on the present marriage market.

Note however that *what* may be exchanged is defined by the society itself. Thus in the Jewish ghetto, a poor young man devoted to learning could count to some extent on his intellectual achievement as a basis for obtaining a wife with money, and this was at least an ideal in Imperial China. On the other hand, our society disapproves of a marriage exchange in which it is the woman who has the brains and talent, and the young man has great beauty; or the woman has social position and money, and the man has youth. In such cases it becomes clear that the society requires the man to achieve some part of his position with his own work and ability. A young man is not disapproved of, for example, if he marries the boss's daughter *but also* works hard to make a success of the company.

From the considerable mass of data demonstrating that generally people marry within the same class, ethnic group, economic level, religion, and age (or at least that they are far more likely to marry within those categories than would occur by chance alone) two major processes ought to be noted here. One is, that though young people in our society insist on making this important family decision, while their elders are somewhat dubious of their ability to make wise choices, the sifting process actually begins at the earliest years of association among children. That is, marriage is the final point in a long

[1] H. J. Habakkuk, "Family Structure and Economic Change in 19th Century Europe", *Journal of Economic History,* 15 (I, 1955), p. 7.

process, and since young people will fall in love with and marry only the people they meet, their parents attempt to control whom they meet.

This process is reflected in the data in Hollingshead's research in Elmtown, where he recorded 1,258 clique ties. Three out of five of these ties were between boys or girls at the same class level, and nearly two out of five between boys and girls only one class removed. In the few instances when a clique tie included a child two classes removed, the child was usually an outstanding one. When boys and girls noted who was their "best friend," 70 percent were with class equals. Somewhat similar patterns were found in dating.[1]

Sussman's analysis of about one hundred middle-class families showed that even in the young adult years before marriage, parents attempt to control their social contacts by inviting marital prospects to the home for a weekend, supervising their parties, choosing schools and so on. Indeed, when these young people expressed some intention of marrying an "inappropriate" person, in 81 percent of the cases the parents used extended persuasion or threats of economic withdrawals in order to break up the relationship.[2]

It is not surprising, then, that in the United States about half of all marriages occur between people who live no more than one mile from one another, and toward the upper strata the distances are much greater — but this means only that those with social and economic advantages can more easily travel longer distances to find similar spouses.

This large process, coupled with the process of market sifting, points to a second pattern, which is that in spite of the research data suggesting an increasing number of marriages between people of different classes, in fact such unions are likely to take place between young people of different class *origins*, but very similar life styles. That is, one of the spouses is socially mobile, and has taken on the cultural patterns, attitudes, and even aspirations common in the class of the potential spouse.

This reflects indeed the pattern of class mobility in many societies in the past. Perhaps the two most striking instances are those of China and eighteenth-century France.[3] In France, the amount of dowry necessary for achieving an upward marriage between the young daughter of a merchant family and a noble family was quite widely known, the amount necessary

rising with each successively higher layer in the hierarchy of nobility. However, it cannot be supposed that such marriages occurred between an uneducated merchant's daughter and an elegant courtier. Rather, the merchant's family began to live "nobly" before such a marriage took place, and might well be interacting socially on fairly intimate terms with noble families, while the young women themselves were of course being educated in all the graces necessary for a high-born lady.

In both France and China one may say that the typical process of upward mobility consisted in the family obtaining its wealth in business or manufacturing, but then moving from such activities into official position and a life style common to the elite of the society. For China, the evidence seems to be that maintenance of a mandarin's status over generations was relatively difficult, once the source of wealth in business has been abandoned.[4]

In any event it seems fairly clear that the upper-class family must maintain a higher control over its young members, especially in the choice of spouse, if the family is not to lose its position.

Choices in marriage seem not to be a major source of upward or downward mobility in any society although all societies seem to exhibit some degree of upward movement of this type. We may, however, present here a few of the major findings now available.

1) Since women depend far more than men upon their mate choice as a basis for their future social position, they tend to be more objective in weighing the characteristics of their potential spouse.

2) Since men derive less benefit from marrying upward socially, they have a wider range of permitted mates; i.e., they can marry downward without losing in prestige. At the same time, the higher their social position, the more they are worth on the marriage market.

3) Consequently, far more men marry downward than upward, whether the index used is education, income, or prestige. Moreover, toward the higher social strata, a higher percentage of men marry eventually, but a lower percentage of women.

4) The average ages at marriage are higher toward the upper social strata, although the differences are not great. However, both men and women who marry upward are likely to marry earlier than those who marry at the same class level.[5]

5) In general, the occupational career of women has little effect on the direction of movement when they marry. However, Danish data suggest that working women who marry downward had experienced some downward occupational mobility before that marriage; and women who move upward occupationally before marriage are more likely to marry upward as well.

Perhaps a parallel association is that the higher a man's father-in-law's social status is, relative to the groom himself, the more likely is the man to be occupationally upwardly mobile.[6]

6) Women who marry upward socially are more

---

[1] A. B. Hollingshead, *Elmtown's Youth* (New York: John Wiley, 1949), p. 212.

[2] M. B. Sussman, "Parental Participation in Mate Selection and Its Effects Upon Family Continuity," *Social Forces*, 32 (October, 1953).

[3] For an excellent description of the French process, see Elinor Barber, *The Bourgeoisie in 18th Century France* (Princeton: Princeton University Press, 1955).

[4] Francis L. K. Hsu, *Under the Ancestor's Shadow* (New York: Columbia University Press), 1948.

[5] Ramkrishna Mukherjee, "Social Mobility and Age at Marriage," in Glass, *op. cit.*, p. 342.

[6] Kaare Svalastoga, "The Family in the Mobility Process," in *Recherches sur la Famille*, ed. Nels Anderson, vol. III, Göttingen: Vandenhoeck and Ruprecht, 1958, pp. 302–304.

likely to have higher than average I.Q. scores, than women who marry within their own stratum; and those who marry within their own social stratum have higher scores than those who marry downward.[1]

Adoption and surrogate parents

Although no systematic data now seem to be available, and the technical resources for pursuing this question would be difficult to muster, it seems worthwhile nevertheless to open a relatively untouched question in the mobility process in certain countries and societies. Perhaps its most extreme form may be found in Japan prior to the Meiji Restoration in 1868. Tokugawa Japan is commonly described as a "closed-class system." It was feudal in that everyone was placed in a hierarchal system, with each person owing allegiance to the person above him and exacting allegiance from the man or men below him. The ideology was — contrary to that of China — that people should remain in their places and do their full duty in that position. Presumably, there was to be no mobility through achievement, except perhaps among the Samurai, during wartime. In this system, too, the merchant or manufacturer had a low social position.

At least among the upper social strata, family property and the family headship descended intact to the eldest male, and so to his eldest son in the next generation in an unbroken chain through the generations. Several interesting facets of this situation are worth mentioning. One is that folklore typically imputed to the younger son or sons the qualities of adventuresomeness, originality and geographic mobility. The family had only a modest economic responsibility for him once he was an adult. If the family was very wealthy it could afford to allow him to set up a junior branch family and would of course help him to obtain some position. However, as in England, he had little claim to either the power or wealth of the family. This may indeed have helped somewhat in the industrialization of Japan, since thereby family capital was not dissolved each generation, as it was in China.

Nevertheless the head of the family had an absolute right to disown his son, whatever the ordinary custom of inheritances, and could bring in an adopted son. This young man cut off all his ties with his family of origin, and was expected to be thenceforth a loyal member of his new family. The consequence of this was, at all economic levels, that talent did have considerable chance, and the ineptitude or disobedience of a blood son was not to be rewarded. (This situation contrasts sharply with China, and again may have had some effect upon the greater success of Japan in the industrializing process.)

In addition, the head of any family had a great obligation to his ancestors to continue the family line intact. Thus, if he had only daughters, he would adopt a son who would become the head of the family after the death of the father.

How widespread was this practice? At present, the data are not available in English sources and a first perusal of major Japanese sources through Takeji Kamiko's annotated bibliography[2] of Japanese sources suggests that the data have not as yet been tabulated by Japanese scholars. On the other hand the Japanese biographical materials suggest that high mobility rates from this source may eventually be discovered. This might also be expected, theoretically, because of the high emphasis on achievement and effectiveness in Japanese culture. Recent work on geographic mobility also suggests that the common picture of family stability over many generations is entirely incorrect, at least for Japanese cities.[3]

Thus we have the interesting possibility that in Japanese society there was little official recognition of mobility as a legitimate aspiration of individuals and families, but a substantial amount of it may have occurred just the same. This is of course in line with my earlier speculation that mobility may be relatively high in many societies where we had previously supposed a high amount of rigidity.

Note, however, that the movement of an individual from one class or social estate to another in Japan did not mean that the sharp boundaries between classes would loosen. The individual who moved simply took over the life style and social patterns of the family to which he moved, and would adopt their attitudes of scorn or deprecation for the classes below.

It seems clear in any event that this line of research needs to be pursued if we are to understand better the interrelations of family and mobility systems.

However we might well add some similar instances in the Western world. We refer now not to the institutions of foster parenthood and adoption in the modern era, but more specifically to the English — and later Puritan — custom among the merchant classes of sending both boys and girls to live with other merchant families or even with noble families in order to acquire manners, learn new skills, and make desirable acquaintances. Noble boys were also sent away. These youngsters, it must be kept in mind, were not being thrust from their homes permanently, and did not lose their property rights. This was a temporary experience, perhaps comparable to going away to college in our time, although it then occurred at the earlier ages of 10 or 11.

Among the Puritans,[4] a further ideological or philosophical element was introduced: the Puritan parent

---

[1] Eileen M. Scott, R. Ilsley, and A. M. Thompson, "A Psychological Investigation of Primigravidae." II — Maternal Social Class, Age, Physique, and Intelligence," *Journal of Obstetrics and Gynaecology of the British Empire*, 63 (June, 1956), pp. 339–340.

[2] *Japanese Bibliography*, University of Minneapolis, 1962 (mimeo).

[3] Robt. J. Smith, "Aspects of Mobility in Pre-Industrial Japanese Cities," *Comparative Studies in Society and History*, 5 (July, 1963), pp. 416–423.

[4] For a good account of the Puritan parental attitudes toward children, see Edmund S. Morgan, *The Puritan Family*, Boston: Boston Public Library, 1944.

knew that he was likely to indulge his children because he loved them so. Consequently, he felt it would be difficult to chastise them adequately, or to apply that objective and relentless discipline necessary to make them into efficient and God-fearing adults. Consequently it would be good to send them to other trusted families, where the attitudes of the surrogate parent would not be so warm as to undermine the socialization process.

It seems likely that this pattern acted to maintain or advance the social position of especially merchant families. Its effects have not been studied. A historical connection seems likely between this fourteenth-century English pattern, the later Puritan pattern, and the upper-class English pattern of sending youngsters away to private schools at early ages. In addition, in a number of primitive societies young men go to the households of their mother's brother to live, where eventually they will very likely marry the daughter of the family (matrilateral, cross-cousin marriage).

In all of these instances, several psychological and social questions are raised. We do not at present have data on the total impact of the surrogate parents, when the social definitions of their duties are fairly well defined (as contrasted with the literary stereotype of the cruel step-parent). In these instances, the family of origin is socially present and can control partially the punitiveness of the surrogate family.

Is the speculation of the Puritan family ideology correct, that such surrogate parents would insist more strongly on adequate performance by the youngster, and thus perhaps create a higher degree of motivation to achieve? And as a side effect, would this mean that the adult, raised under such circumstances, would always feel a lack of emotional security, and develop a drive to achieve? To what extent did this pattern also act as a general process of upward mobility, affording new social opportunities and offering the chance of acquiring social skills that would be useful in moving upward? This historical and cross-cultural area needs considerable attention.

Fertility and mobility patterns

Although we do not propose to investigate this problem thoroughly, we should at least note it in passing, since it may well play a substantial role in large-scale secular trends in the circulation of the elite, the ebb and flow of families from high to low position within the given society. The main elements may be briefly stated.

Prior to the modern era, almost all societies have had high birth and death rates. Only when a civilization becomes highly urbanized does it begin to exhibit a moderate or low fertility. This does not mean, however, that all societies have a high *net* reproduction rate. In periods of epidemic or war, or during famines, and indeed for extended periods of time the population of a given society may drop in spite of a high crude birth rate.

In almost all societies for which we have data, there is a clear inverse relationship between class position and fertility; that is toward the upper strata the fertility is lower. A few exceptions have been recorded: Sweden a generation ago; perhaps polygynous Africa (since upper-class men typically had more wives, and married earlier, than lower-class men); and perhaps imperial China. Whether this modern relationship has always held is not entirely clear although it seems likely that *urban* populations have always had a lower fertility than agricultural populations.

Nevertheless, whatever the differential fertility, it is clear that if the net reproduction rate in *each* class is exactly equal to 100 (i.e. each generation produces enough children to replace itself a generation later) then the form of the class pyramid will not change from this source. However, since typically the lower classes do have a higher net reproduction rate, this means that the lower classes will gradually become a higher proportion of the total pyramid, and the distribution form will alter. Otherwise, there will be increasing pressure from the lower classes to move into the upper classes.

It is possible that in many epochs prior to the modern, the net reproduction rate of the upper classes was higher, however, because of superior food, comfort, warmth, protection, and so on. This meant that there was a continual flow of people downward, unless the society could provide additional places for the more numerous new generation. We know, for example, that the lower classes in the Middle Ages married late, not early, because the man had to have adequate land for his family before he married. Certainly through the seventeenth and possibly the eighteenth centuries in Europe, the nobility married earlier than the bourgeoisie or the peasants, and thus very likely had a higher net reproduction rate. Thus, the flow downward would be substantial, or the stratification pyramid would change its shape.

Of course, the elite often initiated political events that took care of the surplus. We must remember that until the military reforms begun by Frederick the Great and Napoleon, war was mainly the sphere of the upper social classes, if not the nobility. Thus, colonial expansion and war both increased the circulation of the elite — for men of lesser families might sometimes rise high through their military success, and noble sons died — and opened the possibility of new wealth, lands, and governmental posts for the surplus sons of the elite. When such ventures were unsuccessful, the reduction in the numbers of the elite sometimes reduced the pressure for downward mobility, but often the total economic and personnel costs of a series of battles undermined the capacity of a nobility family to survive. Indeed, as noted earlier, few noble families managed to survive over many generations.

And, as noted earlier, the biological capacity of a family to survive is less important than its total *social* reproductiveness, i.e., its ability to produce a next generation of sons with the necessary skills and motivations to maintain the high position of the family.

We do know however, that the net reproduction rate is lower toward the upper social strata in Western countries and that it is possible to calculate the percentage of mobility that must take place if each successively higher stratum is to be replaced in the next generation. In the table below a rough estimate of the mobility from purely populational elements can be made. Thus, for example, the net deficit in the lower middle class is such (for the 1950's) that something like one-fourth must come from a status below. Actually, as we have already noted, this percentage may come from a status above, whereupon the population deficit in the higher status is still greater than appears in the table. It should be added, however, that the present fertility trends in

TABLE 3. *Percent of Social Mobility in American Society by Status**

Social class	Population distribution by status	Population by net rate of reproduction	Net social mobility required	Percent of mobility from status below
Upper class	3.0	2.5	+ 0.5	+ 7.7
Upper middle	9.0	6.5	+ 3.0	+10.7
Lower middle	36.0	28.0	+11.0	+28.2
Upper lower	35.0	39.0	+ 7.0	+29.1
Lower lower	17.0	24.0	—	—
Totals	100.0	100.0	+21.5	—

* Space does not permit explanation of the methods of social mathematics, of the relative reproduction rates employed, or of the projection of trends which indicate an increasing middle-class segment in American society. Similar tables have been calculated independently by Robert J. Havighurst.

To comprehend the table, the figure "+3.0" mobile to upper middle in the third column is the difference between "9.0" in column 1 and the "6.0" left in column 2 when "+0.5" percent of a generation move into upper class. The fourth column indicates the percent of young people in the social class just below (or others from farther down) who will have to move up in class status to maintain the composition of the American status structure.

Western countries are in the direction of a lessening difference among the various social strata, as well as between urban and rural populations. Consequently, we would suppose that the differential net reproduction rate among the various strata may have a lessening effect upon social mobility rates.

Extension of the kin network

The classical and enlightened opinion as to the effect of extended kin networks on mobility was stated by Bacon when he made his pithy comment that a man who marries "gives hostage to fortune." Plato said essentially the same thing by suggesting that equality of social opportunity could best be obtained by getting rid of the family system. This folk wisdom was embodied in a hypothesis of over half a century ago, Dumont's *Theory of Social Capillarity.* The physical analogy was invoked, by noting that a very thin column of liquid would rise higher by capillary action than a tube of wider diameter. Individual people, thus, would rise

higher if they were unencumbered by their family or far more distant kinfolk.

This notion is also given credence by the observations on mobility in China. Far from being unethical or criminal in Imperial China, nepotism was viewed rather as a *duty.* The man who attempted to rise in the imperial bureaucracy unencumbered by his family would encounter great resistance. Under the Confucian ethic, the most respected public value was being *filial.* Obviously, if a man did not carry his parents up with him, he would be unfilial, but if he failed to aid his relatives he was also failing to pay adequate respect to his ancestors. Since a man was given a post or was maintained in his post in part because of a general opinion that he was more or less in harmony with the gods and cosmic forces, a man who was thus unfilial would have forfeited these supports, and thus should not be allowed to hold a position.

In addition, and partly as a consequence, a man simply could not appear in a strange city without proper introductions from his kin. Social relations were highly particularistic; that is, dependent upon particular personal ties, and even an able man would not have been given a chance to show his talents without the backing of his relatives.

However, it has generally been believed that a man's rise upward was hindered somewhat in China, because he was expected to carry along with him as many of his kin as he could afford, and doubtless the pressures from kin were in the direction of asking more than he could indeed produce. However, the Chinese case has further instruction for us, and we shall return to it.

Certainly the Japanese ideology of the family supports the traditional view that extended kin are a burden on mobility, since a major mode of ascent was through adoption, and the adopted son was expected to discard both his extended relatives and his immediate family, a nearly unthinkable act in China. Reports on geographic and occupational mobility among urban sub-Saharan African populations have pointed to what is called "kin parasitism." The obligations to extended relatives are strong even among urban populations, so that a man may feel it his duty to help educate a nephew or to care for adults who are looking for work. Since wages are low, relatives may decide not to work for a long period of time, but to be parasitic on the man who has already moved to the city and established himself. It is thus sometimes difficult for a man to acquire the capital with which to move upward, and at least some kin may become dependent rather than attempt to compete in the job market.

A common complaint among Indians for generations past is that the close dependence of individuals upon one another may permit some young men who are lacking in initiative to stay within the household and avoid the disturbing challenge of upward mobility. The lack of "managerial personalities" in India has been ascribed in part to a family system in which adult brothers must take care of one another's children as well as taking care of one another. In any event, the individual in India had little chance to rise alone, since it was taken for granted that all his land or earnings would go into a common family pool (the joint family system).[1]

However, a closer and theoretical factual analysis of the data has uncovered a number of complexities in these relationships that have not as yet been sufficiently untangled. Our exploration has not been completed, but at least some outline of the direction of inquiry can be presented here. First, as a merely factual matter, almost *all* kinship systems can be called "extended" in some sense. That is, the individual or the individual family must recognize a wide array of obligations to a considerable network of both affinal and blood relatives. For our purposes, it does not matter here whether the blood relatives are traced through the mother's or the father's line. However, mobility may be high even when the network of kin obligations is much wider.

It seems quite clear, for example, that in the eleventh century in Europe, when an enormous number of monasteries, convents, nunneries, and churches were founded, and much economic expansion took place, mobility was relatively high. We know that in the general era between the ninth and the middle of the twelfth centuries, warfare played a substantial role in social mobility, and there was considerable turnover in the social rank of families. Nevertheless, during this period a wide extension of kin was recognized.

We have already noted that, in spite of the obligation of the successful Chinese to carry his relatives upward with him, there was much mobility in Imperial China. Moreover, an examination of the process of mobility reveals to us that the talented Chinese boy could never rise through the successive examinations unless he had much support from his family. If his family was poor, he had to get it from the wider array of relatives. Where clans were strong, as in southeast China, this often meant that the clan itself either established a school, or supported a young man while he laboriously acquired the necessary intellectual and humanistic skills for mobility within the bureaucracy.

Moreover, even within the contemporary United States, common observation will tell us that though the social ideology proclaims that each man must be evaluated individually on the basis of his merit, selection is in fact partly based on family origins, and families themselves may take an active interest in supporting an individual not only through his education but later in his occupational career. This is especially obvious over the post-World-War-II period, when a high proportion of middle-class youngsters may actually marry in the later years of college but continue their professional education for some years afterwards while being supported by a family. Granted, that we are here including the extended kin network *and* the immediate family, but it is important to bring these relationships together.

Perhaps equally important is the considerable amount of research carried out since World War II in an effort to measure how extended *is* the kin network in the United States and other countries. Sussman has recently published a bibliography of such reports, numbering by now well over sixty. They raise serious questions about some of our assumptions concerning the modern industrial family.[2]

Not all of these assumptions concern us now, but it is at least obvious that the supposed "nuclear family," made up only of parents and their children, and without any important kin ties outside that circle, is in fact rare. Parents may *agree* that they *should* not interfere in the lives of their adult married children but in fact they *do*. People may generally assert that their extended or distant kin have no special kinship rights, but if called upon they will respond just the same.

In sheer numbers, the figures may surprise those who have thought of the modern industrial urban family as living in an isolated rootless fashion. Perhaps the following tables will document this point better than any verbal statement. It is sufficient to say, in summary, that most families recognize a large number of affinal and blood kin and interact with them from time to time; and we must expect that a middle-class urban family may well include over a hundred relatives in these categories. Social interaction among relatives is more common than almost any other category of social interaction, and in general, the number of relatives and the amount of exchanges are both somewhat larger toward the upper strata.

This last point has been suggested in other contexts previously in this report, and deserves attention now. We cannot suppose that those who are in the higher social strata have all been mobile, but some have; and in any event the question is raised as to how burdensome could the kin network be, since those who enjoy the most advantages in this industrial urban society clearly take part in much social interaction with relatives. We know that toward the lower strata, family interaction is a larger *percentage* of their total social life interaction — but that is because toward the lower social strata people belong to far fewer voluntary or formal associations and relationships.

Does this mean that over the past generation or so there has been a *return* to "familism"? Surely it could not be maintained that loyalty to kin is greater now than, say, a century ago. The present data do suggest, as a tangential hypothesis, that direct interaction among kin is probably more frequent than a century ago, if only because of the transportational and communicational difficulties of that time.

Does social and geographic mobility undermine these

[1] See M. S. Gore, *The Impact of Industrialization and Urbanization on the Aggarwal Family in Delhi Area*, unpublished Ph.D. Dissertation, Columbia University, 1961.

[2] Marvin B. Sussman and L. Burchinal, "Kin Family Network: Unheralded Structure in Current Conceptualizations of Family Functioning," *Marriage and Family Living*, 24 (August, 1962), p. 231, pp. 235–240. Also see, William J. Goode, *World Revolution and Family Patterns*, (New York: The Free Press of Glencoe, 1963), pp. 70–81.

TABLE 4. *Number of Familiar and Effective Cognatic Kin* (in per cent)*

FAMILIAR COGNATIC KIN — CLIENTS[a]

Number of familiar kin	Nuclear family	Wives	Husbands
0	— (0)	7 (13)	7 (12)
1–15	34 (62)	75 (136)	80 (145)
16–30	49 (90)	16 (29)	12 (21)
31–45	13 (23)	2 (4)	2 (4)
46–60	2 (4)	—	—
61–75	2 (3)	—	—

EFFECTIVE COGNATIC KIN[b]

0	—	1 (2)	—
1–15	11 (20)	46 (83)	34 (61)
16–30	27 (50)	41 (74)	49 (90)
31–45	32 (59)	11 (20)	15 (27)
46–60	20 (37)	2 (3)	1 (2)
61–75	7 (1)	—	1 (2)
76–90	1 (2)	—	—
91–105	1 (2)	—	—

* Hope Jansen Leichter and Candace Rogers, unpub. ms., 1961. Leichter also uses the term "cognatic kin," in a way that cuts across all kin categories included in her study, and refers to the fact that no affines are included; i.e., they are all blood kin.

[a] Kin with whom Ego maintains some form of contact. Includes kin seen at "Big Family Gatherings" or more frequently. This arbitrary criterion was frequently given in interviews as an operationally defined boundary for minimal interaction. Figures extracted from *ibid.*, Table 11. Filial kin — children, grandchildren, and great grandchildren — are excluded.

[b] Kin with whom Ego maintains frequent contact. As defined, it is an "interaction" criterion, although it would probably overlap with a "sentiment" criterion. These are kin that Ego sees more frequently than familiar kin — at weddings, funerals, Bar Mitzvehs, etc. *Ibid.*, p. 2.

large kinship networks? The question cannot be answered fully as yet. Certainly, the continued existence of such networks in a society of high mobility suggests that families must have some procedures or techniques for maintaining the cohesion of kin ties in the face of mobility.

For the moment, however, we are concerned with how such networks may actually affect mobility, and here we have primarily a set of theoretical points

TABLE 5. *Range of Kin for Twelve Households, London**

Households	Recognized kin	Nominated kin
A	246	176
B	231	140
C	223	53
D	209	162
E	167	137
F	160	122
G	157	144
H	126	96
I	113	99
J	52	43
K	45	34
L	37	14

* Raymond Firth (ed.), *Two Studies of Kinship in London,* London School of Economics, Monographs on Social Anthropology, No. 15 (London: The Athlone Press, 1956), p. 42.

buttressed by some few facts, which deserve further research attention. Whatever the complexities of the data when we finally know them, it is at least empirically obvious that the truncated or nuclear family — often without a male head — is more common towards the *bottom* of the social pyramid than toward the *top*. This is

TABLE 6. *Frequency of Social Participation with Relatives* by Family and Economic Status, San Francisco† (in per cent)*

Frequency of participation by group	Low family, low economic status	Low family, high economic status	High family, low economic status	High family, high economic status
About once a week or more	33	30	45	42
A few times a month	10	15	13	13
About once a month	13	13	14	11
A few times a year	10	16	14	19
About once a year	8	12	4	6
Never	26	15	10	8
Total percent answering	100	100	100	99
Number answering	172	191	170	168

* Relatives other than those living with the respondent.
† Wendell Bell and Marion D. Boat, "Urban Neighborhoods and Informal Social Relations," *American Journal of Sociology*, 62 (January, 1957), 294.

most strikingly the situation in the Caribbean nations, where at least one element in the high illegitimacy rates is the lack of extended family controls. Although the nuclear family is sometimes thought of as harmonious adaptation to the needs of the industrial system, it is actually found in the stratum where the individual's

TABLE 7. *Reliance on Individuals for Help in Illness, by Status,* San Francisco†*

	PER CENT NAMING AT LEAST ONE MEMBER OF THAT GROUP			
Whom could you call on for help if you were ill for even as much as a month?	Low family, low economic	Low family, high economic	High family, low economic	High family, high econmic
Relatives	71 (172)	84 (191)	81 (170)	85 (168)
Friends	60 (172)	65 (191)	53 (170)	73 (168)
Neighbors	34 (172)	29 (191)	45 (170)	40 (168)
Co-workers†	40 (145)	46 (166)	24 (149)	44 (156)

* Unemployed persons are excluded. Parenthetical numbers are those upon which percentages are based.
† Bell and Boat, *op. cit.*, p. 396.

family has the least to gain from exchanges of rights and obligations with his own kin. By contrast, toward the upper strata, kin networks can be kept alive because each family within the network has *resources* to exchange with the others. Having at best a small margin above subsistence, the lower-class families are often unable to pool their resources even to help a talented boy get the education that is increasingly necessary for upward mobility. Moreover, they have little reason to suppose that if they did help, they would receive any benefit from it.

The case of China is especially instructive at this point. Families whose sons passed the third (highest) or second examination degrees "were entitled to the erection at their residence of a flagpole on which was hoisted a red silk flag bearing the academic degree written in gold."[1] Even lesser evidence of achievement might well be inscribed on the ancestral tablets, and clans typically attempted, when they became somewhat successful, to initiate historical studies designed to prove that members of their clan had in the past achieved academic and bureaucratic success.

Thus one can say that the Chinese lineage encouraged the support of individual mobility, because in turn it derived benefit from that mobility, both in honor and in material rewards. In blunt terms, they were likely to get their investment back.

The extent to which this is true in modern industrial society is not clear, although at present the evidence would seem to be negative. The maintenance of kin ties may be no more than a reaction to the general impersonality of urban life. We suspect, however, that empirical research will uncover far more actual exchanges of goods and services among kin; and far more pooling of economic resources for mutual advantage, than has been assumed in most analyses of our society. The hypothesis seems tenable, that the members of the extended network are more likely to tender such help if they can be sure that kin obligations will be returned; and that even when a man rises he will continue to recognize his own kin as (in at least some senses) *equal as* kinfolk.

To what extent this can be true in a society with so great a gap between the top and the bottom as in our own, is not yet clear. We believe, however, that we shall be able through research to uncover a number of family mechanisms for blurring or masking considerable differences in prestige or wealth. Finally, we may find it useful to distinguish between the *size* of kin network, that is, how many of affinal and blood kin are included from time to time; and the cohesiveness or *tightness* of the network. Perhaps it is only when this network is relatively tight that it plays a substantial role in upward mobility.

The case of India may have to be examined separately. It is possible that the support of the kin network or individual mobility requires not only that they be guaranteed some part of the spoils, should he rise, but also that he *himself* be permitted to enjoy the larger part of those spoils. The ideology in India, until recently (and sentiment in this regard still remains strong) was that the successful individual should contribute all of his

gains to the family pool, which would not only include everyone in his paternal line upward, but all of his brothers and their children as well. Indeed, it was not until a generation ago, with the passage of the Gains of Learning Act, that the Indian who was helped by his relatives to rise through education, could claim these gains as his own. Thus, it may be that the relatively lesser pressure of the joint family in India toward mobility did not arise so much from a lack of kin cohesion, as from the lack of any provision in the family ideology for an adequate payoff to the man who did work hard to rise.

The impact of social mobility on family structure

Just as it has been long assumed that upward mobility was easiest for those who were unencumbered by kin, so has it been assumed that the consequence of social class mobility would always be the disintegration of the family. The point has been made in essay and story for centuries, and doubtless contains an important truth: even kinfolk who move far away from one another are less likely to continue being intimate together; and those who enter very different ways of life may feel uncomfortable with one another, if not downright hostile. We know too, from a considerable amount of work over the past decade, that lineages and clan systems are dissolving all over the world, at least in part as a consequence of geographic and social mobility.

On the other hand, in a society with very high mobility, not only are the ties close among members of the small conjugal family, and the ties among siblings especially close, but a mounting body of evidence reveals that the extended kin network — whose demise had been announced for some generations — is very much alive and functioning.[2] The new data that demonstrate the aliveness of extended kin networks do give us a better picture of the operation of the family in an industrial society; but they do not prove that mobility has no effect on family patterns. Moreover, they do not tell us which *types* of family ties are maintained or dissolved, or how family members adjust to the strains caused by mobility.

It seems necessary to look at differing and changing patterns of communication, the frequency of interaction among kin under conditions of mobility, and the comparative size of kin networks when some siblings or relatives have been mobile and others not. In addition, it seems necessary to find out which kinds of activities are engaged in with mobile kin as against nonmobile kin; and which areas of social interaction remain, in which relatives attempt to maintain control over one another and to express family sentiment.

Occupational mobility of women

Although the problems of aspiration, motivation to achieve, and choice of occupation are similar among

---

[1] Ping-ti Ho, *op. cit.*, p. 29.

[2] See E. E. Lemasters, "Social Class Mobility and Family Integration," *Marriage and Family Living*, 16 (August, 1954), pp. 226–232 for some empirical evidence of disruption. Among the authors who have noted the disruptive effect of mobility are Talcott Parsons, Ernest W. Burgess and Harvey J. Locke and Carl Zimmerman.

women and several disadvantaged ethnic groups, in that many barriers have been maintained by the society, they are different in one important emphasis: At the same class and I.Q. levels, girls obtain only slightly less education than boys at the college level. Yet, at each successively higher level of training, women become increasingly scarcer, just as they are fewer at successively higher job levels. Although one may debate the issue philosophically, without question our society places the female in an inconsistent position, demanding high levels of achievement through high school, and even through college, but thereafter pressing her not to utilize her talents or skills.[1]

This pattern is common to Western nations, and in fact the percentage of women in the labor force has not increased substantially over the past half century in most of these societies. A largely untapped reservoir of creativity exists in the female population, but it is not yet clear just where the choice points and social or psychological pressures exist, to shape the result — that is, stimulating females to achieve, but then persuading them that they should not bother.

Some attention should be devoted to ascertaining whether a structural analog of the "achievement syndrome" for boys, analyzed earlier, is to be found for girls. Level of motivation, clarity of mobility goals, and pressure from peers, kin, close family, husband, and teacher, should be measured, to learn when and under which structural conditions the talented girl decides to give up. It is especially necessary that both men and women at the same stages in training be compared, since in many fields the rate of attrition among men is *also* high, and one cannot assume that if most women drop out they have done so because of social barriers erected against them.

Conclusion

In analyzing the radical social changes occurring in almost every country of the world, major attention should be given to alterations in stratification patterns. Even where great changes have not yet taken place, ideological and material forces have been set in motion to implement them. However, in every social system these patterns have been maintained through family structures, and the new hopes and goals of an altered stratification system will be embodied in new family behavior. It seems unlikely that either stratification or family variables are wholly dependent: both are independent sets of forces. Even if one set turns out, after careful study, to be less powerful, in understanding how social forces operate, it is important to ascertain *any determinate* relations between them.

In the foregoing analysis, part of a more extended report, attention was focused on one large set of such relationships, the structural points at which stratification and family patterns shape one another. In a broader view, of course, we would separate macrostructural patterns from microstructural ones; and forces that facilitate or hinder social mobility (and its frequent accompaniment, geographical mobility) from the *consequences* of mobility. In addition, with special reference to the microstructural forces, i.e., the patterns *within* the family unit, sociological analysis must be combined with sociopsychological data to explain the formation of motivational syndromes toward achievement and mobility. Space has precluded the inclusion of these materials, but it should be noted that such internal processes within the family are themselves shaped by the larger structural elements outlined in the present paper. It is to be hoped that further steps in both theory and description will yield a still more systematic picture of how these two great sets of forces interact to maintain or alter various types of social systems.

[1] W. J. Goode, *op. cit.*, pp. 54–66. See also E. Peterson, "Working Women," in *Daedalus*, 93 (Spring, 1964), pp. 671–699; A. K. Rossi, "Equality Between the Sexes: An Immodest Proposal," in *Daedalus*, 93 (Spring, 1964), pp. 607–652.

Class and Mobility in a Nineteenth-Century City

A STUDY OF UNSKILLED LABORERS[1]

Stephan Thernstrom

AMERICAN LEGEND has it that the United States has long been "the land of opportunity" for the common man. No other society has so often celebrated social mobility, none has made a folk hero of the self-made man to quite the same degree. The idea of the distinctive fluidity of our social order has been a national obsession for more than a century.

This has been the myth. How has it squared with social reality? The literature on social mobility in contemporary America is abundant, but social scientists have made few efforts to examine the problem in historical depth. One of the most glaring gaps in our knowledge of nineteenth-century America is the absence of reliable information about the social mobility of its population, particularly at the lower and middle levels of society. And ignorance of the past, in this instance,

clouds our understanding of the present as well. Recent scholarly disputes over the charge that the American class structure is becoming increasingly rigid have been heated but inconclusive.[2] The question of whether it is actually more difficult to rise from the bottom social ladder in the United States today than it was in the America of Horatio Alger can hardly be settled when so little is known about the actual extent of social mobility in our society prior to 1900.

The only systematic mobility research in America which extends back into the nineteenth century has examined the social origins of members of the American business elite. Valuable as this research has been, it must be said that very little can be learned about the range of mobility opportunities at the base of the social pyramid from a survey of the class origins of those who climbed to its very pinnacle. "Room at the top" is perhaps less important than room at the middle, and about room at the middle a century ago the business elite studies are silent.

This essay summarizes some of the findings of a small-scale inquiry which ventures into this important but virtually unexplored territory. For some years now I have been analyzing the career patterns of hundreds of obscure workmen living in a small New England city in the latter half of the nineteenth century, using evidence drawn from original manuscript schedules of the U.S. Census, local tax and school records, and a variety of other sources. Rates of intra-generational and inter-generational occupational mobility, property mobility, and geographical mobility were determined for the sample population, and these discoveries were used to reinterpret the social history of the community and to explain the successful integration of its industrial working class. A few of the chief conclusions of the study will be reviewed here, with particular attention to those of special interest to the sociologist.[3]

The site of the research was Newburyport, Massachusetts, a city which already enjoys a certain notoriety as the scene of W. Lloyd Warner's "Yankee City" inquiry. Since Vol. IV of the Yankee City study, *The*

[1] I am indebted to the Joint Center for Urban Studies of the Massachusetts Institute of Technology and Harvard University for generously supporting the research on which this article is based.

[2] Important statements of the blocked mobility hypothesis include: W. Lloyd Warner and J. O. Low, *The Social System of the Modern Factory* (New Haven, 1947), pp. 182–185, 87–89; Robert S. and Helen Merrell Lynd, *Middletown: A Study in American Culture* (New York, 1929), pp. 51, 65–66; *Middletown in Transition: A Study in Cultural Conflicts* (New York, 1937), pp. 67–72, 471; J. O. Hertzler, "Some Tendencies Towards a Closed Class System in the United States," *Social Forces*, XXX (1952), pp. 313–323.

For the opposite view, see Gideon Sjoberg, "Are Social Classes in America Becoming More Rigid?" *American Sociological Review*, XVI (1951), pp. 775–783; Ely Chinoy, "Social Mobility Trends in the United States," *American Sociological Review*, XX (1955), pp. 180–186; William Petersen, "Is America Still the Land of Opportunity? What Recent Studies Show about Social Mobility," *Commentary*, XVI (1953), pp. 477–486; Natalie Rogoff, *Recent Trends in Occupational Mobility* (Glencoe, 1953); Elton F. Jackson and Harry J. Crockett, Jr., "Occupational Mobility in the United States: A Point Estimate and Trend Comparison," *American Sociological Review*, XXIX (1964), pp. 5–15.

[3] It was not possible, in this brief essay, to describe in detail the procedures followed and the sources used. The skeptical reader will find a fully documented account in my book. The notes included here are intended only to clarify and to suggest some connections between my findings and those of other researchers.

This article was written especially for this book and is drawn from the author's *Poverty and Progress: Social Mobility in a Nineteenth Century City* (Cambridge, Mass.: Harvard U. Press, 1964), by permission of the publisher.

Social System of the Modern Factory, is one of the most important sources of the influential "blocked mobility" hypothesis, it seemed particularly appropriate to conduct my own study of social mobility in Newburyport. A full critical discussion of what Warner and his associates failed to understand about the community as a result of their ahistorical, functionalist methodological preconceptions cannot be included in this article, but it is important to point out here that nineteenth-century Newburyport was not the dormant, self-contained "predominantly old American" *Gemeinschaft* village portrayed in the Yankee City volumes. Both Warner's image of the community in the 1930's when his study was carried out, and his assumptions about the city's history were badly distorted. In the latter half of the nineteenth century Newburyport underwent a drastic economic and social transformation and became a booming industrial city with its full quota of factories and immigrants. The point is important, for it means that the data on social mobility reported below pertain not to a deviant community representing a "substitute cultural profile," but to a city exposed to the same massive social forces which were altering the face of hundreds of other American communities in those years.[1] To observe nineteenth-century Newburyport is not to view New York or Chicago in microcosm, of course, but this small New England city can legitimately serve as a case study of the social effects of processes which affected New York and every other American city to a greater or lesser degree. For this reason, these findings concerning social mobility in one nineteenth-century city, though hardly a satisfactory index of the openness of the national class structure of the era, seem to me to provide a useful new starting point for gauging long-term mobility trends in our society.

Sample and procedures

The population studied consisted of all male residents of Newburyport who reported "laborer" as their occupation on a U.S. Census schedule for 1850, 1860, or 1870, and all the sons of these men listed in the Newburyport schedules.[2] These obscure unskilled workmen and their children stood at the very bottom of the community social ladder, suffering from the classic disabilities of a depressed social group: unemployment, illiteracy, bad housing, poor diets. Roughly two-thirds of them were recent immigrants to the United States, uprooted Irish peasants driven to the New World by the terrible famine of the late 1840's. And the native-born Americans in the group were largely newcomers to urban life as well, migrants from the declining marginal farms of rural New England, men lacking capital or useful skills. The limited resources available for the study made it necessary to focus on a relatively small group. The unskilled laborers of the city were chosen as the least favorable case with which to test popular American mythology about mobility

opportunities. This choice imparted certain biases to the findings, of course; downward mobility, for instance, could not be explored, for these were men who could fall no lower on the social scale. But this seemed the most interesting starting point for a mobility inquiry. If many of these impoverished common laborers and their sons actually made significant social gains, it would seem particularly impressive testimony to the fluidity of the social structure.

The career patterns of laborers in the sample were traced through 1880. The selection of the 1850–1880 period was fortuitous (manuscript census schedules were unavailable before 1850 and after 1880) but not unfortunate, for these three decades were of decisive importance in the social and economic history of the community. It was in just these years that Newburyport, still a sleepy pre-industrial town of 7,000 in 1840, experienced the sudden shock of rapid population growth, mass immigration, and economic transformation. By 1880 a modicum of industrial peace and social stability had been restored in Newburyport, a development which cannot be properly understood without some grasp of the mobility patterns disclosed in the sample study.

Men on the move: the problem of geographical mobility

The most common form of mobility experienced by the ordinary laborers of nineteenth-century Newburyport was mobility out of the city. Slightly less than 40 percent of all the unskilled laborers and their children living in the community at mid-century were still listed there in the Census of 1860; of the 454 men in this class in 1860, but 35 percent were to be found in the city a decade later; the comparable figure for 1870–1880 was 47 percent. The first generalization to make about the "typical" Newburyport laborer of this period, it appears, is that he did not live in Newburyport very long! For a majority of these permanent transients, Newburyport provided no soil in which to sink roots. It was only one

---

[1] For the argument that Newburyport embodies a "substitute cultural profile," see Florence Kluckhohn, "Dominant and Substitute Profiles of Cultural Orientations: Their Significance for the Analysis of Social Stratification," *Social Forces*, XVIII (1949–50), pp. 376–393. A host of critics have attacked the assumption that small and seemingly static communities like Newburyport and Morris, Illinois ("Jonesville") are adequate laboratories for observing American social life. The critics are surely right to insist that the city Warner calls "Yankee City" must be considered a deviant case in many respects. My point, however, is that Newburyport was far less deviant than Warner made it out to be. See ch. viii and the appendix to my book for a full discussion of this.

[2] Errors were undoubtedly made in tracing the careers of these hundreds of individuals. For a variety of reasons such errors are most likely to have led to some overestimation of the extent of migration out of the community and perhaps some underestimation of the frequency of upward occupational mobility. However, a cross check against the Newburyport Assessor's lists revealed few mistakes and suggests that the margin of error in gathering data was relatively small.

more place in which to carry on the struggle for existence for a few years, until driven onward again.[1]

Did these men on the move make their fortunes elsewhere, in the Great West or the Great City, as American folklore would have it? It was impossible, regrettably, to trace these individuals and thereby to provide a certain answer as to how many of them were successful in other communities. In the absence of a magical electronic device capable of sifting through tens of millions of names and locating a few hundred there was no way of picking out former residents of Newburyport on later national censuses. It is important to note, however, that in only a handful of these cases was the laborer migrating from Newburyport in a particularly strategic position to take advantage of new opportunities in another community. If, for instance, the son of a laborer, unencumbered as yet with family responsibilities, was fortunate enough to possess a substantial savings account and perhaps a high school education or some experience in a skilled or nonmanual occupation, his employment prospects after migration were obviously excellent. Such cases, however, were rare. The great majority of laborers who left Newburyport departed under less auspicious circumstances. Without

financial resources, occupational skill, or education, frequently with heavy family responsibilities, the range of alternatives open to these men in their new destination was slender. Laborers like these were not lured to leave the city by the prospect of investing their savings and skills more profitably elsewhere; they left when the depressed state of the local labor market made it impossible for them to subsist where they were. As a result of the collapse of 1857, for example, Newburyport suffered a population decline estimated by the local newspaper as "more than one thousand." Most of these departures, it was thought, were cases of workers moving to "locations where work is more abundant."

That the geographical mobility of men in these circumstances dramatically improved their prospects of upward social mobility seems unlikely. The telling objection which has been advanced against the famous "safety valve" theory of the frontier applies here.[2] Migrant laborers from the city rarely had the capital or knowledge necessary to reap the benefits of the supply of "free land" at the frontier. Most often these workmen probably remained within the unskilled labor market centered in Boston and extending out to Lowell, Lawrence, Lynn, and smaller cities like Newburyport and Chicopee. And it is doubtful that a laborer without capital or skills found it notably easier to advance himself in Boston than in Newburyport. The great metropolis offered alluring opportunities at the top to those with the proper requisites, but to the common laborer who drifted there from Newburyport it probably meant more of the same.

The present study necessarily focused on the settled minority of workmen who remained within the community for a decade or more and whose careers could therefore be traced. It is highly improbable, however, that our lack of precise knowledge of the later careers of migrants from Newburyport has led to an underestimation of the upward mobility achieved by local laborers. An inquiry of this kind, indeed, is biased to some degree in the opposite direction. To analyze the social adjustment of workmen who settled in a particular city long enough to be recorded on two or more censuses is to concentrate on laborers who were most resistant to pressures to migrate, and these tended to be men who had already attained a modicum of economic security in the community. Thus four-fifths of the local unskilled laborers who owned real property in 1850 were still living in Newburyport in 1860, a persistence rate of 80 percent; the comparable figure for propertyless laborers in this decade was 31 percent. Migration was, in this sense, a selective process. Masses of unskilled newcomers — from rural areas and from abroad — streamed into the nineteenth-century city. Large numbers of these men were unable to establish a secure place for themselves in the community. Unemployment was always a possibility, and all too often a grim reality. When jobs were too few to go around, the rumor of work in Lawrence, or Lynn or Holyoke was enough to draw these men on. Workmen who remained in a

---

[1] This remarkable volatility of the local population, it should be noted, was not a working class phenomenon. During the three decades studied, Newburyport experienced something very close to a complete turnover of population. Of the 2,025 families recorded in the city directory of 1849, only 360 were listed in the directory of 1879. The social consequences of this are considered at length in ch. vii of my book. Nor is it likely that Newburyport was an exceptionally unstable community. Merle Curti found that less than 50 percent of each of several occupational groups in Trempealeau County, Wisconsin, remained there for as long as a decade in the 1850–1880 period; *The Making of an American Community: A Case Study of Democracy in a Frontier County* (Stanford, 1959), pp. 65–77. The population of Rochester, New York, appears to have been even less stable at this time. Only 47 percent of a sample of 500 names drawn from the 1849 city directory could be located in the 1855 edition, and the figure fell to 20 percent in 1859. See Blake McKelvery, *Rochester, the Flower City, 1855–1890* (Cambridge, 1949), p. 3. The whole question requires systematic study by American social and economic historians. For some valuable methodological suggestions, see Eric E. Lampard, "Urbanization and Social Change: On Broadening the Scope and Relevance of Urban History," in Oscar Handlin and John Burchard, ed., *The Historian and the City* (Cambridge, 1963), pp. 225–247.

[2] Carter Goodrich and Sol Davison, "The Wage Earner in the Westward Movement," *Political Science Quarterly*, L (1935), pp. 161–185, and LI (1936), pp. 61–110; Fred A. Shannon, "A Post Mortem on the Labor Safety Valve Theory," *Agricultural History*, XIX (1945), pp. 31–37; Clarence H. Danhof, "Farm-Making Costs and the 'Safety Valve;' 1850–1860," *Journal of Political Economy*, IL (1941), pp. 317–359. It is impressive that sample surveys conducted in Saskatchewan and Alberta in 1930–1931 revealed that a significant number of the farm operators of the prairie provinces had some previous experience in unskilled or semiskilled employment; see C. A. Dawson and Eva R. Younge, *Pioneering in the Prairie Provinces: The Social Side of the Settlement Process* (Toronto, 1940), pp. 120–123, 318. But many of these men had been born and raised on farms; and it is probable that relatively few of them had ever worked as laborers in cities hundreds of miles from the frontier. For other negative evidence on this point, see Oscar Handlin, *Boston's Immigrants: A Study in Acculturation* (Rev. ed., Cambridge, 1959), p. 159 and the literature cited there.

particular city for any length of time were therefore a somewhat select group, because to find sufficiently stable employment to maintain a settled residence in a community was itself success of a kind to the laborer. In tracing the changing social position of groups of Newburyport workmen we must keep this relationship between geographical mobility and social mobility clearly in mind. The process of internal migration within the unskilled labor market removed many of the least successful laborers from the community; the following analysis of occupational and property mobility in Newburyport applies only to a settled minority from the total unskilled laboring population which passed through the community between 1850 and 1880.

Patterns of intra-generational occupational mobility

In mid-nineteenth-century America there were few dissenters from the proposition that a uniquely open, perfectly competitive social order had emerged in the New World, a social order in which any man, however lowly his origins, could rise to a station befitting his true worth. A note of skepticism about the ideology of mobility, however, occasionally crept into the immigrant press. Thus the *Pilot*, organ of the Boston Irish, observing that "if the school of adversity is the best place to learn, few will be disposed to question the great opportunities enjoyed by us to acquire a knowledge of mankind," mounted a sharp attack on the myth of America as "the paradise of the poor man." Just how was the lot of "the poor man in America superior to the poor man in Austria or Italy?" The trinity of poverty, misery, and vice had been exported to the United States with eminent success. The braggart's "boastful tongue is silenced in hard times like these." And even in times of great prosperity, estimated the editors, 95 out of 100 ordinary workmen were fated to "live and die in the condition in which they were born." These opposed claims may be put to empirical test; this report on the social mobility experiences of laborers in a New England community is one such test.

An overview of the intra-generational occupational mobility of hundreds of unskilled laborers employed in Newburyport between 1850 and 1880 is provided in Table I.[1] Occupational mobility was defined simply as a job shift from one to another of four broad categories: unskilled manual occupations, semiskilled manual occupations, skilled manual occupations, and nonmanual occupations. In the original study more refined categories were employed at a later stage of the analysis, but these crude ones are well suited for this brief report on the chief findings.

The simplest generalization which suggests itself is that less than half of the unskilled workmen in Newburyport at the time of the Census of 1850, 1860 or 1870 remained there for as much as a decade, and that only a minority of those who did climbed up the occupational

ladder at all.[2] On the whole the likelihood of moving into a higher status occupation varied inversely with the status of the occupation. By far the most widespread form of vertical occupational mobility was into positions of only slightly higher status than unskilled labor — such

TABLE I. *Occupational and Geographical Mobility of Three Groups of Laborers, 1850–1880*

	OCCUPATIONAL STATUS ATTAINED					
Year	Un-skilled	Semi-skilled	Skilled	Non-manual	Rate of per-sistence[a]	Number in sample
	1850 census group					
1860	64%	16%	15%	5%	32%	55
1870	36	39	9	15	64	35
1880	57	21	7	14	40	14
	1860 census group					
1870	74	12	8	5	33	74
1880	69	19	6	6	65	48
	1870 census group					
1880	79	6	10	5	41	102

a This column provides a measure of the geographical mobility of workmen in the sample. The rate of persist-ence of a group for a particular decade is defined as that proportion of the group recorded on the census at the start of the decade that is still present in the community at the end of the decade. Thus 32 percent of the unskilled laborers of 1850 still lived in Newburyport in 1860; 64 per-cent of the men in this group as of 1860 still lived in Newburyport in 1870, and so forth.

semiskilled jobs as factory operative, fisherman or watchman. The common workman who resided in Newburyport in this period had only a slight chance of rising into a middle-class occupation, even when "middle class" is generously defined to include a petty clerkship or the proprietorship of a tiny grocery or a

[1] A word of warning is in order here. The discussion which follows is based on a series of tables which display in percentages the changing occupational distribution of several groups of men and boys. Scrutiny of the absolute numbers from which these percentages were calculated will reveal that, in some instances, occupational shifts by relatively few men appear as a rather dramatic percentage change. These changes in the occupational adjustment of even a small group of individuals are suggestive, but the reader must recall that this is an interpretative essay based on fragmentary data, not a large-scale, definitive statistical study.

It must also be remembered that these conclusions refer not to the entire working class population of the community but to *unskilled* laborers and their sons. Recent mobility research suggests the likelihood that an investigation of the career patterns of *skilled* families would have revealed substantially greater movement into nonmanual occupations. Presumably it would also have disclosed evidence of downward occupational mobility, since skilled workmen (unlike common laborers) have status to lose.

[2] The career patterns of three distinct groups of laborers are analyzed here. The first of these groups consists of all Newbury-port residents listed as unskilled laborers on the manuscript schedules of the U.S. Census of 1850. The second consists of men first listed as laborers in Newburyport on the Census of 1860, and the third of unskilled workmen new to the community in 1870.

subsistence farm. Nor was his prospect of entering a skilled craft very great. From 75 to 85 percent of these men remained near the bottom of the job ladder in the low-skill, low-pay occupational universe. The great majority continued to work as day laborers; most of those who did change occupations became semiskilled workmen, performing simple manual tasks at slightly higher wages and with somewhat more regular employment than they had previously enjoyed.

Comparison of the fortunes of the three groups of laborers studied suggests that the mobility prospects of those who arrived in Newburyport after 1850 were somewhat less favorable. Table 1 shows that workmen in the 1860 and 1870 groups tended to cluster more heavily towards the bottom of the occupational scale than laborers already working in the city in 1850. There was in fact a modest tightening of the local opportunity structure after 1850, a point to which we shall return later.[1] But much of this seeming change was an ethnic phenomenon. When the occupational distribution of foreign-born and native-born workmen in these years is tabulated separately it becomes evident that the immigrant was distinctly slower to rise occupationally than his Yankee counterpart, and that the apparent trend registered in Table 1 may be largely attributed to the higher proportion of foreign-born laborers in the two later groups.

Fathers and sons: patterns of inter-generational occupational mobility

If nineteenth-century Americans professed great optimism about the laborer's chances of "pulling himself up by his own bootstraps," they were more optimistic still about his children's prospects of rising in the world. A distinction between the situation of the first-generation immigrant and the second-generation American was frequently drawn in mobility folklore. A promotional book on *The Irish in America*, for example, was careful to say that in the New World "the rudest implements of labor may be the means of advancement to wealth, honour, and distinction, *if not for those who use them*, at least for those who spring from their loins."

Table 2 summarizes the career patterns of youths who sprang from the loins of the common laborers of Newburyport. The data are arranged by age groups, so that the adult occupations of laborers' sons as well as their initial jobs as teen-agers are displayed. Not all of the fathers of these youths actually remained unskilled laborers throughout this entire period, of course, but for the present this variable can be ignored. A majority

[1] It should be pointed out that the overall *shape* of the Newburyport occupational structure changed very little during this thirty-year period. The proportion of the labor force employed in skilled manual trades declined slightly between 1850 and 1880, and the semiskilled and nonmanual categories expanded slightly. It seemed pointless, therefore, to employ special techniques in an effort to control for the effects of changes in the occupational structure and to isolate "pure mobility."

of them did in fact remain laborers, and, as we shall see shortly, those who did climb a notch or two upwards had little success in passing on their advantage to their offspring.

In one important respect the sons of these laborers fared better than their fathers. Unskilled manual laborers in Newburyport during these years characteristically remained common laborers; the odds that one of these men would hold the same lowly position ten years later were at least two to one. But the sons of these unskilled workmen, Table 2 reveals, did not typically gravitate to unskilled jobs. In none of the age cohorts at any of the four censuses between 1850 and 1880 had a majority of these sons inherited their fathers' occupations; no more than one in four, on the average, were employed as common laborers.

TABLE 2. *Occupational and Geographical Mobility of Sons of Laborers, 1850–1880*[a]

	OCCUPATIONAL STATUS ATTAINED					
Year	Un-skilled	Semi-skilled	Skilled	Non-manual	Rate of per-sistence	Number
Youths born 1830–1839						
1850	39%	56%	6%	0%	—	18
1860	10	76	7	7	29%	41
1870	11	48	30	11	56	27
1880	11	42	37	11	63	19
Youths born 1840–1849						
1860	11	84	2	4	54	57
1870	28	45	17	10	32	58
1880	21	46	17	17	33	24
Youths born 1850–1859						
1870	23	59	11	7	54	95
1880	33	40	20	8	44	76
Youths born 1860–1869						
1880	25	60	7	8	56	73

[a] The reader may be surprised to see the number of youths in a group increasing from decade to decade in some instances, at the same time that the persistence rate figure indicates that half to two thirds of the group members left Newburyport each decade. The explanation is that large numbers of youths were coming *into* the city during these years as well, and that these have been included in the analysis.

If most of these youths moved upwards on the occupational ladder, however, few moved very far. The great majority of mobile sons found semiskilled manual employment, and most of the rest entered a skilled trade. The contrast between generations was not at all sharp in the upper ranges of the occupational scale. It is striking that entry into an occupation which carried middle class status was almost as difficult for the son of a common laborer as for his father.

The children of foreign-born workmen suffered from special disabilities in the occupational competition, as did their fathers. As Table 3 clearly shows, the proportion of native youths in skilled and nonmanual positions was consistently higher than the proportion of sons of immigrant stock; the latter clustered heavily near the bottom of the occupational scale. But these ethnic differences in mobility opportunities narrowed somewhat in the post-Civil War years. The popular belief that second generation Americans labored under no special handicaps in the race for occupational status was excessively optimistic, but Table 3 hints at the beginning of a trend towards some equalization of opportunities. It is noteworthy, however, that by 1880 none of these

control for when the sample is so small, or some other variable may have been responsible for the pattern disclosed in Table 4. But it remains impressive that the cross-tabulation provides no positive support for the belief that exceptionally mobile workmen imparted exceptionally high mobility aspirations to their children, nor for the hypothesis that a mobile father was able to ease his son's entry into a higher status occupation.

TABLE 3. *Occupational Distribution of Sons of Native and Foreign-born Laborers, 1850–1880*

Occupational category	1850		1860		1870		1880	
	Native	Foreign	Native	Foreign	Native	Foreign	Native	Foreign
Number in sample	19	14	34	76	37	148	37	158
Unskilled	26%	71%	12%	8%	8%	27%	19%	27%
Semiskilled	53	21	53	88	38	55	38	50
Skilled	21	7	18	3	27	14	24	15
Nonmanual	0	0	18	1	27	5	19	8

youths had advanced through the mobility channels so often stressed in impressionistic accounts of immigrant life – politics and religion. To become a priest required education; to become a ward boss required some education too, and a well-organized, politically conscious constituency. The Irish of Newburyport, and later groups as well, eventually attained these requisites, but only after long years of struggle.

Since these mobility data display the career patterns of two generations of men over a period of some decades, it is possible to explore a question which has rarely been examined by students of social mobility. Was occupational mobility a cumulative process, in the sense that a father's upward mobility positively influenced his son's prospects for occupational advance? A rather surprising, though tentative, answer is suggested by Table 4 which classifies the sons of Newburyport laborers according to the highest occupation held by their father in the 1850–1880 period. No consistent positive relationship between the occupational mobility of fathers and sons appears. The children of laborers mobile into a semiskilled occupation were more successful than the sons of static laborers in both the semiskilled and skilled callings, as we would expect. But workmen who climbed into a skilled trade were unable to transfer higher status to their children; their sons found skilled jobs less often than the sons of semiskilled men, and were the least successful of all the groups at penetrating the nonmanual occupations. And the sons of the small elite of laborers who rose into a nonmanual occupation during this period, paradoxically, clustered in unskilled laboring jobs more heavily than the sons of men still at the bottom of the occupational scale. The children of these highly mobile fathers, it is true, showed up much better than the other groups in the nonmanual category. But even so, only a third of them attained middle class occupational status, and this, for technical reasons, is an inflated estimate.[1] The table, however, is only suggestive. Differences in the age distribution of sons in the four categories, impossible to

Property, savings and status

Occupation, of course, is not the sole determinant of social status; men make certain social advances without changing their occupations at all. Class is not unidimensional; as Weber notes, "only persons who are completely unskilled, without property and dependent on employment without regular occupation, are in a strictly identical class status."[2]

The social group examined here consisted of men who did at one time hold a "strictly identical class status" in a nineteenth-century New England city. By any criterion the unskilled manual laborers of Newburyport at mid-century stood at the bottom of the social

TABLE 4. *Occupational Status Attained by Laborers' Sons According to the Highest Occupation of their Fathers*

Son's occupation at the last census on which he was listed in the 1850–1880 period	FATHER'S HIGHEST OCCUPATION IN THE 1850–1880 PERIOD			
	Unskilled	Semiskilled	Skilled	Nonmanual
Number in sample	234	38	23	24
Unskilled	26%	3%	9%	29%
Semiskilled	54	63	70	29
Skilled	13	24	17	8
Nonmanual	8	10	4	33

ladder. But how permanent was their lowly status? An assessment of the extent of occupational mobility out of the unskilled laboring class has been presented. The other major determinant of class status suggested by Weber – possession of property – should now be considered.

[1] For want of a better place to put them, youths working on farms owned by the fathers were ranked as nonmanual employees. Many of them, it is reasonable to assume, later entered ordinary manual laboring positions. There was no evidence of this, however, during the period studied.

[2] Max Weber, *The Theory of Social and Economic Organization* (New York, 1947), p. 425.

The facile optimism of nineteenth-century celebrants of the American way of life has been viewed with suspicion by twentieth-century historians. Few students of American labor history have expressed much optimism about the economic situation of the urban working class during the 1850–1880 period. Wages for unskilled and semiskilled labor were never very high in the best of times, and unemployment was endemic to the economic system. These three decades were punctuated by a national financial panic in 1857, a post-war slump, and a prolonged depression in the 1870's. A fairly characteristic judgment of working class opportunities for property mobility is Shlakman's verdict for Chicopee, Massachusetts: "Savings accumulated during the good years were eaten up in the frequent and severe depression periods." Another scholar reports that wages

returned by an observer of the Newburyport scene in 1850. And in many respects the lot of the laborer in 1880 seemed little better. Real earnings of unskilled workmen seem to have increased only slightly, if at all, in this period, and efforts to improve wages by collective action were still doomed to failure.

A careful tracing of the economic position of individual working class families through a variety of local records, however, yielded some surprising findings. Table 5, for example, which indicates the extent of real property ownership in the three groups, shows that real estate was strikingly available to working-class men who remained in Newburyport for any length of time. From a third to a half of these workmen were able to report some property holdings on the census schedules after a decade of residence in the city; after twenty years the

TABLE 5. *Property Holdings of Laboring Families*[a]

Year	Number of families	PROPERTY OWNERS		PERCENTAGE DISTRIBUTION BY VALUE			Median holding
		Number	Percent	Under $300	$300–999	$1000 or more	
				1850 census group			
1850	175	18	11%	0%	72%	28%	$600
1860	71	23	32	0	70	30	800
1870	49	38	78	8	47	45	800
1880	34	18	53	0	56	44	950
				1860 census group			
1860	256	28	11	4	86	11	700
1870	105	50	48	8	46	46	800
1880	70	44	63	5	52	43	800
				1870 census group			
1870	256	74	29	5	53	42	700
1880	121	49	41	6	61	33	700

* It may be noticed that the group numbers here are somewhat larger than those in the occupational mobility tables preceding. This is because the unit of study has shifted from the individual to the family. If the father in the 1850 group died in 1868, obviously no occupation would be listed for him in the Census of 1870. But if one of his employed sons continued to live with the family in 1870, the family would still be included in these property calculations.

in Holyoke in this period were "little more than enough to live on."[1]

An equally pessimistic diagnosis of the economic prospects of the laboring class might easily have been

[1] Vera Shlakman, *Economic History of a Factory Town: A Study of Chicopee, Massachusetts* (Northampton, 1936), pp. 193–194; Constance M. Green, *Holyoke, Massachusetts* (New Haven, 1939), pp. 44, 105. Edgar W. Martin's *The Standard of Living in 1860: American Consumption Levels on the Eve of the Civil War* (Chicago, 1942) concludes that the typical urban working-class family of the period had negligible prospects of saving anything but a tiny fraction of its income.

[2] The 1880 figures on Table 5 suggest a slowing of the trend towards more widespread property ownership and larger holdings, but this is a statistical artifact. The estimates for 1850, 1860 and 1870 come from manuscript schedules of the U.S. Census. No question about the ownership of real or personal property was included in the Census of 1880, unhappily, so local tax figures had to be used for that year, and those are notoriously conservative. A comparison of responses to census property questions in 1850, 1860 and 1870 with assessor's lists for the same years indicates that the 1880 figures on Table 5 are some 10 percent lower than they would have been had census data been available.

proportion of owners had risen to 63 percent in one group and 78 percent in another. The typical size of these accumulations, by men who had once lived on the margin of subsistence, was similarly impressive. The range of reported holdings was fairly wide, but the median figure was $600 or more for each group at each census. Only an insignificant fraction of these propertied workmen held less than $300, while a large and rising proportion reported accumulations valued at $1,000 or more.[2] Furthermore, a majority of the laboring families who settled in Newburyport in these years had accounts in local savings banks, and accumulations of several hundred dollars were not uncommon. That an ordinary workman in Newburyport might in time accumulate a sizeable property stake was not a mere possibility: it was a strong probability.

Inferences about the economic position of working-men based on raw wage data and dubious guesses as to "minimum" family budgets, it appears, can be extremely misleading. And confident estimates of the disastrous impact of seasonal and cyclical economic fluctuations on ordinary working-class families may be equally unreliable. In actuality, the depression of the middle and late 1870's, the second most severe and prolonged economic collapse in American history, did little to disturb the patterns of property mobility described here. A random check of 50 of the property-owning laboring families recorded in the Newburyport Assessor's Valuation Lists for 1870, 1873, 1876 and 1880 revealed that one-third of them actually increased their property holdings between 1873 and 1876, during the depths of the slump. In 1880 only 3 of the 50 were substantially poorer than they had been in 1870; 26 had increased their accumulation of taxable property. The depression may well have slowed the pace at which local workmen discharged the mortgages on their homes, but rarely did it reverse the gains already made. The very low rate of foreclosures on mortgages held by local workmen in this period is further testimony of the remarkable ability of settled working-class families to weather hard times.

Three reasons help to explain the striking ability of these families to accumulate property on pittance wages and to preserve it through prolonged depressions. First, it must be remembered that the most impoverished laborers, the working-class families hardest hit in a depression, were forced to go on the road; a study of laborers settled in a particular community deals with a selected minority who tended to be the last to be fired in hard times and the first to be rehired when the economy picked up.

A second point of great importance is that these settled laboring families were rarely dependent on the income of the chief wage earner alone. One member of family might often be out of work, but it was highly unusual for all able-bodied family members to be out of work simultaneously. The local newspaper gave an illuminating instance. Tim Harrington sent his wife and children to work; when they were employed he bought only the family flour out of his weekly wages and deposited the surplus in the savings bank. Unemployment rarely cut off the entire income of such families and ate up their savings; it commonly blocked only a portion of their income, and temporarily prevented further accumulation.

This is not to suggest, however, that these multiple income families could live comfortably and still put money in the bank. It cannot be emphasized too strongly that the real estate holdings and savings accounts of Newburyport laborers depended on ruthless *under-consumption*. Few of these families earned much above the "minimum" subsistence figure estimated by the Massachusetts Bureau of the Statistics of Labor, but they very often managed to consume much less than this "minimum" and to save the difference. A luxury like drinking, for example, was out of the question. The workman who wished to accumulate and maintain a property stake in the community had compelling reasons for sobriety; it was no coincidence that a Roman Catholic Temperance Society was formed in Newbury-

port at just the time that the Irish immigrants began their climb upward into the propertied sector of the working class.

Money in the bank and a place to live without paying rent did provide security against extreme want, and did give a man a certain respectability. Entry into the propertied sector of the working class was thus an important form of social mobility. But it was mobility within narrow limits, mobility which tended to close off future opportunities rather than open them, as Table 6 reveals. Common sense suggests that youths from the thrifty, respectable, home-owning segment of the working class would develop higher ambitions than the children of laborers living at the bare subsistence level, and that they would possess superior resources in the contest for better jobs. Table 6, however, suggests that this was not the case in Newburyport. Property mobility and inter-generational occupational mobility were not necessarily complementary forms of social

TABLE 6. *Occupational Status Attained by Laborers' Sons According to the Property Holdings of their Fathers*

Son's occupation at the last census on which he was listed in the 1850–1880 period	FATHER'S MAXIMUM PROPERTY HOLDING IN THE 1850–1880 PERIOD		
	Less than $300	$300–899	$900 or more
Number in sample[a]	121	65	48
Unskilled	24%	22%	35%
Semiskilled	59	57	38
Skilled	7	18	21
Nonmanual	11	3	6

a The numbers here are smaller than on Table 4, because property data were analyzed only for families resident in Newburyport for a decade or more during the period.

mobility; indeed, in some instances they were mutually exclusive. The sons of property-owning workmen entered skilled manual callings more often than sons of propertyless laborers, but they remained disproportionately concentrated in unskilled positions and, most surprising, somewhat underrepresented in nonmanual positions.

This striking discovery recalls an aspect of working-class property mobility about which the prophets of the nineteenth-century success creed were understandably silent. The ordinary workman of Newburyport could rarely build up a savings account or purchase a home without making severe sacrifices. To cut family consumption expenditures to the bone was one such sacrifice. To withdraw the children from school and to put them to work at the age of ten or twelve was another. As Table 6 shows, the sons of exceptionally prosperous laborers did *not* enjoy generally superior career opportunities; the sacrifice of their education and the constriction of their occupational opportunities, in fact, was often a prime cause of the family's property mobility.

This pattern was particularly characteristic of the Irish working-class families of Newburyport. Immigrants and their children, we saw, moved upwards on the occupational scale with greater difficulty than their Yankee counterparts. When we consider property mobility, however, the roles of the two groups are reversed. More than 60 percent of the foreign-born laborers of the community accumulated significant property holdings within a decade; the comparable figure for native workmen was little more than 40 percent. That Irish working-class families were especially successful in accumulating property but especially unsuccessful in climbing out of the low-status manual occupations was hardly a coincidence. The immigrant laborer received wages no higher than those of the Yankee workman, but he had a greater determination to save and to own. Perhaps the land hunger displayed by the Irish laborers of Newburyport was a manifestation of older peasant values. In any case, it was a hunger which could be satisfied to a remarkable extent by even the lowliest laborer — but only at a price. The price was not only ruthless economy; equally necessary was the employment of every able-bodied member of the family at the earliest possible age. The cotton mill or the shoe factory was not to provide the teen-agers of the second generation with the education a rapidly industrializing economy was making increasingly necessary, as the exceptionally low mobility of Irish youths into non-manual occupations so plainly reveals.[1]

Mobility, class conflict and social control

These findings about working-class social mobility reveal something of importance about the social consequences of urbanization and industrialization in nineteenth-century America. To set them in their proper historical context, and to relate them fully to the problems of disorder and social control which emerged as the forces of change reached into quiet villages and towns across the land cannot be attempted in the limited space available here. A few brief comments, however, may suffice to suggest how these findings can deepen our understanding of social change in the American city.

Until the 1840's, Newburyport had been a compact, stable, tightly-integrated community, dominated, in Henry Adams' phrase, by "a social hierarchy in which respectability, education, property and religion united

[1] Cf. Oscar Handlin's discussion of the differences between the adjustment of the Irish and the Jews in nineteenth-century New York; *The Newcomers: Negroes and Puerto Ricans in a Changing Metropolis* (Cambridge, 1959), pp. 26–27. For other suggestive evidence, see Curti, *The Making of an American Community*, pp. 183–187; Otis Dudley Duncan and Stanley Lieberson, "Ethnic Segregation and Assimilation," *American Journal of Sociology*, LXIV (1959), pp. 364–374.
[2] Cf. the excellent discussion of the Federalist elite of the day in Norman Jacobson, "Class and Ideology in the American Revolution," in the first edition of this Reader.

to defeat and crush the unwise and vicious."[2] The Federalist social system of old Newburyport collapsed when the industrialization and rapid urban growth of the 1840's drastically altered the composition of the Newburyport population and the relationship between the community's social classes. A host of anxieties about "the poor and the working classes of the city" developed then, anxieties reflecting changes both in the character of the local working class and in the institutional setting which had formerly promoted deference and subordination of lower-class elements. The old constraining network of religious, economic, political and personal controls had been drastically weakened; the charitable, educational, and legal institutions on which the burden of social control now fell seemed hopelessly inadequate substitutes.

Community fears focused particularly on the newly-arrived Irish, but in fact the separation of the Irish from Newburyport life was part of a larger social process which severed the entire lower class, foreign and native, from its traditional bonds to the community. The immigrant was naturally the most vulnerable target of the stereotypes. "When the paupers, criminals, and intriguing Jesuits are poured in upon us, then let every true-blue American show all such the way they should be received." The facile coupling suggested the ease with which a further equation could be made. Perhaps the impoverished and the immoral, the immigrants and the drifters, the coal-porters and the gravel-diggers were all part of the same class. If in fact only the foreign-born members of this class were, strictly speaking, "alien," in a deeper sense all were coming to be seen as alien to the traditional values of the community. The deep undercurrents of anxiety beneath the optimistic rhetoric of local politicians, ministers, and newspaper writers at mid-century, sometimes came to the surface, as in the editorial complaining that the imminent exhaustion of America's free land would mean that "the great safety valve of our prosperity will be forever closed." Then, as land became concentrated in the hands of "the strongest class," "the most indolent class" would be driven off the land and forced into the cities. In the sprawling cities, "the strife of competition" would become "a hundred fold more severe," and the gulf between "exaltation" and "degradation" would grow ever wider. In a similar vein, the Fourth of July oration delivered at City Hall in 1850 evoked an apocalyptic vision of a bloody struggle between "the *have-alls* and the *lack-alls*" which would end in either anarchy or tyranny.

These lurid fears rested on the premise that the alienated "lack-alls" of America were a permanent class, with a consciousness of their separate identity and a determination to fight for their interests. That this premise was false soon became clear to Newburyport residents, as the processes of mobility analyzed in this essay began to operate. Before long, the undifferentiated mass of poverty-stricken laboring families, the "lack-alls" who seemed at mid-century to be forming a permanent class, separated into three layers. On top was a small but significant elite of laboring families who had gained a foothold in the lower fringes of the middle-class occupational world. Below them was the large body of families who had attained property mobility while remaining in manual occupations, most often of the unskilled or semiskilled variety; these families constituted the stable, respectable, home-owning stratum of the Newburyport working class. At the very bottom of the social ladder was the impoverished, floating lower class, large in numbers but so transient as to be formless and powerless.

That movement into middle-class occupations inspired commitment to middle-class norms and promoted the integration of mobile working-class families into the community is obvious. But what was the significance of the much more common form of social advance achieved by the laboring families of Newburyport — mobility from the floating group of destitute unskilled families into the respectable, propertied sector of the working class? Nineteenth-century propagandists took a simple view. The property-owning laborer was "a capitalist." If there was a working class in America, as soon as "a man has saved something he ceases to belong to this class"; "the laborers have become the capitalists in this new world." Accumulated funds, however small, were capital, and the possession of capital determined the psychological orientation of the workman. It was the nature of capital to multiply itself; he who possessed capital necessarily hungered for further expansion of his holdings. To save and to invest was the first step in the process of mobility; it inspired a risk-taking, speculative mentality conducive to further mobility. The distinction between the "petty capitalist" workman and the rich merchant was one of degree. To move from the former status to the latter was natural; it happened "every day." Similar assumptions lie behind the still-popular view that "the typical American worker" has been "an expectant entrepreneur."[1]

This was sheer fantasy. A mere handful of the property-owning laborers of Newburyport ventured into business for themselves. More surprising, the property mobility of a laboring man did not even heighten his children's prospects for mobility into a business or professional calling. Indeed, the working-class family which abided by the injunction "spend less than you earn" could usually do so only by sacrificing the children's education for an extra paycheck, and thereby restricting their opportunities for inter-generational occupational mobility.

Furthermore, the use these laborers made of their savings testifies to their search for maximum *security* rather than for *mobility* out of the working class. An economically rational investor in nineteenth-century Newburyport would not have let his precious stock of capital languish in a savings bank for long, and he certainly would not have tied it up in the kind of real estate purchased by these laborers. The social environment of the middle-class American encouraged such

investment for rising profits, but the working-class social milieu did not. The earning capacity of the merchant, professional, or entrepreneur rose steadily as his career unfolded — the very term "career" connotes this. The middle-class family head was ordinarily its sole source of support, and the family was able both to accumulate wealth and to improve its standard of living out of normal increments in the salary (or net profits) accruing to him over the years.

Ordinary workmen did not have "careers" in this sense. Their earning capacity did not increase with age; in unskilled and semiskilled occupations a forty-year-old man was paid no more than a boy of seventeen. Substantial saving by a working-class family thus tended to be confined to the years when the children were old enough to bring in a supplementary income but too young to have married and established households of their own.

The tiny lots, the humble homes, the painfully accumulated savings accounts were the fruits of those years. They gave a man dignity, and a slender margin of security against unpredictable, uncontrollable economic forces which could deprive him of his job at any time. Once the mortgage was finally discharged, home ownership reduced the family's necessary expenses by $60 to $100 a year, and a few hundred dollars in the savings bank meant some protection against illness, old age, or a sluggish labor market. While a cynical observer would have noted the possibility that home ownership served also to confine the workman to the local labor market and to strengthen the hand of local employers, who were thus assured of a docile permanent work force, few laborers of nineteenth-century Newburyport were disposed to think in these terms.

If, however, families belonging to the propertied stratum of the working class had not set their feet upon an escalator which was to draw them up into the class of merchants, professionals and entrepreneurs, they had established themselves as decent, hard-working, church-going members of the community. In this sense, the ordinary workmen of Newburyport could view America as a land of opportunity despite the fact that

[1] For a recent elaboration of the familiar view that the psychology of the American working class has been "entrepreneurial" see Gerald N. Grob, *Workers and Utopia: A Study of Ideological Conflict in the American Labor Movement, 1865–1900* (Evanston, 1961), pp. 165–166, 189. The classic expressions of this approach are to be found in the writings of "the Wisconsin school" of labor history; see John R. Commons *et. al., History of Labor in the United States*, 4 vols. (New York, 1918–1935) and Selig Perlman, *A Theory of the Labor Movement* (New York, 1928). For a perspective on working-class life closer to that taken here, see Richard Hoggart, *The Uses of Literacy: Aspects of Working Class Life, With Special Reference to Publications and Entertainments* (London, 1957); Ely Chinoy, *Automobile Workers and The American Dream* (Garden City, N.Y., 1955); S. M. Miller and Frank Riessman, "Are Workers Middle Class?" *Dissent*, VIII (1961), pp. 507–513 and the works cited there; Miller and Riessman, "The Working Class Subculture: A New View," *Social Problems*, IX (1961), 86–97; Herbert J. Gans, *The Urban Villagers: Group and Class in the Life of Italo-Americans* (Glencoe, 1962).

the class realities which governed their life chances confined most of them to the working class. The gospel of success, it may be suggested, had symbolic truth to these obscure men. Not one rose from rags to riches, but all of them could see that *self-improvement was possible*. This sense of satisfaction, and the conformity to community norms which it inspired, cannot be further documented here,[1] but it provides an essential clue to the social history of Newburyport as the community peacefully adjusted to the challenges of an industrial civilization.

A note on mobility trends in the United States

The U.S. Census of 1850 counted 62 cities of more than 10,000; by the end of the century the number

scattered evidence concerning social mobility in several American cities in the twentieth century, allows us to reappraise the blocked mobility hypothesis. If the level of mobility opportunities open to unskilled workmen and their children in nineteenth-century Newburyport was at all representative of other American cities of the period, the contrast between the boundless opportunities of the past and the constricted horizons of the present drawn by writers like Warner is a romantic illusion. To rise from "the bottom of the social heap" has not become increasingly difficult in modern America; if anything, Tables 7 and 8 suggest, it has become somewhat less difficult.

Studies of the intra-generational occupational mobility rates of unskilled laborers are regrettably scarce; the available evidence, however, is relatively unambiguous. Table 7 compares the Newburyport findings with the

TABLE 7. *Occupational Status Attained by Unskilled Laborers over Ten-year Periods, Selected Cities, 1850–1950*[a]

	Unskilled	Semiskilled	Skilled	Nonmanual	Number in sample
Newburyport					
1850–1860	64%	16%	15%	5%	55
1860–1870	74	12	8	5	74
1870–1880	79	6	10	5	102
Norristown					
1910–1920	70	14	6	10	825
1920–1930	70	12	10	8	925
1930–1940	52	30	10	8	1180
1940–1950	51	26	12	12	1065
Chicago, Los Angeles, New Haven, Philadelphia, St. Paul, San Francisco					
1940–1950	65	26	26	9	—

[a] The Norristown data were drawn from local city directories by Sidney Goldstein; see *Patterns of Mobility, 1910–1950: The Norristown Study* (Philadelphia, 1958), pp. 169, 175, 178, 185. The figures for the six major cities are from Gladys L. Palmer, *Labor Mobility in Six Cities: A Report on the Survey of Patterns and Factors in Labor Mobility, 1940–1950* (New York, 1954), p. 115. Semiskilled, skilled, and service workers are combined in one category in the Palmer report, unfortunately, but the unskilled and nonmanual estimates are acceptable for comparative analysis. The number of unskilled laborers in the sample is not reported, but the survey as a whole is based on some 13,000 work history schedules collected in the six cities.

stood at 440. Can a study of social mobility patterns in one of these communities tell us anything about the others? Is it possible, on the basis of the Newburyport example, to draw any broader conclusions about the social structure of nineteenth-century America? I believe that it is, to some degree. There are good theoretical grounds for believing in certain uniformities in the impact of urbanization and industrialization within a given society, and a few suggestive fragments of evidence gathered by other investigators tend to support the view that the patterns of working-class mobility found in Newburyport in the latter half of the nineteenth century were the result of forces which were operating in much the same way in cities throughout the entire society. The point can only be asserted here; the skeptical reader will find a full discussion of it in the book from which this essay is drawn.

If this be granted, the present study, coupled with

[1] See ch. vii of my book for a full discussion.

results of mobility inquiries dealing with Norristown, Pennsylvania between 1910 and 1950, and with six major metropolitan centers in the decade 1940–1950. The career patterns of common workmen in these cities displayed a striking resemblance, it is clear, and the small differences which can be detected indicate slightly superior opportunities in the twentieth-century community. Only one laborer in twenty from the Newburyport sample rose into a nonmanual position, while the figure for Norristown, Chicago, Los Angeles and the others was approximately one in ten. The tremendous expansion of menial white-collar and sales positions which has produced these new opportunities in the nonmanual occupations has also tended to blur income and status differentials between manual and nonmanual callings, of course, so that upward mobility into a routine white-collar job means less of a status advance than it did a century ago. While this is an important qualification, it remains the case that the rise from an unskilled laboring position to virtually any nonmanual occupation represents significant upward mobility. Mobility of this kind is not being blocked; it appears to be on the increase in the modern American city.

Much more is known about the occupational attainments of the sons of unskilled laborers in the United States, and it is possible to conclude with some confidence that in the past century there has been a mild trend towards greater upward mobility. The available

unskilled laborers working in Norristown in 1952, five out of ten held unskilled or semiskilled positions, while three were in nonmanual callings. The data from San Jose, Indianapolis, New Haven and the other communities listed on Table 8 covering the years 1900–1956, indicate that this contrast reflects a genuine trend. It may be objected that the first column of the table, which shows the extent of direct inheritance of unskilled manual positions in these several cities, does not reveal

TABLE 8. *Occupational Status Attained by Sons of Unskilled Laborers, Selected Samples, 1860–1956*[a]

Sample	Unskilled	Semiskilled	Total of unskilled and semiskilled	Skilled	Nonmanual	Number in sample
Newburyport 1860–1880	22%	49%	71%	19%	10%	245
San Jose, Calif. ca. 1900	60	4	64	16	20	70
Indianapolis 1910	36	20	56	28	16	1195
New Haven 1931	—	—	72	13	15	153
San Jose 1933–34	42	17	59	14	28	242
Indianapolis 1940	30	32	62	16	21	675
U.S. National Sample 1945	38	20	58	17	25	41
Chicago, Los Angeles, San Francisco, Philadelphia 1950	20	34	54	27	20	—
Norristown 1952	14	34	48	24	28	86
U.S. National Sample 1956	25	28	53	28	20	87

a The Newburyport figures represent the distribution of occupations held by laborers' sons aged twenty or over in 1860, 1870, or 1880. The age limitation was essential to avoid an overrepresentation of boys holding their first jobs. Most of the other studies reported made some attempt to eliminate very young males, but the varying age limits of the samples remain an inescapable source of variation between the studies. The San Jose figures were calculated from Percy E. Davidson and H. Dewey Anderson, *Occupational Mobility in an American Community* (Stanford, 1937), pp. 20, 29, The ca. 1900 estimate for San Jose is not very reliable since it depends on a retrospective estimate (in 1933–34) by respondents of the regular occupation of their fathers and grandfathers. Unskilled and semiskilled occupations, unfortunately, were not distinguished in the New Haven survey; John W. McConnell, *The Evolution of Social Classes* (Washington, 1942), p. 216. The Indianapolis figures are for all of Marion County, Indiana, which includes some suburban and rural fringes around Indianapolis as well as the city itself. They were calculated from the detailed mobility tables included in Rogoff's *Recent Trends in Occupational Mobility*. The 1945 sample of the adult white population of the U.S. is reported in Richard Centers, "Occupational Mobility of Urban Occupational Strata," *American Sociological Review*, XIII (1948), pp. 197–203. The 1950 data for Chicago, Los Angeles, San Francisco, and Philadelphia were gathered in the Occupational Mobility Survey carried out under the auspices of the Committee on Labor Market Research of the Social Science Research Council, seven university research centers, and the U.S. Bureau of the Census and were published in Stanley Lieberson, *Ethnic Patterns in American Cities* (Glencoe, Ill., 1963), pp. 186–187; the number in the sample was not reported. The Norristown figures, based on data from the Norristown Household Survey, are for adult whites; see Sidney Goldstein, ed., *The Norristown Study*, p. 109. The 1956 national sample was selected by the Survey Research Center of the University of Michigan; reported in S. M. Miller, "Comparative Social Mobility: A Trend Report and Bibliography," *Current Sociology*, IX (1960), p. 78.

evidence is summarized in Table 8. The occupational categories used in the various studies reported there varied slightly, and there were differences in sampling techniques which could produce artificial variations. The consistency of the findings, given these facts, is impressive.

Of the sons of unskilled laborers employed in nineteenth-century Newburyport, seven out of ten held unskilled or semiskilled jobs themselves and one was in a nonmanual position of some kind; of the sons of

any such clear trend. Neither does the second column, which measures movement in semiskilled occupations. But this should come as no surprise, for the Newburyport evidence showed that the unskilled and semiskilled occupations constituted a common occupational universe; while there were status differences between these two job categories, they were small and movement between the two was very easy. The same held true in other American communities, Table 8 shows clearly; the concentration of laborers' sons in unskilled jobs and in semiskilled jobs fluctuated widely from city to city, but the concentration of sons in the *low-skill occupational universe* (column three) varied relatively little. The unskilled and semiskilled total is a better indicator of mobility trends than either separately, and it shows a modest but definite improvement in the prospects of youths of lowly birth. More than two-thirds of them remained in low-status callings in Newburyport; a figure this high was reported in only one of the nine twentieth-century studies, and the lowest concentration of sons in unskilled and semiskilled work was found in the three post-World War II inquiries.[1]

The converse of this decline in the tendency of youths from unskilled working-class families to remain in the low-skill occupational universe, of course, was their growing representation in the skilled and nonmanual occupations. The skilled column of Table 8 actually presents a rather confused picture; the variation in skilled opportunities from community to community was sizeable, and it is difficult to see any clear trend, though the fact that three of the four highest figures were from the post-war studies should be a valuable reminder that the disappearance of the glassblower and the shoemaker of old must not be confused with a disappearance of the skilled crafts themselves.

The evidence of a modest trend towards increased mobility from the bottom of the occupational scale into business, professional, and white-collar callings is fairly persuasive. A few of the figures seem surprising, but it is surely significant that the six studies covering the 1933–1956 period show two to three times as many laborers' sons in nonmanual positions as the figures for Newburyport in the latter half of the nineteenth century and for Indianapolis in 1910.[2] In recent decades white-collar and professional occupations have made up an ever-increasing segment of the American occupational structure, and during the same period the American

educational system has become markedly more democratic. The fruits of these two developments are graphically displayed here, in the rising proportion of laborers' sons who no longer face the necessity of making a living with their hands. Whatever the effects of mechanization, the closing of the frontier, the narrowing of class differences in fertility, and a host of other factors which have inspired gloomy prophecies of an increasingly rigid class structure in the United States, their combined effect has evidently been insufficient to offset these forces making for improved mobility opportunities for men at the bottom of the occupational ladder.[3]

Nor does it seem likely that a serious case could be made that opportunities for property mobility are declining. If it is not at all clear that the distribution of income in the United States has become markedly more equal in recent decades, it is incontestable that in every occupational class absolute levels of real income have risen dramatically. The extraordinary devotion to home ownership displayed by the Irish working-class families of Newburyport has not been uniformly displayed by American workmen in subsequent decades, but other forms of investment — the automobile, for example, have become increasingly important. The two Middle-town volumes are rich with data concerning these changes in the working-class style of life, and a few later studies supply evidence on property mobility in the post-World War II period. Chinoy's suggestive report, *Automobile Workers and the American Dream*, shows in convincing detail how, for factory workers lacking any reasonable prospects of upward occupational mobility, "the constant accumulation of personal possessions" has provided substitute gratifications which allow them to retain a belief that they are "getting ahead."[4]

Whether our index of the openness of the class structure be the extent of intra-generational occupational mobility, of inter-generational occupational mobility, or property mobility, therefore, it is difficult to resist the conclusion that chances to rise from the very bottom of the social ladder in the United States have not declined visibly since the nineteenth century; they seem, in fact, to have increased moderately in recent decades.

To say this is not to say that opportunities are boundless in present-day America, that ours is a society in which every "deserving" man holds a status in accord with his "true merit." Opportunities are neither boundless nor are they equal in the United States today, as an abundance of sociological research into class differences testifies. The mere fact of being born into a middle-class or a working-class home still profoundly influences the life chances of every American — his prospects of obtaining a college education, finding a good job, living in decent housing, even his prospects of enjoying mental and physical health and living to an advanced age.

All this is true, but we can obtain some true perspective on the present only when we shed the rose-tinted spectacles through which the American past has

---

[1] The high concentration of sons in the low-skill occupational universe in New Haven was probably due largely to the fact that the sample included many more very young men than any of the others; the minimum age for inclusion in the New Haven Sample Family Survey was only sixteen, and all respondents were unmarried and living at home.

[2] Both of the San Jose estimates seem high, but the ca. 1900 figure warrants little confidence for reasons advanced in the note to Table 8. It is quite possible, of course, that California attracts a disproportionately ambitious and talented migrant population, and this may be reflected in both San Jose figures.

[3] It can be objected, of course, that the trend towards somewhat greater access to nonmanual jobs for men of working-class origins has been accompanied by a decline in the relative status of nonmanual as against manual occupations; see C. Wright Mills, *White Collar: The American Middle Classes* (New York, 1951) for a discussion of the dramatic expansion of menial white-collar occupations in recent decades and the consequent blurring of income and other status differentials between blue-collar and white-collar work. This is indeed an important point, but it may be doubted that many white-collar workers evaluate their status as negatively as Mills does. Certainly in present-day America most shifts from manual to nonmanual positions would still be considered upward mobility by most observers.

[4] Chinoy, *Automobile Workers*, 124.

characteristically been viewed. In the United States today the climb upward from the bottom rungs of the social ladder is not often rapid or easy, but *it never was*, if the experiences of the working-class families of nineteenth-century Newburyport are at all representative. Few of these men and few of their children rose very far on the social scale; most of the upward occupational shifts they made left them manual workmen still, and their property mobility, though strikingly widespread, rarely involved the accumulation of anything approaching real wealth. This was not the ladder to the stars that Horatio Alger portrayed and that later writers wistfully assumed to have been a reality in the days of Abraham Lincoln and Andrew Carnegie. It was, however, social advancement of a kind immensely meaningful to men whose horizons of expectations were not those of an Alger hero. Low-level social mobility of this sort does not seem more difficult for the American working-class family today; quite the contrary.

Six

Pending Issues

The Other America: Definitions

Michael Harrington

WHEN I FIRST BEGAN research on the culture of poverty in the United States, I was writing a piece for *Commentary* magazine. The article was in galley proof when I got a call from one of the editors there. Someone, he said, had just run across an analysis in *Fortune* that gave a much more optimistic picture of the income pattern in the United States. How could this be, given the fact that I was arguing that there were 50,000,000 or more poor people in this land?

I read the article. *Fortune* was using the same basic research that I was quoting. The difference was in point of view. The *Fortune* writer focused on the development of the middle third in American society — the organized worker in well-paying industry, those who benefited from rising levels of education, and so on — and there was indeed a heartening rise in standard of living for these people. Yet, in the *Fortune* analysis the bottom group was there. It was simply that these people were not commented upon.

The *Fortune* writer had been looking for improvement in American society, and he had located a very real area of advance. In my book, let it be said candidly, I had been looking for retrogression and stagnation. Those in American society who have been moving up in the world have enough celebrants and chroniclers; they are the stuff of proud boasts and claims. But those who have been omitted from progress have been, over long stretches of time, forgotten.

If my interpretation is bleak and grim, and even if it overstates the case slightly, that is intentional. My moral point of departure is a sense of outrage, a feeling that the obvious and existing problem of the poor is so shocking that it would be better to describe it in dark tones rather than to minimize it. No one will be hurt if the situation is seen from the most pessimistic point of view, but optimism can lead to complacency and the persistence of the other America.

This is not to say that the statistics in my book have been invented or misrepresented. They come from Government sources and they have been confirmed in most cases by my own experiences in walking the streets of the slums and talking to the people, or visiting the broiling-hot fields of the California migrants. Yet there is an understandable and legitimate area in which interpretation and point of view give rise to different conclusions.

In Robert Lampman's Senate study, for instance, the author notes that the estimate of low-income people in the United States could "reasonably range" between 16 per cent and 36 per cent of the population. Stated as percentages, the differences involved in these definitions might not seem to be too huge. But if one translates these figures into numbers of human beings, the discrepancy is huge and obvious: the high figure includes 36,000,000 more people than the low one.

Moreover, the choice of figure will determine one's picture of the kind of people who make up the culture of poverty. The lower the cut-off line by which one establishes poverty, the fewer large families will be included, and the aged will be a higher percentage. This obviously is of great importance, for at least one consequence of a study of poverty should be to point America toward those groups that must be given special help.

In this explanatory note I have presented the statistical assumptions and basic interpretations that underlie the rest of the book. In such a discussion it is inevitable that one gets mixed up with dry, graceless, technical matters. That should not conceal the crucial fact that these numbers represent people and that any tendency toward understatement is an intellectual way of acquiescing in suffering.

I have been guided by two principles: to be as honest and objective as possible about the figures; to speak emotionally in the name of the common humanity of those who dwell in the culture of poverty. If some statistician should find an error in technical approach, if

---

Reprinted from *The Other America* (N.Y.: Macmillan, 1962), pp. 175–191, by permission of the author and the publisher.

he could say, there are 10,000,000 less poor, that would not really be important. Give or take 10,000,000, the American poor are one of the greatest scandals of a society that has the ability to provide a decent life for every man, woman, and child.

I

In the nineteenth century, conservatives in England used to argue against reform on the grounds that the British worker of the time had a longer life expectancy than a medieval nobleman.

This is to say that a definition of poverty is, to a considerable extent, a historically conditioned matter. Indeed, if one wanted to play with figures, it would be possible to prove that there are no poor people in the United States, or at least only a few whose plight is as desperate as that of masses in Hong Kong. There is starvation in American society, but it is not a pervasive social problem as it is in some of the newly independent nations. There are still Americans who literally die in the streets, but their numbers are comparatively small.

This abstract approach toward poverty in which one compares different centuries or societies has very real consequences. For the nineteenth century British conservative, it was a way of ignoring the plight of workers who were living under the most inhuman conditions. The twentieth century conservative would be shocked and appalled in an advanced society if there were widespread conditions like those of the English cities a hundred years ago. Our standards of decency, of what a truly human life requires, change, and they should.

There are two main aspects of this change. First, there are new definitions of what man can achieve, of what a human standard of life should be. In recent times this has been particularly true since technology has consistently broadened man's potential: it has made a longer, healthier, better life possible. Thus, in terms of what is technically possible, we have higher aspirations. Those who suffer levels of life well below those that are possible, even though they live better than medieval knights or Asian peasants, are poor.

Related to this technological advance is the social definition of poverty. The American poor are not poor in Hong Kong or in the sixteenth century; they are poor here and now, in the United States. They are dispossessed in terms of what the rest of the nation enjoys, in terms of what the society could provide if it had the will. They live on the fringe, the margin. They watch the movies and read the magazines of affluent America, and these tell them that they are internal exiles.

To some, this description of the feelings of the poor might seem to be out of place in discussing a definition of poverty. Yet if my book indicates anything about the other America, it is that this sense of exclusion is the source of a pessimism, a defeatism that intensifies the exclusion. To have one bowl of rice in a society where all other people have half a bowl may well be a sign of achievement and intelligence; it may spur a person to

act and to fulfill his human potential. To have five bowls of rice in a society where the majority have a decent, balanced diet is a tragedy.

This point can be put another way in defining poverty. One of the consequences of our new technology is that we have created new needs. There are more people who live longer. Therefore they need more. In short, if there is technological advance without social advance, there is, almost automatically, an increase in human misery, in impoverishment.

And finally, in defining poverty one must also compute the social cost of progress. One of the reasons that the income figures show fewer people today with low incomes than twenty years ago is that more wives are working now, and family income has risen as a result. In 1940, 15 per cent of wives were in the labor force; in 1957 the figure was 30 per cent. This means that there was more money and, presumably, less poverty.

Yet a tremendous growth in the number of working wives is an expensive way to increase income. It will be paid for in terms of the impoverishment of home life, of children who receive less care, love, and supervision. This one fact, for instance, might well play a significant role in the problems of the young in America. It could mean that the next generation, or a part of it, will have to pay the bill for the extra money that was gained. It could mean that we have made an improvement in income statistics at the cost of hurting thousands and hundreds of thousands of children. If a person has more money but achieves this through mortgaging the future, who is to say that he or she is no longer poor?

It is difficult to take all these imponderables together and to fashion them into a simple definition of poverty in the United States. Yet this analysis should make clear some of the assumptions that underlie the assertions in this book:

Poverty should be defined in terms of those who are denied the minimal levels of health, housing, food, and education that our present stage of scientific knowledge specifies as necessary for life as it is now lived in the United States.

Poverty should be defined psychologically in terms of those whose place in the society is such that they are internal exiles who, almost inevitably, develop attitudes of defeat and pessimism and who are therefore excluded from taking advantage of new opportunities.

Poverty should be defined absolutely, in terms of what man and society could be. As long as America is less than its potential, the nation as a whole is impoverished by that fact. As long as there is the other America, we are, all of us, poorer because of it.

II

Probably the simplest way to get an idea of how many poor people there are in the United States is to use the income figures supplied by various Government agencies.

Without question, this approach misses many subtle distinctions. It does not, for example, allow for individual variation: How skilled a cook is a certain wife? What are the foods of a particular ethnic group and how much do they cost? Using this method, the very important issue of the increase in working wives is slighted. But, though it misses the quality of life in the other America, the income test does provide a rough index of poverty in the United States.

In the late forties the low-income studies of special congressional committees fixed a poverty line at $2,000 money income for an urban family of four. If this were brought up to date (that is, if it were simply corrected for inflationary changes that have taken place in the intervening years) it would be around $2,500 a year. However, at the time this figure was set various authorities argued that the definition put the minimum income much too low. And by merely revising it so that it expresses 1961 prices, this test tacitly assumes that there should be no progress over the course of a decade. In short, it leaves out the fact that this was a time when other groups in the society advanced.

Recently, Robert Lampman's study used the $2,500 cut-off as establishing the low-income line for an urban family of four. Lampman then assumed that other family sizes would be in direct proportion to this figure; an urban individual would be low-income if he received $1,157; a six-person family would meet the definition if its annual money take was $3,236, and so on. On this basis, Lampman came to the conclusion that 19 per cent of the American population, 32,000,000 people, were in the low-income classification.

In the same period, the AFL-CIO used a slightly higher definition of what constituted low income. It found that 36,000,000 Americans were living in households of two persons or more with 1958 incomes of less than $3,000. Another 5,500,000 individuals were living on incomes of under $1,500 (which is less than $29 a week before taxes). Thus the AFL-CIO statisticians would argue that there were 41,500,000 Americans — 24 per cent of the population — who had demonstrably substandard incomes.

Since the Lampman and AFL-CIO estimates, the Bureau of Labor Statistics has issued a report that would indicate that both of these studies had a tendency toward understating the problem. Throughout his work Lampman assumed that the "adequate" budget for a four-person urban family in Bureau of Labor Statistics terms would be just over $4,000 a year. The AFL-CIO had the same figure pegged at $4,800 a year.

However, both of these calculations were based on an approach to "adequacy" developed by the Government in the late forties (and adjusted, without changing the basic concepts, for price increases over the intervening years). More recently, the Bureau of Labor Statistics has produced a new budget for an urban family of four. It varies from $5,370 in Houston to $6,567 in Chicago, with Washington, D.C., close to an average at $6,147. According to the Government, these figures define a budget that is above "minimum maintenance" and well below "luxury." It is seen as "modest but adequate," although it is "below the average enjoyed by American families."

This budget is an important attempt at specifying income needs, and it is worth going into a little detail about it before attempting a definition of poverty. The family of four in these Government figures assumes an employed thirty-eight-year-old husband, a wife who is not employed outside the home, a girl of eight and a boy of thirteen. The family lives in a rented dwelling in a large city or its suburbs. The budget is based on prices in the fall of 1959.

Here are some typical examples of the budget items as they were computed in Washington, D.C. (the city closest to the average): the total allotment for food was $1,684, with $1,447 spent on meals at home and $181 on dining out; rent was calculated at $1,226; the wife had $160 to spend on clothing during the year. Clearly, this is not a budget for the gracious living depicted by the American magazines. It is not, in contemporary terms, poverty or anything like it. But such a family would face a serious crisis in the event of a protracted illness or long-term unemployment for the family head.

Another important factor in the Bureau of Labor Statistics budget is the way in which it computes the cost for maintaining families that are smaller or larger than the typical case of four. The two-person budget, for instance, is a little better than 60 per cent of the budget for the family of four.

On this basis, if one were to take approximately half of this budget as the standard for low income or poverty (making all the adjustments for smaller families, for low-income individuals, for lower costs, and for food grown in farm areas), if the cut-off were established somewhere between $3,000 and $3,500 for an urban family of four, then the culture of poverty would be roughly defined in the United States as composed of around 50,000,000 people. (Using Lampman's figures, and taking $4,000 as the cut-off, which is the top level he considers to be a "reasonable" estimate of low-income, it would be over 60,000,000.)

There is no point in getting involved in an endless methodological controversy over the precise point at which a family becomes impoverished. Lampman's estimate of 32,000,000 poor people can be taken as a minimal definition; the AFL-CIO figure of 41,000,000 would be an extremely reasonable definition; and, in view of the revisions made by the Bureau of Labor Statistics, the total of 50,000,000 poor Americans would reflect our latest statement of living standards.

In short, somewhere between 20 and 25 per cent of the American people are poor. They have inadequate housing, medicine, food, and opportunity. From my point of view, they number between 40,000,000 and 50,000,000 human beings.

However, it is important not to be overly cautious. It is quite possible that these figures will require upward revision. In the Department of Commerce statistics, one of the most striking factors is the way in which the number of low-income people vary according to a recession or prosperity situation. In 1947, for instance, Commerce estimated that 34 per cent of the family units had under $3,000 money income as expressed in 1961 dollars. In 1949, a recession year, this moved up to 36 per cent of the families with incomes under $3,000 in 1961 dollars. In 1950, a year of renewed prosperity, the number dropped to 33 per cent of the total. This pattern continued throughout the fifties.

Thus, when using these percentages and numbers, one must understand that they express the conditions of a given time and place. In this case, they describe a time of mild recession and renewed prosperity. (The current, 1961, figures refer to the late fifties.) The direction that the statistics of poverty will take in the future depends in part upon general economic conditions in the United States. The other Americans do not automatically share in the gains of good times, for they tend to be progress-immune; but they do automatically share in the losses of bad times. Millions of people live just above the poverty line. Stagnation, recession, or even continuing high levels of unemployment during prosperity would require an upward revision of all the figures in this chapter.

So far, most of this analysis has been based on an attempt to discover a minimum measure for life at the bottom of American society and to determine how many people live beneath this line. If one moves on to a related question – How has the general-distribution pattern of income been changing in the United States? – the results are even more shocking. The following table is an extremely revealing illustration of what has been happening. (It is taken from an AFL-CIO publication; it was derived from Department of Commerce figures.)

How Total Family Income Was Shared Before Taxes 1935–36, 1944, and 1958

Families by fifths	1935–36 (Per cent)	1944 (Per cent)	1958 (Per cent)	Average income per family 1958
Lowest	4.1%	4.9%	4.7%	$1,460
2nd	9.2	10.9	11.1	3,480
3rd	14.1	16.2	16.3	5,110
4th	20.9	22.2	22.4	7,020
Highest	51.7	45.8	45.5	14,250

How do we interpret these percentages? In 1958 the lowest fifth of families in the United States had 4.7 per cent of total personal income; and the highest fifth, those families with top income, had 45.5 per cent. But even more important than this incredible comparison is the direction that American income distribution took in this period. Between 1935–1936 and 1944, the poor (for the lowest fifth, and more, dwell in the culture of poverty) increased their share of personal income from 4.1 per cent to 4.9 per cent. There was a slow, tortoise-like trend toward bettering the relative position of the

neediest citizens of the United States. But in the postwar period, this trend was reversed. In 1958 the poor had less of a share of personal income than they had in 1944.

Indeed, this chart is one of the statistical keys to the invisibility of poverty in the United States. The third, fourth, and highest groupings are those that contain the college-educated, the politically more active, the writers and editors, and so on. In the middle level there has been steady progress, and the general experience is one of optimism and advance. At the very top there has been a decline, but it must be put into context. Between 1944 and 1958, the average real-income rise of the neediest fifth in America was $80; while the top 5 per cent (with average 1958 incomes of $25,280) rose by $1,900. In short, even though the percentages at the very top indicate a mild decline (and, as will be seen, it is questionable whether this is the reality), the experience has hardly been a traumatic one.

If these figures are shocking, a further qualification must be made that intensifies their affect. Almost all these income statistics are based on Government reports that systematically understate the wealth of the rich. There is no malice in stating this fact. It is simply the result of the ability of top-income families and individuals to conceal income for the pupose of avoiding income taxes. This can be done through the utilization of lavish expense accounts (which are part of a standard of living but not of income figures), through stock transactions that are not included in the Commerce computations, and so on.

It might come as a surprise to some to learn that taxes generally work against the poor. According to a 1960 study of the Tax Foundation, 28.3 per cent of family income under $2,000 is paid out to Federal, state, and local governments, while families earning five to seven times as much surrender only 24 per cent of their income to the public authorities. (One of the reasons for this is the widespread use of property and excise taxes on the state and municipal levels. These, falling "evenly" upon all, take a much greater percentage from the poor.)

Thus, put most modestly and without correcting for the systematic misreporting that goes on at high-income levels, the poor have a worse relative position in American society today than they did a decade and a half ago. As technology has boomed, their share in prosperity has decreased; their participation in recession and misery has increased.

III

The identity of the major groups in the other America has been made fairly clear in the preceding chapters. The main subcultures of poverty are those of the aged, the minorities, the agricultural workers, and the industrial rejects.

What are the proportions of these people in the world of the poor?

Our current myth has two main ways of rationalizing away the importance of poverty in American society.

On the one hand, people speak of "pockets" of poverty, an argument that has already been dealt with. On the other hand, there is a most strange theory. The poor, it says, are rural and nonwhite. This is unfortunate, to be sure, but it means that poverty is something on the fringes of the nation, that it is associated with areas of backwardness, and that it will inevitably be obliterated by advancing technology. (In Australia, I am told, it was once the custom to develop income and standard-of-living statistics by omitting the aborigines. The Negroes and the rural poor often get the same kind of treatment in this country.)

The facts, however, run counter to the notion that poverty in America is primarily nonwhite and rural.

In Robert Lampman's study there is a modest estimate of the total low-income population: 32,000,000 people. One of the consequences of Lampman's definition, as he himself notes, is that it excludes a considerable number of large family units that lie just the other side of his cut-off line. Granted his low estimate in defining poverty, and this one distortion resulting from it, Lampman's work is useful in determining the proportion of the various groups in the culture of poverty.

In Lampman's impoverished population of 32,000,000, 8,000,000 were sixty-five years or older; 6,400,000 were nonwhite; 8,000,000 in consumer units headed by women; 21,000,000 were in units headed by a person with an eighth-grade education or less. Clearly, these figures overlap, for one of the most important single facts about the culture of poverty is that it tends to cluster misery.

Lampman found that 70 per cent of the low-income population had one or more of the characteristics that tend to push a person down. (In the general population, the figure is 50 per cent with one or more of these disabilities.) Consequently, it is common to find a person who is the victim of a whole chain of disadvantages: a Negro, facing job discrimination, with inferior educational training, and living in a family unit headed by a woman, would be a not untypical figure in the racial ghetto.

One of the disabling characteristics noted by Lampman is age. But here a certain refining of terms is necessary. Statistically, "age" is now thought of as beginning in America at sixty-five. Yet, as the chapter on displaced workers and depressed areas makes clear, the actual cut-off in these situations is much younger. The economic definition of age in industry is somewhere between forty and fifty; that is, if a worker between forty and fifty is laid off, his chances of finding a new job at the old level of pay are less whatever his skill may be; and if he is an unskilled or semiskilled worker (or if his skill has been destroyed by technology), the probabilities are against his ever finding a comparable job.

This is an example of the way in which biological facts are made relative to social standards. For along with the fact of discrimination against the blue-collar worker forty years or older goes the terrible psychological experience of rejection and defeat. If, as seems to be the case, this problem intensifies in the immediate period ahead, it may well be necessary to readjust the very definition of what constitutes aging in America.

At the other end of the age scale, Lampman draws a most important conclusion: children are a more significant percentage of the culture of poverty than old people. In his low-income population of 32,000,000, there are 8,000,000 individuals over sixty-five — and 11,000,000 under eighteen. The young are thus one-third of the total. (And once again, it must be emphasized that I regard Lampman's definition as representing a rock-bottom estimate.)

This fact has enormous significance. Among the aged, as was noted in a previous chapter, there are a good many people who become poor after working lives that had a decent standard of living. That is one particular kind of tragedy, one the nation has manufactured by increasing life without providing for its decent maintenance. But with the children of the poor, there is another grim process at work: it is likely that they will become the parents of the next generation of the culture of poverty.

As Lampman remarks, "A considerable number of younger persons are starting life in a condition of 'inherited poverty.'" At the present time, as I have argued elsewhere in this book, this fact may be of greater significance than ever before in the history of the nation. The character of poverty has changed, and it has become more deadly for the young. It is no longer associated with immigrant groups with high aspirations; it is now identified with those whose social existence makes it more and more difficult to break out into the larger society. At the same time, the educational requirements of the economy are increasing.

These millions of poor children are the ones who are going to the most inferior schools. Even when they have educational opportunities, they come from families who have a low opinion of education and who encourage the earliest possible legal leave-taking from school.

The nation is therefore beginning the sixties with a most dangerous problem: an enormous concentration of young people who, if they do not receive immediate help, may well be the source of a kind of hereditary poverty new to American society. If this analysis is correct, then the vicious circle of the culture of poverty is, if anything, becoming more intense, more crippling, and problematic because it is increasingly associating itself with the accident of birth.

In any case, poverty in the United States is not a non-white phenomenon, nor is it confined to the rural areas. The nonwhites constitute about 25 per cent of the other America (that is, to be sure, double their percentage in the nation as a whole); the rural poor are even less of the total (and there is overlap, because poor Negroes in the countryside are an important grouping). The theory that somehow finds comfort in the idea of "marginal" poverty does not stand up against the facts.

In *The Other America*, the special health tragedies of

the aged were documented. Yet it is important to understand that illness is a general disability of everyone in the culture of poverty, young or old. I first noticed this during the Asian-flu problem in New York in the fifties. The newspapers noted that the epidemic hit on a social-class basis, that is, areas like Harlem and the Lower East Side, where people were packed together under unhygienic circumstances, had a much higher incidence of the disease than better-off neighborhoods.

Here are just a few of the statistics from the United States National Health Survey on the way in which the poor are physically victimized in America:

In the age group between five and fourteen, children in families with incomes of $4,000 and over had a rate of dental visits three times that for children in families with a lower income.

The rate for Americans who lose their teeth is directly proportional to family income; the less money a family has, the more likely that there will be a total loss of teeth.

In all age groups, the number of people who suffer limitations of activity or mobility are directly related to income; between the ages of forty-five and sixty-four the families with incomes under $2,000 have six times more limitation of mobility than those with incomes of $7,000 or better.

The consequence of this is that the poor suffer more loss of work than any other group in the society: "Families having incomes under $2,000 experienced 32.4 restricted-activity days per person per year. The corresponding figure for families with incomes between $2,000 and $3,999 was 20.5 restricted-activity days per person, and for families with incomes of $4,000 and over, about 16.5 days of restricted activity."

The last quotation is from a National Health Survey study of conditions between July, 1957, and June, 1958. After citing these facts, the analysis continues, "A possible explanation for this relationship is that persons in lower-income families are more subject to restricting illness because of less utilization of medical care, poorer diet, and other factors."

The facts of health insurance do not give any cause for feeling that this situation will change for the better in the immediate future. The National Health Survey studied a period from July to December, 1959. At this time, the group with incomes under $1,999 constituted 15 per cent of the population, yet they accounted for only 7.4 per cent of hospital insurance, 6.6 per cent of surgical insurance, and 7.0 per cent of doctor-visit insurance. By way of contrast, the group with an income between $4,000 and $6,999 makes up 35.6 per cent of the population, but it possesses 42.1 per cent of the hospital insurance, 43.1 per cent of the surgical insurance, and 40.6 per cent of the doctor-visit insurance.

Finally, another important aspect of the culture of poverty is geographical. According to the Department of Commerce figures, the Northeast and the West had 16 per cent of the families with incomes under $3,000 in 1959; the North Central area had a figure of 21 per cent; and the South had the highest concentration with 34 per cent. The great progress, between 1953 and 1959, was made in the West (the number of families with incomes under $3,000 fell from 23 per cent to 16 per cent), and the area with the least advance was the North Central, where the number of impoverished families declined by only 1 per cent over a six-year period.

In reading these figures (or any statistics dealing with families), it must be remembered that "unattached individuals" who are poor have a much higher percentage who live in cities and who are unconnected with farm life. This would make the relative position of the South just a little less of a scandal than it is when viewed from the criterion of family poverty. (According to AFL-CIO estimates, there are 5,500,000 "single person families" with income under $1,500. This excludes the aged institutional population, which is over 250,000.)

In conclusion, one can draw a summary statistical picture of the other America.

The poor in America constitute about 25 per cent of the total population. They number somewhere between 40,000,000 and 50,000,000, depending on the criterion of low income that is adopted.

The majority of the poor in America are white, although the nonwhite minorities suffer from the most intense and concentrated impoverishment of any single group.

A declining number and percentage of the poor are involved in farm work, and although rural poverty is one of the most important components of the culture of poverty, it does not form its mass base.

In addition to the nonwhite minorities, the groups at a particular disadvantage are: the aged, the migrant workers, the industrial rejects, children, families with a female head, people of low education. These various characteristics of the culture of poverty tend to cluster together. (The large families have had the least gain of all family groups in recent years, and hence more children among the poor.)

The people who are in this plight are at an enormous physical disadvantage, suffering more from chronic diseases and having less possibility of treatment.

The citizens of the culture of poverty also suffer from more mental and emotional problems than any group in American society.

These figures do not confirm any of the complacent theories that poverty is now in "pockets," that it is nonwhite and rural, and so on. Rather, they indicate a massive problem, and one that is serious precisely because it concerns people who are immunized from progress and who view technological advance upside-down.

I would conclude this note as I began it. These are the figures, and there is legitimate reason for sincere men to argue over the details, to claim that a particular interpretation is too high or too low. At this point I would beg the reader to forget the numbers game. Whatever the precise calibrations, it is obvious that these statistics represent an enormous, an unconscionable amount of human suffering in this land. They should be read with a sense of outrage.

For until these facts shame us, until they stir us to action, the other America will continue to exist, a monstrous example of needless suffering in the most advanced society in the world.

What's Happening to Our Social Revolution?
Herman P. Miller

A MYTH has been created in the United States that incomes are gradually becoming more evenly distributed. This view is held by prominent economists of both major political parties. It is also shared by the editors of the influential mass media.

Arthur F. Burns, chief economist for the Eisenhower Administration, stated in 1951 that "the transformation in the distribution of our national income ... may already be counted as one of the great social revolutions of history." Paul Samuelson, one of President Kennedy's leading economic advisers, stated in 1961 that "the American income pyramid is becoming less unequal." Several major stories on this subject have appeared in the *New York Times*, and the editors of *Fortune* magazine announced ten years ago: "Though not a head has been raised aloft on a pikestaff, nor a railway station seized, the U.S. has been for some time now in a revolution."

In the preceding chapter, several basic facts were presented regarding trends in the inequality of income distribution in the United States. It was shown that there has been no appreciable change in income shares for nearly twenty years. This question will now be examined a little more intensively.

Despite the existence of much poverty in the United States, there is general agreement that real levels of living are much higher than they were only ten years ago and that the prospects for future increases are very good. Since conditions are improving you may wonder why it is important to consider the gap between the rich and the poor. Isn't it enough that the *amount* of income received by the poor has gone up substantially? Why be concerned about their share? Many who have thought about this problem seriously regard the *share* as the critical factor. When Karl Marx, for example, spoke about the inevitability of increasing misery among workers under capitalism he had a very special definition of misery in mind. Sumner Slichter, in summarizing the Marxian position on this point, states: "Marx held that wages depend upon the customary wants of the laboring class. Wages, so determined, might rise in the long run. Hence, Marx conceded that real wages *might* rise, but not the relative share of labor. Even if real wages rose, misery would grow, according to Marx, since workers would be worse off relative to capitalists."

Arnold Toynbee has approached the problem of income shares in still another way. He notes that minimum standards of living have been raised considerably and will continue to be raised in the future, but he observes that this rise has not stopped us from "demanding social justice; and the unequal distribution of the world's goods between a privileged minority and an underprivileged majority has been transformed from an unavoidable evil to an intolerable injustice."

In other words "needs" stem not so much from what we lack as from what our neighbors have. Veblen called this trait our "pecuniary standard of living" and modern economists refer to it as the "relative income hypothesis," but it all comes back to the same thing. Except for those rare souls who have hitched their wagons to thoughts rather than things, there is no end to "needs." So long as there are people who have more, others will "need" more. If this is indeed the basis for human behavior, then obviously the gap between the rich and the poor cannot be ignored, however high the *minimum* levels of living may be raised.

Although the figures show no appreciable change in income shares for nearly twenty years, the problem is complex and there is much that the statistics cannot show. It is conceivable, for example, that a proportional increase in everybody's real income means more to the poor than to the rich. The gap in "living levels" may have closed more than the gap in incomes. Even if exact comparisons are not possible, many believe that by satisfying the most urgent and basic needs of the poor, there has been some "leveling up" in the comforts of life.

Other examples of a similar nature can be cited. The extension of government services benefits low-income families more than those who have higher incomes — by

Reprinted from *Rich Man, Poor Man* (N.Y.: Thos. Y. Crowell Co., 1964), pp. 37–55, by permission of the author and the publisher.

providing better housing, more adequate medical care, and improved educational facilities. The increase in paid vacations has surely brought a more equal distribution of leisure time — a good that is almost as precious as money. Finally, improved working conditions — air conditioning, better light, mechanization of routine work — has undoubtedly reduced the painfulness of earning a living more for manual workers than for those who are in higher paid and more responsible positions.

When allowance is made for all of these factors, and for many others not mentioned, it may well be that some progress has been made during recent years in diminishing the inequality of levels of living. But it is hard to know how much allowance to make and our judgments could be wrong. Most opinions regarding changes in inequality, including those held by professional economists, are based on statistical measures of income rather than on philosophical concepts. With all their limitations, the income figures may well serve as a first approximation of changes in welfare. These figures show that the share of income received by the lower income groups has not changed for twenty years. Let us look at some other evidence that supports this view and then examine the implications of the findings.

White–nonwhite income differentials are not narrowing

The narrowing of income differentials between whites and nonwhites (92 per cent of whom are Negroes) is sometimes cited as evidence of a trend toward equalization. Several years ago, Professor Joseph Kahl of Washington University stated: "The poorest section of the country, the South, and the poorest group in the country, the Negroes, made the greatest gains of all."

What are the facts? Surely one would expect a change here in view of the major relocation of the Negro population in recent years. Migration and technological change during the past twenty years have altered the role of the nonwhite from a southern farmhand or sharecropper to an industrial worker. In 1940, about three-fourths of all nonwhites lived in the South and were largely engaged in agriculture. By 1950, the proportion residing in the South had dropped to about two-thirds, and today it is down to a little more than half. Even in the South, nonwhites are now more concentrated in urban areas than ever before.

The change in the occupations of nonwhite males tells the story of their altered economic role even more dramatically. Twenty years ago, four out of every ten nonwhites who worked were laborers or sharecroppers on southern farms. At present, less than two out of every ten are employed in agriculture, and about five out of ten work as unskilled or semiskilled workers at nonfarm jobs. The change in the occupational status of nonwhites has been accompanied by a marked rise in educational attainment, proportionately far greater than for whites. In 1940, young white males averaged four years more of schooling than nonwhites in the same age group.

Today the gap has been narrowed to one and a half years.

The income gap between whites and nonwhites did narrow during World War II. During the last decade, however, it shows some evidence of having widened again (see Table 1 and pictograph). The census statistics demonstrate this dismaying fact.

TABLE I.   *The Income Gap: White vs. Non-white Male Workers Aged 14 and over, in 1939, and 1947 to 1962*

Year	White	Nonwhite	Nonwhite as percent of white
All persons with wage or salary income:			
1939	$1,112	$ 460	41%
1947	2,357	1,279	54
1948	2,711	1,615	60
1949	2,735	1,367	50
1950	2,982	1,828	61
1951	3,345	2,060	62
1952	3,507	2,038	58
1953	3,760	2,233	59
1954	3,754	2,131	57
1955	3,986	2,342	59
1956	4,260	2,396	56
1957	4,396	2,436	55
1958	4,596	2,652	58
1959	4,902	2,844	58
1960	5,137	3,075	60
1961	5,287	3,015	57
1962	5,462	3,023	55
Year-round full-time workers with wage or salary income:			
1939	$1,419	$ 639	45
1955	4,458	2,831	64
1956	4,710	2,912	62
1957	4,950	3,137	63
1958	5,186	3,368	65
1959	5,456	3,339	61
1960	5,662	3,789	67
1961	5,880	3,883	66
1962	6,025	3,799	63

U.S. Bureau of the Census, *Current Population Reports — Consumer Income*, Series P-60, annual issues.

In 1947, the median wage or salary income for non-white workers was 54 percent of that received by the whites. In 1962, the ratio was almost identical (55 per cent). Prior to 1947 there was a substantial reduction in the earnings gap between whites and nonwhites. In view of the stability of the earnings gap during the postwar period, however, the reduction during the war years cannot be viewed as part of a continuing process, but rather as a phenomenon closely related to war-induced shortages of unskilled labor and government regulations such as those of the War Labor Board designed generally to raise the incomes of lower paid workers, and to an economy operating at full tilt.

This conclusion is reinforced by details of the 1960 census which show that in the twenty-six states (including the District of Columbia) which have 100,000 or more Negroes, the ratio of Negro to white income for males increased between 1949 and 1959 in two states

incomes of whites and Negroes and in some cases it was fairly substantial.

Occupational differentials in earnings are not narrowing

One of the most widely and strongly held misconceptions about income concerns the narrowing of the difference in earnings between skilled and unskilled workers. The prevailing view holds that the decrease in the earnings gap between the skilled and the unskilled in the United States is part of a historical process that has been going on since the turn of the century. The Department of Labor reports that in 1907 the median earnings of skilled workers in manufacturing industries was about twice that received by unskilled workers. By the end of World War I, it was only 75 percent greater, and by the end of World War II only 55 percent greater.

TABLE 2a

Men's income by Occupation in 1939, 1950, and 1961

| | Professional and managerial workers | Craftsmen | Semiskilled factory workers | Service workers and nonfarm laborers |
| | 1939 $1,986 / 1950 $3,890 / 1961 $6,821 | 1939 $1,309 / 1950 $3,405 / 1961 $5,527 | 1939 $1,007 / 1950 $2,736 / 1961 $4,344 | 1939 $730 / 1950 $2,041 / 1961 $3,019 |

(District of Columbia and Florida) and it was unchanged in two others (New Jersey and Oklahoma). In every other state there was a widening of the gap between the

TABLE 2b. *Men's Income by Occupation: Percent Change*

Year	Professional and managerial workers	Craftsmen	Semiskilled factory workers	Service workers and nonfarm laborers
1939–61	243%	322%	331%	314%
1939–50	96	160	172	180
1950–61	75	62	59	48

U.S. Bureau of the Census, *Current Population Reports — Consumer Income*, Series P-60, Nos. 9 and 39 (for Tables IV-22 and IV-2b).

Thus, during a forty-year period, this income gap was reduced by about 50 percent, an average of about 1 percent per year.

Recent trends in income differentials between skilled and unskilled workers are shown in the pictograph (Table 2a) and Table 2b. These figures represent the median wages and salaries received during the year in the major occupation groups for men. Women are excluded because their earnings are highly influenced by the fact that a large proportion of them work intermittently rather than full time.

There was not too much variation among occupation groups in the rate of income growth during the entire twenty-two-year period. The average income for most of the occupations quadrupled. But an examination of the growth rates for two different periods, 1939–50, and 1950–61, reveals striking differences.

During the decade that included World War II, the lower paid occupations made the greatest relative gains in average income. Thus, laborers and service workers (waiters, barbers, janitors, and the like), two of the lowest paid groups among nonfarm workers, had increases of about 180 percent. The gains for craftsmen, who are somewhat higher paid, was 160 percent; professional and managerial workers, the highest paid workers of all, had the lowest relative gains – 96 percent.

During the past decade the picture has been reversed. Laborers and service workers made the smallest relative gains, 48 percent; craftsmen had increases of 62 percent, and the professional and managerial workers had the greatest gains of all, 75 percent. The narrowing of the income gap between the skilled and the unskilled, the high-paid and the low-paid workers, which was evident up to and including the war years, has stopped during the past decade and the trend seems to be moving in the opposite direction.

The above figures are national averages in which all industries and regions are combined. They are very useful for identifying major trends, but they can also be very misleading because they average together so many different things. It is important to examine the figures for a particular industry in a particular region to get a better understanding of the underlying trends. The primary and fabricated metals industries have been selected for this purpose. The same analysis was also made for about ten other major American industries and the results are generally the same as those presented below.

About 2,200,000 men were engaged in the production of metals or the fabrication of metal products in 1960. This employment was about equally divided between production and fabrication.

The production of primary metals consists of three major components: blast furnaces and steel mills with about 600,000 men; other primary iron and steel works (mostly foundries) with about 300,000 men; and primary nonferrous metal (mostly aluminium) plants, with about 300,000 men. The iron and steel industry is highly concentrated in the Northeast and North Central states and within these states it can be further pinpointed to the following areas: Pittsburgh-Youngstown, Cleveland-Detroit, and Chicago.

The fabrication industry has a similar geographic distribution. About one-third of the workers are employed in the Northeastern states and a somewhat larger proportion are in the North Central region. This industry is divided into several major components, two of which are dominant and account for about nine-tenths of the employment. The largest component manufactures structural metal products – a miscellany ranging from bridge sections to bins, metal doors, windows, etc. It employs 200,000 men. The second major category, called "miscellaneous fabricated metal products," makes everything from dog chains to missiles and employs 700,000 men.

TABLE 3

| 260,000 | 220,000 | 650,000 | 780,000 | 540,000 | 660,000 | 340,000 | 550,000 |

Men employed in the metal industries: 1950 and 1960

U.S. Census of Population : 1960, Vol. II, *Occupation by Industry*, Table 2; and *U.S. Census of Population : 1950*, Vol. II, Table 84.

An examination of employment in this industry shows that the total number of workers increased by 24 percent between 1950 and 1960. Professional, managerial, and other white-collar workers increased 62 percent; skilled and semiskilled production workers increased by about 20 percent, but unskilled laborers decreased 9 percent. Thus, despite the general rise in employment and output in this industry, there was a drop in the demand for unskilled labor.

In view of these changes in the demand for labor in this industry, what happened to earnings? The figures for the eight major metal-producing and fabricating states are shown in Table 4. The states are shown in order of the size of their employment in this industry. They accounted for nearly three-fourths of the entire employment in this industry in 1960. The actual dollar earnings for unskilled, semiskilled, and all other workers (largely craftsmen and white-collar workers) for 1939, 1949, and 1959 are shown in the first part of the table; percentage changes are shown in the second part. It is the latter figures that are of greatest interest because they show which groups made the greatest relative gains. There are some differences in the definition of earnings for each of the years shown, but they are not believed to create serious distortions in the figures for these workers.

In all states except Ohio and California, unskilled workers in this industry made greater relative gains than the semiskilled between 1939–49. Similar figures are not available for the higher paid "other" workers for 1939. Thus there was a tendency toward a narrowing of earnings differentials in this industry between 1939–49. But, during the decade 1949–59, the reverse was true. In every state there was a widening of differentials, with the highest paid "other" workers making the greatest relative gains, followed by the semiskilled workers and

TABLE 4. *Regional Differences in Income of Men in the Metal Industries in 1939, 1949, and 1959*

AMOUNT OF EARNINGS

State	Laborers			Operatives			Other workers	
	1939	1949	1959	1939	1949	1959	1949	1959
Pennsylvania	$ 947	$2,414	$3,939	$1,153	$2,767	$4,597	$3,220	$5,624
Ohio	1,006	2,403	4,077	1,091	2,841	4,885	3,367	5,920
California	1,056	2,411	4,136	1,231	2,814	5,002	3,639	6,866
Illinois	950	2,506	4,448	1,124	2,931	5,034	3,517	6,321
New York	918	2,503	3,940	1,060	2,703	4,458	3,318	5,796
Michigan	962	2,645	4,134	1,150	2,997	4,726	3,691	6,246
Indiana	1,074	2,526	4,054	1,286	2,918	4,897	3,454	5,792
Alabama	701	2,032	3,565	887	2,316	4,301	3,073	5,864

State	PERCENT INCREASE, 1939–49		PERCENT INCREASE, 1949–59		
	Laborers	Operatives	Laborers	Operatives	Other workers
Pennsylvania	155%	140%	63%	66%	75%
Ohio	139	160	70	72	76
California	128	129	72	78	89
Illinois	164	161	77	72	80
New York	173	155	57	65	75
Michigan	175	161	56	58	69
Indiana	134	127	60	68	68
Alabama	190	161	75	86	91

U.S. Census of Population : 1960, Detailed Characteristics, Tables 124 and 130; *U.S. Census of Population : 1950,* Vol. II, Tables 78 and 86; and *U.S. Census of Population : 1940,* Vol. III, Table 16.

then the unskilled. In Pennsylvania, for example, laborers had a 63 percent increase in earnings between 1949–59, semiskilled operatives had a 66 percent increase, and professional, managerial, and other white-collar workers had a 75 percent increase. The same general pattern of wage movement was found in each of the other states shown.

Where do we go from here?

There was a time, not too long ago, when economists did not look for changes in income distribution because they did not expect to find any. Indeed, the stability of the income curve was so striking that it was given a name, Pareto's Law, in honor of the economist who conducted some of the earliest statistical inquiries in this field.

Pareto believed that the distribution of income is fixed and that regardless of changes in economic conditions, short of a revolutionary change from a competitive to a collectivist society, the distribution of income is the same in all places and at all times.

Statistical studies in recent years have so thoroughly demolished Pareto's notions that we have now come to look for change where no change exists. The facts show that our "social revolution" ended nearly twenty years ago; yet important segments of the American public, many of them highly placed government officials and prominent educators, think and act as though it were a continuing process. Intelligent public policy demands that things be seen as they are, not as they were.

The stability of income distribution, particularly during the fifties, could be related to the fact that the decade was dominated by a political philosophy com-

mitted to stability rather than change. In a different climate income differentials might narrow further. This could be accomplished through legislation designed to raise the levels of living of the poor: expansion of unemployment insurance benefits, federal aid to dependent children of the unemployed, liberalization of social security benefits, increase in the minimum wage and extension of its coverage, federal aid under the Area Redevelopment Act to revitalize the economies of areas with large and persistent unemployment.

In opposition to political factors that seem to favor equalization, there are some very stubborn economic factors that seem to be headed in quite the other direction. For many years now unskilled workers have been a declining part of the American labor force. This fact has been documented over and over again. Between 1940 and 1950 and again between 1950 and 1960 only one nonfarm occupation group for men — laborers — declined in number at a time when all other groups were increasing. Their income changed erratically. Laborers had the greatest relative income gains during the forties and the smallest relative gains during the fifties. This could mean that unskilled labor was in very short supply during World War II, with millions of young men away in the armed forces and the economy working at full steam. This pressure, with a little help from the government, forced wage rates up more for unskilled workers than for other workers. Since the fifties, on the other hand, there is evidence that the supply of unskilled labor has far exceeded the demand. As a result the unskilled are finding it increasingly difficult to locate jobs and many who are employed live in constant fear of being replaced by machines. Moreover, the over-abundance of these workers has prevented their wages from keeping pace with the others; thus the gap between the earnings of skilled and unskilled has widened.

The American economy has been plagued by relatively high unemployment since late 1957. According to the Joint Economic Committee, which has studied this problem in some detail, it is still premature to attribute this unemployment to the technological changes that are rapidly reshaping the economy. However, there can be no doubt that many thousands of unskilled workers in farming, manufacturing, mining, and railroads have been permanently displaced by machines and that this trend will continue. The labor-union leaders who represent these workers certainly tend to view the problem in this light. Even if they do not qualify as impartial observers, they know how these economic developments are interpreted at the grass-roots level. The leader of the Transport Workers Union of America, Michael Quill, is one among many who have spoken out sharply. His words carry a defiant ring that has been virtually absent from the American scene for over twenty years. He stated: "Unless something is done to put people to work despite automation, they may get rough in this country and this country may have a real upheaval, a real turmoil." The increase in racial tension and juvenile delinquency during the past few years may be early manifestations of trouble to come.

Labor-union leaders are not the only ones who have shown a keen awareness of both the bogey and the boon of automation. Many who have given the matter serious thought find it conceivable that, in the absence of remedial action, this nation may soon be faced with an increase in the disparity of incomes. We may then discover that our "social revolution" has not only been marking time for nearly twenty years, but that it is beginning to move backward. Justice William O. Douglas has spoken out eloquently on this subject in the pamphlet *Freedom of the Mind:* "We have a surplus of everything — including unemployed people; and the hundreds of unemployed and unemployable will increase if technology continues to be our master. We have a surplus of food and millions of hungry people at home as well as abroad. When the machine displaces man and does most of the work, who will own the machines and receive the rich dividends? Are we on the threshold of re-entering the world of feudalism which Europe left in the 15th and 16th centuries and which is fastened on much of the Middle East today?"

The Problem of Group Membership

SOME REFLECTIONS ON THE JUDICIAL VIEW OF INDIAN SOCIETY

Marc Galanter

THE CONSTITUTION authorizes the Government to provide special benefits and preferences to previously disadvantaged sections of the population.[1] Reserved posts in government, reserved seats in legislatures and on local political bodies, reserved places in public educational institutions and an array of preferences and welfare measures have been made available to Scheduled Castes and Tribes and, to a lesser extent, to Backward Classes.[2]

With membership in these groups a qualification for preferment of various kinds, it is not surprising that disputes have arisen concerning such membership. In a number of cases over the past twelve years, the courts have had to pass on the question of whether a person was in fact a member of such a preferred group. The cases raise many puzzling questions: Is membership in a caste or tribe to be determined solely by birth, or by allegiance or by the opinion of its members or of the general neighbourhood? Does one lose caste by conversion? By excommunication? By assimilation? Does one lose tribal membership by claiming or achieving caste status? Who is a communicant of a particular religion? Those born into it? Those who have been

[1] It is a "Directive Principle of State Policy" that: "The State shall promote with special care the educational and economic interests of the weaker sections of the people, and, in particular, of the Scheduled Castes and the Scheduled Tribes, and shall protect them from social injustice and all forms of exploitation." Art. 46. Consonant with this directive, Article 15 and Article 29(2) are qualified by Art. 15(4), which provides that the State may make " . . . any special provision for the advancement of any socially and educationally backward classes of citizens or for the Scheduled Castes and the Scheduled

Reprinted from *The Journal of the Indian Law Institute*, V. 4 (July–September, 1962, pp. 331–358.

THE PROBLEM OF GROUP MEMBERSHIP *Marc Galanter*

converted to it? Those who adhere to its precepts? What is the effect of unorthodoxy? Of excommunication? Are the tests used for the application of personal law appropriate in the area of preferences?

Prior to Independence and to a diminishing extent since, the courts have faced problems of determining membership in social groups for the purpose of applying appropriate rules of personal law in such fields as marriage, divorce and inheritance. The recent judicial treatment of group affiliation represents an adaptation of this older jurisprudence to a new purpose. More notably, it reveals some of the assumptions, explicit and implicit, about the structure of Indian society, which guide the courts. It is proposed to examine these assumptions from the viewpoint of their consonance with the principles of the Constitution and with empirical knowledge of Indian social organization.

Where a nation's fundamental law envisages a far-reaching reconstruction of society, the judiciary are inevitably engaged in the delicate task of mediating between social actualities and the avowed goals of the polity. They are both authoritative interpreters of these goals and assessors of the changing actuality in which these are to be realized. These are not wholly separate undertakings, for the interpretation of goals and values takes on content and color from one's picture of what is; and the perception of the latter tends to be informed by an awareness of one's goals. What one imagines to be desirable and attainable and what one imagines to be real are interdependent and interpenetrated. In examining judicial methods of solving problems of group membership we can discern competing views of Indian society and divergent proposals for the implementation of the principles of the Indian Constitution.

I. Caste, sect and tribe

A. CASTE AND SECT

The Constitution does not itself define the groups which may receive preferences nor does it provide standards by which such groups are to be designated. It provides for the initial designation of Scheduled Castes and Scheduled Tribes by Presidential order[1] with subsequent modification only by act of Parliament.[2] The wider and more inclusive group of backward classes is not only undefined in the constitution, but no such method or agency for their determination is provided.[3] Unlike Scheduled Castes and Tribes, backward classes may be designated by state and local as well as central government and by administrative as well as legislative authorities.[4] Although there is a growing tendency to substitute economic criteria of backwardness,[5] for the most part the backward classes designated by the states have been caste groups.[6]

In order to qualify for preferences, one must be a member of a listed caste or tribe. The tests for determining membership were given extensive consideration by the Supreme Court in *Chatturbhuj Vithaldas Jasani* v.

Moreshwar Parashram.[7] An Election Tribunal had rejected the nomination papers for a reserved seat submitted by a Mahar who had joined the Mahanubhava Panth, a Hindu sect which repudiated the multiplicity of gods and the caste system. Reversing the Tribunal, the Supreme Court held that the candidate remained a Mahar and was thus entitled to stand for the seat reserved for Scheduled Castes. To determine whether adherence to this sect made the candidate cease to be a Mahar, the Court specified three factors to be considered: "(1) the reactions of the old body, (2) the

[1] Art. 341(1) empowers the President to specify, after consulting the Governor of a State, those "castes or races or tribes or parts of or groups within castes, races or tribes which shall for purposes of this Constitution be deemed to be Scheduled Castes in relation to that State." See Constitution (Scheduled Castes) Order, 1950. Art. 342(2) provides that the President may similarly specify "tribes and tribal communities or parts of or groups within tribes or tribal communities" to be Scheduled Tribes. See Constitution (Scheduled Tribes) Order, 1950.

[2] Art. 341(2), Art. 342(2). The list of Scheduled Castes was revised by Parliament in 1956. Scheduled Castes and Scheduled Tribes (Amendment) Act, 1956.

[3] Article 340 provided for the establishment of a Backward Classes Commission to be appointed by the President to investigate the conditions of the Backward Classes and recommend measures for improvement. This Investigative Commission, established in 1953, was directed to determine criteria for designating Backward Classes but its report did not meet a favourable response. For a discussion of difficulties in designating Backward Classes, see my article cited in note 6, p. 637.

[4] *Kesava Iyengar* v. *State of Mysore*, A.I.R. 1956 Mys. 20; *Ramakrishna Singh* v. *State of Mysore*, A.I.R. 1960 Mys. 338; Cf. *Venkataramana* v. *Madras*, [1951] S.C.J. 318.

[5] See Report of the Commissioner for Scheduled Castes and Scheduled Tribes, 1958–59, p. 12.

[6] The use of caste as a criterion has been upheld in *Ramakrishna* v. *State of Mysore*, *op. cit. supra* note 4 (above). *S. A. Partha* v. *State of Mysore*, A.I.R. 1961 Mys. 220. See also *Venkataramana* v. *Madras*, *op. cit. supra* note 4 (above).

[7] [1954] S.C.R. 817. Hereafter referred to as *Jasani*.

Tribes." Article 16 is qualified in Article 16(4) to permit the State to make "any provision for the reservation of appointments or posts in favour of any backward class of citizens which, in the opinion of the State, is not adequately represented in the services under the State." Cf. Art. 335.

In the sequel, unless the context otherwise requires, the word "reservations" is used to refer to reserved posts in government service authorized by Art. 16(4); the word "benefits" is used to refer to all special provisions authorized by Art. 15(4); the word "preferences" is used as a general term including both of the above.

[2] Arts. 330 and 332 specifically provide reserved seats in Parliament and Legislature for Scheduled Castes and Scheduled Tribes. Backward Classes do not enjoy this preference. Art 334 provided that such reservations should expire ten years after the commencement of the Constitution. They were extended for another ten years by the Constitution (8th Amendment) Act, 1959.

The term backward Classes is sometimes used in the broader sense of including the former two groups as well. In the sequel it is used in the narrower sense. Preferences for a fourth group, Anglo Indians, are explicitly provided in the Constitution. Arts. 331, 333, 336, 337.

For description of the various schemes of preference employed see the annual reports of the Commissioner for Scheduled Castes and Scheduled Tribes. (Delhi, 1950).

intentions of the individual himself and (3) the rules of the new order."[1]

The candidate was admitted to all Mahar caste functions and had been allowed to marry within the community. He twice married Mahar girls, neither of whom were Panth members at the time of the marriage. He always identified himself as a Mahar. The Panth, in spite of its doctrinal repudiation of caste, had not penalized him for his adherence to the caste.

The Supreme Court concluded that "conversion to this sect imports little beyond an intellectual acceptance of certain ideological tenets and does not alter the convert's caste status."[2] It is clear that the primary consideration was the second test — *i.e.*, the intentions of the convert himself — intention not in the sense of mere declaration but as evidenced by a consistent course of conduct and dealings. The Court applies the "broad underlying principle" of *Abraham* v. *Abraham*,[3] decided a century before by the Privy Council in determining the law of inheritance applicable to a Hindu convert to Christianity: "[h]e may renounce the old law by which he was bound, as he has renounced his old religion, or, if he thinks fit, he may abide by the old law, notwithstanding he has renounced his religion."[4] Applying this principle, the Supreme Court found that "if the individual . . . desires and intends to retain his old social and political ties" and if the old order is tolerant of the new faith and does not expel the convert, the conversion has no effect. "On the other hand, if the convert has shown by his conduct and dealings that his break from the old order is so complete and final that he no longer regards himself as a member of the old body and there is no reconversion and readmittance to the old fold . . . [he cannot] claim temporal privileges and political advantages which are special to the old order."[5]

---

[1] [1954] S.C.R. at 838.

[2] *id.* at 840.

[3] *Abraham* v. *Abraham*, 9 M.I.A. 199, (1863). The rule was subsequently overturned by the Indian Succession Act, 1865, (now Indian Succession Act, 1925, s. 58). But the courts are still divided over whether the Hindu rule of survivorship is applicable to Christian families who continue to be joint after conversion.

[4] Reporter's note at 9 M.I.A. 196. Cf. pp. 242–244.

[5] [1954] S.C.R. at 838.

[6] *id.* at 839.

[7] Separate electorates are barred by Art. 325. Since seats are not reserved for particular Scheduled Castes but for the Scheduled Castes as a whole, one might question the relevance of looking specifically to the Mahar community to see whether he was accepted. E.g. if the privileged group is comprised of A's, B's, and C's and X, a member of A converts to sect S, the question of whether X is a scheduled caste might equally well depend not only on whether the A's accept him as an A but whether the B's and C's do as well or instead.

[8] [1954] S.C.R. at 838.

[9] *id.*

[10] *id.* at 840. For a situation in which the rules of the new order played a more prominent role, see *Rhagava Dass* v. *Sarju Bayamina*, A.I.R. 1942 Mad. 413, where by joining the *Byragi* sect a person ceased to belong to his original caste.

[11] A.I.R. 1960 Mys. 27.

Although the test is primarily one of the convert's intention or behaviour this intention must be confirmed by acceptance by the old group. The inclusion of this additional test is important because as the court says, "the only modification here is that it is not only his choice which must be taken into account but also the views of the body whose religious tenets he has renounced, because here the right we are considering is the right of the old body, the right conferred on it as a special privilege to send a member of its own fold to Parliament."[6] Since the general electorate chooses among the candidates standing for the reserved seat, the only way such representation can be assured is by seeing that only those accepted by the "privileged" group are permitted to stand for these seats.[7] If the preference were not in the political area, if it did not devolve on the Scheduled Castes collectively but on their members individually, the primary test of intention and conduct would apparently be conclusive and it would not be necessary to confirm this by acceptability to the privileged group. It seems doubtful whether ostracism or excommunication by the old group would effectively deprive one of group membership for the purpose of qualification for benefits not directed to the group collectively. For such benefits as education and housing do not devolve on the group in any corporate or collective capacity; membership in the group is merely a convenient device for identifying deserving beneficiaries. In such a case the relevant question would be whether the purported membership elsewhere had effectively dispelled the disabilities or other backwardness which had caused the group's members to be singled out for preferential treatment. Presumably if the individual still suffers these disadvantages he would remain a member of the privileged group in the sense of being a legitimate recipient of these preferences.

The third test, "the rules of the new order," is of minor significance. Since it is the legal and political rights of the old body that are being considered "the views of the new faith hardly matter."[8] "The new body is free to ostracise and outcaste the convert from its fold if he does not adhere to its tenets but it can hardly claim the right to interfere in matters which concern the political rights of the old body, when neither the old body nor the convert is seeking legal or political favours from the new body as opposed to purely spiritual advantages."[9] If this test has to be taken into account at all, it is only as indirect evidence of the intentions and conduct of the convert. For example, continued acceptance by a new group which was notoriously intolerant of the retention of the old ties might well evince an intention to break with the old group. But here the Court found it "evident that present day Mahanubhavas admit to their fold persons who elect to retain their old caste customs."[10]

In *Shyamsundar* v. *Shahkar Deo*,[11] the principles of the *Jasani* case were applied to decide whether a candidate for a reserved seat had lost his membership in the Samgar caste by joining the Arya Samaj, a Hindu sect which rejects idolatry and ascription of caste by birth. He had been accepted for membership in a local Arya Samaj organization, had paid membership dues, had married a girl of Sonar caste in accordance with Arya Samaj rites and had reported himself as an "Arya" in the 1951 census. The Mysore High Court, citing the *Jasani* case, announced that there would be no deprivation of caste unless there was either 1) expulsion by the old caste or 2) intentional abandonment or renunciation by the convert. There being no evidence of expulsion or ostracism by the old caste, the question was whether there had been a break from the old order "so complete and final that . . . he no longer regarded himself as a member of the Samgar caste."[1] The Court found that his activities evinced that he regarded himself as a Samgar, as did his testimony that he believed in idolatry and in texts repudiated by the Samajists. The Court found no evidence that he could not have married the Sonar girl "in the ordinary way" and thus the marriage was not inconsistent with his membership in the caste, nor was the census report since the Court refused to accept Arya as equivalent to Arya Samajist. Almost as an afterthought, the Court notes that the Samaj did not expel him for departure from their tenets. Such expulsion would only have reinforced the Court's conclusion, where the absence of it (if there ever were expulsions) might indicate an acceptance inconsistent with his remaining in the caste. The test that emerges, somewhat inchoately, is that so long as the person identifies himself with the old caste and is accepted by the caste — no matter if he is accepted by the new group or not — he remains a member of the caste for purposes of qualification for nomination to a reserved seat.

In *Wilson Reade* v. *C. S. Booth*[2] an Election Commission had rejected nomination papers for a Scheduled Tribe seat from a candidate whose father was English and whose mother was a Khasi. In pre-independence days he had accepted for himself and his children (his wife was a Khasi) privileges restricted to Anglo-Indians. But he was accepted as a Khasi by the tribespeople, the group being matrilineal and anyone born of a Khasi mother being regarded as a member of the tribe; he had followed "the customs and the way of life of the tribe," was treated by them as one of themselves and had been active in Khasi politics. The Assam High Court found that even though he was an Anglo-Indian within the Constitutional definition,[3] this did not prevent him from being a member of this tribe or some other community. Whether he was in fact a Khasi depended not on purity of blood but on his conduct and on the acceptance of the community.

The situation in the *Wilson Reade* case is the reverse of that in the *Jasani* and *Shyamsundar* cases. Here, it is the "new" group that is the politically privileged group rather than the "old" one. The question is not whether the new identification precludes the old, but whether the old precludes the new. In *Wilson Reade* as in the other two cases, the Court looked to the views of the privileged group to confirm the individual's claimed

membership. It was the Khasis who were entitled to special representation and it was their acceptance of him that was determinative. Neither birth nor the possibility that the Anglo-Indian community might also have accepted him was considered relevant. Thus all of these cases permit overlapping and multiple group affiliations. The possibility that an individual might be accepted by a second group is not taken to automatically remove him from the first.

B. TRIBE AND CASTE

The empirical approach of the *Jasani* case has not been applied in the problem of tribals attaining caste status. The case of *V. V. Giri* v. *D. Suri Dora*[4] arose out of an election to a seat in Parliament reserved for a member of a Scheduled Tribe. The candidate was born a Moka Dora and his family had described itself as such in all documents from 1885 to 1928. Since that time they had described themselves as Kshatriyas. There was evidence that the family had adopted Kshatriya customs, celebrated marriages in Kshatriya style, was connected by marriage to Kshatriya families, employed Brahmin priests and wore the sacred thread in the manner of Kshatriyas. His election was challenged on the ground that he was no longer a Moka Dora and was therefore ineligible to stand for the seat.

Applying the tests set forth in the *Jasani* case the Election Tribunal concluded that the candidate was no longer a Moka Dora, finding that "he has expressed unequivocal intention of drifting away from the clan, has totally given up feeling himself to be a member of the Moka Dora tribe and considers himself a Kshatriya."[5] Apparently the candidate's family was one of a number of families of Mokasadars or large landowners who, according to the Tribunal, "would not like to be called Moka Doras but considered themselves Kshatriyas."[6] The Tribunal found support for its finding in the observation that "persons of [this] type . . . who have drifted away from their old clan and renounced the tribal customs and manners and chosen to adopt the prevailing practices of the higher caste [sic] of the Hindu community could not be entrusted with the task of representing the genuine grievances" of the tribal communities; to do so would amount to a denial of the benefit of special representation conferred on the tribals by the Constitution.[7] Since the Tribunal had found against the candidate on the question of his intention to remain a Moka Dora, it was not necessary to go into the

[1] A.I.R. 1960 at 32.
[2] A.I.R. 1958 Ass. 128.
[3] Art. 366(2) defines an Anglo-Indian as "a person whose father or any of whose other male progenitors in the male line is or was of European descent but who is domiciled within the territory of India and is or was born within such territory of parents habitually resident therein. . . ."
[4] A.I.R. 1959 S.C. 1318. Hereafter referred to as the *Dora* case.
[5] XV E.L.R. 1 at 38 (1957).
[6] id.
[7] id.

question of acceptance by either the tribe or the Kshatriyas.

So far the case, although reaching the opposite result, proceeded along the lines laid down in the *Jasani* case. However, the case took a radically different turn when it reached the High Court of Andhra Pradesh[1] which addressed itself not to the question of whether he had remained a Moka Dora but to the quite distinct question of whether he had become a Kshatriya. Starting with the principle that caste is a matter of birth rather than choice and that higher caste cannot be gained[2] the Court conceded that "it is possible that a member of a Scheduled Tribe may in course of time adopt certain customs and practices in vogue among the Hindus, but in order to bring them within the fold of Hinduism it would take generations. Even if they came within the fold of Hinduism, [a] question would arise whether they have formed a separate sect among themselves, or [whether] they would belong to the ... [Sudras] or to the twice-born class."[3] Having thus indicated the severe limitations of possible mobility, the Court proceeded to lay down as requirements for proving that such movement had taken place its version of the tests employed in the *Jasani* case. These tests — intention, reaction of the old group, rules of the new group — are used in the *Jasani* case to test whether the individual has remained in his old group. But here the Court uses them as tests of assimilation in the new group. They become in effect a set of binding requirements, which must all be satisfied in order to prove a case of successful mobility.

The High Court found no evidence of the reaction of the old tribe (which, by the *Jasani* approach, would have been irrelevant had he failed on the test of intention) and "no evidence as regards the reaction of the new fold, except that some of the Kshatriyas recognize appellant as a Kshatriya. We can understand this if this had been the result of generations, but the acceptance of the appellant as a Kshatriya by one or two families would not ... be sufficient."[4] Having thus failed to attain Kshatriya status the High Court, assuming that

---

[1] A.I.R. 1958 A.P. 724.

[2] The cases cited by the High Court in support of this point, *id.* at 735, are easily distinguishable. *Sahdeonarain* v. *Kusumkumari*, A.I.R. 1923 P.C. 21, and *Chunku Manjhi* v. *Bhabani Majhan*, A.I.R. 1946 Pat. 218, are concerned with whether tribals are governed by Hindu personal law. *Maharajah of Kolhapur* v. *Sundaram Iyer*, A.I.R. 1925 Mad. 497 is concerned with varna status for purposes of finding the applicable rule of inheritance.

[3] A.I.R. 1958 A.P. at 735.

[4] *id.* at 736.

[5] A.I.R. 1959 S.C. 1318 at 1327.

[6] *id.*

[7] Another election tribunal dealing with a similar Mokhasadar family reached the same conclusion by anticipating the approach followed by the Supreme Court. The candidate remained a tribal since "there was no evidence that the Kshatriya community as a whole recognized him as belonging to their class." *Gadipalli Parayya* v. *Boyina Rajayya*, XII E.L.R. 93 (1956). One may wonder who are "the Kshatriya community as a whole" — whether this is defined in terms of the locality, the district, the state or all-India?

he therefore remained a Moka Dora, found him eligible for nomination to the reserved seat.

The Supreme Court, rather than reasserting the *Jasani* tests and disengaging them from the High Court's theories about caste mobility, took a third tack. Where the Election Tribunal had addressed itself primarily to the "intention" test laid down by *Jasani*, and the High Court had insisted that all three factors mentioned in *Jasani* were required to prove mobility, the Supreme Court fixed its attention only on the third — and originally least important — of the *Jasani* tests: the reactions of the new group.

The Supreme Court found the evidence insufficient to demonstrate that the candidate was a Kshatriya, since "the caste status of a person in this context would necessarily have to be determined in the light of the recognition received by him from the members of the caste into which he seeks an entry."[5] Finding no evidence of such recognition, the Court said "unilateral acts cannot be easily taken to prove that the claim for the higher status which the said acts purport to make is established."[6] The Court concluded that the candidate had not become a Kshatriya and had therefore remained a Moka Dora, eligible for the reserved seat.[7] In spite of the similarity in outcome, the course of reasoning taken by the Supreme Court here is in sharp contrast to that in the cases discussed earlier. The *Dora* case agrees with its predecessors that neither birth nor mere intention is determinative of group membership; the conduct of the individual and the attitudes of the groups must be considered. But which groups? And their attitudes about what? In the earlier cases, when the question was whether X had, by joining a new group B, ceased to be a member of privileged group A, it was the group A whose reactions were consulted — the Mahars in the *Jasani* case and the Samgars in the *Shyamsundar* case. But when the question was whether a person had become a member of a privileged group B, then the views not of the old group A but only of group B were pertinent — the Khasis in the *Wilson Reade* case. It was irrelevant what the Anglo-Indians might have thought of Reade, just as the views of the Mahanubhava Panth and the Arya Samaj received only a passing glance. Had the courts in these cases seriously considered acceptance by the non-privileged group as incompatible with membership in the privileged group, the cases would most probably have had different outcomes. Following on these lines one would have expected the Supreme Court in the *Dora* case to address itself to the views of the Moka Doras. But like the High Court below, they consider only the views of Kshatriyas.

True, the *Jasani* case did mention "the rules of the new order" as one of the factors to be considered. But it is clear that this was not only the least important factor, but was intended to mean the rules of the new order respecting the retention by X of his membership in the old group. It was not the views of the B's as to his membership in the B's that counted, but their views as to his membership in the A's. In the *Dora* case when the

Supreme Court consults the attitudes of the new group, it is on the question of X's membership in the B's.[1]

Since the Court never discusses the question of his membership in the Moka Doras, one can only gather that there is implicit in the Court's view a logical incompatibility between membership in the two groups. Had his Kshatriya status been upheld, he would *ipso facto* have not been a member of the Moka Doras for the purpose of standing for the reserved seat. Faced with the question of whether X remained an A, the Court addressed itself to the question of whether he had become a B. But this course of reasoning is only plausible if it is assumed first, that the two memberships exhaust the possibilities and second, that they are mutually exclusive.

In assuming that they exhausted the possibilities the Court seems to deny the possibility that the candidate's family had, although failing in some sense to become Kshatriyas, so separated themselves from the Tribe as to lose acceptance as members. Such an intermediate possibility was considered by the Election Tribunal and to some extent by the High Court.[2] Such splitting off is one of the classic and well documented methods by which new castes are formed.[3]

The *Jasani* line of cases had allowed overlapping and multiple affiliations. It was possible to be simultaneously a Mahar and a member of the Mahanubhava Panth; a Samgar and an Arya Samajist, an Anglo-Indian and a Khasi. Why is it not possible to be both a Moka Dora and a Kshatriya? The Court does not indicate the source of its notion that these affiliations are mutually exclusive. But it seems that this incompatibility is felt because Indian society is visualized as consisting of groups with unique corporate ranks in some definite rank ordering. Thus membership in one such group entails occupying such a rank and is inconsistent with membership in another group, which would mean simultaneously holding a lower rank in the same system of ranks. The Court refers to the claim here as one for "higher status," which presumably cannot be achieved without giving up membership in the group with lower status.

In part this notion of Indian society as consisting of mutually exclusive groups ranked in a definite and unique order is a carry-over from the area of personal law. The courts have long applied to members of different religious communions their respective laws in matters of marriage, divorce, inheritance, succession and religious endowments. Since in Hindu law, there were some differences in the rules applicable to the three higher varnas on the one hand and Sudras on the other,[4] the courts had from time to time to determine which rules were applicable to particular persons or groups. For this purpose Hindu society was visualized as if it consisted of four ranked compartments — the lowest being residual — and any of the actually existing caste groups would be assigned, if need be, to one of these theoretical compartments.[5] Since the Constitution, the courts have continued to make such varna assignments when necessary.[6] Now that the various Hindu Code acts of 1955–56 have eliminated almost all of the instances

in which varna might make a difference in applicable

[1] The practical effect of these divergent approaches can be easily seen in tabular form. Let us imagine X, a member of privileged Group A, has somehow aspired to membership in Group B.

	Test I Did X intend to remain an A?	Test II Did the A's accept X as an A?	Test III Did the B's accept X as a B?	Is X an A? Jasani	Is X an A? Dora
1)	yes	yes	yes	yes	no
2)	yes	yes	no	yes	yes
3)	yes	no	yes	no	no
4)	yes	no	no	no	yes
5)	no	yes	yes	no	no
6)	no	yes	no	no	yes
7)	no	no	yes	no	no
8)	no	no	no	no	yes

This table merely restates the requirement of *Jasani* that to be an A (for purpose of filling a reserved seat) X must fulfill both tests I and II. This occurs only in lines 1 and 2. It is clear that according to the *Dora* court the yes on test III in line 1 would make the answer "no". And in lines 4 and 6 and 8 the *Dora* method would make him an A by virtue of his not being a B (*i.e.*, failing test III) whereas the *Jasani* method would find him not an A because of failing either test I (line 6), test II (line 4) or both tests (line 8).

It should be noted that using the approach of the *High Court* in the *Dora* case the answer would be yes in every case except for line 7 and then only upon the additional condition that the A's accepted X as a B.

[2] XVI E.L.R. at 38; A.I.R. 1958 A.P. at 735.

[3] E.g., *Muthasami Mudaliar v. Masilamani*, I.L.R. 33 Mad. 342 (1919); Hutton, *Caste in India* (3d Ed., 1961), pp. 50 ff.

[4] These differences are concisely summarized by Derrett, "Statutory Amendments of the Personal Law of the Hindus since Indian Independence" 7 *Am. J. of Compar. Law*, 380, 383–385 (1958).

[5] In order to make such assignments, the courts evolved various tests: lists of diagnostic customs (see e.g., *Gopal v. Hanmant*, I.L.R. 3 Bom. (273, 1879) where the tests of Sudra status are widow remarriage and admission of illegitimate sons to dine and marry within the caste and to inheritance), or alternatively, tests of reputation (see e.g., *Subrao v. Radha*, I.L.R. 52 Bom. 497 (1928) where it is held that varna depends on the consciousness of the caste as to its status and the acceptance of this estimate by other castes).

According to the theory of varna, Hinduism was comprised of the four varnas and every caste group could be assigned to one of these; caste and varna were co-extensive with Hinduism. But departures from the symmetry of this scheme are found in many instances where courts modified it to account for the actualities of the situations before them. Thus it is possible to have varna standing without belonging to a caste group. *Sunder Devi v. Jheboo Lal* A.I.R. 1957 All. 215 (convert to Hinduism); *Upoma Kuchain v. Bholaram* I.L.R. 15 Cal. 708 (1888) (daughter of outcaste); cf *Ratansi v. Administrator General*, A.I.R. 1928 Mad. 1279 (convert to Hinduism). For some purposes at least, Hindu caste groups may fall outside of or below the four varnas. *Sankaralinga Nadan v. Raja Rajeswara Dorai*, 35 I.A. 176 (1908). Possibly one can be a Hindu without either caste or varna. See *Ratansi v. Administrator General, supra.* Caste and varna may apply to persons, who are not strictly Hindus, *Inder Singh v. Sadhan Singh*, I.L.R. (1944) 1 Cal. 233 (Sikh Brahmins). Caste groups have been recognized which have no varna nor are Hindu in any sense. *Abdul Kadir v. Dharma* I.L.R. 20 Bom. 190 (1895). Again, members of the same caste may hold different varna statuses. *Subrao v. Radha, op. cit. supra.*

[6] After the advent of the Constitution the administration of separate personal law to the respective religious communities was challenged as discriminatory and ultra vires Art. 15.

law,[1] the courts can look forward to the day when they will no longer be faced with the task of making these imponderable and often fictitious varna identifications.

In personal law cases the question was not whether an individual was or was not a member of some existing social group, but whether he should be assigned the status of one or the other varna.[2] Ordinarily the individual was indisputably a member of some actual caste or group and the proceedings took the form of determining the varna of this group. It was assumed for this purpose that all caste groups could be assigned to one or the other of the varnas. Since the purpose of determining varna was to ascertain the appropriate rule of law, and since varnas clearly stood in a ranked order, the whole object of the proceeding was to arrive at a unique determination of status.

The question before the courts in these election cases is quite different in kind. It is whether in fact a person is for a particular purpose to be considered a member of some existing group. There is no necessary incompati-

---

[1] *i.e.*, the Hindu Marriage Act of 1955, the Hindu Succession Act of 1956, the Hindu Minority and Guardianship Act of 1956 and the Hindu Adoptions and Maintenance Act of 1956. Derrett, *op. cit. supra* note 4, p. 633 suggests that the only instances in which varna might continue to have effect are succession to sanyasis and determination of the maximum age for adoption.

[2] The judicial treatment of the relation between varna and caste was plagued by confusion, engendered in part by the use of "caste" to refer both to the four great classes or *varnas* into which Hindu Society is theoretically divided by the Sanskrit lawbooks and to the multitude of existing endogamous groups or *jatis*. In the sequel caste is used only in latter sense.

[3] *cf. Mulai* v. *Lal Dan Bahadur Singh*, IX E.L.R. 9 (1952) where an Election Tribunal found that the proclamation of a former prince had not transformed the Gonds of Rewa state into Kshatriyas. "But even if the Gonds . . . could be deemed to be Kshatriyas, they would not cease to be members of Scheduled Tribes." Even "their aristocratic sub-division known as Raj Gonds, still continue to be Gonds and . . . belong to the Scheduled Tribes."

[4] See note 5, p. 633.

[5] A.I.R. 1959 S.C. at 1327.

[6] *id.*

[7] This tendency to picture Indian Society as series of graded corporate ranks seems congenial to the courts, perhaps because of the felt necessity of having some conceptual means for reducing the immense variability of Indian society to terms which could be applied without extensive investigation in each individual instance. Cf. Marriott's suggestion that urban and educated Indians (and foreigners) tend to conceive of caste in terms of criteria which constitute or imply a scale of Hindu ritual values rather than according to the structure of interaction among various groups. "Interactional and Attributional Theories of Caste Ranking," 39 *Man in India* 92, 104 (1959).

[8] A.I.R. 1959 S.C. at 1327.

[9] *id.* at 1331.

Although Art. 44 directs the eventual elimination of separate personal laws, the continuing validity of disparate rules of personal law and the power of the state to create new rules applicable to particular religious communities has been upheld. *State of Bombay* v. *Narasu Appa*, A.I.R. 1952 Bom. 84. The assignment of a community to a varna has been held not to constitute a deprivation of rights to equality before the law, nor is it religious discrimination. *Sangannagonda* v. *Kallangonda*, A.I.R. 1960 Mys. 147.

bility between membership in such a group and holding of varna status.[3] Apparently the candidate in the *Dora* case — and his family and possibly the whole group of Mokasadars — claimed to be Kshatriyas. It is unclear whether they were merely asserting Kshatriya varna status or whether they were claiming membership in some particular endogamous group of Kshatriya families. It would seem possible to achieve varna status without necessarily becoming effective members of a caste with that status.[4] In any event, it is unclear whether attainment of the varna status claimed in the *Dora* case would have been felt by the tribe to be incompatible with continued membership. Whatever theoretical incompatibility there may be in belonging to two varnas, it is not impossible to be accepted as a member of two actual social groups.

But varna theory is not the sole source of the Supreme Court's notion of mutually exclusive group membership. This notion is supported by its picture of Indian society. The Court indicates that it bears in mind "the recognized features of the hierarchical social structure prevailing amongst the Hindus" and the "inflexible and exclusive nature of the caste system."[5] The Court is, of course, only giving its view of the conditions that obtain; it expresses the hope "that this position will change, and in course of time the cherished ideal of a casteless society . . . will be attained."[6] Nevertheless, in its anxiety not to be "unrealistic and utopian," the Court seems unnecessarily to give currency to the view that all groups in Indian society are ranked in some unique and definite order.[7] Thus the Court is impelled to formulate a general standard for assigning standing in such a rank ordering. Noting that whatever may have been the case in ancient times "status came to be based on birth alone . . .," the Court says "it is well known that a person who belongs by birth to a depressed class or tribe would find it very difficult, if not impossible, to attain the status of a higher caste amongst the Hindus by virtue of his volition, education, culture and status."[8] Thus Hindu society is not only hierarchic but inflexible as well. If the Court meant literally that caste status was determined by birth alone, it would of course be redundant to consider the views of any group in order to determine it. But the Court apparently means that birth is determinative in the first instance and that this can be varied — but not by an individual's conduct but only by the unanimous recognition of his claims by members of the higher group. J. L. Kapur, J., dissenting, vigorously rejected the primacy of birth, put forward another general theory of assignment of rank. Holding that caste varies as a consequence of the gunas, karma and subhavana and is dependent on actions, he found that the candidate had "by his actions raised himself to the position of a Kshatriya and he was no longer a member of the Scheduled . . . Tribe . . ."[9]

Either of these general theories may prove embarrassing. Acceptance of the dissenting judge's theory that caste (or varna) status may be gained by entirely individual action would expose the courts to a torrent of litigation in which they would be faced with the necessity of setting up legal tests for caste standing and assigning it to individuals and communities. The majority's acceptance of birth as the primary determinative of group membership avoids this difficulty and is no doubt accurate in the overwhelming majority of instances. But by making membership in the old group dependent on failure to achieve the purported membership in the new group, the majority's theory may disincline the courts from giving legal recognition to existing patterns of mobility, which ordinarily involve a period of conflicting claims and overlapping identifications. Successful separation from an old group may be overlooked, with the result of imposing on a privileged group a candidate who is not an accepted member of it. More generally, existing channels of mobility may be discredited. For if acceptance by a new group remove one from the old, the Hinduization of tribals and the formation of new sects would be accompanied by the danger of disqualification for receipt of preferences. Since the system of preferences is designed to increase flexibility and mobility within Indian society, there seems little reason to make abandonment of older and slower methods of mobility a condition for the utilization of the new ones.

The dilemma posed by these opposing theories can be solved by eschewing any general theory of assignment and deciding questions of group membership by the pragmatic approach of the *Jasani* case. Since this permits multiple identifications, the courts would not pose for themselves the kind of either/or puzzles that have no satisfactory answer. They would be concerned only with whether for the purpose of the particular measure the individual concerned ought to be counted a member of the privileged group.[1] As far as it is compatible with the particular legislative policy, membership would depend entirely on the voluntary affiliation of the individual — as confirmed, where necessary, by voluntary acceptance by the group's members. Consonant with the constitutional principles of freedom of association and the autonomy of social groups, state imposition of standards of membership would be minimized,[2] and judicial determination of the relative status of groups would be eliminated.

II. Religion

The Constitution is openly and determinedly secular. Religious discrimination on the part of the State is forbidden.[3] Freedom of religion is guaranteed.[4] Taxation for support of religious institutions is prohibited.[5] The courts have been vigilant in invalidating governmental measures framed along religious lines.[6] Nevertheless, in some instances religion has been made a qualification for preferential treatment. The President's order specifying Scheduled Castes provides that "no person professing a religion different from Hinduism shall be deemed a member of a Scheduled Caste."[7]

Who is a Hindu? The legal definition of Hinduism, developed for the purpose of applying appropriate personal law, was neither a measure of religious belief nor a description of social behavior as much as a civil status describing everyone subjected to the application of "Hindu law" in the areas reserved for personal law.[8] Heterodox practice, lack of belief, active support of non-Hindu religious groups,[9] expulsion by a group within Hinduism[10] — none of these removed one from the Hindu category, which included all who did not openly renounce it or explicitly accept a hostile religion. The individual could venture as far as he wished over any doctrinal or behavioral borders; the gates would not shut behind him if he did not explicitly adhere to another communion.[11]

[1] In *Jankilal* v. *Jabarsingh*, A.I.R. 1957 Nag. 87 the Court found that "a person can be a Hindu and also be deemed a member of an aboriginal tribe" for the purposes of the provisions of the Central Provinces Land Alienation Act which outlawed conditional sale provisions in mortgages made by listed tribes.

[2] It has been argued with some persuasiveness that the Constitution withdraws all governmental power to determine whether an individual is a member of a particular caste. "Can a secular government force a citizen to belong or not to belong to a particular caste?" queries the Chairman of the Backward Classes Commission in considering whether census clerks may put down the caste of an individual according to their conception of it or whether the individual's conception is determinative. The Chairman contends that if caste is to be a voluntary affiliation, government must refrain from assigning it. Report of the Backward Classes Commission, 1956, Vol. I, p. xviii. But once caste and tribe have been accepted as appropriate units for the distribution of preferences, some governmental determinations, in order to prevent abuses, are unavoidable. It would seem possible to have more or less objective standards, even for determining a voluntary affiliation, and to refrain from any assignments other than the determination whether or not he is within the group he claims.

[3] Art. 15, 16, 29(2), 30(2), 325. See Alexandrowics, "The Secular State in India and the United States," 2 *J.I.L.I.* 273 (1960).

[4] Arts. 25, 26, 28, 30(1).

[5] Art. 27.

[6] *State of Rajasthan* v. *Pratap Singh*, A.I.R. 1960 S.C. 1208; *Nain Sukh Das* v. *State of U.P.*, A.I.R. 1953 S.C. 384; *State of Jammu and Kashmir* v. *Jagar Nath*, A.I.R. 1958 J. & K. 14.

[7] Constitution (Scheduled Caste) Order, 1950, para. 3. *Cf.* the Government of India (Scheduled Caste) Order, 1936, para. 3, which provided that "No Indian Christian shall be deemed a member of a Scheduled Caste." The Constitution (Scheduled Tribes) Order, 1950 contains no analogous provision.

[8] Or, more accurately, all who would be subject to Hindu law in the absence of proved special custom or of a contingency such as marriage under the Special Marriage Act (III of 1872).

[9] *Bhagwan Koer* v. *Bose*, 30 I.A. 249 (1903). A similar latitudinarianism may be observed in the tests for whether a tribe is sufficiently Hinduized to attract the application of Hindu law. Orthodoxy is unnecessary; it is sufficient that the tribe acknowledge themselves as Hindus and adopt some Hindu social usages, notwithstanding retention of non-Hindu usages. *Chunku Manjhi* v. *Bhabani Majhan*, A.I.R. 1946 Pat. 218.

[10] *Ratansi D. Morarji* v. *Admr. General of Madras*, A.I.R. 1928 Mad. 1279, 1283.

[11] No proof of formal abandonment of his new religion is necessary for the convert to effect a successful reconversion to Hinduism. While a mere declaration is not sufficient to restore him to Hinduism, acceptance by a Hindu community with whatever formalities it deems proper — even none at all — is sufficient. *Durgaprasada Rao* v. *Sundarsanaswami*, A.I.R. 1940

In the post-constitutional cases involving preferences the same broad conception of Hinduism has been carried over from the area of personal law. To "profess" Hinduism, merely means to be a Hindu by birth or conversion.[1] Unorthodoxy or lack of personal belief in its tenets does not mean lack of profession for this purpose — one may eat beef and deny the authority of the Vedas. In effect the test seems to amount to a willing-

[1] *Michael* v. *Venkataswaran*, A.I.R. 1952 Mad. 474.

[2] *Karwadi* v. *Shambharkar*, A.I.R. 1958 Bom. 296, 297.

[3] *id.* at 299. The vagaries of the declaration test are illustrated in *Rattan Singh* v. *Devinder Singh*, VII E.L.R. 234 (1953), XI E.L.R. 67 (1955), where the candidate had at various times described himself as a Mazhabi Sikh, a Harijan Hindu, a Balmiki, and a Balmiki Hindu. The Tribunal, holding that the minimum qualification for being a Sikh is willingness to declare "I solemnly affirm that I believe in the ten gurus and that I have no other religion," found him to be a Balmiki Hindu in 1953 and a Mazhabi Sikh in 1955. Any objective evidence was rigorously excluded since "the question of . . . religion . . . is a matter of personal faith and cannot be the subject matter of any evidence of a third party."

[4] *Michael* v. *Venkataswaran*, *op. cit. supra* note 1 (above). But Hindu personal law has sometimes been applied to Christians (see, *e.g.*, *Abraham* v. *Abraham*, *op. cit. supra* note 3, p. 630) and to Muslims (until the passage of the Muslim Personal law (Shariat) Application Act (XXVI of 1937)).

[5] These groups are Hindu for purposes of personal law. But their separateness has been recognized in other contexts. *E.g.*, Jains are not Hindus for purposes of temple-entry legislation. *State* v. *Puranchand*, A.I.R. 1958 M.P. 352; *Devarajiah* v. *Padmanna*, A.I.R. 1958 Mys. 84.

[6] *Gurmukh Singh* v. *Union of India*, A.I.R. 1952 Pun. 143; *Rattan Singh* v. *Devinder Singh*, *op. cit. supra* note 3 (above). Sikh members of four of the thirty-four Scheduled Castes listed for the Punjab, were included in the Scheduled Castes. See Constitution (Scheduled Castes) Order, 1950, sec. 3 and cases cited *supra*.

[7] Report of the Commissioner of Scheduled Castes and Scheduled Tribes, 1957–58, Vol. I, p. 25. This ruling is based squarely on the "Hinduism" requirement of the President's Order. See the statement of Pandit Pant, Times of India, Aug. 21, 1957, p. 12, col. 3.

[8] Report of the Commissioner of Scheduled Castes and Scheduled Tribes, 1957–58, Vol. I, p. 25, Vol. II, p. 60. While some states have included neo-Buddhists within backward classes, others have continued to treat them like scheduled castes for some purposes and still others have withdrawn all preferential treatment.

[9] A bill to this effect was recently defeated in the Lok Sabha. New York Times, Apr. 30, 1961, p. 2, col. 6.

[10] A.I.R. 1952 Punj. 143.

[11] *op. cit. supra* note 1 (above).

Mad. 513; *Gurusami Nadar* v. *Irulappa Konar*, A.I.R. 1934 Mad. 630. However, *Cf. Marthamma* v. *Munuswami*, A.I.R. 1951 Mad. 888, 890, where the primary test is the "intention" of the re-convert; the court says "the religious persuasion of a man now-a-days depends on his 'subjective preference' for any religion." *Cf.* the declaration test discussed note 3, p. 636.

For purposes of at least certain preferences, re-converts to Hinduism who were born in Scheduled Castes are deemed members of the Scheduled Castes. But those born in another religion (*e.g.*, whose fathers were converts) are not treated as members of Scheduled Castes "whatever may be their original family connections." Report of the Commissioner for Scheduled Castes and Scheduled Tribes, 1953, p. 132. In the personal law cases, acceptance by the community was a measure of one's success in re-entering Hinduism; here, Hindu birth is the condition of gaining membership in the community.

ness to refrain from calling oneself something else. Thus where the election to a reserved seat of an active supporter of Dr. Ambedkar's neo-Buddhist movement was challenged on the ground that he was not a Hindu, the Court found that "it has to be established that the person concerned has publicly entered a religion different from the Hindu . . . religion. Mere declarations falling short of this would not be sufficient.[2] The candidate had supported the movement for mass conversion by serving on the reception committee, editing a newspaper supporting the movement and attending a rally where an oath "I abandon the Hindu religion and accept the Buddha [sic] religion" was administered by Dr. Ambedkar. When those who wished to convert were asked to stand, the candidate stood. But there was no evidence that he did in fact take the oath; the Court held that absent evidence of such a declaration, he remained a Hindu.[3]

Converts to Christianity and Islam are, of course, non-Hindus.[4] Although Buddhists, Sikhs and Jains are treated as Hindus for some purposes, they are considered non-Hindus for purposes of preferences.[5] Sikhs are excluded from the Scheduled Castes.[6] Neo-Buddhists lose their right to preferences. "As Buddhism is different from the Hindu religion, any person belonging to a Scheduled Caste ceases to be so if he changes his religion. He is not, therefore, entitled to the facilities provided under the Constitution specifically for the Scheduled Castes."[7] The central Government, recognizing that conversion itself is unlikely to improve the condition of the converts, has recommended that the State Governments accord the neo-Buddhists the concessions available to the Backward Classes. Such preferences, less in scope and in quantity than those for Scheduled Castes, have been granted in some cases.[8] Persistent efforts by neo-Buddhists to be treated as members of Scheduled Castes have proved unavailing.[9]

The "Hinduism" test for recipients of preferences has been challenged as an infringement of the ban on religious discrimination by the State in two sorts of factual situations: first, where a group straddles the Hindu/non-Hindu border and includes among its members both Hindus and non-Hindus; second, in instances of individual conversions by members of a privileged Hindu group.

In *S. Gurmukh Singh* v. *Union of India*[10] a Bawaria Sikh protested his exclusion from the Scheduled Castes in which the President had included Hindu Bawarias. The Court conceded that Scheduled Castes were to be designated on the basis of their backwardness. But, finding that the Constitution vested in the President entire power to make such determinations, the Court refused to review his order by considering whether the Sikh Bawarias were in fact sufficiently backward to be included.

In *Michael* v. *Venkataswaran*[11] the religious requirement was upheld against a Paraiyan convert to Christianity who wished to stand for a reserved seat. Even if there are cases in which both the convert and his castefellows consider him as still being a member of the caste, the

Court found, "the general rule, is [that] conversion operates as an expulsion from the caste ... a convert ceases to have any caste."[1] The presidential order, according to the Court, proceeds on this assumption and takes note of a few exceptions. The Court declined to sit in judgment on the President's determination that similar exceptional conditions do not prevail in other instances. Thus the Presidential order was upheld not because of an absence of judicial power to review it but because of its accuracy in the general run of cases.

In *In re Thomas*[2] another bench of the Madras Court considered a convert case which did not involve the Presidential order. The Madras government had extended school-fee concessions to converts from Scheduled Castes "provided ... that the conversion was of the ... student or of his parent ..." A Christian student whose grandfather had converted could not, it was held, complain of discrimination since converts did not belong to the Harijan community. By conversion they had "ceased to belong to any caste because the Christian religion does not recognize a system of castes."[3] The concessions to recent converts were merely an indulgence and the State could determine the extent of this indulgence.

These cases indicate the two distinct grounds on which religious classification has been upheld: first, the inappropriateness of reviewing the President's order; second, the theory that non-Hindus have no caste. Unreviewability has been emphasized in the instance of Hindu/non-Hindu groups; the castelessness of non-Hindus has been more prominent in cases involving individual conversions.

Is the President's order unreviewable? There is no indication in the Constitution that executive action, even in pursuance of expressly granted and exclusive constitutional powers, is immune from judicial review for conformity with constitutional guarantees of fundamental rights.[4] The position in the *Gurmukh Singh* case was one of judicial restraint rather than judicial powerlessness.[5] Is such restraint appropriate? Since that case was decided judicial power to review the government's designation of beneficiaries of preferences has been firmly established. In recent cases the courts have subjected the standards used by government to designate backward classes to close and detailed scrutiny.[6] There is no indication that the power of the President and Parliament to delineate Scheduled Castes stands on a different footing than that of Government to name backward classes.[7]

Caste and religion are normally forbidden bases of classification.[8] Constitutional authorization for special provisions for disadvantaged groups has been held to authorize the use of such otherwise forbidden classifications.[9] However their use is still subject to the standards applicable to any governmental classification of citizens. The classification "must be founded upon an intelligible differentia which distinguishes persons or things that have been grouped together from those left out ... and ... the differentia must have a rational relationship to

the object sought to be achieved."[10] Although the constitutionality of the use of religion as a criterion for selecting backward classes has never been explicitly rejected the courts have shown a pronounced tendency to reject its application in practice.[11] It would appear that

---

[1] *id.* at 478.

[2] A.I.R. 1953 Mad. 21.

[3] *id.* at 22. The exclusion of neo-Buddhists from the preferences for Scheduled Castes has been similarly justified by the notion that "Buddhism [does] not recognize castes." Statement of Mr. B. N. Datar in Rajya Sabha, Aug. 26, 1957. Reported in Times of India, Aug. 27, 1957, p. 10, col. 1.

[4] In *Karkare* v. *Shevde*, A.I.R. 1952 Nag. 330, the Court found that the immunity conferred on President and State governors by Art. 361 "does not place the actions of the Governor purporting to be done in pursuance of the Constitution beyond the scrutiny of the Courts. ... Unless there is a provision excluding a particular matter from the purview of the Courts [as in Arts. 122, 212, 263, 329(a)] it is for the Courts to examine how far any act done in pursuance of the Constitution is in conformity with it." But *cf. Biman Chandra* v. *Governor*, A.I.R. 1952 Cal. 799, holding that Art. 361 removes the acts of a governor from judicial review unless there is evidence of dishonesty or bad faith.

[5] Art. 12 provides that for purposes of the Fundamental Rights provisions of the Constitution, " 'the State' includes the Government and Parliament of India and the Government and the Legislature of each of the States and all local or other authorities. ..." In *Gurmukh Singh* the court concedes that the President is included and that therefore his action is governed by the requirements of the chapter on fundamental rights.

[6] *Ramakrishna Singh* v. *State of Mysore*, A.I.R. 1960 Mys. 338; *S. A. Partha* v. *State of Mysore*, A.I.R. 1961 Mys. 220. These were foreshadowed by *Venkataramana* v. *State of Madras*, [1951] S.C.J. 318. But *cf. Keseva Iyengar* v. *State of Mysore*, A.I.R. 1956 Mys. 20, where the Court refused to review the government's designation. For a detailed discussion of the scope of review in this area, see my article " 'Protective Discrimination' for Backward Classes," 3 *J.I.L.I.* 39 (1961) and Comment, 3 *J.I.L.I.* 459 (1961).

[7] See Art. 12, note 2 (above). The Hinduism requirement is an expression of the power conferred by Art. 341 to select "castes, races or tribes or *parts of or groups within* castes, races or tribes." (Emphasis supplied.) Is the power of the President and of Parliament (which has exclusive power to modify the list) subject to review on the question of whether the delineation of "parts" or "groups" is reasonably related to the object of the classification? There is no indication that this power is exempt from such review. See Art. 13(2) and (3)a.

[8] On the religiou sclassification, see cases cited note 6, p. 635. For striking down of caste classifications see *Sanghar Umar* v. *State*, A.I.R. 1952 Saur. 124; *Bhopalsingh* v. *State*, A.I.R. 1958 Raj. 41; *State of Madras* v. *Champakam Dorairajan*, [1951] S.C.J. 313.

[9] The power to designate "classes" in Art. 15(4) and Art. 16(4) operates as an exception to the prohibition on the use of all the grounds of classification in Arts. 15(1) and 16(2) respectively. See *Ramakrishna Singh* v. *State of Mysore*, *op. cit. supra* note 6 (above), cases cited note 6, p. 629.

[10] A.I.R. 1960 Mys. at 346–48, A.I.R. 1961 Mys. at 229. These cases represent the application to the field of preferences of the general standards for the constitutionality of preferences, firmly established by numerous rulings of the Supreme Court, See, *e.g.*, *Budhan Chaudhry* v. *State of Bihar*, A.I.R. 1955 S.C. 191; *Bidi Supply Co.* v. *Union of India*, A.I.R. 1956 S.C. 479.

[11] In *Venkataramana* v. *State of Madras*, *op. cit. supra* note 6 (above) the Supreme Court rejected the inclusion of Muslims and Christians as backward classes. *State of Jammu and Kashmir* v. *Jagar Nath*, A.I.R. 1958 J. and K. 14 a cabinet order authorizing appointment of Muslims to certain posts "to remove the

non-Hindus cannot be made the recipients of benefits on the basis of purely religious classification; one wonders why they can be excluded from preferences on the same basis.[1]

If the standards of reasonable classification are to be

[1] Perhaps the State's power to define backward classes is not as broad as the President's to define Scheduled Castes. And perhaps the relevance of religion to untouchability, notwithstanding its inappropriateness in marginal cases, is more apparent than to defining backwardness. But it cannot be inferred that this exempts the power from review in those cases where the use of such standards is inappropriate.

[2] The *Jasani* case might seem to suggest the case of political preferences, the appropriateness of considering whether the whole privileged group would find representation by a non-Hindu acceptable. Should the unwillingness of the other privileged groups be a bar to qualification for reserved seats for members of minority religions any more than for Hindu groups which may be unpopular among other Scheduled Caste groups? Presumably the political process can deal with this without intervention by the courts.

[3] E.g., *Michael Pillai* v. *Barthe*, A.I.R. 1917 Mad. 431 (Christians); *Abdul Kadir* v. *Dharma*, I.L.R. 20 Bom. 190 (1895) (Muslims); *Inder Singh* v. *Sadhan Singh*, 1944 (I) Cal. 233, *Gurmukh Singh* v. *Union of India*, op. cit. supra note 10, p. 636 (Sikhs). See also the Report of the Backward Classes Commission, Vol. I, p. 28 ff.

[4] The reports are replete with cases in which converts have lived so indistinguishably with their caste-fellows that the courts retrospectively infer a tacit reconversion without either formal abjuration of the new religion or formal expiation and readmittance to Hinduism. *Durgaprasada Rao* v. *Sundarsauaswaram*, A.I.R. 1940 Mad. 513; *Gurusami Nadar* v. *Irulappa Konar*, A.I.R. 1934 Mad. 630; *Venkatramayya* v. *Seshayya*, A.I.R. 1942 Mad. 193. The "indulgence" extended by the State in the *Thomas* case, op. cit. supra note 1, p. 637 seems to reflect an awareness that recent converts, if not effective members of their old castes, are at least subject to similar disabilities. And cf. *Muthasami Mudaliar* v. *Masitami*, I.L.R. 33 Mad. 342 (1909) where non-convert Christians were accepted as members of a Hindu caste.

[5] In the *Jasani* case the Supreme Court undertook to determine "the social and political consequences of such conversion ... in a commonsense practical way rather than on theoretical or theocratic grounds." [1954] S.C.J. at 326.

[6] Where an Election Tribunal had to decide whether a Konda Dora who had converted to Christianity at the age of ten "for purposes of his education" was a member of the Tribe and thus qualified to stand for a reserved seat, they applied the empirical approach laid down in the *Jasani* case. There was no evidence that the convert had been excommunicated by the Tribe and finding that converts observe the same customs and habits, intermarry and are treated as members of the tribe, the Tribunal held that "mere acceptance of Christianity is not sufficient to make him cease to be a member." *Gadipalli Parayya* v. *Boyina Rajayya*, XII E.L.R. 83 (1956).

[7] [1954] S.C.J. at 326.

[8] See *e.g.*, *Michael Pillai* v. *Barthe*, supra note 3 (above). This reluctance was not so pronounced when the rights claimed concerned internal management rather than claims against outsiders. See *Abdul Kadir* v. *Dharma*, supra note 3 (above).

applied the crucial consideration would be whether the division of the group into Hindu and non-Hindu corresponds to some difference in conditions, resources or the incidence of disabilities so that the division is rationally related to the object of the preferences.[2] Existing precedents would not seem to foreclose such an approach, since the cases upholding religious tests were all decided before judicial review was established in the preference area and before *Jasani* and others had developed an empirical approach to questions of group membership.

Is the second ground — that acceptance of a non-Hindu religion operates as loss of caste — more substantial? The existence of caste among non-Hindu groups in India is well known and has long been recognized by the judiciary.[3] Does an individual convert's acceptance of Christianity, Islam or neo-Buddhism invariably evidence a loss of membership in the caste group to which he belonged at the time of the conversion? This is a double faced question of both fact and law — a question about his observable interactions with others and about his legal status. There is evidence that in some cases at least the convert continues to regard himself and to be regarded by others as a member of the old caste.[4] Why in such cases do the courts insist that the act of conversion has as a matter of law deprived him of membership? In other instances of conversion by members of privileged groups, the courts have addressed themselves to the factual side of the question.[5] Thus in the *Jasani* and *Shyamsundar* cases the courts addressed themselves to whether the adherence to sects within Hinduism had actually removed the person from his caste. A similar empirical approach has been applied to conversions among Scheduled Tribes.[6] One wonders why the courts have forsaken this empirical approach when dealing with religious classification among the Scheduled Castes. Why, rather than look to the facts of the individual case, have they chosen to apply this theoretical statement about loss of caste? As the Supreme Court observed in the *Jasani* case, "conversion ... imports a complex composite composed of many ingredients. Religious beliefs, spiritual experience and emotion and intellectual conviction mingle with more material considerations such as severance of family and social ties and the casting off or retention of old customs and observances. The exact proportions of the mixture vary from person to person."[7] It is surprising that the courts have accepted a picture of conversion which corresponds more closely to missionary aspirations than to observable consequences. This acceptance may derive from the long-standing reluctance of the courts to give legal effect to caste divisions among non-Hindu communities.[8] However, the problem in the convert cases is not analogous — the question is not the recognition of castes as corporate groups among non-Hindus but whether non-Hindu individuals are effective members of particular caste groups whose existence is already officially recognized.

Preferences are designed to remedy certain conditions

communal disparity" was held void. Reserved seats for Muslims and Indian Christians on the Madras Corporation Council were held invalid in *A. R. V. Achar* v. *State of Madras*, Writ Petition No. 568, High Court at Madras, Aug. 25, 1952, aff'd on other grounds A.I.R. 1954 Mad. 563. In *Ramakrishna Singh* v. *State of Mysore*, supra note 6, p. 637, the court invalidated a scheme of educational reservations under which Sikh, Jains, Muslims and Indian Christians were among the beneficiaries. But cf. *Keseva Iyengar* v. *State of Mysore*, op. cit. supra note 6, p. 637.

— particularly to offset or dispel the disadvantages created by the imposition of social disabilities and the lack of economic and educational resources. The usefulness of the theory that converts are casteless in describing these conditions is questionable. Where the preference is one that devolves on the members of the group as individuals, surely the appropriate question is whether the disabilities and disadvantages have, in the particular case, been effectively dispelled by the conversion. Where the preference is a political one that devolves on the group corporately, the appropriate question would be whether the group still accepts the convert as a member and is willing to have him as a representative. In neither instance would it be necessary to decide whether he is a member of the group for all purposes or whether he is a Hindu.

This Hindu requirement seems to reflect a hostility toward conversions which is anachronistic.[1] There is little reason to expect large-scale conversions at this point in Indian history and anxieties inspired by the threat of separate electorates is similarly out of date. The test is certainly not designed to bolster Hindu orthodoxy since one can remain a Hindu while embracing the most heterodox beliefs and practices. Not only is the test inconsistent with the avowed lack of religious discrimination but, ironically, it seems to impose on Hinduism the notion of a hard and fast line between creeds and communions. This is neither historically nor philosophically a Hindu notion but is more consonant with the exclusivist creeds of the West, which require the convert to abjure his previous faith. It is rather surprising that Indian jurisprudence should give currency to this notion instead of more cosmopolitan views that are more congenial to the Indian tradition of religious tolerance.

Conclusion

In surveying the judicial treatment of the group membership problem, we find in the case law two divergent tendencies, each with some support from the Supreme Court. The first, which might be called the pragmatic or empirical approach is represented in the *Jasani*, *Shyamsundar* and *Wilson Reade* cases. The second, which might be called the formal or fictional approach is represented in the *Dora* case and in the cases dealing with the Hinduism test for Scheduled Castes.

Both approaches recognize the "compartmental" nature of Indian society. But the empirical approach is willing to give recognition to the areas of blurring and overlap that are found within it. The fictional approach, emphasizing theoretical symmetry, tends to picture the society as one of mutually exclusive and hierarchically-ranked compartments; where in fact individuals straddle compartments, the Court sees its task as assigning them to one or the other. The pragmatic approach does not share this notion of resolving the ambiguity into a single identification but is congenial to multiple and overlapping affiliations; it addresses itself to whether, in the light of the policy of the particular legislation involved, the individual can be said to be a member of the group concerned.

The fictional approach concentrates on the theoretical consequences of certain acts — one who attains caste status loses his tribal affiliation, one who declares himself a non-Hindu loses caste membership. The pragmatic approach pays less attention to such theoretical incompatibility and gives greater weight to the facts of intention and acceptance. Thus sect members can retain their caste memberships, an Anglo-Indian can become a tribal and a convert can remain a tribal.

Is one of these approaches preferable or constitutionally incumbent upon the courts? The pragmatic approach is clearly more consonant with empirical knowledge of Indian society. It avoids the encumbrance of theories of caste which reflect perceptions of Indian society current among observers a generation or more ago. Modern students of Indian society have modified older notions of the caste-system which emphasized varna and inflexibility and have achieved a new understanding of its complexity which includes its local variability, the ambiguity of caste-ranking, the existence of mobility, and the limitations of varna theory.[2] The courts have long recognized the deficiencies of the older notions.[3] Now that courts are no longer hampered by the necessity of giving legal effect to a picture of society consisting of the four varnas,[4] they may appropriately employ the new perspectives in an attempt to confront the actualities of Indian society in order to felicitously implement the principles of the constitution.

It is submitted that the empirical approach is also to be preferred because of its consonance with the ideals and principles of the Constitution, while the fictional approach contravenes these and should be discarded. The Constitution sets forth a general program for the reconstruction of Indian society. In spite of its length, it is surprisingly undetailed in its treatment of the institution of caste and of existing group structure of Indian society. But it clearly sets out to secure to individuals equality of status and opportunity,[5] to abolish invidious

---

[1] *Cf.* the disabilities imposed upon converts from Hinduism in the various Hindu code acts. Derrett, *op. cit. supra* note 4, p. 633, remarks that it is "strangely inconsistent with the claim to be a secular state" that a Hindu who changes his religion is liable to be divorced by his wife, may forfeit an exꞁing claim to maintenance, may lose the right to give his child in adoption, may lose the right to be the guardian of his own issue and may have his issue deprived of the right of inheritance from unconverted relations.

[2] For a survey of recent research on caste see Srinivas, et al., "Caste: A Trend Report and Bibliography", VIII *Current Sociology/La Sociologie Contemporaine* No. 3 (1959).

[3] On the limitations of the varna model, see note 5, p. 633. For instructive discussion of the complexity of the caste-system, see *Muthusami Mudaliar v. Masilamani, op. cit. supra* note 4, p. 638.

[4] The enactment of the various Hindu Code acts in 1955–56 virtually eliminates varna as an effective legal concept and discredits it as a source of analogy. Although its use as a distinct legal status is still permissible for limited purposes, (see notes 6, pp. 633–34; 1, p. 634), the Constitution surely provides a mandate to confine it within the narrowest limits.

[5] Preamble, Arts. 14, 15, 16, 17, 18, 23, 46.

distinctions among groups,[1] to protect the integrity of a variety of groups — religious, linguistic and cultural,[2] to give free play to voluntary associations,[3] the widest freedom of association to the individual[4] and generally the widest personal freedom consonant with the public good.[5] Without pursuing all of these in detail, it is clear that the following general principles are consistently in evidence: *1)* a commitment to the replacement of ascribed status by voluntary affiliations; *2)* an emphasis on the integrity and autonomy of groups within society; *3)* a withdrawal of governmental recognition of rank ordering among groups.[6]

[1] Arts. 14–17, 25–30.
[2] Arts. 25–30, 347, 350A, 350B.
[3] Arts. 19(I)c, 25, 26, 30.
[4] *id.*
[5] See generally, Parts III and IV of the Constitution.
[6] It is not asserted here that these three principles are always mutually compatible. In most of the situations involved in these group membership cases they seem to be entirely compatible, but it is easy to imagine conflicts especially between the first and second. *E.g.,* should expulsion or excommunication remove one from a group for purposes of benefiting from preferences? It is suggested that our principles can be reconciled to some extent by invoking the distinction between preferences which are corporate and those which are distributive (*i.e.,* devolve on the members individually). Clearly the group's opinion as to membership should be decisive in the first, but in the second the state may more legitimately intervene to protect the individual from group power. In the latter instance the appropriate question would be whether his condition had changed from that which caused the members of the group to be given the preferences.
[7] *Cf.* Derrett's criticism of the occasional readiness of courts to decide what is religious on the basis of orthodox and literary sources without reference to the custom or actual belief of the group involved. "The Definition of Religion in Indian Law," LXI *Bombay Law Reporter* 17 (1959). Just as the correct test of a community's religion is its usage, so the test of an individual's membership in it is his and the community's conduct and usage. As to the relative emphasis between these, see the previous note.

In all of these, the pragmatic approach seems more congenial to the constitutional design. Its emphasis on the actual conduct of the individual and the actual acceptance by members of the group gives greater play to the voluntary principle. The control this gives the group over determination of its own membership seems implicit in the recognition of the integrity of the group.[7] Finally it avoids the necessity of giving official recognition to the ranking of groups.

The fictional approach, on the other hand, severely limits the voluntary principle and the autonomy of the group by giving conduct unintended consequences on theoretical grounds and by determining the question of membership without consulting the views of the relevant groups. It gives, if unwillingly, legal effectiveness to the notions of rank order among groups and mutual exclusiveness among them. The appearance and persistence of such an approach at this time should be regarded as an anachronism and one expects that before long the Supreme Court will refine and extend the empirical approach it pioneered in the *Jasani* case.

The courts have an opportunity to demonstrate how principles of equality and voluntarism can be implemented in a plural society with a social structure that is mainly traditional and where status is mainly ascribed. By the thoughtful and coherent treatment of these problems of group membership and group preferences, Indian jurisprudence can contribute much-needed guidance both to new nations attempting to construct a viable plural society and to older nations which have been unable to resolve the problems of diversity. By such guidance the courts may play a crucial role in assuring that the world-wide transformation from traditional to modern society takes place in conformity to the principles of freedom and equality.

Social Selection in the Welfare State[1]

T. H. Marshall

I WILL BEGIN by defining my terms. There need be little ambiguity about "social selection". I take it to refer to the processes by which individuals are sifted, sorted and distributed into the various positions in the

[1] The Galton Lecture delivered at a meeting of the Eugenics Society on 18 February 1953.

social system which can be distinguished one from another by their function, status, or place in the social hierarchy. I shall be considering, in this lecture, social selection through the educational system.

The Welfare State is a tougher proposition, because it would be difficult to find any definition acceptable

Reprinted from *Class, Citizenship and Social Development* (Garden City, N.Y.: Doubleday and Co., Inc., 1964), pp. 236–255, by permission of the author and the publisher.

both to its friends and to its enemies — or even to all its friends. Fortunately I needn't try to define it; I have only to explain what are the characteristics of the Welfare State which seem to me to provide a distinctive setting to the problem of social selection. I take the most relevant aspects of the Welfare State, in this context, to be the following.

First, its intense individualism. The claim of the individual to welfare is sacred and irrefutable and partakes of the character of a natural right. It would, no doubt, figure in the new Declaration of the Rights of Man if the supporters of the Welfare State were minded to issue anything so pithily dramatic. It would replace property in those early French and American Testaments which speak of life, liberty and property; this trinity now becomes life, liberty and welfare. It is to be found among the Four Freedoms in the guise of "Freedom from Want" — but that is too negative a version. The welfare of the Welfare State is more positive and has more substance. It was lurking in the Declaration of Independence, which listed the inalienable rights of man as "Life, Liberty and the Pursuit of Happiness." Happiness is a positive concept closely related to welfare, but the citizen of the Welfare State does not merely have the right to pursue welfare; he has the right to receive it, even if the pursuit has not been particularly hot. And so we promise to each child an education suited to its individual qualities, we try to make the punishment (or treatment) fit the individual criminal rather than the crime, we hold that in all but the simplest of the social services individual case study and family case work should precede and accompany the giving of advice or assistance, and we uphold the principle of equal opportunity, which is perhaps the most completely individualistic of all.

But if we put individualism first, we must put collectivism second. The Welfare State is the responsible promoter and guardian of the welfare of the whole community, which is something more complex than the sum total of the welfare of all its individual members arrived at by simple addition. The claims of the individual must always be defined and limited so as to fit into the complex and balanced pattern of the welfare of the community, and that is why the right to welfare can never have the full stature of a natural right. The harmonizing of individual rights with the common good is a problem which faces all human societies.

In trying to solve it, the Welfare State must choose means which are in harmony with its principles. It believes in planning — not of everything but over a wide area. It must therefore clearly formulate its objectives and carefully select its methods with a full sense of its power and its responsibility. It believes in equality, and its plans must therefore start from the assumption that every person is potentially a candidate for every position in society. This complicates matters; it is easier to cope with things if society is divided into a number of non-competing social classes. It believes in personal liberty because, as I choose to define it, it is a

democratic form of society. So although, of course, like all States, it uses some compulsion, it must rely on individual choice and motivation for the fulfilment of its purposes in all their details.

How do these principles apply to selection through the educational system? The general social good, in this context, requires a balanced supply of persons with different skills and aptitudes who have been so trained as to maximize the contribution they can make to the common welfare. We have, in recent years, seen the Welfare State estimating the need for natural scientists, social scientists and technicians, for doctors, teachers and nurses, and then trying to stimulate the educational system to produce what is required. It must also be careful to see that the national resources are used economically and to the best advantage, that there is no waste of individual capacities, by denying them the chance of development and use, and no waste of money and effort, by giving education and training to those who cannot get enough out of them to justify the cost.

On the other side, the side of individualism, is the right of each child to receive an education suited to its character and abilities. It is peculiar, in that the child cannot exercise the right for itself, because it is not expected to know what its character and abilities are. Nor can its parents wholly represent its interests, because they cannot be certain of knowing either. But they have a rather ambiguous right at least to have their wishes considered, and in some circumstances to have them granted. The status of parental rights in the English educational system is somewhat obscure at the moment. There is no reason to assume that the independent operation of the two principles, of individual rights and general social needs, would lead to the same results. The State has the responsibility of harmonizing the one with the other.

So far I have merely been trying to explain the general meaning which I have discovered in the title of this lecture. As I have already said, I shall first limit this broad field by concentrating on selection through the educational system. I shall then limit it further to the two following aspects of the problem. I shall look first at the selection of children for secondary education and try to see what is involved in bringing it into harmony with the principles of the Welfare State. I choose this particular point in the selection process partly because of its intrinsic and often decisive importance, and partly because so much has recently been written about it. I shall look in the second place rather at the social structure and consider how far it is possible to achieve the aims of the Welfare State in this field — particularly the aim of equal opportunity — in a society in which there still exists considerable inequality of wealth and social status. In doing this I shall be able to draw on some of the still unpublished results of researches carried out at the London School of Economics over the past four years, chiefly with the aid of a generous grant from the Nuffield Foundation.

Selection for secondary schools

We are all, I expect, aware that for some time past educationists (both teachers and administrators), and psychologists and statisticians (I sometimes find it hard to distinguish the one from the other) have been hurling themselves at the problem of selection for secondary schools with a determination and a ferocity of purpose which are positively terrifying. A good general survey of the campaign can, I think, be extracted from four sources. There is first the Report of the Scottish Council for Research in Education, *Selection for Secondary Education*, presented by William McClelland in 1942. This is an impressive document which might be described as a bold and challenging advance by the forces of pure science and exact measurement. It was met and held in check by a counter-attack delivered by the National Union of Teachers in its Report *Transfer from Primary to Secondary Schools*, published in 1949. Meanwhile there had opened, in June 1947, a friendly contest conducted under strict tournament rules in *The British Journal of Educational Psychology*, in the form of the "Symposium on the Selection of Pupils for Different Types of Secondary Schools," which continued until February 1950. It was richly informative, and contained a little bit of everything. Finally we have the two Interim Reports of the Committee of the National Foundation of Educational Research: *The Allocation of Primary School Leavers to Courses of Secondary Education*, published in 1950 and 1952. It is too soon to say exactly what position this new detachment will take up on the battlefield, but the wording of its title is highly significant when compared with that of the Symposium. "Selection" has been replaced by "allocation" and "types of secondary school" by "courses of secondary education."

The first point to note is that, in this matter of selection for secondary education, the State is in full command of the whole situation. It provides the primary schools which prepare children for the examination, it designs the secondary school system for which they are being selected, and therefore determines the categories into which they are to be sorted, and it invents and administers the tests. Such power is dangerous. It is easy in these circumstances to make sure that one will find what one is looking for, and it is, no doubt, gratifying to discover that one's artistic masterpiece has been faithfully copied by Nature. I find it unfortunate that, just as there are three main types of secondary school, so there are three types of ability with which educational psychologists juggle — *g* or general, *F* or technical and *k* or spatial. I am afraid people may come to regard this as evidence of collusion, when in fact, of course, the two trinities do not correspond.

The second point to note is that the principles of the 1944 Act, which I take to be the principles of the Welfare State, have not yet been put into effect. The Act, according to the N.U.T. Report, "has given the

[1] *Social Progress and Educational Waste*, p. 28.
[2] *The British Journal of Educational Psychology*, Vol. XVII, June 1947, p. 57.

problem of transference from the primary to the secondary school an entirely new form", which necessitates a thorough reassessment of our old methods of selection (p. 16). The profound change referred to is that from competitive selection of a few for higher things to allocation of all to suitable schools, or, as Kenneth Lindsay phrased it nearly twenty years before the Act, from "selection by elimination" to "selection by differentiation".[1] When allocation is working fully, says the N.U.T., "the situation ought not to arise in which it is impossible to send a child to the school most suited to his needs because there is no place available for him in a school of this kind" (p. 20). We are still a long way from this, and "for the time being the sole certain indication for a modern school is unsuitability for a grammar or technical school" (p. 18).

I see danger lurking here too. If too long a time passes during which an ideal cannot be realized, it may become unrealizable — a myth, as it were, which has lost contact with the world of experience, and which has never been through the testing which must lie between the blueprint and the finished machine. There is a danger, too, that we may imagine we are preparing the instruments for use in the new operation when in fact we are only perfecting those which are suited for use in the old. In the first Interim Report of the National Foundation there occurs the sentence: "It is the procedure of competitive entry to grammar schools that has been responsible for the undue importance which has been attached to objective tests and to external examinations" (p. 62). Note "external examinations", for there is something pretty fundamental there.

But the principle of allocation is not a new idea. It was implicit in the Act of 1918, which stated that sufficient provision must be made to ensure that no children are "debarred from receiving the benefits of any form of education by which they are capable of profiting through inability to pay fees," and it has been steadily developing since that date. And the importance attached to objective tests and external examinations is not an old phenomenon which happens to have survived into the new age. It has grown side by side with the growth of the idea of allocation, and continued to grow after the passing of the 1944 Act.

The movement in the field of ideas towards allocation instead of selection, and the movement in the field of practice towards uniform general standardized testing have been contemporaneous. I think, too, that any reader of the Symposium must be struck by the intense interest shown in the possibility of devising objective tests accurate enough to be used for allocation on the basis of special aptitudes, as well as for selection on the basis of general ability. There are, of course, signs of movement in other directions among education authorities, such as the greater use made of cumulative school records and so on; and, as regards the Symposium, it must not be overlooked that Sir Cyril Burt opened boldly with the statement that the problem was "administrative rather than psychological".[2] This sounded very much like the old-fashioned rebuking the newfangled, and no doubt some psychologists thought that he was letting the side down.

In all this I seem to see evidence of a clash between what I earlier referred to as the collectivist and individualist elements in the Welfare State. Allocation, interpreted along N.U.T. lines, represents unqualified individualism. The right of each child to receive the education best suited to its unique individual needs should not be inhibited by reference to the cost of providing the necessary schools and teachers nor to the demand in society at large for particular numbers of persons educated and trained in particular ways. But to the collectivist principle these limiting factors arise from rights of the community as a whole, which the Welfare State cannot ignore. And they may favour a provision of grammar school places which is less than the provision needed to accommodate all who could benefit from a grammar school education. As long as this happens, competitive selection will remain with us. How long that will be, I do not propose to guess. But, when selection is competitive, the authorities must reach a decision somehow, using the best means at their disposal. And they must be able to enforce the decision negatively (that is to say, the decision not to admit) against the wishes of the parent. When faced with the necessity of filling the last five places in a grammar school from twenty applicants, all backed by ambitious and determined parents, you may feel that the best means of selection are either to follow the mark order or to toss up. The public may prefer you to follow the marks, even though you know that in this border zone the verdict of the marks has no real validity. So the use of imperfect selection methods can be justified by the inadequacy of the educational system, as judged by the ideal of allocation.

But in my view, if allocation replaced selection, then no amount of improvement would make the tests sufficiently exact to carry the weight of decisions enforceable against parental wishes. For the question to be answered in each case would not be: "Is this child better suited to a grammar school than the other applicants? If so, we must tell the others we are full up." But: "What, as judged by absolute standards and without reference to competing claims, is the education best suited to this child's needs?" I feel convinced that, in the majority of cases, questions in this form will remain unanswerable by tests and examinations — unanswerable, that is, with the degree of assurance necessary before the answer can be made the basis of administrative action. So we should find, I think, that instead of allocation in the sense of the definitive assignment of each child to an appropriate school or course, we should have something more like an advisory service which left the responsibility of decision to the parents. And that, I understand, is what happens now in so far as the principle of allocation already enters into our system. And in support of the view that it *should* be so, I can quote, from the Symposium, Mr. Dempster of Southampton, who writes: "The wishes of the parents are possibly the best guide at present available to selectors in deciding between grammar and technical school education."[1]

This sounds in many ways a very attractive prospect, though we ought to know a little more about how parental wishes work before we acclaim it, and I shall have something to say on that later. But I fancy it conflicts with another aspect of the collectivist element in the Welfare State. The principle I have in mind is the one which says that all should be judged by the same procedure, as impartially and impersonally as possible, that favouritism and privilege must be eradicated, and also the effects of differing social environments on the critical turning-points in life. So far so good. The principle must be allowed to have full weight. There is one obvious point at which it favours objective tests. Because children come to their examination at 11 + from schools and neighbourhoods of very different quality, they cannot be judged by their attainments only; an attempt must be made to discover natural abilities which may have been frustrated by circumstances but may still be able to come to fruition if given a fair chance. But latent capacities are concealed, and something more scientific than a teacher's judgement or a school record is needed to reveal them.

But the collectivist principle goes farther, and sometimes assumes shapes which are more open to question. The doctrine of fair shares and equal opportunity sounds admirable, but it may become so distorted as to merit the cynical comment that fair shares means "if we can't all have it, nobody shall," and that equal opportunity means "we must all have an equal chance of showing that we are all equally clever". And the present situation may encourage this type of distortion, if it leads us to regard competitive selection as a necessary evil. If the Welfare State is to bring its two principles into harmony, it must conceive of the basic equality of all as human beings and fellow-citizens in a way which leaves room for the recognition that all are not equally gifted nor capable of rendering equally valuable services to the community, that equal opportunity means an equal chance to reveal differences, some of which are superiorities, and that these differences need for their development different types of education, some of which may legitimately be regarded as higher than others. The notion, therefore, that selection, even competitive selection, can be eliminated from our educational system seems to me to be a pipe-dream and not even a Utopian one.

Obstacles to equal opportunity

I will defer making any general comment until I have considered my second question, to which I now turn. This relates to another dilemma or antithesis inherent in the principles and structure of the Welfare State. It is the problem of establishing equal opportunity

[1] *The British Journal of Educational Psychology*, Vol. XVIII, November 1948, p. 130.

without abolishing social and economic inequality. I say this is inherent in the nature of the Welfare State because it is my opinion — which I do not propose to argue here — that the Welfare State, as we know it, must necessarily preserve a measure of economic inequality. This problem, therefore, is a permanent and not a transitory one.

One of the most striking passages in Kenneth Lindsay's well-known and far-sighted study of this question in the inter-war period is the quotation from Lord Birkenhead which runs: "There is now a complete ladder from the elementary school to the university, and the number of scholarships from the elementary to the secondary school is not limited, awards being made to all children who show capacity to profit."[1] This fantastic illusion was blown sky-high by Lindsay's book, and later studies showed that equality of educational opportunity was still a distant ideal at the outbreak of World War II. The research carried out at L.S.E. during the past four years, to which I have already referred, has drawn in more firmly the outlines of the picture and added some details. We can see pretty clearly what the situation was when the Welfare State took over and what were the obstacles it had to overcome.

This research included a 10,000 sample survey of persons aged 18 and over in Great Britain in 1949. Mobility was examined on the basis of the seven-point scale of occupational status, widely known as the Hall-Jones scale, which had been prepared for this study. Groups 1 and 2 include the professional and managerial occupations, and groups 3 and 4 the supervisory and clerical — to give a rough idea of their character. Together they comprised about 30 per cent. of the sample, which can be called the middle-class section (the upper class is too small to appear in a sample of this size). Group 5, including routine non-manual and skilled manual jobs, was a very large one comprising 40 per cent., while groups 6 and 7, semi-skilled and unskilled manual, provided approximately another 30 per cent. Of the general picture I will say little; I would rather wait for the papers to be published with full statistical tables. But one or two points may be noted. We find that the social forces holding a son to the occupational group of his father are significantly strongest in groups 1 and 2 and weakest in group 5. We can summarize crudely by saying that money and influence count for most at the top, and life's chances lie most widely open, for good or ill, in the melting-pot in the middle of the scale. This is interesting, because it is at this middle point in the scale that we might expect to find many families ambitious for their children's future and ready to forgo their earnings while they get secondary and further education, but not in a position to pay fees. It is precisely among such families that the building of an educational ladder is likely to have the greatest effect.

The second point of relevance in the general picture is that the returns show what to many may be a surprising amount of downward movement. There is a

[1] Kenneth Lindsay: *Social Progress and Educational Waste*, p. 9.

common saying, which in the United States has had the force of a political dogma, that "there is plenty of room at the top". And one remembers benevolent members of the upper layers of society who have strongly advocated the building of a social and educational ladder under the impression, apparently, that it could carry one-way traffic only, and that the ascent of the deserving from below would not have to be accompanied by a descent on the part of any of their own children to make room for the newcomers. But if we take all the male subjects in the sample, we find that 35.2 per cent. had the same occupational status as their father, 29.3 per cent. had risen and 35.5 per cent. had fallen. These figures probably exaggerate the falls because they include the young men in the sample who had not yet reached their final occupational level, and, of course, they tell us nothing of the distance risen or fallen, which is an important factor. The believers in one-way traffic thought that upper- and middle-class jobs were increasing faster than jobs in general, while upper- and middle-class families were producing fewer children than families in general. But it seems clear, and the 1951 census sample confirms this, that this was true, as regards middle-class jobs in general, only of women's employment. The proportion of occupied men in such jobs showed no significant increase from 1911 to 1951, while the proportion of occupied women in such jobs rose approximately from 24.5 per cent. to 45.5 per cent. There was some increase in clerical jobs for men, but even here the spectacular advance was in the employment of women. In 1947, to quote one illustrative case, of those leaving secondary grammar schools at the age of sixteen to go straight into jobs, just about 43 per cent. of the boys went into the "clerical and professional" category and of the girls 68 per cent., or, if nursing is included, nearly 77 per cent. Since there was an expansion of grammar schools during this period, and since grammar schools were largely an avenue to middle-class jobs, these facts are interesting. There may have been many boys who hitched their wagon to a white collar without realizing that their most serious competitors were their own sisters.

The educational data in the survey confirm and extend the picture presented in 1926 by Kenneth Lindsay. The most interesting general lesson to be drawn is that it is harder than one might suppose to ensure that the new opportunities created go to the people for whom they are intended, provided the fundamental principles of a free democracy are preserved. The survey covered the period of the introduction and expansion of the Free Place system in secondary schools, and its successor, the Special Place system, and it is possible to compare the experience of the first wave of entrants following the Act of 1902 (those born from 1890 to 1899) with the last pre-war wave (those born from 1920 to 1929). In the period covered by this comparison the percentage of boys in families belonging to the top three occupational groups who went to grammar schools rose from 38.4 to 45.7, and the corresponding figures for group 5 (the skilled manual and routine non-manual workers) are 4.1 and 10.7. The percentage increase for the working-class group is much greater than for the middle-class group, but the inequality that remains is enormous. And it is still greater if one includes boarding schools. The reason for this was not only that the total provision was insufficient, but also that a considerable part of the benefit went to the middle classes. It is true that the proportion of children in grammar schools who are occupying free places increases as you go down the social scale. But the proportion of the whole company of children of an occupational group who hold free places in grammar schools is highest at the top, 13.2 per cent. in status groups 1 and 2 (upper middle class) and 5 per cent. in group 5 (upper working class). I have picked these pieces of information from the analysis which Mrs. Floud has made of this part of the survey and which contains many more points of equal interest.

My point is this. It may look at first sight as if the *bourgeoisie* had, as usual, filched what should have gone to the workers. But, in the circumstances, that was bound to happen in a free democracy and is bound to go on happening in the Welfare State. For the Welfare State is not the dictatorship of the proletariat and is not pledged to liquidate the *bourgeoisie*. Of course more and more middle-class families made use of the public elementary schools as the quality of these improved, and of course more and more of them competed for admission to secondary schools through free and special places. And since the children were backed by a better educational tradition and stronger parental support, because more of their families could afford to forgo the earnings of the children, because they came from more comfortable homes, where it was easier to work, and from smaller families, they were certain to be more successful. And when it came to deciding as to remission of fees for special places, many of the middle-class families had a genuine claim. Today, with the 100 per cent. free place system in maintained schools, there can be no question of discriminating against middle-class families, and the competitive advantages of social and economic status can operate without check. Other inquiries conducted at the L.S.E., either within or in close relation to the main project, have begun to throw some light on the nature and extent of these competitive advantages.[1]

That there is a greater preponderance of working-class children in the modern schools today and of middle-class children in the grammar schools is a fact which no one is likely to dispute. In an article in the March 1953 issue of *The British Journal of Sociology*, Messrs. Halsey and Gardner produce evidence to show that, in the London areas they studied, this uneven distribution could not be attributed solely to the intelligence of the children, but must be in large part the result of social forces. When, for instance, comparison was made of two groups with the same mean I.Q., one of which had been assigned to a grammar school and the other to a modern school, it was found that the middle classes were heavily over-represented and the working classes, especially the unskilled families, heavily under-represented in the grammar school group. It is also interesting that of working-class children in grammar schools in the areas studied 63 per cent. came from small families with one or two children and 37 per cent. from larger families with three or more. Among working-class children in modern schools the proportions were almost exactly the reverse, and among middle-class children there was no significant relation between type of school and size of family. No known correlation between fertility and intelligence could possibly explain this, and it is clear that powerful social influences are at work. And they show themselves in other ways. A similar, though less marked, correlation with size of family appears when we ask how much thought parents give to their children's school career, how much interest they show in their work and progress, and how ambitious they feel about their future. Here, then, is a social factor causing what might be called "unfairness" in social selection about which the Welfare State can do very little. Positive action, by improving the physical conditions in poorer families and by stimulating greater interest and ambition among apathetic parents, can only be a very slow process. Family differences will continue to have their influence as long as the family is the basic cell in the social structure.

Social ambition and educational achievement

The interest of parents may be shown by their giving thought to the matter of secondary schooling for their children. In one county area parents of children about to sit for the examination for secondary schools were asked whether they had thought a lot, a little, or not at all about the matter. The proportion claiming to have thought a lot declined steadily as one moved down the social scale and was little over a third among the unskilled workers. But the preference for a grammar school education, though it showed the same trend, did not fall so low. The lowest proportion preferring the grammar school was 43.4 per cent. and the highest preferring the modern school 23.9 per cent. — these figures being those for unskilled workers. But over two-thirds of the unskilled worker parents preferring the grammar school did not want their child to stay there after the age of sixteen. Their ambitions were limited. And about half the professional and a quarter of the clerical families said that if their child did not get a grammar school place they would not send it to a modern school.

The picture is slightly distressing. It suggests that those who care about education, and some who do not care much, almost automatically aspire to a grammar school for their children; but the aspiration may vary from the

[1] The work has been done by Dr Hilde Himmelweit, Mr Martin and their associates. Since the information has been collected in intensive local studies it cannot be used for generalization of any kind as yet.

desire of a steady job, with good prospects, to be entered at sixteen, to the hope of admission to a university and a professional career. There cannot be much homogeneity of purpose in a grammar school population. And, looking at the other side of the picture, we find a low opinion of the modern school which to many appears as a catastrophe and a disgrace. Talk of "parity of esteem" is a little premature.

Now these likes and dislikes owe something, no doubt, to real or supposed differences in the quality of education received in the different types of school. But I doubt whether most parents are following the advice of the N.U.T. to concentrate on the "present educational needs of the child" and not to think too much "what these needs may be at some later stage in his development".[1] They are thinking of what the school may lead to in the way of employment or further education, and perhaps of what it stands for in terms of social prestige. This last point is one on which it is extremely hard to get reliable information, since much of the mental process involved may be only semi-conscious. If social status is not offered by the questioner as a possible reason for aiming at a particular school or job, it is not likely to be put down spontaneously; if it is offered, it may score a fair number of votes, but less than such job attributes as good prospects, security and interesting work. Another cause of difficulty is the lack of uniformity in the use of class names. People differ widely in the way they classify themselves or typical occupations as middle or working class, and it is clear that the term "lower middle class" is becoming abhorrent. But, in spite of this, there is fairly close agreement as to the order in which jobs should be ranked, even though there is disagreement as to the social class to which they should be assigned.

The material dealing with job ambitions is too complicated to be briefly surveyed in an intelligible form. So I shall confine myself to two points. In a sample of adults in two urban areas who were asked what occupation they would like their son to enter, more than a fifth of the working-class subjects chose a profession and less than 8 per cent. a clerical job; the commonest choice (about 36 per cent.) was for a skilled trade. The figures are not complete, as a good many said their son must choose for himself. In the middle-class section of the sample, clerical jobs were even less popular, and the total vote for independent business was practically negligible. A similar dislike of the sound of clerical and office jobs was found by Dr Jahoda among school-leavers in Lancashire — that is to say, among the boys. The girls put office work at the top of the list. When boys were asked what jobs they most definitely rejected, office work was the one most often chosen, but half of those who named it did so because they did not think they were qualified for it.[2] It would be very rash to jump to conclusions from such fragmentary evidence,

but it does seem possible that office work is losing its charm. It is often described as dull and monotonous, and perhaps the rise in wages for manual work and familiarity with conditions of full employment are robbing it of some of its other former attractions.

The second point of interest is the clear evidence, at present confined to one area, that working-class boys who get into grammar schools have very high expectations that they will rise in the world, while middle-class boys in modern schools are inclined to expect to fall below the position of their parents. No less than 63 per cent. of the boys of lower working-class origin in grammar schools expected to rise at least two steps on a five-point status scale above their fathers; only 12 per cent. of their comrades in the modern schools were equally ambitious. But, if we measure the rise by the boys' own estimate of it and not by objective standards, the percentage falls from 63 to 21. This inquiry was reported in Dr Himmelweit's article in *The British Journal of Sociology*, June 1952. It suggests that the boys themselves feel that selection for secondary schooling has a decisive effect on future careers, and that boys from the humbler working-class families who get into grammar schools may overrate their chances without fully realizing how ambitious their success has made them. So long as this is the case, "parity of esteem" is hardly possible.

Effects of social distance

My last point relates to the possible effects of social distance on life in a grammar school. Grammar schools, one might say, have a tradition, an educational atmosphere, and contacts with the world outside which have for some time past belonged to the way of life of the middle classes. And the middle classes are over-represented in the school population, even though the skilled working-class families may supply the largest absolute numbers. If, then, we introduce boys and girls from outside this circle, can they fit in? Can they become sufficiently assimilated to enter into the life of the school and get out of it what it has to give, and yet retain enough of their identity to break down, in the course of time, any class barriers which exist, and thus make the way easier for their successors, and for the Welfare State? Much study is needed before this question can be fully answered. We have evidence to show that middle-class boys in grammar schools (in the area studied) do better on average in class examinations in pretty well all subjects than working-class boys, and that, when teachers are asked to rank the boys in their class in terms of such things as industry, responsibility, interest in school affairs, good behaviour, and popularity, the middle-class boys do definitely better than the rest. And working-class boys are inclined to care less about their marks and to take less part in general school activities, and yet, as we have seen, they expect great results from their grammar school status when the time comes for them to get a job. On the other hand may

---

[1] Report of the National Union of Teachers: *Transfer from Primary to Secondary Schools*, p. 20.

[2] *Occupational Psychology*, Vol. XXVI, pp. 132–134.

not a school have an assimilating influence and mould its members into a more homogeneous group than they were to start with, thus producing in reality the category of children which until then existed only in the imagination of the selectors? That is a question which points the way to a fascinating piece of research which has hardly yet been begun.

The Americans have similar problems today, and there is much evidence of status-consciousness in the high schools of the United States. The book, *Who Shall Be Educated?*, by Lloyd Warner, Havighurst and Loeb (1946), is a revelation on this point. We hear a junior high school principal say: "You generally find the children from the best families do the best work. The children from the lower class seem to be not as capable as the others," and on this the authors comment that "this correlation holds true. There is a strong relationship between social status and rank in school." A teacher then says that there is a lot of class feeling in the schools. "Sections [i.e. streams] are supposed to be made up just on the basis of records in school but it isn't [sic] and everybody knows it isn't. I know right in my own A section I have children who ought to be in B section, but they are little socialites and so they stay in A", and there is much more in the same strain (p. 73). But the problem there is allocation between streams or courses, rather than between schools.

It was on this general question that Sir Cyril Burt made one of his most challenging remarks. "A realistic policy," he wrote, "must take frankly into consideration the fact that a child coming from this or that type of home may as a result be quite unsuited for a type of education, occupation or profession, which lies at an excessive "social distance" from those of his parents and friends."[1] Whereupon Dr Alexander descended on him like a ton of bricks, saying that no Authority could act on the view "that the present social circumstances of a child should be a criterion limiting his future opportunity."[2] Undoubtedly he is right. No Authority can act on the principle that social circumstances must limit educational opportunity, but in fact they do, and the accepted methods of educational selection cannot wholly prevent this. The remedy lies in the reduction of "social distance."

Conclusions

I must now try to sum up. The Welfare State, as I see it, is in danger of tying itself in knots in an attempt to do things which are self-contradictory. One example, I submit, is the proposal to assign children to different schools, largely on the basis of general ability, and then to pretend that the schools are all of equal status. If this means that we shall take equal trouble to make all schools as good as possible, treat all the children with equal respect and try to make them all equally happy, I heartily endorse the idea. But the notion of parity of esteem does not always stop there; and I feel it really is necessary to assert that some children are more able than

others, that some forms of education are higher than others, and that some occupations demand qualities that are rarer than others and need longer and more skilled training to come to full maturity, and that they will therefore probably continue to enjoy higher social prestige.

I conclude that competitive selection through the educational system must remain with us to a considerable extent. The Welfare State is bound to pick the children of high ability for higher education and for higher jobs, and to do this with the interests of the community as well as the rights of the children in mind. But the more use it can at the same time make of allocation to courses suited to special tastes and abilities the better. It further seems to me that, for the purpose of selection on grounds of general ability, the objective tests are already accurate enough to do all that we should ever ask them to do, while, so far as "allocation" is concerned, they will never be able to give a decisive verdict in more than a minority of cases, although they can be of great value in helping to decide what advice to give.

So I agree with Sir Cyril Burt that the problem which now faces us is more administrative than psychological. There is less to be gained by trying to perfect the tests and examinations than by thinking how to shape the structure of our educational and employment systems. It is better to minimize the effects of our decisions in doubtful cases than to imagine that, if we only try hard enough, we can ensure that all our decisions in such cases are correct. The word "correct" has no meaning in this context; it is a bureaucratic fiction borrowed from the office where there is a correct file for every document.

By "minimize the effects of our decisions" I mean refrain from adding unnecessary and artificial consequences to acts whose real meaning and necessary consequences I have been urging that we should frankly recognize. A system of direction into distinct "types of secondary school" rather than "courses of secondary education" (to use the titles I quoted earlier) must, I think, intensify rather than minimize the consequences. I am aware of the educational arguments on the other side, but do not intend to enter into a controversy for which I have no equipment. The other point at which artificial consequences may be added is the point of passage from education to employment. The snobbery of the educational label, certificate or degree when, as often, the prestige of the title bears little or no relation to the value of the content, is a pernicious thing against which I should like to wage a major war.

There is another matter on which the Welfare State can easily try to follow contradictory principles. It relates to occupational prestige, social class and the distribution of power in society. All I can do is to throw one or two raw ideas at your heads as a parting gift.

[1] *The British Journal of Educational Psychology*, Vol. XVII, June 1947, p. 67.
[2] Ibid., November 1947, p. 123.

Although the Welfare State must, I believe, recognize some measure of economic inequality as legitimate and acceptable, its principles are opposed to rigid class divisions, and to anything which favours the preservation or formation of sharply distinguished culture patterns at different social levels. The segregation when at school of those destined for different social levels is bound to have some effect of this kind and is acceptable only if there are irrefutable arguments on the other side. Further, a system which sorts children by general ability and then passes them through appropriate schools to appropriate grades of employment will intensify the homogeneity within each occupational status group and the differences between groups. And, in so far as intelligence is hereditary and as educational chances are influenced by family background (and I have produced evidence to show that they are), the correlation between social class and type of school will become closer among the children.

Finally, the Welfare State, more than most forms of democracy, cannot tolerate a governing class. Leadership and power are exercised from many stations in life, by politicians, judges, ecclesiastics, business men, trade unionists, intellectuals and others. If these were all selected in childhood and groomed in the same stable, we should have what Raymond Aron calls the characteristic feature of a totalitarian society – a unified *élite*.[1] These leaders must really belong to and represent in a distinctive way the circles in and through which their power is exercised. We need politicians from all classes and occupational levels, and it is good that some captains of industry should have started life at the bench, and that trade unions should be led by genuine members, men of outstanding general ability who have climbed a ladder other than the educational one. It is important to preserve these other ladders, and it is fortunate that the selection net has some pretty big holes in it. It is fortunate too, perhaps, that human affairs cannot be handled with perfect mechanical precision, even in the Welfare State.

[1] *The British Journal of Sociology*, March 1950, p. 10.

Social Stratification in Industrial Society
John H. Goldthorpe

FOR A DECADE or so now, a growing interest has been apparent, chiefly among American sociologists, in the pattern of long-term social change within relatively mature industrial societies. This interest appears to derive from two main sources.

In the first place, it can be seen as resulting from broadly based studies of the sociology of industrialization, concentrating originally on the underdeveloped or developing countries of the world. For example, work conducted as part of the Inter-University Study of Labour Problems in Economic Development led up to the theoretical statement on the "logic" of industrialism attempted by Clark Kerr and his associates in their book, *Industrialism and Industrial Man*.[1] Secondly, this interest has undoubtedly been stimulated by the revival in comparative studies of social structure and social processes in economically advanced countries. Important here, for example, has been the work of Professor Lipset and a number of other members of the Berkeley campus of the University of California; and even more so, perhaps, studies which have chiefly involved comparisons between Western and Communist societies, such as those produced in connection with the Harvard Project on the Soviet Social System by Professor Inkeles and his colleagues.[2]

However, it is notable that in spite of possibly different origins, current American interpretations of the development of industrial societies often reveal marked similarities. Basically, it may be said, they tend to be alike in stressing the standardizing effects upon social structures of the exigencies of modern technology and of an advanced economy. These factors which make for uniformity in industrial societies are seen as largely overriding other factors which may make for possible diversity, such as different national cultures or different political systems. Thus, the overall pattern of development which is suggested is one in which, once countries enter into the advanced stages of industrialization, they tend to become increasingly comparable in their major

[1] Clark Kerr, J. T. Dunlop, F. H. Harbison and C. A. Myers, *Industrialism and Industrial Man*, 1960.

[2] See, e.g., Raymond A. Bauer, Alex Inkeles and Clyde Kluckhohn, *How the Soviet System Works*, 1956; Inkeles and Bauer, *The Soviet Citizen*, 1959.

Reprinted from *The Development of Industrial Society*, Paul Halmos, ed. (*The Sociological Review*, Monograph No. 8, 1964), pp. 97–122, by permission of the author, the editor, and the publisher.

institutional arrangements and in their social systems generally. In brief, a *convergent* pattern of development is hypothesized.

Kerr and his associates have been the most explicit in this connection — and also in the matter of specifying the type of society on which the process of convergence is focussed. In their conception, "the road ahead" for all advanced societies leads in the direction of what they call "pluralistic" industrialism. By this they mean a form of industrial society in which the distribution of power is neither "atomistic" nor "monistic", nor yet radically disputed by warring classes; but rather a social order in which an "omnipresent State" regulates competition and conflict between a multiplicity of interest groups on the basis of an accepted "web of rules," and at the same time provides the means through which a degree of demo-cratic control can be exercised over the working of the economy and over other key social processes such as the provision of welfare and public services, education and so on.[1] Other theorists have usually been a good deal more guarded than this in their formulations; but it would nonetheless be fair to say that, in the main, they have adopted views which have been broadly consistent with the Kerr thesis. In general, the "logic" of industrial-ism has been regarded as powerfully encouraging, even if not compelling, the emergence of a new type of society from out of former "class" and "mass" societies alike.[2]

Clearly, then, a central theme in the interpretations in question concerns the development in advanced societies of systems of social stratification. And it is perhaps indicative of the importance of this theme that it has on several occasions been singled out for special discussion. In this paper[3] my main purpose will be to consider this particular aspect of current theories of industrialism and, further, to raise certain doubts and objections which seem to me to be of a serious kind and to have negative implications for these theories *in toto*. But at the outset I should say that I in no way intend to criticize the *kind* of sociological endeavour which is here represented. On the contrary, we are, I believe, much indebted to the authors of these theories for showing us a way to escape from the cramped quarters of trivialized empiricism without falling victim to highly speculative building with "empty boxes."

The arguments concerning the development of social stratification which form a core element in American interpretations of industrialism can be usefully stated under three main heads: differentiation, consistency and mobility.[4] To begin with, I would like to consider these three sets of arguments in turn.

Differentiation

In regard to differentiation, the major proposition that is put forward is that, in course of industrial advance, there is a decrease in the degree of differentiation in all stratification subsystems or orders. In other words, to follow Inkeles' formulation: "a process of relative homo-genization takes place, reducing the gap or range separating the top and bottom of the scale" — in income and wealth, in status formal and informal, and in political power.[5] As a result of this process, a marked increase occurs within each stratification order in the proportion of the total population falling into the middle ranges of the distribution. The "shape" of the stratifica-tion hierarchy thus ceases to be pyramidal and approxi-mates, rather, to that of a pentagon or even of a diamond.

This trend is related to the "logic" of industrialism in several different ways. But, primarily, the connection is seen as being through the changing division of labour. An advancing technology and economy continually repattern the occupational structure, and in ways which progressively increase the number of higher level occupational rôles; that is to say, rôles requiring rela-tively high standards of education and training and at the same time commanding relatively high economic rewards and social status. Thus, the middle of the stratification hierarchy becomes considerably expanded.

So far as Western societies are concerned, a further factor in this homogenizing process is also recognized in the growing intervention of the state in economic affairs; particularly in governmental policies which lead to the redistribution and control of economic power. For example, it is observed that policies of progressive taxation and of social welfare in various ways modify for the benefit of the less privileged the division of

---

[1] *Op. cit.*, Chs. 1, 2 and 10 especially.

[2] The issue on which, of course, there has been greatest doubt and discussion is that of whether totalitarian régimes will *inevitably* become less "monistic" with continuing industrial advance. As emerges later in this paper, Inkeles appears some-what uncertain on this point. Another leading American theorist of industrialism, W. E. Moore, has expressly rejected the idea that industrialization necessarily engenders increased political participation and more representative government. See his section, "Industrialisation and Social Change" in B. F. Hoselitz and W. E. Moore (eds.), *Industrialisation and Society*, 1963, pp. 357–359 especially. Nevertheless, the greater part of this section is written in terms of the social exigencies of an industrial technology and economy.

[3] I am indebted to my friend M. Alfred Willener for his criticisms of an earlier draft of this paper and also to colleagues in the Faculty of Economics and Politics of the University of Cambridge who have discussed many specific points with me.

[4] The following exposition is derived chiefly from Kerr *et al.*, *op. cit.*; Inkeles, "Social Stratification in the Modernization of Russia" in Cyril E. Black (ed.), *The Transformation of Russian Society*, 1960; and Moore, *loc. cit.*, pp. 318–322, 353–359 especially. It is, however, important to note the very marked differences in tone and style between these contributions. Kerr and his colleagues are most dogmatic and "prophetic", but also the most diffuse in their arguments; Inkeles, on the other hand, is the most explicit yet is clearly writing, as he says, "not to settle a point but to open a discussion"; while Moore, aiming at the summing-up of a body of research data, puts forward by far the most cautious and qualified statements.

[5] *Loc. cit.*, p. 341. Cf. Kerr *et al.*, pp. 286–294. Moore (p. 354), claims that during early industrialization "differences in social origin, education and power of managers and workers are likely to be widest" and the following paragraph appears to support the "relative homogenization" thesis. It is not clear, however, how far Moore is prepared to regard the trend towards reduced differentiation as one which has so far continued progressively with industrial advance.

income and balance of social advantage which would have resulted from the free operation of market mechanisms. However, in this case great stress is placed on the close relationship that exists between this expansion in the regulatory functions of government and the direct requirements of the industrialization process. The state, it is argued, *must* be the key regulatory organization in any advanced society: the complexity of its technology and economy demand this. At minimum, the state must be responsible for the general rate of economic progress, and thus ultimately, for the overall allocation of resources between uses and individuals, for the quality of the national labour force, for the economic and social security of individuals and so on.[1]

In other words, even where greater social equality results directly from the purposive action of governments, the tendency is to see behind this action not a particular complex of socio-political beliefs, values or interests but rather the inherent compulsions of "industrialism" itself.[2] For example, on the subject of the development of education and its consequences, Kerr and his associates write as follows:

> Education is intended to reduce the scarcity of skilled persons and this after a time reduces the wage and salary differentials they receive; it also pulls people out of the least skilled and most disagreeable occupations and raises wage levels there. *It conduces to a new equality which has nothing to do with ideology.* . . .[3]

Furthermore, one should note, a similar viewpoint is

taken in arguing that greater equality in political power – in the form of a pluralistic system – will tend to emerge in societies which now have totalitarian (or autocratic) regimes. In the first place, it is held, the production technology of an industrial society is such that any regime must become increasingly interested in the consent of the mass of the labour force; for the efficient use of this technology requires responsible initiative and freely given co-operation on the part of those who operate it. Secondly, the growing complexity of technical problems arising in the process of government itself necessitates the greater involvement in decision-making of experts and professionals, and in this way the latter come to acquire some independent authority. Thus, a monolithic structure gives way to one in which there are a number of "strategic" elites and of different foci of power. In brief, industrialism is regarded as being ultimately inimical to any form of monistic political order.[4]

Consistency

In this respect, the central argument is that as societies become increasingly industrial, there is a growing tendency within the stratification system towards what Inkeles terms "equilibration"; that is, a tendency for the relative position of an individual or group in any one stratification order to be the same as, or similar to, their position in other orders.[5] In traditional societies, it is observed, inconsistencies in the stratification system may have been contrary to the prevailing ideology but were nonetheless frequent because of the rigidity of the levels within the different subsystems and the relatively low degree of interaction between them. For example, a merchant might become extremely wealthy yet be debarred from "noble" status; in fact, legally, he could be of peasant status and might be treated as such in certain circumstances in spite of his wealth. In industrial societies, by contrast, there are far fewer difficulties in the way of "adjustments" which serve to bring the position of individuals and groups more or less into line from one stratification order to another. Moreover, there is also a shift away from the relative diversity of the bases of stratification which is characteristic of traditional society. With industrialism, the occupational structure takes on overwhelming primacy in this respect. The occupational rôle of the individual is in general in close correlation with most of his other attributes which are relevant to his position in the stratification hierarchy as a whole: his economic situation, his educational level, his prestige in the local community and so on.[6]

In the same way as the trend towards greater equality, the trend towards greater consistency in stratification systems is also treated as an integral part of the industrialization process and as being directly linked to technological and economic advance. In industrial society, it is argued, the distribution of both economic rewards and prestige must come into a close relationship with

---

[1] Cf. Kerr *et al.*, pp. 31, 40–41, 273–274, 290–292; Moore, pp. 357–359.

[2] For a discussion of the strengths and weaknesses of attempts to apply this approach to the explanation of the development of social policy in 19th century England, see John H. Goldthorpe, 'Le développment de la politique sociale en Angleterre de 1800 à 1914", *Sociologie du Travail*, No. 2, 1963. (English version forthcoming in *Transactions of the Vth World Congress of Sociology*, Vol. IV, 1964.)

[3] *Op. cit.*, p. 286 (my italics). The theme of "the end of ideology" – in the West at least – runs strongly throughout *Industrialism and Industrial Man*. Moore, by contrast, is sufficiently detached and sophisticated to recognize "the ideology of a pluralistic society".

[4] Cf. Kerr *et al.*, pp. 274–276, 288–290; Inkeles, p. 346. As earlier noted, Moore diverges here. He notes (p. 359) the empirical probability of increased political participation as societies become industrial, but argues that so far there is no evidence of a *necessary* incompatibility between industrialism and totalitarianism.

[5] Inkeles' "equilibration" (following E. Benoit-Smullyan, "Status Types and Status Interrelations", *Am. Soc. Rev.*, Vol. 9, 1944) thus largely corresponds to what Lenski and Landecker have referred to as "crystallization" and Adams and Homans as "congruence". See Gerhard E. Lenski, "Status Crystallization: a Non-Vertical Dimension of Social Status", *Am. Soc. Rev.*, Vol. 19, 1954; Werner S. Landecker, "Class Crystallization and Class Consciousness", *Am. Soc. Rev.*, Vol. 28, 1963; Stuart Adams, "Social Climate and Productivity in Small Military Groups", *Am. Soc. Rev.*, Vol. 19, 1954; G. C. Homans, "Status Congruence" in *Sentiments and Activities*, 1962. Moore refers simply to "consistency" or "coalescence".

[6] Cf. Kerr et al., pp. 272–273, 284, 292–293; Inkeles, pp. 341–342; Moore, pp. 356–357.

occupational performance since this type of society in fact presupposes an overriding emphasis upon achievement, as opposed to ascription, as the basis of social position — and specifically upon achievement in the sphere of production. At the same time, though, as a result of technological progress, occupational achievement becomes increasingly dependent upon education, and in this way closer ties are formed between economic standing on the one hand and life-styles and subculture on the other. The ignorant and vulgar tycoon and the poor scholar are seen alike as figures of declining importance. In other words, the argument is that inevitably in modern societies, the various determinants of an individual's placing in the overall stratification hierarchy come to form a tight nexus; and that in this nexus occupation can be regarded as the central element — providing as it does the main link between the "objective" and "subjective" aspects of social inequality.

Implicit, then, in this interpretation is the view that in industrial societies stratification systems tend to become relatively highly integrated, in the sense that specifically class differences (i.e. those stemming from inequalities in the economic order) are generally paralleled by status differences (i.e. those based on inequalities in social evaluation); and, thus, that changes in the pattern of the former will automatically result in changes in the pattern of the latter. For example, Kerr and his associates see the growth of "middle incomes" as making for a "middle class society"; that is, a society in which middle class values are widely accepted, both among manual workers and elite groups, and in which the bulk of the population share in "middle class" status.[1]

Mobility

In regard to mobility, the central proposition that is made is one which complements the previous arguments concerning differentiation and consistency. It is that once societies have reached a certain level of industrialization, their overall rates of social mobility tend to become relatively high — higher that is, than is typical in pre-industrial or traditional societies. The increasing number of intermediate positions in the stratification hierarchy widens the opportunity for movement upward from the lower levels, while the emphasis upon occupational achievement rather than on the ascription of social positions means that intergenerationally the talented will tend to rise at the expense of those whose talent is unequal to their birth. In this respect, the educational system is seen as the crucial allocative mechanism, sieving ability and matching capacity to the demands and responsibilities of occupational rôles.[2]

In other words, then, industrial society is regarded as being essentially "open" and "meritocratic". And once more, one should note, the interpretation derives from a conception of the structural and functional imperatives of this type of social order. The high level of mobility is taken as an inevitable consequence of the technologically and economically determined division of labour and of the necessary pressure within a highly dynamic form of society for the increasingly efficient use of talent. To quote again from the authors of *Industrialism and Industrial Man*:

> The industrial society is an open community encouraging occupational and geographic mobility and social mobility. In this sense industrialism *must* be flexible and competitive; it is against tradition and status based upon family, class, religion, race or caste.[3]

In this approach, thus, there is little room for consideration of institutional variations or of value differences between industrial societies which might be associated with *differing* patterns of mobility. It is taken that the overall similarities in this respect are, or at any rate are certainly becoming, the feature of major significance.

These, then, in a necessarily abbreviated form, are the main arguments concerning the development of stratification systems which figure, with varying degrees of refinement or crudity, in current American theories of industrialism. I would now like to turn to what I have to say by way of criticism of these arguments and, to begin with, I would like to comment on each of the three themes on which I based the foregoing exposition. My main purpose here will be to indicate that the views which I have outlined are not always in entire accord with empirical data, and in this connection I shall refer primarily to the industrial societies of the West. Subsequently, however, I shall offer certain more basic, theoretical criticisms which are suggested by a consideration of social stratification in modern Communist society.

On the question of reduced differentiation — or greater equality — in stratification systems, my remarks at this stage will be largely confined to the economic order. This is because it is chiefly in this regard that we have data which will permit, at least in principle, some test of the arguments involved; that is, data on the distributions of income and wealth.[4]

[1] *Op. cit.*, pp. 272–273, 286.
[2] Cf. Kerr *et al.*, pp. 35–37; Moore, pp. 319–321, 343–344. Inkeles does not include the factor of increased mobility as a separate element in his model of the "modernization" of stratification systems. It is, however, incorporated in his discussion of both decreasing differentiation and growing consistency. E.g., in modern societies, "Movement from one to another position on the scale . . . will not be sharply proscribed. Fluidity will characterize the [stratification] system as a whole . . .' *Loc. cit.*, p. 341.
[3] P. 35 (my italics).
[4] It should be acknowledged, however, that for the West, at least, there is clear evidence on one other important point; that is, on the reduction, indeed virtual elimination, of *formal* inequalities of status. This has been the concomitant of the growth of "citizenship" through which all members of national communities have been granted equal civil, political and social rights. Cf. T. H. Marshall, "Citizenship and Social Class" in *Sociology at the Crossroads*, 1963.

At the outset it may be said that, although the evidence is often very patchy, a broad trend towards greater economic equality *does* seem to be discernible in the case of all those societies which have so far progressed from a traditional to an industrial form. Myths of "golden ages" of economic equality in pre-industrial times are now little heeded, and, as a rough generalization, it would, I think, be widely accepted that the poorer the society, the greater the "skew" one may expect in its distributions of income and wealth alike.[1] With this view I would not wish to quarrel — provided that it is taken merely as a formula summing up historical experience, and as one which is subject to exceptions. But there are no grounds at all, in my view, for regarding the regularity in question as manifesting the operation of some process inherent in industrialism — of some general economic law — which will necessarily persist in the future and ensure a continuing egalitarian trend. Rather, the possibility must be left quite open that where such a trend exists, it may at some point be checked — and at a point, moreover, at which considerable economic *in*equality remains. In fact, in my assessment, the relevant data suggest that such a check may already be occurring in some of the more advanced societies of the West; or, at any rate, I would say that on present evidence *this* conclusion is indicated as much as any other.

For the distributions of income and wealth alike, it is true that figures exist to show a movement towards greater equality in most western industrial societies over the years for which adequate time-series are available; that is, from the late inter-war or early post-war period onwards.[2] However, it is now becoming increasingly clear that these figures, which are largely based on tax returns, are not always to be taken at their face value. And, in general, their defects appear to be such that they tend on balance to underestimate the income and wealth which accrue to the economically more favoured groups and in this and other ways to give a somewhat exaggerated idea of the degree of "levelling" that has taken place. In fact, for some western societies at least, there are now grounds for believing that during the last twenty years or so, overall economic inequality has in reality declined only very little, if at all. And particularly so far as wealth is concerned, it is likely that such changes as have occurred have been virtually negligible in their implications for social stratification.[3] Such conclusions have been suggested for the United Kingdom, for example, in Professor Titmuss' recent study, *Income Distribution and Social Change*. It must, of course, be admitted that the whole matter remains a highly controversial one,[4] and it is not possible here to enter into all its complexities. But what is, I think, justified by the evidence, and what is certainly most relevant to my general argument, is Titmuss' contention that "we should be much more hesitant in suggesting that any equalising forces at work in Britain since 1938 can be promoted to the status of a 'natural law' and projected into the future.... There are other forces, deeply rooted in the social structure and fed by many complex institutional factors inherent in large-scale economies, operating in reverse directions."[5]

A similar point of view is maintained, with reference to the United States, in Gabriel Kolko's somewhat neglected book, *Wealth and Power in America*. This study involves not only a critique of previous findings on the distribution of income and wealth in the USA but also a positive reappraisal of the situation. This is particularly important in regard to income. Kolko supplements material from official sources with generally more reliable survey data, and on this basis suggests that over as long a period as 1910 to 1959 there has been no significant *general* trend in the USA towards greater income equality.[6]

Kolko's study prompts one to note the often overlooked point that simply because there may be some levelling of incomes going on in *certain ranges* of the total income distribution, this does not necessarily mean that *overall* equality is increasing; for in other ranges inegalitarian trends may simultaneously be operating. For example, there may be a tendency towards greater equality in that the number of middle-range incomes is growing; but at the same time the position of the lower income groups, relative to the upper and middle groups alike, may be worsening.

In fact, it seems more than possible that a pattern of change of this kind is now going on in the United States. This is indicated by a good deal of recent investigation, apart from that of Kolko, and particularly by

---

[1] Cf. United Nations, *Preliminary Report on the World Social Situation*, 1952, pp. 132–134; and *Report on the World Social Situation*, 1961, pp. 58–61.

[2] See, e.g., United Nations, *Economic Survey of Europe in 1956*, 1957, Ch. VII; R. M. Solow, "Income Inequality since the War" in Ralph E. Freeman (ed.), *Postwar Economic Trends in the United States*, 1960. Recent studies relating specifically to Great Britain are H. F. Lydall, "The Long-term Trend in the Size Distribution of Income", *Journ. Royal Stat. Soc.*, Vol. 122, Part I, 1959, and H. F. Lydall and D. C. Tipping, "The Distribution of Personal Wealth in Britain", *Oxford Inst. Stat. Bull.*, Vol. 23, 1961.

[3] Chiefly, this is because much levelling which appears to have gone on at the top of the distribution has in fact taken place simply *within* families — particularly between parents and children and generally as a means of avoiding taxation. E.g., Lydall and Tipping (*op. cit.*), note the "growing tendency for owners of large properties to distribute their assets amongst the members of their families well in advance of death." (p. 85). However, it is, of course, the family, not the individual, that must be regarded as the basic unit of stratification.

[4] See, e.g., the critical review of Titmuss' book by A. R. Prest, and Titmuss' reply, in *British Tax Review*, March–April, 1963.

[5] *Income Distribution and Social Change*, 1962, p. 198. In this connection it should also be remembered that certain major developments which have made for greater equality in incomes in the recent past are of a non-repeatable kind — notably, the ending of large scale unemployment and the considerable expansion in the number of working class wives in gainful employment.

[6] *Wealth and Power in America*, 1962, Ch. 1. The data in question refer to pre-tax incomes, but Kolko is prepared to argue (Ch. 2) that "Taxation has not mitigated the fundamentally unequal distribution of income ...'

the growing volume of work on the extent of poverty. Gunnar Myrdal, for example, has argued in his book, *Challenge to Affluence*, that while many Americans in the intermediate social strata may well be benefiting from a levelling upwards of living standards, at the base of the stratification hierarchy there is increasing inequality, manifested in the emergence of an "underclass" of unemployed and unemployable persons and families. In other words, the middle ranks of the income distribution may be swelling, but the gap between the bottom and the higher levels is, if anything, tending to widen.[1]

Moreover, what is also significant in Myrdal's study for present purposes is the way in which he brings out the *political* aspects of the problem. Myrdal observes that structural unemployment, resulting from technological innovation in industry, is a basic, and increasingly serious, cause of poverty in America, whereas, in a country like Sweden, in which technological advance is also proceeding rapidly, full employment has been steadily maintained. Again, he notes the relative failure of the United States, compared with most western European countries, to stabilize aggregate demand in its economy on a high and rising level.[2] The explanation of these differences, Myrdal then argues, while not of course entirely political, must nonetheless be regarded as being significantly so. In particular, he stresses the inadequate achievement of government in America in long-range economic planning, in redistributional reforms, and in the provision of public services and advanced social welfare schemes. And the sources of this governmental inadequacy he traces back to certain basic American socio-political dispositions and also to a relative lack of "democratic balance" in the institutional infrastructure of the American policy. On the one hand, Myrdal claims, there is among the powerful business community and within government itself a reluctance to take the long view and to envisage more central direction and control of the economy; also "a serious and irrational bias against public investment and consumption." On the other hand, among the lower strata of American society there is an unusual degree of political apathy and passivity which is most clearly seen in the general failure of the poorer sections of the population to organize themselves effectively and to press for the fundamental social reforms that would be in their interest. In this way an imbalance in organized power is brought about within the "plural society" which makes the need for initiative on the part of government all the more pressing — at the same time as it seems to paralyse this.[3]

If, then, Myrdal's analysis has any general validity — and it has yet, I think, to be seriously disputed — it follows that we should look somewhat doubtfully on arguments about a new equality which "has nothing to do with ideology" but which is the direct outcome of technological and economic advance. Such new equality there may be for some. But for those at the base of stratification hierarchies at least — how "equal" they are likely to become seems to have a good deal to do with ideology, or at any rate with purposive social action,

or lack of this, stemming from specific social values and political creeds as well as from interests.[4] And differences between some industrial societies in these respects may well be giving rise to divergent, rather than convergent, patterns of change in their stratification systems.

On the second set of arguments — those concerning growing consistency between different stratification orders — I shall have relatively little to say for the good reason that there is little empirical data which directly bears on the crucial issue here; that is, the issue of whether there really is a *continuing* increase in the degree of integration of the stratification systems of *advanced* societies. About the long-term historical trend, one would not wish to argue; but again it is a question of whether such a trend is a reliable guide to the present and the future.

My main comment is that such evidence as does appear relevant to this issue indicates that in some industrial societies, at least, on-going economic progress is resulting in stratification systems becoming, if anything, somewhat *less* well integrated in certain respects. This evidence refers to what has become known as the "new working class." It suggests that the appreciable gains in income and in general living standards recently achieved by certain sections of the manual labour force have not for the most part been accompanied by changes in their life-styles of such a kind that their *status* position has been enhanced commensurately with their *economic* position. In other words, there is evidence of cultural and, in particular, of "social" barriers still widely exist-

---

[1] *Challenge to Affluence*, 1963, Ch. 3. The data assembled by the Conference on Economic Progress, *Poverty and Deprivation in the United States*, 1962, suggest that there was real improvement in the income position of low-income groups during World War II but that since then the economy has not greatly enhanced the living standards of the low-income population. In regard to the distribution of wealth, Robert J. Lampman, *The Share of Top Wealth-Holders in National Wealth*, 1962, has produced data to show that the share of personal sector wealth held by the wealthiest 1% of adults in the USA has steadily increased from 1949 to 1956.

[2] *Op. cit.*, pp. 13–15, 27–30.

[3] *Ibid.*, Chs. 4, 6 and 7. A basically similar view is presented in Michael Harrington, *The Other America*, 1962. On the organizational, and thus political, weakness of the poor, see pp. 13–17; on the past failure and present responsibility of the Federal Government, pp. 163–170. Cf. also Stephen W. Rousseas and James Farganis, "American Politics and the End of Ideology", *Brit. Journ. Soc.*, Vol. XIV, No. 4, 1963.

[4] Cf. Harrington's emphasis on the fact that "If there is to be a way out (of poverty) it will come from human action, from political change, not from automatic processes," (p. 162). Similarly, Raymond Aron has observed that the present problem of poverty in the USA is not that of the "pauperization" envisaged by Marx but that "Il n'en existe pas moins et il rappelle opportunément, à ceux qui seraient enclins à oublier, que la croissance économique ou les progrès techniques ne sont pas des recettes miraculeuses de paix sociale ou de relations authentiques humaines"; and further that "... ni la croissance économique livrée à elle-même, ni le progrès technique, emporté par son dynamisme, ne garantissent un ordre juste ni, moins encore, des conditions de vie conformes aux aspirations d'une humanité qui a transformé le monde plus qu'elle ne c'est transformée elle-même." *La Lutte des Classes*, 1964, pp. 15–16.

ing between "working class" and "middle class" even in cases where immediate material differences have now disappeared.[1] Thus it seems that, contrary to the expectations of Kerr and his associates, "middle incomes" have not resulted, as yet at least, in the generalization of "middle class" ways of life or of "middle class" status.

Moreover, there are grounds for believing that notable discrepancies in stratification will persist in industrial societies. As Kerr himself recognizes, there will still exist in the foreseeable future in such societies a division between "managers" and "managed" — between those who are in some way associated with the exercise of authority in productive and administrative organizations and those who are not. And this division, one would suggest, will remain associated with differences in prestige, as well as in power, while at the same time managers and managed overlap to some extent in terms of living standards. One would agree that in an economically advanced society a broad stratum of workers, performing skilled or, one would add, particularly arduous or irksome jobs, are likely to earn middle-range incomes. But there are no grounds for automatically assuming that they will thereby become socially accepted and assimilated into even the lower levels of what Renner has usefully termed the "service class".[2] After all, it must be recognized that groups which have some serious basis for claiming superior status generally take advantage of this. And further, it should be borne in mind that, increasingly, the members of this "service class" will be selected through their educational attainments rather than being recruited from the rank and file. Thus, if anything, they are likely to become more set apart from the latter in terms of culture and lifestyles than they are at present.

In sum, one might suggest that the "increasing consistency" argument is flawed because it fails to take into account first, that occupational rôles with similar economic rewards may in some instances be quite differently related to the exercise of authority; and secondly, that relatively high income may serve as recompense for work of otherwise high "disutility" to the operative as well as for work involving expertise and responsibility.

Lastly, then, we come to the matter of social mobility. In this case, the first question which arises is that of whether it is in fact valid to regard industrial societies as having regularly higher rates of mobility than pre-industrial societies. Several writers, one should note, have recently argued that this view should not be too readily taken and have produced evidence to suggest that certain pre-industrial societies were far less rigidly stratified than seems generally to have been supposed.[3] Nevertheless, I would not wish to argue here against the more orthodox view, except to make the point that an increased rate of *inter*generational mobility in advanced societies is likely to be associated with some limitation of *intra*generational or "career" mobility. To the extent that education becomes a key determinant of occupational achievement, the chances of "getting ahead" for those who start in a lowly position are inevitably diminished. This fact is most clearly demonstrated in recent studies of the recruitment of industrial managers. These show that as the educational standards of managers have risen, the likelihood of shop floor workers being promoted above supervisory level has been reduced.[4] Furthermore, in an advanced society, increasingly dominated by large scale organizations, the possibilities for the "little man" of starting up a successful business of his own also tend to be more limited than they were at an earlier phase in the industrialization process. Thus, for that large proportion of the population at least, with rank-and-file jobs and "ordinary" educational qualifications, industrial society appears to be growing significantly *less* "open" than it once was.

However, other, and perhaps more basic, issues arise from the arguments concerning mobility which I earlier outlined; in particular issues relating to the determinants of mobility patterns and rates. What are the grounds, one might ask, for believing that in advanced societies the crucial factor here is the occupational distribution, and thus that from one such society to another social mobility will tend to be much the same? Support for this view can be found in the well-known Lipset and Zetterberg study which led, in fact, to the conclusion that Western industrial societies have broadly similar rates of intergenerational mobility, and which produced no evidence to suggest that factors other than the "standardizing" one of the occupational structure were of major significance.[5] Their data, the authors claim, give no backing for the idea that differences in social ideologies, religious beliefs or other aspects of national cultures exercise a decisive influence on mobility. But it has to be noted that, as Lipset and Zetterberg themselves make quite clear, their findings in this respect refer only to "mass" mobility; that is,

[1] See, e.g., for Great Britain, John H. Goldthorpe and David Lockwood, "Affluence and the British Class Structure," *Soc. Rev.*, Vol. 11, No. 2, 1963; for the USA, Bennet Berger, *Working Class Suburb: a study of Auto Workers in Suburbia*, 1960; for France, A. Andrieux and J. Lignon, *L'Ouvrier D'Aujourd'hui*, 1960. In all these contributions a common emphasis is that on the growing *disparity* between the situation of the manual worker as *producer* and *consumer*.

[2] Karl Renner, *Wandlungen der modernen Gesellschaft; zwei Abhandlungen über die Probleme der Nachkriegzeit*, 1953.

[3] See, e.g., for China, Robert M. Marsh, *The Mandarins: the Circulation of Elites in China, 1600–1900*, 1961, and "Values, Demand and Social Mobility," *Am. Soc. Rev.*, Vol. 28, 1963; also, Ping-ti Ho, *The Ladder of Success in Imperial China: aspects of Social Mobility, 1368–1911*, 1963.

[4] For Great Britain, see Acton Society Trust, *Management Succession*, 1965, and R. V. Clements, *Managers: a study of their careers in industry*, 1958. For the USA, see W. Lloyd Warner and James C. Abegglen, *Occupational Mobility in American Business and Industry*, 1955.

[5] See S. M. Lipset and Hans L. Zetterberg, "A Theory of Social Mobility," *Transactions of the Third World Congress of Sociology*, 1956, Vol. III, pp. 155–177, and Ch. II, "Social Mobility in Industrial Society" in S. M. Lipset and R. Bendix, *Social Mobility in Industrial Society*, 1959.

simply to movements across the manual–nonmanual line. And indeed they point out that the investigation of some aspects of "élite" mobility — for example, the recruitment of higher civil servants — has indicated some important national variations.[1]

Moreover, we have more recently the outstanding study of comparative social mobility made by Professor S. M. Miller.[2] This covers a still greater amount of data than Lipset and Zetterberg's work and demonstrates fairly conclusively that when *range* as well as frequency of mobility is taken into consideration, industrial societies do reveal quite sizeable differences in their mobility patterns. Such differences tend to be most evident in the case of long-range mobility. This is generally low — another reason for querying just how "open" and "meritocratic" industrial societies have so far become — but certain countries, the USA and USSR, for example, appear to have attained quite significantly higher rates of "élite" mobility than do others, such as many in western Europe. Further, though, Miller shows that countries with low long-range mobility may still have relatively high short-range mobility — as, for instance, does Great Britain: there is no correlation between rates of mobility of differing distance. Thus, industrial societies have quite various "mobility profiles"; the overall similarity indicated by the study of "mass" mobility turns out to be somewhat spurious.

On this basis, then, Miller is able to argue very strongly that patterns of social mobility in advanced societies cannot be understood *simply* in terms of occupational structure[3] — or, one would add, in terms of any "inherent" features of industrialism. Their diversity precludes this. It appears necessary, rather, to consider also the effects on mobility of other, and more variable, aspects of social structure — educational institutions, for example, and their articulation with the stratification hierarchy itself — and further, possibly, *pace* Lipset and Zetterberg, the part played by cultural values.[4] As Miller points out, what is perhaps most surprising about his data is the *lack* of convergence in mobility patterns that is indicated between societies at broadly comparable levels of economic development. The "logic" of industrialism, it appears, is often confused by "extraneous" factors.

These, then, are some of the objections that may be made on empirical grounds to the hypotheses concerning changes in stratification systems which I previously outlined. Accepting the arguments in question on their own terms, as it were, it is possible to indicate a number of points at which they do not appear to fit well with the findings of empirical research in western industrial societies or, at least, at which they remain unproven. However, in conclusion of this paper, I would like to make a more basic objection which relates to the theoretical position underlying these arguments. Specifically, I would like to question the idea that the stratification systems of all industrial societies are *ipso facto* of the same generic type, and thus that they may in principle be expected to follow convergent or parallel lines of development. Against this view, I would like to suggest that social stratification in the advanced societies of the Communist world — or at any rate in the USSR and its closer satellites — is *not* of the same generic type as in the West and that, because of this, the hypotheses earlier discussed cannot in this case really apply.

Soviet society is, of course, stratified; and, furthermore, it is true that in spite of the absence of private property in production, it appears to be stratified on an often similar pattern to the capitalist or post-capitalist societies of the West. For example, to a large degree there is apparent similarity in the connections between occupational rôle, economic rewards and social prestige, in the part played by education in determining occupational level, in the operation of an informal status system, and so on. But, I would argue, this similarity is only of a phenotypical kind: genotypically, stratification in Soviet society is significantly different from stratification in the West.

Primarily, it may be said, this difference derives from the simple fact that in Soviet society the economy operates within a "monistic", or totalitarian, political order and is, in principle at least, totally planned, whereas in advanced Western societies political power is significantly less concentrated and the economy is planned in a far less centralized and detailed way. From this it results that in the West economic, and specifically market forces act as the crucial stratifying agency within society. They are, one could say, the major source of social inequality. And consequently, the *class* situation of individuals and groups, understood in terms of their economic power and resources, tends to be the most important single determinant of their general life-chances. This is why we can usefully speak of Western industrial society as being "class" stratified. However, in the case of Soviet society, market forces cannot be held to play a comparable rôle in the stratification process. These forces operate, of course, and differences in economic power and resources between individuals and groups have, as in the West, far-reaching social and human consequences. But, one would argue, to a significantly greater extent than in the West, stratification in Soviet society is subjected to *political* regulation; market forces are not permitted to have the primacy or the degree of autonomy in this respect that they have

[1] *Ibid.*, pp. 38–42.
[2] S. M. Miller, "Comparative Social Mobility," *Current Sociology*, Vol. IX, No. 1, 1960.
[3] *Ibid.*, pp. 22–23, 57–58.
[4] As an example of the kind of study which would seem particularly relevant and valuable, see Ralph H. Turner, "Modes of Social Ascent through Education: Sponsored and Contest Mobility" in A. H. Halsey, Jean Floud and C. Arnold Anderson (eds.), *Education, Economy and Society*, 1961. This paper is concerned with the relation between differences in the American and English educational systems and differences in the prevailing norms in the two societies pertaining to upward mobility. More specifically, the aim is to investigate how the *accepted mode* of upward mobility shapes the pattern of educational institutions.

even in a "managed" capitalist society. Undoubtedly, the functional requirements of the economy exert pressures upon the system of stratification, and these pressures may in some cases prove to be imperative. But the nature of the political order means that far more than with Western democracy, the pattern of social inequality can be shaped through the purposive action of the ruling party, and still more so, of course, the "life-fates" of particular persons.[1]

For example, during the years of Stalin's rule, economic inequality in the USSR generally increased. Numerous writers have in fact commented upon the progressive abandonment over this period of the egalitarian aspects of Marxist-Leninist ideology and of post-revolutionary attempts to operate egalitarian economic and social policies.[2] From the early 1930's differential rewards in relation to skill, effort and responsibility were introduced into industry and administration, and thus from this point the range of wages and salaries tended to widen. Further, changes in the 1940's in the income tax and inheritance laws were conducive to greater inequalities in incomes and personal wealth alike. Then again, high ranking officials and other favoured persons appear to have received increasingly important non-monetary rewards in the form of cars, apartments, villas, free holidays and so on. By the end of the war decade, these developments had led to a degree of inequality in Soviet society which, in the view of many commentators, was greater than that which was generally to be found in the industrial societies of the West.[3] However, in more recent years it has become clear that contrary to most expectations, this inegalitarian trend in the USSR has been checked and, moreover, that in certain respects at least it has even been reversed. Minimum wages in industry have been increased several times since the late 1950's and the incomes of the *kolkhozy* have for the most part risen

quite considerably. This latter development has had the effect of closing somewhat the income gap between industrial and agricultural workers and has also been associated with a reduction in differentials in the earnings of the *kolkhoz* peasants themselves. At the same time, there is evidence of limitations being placed on the more excessive salaries of higher officials and of more stringent measures being taken against the abuse of privileges. Finally, tax changes in the past few years have tended to favour the poorer against the richer groups, and various kinds of welfare provision have been substantially improved. In these ways, then, economic differences between the manual and nonmanual categories overall have almost certainly been reduced to some extent, as well as differences within these categories.[4]

Now these changes can, of course, be rightly regarded as being in some degree economically conditioned. Clearly, for instance, the increased differentiation in wages and salaries in the Stalin era must in part be understood in terms of the exigencies and consequences of rapid industrialization. But, I would argue, there can be little question that at the same time these changes were the outcome of political decisions — of choices made between realistic alternatives — and, furthermore, that frequently they were brought about with political as well as with specifically economic ends in view. Stalin, it is true, wanted rapid industrialization: but he had the further political objective that this process should be carried through under his own absolute control. Thus, this entailed not only depriving a large section of the population of material returns from their labour in order to achieve maximum expansion of industrial capacity, but also the building-up of a group of exceptionally favoured administrators and managers who would be highly motivated to retain their enviable positions through loyalty to Stalin and through high level performance. To this latter end, in fact, appropriate status as well as economic inequalities were also developed. For example, during and after the war years, formal titles, uniforms and insignia of rank were introduced into various branches of industry and the governmental bureaucracy. Moreover, the wide social distance which was in this way created between the top and bottom of the stratification hierarchy had the manifest function of insulating the "élite" from the masses and from their needs and wishes. And thus, as Professor Feldmesser has pointed out, those in high positions were helped to learn "that success was to be had by winning the favour not of those below them but of those above them, which was exactly what Stalin wanted them to learn."[5]

Similarly, the more recent moves towards reducing inequalities have again fairly evident political aims, even though, in some cases, they may also have been economically required.[6] On the one hand, it seems clear that the present Soviet leadership is working towards a future Communist society which will be characterized by a high level of social welfare, and indeed eventually by private affluence, while still remaining under the

[1] Also relevant here, of course, is a further distinctive feature of a totalitarian political system — the absence of the "rule of law".

[2] Probably the best analysis in this respect is that provided by Barrington Moore Jnr., *Soviet Politics — the Dilemma of Power*, 1950.

[3] See, e.g., Alex Inkeles, "Social Stratification and Mobility in the Soviet Union: 1940–1950," *Am. Soc. Rev.*, Vol. 15, 1950. (Reprinted in this book.) This paper contains an excellent factual account of the ways through which both economic and status inequality was increased during the Stalin era.

[4] For a general discussion of these changes, see Robert A. Feldmesser, "Towards the Classless Society?" (reprinted in this book.) Cf. also Alec Nove, "Is the Soviet Union a Welfare State?", in Alex Inkeles and Kent Geiger (eds.), *Soviet Society*, 1961.

[5] *Op. cit.*, p. 579. This political subordination of members of the "élite", concomitant with their economic and status elevation, is the reason for using inverted commas. As Feldmesser notes, the "élite" created by Stalin is surely distinctive by virtue of its general lack of autonomy.

[6] As, e.g., in the case of the increase in peasant incomes which was essential if genuine incentives to improve production were to be offered in agriculture. Cf. Seweryn Bialer, "But Some are More Equal than Others," *Problems of Communism*, Vol. IX, No. 2, 1960.

undisputed dominance of the Party. In other words, the creation of the "good life" for all appears destined to become one of the régime's most important sources of legitimacy. In fact, as Professor Shapiro has noted, the 1961 Programme of the CPSU makes this more or less explicit. The Programme, he writes,

> enunciates squarely the concrete fact that party rule has come to stay. It calls upon the Soviet citizen to recognize and accept this fact, and to abandon the illusion that in this respect, things are going to change. In return, it promises him great material benefits and prosperity.[1]

On the other hand, the security of the régime also requires that the bureaucratic and managerial "élite" does not become so well established as to gain some measure of independence from the Party chiefs. Thus, Krushchev has been concerned to show the members of this group that they remain the creatures of the Party and that their privileges are not permanent but still rest upon their obedience and service to the Party. Those whom Djilas has referred to as the "new class" in Communist society[2] cannot in fact be allowed by the Party leadership to become a class — in the sense of a collectivity which is capable of maintaining its position in society (and that of its children) through its own social power, and which possesses some degree of group consciousness and cohesion. For the emergence of such a class would constitute a serious threat to the Party's totalitarian rule, different only in degree from the threat that would be posed by the emergence of an independent trade union, professional body or political organization. It is awareness of this danger, one would suggest, which chiefly lies behind the recent attacks — verbal as well as material — which have been made upon higher officialdom and the top industrial personnel. For apart from the curtailment of economic rewards in some cases, it is interesting to note that the quasi-military status distinctions of the war decade have now been largely abolished and that the Party has actually encouraged rank and file employees in industry and agriculture to expose inadequacy and inefficiency on the part of their superiors.[3] Furthermore, there has been some weeding out of superfluous posts, and demotions appear to have become much more common.[4] Finally, though, it is probably Krushchev's educational reforms which have been of greatest significance. These were carried through at a time when pressure on the institutions of secondary and higher education was reaching a peak; yet they were designed to make access to these institutions less dependent than previously upon economic resources and the new rules for competitive entry which were introduced seem, if anything, to shift the balance of "social" advantage away from the children of the "élite" and towards candidates from worker or peasant families. As Feldmesser notes, if a "new class" — a "state bourgeoisie" — were in fact in existence in the USSR, then exactly the reverse of this might have been expected;

that is, a move to make access to these scarce facilities *more*, rather than less, dependent upon the ability to pay.[5]

It is then not too much to say that in Soviet society hierarchical differentiation is an instrument of the régime. To a significant degree stratification is *organized* in order to suit the political needs of the régime; and, as these needs change, so too may the particular structure of inequality. In other words, the Soviet system of stratification is characterized by an important element of "deliberateness", and it is this which basically distinguishes it from the Western system, in spite of the many apparent similarities. In the industrial societies of the West, one could say, the action of the state sets limits to the extent of social inequalities which derive basically from the operation of a market economy: in Soviet society the pattern of inequality also results in part from "market" forces, but in this case these are subordinated to political control up to the limits set by the requirements of the industrial system.[6] For this reason, one may conclude, Soviet society is not, in the same way as Western society, *class* stratified. As Raymond Aron has observed, class stratification and a monistic political system are to be regarded as incompatibles.[7]

If, then, the foregoing analysis is accepted, it follows that the arguments I earlier outlined on the development of stratification systems can have no general validity. Their underlying rationale, in terms of the exigencies of an advanced industrial technology and economy, is destroyed. The experience of Soviet society can be taken

[1] Leonard Shapiro, "From Utopia towards Realism" in Shapiro (ed.), *The USSR and the Future: an Analysis of the New Program of the CPSU*, 1963. See also in this volume Erik Boettcher, "Soviet Social Policy in Theory and Practice". The text of the Programme itself is printed as an Appendix; note, in particular, Part Two, Sections II, III, V and VII.

[2] Milovan Djilas, *The New Class*, 1957.

[3] Feldmesser, *op. cit.*, pp. 573–575.

[4] Bialer, *op. cit.*, pp. 576–578.

[5] *Op. cit.*, pp. 576–578.

[6] This assessment is consistent with the more general interpretations of the Soviet social system advanced by writers such as Brzezinski and Daniel Bell, in some opposition to the interpretation of Inkeles and his associates. "The important thing is that those in charge of Soviet society have assumed that economic and social development in all its aspects can be purposefully steered by man in the direction of an ideal solution. This produces consequences that are not only economic but also political, quite different from those induced by other equally technologically advanced economic systems where, to a large extent, economic life is self-directive and ultimate goals, such as plenty and progress, are purposely vague." Zbigniew K. Brzezinski, *Ideology and Power in Soviet Politics*, 1962, p. 31. "The Harvard group . . . shrinks from seeking to specify the motor forces in the social system as they have conceived it. . . . Is it not quite clear, really, that the Soviet system is characterized, essentially, by the centralized control of political power, that it is a *command* system, with few institutional checks. . . . In a society like Russia, where institutional and behaviour patterns are not autonomous, a 'social system' has no meaning unless it can be defined within the context of politics." Daniel Bell, "Ten Theories in Search of Reality: the Prediction of Soviet Behaviour" in *The End of Ideology*, 1961, pp. 340–341.

[7] See his "Social Structure and the Ruling Class," *Brit. Journ. Soc.*, Vol. I, 1950.

as indicating that the structural and functional imperatives of an industrial order are not so stringent as to prevent quite wide variations in patterns of social stratification, nor to prohibit the systematic manipulation of social inequalities by a régime commanding modern administrative resources and under no constraints from an organized opposition or the rule of law.

The crucial point, in fact, at which the rationale breaks down is in the supposition that industrialism and totalitarianism cannot "in the long run" co-exist; that is, in the idea that with industrial advance a progressive diffusion of political power must of necessity occur. Were this idea valid, then it would become difficult to maintain the claim that differences between the stratification systems of the Western and Communist worlds are of a generic kind. However, it may be said that no serious grounds exist for believing that within Soviet society any such diffusion of power is taking place, or, at least, not so far as the key decision-making processes are concerned.[1] The régime may be compelled to give more consideration to the effect of its decisions on popular morale and to rely increasingly on the expertise of scientists, technicians and professionals of various kinds; it may also find it desirable to decentralize administration and to encourage a high degree of participation in the conduct of public affairs at a local level. But the important point is that all these things can be done, and in recent years *have* been done, without the Party leadership in any way yielding up its position of ultimate authority and control. Indeed, it is far more arguable that since the end of the period of "collective" rule, the power of the Party leadership has become still more absolute and unrivalled. This situation, one would suggest, has been brought about as a result of Krushchev's success in reducing the power and independence, relative to the Party machine, of the other major bureaucratic structures within Soviet society — those of the political police, of the military and of government and industry. In some cases, it might be noted, the changes involved here can be seen as aspects of "de-stalinization" — for example, the mitigation of the terror or the dissolution of a large part of the central state apparatus. Yet at the same time these changes have had the effect of accentuating still further the totalitarian nature of Party rule. As Bialer points out:

> The party bureaucracy is at present the only remaining apparatus which is centralized in its organization, which operates at all levels of the society, and which "specializes" in every sphere of societal activity. In its functions of communicating, controlling and to an ever greater degree directly organizing the tasks set forth by the leadership, it influences the operation of the other bureaucratic apparatuses, but is not in turn subject to any outside interference. It is subordinate only to the top leadership and to its own hierarchical line of authority.[2]

It is, I think, significant that Inkeles himself sees the weakest spot in the entire thesis of "declining differentiation" as being in the application of this to the "realm of power" within Communist society. He acknowledges the distinct possibility that here his model of stratification change may have to be revised and the prediction of increased homogenization restricted to realms other than that of power.[3] Moreover, Inkeles has elsewhere stated quite explicitly that

> ... there is no necessary, or even compelling, force in the modern industrial social order which clearly makes it incompatible with totalitarianism.

and again that

> ... the modern industrial order appears to be compatible with either democratic or totalitarian political and social forms.[4]

What one would wish to stress, then, is that if such views as these are sound (as I believe they are), it becomes difficult to see how one can formulate *any* general and comprehensive propositions concerning stratification change as part of a "logic" of industrial development. For the essential assumption involved in such propositions — that of some necessary "primacy" of the economic system over the political — is no longer a reliable one. It has to be recognized, rather, that stratification systems are not to be understood as mere "reflections" of a certain level of technology and industrial organization but are shaped by a range of other factors, important among which may be that of purposive political action; and further, that the importance of this latter factor in societies in which political power is highly concentrated is such as to create a distinctive type of stratification which is difficult even to discuss in terms of concepts developed in a Western, capitalist context.[5]

---

[1] For recent discussion of the issue of the compatibility of industrialism and totalitarianism from both empirical and theoretical points of view, see Brzezinski, *op. cit.*, Chs. I and III, and R. Aron (ed.), *World Technology and Human Destiny*, 1963.

[2] *Op. cit.*, pp. 48–49. In addition to Bialer's paper, see also on the strengthening of Party rule under Krushchev, Brzezinski, *op. cit.*, Ch. III, and Edward Crankshaw, *Krushchev's Russia*, 1957, pp. 69, 76–79. Crankshaw shows how this process is in no way inconsistent with the widening of opportunities for popular participation in administrative work at a local level via the "public organizations". See pp. 94–98.

[3] "Social Stratification in the Modernization of Russia," *loc. cit.*, pp. 345–347.

[4] Inkeles and Bauer, *op. cit.*, p. 390.

[5] As Feldmesser has indicated, the argument that Soviet society is not "class" stratified in the manner of Western industrial societies can also be supported from the "subjective" point of view. See his paper, "Social Classes and the Political Structure" in Black (ed.), *op. cit.*, pp. 235–252. The available evidence suggests that Soviet citizens exhibit a relatively low level of class consciousness in the sense that their class situation is not of fundamental importance in patterning their dominant modes of thought and action. Members of different social strata in Soviet society seem more alike in their social ideologies and attitudes than their counterparts in the West, while the feature of the social structure which is most strongly reflected

To end with, it might be observed that the arguments pursued in the latter part of this paper have negative implications not only for the model of stratification change with which I have been specifically concerned, but also for the kind of general theory of industrialism with which this model may be associated. The rejection of the particular hypotheses on stratification on the grounds that have been suggested obviously entails a rejection too of the idea of the convergent development of advanced societies focussed on "pluralistic industrialism", and equally of the key notion of a rigorous "logic" of industrialism which is the engine of such development.

At least as expressed in the somewhat brash manner of Kerr and his colleagues, these ideas would seem to amount to little more than what might be called an evolutionary para-Marxism; and, as such, one would say, they share certain major flaws with the developmental theories of Marx and of the social evolutionists alike. In the first place, there is the exaggeration of the degree of determinism which is exercised upon social structures by "material" exigencies, and, concomitantly with this, the underestimation of the extent to which a social order may be shaped through purposive action within the limits of such exigencies. Secondly, and relatedly, there is the further underestimation of the diversity of values and ideologies which may underlie

purposive action; and thus, from these two things together, there results the tendency to envisage a future in which the complex patterns of past development will become increasingly orderly and aligned — the tendency, in fact, to think in terms of "*the* road ahead" rather than in terms of a variety of roads.[1] And then finally, and perhaps most culpably, there is the ethnocentric bias; that failure of the imagination which leads the sociologist to accept his own form of society, or rather some idealized version of this, as the goal towards which all humanity is moving.

[1] More radically, it may be objected that, if a long-run view is to be taken, the very concept of "industrial society" will eventually cease to be useful. As the Spanish social scientist, Luis Diez del Corral, has pointed out, the concept remains of some significance while societies exist in which highest priority is assigned to industrial and economic values generally. During this phase, "this secularization and concentration of values helps explain the lessening of ideological conflicts ..." But, Del Corral goes on, "This *élan* will only be temporary, and this standardization, this secularization of values which results in economic growth will one day enable all values to flower, all constraints to be forgotten, unless it ends in the apocalyptic destruction of mankind. These two possibilities underline both the grandeur and the misery of our destiny." See R. Aron (ed.) *op. cit.*, p. 68.

---

in their social consciousness at all levels is that of the division between "Party people" and "non-Party people". On this latter point see Inkeles and Bauer, *op. cit.*, Ch. XIII.

LIST OF SOME CONTRIBUTORS AS OF 1965-66

Raymond Aron, Sociology, University of Paris

E. Digby Baltzell, Sociology, University of Pennsylvania

Zygmunt Bauman, Sociology, University of Warsaw

Joseph Ben-David, Sociology, Hebrew University, Jerusalem

Reinhard Bendix, Sociology, University of California, Berkeley

Robert Blauner, Sociology, University of California, Berkeley

Urie Bronfenbrenner, Psychology, Cornell University

Howard Brotz, Sociology, New School for Social Research

Kingsley Davis, Sociology, University of California, Berkeley

N.J. Demerath III, Sociology, University of Wisconsin

Wolfram Eberhard, Sociology, University of California, Berkeley

Lloyd A. Fallers, Anthropology, University of Chicago

Robert A. Feldmesser, Sociology, Dartmouth College

Irving A. Fowler, School of Social Welfare, State University of N.Y. at Buffalo

Thomas Fox, Sociology, Syracuse University

Marc Galanter, The Law School, University of Chicago

Charles H. and Katherine George, Sociology, United College, Winnipeg

John H. Goldthorpe, Sociology, Kings College, Cambridge University

William J. Goode, Sociology, Columbia University

Michael Harrington, Journalism, League for Industrial Democracy

Robert W. Hodge, Sociology, University of Chicago

Herbert H. Hyman, Sociology, Columbia University

Alex Inkeles, Sociology, Harvard University

Charles Kadushin, Sociology, Columbia University

Carl Kaysen, Economics, Harvard University

William Kornhauser, Sociology, University of California, Berkeley

Seymour Martin Lipset, Sociology, Harvard University

Jackson T. Main, History, San Jose State College

* Andrzej Malewski, Sociology, University of Warsaw

T. H. Marshall, Sociology, London School of Economics

David Matza, Sociology, University of California, Berkeley

Kurt B. Mayer, Sociology, University of Berne, Switzerland

Robert K. Merton, Sociology, Columbia University

Herman P. Miller, Demography, U.S. Bureau of the Census

S. M. Miller, Sociology, Syracuse University

* C. Wright Mills, Sociology, Columbia University

Wilbert E. Moore, Sociology, The Russell Sage Foundation

Kunio Odaka, Sociology, University of Tokyo

* Stanislaw Ossowski, Sociology, University of Warsaw

Talcott Parsons, Sociology, Harvard University

Alice Kitt Rossi, Sociology, University of Chicago

Peter H. Rossi, Sociology, University of Chicago

Paul M. Siegel, Sociology, University of Chicago

Thomas C. Smith, History, Stanford University

Glaucio A. D. Soares, Sociology, UNESCO Graduate Faculty of Sociology, Santiago, Chile

William Spinrad, Sociology, Paterson State College

M. N. Srinivas, Sociology, University of Delhi, Delhi, India

Arthur L. Stinchcombe, Sociology, The Johns Hopkins University

Stephan Thernstrom, History, Harvard University

Donald J. Treiman, Sociology, University of Chicago

Martin Trow, Sociology, University of California, Berkeley

Melvin M. Tumin, Sociology, Princeton University

Ralph H. Turner, Sociology, University of California, Los Angeles

Morris Watnick, Political Science, Brandeis University

Wlodzimierz Wesolowski, Sociology, University of Warsaw

Alan B. Wilson, Educational Sociology, University of California, Berkeley

* R. Richard Wohl, History, University of Chicago

Dennis H. Wrong, Sociology, New York University

Hans L. Zetterberg, Sociology, State Bank Foundation, Stockholm, Sweden

* Deceased

Name Index

Abbot, W. W., 120
Abegglen, James C., 155, 457, 654
Acton, John E. D., 470
Adalbald, St., 398
Adams, Brooks, 268
Adams, Charles Francis, 270
Adams, D. K., 496
Adams, G. B., 534
Adams, Stuart, 308
Adelman, M. A., 232
Adloff, R., 433
Albert, Ethel, 145
Alembert, Jean le Rond d', 87
Alexander II, 125
Aleksandrov, A. V., 520
Alexandrov, B., 521, 524
Alford, Robert R., 150
Alger, Horatio, 501-506, 602, 615
Allardt, Erik, 386, 419, 427
Allen, Frederick Lewis, 269
Allinsmith, Wesley, 362
Almond, Gabriel, 86, 162
Amory, Cleveland, 268, 344
Anderson, C. A., 166, 309, 450, 460, 655
Anderson, H. E., 363-364, 413, 613
Anderson, John E., 362
Anderson, Nels, 594
Andrieux, A., 654
Arens, F., 105
Argyle, Michael, 421
Aristotle, 1-2
Arnold, Rosemary, 147
Arnold, Thomas, 164
Aron, Raymond, 84, 201-210
Arond, H., 497
Asch, S. E., 336
Ashburn, Frank D., 271
Ashby, Sir Eric, 462, 469
Assorodobraj, N., 88
Atkinson, J. W., 66
Atlee, Clement, 165
Aymes, Joseph, 563

Babeuf, François Emile, 87, 95
Bacon, Nathaniel, 111
Bagehot, Walter, 162, 164
Bailey, F. G., 557
Bain, R. K., 445
Baker, George Fales, 269
Balasz, E., 181
Baldwin, Alfred L., 362-364
Balfour, W., 404
Baltzell, E. Digby, 266-275
Banfield, Edward C., 220-221, 224, 228, 230, 240
Barber, Bernard, 402, 590
Barber, Elinor, 594
Barker, Ernest, 82

Barnard, C. I., 241, 248
Barnes, H. E., 76
Baron, George, 166, 455
Bascom, W. R., 143
Basset, John Spencer, 117
Bauer, Otto, 429
Bauman, Zygmunt, 534-540
Baykov, Alexander, 516, 518-519
Bayley, Nancy, 362-363
Bayton, J., 496
Beard, Charles A., 268-269
Becker, Howard, 450
Beecher, Henry Ward, 393
Beegle, J. Allen, 417
Bell, Daniel, 85, 163, 166, 571-572, 657
Bell, Howard M., 476, 479
Bell, Landon C., 112
Bell, Wendell, 218, 599
Below, G. von, 103
Ben-David, Joseph, 459-472
Bendix, Reinhard, 5-11, 73-86, 92, 164, 183, 192-193, 267, 298, 307, 327, 335, 341, 402, 419, 425-427, 450, 457, 473, 477, 493, 498, 567, 570, 573, 575, 583, 591, 654
Benedict, R., 372
Benney, M., 421, 423
Benoit-Smullyan, E., 650
Bensman, Joseph, 224
Benson, E. G., 420
Berdayev, Nicholas, 470
Berelson, B., 423
Berenda, R. W., 336
Berger, Bennett, 81
Berger, Peter, 393
Bergson, Abram, 518
Berle, A. A., Jr., 239
Bernard, Jessie, 378, 387, 451
Bernstein, Basil, 192, 447
Berreman, G. D., 445
Bertillon, Jacques, 354
Bialer, Seweryn, 656-658
Bielenstein, H., 181
Bienstock, Gregory, 518
Bierstedt, R., 65
Birch, A. H., 421
Black, C. E., 649
Black, Max, 161-162
Blau, Peter, 575
Blauner, Robert, 183, 419, 473-487
Bloch, Marc, 534-535
Bloomberg, Warner, 222-223
Blum, Fred H., 480, 487
Blum, Jerome, 185
Blumberg, Leonard U., 222
Boalt, Gunnar, 567
Boat, Marion D., 599
Boehlau, Hermann, 470
Boek, W. E., 363-364
Bogue, Donald J., 438

Bohannan, Paul, 144
Boinebroke, Jehan, 105
Bolte, K. M., 313
Bonham, John, 415
Borrie, W. D., 149, 357
Borrowman, Merle L., 439
Bottomore, T. B., 473
Boulding, Kenneth, 291
Bowman, Mary Jean, 472
Brace, Charles Loring, 302, 504
Bremmer, Robert H., 289
Brennan, T., 564
Bressard, M., 569
Briggs, Asa, 163
Bright, A. A., Jr., 236
Brinton, Crane, 470
Britt, George, 506
Britten, R. H., 409
Brodbeck, A., 261, 414
Brogan, Denis, 163, 457
Bronfenbrenner, Urie, 362-377
Brooke, E., 408
Broom, Leonard, 150, 156, 189, 304, 377
Brotz, Howard, 342-352
Brown, E. E., 438
Brown, Herbert Ross, 505
Brown, J. C., 474-477
Brown, K. E., 446
Brown, Newell, 443
Brown, Robert E., 111
Bruce, Maurice, 297
Brunner, Otto, 79, 85
Brunt, Maureen, 154, 157-158
Brutzkus, Boris, 121-135
Bryce, Herrington C., 576, 581
Bryce, James, 345
Brzezinski, Zbigniew K., 657
Bücher, Karl, 98
Buckley, W., 64
Bukharin, Nikolai, 290-291
Bull, E., 417
Bultena, Louis, 389
Burchard, John, 604
Burchinal, L., 598
Burckhardt, Jacob, 392
Burdick, E., 261, 414
Burgess, Ernest W., 378-379, 600
Buriks, P., 176-177
Burke, Edmund, 299
Burnham, James, 215
Burns, Arthur F., 623
Burrell, S. A., 162
Burt, Sir Cyril, 642, 647
Butler, Alban, 394-396
Butler, E. E., 465

Cahalan, Don, 490
Campbell, A., 192

Campbell, John D., 316, 329
Campbell, P., 423
Campbell, Zoe, 509
Cantril, Hadley, 417, 420, 456, 478, 490-491, 494-495
Caplow, Theodore, 476, 484
Capwell, Dora P., 474
Carlsson, Gösta, 316
Carman, Harry J., 117
Carnegie, Andrew, 615
Carroll, Charles, 117, 120
Carr-Saunders, A. M., 355
Carter, Landon, 117
Carter, Roy E., Jr., 313
Castlemon, Henry, 505
Catherine II, 131
Centers, Richard, 341, 418, 420, 424, 475, 489, 492, 494, 547, 562, 569, 573, 575, 613
Chandler, Gardner, 113
Chang Chung-li, 179-180
Chan Han-seng, 185
Chapman, S. J., 496, 567
Charlemagne, 398
Charles II, 350
Chauncey, Henry, 444
Ch'en Tu-hsu, 432
Chernev, Victor, 291
Chinoy, Ely, 360, 478-479, 489, 496, 602, 611, 614
Christensen, C. R., 482
Christie, R., 414
Chubei, Ito, 139
Clark, Burton R., 447-448
Clark, H. F., 494
Clark, Joseph S., Jr., 274
Clark, J. V., 308
Clausen, John A., 362, 375
Cleland, S., 424
Clements, R. U., 654
Clignet, Remi, 316
Coates, Charles H., 224
Cockerill, John, 106
Coeur, Jacques, 105
Cohen, Albert K., 448, 452
Coke, Ricardo Cruz, 418
Cole, G. D. H., 537, 542
Coleman, James S., 86, 162, 182, 305, 321, 449, 483, 564
Coleman, Peter, 152
Collins, S. D., 408
Colson, E., 142
Commager, Henry Steele, 502
Commons, John R., 611
Comte, Auguste, 201, 205
Conant, James B., 167, 439-440
Congalton, Athol A., 158-159
Converse, P. E., 192
Cook, David R., 313
Coombs, Philip, 442
Cooper, James G., 313
Corey, Lewis, 150
Correa, H., 460
Cottrell, Leonard S., 304, 377-378, 510
Coulanges, Fustel de, 534
Coulborn, Rushton, 534
Coulton, G. G., 395, 401

Counts, George S., 329-330
Cousin, Victor, 555
Cowhig, J. D., 411
Creel, H. G., 176
Cremin, Lawrence A., 440
Crittenden, Charles C., 119
Crockett, Harry J., Jr., 602
Cromwell, Oliver, 350
Crosland, C. A. R., 164, 166, 190
Crouse, Russel, 502, 506
Cubberley, Ellwood P., 438
Cuber, J. F., 64

Dagobert I, 398
Dahl, Robert, 218-219, 221-222, 229-230, 240, 245
Dahrendorf, R., 193
Daiches, David, 347
Daley, Richard, 221
Dallen, David, 517
Danev, A. M., 523
Dangerfield, George, 119
Danhof, Clarence H., 604
D'Antonio, William V., 219, 224, 229
Davidson, Percy E., 98, 413, 613
Davies, A. F., 159
Davis, A., 92, 362, 366, 489
Davis, Harry R., 224
Davis, Jerome, 191, 309
Davis, Kingsley, 46-52, 54, 56, 58-62, 64-67, 69, 195, 353, 355, 375, 378, 570
Davison, Sol, 604
Dawson, C. A., 604
Deane, P., 196
De Charms, R., 363
Deeg, M. E., 497
De Lancey, James, 120
De Man, Henri, 477-478, 484
Dembo, T., 496
Demerath, N. J. III, 388-394
Dentler, Robert A., 224
de Staël-Holstein, A., 343
Deutsch, Karl W., 162, 246
Deutsch, Morton, 260
Deverall, Richard, 430
Dewey, John, 440-441
Dewey, Thomas E., 260
Dewhurst, J. F., 168
De Witt, Nicholas, 468, 530
Dexter, Franklin P., 119
Dickson, W. J., 482
Diderot, Denis, 87-88
Diez del Corral, Luis, 659
Dilworth, Richardson, 274
Dirlam, J., 239
Disraeli, Benjamin, 93, 349
Di Tella, Torcuato, 199
Dittmann, W., 420
Djilas, Milovan, 657
Dobb, Maurice, 516, 518
Dollard, J., 92, 375
Donnison, D., 423
Doob, L. W., 93
Dopsch, A., 100
Dore, Ronald P., 186

Doren, A., 98
Dovring, Folke, 187
Dowling, George, 291
Dressel, R. J., 445
Dreyfuss, C., 424
Drucker, Peter, 485
Dubin, Robert, 476, 479, 483
Dubois, Abbé, 555
Dubos, René, 333
Ducci, Gaspar, 106
Duchesne, A., 104
Duke, Antera, 147
Dumont, Arsène, 360, 597
Duncan, Dudley, 575
Duncan, Otis D., 195, 311
Dunlop, J. T., 648
Durant, Henry, 484
Durkheim, Emile, xiii, 74-76, 80-82, 84, 252, 264, 450, 483-484
Dutte, R. Palme, 430
Duvall, E. M., 363-364
Duverger, M., 414
D'yachenko, V. P., 521
Dynes, Russell, 393

Easton, David, 242
Eberhard, Wolfram, 171-182
Eckleberry, R. H., 456
Eckstein, Harry, 167, 246
Eckstein, Otto, 234
Eden, Karl A., 355
Edward III, 104-105
Edwards, Alba, 382
Eels, K., 69
Egerton, Hugh, 119
Ehrenberg, R., 106
Ehrlich, Howard J., 219
Eisenhower, Dwight D., 206
Eldersveld, S. J., 418
Elinson, J., 407
Elkan, Walter, 148
Elkin, A. P., 157
Ellis, Edward, 505
Ellis, Howard S., 579
Elwes, R. H. M., 87
Ely, Richard T., 504
Emmerij, L. T., 460
Encel, S., 149, 155-156, 158-159
Engels, Friedrich, 6-7, 10, 69, 89, 93, 171, 192
Epstein, A. L., 313, 424
Erickson, M. C., 489
Ernst, Robert, 295
Espinas, G., 105
Etzioni, Amitai, 182, 224
Evan, William M., 162, 260
Eysenck H. J., 421

Fainsod, Merle, 521
Fallers, Lloyd A., 141-149, 402-405
Fararo, Thomas J., 222-223
Farganis, James, 653
Faunce, William A., 481
Feld, Sheila, 389
Feldman, Arnold J., 148
Feldmesser, Robert A., 527-533, 569, 578-579, 656-658

Ferguson, A. L., 9
Festinger, L., 496
Feuer, Lewis S., 192
Field, James A., 355
Field, Mark G., 532
Fielding, Joseph, 140
Firth, Raymond, 599
Fitzpatrick, Brian, 152
Flanders, Ralph E., 260
Flechtheim, O. K., 418
Florence, P. S., 166
Floud, Jean, 166, 449-450, 454, 457, 591, 645
Fogarty, Michael, 418
Foote, Nelson, 360
Forbes, Abner, 505
Ford, Thomas R., 185, 189
Forde, Daryll, 143, 147, 378
Foster, Philip, 316
Fox, Thomas, 574-581
Francis of Assisi, St., 399
Frederick the Great, 596
Freedman, M., 343
Freeman, H. E., 412
Freeman, Linton C., 222-224
Freeman, Ralph E., 652
Freud, Sigmund, 485, 487
Friedland, S., 233
Friedmann, E. A., 476, 478, 480-483
Friedrich, C. J., 74, 240, 243
Friese, H., 181
Fris, V., 105
Fuchs, Lawrence A., 572
Fukuyama, Yoshio, 389
Furtado, C., 196

Galanter, Marc, 628-640
Gadgil, D. R., 431
Galbraith, J. K., 282, 287
Gale, James, 280
Galenson, Walter, 193, 419, 473, 481
Galler, E. H., 489, 492, 494
Gallup, George, 420
Gandhi, Mohandas K., 148, 555
Gans, Herbert J., 611
Ganshof, F. L., 535
Gapon, Father Georgi, 134
Gardner, B. B., 489
Gardner, M. R., 375, 489
Gaskell, P., 106
Gaudet, H., 423
Gebr, N. V., 417
Geertz, Clifford, 141
Geiger, Kent, 656
Geiger, Theodore, 193, 419-420, 561, 567, 575
Geis, Gilbert, 313
George, Charles and Katherine, 394-401
George, Wilma, 418
Gerhard, Dietrich, 77
Germani, G., 196-197
Gernet, Jacques, 182
Gerth, H. H., 20, 27, 69, 82, 222, 347, 525
Gertrude, St., 398

Ghurye, G. S., 560
Gibbon, Edward, 396
Gibbs, P. K., 362
Gierke, Otto, 77
Ginsburg, Norton, 319
Girod, Roger, 569
Gittler, Joseph B., 377
Gladstone, P., 418
Gladwin, Thomas, 290
Glass, Bentley, 446
Glass, D. V., 322, 355, 357, 453, 561, 563, 565, 567, 575, 591
Glazer, Nathan, 214, 299, 572
Glock, Charles Y., 389
Gluckman, Max, 147
Glueck, Eleanor and Sheldon, 381
Godric of Finchale, St., 101, 105
Goffman, I. W., 304, 306
Goldsmith, Selma, 563
Goldstein, Sidney, 612
Goldthorpe, John H., 648-659
Goode, W. J., 52, 377-387, 582-601
Goodrich, Carter, 604
Gordon, Joan, 573
Gordon, Milton M., 64, 266
Gordon, R. A., 232
Gore, M. S., 598
Gorer, Geoffrey, 451, 453
Goretti, Maria, 400
Gorky, Maxim, 291
Gosnell, H. F., 418
Gould, R., 494
Gouldner, Alvin W., 214, 480
Gower, L. C. B., 166, 168
Graham, S., 409, 412
Grant, Andrew, 542
Grant, Charles S., 112
Grant, Ulysses S., 70
Gratian, Emperor, 101
Gray, A. P., 421, 423
Gray, Lewis Cecil, 117
Gray, William S., 440
Grebenik, E., 355
Green, Constance M., 608
Greenblum, Joseph, 573
Greene, Lorenzo Johnston, 117
Greenhalgh, John, 348
Greenstein, Fred I., 426
Greer, Scott, 224, 228
Griaule, Marcel, 142
Griewank, Karl, 470
Griscom, John, 289
Grob, Gerald N., 611
Gross, Edward, 479
Gross, Llewellyn, 81
Grotjahn, A., 357
Grundmann, Herbert, 79
Gsovski, V., 520, 524
Gubariev, T., 93
Guesnon, A., 103
Guest, Robert H., 479, 481, 486
Guizot, François P., 88
Gurin, G., 411

Habakkuk, H. J., 593
Hacker, Andrew, 162

Hagen, Elizabeth, 445
Hagood, Margaret Jarman, 358
Hagstrom, Warren O., 444
Hailman, D. E., 409
Hajda, Jan, 182
Hajnal, John, 358-359
Haldane, Richard, 165
Halévy, Elie, 77
Hall, G. Stanley, 440
Hall, J. R., 313, 322
Haller, A. O., 316, 335
Hall-Quest, Alfred L., 440
Halmos, Paul, 648
Halsey, A. H., 166, 450, 454, 457, 460, 591, 645, 655
Hamburger, Joseph, 168
Hammond, S. B., 159
Hamrick, Lillian A., 111
Hamsun, Knut, 188
Hancock, W. K., 152
Handlin, Oscar, 293, 604, 610
Hansen, Georg, 103, 105
Hansen, Marcus Lee, 297
Hanson, Alexander C., 117
Harbison, F. H., 476, 648
Harley, Robert, 292
Harriman, Edward H., 269
Harrington, Michael, 289, 617-623, 653
Harris, L., 420
Harrison, Paul M., 389
Harrison, S. S., 423
Harrison, Tom, 165, 167
Hartley, E. L., 336, 362
Hartmann, G. W., 425
Harvey, Maurice, 119
Harwitz, Mitchell, 141
Haslewood, H. L., 181
Hastad, Elis, 420, 569
Hastings, Hugh, 117
Hatt, Paul K., 360
Havemann, Ernest, 358
Havighurst, Robert J., 362, 365-366, 441, 450, 476-478, 480-483, 494, 647
Hayashi, Chikio, 548
Heberle, Rudolf, 186, 358, 360, 417
Hegel, Georg Wilhelm Friedrich, 205, 207
Heist, Paul, 447, 449
Hellevuo, Tauno, 569
Helling, George, 316
Henderson, A. M., 242, 517
Heron, Alexander R., 475, 485
Herskovits, Melville J., 141, 146-147
Hertzler, J. O., 602
Herzberg, Frederick, 474, 486
Herzen, Alexander I., 88
Heynen, R., 98
Hicks, J. D., 417
Hilferding, Rudolf, 429
Hill, Charles J., 218
Hill, Reuben, 377
Hillman, Karen G., 383
Himmelfarb, Milton, 342
Himmelweit, Hilde, 449, 454, 645
Hinkle, L. E., Jr., 408
Hintze, Otto, 77
Hobsbawm, E. J., 85, 294

Ho Chi Minh, 430
Hodge, Robert W., 309-334
Hofstadter, Richard, 571
Hoggart, Richard, 611
Hollingshead, August B., 457, 489, 494, 594
Holweck, F. G., 394
Homans, George C., 186, 303, 308, 378, 566, 650
Ho Ping-ti, 177-178, 181
Hopkins, W., 33
Hoppock, Robert, 474-475, 487
Horelick, Arnold, 516
Hoslett, S. D., 474
House, Albert V., 188
Howes, Frederick G., 119
Hsu, F. L. K., 594
Hsü Cho-yün, 174
Hughes, E. C., 304, 478
Huizinga, J., 392
Hummel, A. W., 179
Hunt, Mc V., 496
Hunter, Alex, 154
Hunter, Floyd, 218-219
Hunter, Robert, 292
Hurst, W. L., 248
Hutchinson, B., 192
Hutchinson, Edward P., 355
Hyamson, Albert, 343, 350
Hyman, Herbert H., 166, 335-336, 488-499

Ibi, A. G., 567
Ieyasu, Tokugawa, 137
Ilsey, Raymond, 381, 595
Inkeles, A., 191, 309-310, 316-317, 525, 562, 570, 650, 656
Innes, J. W., 353-354
Iutaka, S., 194
Ivan III, 129
Ivan IV, 129

Jackson, Elton F., 602
Jackson, John A., 299
Jacob, P. E., 336
Jacobson, Norman, 610
Jacobson, Paul H., 355, 357
Jacoby, Erich H., 185-186, 189
Jahoda, M., 414, 485
James, E., 167
James, William, 389
Jameson, J. F., 106
Jamieson, S., 418
Jasny, N., 518
Jenkins, William S., 111
Jenkinson, H., 102
Jones, D. C., 313
Jones, W. O., 141
Jong, J. J. de, 417, 423
Jordan, Alice M., 502
Jowett, Benjamin, 1

Kadushin, Charles, 406-412
Kahl, Joesph A., 64, 191, 194, 294, 335, 457, 624
Kahler, Wilfried, 187

Kaftanov, S., 522
Kalven, Harry, 169
Kane, P. V., 386
Kann, R. A., 162
Kantorowicz, Ernst, 78
Kaplan, A. D. H., 239, 255
Kaplan, Sidney, 117
Kandel, I. L., 446
Kapur, J. L., 634
Karbyshev, D. M., 520
Karlsson, Georg, 378
Karmel, P. H., 155-158
Karpinos, Bernard D., 355
Kassof, A., 569
Katz, Donald, 483
Katz, Elihu, 219, 305, 335, 341
Kaufman, Herbert, 229
Kaysen, Carl, 231-239
Keay, J. Seymour, 555
Keene, James R., 269
Kelly, Bernard, 400
Kelsall, R. K., 591
Kenkel, W. F., 64, 304
Kenyatta, Jomo, 144
Kerr, C., 483, 648-659
Keutgen, F., 98
Key, V. O., Jr., 417
Keynes, J. M., 262
Khrushchev, Nikita S., 528-533, 657
Kierkegaard, Soren, 390
Kilpatrick, W. H., 441
King, E. J., 168
Kirkpatrick, Clifford, 378
Kiser, Clyde V., 355, 358-359, 361
Kitagawa, Evelyn M., 355, 359
Kitaro, Okano, 139
Klapprodt, Carol, 360
Klatskin, E. H., 363, 365-366
Klein, Sidney, 185
Klingberg, Frank J., 117
Kluckhohn, Florence, 603
Knox, Henry, 117
Knupfer, Genevieve, 294, 489
Koff, Stephen S., 223
Kohn, Hans, 470
Kohn, Melvin L., 362-363, 374
Kolakowski, Leszek, 87
Kolko, Gabriel, 652
Komarovsky, Mirra, 485
Koos, E. L., 412
Kornhauser, Arthur, 212, 425, 474-476, 483, 489, 495
Kornhauser, Ruth, 423
Kornhauser, William, 210-218
Kotschnig, W. M., 463-464, 467
Kracke, E., 177-178
Kravis, Irving, 510
Kroese, H. E. S., 313
Kruijt, J. P., 422
Kulischer, J., 104
Kuznets, S. S., 194, 509

Labedz, Leopold, 416
Lampard, Eric E., 604
Lampman, Robert J., 121, 617, 619, 621, 653

Landecker, Werner S., 650
Landis, Paul H., 381
Landry, Adolphe, 357
Landsberger, Henry A., 483
Langer, P., 423
Laski, Harold, 502
Lasswell, Harold, 67, 222, 255
Latourette, Kenneth Scott, 401
Laughton, K. B., 407
Lawrence, D. H., 158
Lawrence, P. S., 408
Lawson, E. D., 363-364
Lazarsfeld, Paul F., 191, 335, 341, 423, 510-511
Lebergott, Stanley, 290
Le Bras, G., 171
Lee, F. C., 435
Lee, M., Jr., 162
Lee, Richard, 220-221
Leger, B., 418
Leichter, Hope Jansen, 599
Leighton, A. H., 408
Leinenweber, Charles, xviii
Lelewel, Joachim, 88
Lemaire, Isaac, 106
Lemaster, E. E., 600
Lenin, Nikolai, 89, 425, 434
Lenski, G., 304, 306, 389, 562, 650
Lerner, Daniel, 186
Lesniewski, Victor, 188
Lessing, Gotthold Ephraim, 351
Lever, Philip, 522-523
Levin, Harry, 362-363
Levine, G. N., 411
Levi-Strauss, Claude, 377, 534
Levy, M. J., 146
Lewin, K., 496
Lewis, David M., 316
Lewis, Oscar, 293
Lewis, Roy, 166, 542
Lewis-Fanning, E., 358-359
Li Chi, 181
Lichterman, M., 162
Lieberson, Stanley, 150, 613
Lignon, J., 654
Lincoln, Abraham, 94, 210, 508, 615
Linde, Bogumil, 88
Lindgren, R. E., 162
Lindsay, Kenneth, 642, 644
Lindsay, M., 436
Lindzey, G., 341, 562, 566
Linz, J., 307, 423-424, 561
Lipman, V. D., 350
Lipset, Seymour Martin, 5-10, 84-85, 92, 161-171, 183, 186, 192, 210, 216, 267, 302, 307, 327, 341, 360, 402, 413-428, 450, 457, 473, 477, 481, 483-484, 493, 498, 561-573, 575, 583, 591, 654-655
Lipson, E., 166
Lipton, Lawrence, 452
List, F., 4
Li Ta-chao, 432
Littman, Richard A., 362-363
Liu Shao-chi, 430, 435-436
Livi, L., 569
Livingstone, Robert, 120

Lobel, Lyle S., 402
Locke, Harvey J., 378-379, 600
Lockwood, David, 654
Loeb, M. B., 450, 647
Loewenheim, F. L., 162
Logan, W. P. D., 408
Loginov, A., 518
Lombard, George F., 482
Loomis, Charles P., 161, 219, 417
Lot, F., 535
Low, J. O., 573, 602
Lowenthal, Leo, 163, 210, 216, 561
Löwith, Karl, 75
Lowrie, Walter, 390
Lubell, Samuel, 426
Lucci, Yorke, 561
Luethy, Herbert, 360
Lumsdaine, A., 510
Lumsdaine, M., 510
Lundberg, Ferdinand, 269
Lundquist, Agne, 564
Lunt, P. S., 375, 389
Lydall, H. F., 652
Lynd, Helen M. and Robert S., 191, 218, 222, 266-267, 389, 440, 602

McAlister, Ward, 271, 274
McBride, George M., 184
McCarthy, Joseph R., 259-260
McClelland, D. C., 363-365
McClelland, William, 642
Maccoby, E. E., 336, 362-363, 573
McConnell, T. R., 447, 449
McCormack, Col. Robert, 221
Machiavelli, Niccoló, 74, 84
MacIntosh, A., 496
MacIver, Robert M., 74, 84, 413
McKee, James B., 230
McKelvery, Blake, 604
Mackenroth, G., 313
Mackenzie, H. C., 423, 426
MacKenzie, Jean, 157
Maclaurin, R., 236
McMurray, Robert N., 483
McPhee, W. N., 191, 423-424
MacPherson, C. B., 417
Madison, James, 90, 93
Mahaim, E., 106
Main, Jackson T., 111-121
Maine, H. S., 15
Mairano, Romano, 98
Malenkov, G. M., 528
Malewski, Andrzej, 303-308, 416
Malleson, Nicolas, 455
Malthus, T. R., 406, 408
Manis, Jerome G., 426
Manuel, Frank E., 74
Mao Tse-tung, 430, 432, 435
Maquet, J., 147
Marquis, F. J., 567
Marriott, McKim, 145, 557
Marsh, Robert M., 179, 654
Marshall, Alfred, 242
Marshall, Lorna, 141
Marshall, T. H., 73, 85, 640-648, 651

Martin, Alfred von, 392
Martin, Edgar W., 608
Martin, F. M., 450, 454
Martin, Jean I., 157-158
Martin, Kingsley, 165
Martin, W. E., 362
Martindale, Don, 28, 451
Martineau, Harriet, 292, 297, 388
Marvin, Donald, 565
Marx, Karl, 4-10, 69, 75, 93-94, 143, 171, 182-183, 192, 201, 215, 298, 473, 484, 487, 534, 623, 653
Mary Magdalen, 396-397
Masani, M. R., 433
Mason, Edward S., 231, 239
Mason, Frances Norton, 119
Mason, W. S., 445
Masters, N. A., 424
Matsushita, Keiichi, 546
Matthews, Donald R., 561
Matza, David, 289-302, 448
Maud, Angus, 542
Mausner, Bernard, 474
Mauss, Marcel, 76
May, Henry F., 393, 504
Mayer, Adrian, 559
Mayer, Albert, 360
Mayer, Kurt B., 149-161, 438
Mayes, Herbert R., 502
Maynard, Sir John, 519
Mayntz, Renate, 69
Mayo, Elton, 482-483
Mazzini, Giuseppe, 88
Mboria, Lester, 386
Mead, Margaret, 378
Meeker, M., 69, 365, 375
Meinecke, Friedrich, 74
Menzel, H., 305, 307
Mencken, H. L., 344
Merton, Robert K., 68, 304, 335, 377-379, 403, 424, 448, 477, 488, 490-491, 510-515
Meyers, C. A., 648
Michels, Robert, 164, 215, 422, 571-572
Middleton, Drew, 163
Middleton, J. F. M., 144
Milic, Vojin, 385
Mill, John Stuart, 348
Miller, Daniel R., 362-365, 375, 411
Miller, Delbert, 219, 221
Miller, F. J. W., 408
Miller, Herman P., 506-510, 623-628
Miller, S. M., 574-581, 584, 611, 613, 655
Miller, W. E., 192, 229-230, 294, 423
Mills, C. Wright, 20, 69, 82, 150, 193, 210-218, 222, 254-255, 275-283, 286, 347, 419, 508, 525, 542, 614
Mills, L., 431
Mills, Werner E., Jr., 224
Milne, R. S., 423, 426
Minobe, Ryokichi, 546
Mitchell, B., 196
Mitchell, William, 163
Mitra, K., 357
Moberg, Soen, 358

Mohr, J. C. B., 78, 420
Monachesi, Elso, 451
Monier-Williams, M., 554
Montefiore, Claude, 350
Montesquieu, Charles de Secondat, Baron de la Brède et de, 74, 76
Moore, Barrington, Jr., 521, 525, 656
Moore, R. A., 363
Moore, Wilbert E., 45-51, 53, 55, 60, 63-66, 68, 148, 282, 486, 570, 649
Moos, Malcolm, 418
Morgan, Edmund S., 595
Morgan, J. P., 269
Morison, Samuel Eliot, 268, 271
Morris, J. N., 407
Morse, Nancy C., 475, 485, 562
Morsell, J. A., 423
Mosca, G., 70, 204, 215
Moser, C. A., 322
Moses, Robert, 227
Mott, Frank Luther, 502
Moucheron, Balthazar de, 106
Moynihan, Daniel P., 299
Mukherjee, Ramkrishna, 594
Müller, Max, 555
Munger, C. L., 502
Munro, Col. Thomas, 555
Munsey, Frank, 505-506
Murdock, George P., 377, 380
Murray, Henry A., 379
Murray, M. A., 401
Myers, Gustavus, 269-270
Myrdal, Gunnar, 92, 653

Nadel, S. F., 144
Nahirny, Vladimir C., 470
Napoleon Bonaparte, 596
Nasmyth, Jenny, 165
Nehru, Jawaharlal, 556
Neill, Stephen, 401
Nietzsche, Friedrich, 24
Neumann, Franz, 571
Newcomb, T. M., 66, 336, 362, 425
Nicholas, H. G., 167, 418
Niebuhr, H. Richard, 388
Nilson, S. S., 417
Nisbet, Robert A., 82, 379
Nishihira, Shigeki, 545, 575
Norbeck, Edward, 189
Normano, J. F., 431
Notestein, Frank W., 354-355
Nove, Alec, 656

Obourn, E. S., 646
Odaka, Kunio, 541-551
Oeser, O. A., 159
Oldenburgh, Henry, 347
Olschki, Leonard, 74
Opie, Redvers, 256
Oppenheim, A. N., 457
Optic, Oliver, 505
Orwell, George, 165
Osborn, Frederick, 357-358
Ossowski, Stanislaw, 86-96, 191

Overacker, Louise, 421
Oxtoby, Toby, 444

Packard, Vance, 542, 551
Page, Charles H., 93
Palmer, Gladys L., 475, 612
Palmer, R. R., 75, 83
Pareto, Vilfredo, 204, 208, 215, 451
Parker, Benjamin Franklin, 113
Parker, R. S., 153
Parkes, James, 343
Parry, L. J., 456
Parsons, Talcott, 76, 84, 141, 162-163,
   170, 182, 217, 240-265, 378, 388,
   402, 413, 448, 517, 561, 570, 600
Patchen, M., 308
Paterson, D. G., 497
Patterson, M. W., 344
Paulinus, St., 399
Peabody, Endicott, 271
Peabody, Joseph, 271
Pear, R. H., 421, 423
Pearson, Richard, 446
Péguy, Charles, 508
Pellegrin, Ronald J., 224
Pemberton, Joseph, 117
Perlman, Selig, 611
Perrott, G. T., 409
Perry, Oliver Hazard, 135-137
Peter the Great, 121-124, 130
Petersen, William, 360, 602
Peterson, E., 601
Peterson, Richard O., 393, 474
Phillips, John C., 358
Pidgeon, D. A., 454
Pierce-Jones, J., 363
Pierson, George W., 81
Ping Ti-ho, 590, 600
Pipes, A. Richard, 470
Pirenne, Henri, 97-107
Plantin, Christophe, 106
Plato, 584
Plotnikov, K. N., 521-522
Polanyi, Karl, 292, 297
Pollock, J. K., 418
Ponikowski, Waclaw, 188
Pope, Liston, 393
Potter, A., 423
Potter, George, 299
Pound, Roscoe, 248
Pratt, S., 419, 424
Preble, Jeremiah, 116
Presthus, Robert, 538
Price, Leolin, 166, 168
Pringle, John Douglas, 156
Pugachev, Emeljan, 125

Quattlebaum, C. A., 456

Radcliffe-Brown, A. R., 378
Radford, W. C., 157
Ramsey, Charles E., 313
Raumer, Kurt von, 79
Razin, Stenka, 125, 135

Redfield, Robert, 145
Redlich, Frederick C., 457
Reiss, Albert J., Jr., 195, 311, 316,
   322, 325, 327
Remmenga, Albin J., 228
Renier, G. J., 163
Renner, Karl, 654
Reynolds, Lloyd G., 475, 481, 579
Rice, A. K., 483
Rice, Stuart A., 413, 417
Richardson, Stephen, 169
Riecken, H. W., 566
Riesman, David, 210-218, 480, 542,
   572
Riessman, Frank, 611
Rigby, T. H., 528
Riis, Jacob, 289
Rindlisbacker, A., 363
Ringer, Benjamin B., 307, 389
Roberts, Henry L., 186
Robertson, Douglas S., 119
Robinson, H. Alan, 474
Rockefeller, John D., 269
Rockefeller, William, 269
Roethlisberger, F. J., 482
Rogers, Candace, 599
Rogers, Henry H., 269, 494
Rogger, Hans, 516
Rogoff, Natalie, 360, 426, 561, 563,
   565-567, 575, 591, 602
Rokkan, Stein, 251
Roman, Richard, xviii
Roper, Elmo, 477, 491-493, 495
Rose, Arnold M., 150
Rosenberg, M., 93
Rosenstein, Eliezer, xviii
Ross, Arthur, 476, 483
Ross, J. F. S., 418
Rossi, A. K., 510-517, 562, 601
Rossi, F., 191
Rossi, Peter H., 224, 309-334
Rosten, Leo, 477
Roth, Cecil, 343, 347-348, 350
Rothschild, Baron Lionel de, 346
Rousseas, Stephen W., 653
Rousseau, Jean-Jacques, 75
Roy, M. N., 431-432
Rubel, Maximilien, 473
Russell, Bertrand, 222

Saint-Simon, Claude Henri, Comte
   de, 74, 87, 95, 201-202, 208
Salisbury, Robert, 222, 230
Salomon, Sidney, 343
Sampson, Anthony, 164
Samuelson, Kurt, 392
Samuelson, Paul, 506, 623
Sanford, N., 447
Sarapata, A., 67, 313, 538
Sayre, Wallace S., 229
Scarrow, H. A., 155
Schaefer, E. S., 363
Schaube, A., 98, 104
Schelting, Alexander von, 470
Schiff, Jacob H., 269
Schiff, Tevele, 349

Schlesinger, Rudolph, 517
Schneider, David L., 381
Schneider, Herbert, 389
Schnore, L. F., 411
Schoepf, Johann David, 120
Schram, Stuart R., 422
Schulze, Robert O., 222, 224
Schumer, William, 518
Schumpeter, Joseph A., 41-47, 92,
   256, 403, 470
Schwartz, Benjamin, 432
Schwarz, Solomon M., 518, 524
Scott, Eileen, 595
Scott, W. H., 591
Sears, R. R., 362, 496
Seebohm, F., 534
Segerstedt, Torgny, 564
Seidman, Joel, 478, 480
Selezner, K., 518
Sellers, Charles, 163
Selvin, H. C., 444
Selznick, Philip, 85, 189
Sepulveda, Orlando, 313
Servat of Cahors, Guillaume, 105
Seton-Watson, Hugh, 527
Sewell, W. H., 335
Shannon, Fred A., 604
Shapiro, Leonard, 657
Shastri, H., 431
Shils, E. A., 84-85, 165-166, 260, 414,
   470
Shister, Joseph, 475, 481
Shlakman, Vera, 608
Sibley, Elbridge, 192, 360, 565
Siebeck, Paul, 420
Siegel, A., 483
Siegel, Paul M., 316, 322-334
Siegfried, A., 417
Sieveking, H., 98
Sieyès, Abbé Emmanuel Joseph, 87
Sigourney, Andrew, 118
Sills, D., 307
Simeon Stylites, St., 398
Simon, Walter B., 418, 421
Simpson, Richard L., 377
Singh, Mohindar, 386
Sjahrir, S., 431
Sjoberg, Gideon, 602
Sklare, Marshall, 448
Sluiter, Greet, 144
Small, Albion, 74, 90
Smelser, Neil J., 165, 241, 298
Smith, Abbot Emerson, 117
Smith, Adam, 87-88, 90
Smith, Mapheus, 329
Smith, Marion B., 503, 510
Smith, Robert J., 313, 595
Smith, Warren B., 117
Smythe, Hugh and Mabel, 149
Soares, Glaucio Ary Dillon, 190-199
Socha, Zeigniew, 416
Soda, T., 409
Soloviev, L., 429
Solow, R. M., 652
Sombart, W., 98
Sorokin, Pitirim, 395, 565, 567
Speier, Hans, 567, 573

Spencer, Herbert, 269
Spengler, Joseph J., 354
Spier, John, 480
Spinley, B. M., 375
Spinoza, Benedictus de, 87
Spinrad, William, 218-231
Spock, Benjamin, 369, 376
Srinivas, M. N., 552-560
Srole, Leo, 302
Stalin, Joseph V., 516-517, 527
Stamler, J. M., 407
Standler, C. B., 362
Stead, M. T., 102
Stendler, C. B., 368
Stephan, W., 420
Stephens, Tom, 293
Stephenson, C., 535
Stevenson, Alexander, 357
Stewart, Rosemary, 166
Stillman, James, 269
Stinchcombe, Arthur L., 69-73, 182-190
Stine, Leo C., 426
Stoetzel, J., 414
Stokes, D. E., 192
Stolypin, Pĕtr A., 127, 132, 134
Stonequist, E. V., 512
Straus, M. A., 335
Streib, Gordon F., 485
Strodtbeck, Fred L., 362-364
Strunk, M., 490
Suchkova, A. K., 521
Suchman, E. A., 409, 510
Sumner, W. G., 84
Sunshine, Morris H., 222-223
Sun Yat-sen, 435
Super, Donald, 475
Sussman, Marvin B., 594, 598
Sutton, Francis X., 282
Svalastoga, Kaare, 313, 316, 322, 416, 590, 594
Swanson, Guy E., 362-365, 375, 411
Swearingen, R., 423
Sydenstricker, Edgar, 354
Sykes, Gresham, 448

Ta Chen, 355
Taeuber, Irene, 387
Taft, Ronald, 159, 313
Taine, Hippolyte, 165
Talbot, P., 431
Tangri, Shanti S., 470
Tannenbaum, Arnold, 573
Tannenbaum, Frank, 185
Tawney, R. H., 88, 392, 508
Terman, Lewis M., 378
Tertullian, 396
Thernstrom, Stephan, 602-615
Thomas, E. Murray, 141, 310, 313
Thomas, Hugh, 163
Thomas, Lawrence G., 475
Thomas, William I., 292
Thomas Aquinas, St., 397
Thompson, A. M., 595
Thompson, Barbara, 381
Thompson, Edgar T., 189

Thompson, V., 433
Thompson, Wayne E., 485
Thorndike, R. L., 445
Thurston, E., 552
Thurston, Herbert, 394
Tilgher, Adriano, 484
Tilghman, Tench, 117
Timasheff, Nicholas S., 517
Tinbergen, J., 460
Ting Wen-chieng, 174
Tipping, D. C., 652
Tiryakian, Edward A., 310-311, 313, 316
Toby, Jackson, 448
Tocqueville, Alexis de, xvi, 76, 79-83, 107-110, 135, 162, 164, 186, 201, 214, 344-345, 347, 388, 390, 455, 470
Toennies, Ferdinand, 11-20, 161
Tomasevich, Jozo, 186
Toynbee, Arnold, 623
Treiman, Donald J., 309-321
Troeltsch, Ernst, 391
Tropp, Asher, 166
Trow, Martin, 419, 437-449, 483, 564
Truman, Harry S., 428
Truman, T. C., 418
Trussel, R. E., 407, 411
Tuckman, Jacob, 313, 316
Tumin, Melvin M., 51-61, 63, 570
Turberville, A. S., 590
Turner, D. F., 233, 239
Turner, Ralph H., 166, 449-458, 655

Uhrbock, R. S., 475
Ulmer, Melville J., 282-283, 286
Usselinx, Willem, 106

Vailland, Roger, 85
Vaizey, John, 163
Vanderbilt, William K., 269
van der Kroef, J. M., 431
van der Sprenckel, H., 181
Van Heek, F., 313
van Tulder, Johannes, 575
Van Wagenen, R. W., 162
Veblen, Thorstein, 35-41, 215, 291, 566, 571, 623
Vernon, P. E., 454-455
Veroff, Joseph, 389
Vidich, Arthur J., 224
Vincent de Paul, St., 400
Vinogradoff, Paul, 185
Vogel, W., 101
Volin, Lazar, 529
Volkov, A., 529
Voltaire, 74
Voragine, Jacobus de, 397

Wagley, Charles, 450
Waithman, Robert, 503
Walker, Charles R., 479, 482, 486
Walker, Kenneth, 154
Waller, Willard, 70
Wallich, Henry, 508

Wallin, Paul W., 378
Wang Tse-tsiu, 386
Wang, Y. C., 460, 470
Ward, Barbara, 434
Ward, Russel, 90, 153, 168
Warner, W. Lloyd, 69, 155, 266, 268, 290, 302, 365, 375, 389, 402, 450, 457, 572-573, 602-603, 612, 647
Warriner, Doreen, 186
Watnick, Morris, 428-436
Waugh, Evelyn, 584
Weaver, Glenn, 119
Webb, Leicester, 421
Webb, Beatrice and Sidney, 298
Weber, Max, 19-25, 26-34, 41, 66, 77-78, 81-84, 93-94, 161, 185, 189, 215, 221, 242, 253, 260, 347, 391, 450, 478, 517, 525, 538, 561, 607
Wecter, Dixon, 267, 269, 344
Weinberg, S. K., 497
Weiss, Robert S., 475, 485, 562
Wesolowski, Wlodzimierz, 64-69, 313
West, Patricia Salter, 358
Westoff, Charles F., 358, 360
Weston, J. F., 233
Wharton, Edith, 268
Wheelwright, E. L., 158
Whelpton, P. K., 358-359, 361
White, Albert B., 79
White, Martha S., 362-363
White, Winston, 163
Whyte, William Foote, 478-479
Whyte, William H., 426
Wicoff, Evelyn, 420
Widerszpil, Stanislaw, 537
Wiens, H., 181
Willener, M. Alfred, 649
Williams, Raymond, 164
Williams, Robin M., Jr., 163, 282, 287, 510
Willie, C. U., 410
Willing, Matthew H., 440
Wilner, D. M., 410
Wilson, Alan B., 335-342, 449
Wilson, Mary D., 454
Winch, Robert F., 377, 379
Witte, Sergei Julevic, 132
Wittfogel, K. A., 176
Wohl, R. Richard, 501-506
Wolfenstein, M., 368-369
Wolff, H. G., 408
Wolff, Kurt, 252
Wolfinger, Raymond E., 222, 426
Wolfle, Dael, 444, 468
Wolin, Sheldon S., 84
Wood, Robert C., 224
Woodham-Smith, Cecil, 299
Woodmason, Charles, 119
Woolsey, T. D., 411
Worthy, James C., 485
Wright, Charles R., 218
Wright, D. S., 424
Wright, David McCord, 502
Wright, Quincy, 260
Wrong, Dennis H., 63, 353-361
Wu Min, 435
Wurzbacher, Gerhard, 313

Xydias, N., 313

Yang Lien-sheng, 174
Yates, Alfred, 454
Young, Michael, 165-167
Young, Roland, 261

Younge, Eva R., 604
Yugow, A., 517-518

Zaleznik, A., 482-483
Zborowski, M., 407
Zeisel, H., 485

Zeromski, Stefan, 93
Zetterberg, Hans L., 377, 419, 426, 561-573, 575, 654-655
Zimbe, Batulumayo Musoke, 147
Zimmerman, Carl, 600
Zloczower, Awraham, 469
Znaniecki, Florian, 292
Zubrzycki, J., 149

Subject Index

achievement, education and, 339-341; *see also* motivation and social mobility

adoption, social mobility and, 595-596

AFL-CIO, 278, 619-620, 622

Africa, agriculture in, 148; commercialization of land and labor in, 148; crafts in, 143; cultures in, 142-143; developing areas of, 85; division of labor in, 142-143; food problem in, 141; kin parasitism in, 597; kingdoms and rulers of, 147; occupational prestige, 318, 320; "peasantry" in, 145; religions in, 142; role differentiation in, 144-145, 148; social stratification in, 141-149; trader-chiefs in, 147; wants and needs in, 148; well-being in, 141, 144

agrarian reform, Poland, 536; Russia, 127-128

agricultural enterprise, and rural class, 182-190

agricultural life, Middle Ages, 101

agricultural workers, fertility of, 356-357

agriculture, plantation, 188-189; property and enterprise in, 183-184; *see also* farms

alus, concept of, 142

America, "other," 617-623; *see also* United States

American Jewry, 349

American Medical Association, 466

American society, class structure in, 89, 111-121, 150-151

American sociology, xiv-xv

American Soldier, The, 510

ancien régime, France, 79-80, 202, 209

ancient civilization, estates and cities in, 14-15

Anglo-Jewry, 342-350

Anglo-Saxons, social mobility of, 571

anomie, 77, 488

anti-Semitism, 343, 348-349

apathy, political, 214

Argentina, middle class in, 194

aristocracy, British, 164, 344; Chinese, 175; democracy and, 108; Japanese, 135-140; Polish, 535

artisans, in Revolutionary era, 118

Asia, communism in, 432-436; developing areas of, 85; social mobility in, 584

Australia, beginnings of, 151; civil service in, 155; convict labor in, 151; divorce rate in, 383; education in, 155-157; egalitarianism in, 155; fertility in, 357; gold discovery in, 152; immigration policy of, 159; income distribution in, 156; labor unions in, 153; landholders in, 157-158; living standards, 157; stratification in, 149-161; voting behavior, 160-161, 421, 425; wool culture, 151, 189; working class, 154, 159

Australian Labour Party, 152, 160

authoritarianism, 167

authority roles, 144

baby boom, 358-360

banking, Jews in, 346; money and, 255-256

beatniks, 452

Belgium, divorce rate in, 384; occupational inheritance in, 587

Bible, 396

big business, *see* corporation

birth, estate of, 13-14

birth-rate, decline of, 354

blue-collar workers, 192; Japan, 541, 545-546, 551; job satisfaction among, 475; occupational prestige among, 318

bohemians, 295-296

bourgeoisie, democracy and, 204; emergence of, 103; Marx on, 4-7, 182

Brahmans and Brahmanization, 30, 552-560

Brazil, class structure in, 196-197

breast feeding, social class and, 367-370

British Labour Party, 164

British Psychological Society, 454

British Socialism, 572

Brock Committee, 293

bureaucracy, 172, 179; Soviet Union, 517; Weber's concept of, 82

Bureau of Labor Statistics, 619

businessman, occupation and, 16-17; power position of, 228-239; small, 276-277

"business society," 238

Byzantine Empire, 128-129

Canada, sociology in, xiv

canonization, 401

capital, in power structure, 243

capitalism, classic period of, 89; Marxism and, 9, 182; *rentier* system in, 186; Russian, 127-128; social history and, 97-107

capitalist class, permanence of, 98; as power elite, 206

cartels, 106

caste, class and, 90; development of, 27-35; estate and, 89; in India, 13-14, 553-557, 629-635; sib and, 32-35

Catholic Church, Jewry and, 351; sainthood in, 394-401; voting behavior and, 421-422; *see also* Roman Catholic Church

cattle, as status symbol, 147

celibacy, fertility and, 355

centralization, in political community, 81-82

Centre d'Etude Sociologique, xiv

Chambers of Commerce, 278

charisma, 32

Chicago, power structure in, 220

child labor, education and, 439

child rearing, 362-365, 376-377, 489-490

Chile, economic development of, 197, 199; graduates in, 459

China, aristocracy in, 175; bureaucracy in, 179; classes in, 172; Communism in, 430; divorce rate, 386; early history, 171-172; family tenancy in, 185; as history-less people, 429; kinship in, 600; medieval period, 174-175; Mongol rule, 177; sib glorification in, 33; social mobility in, 171-182, 583-585, 590, 595, 597

Christianity, Jewry and, 347; sainthood in, 396; *see also* Catholic Church

church, leadership in, 391

church-sect dichotomy, 391

CIO-AFL, see AFL-CIO

cities, estates and, 14-15; in Middle Ages, 98-102; middle-sized, 275-281; in Revolutionary era, 114-116

Civil War, 82, 89, 163, 212, 268-269, 272, 437-438, 607

clan, 34

class, Aristotle on, 1-2; biological criteria for, 91; breast feeding and, 365-368; capitalist, *see* capitalist class; caste and, 90; in China, 172; comparable groupings in, 365; concept of, 87; defined, 41; deviation from model, 95; different conceptions of, 86-96; differential behavior in, 353-361; estates and, 11-20; exhaustive and nonexhaustive divisions of, 95; fertility of in Western societies, 353-361; formation of, 42; in French army, 109; in Great Britain, 164-165; group system and, 90; history of term, 87; labor market and, 20; Marxist or Leninist concept of,

4-10, 89, 92, 95; mobility and, 563, 610-612 (see also social mobility); model of as basic group, 94-95; occupation and, 274; parent-child relationships in, 370-375; power and, 201-210; problem of, 41-45; professions and, 459-472; residential segregation of, 335-342; socialization and, 362-377; superordinate concept of, 89; threefold denotation of, 88-89

class conflict, 610-612

class consciousness, 15-16, 92-94, 163; Marx on, 10; parties and, 18-19

classless society, 527-533

class-society, concept of, 73, 86, 91

class structure, concepts of, 86-96; criteria and common assumptions of, 92-93; defined, 44-45; economic development and, 190-199; interdependence of characteristics in, 93-94; openness of, 360; theories of, 1-96

class struggle, 19-23, 41; elections and, 413-428

clergymen, in Revolutionary era, 119

clerical estate, 13

collective action, 252-253

college, economic level and, 490; failure and, 447, 592; I.Q. and, 340; number of degrees granted, 468; occupational choice and, 495; percentages aspiring to, 336-338; preference for by economic and age-sex levels, 490-492; preparatory programs, 441-445; research vs. teaching in, 72; in Revolutionary era, 118; sex and age composition in, 491-492

Cold War, 85-86

Comintern, 428, 431-432

Commonwealth Public Service, Australia, 155

communal action, 21-22

Communism, appeal of, 428-436; driving force of, 434; sociology and, xiv; in Soviet Union, 656-657

Communist party, 204, 207, 428; Germany, 424; Poland, 540; Soviet Union, 128, 135, 518, 521, 525

Communists, voting for, 418, 427

community, group power in, 224 (see also community power); "law" type, 82

community power, 218-231; defined, 221-223; formal features of, 226-227; personal factors in, 225-226

community welfare, 282-288

competition, rise of, 105

complementarity, in marriage, 379

conformity, 213

Constitution, U.S., 2

consumption rankings, 562-563

contest mobility, 451-452

control, of work conditions, 478-481

corporation, power of, 231-239

Cossacks, revolt of, 125

court cases, in India caste problems, 630-640

craft guilds, 104

crafts and craftsmen, Africa, 143; in Revolutionary era, 118; work satisfaction and, 484

Crimean War, 125

decision-making, by corporations, 234; power and, 215-216, 223-231, 248

democracy, aristocracy and, 108; Australian and U.S. compared, 153; elections in, 413-428; master and servant in, 107-110; oligarchy and, 208; power structure and, 214-215; "revival" of, 527-528; snobbery in, 344; stratification and, 23; "unmasking" of, 208-209

Democracy in America (de Tocqueville), xvi, 107-110, 162-163

Democratic party, voting behavior and, 426

democratic process, values and, 169-171

Democratic-Socialist Party, Japan, 549-550

depersonalization, of government, 82, 84

"developing areas," study of, 83-86

dharma, 554

differentiation, social stratification and, 649-650

discipline, love-oriented, 373

disreputable poverty, 290-296

dissatisfaction, of worker, 473

division of labor, 77, 142

divorce, causes and decisions in, 382; "easy," 386-387; social class and, 381-382

divorce rates, 377-387; differentials in, 381; social strata and, 583; world, 383-386

doctors, in Revolutionary era, 119

échevinage, 103

economic development, biology and, 141; class structure and, 190-199; differences in among nations, 196-199; local, 282-288

education, 437-449; achievement and, 339-341; attainment in, 460-461; authority and, 67; "failure" in not going to college, 447; Great Britain, 166-168, 456; higher-institution enrollment by countries, 463; Japan, 470-472; Poland, 67; "position" and, 66; poverty and, 294; power structure and, 220; religion and, 337; segregation and aspirations in, 335-342; social ambition and, 449-458, 645-646; social class and, 490-491; social mobility and, 592; Soviet Union, 462-463, 468-469, 522-524, 530-531; terminal, 447-448; transformation in, 438-449; United States, 166, 168, 339-341, 437-449, 592; values and, 66; world figures on, 168

egalitarianism, Australia, 155; Great Britain, 167; Soviet Union, 527-528; United States, 162-163

ego, power and, 245

ego-needs, 566

Egypt, divorce rate in, 385

elite, 163, 170, 202, 267, 382; China, 174; divorce rate and, 386; Great Britain, 471-472; list of individuals, 270; mobility of, 451-453, 577-578, 655; Poland, 534-540; power and, 206 (see also power elite); ruling class and, 11, 201-210, 517; Social Register and, 272-274; Soviet Union, 517, 656-657

employment, concentration of, 283; stability of, 235

Encyclopedia, French, 87-88

England, divorce rate in, 384; kinship relations, 599; mobility in, 454-455; Poor Laws, 299-300; religion in, 346-347; secondary education, 454-455; society and culture, 343-346; see also Great Britain

Enlightenment, 74

enterprise, in agriculture, 183

equalitarianism, see egalitarianism

equality, 46-52; and feudal order, 81; freedom and, 80; in French Revolution, 79-80; in Great Britain, 643-645; indices of, 580; prestige and, 68; principle of, 252

"establishment," 169

estates, caste and, 89; in Muscovite Russia, 124; occupational, 17-18; social classes and, 11-20

ethnic segregation, 24

Europe, agriculture in, 185-186; educational statistics for, 460-468; nationalism in, 429; new social classes in, 85; social mobility in, 566-569, 572, 575-576

fairs, medieval, 103

family, Africa, 146; disruption of in Russia, 133; divorce rate and, 377-387; income levels and, 507-508, 619-621, 625; kinship and, 598; marital instability and, 379-380; Marx on, 7; nuclear, 598; problems of, 290, 362-377; in Revolutionary era, 116-117; size-fertility relationships in, 357; social mobility and, 582-601; stratification and, 583; tenancy and, 185-187; tyranny of, 81; wage-worker's, 277

family smallholding, 187-188

farms, in Revolutionary era, 111, 117; fertility on, 355; size of, 113; small-holding, 186-187

fascism, 414

father's occupation, school grades and, 340

father-son relationship, and occupational mobility, 576-578, 606-608, 613; skill inheritance and, 585

Federal Housing Act, 227

Federalist, The, 2-5

feedback, illness and, 407-408

fertility, class structure and, 354-355; illegitimacy and, 358; social mobility and, 596-597; status and, 355

Fescobaldi family, 106

feudal order, equality and, 81

field-community, Russia, 127

financiers, in Middle Ages, 105-106

Finland, divorce rate in, 386; social mobility in, 572-573

Five-Year Plan, India, 557; Soviet Union, 516, 521, 523-524

Ford Foundation, 442, 561

formal position, power and, 226-227

Fortune, 491-493, 617

four freedoms, 641

"Four Hundred," 274

France, *ancien régime* in, 79-80, 202, 209; class in, 109; divorce rate, 384; political party support vs. occupations, 414; sociology in, xiv; voting behavior in, 414, 419, 422, 424

franchise, equalization of, 254

fraternal organizations, 280

freedom, in French Revolution, 79-80; power and, 246

Free Place system, 644

French Revolution, 79-81, 83, 161-162, 201

frontier, Australia, 151; U.S., 111, 151

Fugger family, 105-106

functional analysis, 47-52, 65, 68

gain, love of, 101

Gemeinschaft and *Gesellschaft,* 161

General Social Welfare Index, 284

gentleman, concept of, 345

geographical mobility, 603-604

Germany, class in, 43; manufacturing in, 193; occupational inheritance in, 589; social mobility in, 566-570; sociology in, xiv; voting behavior in, 420-425; white-collar workers in, 573

Gilded Age, 269, 272

goods and services, as status symbol, 146

government, centralization of, 84-85; depersonalization of, 82, 84; vs. society, 83; stratification of, 50

Gratian, Decretum of, 101

Great Britain, aristocracy in, 163-164; class system, 164; economy and polity in, 164; education, 166-167, 456; elite in, 471-472; equal opportunity in, 643-645; fertility in, 359; graduates in, 459; India, rule of, 555-556; Jewish society in, 342-344; secondary education in, 454-455; social distance in, 646-647; social mobility in, 454-455, 571-572, 576, 591; social selection in, 640-648; value patterns in, 161-

171; as Welfare State, 640-648; *see also* England

Great Depression, 393, 419, 425

Greenwich Village, 293

gross national product, 319-321, 460

group, institutions and, 84; membership of, 628-640; in Middle Ages, 79; moral norms and, 75-77; non-membership, 511-515; secular transformation of, 76

group mobility, caste system and, 558

group power, 224

group relations, status incongruence and, 307-308

guilds, in Middle Ages, 28-30, 102

hacienda system, 184-185

Hall-Jones scale, 644

Han Dynasty, 174

Harvard Business School, 482-483

Harvard University, 271

Haug family, 106

Hawthorne experiment, 482

Hell's Kitchen, 292

heterogamy, 593-595

hierarchy, in British society, 165; India, 553; of individual, 404; in occupational prestige, 316-319, 322; in power structure, 215, 248-249

higher education, growth of, 441-443; *see also* education

high school, statistics on, 335-342, 592

high society, 90

Hinduism, defined, 635-640

Hindu religion, 32, 560, 635-640

Hindu society, 552-558, 630-635

history-less peoples, 428, 430

Homestead Act, 152

homography, 379, 593-595

Horatio Alger story, 447, 501-506

human associations, two types of, 84

humanitarianism, in English society, 348

"human nature," motivation and, 66

Hungary, social orders in, 185, 189, 386

illegitimacy, fertility and, 358; marital instability and, 380

Illinois, University of, 220

illness, employment status and, 409; household income and, 409; mental and physical, 406-412; social class and, 410-411

immunity, of ruler, 78

income, family, 507-508, 619-621, 625; leftist voting and, 417-418; talent and, 72

income distribution, 506-510; Australia and U.S. compared, 156; Japan, 547; Soviet Union, 528-529

income level, 507-508, 619-620

incongruence, of status factors, 303-308

India, Brahmans in, 552-558; caste in, 14, 28-32, 553-558, 590, 629-635; commensalism in, 30-31; court cases in, 630-640; divorce in, 386; guilds in, 28-30; Hindu society, 553-558, 630-635; movies, 555; occupational inheritance in, 588; religion, 32, 560, 635-640; social mobility, 590; social problems of, 628-640; society in, 628-640; stratification in, 552-558; Supreme Court, 630-632; tribe and caste in, 631-635; *varna* theory, 634; Westernization of, 552-558

Indian Communist Party, 433

individual, vs. society, 76

individualism, concept of, 16; in English society, 347-348; U.S. and Australia compared, 153

Indonesia, Communism in, 433; occupational prestige in, 310

industrial class, 87

industrialization, and occupational prestige, 309-310, 319-320; rate of, 194

industrial society, stratification in, 648-659

industry, local, 282-288; work satisfaction in, 473-487

infant care, social class and, 366-370

infirm, poverty and, 296

influence, in political process, 243; power and, 250-253, 258

"influentials," 222

inheritance, of land, 103; occupational, 576-578, 585-586, 606-608, 613

institutions, "crescive" vs. "enacted," 84

interchange system, in power structure, 262

interclass relationships, 91

interests, diversity of, 213

inter-group relations, 93

International Congress of Historical Studies, 97

investment, interchange and, 263

involvement, degree of, 390

IQ, 340; social class and, 591; social mobility and, 601; stratification and, 583

Irish, emigration of, 300

Irish famine, 299

Irish farmers, as tenants, 300

Irish Poor Laws, 300

Italy, occupational inheritance in, 588; voting behavior in, 415, 424

Jacksonian era, 211

Japan, aristocracy in, 135-140; family tenancy in, 185; divorce rate, 383, 386; education, 470, 472; illness, 409; job opportunity in, 579; middle class, 541-551; occupational inheritance, 589; occupational pat-

terns, 576; political parties, 549-550; social mobility, 567, 595; sociology in, xiv; status-consciousness in, 140; status symbols, 543-547; superficial social homogeneity of, 542-543; warrior class, 136-139; working class, 544, 547
Japan Sociological Society, 541
Java, 142, 189
Jesuits, 399
Jews, aristocracy and, 345-346; community character of, 349-350; in English society, 342-352; ethnic segregation of, 24; hatred of, 343, 348, 351; humanitarianism and, 348; number of in New York and London, 349; occupation and, 17
job, *see* occupation
job satisfaction, *see* work satisfaction
Jordan, divorce rate for, 385
jury system, 169

Karma, 554
kasar, concept of, 142
king, in democratic monarchies, 71; loyalty to, 79, 82
kinship, Africa, 145-146; loyalties in, 81; social mobility and, 597-600; stratification and, 62
kolkhoz, 95, 184, 521, 656
Komsomol, 531
Korea, Communist power in, 435

labor, alienation of, 473; division of, 77, 142; occupational mobility and, 605-606; property holdings and, 608
labor market, class and, 20
labor unions, 278; Australia and U.S. compared, 153; Communism and, 431; power and, 228; white-collar workers and, 280; work satisfaction and, 478
lackey, 108-109
laissez-faire, Africa, 149; and giant corporations, 237; origin of, 106; social reform and, 414; in U.S. and Australia, 152
land, Africa, 144; aristocracy and, 99; Australia, 151, 157; inheritance of, 103; and Japanese warrior class, 137; manorial or hacienda system, 184-185; in Middle Ages, 99-100, 103; Poland, 535; redistribution of in Russia, 124; *rentier* capitalists and, in Revolutionary era, 111-112, 120; *see also* property
Latin America, agricultural classes, 184-185, 189; occupational prestige, 311-312, 318; social class and economic development in, 193-199; social mobility in, 585, 587
law, equal protection of, 252
"law communities," 82

lawlessness, 168
lawyers, 119
leadership, power and, 219
leftist voting behavior, 417-423; social conditions and, 423-428
leisure class, 35-41
lex terrae, 78
liberty, commerce and, 106
Lives of the Saints (Butler), 394-401
living standards, Australia and U.S., 157
local government, power of, 228-229
local industry, 282-288
Lonely Crowd, The (Riesman), 210-218
lower class, 156, 506-510, 528, 547, 619-620; religion of, 389; sainthood and, 395; voting behavior of, 427
lumpenproletariat, 95, 290

McCarthyism, 163, 259-261
Mafia, 85
Maine, landowning in, 116
Malaya Communist Party, 433-434
Manlich family, 106
manorial system, 184-185
manual-nonmanual dichotomy, 575, 585
manufacturing, oligopoly in, 233; rise of, 103
marital satisfaction, 377-387
market economy, emergence of, 84
marriage, complementarity in, 379; divorce and, 378; instability in, 379-381; social mobility and, 563, 594; "trial," 383
marriage counselors, 378
Marshall Plan, 428-429
Marxism, xvii, 88, 543; and *ancien régime*, 202; class theory in, 5-11, 191; internal contradictions of, 202; money in, 255; Russian, 133-134; stratification and, 516; work satisfaction and, 483, 485
Massachusetts, landowning in, 114
mass education, growth of, 441-443
master-servant relationship, 107-110
mateship, 152
Medici family, 105
medieval political life, 77-79; *see also* Middle Ages
mental illness, 406-412
merchant class, 101-103, 136
merchant marine, 169
Middle Ages, agricultural life in, 101; Catholicism in, 392; cities in, 98-100; class struggle in, 22; and development of capitalism, 97; economic organization of, 98; guilds in, 28-30; in India, 27, 34; landed proprietors in, 99-100; limitations on commerce during, 104-105; manufacturing in, 103; peasant revolts, 186; political life in, 77-79; sainthood in, 398-399; towns and cities in, 98-100, 102; "unions" in, 8; vocation in, 13

middle class, 88; Australian, 159; education for, 454; equality of opportunity in, 579; fertility differences and, 360; Horatio Alger story for, 503; infant care in, 366-368; in Japan, 541-551; in Latin America, 193-194; living standards of, 360; in middle-sized cities, 275-281; mobility and, 470, 578; permissiveness in, 363, 371; proletariat and, 191-192; religion of, 389; in Revolutionary era, 118; sainthood and, 395; secondary school education for, 438; social mobility of, 470, 578; stratum inheritance in, 580; voting behavior of, 421; *see also* stratification
military career, advancement in, 510-511
military officials, importance of, 71
miners, voting behavior of, 418; work satisfaction in, 476
Ming Dynasty, 177, 181
ministeriales, 99
mobility, downward, 575-576, 585; elite and, 451-453; social, *see* social mobility
Modjokuto, Java, 141-142
Moka Dora tribe, India, 631-632
money, banking and, 255-256; circular flow of, 256-257; power and, 243-244; productivity and, 256; reserves and, 255; as symbol, 246
money lenders, Middle Ages, 105-106
Mongol rule, China, 177
moots, Africa, 144
mother, working-class, 363
motivation, advancement and, 492-495; hypothesis of, 65; material advantages and, 67; mechanism of, 65-68; prestige and, 67-68; stratification and, 55-60
Muscovite Empire, rise of, 122; *see also* Russia
Mysore, India, 553-558, 560, 629, 631

National Council of Churches, 389
National Health Survey, 622
National Industrial Conference Board, 509
nationalism, 429
National Opinion Research Center (NORC), 488, 490, 562; *see also* NORC prestige study scores
National Science Foundation, 232, 446
National Union of Teachers, 642-648
nature, state of, 75, 246
navigation, commerce and, 105
Nazi party, 420
negative interchange, 85
negociatores, 99
négritude, 148
Negro, aspiration level in, 496; child rearing among, 490; as college stu-

dents, 496; divorce rate for, 382; as doctors, 304; educational level of, 337; family income of, 621, 625; middle-class, 307; pauperization of, 301-302; as soldier, 513; religion and, 170

Netherlands, divorce rate in, 384; job opportunity in, 579-580; manual-nonmanual mobility in, 575-576; skill inheritance in, 580; voting behavior in, 422

Newburyport, Mass., mobility in, 602-605

New Deal, 212

New Haven, Conn., power structure in, 219

new nations, *see* developing areas

New Testament, 396

New Zealand, divorce rate in, 383

nobility, in Muscovite Russia, 124

NORC prestige study scores, 311-312, 316-319, 326-328, 331-333, 494-495, 497

Norman conquest, 79

Norristown, Pa., social mobility in, 612

North-Hatt occupational prestige study, 480, 490

Norway, fertility in, 358; voting behavior in, 420

nuclear family, 598

obligations, power and, 254

occupation, business and, 16-17; deviant goals in, 497; estate of, 13-14; income and, 625; knowledge about, 328-329; social class and, 473-487, 493; social psychology and, 473-487; structural trends in, 191-196

occupational class, social mobility and, 562

occupational mobility, 562, 566, 574-581, 605-606

occupational prestige, 309-321; education and, 338; hierarchies in, 316-319; Japan, 543-546, 549; methodological aspects of, 312-313; United States, 316-317, 322-334; work satisfaction and, 477-478

Office of Education, 444

off-the-job satisfaction, 483

oligarchy, modern, 206-208, 233

open class value system, 570

"open" society, xv

opportunity, equality of, 253-255, 578

order, class and, 88-89; *see also* rank

organizing norms, 450

"other America," poverty in, 617-623

Panama, economic development and class structure in, 195

papal infallibility, 401

parent, surrogate, 595

parental discipline, 371-373

parent-child relationships, 370-378

parent's education, college aspirations and, 339

Pareto's Law, 627

party, class and status in, 20-27

pattern variables, 161

pauperization, process of, 296-302

"pay-off," power and, 242, 258

peasantry, Africa, 145; as class, 95; emancipation of in Russia, 125-126; Marx on, 10; rebellions of, 186; Russian, 127-130

pecuniary emulation, 35-37

Penal Laws, 299-300

"people," in Middle Ages, 77

permissiveness, social class and, 363, 371

personality, mobility and, 457-458

personal law, 78

Philippines, occupational prestige in, 310-311

phyle, 27

physician, status of, 304-305

plantation agriculture, 188-189

Poland, agrarian reform in, 536; aristocracy in, 535; class and estate in, 88; Communist party, 540; economic growth in, 534-540; education, 67; industrialization of, 537; landowners in, 535; power elite, 539; prewar conditions, 535; sociology in, xiv; social structure of, 534-540; stratification in, 537-538; wage scales in, 93

political attitudes, behavior and, 413-428

political career, 498

political class, 201-210

political community, 73-86

political life, 77-80

political power, 240-265; *see also* power

political process, 241-243

polity, concept of, 83, 241; interchanges of, 262

polylith, in power structure, 230

poor, "disreputable," 298-302; *see also* poverty

Poor Law Reform, 298

population, Malthus' theory of, 406; social mobility and, 568-569

populist society, 165

position, "importance" of, 64-66

poverty, defined, 618; disreputable, 290-296; "dregs" of, 292-293; fractional selection in, 296, 301-302; penalization of, 298-301; newcomers to, 294-295; social mobility and, 610; United States, 617-623

power, authority and, 249-250; class and, 201-210; concentration of, 214; concept of, 243-248; of corporation, 231-237; decision-making and, 229-231, 259; defined, 242; differentials in, 217; ego in, 245; and equality of opportunity, 253-255;

formal limitations to, 227; group, 224; hierarchy in, 215, 248-249; interests and, 213; intrinsic importance of, 247; as key concept, 240; of king, 79; legitimation and, 243-244, 248; in local communities, 218-231; Machiavellian, 222; money and, 243-245; obligations and, 254; patterns of, 201-210; personal factors in, 225-226; political, 240-265; polyliths and monoliths in, 230; religion and, 213; social order and, 20; solidarity and, 250-253; status and, 201-210; stratification and, 68-69; structure of, 211-218; as symbol, 259; value systems and, 227-228

power elite, 206, 210-218, 564

Power Elite, The (Mills), 210-218

power variable, 218

prestige, hierarchy of, 322; Japan, 543-546; national by countries (table), 314-315; occupational, *see* occupational prestige; stratification and, 60

Princeton University, 271

private school, 336

productivity, interchange of, 264; leisure and, 37-41; status symbol and, 404

professions, growth of, 459-472

profit maximization, 232

proletariat, as "chevroletariat," 93; defined, 14; derivation of, 95-96; model of, 95; Poland, 536; ruling class and, 204, 208; Russian, 135, 201

property, in agriculture, 183-184; class and, 90; division of, 592-593; occupation and, 607-610; in Revolutionary era, 115-116; self-respect and, 36; stratification and, 50

property systems, 183

Protestantism, U.S., 393; voting behavior of, 421-422

purchasing power, income and, 508

putting-out system, Russia, 132

rags-to-riches myth, 447, 501-506

railroading, work satisfaction in, 484

Rama, 554

ranch system, 189-190

rank, determinants of, 47-52; inherited, 570; interchange of, 565; social mobility and, 566

redistributive communities, Russia, 126

reference-group theory, 510-515

religion, church-set dichotomy in, 391-394; education and, 337; in England, 346-347; India, 553-557; power and, 213; social class and, 388-394; stratification and, 48-49; in value systems, 170; voting behavior and, 421-422; *see also* Catholic Church

Renaissance, 74, 392

rentier capitalists, 186
representation, demand for, 83
Republican party, 342, 426
research, vs. teaching, 72
Revolutionary era, artisans and craftsmen in, 118; class structure during, 111-121; economic class, 120; money value in, 116; stratification in, 150; upper class in, 268
role differentiation, Africa, 144, 148
Roman Catholic Church, 157, 351, 394, 401, 421-422
Roman Law, 124
Rome, estates in, 14-15
royal power, 79
rubber culture, 189
ruler, immunity of, 78; *see also* king
ruling class, 11, 201-210, 517; *see also* elite; power elite
Rumania, agriculture in, 186
rural class relations, 184
Russia, agrarian development in, 122-128; agriculture in, 129; cities in, 128-130; Communist power seizure in, 128; emancipation of peasants, 125-126; family disruption in, 133; geographic environment of, 121-122; industry in, 130-133; iron and steel production, 131; labor force, 131; labor legislation, 133; land redistribution in, 124; overpopulation in, 126; proletariat in, 134-135; rural society under Empire, 122-123; serfdom basis of, 131; social and economic development of, 121-135; working class in, 132-135; *see also* Soviet Union
Russian Revolution, 431
Russo-Japanese War, 127

sainthood, social status and, 394-401
samurai class, Japan, 136, 138
Sanskritization, concept of, 552-560
savings, occupational mobility and, 607-610
schizophrenia, 407
school grades, father's occupation and, 340
school norms, value system and, 341-342
science and technology, 461, 466-467
secondary schools, 436-441, 642; *see also* education
sect, church and, 391-394
Seiler family, 106
self-hatred, value systems and, 170, 571
self-identification, 544
Senate Small Business Committee, 282
serfdom, Russian, 125, 131
servants, in democratic society, 107-110; indentured, 117
service, power and, 242
service clubs, 278, 280
SES (sociometric status) index, 364-365

sex play, 365
sheepherding, Australia, 151
"skidders," 295-296
skilled labor, occupational mobility and, 576-577, 605; Soviet Union, 518-519; work satisfaction and, 476
slavery, U.S., 109-112, 114
small business, social welfare and, 284-285; stratification in, 276-279
social class, *see* class
social collectives, 11
social distance, 92, 646-647
social isolation, 92
socialization, anticipatory, 512; social class and, 362-377
social mobility, 501-506; adoption and, 595-596; causes of, 565-570; class conflict and, 503, 610-612; education and, 449-450, 592; Europe, 566-569, 572, 575-576; family and, 582-601; fertility and, 596-597; heterogamy and homogamy in, 593-595; India, 590; Japan, 543-545, 567, 597; kinship and, 597-600; marriage and, 563, 594; of middle class, 470; Newburyport, Mass., 602-615; nineteenth century, 602-615; occupational, 562, 566, 574-581, 605-606; personality and, 457-458; political consequences of, 570-573; rank and, 566; Soviet Union, 516-526, 532, 570; sponsored and contest, 449-458; status and, 597; stratification and, 564, 574-581, 651-659; theory of, 561-573; uni-geniture and, 592-593; United States, 501-506, 565-570, 612-615, 623-628; of upper class, 571; upward, 458, 575; value systems and, 170, 570; voting behavior and, 425; white-collar workers, 564-566, 614
social order, power and, 20
Social Register, 266-275, 563
social revolution, U.S., 623-628
social selection, 640-648
social stratification, *see* stratification
social structure, "class" and, 90; comparative study of, 83-86; conceptual content of, 91-92; government and, 75-76, 83
society, vs. individual, 76; secondary groups in, 77; state and, 75, 84; upper class and, 268; in Western tradition, 74; *see also* Social Register
sociology, American, xiv-xv; in other countries, xiv; terminology of, xv-xvi, 90-91
soldier, advancement of, 510-511
solidarity, power and, 250-253
South, family smallholdings in, 187; social order in, 163
South Africa, divorce rate in, 384
South Carolina, landowning in, 115
Soviet Union, college degrees in, 468; Communism in, 429; education in, 462-463, 468-469, 522-524, 530-531; equality in, 527; elite, 517,

656-657; Five-Year Plan, 516, 521-524; graduates in, 459; income structure, 528-529; inequality in, 656; occupational prestige in, 310; power elite in, 208; purges in, 519; rank insignia in, 520; ruling class in, 204-205; social mobility in, 516-526, 532, 570; sociology in, xiv; stratification in, 516-526; 648; students' rewards in, 522-523; women in, 519; *see also* Russia
Speenhamland, England, 297-299
sponsored mobility, 451-452
Stakhanovites, 517, 526
Stalinism, 532
Stalin Prize, 520
state, concept of, 86; as political identity, 83; "reverse interchange" with society, 85; ruling class and, 205; society and, 75, 84-85; tyranny of, 81
status, class and, 20-27; concept of, xv; estates and, 12; occupational mobility and, 607-610; power and, 201-210; social mobility and, 597
status-consciousness, 140
status-group, caste and, 30-32, in political community, 81
status honor, 13-14, 23
status incongruence, 303-308
status privileges, 24-25
status stratification, 23-24; *see also* stratification
status symbol, goods and services as, 146; individual hierarchy and, 404
steel worker, work satisfaction of, 476-477, 480-481
stratification, Africa, 141-149; Australia and U.S. compared, 149-161; China, 171-182; class structure and, 92; composite types in, 51-52; consistency in, 650-651; cultural and social factors in, 142; Davis-Moore theory of, 65-72; democracy and, 23; determinants of, 48-51; differentiation in, 649-650; economic conditions of, 25-26, 141-149; empirical consequence of, 69-72; English society, 344-345; functional theory of, 45-46, 64-69; "heart" of, 141; industrial society, 648-659; intra-country, 574-581; kinship and, 61-62, 146; Marxist theory and, 182; in middle class, 275-281; motivation and, 65-67; occupational, 574-581; opportunity and, 54; Poland, 537-538; political community and, 73-86; power and, 68-69; principle of, 46-52, 57; rural, 184; secondary cultures of, 145; social mobility and, 564, 574-578, 651-659; social structure and, 488; in Soviet Union, 516-526, 648; status and, 23-26; talent and, 55, 59; value systems and, 488-499; variation in, 51
striving, 496-498
students, world figures on, 460-468

success, striving for, 496-498
suicide, 75
Sung Dynasty, 176
superiority-subordination relationship, 69
support system (Parsons), 252
Sweden, divorce rate, 384; fertility, 357-358; middle class, 194
Syracuse, N.Y., power structure in, 223

talent, complementarity factor in, 71; productivity and, 70; rewards and, 71; stratification and, 55, 59
T'ang Dynasty, 175
Tavistock Institute, 483
teachers, for mass secondary education, 444-446
technical knowledge, stratification and, 50
technology, labor productivity and, 193
television, vulgarity and, 405
tenancy, family, 185-187
terms, in sociology, xv-xvi
Theory of the Leisure Class, The (Veblen), 35-41
third estate, 87
Thorndike G score, 282
toilet training, 366, 376
Tokyo, Japan, 136
totemism, 34
towns and cities, Middle Ages, 98-102; middle-sized, 275-281; Revolutionary era, 114-116
trade unions, 153, 564; see also labor unions
training, education and, 65-67; see also education
tribe, caste and, 27-28
trickle effect, 402-405
Tuxedo Park, N.Y., 271, 344

underconsumption, 609
underdeveloped areas, 428-436
unemployment, voting behavior and, 418
UNESCO, 569, 573
unigeniture, 592-593
United Nations, 509
United States, aristocracy in, 344; class structure in, 89, 111-121, 150-151; college degrees, 118, 468, 490-492, 495; colonial society, 150; community power, 229-231; di-
vorce rate, 383; dominant cultural standards, 538; education, 166-168, 339-341, 437-449, 592; economic development of certain states in, 198-199; egalitarianism in, 162-163; factions in, 1-4; family income, 507-508, 619-620, 625; fertility, 359; giant corporations, 232-233; graduates, 459-460; high school attendance, 335-342, 438-449, 592; illness in, 409-410; income distribution, 156, 506-510; kinship relationships in, 599-600; labor unions, 153, 228, 280; manufacturing industries, 193; mass higher education, 441-443; middle class, 150, 421, 438; occupational inheritance in, 586; occupational prestige, 316-317, 322-334; populist culture, 165; poverty, 617-623; power elite, 206-207, 211-219; prestige-rating distributions, 324-325; Protestantism, 393; religion and social class, 388-393; secondary education, 437-449; slavery, 109-114; social revolution in, 623-628; Tocqueville on, 107-110, 162-163; transformation of, 437-438; value systems in, 161-171; voting behavior, 425; wage averages in, 619; work-force distribution, 154; see also Revolutionary era
United States Children's Bureau, 376
unskilled labor, 476, 576-577, 602-615
Untouchables, India, 552, 557-559
upper class, Australia, 158; elite and, 267; family mobility and, 590; Great Britain, 164; Japan, 546-548; in middle-sized cities, 276-277; power of, 202; religion of, 389; sainthood and, 395; social mobility of, 571; and white-collar workers, 279
urbanization, mobility and, 582
urban renewal, 224
U.S.S.R., see Soviet Union
utilitarianism, 75

vacant statuses, 565
value systems, class history and, 498-499; and democratic system, 169-171; education and, 67; mobility and, 170, 570; money and, 243-244; open-class, 570; power and, 227-228; school norms and, 341-342; social class and, 488-499; U.S. and Great Britain compared, 161-167
varna theory, India, 634

Venezuela, 195-198
Vietnam, 435
Virginia, landowning in, 114
voting behavior, Australia, 160; class and, 191; communication channels and, 423-425; leftist, 417-423; trade unions and, 573

wage workers, 120, 277, 619
War Labor Board, 625
Warner occupation scale, 364-366
warrior class, Japan, 136-139
wealth, occupational choice and, 494; in Revolutionary period, 114; stratification and, 49-50
welfare-state, xvii, 74, 85, 225; Great Britain as, 640-648
West Germany, occupational inheritance in, 589; see also Germany
white-collar workers, 192, 275, 279-281, 586; Germany, 573; Great Britain, 591; inheritance in, 585; Japan, 541, 545-546, 551; occupational prestige of, 312, 318; proportion of, 438; social mobility and, 564, 566, 614; work satisfaction among, 475
Who's Who in America, 266-275, 583
women, occupational mobility of, 600-601
wool culture, 104, 151, 189
work groups, integrated, 481
work satisfaction, 473-487; control of conditions in, 478-481; factors in, 476-484; methodology of research in, 486-487; occupational differences in, 474-476; occupational prestige and, 477-478
World War I, xiii, 128, 132, 134, 187, 292, 354, 462, 467, 584
World War II, xiii, xvi, 72, 85, 155, 158, 185-186, 189, 212, 230, 376, 441, 445, 462, 467, 471, 527, 541-542, 547, 557, 584, 598, 614, 624, 626-627, 644, 653

Yale University, 271
Yoruba, Africa, 143
Yugoslavia, divorce rate in, 385; sociology in, xiv

zero-sum problem and occupational prestige, 325; power and, 255-260
Zulu kingdom, 147